Peterson's
Short-Term
Study Abroad
2007

PETERSON'S

A ⓝelnet. COMPANY

PETERSON'S

A ⓝelnet. COMPANY

About Peterson's, a Nelnet company

Peterson's (www.petersons.com) is a leading provider of education information and advice, with books and online resources focusing on education search, test preparation, and financial aid. Its Web site offers searchable databases and interactive tools for contacting educational institutions, online practice tests and instruction, and planning tools for securing financial aid. Peterson's serves 110 million education consumers annually.

For more information, contact Peterson's, 2000 Lenox Drive, Lawrenceville, NJ 08648; 800-338-3282; or find us on the World Wide Web at www.petersons.com/about.

Editor: Linda Seghers; Production Editor: Mark D. Snider; Copy Editor: Sally Ross; Research Project Manager: Christine Lucas; Research Associates: James Feichthaler, Amy L. Weber; Programmer: Alex Lin; Manufacturing Manager: Ivona Skibicki; Composition Manager: Gary Rozmierski; Client Relations Representatives: Danielle Groncki, Mimi Kaufman, Karen D. Mount, Eric Wallace.

ISBN-13: 978-0-7689-2176-2
ISBN-10: 0-7689-2176-7

Printed in the United States of America

10 9 8 7 6 5 4 3 2 1   09 08 07

Tenth Edition

CONTENTS

A Note from the Peterson's Editors

If you're planning to become one of the nearly 200,000 American students who annually spend a semester or year studying abroad, you've probably begun to collect brochures on various programs and examined the beautiful travel posters that cover bulletin boards across your campus. At this point you may also be wondering how you will ever sort out which program is best for you, how you will afford it, how you will convince your parents and advisers to let you go, and how you will finalize all the details involved.

Many students abandon the idea of going abroad when faced with these issues. You don't have to be one of them! *Peterson's Short-Term Study Abroad 2007* is designed to walk you step-by-step through the process of selecting a program and preparing for what may be the most enriching time of your academic life.

This guide is divided into three main parts. **The Ins and Outs of Studying Abroad** section provides insight into the following:

- How to decide if you are a good candidate for a study-abroad program

- Avoiding culture shock, traveling smart, and living within your budget

- Transferring credits and finding and securing financial aid

- Obtaining passports and visas

- What nontraditional destinations have to offer

- Study-abroad programs for students with disabilities

The "How to Use This Guide" article provides in-depth explanations about each element contained in the **Profiles,** the criteria used to select the programs, and data collection procedures.

A NOTE FROM THE PETERSON'S EDITORS

The **Profiles of Short-Term Study-Abroad Programs** section lists more than 1,400 programs. These **Profiles** contain all the details you'll need to make a list of preliminary program choices.

Finally, the three **Indexes** contained in this guide—**Field of Study**, **Program Sponsors**, and **Host Institutions**—are invaluable resources for narrowing your choice of programs.

Peterson's publishes a full line of resources to help guide you and your family through the college admission process. Peterson's publications can be found at your local bookstore, library, and high school guidance office, and you can access us online at www.petersons.com.

We welcome any comments or suggestions you may have about this publication and invite you to complete our online survey at www.petersons.com/booksurvey. Your feedback will help us to provide personalized solutions for your educational advancement.

Like anything worthwhile, you'll get out of your study-abroad experience what you put into it. Peterson's is dedicated to helping you gather all the information you need to make a sound decision. We wish you the best of luck in your search for the perfect study-abroad program for you!

THE INS AND OUTS OF STUDYING ABROAD

Credit for Study Abroad

Stephen Cooper, Ph.D.
Former Director of Academic Programs Abroad, Louisiana State University

Parents encourage it. The financial aid office insists on it. The United States Congress even authorizes money for students who go for it—college credit.

It increasingly matters to students that they earn maximum credit for an overseas experience as the costs of a college education increase. While it may be tempting to set up your own trip or sign up for an adventurous tour, most students seek an international experience that will strengthen their academic record. Credit programs provide significant structure, educational gains, and other benefits, not the least of which is the academic credit itself.

This guide includes only credit-granting study-abroad programs. Here we'll discuss the kinds of credit possible and the best ways to ensure that you get the credit you want. Unless you are going on a program run by your own university, you will probably earn credit *by transfer.* That means your home university will evaluate the courses you took and decide whether to accept them and then how to put them on your transcript.

CREDIT FOR WHAT?

Depending on your home university, you could earn credit in general education courses, electives, your major and minor subjects, and foreign languages (possibly even for languages not taught at your home school). While you may be able to get credit that will appear on your transcript, you may also want to know if that credit can be applied toward your degree.

Also consider the personal benefits of taking a course that won't satisfy any degree requirement but that could provide you with rewarding cultural enrichment. For example, an engineering major who has already "maxed out" in electives might find the value of an art history course in Paris, a political science course in Germany, or a theater course in London too rich a treat to pass up—a healthy attitude for a student who might not return overseas for decades.

WHO GIVES THE CREDIT?

Be certain of the source of the credit offered before you sign up for a program. If you are going on your own school's program, find out if the courses actually appear in your college course catalog. If they are extramural courses, verify that your academic advisers will accept them and that you will not exceed any limits on taking such courses.

If you decide to join a program set up by another U.S. university, more care is required. You'll probably need more information than appears in the program brochure. Will the sponsoring U.S. school issue the transcript, or will a foreign university or some agency do so? *Find this out before you sign up!* Either way, you may need more details on the courses offered to satisfy your college's academic counselors that you can earn *credit by transfer.*

HOW MUCH CREDIT CAN I EARN?

The amount of credit you can earn will depend on policies of the host institution and your school, as well as what you take abroad and (often) whether or not you get written prior approval. Of course, *you have to pass all those courses.* In fact, your home school may require that you earn a C or better in a course before accepting the credits.

Your home advisers may require a lot of information on the courses you want to take to help estimate how much credit you will earn. If a foreign university will issue your final transcript, some admissions officers and registrars will look closely at the number of contact hours in a particular course—that is, the actual number of

hours you will have in lectures, labs, field experiences, and tutorials. If a U.S. university will provide the official transcript, the transfer may be simpler because of similarities in credit systems here.

As you look at programs offered by other U.S. universities, remember that some offer credit on the *quarter system,* others on a *semester credit* basis. If your college and the sponsoring school differ, another transfer issue may arise. For example, some U.S. universities use a ratio of 3:2 in transferring quarter credit hours to semester credits. How would this affect you? Get your admissions office or registrar to help you calculate credit-hour transfer potential.

Many U.S. students choose *direct enrollment* in foreign universities for a semester or a year, some going on exchanges. Again, it is important to get course descriptions in advance and, sometimes just as important, to demonstrate to your home school that the foreign university has some kind of accreditation or official standing with the country's ministry of education.

Getting course information in adequate detail sometimes proves difficult, for example, in Europe, where the U.S. practice of publishing comprehensive course catalogs is rare. However, with persistence, the right contacts, help from your study-abroad adviser, and the use of faxes and e-mails, you can usually get enough advance information to determine if you will be able to earn desired credit, again by transfer, from the overseas school. Even if the descriptive course material given is in the language of the host country, you can usually get it translated for your school officials who will rule on its acceptability.

PRIOR APPROVAL—GET IT IN WRITING!

Most students should know before they take off for a particular study-abroad experience whether or not they will earn credit. In fact, many universities require a process of prior approval and will not accept any credit earned abroad that was not authorized beforehand. Indeed, part of the process of obtaining financial aid via your home school for your overseas study may include seeking signatures from persons who can approve your anticipated selections. Usually, your study-abroad adviser, registrar, or admissions office will guide you through the process. Keep in mind that if you fail to get that approval in writing, you could return with little to show for your academic efforts abroad.

You might also have to seek from the host university such items as course outlines and reading lists, information on the level of the course (first year, advanced, etc.), prerequisites, the number of contact hours, and the format of the course, such as lecture, seminar, lab, or field study.

Different universities in the United States handle the acceptance or transfer of credit in different ways. Some have already set up exact matches or direct equivalents, which pair foreign university courses with courses in your home school's catalog. More commonly, though, the home university will receive the overseas courses as substitutes for some of your required courses or as electives that can still fulfill degree requirements. Find out in each case how your institution will handle each of your chosen courses.

DOCUMENTING CREDIT EARNED ABROAD

Note that some overseas institutions do not create transcripts; instead, you may have to get other kinds of documentation, including letters from the professors who taught you. Find out in advance what to expect and how to get what you will need. Also, be sure that the transcript or other materials are sent to the proper person at your home school. At some U.S. colleges, a good way to handle this is to have everything sent to your study-abroad adviser, as that person will know how to route everything to avoid delays or loss. Find out before you leave so you can tell your host school administrators.

Upon return, in addition to the transcript, be prepared to show your home school other items related to the courses you took, including course syllabi, reading lists, returned exams, papers you did, your lecture notes, and the like. These can help document the nature and level of the course work and ensure that you earn full credit.

OTHER CREDIT OPTIONS

So far, we have focused on traditional course work. But some students earn credit for study abroad in other ways. Some colleges offer what is called credit for experiential education, sometimes for work experience or for public service projects, and sometimes for travel abroad. If this is a possibility at your school, find out what is required to document the experience to earn credit.

More and more U.S. universities encourage internships and may give credit for them alone or in combination with course work taken abroad. Check with your home school in advance to see if credit applies. See the article on "International Internships" in this guide to explore this possibility.

Many U.S. schools give credit by exam, especially in foreign languages but also in other

subjects. It works like this: You take a course abroad, return home, and sit for a formal examination on your campus to see how much knowledge you gained. The exam might be oral, written, or both and is almost always designed by your own home campus faculty. You can find out before departure if this is an option and how to prepare for the exam.

Independent study provides another avenue for credit. An independent study or readings course is an individualized course for credit agreed upon between a student and a professor, one that usually allows the student to pursue some special research topic or do selected work in depth in a specialized area, usually in the student's major field of study. Some students set up independent readings or project courses with cooperative host or home campus faculty members prior to leaving on an overseas study program. You may also get to take such courses in the host university's program. Doing so may be limited in terms of credits that may be earned and will usually require formal enrollment in those courses. Nevertheless, independent study for credit provides valuable possibilities for carrying out research projects and doing work that could not be done for credit in an overseas institution or program offered by another U.S. school. If you can take advantage of this option, be sure to make precise arrangements with your sponsoring professor(s) so that you meet required deadlines and satisfy established expectations. Then, keep in touch with your sponsoring faculty members while you are abroad to advise them of your progress and to seek guidance. Save copies of anything you

mail back to them, as not all international postal systems are perfect, nor is our own!

Graduate students may need credit for their overseas study. In addition to the options discussed above, some graduate schools in the United States allow thesis or dissertation credit for research done abroad. In fact, some universities will enroll graduate students for credit concurrently with the foreign experience, and indeed this may be a requirement for maintaining fellowships or other awards from the home school.

Now, you may also have the option of telecommunication course work or using e-mail, the Internet, and television via satellite transmission.

CREDIT AND FINANCIAL AID

The federal government has made it clear that U.S. college students who are eligible for federal loans, grants, and scholarships may use their aid in overseas programs approved by their home universities, but the programs have to be for credit. Carefully read the article "Paying for Study Abroad" for details, and study your home school's rules.

WHAT ABOUT GRADES?

In addition to granting credits for courses taken abroad, many U.S. colleges accept grades and post them on the home transcript. Specialists in your office of admissions or your registrar will know how to do this, but you will want to understand what will happen, too.

Different universities have different grading systems. In some countries, numbers are used rather than letter grades. Some foreign universities give comments but no grades of any kind. Your home university may or may not convert the grades received to your own school's grading scale, post the foreign grades on your transcript, or average the grades into your personal grade point average.

Furthermore, some overseas university systems tend to grade more severely than those in the United States. For that reason, many U.S. students take advantage of a pass/fail grading option in order to protect their averages. If you seek that option, do so officially, in writing, and before departure to ensure acceptability by your home school; you may have to petition your dean in writing. Once abroad, it is difficult to change a course to pass/fail.

If you get a foreign university transcript or one from the U.S. institution that provided your program abroad, save original copies or find out how to get them; you may decide to apply to graduate or a professional school after graduation, and you will probably have to provide original transcripts from all the institutions you have attended.

SOLVING PROBLEMS

Clearly, the best way to avoid difficulty in earning credit for your experience abroad is to seek formal prior approval of the course work you want to take. On most campuses, this requires patience, legwork, research, diplomacy, and attention to detail. Your study-abroad adviser and other personnel will assist you as much as they can, but you will have full responsibility for providing what is needed before you go and when you return.

Once abroad, expect surprises. You may have to change some courses, and you may run into other unanticipated difficulties. Act quickly and resourcefully. Use e-mail and faxes as well as the telephone to keep in touch with your advisers back home. This contact will pay for itself when you get back home and the final credit evaluation begins. Also, provide your home university with your foreign address once you get settled.

Students who understand the kinds of credit available in study abroad and how to arrange for that credit usually do quite well, returning home not only with fond memories, increased global awareness, and personal growth but also with a vital addition to their academic records. May all of this happen to you, and more!

Stephen Cooper, Ph.D., was Director of Academic Programs Abroad at Louisiana State University from 1980–1990. A frequent presenter at professional conferences, he has also written articles and chapters on study abroad for various publications. He coedited Financial Aid for Study Abroad: A Manual for Advisers and Administrators *(NAFSA, 1989). In 1993 he received the Lily von Klemperer Award from the study-abroad section of NAFSA for his service to the field.*

Paying for Study Abroad

Nancy Stubbs

Director of Study Abroad Programs, University of Colorado at Boulder

So, you've found the perfect study-abroad program, and you have the information you need. You even found out that the credit earned abroad will transfer back to your home institution. What's next? Paying for it. This article is designed to help you get the most for your money as well as guide you through the financial aid issues that may concern you.

HOW MUCH WILL IT REALLY COST?

Study-abroad costs vary greatly from program to program. Even at the same site, three or four different programs can charge different fees. There are a variety of reasons for this. When shopping around for the best price, you should think about what the program offers.

When you study abroad (as opposed to enrolling directly in a foreign institution to pursue a degree), you pay for a certain amount of service and expertise. A faculty member at the sponsoring U.S. institution may be hired as program director. He or she will speak the language of the country, be familiar with the educational system and local customs, and be on-site during the program to help you get oriented, fill out forms, register for courses, and deal with emergencies.

The program may schedule special events that aren't open to others at the program site. Field trips, special orientations, or language classes are good examples. The cost of these events could be built into the fee you pay. They might also be optional events, allowing you to choose and pay for those that interest you. It's important to have a good idea of *all* costs, since it is impossible to create a reasonable budget if you keeping running across unexpected expenses.

You may also pay tuition to the sponsoring institution as a way of allowing the course work to be transferred and transcripted. Normally, at least part of this tuition is used to pay program costs; some of it may be kept by the sponsor to cover the cost of administering the program.

As you can see, the cost of programs can vary even at the same site because of the number of persons hired to assist you, the cost of extra events planned for the program, administrative costs at the home institution, or even things like the type of housing available. You've probably figured out that study abroad will cost more in a country with a higher cost of living. But, you can also pay a lot in a country where living costs are low if you choose to attend a private school with no subsidized tuition.

WHY DO I NEED A BUDGET?

There are several reasons to assemble a good estimate of your program costs. Most obvious is the need to know how much money you will need. Unless you have been abroad on your own before, you will probably not think of all costs associated with study abroad.

For instance, you don't need to worry about passport and visa costs, airport taxes, customs fees, the cost of changing currency, currency fluctuations, and so on to be a college student in the United States. All of these, however, could be part of your budget for study abroad.

While vacation travel, shopping, or recreational activities may not fit the definition of "required education costs," you will surely want to have enough money for some fun while you are abroad. If you do succeed in finding an outside source of funding, you may need a budget so that the aid administrator can determine your award. It is in your best interest to be sure that all reasonable costs are included in this budget.

Always ask for an estimate of total costs for the program, preferably broken down into categories. The program administrator should be able to provide this for you. If not, ask for a list of alumni willing to speak to interested persons. You can ask them what they spent. Be sure to check with your home school study-abroad adviser, too. He or she may have information about budgets and transferring funds that will help you determine the real cost of study abroad. Here are typical categories for the study-abroad budget:

- **Tuition and fees at the study-abroad site**

- **Tuition due to the institution administering the program**

- **Books, paper, and other school supplies**

- **Room and meal costs, including those during vacation periods**

- **Typical living costs, including local commuting, laundry, telephone, postage, and entertainment**

- **Medical and other insurance (lost baggage, trip cancellation, etc.)**

- **Passport, visa, and airport tax fees**

- **Round-trip transportation to and from the program site**

- **Travel on weekends and vacation**

- **Optional program activities, such as field trips and cultural events**

HOW CAN I PAY FOR IT?

There is, unfortunately, no huge source of private scholarships available for undergraduate study abroad. Most private funding is dedicated to graduate, or even postgraduate, study and research. Still, there are a variety of places you can look for outside help:

- **Federal or state financial aid**

- **Institutional, private, and other types of government aid for education**

- **Scholarships for undergraduate study abroad**

FEDERAL AND STATE FINANCIAL AID

By far the largest pool of funding available to U.S. college students is federal and state financial aid. You may be using financial aid already. If so, you might be able to use that aid to study abroad.

Federal and state aid is divided into three categories:

- **Grants and scholarships,** which do not have to be repaid. The most common federal grants are Federal Pell Grants and Federal Supplemental Educational Opportunity Grants. State grants can include various diversity grants for nontraditional students and state-funded scholarship programs for residents who attend public or private institutions.

- **Work-study funds,** which partially pay your salary for certain jobs. Work-study programs can be funded by both the federal and state governments.

- **Education loans,** which you can obtain without a credit rating, and which usually do not have to be repaid until you graduate. Some of the loans have an added advantage— the government pays the interest while you are in school. The Federal Perkins Loan program is one of the most familiar of these. The federal government also offers the Stafford Loan, the PLUS Loan for parents, and Direct Loans. Some states also have loan programs for students attending state institutions.

Check with your financial aid office to determine which state aid programs are available at your institution. This office can also assist you in learning about federal aid, institutional scholarships, and often even private scholarships.

CAN I USE MY FINANCIAL AID TO STUDY ABROAD?

The answer is—sometimes. Federal aid can legally be used to study abroad as long as the program you attend has been approved for credit by your home institution.

Many state aid programs follow the same rules and regulations as the federal government. If your state does this, you should be able to use state aid for study-abroad programs approved by your home campus. In some cases, state grants or scholarships may be restricted to use in that state.

If you already get federal or state aid, you know that both are governed by a multitude of rules and regulations. Each institution is allowed some latitude in deciding how aid programs will be administered and how certain things, like the cost of attending school, will be determined. This is good—it allows aid administrators to take into account special circumstances when awarding aid. Here are some things to know if you are investigating whether state or federal aid can be used for study abroad:

- **It is legal to use federal grants, work-study, or loans for study abroad, but you can only get aid from a school where you are enrolled in a degree program, and you must be enrolled at least half-time (or full-time in some cases) while you get the aid.** So, you have to maintain enrollment at your "home" campus (where you plan to get your degree), and your home campus must agree that the credit earned abroad is "approved." Under these circumstances, your home campus can award federal aid even if you are going abroad on a program sponsored by another U.S. school or by a foreign institution.

- **It may not be possible to use your work-study award abroad because of restrictions on where you can work and how your time must be reported.**

- **You will find it easiest to use federal or state aid if you go on a study-abroad program run by your school.** The programs are already academically approved, and your school has devised some mechanism to keep you enrolled while you study abroad. The credit does not have to satisfy major requirements, but you need to be able to use it for general education or elective credit.

- **If your perfect program is administered by another U.S. institution or if you wish to enroll directly in a foreign school's program, you can still arrange to use your federal or state aid.** Your home school must have a mechanism for examining the courses you will take and for approving them for transfer. Again, the credit does not have to satisfy major requirements, but you need to be able to use it for general education or elective credit.

- **Once the program is approved by your home institution, it is necessary to have a written agreement between your school and the school or organization that administers it.** Ask your home school study-abroad office or your financial aid office about this agreement.

- **Your financial aid office may require a budget for your study-abroad program to ensure that you are not awarded too much aid (more than the cost of your education).** Federal law allows the use of aid to cover all "reasonable" costs of study abroad, including round-trip transportation, tuition and fees for the program, living costs, passport and visa fees, health insurance, etc.

- **If your study-abroad program costs more than what you normally pay, ask your financial aid office to consider the higher costs and give you more aid.** If studying abroad costs less, you should expect the normal aid award to be reduced.

- **If you have never applied for a federal loan, federal law requires that you attend school for at least thirty days before you can get your loan money.** You are also required to have special counseling about borrowing money for college; your first loan cannot be disbursed to you until you have received this counseling.

- **You have extra responsibilities if you receive federal or state aid for study abroad. You may have to gather information about the cost of your program.** You must take responsibility for ensuring that all forms, documents, and other materials are filled out and turned in so you can get your aid award. You will have to arrange for someone you trust to "watch over" your aid, perhaps pick up refund checks, and contact your financial aid officer if problems arise, since it is very hard to sort out problems when you are away from your campus. This can often be done with a "power of attorney." Most importantly, you must be sure you take enough courses and earn satisfactory grades while abroad.

- **If you think you might be eligible for state or federal financial aid, talk to your study-abroad adviser and your financial aid officer.** Find out what policies exist for using aid to study abroad, and be sure you follow instructions so you won't be denied aid at the last minute or have difficulties getting the money that has been awarded.

INSTITUTIONAL, PRIVATE, AND OTHER TYPES OF GOVERNMENT AID FOR EDUCATION

You may be receiving other assistance for your education that can be used for a study-abroad

program. For instance, if you are in an ROTC program or if you receive veteran's benefits or vocational-rehabilitation benefits, it may be possible to use these funds for study abroad. Since these are all government programs, you must work carefully with your campus representative to see how the benefits might be applied to study abroad. It will be important for your home school to approve the program so credit can be transferred back toward your degree. You will undoubtedly have to make extra arrangements to ensure that the benefits are properly awarded and tracked.

Many universities award institutional aid to their students. This may be a tuition scholarship, a merit award for good grades, or some other nongovernment scholarship or loan. If you plan to go on a study-abroad program run by your institution, ask if you can use these funds. If the answer is "no," ask why, since you are going on a program that is an extension of your institution. Some institutions will not allow such scholarships to be used for programs sponsored by others, but some will. Again, it never hurts to ask.

You can look for private aid that is awarded to you to be used wherever you go to school. You have undoubtedly heard about the "millions of

dollars in private aid" that can be located by various scholarship search companies. It isn't necessary to pay someone to look for scholarships. Most college reference libraries have private funding sourcebooks that list hundreds of scholarships. This is especially useful if you are a member of an ethnic minority or if you are a "nontraditional" (i.e., older, married, disabled, etc.) student. An excellent resource for this type of information is *Peterson's Scholarships, Grants & Prizes 2007*. You can also search for scholarships on the Internet at www.petersons.com/.

SCHOLARSHIPS FOR UNDERGRADUATE STUDY ABROAD

There are a few scholarships specifically for undergraduate study abroad. You must apply at least a year in advance for some, so it is wise to plan ahead if you want to apply for these scholarships.

Perhaps the best-known undergraduate scholarships are provided by Rotary International. This service organization has a yearly nationwide competition for high school, graduate, and undergraduate students. Awards range from travel grants to full-cost grants. The application deadline for the national competition is usually in the early fall preceding the year that you will study abroad. Check with your local Rotary Club.

The U.S. government now provides scholarships specifically for undergraduate and graduate study abroad. The National Security Education Program (NSEP) provides scholarships for study in nontraditional countries. Awards are made after a highly competitive national process. If you get a scholarship from NSEP, you will be expected to complete a service requirement. Your campus should have an NSEP representative who can give you more information about this program. Check with your study-abroad office for details.

Other scholarships for study abroad will not cover all costs but can be used to supplement other funding. Some study-abroad programs have scholarships for their students. Your campus might provide scholarships if you go on an approved program or one run by your institution. A few scholarships are provided to U.S. students by foreign governments, and there is an increasing number of scholarships available to minority and nontraditional students. Information about these types of scholarships can be found by contacting your study-abroad office.

WHERE DO I START?

Begin your search by taking a realistic look at the cost of your perfect program. Compare that to your own resources. How much money can you or your family devote to study abroad? Don't assume you can earn money while you study; it is illegal for foreign students to work in many countries. Don't decide you can sell all your earthly possessions if it means you will return home destitute and unable to continue your education. Also, think about owing thousands in student loans if you plan to borrow your way abroad. Is it realistic to think you can repay all of those loans, or would it be better to wait a semester or year so funds can be saved?

After you have a clear picture of the program's costs and your ability to pay them, begin to look for other sources of money. Check with your study-abroad and financial aid offices to see if you might qualify for federal, state, or institutional aid. Look at private funding resource books to see if there are scholarships you can use. Ask your study-abroad office about the NSEP and Rotary scholarships or any other source of funding for study-abroad, and ask the program sponsor if you qualify for scholarships, work, or other types of assistance.

Most students still fund study abroad with individual or family funds. An increasing number of people, however, are finding support from the aid sources mentioned above. If you will need help funding your study-abroad program, begin early, look carefully, and remember that you won't get funding if you don't ask. Good luck!

Nancy Stubbs is Director of Study Abroad Programs at the University of Colorado at Boulder. She is coeditor of Financial Aid for Study Abroad: A Manual for Advisers and Administrators. *She has written many articles and given presentations on funding for study abroad. She is past chair of a subcommittee of study-abroad professionals who work to make federal financial aid available to students who study abroad.*

The Essentials: Passports, Visas, ID Cards, Money, and More

Rob Becker

Vice President of Sales and Marketing, Travel CUTS

When planning your departure from the United States to study in another country, there's more to it than simply packing your bags and heading to the airport with ticket in hand. The length of your stay means you'll need to give a bit more consideration to things like your passport, any necessary visas, and what form of money (ATM card, credit cards, traveler's checks, etc.) you will bring.

PASSPORTS

U.S. citizens are required to have a passport for entry into almost any country. Even the easy old stand-bys like Canada, Mexico, and the Caribbean are slowly phasing in a passport requirement. If your destination doesn't currently require a passport, for the sake of ease if nothing else, it's recommended that you obtain one.

The cost of a U.S. passport (for an adult, 16 years and older) is $97. This includes the passport fee of $55, a security fee of $12, and an execution fee of $30. An expedited service is also available for an additional $60. There is usually a higher demand for passports between March and August, so allow yourself at least a few months to apply for your passport. If you are required to obtain any visas, you'll need your passport even further in advance. U.S. passports are valid for ten years from date of issue, so there is certainly no harm in getting your passport well in advance.

All first-time applicants must apply in person. You'll be required to set up an appointment in advance at one of 7,000 passport acceptance offices located throughout the United States. To find the location nearest to you, visit www.travel.state.gov. Applications can often be obtained from your local post office.

You may be required to present your passport for identification at various times when you're abroad. It's a good idea to keep it with you in a secure place. There are a number of products on the market that are small and discreet and allow you to keep your passport on your person and wear it with comfort underneath your clothes. There's one that goes around your waist and one for around your neck. Whichever you choose, make sure it's secure and comfortable. Should your passport be lost or stolen, immediately file a police report with the local authorities and contact the nearest U.S. Embassy or Consulate for assistance with a replacement.

VISAS

With the exception of a short tourist visit, most countries require that you obtain a visa for entry into their country. A visa is simply a stamp or endorsement placed in your passport by a foreign government that permits you to visit that country for a specified time, for a specified purpose. If you are studying abroad, you will likely be required to obtain a special student visa. Unless your study-abroad department is facilitating this process on your behalf, you will need to contact the nearest embassy or consulate of the countries that you will be visiting to find out what their visa requirements and/or process are. For an extra fee, you can also use a visa service to expedite your visa. Either system will require you to fill out an application form and submit it along with official passport photos and your passport. When you are getting your initial passport pictures taken, simply get some extras for this use. Depending on the country, it can take several weeks to process your visa, so be sure to allow for plenty of time.

INTERNATIONAL STUDENT IDENTITY CARD

The International Student Identity Card, or ISIC, is a basic travel card for students going abroad. The ISIC is issued to more than 5 million students each year by academic and student travel organizations in more than eighty countries around the world. It is the product of the International Student Travel Confederation (ISTC),

based in Amsterdam. Information about ISTC can be found at www.istc.org. The concept of the ISIC is basic: it provides a consistent form of proof of student status that is internationally recognized, regardless of the country you're in. It provides you with a variety of discounts, including special student airfare, international phone calls, local discounts at tourist attractions and restaurants, and more. The special student airfares cannot be obtained through the airlines directly; they are only offered through specially authorized student travel companies such as Travel CUTS.

U.S. International Student Identity Cards also provide the cardholder with free basic medical and accident insurance while traveling abroad, along with a toll-free hotline for travelers in need of financial or medical assistance.

International Student Identity Cards are valid from September 1 to December 1 of the following year. Although there is no age limit for cardholders, some special student airfares may have a maximum age allowed for the applicable discount. Your travel adviser can inform you of the eligibility restrictions for your specific student airfare.

Many college and university campuses issue the cards, and you can also get one through a student travel agency, such at Travel CUTS (www.travelcuts.com/usa).

MONEY

Traveler's checks still provide the safest method for carrying your money while abroad. If they are lost or stolen, they can be replaced. The cost of traveler's checks varies and generally runs about 1 percent of the total cost you are purchasing. However, some banks provide them free of charge as a service to their customers. Do your research.

Many travelers purchase U.S. dollar traveler's checks because they are widely accepted around the world. You may also purchase traveler's checks in the foreign currency of your destination, such as euros, British pounds, or Japanese yen. By doing so you will not be subject to any further currency fluctuations once you're there.

If you do end up with U.S. dollar traveler's checks, you can exchange them at most banks or foreign currency exchange bureaus. Note however, that most charge a commission for the exchange and may also add a service charge. So, you may want to do larger exchanges less frequently as opposed to many smaller exchanges. *Never* exchange your money with a street vendor. Make sure you are exchanging your funds through a recognized currency exchange bureau, such as Thomas Cook. If you run out of cash, you can usually receive money within a day or so from friends or family back in the United States by wire through Western Union.

ATMs are almost everywhere now. Using a foreign ATM means your account is debited in a foreign currency and billed in U.S. dollars at fluctuating rates of exchange. The exchange rates can often be favorable if they follow the exchange rates that the banks use amongst themselves. Check with your local bank for their specific exchange guidelines.

Most ATMs in the United States are connected to international networks such as Cirrus and the Plus System. This makes it easy to get cash from your U.S. account from almost anywhere.

DO YOUR HOMEWORK!

If you want to get the most out of your travel experience, do some basic research on your destination in advance. There's nothing worse than an American in a foreign country coming across as clueless about his or her host country. There are myriad guidebooks, blogs, travel discussion boards, novels, etc., that you can review in advance. Your "hosts" will appreciate your effort.

In addition, you can almost be guaranteed that you'll be asked about U.S. foreign policy. This will be of even more significance if the country you are visiting is being affected by a current U.S. policy. Once again, the best advice is to do your homework. Be informed about current U.S. policy, even if you don't agree with it. Do some general reading of the *New York Times* or *Washington Post*, newspapers known for their coverage of international affairs. And of course there is the Internet, with its countless informative sites. There is also an annual publication called *Great Decisions* that is published through the Foreign Policy Association. They can be reached by calling 212-481-8100 or by visiting their Web site at www.fpa.org.

CUSTOMS

When you arrive back in the United States, you'll have to clear customs. The U.S. government limits the amount of duty-free goods you may bring back and prohibits certain items entirely. For up-to-date customs regulations visit www.cbp.gov, the official site of the U.S. Customs and Border Protection, an agency within the Department of Homeland Security.

Rob Becker, whose career includes more than twenty years in the student travel business, has extensive travel experience in Asia, Australia, Europe, and the Americas. He is currently Vice President of Sales and Marketing at Travel CUTS (www.travelcuts.com), a North American student travel company.

Options in International Educational Exchange for People with Disabilities

Mobility International USA and the National Clearinghouse on Disability and Exchange

There are few things in life as exciting, challenging, and transforming as studying, living, working, or volunteering abroad. While relatively few people with disabilities take advantage of these life-changing opportunities, more and more people with all types of disabilities are becoming aware that they too can participate in international programs. People who use wheelchairs or crutches, are blind or partially sighted, are deaf or hard of hearing, or are learning disabled have all been successful participants in international exchange, volunteer, and work programs.

People with disabilities benefit from international programs by being able to share experiences with others. At the same time, international exchange, volunteer, and work programs create leadership skills essential in our increasingly global society.

With the passage of the Americans with Disabilities Act in 1990, international exchange programs, study-abroad offices, and international community service projects are now mandated to offer the same services to people with disabilities as they do to nondisabled individuals. Although this does not mean they can guarantee accessible services and sites abroad, it does mean that they need to assist qualified disabled applicants in making international programs as accessible as possible. A world of opportunities awaits people with disabilities!

Including people with disabilities in international programs creates a multicultural atmosphere for all participants. Encouraging and facilitating the participation of people with disabilities is as important to diversity as including people with a range of economic, social, and ethnic backgrounds in international programs. These types of experiences also provide participants with the opportunity to share their unique perspective with others around the world.

It is the mission of Mobility International USA (MIUSA) and the National Clearinghouse on Disability and Exchange to promote the inclusion of individuals with disabilities in international programs and assist international exchange organizations in the process of increasing general program accessibility.

The Clearinghouse provides information and referral services free of charge for anyone with a disability who is interested in academic, volunteer, or work opportunities abroad. MIUSA and the Clearinghouse also can provide consultation and training to international organizations interested in including more people with disabilities in exchange, volunteer, and work programs.

STUDY ABROAD

As more universities around the world are learning about accommodating students with disabilities, an increasing number of accessible study-abroad programs are becoming available for students. In England, for instance, Lancaster University actively recruits international students with disabilities to its program. Many other universities also provide fully accessible programs for foreign students.

Universities and independent exchange organizations should not wait until they have disabled applicants to reach out to students with disabilities. Programs can prepare in advance to include people with disabilities by making simple modifications. These adaptations might include building ramps, arranging for notetakers or interpreters, and linking international students with disabled peers on campus.

Some ways in which international programs can work toward accommodating students with disabilities include program modifications (such as making classrooms more accessible), building ramps, arranging for notetakers or interpreters, and linking international students with other students with disabilities on campus.

Advance planning and good communication are essential to organizing a successful experience abroad. Providing advisers with information about specific accessibility requirements well in advance is the key to finding an appropriate program. People with disabilities need to be advocates for themselves at every step in the process, as well as being creative and flexible in approaching international experiences.

WORK AND VOLUNTEER ABROAD

Work and volunteer programs are other types of international opportunities available for students with disabilities. International community service projects are a great way to volunteer in another country and participate in a wide variety of projects. They offer a wide range of opportunities and last from a few weeks to as long as one or two years.

Each individual has his or her own unique skills to contribute, and with a little creativity, many sites and activities can be adapted to suit anyone.

General volunteer opportunities range from working with homeless children in Peru to participating in environmental projects in Nepal. Exciting volunteer opportunities also exist, which are directly related to disability issues—for example, helping to build wheelchairs in Latin America or teaching sign language in Malaysia.

Many long-term service activities are also open to people with disabilities. The Peace Corps, for example, has placed a number of disabled individuals in two-year assignments throughout the world.

Work opportunities are available through organizations like the Council on International Educational Exchange (Council). Work programs often include assistance in identifying an employment location, securing work permits, and adapting to a new environment.

SURVIVAL ABROAD

People with disabilities often need to be innovative in solving problems of accessibility and communication when traveling or living abroad. It is very helpful to contact disability-related organizations in your host country well in advance. These organizations can provide information on local services such as wheelchair repair, accessible lodging, sign language interpreters, and mobility training, as well as firsthand information about conditions for people with disabilities in specific countries.

FINANCIAL AID

Financing an international experience can be a challenge for anyone. People with disabilities can take advantage of general scholarships as well as financial aid directly related to disability. Other resources include service clubs like Rotary International, as well as vocational rehabilitation departments and friends and family.

Contact the National Clearinghouse on Disability and Exchange for a list of international and disability-related scholarships and grants.

AIRLINE AND RAIL TRAVEL

Those traveling on U.S. airlines are covered by the Air Carriers Access Act, as well as the Americans with Disabilities Act. On non-U.S. carriers, check the policy with the airline and let them know about your needs in advance. Gathering a little information before you fly can make problem solving much easier. Give foreign airlines as much information as necessary on your disability well in advance.

Train travel in Europe is easier than ever for people with disabilities, but, again, be proactive about your needs. Contact local disability organizations in advance for information on how to best navigate each country's transportation system.

GO FOR IT!

Many people with disabilities have found that international programs provide tremendously enriching experiences. Those willing to be assertive about finding an accessible program will discover that there are many interesting options available for people with disabilities.

Where in the World? Nontraditional Destinations

Karen Jenkins

Former President, Brethren Colleges Abroad

If you are interested in studying in a nontraditional location, you have nearly the whole world to choose from. You can study in Asia, Africa, Latin America, the Caribbean, the Middle East, or the nations and territories of the South Pacific. More than 80 percent of the world's population resides in these areas, with many of the countries showing striking contrasts between rich and poor and modern and traditional.

These areas also boast cultures that are among the oldest, including many that have cradled some of the great religions of the world and provided the basis for modern learning and technology. These countries reveal the global interconnectedness of problems once thought to be national—from the environment, population growth, and immigration to human rights and the use of force and weapons of warfare.

Perhaps you think that the most difficult part of a study-abroad experience in a nontraditional location is leaving the familiar, stepping into the unknown, and traveling to a remote place where every aspect of life seems different. But it is that very difference that makes study in a nontraditional location so exciting and attractive. You can examine political change in South Africa, rural health care in India, wildlife conservation in Botswana, economic development in Japan, Arabic in Egypt, agriculture in Cuba, or urban planning in Mexico City. If you know some French, why not study it in Morocco? If you are interested in learning about post-colonial nations, Ghana and Indonesia are living laboratories. What better place than Jordan to study early Christianity, Islam, or Judaism? The art collection at your college or university may be excellent, but imagine viewing Chinese art in its intended lodgings—the imperial palace in Beijing.

Your desire to study in a nontraditional location may require additional preparatory work, from finding a suitable program to predeparture reading.

Remember that there are fewer academic programs in nontraditional locations than in Western Europe, where the overwhelming majority of American undergraduates study abroad.

HOW CAN I FIND AN ACADEMIC PROGRAM OUTSIDE OF WESTERN EUROPE?

Over the past decade more colleges, universities, and educational exchange organizations have been offering an increasing array of programs in parts of the world beyond Europe; this guide lists many such programs. Start by visiting your campus study-abroad office for information about programs, admission requirements, and application deadlines. Seek out faculty members who specialize in your country or geographic area of interest. They are likely to have traveled in that part of the world, maintained contacts with colleagues at universities, and have information about academic programs for international students.

WHY DO I WANT TO STUDY IN THIS KIND OF PLACE?

Perhaps you are adventuresome and seek a study experience that offers independence. Or you want to test yourself by going somewhere different. Maybe you're a romantic with the desire to see Ankara, Lima, or Mbabane instead of Paris, London, or Geneva. That spirit of adventure and independence will reward you when you learn to speak Swahili in Kenya, study agricultural development in India, or visit the Buddhist temple of Borobudur in Java, Indonesia.

WILL THE PROGRAM FIT MY MAJOR?

Early planning is important when pursuing any study-abroad program, no matter what the academic discipline or geographic location. The sooner you decide you want to study abroad, the more likely you are to find a program that either fits your major or fulfills core requirements. Talk to your faculty academic adviser about what courses you can take abroad, what courses can be accepted toward graduation requirements, and

what additional expenses to anticipate. Early planning is especially important if you are a science major with limited options for the number of classes you can take away from your campus. You may be able to fulfill art, history, or language requirements in a program abroad.

DO I NEED TO SPEAK THE LANGUAGE?

If language is not a requirement for admission to a program, don't let your lack of knowledge of a specific language stop you from applying. Undoubtedly, your access to people and their culture is best facilitated by fluency in their language, which will allow you to learn about your hosts and to share in their lives and customs. Many good programs, however, will offer a language component. While you may only acquire "survival" language skills, with diligence you should be able to learn to communicate your basic needs in a short time. Your sincere attempt to learn and use the language of your chosen country will be appreciated and applauded by your hosts. You are likely to be rewarded by sincere gestures of friendship and with more opportunities to gain even greater language proficiency.

WHOM DO I TALK TO ONCE I'VE FOUND A PROGRAM?

Support for international study programs varies from campus to campus. If you are enrolled at a college or university that sends a large number of students abroad, there is likely to be a study-abroad office on campus that is staffed by advisers who will answer questions on issues such as transferring academic credit, financial aid, and

required immunizations. If your campus does not have a study-abroad office, your faculty academic adviser, department chair, and registrar should all be consulted. You will want to talk to the registrar at your school to ensure that credit you earn abroad will be accepted by your school.

Next, check with the financial services office for information about how the program will be financed, especially if you are receiving any type of financial assistance. Some colleges and universities charge full tuition and make payments to programs abroad on behalf of their students. Others expect students to be responsible for making financial arrangements once they are accepted into a program. Many institutions allow students to apply part of their financial aid to study abroad, so be sure to ask. However the finances are arranged, it is usually preferable to remain a registered student at your institution during the time you are studying abroad.

HOW DEEPLY WILL I BE INVOLVED WITH OTHER PEOPLE AND CULTURES?

It may be difficult for you to find a program that offers practical applications of your classroom work. First, you will be on a student visa, which will prohibit you from engaging in paid employment. Second, it is unlikely that you will possess the skills needed by the host country, such as animal husbandry, engineering, teaching, or auto mechanics. A well-designed study-abroad program, however, might include field trips, volunteer work projects, or language instruction, all of which will provide you with opportunities to interact with people outside of the classroom. Look for a program that is affiliated with a university in the host country. That will enable you to learn about a different educational system, take classes taught by local professors, and make friends with students. Many countries have a rich tradition of learning and higher education. Studying at a university or institute in Japan or Mali will prove to be a unique experience that will involve you with another people and culture.

WHAT MIGHT THE PROGRAM STRUCTURE BE LIKE IN A NONTRADITIONAL COUNTRY?

Programs will be different, but you should still look for a few standard elements. A knowledgeable and experienced on-site coordinator who oversees the academic program, coordinates the logistics, and negotiates the local bureaucracy can make the program run smoothly and allay concerns of your family and friends. If English is not the national language, look for a language component in the program. Acquiring even limited language ability will enable you to enjoy your experience more fully and to learn much more about the culture.

Be sure that the program has a strong academic focus. Do not be misled by descriptions that emphasize the experiential nature of the program at the expense of the academic work. The experiential aspect of any program abroad should be integrated into academic objectives. In a developing country where more hours may be spent outside of the classroom, there should be a structured academic schedule for that time.

WHAT SHOULD I DO WHEN PEOPLE SAY "YOU WANT TO GO WHERE?"

Your family and friends may be reluctant to see you enroll in a program in a nontraditional location, since you will more than likely be living in a developing nation. These are places that few Americans know anything about except through sensational and often unflattering news stories. If you are a member of an ethnic minority, going to a nontraditional location—an African American in China, a Korean American in Ecuador, a Native American in South Africa, or a Hispanic American in Russia—may seem doubly complicated.

However, none of these are insurmountable obstacles, yet all require extra planning, research, and persistence. Your determination will be rewarded when you embark on your adventure better prepared for an encounter with a different culture, when your college or university opens its doors to a different type of program, and when your family and friends help you engage in preparations and become more knowledgeable about the place you will be living. Furthermore, when you seek your first professional position after completing your education, the time you spent in a nontraditional location will prove to be an asset. Employers are always looking for young people who are adaptable but focused, and a successful experience abroad, especially in a place not many other students have been, is evidence of that.

Most important, you will spend part of your college years participating in a community that few Americans visit. You will attach names and faces to the news stories you've heard and will be able to decide for yourself how accurate they are. You will learn that many of the world's problems can be solved by knowledgeable citizens willing to actively engage their friends and neighbors in the search for creative solutions, no matter where they live.

If you have chosen your program for sound academic reasons, your family is likely to be more accepting. They should also be reassured if the program is well organized and supervised. Their surprise at your chosen location is probably because of one-sided information and scanty knowledge about your chosen country. If you are from a racial minority in the United States, your family may believe you will be subjected to discrimination while abroad. Or perhaps you are from a family of recent immigrants who do not understand why you would want to go to a place they left because of conflict or harsh economic conditions.

Use your family's skepticism as an opportunity not only to prepare for your departure but also to help inform and educate them about another part of the world and its changing conditions. Involve them by sharing program literature, maps, encyclopedia articles, newspaper stories, novels, and tourist information. Your family and friends will appreciate knowing that you are preparing seriously for your journey and will enjoy learning about the people and culture of your destination.

If you have chosen a place that is not often in the news, your task may be easier than if you'd

decided to go somewhere that has received a lot of negative attention. Start by asking your family what they know about the country. If all their knowledge is from provocative and disturbing news reports, try to provide information to help them understand that the majority of people in the country work hard and are proud of their culture and national achievements. Take the concerns of your family and friends seriously, and work in an informed and determined way to overcome them.

HOW DO I GET READY TO GO? ARE THERE ANY SPECIAL HEALTH ISSUES TO CONSIDER ONCE I'M THERE?

While you are obtaining your passport and any required visas, you should also be preparing for different food, customs, climate, and time zones to help you stay safe and healthy. Check with your physician about required immunizations such as yellow fever and recommendations for

medication if you are traveling in an area where, for instance, malaria is prevalent. If you live near a large city or university, you may find a travel clinic staffed by physicians and health-care workers who specialize in tropical medicine. You can find valuable information on the Web site of the Centers for Disease Control and Prevention (CDC) at www.cdc.gov. There is a link to "Travelers' Health" which gives up-to-date information and advice on health conditions as well as immunizations and medications for specific countries.

Staying safe and healthy, even in a developing country, is not impossible. Prepare, remain alert, and follow the advice of friends who live there or who have traveled there.

Perhaps the biggest danger to your health and safety is a motor vehicle accident. Traffic patterns and driving habits are different all over the world, and you must be aware of them. Don't rent a motor scooter in a city where thousands are on the street if you are not an experienced driver and prepared to observe the country's driving rules. The enforcement of motor vehicle standards may be lax and, in some places, it is not uncommon for operators to overcrowd buses. It is important that you remain alert when you are walking and when choosing your mode of transportation.

Always try to get plenty of rest and, if you drink alcohol, do not drive! Remember, too, that alcohol can affect your mental control even on foot. Be careful, or you'll make the common mistake of looking in the wrong direction when crossing a street in a country where the traffic flows in the opposite direction.

Much is often made of what not to eat or drink in a tropical country. You will miss an important aspect of your experience if you are afraid to consume the food; you'll also spend needless time looking for something familiar. Some of the best food in the world is outside the United States—recently picked, harvested with little chemical preservatives, and prepared fresh from the market.

It is important that you consume adequate liquids to remain healthy. Get in the habit of looking around and observe what others are drinking. Throughout Indonesia, for instance, where in some places the water supply is undrinkable, Indonesians drink bottled water, which is cheap and easily obtainable. Hotels and restaurants routinely boil water, wash their vegetables in it, and offer bottled water. Indonesians at home do likewise. If you are unsure about the food or water supply, find local students and friends and do as they do. Your friends and their families will be just as concerned about their health as you are about yours.

WHAT IF THERE IS A CRISIS IN THE COUNTRY WHERE I'M TRAVELING?

Remember that your family may be concerned about your safety while you're away from home, especially when you are in place that seems so different and remote. This is especially true during times of heightened international tension. The possibility of war or terrorist attacks is a growing concern. Therefore, it is important that you pay close attention to the organizers of your program and read all materials they send before your departure. Upon arrival, you should receive an on-site orientation with information on how to travel, where to travel, what precautions to take, and the importance of taking responsibility for good decision-making when it comes to your personal safety.

The officials of your program and your host university will be experienced and sensitive to student concerns. They will provide accurate updates in the event of a crisis situation. They will also be familiar with local security procedures and be in close contact with the civil authorities and health professionals. Should a crisis arise or a situation deteriorate, the staff will advise you on appropriate actions to take.

You can take responsibility for your safety by being aware of your local surroundings just as you would if you were in the U.S. or on your home campus. You should keep a low profile and not call unnecessary attention to yourself. Do not carry a large backpack, an expensive camera, or computer equipment and do not wear excessive or expensive jewelry. Your behavior is just as important to keeping a low profile.

- **Avoid speaking on a cell phone in public places.** Not only is it impolite, but you will call unnecessary attention to yourself.

- **When talking in public, do not speak in a loud voice with expansive gestures.**

- **Do not espouse your political views either about the United States or your host country.** You do not want to easily distinguish yourself from local students and young people.

In the unlikely event that the U.S. government recommends an evacuation of students, the first concern of your program providers will be to ensure that arrangements are made for you and your fellow students to travel to a secure location. Every effort will be made to facilitate the completion of the academic program in cooperation with the students' home institution.

CAN I LIVE IN A PLACE THAT SEEMS SO REMOTE AND FAR FROM HOME?

Today, no place is really remote. E-mail, cell phones, satellite communication, and air transportation make it easy to communicate and travel quickly over long distances. There are familiar fast-food stores in Beijing, Rio de Janeiro, and Abidjan. Yet many parts of the world retain their distinctive character and confront visitors with what may seem like overwhelming differences in culture and customs. These differences are exactly what you are seeking!

Moving to any new place requires a period of adjustment, especially if you are faced with new food, customs, language, and climate. Be prepared for "culture shock," which can range from homesickness to extreme feelings of dislike for your new place of residence. It is normal to miss the familiar but you can overcome such feelings by reading as much as possible about your destination and talking with students, faculty members, or friends who have been there before you depart. Once you have arrived, keep in contact with family and friends back home. E-mail and inexpensive calling cards makes that easy!

Make friends with other students and their families in your new host country. The best way to learn about others is to spend time with them. Keep a journal and record your feelings and observations. Most importantly go out and experience the people and culture. You wanted to study in a nontraditional destination because it is different! That is what you sought, so let the differences hit you; soak them up, enjoy them, and learn from them!

HOW WILL I COPE IN A POOR COMMUNITY?

If you expect to observe extreme poverty for the first time in your life when abroad, then you certainly haven't been inquisitive or observant enough about the United States. Extreme poverty exists here, although its location off well-built interstate highways, in segregated inner cities, and in rural areas may make it easy to miss. Poverty in developing countries will be more apparent, as the majority of people live below the standards of the average American. Many developing countries have initiated innovative programs to deter deforestation, alleviate hunger, improve crop yields, lower the birth rate, bring health care to rural areas, increase literacy, introduce appropriate technologies, or make microbusiness loans available. Your quiet and respectful observations will be more appropriate to people working hard to overcome poverty. You might also learn some useful techniques that are adaptable to your community in the United States.

Your respectful observation should also include dressing neatly. American students often assume that jeans, T-shirts, and sandals are appropriate in poor and developing countries. They are often surprised that people abroad tend to dress very neatly, with men rarely in shorts and women rarely in short tops or sleeveless dresses. People in developing countries are very proud of their progress in literacy and education, alleviation of disease and poverty, stable governments, and rural development. So be respectful of the issues impacting the country in which you choose to study.

WHAT DO I DO WHEN IN A COUNTRY WITH A REPUTATION FOR OPPRESSION OR HUMAN RIGHTS VIOLATIONS?

You are traveling to another country to learn, and your objectives should be to just that. If you have selected a country because you want to try to change conditions or to encourage others to take action against conditions you think are objectionable, you should reconsider your choice. If after you've been in a country for a period of time you encounter social, political, environmental, or economic conditions that offend you, remember that it's not your place to express opposition or disapproval. That doesn't mean you're not entitled to your opinion—just keep it to yourself. Write down your feelings in a journal or discuss them with those in your academic program. You don't want to embarrass your hosts or create a situation that could get them into trouble by speaking inappropriately. Nor do you want to jeopardize your study program. When you return home your observations and firsthand accounts might provide the basis for an independent study project. You may decide to work for an organization with a mission to alleviate the conditions you observed, and your experience abroad could prove to be invaluable.

WILL I BE DIFFERENT WHEN I RETURN?

You will meet people who will welcome you to their countries and teach you a new definition of hospitality, friendship, and beauty. Victoria Falls between Zambia and Zimbabwe is majestic, the variety of flora and fauna in Indonesia overwhelming, the food in Thailand exquisite, the rain forests of Brazil magnificent, the blueness of the Caribbean Sea awesome, and the religious architecture of Turkey inspiring.

Whether you are different when you return to your campus and familiar surroundings after studying and living in a nontraditional destination will depend on your willingness to embrace new places, people, and customs with openness and enthusiasm.

_____

Karen Jenkins is a former president of Brethren Colleges Abroad. Brethren Colleges Abroad offers study-abroad programs around the world for undergraduate students and is committed to global education with an emphasis on studying issues of peace and justice. Ms. Jenkins has lived, worked, and traveled extensively in southern Africa; has taught graduate-level courses; and has undertaken development consultant contracts with international agencies in more than twenty developing nations.

International Internships

Charles A. Gliozzo, Ph.D.

Assistant to the Dean of International Studies and Programs at Michigan State University

A report of The American Council of Education, *Educating Americans for a World In Flux*, listed ten ground rules for internationalizing educational institutions. Ground rule number five is "to expand study-abroad and internship opportunities for all students." The Council concluded, "international internships are among the most valuable educational experience any student can receive."

WHAT IS AN INTERNATIONAL INTERNSHIP?

An international internship is an academic and organizational off-campus learning experience that maximizes the cross-cultural and professional development of students, practitioners, employers/employees, and faculty with respective institutions, government agencies, and private sector organizations. International internships cannot be underestimated. They will acquaint you with career options in your field of study, offering practical activities that supplement academic work.

An international internship allows you to test the validity of academic or career choices while making a contribution to an organization. You will obtain greater marketability in the future, and your employer will benefit in the short term with additional assistance, as well as in the long term through early identification and training of a potential future employee.

International internships offer the opportunity to learn about the role of the United States in the world. Your internship is a bridge between your education and preparation for career opportunities. Internships in other countries allow you to understand firsthand how our society is part of a larger world system encompassing economics, education, business, and politics.

If these opportunities sound inviting or if you have been considering the possibility of interning overseas, there are a lot of questions to ask yourself and many issues to consider. The information that follows will help you sort out whether an international internship is right for you and how to go about finding the right one. Don't try to go it alone! Talk to your study-abroad adviser, your teachers, and career guidance counselors who are professionally trained and can help you make the right choices and avoid many pitfalls.

BEGINNING YOUR SEARCH

As the popularity of international internships increases every year, so does competition for the limited number of openings. A careful and thorough search is important, not only to find an internship, but to identify one that will be enjoyable and challenging. If you are fairly convinced you want to pursue an internship abroad, your next step is to answer these questions:

- **What realistic expectations do you have?**

- **Is it worth your time and effort to carry out the necessary preliminary work, such as processing the application, writing cover letters, completing your resume, filling out forms, writing follow-up letters, and numerous other tasks?**

- **Are you able to afford going overseas?**

- **Does your academic institution endorse participation in an international internship program?** If it does, does your school have its own program or does it allow you to obtain an international internship with another university or organization?

- **Will you receive academic credit for the internship and how will your internship be evaluated for credit?**

- **Do you need a visa or work permit?**

- **Where are internships and how do you obtain information about them?**

- **Would your objectives be better served by pursuing an internship in the United States?**

Once you have answered these questions, make a list of your preferences and goals. Be as realistic and honest with yourself as possible, as you consider these questions:

- **What is your preferred internship location?**

- **How many hours are you willing to work?**

- **What is the exact nature of the work you are seeking?**

- **What specific working conditions would be acceptable?** Close supervision or independent work? A structured or relaxed environment? A social atmosphere or a solitary one?

- **What do you need to earn, if anything?** Salary? Stipend? Room and board? College credit?

- **Are job contacts or permanent employment priorities available?**

An international internship could be a rewarding experience, but consider both the benefits and disadvantages.

THE BENEFITS

Following are some benefits of international internships:

- **A cross-cultural exposure.** An international internship will give you a living-learning experience in another society.

- **The possibility of obtaining academic credit to satisfy graduation requirements.** Many institutions will supplement their internship programs with academic courses on the history/culture, etc., of the host country. Note, not all international internships give academic credit.

- **Develop foreign language competency.** Many international jobs require knowledge of a foreign language. Foreign language competency is gaining significance as more students seek overseas positions in the face of a restrictive U.S. job market.

- **Increase your chances for career placement in multinational and international companies, in government agencies, and in educational institutions.**

- **Establish contacts for developing future career goals.** In today's competitive job market, knowing key individuals is a plus.

- **Challenges of adapting to a variety of environments; this skill will be very useful in any international job you'll undertake in the future.**

BE AWARE OF THE DISADVANTAGES

Following are some disadvantages of international internships:

- **Restrictions that an intern may encounter in an international setting.** Linguistic and cultural barriers may limit expectations. For example, you may assume that the internship is an entry-level career position only to discover that it provides substantially less work.

- **The expense of travel, housing, and overseas administration and other fees.** Some international internships are paid, but many do not offer stipends.

- **Accommodations, which may be difficult to secure or are substandard.**

FINDING THE RIGHT INTERNSHIP

Once you know what you want from your internship, it is important to find the right internship. Examine your personal job-related strengths and weaknesses. Be sure to analyze your past academic and work performances. If you want to emphasize your strong points to a prospective internship sponsor, you have to know what they are. Are your skills analytical, verbal, or quantitative? Are you a self-starter with initiative? Are you qualified to do a research project requiring organization and attention to detail? Are you better working on a group project, where communication skills are essential?

This guide lists many study-abroad programs that offer internships. Once you have narrowed your search to a particular geographic region, you can use the **Field of Study** index to identify programs that interest you. When you develop your "short list" of possibilities, you can begin to contact institutions and organizations to request more information. Learn about the structure of the program and whether the program is well organized.

An internship can consist of one specific job or many. In any case, you should closely examine the internship requirements. You must be prepared to make whatever adjustments are necessary to comply with the policies, regulations, and standards of the host organization and country. What may seem like the perfect internship may end up being a job filling out forms in triplicate. To avoid this problem, your duties should be decided in advance. A good way to learn about the quality of the internship is to contact previous

You may be required to keep a journal or write an evaluative paper. If an academic project is required, it will be evaluated by the faculty supervisor. Your intern coordinator should contact the host employer during your internship to assess your progress. A formal evaluation should be completed by the employer, and debriefing meetings should be held with all parties involved in your internship.

THE BOTTOM LINE . . .

You should not jump haphazardly into an internship, whether it's in the United States or abroad. Interns should be motivated and self-directed to complete a series of assignments in preparing for an internship. Interns must have the qualifications required by the host organization, language competency, and an understanding of the culture. You should work closely with the intern coordinator to determine internship goals and to identify organizations. This process requires serious thought and commitment.

Remember, you will be investing your time and energy—often with no financial compensation—so it pays to do some research. Your search for the best internship should follow the basic approaches of looking for a full-time job. College career placement and overseas study offices are invaluable resources in assisting you.

interns. The organization to which you are applying, in most cases, will give you the names of former interns if you request them.

EVALUATION

The evaluation process is important in any internship. Content and quality must be monitored closely by the sponsoring organization to preserve the integrity of the program and ensure maximum learning experience.

Charles A. Gliozzo is a Professor and Assistant to the Dean of International Studies and Programs at Michigan State University and Director Emeritus of the Office of Overseas Study.

Volunteering Abroad

Gina Chase

Associate Dean of International Programs, Endicott College, and Former Director of International Voluntary Service, Council on International Educational Exchange

If you're looking for a way to learn by doing, to expand your awareness of another population and culture while making a worthwhile contribution, then volunteering abroad may be for you. There's a lot to gain. By helping out in another country, you'll get to learn firsthand about local issues, lifestyles, and politics. You'll get to develop the kind of cross-cultural communication and language skills many international businesses now seek. You'll get practical experience working with others and accomplishing goals through teamwork. And, most important, you'll get the opportunity to contribute and play a role in something that has meaning and importance.

How can you help? Plant trees to slow erosion in South America. Dig for archaeological treasures in the Middle East. Help a medical team distribute food and medicine in Africa. Build a school, community center, or irrigation system in Asia. Whatever your interest, chances are there's a community service project somewhere in the world that needs your time, energy, and commitment.

FINDING THE RIGHT PROGRAM

The study-abroad office on your campus is a good place to start. Even if staff members don't have information on volunteer programs, they can help you prepare for life in another country. As you do your research, keep in mind that many volunteer activities are also called unpaid internships. The career services office may be helpful in finding opportunities related to your area of study.

Ask around. Professors and faculty advisers can help you evaluate programs, as well as your own motivation and expectations. Here are some questions to help you choose a program that's right for you:

- **Who is the sponsoring organization and how long has it run the program?**

THE RIGHT STUFF?

Volunteering abroad isn't for everyone. Flexibility and the ability to take initiative and work independently are important traits in a volunteer, as is the willingness to work with others with different views.

International projects present special challenges. If you're considering this type of work, you'll need to have realistic expectations of what you can accomplish and what you will get in return. To give you a better idea about the stops and starts you'll likely encounter, imagine that you have gone to Ghana to help build a water irrigation system in a rural village. There aren't enough shovels for all the volunteers, so you take turns digging and shoveling. The project progresses rapidly, but to complete the job, the team will need pipes. Halfway through your stay, you find out that the needed pipes will not arrive in time for you to see the project to its end. You spend the rest of your time playing games with the village children and helping the women carry water in buckets from the nearest stream.

In this scenario, you may not have completed the irrigation system, but you did demonstrate the ability to adapt to a difficult situation. You got to join in the daily lives of people very different from yourself. Although you didn't accomplish the stated goal of building an irrigation system, the village is that much closer to having a completed solution and you came away with an experience that will stay with you forever.

- **With whom and for whom will you be working?**

- **What kind of supervision will be provided?** This varies widely from program to program, and it's important to be clear about the resources you can depend on while out of the country.

- **What are the living arrangements?** On most projects, you can't expect luxury, but you'll want to be prepared. Are room and board provided, included in the program fee, or something you'll have to provide for yourself when you get there? Again, what you must cover varies greatly from program to program.

- **Is health insurance provided or must you provide your own?** Either way is acceptable, but you must be sure you're covered.

- **What do former participants say about the program?** Contacting former participants is probably the best way to get a feel for the program, and most organizations are willing to provide a list to you.

- **Will you be able to get academic credit for your participation?** On some programs the academic credit is built in. If it's not, you might still want to check with your advisers on campus to see if you can work out an independent study credit.

- **What is the total cost to you for participating in the program?** Before signing up, find out about airfare and ground transportation costs, recommended pocket money, etc. It's important to get a sense of all the resources you will need for the experience.

Getting There and Getting Around on a Budget

Rob Becker

Vice President of Sales and Marketing, Travel CUTS

The opportunity to travel, experience different cultures, and meet locals and like-minded travelers is a unique experience that will stay with you forever. But before you head out on your study-abroad adventure, there are a number of practical things you'll need to know in order to take full advantage of your travel opportunities.

Research your airfare options and make sure you have a *flexible, round-trip airline ticket*. Even students with the most detailed, laid-out plans can change their minds once they're abroad. Being a student also allows you to benefit from special airfares that are *only for students*. Most of these student airfares have a validity of up to one year and allow you to make a date change to your return flight for a nominal fee. Other airfares will likely only allow for a three- to six-month maximum stay, and if a date change to your return is allowed it will be expensive. Travel CUTS, STA Travel, and Student Universe all offer student airfare options. Given the unique nature of your plans, it is recommended that you call or stop in rather than purchase your tickets online.

In addition to a long-stay and flexible return date, these special student fares come with some added features. Many allow for what is termed an "open jaw" in the travel industry. In laymen's terms this means you can fly into one city and home from another. For example, you may plan on studying in Paris and then traveling south to Greece upon completion of your course, before heading back home to the United States. Purchasing a ticket for a flight to Paris and home from Athens may only be about $50 more than a ticket to Paris and back, and it will save you the hassle of having to get back to Paris for your flight home and save you the cost of getting back to Paris (with either a separate air ticket, or additional days on a rail pass). In addition to this open jaw feature, many student airfares also allow for free or cheap stopovers en route. For example, a student airfare through British Airways into Paris and home from Athens may also allow you to stopover

WHAT IF YOU LOSE YOUR AIRLINE TICKETS?

Fortunately, most tickets are now e-tickets, so you may not be carrying a physical ticket. However, some special student airfares are still printed on paper ticket stock. If you happen to have a paper ticket and lose it, have a family member back in the United States follow up with the agency through which you've purchased it for instructions on obtaining a replacement. Generally speaking, expect to pay about $100 in fees, plus the cost of a replacement ticket, and then wait for six months to receive a refund for the ticket you lost.

As an ISIC (International Student Identity Card) holder, you receive a free feature with your card that allows you to scan and store copies of your important travel documents, such as passport and airline tickets. You can retrieve them online from anywhere in the world. This will help facilitate the replacement process. For more information, go to www.travelcuts.com/isiconnect and click on "Travel Safe."

- **Research options for getting around in the country(ies) you will be visiting in advance.** With fluctuating currencies and a need for budget planning, it is often much cheaper and more convenient to obtain your rail and/or bus options in advance. Many rail passes, such as BritRail and Eurail, are only valid for sale outside of Europe and are less expensive. Ask your travel adviser for more information.

- **Sleep cheap.** Generally speaking, youth hostels are the accommodation of choice for most budget student travelers. It is recommended that you book your accommodation for at least the first night after your arrival to allow you to get settled in. After that, you can wing it as you go with your Youth Hostel Membership or by simply booking online. All student travel companies now have budget accommodation available for you to prebook online. You can do so either before you leave or, once you are in your destination, as you go.

- **Have ISIC (International Student Identity Card) in hand.** Most of the special student airfares referenced here require that you have the ISIC card. In addition to the special airfare, the card also will provide you with a wide variety of local discounts. Many college and university campuses issue the cards, and you can also purchase it from Travel CUTS by faxing, mailing, or e-mailing your application. It can be downloaded at www.travelcuts.com/usa.

- **Check current baggage restrictions.** As airlines eliminate food service and enhancements in an effort to control costs, all aspects of their operating costs are reviewed, including luggage. The standard allotment to/from the United States is two checked pieces with a maximum dimension of 63 combined inches. The weight restriction varies however, and exceeding it will cost you. Pack smart and check out your

in London on the way home. Note again however, that you will likely not be able to book something like this online and as such, it is recommended that you call. Don't bother calling the airlines directly either; these are special fares that are unique to student travel companies. Travel CUTS also has partner organizations that can assist you abroad.

You may be tempted to simply book a one-way flight to your destination and deal with the flight back home locally when you're ready. Don't! Due to many new security regulations, countries often will not allow you entry without a return ticket home, or proof of onward travel out of their country. In fact, since it is the airline's responsibility to ensure that you meet the requirements of your point-of-entry country, the airline might simply deny you a seat on the plane. Avoid the potential hassle.

maximum allowance in advance. If necessary have lesser-needed items shipped to you from home.

- **Leave copies of important travel documents with family or friends.** In addition to Travel Safe (previously referenced), it is always a good idea for your family or friends back home to have a copy of all important travel documents, especially your passport. You may also want to carry a copy with you, separate from the real thing.

- **Credit cards, ATM cards, and traveler's checks are all safer than cash.** It's always a bit of debate as to which of these options works out to be most favorable. Here are some guidelines for you to consider. Credit cards debited in a foreign currency are billed in the United States at fluctuating rates of exchange. The same holds true for service fees and exchange rates at ATMs. Traveler's checks generally provide a better rate of exchange than cash at a currency exchange kiosk but may prove to be cumbersome to use on a regular basis. The growing trend is to prepurchase a small amount of the local currency in advance (at the airport before you leave) to have for use upon arrival. Use your ATM card as you go along and have a credit card for emergencies. You may also want to have a small amount of large-denomination traveler's checks, should you end up making a larger-than-normal purchase, such as an irresistible leather jacket from Italy.

Rob Becker, whose career includes more than twenty years in the student travel business, has extensive travel experience in Asia, Australia, Europe, and the Americas. He is currently Vice President of Sales and Marketing at Travel CUTS (www.travelcuts.com), a North American student travel company.

Staying Healthy Abroad

Joan Elias Gore

Former Director of Institutional Relations at Denmark's International Study Program

Study abroad is an adventure of the mind and spirit. It is also an adventure of and for the body. Traveling overseas is an exhilarating experience—it should be a healthy one, too.

In most regions there are no special health procedures about which you should be concerned. Health-care systems and facilities in many overseas locations are quite similar to what we have in the United States. In other regions, however, there are differences and specifically recommended health procedures that you should know about.

The following will acquaint you with health matters related to the different phases of your study abroad experience. Although help is available both in the United States and abroad, you must take an active and responsible role in planning for and maintaining a healthful approach to your overseas experience.

HEALTH AND YOUR STUDY-ABROAD APPLICATION

Application forms will ask you about your current health status. They will probably ask for a doctor's recommendation. Be honest in your application forms and with your doctor. The information being sought will determine how best to provide you with service and support in your overseas program.

Housing forms can also be important for health. Remember to include information about any allergies, physical challenges, or other health issues that might affect where you can live comfortably.

Students should ask program operators about any health or safety concerns they may have.

PREDEPARTURE HEALTH CHECKLIST

Once you've been accepted into a program, you will need to take appropriate health measures as dictated by your overseas location. Although many countries

require no special procedures, you should find out if any apply in the area(s) in which you will be traveling and studying. L. Robert Kohls' *Survival Kit for Overseas Living: For Americans Planning to Live and Work Abroad* (Nicholas Brealey Publishing/Intercultural Press, 2001) includes an excellent checklist that discusses many of the items that follow.

- **Predeparture medical appointments.** Make all medical appointments well in advance of your travel date. Begin at least three months ahead to allow for completion of immunizations, for gamma globulin shots (a preventive against hepatitis A), and for assessments of any special medical problems you may have. You can consult your doctor, your public health service office, or your school's international health advisory service to find out what immunizations you'll need for the areas to which you're traveling. Also ask about the advisability of hepatitis B protection. Note that children and pregnant women often receive different recommendations than the rest of the population.

- **Health records.** Update your health records, including eyeglass and contact lens prescriptions and prescriptions for any medications you routinely take. Have prescriptions written using generic names to facilitate getting them filled overseas, where U.S. brand names might not be available. If relevant to your medical condition, EKGs and X-rays should also be included in these updated records. A doctor's statement about your prescriptions and how they are to be used,

along with statements about any special medical conditions you have, should also be included. Dental records should be included if special procedures or medications are indicated for you. You should carry all of these records in a safe place during travel.

- **Routine check-ups.** Prior to departure, complete all routine medical examinations such as gynecological and dental checkups that might fall within your time abroad.

- **Prescription drugs.** Take extra prescription drugs. Pack them in different places, but avoid putting them in luggage that might get misplaced or stolen. It's best to put them in carry-on luggage.

- **Instruments for self-administered medication.** Take instruments necessary for self-administration of medications. Diabetic persons should carry a supply of disposable syringes and needles to help protect against HIV infection and other communicable diseases in areas where medical personnel do not use disposable materials. If you plan to study in an area where AIDS is endemic, ask about the advisability of carrying a supply of needles and syringes (even if you do not need them for routine medication) in the event of an accident or illness that requires injections.

- **Extra appliances.** Take extra glasses or contact lenses and extra dental appliances if you use them.

- **Medical kit.** Take a medical kit containing such items as bandages, adhesive tape, gauze, sterile cleansers, antibacterial ointment and antiseptic cream, sunburn ointment, aspirin or other painkillers, and anti-diarrheal medicine. Depending on the region, take water purification tablets, antihistamines for allergy relief, salt tablets, skin moisturizers, and insect repellants. Check with your doctor or health service about the best insect repellant to take for the region.

HEALTH ADVISORIES

If you have special medical needs or if you are going to an area where there may be special medical requirements, it is important to seek authoritative advice. Your family physician, student health service, public health service, and school may have specializations in geographic medicine or may operate travel clinics. Contact one of these offices and ask which vaccinations are indicated—both the recommended and the required—prior to your departure. In addition, ask your doctor to help you determine if any special conditions apply to your travel overseas because of any particular health needs.

- **Regional problems.** Are there particular health problems in the region to which you're going? You can phone the U.S. State Department's Overseas Citizens Services at 202-647-5225 between 8 a.m. and 5 p.m. Eastern Standard Time Monday–Saturday and at 202-647-4000 after hours for information on current health conditions worldwide. The U.S. Department of Health and Human Services Centers for Disease Control publishes *Health Information for International Travel* every other year with updates on vaccinations and other health issues. For a fee, the information can be ordered by calling toll-free 877-252-1200. You can also find much of this information online by visiting the Web site for the Centers for Disease Control at www.cdc.gov.

- **Medical insurance.** Check with your insurance company to determine whether your insurance policy covers you when you are outside the United States. Medical insurance policies do not always provide this coverage. If you are going overseas through a U.S.-operated study-abroad program, check with the program to determine what health and accident coverage is provided.

  The International Student Identity Card provides accident and sickness insurance for travel outside the United States, as well as discounts on transportation and housing accommodations. This insurance is in effect for overseas travel from the time of purchase until the expiration date. The card includes a toll-free emergency number as well as other information. You may obtain this card by contacting the Council on International Educational Exchange. You may be able to obtain the card at your school or at any Council Travel office in the United States.

REGIONAL HEALTH ISSUES

In areas of the world where there are special health issues, you need to be informed in advance about what to expect. The following list should help you anticipate these issues and prepare you to deal with them.

- **Medical requirements for admission to the country.** Find out if any exist. Many countries have very strict requirements, and you may experience serious delays if you have not met them.

- **Regional diseases.** Ask about the nature, prevention, and treatment of the region's specific illnesses. You will find that malaria and diarrhea are the two most prevalent diseases afflicting travelers, particularly in developing regions. You should take an antidiarrheal medication with you on your travels. Ask your physician about which one is appropriate for you. If you are going to an area where malaria is prevalent, you may be advised to begin a program of antimalarial medication, which begins before you leave the United States and continues for a short period after you return.

- **Regions where AIDS is prevalent.** Know how to handle injections, emergencies, and blood transfusions in regions affected by AIDS.

- **Diet and eating patterns.** Inquire about local diet and eating patterns, including the need for and availability of nutritional supplements.

- **Laws about medications.** Find out about laws regulating the import and possession of medications, hypodermic needles and syringes, and condoms and other contraceptives.

- **Recommended medical kit items.** Research any recommended medications and materials that you should take along in a medical kit.

- **Health-care delivery systems.** Find out about the health-care delivery in the region, especially if it differs from that in the United States. Ask how patients are likely to be treated, what kinds of facilities will be found, how payments for services are handled, and what your legal right will be to obtain services in the country.

- **Jet lag.** Ask your physician about ways you can anticipate and possibly reduce the effects of jet lag. Some precautions are dietary; no alcohol en route but drinking plenty of other fluids is a good example.

All the above information should be available from the advisory service where you are inquiring about predeparture immunizations. Your study-abroad program director should also be able to provide you with answers to these questions.

HEALTH QUESTIONS ON-SITE

Taking the following basic health precautions once you arrive in the country you're traveling to will complete your efforts to have a healthy and happy experience overseas.

- **How to get medical help.** Learn how to find a doctor overseas. If you are with a study-abroad program, your director should be able to tell you where to find a reliable doctor. There may be a specific doctor serving your group. Acquaint yourself with emergency phone numbers (some countries have systems similar to 911 in the United States), special medical services for which you may be eligible in the country, and information about organizations that can provide you with assistance for special medical needs.

Prior to your arrival, you should let program directors know about any special requirements you might have so that you can be accommodated upon arrival. If you find yourself traveling alone in a developing area, you might contact a Western-style hotel and ask for the doctor to whom guests are referred. You might also go to a university hospital or contact a U.S. Consulate office for a list of doctors. The International Association for Medical Assistance to Travelers (IAMAT) provides a list of English-speaking doctors all over the world. There is no fee, but donations to this nonprofit organization are welcomed.

- **Jet lag and culture shock.** As surprising as it may seem, jet lag and culture shock are real health issues. Traveling through time zones and traveling for long periods of time, facing new values, habits, and methods of daily life—all this can leave travelers impatient, bewildered, and depressed. Your study-abroad program director should provide you with information about how to function in your new culture—how to make phone calls, how to make travel arrangements within the country, how to receive basic services, and how to get information and assistance.

Armed with all this information, you may still find yourself alternately exhilarated and exasperated, thrilled at the experiences the new culture offers you and frustrated with the culture's differences from your own. In the first few weeks of your experience, you will likely experience these ups and downs. The feelings you experience are natural. If you are angry, impatient, homesick, or depressed your first few days, remind yourself that these things will pass once you have rested and are eating normally. If homesickness or depression persists, however, look upon them as the medical problems that they indeed may be and seek professional assistance from counselors or doctors.

- **Diet.** Food overseas may be quite different from what you are used to in the United States. They may be "healthier" in some instances (more vegetables and fruits) or "less healthy" in others (more fried foods than you may usually eat), but most often they will just be different from what you are used to—eel soup, for example! Make sure that you take special dietary needs into account, if you have any, and make arrangements in advance with your program director so that your special needs will be met.

  Follow recommended precautions if there are any. For example, in some areas you will be told to avoid eating foods at public stands on the street or to avoid eating uncooked or unwashed foods. Listen closely to precautions given in the health advisories you gather before departure and on-site in your region from program directors.

- **Exercise.** Exercise is important for both physical and mental health. You will probably find yourself walking more while overseas than in America, partly because you may not be driving a car, but also because student housing overseas is often not as close to class meeting places as it is in the United States. Find out in advance from program directors about safe routes to class, and follow the recommendations. Try to exercise. It is an excellent counterbalance to dietary change and to the emotional ups and downs associated with culture shock.

- **Substance abuse problems.** One of the most typical health problems students can experience overseas is alcohol abuse. Alcohol may be more readily available overseas; laws regarding minimum age are more lenient, and traditions concerning alcohol consumption as a part of everyday social life are different from those in the United States. Students often find themselves with accustomed rules gone and new rules unknown. The damage from alcohol abuse to the body can be considerable but moreover, legal implications can be quite severe in some countries. Drunk driving laws, for example, may be far more severe abroad than they are in the United States.

  The same precautions apply to drug use. Not only is drug abuse damaging to the body but it can also have legal consequences that will affect you as a student visiting another country. Some countries provide very stiff penalties for drug use; these penalties are not any less severe simply because the offender is a student.

- **Emotional problems.** If you are experiencing emotional problems in the United States, you will find that overseas travel and study will not do away with your condition. *Do not* plan to go abroad to "get away from it all"! Rarely does genuine emotional illness lessen overseas, where culture shock and different dietary and exercise patterns exist. Indeed, study overseas may exacerbate a condition. It is not unusual for people at some time in their lives to need professional counseling. If you find yourself experiencing emotional stress while overseas, take advantage of counseling and support systems. Organizations such as Alcoholics Anonymous exist worldwide, as do other groups with various emotional and development goals. Your program director should be able to help you locate such groups and give you information about them.

- **Sexually transmitted diseases and AIDS.** Diseases such as gonorrhea, herpes, and syphilis continue to pose health threats for travelers in virtually all countries in the world. HIV, the virus responsible for AIDS, can be transmitted sexually and presents grave health risks everywhere. HIV is also transmitted by poor medical practices, such as the use of unsterilized needles for vaccinations, allergy shots, medications, and blood transfusions and by use of contaminated blood in transfusions. Take the same precautions you would in the United States to avoid exposure to sexually transmitted diseases. Follow health advisories, especially in areas where AIDS is endemic. If you feel it is appropriate, take latex condoms with you overseas, as those available abroad may be inferior or offer poor protection. If you become pregnant while overseas, consult a physician immediately.

- **Accidents.** Accidents can be a matter of concern for travelers, who should take special precautions overseas. To help avoid them you should, of course, follow traffic rules and use seat belts whenever possible. Make sure the equipment you use (bicycles, mopeds, motorcycles, or cars) is operationally safe. Inquire about driving regulations, and make sure you can legally drive in the country. Study symbols and signs so that you can drive safely. Be very cautious while swimming, especially in large bodies of water. Find out about tides and currents before you jump in. Electrical appliances overseas may operate differently than those in the United States. Be aware of the different voltages in other countries, and make sure the equipment you use is suited to the local voltage.

- **International medical differences.** Health-care delivery in many countries is different from what you'll find in the United States. Try to get information about health-care delivery in the country in which you'll be studying. Keep in mind that value differences can play a part in medical practice abroad; in some countries patients are expected simply to follow the doctor's advice and never to question what they are told, while in other countries patients are invited to ask questions.

- The hotline number on your student ID can help you get information on services overseas, as can emergency numbers you obtain from your own insurance program. You may also be able to call your physician in the United States to get advice.

BEFORE YOU LEAVE THE U.S.

The U.S. State Department has a Web site that monitors travel, health, and crime and security issues and reports on unusual immigration practices, unusual currency and entry regulations, drug possession and use penalties, and terrorist activity for every country in the world. It is a good idea to check this site before you leave so that you'll know what to expect when you arrive (or whether or not you should go at all). Visit www.state.gov for more information.

RE-ENTRY ISSUES

Many students returning from overseas study fail to consider jet lag and the culture shock associated with returning to the United States to be potential health issues and are surprised to find themselves drained emotionally and enervated physically shortly after they return. You need to adjust to your own native culture, just as you did to the foreign. Your body will need to adjust to the time difference, too. Take time to relax and absorb all the changes.

Returning home may result in other emotional stresses, too. You may find that problems you left behind when you went overseas have not been resolved. You may find it a little hard to fit back into a social group that has gone on without you for some time. You may find that friends have changed. The bad feelings associated with these things are usually temporary. But if you continue to feel stress because of them, you should seek professional counseling.

THE BOTTOM LINE . . .

Your health is partly an issue of where you are and, in many regions of the world, health issues are no different than those in the United States. But your health is equally an issue of your own responsibility. Take reasonable precautions before you go, seek advice from authoritative sources about special health needs you might face, concern yourself with how to care for yourself, and take care of yourself when you return home. These things will all add up to a healthy experience in most parts of the world.

Joan Elias Gore is the former Director of Institutional Relations at Denmark's International Study Program. Over the span of her career, she has worked with agencies that have developed and managed programs worldwide, functioned as resident director for overseas programs, and worked as a study-abroad adviser and administrator within the university setting.

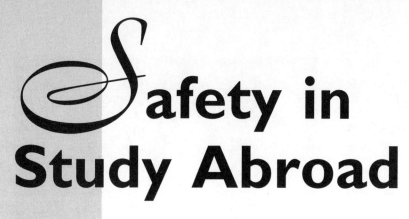

Safety in Study Abroad

William L. Gertz

President and CEO, American Institute for Foreign Study

Every year, hundreds of thousands of U.S. citizens travel abroad for business, pleasure, or study. For most people, travel abroad is a positive, rewarding, and educational experience. For the few who experience safety-related problems, a lack of planning and general awareness are often contributing factors. Whether you are an experienced traveler or traveling abroad for the first time you should pay special attention to your personal safety and security. This will make your study-abroad experience satisfying and rewarding. Don't lose any sleep over sensational headlines. You probably face as much danger on your home campus as in any major westernized city in the world. The real danger when traveling abroad is casting off all inhibitions and ignoring normal precautions that common sense dictates no matter where you are.

Cautious students may say to themselves, "I'm staying home!" However, the reality is that the risks of studying abroad are small compared to the benefits of the overseas experience. If you prepare adequately for your study-abroad experience, you will greatly minimize the risks associated with foreign travel. At the very least, your research on safety should include the following:

- **General country conditions**. Learn about the place where you plan to study. The U.S. State Department issues periodic Travel Warnings, which may recommend that Americans defer travel to a particular country. Public Announcements are a means to disseminate information about terrorist threats and other significant risks to the security of American travelers. Check all-news channels, such as CNN, frequently to keep abreast of international events.

- **Local laws and customs**. Although you are an American citizen, you are subject to the laws of the country in which you are studying. This cannot be stressed enough. What you consider to be your basic rights is an American concept that does not necessarily apply abroad. Don't assume that what is acceptable in the U.S. is acceptable abroad.

- **The study-abroad program**. As you search through this book for a study-abroad program, ask yourself these questions:

1. What kind of track record does the program have?

2. Is there information available on health and safety issues?

3. Are the medical facilities acceptable and what currency will they accept?

4. Is your medical insurance valid?

5. Are local excursions well planned and are third-party providers, such as bus companies, selected with care?

6. Is there a homestay option? Have the families been carefully screened?

7. In a university residence, is security adequate and are there locks on the doors?

8. How safe is the neighborhood where you will be living?

9. What is the attitude of the local police toward visiting students?

Don't be shy! Ask these questions before you enroll in a program.

As you carefully consider the country and the local environment, there is still one more piece to the safety in study-abroad puzzle. That piece is you! How will you act in your new environment? Here is some advice given to students enrolled in programs offered by the American Institute for Foreign Study.

- **Blend in.** It is not a good idea to attract undue attention to yourself. For example, don't wear a baseball cap backwards—it says "American." Women often receive more than their fair share of unwanted attention. Dressing conservatively is the best way to play it safe from the start. Leave provocative

clothing at home. In some places, you may be harassed, pinched, or even grabbed. Observe the strategy of local women for fending off unwanted attention.

- **Exercise caution.** Always be aware of your surroundings and remain alert. Don't stumble through unknown streets alone. Would you do this in New York or Boston?

- **Drink wisely.** If you are going to drink alcohol, do so only with trusted friends and make sure one friend remains sober. Of course, never drink and drive.

- **Be aware of cultural behavior.** What may be customary in the U.S. may send the wrong signals abroad.

- **Avoid illegal drugs.** If you are caught, you are subject to local laws.

- **Watch your bags.** Don't carry or flash large sums of money, and leave your valuables at home. Never leave your wallet or purse unattended. Passports are a primary target for pickpockets.

- **Protect your passport.** The passport is the most significant identification you carry so take extra precautions, since passport theft is on the rise. Use discretion when displaying it since it can draw unwanted attention. If it is lost or stolen, report it immediately.

- **Use the "buddy" system.** Whenever possible, travel with a friend or a group. If you are out at night, walk on well-lighted, heavily traveled streets and never go out alone. Avoid high crime areas, parks, and shortcuts through alleys and side streets. Use caution as a pedestrian, especially in countries where they drive on the "other" side of the road.

- **Choose vehicles wisely.** Use only official taxis and agree on the rate before you drive off.

- **Exercise.** If you plan to exercise, do it in daylight. Be careful of local drivers who may not be used to people running along the road.

- **Avoid civil disturbances.** Avoid demonstrations, rallies, and other disputes with local citizens. Should violence break out, arrests are sometimes made indiscriminately. You don't want to be arrested or detained as an "innocent bystander."

If you feel you are in a dangerous situation, head for a hotel or restaurant and ask for help.

Additional Study-Abroad Resources

For your convenience, we have created a comprehensive list, with contact information, of organizations involved in various aspects of study abroad.

DISABILITY AND EXCHANGE

Disability Rights and Education Defense Fund (DREDF) provides information on the Americans with Disabilities Act.

> 2212 Sixth Street
> Berkeley, CA 94710
> Phone: 510-644-2555 V/TTY
> Fax: 510-841-8645
> Web site: www.dredf.org

Mobility International USA/National Clearinghouse on Disability and Exchange empowers people with disabilities around the world through international exchange and international development to achieve their human rights.

> 132 E. Broadway, Suite 343
> Eugene, OR 97401
> Phone: 541-343-1284 V/TTY
> Fax: 541-343-6812
> Web site: www.miusa.org

Service Civil International (SCI) provides information on volunteer and work camp opportunities.

> 5505 Walnut Level Road
> Crozet, VA 22932
> Phone: 434-823-9003
> Fax: 206-350-6585
> Web site: www.sci-ivs.org

Society for Accessible Travel & Hospitality (SATH) provides travel and accessibility information for people with disabilities.

> 347 Fifth Avenue, Suite 610
> New York, NY 10016
> Phone: 212-447-7284
> Fax: 212-725-8253
> Web site: www.sath.org

University of New Orleans Training, Resource, and Assistive-Technology Center provides quality services to persons with disabilities, rehabilitation professionals, educators, and employers.

> P.O. Box 1051
> Lakefront Campus
> New Orleans, LA 70148
> Phone: 504-280-5700
> Fax: 504-280-5707
> Web site: www.uno.edu/trac

HEALTH AND SAFETY

Association for Safe International Road Travel (road travel reports for 150 countries) promotes road travel safety through education and advocacy and provides travelers with road safety information, enabling them to make informed travel choices.

> 11769 Gainsborough Road
> Potomac, MD 20854
> Phone: 301-983-5252
> Fax: 301-983-3663
> Web site: www.asirt.org

Centers for Disease Control and Prevention (travel health advisories) provides warnings about potential health risks in foreign countries.

> 1600 Clifton Road, NE
> Atlanta, GA 30333
> Phone: 404-639-3311
> Web site: www.cdc.gov/travel

Cultural Insurance Services International offers 24-hour telephone help with medical, legal, financial, language, and other travel-related problems. It also offers group and individual insurance plans for study abroad, including medical, accident, accidental death, baggage, etc.

> River Plaza
> 9 West Broad Street
> Stamford, CT 06902-3788
> Phone: 800-303-8120
> Fax: 203-399-5596
> Web site: www.culturalinsurance.com

CultureGrams™ is a widely used cultural reference product in the education, government, and nonprofit arenas.

> Proquest Information and Learning
>   Company
> 300 North Zeeb Road
> P.O. Box 1346
> Ann Arbor, MI 48106-1346
> Phone: 800-528-6279
> Fax: 800-864-0019
> Web site: www.culturegrams.com

International Association for Medical Assistance to Travelers (IAMAT) advises travelers about health risks, the geographical distribution of diseases worldwide, and immunization requirements for all countries.

> 1623 Military Road #279
> Niagara Falls, NY 14304-1745
> Phone: 716-754-4833
> Web site: www.iamat.org

NAFSA: Association of International Educators promotes the exchange of students and scholars to and from the United States.

> 1307 New York Avenue, NW, 8th Floor
> Washington, D.C. 20005
> Phone: 202-737-3699
> Fax: 202-737-3657
> Web site: www.nafsa.org

U.S. State Department (for advisories) issues travel warnings when the State Department recommends that Americans avoid a certain country.

> 2201 C Street, NW
> Washington, D.C. 20520
> Phone: 202-647-4000
>   800-647-5225 (Hotline for American Travelers)
> Web site: www.travel.state.gov/travel

INTERNATIONAL VOLUNTEER AND STUDY ABROAD ORGANIZATIONS

American Friends Service Committee carries out service, development, social justice, and peace programs throughout the world.

> 1501 Cherry Street
> Philadelphia, PA 19102
> Phone: 215-241-7000
> Fax: 215-567-7275
> Web site: www.afsc.org

Amigos de las Americas creates opportunities for young people to excel in leadership roles promoting public health, education, and community development.

> 5618 Star Lane
> Houston, TX 77057
> Phone: 800-231-7796
> Fax: 713-782-9267
> Web site: www.amigoslink.org

Community Service Volunteers works to reconnect people to their community through volunteering and training.

> 237 Pentonville Road
> London N1 9NJ
> United Kingdom
> Web site: www.csv.org.uk

Council on International Educational Exchange offers exchange, volunteer, and work opportunities throughout the world.

> 7 Custom House Street, Third Floor
> Portland, ME 04101
> Phone: 800-40-STUDY
> Fax: 207-553-7699
> Web site: www.ciee.org

Earthwatch engages people worldwide in scientific field research and education to promote the understanding and action necessary for a sustainable environment.

> 3 Clock Tower Place, Suite 100
> Box 75
> Maynard, MA 01754
> Phone: 800-776-0188
> Fax: 978-461-2332
> Web site: www.earthwatch.org

Foreign Policy Association provides independent publications, programs, and forums to increase public awareness of, and foster popular participation in, matters relating to those policy issues.

> 470 Park Avenue, North
> New York, NY 10016-6819
> Phone: 212-481-8100
> Web site: www.fpa.org

Global Volunteers provides short-term service opportunities on community development programs in host communities abroad.

> 375 East Little Canada Road
> Saint Paul, MN 55117-1628
> Phone: 800-487-1074
> Fax: 651-482-0915
> Web site: www.globalvolunteers.org

Habitat for Humanity International is a nonprofit, nondenominational Christian housing organization that builds simple, decent, affordable houses in partnership with those who lack adequate shelter.

> 121 Habitat Street
> Americus, GA 31709-3498
> Phone: 800-HABITAT, Ext. 2652
> Web site: www.habitat.org

Institute of International Education offers information on international study and volunteer opportunities.

> 809 United Nations Plaza
> New York, NY 10017-3580
> Phone: 212-984-5400
> Fax: 212-984-5452
> Web site: www.iie.org

The International Partnership for Service Learning unites academic study and volunteer service, giving students a fully integrated study abroad experience.

> 815 Second Avenue, Suite 315
> New York, NY 10017
> Phone: 212-986-0989
> Fax: 212-986-5039
> Web site: www.ipsl.org

Lisle, Inc. broadens global awareness and cultural understanding worldwide through opportunities that integrate learning with experience.

> 900 County Road 269
> Leander, TX 78641
> Phone: 800-477-1538
> Fax: 512-259-0392
> Web site: www.lisle.utoledo.edu

The Rotary Foundation of Rotary International is a worldwide organization of business and professional leaders that provides humanitarian service, encourages high ethical standards in all vocations, and helps build goodwill and peace in the world.

> One Rotary Center
> 1560 Sherman Avenue
> Evanston, IL 60201
> Phone: 847-866-3000
> Fax: 847-328-8554
> Web site: www.rotary.org

University Research Expeditions Program (UREP) invites students to explore new intellectual and professional worlds, with hundreds of classes, workshops, seminars, and specialized training for schools, organizations, individuals, and businesses.

> UREP
> UC Davis Extension
> 1333 Research Park Drive
> Davis, CA 95616-4852
> Phone: 530-752-8811
> Fax: 530-757-8596
> Web site: www.extension.ucdavis.edu/urep

Volunteers for Peace offers information on a variety of volunteer opportunities.

> 1034 Tiffany Road
> Belmont, VT 05730
> Phone: 802-259-2759
> Fax: 802-259-2922
> Web site: www.vfp.org

INTERNSHIPS

AIESEC/US facilitates international exchange of thousands of students and recent graduates each year.

> 127 West 26th Street, 10th Floor
> New York, NY 10001
> Phone: 212-757-3774
> Fax: 212-757-4062
> Web site: www.aiesecus.org

ADDITIONAL STUDY-ABROAD RESOURCES

American Scandinavian Foundation promotes international understanding through educational and cultural exchange between the United States and Denmark, Finland, Iceland, Norway, and Sweden.

> 58 Park Avenue
> New York, NY 10016
> Phone: 212-879-9779
> Web site: www.amscan.org

Association for International Practical Training (AIPT) provides international human resource development through practical training programs.

> 10400 Little Patuxent Parkway, Suite 250
> Columbia, MD 21044-3519
> Phone: 410-997-2200
> Fax: 410-992-3924
> Web site: www.aipt.org

CARE works with poor communities in more than 70 countries around the world to find lasting solutions to poverty.

> 151 Ellis Street
> Atlanta, GA 30303
> Phone: 800-521-CARE
> Fax: 404-589-2651
> Web site: www.careusa.org

CDS International is a non-profit organization committed to the advancement of international practical training opportunities for young professionals, students, educators, as well as labor, business, and government representatives.

> 871 United Nations Plaza
> New York, NY 10017-1814
> Phone: 212-497-3500
> Fax: 212-497-3535
> Web site: www.cdsintl.org

InterExchange, Inc. provides valuable cross-cultural life and work experiences for young adults.

> 161 Sixth Avenue
> New York, NY 10013
> Phone: 212-924-0446
> Fax: 212-924-0575
> Web site: www.interexchange.org

International Cooperative Education (ICE) provides American college and university students with the opportunity to gain practical work experience abroad. Each summer ICE arranges for students to travel to Europe, Australia, Asia, and South America to work as paid interns.

> 15 Spiros Way
> Menlo Park, CA 94025
> Phone: 650-323-4944
> Fax: 650-323-1104
> Web site: www.icemenlo.com

U.S. Department of State Internship Coordinator, Student Intern Program enables students to obtain job experience in a foreign affairs environment. Students work in Washington, D.C., while others have the opportunity to work at U.S. embassies and consulates abroad.

> 2401 E Street NW, Suite 518 H
> Washington, D.C. 20522
> Web site: www.careers.state.gov/student

PASSPORTS, VISAS, AND STUDENT ID CARDS

CIEE

3 Copley Place
2nd Floor
Boston, MA 02116
Phone: 617-247-0350
Fax: 617-247-2911
Web site: http://us.councilexchanges.org

TRAVEL

STA Travel

Phone: 800-781-4040
Web site: www.statravel.com

Searching for Study-Abroad Programs Online

Thinking about studying abroad? The Internet can be a great tool for gathering information about institutions and their study-abroad programs. There are many worthwhile sites that are ready to help guide you through the various aspects of the selection process, including Peterson's Study-Abroad Channel at www.petersons.com/stdyabrd.

HOW PETERSON'S STUDY-ABROAD CHANNEL CAN HELP

If you want to see the world and get college credit for it, Peterson's has everything you need to know about studying overseas at leading universities.

Choosing a study-abroad program involves a serious commitment of time and resources. Therefore, it is important to have the most up-to-date information about prospective institutions and their programs at your fingertips. That is why Peterson's Study-Abroad Channel is a great place to start the process!

STUDY-ABROAD PROGRAMS DETAILED SEARCH

Explore more than 1,400 short-term study abroad programs! To search by sponsoring institution, select a letter from the alphabetical list of sponsor names. If you're interested in studying in a certain country, click on "Location" and then the country you're interested in to find the institutions that sponsor a program there. If field of study is your top priority, click on "Program" and scroll through the list of major areas of study to find out who is sponsoring programs in that area.

Once you have found a program of your choice, simply click on it to get more in-depth information, including venue, academic focus, admission requirements, contact information, and more.

Get Free Info

If, after looking at the information provided on Peterson's Study-Abroad Channel, you still have questions, you can send an e-mail directly to the school. Just click on "Get Free Info" and send your message. In most instances, if you keep your questions short and to the point, you will receive an answer in no time at all.

Web Site Visit

For programs that have provided their Web sites, simply click on "Web Site Visit" and you will be taken directly to that program's Web page.

USE THE TOOLS TO YOUR ADVANTAGE

Choosing to study abroad is an important decision. The tools available to you at www. petersons.com/stdyabrd can help you make an informed decision. So, what are you waiting for? Log on; a study-abroad program is just a click away!

How to Use This Guide

PROFILES OF SHORT-TERM STUDY-ABROAD PROGRAMS

Profiles of more than 1,400 short-term study-abroad programs are divided into three sections: **Country-to-Country Programs, Programs at Sea,** and **Programs by Country.** These profiles contain all the details you'll need to make a list of preliminary program choices.

The **Country-to-Country Programs** section lists those academic programs that incorporate traveling as a major emphasis of the curriculum. For example, students might spend a few weeks in each of several European countries visiting museums as part of an art program or corporations for a business class. This section is organized alphabetically by the sponsoring institution.

The **Programs at Sea** section contains programs that are held aboard research vessels, schooners, and yachts. Students sail to and from various locations and can become working members of the crew while studying and earning academic credit in these unique study-abroad programs.

The **Programs by Country** section contains most of the study-abroad programs in the guide. This section is divided alphabetically by country in which the programs take place. Country listings are further subdivided alphabetically by city. If a program takes place in more than one city, it appears at the beginning of the country listing under the City-to-City heading.

Note that for ease of use, this book divides the United Kingdom into its constituent countries—England, Scotland, and Wales. Also note that this book contains two separate sections for Ireland and Northern Ireland.

INDEXES

Field of Study. Consult this index if you want to know which colleges or universities offer course work in the academic area you're pursuing. Each subject

area is subdivided by country; all relevant programs and their profile page numbers are listed. By using this index you can find out, for example, which Spanish programs are available in Mexico or where you can study African art and culture.

Program Sponsors. This index lists each program in the book by its sponsoring institution. Use this index to find out about your school's offerings as well as those of any other school.

Host Institutions. Perhaps you've always wanted to study at the American University in Cairo or LaTrobe University in Australia. These institutions act as "hosts," and a U.S. school makes arrangements for students to take courses at these foreign institutions. The index lists host institutions alphabetically by country.

DATA COLLECTION PROCEDURES

Peterson's obtained program information through a questionnaire sent to study-abroad directors in spring and summer 2006. While the editors believe the information in this book is accurate, Peterson's does not assume responsibility for the quality of the programs or the practices of the sponsoring institutions. You are encouraged to obtain as much information as possible from the sponsors themselves.

CRITERIA FOR INCLUSION IN THIS GUIDE

The programs in this book have met the following criteria:

The sponsoring college, university, or group of schools (consortium) has been accredited by one of the national, regional, or international organizations that review undergraduate and graduate degree–granting institutions in the United States and abroad. The guide also lists programs sponsored by third-party organizations who have arranged for an accredited college or university to transfer credit.

The program must be regularly accepted for undergraduate credit at U.S. colleges and universities. You will still need to get approval from your own school, however, to receive credit for the program you choose.

The program's enrollment cannot be limited to students from the sponsoring school; students from other schools must be able to participate. This means that you should also check with your own school to see if they offer limited-enrollment programs that do not appear in this guide.

PROFILES OF SHORT-TERM STUDY-ABROAD PROGRAMS

Country-to-Country Programs

AMERICAN INSTITUTE FOR FOREIGN STUDY (AIFS)
AIFS–BUSINESS AND POLITICS IN THE EUROPEAN UNION, THE AMERICAN INTERNATIONAL UNIVERSITY IN LONDON

Academic Focus • Business administration/management, marketing, political science and government.

Program Information • Program takes place in Belgium; Czech Republic; Germany; France; England. Scheduled travel to London (9 nights), Paris (4 nights), Brussels (3 nights), Prague (4 nights), Berlin (3 nights); field trips to Strasbourg (2 nights), Frankfurt (1 night), welcome dinner in London. Students typically earn 4 semester credits per term.

Sessions • Jun–Jul (summer).

Eligibility Requirements • Minimum age 20; open to juniors, seniors; 2.0 GPA; good academic standing at home school; Formal classroom teaching in London with extensive field trips in all cities.

Living Arrangements • Students live in hotels. Quarters are shared with host institution students. Meals are taken as a group, in residences.

Costs (2007) • $6399; includes tuition, housing, some meals, insurance, excursions, student support services, entrances/transfers, accompanying faculty and travel manager, phone card to call the U.S. $95 application fee. $395 nonrefundable deposit required. Financial aid available for all students: scholarships.

For More Information • Mr. David Mauro, Admissions Advisor, American Institute For Foreign Study (AIFS), 9 West Broad Street, Stamford, CT 06902-3788; *Phone:* 800-727-2437 Ext. 5163; *Fax:* 203-399-5597. *E-mail:* dmauro@aifs.com. *World Wide Web:* http://www.aifsabroad.com/

AMERICAN INSTITUTE FOR FOREIGN STUDY (AIFS)
AIFS–EUROPEAN ART AND ARCHITECTURE, THE AMERICAN INTERNATIONAL UNIVERSITY IN LONDON

Academic Focus • Art history.

Program Information • Program takes place in Switzerland; Czech Republic; France; Italy; England. Scheduled travel to London (7 nights), Amsterdam (3 nights), Paris (5 nights), Venice (4 nights), Florence (4 nights), Rome (3 nights); field trips to Lucerne (1 night), welcome dinner in London. Students typically earn 4 semester credits per term.

Sessions • Jun–Jul (summer).

Eligibility Requirements • Minimum age 18; open to freshmen, sophomores, juniors, seniors; 2.0 GPA; Formal classroom teaching in London with extensive field trips in all cities.

Living Arrangements • Students live in hotels. Quarters are shared with host institution students. Meals are taken as a group, in residences.

Costs (2007) • $6199; includes tuition, housing, some meals, insurance, excursions, student support services, entrances/transfers, accompanying faculty and travel manager, phone card to call the U.S. $95 application fee. $395 nonrefundable deposit required. Financial aid available for all students: scholarships.

For More Information • Mr. David Mauro, Admissions Advisor, American Institute For Foreign Study (AIFS), 9 West Broad Street, Stamford, CT 06902-3788; *Phone:* 800-727-2437 Ext. 5163; *Fax:* 203-399-5597. *E-mail:* dmauro@aifs.com. *World Wide Web:* http://www.aifsabroad.com/

BOWLING GREEN STATE UNIVERSITY
SUMMER IN FRANCE AND/OR BURKINA FASO

Hosted by Institut d'Etudes Françaises de Touraine

Academic Focus • African studies, French studies.

Program Information • Students attend classes at Institut d'Etudes Françaises de Touraine (Tours, France). Classes are also held on the campus of University of Ouagadougou (Ouagadougou, Burkina Faso). Field trips to châteaux of the Loire Valley, various sites in and around Ouagadougou. Students typically earn 14–17 semester credits per term.

Sessions • May–Jul (summer).

Eligibility Requirements • Minimum age 17; open to precollege students, freshmen, sophomores, juniors, seniors, graduate students, adults; 2.5 GPA; 1 letter of recommendation; good academic standing at home school; essay; no foreign language proficiency required.

Living Arrangements • Students live in host institution dormitories, locally rented apartments, host family homes. Meals are taken with host family, in residences.
Costs (2004) • $5521 for Ohio residents; $9000 for nonresidents; includes tuition, housing, all meals, excursions, books and class materials, local transportation, airport pick-up, access to medical clinic in Burkina Faso. $25 application fee. Financial aid available for students from sponsoring institution: scholarships, loans, travel grants from Center for International Programs.
For More Information • Ms. Cynthia Whipple, Director, AYA France/Burkina Faso, Bowling Green State University, Department of Romance Languages, 102 Shatzel Hall, Bowling Green, OH 43403; *Phone:* 419-372-8053; *Fax:* 419-372-7332. *E-mail:* ayafran@bgsu.edu. *World Wide Web:* http://www.bgsu.edu/

CIEE
CIEE STUDY CENTER IN TRANSYLVANIA, HUNGARY AND ROMANIA–FIELD SEMINAR

Held at CIEE Eastern Europe Study Center

Academic Focus • Anthropology, architecture, art, art history, history, religious studies, sociology.
Program Information • Classes are held on the campus of CIEE Eastern Europe Study Center (Budapest, Hungary), CIEE Eastern Europe Study Center (Transylvania, Romania). Faculty members are local instructors hired by the sponsor. Field trips to towns throughout the Transylvania region. Students typically earn 3 semester credits per term.
Sessions • Jun–Jul (summer).
Eligibility Requirements • Minimum age 18; open to sophomores, juniors, seniors; 2.75 GPA; 1 letter of recommendation; good academic standing at home school; no foreign language proficiency required.
Living Arrangements • Students live in host institution dormitories, host family homes. Quarters are shared with host institution students. Meals are taken as a group, on one's own, in residences, in restaurants.
Costs (2006) • $1900; includes tuition, housing, some meals, excursions, student support services, optional on-site pick-up, orientation, pre-departure advising, resident director, cultural activities. $30 application fee. $300 nonrefundable deposit required. Financial aid available for all students: scholarships, minority student scholarships.
For More Information • Information Center, CIEE, 7 Custom House Street, 3rd Floor, Portland, ME 04101; *Phone:* 800-40-STUDY; *Fax:* 207-553-7699. *E-mail:* studyinfo@ciee.org. *World Wide Web:* http://www.ciee.org/isp/

COOPERATIVE CENTER FOR STUDY ABROAD
LONDON/DUBLIN WINTER

Academic Focus • Drama/theater, literature, psychology.
Program Information • Program takes place in Dublin, Ireland; London, England. Faculty members are drawn from the sponsor's U.S. staff. Field trips. Students typically earn 3 semester credits per term.
Sessions • Dec–Jan (winter).
Eligibility Requirements • Minimum age 18; open to freshmen, sophomores, juniors, seniors, graduate students, adults; 1 letter of recommendation; good academic standing at home school.
Living Arrangements • Students live in hotels. Quarters are shared with host institution students. Meals are taken as a group, on one's own, in central dining facility, in restaurants.
Costs (2006–2007) • $3195; includes housing, some meals, insurance, excursions, international airfare, student support services, airport transfers. $200 nonrefundable deposit required. Financial aid available for students from sponsoring institution: scholarships, loans.
For More Information • Dr. Michael A. Klembara, Executive Director, Cooperative Center for Study Abroad, Northern Kentucky University, Nunn Drive, Founders Hall 301, Highland Heights, KY 41099; *Phone:* 800-319-6015; *Fax:* 859-572-6650. *E-mail:* ccsa@nku.edu. *World Wide Web:* http://www.ccsa.cc/

KENTUCKY INSTITUTE FOR INTERNATIONAL STUDIES
ATHENS AND ROME

Academic Focus • History, literature.
Program Information • Program takes place in Athens, Greece; Rome, Italy. Faculty members are drawn from the sponsor's U.S. staff. Scheduled travel to Greek Islands; field trips to sites of local interest. Students typically earn 3-6 semester credits per term.
Sessions • May–Jul (summer).
Eligibility Requirements • Minimum age 18; open to freshmen, sophomores, juniors, seniors, graduate students, adults; 2.0 GPA; 1 letter of recommendation; no foreign language proficiency required.
Living Arrangements • Students live in hotels. Meals are taken as a group, in restaurants.
Costs (2006) • $4200; includes housing, some meals, insurance, excursions, international airfare, international student ID, instructional expenses. $150 application fee. Financial aid available for all students: scholarships.
For More Information • Ms. Nancy Martin, Coordinator, Kentucky Institute for International Studies, PO Box 9, Murray, KY 42071-0009; *Phone:* 270-762-3091; *Fax:* 270-762-3434. *E-mail:* kiismsu@murraystate.edu. *World Wide Web:* http://www.kiis.org/

KNOWLEDGE EXCHANGE INSTITUTE (KEI)
AFRICAN SAFARI PROGRAM

Hosted by United States International University–Nairobi
Academic Focus • African studies, conservation studies, cultural studies, earth sciences, ecology, environmental science/studies, ethnic studies, geography, geology, intercultural studies, meteorology, natural resources, public health, public policy, Swahili, wildlife studies, zoology.
Program Information • Students attend classes at United States International University–Nairobi (Nairobi, Kenya). Scheduled travel to Masai Mara Reserve, Tsavo Wildlife Park, Amboseli Reserve; field trips to Lake Victoria, Great Rift Valley, Nairobi National Park. Students typically earn 6 semester credits per term.
Sessions • Jun–Jul (summer).
Eligibility Requirements • Open to precollege students, freshmen, sophomores, juniors, seniors; 2.2 GPA; good academic standing at home school; no foreign language proficiency required.
Living Arrangements • Students live in host institution dormitories, campsites. Quarters are shared with host institution students, students from other programs. Meals are taken as a group, in central dining facility, in restaurants.
Costs (2006) • $5350; includes tuition, housing, all meals, insurance, excursions, books and class materials, student support services, mobile telephone. $50 application fee. $500 nonrefundable deposit required. Financial aid available for all students: scholarships, loans.
For More Information • Mr. Eduard Izraylovsky, Director, Knowledge Exchange Institute (KEI), 111 John Street, Suite 800, New York, NY 10038; *Phone:* 800-831-5095; *Fax:* 212-528-2095. *E-mail:* info@knowledgeexchange.org. *World Wide Web:* http://www.knowledgeexchange.org/

KNOWLEDGE EXCHANGE INSTITUTE (KEI)
DISCOVER SPAIN AND PORTUGAL

Hosted by Moreruela: Escuela de Espanol
Academic Focus • Area studies, cultural studies, intercultural studies, Portuguese studies, Spanish language and literature, Spanish studies.
Program Information • Students attend classes at Moreruela: Escuela de Espanol (Moreruela, Spain). Scheduled travel to Madrid, Salamanca, Valencia, Aranjuez; Leon; Toledo; field trips to Zamora, Sanabria, Segovia, Zaragoza; Barcelona; Granada. Students typically earn 6 semester credits per term.
Sessions • Jun–Jul (summer).
Eligibility Requirements • Open to precollege students, freshmen, sophomores, juniors, seniors; 2.2 GPA; good academic standing at home school; no foreign language proficiency required.
Living Arrangements • Students live in host institution dormitories, host family homes, hotels. Quarters are shared with host institution students, students from other programs. Meals are taken as a group, on one's own, with host family, in residences, in restaurants.

COUNTRY-TO-COUNTRY PROGRAMS

Costs (2006) • $6350; includes tuition, housing, all meals, insurance, excursions, books and class materials, student support services, mobile phone. $50 application fee. $500 nonrefundable deposit required. Financial aid available for all students: scholarships, loans.
For More Information • Mr. Eduard Izraylovsky, Director, Knowledge Exchange Institute (KEI), 111 John Street, Suite 800, New York, NY 10038; *Phone:* 800-831-5095; *Fax:* 212-528-2095. *E-mail:* info@knowledgeexchange.org. *World Wide Web:* http://www.knowledgeexchange.org/

KNOWLEDGE EXCHANGE INSTITUTE (KEI)
EUROPEAN CAPITALS PROGRAM
Hosted by International Management Institute
Academic Focus • Area studies, British studies, comparative history, cultural studies, Dutch, economics, European studies, French language and literature, French studies, German language and literature, German studies, history, intercultural studies, interdisciplinary studies, international affairs, liberal studies, political science and government.
Program Information • Students attend classes at International Management Institute (Brussels, Belgium). Scheduled travel to London, Paris, Berlin, Vienna; Geneva; Prague; field trips to Brussels, Antwerp, Bruges, Luxembourg. Students typically earn 6 semester credits per term.
Sessions • Jun–Jul (summer).
Eligibility Requirements • Open to precollege students, freshmen, sophomores, juniors, seniors; 2.2 GPA; 2 letters of recommendation; good academic standing at home school; no foreign language proficiency required.
Living Arrangements • Students live in host institution dormitories, program-owned apartments, program-owned houses, hotels. Quarters are shared with host institution students, students from other programs. Meals are taken as a group, on one's own, in residences, in restaurants.
Costs (2006) • $6350; includes tuition, housing, insurance, excursions, books and class materials, student support services, mobile telephones. $50 application fee. $500 nonrefundable deposit required. Financial aid available for all students: scholarships, loans.
For More Information • Mr. Eduard Izraylovsky, Director, Knowledge Exchange Institute (KEI), 111 John Street, Suite 800, New York, NY 10038; *Phone:* 800-831-5095; *Fax:* 212-528-2095. *E-mail:* info@knowledgeexchange.org. *World Wide Web:* http://www.knowledgeexchange.org/

LEXIA INTERNATIONAL
LEXIA INTERNATIONAL–SUMMER PROGRAM: MINORITY ISSUES IN CENTRAL EUROPE: HUNGARY AND ROMANIA
Hosted by Babes Bolyai' University of Cluj Napoca, Eötvös Loránd University Budapest (ELTE)
Academic Focus • Anthropology, area studies, Central European studies, civilization studies, comparative history, cultural studies, Eastern European studies, economics, ethnic studies, geography, Hungarian studies, international affairs, literature, political science and government, social sciences.
Program Information • Students attend classes at Babes Bolyai' University of Cluj Napoca (Cluj-Napoca, Romania), Eötvös Loránd University Budapest (ELTE) (Budapest, Hungary). Field trips to Budapest, Cluj-Napoca, Batya, Visegrad; Transylvania.
Sessions • Jun–Aug (summer).
Eligibility Requirements • Minimum age 18; open to freshmen, sophomores, juniors, seniors, graduate students, adults; 2.5 GPA; 2 letters of recommendation; good academic standing at home school; no foreign language proficiency required.
Living Arrangements • Students live in host institution dormitories, host family homes. Quarters are shared with host institution students. Meals are taken on one's own, in residences, in central dining facility, in restaurants.
Costs (2006) • $5950; includes tuition, housing, insurance, excursions, international student ID, student support services. $40 application fee. $300 nonrefundable deposit required. Financial aid available for all students: scholarships, work study.

For More Information • Lexia International, 23 South Main Street, Hanover, NH 03755; *Phone:* 800-775-3942; *Fax:* 603-643-9899. *E-mail:* info@lexiaintl.org. *World Wide Web:* http://www.lexiaintl.org/

MICHIGAN STATE UNIVERSITY
ADVERTISING AND PUBLIC RELATIONS A LA MEDITERRANEAN
Hosted by The American University of Rome
Academic Focus • Advertising and public relations.
Program Information • Students attend classes at The American University of Rome (Rome, Italy). Scheduled travel to the Cannes Advertising Festival; field trips to Rome, Milan, Monte Carlo. Students typically earn 8 semester credits per term.
Sessions • May–Jul (summer).
Eligibility Requirements • Minimum age 18; open to freshmen, sophomores, juniors, seniors, graduate students; 2.0 GPA; good academic standing at home school; background in advertising or public relations; no foreign language proficiency required.
Living Arrangements • Students live in locally rented apartments, hotels. Meals are taken as a group, on one's own, in residences, in restaurants.
Costs (2005) • $3699 (estimated); includes housing, some meals, insurance, excursions, books and class materials, student support services. $100 application fee. $200 nonrefundable deposit required. Financial aid available for students from sponsoring institution: scholarships, loans.
For More Information • Ms. Yvonne Squiers, Secretary, Michigan State University, Office of Study Abroad, 109 International Center, East Lansing, MI 48824-1035; *Phone:* 517-353-8920; *Fax:* 517-432-2082. *E-mail:* squiers@msu.edu. *World Wide Web:* http://studyabroad.msu.edu/

MICHIGAN STATE UNIVERSITY
ADVERTISING IN ASIA
Academic Focus • Advertising and public relations.
Program Information • Program takes place in Beijing, China; Hong Kong, China; Tokyo, Japan. Faculty members are drawn from the sponsor's U.S. staff. Field trips to advertising agencies, local companies. Students typically earn 6 semester credits per term.
Sessions • May–Jun (summer).
Eligibility Requirements • Minimum age 18; open to sophomores, juniors, seniors; 2.0 GPA; good academic standing at home school; essay; no foreign language proficiency required.
Living Arrangements • Students live in host institution dormitories, hotels. Meals are taken as a group, in restaurants.
Costs (2005) • $3104; includes housing, some meals, insurance, excursions, student support services. $100 application fee. $200 nonrefundable deposit required. Financial aid available for students from sponsoring institution: scholarships, loans.
For More Information • Ms. Darla Conley, Secretary, Michigan State University, Office of Study Abroad, 109 International Center, East Lansing, MI 48824-1035; *Phone:* 517-355-4654; *Fax:* 517-353-8727. *E-mail:* stackma1@msu.edu. *World Wide Web:* http://studyabroad.msu.edu/

MICHIGAN STATE UNIVERSITY
ECONOMIC AND POLITICAL TRANSITION IN EASTERN EUROPE
Hosted by Babes Bolyai' University of Cluj Napoca, Corvinus University of Budapest
Academic Focus • International affairs, political science and government.
Program Information • Students attend classes at Babes Bolyai' University of Cluj Napoca (Cluj-Napoca, Romania), Corvinus University of Budapest (Budapest, Hungary). Classes are also held on the campus of American University in Bulgaria (Blagoevgrad, Bulgaria). Scheduled travel to Budapest, Cluj; field trips to universities and institutes. Students typically earn 8 semester credits per term.
Sessions • May–Jun (summer).

Eligibility Requirements • Minimum age 18; open to freshmen, sophomores, juniors, seniors; 2.3 GPA; good academic standing at home school; faculty approval; no foreign language proficiency required.
Living Arrangements • Students live in host institution dormitories, hotels. Meals are taken as a group, on one's own, in central dining facility, in restaurants.
Costs (2005) • $1450 (estimated); includes housing, insurance, excursions, student support services. $100 application fee. $200 nonrefundable deposit required. Financial aid available for students from sponsoring institution: scholarships, loans.
For More Information • Ms. Yvonne Squiers, Secretary, Michigan State University, Office of Study Abroad, 109 International Center, East Lansing, MI 48824-1035; *Phone:* 517-353-8920; *Fax:* 517-432-2082. *E-mail:* squiers@msu.edu. *World Wide Web:* http://studyabroad.msu.edu/

MICHIGAN STATE UNIVERSITY
EDUCATION AND SOCIETY IN EUROPE

Held at Maastricht University
Academic Focus • Education, teaching.
Program Information • Classes are held on the campus of Maastricht University (Maastricht, Netherlands). Faculty members are drawn from the sponsor's U.S. staff. Scheduled travel to Aachen, Liege; field trips to schools, community organizations in Maastricht, historic and cultural sites in the Netherlands. Students typically earn 4 semester credits per term.
Sessions • May–Jun (summer).
Eligibility Requirements • Minimum age 18; open to freshmen, sophomores, juniors, seniors, graduate students; course work in education; 2.75 GPA; good academic standing at home school; faculty approval; no foreign language proficiency required.
Living Arrangements • Students live in host institution dormitories. Meals are taken as a group, on one's own, in central dining facility, in restaurants.
Costs (2004) • $2881 (estimated); includes housing, some meals, insurance, excursions, student support services. $100 application fee. $200 nonrefundable deposit required. Financial aid available for students from sponsoring institution: scholarships, loans.
For More Information • Ms. Yvonne Squiers, Secretary, Michigan State University, Office of Study Abroad, 109 International Center, East Lansing, MI 48824-1035; *Phone:* 517-353-8920; *Fax:* 517-432-2082. *E-mail:* squiers@msu.edu. *World Wide Web:* http://studyabroad.msu.edu/

MICHIGAN STATE UNIVERSITY
ENVIRONMENTAL PLANNING AND MANAGEMENT

Academic Focus • Economics, environmental science/studies, natural resources, urban studies, urban/regional planning.
Program Information • Program takes place in Brussels, Belgium; Paris, France; Netherlands. Faculty members are drawn from the sponsor's U.S. staff. Scheduled travel to Amsterdam, Paris, Brussels; field trips to universities, recycling facilities, historic sites. Students typically earn 3 semester credits per term.
Sessions • May (summer).
Eligibility Requirements • Minimum age 18; open to seniors, graduate students; major in natural resources, urban development; 2.0 GPA; good academic standing at home school; faculty approval; no foreign language proficiency required.
Living Arrangements • Students live in host institution dormitories, hotels. Meals are taken on one's own, in restaurants.
Costs (2004) • $3094 (estimated); includes housing, some meals, insurance, excursions, student support services. $100 application fee. $200 nonrefundable deposit required. Financial aid available for students from sponsoring institution: scholarships, loans.
For More Information • Ms. Yvonne Squiers, Secretary, Michigan State University, Office of Study Abroad, 109 International Center, East Lansing, MI 48824-1035; *Phone:* 517-353-8920; *Fax:* 517-432-2082. *E-mail:* squiers@msu.edu. *World Wide Web:* http://studyabroad.msu.edu/

MICHIGAN STATE UNIVERSITY
FOOD, AGRICULTURE, AND ENVIRONMENTAL SYSTEMS IN THE UNITED KINGDOM AND IRELAND

Academic Focus • Agriculture, food science, natural resources.
Program Information • Program takes place in Ireland; England; Scotland. Faculty members are drawn from the sponsor's U.S. staff and local instructors hired by the sponsor. Scheduled travel to Dublin, Edinburgh, London, Belfast; field trips to farms, food processing plants, cultural sites. Students typically earn 6 semester credits per term.
Sessions • May (summer).
Eligibility Requirements • Minimum age 18; open to freshmen, sophomores, juniors, seniors; 2.0 GPA; good academic standing at home school; faculty approval.
Living Arrangements • Students live in host institution dormitories, host family homes, hotels. Meals are taken as a group, on one's own, in restaurants.
Costs (2004) • $2617; includes housing, some meals, insurance, excursions, student support services. $100 application fee. $200 nonrefundable deposit required. Financial aid available for students from sponsoring institution: scholarships, loans.
For More Information • Mrs. Meghan Hock, Educational Programs Coordinator, Michigan State University, Office of Study Abroad, 109 International Center, East Lansing, MI 48824-1035; *Phone:* 517-353-8920; *Fax:* 517-432-2082. *E-mail:* hock@msu.edu. *World Wide Web:* http://studyabroad.msu.edu/

MICHIGAN STATE UNIVERSITY
FOOD, AGRICULTURE, AND NATURAL RESOURCE SYSTEMS

Academic Focus • Agriculture, natural resources, veterinary science, zoology.
Program Information • Program takes place in Swaziland; South Africa. Faculty members are drawn from the sponsor's U.S. staff. Scheduled travel to Johannesburg; Pretoria; Durban; Port Elizabeth; Cape Town, Mbabane, Swaziland; field trips to mountains, a farm family visit, universities, agricultural facilities; parks. Students typically earn 6 semester credits per term.
Sessions • May–Jun (summer).
Eligibility Requirements • Minimum age 18; open to sophomores, juniors, seniors, graduate students; 2.0 GPA; good academic standing at home school; faculty approval; no foreign language proficiency required.
Living Arrangements • Students live in hotels. Meals are taken as a group, on one's own, in restaurants.
Costs (2005) • $3492; includes housing, all meals, insurance, excursions, student support services. $100 application fee. $200 nonrefundable deposit required. Financial aid available for all students: scholarships, loans.
For More Information • Ms. Cindy Felbeck Chalou, Assistant Director, Michigan State University, Office of Study Abroad, 109 International Center, East Lansing, MI 48824-1035; *Phone:* 517-432-4345; *Fax:* 517-432-2082. *E-mail:* chalouc@msu.edu. *World Wide Web:* http://studyabroad.msu.edu/

MICHIGAN STATE UNIVERSITY
INTERNATIONAL BUSINESS MANAGEMENT IN EASTERN EUROPE

Academic Focus • Business administration/management, international business.
Program Information • Program takes place in Austria; Czech Republic; Hungary. Faculty members are drawn from the sponsor's U.S. staff and local instructors hired by the sponsor. Students typically earn 6 semester credits per term.
Sessions • May (summer).
Eligibility Requirements • Open to sophomores, juniors, seniors; 3.0 GPA; good academic standing at home school; no foreign language proficiency required.
Living Arrangements • Students live in host institution dormitories, hotels. Meals are taken as a group, on one's own, in restaurants.
Costs (2005) • $3556 (estimated); includes housing, some meals, insurance. $100 application fee. $200 nonrefundable deposit required. Financial aid available for students from sponsoring institution: scholarships, loans.
For More Information • Ms. Yvonne Squiers, Secretary, Michigan State University, Office of Study Abroad, 109 International Center,

East Lansing, MI 48824-1035; *Phone:* 517-353-8920; *Fax:* 517-432-2082. *E-mail:* squiers@msu.edu. *World Wide Web:* http://studyabroad. msu.edu/

MICHIGAN STATE UNIVERSITY
INTERNATIONAL BUSINESS MANAGEMENT IN WESTERN EUROPE

Academic Focus • International business.

Program Information • Program takes place in Belgium; Luxembourg; Netherlands. Faculty members are drawn from the sponsor's U.S. staff. Scheduled travel to Belgium, the Netherlands, Luxembourg; field trips to manufacturing sites, educational institutions, businesses. Students typically earn 9 semester credits per term.

Sessions • Jun (summer).

Eligibility Requirements • Minimum age 18; open to juniors, seniors; major in business; 3.0 GPA; good academic standing at home school; faculty approval; résumé; selection interview; no foreign language proficiency required.

Living Arrangements • Students live in host institution dormitories, hotels. Meals are taken as a group, on one's own, in restaurants.

Costs (2005) • $3683 (estimated); includes housing, some meals, insurance, excursions, books and class materials, student support services. $100 application fee. $200 nonrefundable deposit required. Financial aid available for students from sponsoring institution: scholarships, loans.

For More Information • Ms. Yvonne Squiers, Secretary, Michigan State University, Office of Study Abroad, 109 International Center, East Lansing, MI 48824-1035; *Phone:* 517-353-8920; *Fax:* 517-432-2082. *E-mail:* squiers@msu.edu. *World Wide Web:* http://studyabroad. msu.edu/

MICHIGAN STATE UNIVERSITY
INTERNATIONAL FOOD LAWS

Held at Wageningen University

Academic Focus • Agriculture, food science.

Program Information • Classes are held on the campus of Wageningen University (Wageningen, Netherlands). Faculty members are drawn from the sponsor's U.S. staff. Field trips to cultural and historic sites in Amsterdam, Brussels, Geneva, Rome. Students typically earn 3 semester credits per term.

Sessions • May (summer).

Eligibility Requirements • Minimum age 18; open to juniors, seniors, graduate students; major in agriculture and natural resources; course work in food science; 2.5 GPA; good academic standing at home school; faculty approval; no foreign language proficiency required.

Living Arrangements • Students live in host institution dormitories, hotels. Meals are taken on one's own, in restaurants.

Costs (2005) • $3020 (estimated); includes housing, some meals, insurance, excursions, books and class materials, student support services. $100 application fee. $200 nonrefundable deposit required. Financial aid available for students from sponsoring institution: scholarships, loans.

For More Information • Ms. Yvonne Squiers, Secretary, Michigan State University, Office of Study Abroad, 109 International Center, East Lansing, MI 48824-1035; *Phone:* 517-353-8920; *Fax:* 517-432-2082. *E-mail:* squiers@msu.edu. *World Wide Web:* http://studyabroad. msu.edu/

MICHIGAN STATE UNIVERSITY
INTERNATIONAL FOOD LAWS IN ASIA

Academic Focus • Agriculture, food science, natural resources.

Program Information • Program takes place in Japan; Korea; Thailand. Faculty members are drawn from the sponsor's U.S. staff. Scheduled travel to Tokyo, Hong Kong, Seoul; field trips to research institutes, food corporations, universities, cultural sites. Students typically earn 3 semester credits per term.

Sessions • May (summer), Program runs every other year.

Eligibility Requirements • Minimum age 18; open to juniors, seniors, graduate students; course work in food science; 2.5 GPA; good academic standing at home school; faculty approval; no foreign language proficiency required.

Living Arrangements • Students live in hotels. Meals are taken as a group, in central dining facility, in restaurants.

Costs (2004) • $2095 (estimated); includes housing, some meals, insurance, excursions, student support services. $100 application fee. $200 nonrefundable deposit required. Financial aid available for students from sponsoring institution: scholarships, loans.

For More Information • Ms. Darla Conley, Office Assistant, Michigan State University, Office of Study Abroad, 109 International Center, East Lansing, MI 48824-1035; *Phone:* 517-355-4654; *Fax:* 517-353-8727. *E-mail:* stackma1@msu.edu. *World Wide Web:* http://studyabroad.msu.edu/

MICHIGAN STATE UNIVERSITY
INTERNATIONAL VETERINARY FOCAL STUDIES IN THE U.K. AND WESTERN EUROPE

Academic Focus • Veterinary science.

Program Information • Program takes place in Germany; Ireland; Netherlands; England; Scotland. Faculty members are drawn from the sponsor's U.S. staff. Scheduled travel to biosafety research stations, veterinary schools; field trips to Canterbury, veterinary schools, corporate entities. Students typically earn 3 semester credits per term.

Sessions • May–Jun (summer).

Eligibility Requirements • Minimum age 18; open to seniors, graduate students; major in veterinary medicine; 2.5 GPA; faculty approval; no foreign language proficiency required.

Living Arrangements • Students live in host institution dormitories, hotels. Meals are taken as a group, in residences.

Costs (2005) • $2265; includes housing, some meals, insurance, excursions, student support services. $100 application fee. $200 nonrefundable deposit required. Financial aid available for students from sponsoring institution: scholarships, loans.

For More Information • Ms. Yvonne Squiers, Secretary, Michigan State University, Office of Study Abroad, 109 International Center, East Lansing, MI 48824-1035; *Phone:* 517-353-8920; *Fax:* 517-432-2082. *E-mail:* squiers@msu.edu. *World Wide Web:* http://studyabroad. msu.edu/

MICHIGAN STATE UNIVERSITY
IS THIS A POSTMODERN WORLD?

Held at Utrecht University

Academic Focus • American studies, civilization studies, European studies.

Program Information • Classes are held on the campus of Utrecht University (Utrecht, Netherlands). Faculty members are drawn from the sponsor's U.S. staff. Scheduled travel to Paris; field trips to surrounding areas, Amsterdam. Students typically earn 8 semester credits per term.

Sessions • May–Jun (summer).

Eligibility Requirements • Minimum age 18; open to juniors, seniors; major in arts and letters; 2.0 GPA; good academic standing at home school; faculty approval; good physical condition; interview; no foreign language proficiency required.

Living Arrangements • Students live in host institution dormitories, hotels, hostels. Meals are taken as a group, on one's own, in central dining facility, in restaurants.

Costs (2005) • $2854 (estimated); includes housing, insurance, excursions, student support services. $100 application fee. $200 nonrefundable deposit required. Financial aid available for students from sponsoring institution: scholarships, loans.

For More Information • Ms. Yvonne Squiers, Secretary, Michigan State University, Office of Study Abroad, 109 International Center, East Lansing, MI 48824-1035; *Phone:* 517-353-8920; *Fax:* 517-432-2082. *E-mail:* squiers@msu.edu. *World Wide Web:* http://studyabroad. msu.edu/

MICHIGAN STATE UNIVERSITY
LAND OF THE INCAS

Held at Academia Latinoamericana, La Molina National University of Agriculture, University Privada Boliviana

Academic Focus • Agriculture, Latin American studies, social sciences.

Program Information • Classes are held on the campus of University Privada Boliviana (La Paz, Bolivia), La Molina National University of Agriculture (Lima, Peru), Academia Latinoamericana (Cusco, Peru). Faculty members are drawn from the sponsor's U.S.

staff. Scheduled travel to Lake Titicaca; field trips to Pisaq, the Sacred Valley, the Inca trail, Machu Picchu. Students typically earn 4 semester credits per term.

Sessions • Dec–Jan (winter break).

Eligibility Requirements • Minimum age 18; open to freshmen, sophomores, juniors, seniors; 2.5 GPA; good academic standing at home school; faculty approval; no foreign language proficiency required.

Living Arrangements • Students live in host family homes, hotels. Meals are taken with host family, in residences.

Costs (2004–2005) • $2262 (estimated); includes housing, some meals, insurance, excursions. $100 application fee. $200 deposit required. Financial aid available for students from sponsoring institution: scholarships, loans.

For More Information • Mr. Mark Davis, Coordinator, Michigan State University, Office of Study Abroad, 109 International Center, East Lansing, MI 48824-1035; *Phone:* 517-432-1315; *Fax:* 517-432-2082. *E-mail:* mdavis@msu.edu. *World Wide Web:* http://studyabroad.msu.edu/

MICHIGAN STATE UNIVERSITY
MARKETING AND MANAGEMENT OF FOOD AND AGRICULTURAL SYSTEMS IN WESTERN EUROPE

Academic Focus • Agriculture, environmental science/studies.

Program Information • Program takes place in Switzerland; Germany; Netherlands. Faculty members are drawn from the sponsor's U.S. staff. Field trips to agricultural firms. Students typically earn 6 semester credits per term.

Sessions • May–Jun (summer).

Eligibility Requirements • Minimum age 18; open to juniors, seniors; major in agriculture and natural resources; 2.0 GPA; good academic standing at home school; faculty approval; no foreign language proficiency required.

Living Arrangements • Students live in host institution dormitories, hotels, hostels. Meals are taken as a group, in central dining facility, in restaurants.

Costs (2005) • $2783; includes housing, some meals, insurance, excursions, student support services. $100 application fee. $200 nonrefundable deposit required. Financial aid available for students from sponsoring institution: scholarships, loans.

For More Information • Ms. Yvonne Squiers, Secretary, Michigan State University, Office of Study Abroad, 109 International Center, East Lansing, MI 48824-1035; *Phone:* 517-353-8920; *Fax:* 517-432-2082. *E-mail:* squiers@msu.edu. *World Wide Web:* http://studyabroad.msu.edu/

MICHIGAN STATE UNIVERSITY
MASS MEDIA

Academic Focus • Advertising and public relations, communications, telecommunications.

Program Information • Program takes place in London, England; Edinburgh, Scotland. Faculty members are drawn from the sponsor's U.S. staff and local instructors hired by the sponsor. Scheduled travel to Edinburgh, the University of Edinburgh; field trips to the BBC, Cambridge University, the London Times, Wales, SKY-TV. Students typically earn 6 semester credits per term.

Sessions • Jun–Jul (summer).

Eligibility Requirements • Minimum age 18; open to juniors, seniors, graduate students; 2.5 GPA; good academic standing at home school; faculty approval.

Living Arrangements • Students live in host institution dormitories. Quarters are shared with students from other programs. Meals are taken as a group, on one's own, in residences, in central dining facility, in restaurants.

Costs (2005) • $3374; includes housing, some meals, insurance, excursions, student support services. $100 application fee. $200 nonrefundable deposit required. Financial aid available for students from sponsoring institution: scholarships, loans.

For More Information • Mrs. Meghan Hock, Educational Programs Coordinator, Michigan State University, Office of Study Abroad, 109 International Center, East Lansing, MI 48824-1035; *Phone:* 517-353-8920; *Fax:* 517-432-2082. *E-mail:* hock@msu.edu. *World Wide Web:* http://studyabroad.msu.edu/

MICHIGAN STATE UNIVERSITY
A MULTIDISCIPLINARY PROGRAM IN RUSSIA: ENGINEERING, EDUCATION, AND RUSSIAN LANGUAGE

Held at Volgograd State Architectural and Civil Engineering Academy

Academic Focus • Education, engineering, Russian language and literature.

Program Information • Classes are held on the campus of Volgograd State Architectural and Civil Engineering Academy (Volgograd, Russia). Faculty members are drawn from the sponsor's U.S. staff and local instructors hired by the sponsor. Scheduled travel to St. Petersburg, Moscow; field trips to the opera, museums, concerts. Students typically earn 6 semester credits per term.

Sessions • May–Jul (summer).

Eligibility Requirements • Minimum age 18; open to juniors, seniors, adults; major in civil or environmental engineering; 2.0 GPA; good academic standing at home school; faculty approval; no foreign language proficiency required.

Living Arrangements • Students live in hotels. Meals are taken on one's own, in restaurants.

Costs (2005) • $2197 (estimated); includes housing, some meals, insurance, excursions, student support services. $100 application fee. $200 nonrefundable deposit required. Financial aid available for students from sponsoring institution: scholarships, loans.

For More Information • Ms. Yvonne Squiers, Secretary, Michigan State University, Office of Study Abroad, 109 International Center, East Lansing, MI 48824-1035; *Phone:* 517-353-8920; *Fax:* 517-432-2082. *E-mail:* squiers@msu.edu. *World Wide Web:* http://studyabroad.msu.edu/

MICHIGAN STATE UNIVERSITY
NATURAL SCIENCE IN THE VIRGIN ISLANDS

Academic Focus • Earth sciences, environmental science/studies.

Program Information • Program takes place in British Virgin Islands; U.S. Virgin Islands. Faculty members are drawn from the sponsor's U.S. staff. Scheduled travel to Tortola, Virgin Gorda, St. John, Puerto Rico; field trips to coral reefs, beaches, rainforests. Students typically earn 6 semester credits per term.

Sessions • Dec–Jan (winter break).

Eligibility Requirements • Minimum age 18; open to freshmen, sophomores, juniors, seniors; 2.0 GPA; good academic standing at home school; faculty approval; good physical condition.

Living Arrangements • Students live in hotels, campsites. Meals are taken as a group, on one's own, in central dining facility, in restaurants.

Costs (2004–2005) • $2220 (estimated); includes housing, insurance, excursions, student support services. $100 application fee. $200 nonrefundable deposit required. Financial aid available for students from sponsoring institution: scholarships, loans.

For More Information • Mr. Mark Davis, Coordinator, Michigan State University, Office of Study Abroad, 109 International Center, East Lansing, MI 48824-1035; *Phone:* 517-432-1315; *Fax:* 517-432-2082. *E-mail:* mdavis@msu.edu. *World Wide Web:* http://studyabroad.msu.edu/

MICHIGAN STATE UNIVERSITY
PHOTO COMMUNICATION IN THE UNITED KINGDOM AND CZECH REPUBLIC

Academic Focus • Photography.

Program Information • Program takes place in Prague, Czech Republic; Bath, England; Bradford, England; London, England; Edinburgh, Scotland. Faculty members are drawn from the sponsor's U.S. staff and local instructors hired by the sponsor. Scheduled travel to sites in Wales, Edinburgh, Glasgow, Bath, York, Dublin, Ireland; field trips to photography schools, museums, studios, workshops. Students typically earn 6 semester credits per term.

Sessions • Jun–Aug (summer).

Eligibility Requirements • Minimum age 18; open to freshmen, sophomores, juniors, seniors, graduate students; 2.0 GPA; good academic standing at home school; faculty approval.

Living Arrangements • Students live in host institution dormitories, hotels. Meals are taken as a group, on one's own, in central dining facility, in restaurants.

Costs (2005) • $3947; includes housing, some meals, insurance, excursions, student support services. $100 application fee. $200 nonrefundable deposit required. Financial aid available for students from sponsoring institution: scholarships, loans.

For More Information • Mrs. Meghan Hock, Educational Programs Coordinator, Michigan State University, Office of Study Abroad, 109 International Center, East Lansing, MI 48824-1035; *Phone:* 517-353-8920; *Fax:* 517-432-2082. *E-mail:* hock@msu.edu. *World Wide Web:* http://studyabroad.msu.edu/

MICHIGAN STATE UNIVERSITY
PRODUCTION AND MARKETING OF CONVENTIONAL, ORGANIC, AND GENETICALLY MODIFIED CROPS IN WESTERN EUROPE

Academic Focus • Agriculture, natural resources.

Program Information • Program takes place in Austria; Germany; France; Netherlands. Faculty members are drawn from the sponsor's U.S. staff. Field trips to government, industry, farms. Students typically earn 4 semester credits per term.

Sessions • May (3 weeks).

Eligibility Requirements • Minimum age 18; open to juniors, seniors, graduate students; course work in crop and soil sciences; 2.5 GPA; good academic standing at home school; faculty approval; no foreign language proficiency required.

Living Arrangements • Students live in hotels. Meals are taken as a group, in restaurants.

Costs (2005) • Contact sponsor for cost. $100 application fee. $200 nonrefundable deposit required. Financial aid available for students from sponsoring institution: scholarships, loans.

For More Information • Ms. Yvonne Squiers, Secretary, Michigan State University, Office of Study Abroad, 109 International Center, East Lansing, MI 48824-1035; *Phone:* 517-353-8920; *Fax:* 517-432-2082. *E-mail:* squiers@msu.edu. *World Wide Web:* http://studyabroad.msu.edu/

MICHIGAN STATE UNIVERSITY
PRODUCTION, MARKETING, AND USE OF ORNAMENTAL PLANTS IN WESTERN EUROPE

Held at Wageningen University

Academic Focus • Agriculture.

Program Information • Classes are held on the campus of Wageningen University (Wageningen, Netherlands). Faculty members are drawn from the sponsor's U.S. staff. Scheduled travel to greenhouses, nurseries, arboreta, research stations; field trips to greenhouses, nursey, arboreta. Students typically earn 5 semester credits per term.

Sessions • May-Jun (summer).

Eligibility Requirements • Minimum age 18; open to juniors, seniors; 2.0 GPA; good academic standing at home school; faculty approval; no foreign language proficiency required.

Living Arrangements • Students live in host institution dormitories, hotels. Meals are taken as a group, in central dining facility, in restaurants.

Costs (2005) • Contact sponsor for cost. $100 application fee. $200 nonrefundable deposit required. Financial aid available for students from sponsoring institution: scholarships, loans.

For More Information • Ms. Yvonne Squiers, Secretary, Michigan State University, Office of Study Abroad, 109 International Center, East Lansing, MI 48824-1035; *Phone:* 517-353-8920; *Fax:* 517-432-2082. *E-mail:* squiers@msu.edu. *World Wide Web:* http://studyabroad.msu.edu/

MICHIGAN STATE UNIVERSITY
REPORTING IN THE BRITISH ISLES

Academic Focus • Journalism.

Program Information • Program takes place in Dublin, Ireland; London, England; Edinburgh, Scotland. Faculty members are drawn from the sponsor's U.S. staff and local instructors hired by the sponsor. Field trips to news organizations around Ireland, Northern Ireland, Scotland. Students typically earn 6 semester credits per term.

Sessions • May-Jun (summer).

Eligibility Requirements • Minimum age 18; open to sophomores, juniors, seniors, graduate students; course work in journalism; 2.0 GPA; good academic standing at home school; faculty approval.

Living Arrangements • Students live in host institution dormitories, locally rented apartments, hotels. Quarters are shared with students from other programs. Meals are taken on one's own, in residences, in central dining facility.

Costs (2005) • $3695; includes housing, some meals, insurance, excursions, student support services. $100 application fee. $200 nonrefundable deposit required. Financial aid available for students from sponsoring institution: scholarships, loans.

For More Information • Mrs. Meghan Hock, Educational Programs Coordinator, Michigan State University, Office of Study Abroad, 109 International Center, East Lansing, MI 48824-1035; *Phone:* 517-353-8920; *Fax:* 517-432-2082. *E-mail:* hock@msu.edu. *World Wide Web:* http://studyabroad.msu.edu/

MICHIGAN STATE UNIVERSITY
RETAIL DISTRIBUTION

Academic Focus • Fashion merchandising, marketing.

Program Information • Program takes place in Warsaw, Poland; Pushkin, Russia. Faculty members are drawn from the sponsor's U.S. staff. Scheduled travel to Warsaw, Pushkin; field trips to wholesalers, manufacturers, retailers. Students typically earn 4 semester credits per term.

Sessions • May (summer).

Eligibility Requirements • Minimum age 18; open to freshmen, sophomores, juniors, seniors, graduate students; major in human ecology, business, commercial arts; 2.0 GPA; good academic standing at home school; faculty approval; valid passport; no foreign language proficiency required.

Living Arrangements • Students live in host institution dormitories, host family homes. Meals are taken as a group, on one's own, with host family, in residences, in restaurants.

Costs (2005) • $1175 (estimated); includes housing, some meals, insurance, excursions, student support services. $100 application fee. $200 nonrefundable deposit required. Financial aid available for students from sponsoring institution: scholarships, loans.

For More Information • Ms. Yvonne Squiers, Secretary, Michigan State University, Office of Study Abroad, 109 International Center, East Lansing, MI 48824-1035; *Phone:* 517-353-8920; *Fax:* 517-432-2082. *E-mail:* squiers@msu.edu. *World Wide Web:* http://studyabroad.msu.edu/

MICHIGAN STATE UNIVERSITY
SOCIAL SCIENCE

Academic Focus • Social sciences.

Program Information • Program takes place in Belgium; France; London, England. Faculty members are drawn from the sponsor's U.S. staff. Scheduled travel to Brussels, Strasbourg, the Black Forest; field trips to museums, local government, Parliament, Cambridge. Students typically earn 8 semester credits per term.

Sessions • Jun-Aug (summer).

Eligibility Requirements • Minimum age 18; open to freshmen, sophomores, juniors, seniors; 2.0 GPA; good academic standing at home school; faculty approval; no foreign language proficiency required.

Living Arrangements • Students live in host institution dormitories, hotels. Meals are taken as a group, on one's own, in central dining facility, in restaurants.

Costs (2005) • $4476; includes housing, some meals, insurance, excursions, student support services. $100 application fee. $200 nonrefundable deposit required. Financial aid available for students from sponsoring institution: scholarships, loans.

For More Information • Mrs. Meghan Hock, Educational Programs Coordinator, Michigan State University, Office of Study Abroad, 109 International Center, East Lansing, MI 48824-1035; *Phone:* 517-353-8920; *Fax:* 517-432-2082. *E-mail:* hock@msu.edu. *World Wide Web:* http://studyabroad.msu.edu/

MICHIGAN STATE UNIVERSITY
TELECOMMUNICATION

Held at Institut National des Télécommunications

Academic Focus • Telecommunications.

Program Information • Classes are held on the campus of Institut National des Télécommunications (Evry, France). Faculty members are drawn from the sponsor's U.S. staff and local instructors hired by the sponsor. Scheduled travel to London, Brussels, Geneva, Bonn; field trips to various organizations. Students typically earn 4 semester credits per term.

Sessions • Jun–Jul (summer).

Eligibility Requirements • Minimum age 18; open to juniors, seniors, graduate students; course work in telecommunication; 2.0 GPA; good academic standing at home school; faculty approval; no foreign language proficiency required.

Living Arrangements • Students live in locally rented apartments, hotels. Meals are taken as a group, on one's own, in residences, in restaurants.

Costs (2005) • $2182 (estimated); includes housing, insurance, books and class materials, student support services, Eurostar pass. $100 application fee. $200 nonrefundable deposit required. Financial aid available for students from sponsoring institution: scholarships, loans.

For More Information • Ms. Yvonne Squiers, Secretary, Michigan State University, Office of Study Abroad, 109 International Center, East Lansing, MI 48824-1035; *Phone:* 517-353-8920; *Fax:* 517-432-2082. *E-mail:* squiers@msu.edu. *World Wide Web:* http://studyabroad.msu.edu/

MICHIGAN STATE UNIVERSITY
URBAN DEVELOPMENT IN AUSTRIA AND GERMANY

Held at University of Dortmund, University of Technology Vienna

Academic Focus • Urban/regional planning.

Program Information • Classes are held on the campus of University of Dortmund (Dortmund, Germany), University of Technology Vienna (Vienna, Austria). Faculty members are drawn from the sponsor's U.S. staff. Scheduled travel to Vienna; field trips to Cologne, Berlin. Students typically earn 4 semester credits per term.

Sessions • May (summer).

Eligibility Requirements • Minimum age 18; open to seniors, graduate students; course work in urban development land use palnning; 2.0 GPA; good academic standing at home school; faculty approval; no foreign language proficiency required.

Living Arrangements • Students live in with local students. Quarters are shared with host institution students. Meals are taken on one's own, in residences.

Costs (2005) • $943 (estimated); includes housing, insurance, excursions, student support services. $100 application fee. $200 nonrefundable deposit required. Financial aid available for students from sponsoring institution: scholarships, loans.

For More Information • Ms. Yvonne Squiers, Secretary, Michigan State University, Office of Study Abroad, 109 International Center, East Lansing, MI 48824-1035; *Phone:* 517-353-8920; *Fax:* 517-432-2082. *E-mail:* squiers@msu.edu. *World Wide Web:* http://studyabroad.msu.edu/

MICHIGAN STATE UNIVERSITY
THE U.S. AND WORLD WAR II EUROPE: MEMORY AND MEMORIALS

Academic Focus • American studies, creative writing.

Program Information • Program takes place in Belgium; Germany; France; United Kingdom; Luxembourg. Faculty members are drawn from the sponsor's U.S. staff. Scheduled travel to London, Portsmouth, Normandy, Paris, Berlin. Students typically earn 7 semester credits per term.

Sessions • May–Jun (summer).

Eligibility Requirements • Minimum age 18; open to sophomores, juniors, seniors; 2.0 GPA; good academic standing at home school; faculty approval; no foreign language proficiency required.

Living Arrangements • Students live in locally rented apartments, hotels. Meals are taken on one's own, in restaurants.

Costs (2005) • Contact sponsor for cost. $100 application fee. $200 nonrefundable deposit required. Financial aid available for students from sponsoring institution: scholarships, loans.

For More Information • Ms. Yvonne Squiers, Secretary, Michigan State University, Office of Study Abroad, 109 International Center, East Lansing, MI 48824-1035; *Phone:* 517-353-8920; *Fax:* 517-432-2082. *E-mail:* squiers@msu.edu. *World Wide Web:* http://studyabroad.msu.edu/

NEW YORK UNIVERSITY
DRAMA IN EDUCATION

Hosted by NYU at Dublin, NYU at London

Academic Focus • Drama/theater.

Program Information • Students attend classes at NYU at Dublin (Dublin, Ireland), NYU at London (London, England). Field trips to Stratford-upon-Avon, Globe Theatre, West End theatre, the Abbey.

Sessions • Jun–Aug (summer).

Eligibility Requirements • Minimum age 18; open to graduate students; major in Educational Theatre; good academic standing at home school; advisor approval.

Living Arrangements • Students live in locally rented apartments. Meals are taken on one's own.

Costs (2005) • $5634; includes tuition, registration fees. $50 application fee. Financial aid available for students from sponsoring institution: scholarships.

For More Information • Mr. Daniel Young, Program Associate, New York University, 82 Washington Square East, New York, NY 10003; *Phone:* 212-992-9380. *E-mail:* dy14@nyu.edu. *World Wide Web:* http://www.nyu.edu/global/studyabroad.html

NORTHERN ILLINOIS UNIVERSITY
INTERNATIONAL BUSINESS SEMINARS

Academic Focus • Business administration/management, finance, international business, marketing.

Program Information • Program takes place in Geneva, Switzerland; Cologne, Germany; Heidelburg, Germany; Paris, France; Amsterdam, Netherlands; London, England. Faculty members are drawn from the sponsor's U.S. staff. Students typically earn 3 semester credits per term.

Sessions • Dec–Jan (regular winter session or winter MBA seminar).

Eligibility Requirements • Minimum age 18; open to sophomores, juniors, seniors, graduate students, adults; course work in management; 2.5 GPA; good academic standing at home school; no foreign language proficiency required.

Living Arrangements • Students live in hotels. Quarters are shared with students from other programs. Meals are taken on one's own, in restaurants.

Costs (2005) • $4015–$4915; includes tuition, housing, some meals, insurance, excursions, international airfare, international student ID. $200 nonrefundable deposit required. Financial aid available for students from sponsoring institution: loans.

For More Information • Ms. Rita Withrow, Program Assistant, Northern Illinois University, Study Abroad Office, Williston Hall 417, DeKalb, IL 60115; *Phone:* 815-753-0700; *Fax:* 815-753-0825. *E-mail:* niuabroad@niu.edu. *World Wide Web:* http://www.niu.edu/niuabroad/

NORTHERN ILLINOIS UNIVERSITY
INTERNATIONAL BUSINESS SEMINARS

Academic Focus • Business administration/management, finance, international business, marketing.

Program Information • Program takes place in Innsbruck, Austria; Brussels, Belgium; Geneva, Switzerland; Heidelberg, Germany; Stuttgart, Germany; Avignon, France; Nice, France; Paris, France; Florence, Italy; Rome, Italy; London, England. Faculty members are drawn from the sponsor's U.S. staff. Students typically earn 3 semester credits per term.

Sessions • May–Jun (summer MBA seminars).

Eligibility Requirements • Minimum age 18; open to sophomores, juniors, seniors, graduate students, adults; course work in management; 2.5 GPA; good academic standing at home school; no foreign language proficiency required.

Living Arrangements • Students live in hotels. Quarters are shared with students from other programs. Meals are taken on one's own, in restaurants.

Costs (2005) • $4390–$6140; includes tuition, housing, some meals, insurance, excursions, international airfare, international student ID. $200 nonrefundable deposit required. Financial aid available for students from sponsoring institution: loans.

For More Information • Ms. Rita Withrow, Program Assistant, Northern Illinois University, Study Abroad Office, Williston Hall 417, DeKalb, IL 60115; *Phone:* 815-753-0700; *Fax:* 815-753-0825. *E-mail:* niuabroad@niu.edu. *World Wide Web:* http://www.niu.edu/niuabroad/

COUNTRY-TO-COUNTRY PROGRAMS

QUEEN'S UNIVERSITY AT KINGSTON–INTERNATIONAL STUDY CENTER AT HERSTMONCEUX CASTLE
INTERNATIONAL STUDY CENTER, HERTSMONCEUX CASTLE

Hosted by IESEG School of Management
Academic Focus • Art, business administration/management, law and legal studies, social sciences.
Program Information • Students attend classes at IESEG School of Management (Lille, France). Classes are also held on the campus of Queen's University at Kingston–International Study Center at Herstmonceux Castle (Hailsham, England). Scheduled travel to Brussels, Paris, Ypres, Edinburgh; Liverpool; Oxford; field trips to London, Bath, Stratford, Birmingham; Portsmouth; Brighton; optional travel to London, Normandy, Cornwall, Wales at an extra cost. Students typically earn 1-2 Queen's University Credit per term.
Sessions • Jun-Jul (summer), Jan-Apr (winter).
Eligibility Requirements • Open to freshmen, sophomores, juniors, seniors, graduate students; good academic standing at home school; letter of permission for students from non-partner institutions.
Living Arrangements • Students live in host institution dormitories. Meals are taken as a group, in central dining facility.
Costs (2005–2006) • Can$3925; includes tuition, all meals, excursions, student support services, library services, computer facilities, athletic facilities, airport shuttle service. Can$45 application fee. Can$1000 nonrefundable deposit required. Financial aid available for all students: bursaries.
For More Information • Student Recruitment and International Initiatives, Queen's University at Kingston–International Study Center at Herstmonceux Castle, Stauffer Library, lower level, Kingston, Ontario K7L 5C4, Canada; *Phone:* 613-533-2217; *Fax:* 613-533-6754. *E-mail:* iscinfo@queensu.ca. *World Wide Web:* http://www.queensu.ca/isc

SAINT MARY'S COLLEGE
EUROPEAN STUDY PROGRAM

Academic Focus • European studies, history.
Program Information • Program takes place in Belgium; France; Ireland; England; Scotland. Faculty members are drawn from the sponsor's U.S. staff. Scheduled travel to Paris, London, Dublin, Edinburgh; Brussels; field trips to Bath, Stonehenge, Kilarney, Blarney. Students typically earn 3-6 semester credits per term.
Sessions • May-Jun (summer).
Eligibility Requirements • Minimum age 18; open to freshmen, sophomores, juniors, seniors, adults; 2.0 GPA; 3 letters of recommendation; good academic standing at home school; no foreign language proficiency required.
Living Arrangements • Students live in hotels. Meals are taken as a group, in restaurants.
Costs (2005) • $4840; includes housing, some meals, excursions, student support services. $30 application fee.
For More Information • Dr. David Stefanuc, Faculty Director, Saint Mary's College, Department of History, Notre Dame, IN 46556; *Phone:* 574-284-4462; *Fax:* 574-284-4141. *E-mail:* dstefanc@saintmarys.edu. *World Wide Web:* http://www.saintmarys.edu/~cwil

SANN RESEARCH INSTITUTE
NUTRACEUTICAL AND NON-PRESCRIPTION CARE

Hosted by Sann International College, Sann Research Institute
Academic Focus • Pharmacology.
Program Information • Students attend classes at Sann International College (Kathmandu, Nepal), Sann Research Institute (Jaipur, India). Field trips to safari park, religious, cultural and historical sites, botanical gardens; optional travel to Bangkok, India at an extra cost. Students typically earn 3 semester credits per term.
Sessions • Summer, winter break.
Eligibility Requirements • Minimum age 18; open to freshmen, sophomores, juniors, seniors; 2.5 GPA; 2 letters of recommendation; good academic standing at home school; good health; no foreign language proficiency required.
Living Arrangements • Students live in host family homes, hotels. Meals are taken as a group, with host family, in residences, in restaurants.
Costs (2005–2006) • $4000. $225 application fee. $500 nonrefundable deposit required.

For More Information • Narayan Shrestha, President, Sann Research Institute, 948 Pearl Street, Boulder, CO 80302; *Phone:* 303-449-4279; *Fax:* 303-440-7328. *E-mail:* info@sannr.com. *World Wide Web:* http://www.sannr.com/

SCHOOL FOR INTERNATIONAL TRAINING, SIT STUDY ABROAD
ISLAMIC DIASPORA IN EUROPE

Academic Focus • European studies, Islamic studies.
Program Information • Program takes place in Berlin, Germany; Toulouse, France; Amsterdam, Netherlands. Faculty members are drawn from the sponsor's U.S. staff and local instructors hired by the sponsor. Scheduled travel to Paris, Berlin, the Netherlands; field trips to cultural events. Students typically earn 8 semester credits per term.
Sessions • Jun-Jul (summer).
Eligibility Requirements • Open to freshmen, sophomores, juniors, seniors; 2.5 GPA; 2 letters of recommendation; good academic standing at home school; no foreign language proficiency required.
Living Arrangements • Students live in hotels, guest houses. Meals are taken as a group, in residences, in restaurants.
Costs (2005–2006) • $7574; includes tuition, housing, all meals, insurance, excursions. $50 application fee. $400 nonrefundable deposit required. Financial aid available for all students: scholarships.
For More Information • SIT Study Abroad, School for International Training, SIT Study Abroad, PO Box 676, Kipling Road, Brattleboro, VT 05302-0676; *Phone:* 888-272-7881; *Fax:* 802-258-3296. *E-mail:* studyabroad@sit.edu. *World Wide Web:* http://www.sit.edu/studyabroad/

SCHOOL FOR INTERNATIONAL TRAINING, SIT STUDY ABROAD
JAMAICA AND BELIZE: AFRICAN SPIRITUALITY IN THE CARIBBEAN

Academic Focus • African studies, religious studies.
Program Information • Program takes place in Belize City, Belize; Kingston, Jamaica. Faculty members are drawn from the sponsor's U.S. staff and local instructors hired by the sponsor. Scheduled travel to Punta Gorda area, a former Maroon Colony, a Rastafari Boboshanti Camp; field trips to cultural events. Students typically earn 8 semester credits per term.
Sessions • Jun-Jul (summer).
Eligibility Requirements • Open to freshmen, sophomores, juniors, seniors; 2.5 GPA; 2 letters of recommendation; good academic standing at home school; background in religious studies, Black or African Diaspora studies, Caribbean studies; no foreign language proficiency required.
Living Arrangements • Students live in hotels, guest houses. Meals are taken as a group, in residences, in restaurants.
Costs (2005–2006) • $7041; includes tuition, housing, all meals, insurance, excursions. $50 application fee. $400 nonrefundable deposit required. Financial aid available for all students: scholarships.
For More Information • SIT Study Abroad, School for International Training, SIT Study Abroad, PO Box 676, Kipling Road, Brattleboro, VT 05302-0676; *Phone:* 888-272-7881; *Fax:* 802-258-3296. *E-mail:* studyabroad@sit.edu. *World Wide Web:* http://www.sit.edu/studyabroad/

SEMESTER AT SEA, INSTITUTE FOR SHIPBOARD EDUCATION
SEMESTER AT SEA

Held at MV Explorer
Academic Focus • Anthropology, art, biological/life sciences, economics, English, geography, history, marine sciences, music, philosophy, political science and government, psychology, religious studies, sociology.
Program Information • Classes are held aboard MV Explorer (At Sea). Faculty members are drawn from the sponsor's U.S. staff. Scheduled travel to Vancouver, Sitka, Vladivostok, Pusan, Shanghai, Hanoi, Hong Kong, Taipei, Osaka; field trips to museums, local

universities, historic sites, religious sites, businesses; optional travel at an extra cost. Students typically earn 9–12 semester credits per term.

Sessions • Jun–Aug (summer).

Eligibility Requirements • Minimum age 18; open to sophomores, juniors, seniors; 2.75 GPA; good academic standing at home school; essay; full-time enrollment in a degree program; no foreign language proficiency required.

Living Arrangements • Students live aboard MV Explorer. Meals are taken on one's own, in central dining facility.

Costs (2005) • $9575; includes tuition, housing, some meals, insurance, student support services. $35 application fee. $1000 refundable deposit required. Financial aid available for all students: scholarships, work study, loans, grants.

For More Information • Mr. Michael J. Zoll, Director of Admissions and Student Services, Semester at Sea, Institute for Shipboard Education, University of Virginia, PO Box 400885, Charlottesville, VA 22904; *Phone:* 800-854-0195; *Fax:* 412-648-2298. *E-mail:* info@semesteratsea.com. *World Wide Web:* http://www. semesteratsea.com/

STATE UNIVERSITY OF NEW YORK AT NEW PALTZ
BUSINESS IN EUROPE: SUMMER PROGRAM IN BELGIUM, SPAIN, FRANCE, HOLLAND

Held at Flemish Business School, Haarlem Business School, Normandy Business School, Technical University of Catalonia

Academic Focus • International business.

Program Information • Classes are held on the campus of Flemish Business School (Brussels, Belgium), Technical University of Catalonia (Barcelona, Spain), Normandy Business School (Caen, France), Haarlem Business School (Amsterdam, Netherlands). Scheduled travel to Barcelona, Brussels, Amsterdam, Bruges; field trips to Le Havre, Brussels, Caen. Students typically earn 3 semester credits per term.

Sessions • Jun–Jul (summer).

Eligibility Requirements • Minimum age 18; open to seniors; course work in business for 2 years; 2.5 GPA; 1 letter of recommendation; no foreign language proficiency required.

Living Arrangements • Students live in hotels. Quarters are shared with host institution students. Meals are taken on one's own, in restaurants.

Costs (2006) • $4200 for New York residents; $5000 for nonresidents; includes tuition, housing, some meals, insurance, excursions, administrative fees, PC and internet access. $25 application fee. $300 nonrefundable deposit required. Financial aid available for all students: scholarships, loans.

For More Information • Center for International Programs, State University of New York at New Paltz, 1 Hawk Drive, New Paltz, NY 12561-2443; *Phone:* 845-257-3125; *Fax:* 845-257-3129. *E-mail:* studyabroad@newpaltz.edu. *World Wide Web:* http://www.newpaltz. edu/studyabroad/

STERLING COLLEGE
ICELAND AND THE SCOTTISH ISLES

Academic Focus • Ancient history, earth sciences, ecology, geography, Scottish studies, sociology.

Program Information • Program takes place in Iceland; Scotland. Faculty members are drawn from the sponsor's U.S. staff and local instructors hired by the sponsor. Scheduled travel to coastal villages; field trips. Students typically earn 3 semester credits per term.

Sessions • May (2 weeks).

Eligibility Requirements • Minimum age 18; open to freshmen, sophomores, juniors, seniors, graduate students, adults; 2 letters of recommendation; good academic standing at home school; no foreign language proficiency required.

Living Arrangements • Students live in host family homes, hotels, hostels. Meals are taken as a group, with host family, in residences, in restaurants.

Costs (2005) • $3835; includes tuition, housing, all meals, excursions, international airfare. $35 application fee. Financial aid available for all students: scholarships, loans.

For More Information • Mr. Erik Hansen, Director of Global Field Studies, Sterling College, PO Box 72, Craftsbury Common, VT

05827; *Phone:* 802-586-7711 Ext. 128; *Fax:* 802-586-2596. *E-mail:* admissions@sterlingcollege.edu. *World Wide Web:* http://www. sterlingcollege.edu/

STERLING COLLEGE
LAPLAND

Academic Focus • Botany, Scandinavian studies, wildlife studies.

Program Information • Program takes place in Finland; Norway; Sweden. Faculty members are drawn from the sponsor's U.S. staff and local instructors hired by the sponsor. Scheduled travel to explore traditional reindeer herder lifestyles, visits to rock art sites and cultural centers; field trips. Students typically earn 3 semester credits per term.

Sessions • Sep (2 weeks).

Eligibility Requirements • Minimum age 18; open to freshmen, sophomores, juniors, seniors, graduate students, adults; 2 letters of recommendation; good academic standing at home school; no foreign language proficiency required.

Living Arrangements • Students live in host family homes, hotels, hostels; campsites. Meals are taken as a group, with host family, in residences, in restaurants.

Costs (2004) • $3970; includes tuition, housing, all meals, excursions, international airfare. $35 application fee. Financial aid available for all students: scholarships, loans.

For More Information • Mr. Erik Hansen, Director of Global Field Studies, Sterling College, PO Box 72, Craftsbury Common, VT 05827; *Phone:* 802-586-7711 Ext. 128; *Fax:* 802-586-2596. *E-mail:* admissions@sterlingcollege.edu. *World Wide Web:* http://www. sterlingcollege.edu/

STERLING COLLEGE
SUSTAINABLE SCANDINAVIAN SYSTEMS

Academic Focus • Danish, environmental science/studies, natural resources, political science and government, Scandinavian studies, sociology, Swedish.

Program Information • Program takes place in Denmark; Iceland; Norway; Sweden. Faculty members are drawn from the sponsor's U.S. staff and local instructors hired by the sponsor. Scheduled travel to alternative energy sites, eco-villages, industries featuring green technology; field trips. Students typically earn 3 semester credits per term.

Sessions • May (2 weeks).

Eligibility Requirements • Minimum age 18; open to freshmen, sophomores, juniors, seniors, graduate students, adults; 2 letters of recommendation; good academic standing at home school; no foreign language proficiency required.

Living Arrangements • Students live in host family homes, hotels, hostels. Meals are taken as a group, with host family, in residences, in restaurants.

Costs (2005) • $3370; includes tuition, housing, all meals, excursions, international airfare, transportation in-country. $35 application fee. Financial aid available for all students: scholarships, loans.

For More Information • Mr. Erik Hansen, Director of Global Field Studies, Sterling College, PO Box 72, Craftsbury Common, VT 05827; *Phone:* 802-586-7711 Ext. 128; *Fax:* 802-586-2596. *E-mail:* admissions@sterlingcollege.edu. *World Wide Web:* http://www. sterlingcollege.edu/

SYRACUSE UNIVERSITY
BODIES IN MOTION: FASHION IN PARIS AND MILAN

Academic Focus • Fashion design.

Program Information • Program takes place in Paris, France; London, England. Faculty members are drawn from the sponsor's U.S. staff. Scheduled travel to Paris from London. Students typically earn 6 semester credits per term.

Sessions • May–Jun (summer).

Eligibility Requirements • Open to freshmen, sophomores, juniors, seniors, graduate students; 1 letter of recommendation; good academic standing at home school; no foreign language proficiency required.

Living Arrangements • Students live in hotels. Meals are taken on one's own, in restaurants.

COUNTRY-TO-COUNTRY PROGRAMS

Costs (2005) • $8035; includes tuition, housing, some meals, excursions, international student ID, student support services. $55 application fee. $350 nonrefundable deposit required. Financial aid available for all students: loans, need-based tuition grants.
For More Information • Mrs. Daisy Fried, Associate Director, Syracuse University, 106 Walnut Place, Syracuse, NY 13244-4170; *Phone:* 315-443-9420; *Fax:* 315-443-4593. *E-mail:* dipasum@syr.edu. *World Wide Web:* http://suabroad.syr.edu/

SYRACUSE UNIVERSITY
COMPARATIVE HEALTH POLICY AND LAW

Academic Focus • Law and legal studies, medicine, political science and government, premedical studies, social sciences.
Program Information • Program takes place in Geneva, Switzerland; Amsterdam, Netherlands; London, England. Faculty members are drawn from the sponsor's U.S. staff. Scheduled travel; field trips. Students typically earn 6 semester credits per term.
Sessions • May–Jun (summer).
Eligibility Requirements • Open to sophomores, juniors, seniors, graduate students, adults; 1 letter of recommendation; good academic standing at home school; no foreign language proficiency required.
Living Arrangements • Students live in hotels. Meals are taken on one's own, in restaurants.
Costs (2005) • $8605; includes tuition, housing, some meals, international student ID, student support services. $55 application fee. $350 nonrefundable deposit required. Financial aid available for all students: loans, need-based tuition grants.
For More Information • Mrs. Daisy Fried, Associate Director, Syracuse University, 106 Walnut Place, Syracuse, NY 13244-4170; *Phone:* 800-251-9674; *Fax:* 315-443-4593. *E-mail:* dipasum@syr.edu. *World Wide Web:* http://suabroad.syr.edu/

SYRACUSE UNIVERSITY
GLOBALIZATION AND ITS CRITICS: RACE FOR THE WORLD

Academic Focus • Business administration/management, marketing.
Program Information • Program takes place in Belgium; Switzerland; Germany; France; Italy; Netherlands; England. Faculty members are local instructors hired by the sponsor. Students typically earn 6 semester credits per term.
Sessions • May–Jun (summer).
Eligibility Requirements • Minimum age 18; open to sophomores, juniors, seniors, graduate students, adults; 1 letter of recommendation; good academic standing at home school; no foreign language proficiency required.
Living Arrangements • Students live in hotels. Meals are taken on one's own, in restaurants.
Costs (2005) • $8830; includes tuition, housing, some meals, excursions, international student ID, student support services. $55 application fee. $350 nonrefundable deposit required. Financial aid available for all students: loans, need-based tuition grants.
For More Information • Mrs. Daisy Fried, Associate Director, Syracuse University, 106 Walnut Place, Syracuse, NY 13244-4170; *Phone:* 800-251-9674; *Fax:* 315-443-4593. *E-mail:* dipasum@syr.edu. *World Wide Web:* http://suabroad.syr.edu/

TWO WORLDS UNITED
TWO WORLDS UNITED SUMMER PROGRAM

Academic Focus • Full curriculum.
Program Information • Program takes place in Australia; Austria; Belgium; Brazil; Canada; Chile; China; Costa Rica; Germany; Denmark; Ecuador; Spain; Finland; France; Greece; Hong Kong; Ireland; Italy; Japan; Mexico; Netherlands; Norway; New Zealand; Puerto Rico; Portugal; Russia; Sweden; England; South Africa.
Sessions • Jun–Aug (summer).
Eligibility Requirements • Open to precollege students, freshmen, sophomores, juniors, seniors; 2.5 GPA; good academic standing at home school.
Living Arrangements • Students live in host family homes.
Costs (2007) • Contact sponsor for cost.
For More Information • Two Worlds United, *World Wide Web:* http://www.twoworldsunited.com/

UNIVERSITY OF CALIFORNIA, SANTA BARBARA, WILDLANDS STUDIES
ENVIRONMENTS OF THE HIMALAYA

Academic Focus • Ecology, environmental science/studies, geography, Indian studies, Nepali studies, wildlife studies.
Program Information • Program takes place in India; Nepal. Faculty members are drawn from the sponsor's U.S. staff. Scheduled travel to wildlife field locations. Students typically earn 15 quarter credits per term.
Sessions • Jul–Aug (summer), Oct–Nov (fall).
Eligibility Requirements • Minimum age 18; open to freshmen, sophomores, juniors, seniors; course work in biology or environmental studies; good academic standing at home school; application essay; no foreign language proficiency required.
Living Arrangements • Students live in field study sites. Meals are taken as a group.
Costs (2006–2007) • $1995; includes tuition. $75 application fee.
For More Information • Mr. Crandall Bay, Director, Wildlands Studies Program, University of California, Santa Barbara, Wildlands Studies, 3 Mosswood Circle, Cazadero, CA 95421; *Phone:* 707-632-5665; *Fax:* 707-632-5665. *E-mail:* wildlands@sonic.net. *World Wide Web:* http://www.wildlandsstudies.com/

UNIVERSITY OF DELAWARE
SWISS-ITALIAN HOSPITALITY SUMMER SESSION

Hosted by Swiss School of Hotel and Restaurant Management
Academic Focus • German language and literature, hotel and restaurant management.
Program Information • Students attend classes at Swiss School of Hotel and Restaurant Management (Chur, Switzerland). Scheduled travel to Munich, Italy; field trips to hotels, wineries, cheese factory; optional travel to Europe at an extra cost. Students typically earn 7 semester credits per term.
Sessions • Jun–Jul (summer).
Eligibility Requirements • Open to freshmen, sophomores, juniors, seniors, adults; 2.0 GPA; 1 letter of recommendation; no foreign language proficiency required.
Living Arrangements • Students live in host institution dormitories, hotels. Meals are taken as a group, in central dining facility, in restaurants.
Costs (2005) • Contact sponsor for cost. $200 nonrefundable deposit required. Financial aid available for all students: scholarships.
For More Information • Center for International Studies, University of Delaware, 186 South College Avenue, Newark, DE 19716-1450; *Phone:* 888-831-4685; *Fax:* 302-831-6042. *E-mail:* studyabroad@udel.edu. *World Wide Web:* http://www.udel.edu/studyabroad/

UNIVERSITY OF DELAWARE
WINTER SESSION IN AUSTRALIA AND NEW ZEALAND: COMMUNICATIONS AND CONSUMER STUDIES

Held at St. John's College, University of Otago
Academic Focus • Communications.
Program Information • Classes are held on the campus of St. John's College (Sydney, Australia), University of Otago (Dunedin, New Zealand). Faculty members are drawn from the sponsor's U.S. staff. Scheduled travel to Fiji, Christchurch; field trips; optional travel to Australia at an extra cost. Students typically earn 6 semester credits per term.
Sessions • Jan–Feb (winter).
Eligibility Requirements • Open to freshmen, sophomores, juniors, seniors, adults; 2.0 GPA; 1 letter of recommendation.
Living Arrangements • Students live in host institution dormitories. Quarters are shared with host institution students. Meals are taken as a group, on one's own, in central dining facility.
Costs (2005) • Contact sponsor for cost. $200 nonrefundable deposit required. Financial aid available for all students: scholarships.
For More Information • Center for International Studies, University of Delaware, 186 South College Avenue, Newark, DE 19716-1450; *Phone:* 888-831-4685; *Fax:* 302-831-6042. *E-mail:* studyabroad@udel.edu. *World Wide Web:* http://www.udel.edu/studyabroad/

"**I'd like to**" See the Golden Pavilion, Nijo Castle, Sanjusangendo, & Kiyomizu Temple in Kyoto

See the Future in Dubai

Book a Quick Summer Getaway

Explore Secret European Villages   *Stay in an Overwater Bungalow*

Make an Architectural Pilgrimage   Find My Roots

Photograph Monet's Garden

campustravel.org

SPAIN, JAPAN, ITALY, AUSTRALIA, FRANCE, NEW ZEALAND, UNITED KINGDOM, GERMANY, GREECE, PORTUGAL, CHINA, MEXICO, COSTA RICA, PUERTO RICO, SWEDEN, ARGENTINA, BRAZIL, CHILE...

✓ Summer Abroad	✓ Trimester Abroad	✓ Sports Breaks	✓ Language Travel
✓ Semester Abroad	✓ Short term Travel	✓ Spring Breaks	✓ Language Study
✓ Year Abroad	✓ Multi Country Programs	✓ Budget Breaks	✓ Language Immersion

For Information contact: 1 800 985-2236 > www.campustravel.org > info@campustravel.org

COUNTRY-TO-COUNTRY PROGRAMS

UNIVERSITY OF DELAWARE
WINTER SESSION IN AUSTRALIA AND NEW ZEALAND: ECONOMICS

Hosted by University of South Australia

Academic Focus • Economics.

Program Information • Students attend classes at University of South Australia (Adelaide, Australia). Scheduled travel to Adelaide, Melbourne, Sydney, Cairns, Christchurch; field trips to cultural and historic sites; optional travel to Australia, the Great Barrier Reef at an extra cost. Students typically earn 6 semester credits per term.

Sessions • Dec–Feb (winter).

Eligibility Requirements • Open to freshmen, sophomores, juniors, seniors, adults; 2.0 GPA; 1 letter of recommendation.

Living Arrangements • Students live in hotels. Meals are taken on one's own, in restaurants.

Costs (2005) • Contact sponsor for cost. $200 nonrefundable deposit required. Financial aid available for all students: scholarships.

For More Information • Center for International Studies, University of Delaware, 186 South College Avenue, Newark, DE 19716-1450; *Phone:* 888-831-4685; *Fax:* 302-831-6042. *E-mail:* studyabroad@udel. edu. *World Wide Web:* http://www.udel.edu/studyabroad/

UNIVERSITY OF DELAWARE
WINTER SESSION IN AUSTRALIA/NEW ZEALAND–NURSING AND ENGLISH

Academic Focus • English, nursing.

Program Information • Program takes place in Melbourne, Australia; New Zealand. Faculty members are drawn from the sponsor's U.S. staff. Scheduled travel to Sydney, Auckland, Christchurch; optional travel to Australia, New Zealand at an extra cost. Students typically earn 6 semester credits per term.

Sessions • Jan–Feb (winter).

Eligibility Requirements • Open to freshmen, sophomores, juniors, seniors; 2.0 GPA; 1 letter of recommendation.

Living Arrangements • Students live in host institution dormitories, locally rented apartments. Meals are taken on one's own, in restaurants.

Costs (2005) • Contact sponsor for cost. $200 nonrefundable deposit required. Financial aid available for all students: scholarships.

For More Information • Center for International Studies, University of Delaware, 186 South College Avenue, Newark, DE 19716-1450; *Phone:* 888-831-4685; *Fax:* 302-831-6042. *E-mail:* studyabroad@udel. edu. *World Wide Web:* http://www.udel.edu/studyabroad/

UNIVERSITY OF DELAWARE
WINTER SESSION IN EUROPE: BUSINESS

Academic Focus • Business administration/management, marketing.

Program Information • Program takes place in Vienna, Austria; Prague, Czech Republic; Frankfurt, Germany; Munich, Germany; Budapest, Hungary. Faculty members are drawn from the sponsor's U.S. staff. Scheduled travel to Prague, Frankfurt, Budapest, Munich; field trips to company visits; optional travel to Europe at an extra cost. Students typically earn 6 semester credits per term.

Sessions • Dec–Jan (winter).

Eligibility Requirements • Open to freshmen, sophomores, juniors, seniors, adults; 2.0 GPA; 1 letter of recommendation; no foreign language proficiency required.

Living Arrangements • Students live in hotels. Meals are taken as a group, on one's own, in restaurants.

Costs (2005) • Contact sponsor for cost. $200 nonrefundable deposit required. Financial aid available for all students: scholarships.

For More Information • Center for International Studies, University of Delaware, 186 South College Avenue, Newark, DE 19716-1450; *Phone:* 888-831-4685; *Fax:* 302-831-6042. *E-mail:* studyabroad@udel. edu. *World Wide Web:* http://www.udel.edu/studyabroad/

UNIVERSITY OF IDAHO
INTERNATIONAL EXPEDITIONS–SOUTH AFRICA AND SWAZILAND

Hosted by University of Pretoria

Academic Focus • African studies, anthropology, conservation studies, ecology, parks and recreation, wildlife studies.

Program Information • Students attend classes at University of Pretoria (Pretoria, South Africa). Scheduled travel to reserves and national parks in South Africa and Swaziland. Students typically earn 8 semester credits per term.

Sessions • May–Jun (winter).

Eligibility Requirements • Open to freshmen, sophomores, juniors, seniors, graduate students, adults; major in a related field; 2.5 GPA; good academic standing at home school; no foreign language proficiency required.

Living Arrangements • Students live in tents. Quarters are shared with host institution students, students from other programs. Meals are taken as a group, in central dining facility.

Costs (2006) • $3150–$3670; includes tuition, housing, all meals, excursions, books and class materials, student support services. $150 application fee. $200 refundable deposit required. Financial aid available for students from sponsoring institution: scholarships, loans.

For More Information • Ms. Kate Peterson, Program Advisor, University of Idaho, 901 Paradise Creek Street, LLC 3, Ground Floor, Moscow, ID 83844-1250; *Phone:* 208-885-4075; *Fax:* 208-885-2859. *E-mail:* abroad@uidaho.edu. *World Wide Web:* http://www.webs. uidaho.edu/ipo/abroad/

UNIVERSITY OF KANSAS
EMERGING TECHNOLOGIES

Academic Focus • Architecture.

Program Information • Program takes place in Switzerland; Germany; Italy. Faculty members are drawn from the sponsor's U.S. staff. Scheduled travel to Genoa, Turin, Basel, Chur; Davos; Vals; Lucene; Zurich; Berlin; Munich. Students typically earn 9 semester credits per term.

Sessions • Jun–Jul (summer).

Eligibility Requirements • Open to sophomores, juniors, seniors, graduate students; 2.5 GPA; 2 letters of recommendation; good academic standing at home school; sketching experience; no foreign language proficiency required.

Living Arrangements • Students live in hotels. Meals are taken as a group, on one's own, in restaurants.

Costs (2005) • $6970; includes tuition, housing, some meals, excursions, student support services, emergency medical evacuation and repatriation insurance, ground transportation in each program city. $38 application fee. $300 nonrefundable deposit required. Financial aid available for students from sponsoring institution: scholarships.

For More Information • Ms. Renée Frias, Program Coordinator, University of Kansas, Office of Study Abroad, Lippincott Hall, 1410 Jayhawk Boulevard, Room 108, Lawrence, KS 66045-7515; *Phone:* 785-864-3742; *Fax:* 785-864-5040. *E-mail:* osa@ku.edu. *World Wide Web:* http://www.ku.edu/~osa/

UNIVERSITY OF KANSAS
EUROPEAN STUDIES: BRUSSELS, BELGIUM AND PARIS, FRANCE; BUDAPEST, HUNGARY AND VIENNA, AUSTRIA

Academic Focus • European studies, history, political science and government.

Program Information • Program takes place in Vienna, Austria; Brussels, Belgium; Paris, France; Strasbourg, France; Budapest, Hungary. Faculty members are drawn from the sponsor's U.S. staff and local instructors hired by the sponsor. Field trips to multinational corporations, Ghent, Antwerp, OSCE headquarters, OPEC headquarters, the United Nations office at Vienna, NATO headquarters, the European Parliament. Students typically earn 6 semester credits per term.

Sessions • Jun (summer).

Eligibility Requirements • Minimum age 18; open to freshmen, sophomores, juniors, seniors, graduate students; 2.5 GPA; 2 letters of recommendation; good academic standing at home school; no foreign language proficiency required.

Living Arrangements • Students live in hotels. Meals are taken as a group, on one's own, in restaurants.

Costs (2005) • $5400; includes tuition, housing, some meals, excursions, student support services, medical evacuation and repatriation services. $38 application fee. $300 nonrefundable deposit required. Financial aid available for students from sponsoring institution: scholarships, loans.

For More Information • Ms. Ingrid Horton, Program Coordinator, University of Kansas, Office of Study Abroad, Lippincott Hall, 1410 Jayhawk Boulevard, Room 108, Lawrence, KS 66045-7515; *Phone:* 785-864-3742; *Fax:* 785-864-5040. *E-mail:* osa@ku.edu. *World Wide Web:* http://www.ku.edu/~osa/

UNIVERSITY OF MIAMI
GRAND TOUR OF EUROPE SUMMER PROGRAM

Academic Focus • Architecture.

Program Information • Program takes place in Madrid, Spain; Paris, France; Athens, Greece; Florence, Italy; Rome, Italy; Venice, Italy. Faculty members are drawn from the sponsor's U.S. staff. Scheduled travel. Students typically earn 3-6 semester credits per term.

Sessions • May–Jun (summer).

Eligibility Requirements • Minimum age 18; open to sophomores, juniors, seniors, graduate students; good academic standing at home school; no foreign language proficiency required.

Living Arrangements • Students live in hotels. Quarters are shared with students from other programs. Meals are taken as a group, on one's own, in restaurants.

Costs (2005) • $2505–$5022; includes tuition. Financial aid available for students from sponsoring institution: scholarships, loans.

For More Information • Ms. Amy Cosan, Coordinator, University of Miami, International Education and Exchange Programs, 5050 Brunson Drive, Allen Hall Room 212, PO Box 248005, Coral Gables, FL 33124-1610; *Phone:* 305-284-3434; *Fax:* 305-284-4235. *E-mail:* ieep@miami.edu. *World Wide Web:* http://www.studyabroad.miami.edu/

UNIVERSITY OF SOUTHERN MISSISSIPPI
AUSTRALIAN AND NEW ZEALAND EXPEDITION

Academic Focus • Geography.

Program Information • Program takes place in Australia; New Zealand. Faculty members are drawn from the sponsor's U.S. staff and local instructors hired by the sponsor. Scheduled travel; field trips. Students typically earn 4 semester credits per term.

Sessions • Jul–Aug (summer).

Eligibility Requirements • Minimum age 18; open to sophomores, juniors, seniors, graduate students, adults; 2.0 GPA; good academic standing at home school.

Living Arrangements • Students live in host institution dormitories, hotels, hostels. Quarters are shared with students from other programs. Meals are taken as a group, on one's own, in restaurants.

Costs (2005) • $4999; includes tuition, housing, excursions, international airfare, student support services. $200 nonrefundable deposit required. Financial aid available for students from sponsoring institution: scholarships, loans.

For More Information • Director, Australian Studies, University of Southern Mississippi, 118 College Drive #10047, Hattiesburg, MS 39406-0001; *Phone:* 601-266-4344; *Fax:* 601-266-5699. *E-mail:* holly.buckner@usm.edu. *World Wide Web:* http://www.usm.edu/internationaledu/

Programs at Sea

SEA EDUCATION ASSOCIATION
SEA SUMMER SESSION-WOODS HOLE, MA

Hosted by Research Vessel Corwith Cramer, Research Vessel Robert C. Seamans, SSV

Academic Focus • American studies, biological/life sciences, conservation studies, earth sciences, ecology, environmental science/studies, fisheries studies, history, interdisciplinary studies, marine sciences, oceanography, physical sciences, public policy.

Program Information • Classes are held aboard the Research Vessel Corwith Cramer, Research Vessel Robert C. Seamans, SSV. Scheduled travel to 4-week stay as crew on an oceanographic sailing vessel in the North Atlantic or Northeast Pacific; field trips to New Bedford Whaling Museum, Mystic Seaport. Students typically earn 12 semester credits per term.

Sessions • Jun–Aug (summer).

Eligibility Requirements • Minimum age 18; open to freshmen, sophomores, juniors, seniors, graduate students, adults; 2 letters of recommendation; good academic standing at home school; must be able to stay afloat for 30 minutes.

Living Arrangements • Students live in program-owned houses, on 134-foot sailing/research vessels. Meals are taken as a group, in residences.

Costs (2006) • $14,195; includes tuition, housing, some meals, books and class materials, lab equipment, student support services. $45 application fee. $750 nonrefundable deposit required. Financial aid available for all students: scholarships, loans, grants.

For More Information • Ms. Judith M. Froman, Dean of Enrollment, Sea Education Association, Box 6, Woods Hole, MA 02543; *Phone:* 800-522-3633 Ext. 770; *Fax:* 508-540-0558. *E-mail:* admission@sea.edu. *World Wide Web:* http://www.sea.edu/

SEA-MESTER PROGRAMS
SEA-MESTER PROGRAMS–CARIBBEAN MINI-MESTERS

Academic Focus • Community service, marine sciences, oceanography.

Program Information • Faculty members are drawn from the sponsor's U.S. staff. Scheduled travel to British Virgin Islands, St. Martin, Anguilla, St. Barts, Saba, St. Kitts, Nevis, Antigua, Montserrat, Dominica; field trips to British Virgin Islands, St. Martin, Anguilla, St. Barts, Saba, St. Kitts, Nevis, Antigua, Montserrat, Dominica. Students typically earn 3-7 semester credits per term.

Sessions • Jul–Aug (summer), Jun–Jul (summer 2).

Eligibility Requirements • Minimum age 17; open to freshmen, sophomores, juniors, seniors; 2 letters of recommendation; no foreign language proficiency required.

Living Arrangements • Students live on an 88-foot schooner or a 50-foot sailing yacht. Meals are taken as a group, in central dining facility.

Costs (2007) • $3970-$7170; includes tuition, housing, all meals, excursions, books and class materials, lab equipment. $50 application fee. $500 refundable deposit required.

For More Information • Mr. Mike Meighan, Program Director, Sea-mester Programs, PO Box 5477, Sarasota, FL 34277; *Phone:* 941-924-6789; *Fax:* 941-924-6075. *E-mail:* info@seamester.com. *World Wide Web:* http://www.seamester.com/

SEA-MESTER PROGRAMS
SEA-MESTER PROGRAMS–OCEAN MINI-MESTERS

Academic Focus • Oceanography.

Program Information • Faculty members are drawn from the sponsor's U.S. staff. Scheduled travel to Nice, Cannes, Monaco, Corsica, Elba, Rome, Athens; field trips to Nice, Cannes, Monaco, Corsica, Elba, Rome, Athens. Students typically earn 7 semester credits per term.

Sessions • Jul–Aug (summer), May–Aug (summer 2); Jun–Aug (summer 3); late spring 40-day voyage Apr-Jun.

Eligibility Requirements • Minimum age 17; open to freshmen, sophomores, juniors, seniors, graduate students; 2 letters of recommendation.

Living Arrangements • Students live on a 110-foot schooner. Meals are taken as a group, in central dining facility.

Costs (2007) • $6870–$7670 for mini-mester; contact sponsor for regular summer program; includes tuition, housing, all meals, excursions, books and class materials, lab equipment. $50 application fee. $500 refundable deposit required.

For More Information • Mr. Mike Meighan, Program Director, Sea-mester Programs, PO Box 5477, Sarasota, FL 34277; *Phone:* 941-924-6789; *Fax:* 941-924-6075. *E-mail:* info@seamester.com. *World Wide Web:* http://www.seamester.com/

Programs by Country

Antarctica

CITY-TO-CITY

MICHIGAN STATE UNIVERSITY
STUDIES IN ANTARCTIC SYSTEM SCIENCE

Academic Focus • Agriculture, fisheries studies, natural resources, wildlife studies.

Program Information • Faculty members are drawn from the sponsor's U.S. staff. Scheduled travel to Antarctica, surrounding waters/islands, Patagonia. Students typically earn 4 semester credits per term.

Sessions • Dec–Jan (winter break).

Eligibility Requirements • Minimum age 18; open to freshmen, sophomores, juniors, seniors; 2.0 GPA; good academic standing at home school; faculty approval.

Living Arrangements • Students live in an expedition ship. Meals are taken as a group, in central dining facility.

Costs (2004–2005) • $5335 (estimated); includes housing, some meals, insurance, excursions. $100 application fee. $200 nonrefundable deposit required. Financial aid available for students from sponsoring institution: scholarships.

For More Information • Mr. Mark Davis, Coordinator, Michigan State University, Office of Study Abroad, 109 International Center, East Lansing, MI 48824-1035; *Phone:* 517-432-1315; *Fax:* 517-432-2082. *E-mail:* mdavis@msu.edu. *World Wide Web:* http://studyabroad.msu.edu/

ARGENTINA

BARILOCHE

ARGENTINA I.L.E.E.
SPANISH SCHOOL IN PATAGONIA, ARGENTINA

Hosted by Argentina I.L.E.E.
Academic Focus • Spanish language and literature.
Program Information • Students attend classes at Argentina I.L.E.E. (Bariloche, Argentina). Field trips to social activities, tourist sites; optional travel to Patagonia at an extra cost.
Sessions • 2 weeks or more, year-round.
Eligibility Requirements • Open to precollege students, freshmen, sophomores, juniors, seniors, graduate students, adults; no foreign language proficiency required.
Living Arrangements • Students live in host family homes, hotels. Quarters are shared with host institution students. Meals are taken on one's own, with host family, in central dining facility, in restaurants.
Costs (2004–2005) • $210 per week; includes tuition, housing, all meals, books and class materials, lab equipment, international student ID, student support services. $50 application fee.
For More Information • Mr. Daniel Korman, International Director, Argentina I.L.E.E., Avenida Callao 339, 3et piso (1022), 1022 Buenos Aires, Argentina; *Phone:* +54 11-47827173; *Fax:* +54 11-47827173. *E-mail:* info@argentinailee.com. *World Wide Web:* http://www.argentinailee.com/

LINGUA SERVICE WORLDWIDE
VACATION 'N LEARN SPANISH AT COINED ARGENTINA

Hosted by Comision de Intercambio Educativo (COINED)
Academic Focus • Spanish language and literature, Spanish studies.
Program Information • Students attend classes at Comision de Intercambio Educativo (COINED) (Bariloche, Argentina). Optional travel at an extra cost. Students typically earn 3 semester credits for 3 weeks, 6 semester credits for 5 weeks.
Sessions • Year-round sessions of 2 or more weeks.
Eligibility Requirements • Minimum age 18; open to freshmen, sophomores, juniors, seniors, graduate students, adults; no foreign language proficiency required.
Living Arrangements • Students live in locally rented apartments, host family homes, hotels. Meals are taken on one's own.
Costs (2006–2007) • Contact sponsor for cost. $100 application fee.
For More Information • Assistant Director, Lingua Service Worldwide, 75 Prospect Street, Suite 4, Huntington, NY 11743; *Phone:* 800-394-5327; *Fax:* 631-271-3441. *E-mail:* linguaservice@att.net. *World Wide Web:* http://www.linguaserviceworldwide.com/

BUENOS AIRES

ARGENTINA I.L.E.E.
SPANISH LANGUAGE SCHOOL FOR FOREIGNERS

Hosted by Argentina I.L.E.E.
Academic Focus • Spanish language and literature.
Program Information • Students attend classes at Argentina I.L.E.E. (Buenos Aires, Argentina). Optional travel at an extra cost. Students typically earn 3-15 credits per term.
Sessions • 2 weeks or more, year-round.
Eligibility Requirements • Open to precollege students, freshmen, sophomores, juniors, seniors, graduate students, adults; no foreign language proficiency required.
Living Arrangements • Students live in locally rented apartments, program-owned apartments, host family homes, hotels. Quarters are shared with host institution students. Meals are taken on one's own, with host family, in central dining facility.
Costs (2004–2005) • $210 per week; includes tuition, housing, some meals, books and class materials, lab equipment, international student ID, student support services. $50 application fee.
For More Information • Mr. Daniel Korman, International Director, Argentina I.L.E.E., Avenida Callao 339, 3et piso (1022), 1022 Buenos Aires, Argentina; *Phone:* +54 11-47827173; *Fax:* +54 11-47827173. *E-mail:* info@argentinailee.com. *World Wide Web:* http://www.argentinailee.com/

ARGENTINA
Buenos Aires

COLLEGE CONSORTIUM FOR INTERNATIONAL STUDIES–CENTRAL WASHINGTON UNIVERSITY
SUMMER SPANISH LANGUAGE PROGRAM IN BUENOS AIRES, ARGENTINA

Hosted by University of Belgrano

Academic Focus • Spanish language and literature.

Program Information • Students attend classes at University of Belgrano (Buenos Aires, Argentina). Field trips to Teatro Colon, La Boca, markets. Students typically earn 10 quarter credits per 4 week session.

Sessions • May–Jun; Jun–Jul; Jul–Aug (4 weeks).

Eligibility Requirements • Open to sophomores, juniors, seniors, adults; 2.5 GPA; 2 letters of recommendation; good academic standing at home school; essay; transcript; no foreign language proficiency required.

Living Arrangements • Students live in host family homes. Quarters are shared with students from other programs. Meals are taken with host family, in residences.

Costs (2006) • $1025; includes tuition, insurance, excursions, student support services. $50 application fee. $300 refundable deposit required. Financial aid available for students from sponsoring institution: scholarships, loans.

For More Information • Ms. Heather Barclay Hamir, Director, Study Abroad and Exchange Programs, College Consortium for International Studies–Central Washington University, 400 East University Way, Ellensburg, WA 98926-7408; *Phone:* 509-963-3612; *Fax:* 509-963-1558. *E-mail:* goabroad@cwu.edu. *World Wide Web:* http://www.ccisabroad.org/

ENFOREX–SPANISH IN THE SPANISH WORLD
SPANISH INTENSIVE COURSE BUENOS AIRES

Hosted by ENFOREX

Academic Focus • Spanish language and literature, Spanish studies.

Program Information • Students attend classes at ENFOREX (Buenos Aires, Argentina). Field trips to a city tour; optional travel to Córdoba at an extra cost. Students typically earn 4 semester credits per term.

Sessions • Year-round.

Eligibility Requirements • Minimum age 18; open to freshmen, juniors, seniors, graduate students, adults; no foreign language proficiency required.

Living Arrangements • Students live in host family homes, hotels. Meals are taken as a group, on one's own, with host family.

Costs (2005) • $1260 per month; includes tuition, housing, all meals, excursions, books and class materials, lab equipment, international student ID, student support services. $100 application fee. $250 nonrefundable deposit required.

For More Information • Mr. Antonio Anadón, Director of Spanish Department, ENFOREX-Spanish in the Spanish World, Alberto Aguilera, 26, 28015 Madrid, Spain; *Phone:* +34 91-594-3776; *Fax:* +34 91-594-5159. *E-mail:* promotion@enforex.es. *World Wide Web:* http://www.enforex.com/

INSTITUTE FOR STUDY ABROAD, BUTLER UNIVERSITY
SUMMER LANGUAGE AND CULTURE PROGRAM IN ARGENTINA

Hosted by University of Buenos Aires

Academic Focus • Argentine studies, Spanish language and literature.

Program Information • Students attend classes at University of Buenos Aires (Buenos Aires, Argentina). Scheduled travel to visit to working ranch; field trips to Casco Historico, Recoleta, San Isidro, Museo de Bellas Artes; Teatro Colón; optional travel to Colonia, Uruguay at an extra cost. Students typically earn 6-9 semester credits per term.

Sessions • Jun–Jul (summer).

Eligibility Requirements • Open to sophomores, juniors, seniors; 3.0 GPA; 1 letter of recommendation; good academic standing at home school; enrollment at an accredited American college or university; Spanish language evaluation; 1-2 years of college course work in Spanish.

Living Arrangements • Students live in host family homes. Meals are taken with host family, in residences.

Costs (2005) • $3780; includes tuition, housing, some meals, excursions, student support services, cultural and sporting events, pre-departure advising. $40 application fee. $500 nonrefundable deposit required. Financial aid available for all students: scholarships.

For More Information • Institute for Study Abroad, Butler University, 1100 West 42nd Street, Suite 305, Indianapolis, IN 46208-3345; *Phone:* 800-858-0229; *Fax:* 317-940-9704. *E-mail:* pilas@butler.edu. *World Wide Web:* http://www.ifsa-butler.org/

INTERNATIONAL STUDIES ABROAD
BUENOS AIRES, ARGENTINA–INTENSIVE SPANISH LANGUAGE

Hosted by University of Belgrano

Academic Focus • Spanish language and literature.

Program Information • Students attend classes at University of Belgrano (Buenos Aires, Argentina). Field trips to Iguazú Falls, El Tigre; optional travel to Bariloche, Chile, Mendoza, Peninsula Valdes (Patagonia); The Andean Northwest; Ranch in Córdoba at an extra cost. Students typically earn 6 semester credits per term.

Sessions • May–Jun (summer), Jun–Jul ((intensive month programs are also held at beginning of each month)).

Eligibility Requirements • Minimum age 18; open to freshmen, sophomores, juniors, seniors, graduate students, adults; 2.5 GPA; good academic standing at home school; transcripts; no foreign language proficiency required.

Living Arrangements • Students live in host institution dormitories, host family homes. Quarters are shared with host institution students. Meals are taken with host family, in residences.

Costs (2005) • Contact sponsor for cost. $200 refundable deposit required. Financial aid available for all students: scholarships, loans, U.S. federal financial aid.

For More Information • Argentina Site Specialist, International Studies Abroad, 901 West 24th Street, Austin, TX 78705; *Phone:* 800-580-8826; *Fax:* 512-480-8866. *E-mail:* isa@studiesabroad.com. *World Wide Web:* http://www.studiesabroad.com/

INTERNATIONAL STUDIES ABROAD
BUENOS AIRES, ARGENTINA–INTENSIVE SPANISH LANGUAGE

Hosted by University of Belgrano

Academic Focus • Spanish language and literature.

Program Information • Students attend classes at University of Belgrano (Buenos Aires, Argentina). Optional travel to Uruguay, El Tigre, Iguazu Falls, Bariloche; Peninsula Valdés; Ranch in Cordoba; The Andean Northwest (Patagonia) at an extra cost. Students typically earn 6 semester credits per term.

Sessions • Jan, Feb, Mar–Apr, Aug (intensive Month Programs held throughout the year).

Eligibility Requirements • Minimum age 18; open to freshmen, sophomores, juniors, seniors, graduate students, adults; 2.5 GPA; good academic standing at home school; transcripts; no foreign language proficiency required.

Living Arrangements • Students live in host institution dormitories, host family homes. Quarters are shared with host institution students. Meals are taken with host family, in residences.

Costs (2005) • Contact sponsor for cost. $200 refundable deposit required. Financial aid available for all students: scholarships, loans, US federal financial aid.

For More Information • Argentina Site Specialist, International Studies Abroad, 901 West 24th Street, Austin, TX 78705; *Phone:* 800-580-8826; *Fax:* 512-480-8866. *E-mail:* isa@studiesabroad.com. *World Wide Web:* http://www.studiesabroad.com/

JAMES MADISON UNIVERSITY
SUMMER IN ARGENTINA

Academic Focus • Argentine studies, political science and government, Spanish language and literature.

Program Information • Faculty members are drawn from the sponsor's U.S. staff and local instructors hired by the sponsor. Field trips. Students typically earn 9 semester credits per term.

Sessions • Jun–Aug (summer).

Eligibility Requirements • Minimum age 18; open to sophomores, juniors, seniors; 2.0 GPA; 1 letter of recommendation; good academic standing at home school; 2 years of college course work in Spanish.

Living Arrangements • Students live in hotels. Meals are taken as a group, in restaurants.

Costs (2005) • $3362 for Virginia residents; $5882 for nonresidents; includes tuition, housing, some meals, excursions, books and class materials, international student ID. $400 nonrefundable deposit required.

For More Information • Mr. Felix Wang, Director, James Madison University, Office of International Programs, MSC 5731, 1077 South Main Street, Harrisonburg, VA 22807; *Phone:* 540-568-6419; *Fax:* 540-568-3310. *E-mail:* studyabroad@jmu.edu. *World Wide Web:* http://www.jmu.edu/international/

LANGUAGE LIAISON
LEARN SPANISH IN BUENOS AIRES, ARGENTINA

Hosted by Language Liaison

Academic Focus • Spanish language and literature.

Program Information • Students attend classes at Language Liaison (Buenos Aires, Argentina). Field trips; optional travel at an extra cost. Students typically earn 3–15 semester credits per term.

Sessions • New programs begin weekly, year-round.

Eligibility Requirements • Minimum age 18; open to precollege students, freshmen, sophomores, juniors, seniors, graduate students, adults; no foreign language proficiency required.

Living Arrangements • Students live in locally rented apartments, host family homes, hotels. Meals are taken on one's own, with host family, in residences, in restaurants.

Costs (2005) • Contact sponsor for cost. $175 application fee. Financial aid available for all students: scholarship research service.

For More Information • Ms. Nancy Forman, President, Language Liaison, PO Box 1772, Pacific Palisades, CA 90272; *Phone:* 800-284-4448; *Fax:* 310-454-1706. *E-mail:* learn@languageliaison. com. *World Wide Web:* http://www.languageliaison.com/

LANGUAGE LINK
I.L.E.E. OF BUENOS AIRES, ARGENTINA

Hosted by Argentina I.L.E.E., Argentina I.L.E.E.

Academic Focus • Spanish language and literature.

Program Information • Students attend classes at Argentina I.L.E.E. (Bariloche, Argentina), Argentina I.L.E.E. (Córdoba, Argentina), Argentina I.L.E.E. (Buenos Aires, Argentina). Field trips to places of cultural/historic interest in and around Buenos Aires. Students typically earn 6–15 semester credits per term.

Sessions • Classes begin every Monday, year-round.

Eligibility Requirements • Minimum age 17; open to freshmen, sophomores, juniors, seniors, graduate students, adults; no foreign language proficiency required.

Living Arrangements • Students live in program-owned apartments, host family homes, hotels. Quarters are shared with host institution students. Meals are taken on one's own, with host family, in residences, in restaurants.

Costs (2005) • $360 per week; includes tuition, housing, some meals, books and class materials, student support services.

For More Information • Ms. Kay G. Rafool, Director, Language Link, PO Box 3006, Peoria, IL 61612-3006; *Phone:* 800-552-2051; *Fax:* 309-692-2926. *E-mail:* info@langlink.com. *World Wide Web:* http://www.langlink.com/

LEXIA INTERNATIONAL
LEXIA SUMMER IN BUENOS AIRES

Hosted by University of Buenos Aires

Academic Focus • Anthropology, area studies, Argentine studies, art history, civilization studies, comparative history, cultural studies, economics, ethnic studies, geography, history, interdisciplinary studies, international affairs, Latin American literature, Latin American studies, liberal studies, literature, political science and government, social sciences, sociology, Spanish language and literature.

Program Information • Students attend classes at University of Buenos Aires (Buenos Aires, Argentina). Field trips to Colonia, La Plata, Montevideo, Estancia. Students typically earn 8–10 semester credits per term.

Sessions • Jun–Aug (summer).

Eligibility Requirements • Minimum age 18; open to freshmen, sophomores, juniors, seniors, graduate students, adults; 2.5 GPA; 2 letters of recommendation; no foreign language proficiency required.

Living Arrangements • Students live in host institution dormitories, host family homes. Quarters are shared with host institution students. Meals are taken on one's own, with host family, in residences, in central dining facility, in restaurants.

Costs (2006) • $6450; includes tuition, some meals, insurance, excursions, international student ID, student support services, computer access, transcript. $40 application fee. $300 nonrefundable deposit required. Financial aid available for all students: scholarships, work study.

For More Information • Lexia International, 23 South Main Street, Hanover, NH 03755; *Phone:* 800-775-3942; *Fax:* 603-643-9899. *E-mail:* info@lexiaintl.org. *World Wide Web:* http://www.lexiaintl. org/

LINGUA SERVICE WORLDWIDE
VACATION 'N LEARN SPANISH AT COINED ARGENTINA

Hosted by Comision de Intercambio Educativo (COINED)

Academic Focus • Spanish language and literature, Spanish studies.

Program Information • Students attend classes at Comision de Intercambio Educativo (COINED) (Buenos Aires, Argentina). Optional travel at an extra cost. Students typically earn 3 semester credits for 3 weeks, 6 semester credits for 5 weeks.

Sessions • Year-round sessions of 2 or more weeks.

Eligibility Requirements • Minimum age 18; open to freshmen, sophomores, juniors, seniors, graduate students, adults; no foreign language proficiency required.

Living Arrangements • Students live in locally rented apartments, host family homes, hotels. Meals are taken on one's own.

Costs • Contact sponsor for cost. $100 application fee.

For More Information • Assistant Director, Lingua Service Worldwide, 75 Prospect Street, Suite 4, Huntington, NY 11743; *Phone:* 800-394-5327; *Fax:* 631-271-3441. *E-mail:* linguaservice@att. net. *World Wide Web:* http://www.linguaserviceworldwide.com/

LINGUA SERVICE WORLDWIDE
VACATION 'N LEARN SPANISH IN ARGENTINA

Hosted by Argentina I.L.E.E.

Academic Focus • Spanish language and literature, Spanish studies.

Program Information • Students attend classes at Argentina I.L.E.E. (Buenos Aires, Argentina). Optional travel to cultural sites throughout Argentina at an extra cost. Students typically earn 3 semester credits for 3 weeks, 6 semester credits for 5 weeks.

Sessions • Sessions of 2 or more weeks begin Tuesdays, year-round.

Eligibility Requirements • Minimum age 16; open to precollege students, freshmen, sophomores, juniors, seniors, graduate students, adults; no foreign language proficiency required.

Living Arrangements • Students live in host family homes, hotels. Meals are taken on one's own.

Costs (2006–2007) • Contact sponsor for cost. $100 application fee.

For More Information • Assistant Director, Lingua Service Worldwide, 75 Prospect Street, Suite 4, Huntington, NY 11743; *Phone:* 800-394-5327; *Fax:* 631-271-3441. *E-mail:* linguaservice@att. net. *World Wide Web:* http://www.linguaserviceworldwide.com/

MICHIGAN STATE UNIVERSITY
GLOBALIZATION, THE ENVIRONMENT, AND SOCIAL CAPITAL IN ARGENTINA

Held at Salvador University Buenos Aires

Academic Focus • Latin American studies, natural resources, social sciences.

Program Information • Classes are held on the campus of Salvador University Buenos Aires (Buenos Aires, Argentina). Faculty members

ARGENTINA
Buenos Aires

are drawn from the sponsor's U.S. staff. Field trips to Pampas, Patagonia, Salta, Iguazú. Students typically earn 4 semester credits per term.

Sessions • May–Jun (summer).

Eligibility Requirements • Minimum age 18; open to freshmen, sophomores, juniors, seniors, graduate students; 2.0 GPA; good academic standing at home school; faculty approval; statement of purpose at application; no foreign language proficiency required.

Living Arrangements • Students live in host family homes. Meals are taken with host family, in residences.

Costs (2005) • $2695 (estimated); includes housing, all meals, insurance, excursions, student support services. $100 application fee. $200 nonrefundable deposit required. Financial aid available for students from sponsoring institution: scholarships, loans.

For More Information • Mr. Mark Davis, Coordinator, Michigan State University, Office of Study Abroad, 109 International Center, East Lansing, MI 48824-1035; *Phone:* 517-432-1315; *Fax:* 517-432-2082. *E-mail:* mdavis@msu.edu. *World Wide Web:* http://studyabroad.msu.edu/

ST. JOHN'S UNIVERSITY
SUMMER PROGRAM IN ARGENTINA

Held at University of Buenos Aires, University of Cuenca del Plata

Academic Focus • Spanish language and literature.

Program Information • Classes are held on the campus of University of Cuenca del Plata (Corrientes, Argentina), University of Buenos Aires (Buenos Aires, Argentina). Faculty members are drawn from the sponsor's U.S. staff. Field trips to Iguazú Falls. Students typically earn 3–6 semester credits per term.

Sessions • Jul (summer).

Eligibility Requirements • Minimum age 18; open to freshmen, sophomores, juniors, seniors, graduate students; 2.75 GPA; 2 letters of recommendation; good academic standing at home school; interview; 1 year of college course work in Spanish.

Living Arrangements • Students live in host institution dormitories, locally rented apartments, hotels. Quarters are shared with host institution students. Meals are taken on one's own, in residences, in restaurants.

Costs (2004) • $2275; includes housing, some meals, excursions, international airfare, student support services, bus trip between Corrientes and Buenos Aires, transportation to and from Argentina airports, guided tours, guest lectures. $30 application fee. $750 nonrefundable deposit required. Financial aid available for students from sponsoring institution: scholarships, loans, students must be enrolled for at least 6 credits to receive aid.

For More Information • Dr. Ruth De Paula, Director, Office of Study Abroad Programs, St. John's University, 8000 Utopia Parkway, Jamaica, NY 11439; *Phone:* 718-990-6105; *Fax:* 718-990-2321. *E-mail:* intled@stjohns.edu. *World Wide Web:* http://www.stjohns.edu/studyabroad/

UNIVERSITY OF DELAWARE
WINTER SESSION IN ARGENTINA

Hosted by Palermo University Buenos Aires

Academic Focus • Political science and government, Spanish language and literature.

Program Information • Students attend classes at Palermo University Buenos Aires (Buenos Aires, Argentina). Field trips to Iguazú Falls, Colonia, a tango performance, a ranch visit, Mar del Plata; optional travel to sites throughout Argentina at an extra cost. Students typically earn 6 semester credits per term.

Sessions • Jan (winter).

Eligibility Requirements • Open to freshmen, sophomores, juniors, seniors, adults; 2.0 GPA; 1 letter of recommendation; no foreign language proficiency required.

Living Arrangements • Students live in host family homes. Meals are taken with host family, in residences.

Costs (2005) • Contact sponsor for cost. $200 nonrefundable deposit required. Financial aid available for all students: scholarships.

For More Information • Center for International Studies, University of Delaware, 186 South College Avenue, Newark, DE 19716-1450; *Phone:* 888-831-4685; *Fax:* 302-831-6042. *E-mail:* studyabroad@udel.edu. *World Wide Web:* http://www.udel.edu/studyabroad/

UNIVERSITY OF MINNESOTA
CULTURE AND HISTORY IN BUENOS AIRES

Academic Focus • Area studies, art history, cultural studies.

Program Information • Field trips to Colonia, Uruguay. Students typically earn 3 semester credits per term.

Sessions • May–Jun (summer).

Eligibility Requirements • Minimum age 18; open to freshmen, sophomores, juniors, seniors, adults; 2.5 GPA; good academic standing at home school; no foreign language proficiency required.

Living Arrangements • Students live in host institution dormitories, hotels. Quarters are shared with students from other programs. Meals are taken as a group, on one's own, in central dining facility, in restaurants.

Costs (2006) • Contact sponsor for cost; includes tuition, housing, some meals, insurance, excursions, international airfare, student support services. Financial aid available for students from sponsoring institution: scholarships, loans.

For More Information • Learning Abroad Center, University of Minnesota, 230 Heller Hall, 271 19th Avenue South, Minneapolis, MN 55455; *Phone:* 888-700-UOFM; *Fax:* 612-626-8009. *E-mail:* umabroad@umn.edu. *World Wide Web:* http://www.umabroad.umn.edu/

UNIVERSITY OF PENNSYLVANIA
PENN-IN-BUENOS AIRES, ARGENTINA

Hosted by San Andres University, Victoria

Academic Focus • Argentine studies, Latin American studies, Spanish language and literature.

Program Information • Students attend classes at San Andres University, Victoria (Buenos Aires, Argentina). Scheduled travel. Students typically earn 2 course units per term.

Sessions • Jul–Aug (summer).

Eligibility Requirements • Open to freshmen, sophomores, juniors, seniors, graduate students; 1 letter of recommendation; good academic standing at home school; language proficiency requirement is dependent on course chosen.

Living Arrangements • Students live in host family homes. Meals are taken with host family.

Costs (2005) • $5700; includes tuition, housing, all meals, insurance, excursions. $50 application fee. $300 nonrefundable deposit required. Financial aid available for students from sponsoring institution: scholarships, loans.

For More Information • Penn Summer Abroad, University of Pennsylvania, 3440 Market Street, Suite 100, Philadelphia, PA 19104-3335; *Phone:* 215-746-6900; *Fax:* 215-573-2053. *E-mail:* summerabroad@sas.upenn.edu. *World Wide Web:* http://www.sas.upenn.edu/summer/

CÓRDOBA

ARGENTINA I.L.E.E.
SPANISH SCHOOL FOR FOREIGNERS

Hosted by Argentina I.L.E.E.

Academic Focus • Spanish language and literature.

Program Information • Students attend classes at Argentina I.L.E.E. (Córdoba, Argentina). Scheduled travel to Buenos Aires Province locations, Córdoba; field trips to social/cultural activities; optional travel to Buenos Aires Province, Córdoba at an extra cost.

Sessions • 2 weeks or more, year-round.

Eligibility Requirements • Open to precollege students, freshmen, sophomores, juniors, seniors, graduate students, adults; no foreign language proficiency required.

Living Arrangements • Students live in host family homes, hotels. Quarters are shared with host institution students. Meals are taken on one's own, with host family, in central dining facility.

Costs (2004–2005) • $210 per week; includes tuition, housing, all meals, books and class materials, lab equipment, international student ID, student support services, cafeteria access. $50 application fee.

For More Information • Mr. Daniel Korman, International Director, Argentina I.L.E.E., Avenida Callao 339, 3et piso (1022), 1022 Buenos Aires, Argentina; *Phone:* +54 11-47827173; *Fax:* +54 11-47827173. *E-mail:* info@argentinailee.com. *World Wide Web:* http://www.argentinailee.com/

THE CENTER FOR CROSS-CULTURAL STUDY
CC-CS SUMMER TERM IN CÓRDOBA, ARGENTINA

Hosted by University Blas Pascal
Academic Focus • Cultural studies, Spanish language and literature.
Program Information • Students attend classes at University Blas Pascal (Córdoba, Argentina). Field trips to Buenos Aires, Las Estancia Jesuitas. Students typically earn 4 semester credits per term.
Sessions • Jul–Aug (summer).
Eligibility Requirements • Minimum age 18; open to freshmen, sophomores, juniors, seniors, graduate students, adults; 1 letter of recommendation; good academic standing at home school; minimum 3.0 GPA in Spanish; 1.5 years of college course work in Spanish.
Living Arrangements • Students live in host family homes. Quarters are shared with host institution students. Meals are taken with host family, in residences.
Costs (2007) • $2685; includes tuition, housing, all meals, insurance, excursions, lab equipment, student support services, activities, study tours, laundry, email and high-speed Internet access. $50 application fee. $300 deposit required. Financial aid available for all students: scholarships.
For More Information • Dr. Judith M. Ortiz, Director, U.S., The Center for Cross-Cultural Study, 446 Main Street, Amherst, MA 01002-2314; *Phone:* 413-256-0011; *Fax:* 413-256-1968. *E-mail:* admin@cccs.com. *World Wide Web:* http://www.cccs.com/

ENFOREX–SPANISH IN THE SPANISH WORLD
SPANISH INTENSIVE COURSE CÓRDOBA

Hosted by ENFOREX
Academic Focus • Sociology, Spanish language and literature.
Program Information • Students attend classes at ENFOREX (Córdoba, Argentina). Field trips to Córdoba; optional travel to Rosario at an extra cost. Students typically earn 4 semester credits per term.
Sessions • Year-round.
Eligibility Requirements • Minimum age 18; open to freshmen, juniors, seniors, graduate students, adults; no foreign language proficiency required.
Living Arrangements • Students live in host family homes. Meals are taken as a group, on one's own, with host family.
Costs (2005) • $920 per month; includes tuition, housing, all meals, excursions, books and class materials, lab equipment, international student ID, student support services. $100 application fee. $250 nonrefundable deposit required.
For More Information • Mr. Antonio Anadón, Director of Spanish Department, ENFOREX–Spanish in the Spanish World, Alberto Aguilera, 26, 28015 Madrid, Spain; *Phone:* +34 91-594-3776; *Fax:* +34 91-594-5159. *E-mail:* promotion@enforex.es. *World Wide Web:* http://www.enforex.com/

LINGUA SERVICE WORLDWIDE
VACATION 'N LEARN SPANISH AT COINED ARGENTINA

Hosted by Comision de Intercambio Educativo (COINED)
Academic Focus • Spanish language and literature, Spanish studies.
Program Information • Students attend classes at Comision de Intercambio Educativo (COINED) (Córdoba, Argentina). Optional travel at an extra cost. Students typically earn 3 semester credits for 3 weeks, 6 semester credits for 5 weeks.
Sessions • Year-round sessions of 2 or more weeks.
Eligibility Requirements • Minimum age 18; open to freshmen, sophomores, juniors, seniors, graduate students, adults; no foreign language proficiency required.
Living Arrangements • Students live in locally rented apartments, host family homes, hotels. Meals are taken on one's own.
Costs (2006–2007) • Contact sponsor for cost. $100 application fee.
For More Information • Assistant Director, Lingua Service Worldwide, 75 Prospect Street, Suite 4, Huntington, NY 11743; *Phone:* 800-394-5327; *Fax:* 631-271-3441. *E-mail:* linguaservice@att.net. *World Wide Web:* http://www.linguaserviceworldwide.com/

ROSARIO

AHA INTERNATIONAL AN ACADEMIC PROGRAM OF THE UNIVERSITY OF OREGON
ROSARIO, ARGENTINA: NORTHWEST COUNCIL ON STUDY ABROAD

Hosted by National University of Rosario
Academic Focus • Spanish language and literature.
Program Information • Students attend classes at National University of Rosario (Rosario, Argentina). Field trips to Espinillo Island, local "estancia," museums, monuments, parks. Students typically earn 6–12 quarter credits per session.
Sessions • Jun–Jul (summer), Jul–Aug (summer 2).
Eligibility Requirements • Open to sophomores, juniors, seniors; 2 letters of recommendation; good academic standing at home school; official transcript; no foreign language proficiency required.
Living Arrangements • Students live in host family homes. Meals are taken with host family, in residences.
Costs (2005–2006) • $2400; includes tuition, housing, all meals, insurance, excursions, books and class materials, student support services, local transportation, on-site orientation. $50 application fee. $200 refundable deposit required. Financial aid available for all students: scholarships, loans, home institution financial aid.
For More Information • Mr. Richard Browning, Associate Director for University Programs, AHA International An Academic Program of the University of Oregon, 221 NW 2nd Avenue, Suite 200, Portland, OR 97209; *Phone:* 503-295-7730; *Fax:* 503-295-5969. *E-mail:* mail@aha-intl.org. *World Wide Web:* http://www.aha-intl.org/

USTRALIA

CITY-TO-CITY

COOPERATIVE CENTER FOR STUDY ABROAD
AUSTRALIA WINTER

Academic Focus • Biological/life sciences.
Program Information • Faculty members are drawn from the sponsor's U.S. staff. Field trips. Students typically earn 3 semester credits per term.
Sessions • Dec–Jan (winter).
Eligibility Requirements • Minimum age 18; open to freshmen, sophomores, juniors, seniors, graduate students, adults; good academic standing at home school.
Living Arrangements • Students live in host institution dormitories, hotels. Quarters are shared with host institution students. Meals are taken as a group, on one's own, in central dining facility, in restaurants.
Costs (2006–2007) • $4895; includes housing, some meals, insurance, excursions, international airfare, student support services, airport transfers. $200 nonrefundable deposit required. Financial aid available for students from sponsoring institution: scholarships, loans.
For More Information • Dr. Michael A. Klembara, Executive Director, Cooperative Center for Study Abroad, Northern Kentucky University, Nunn Drive, Founders Hall 301, Highland Heights, KY 41099; *Phone:* 800-319-6015; *Fax:* 859-572-6650. *E-mail:* ccsa@nku.edu. *World Wide Web:* http://www.ccsa.cc/

MICHIGAN STATE UNIVERSITY
ENVIRONMENTAL MANAGEMENT IN NORTHWESTERN AUSTRALIA

Academic Focus • Wildlife studies, zoology.
Program Information • Faculty members are drawn from the sponsor's U.S. staff. Field trips to Darwin, Kakadu National Park, Kununarra, Broome, Exmouth, Perth. Students typically earn 8 semester credits per term.
Sessions • May–Jun (summer).
Eligibility Requirements • Minimum age 18; open to juniors, seniors, graduate students; major in fisheries and wildlife, zoology, biology, environmental science; 2.5 GPA; good academic standing at home school; faculty approval; letter of interest.
Living Arrangements • Students live in host institution dormitories, hotels, campsites. Meals are taken as a group, on one's own, in central dining facility, in restaurants.
Costs (2005) • Contact sponsor for cost. $100 application fee. $200 nonrefundable deposit required. Financial aid available for students from sponsoring institution: scholarships, loans.
For More Information • Ms. Sandy Tupper, Educational Programs Coordinator, Michigan State University, Office of Study Abroad, 109 International Center, East Lansing, MI 48824-1035; *Phone:* 517-353-8920; *Fax:* 517-432-2082. *E-mail:* tuppers@msu.edu. *World Wide Web:* http://studyabroad.msu.edu/

MICHIGAN STATE UNIVERSITY
FOOD, ENVIRONMENTAL, AND SOCIAL SYSTEMS IN AUSTRALIA

Academic Focus • Agriculture, environmental science/studies, food science, social sciences.
Program Information • Faculty members are drawn from the sponsor's U.S. staff. Scheduled travel to Tasmania; field trips to farms, agri-businesses, wildlife sanctuaries, national parks; optional travel to Hawaii at an extra cost. Students typically earn 6 semester credits per term.
Sessions • May–Jun (summer).
Eligibility Requirements • Minimum age 18; open to freshmen, sophomores, juniors, seniors, graduate students; 2.75 GPA; good academic standing at home school; faculty approval; good physical condition.
Living Arrangements • Students live in host institution dormitories, hotels. Meals are taken as a group, on one's own, in restaurants.
Costs (2004–2005) • $2651; includes housing, some meals, insurance, excursions, student support services. $100 application fee. $200 nonrefundable deposit required. Financial aid available for students from sponsoring institution: scholarships, loans.
For More Information • Ms. Sandy Tuppers, Educational Programs Coordinator, Michigan State University, Office of Study Abroad, 109 International Center, East Lansing, MI 48824-1035; *Phone:* 517-353-8920; *Fax:* 517-432-2082. *E-mail:* tuppers@msu.edu. *World Wide Web:* http://studyabroad.msu.edu/

MICHIGAN STATE UNIVERSITY
SUMMER SPORTS PROGRAM AT MACQUARIE UNIVERSITY

Held at Macquarie University
Academic Focus • Communications, economics, interdisciplinary studies, sociology.

Program Information • Classes are held on the campus of Macquarie University (Sydney). Faculty members are drawn from the sponsor's U.S. staff and local instructors hired by the sponsor. Scheduled travel to Melbourne, Canberry; field trips to Blue Mountains, sporting events, cultural events.
Sessions • Jun–Aug (summer).
Eligibility Requirements • Minimum age 18; open to freshmen, sophomores, juniors, seniors, graduate students; 2.5 GPA; 2 letters of recommendation; good academic standing at home school; faculty approval, good physical condition.
Living Arrangements • Students live in host institution dormitories. Meals are taken as a group, on one's own, in residences, in central dining facility.
Costs (2004–2005) • $3990; includes housing, some meals, insurance, excursions, student support services, use of sport/training facilities. $100 application fee. $200 nonrefundable deposit required. Financial aid available for students from sponsoring institution: loans.
For More Information • Ms. Sandy Tupper, Educational Programs Coordinator, Michigan State University, Office of Study Abroad, 109 International Center, East Lansing, MI 48824-1035; *Phone:* 517-353-8920; *Fax:* 517-432-2082. *E-mail:* tuppers@msu.edu. *World Wide Web:* http://studyabroad.msu.edu/

STATE UNIVERSITY OF NEW YORK AT NEW PALTZ
SUMMER AUSTRALIAN ECO-TOUR
Held at University of New England

Academic Focus • Aboriginal studies, anthropology, ecology, education, wildlife studies.
Program Information • Classes are held on the campus of University of New England (Armidale). Faculty members are drawn from the sponsor's U.S. staff. Scheduled travel to many national parks, Noulangie Rock, the Mangarre monsoon forest, the Great Barrier Reef, the most remote roadhouses in the world; field trips to local attractions of Sydney. Students typically earn 6 semester credits per term.
Sessions • Jun–Jul (summer).
Eligibility Requirements • Minimum age 18; open to freshmen, sophomores, juniors, seniors, graduate students; 2.5 GPA; 1 letter of recommendation; good academic standing at home school.
Living Arrangements • Students live in hotels, campgrounds; bunk houses; roadhouses. Meals are taken on one's own, in central dining facility, in restaurants.
Costs (2006) • $3200 for New York residents; $4800 for nonresidents; includes tuition, housing, some meals, excursions, administrative fee. $25 application fee. $300 nonrefundable deposit required. Financial aid available for students from sponsoring institution: scholarships, loans.
For More Information • Center for International Programs, State University of New York at New Paltz, 1 Hawk Drive, New Paltz, NY 12561-2443; *Phone:* 845-257-3125; *Fax:* 845-257-3129. *E-mail:* studyabroad@newpaltz.edu. *World Wide Web:* http://www.newpaltz.edu/studyabroad/

UNIVERSITY OF DELAWARE
WINTER SESSION IN AUSTRALIA–ACCOUNTING AND MIS

Academic Focus • Accounting, management information systems.
Program Information • Faculty members are drawn from the sponsor's U.S. staff. Scheduled travel to Sydney; field trips to the Great Barrier Reef; optional travel to Australia at an extra cost. Students typically earn 6 semester credits per term.
Sessions • Jan–Feb (winter).
Eligibility Requirements • Open to freshmen, sophomores, juniors, seniors; 2.0 GPA; 1 letter of recommendation.
Living Arrangements • Students live in host institution dormitories. Meals are taken as a group, on one's own, in central dining facility, in restaurants.
Costs (2005) • Contact sponsor for cost. $200 nonrefundable deposit required. Financial aid available for all students: scholarships.
For More Information • Center for International Studies, University of Delaware, 186 South College Avenue, Newark, DE 19716-1450; *Phone:* 888-831-4685; *Fax:* 302-831-6042. *E-mail:* studyabroad@udel.edu. *World Wide Web:* http://www.udel.edu/studyabroad/

UNIVERSITY OF DELAWARE
WINTER SESSION IN AUSTRALIA: MECHANICAL AND CIVIL ENGINEERING

Academic Focus • Mechanical engineering.
Program Information • Faculty members are drawn from the sponsor's U.S. staff and local instructors hired by the sponsor. Field trips to Sydney; optional travel to Australia, New Zealand at an extra cost. Students typically earn 6 semester credits per term.
Sessions • Jan–Feb (winter).
Eligibility Requirements • Open to freshmen, sophomores, juniors, seniors, adults; 2.0 GPA; 1 letter of recommendation.
Living Arrangements • Students live in host institution dormitories. Meals are taken as a group, on one's own, in central dining facility.
Costs (2005) • Contact sponsor for cost. $200 nonrefundable deposit required. Financial aid available for all students: scholarships.
For More Information • Center for International Studies, University of Delaware, 186 South College Avenue, Newark, DE 19716-1450; *Phone:* 888-831-4685; *Fax:* 302-831-6042. *E-mail:* studyabroad@udel.edu. *World Wide Web:* http://www.udel.edu/studyabroad/

ATHERTON TABLELANDS

THE SCHOOL FOR FIELD STUDIES
TROPICAL RAINFOREST MANAGEMENT STUDIES
Hosted by Center for Rainforest Studies

Academic Focus • Australian studies, biological/life sciences, conservation studies, ecology, economics, environmental science/studies, forestry, natural resources.
Program Information • Students attend classes at Center for Rainforest Studies (Tropical North Queensland, Australia). Field trips to Atherton Tablelands rainforest, Lake Tinaroo. Students typically earn 4 semester credits per term.
Sessions • Sep–Dec (summer), Jan–May (summer 2).
Eligibility Requirements • Minimum age 16; open to precollege students, freshmen, sophomores, juniors, seniors; 2.5 GPA; 2 letters of recommendation; personal statement.
Living Arrangements • Students live in cabins in the rainforest. Quarters are shared with host institution students. Meals are taken as a group, in central dining facility.
Costs (2007) • $4080; includes tuition, housing, all meals, excursions, lab equipment. $45 application fee. $450 nonrefundable deposit required. Financial aid available for all students: scholarships, loans.
For More Information • Admissions Department, The School for Field Studies, 10 Federal Street, Suite 24, Salem, MA 01970-3876; *Phone:* 800-989-4418; *Fax:* 978-741-3551. *E-mail:* admissions@fieldstudies.org. *World Wide Web:* http://www.fieldstudies.org/

BRISBANE

AMERICAN UNIVERSITIES INTERNATIONAL PROGRAMS (AUIP)
AUSTRALIA: HUMANS AND THE ENVIRONMENT
Hosted by University of Queensland

Academic Focus • Anthropology, conservation studies, ecology, forestry, geography, natural resources, parks and recreation.
Program Information • Students attend classes at University of Queensland (Brisbane, Australia). Scheduled travel to Lamington National Park, Lady Elliot Island (Great Barrier Reef), Outback, Carnarvon Gorge; field trips to Lamington National Park, Lady Elliot Island (Great Barrier Reef), Outback, Carnarvon Gorge. Students typically earn 6 semester credits per term.
Sessions • May–Jun (summer), Jun–Jul (summer 2), Dec–Jan (winter).
Eligibility Requirements • Minimum age 18; open to sophomores, juniors, seniors, graduate students, adults; 2.0 GPA; 2 letters of recommendation; good academic standing at home school; essay; official transcript.
Living Arrangements • Students live in hotels, hostels. Meals are taken as a group, on one's own, in residences, in restaurants.

AUSTRALIA
Brisbane

Costs (2006) • $2450; includes housing, some meals, insurance, excursions, student support services, all in-country travel and activities. $300 application fee.
For More Information • Dr. Michael Tarrant, Director, American Universities International Programs (AUIP), 108 South Main Street, Winterville, GA 30683; *Phone:* 706-742-9285. *E-mail:* info@auip.com. *World Wide Web:* http://www.auip.com/

AUSTRALEARN: STUDY IN AUSTRALIA, NEW ZEALAND, AND THE SOUTH PACIFIC
TROPICAL MARINE SCIENCE ON THE GREAT BARRIER REEF (LONG ISLAND UNIVERSITY)

Academic Focus • Biological/life sciences, ecology, marine sciences, wildlife studies, zoology.
Program Information • Faculty members are local instructors hired by the sponsor. Scheduled travel to Stradbroke Island, Orpheus Island, Heron Island, Cairns; field trips to local attractions at many coastal sites. Students typically earn 4 semester credits per term.
Sessions • May–Jun (summer).
Eligibility Requirements • Minimum age 18; open to sophomores, juniors, seniors, graduate students, adults; 2.5 GPA; 1 letter of recommendation; good academic standing at home school; at least two 100-level biology courses.
Living Arrangements • Students live in host institution dormitories, locally rented apartments, hotels. Meals are taken as a group, in central dining facility, in restaurants.
Costs (2007) • $3990; includes tuition, housing, some meals, excursions, books and class materials, lab equipment, international student ID, student support services. $30 application fee. $300 refundable deposit required. Financial aid available for students from sponsoring institution: loans.
For More Information • AustraLearn: Study in Australia, New Zealand, and the South Pacific, 12050 North Pecos Street, Suite 320, Westminster, CO 80234; *Phone:* 800-980-0033; *Fax:* 303-446-5955. *E-mail:* studyabroad@australearn.org. *World Wide Web:* http://www.australearn.org/

INSTITUTE FOR STUDY ABROAD, BUTLER UNIVERSITY
UNIVERSITY OF QUEENSLAND GREAT BARRIER REEF SUMMER PROGRAM

Hosted by University of Queensland
Academic Focus • Marine sciences.
Program Information • Students attend classes at University of Queensland (Brisbane, Australia). Scheduled travel to Moreton Bay or Heron Island. Students typically earn 4–8 semester credits per term.
Sessions • Jun–Aug (summer).
Eligibility Requirements • Open to sophomores, juniors, seniors; course work in 1 year of biology; 1 letter of recommendation; good academic standing at home school; enrollment at an accredited American college or university.
Living Arrangements • Students live in research stations. Quarters are shared with host institution students. Meals are taken as a group, in central dining facility.
Costs (2005) • $3200–$3800; includes tuition, housing, all meals, insurance, books and class materials, lab equipment, student support services, pre-departure advising. $40 application fee. $500 nonrefundable deposit required. Financial aid available for all students: scholarships.
For More Information • Institute for Study Abroad, Butler University, 1100 West 42nd Street, Suite 305, Indianapolis, IN 46208-3345; *Phone:* 800-858-0229; *Fax:* 317-940-9704. *E-mail:* study-abroad@butler.edu. *World Wide Web:* http://www.ifsa-butler.org/

CAIRNES

AMERICAN INSTITUTE FOR FOREIGN STUDY (AIFS)
AIFS–CAIRNS, AUSTRALIA–JAMES COOK UNIVERSITY

Hosted by James Cook University–Cairns Campus
Academic Focus • Ecology.

Program Information • Students attend classes at James Cook University–Cairns Campus (Cairns, Australia). Field trips to Sydney, Great Barrier Reef and the Outback. Students typically earn 3 semester credits per term.
Sessions • Jun–Jul (summer).
Eligibility Requirements • Minimum age 17; open to precollege students, freshmen, sophomores, juniors, seniors; 2.5 GPA.
Living Arrangements • Students live in program-owned apartments, hotels, Nature Lodges. Quarters are shared with host institution students. Meals are taken as a group, in residences.
Costs (2007) • $5599; includes tuition, housing, some meals, insurance, excursions, student support services, Entrances/transfers, accompanying travel manager, Phone Card to call the U.S. $95 application fee. $395 nonrefundable deposit required. Financial aid available for all students: scholarships.
For More Information • Ms. David Mauro, Admissions Advisor, American Institute For Foreign Study (AIFS), 9 West Broad Street, Stamford, CT 06902-3788; *Phone:* 800-727-2437 Ext. 5163; *Fax:* 203-399-5597. *E-mail:* dmauro@aifs.com. *World Wide Web:* http://www.aifsabroad.com/

CAIRNS

INSTITUTE FOR STUDY ABROAD, BUTLER UNIVERSITY
JAMES COOK UNIVERSITY SUMMER STUDY IN UNDERWATER PHOTOGRAPHY AND VIDEOGRAPHY

Hosted by James Cook University–Cairns Campus
Academic Focus • Photography.
Program Information • Students attend classes at James Cook University–Cairns Campus (Cairns, Australia). Field trips to Great Barrier Reef. Students typically earn 4 semester credits per term.
Sessions • Jun–Jul (summer), Jul (summer 2).
Eligibility Requirements • Open to sophomores, juniors, seniors; 2.8 GPA; 1 letter of recommendation; good academic standing at home school; enrollment at an accredited American college or university; basic open water diving certificate; minimum 15 hours logged diving time; current dive medical certificate.
Living Arrangements • Students live in host institution dormitories. Quarters are shared with host institution students, students from other programs. Meals are taken as a group, on one's own, in residences, in central dining facility.
Costs (2005) • $4175 for 1 term; $6795 for 2 terms; includes tuition, housing, all meals, insurance, excursions, books and class materials, lab equipment, student support services, pre-departure advising. $40 application fee. $500 nonrefundable deposit required. Financial aid available for all students: scholarships.
For More Information • Institute for Study Abroad, Butler University, 1100 West 42nd Street, Suite 305, Indianapolis, IN 46208-3345; *Phone:* 800-858-0229; *Fax:* 317-940-9704. *E-mail:* study-abroad@butler.edu. *World Wide Web:* http://www.ifsa-butler.org/

GOLD COAST

ARCADIA UNIVERSITY
BOND UNIVERSITY

Hosted by Bond University
Academic Focus • Business administration/management, communications, film and media studies, law and legal studies, liberal studies, social sciences.
Program Information • Students attend classes at Bond University (Gold Coast, Australia). Scheduled travel to Melbourne, Moreton Island. Students typically earn 12–16 semester credits per term.
Sessions • May–Aug (summer).
Eligibility Requirements • Open to freshmen, sophomores, juniors, seniors, graduate students; 2.5 GPA; 1 letter of recommendation.
Living Arrangements • Students live in host institution dormitories, program-owned apartments. Quarters are shared with host institution students. Meals are taken on one's own, in residences, in central dining facility.
Costs (2005) • $13,450; includes tuition, housing, insurance, international student ID, student support services, transcripts,

pre-departure guide, on-site orientation. $35 application fee. $500 nonrefundable deposit required. Financial aid available for all students: scholarships, loans.

For More Information • Arcadia University, Center for Education Abroad, 450 South Easton Road, Glenside, PA 19038-3295; *Phone:* 866-927-2234; *Fax:* 215-572-2174. *E-mail:* cea@arcadia.edu. *World Wide Web:* http://www.arcadia.edu/cea/

AUSTRALEARN: STUDY IN AUSTRALIA, NEW ZEALAND, AND THE SOUTH PACIFIC
THE AUSTRALIAN EXPERIENCE

Hosted by Bond University

Academic Focus • Civilization studies, ecology, geography, history, international affairs, social sciences, sociology.

Program Information • Students attend classes at Bond University (Gold Coast, Australia). Scheduled travel; field trips to outback Australia, Great Barrier Reef. Students typically earn 3-6 semester credits per term.

Sessions • Jul-Aug (summer), 6 weeks: Jun-Jul.

Eligibility Requirements • Minimum age 18; open to sophomores, juniors; seniors; 2.5 GPA; 1 letter of recommendation; good academic standing at home school.

Living Arrangements • Students live in program-owned houses, hotels. Meals are taken as a group, in restaurants.

Costs (2007) • $5700 for 4 weeks; $9285 for 6 weeks; includes tuition, housing, some meals, insurance, excursions, student support services. $20 application fee. $300 deposit required.

For More Information • AustraLearn: Study in Australia, New Zealand, and the South Pacific, 12050 North Pecos Street, Suite 320, Westminster, CO 80234; *Phone:* 800-980-0033; *Fax:* 303-446-5955. *E-mail:* studyabroad@australearn.org. *World Wide Web:* http://www.australearn.org/

CENTER FOR INTERNATIONAL STUDIES
BOND UNIVERSITY

Hosted by Bond University

Academic Focus • Full curriculum.

Program Information • Students attend classes at Bond University (Gold Coast, Australia). Field trips to a hinterland excursion; optional travel to the Great Barrier Reef, Sydney at an extra cost. Students typically earn 12-16 semester credits per term.

Sessions • May-Aug (summer).

Eligibility Requirements • Minimum age 18; open to freshmen, sophomores, juniors, seniors, graduate students, adults; 2.5 GPA; 1 letter of recommendation; good academic standing at home school; personal essay

Living Arrangements • Students live in host institution dormitories. Quarters are shared with host institution students, students from other programs. Meals are taken on one's own, in central dining facility.

Costs (2005) • $12,400; includes tuition, housing, some meals, insurance, excursions, international student ID, student support services, airport reception. $50 application fee. $500 nonrefundable deposit required. Financial aid available for all students: scholarships.

For More Information • Mr. Jeff Palm, Program Director, Center for International Studies, 25 New South Street, #105, Northampton, MA 01060; *Phone:* 413-582-0407; *Fax:* 413-582-0327. *E-mail:* jpalm@cisabroad.com. *World Wide Web:* http://www.cisabroad.com/

COLLEGE CONSORTIUM FOR INTERNATIONAL STUDIES–ST. BONAVENTURE UNIVERSITY AND TRUMAN STATE UNIVERSITY
SUMMER PROGRAM IN AUSTRALIA

Hosted by Bond University

Academic Focus • Full curriculum.

Program Information • Students attend classes at Bond University (Gold Coast, Australia). Field trips to a nearby camp (during orientation); optional travel to New Zealand, the Great Barrier Reef, New Caledonia, Fiji at an extra cost. Students typically earn 12-16 semester credits per term.

Sessions • May-Aug (summer).

Eligibility Requirements • Minimum age 18; open to freshmen, sophomores, juniors, seniors; 2.5 GPA; 3 letters of recommendation; good academic standing at home school; statement of purpose.

Living Arrangements • Students live in host institution dormitories, program-owned apartments. Quarters are shared with host institution students, students from other programs. Meals are taken as a group, on one's own, in residences, in central dining facility.

Costs (2006) • $9700; includes tuition, insurance, student support services, instructional and administrative fees. $30 application fee. $200 nonrefundable deposit required. Financial aid available for students from sponsoring institution: scholarships, loans.

For More Information • Center for International Education, College Consortium for International Studies–St. Bonaventure University and Truman State University, 100 East Normal, Kirk Building 114, Kirksville, MO 63501; *Phone:* 660-785-4076; *Fax:* 660-785-7476. *E-mail:* ciea@truman.edu. *World Wide Web:* http://www.ccisabroad.org/. Students may also apply through St. Bonaventure University, St. Bonaventure, NY 14778.

MAGNETIC ISLAND

ARCADIA UNIVERSITY
ENVIRONMENTAL MANAGEMENT OF TROPICAL REEFS AND ISLAND ECOSYSTEMS

Academic Focus • Ecology, marine sciences.

Program Information • Faculty members are local instructors hired by the sponsor. Scheduled travel; field trips to Lizard Island, Orpheus Island. Students typically earn 4 semester credits per term.

Sessions • Jun-Jul (summer).

Eligibility Requirements • Open to freshmen, sophomores, juniors, seniors, graduate students; 2.5 GPA; 1 letter of recommendation.

Living Arrangements • Students live in hotels. Quarters are shared with students from other programs. Meals are taken as a group, on one's own, in central dining facility.

Costs (2005) • $4290; includes tuition, housing, some meals, insurance, lab equipment, international student ID, student support services, transcript, pre-departure guide, orientation. $35 application fee. $500 nonrefundable deposit required. Financial aid available for all students: loans.

For More Information • Arcadia University, Center for Education Abroad, 450 South Easton Road, Glenside, PA 19038-3295; *Phone:* 866-927-2234; *Fax:* 215-572-2174. *E-mail:* cea@arcadia.edu. *World Wide Web:* http://www.arcadia.edu/cea/

MELBOURNE

AUSTRALEARN: STUDY IN AUSTRALIA, NEW ZEALAND, AND THE SOUTH PACIFIC
AUSTRALIAN BEYOND THE CITIES

Hosted by La Trobe University Albury-Wodonga

Academic Focus • Aboriginal studies, Australian studies, comparative history, cultural studies, geography, history, sociology.

Program Information • Students attend classes at La Trobe University Albury-Wodonga (Wodonga, Australia). Field trips to Murray River, surrounding cultural locations. Students typically earn 3 semester credits per term.

Sessions • J-term: Jan.

Eligibility Requirements • Minimum age 18; open to sophomores, juniors, seniors, graduate students; 2.5 GPA; 1 letter of recommendation.

Living Arrangements • Students live in host institution dormitories. Quarters are shared with host institution students. Meals are taken as a group, in central dining facility.

Costs (2007) • $4335; includes tuition, housing, some meals, insurance, excursions, student support services. $20 application fee. $300 deposit required.

For More Information • AustraLearn: Study in Australia, New Zealand, and the South Pacific, 12050 North Pecos Street, Suite 320, Westminster, CO 80234; *Phone:* 800-980-0033; *Fax:* 303-446-5955. *E-mail:* studyabroad@australearn.org. *World Wide Web:* http://www.australearn.org/

AUSTRALIA
Melbourne

AUSTRALEARN: STUDY IN AUSTRALIA, NEW ZEALAND, AND THE SOUTH PACIFIC
CIRQUE DE LA VILLE VIVANT–CONTEMPORARY PERFORMANCE

Hosted by Swinburne University
Academic Focus • Dance, drama/theater, performing arts.
Program Information • Students attend classes at Swinburne University (Melbourne, Australia). Field trips to cultural venues and events in Melbourne. Students typically earn 3 semester credits per term.
Sessions • Jun–Jul (summer).
Eligibility Requirements • Minimum age 18; open to sophomores, juniors, seniors; 2.5 GPA; 1 letter of recommendation.
Living Arrangements • Students live in host institution dormitories, locally rented apartments. Quarters are shared with host institution students. Meals are taken as a group, on one's own, in central dining facility, in restaurants.
Costs (2007) • $4335; includes tuition, housing, some meals, insurance, excursions, lab equipment, student support services. $20 application fee. $300 deposit required.
For More Information • AustraLearn: Study in Australia, New Zealand, and the South Pacific, 12050 North Pecos Street, Suite 320, Westminster, CO 80234; *Phone:* 800-980-0033; *Fax:* 303-446-5955. *E-mail:* studyabroad@australearn.org. *World Wide Web:* http://www.australearn.org/

INSTITUTE FOR STUDY ABROAD, BUTLER UNIVERSITY
UNIVERSITY OF MELBOURNE SUMMER STUDY

Held at University of Melbourne
Academic Focus • Australian studies.
Program Information • Classes are held on the campus of University of Melbourne (Melbourne, Australia). Students typically earn 8 semester credits per term.
Sessions • Jun–Jul (summer).
Eligibility Requirements • Open to sophomores, juniors, seniors; 3.0 GPA; 1 letter of recommendation; good academic standing at home school; enrollment at an accredited American college or university.
Living Arrangements • Students live in locally rented apartments. Quarters are shared with host institution students, students from other programs. Meals are taken on one's own, in residences.
Costs (2005) • $4300; includes tuition, housing, insurance, student support services, pre-departure advising. $40 application fee. $500 nonrefundable deposit required. Financial aid available for all students: scholarships.
For More Information • Institute for Study Abroad, Butler University, 1100 West 42nd Street, Suite 305, Indianapolis, IN 46208-3345; *Phone:* 800-858-0229; *Fax:* 317-940-9704. *E-mail:* study-abroad@butler.edu. *World Wide Web:* http://www.ifsa-butler.org/

JAMES MADISON UNIVERSITY
SUMMER STUDY IN AUSTRALIA

Academic Focus • Education.
Program Information • Faculty members are drawn from the sponsor's U.S. staff. Field trips. Students typically earn 3 semester credits per term.
Sessions • May–Jun (summer).
Eligibility Requirements • Minimum age 18; open to juniors, seniors; major in education; 2.0 GPA; good academic standing at home school.
Living Arrangements • Students live in locally rented apartments. Meals are taken as a group, on one's own, in central dining facility, in restaurants.
Costs (2005) • $3754 for Virginia residents; $4594 for nonresidents; includes tuition, housing, some meals, excursions, books and class materials, international student ID. $400 nonrefundable deposit required.
For More Information • Mr. Felix Wang, Director, James Madison University, Office of International Programs, MSC 5731, 1077 South Main Street, Harrisonburg, VA 22807; *Phone:* 540-568-6419; *Fax:* 540-568-3310. *E-mail:* studyabroad@jmu.edu. *World Wide Web:* http://www.jmu.edu/international/

PERTH

AUSTRALEARN: STUDY IN AUSTRALIA, NEW ZEALAND, AND THE SOUTH PACIFIC
WANJU BOODJAH–ABORIGINAL STUDIES

Hosted by Murdoch University
Academic Focus • Aboriginal studies, Australian studies, cultural studies, geography, intercultural studies, interdisciplinary studies, liberal studies, peace and conflict studies, political science and government, public policy, social sciences.
Program Information • Students attend classes at Murdoch University (Murdoch, Australia). Field trips to Fremantle, Rottnest Island, Yallingup, Maarli Mia; optional travel to western Australia. Students typically earn 6 semester credits per term.
Sessions • Jun–Jul (summer).
Eligibility Requirements • Minimum age 18; open to sophomores, juniors, seniors, graduate students, adults; 2.5 GPA; 1 letter of recommendation; one year of college/university on an official transcript.
Living Arrangements • Students live in locally rented apartments. Quarters are shared with host institution students, students from other programs. Meals are taken on one's own, in residences, in restaurants.
Costs (2007) • $4460; includes tuition, housing, insurance, excursions, student support services. $20 application fee. $300 deposit required.
For More Information • AustraLearn: Study in Australia, New Zealand, and the South Pacific, 12050 North Pecos Street, Suite 320, Westminster, CO 80234; *Phone:* 800-980-0033; *Fax:* 303-446-5955. *E-mail:* studyabroad@australearn.org. *World Wide Web:* http://www.australearn.org/

MICHIGAN STATE UNIVERSITY
CULTURAL AND COMMUNITY CONTEXT OF INDIGENOUS PEOPLE IN WESTERN AUSTRALIA

Academic Focus • Aboriginal studies, social sciences.
Program Information • Faculty members are drawn from the sponsor's U.S. staff. Scheduled travel to gold fields; field trips to museums, historical sites, cultural centers. Students typically earn 6 semester credits per term.
Sessions • May–Jun (summer).
Eligibility Requirements • Open to sophomores, juniors, seniors, graduate students; 2.4 GPA; good academic standing at home school; completed 2-3 courses in one or more of the following areas; child development; family studies; anthropology; social work or early childhood education.
Living Arrangements • Students live in locally rented apartments. Meals are taken as a group, on one's own, in residences, in restaurants.
Costs (2004–2005) • $1930; includes housing, some meals, insurance, excursions, books and class materials, student support services. $100 application fee. $200 nonrefundable deposit required. Financial aid available for students from sponsoring institution.
For More Information • Ms. Sandy Tupper, Educational Programs Coordinator, Michigan State University, Office of Study Abroad, 109 International Center, East Lansing, MI 48824-1035; *Phone:* 517-353-8920; *Fax:* 517-432-2082. *E-mail:* tuppers@msu.edu. *World Wide Web:* http://studyabroad.msu.edu/

QUEENSLAND

LIVING ROUTES–STUDY ABROAD IN ECOVILLAGES
LIVING ROUTES–AUSTRALIA: PERMACULTURE AT CRYSTAL WATERS

Hosted by Crystal Waters Permaculture Village
Academic Focus • Agriculture, community service, conservation studies, ecology, environmental health, environmental science/studies, interdisciplinary studies, peace and conflict studies, social sciences, urban/regional planning.
Program Information • Students attend classes at Crystal Waters Permaculture Village (Queensland, Australia). Scheduled travel to

Fraser Island, a World Heritage sand island; field trips to a rainforest, a crocodile farm, the Mary River; optional travel to the Sunshine Coast, horseback riding at an extra cost. Students typically earn 4 semester credits per term.
Sessions • Jun–Jul (summer), Jan (winter).
Eligibility Requirements • Minimum age 17; open to precollege students, freshmen, sophomores, juniors, seniors, graduate students, adults; 2.5 GPA; good academic standing at home school.
Living Arrangements • Students live in host institution dormitories. Quarters are shared with host institution students. Meals are taken as a group, in central dining facility.
Costs (2006) • $3035; includes tuition, housing, all meals, excursions, student support services. $25 application fee. $300 nonrefundable deposit required. Financial aid available for all students: scholarships.
For More Information • Mr. Gregg Orifici, Director of Admissions, Living Routes–Study Abroad in Ecovillages, 79 South Pleasant Street, Suite A5, Amherst, MA 01002; *Phone:* 888-515-7333; *Fax:* 413-259-9355. *E-mail:* programs@livingroutes.org. *World Wide Web:* http://www.LivingRoutes.org/

STATE UNIVERSITY OF NEW YORK COLLEGE AT CORTLAND
SUMMER STUDY ABROAD AT THE UNIVERSITY OF THE SUNSHINE COAST

Hosted by University of the Sunshine Coast
Academic Focus • Australian studies, education, environmental science/studies, international business, sports management.
Program Information • Students attend classes at University of the Sunshine Coast (Maroochydore, Australia). Field trips to Fraser Island, the Australia Zoo, Aboriginal Culture Center; optional travel to Sydney, Uluru, the Great Barrier Reef, the Outback, Melbourne at an extra cost. Students typically earn 6 semester credits per term.
Sessions • May–Jul (summer).
Eligibility Requirements • Minimum age 18; open to freshmen, sophomores, juniors, seniors, adults; 2.5 GPA; 2 letters of recommendation; good academic standing at home school.
Living Arrangements • Students live in program-owned apartments. Quarters are shared with students from other programs. Meals are taken on one's own, in residences.
Costs (2005) • $6356; includes tuition, housing, all meals, insurance, excursions, international airfare, books and class materials, international student ID, student support services, passport fees, social activities program. $20 application fee. $200 nonrefundable deposit required. Financial aid available for students from sponsoring institution: scholarships, loans.
For More Information • Ms. Liz McCartney, Assistant Director, Office of International Programs, State University of New York College at Cortland, PO Box 2000, Cortland, NY 13045; *Phone:* 607-753-2209; *Fax:* 607-753-5989. *E-mail:* cortlandabroad@cortland.edu. *World Wide Web:* http://www.cortlandabroad.com/. Students may also apply through University of the Sunshine Coast, Office of Study Abroad and International Education, Maroochydore, DC, Queensland 4558, Australia.

SALZBURG

COLLEGE CONSORTIUM FOR INTERNATIONAL STUDIES–MIAMI DADE COLLEGE
SUMMER IN AUSTRIA

Hosted by Salzburg College
Academic Focus • Art history, dance, German language and literature, music, social sciences.
Program Information • Students attend classes at Salzburg College (Salzburg, Austria). Scheduled travel to Vienna, Germany; field trips to local excursions; optional travel at an extra cost. Students typically earn 6 semester credits per term.
Sessions • May–Jun (summer).
Eligibility Requirements • Minimum age 18; open to freshmen, sophomores, juniors, seniors, adults; 2.7 GPA; 2 letters of recommendation; good academic standing at home school.

Living Arrangements • Students live in host family homes. Quarters are shared with students from other programs. Meals are taken with host family, in central dining facility.
Costs (2005) • $4350; includes tuition, housing, all meals, insurance, excursions, books and class materials, student support services. $30 application fee. $300 nonrefundable deposit required. Financial aid available for students from sponsoring institution: loans.
For More Information • Center for International Education, College Consortium for International Studies–Miami Dade College, 100 East Normal, Kirk Building 114, Kirksville, MO 63501; *Phone:* 660-785-4076; *Fax:* 660-785-7473. *E-mail:* ciea@truman.edu. *World Wide Web:* http://www.ccisabroad.org/. Students may also apply through Miami Dade College, Office of International Education, 300 NE 2nd Avenue, Suite 1450, Miami, FL 33132.

SYDNEY

ARCADIA UNIVERSITY
SYDNEY SUMMER INTERNSHIP

Held at Australian Catholic University–Sydney
Academic Focus • Full curriculum.
Program Information • Classes are held on the campus of Australian Catholic University–Sydney (Sydney, Australia). Faculty members are local instructors hired by the sponsor. Scheduled travel to Sydney CBD, museums; optional travel to Sydney at an extra cost. Students typically earn 6 semester credits per term.
Sessions • Jun–Jul (summer).
Eligibility Requirements • Open to sophomores, juniors, seniors; 3.0 GPA; 2 letters of recommendation; good academic standing at home school.
Living Arrangements • Students live in locally rented apartments. Quarters are shared with host institution students. Meals are taken on one's own, in residences, in restaurants.
Costs (2005) • $4275; includes tuition, housing, some meals, insurance, excursions, international student ID, student support services, pre-departure guide, transcript, orientation. $35 application fee. $500 nonrefundable deposit required. Financial aid available for all students: loans.
For More Information • Arcadia University, Center for Education Abroad, 450 South Easton Road, Glenside, PA 19038-3295; *Phone:* 866-927-2234; *Fax:* 215-572-2174. *E-mail:* cea@arcadia.edu. *World Wide Web:* http://www.arcadia.edu/cea/

BOSTON UNIVERSITY
SYDNEY FILM STUDIES PROGRAM

Academic Focus • Australian studies, film and media studies.
Program Information • Faculty members are local instructors hired by the sponsor. Field trips to Sydney Film Festival. Students typically earn 8 semester credits per term.
Sessions • Jun–Jul (summer).
Eligibility Requirements • Open to sophomores, juniors, seniors, adults; 3.0 GPA; 1 letter of recommendation; good academic standing at home school; essay; approval of participation; transcript.
Living Arrangements • Students live in host institution dormitories. Meals are taken on one's own, in residences, in restaurants.
Costs (2005) • $6000; includes tuition, housing, insurance. $50 application fee. $400 nonrefundable deposit required. Financial aid available for all students: scholarships, loans.
For More Information • Division of International Programs, Boston University, 232 Bay State Road, Boston, MA 02215; *Phone:* 617-353-9888; *Fax:* 617-353-5402. *E-mail:* abroad@bu.edu. *World Wide Web:* http://www.bu.edu/abroad/

BOSTON UNIVERSITY
SYDNEY INTERNSHIP PROGRAM

Academic Focus • Australian studies, communications, political science and government.
Program Information • Faculty members are local instructors hired by the sponsor. Scheduled travel to Canberra, the Snowy Mountains; field trips to historic sites, museums. Students typically earn 16 semester credits per term.
Sessions • May–Aug (summer).

AUSTRALIA
Sydney

Eligibility Requirements • Open to sophomores, juniors, seniors, adults; 1 letter of recommendation; good academic standing at home school; essay; approval of participation; transcript; minimum GPA of 3.0 in major and overall.

Living Arrangements • Students live in host institution dormitories. Meals are taken on one's own, in residences, in restaurants.

Costs (2005) • $12,700; includes tuition, housing, insurance, internship placement. $50 application fee. $400 nonrefundable deposit required. Financial aid available for all students: scholarships, loans, resident assistant positions.

For More Information • Division of International Programs, Boston University, 232 Bay State Road, Boston, MA 02215; *Phone:* 617-353-9888; *Fax:* 617-353-5402. *E-mail:* abroad@bu.edu. *World Wide Web:* http://www.bu.edu/abroad/

COOPERATIVE CENTER FOR STUDY ABROAD
AUSTRALIA SUMMER

Academic Focus • Biological/life sciences.

Program Information • Faculty members are drawn from the sponsor's U.S. staff. Students typically earn 3 semester credits per term.

Sessions • Jun–Jul (summer).

Eligibility Requirements • Minimum age 18; open to freshmen, sophomores, juniors, seniors, adults; good academic standing at home school.

Living Arrangements • Students live in host institution dormitories, hotels. Quarters are shared with host institution students. Meals are taken as a group, on one's own, in central dining facility, in restaurants.

Costs (2007) • $5195; includes housing, some meals, insurance, excursions, international airfare, airport transfers; Sydney Transit Pass. $200 nonrefundable deposit required. Financial aid available for students from sponsoring institution: scholarships, loans.

For More Information • Dr. Michael A. Klembara, Executive Director, Cooperative Center for Study Abroad, Northern Kentucky University, Nunn Drive, Founders Hall 301, Highland Heights, KY 41099; *Phone:* 800-319-6015; *Fax:* 859-572-6650. *E-mail:* ccsa@nku.edu. *World Wide Web:* http://www.ccsa.cc/

COOPERATIVE CENTER FOR STUDY ABROAD
INTERNSHIPS IN SYDNEY

Academic Focus • Full curriculum.

Sessions • Year-round.

Eligibility Requirements • Minimum age 18; open to freshmen, sophomores, juniors, seniors, graduate students, adults; 2 letters of recommendation.

Living Arrangements • Students live in host family homes. Quarters are shared with students from other programs. Meals are taken on one's own, with host family, in residences, in restaurants.

Costs (2007) • $4295–$4595; includes housing, some meals, insurance, international student ID, student support services, internship placement. $200 nonrefundable deposit required. Financial aid available for students from sponsoring institution: scholarships, loans.

For More Information • Dr. Michael A. Klembara, Executive Director, Cooperative Center for Study Abroad, Northern Kentucky University, Nunn Drive, Founders Hall 316, Highland Heights, KY 41099; *Phone:* 800-319-6015; *Fax:* 859-572-6650. *E-mail:* ccsa@nku.edu. *World Wide Web:* http://www.ccsa.cc/

INSTITUTE FOR STUDY ABROAD, BUTLER UNIVERSITY
UNIVERSITY OF NEW SOUTH WALES LIBERAL ARTS SUMMER STUDY

Hosted by University of New South Wales

Academic Focus • Australian studies.

Program Information • Students attend classes at University of New South Wales (Sydney, Australia). Scheduled travel to Darwin, Kakadu National Park, Canberra, Cairns. Students typically earn 8 semester credits per term.

Sessions • Jun–Aug (summer).

Eligibility Requirements • Open to sophomores, juniors, seniors; 2.8 GPA; 1 letter of recommendation; good academic standing at home school; enrollment at an accredited American college or university.

Living Arrangements • Students live in host institution dormitories, locally rented apartments, hotels. Quarters are shared with students from other programs. Meals are taken as a group, on one's own, in residences, in central dining facility.

Costs (2005) • $5100; includes tuition, housing, some meals, insurance, excursions, books and class materials, international student ID, student support services, pre-departure advising. $40 application fee. $500 nonrefundable deposit required. Financial aid available for all students: scholarships.

For More Information • Institute for Study Abroad, Butler University, 1100 West 42nd Street, Suite 305, Indianapolis, IN 46208-3345; *Phone:* 800-858-0229; *Fax:* 317-940-9704. *E-mail:* study-abroad@butler.edu. *World Wide Web:* http://www.ifsa-butler.org/

INSTITUTE FOR STUDY ABROAD, BUTLER UNIVERSITY
UNIVERSITY OF NEW SOUTH WALES TOURISM AND RECREATION MANAGEMENT SUMMER PROGRAM

Hosted by University of New South Wales

Academic Focus • Tourism and travel.

Program Information • Students attend classes at University of New South Wales (Sydney, Australia). Scheduled travel to Darwin, Kakadu National Park, Gold Coast, Cairns; Alice Springs; field trips. Students typically earn 8 semester credits per term.

Sessions • 4 to 6 week courses, Jun to Aug.

Eligibility Requirements • Open to sophomores, juniors, seniors; 2.8 GPA; 1 letter of recommendation; good academic standing at home school; enrollment at an accredited American college or university.

Living Arrangements • Students live in host institution dormitories, locally rented apartments, hotels. Quarters are shared with students from other programs. Meals are taken as a group, on one's own, in residences, in central dining facility.

Costs (2005) • $5100; includes tuition, housing, some meals, insurance, excursions, books and class materials, international student ID, student support services, pre-departure advising. $40 application fee. $500 nonrefundable deposit required. Financial aid available for all students: scholarships.

For More Information • Institute for Study Abroad, Butler University, 1100 West 42nd Street, Suite 305, Indianapolis, IN 46208-3345; *Phone:* 800-858-0229; *Fax:* 317-940-9704. *E-mail:* study-abroad@butler.edu. *World Wide Web:* http://www.ifsa-butler.org/

MICHIGAN STATE UNIVERSITY
CIC/AESOP INTERNSHIPS IN AUSTRALIA

Hosted by Macquarie University, University of New South Wales

Academic Focus • Full curriculum.

Program Information • Students attend classes at Macquarie University (Sydney, Australia), University of New South Wales (Sydney, Australia). Students typically earn 8–10 semester credits per term.

Sessions • May–Aug (summer), Feb–May (summer 2).

Eligibility Requirements • Minimum age 18; open to juniors, seniors; 3.0 GPA; 2 letters of recommendation; good academic standing at home school; résumé; personal statement.

Living Arrangements • Students live in host institution dormitories, locally rented apartments. Quarters are shared with host institution students, students from other programs. Meals are taken on one's own, in residences, in restaurants.

Costs (2005) • $4725; includes tuition, housing, insurance, student support services, administrative fees. $100 application fee. $200 nonrefundable deposit required. Financial aid available for students from sponsoring institution: scholarships, loans.

For More Information • Ms. Sandy Tupper, Educational Programs Coordinator, Michigan State University, Office of Study Abroad, 109 International Center, East Lansing, MI 48824-1035; *Phone:* 517-353-8920; *Fax:* 517-432-2082. *E-mail:* tuppers@msu.edu. *World Wide Web:* http://studyabroad.msu.edu/

MICHIGAN STATE UNIVERSITY
MEDIA, ENVIRONMENT, AND CULTURE

Hosted by University of New South Wales

Academic Focus • Journalism, natural resources.

Program Information • Students attend classes at University of New South Wales (Sydney, Australia). Scheduled travel to Uluru, Cairns; field trips to Darwin, Canberra. Students typically earn 7 semester credits per term.

Sessions • Jun–Aug (summer).

Eligibility Requirements • Minimum age 18; open to juniors, seniors, graduate students; 2.5 GPA; good academic standing at home school; faculty approval.

Living Arrangements • Students live in host institution dormitories, hotels. Meals are taken as a group, on one's own, in central dining facility, in restaurants.

Costs (2004–2005) • $4419; includes housing, some meals, insurance, excursions, student support services. $100 application fee. $200 nonrefundable deposit required. Financial aid available for students from sponsoring institution: scholarships, loans.

For More Information • Ms. Sandy Tupper, Educational Programs Coordinator, Michigan State University, Office of Study Abroad, 109 International Center, East Lansing, MI 48824-1035; *Phone:* 517-353-8920; *Fax:* 517-432-2082. *E-mail:* tuppers@msu.edu. *World Wide Web:* http://studyabroad.msu.edu/

MICHIGAN STATE UNIVERSITY
TEACHING AND TEACHER LEADERSHIP

Academic Focus • Education, teaching.

Program Information • Faculty members are drawn from the sponsor's U.S. staff and local instructors hired by the sponsor. Field trips to the Blue Mountains, New South Wales, an Aboriginal community in the Outback. Students typically earn 6 semester credits per term.

Sessions • May–Jun (summer).

Eligibility Requirements • Minimum age 18; open to juniors, seniors, graduate students; major in education; 2.0 GPA; good academic standing at home school.

Living Arrangements • Students live in host institution dormitories, host family homes. Meals are taken as a group, with host family, in residences.

Costs (2004–2005) • $2453; includes housing, some meals, insurance, excursions, student support services. $100 application fee. $200 nonrefundable deposit required. Financial aid available for students from sponsoring institution: scholarships, loans.

For More Information • Ms. Sandy Tupper, Educational Programs Coordinator, Michigan State University, Office of Study Abroad, 109 International Center, East Lansing, MI 48824-1035; *Phone:* 517-353-8920; *Fax:* 517-432-2082. *E-mail:* tuppers@msu.edu. *World Wide Web:* http://studyabroad.msu.edu/

STATE UNIVERSITY OF NEW YORK AT OSWEGO
SUMMER INTERNSHIPS IN SYDNEY, AUSTRALIA

Hosted by Centers for Academic Programs Abroad (CAPA)

Academic Focus • Australian studies.

Program Information • Students attend classes at Centers for Academic Programs Abroad (CAPA) (Sydney, Australia). Scheduled travel to surrounding areas; field trips to surrounding areas; optional travel at an extra cost. Students typically earn 6 semester credits per term.

Sessions • Jun–Jul (summer).

Eligibility Requirements • Open to freshmen, sophomores, juniors, seniors; 2.5 GPA; 1 letter of recommendation; good academic standing at home school.

Living Arrangements • Students live in host institution dormitories, locally rented apartments. Meals are taken on one's own, in residences, in central dining facility, in restaurants.

Costs (2005) • $3700; includes tuition, housing, some meals, insurance, excursions, books and class materials, student support services. $250 nonrefundable deposit required. Financial aid available for students: home university financial aid; loan processing and scholarships for Oswego students.

For More Information • Mr. Ryan Lemon, Program Specialist, State University of New York at Oswego, 122A Swetman Hall, Oswego, NY 13126-3599; *Phone:* 888-4-OSWEGO; *Fax:* 315-312-2477. *E-mail:* intled@oswego.edu. *World Wide Web:* http://www.oswego.edu/intled/

STUDY AUSTRALIA
THE ATTRACTION OF AUSTRALIA: TOURISM AND RECREATION MANAGEMENT

Hosted by University of New South Wales

Academic Focus • Business administration/management, tourism and travel.

Program Information • Students attend classes at University of New South Wales (Sydney, Australia). Scheduled travel to Darwin, Cairns, Sydney, Alice Springs, Gold Coast; field trips to composites in Kakadu National Park, the Great Barrier Reef; optional travel to Fiji, New Zealand, Hawaii at an extra cost. Students typically earn 6 semester credits per term.

Sessions • Jun–Aug (summer).

Eligibility Requirements • Minimum age 18; open to sophomores, juniors, seniors; major in business, tourism, management; 2.5 GPA; good academic standing at home school.

Living Arrangements • Students live in host institution dormitories, locally rented apartments, hotels. Quarters are shared with host institution students, students from other programs. Meals are taken as a group, on one's own, in residences, in central dining facility, in restaurants.

Costs (2005) • $4995; includes tuition, housing, some meals, excursions, books and class materials, student support services. $30 application fee. $500 refundable deposit required.

For More Information • Mr. Chris Shepherd, Director of Programs and Services, Study Australia, 54515 State Road 933 North, PO Box 1004, Notre Dame, IN 46556-1004; *Phone:* 800-585-9658; *Fax:* 509-357-9457. *E-mail:* info@study-australia.com. *World Wide Web:* http://www.study-australia.com/

STUDY AUSTRALIA
AUSTRALIAN WILDLIFE AND CONSERVATION

Hosted by University of New South Wales

Academic Focus • Cultural studies, economics, environmental science/studies, political science and government.

Program Information • Students attend classes at University of New South Wales (Sydney, Australia). Scheduled travel to Darwin, Cairns, Sydney, Alice Springs; field trips to campsites in Kakadu National Park, the Great Barrier Reef; optional travel to Fiji, New Zealand, Hawaii at an extra cost. Students typically earn 6–8 semester credits per term.

Sessions • Jun–Aug (summer).

Eligibility Requirements • Minimum age 18; open to sophomores, juniors, seniors; 3.0 GPA; good academic standing at home school.

Living Arrangements • Students live in host institution dormitories, locally rented apartments, hotels. Quarters are shared with host institution students, students from other programs. Meals are taken as a group, on one's own, in residences, in central dining facility, in restaurants.

Costs (2005) • $4895; includes tuition, housing, some meals, excursions, books and class materials, student support services. $30 application fee. $500 refundable deposit required.

For More Information • Mr. Chris Shepherd, Director of Programs and Services, Study Australia, 54515 State Road 933 North, PO Box 1004, Notre Dame, IN 46556-1004; *Phone:* 800-585-9658; *Fax:* 509-357-9457. *E-mail:* info@study-australia.com. *World Wide Web:* http://www.study-australia.com/

STUDY AUSTRALIA
STUDY AUSTRALIA SYDNEY INTERNSHIP

Academic Focus • Full curriculum.

Program Information • Field trips to the Blue Mountains; optional travel to Fiji, Hawaii, New Zealand at an extra cost. Students typically earn 6–8 semester credits per term.

Sessions • 4 to 52 week internships.

Eligibility Requirements • Minimum age 18; open to freshmen, sophomores, juniors, seniors, graduate students; 2.0 GPA.

Living Arrangements • Students live in locally rented apartments. Meals are taken on one's own, in residences.

AUSTRALIA
Sydney

Costs (2006) • Contact sponsor for cost. $100 application fee. $300 refundable deposit required. Financial aid available for all students: scholarships, loans.
For More Information • Mr. Chris Shepherd, Director of Programs and Services, Study Australia, 54515 State Road 933 North, PO Box 1004, Notre Dame, IN 46556-1004; *Phone:* 800-585-9658; *Fax:* 509-357-9457. *E-mail:* info@study-australia.com. *World Wide Web:* http://www.study-australia.com/

STUDY AUSTRALIA
SYDNEY INTERNSHIP PROGRAM

Academic Focus • Full curriculum.
Program Information • Field trips to the Blue Mountains; optional travel to Fiji, New Zealand, Hawaii, the Great Barrier Reef at an extra cost. Students typically earn 6 semester credits per term.
Sessions • Jun–Jul (summer).
Eligibility Requirements • Minimum age 18; open to sophomores, juniors, seniors; 2.5 GPA; 2 letters of recommendation; good academic standing at home school.
Living Arrangements • Students live in locally rented apartments. Meals are taken on one's own, in residences, in restaurants.
Costs (2005) • $3900; includes housing, excursions, student support services, internship placement. $100 application fee. $300 refundable deposit required. Financial aid available for all students: scholarships, loans.
For More Information • Mr. Chris Shepherd, Director of Programs and Services, Study Australia, 54515 State Road 933 North, PO Box 1004, Notre Dame, IN 46556-1004; *Phone:* 800-585-9658; *Fax:* 509-357-9457. *E-mail:* info@study-australia.com. *World Wide Web:* http://www.study-australia.com/

STUDY AUSTRALIA
UNIVERSITY OF SYDNEY

Hosted by University of Sydney
Academic Focus • Full curriculum.
Program Information • Students attend classes at University of Sydney (Sydney, Australia). Optional travel to Fiji, New Zealand, Hawaii at an extra cost. Students typically earn 6 semester credits per term.
Sessions • Jan–Feb (winter).
Eligibility Requirements • Minimum age 18; open to freshmen, sophomores, juniors, seniors, graduate students; good academic standing at home school.
Living Arrangements • Students live in host institution dormitories, locally rented apartments. Quarters are shared with host institution students, students from other programs. Meals are taken on one's own, in residences, in restaurants.
Costs (2005) • Contact sponsor for cost. $30 application fee. $500 refundable deposit required.
For More Information • Mr. Chris Shepherd, Director of Programs and Services, Study Australia, 54515 State Road 933 North, PO Box 1004, Notre Dame, IN 46556-1004; *Phone:* 800-585-9658; *Fax:* 509-357-9457. *E-mail:* info@study-australia.com. *World Wide Web:* http://www.study-australia.com/

UNIVERSITY OF DELAWARE
WINTER SESSION IN AUSTRALIA: BUSINESS ADMINISTRATION

Held at University of Sydney
Academic Focus • Business administration/management, marketing.
Program Information • Classes are held on the campus of University of Sydney (Sydney, Australia). Faculty members are drawn from the sponsor's U.S. staff. Field trips to Canberra; optional travel to sites throughout Australia at an extra cost. Students typically earn 6 semester credits per term.
Sessions • Dec–Jan (winter).
Eligibility Requirements • Open to freshmen, sophomores, juniors, seniors, adults; 2.0 GPA; 1 letter of recommendation.
Living Arrangements • Students live in locally rented apartments. Meals are taken on one's own, in residences, in restaurants.
Costs (2005) • Contact sponsor for cost. $200 nonrefundable deposit required. Financial aid available for all students: scholarships.

For More Information • Center for International Studies, University of Delaware, 186 South College Avenue, Newark, DE 19716-1450; *Phone:* 888-831-4685; *Fax:* 302-831-6042. *E-mail:* studyabroad@udel. edu. *World Wide Web:* http://www.udel.edu/studyabroad/

UNIVERSITY OF MINNESOTA
STUDY AND INTERNSHIPS IN SYDNEY

Hosted by Billy Blue School
Academic Focus • Anthropology, art history, business administration/management, film and media studies, psychology, social sciences, sports management.
Program Information • Students attend classes at Billy Blue School (Sydney, Australia). Field trips to the Blue Mountains. Students typically earn 6 semester credits per term.
Sessions • Jun–Jul (summer).
Eligibility Requirements • Minimum age 18; open to freshmen, sophomores, juniors, seniors; 2.5 GPA; junior status preferred for internship.
Living Arrangements • Students live in host family homes, hotels. Quarters are shared with host institution students. Meals are taken as a group, on one's own, in residences, in central dining facility, in restaurants.
Costs (2006) • Contact sponsor for cost; includes tuition, housing, some meals, insurance, excursions, student support services. $50 application fee. $400 nonrefundable deposit required. Financial aid available for students from sponsoring institution: scholarships, loans.
For More Information • Learning Abroad Center, University of Minnesota, 230 Heller Hall, 271 19th Avenue South, Minneapolis, MN 55455; *Phone:* 888-700-UOFM; *Fax:* 612-626-8009. *E-mail:* umabroad@umn.edu. *World Wide Web:* http://www.umabroad.umn. edu/

WIDENER UNIVERSITY SCHOOL OF LAW
SYDNEY SUMMER INTERNATIONAL LAW INSTITUTE

Held at University of Technology Sydney
Academic Focus • Law and legal studies.
Program Information • Classes are held on the campus of University of Technology Sydney (Sydney, Australia). Faculty members are drawn from the sponsor's U.S. staff and local instructors hired by the sponsor. Field trips to trips to legal institutions, Sydney Harbor Cruise; optional travel at an extra cost. Students typically earn 6 semester credits per term.
Sessions • Jun–Jul (summer).
Eligibility Requirements • Open to graduate students; good academic standing at home school; students must be enrolled in an accredited law school or be a law school graduate.
Living Arrangements • Students live in host institution dormitories, locally rented apartments, hotels. Quarters are shared with students from other programs. Meals are taken on one's own, in residences, in restaurants.
Costs (2005) • $8300; includes tuition, housing, all meals, excursions, international airfare, books and class materials, student support services. $100 application fee. Financial aid available for all students: loans.
For More Information • Ms. Peggie Wyant, Coordinator, International Programs, Widener University School of Law, 4601 Concord Pike, Box 7474, Room 418 Law Building, Wilmington, DE 19803; *Phone:* 302-477-2248; *Fax:* 302-477-2257. *E-mail:* mawyant@mail. widener.edu. *World Wide Web:* http://www.law.widener.edu/go/ summer/

WAGGA WAGGA

UNIVERSITY OF DELAWARE
WINTER SESSION IN AUSTRALIA: ANIMAL SCIENCE

Hosted by Charles Sturt University–Wagga Wagga Campus
Academic Focus • Agriculture.
Program Information • Students attend classes at Charles Sturt University–Wagga Wagga Campus (Wagga Wagga, Australia). Scheduled travel to Sydney; field trips to landforms. Students typically earn 6 semester credits per term.
Sessions • Jan–Feb (winter).

Eligibility Requirements • Open to freshmen, sophomores, juniors, seniors, adults; 2.0 GPA; 1 letter of recommendation.
Living Arrangements • Students live in host institution dormitories. Meals are taken as a group, in central dining facility.
Costs (2005) • Contact sponsor for cost. $200 nonrefundable deposit required. Financial aid available for all students: scholarships.

For More Information • Center for International Studies, University of Delaware, 186 South College Avenue, Newark, DE 19716-1450; *Phone:* 888-831-4685; *Fax:* 302-831-6042. *E-mail:* studyabroad@udel.edu. *World Wide Web:* http://www.udel.edu/studyabroad/

USTRIA

CITY-TO-CITY

UNIVERSITY OF MIAMI
GERMAN LANGUAGE AND EUROPEAN STUDIES PROGRAM IN VIENNA

Hosted by University of Vienna, Strobl Campus

Academic Focus • European studies, German language and literature, international affairs, political science and government.

Program Information • Students attend classes at University of Vienna, Strobl Campus (Strobl). Field trips to Salzburg. Students typically earn 6 semester credits per term.

Sessions • Jul–Aug (summer).

Eligibility Requirements • Minimum age 18; open to juniors, seniors; 3.0 GPA; 2 letters of recommendation; good academic standing at home school; transcripts; phone interview; no foreign language proficiency required.

Living Arrangements • Students live in host institution dormitories. Quarters are shared with host institution students. Meals are taken as a group, in central dining facility.

Costs (2005–2006) • $4820; includes tuition, housing, all meals. $40 application fee. $500 nonrefundable deposit required. Financial aid available for students from sponsoring institution: loans.

For More Information • Ms. Elyse Resnick, Assistant Director, University of Miami, International Education and Exchange Programs, 5050 Brunson Drive, Allen Hall 212, PO Box 248005, Coral Gables, FL 33124-1610; *Phone:* 305-284-3434; *Fax:* 305-284-4235. *E-mail:* ieep@miami.edu. *World Wide Web:* http://www.studyabroad.miami.edu/

BREGENZ

KENTUCKY INSTITUTE FOR INTERNATIONAL STUDIES
BREGENZ, AUSTRIA

Academic Focus • Communications, German language and literature, international business, marketing.

Program Information • Faculty members are drawn from the sponsor's U.S. staff. Field trips to local points of interest, Munich; optional travel to European capitals at an extra cost. Students typically earn 3–6 semester credits per term.

Sessions • May–Jul (summer).

Eligibility Requirements • Minimum age 18; open to freshmen, sophomores, juniors, seniors, graduate students, adults; 2.0 GPA; 1 letter of recommendation; no foreign language proficiency required.

Living Arrangements • Students live in host family homes. Meals are taken as a group, with host family, in restaurants.

Costs (2006) • $3520; includes housing, some meals, insurance, excursions, international airfare, international student ID, 10-day Eurail Flexipass, instructional expenses. $150 application fee. Financial aid available for all students: scholarships.

For More Information • Ms. Nancy Martin, Coordinator, Kentucky Institute for International Studies, PO Box 9, Murray, KY 42071-0009; *Phone:* 270-762-3091; *Fax:* 270-762-3434. *E-mail:* kiismsu@murraystate.edu. *World Wide Web:* http://www.kiis.org/

KENTUCKY INSTITUTE FOR INTERNATIONAL STUDIES
ENVIRONMENTAL EDUCATION IN BREGENZ, AUSTRIA

Academic Focus • Education, environmental science/studies.

Program Information • Faculty members are drawn from the sponsor's U.S. staff. Scheduled travel to Germany, Switzerland; field trips. Students typically earn 3 semester credits per term.

Sessions • Jul–Jun (summer).

Eligibility Requirements • Minimum age 18; open to freshmen, sophomores, juniors, seniors, graduate students, adults; 3.0 GPA; 1 letter of recommendation; no foreign language proficiency required.

Living Arrangements • Students live in host family homes. Meals are taken with host family, in residences.

Costs (2006) • $2510; includes housing, some meals, insurance, excursions, international airfare, international student ID, instructional expenses. $150 application fee. Financial aid available for all students: scholarships.

For More Information • Ms. Nancy Martin, Coordinator, Kentucky Institute for International Studies, PO Box 9, Murray, KY 42071-0009; *Phone:* 270-762-3091; *Fax:* 270-762-3434. *E-mail:* kiismsu@murraystate.edu. *World Wide Web:* http://www.kiis.org/

nyu

SUMMER 2007

take the summer on

- Choose from over 40 programs in 25 international locations.
- Earn credits as you explore the world's cultural centers.
- Courses taught in English—or learn a new language.

For more information about our Summer 2007 programs: Visit

NEW YORK UNIVERSITY
A private university in the public service

www.nyu.edu/summer2007

New York University is an affirmative action/equal opportunity institution.

MICHIGAN STATE UNIVERSITY
MUSIC, ART, AND LANGUAGE

Academic Focus • Art history, Austrian studies, music.
Program Information • Faculty members are drawn from the sponsor's U.S. staff. Field trips to the Bregenz Opera Festival, Munich, Verona. Students typically earn 7 semester credits per term.
Sessions • Jul (summer).
Eligibility Requirements • Minimum age 18; open to freshmen, sophomores, juniors, seniors; major in arts and letters; 2.5 GPA; good academic standing at home school; faculty approval; no foreign language proficiency required.
Living Arrangements • Students live in host family homes, hotels. Meals are taken with host family, in residences.
Costs (2005) • $2258 (estimated); includes housing, some meals, insurance, excursions, student support services, opera tickets. $100 application fee. $200 nonrefundable deposit required. Financial aid available for students from sponsoring institution: scholarships, loans.
For More Information • Ms. Yvonne Squiers, Secretary, Michigan State University, Office of Study Abroad, 109 International Center, East Lansing, MI 48824-1035; *Phone:* 517-353-8920; *Fax:* 517-432-2082. *E-mail:* squiers@msu.edu. *World Wide Web:* http://studyabroad.msu.edu/

INNSBRUCK

UNIVERSITY OF NEW ORLEANS
THE INTERNATIONAL SUMMER SCHOOL

Hosted by University of Innsbruck
Academic Focus • Full curriculum.
Program Information • Students attend classes at University of Innsbruck (Innsbruck, Austria). Scheduled travel to Italy, Austria; field trips to Munich, Vienna, Venice, South Tirol; optional travel at an extra cost. Students typically earn 6 semester credits per term.
Sessions • Jul–Aug (summer).
Eligibility Requirements • Minimum age 18; open to freshmen, sophomores, juniors, seniors, graduate students, adults; 2.5 GPA; 1 letter of recommendation; good academic standing at home school; home institution approval; no foreign language proficiency required.
Living Arrangements • Students live in host institution dormitories. Meals are taken as a group, in central dining facility.
Costs (2005) • $4295; includes tuition, housing, some meals, insurance, excursions, student support services. $150 application fee. $150 refundable deposit required. Financial aid available for students from sponsoring institution: scholarships, loans.
For More Information • Mr. Peter Alongia, Coordinator, University of New Orleans, PO Box 1315, New Orleans, LA 70148; *Phone:* 504-280-7116; *Fax:* 504-280-7317. *E-mail:* palongia@uno.edu. *World Wide Web:* http://inst.uno.edu/

KLAGENFURT

LANGUAGE LIAISON
GERMAN IN KLAGENFURT

Hosted by Language Liaison
Academic Focus • German language and literature.
Program Information • Students attend classes at Language Liaison (Klagenfurt, Austria). Field trips; optional travel at an extra cost. Students typically earn 3–15 semester credits per term.
Sessions • Classes begin weekly, year-round.
Eligibility Requirements • Open to precollege students, freshmen, sophomores, juniors, seniors, graduate students, adults; no foreign language proficiency required.
Living Arrangements • Students live in locally rented apartments, host family homes, hotels. Meals are taken on one's own, with host family, in residences, in restaurants.
Costs (2005) • Contact sponsor for cost. $175 application fee. Financial aid available for all students: scholarship research service.
For More Information • Ms. Nancy Forman, President, Language Liaison, PO Box 1772, Pacific Palisades, CA 90272; *Phone:* 800-284-4448; *Fax:* 310-454-1706. *E-mail:* learn@languageliaison.com. *World Wide Web:* http://www.languageliaison.com/

UNIVERSITY OF ALABAMA
ALABAMA IN AUSTRIA

Hosted by University of Klagenfurt
Academic Focus • German language and literature, German studies.
Program Information • Students attend classes at University of Klagenfurt (Klagenfurt, Austria). Scheduled travel to Vienna, Salzburg; field trips to the Carinthian Mountains, Vienna, Venice, Salzburg. Students typically earn 6 semester credits per term.
Sessions • Jul–Aug (summer).
Eligibility Requirements • Open to freshmen, sophomores, juniors, seniors, graduate students, adults; 2.5 GPA; good academic standing at home school.
Living Arrangements • Students live in host institution dormitories. Quarters are shared with host institution students. Meals are taken as a group, in central dining facility, in restaurants.
Costs (2005) • $3600; includes tuition, housing, some meals, insurance, excursions, books and class materials, international student ID, student support services. $100 application fee. $500 nonrefundable deposit required. Financial aid available for all students: scholarships, loans.
For More Information • Ms. Angela L. Channell, Director of Overseas Study, University of Alabama, Box 870254, Tuscaloosa, AL 35487-0254; *Phone:* 205-348-5256; *Fax:* 205-348-5298. *E-mail:* achannel@aalan.ua.edu. *World Wide Web:* http://www.overseas-study.ua.edu/

PORTSCHACH

LANGUAGE LIAISON
GERMAN IN PORTSCHACH

Hosted by Language Liaison
Academic Focus • German language and literature.
Program Information • Students attend classes at Language Liaison (Portschach, Austria). Field trips; optional travel at an extra cost. Students typically earn 3–15 semester credits per term.
Sessions • Classes begin weekly, year-round.
Eligibility Requirements • Minimum age 17; open to precollege students, freshmen, sophomores, juniors, seniors, graduate students, adults; no foreign language proficiency required.
Living Arrangements • Students live in locally rented apartments, host family homes, hotels. Meals are taken on one's own, with host family, in residences, in restaurants.
Costs (2005) • Contact sponsor for cost. $175 application fee. Financial aid available for all students: scholarship research service.
For More Information • Ms. Nancy Forman, President, Language Liaison, PO Box 1772, Pacific Palisades, CA 90272; *Phone:* 800-284-4448; *Fax:* 310-454-1706. *E-mail:* learn@languageliaison.com. *World Wide Web:* http://www.languageliaison.com/

SALZBURG

AMERICAN INSTITUTE FOR FOREIGN STUDY (AIFS)
AIFS–SALZBURG, AUSTRIA–UNIVERSITY OF SALZBURG

Hosted by University of Salzburg
Academic Focus • Anthropology, art history, German language and literature, history, music, sociology.
Program Information • Students attend classes at University of Salzburg (Salzburg, Austria). Scheduled travel to 3-day visit to Vienna; field trips to 2-day visit to Munich, Cultural Activities. Students typically earn 6 semester credits per term.
Sessions • May–Jun (summer).
Eligibility Requirements • Minimum age 17; open to precollege students, freshmen, sophomores, juniors, seniors; 2.0 GPA; no foreign language proficiency required.
Living Arrangements • Students live in host institution dormitories, program-owned apartments, hotels. Quarters are shared with host institution students. Meals are taken as a group, in residences.
Costs (2007) • $4399; includes tuition, housing, some meals, insurance, excursions, student support services, On-site Resident Director, Phone Card to call the U.S., Computer Facilities. $95 application fee. $395 nonrefundable deposit required. Financial aid available for all students: scholarships.

AUSTRIA
Salzburg

For More Information • Mr. David Mauro, Admissions Advisor, American Institute For Foreign Study (AIFS), 9 West Broad Street, Stamford, CT 06902-3788; *Phone:* 800-727-2437 Ext. 5163; *Fax:* 203-399-5597. *E-mail:* dmauro@aifs.com. *World Wide Web:* http://www.aifsabroad.com/

BOWLING GREEN STATE UNIVERSITY
SUMMER PROGRAM IN SALZBURG
Hosted by University of Salzburg

Academic Focus • German language and literature, German studies.
Program Information • Students attend classes at University of Salzburg (Salzburg, Austria). Field trips to Munich, areas of interest in Salzburg region. Students typically earn 4–5 semester credits per 3 week session.
Sessions • Jul (summer), Jul–Aug (summer 2).
Eligibility Requirements • Minimum age 18; open to precollege students, freshmen, sophomores, juniors, seniors, graduate students, adults; good academic standing at home school; no foreign language proficiency required.
Living Arrangements • Students live in host institution dormitories, host family homes. Quarters are shared with host institution students. Meals are taken as a group, on one's own, with host family, in residences.
Costs (2005) • $1568 for Ohio residents; $2564 for nonresidents; includes tuition, housing, excursions, books and class materials, student support services. $120 application fee. Financial aid available for all students: scholarships.
For More Information • Ms. Sue Sidor, Austria Programs Assistant, Bowling Green State University, 103 Shatzel Hall, Bowling Green, OH 43403; *Phone:* 419-372-6815; *Fax:* 419-372-2571. *E-mail:* sidors@bgnet.bgsu.edu. *World Wide Web:* http://www.bgsu.edu/

COLLEGE CONSORTIUM FOR INTERNATIONAL STUDIES–TRUMAN STATE UNIVERSITY
SUMMER IN AUSTRIA
Hosted by Salzburg College

Academic Focus • Art history, dance, German language and literature, music, social sciences.
Program Information • Students attend classes at Salzburg College (Salzburg, Austria). Scheduled travel to Vienna, Germany; field trips to local excursions; optional travel at an extra cost. Students typically earn 6 semester credits per term.
Sessions • May–Jun (summer).
Eligibility Requirements • Minimum age 18; open to freshmen, sophomores, juniors, seniors, adults; 2.7 GPA; 2 letters of recommendation; good academic standing at home school; no foreign language proficiency required.
Living Arrangements • Students live in host family homes. Quarters are shared with students from other programs. Meals are taken with host family, in central dining facility.
Costs (2007) • $4500; includes tuition, housing, all meals, insurance, excursions, books and class materials, student support services. $500 nonrefundable deposit required. Financial aid available for students from sponsoring institution: loans.
For More Information • Center for International Education, College Consortium for International Studies–Truman State University, 100 East Normal, Kirk Building 114, Kirksville, MO 63501; *Phone:* 660-785-4076; *Fax:* 660-785-7473. *E-mail:* ciea@truman.edu. *World Wide Web:* http://www.ccisabroad.org/. Students may also apply through Miami Dade College.

ILLINOIS STATE UNIVERSITY
SUMMER PROGRAM–SALZBURG, AUSTRIA
Hosted by Salzburg College

Academic Focus • Austrian studies, German language and literature, music, music history.
Program Information • Students attend classes at Salzburg College (Salzburg, Austria). Scheduled travel to Vienna; field trips to local sites. Students typically earn 6 semester credits per term.
Sessions • May–Jun (summer).

Eligibility Requirements • Minimum age 18; open to sophomores, juniors, seniors; 2.7 GPA; 2 letters of recommendation; good academic standing at home school; essay; no foreign language proficiency required.
Living Arrangements • Students live in host family homes. Quarters are shared with host institution students. Meals are taken as a group, with host family, in residences, in central dining facility.
Costs (2005) • $5975; includes tuition, housing, all meals, insurance, excursions, international airfare, international student ID, student support services, personal expenses. $150 application fee. Financial aid available for students from sponsoring institution: scholarships, loans.
For More Information • Study Abroad Coordinator, Illinois State University, Office of International Studies and Programs, Campus Box 6120, Normal, IL 61790-6120; *Phone:* 309-438-5276; *Fax:* 309-438-3987. *World Wide Web:* http://www.internationalstudies.ilstu.edu/

KENTUCKY INSTITUTE FOR INTERNATIONAL STUDIES
SALZBURG, AUSTRIA

Academic Focus • Music, music history, music performance, music theory.
Program Information • Faculty members are drawn from the sponsor's U.S. staff and local instructors hired by the sponsor. Field trips to Vienna, local points of interest; optional travel to European capitals at an extra cost. Students typically earn 6 semester credits per term.
Sessions • May–Jul (summer).
Eligibility Requirements • Minimum age 18; open to freshmen, sophomores, juniors, seniors, graduate students; 2.0 GPA; 1 letter of recommendation; no foreign language proficiency required.
Living Arrangements • Students live in hotels. Meals are taken as a group, on one's own, in central dining facility, in restaurants.
Costs (2006) • $3620; includes housing, some meals, insurance, excursions, international airfare, international student ID, instructional expenses. $150 application fee. Financial aid available for all students: scholarships.
For More Information • Ms. Nancy Martin, Coordinator, Kentucky Institute for International Studies, PO Box 9, Murray, KY 42071-0009; *Phone:* 270-762-3091; *Fax:* 270-762-3434. *E-mail:* kiismsu@murraystate.edu. *World Wide Web:* http://www.kiis.org/

NORTHERN ILLINOIS UNIVERSITY
SALZBURG COLLEGE SUMMER SESSION
Hosted by Salzburg College

Academic Focus • Austrian studies, European studies, German language and literature, music history, music performance.
Program Information • Students attend classes at Salzburg College (Salzburg, Austria). Scheduled travel to Vienna; field trips to Vienna, Trier, Cologne, Bonn; Heidelberg; Nuremberg; the Rhine. Students typically earn 6 semester credits per term.
Sessions • May–Jun (summer).
Eligibility Requirements • Open to sophomores, juniors, seniors; 2.75 GPA; 2 letters of recommendation; good academic standing at home school; application essay; no foreign language proficiency required.
Living Arrangements • Students live in host family homes. Meals are taken as a group, in residences, in central dining facility.
Costs (2005) • $4215; includes tuition, housing, some meals, insurance, excursions, international student ID, student support services, social and cultural activities. $45 application fee. $500 refundable deposit required. Financial aid available for students from sponsoring institution: regular financial aid.
For More Information • Ms. Emily Gorlewski, Program Assistant, Northern Illinois University, Study Abroad Office, Williston Hall 417, DeKalb, IL 60115; *Phone:* 815-753-0420; *Fax:* 815-753-0825. *E-mail:* niuabroad@niu.edu. *World Wide Web:* http://www.niu.edu/niuabroad/. Students may also apply through Salzburg College, Ursulinenplatz 4, 5020 Salzburg, Austria.

VIENNA

EMORY UNIVERSITY
GERMAN STUDIES

Held at University of Vienna
Academic Focus • German language and literature, history, music.
Program Information • Classes are held on the campus of University of Vienna (Vienna, Austria). Faculty members are drawn from the sponsor's U.S. staff and local instructors hired by the sponsor. Scheduled travel to Prague, Budapest. Students typically earn 8-16 semester credits per term.
Sessions • May-Jul (summer).
Eligibility Requirements • Minimum age 18; open to freshmen, sophomores, juniors, seniors; 2.0 GPA; good academic standing at home school; no foreign language proficiency required.
Living Arrangements • Students live in host family homes. Meals are taken on one's own.
Costs (2005) • $7550; includes tuition, housing, some meals, insurance, excursions. $350 nonrefundable deposit required. Financial aid available for students from sponsoring institution: scholarships, loans.
For More Information • Ms. Gail Scheu, Study Abroad Coordinator, Emory University, 1385 Oxford Road, Atlanta, GA 30322; *Phone:* 404-727-2240; *Fax:* 404-727-6724. *E-mail:* lscheu@emory.edu. *World Wide Web:* http://www.cipa.emory.edu/

EUROPEAN HERITAGE INSTITUTE
SUMMER PROGRAM IN VIENNA

Hosted by University of Vienna
Academic Focus • German language and literature, German studies.
Program Information • Students attend classes at University of Vienna (Vienna, Austria). Field trips to the Vienna Woods, Lake Neusiedl, Wachau. Students typically earn 3-6 semester credits per term.
Sessions • Jul, Aug, Sep (4 week sessions); Feb (3 weeks).
Eligibility Requirements • Minimum age 18; open to freshmen, sophomores, juniors, seniors, graduate students, adults; 2.25 GPA; 2 letters of recommendation; no foreign language proficiency required.
Living Arrangements • Students live in host institution dormitories, locally rented apartments. Quarters are shared with host institution students. Meals are taken on one's own, in residences, in central dining facility, in restaurants.
Costs (2006) • $1230-$1350 for Jul, Aug, and Sep sessions; $900 for Feb session; includes tuition, housing, student support services. $300 refundable deposit required.
For More Information • Dr. Antonio Masullo, Professor, European Heritage Institute, 2708 East Franklin Street, Richmond, VA 23223; *Phone:* 804-643-0661; *Fax:* 804-648-0826. *E-mail:* info@europeabroad.org. *World Wide Web:* http://www.europeabroad.org/

LANGUAGE LIAISON
GERMAN IN VIENNA

Hosted by Language Liaison
Academic Focus • German language and literature.
Program Information • Students attend classes at Language Liaison (Vienna, Austria). Field trips; optional travel at an extra cost. Students typically earn 3-15 semester credits per term.
Sessions • New programs begin weekly, year-round.
Eligibility Requirements • Minimum age 14; open to precollege students, freshmen, sophomores, juniors, seniors, graduate students, adults; no foreign language proficiency required.
Living Arrangements • Students live in locally rented apartments, host family homes, hotels. Meals are taken on one's own, with host family, in residences, in restaurants.
Costs (2005) • Contact sponsor for cost. $175 application fee. Financial aid available for all students: scholarship research service.
For More Information • Ms. Nancy Forman, President, Language Liaison, PO Box 1772, Pacific Palisades, CA 90272; *Phone:* 800-284-4448; *Fax:* 310-454-1706. *E-mail:* learn@languageliaison.com. *World Wide Web:* http://www.languageliaison.com/

UNIVERSITY OF ILLINOIS AT URBANA-CHAMPAIGN
INTERMEDIATE GERMAN

Held at Vienna University of Economics and Business Administration
Academic Focus • German language and literature.
Program Information • Classes are held on the campus of Vienna University of Economics and Business Administration (Vienna, Austria). Faculty members are drawn from the sponsor's U.S. staff. Field trips to Vienna and environs. Students typically earn 5-6 semester credits per term.
Sessions • May-Jun (summer).
Eligibility Requirements • Open to freshmen, sophomores, juniors, seniors, graduate students, adults; good academic standing at home school; 1 year of college course work in German.
Living Arrangements • Students live in host institution dormitories. Quarters are shared with host institution students, students from other programs. Meals are taken on one's own, in residences.
Costs (2005) • $2700; includes tuition, housing, all meals, insurance, books and class materials, student support services, local transportation. $250 deposit required. Financial aid available for all students: loans.
For More Information • Ms. Claudia Bornholdt, Professor, University of Illinois at Urbana-Champaign, Department of Germanic Languages and Literature, 2090 FLB MC-178, 707 South Mathews Avenue, Urbana, IL 61801; *Phone:* 217-333-8777; *Fax:* 217-244-3242. *E-mail:* bornholdt@uiuc.edu. *World Wide Web:* http://www.ips.uiuc.edu/sao/index.shtml

UNIVERSITY OF SOUTHERN MISSISSIPPI
AUSTRIAN STUDIES PROGRAM

Academic Focus • History, social sciences.
Program Information • Faculty members are drawn from the sponsor's U.S. staff and local instructors hired by the sponsor. Scheduled travel; field trips. Students typically earn 4 semester credits per term.
Sessions • Jun (summer).
Eligibility Requirements • Minimum age 18; open to sophomores, juniors, seniors, graduate students, adults; 2.0 GPA; good academic standing at home school; no foreign language proficiency required.
Living Arrangements • Students live in host institution dormitories, locally rented apartments, hotels. Meals are taken as a group, on one's own, in residences, in central dining facility, in restaurants.
Costs (2005) • $3599 for undergraduate students; $3799 for graduate students; includes tuition, housing, some meals, excursions, international airfare, student support services. $200 nonrefundable deposit required. Financial aid available for students from sponsoring institution: scholarships, loans.
For More Information • Director, Austrian Studies Program, University of Southern Mississippi, 118 College Drive #10047, Hattiesburg, MS 39406-0001; *Phone:* 601-266-4344; *Fax:* 601-266-5699. *E-mail:* holly.buckner@usm.edu. *World Wide Web:* http://www.usm.edu/internationaledu/

BAHAMAS

NASSAU

LOYOLA UNIVERSITY NEW ORLEANS
LOYOLA IN THE BAHAMAS

Hosted by College of the Bahamas
Academic Focus • Full curriculum.
Program Information • Students attend classes at College of the Bahamas (Nassau, Bahamas). Field trips to museums, historic areas. Students typically earn 6 semester credits per term.
Sessions • Jul–Aug (summer).
Eligibility Requirements • Open to freshmen, sophomores, juniors, seniors; 2.5 GPA; 2 letters of recommendation; good academic standing at home school.
Living Arrangements • Quarters are shared with host institution students. Meals are taken on one's own, in residences.
Costs (2005) • $3500; includes tuition, housing, insurance, excursions, international airfare.
For More Information • Center for International Education, Loyola University New Orleans, 6363 St. Charles Avenue, Box 205, New Orleans, LA 70118; *Phone:* 504-864-7550; *Fax:* 504-864-7548. *E-mail:* cie@loyno.edu. *World Wide Web:* http://www.loyno.edu/cie/

UNIVERSITY OF ALABAMA
ALABAMA IN BAHAMAS

Held at College of the Bahamas
Academic Focus • Biological/life sciences, ecology.
Program Information • Classes are held on the campus of College of the Bahamas (Nassau, Bahamas). Faculty members are drawn from the sponsor's U.S. staff. Students typically earn 3 semester credits per term.
Sessions • May (summer).
Eligibility Requirements • Minimum age 18; open to sophomores, juniors, seniors, graduate students; course work in biology; 3.0 GPA; good academic standing at home school; permission of instructor.
Living Arrangements • Students live in the BERC research center. Quarters are shared with host institution students. Meals are taken as a group, in central dining facility.
Costs (2005) • $2465; includes tuition, housing, all meals, international airfare, books and class materials, lab equipment, international student ID, student support services. $100 application fee. $500 nonrefundable deposit required. Financial aid available for all students: scholarships, work study, loans.
For More Information • Ms. Angela L. Channell, Director of Overseas Study, University of Alabama, Box 870254, Tuscaloosa, AL 35487-0254; *Phone:* 205-348-5256; *Fax:* 205-348-5298. *E-mail:* achannel@aalan.ua.edu. *World Wide Web:* http://www.overseas-study.ua.edu/

SAN SALVADOR

MICHIGAN STATE UNIVERSITY
TROPICAL ECOLOGY AND MANAGEMENT

Academic Focus • Agriculture, ecology, fisheries studies, natural resources, zoology.
Program Information • Faculty members are drawn from the sponsor's U.S. staff. Field trips to lakes, marsh areas, reefs, historic sites. Students typically earn 6 semester credits per term.
Sessions • May (summer).
Eligibility Requirements • Minimum age 18; open to juniors, seniors, graduate students; course work in ecology; 2.5 GPA; good academic standing at home school; faculty approval; swimming proficiency; diving equipment.
Living Arrangements • Students live in host institution dormitories. Meals are taken as a group, on one's own, in central dining facility, in restaurants.
Costs (2004) • $1800 (estimated); includes housing, all meals, insurance, excursions, student support services, boat rental. $100 application fee. $200 nonrefundable deposit required. Financial aid available for students from sponsoring institution: scholarships, loans.
For More Information • Mr. Mark Davis, Coordinator, Michigan State University, Office of Study Abroad, 109 International Center, East Lansing, MI 48824-1035; *Phone:* 517-432-1315; *Fax:* 517-432-2082. *E-mail:* mdavis@msn.edu. *World Wide Web:* http://studyabroad.msu.edu/

BELGIUM

CITY-TO-CITY

INTERNATIONAL MANAGEMENT INSTITUTE
BACHELOR OF BUSINESS ADMINISTRATION

Hosted by International Management Institute, International Management Institute
Academic Focus • Business administration/management.
Program Information • Students attend classes at International Management Institute (Brussels), International Management Institute (Antwerp). Field trips to Paris, Amsterdam, London, Antwerp, Brussels; optional travel to Berlin, Prague, Rome, Barcelona at an extra cost. Students typically earn 3–21 semester credits per term.
Sessions • New sessions begin every 5 weeks.
Eligibility Requirements • Minimum age 18; open to precollege students, freshmen, sophomores, juniors, seniors; 2 letters of recommendation; no foreign language proficiency required.
Living Arrangements • Students live in host institution dormitories, locally rented apartments, program-owned apartments, hotels. Quarters are shared with host institution students. Meals are taken on one's own, in residences.
Costs (2002–2003) • €3750; includes tuition, student support services. €150 application fee. €750 refundable deposit required.
For More Information • Mr. Luc Van Mele, Director, International Management Institute, Rue de Livourne 116-120, 1000 Brussels, Belgium; *Phone:* +32 3-2185431; *Fax:* +32 3-2185868. *E-mail:* info@timi.edu. *World Wide Web:* http://www.timi.edu/

INTERNATIONAL MANAGEMENT INSTITUTE
MASTER OF BUSINESS ADMINISTRATION

Hosted by International Management Institute, International Management Institute
Academic Focus • International business.
Program Information • Students attend classes at International Management Institute (Brussels), International Management Institute (Antwerp). Field trips to Paris, Amsterdam, Antwerp, Brussels, London; optional travel to London, Berlin, Prague, Rome, Barcelona at an extra cost. Students typically earn 3–21 semester credits per term.
Sessions • New sessions begin every 5 weeks.
Eligibility Requirements • Minimum age 21; open to seniors, graduate students, adults; 2 letters of recommendation; good academic standing at home school; no foreign language proficiency required.
Living Arrangements • Students live in host institution dormitories, locally rented apartments, program-owned houses. Quarters are shared with host institution students. Meals are taken on one's own, in residences.
Costs (2002–2003) • €4500; includes tuition, lab equipment, student support services. €150 application fee. €750 refundable deposit required.
For More Information • Mr. Luc Van Mele, Director, International Management Institute, Rue de Livourne 116-120, 1000 Brussels, Belgium; *Phone:* +32 3-2185431; *Fax:* +32 3-2185868. *E-mail:* info@timi.edu. *World Wide Web:* http://www.timi.edu/

ANTWERP

JAMES MADISON UNIVERSITY
BUSINESS ENVIRONMENT IN EUROPE

Hosted by University of Antwerp
Academic Focus • Economics, marketing.
Program Information • Students attend classes at University of Antwerp (Antwerp, Belgium). Scheduled travel to Strasbourg, Luxembourg; field trips to Bruges, Ghent, Brussels. Students typically earn 3 semester credits per term.
Sessions • May (summer).
Eligibility Requirements • Minimum age 18; open to sophomores, juniors, seniors; 2.0 GPA; good academic standing at home school; no foreign language proficiency required.
Living Arrangements • Students live in hotels. Meals are taken as a group, on one's own, in central dining facility, in restaurants.
Costs (2005) • $2953 for Virginia residents; $3793 for nonresidents; includes tuition, housing, some meals, excursions, books and class materials, international student ID. $400 nonrefundable deposit required. Financial aid available for students from sponsoring institution: work study.
For More Information • Mr. Felix Wang, Director, James Madison University, Office of International Programs, MSC 5731, 1077 South Main Street, Harrisonburg, VA 22807; *Phone:* 540-568-6419; *Fax:* 540-568-3310. *E-mail:* studyabroad@jmu.edu. *World Wide Web:* http://www.jmu.edu/international/

BELGIUM
Antwerp

JAMES MADISON UNIVERSITY
SUMMER PROGRAM IN ANTWERP

Hosted by University of Antwerp

Academic Focus • Business administration/management, marketing.

Program Information • Students attend classes at University of Antwerp (Antwerp, Belgium). Scheduled travel to Strasbourg, France, Luxembourg; field trips to Bruges, Ghent, Brussels. Students typically earn 15 semester credits per term.

Sessions • May–Aug (summer).

Eligibility Requirements • Minimum age 18; open to sophomores, juniors, seniors; 2.0 GPA; 1 letter of recommendation; good academic standing at home school; no foreign language proficiency required.

Living Arrangements • Students live in program-owned apartments. Meals are taken on one's own, in restaurants.

Costs (2005) • $10,170 for Virginia residents; $14,370 for nonresidents; includes tuition, housing, some meals, excursions, books and class materials, international student ID. $400 nonrefundable deposit required. Financial aid available for students from sponsoring institution: scholarships, work study, loans.

For More Information • Mr. Felix Wang, Director, James Madison University, Office of International Programs, MSC 5731, 1077 South Main Street, Harrisonburg, VA 22807; *Phone:* 540-568-6419; *Fax:* 540-568-3310. *E-mail:* studyabroad@jmu.edu. *World Wide Web:* http://www.jmu.edu/international/

BRUSSELS

CIEE
CIEE STUDY CENTER AT VESALIUS COLLEGE AT VRIJE UNIVERSITEIT BRUSSEL, BRUSSELS, BELGIUM

Hosted by Vesalius College

Academic Focus • Art history, business administration/management, communications, economics, European studies, international affairs, marketing, political science and government, statistics.

Program Information • Students attend classes at Vesalius College (Brussels, Belgium). Field trips to Bruges, Caves of Han, France, The Netherlands; Germany. Students typically earn 6 semester credits per term.

Sessions • Jun–Jul (summer).

Eligibility Requirements • Minimum age 18; open to sophomores, juniors, seniors; 2.75 GPA; 1 letter of recommendation; good academic standing at home school; no foreign language proficiency required.

Living Arrangements • Students live in locally rented apartments, host family homes. Quarters are shared with host institution students. Meals are taken on one's own, in residences, in central dining facility, in restaurants.

Costs (2007) • Contact sponsor for cost. $30 application fee. $300 nonrefundable deposit required. Financial aid available for all students: scholarships, minority student scholarships.

For More Information • Information Center, CIEE, 7 Custom House Street, 3rd Floor, Portland, ME 04101; *Phone:* 800-40-STUDY; *Fax:* 207-553-7699. *E-mail:* studyinfo@ciee.org. *World Wide Web:* http://www.ciee.org/isp/

IEBA
EUROPEAN-U.S. BUSINESS CERTIFICATE IN EUROPEAN AFFAIRS

Held at IEBA

Academic Focus • Business administration/management, commerce, European studies, international affairs, international business.

Program Information • Classes are held on the campus of IEBA (Brussels, Belgium), IEBA (Gent, Belgium). Faculty members are local instructors hired by the sponsor. Optional travel to Paris, Amsterdam, London at an extra cost. Students typically earn 6 per term.

Sessions • Jul (summer).

Eligibility Requirements • Minimum age 18; open to sophomores, juniors, seniors, graduate students, adults; good academic standing at home school; no foreign language proficiency required.

Living Arrangements • Students live in hotels. Quarters are shared with host institution students. Meals are taken on one's own, in residences.

Costs (2005) • $1950; includes tuition, housing, some meals, excursions, books and class materials.

For More Information • Prof. Pierre Heyndrickx, President, IEBA, Sint Pietersnieuwstraat 202, 9000 Gent, Belgium; *Phone:* +0032 922-34436; *Fax:* +0032 922-44973. *E-mail:* ieba@iebaeurope.com. *World Wide Web:* http://www.iebaeurope.com

KNOWLEDGE EXCHANGE INSTITUTE (KEI)
BRUSSELS INTERNSHIP PROGRAM

Hosted by International Management Institute

Academic Focus • Accounting, actuarial science, advertising and public relations, brokerage, business administration/management, commerce, communication services, communications, community service, criminal justice, economics, entrepreneurship, European studies, finance, hospitality services, hotel and restaurant management, human resources, information science, international affairs, international business, law and legal studies, management information systems, marketing, political science and government, public administration, social services, social work, tourism and travel.

Program Information • Students attend classes at International Management Institute (Brussels, Belgium). Field trips to Brussels, Antwerp, Bruges. Students typically earn 6 semester credits per term.

Sessions • Jun–Aug (summer).

Eligibility Requirements • Open to freshmen, sophomores, juniors, seniors, graduate students, adults; 2.2 GPA; good academic standing at home school; no foreign language proficiency required.

Living Arrangements • Students live in host institution dormitories, program-owned apartments, host family homes. Quarters are shared with host institution students, students from other programs. Meals are taken on one's own, with host family, in residences, in restaurants.

Costs (2006) • $4845; includes tuition, housing, insurance, excursions, student support services, mobile telephone. $50 application fee. $500 nonrefundable deposit required. Financial aid available for all students: scholarships, loans.

For More Information • Mr. Eduard Izraylovsky, Director, Knowledge Exchange Institute (KEI), 111 John Street, Suite 800, New York, NY 10038; *Phone:* 800-831-5095; *Fax:* 212-528-2095. *E-mail:* info@knowledgeexchange.org. *World Wide Web:* http://www.knowledgeexchange.org/

KNOWLEDGE EXCHANGE INSTITUTE (KEI)
EUROPEAN BUSINESS, LAW, AND DIPLOMACY

Hosted by International Management Institute

Academic Focus • Accounting, business administration/management, commerce, community service, cultural studies, economics, entrepreneurship, European studies, finance, human resources, information science, intercultural studies, interdisciplinary studies, international affairs, international business, labor and industrial relations, management information systems, marketing, political science and government, public administration, public policy, Spanish language and literature, Spanish studies, statistics, telecommunications.

Program Information • Students attend classes at International Management Institute (Brussels, Belgium). Scheduled travel to London, Paris, Berlin; field trips to Brussels, Antwerp, Bruges, Amsterdam. Students typically earn 12 semester credits per term.

Sessions • Jun–Aug (summer).

Eligibility Requirements • Open to freshmen, sophomores, juniors, seniors, graduate students, adults; 2.2 GPA; 2 letters of recommendation; good academic standing at home school; no foreign language proficiency required.

Living Arrangements • Students live in program-owned houses. Quarters are shared with host institution students, students from other programs. Meals are taken on one's own, in residences, in restaurants.

Costs (2006) • $5870; includes tuition, housing, insurance, excursions, books and class materials, lab equipment, student support services, mobile phone, internet access. $50 application fee. $500 nonrefundable deposit required. Financial aid available for all students: scholarships, loans.

For More Information • Mr. Eduard Izraylovsky, Director, Knowledge Exchange Institute (KEI), 111 John Street, Suite 800, New York, NY 10038; *Phone:* 800-831-5095; *Fax:* 212-528-2095. *E-mail:* info@knowledgeexchange.org. *World Wide Web:* http://www. knowledgeexchange.org/

KNOWLEDGE EXCHANGE INSTITUTE (KEI)
EUROPEAN LANGUAGES AND CULTURES
Hosted by International Management Institute

Academic Focus • Area studies, community service, cultural studies, Dutch, economics, ethics, European studies, French language and literature, French studies, German language and literature, history, intercultural studies, interdisciplinary studies, liberal studies, psychology, social work, Spanish language and literature.

Program Information • Students attend classes at International Management Institute (Brussels, Belgium). Scheduled travel to London, Paris, Berlin; field trips to Brussels, Antwerp, Bruges, Amsterdam. Students typically earn 12 semester credits per term.

Sessions • Jun–Aug (summer).

Eligibility Requirements • Open to freshmen, sophomores, juniors, seniors, graduate students, adults; 2.2 GPA; 2 letters of recommendation; good academic standing at home school; no foreign language proficiency required.

Living Arrangements • Students live in program-owned houses. Quarters are shared with host institution students, students from other programs. Meals are taken on one's own, in residences, in restaurants.

Costs (2006) • $5870; includes tuition, housing, insurance, excursions, books and class materials, lab equipment, student support services, mobile phone and internet access. $50 application fee. $500 nonrefundable deposit required. Financial aid available for all students: scholarships, loans.

For More Information • Mr. Eduard Izraylovsky, Director, Knowledge Exchange Institute (KEI), 111 John Street, Suite 800, New York, NY 10038; *Phone:* 800-831-5095; *Fax:* 212-528-2095. *E-mail:* info@knowledgeexchange.org. *World Wide Web:* http://www. knowledgeexchange.org/

KNOWLEDGE EXCHANGE INSTITUTE (KEI)
EUROPEAN TOURISM AND HOSPITALITY MANAGEMENT
Hosted by The International Management Institute

Academic Focus • Business administration/management, communications, cultural studies, economics, European studies, hospitality services, hotel and restaurant management, intercultural studies, interdisciplinary studies, international business, Spanish language and literature, Spanish studies, tourism and travel.

Program Information • Students attend classes at The International Management Institute (Brussels, Belgium). Scheduled travel to London, Paris, Berlin; field trips to Brussels, Antwerp, Bruges, Amsterdam. Students typically earn 12 semester credits per term.

Sessions • Jun–Aug (summer).

Eligibility Requirements • Open to freshmen, sophomores, juniors, seniors, graduate students, adults; 2.5 GPA; 2 letters of recommendation; good academic standing at home school; no foreign language proficiency required.

Living Arrangements • Students live in program-owned houses. Quarters are shared with host institution students, students from other programs. Meals are taken on one's own, in residences, in restaurants.

Costs (2006) • $5870; includes tuition, housing, insurance, excursions, international airfare, books and class materials, lab equipment, student support services, mobile phone, internet access. $50 application fee. $500 nonrefundable deposit required. Financial aid available for all students: scholarships, loans.

For More Information • Mr. Eduard Izraylovsky, Director, Knowledge Exchange Institute (KEI), 111 John Street, Suite 800, New York, NY 10038; *Phone:* 800-831-5095; *Fax:* 212-528-2095. *E-mail:* info@knowledgeexchange.org. *World Wide Web:* http://www. knowledgeexchange.org/

KNOWLEDGE EXCHANGE INSTITUTE (KEI)
GLOBAL SYSTEMS, COMMUNICATIONS, AND E-COMMERCE
Hosted by International Management Institute

Academic Focus • Advertising and public relations, business administration/management, commerce, communication services, communications, economics, information science, interdisciplinary studies, international affairs, international business, liberal studies, management information systems, statistics.

Program Information • Students attend classes at International Management Institute (Brussels, Belgium). Scheduled travel to Paris, London, Berlin; field trips to Brussels, Antwerp, Bruges, Amsterdam. Students typically earn 12 semester credits per term.

Sessions • Jun–Aug (summer).

Eligibility Requirements • Open to freshmen, sophomores, juniors, seniors, graduate students, adults; 2.2 GPA; 2 letters of recommendation; good academic standing at home school; no foreign language proficiency required.

Living Arrangements • Students live in program-owned houses. Quarters are shared with host institution students, students from other programs. Meals are taken on one's own, in residences, in restaurants.

Costs (2006) • $5870; includes tuition, housing, insurance, excursions, books and class materials, lab equipment, student support services, mobile phone, internet access. $50 application fee. $500 nonrefundable deposit required. Financial aid available for all students: scholarships, loans.

For More Information • Mr. Eduard Izraylovsky, Director, Knowledge Exchange Institute (KEI), 111 John Street, Suite 800, New York, NY 10038; *Phone:* 800-831-5095; *Fax:* 212-528-2095. *E-mail:* info@knowledgeexchange.org. *World Wide Web:* http://www. knowledgeexchange.org/

MICHIGAN STATE UNIVERSITY
INTERNATIONAL RELATIONS IN BRUSSELS
Held at Free University of Brussels

Academic Focus • International affairs, peace and conflict studies, political science and government.

Program Information • Classes are held on the campus of Free University of Brussels (Brussels, Belgium). Faculty members are drawn from the sponsor's U.S. staff and local instructors hired by the sponsor. Field trips to NATO headquarters, Commission of the European Union, SHAPE; European Parliament; optional travel to Eastern Europe at an extra cost. Students typically earn 8 semester credits per term.

Sessions • Jul (summer).

Eligibility Requirements • Minimum age 18; open to freshmen, sophomores, juniors, seniors; 2.3 GPA; good academic standing at home school; faculty approval; no foreign language proficiency required.

Living Arrangements • Students live in locally rented apartments. Meals are taken as a group, on one's own, in restaurants.

Costs (2005) • $1231 (estimated); includes housing, insurance, excursions, student support services. $100 application fee. $200 nonrefundable deposit required. Financial aid available for students from sponsoring institution: scholarships, loans.

For More Information • Ms. Yvonne Squiers, Secretary, Michigan State University, Office of Study Abroad, 109 International Center, East Lansing, MI 48824-1035; *Phone:* 517-353-8920; *Fax:* 517-432-2082. *E-mail:* squiers@msu.edu. *World Wide Web:* http://studyabroad. msu.edu/

UNIVERSITY OF ROCHESTER
INTERNSHIPS IN EUROPE–BELGIUM

Academic Focus • Business administration/management, European studies, international affairs, political science and government.

Program Information • Scheduled travel to Strasbourg. Students typically earn 8 semester credits per term.

Sessions • May–Jul (summer).

Eligibility Requirements • Open to sophomores, juniors, seniors; 3.0 GPA; 2 letters of recommendation; good academic standing at home school; .5 years course work in French.

Living Arrangements • Students live in locally rented apartments. Meals are taken on one's own, in residences, in restaurants.

Costs (2005) • $6450; includes tuition, housing, some meals, student support services. $30 application fee. $300 nonrefundable deposit required. Financial aid available for students from sponsoring institution: loans.

BELGIUM
Brussels

For More Information • Ms. Jacqueline Levine, Study Abroad Director, University of Rochester, Center for Study Abroad, PO Box 270376, Lattimore 206, Rochester, NY 14627-0376; *Phone:* 585-275-7532; *Fax:* 585-461-5131. *E-mail:* abroad@mail.rochester.edu. *World Wide Web:* http://www.rochester.edu/college/study-abroad/

LEUVEN

LOYOLA UNIVERSITY NEW ORLEANS
LOYOLA IN BELGIUM

Hosted by Loyola International House
Academic Focus • History, philosophy, religious studies.
Program Information • Students attend classes at Loyola International House (Leuven, Belgium). Field trips to Amsterdam, Verdun, Bruges, Brussels, Aachen, Cologne, Ypres, Ghent; optional travel to Paris, London, Amsterdam at an extra cost. Students typically earn 6 semester credits per term.
Sessions • Jul–Aug (summer).
Eligibility Requirements • Minimum age 18; open to freshmen, sophomores, juniors, seniors; 2.0 GPA; good academic standing at home school; no foreign language proficiency required.
Living Arrangements • Students live in host institution dormitories. Quarters are shared with host institution students. Meals are taken on one's own, in residences, in restaurants.
Costs (2006) • $3895 (estimated); includes tuition, housing, some meals, insurance, excursions, international airfare. $500 nonrefundable deposit required. Financial aid available for students from sponsoring institution: loans.
For More Information • Dr. Bernard Cook, Professor of History, Loyola University New Orleans, 6363 Saint Charles Avenue, New Orleans, LA 70118; *Phone:* 504-865-3537; *Fax:* 504-865-2010. *E-mail:* cook@loyno.edu. *World Wide Web:* http://www.loyno.edu/cie/

LOUVAIN-LA-NEUVE

LOYOLA UNIVERSITY NEW ORLEANS
INTERNATIONAL BUSINESS IN EUROPE

Hosted by Catholic University of Louvain
Academic Focus • International business, international business.
Program Information • Students attend classes at Catholic University of Louvain (Louvain-la-Neuve, Belgium). Scheduled travel to Paris, Amsterdam; field trips to businesses in Belgium and France. Students typically earn 6 semester credits per term.
Sessions • Jul (summer).
Eligibility Requirements • Open to juniors, seniors, graduate students; major in business; course work in economics, marketing, management; good academic standing at home school; no foreign language proficiency required.
Living Arrangements • Students live in program-owned apartments. Meals are taken as a group, on one's own, in restaurants.
Costs (2005) • $3375 for undergraduate students; $3575 for graduate students; includes tuition, housing, insurance, excursions, lab equipment, student support services. $200 refundable deposit required. Financial aid available for students from sponsoring institution: scholarships, loans.
For More Information • Dr. Brenda Joyner, Associate Dean, College of Business, Loyola University New Orleans, College of Business, New Orleans, LA 70118; *Phone:* 504-864-7978; *Fax:* 504-864-7970. *E-mail:* dauteriv@loyno.edu. *World Wide Web:* http://www.loyno.edu/cie/

BELIZE

CITY-TO-CITY

COOPERATIVE CENTER FOR STUDY ABROAD
BELIZE

Academic Focus • Biological/life sciences, women's studies.
Program Information • Faculty members are drawn from the sponsor's U.S. staff. Field trips. Students typically earn 3 semester credits per term.
Sessions • May–Jun (summer).
Eligibility Requirements • Minimum age 18; open to freshmen, sophomores, juniors, seniors, graduate students, adults; good academic standing at home school.
Living Arrangements • Quarters are shared with host institution students. Meals are taken as a group, on one's own, in central dining facility, in restaurants.
Costs (2007) • $3595; includes housing, some meals, insurance, excursions, international airfare, airport transfers. $200 nonrefundable deposit required. Financial aid available for students from sponsoring institution: scholarships, loans.
For More Information • Dr. Michael A. Klembara, Executive Director, Cooperative Center for Study Abroad, Northern Kentucky University, Nunn Drive, Founders Hall 301, Highland Heights, KY 41099; *Phone:* 859-572-6512; *Fax:* 859-572-6650. *World Wide Web:* http://www.ccsa.cc/

STERLING COLLEGE
BELIZE

Academic Focus • Belizean studies, botany, conservation studies, forestry, marine sciences, natural resources, wildlife studies.
Program Information • Faculty members are drawn from the sponsor's U.S. staff and local instructors hired by the sponsor. Scheduled travel to Wee Wee Caye Marine Lab, Barrier Reef, Maya Mountains, Bladen and Mar Key Rivers; field trips. Students typically earn 3 semester credits per term.
Sessions • Jan (2 weeks).
Eligibility Requirements • Minimum age 18; open to freshmen, sophomores, juniors, seniors, graduate students, adults; 2 letters of recommendation; good academic standing at home school; no foreign language proficiency required.
Living Arrangements • Students live in host family homes, hotels. Meals are taken as a group, with host family, in residences, in restaurants.
Costs (2005) • $4470; includes tuition, housing, all meals, excursions, international airfare, lab equipment, student support services, in-country transportation, guiding. $35 application fee. Financial aid available for all students: scholarships, loans.
For More Information • Mr. Erik Hansen, Director of Global Field Studies, Sterling College, PO Box 72, Craftsbury Common, VT 05827; *Phone:* 802-586-7711 Ext. 128; *Fax:* 802-586-2596. *E-mail:* admissions@ sterlingcollege.edu. *World Wide Web:* http://www.sterlingcollege.edu/

UNIVERSITY OF CALIFORNIA, SANTA BARBARA, WILDLANDS STUDIES
ECOSYSTEMS AND CULTURES OF BELIZE

Academic Focus • Ecology, environmental science/studies, geography, wildlife studies.
Program Information • Faculty members are drawn from the sponsor's U.S. staff. Scheduled travel to ecological field locations. Students typically earn 15 quarter credits per term.
Sessions • Jun–Aug (summer), Jan–Feb (winter).
Eligibility Requirements • Minimum age 18; open to freshmen, sophomores, juniors, seniors; course work in biology or geography; good academic standing at home school; application essay; no foreign language proficiency required.
Living Arrangements • Students live in host family homes, tents. Meals are taken as a group.
Costs (2006–2007) • $1995; includes tuition. $75 application fee.
For More Information • Mr. Crandall Bay, Director, Wildlands Studies Program, University of California, Santa Barbara, Wildlands Studies, 3 Mosswood Circle, Cazadero, CA 95421; *Phone:* 707-632-5665; *Fax:* 707-632-5665. *E-mail:* wildlands@sonic.net. *World Wide Web:* http://www.wildlandsstudies.com/

UNIVERSITY OF SOUTHERN MISSISSIPPI
FIELD RESEARCH IN BELIZE

Academic Focus • International affairs.
Program Information • Faculty members are drawn from the sponsor's U.S. staff. Scheduled travel; field trips; optional travel. Students typically earn 6 semester credits per term.

BELIZE

City-to-City

Sessions • Jun (summer).
Eligibility Requirements • Minimum age 18; open to graduate students; 2.0 GPA; good academic standing at home school; interview with program director; no foreign language proficiency required.
Living Arrangements • Students live in hotels. Meals are taken as a group, on one's own, in restaurants.
Costs (2005) • $2899; includes tuition, housing, books and class materials. $200 nonrefundable deposit required. Financial aid available for students from sponsoring institution: scholarships, loans.
For More Information • Director, Field Research in Belize, University of Southern Mississippi, 118 College Drive #10047, Hattiesburg, MS 39406-0001; Phone: 601-266-4344; Fax: 601-266-5699. E-mail: holly.buckner@usm.edu. World Wide Web: http://www.usm.edu/internationaledu/

BELIZE CITY

AMERICAN UNIVERSITIES INTERNATIONAL PROGRAMS (AUIP)
BELIZE: MARINE ECOSYSTEMS

Hosted by University of Belize
Academic Focus • Anthropology, conservation studies, ecology, forestry, geography, natural resources, parks and recreation.
Program Information • Students attend classes at University of Belize (Belize City, Belize). Scheduled travel to Calabash Caye, Mayan villages and ruins; field trips. Students typically earn 3 semester credits per term.
Sessions • Mar (summer), Apr (summer 2).
Eligibility Requirements • Minimum age 18; open to freshmen, sophomores, juniors, seniors, graduate students, adults; 2.0 GPA; 2 letters of recommendation; good academic standing at home school; essay; transcript; no foreign language proficiency required.
Living Arrangements • Students live in host family homes, hotels. Meals are taken as a group, in residences, in central dining facility, in restaurants.
Costs (2006) • $1150; includes tuition, housing, some meals, insurance, excursions, student support services, all in-country travel and activities. $300 application fee.
For More Information • Dr. Michael Tarrant, Program Director, American Universities International Programs (AUIP), 108 South Main Street, Winterville, GA 30683; Phone: 706-742-9285. E-mail: info@auip.com. World Wide Web: http://www.auip.com/

AMERICAN UNIVERSITIES INTERNATIONAL PROGRAMS (AUIP)
BELIZE: RAINFOREST TO REEF

Hosted by University of Belize
Academic Focus • Anthropology, conservation studies, ecology, forestry, geography, natural resources, parks and recreation.
Program Information • Students attend classes at University of Belize (Belize City, Belize). Scheduled travel to Calabash Caye, Punta Gorda, Cockscomb Jaguar Preserve, San Ignacio, Mountain Pine Reserve, Mayan ruins at Tikal, Guatemala; field trips. Students typically earn 6 semester credits per term.
Sessions • May–Jun (summer), Dec–Jan (winter).
Eligibility Requirements • Minimum age 18; open to freshmen, sophomores, juniors, seniors, graduate students, adults; 2.0 GPA; 2 letters of recommendation; good academic standing at home school; essay; transcript; no foreign language proficiency required.
Living Arrangements • Students live in host family homes, hotels. Meals are taken as a group, in residences, in restaurants.
Costs (2006) • $3050; includes tuition, housing, some meals, excursions, all in-country travel and activities. $300 application fee.
For More Information • Dr. Michael Tarrant, Program Director, American Universities International Programs (AUIP), 108 South Main Street, Winterville, GA 30683; Phone: 706-742-9285. E-mail: info@auip.com. World Wide Web: http://www.auip.com/

STATE UNIVERSITY OF NEW YORK COLLEGE AT CORTLAND
BELIZE DEVELOPMENT INTERNSHIPS (SUMMER)

Academic Focus • Full curriculum.
Program Information • Faculty members are local instructors hired by the sponsor. Field trips to national parks, Mayan ruins, Belizean cayes; optional travel to Mexico, the Caribbean, the barrier reef and cayes, Guatemala at an extra cost. Students typically earn 8–12 semester credits per term.
Sessions • May–Aug (summer).
Eligibility Requirements • Minimum age 19; open to juniors, seniors, graduate students; course work in field related to internship placement; 2.5 GPA; 2 letters of recommendation; good academic standing at home school; strong performance in major; maturity; adaptability; no foreign language proficiency required.
Living Arrangements • Students live in host family homes. Meals are taken with host family, in residences.
Costs (2005) • $5008; includes tuition, housing, all meals, insurance, international airfare, books and class materials, international student ID, student support services. $20 application fee. $200 nonrefundable deposit required. Financial aid available for students from sponsoring institution: scholarships, loans.
For More Information • Ms. Liz McCartney, Assistant Director, Office of International Programs, State University of New York College at Cortland, PO Box 2000, Cortland, NY 13045; Phone: 607-753-2209; Fax: 607-753-5989. E-mail: cortlandabroad@cortland.edu. World Wide Web: http://www.cortlandabroad.com/

HOPKINS

PROWORLD SERVICE CORPS
PROWORLD SERVICE CORPS

Academic Focus • Belizean studies, community service, cultural studies, environmental science/studies, Latin American studies, marine sciences, Mayan studies, public policy, social sciences, social work, Spanish language and literature.
Program Information • Faculty members are drawn from the sponsor's U.S. staff and local instructors hired by the sponsor. Field trips to Mayan ruins, snorkeling, cultural events; optional travel at an extra cost. Students typically earn 3 semester credits per term.
Sessions • 4 week sessions begin every month year-round.
Eligibility Requirements • Minimum age 18; open to freshmen, sophomores, juniors, seniors, graduate students, adults; good academic standing at home school; desire to learn and help others; no foreign language proficiency required.
Living Arrangements • Students live in host family homes. Meals are taken with host family, in residences.
Costs (2005) • $1950 for 4 weeks; $300 for each additional week; includes tuition, housing, all meals, insurance, excursions, books and class materials, lab equipment, international student ID, student support services. $200 nonrefundable deposit required. Financial aid available for all students: scholarships.
For More Information • Ms. Anne Connolly, Marketing and Placement Advisor, ProWorld Service Corps, PO Box 21121, Billings, MT 59104-1121; Phone: 877-429-6753; Fax: 406-252-3873. E-mail: info@proworldsc.org. World Wide Web: http://www.proworldsc.org

LAMANAI

UNIVERSITY OF NORTH CAROLINA AT WILMINGTON
SUMMER STUDY IN BELIZE

Academic Focus • Anthropology, archaeology.
Program Information • Faculty members are drawn from the sponsor's U.S. staff. Field trips to Mayan ruins, archaeological field excavation sites; optional travel at an extra cost. Students typically earn 6 semester credits per term.
Sessions • May–Jun (summer).

Eligibility Requirements • Minimum age 18; open to freshmen, sophomores, juniors, seniors, adults; course work in anthropology; 2.0 GPA; permission of instructor; no foreign language proficiency required.
Living Arrangements • Students live in field camp. Meals are taken as a group, on one's own.
Costs (2005) • $4550 for North Carolina residents; $6830 for nonresidents; includes tuition, housing, all meals, insurance, excursions, international airfare, books and class materials. $200 nonrefundable deposit required. Financial aid available for students from sponsoring institution: scholarships, loans, grants.
For More Information • Ms. Elizabeth A. Adams, Director, Education Abroad, University of North Carolina at Wilmington, 601 South College, Wilmington, NC 28403; *Phone:* 910-962-3685; *Fax:* 910-962-4053. *E-mail:* adamse@uncw.edu. *World Wide Web:* http://www.uncw.edu/intprogs/

SAN IGNACIO

COLLEGE CONSORTIUM FOR INTERNATIONAL STUDIES–UNIVERSITY OF INDIANAPOLIS
SUMMER STUDY ABROAD

Hosted by Galen University
Academic Focus • Full curriculum.
Program Information • Students attend classes at Galen University (San Ignacio, Belize). Scheduled travel to archeology sites; field trips to archeology sites; optional travel to tourist areas and archeology sites at an extra cost.
Sessions • May–Aug (summer).
Eligibility Requirements • Open to sophomores, juniors, seniors, graduate students; 2.0 GPA; 3 letters of recommendation; good academic standing at home school; no foreign language proficiency required.
Living Arrangements • Students live in hotels. Quarters are shared with students from other programs. Meals are taken on one's own, in residences.

Costs (2005–2006) • Contact sponsor for cost; includes tuition, insurance, excursions, student support services, local transportation. $30 application fee. Financial aid available for all students: loans, Grants.
For More Information • Breezy Anne Wente, Study Abroad Advisor, College Consortium for International Studies–University of Indianapolis, 1400 E. Hanna Avenue, Indianapolis, IN 46227; *Phone:* 317-788-3394; *Fax:* 317-788-3383. *E-mail:* bwente@windy.edu

PROWORLD SERVICE CORPS
PROWORLD SERVICE CORPS

Academic Focus • Belizean studies, community service, cultural studies, environmental science/studies, Latin American studies, marine sciences, Mayan studies, public health, public policy, social sciences, social work.
Program Information • Faculty members are drawn from the sponsor's U.S. staff and local instructors hired by the sponsor. Field trips to Mayan ruins, snorkeling, cultural events. Students typically earn 3 semester credits per term.
Sessions • 4 week sessions begin every month, year-round.
Eligibility Requirements • Minimum age 18; open to freshmen, sophomores, juniors, seniors, graduate students, adults; good academic standing at home school; desire to learn and help others; no foreign language proficiency required.
Living Arrangements • Students live in host family homes. Meals are taken with host family, in residences.
Costs (2005) • $1950 for 4 weeks; $300 for each additional week; includes tuition, housing, all meals, insurance, excursions, books and class materials, lab equipment, international student ID, student support services. $200 nonrefundable deposit required. Financial aid available for all students: scholarships.
For More Information • Ms. Anne Connolly, Marketing and Placement Advisor, ProWorld Service Corps, PO Box 21121, Billings, MT 59104-1121; *Phone:* 877-429-6753; *Fax:* 406-252-3973. *E-mail:* info@proworldsc.org. *World Wide Web:* http://www.proworldsc.org

BOLIVIA

COCHABAMBA

SCHOOL FOR INTERNATIONAL TRAINING, SIT STUDY ABROAD
BOLIVIA: LENS ON LATIN AMERICA

Academic Focus • Cinematography, film and media studies, Latin American studies, Spanish language and literature.
Program Information • Faculty members are drawn from the sponsor's U.S. staff and local instructors hired by the sponsor. Scheduled travel to La Paz; field trips to cultural events. Students typically earn 8 semester credits per term.
Sessions • Jun–Jul (summer).
Eligibility Requirements • Open to freshmen, sophomores, juniors, seniors; course work in Latin American studies and/or anthropology recommended; 2.5 GPA; 2 letters of recommendation; good academic standing at home school; a background in some form of media production recommended; 1 year of college course work in Spanish.
Living Arrangements • Students live in hotels, guest houses. Meals are taken as a group, in residences, in restaurants.
Costs (2005–2006) • $6693; includes tuition, housing, all meals, insurance, excursions. $50 application fee. $400 nonrefundable deposit required. Financial aid available for all students: scholarships.
For More Information • SIT Study Abroad, School for International Training, SIT Study Abroad, PO Box 676, Kipling Road, Brattleboro, VT 05302-0676; *Phone:* 888-272-7881; *Fax:* 802-258-3296. *E-mail:* studyabroad@sit. edu. *World Wide Web:* http://www.sit.edu/studyabroad/

SUCRE

ALMA COLLEGE
SUMMER PROGRAM OF STUDIES IN BOLIVIA

Hosted by Academia Latinoamericana
Academic Focus • Cultural studies, Spanish language and literature.
Program Information • Students attend classes at Academia Latinoamericana (Sucre, Bolivia). Field trips to Potosí, Caminos, Callejon. Students typically earn 3–12 semester credits per term.
Sessions • Apr–Aug (1 to 4 months).
Eligibility Requirements • Minimum age 18; open to sophomores, juniors, seniors, graduate students, adults; 2.5 GPA; 2 letters of recommendation; no foreign language proficiency required.
Living Arrangements • Students live in host family homes. Meals are taken with host family, in residences.
Costs (2005) • $2200–$6600; includes tuition, housing, some meals, insurance, excursions, books and class materials, international student ID, student support services, on-site orientation, airport pick-up. $50 application fee. $200 refundable deposit required.
For More Information • Ms. Julie Elenbaas, Office Associate, International Education, Alma College, 614 West Superior Street, Alma, MI 48801-1599; *Phone:* 989-463-7055; *Fax:* 989-463-7126. *E-mail:* intl_studies@alma.edu. *World Wide Web:* http://international.alma.edu/

ENFOREX–SPANISH IN THE SPANISH WORLD
SPANISH INTENSIVE COURSE SUCRE

Hosted by ENFOREX
Academic Focus • Spanish language and literature, Spanish studies.
Program Information • Students attend classes at ENFOREX (Sucre, Bolivia). Field trips to Sucre Colonial; optional travel to Titicaca Lake, the Amazon basin at an extra cost. Students typically earn 4 semester credits per term.
Sessions • Year-round.
Eligibility Requirements • Minimum age 18; open to freshmen, juniors, seniors, graduate students, adults; no foreign language proficiency required.
Living Arrangements • Students live in host family homes, hotels. Meals are taken as a group, on one's own, with host family.
Costs (2005) • $825 per month; includes tuition, housing, all meals, excursions, books and class materials, lab equipment, international student ID, student support services. $100 application fee. $250 nonrefundable deposit required.
For More Information • Mr. Antonio Anadón, Director of Spanish Department, ENFOREX–Spanish in the Spanish World, Alberto Aguilera, 26, 28015 Madrid, Spain; *Phone:* +34 91-594-3776; *Fax:* +34 91-594-5159. *E-mail:* promotion@enforex.es. *World Wide Web:* http://www.enforex.com/

# BRAZIL

GOIANIA

KENTUCKY INSTITUTE FOR INTERNATIONAL STUDIES
BRAZIL

Academic Focus • Anthropology, geology.
Program Information • Faculty members are drawn from the sponsor's U.S. staff. Scheduled travel; field trips. Students typically earn 3-6 semester credits per term.
Sessions • Jun-Jul (summer).
Eligibility Requirements • Minimum age 18; open to freshmen, sophomores, juniors, seniors, graduate students, adults; 2.0 GPA; 1 letter of recommendation; no foreign language proficiency required.
Living Arrangements • Students live in hotels. Meals are taken on one's own, in restaurants.
Costs (2006) • $3130; includes housing, some meals, insurance, excursions, international airfare, international student ID, instructional expenses. $150 application fee. Financial aid available for all students: scholarships.
For More Information • Ms. Nancy Martin, Coordinator, Kentucky Institute for International Studies, PO Box 9, Murray, KY 42071-0009; *Phone:* 270-762-3091; *Fax:* 270-762-3434. *E-mail:* kiismsu@murraystate.edu. *World Wide Web:* http://www.kiis.org/

JOÃO PESSOA

UNIVERSITY OF DELAWARE
WINTER SESSION IN BRAZIL

Held at Cultura Inglesia Institute
Academic Focus • Brazilian studies, Portuguese.
Program Information • Classes are held on the campus of Cultura Inglesia Institute (João Pessoa, Brazil). Faculty members are drawn from the sponsor's U.S. staff and local instructors hired by the sponsor. Field trips to Rio de Janeiro, Recife, Pernambuco, Olinda. Students typically earn 6 semester credits per term.
Sessions • Jan-Feb (winter).
Eligibility Requirements • Open to freshmen, sophomores, juniors, seniors; 2.0 GPA; 1 letter of recommendation; 2 years of college course work in Spanish or Portuguese.
Living Arrangements • Students live in host family homes. Meals are taken with host family, in residences.
Costs (2005) • Contact sponsor for cost. $200 nonrefundable deposit required. Financial aid available for all students: scholarships.
For More Information • Center for International Studies, University of Delaware, 186 South College Avenue, Newark, DE 19716-1450; *Phone:* 888-831-4685; *Fax:* 302-831-6042. *E-mail:* studyabroad@udel.edu. *World Wide Web:* http://www.udel.edu/studyabroad/

MACEIÓ

LANGUAGE LIAISON
PORTUGUESE IN MACEIÓ

Hosted by Language Liaison
Academic Focus • Portuguese.
Program Information • Students attend classes at Language Liaison (Maceió, Brazil). Field trips; optional travel at an extra cost. Students typically earn 3-15 semester credits per term.
Sessions • Classes begin weekly, year-round.
Eligibility Requirements • Minimum age 17; open to precollege students, freshmen, sophomores, juniors, seniors, graduate students, adults; no foreign language proficiency required.
Living Arrangements • Students live in locally rented apartments, host family homes, hotels. Meals are taken on one's own, with host family, in residences, in restaurants.
Costs (2005) • Contact sponsor for cost. $175 application fee. Financial aid available for all students: scholarship research service.
For More Information • Ms. Nancy Forman, President, Language Liaison, PO Box 1772, Pacific Palisades, CA 90272; *Phone:* 800-284-4448; *Fax:* 310-454-1706. *E-mail:* learn@languageliaison.com. *World Wide Web:* http://www.languageliaison.com/

BRAZIL
Maceió

LINGUA SERVICE WORLDWIDE
VACATION 'N LEARN PORTUGUESE IN BRAZIL

Hosted by Fast Forward Institute

Academic Focus • Brazilian studies, Portuguese.

Program Information • Students attend classes at Fast Forward Institute (Maceió, Brazil). Optional travel to cultural sites throughout Brazil at an extra cost. Students typically earn 3 semester credits for 3 weeks, 6 semester credits for 5 weeks.

Sessions • Sessions of 2 or more weeks begin on Mondays, year-round.

Eligibility Requirements • Minimum age 16; open to precollege students, freshmen, sophomores, juniors, seniors, graduate students, adults; no foreign language proficiency required.

Living Arrangements • Students live in host family homes, hotels. Meals are taken with host family.

Costs (2006–2007) • Contact sponsor for cost. $100 application fee.

For More Information • Assistant Director, Lingua Service Worldwide, 75 Prospect Street, Suite 4, Huntington, NY 11743; *Phone:* 800-394-5327; *Fax:* 631-271-3441. *E-mail:* linguaservice@att.net. *World Wide Web:* http://www.linguaserviceworldwide.com/

PIRENÓPOLIS

LIVING ROUTES–STUDY ABROAD IN ECOVILLAGES
LIVING ROUTES–BRAZIL: PERMACULTURE AT ECOVERSIDADE

Hosted by Ecoversidade

Academic Focus • Agriculture, community service, conservation studies, ecology, environmental health, environmental science/studies, interdisciplinary studies, peace and conflict studies, social sciences, urban/regional planning.

Program Information • Students attend classes at Ecoversidade (Pirenópolis, Brazil). Field trips to ecological homesteads, colonial and indigenous villages; optional travel to Bioconstruindo Natural Building Workshop at an extra cost. Students typically earn 4 semester credits per term.

Sessions • Jun-Jul (summer).

Eligibility Requirements • Minimum age 17; open to precollege students, freshmen, sophomores, juniors, seniors, graduate students, adults; 2.5 GPA; good academic standing at home school; no foreign language proficiency required.

Living Arrangements • Students live in host institution dormitories, program-owned houses. Quarters are shared with host institution students. Meals are taken as a group, in central dining facility.

Costs (2006) • $2250; includes tuition, housing, all meals, excursions, student support services. $25 application fee. $300 nonrefundable deposit required. Financial aid available for all students: scholarships.

For More Information • Mr. Gregg Orifici, Director of Admissions, Living Routes–Study Abroad in Ecovillages, 79 South Pleasant Street, Suite A5, Amherst, MA 01002; *Phone:* 888-515-7333; *Fax:* 413-259-9355. *E-mail:* programs@livingroutes.org. *World Wide Web:* http://www.LivingRoutes.org/

RIO DE JANEIRO

EMORY UNIVERSITY
BRAZILIAN STUDIES

Hosted by Pontifical Catholic University of Rio de Janeiro

Academic Focus • Brazilian studies, Latin American studies, Portuguese.

Program Information • Students attend classes at Pontifical Catholic University of Rio de Janeiro (Rio de Janeiro, Brazil). Scheduled travel to Sao Paulo, Ouro Preto; field trips to Sugarloaf. Students typically earn 8 semester credits per term.

Sessions • Jun-Jul (summer).

Eligibility Requirements • Minimum age 18; open to freshmen, sophomores, juniors, seniors; 3.0 GPA; good academic standing at home school; phone interview; 1 year college course work in Portuguese or 2 years in Spanish.

Living Arrangements • Students live in host family homes. Meals are taken on one's own, with host family, in residences.

Costs (2005) • $7450; includes tuition, housing, some meals, insurance, excursions. $350 nonrefundable deposit required. Financial aid available for students from sponsoring institution: scholarships, loans.

For More Information • Ms. Gail Scheu, Study Abroad Coordinator, Emory University, 1385 Oxford Road, Atlanta, GA 30322; *Phone:* 404-727-2240; *Fax:* 404-727-6724. *E-mail:* lscheu@emory.edu. *World Wide Web:* http://www.cipa.emory.edu/

LANGUAGE LIAISON
LEARN PORTUGUESE IN RIO DE JANEIRO

Hosted by Language Liaison

Academic Focus • Portuguese.

Program Information • Students attend classes at Language Liaison (Rio de Janeiro, Brazil). Field trips; optional travel at an extra cost. Students typically earn 3-15 semester credits per term.

Sessions • Classes begin weekly, year-round.

Eligibility Requirements • Minimum age 17; open to precollege students, freshmen, sophomores, juniors, seniors, graduate students, adults; no foreign language proficiency required.

Living Arrangements • Students live in locally rented apartments, host family homes, hotels. Meals are taken on one's own, with host family, in residences.

Costs (2005) • Contact sponsor for cost. $175 application fee. Financial aid available for all students: scholarship research service.

For More Information • Ms. Nancy Forman, President, Language Liaison, PO Box 1772, Pacific Palisades, CA 90272; *Phone:* 800-284-4448; *Fax:* 310-454-1706. *E-mail:* learn@languageliaison.com. *World Wide Web:* http://www.languageliaison.com/

NEW YORK UNIVERSITY
HUMAN RIGHTS IN BRAZIL

Hosted by NYU at Rio

Academic Focus • Political science and government, sociology.

Program Information • Students attend classes at NYU at Rio (Rio de Janeiro, Brazil). Scheduled travel; field trips. Students typically earn 4 semester credits per term.

Sessions • Jun-Jul (summer).

Eligibility Requirements • Minimum age 18; open to freshmen, sophomores, juniors, seniors; 3.0 GPA; good academic standing at home school; no foreign language proficiency required.

Living Arrangements • Students live in host institution dormitories. Quarters are shared with host institution students. Meals are taken on one's own, in restaurants.

Costs (2007) • $5000; includes tuition, housing, some meals, excursions. $25 application fee. $300 nonrefundable deposit required.

For More Information • Office of Summer Sessions, New York University, 7 E 12th Street, 6th Floor, New York, NY 10003; *Phone:* 212-998-2292; *Fax:* 212-995-4642. *E-mail:* summer.info@nyu.edu. *World Wide Web:* http://www.nyu.edu/global/studyabroad.html

ST. JOHN'S UNIVERSITY
BRAZIL–SUMMER IN RIO

Hosted by Pontifical Catholic University of Rio de Janeiro

Academic Focus • Brazilian studies, Portuguese.

Program Information • Students attend classes at Pontifical Catholic University of Rio de Janeiro (Rio de Janeiro, Brazil). Students typically earn 3-6 semester credits per term.

Sessions • Jul-Aug (summer).

Eligibility Requirements • Open to sophomores, juniors, seniors; 2.75 GPA; 2 letters of recommendation; good academic standing at home school; interview; 1 year college course work in Portuguese or fluency in Spanish.

Living Arrangements • Students live in host institution dormitories, locally rented apartments, host family homes. Quarters are shared with host institution students. Meals are taken on one's own, in residences, in central dining facility, in restaurants.

Costs (2004) • $2750–$3000; includes student support services, administrative fee. $30 application fee. $750 nonrefundable deposit required. Financial aid available for students from sponsoring institution: scholarships, loans, students must be enrolled in 6 credits to receive aid.

For More Information • Dr. Ruth De Paula, Director, Office of Study Abroad Programs, St. John's University, 8000 Utopia Parkway, Jamaica, NY 11439; *Phone:* 718-990-6105; *Fax:* 718-990-2321. *E-mail:* intled@stjohns.edu. *World Wide Web:* http://www.stjohns.edu/studyabroad/

STATE UNIVERSITY OF NEW YORK AT NEW PALTZ
SUMMER PORTUGUESE LANGUAGE STUDIES IN BRAZIL

Hosted by Pontifical Catholic University of Rio de Janeiro
Academic Focus • Portuguese.

Program Information • Students attend classes at Pontifical Catholic University of Rio de Janeiro (Rio de Janeiro, Brazil). Students typically earn 6 semester credits per term.

Sessions • Jul–Aug (summer).

Eligibility Requirements • Minimum age 18; open to sophomores, juniors, seniors; 2.5 GPA; 1 letter of recommendation; good academic standing at home school; 2 years college course work in Spanish or Portuguese.

Living Arrangements • Students live in host family homes. Meals are taken on one's own, with host family, in residences, in restaurants.

Costs (2006) • $1548 for New York residents; $3115 for nonresidents; includes tuition, housing, some meals, insurance, student support services. $25 application fee. $300 nonrefundable deposit required. Financial aid available for students from sponsoring institution: scholarships, loans.

For More Information • Center for International Programs, State University of New York at New Paltz, 1 Hawk Drive, New Paltz, NY 12561; *Phone:* 845-257-3125; *Fax:* 845-257-3129. *E-mail:* studyabroad@newpaltz.edu. *World Wide Web:* http://www.newpaltz.edu/studyabroad/

UNIVERSITY OF MIAMI
INTERNATIONAL STUDIES COURSE IN BRAZIL

Academic Focus • International affairs, political science and government.

Program Information • Faculty members are drawn from the sponsor's U.S. staff. Field trips. Students typically earn 3 semester credits per term.

Sessions • May–Jun (summer).

Eligibility Requirements • Minimum age 18; open to sophomores, juniors, seniors, graduate students; good academic standing at home school; no foreign language proficiency required.

Living Arrangements • Students live in hotels. Meals are taken as a group, on one's own, in residences, in central dining facility, in restaurants.

Costs (2005) • $3511; includes tuition, housing, some meals, excursions, student support services. $40 application fee. $500 nonrefundable deposit required. Financial aid available for students from sponsoring institution: scholarships, loans.

For More Information • Ms. Glenda Hayley, Director, International Education and Exchange Programs, University of Miami, 5050 Brunson Drive, Allen Hall Room 212, PO Box 248005, Coral Gables, FL 33124-1610; *Phone:* 305-284-3434; *Fax:* 305-284-4235. *E-mail:* ieep@miami.edu. *World Wide Web:* http://www.studyabroad.miami.edu/

SALVADOR

CIEE
CIEE STUDY CENTER AT THE UNIVERSIDADE FEDERAL DE BAHIA, SALVADOR DA BAHIA, BRAZIL–INTENSIVE LANGUAGE AND CULTURE PROGRAM

Hosted by Federal University of Bahia
Academic Focus • Brazilian studies, Portuguese.

Program Information • Students attend classes at Federal University of Bahia (Salvador, Brazil). Field trips to city tours, museums, concerts. Students typically earn 6 semester credits per term.

Sessions • Jun–Jul (summer).

Eligibility Requirements • Minimum age 18; open to sophomores, juniors, seniors; 2.75 GPA; 1 letter of recommendation; 2 years of college course work in Portuguese or Spanish.

Living Arrangements • Students live in host family homes. Meals are taken with host family, in residences, in central dining facility.

Costs (2006) • $3800; includes tuition, housing, all meals, insurance, excursions, books and class materials, student support services, computer and library access at host institution, pre-departure advising, cultural activites, optional onsite orientation, and pickup, resident directo. $30 application fee. $300 nonrefundable deposit required. Financial aid available for all students: minority student scholarships, travel grants.

For More Information • Information Center, CIEE, 7 Custom House Street, 3rd Floor, Portland, ME 04101; *Phone:* 800-40-STUDY; *Fax:* 207-553-7699. *E-mail:* studyinfo@ciee.org. *World Wide Web:* http://www.ciee.org/isp/

LANGUAGE LIAISON
LEARN PORTUGUESE IN SALVADOR BAHIA

Hosted by Language Liaison
Academic Focus • Portuguese.

Program Information • Students attend classes at Language Liaison (Salvador, Brazil). Field trips; optional travel at an extra cost. Students typically earn 3–15 semester credits per term.

Sessions • Classes begin weekly, year-round.

Eligibility Requirements • Minimum age 17; open to precollege students, freshmen, sophomores, juniors, seniors, graduate students, adults; no foreign language proficiency required.

Living Arrangements • Students live in locally rented apartments, host family homes, hotels. Meals are taken on one's own, with host family, in residences, in restaurants.

Costs (2005) • Contact sponsor for cost. $175 application fee. Financial aid available for all students: scholarship research service.

For More Information • Ms. Nancy Forman, President, Language Liaison, PO Box 1772, Pacific Palisades, CA 90272; *Phone:* 800-284-4448; *Fax:* 310-454-1706. *E-mail:* learn@languageliaison.com. *World Wide Web:* http://www.languageliaison.com/

LINGUA SERVICE WORLDWIDE
VACATION 'N LEARN PORTUGUESE IN BRAZIL

Hosted by Dialago Language School
Academic Focus • Brazilian studies, Portuguese.

Program Information • Students attend classes at Dialago Language School (Salvador, Brazil). Optional travel to cultural sites throughout Brazil at an extra cost. Students typically earn 3 semester credits for 3 weeks, 6 semester credits for 5 weeks.

Sessions • Sessions of 2 or more weeks begin on Mondays, year-round.

Eligibility Requirements • Minimum age 16; open to precollege students, freshmen, sophomores, juniors, seniors, graduate students, adults; no foreign language proficiency required.

Living Arrangements • Students live in host family homes, hotels. Meals are taken with host family.

Costs (2006–2007) • Contact sponsor for cost. $100 application fee.

For More Information • Assistant Director, Lingua Service Worldwide, 75 Prospect Street, Suite 4, Huntington, NY 11743; *Phone:* 800-394-5327; *Fax:* 631-271-3441. *E-mail:* linguaservice@att.net. *World Wide Web:* http://www.linguaserviceworldwide.com/

LINGUA SERVICE WORLDWIDE
VACATION 'N LEARN PORTUGUESE IN BRAZIL

Hosted by Dialago Language School
Academic Focus • Brazilian studies, Portuguese.

Program Information • Students attend classes at Dialago Language School (Salvador, Brazil). Optional travel to cultural sites throughout Brazil at an extra cost. Students typically earn 3 semester credits for 3 weeks, 6 semester credits for 5 weeks.

BRAZIL
Salvador

Sessions • Sessions of 2 or more weeks begin on Mondays, year-round.
Eligibility Requirements • Minimum age 16; open to precollege students, freshmen, sophomores, juniors, seniors, graduate students, adults; no foreign language proficiency required.
Living Arrangements • Students live in host family homes, hotels. Meals are taken with host family.
Costs (2006–2007) • Contact sponsor for cost. $100 application fee.
For More Information • Assistant Director, Lingua Service Worldwide, 75 Prospect Street, Suite 4, Huntington, NY 11743; *Phone:* 800-394-5327; *Fax:* 631-271-3441. *E-mail:* linguaservice@att. net. *World Wide Web:* http://www.linguaserviceworldwide.com/

TEMPLE UNIVERSITY
TEMPLE IN BRAZIL

Hosted by State University of Bahia
Academic Focus • Portuguese, Portuguese studies.
Program Information • Students attend classes at State University of Bahia (Salvador, Brazil). Field trips to Salvador, Cachoeira. Students typically earn 6 semester credits per term.
Sessions • Jul–Aug (summer).
Eligibility Requirements • Open to sophomores, juniors, seniors, graduate students; 2.5 GPA; 1 letter of recommendation; good academic standing at home school; official transcripts; essay; no foreign language proficiency required.
Living Arrangements • Students live in locally rented apartments. Quarters are shared with host institution students. Meals are taken on one's own, in residences.
Costs (2005) • $2750–$4200; includes tuition, housing, program fee, local travel. $30 application fee. $200 nonrefundable deposit required. Financial aid available for students from sponsoring institution: scholarships, loans.
For More Information • Ms. Erin Joslyn, Study Abroad Coordinator, Temple University, International Programs, 200 Tuttleman Learning Center, 1809 North 13th Street, Philadelphia, PA 19122; *Phone:* 215-204-0720; *Fax:* 215-204-0729. *E-mail:* study.abroad@temple.edu. *World Wide Web:* http://www.temple.edu/studyabroad/

SÃO PAULO

CIEE
CIEE STUDY CENTER AT THE PONTIFICIA UNIVERSIDADE CATÓLICA DE SÃO PAULO, BRAZIL–INTENSIVE LANGUAGE AND CULTURE PROGRAM

Hosted by Pontifical Catholic University of São Paulo
Academic Focus • Brazilian studies, Portuguese.
Program Information • Students attend classes at Pontifical Catholic University of São Paulo (São Paulo, Brazil). Field trips to museums, a city tour, concerts. Students typically earn 6 semester credits per term.
Sessions • Jan–Feb (winter).
Eligibility Requirements • Minimum age 18; open to sophomores, juniors, seniors; 2.75 GPA; 1 letter of recommendation; good academic standing at home school; 1 year college course work in Portuguese or 2 years in Spanish.
Living Arrangements • Students live in host family homes. Meals are taken with host family, in residences, in central dining facility.
Costs (2006) • $3800; includes tuition, housing, all meals, insurance, excursions, student support services, computer access, pre-departure advising, resident director, orientation, cultural activities, on-site pick-up. $30 application fee. $300 nonrefundable deposit required. Financial aid available for all students: minority student scholarships, travel grants.
For More Information • Information Center, CIEE, 7 Custom House Street, 3rd Floor, Portland, ME 04101; *Phone:* 800-40-STUDY; *Fax:* 207-553-7699. *E-mail:* studyinfo@ciee.org. *World Wide Web:* http://www.ciee.org/isp/

LANGUAGE LIAISON
PORTUGUESE IN SÃO PAULO

Hosted by Language Liaison
Academic Focus • Portuguese.

Program Information • Students attend classes at Language Liaison (São Paulo, Brazil). Field trips; optional travel at an extra cost. Students typically earn 3–15 semester credits per term.
Sessions • Classes begin weekly, year-round.
Eligibility Requirements • Minimum age 16; open to precollege students, freshmen, sophomores, juniors, seniors, graduate students, adults; no foreign language proficiency required.
Living Arrangements • Students live in locally rented apartments, host family homes, hotels. Meals are taken on one's own, with host family, in residences, in restaurants.
Costs (2005) • Contact sponsor for cost. $175 application fee. Financial aid available for all students: scholarship research service.
For More Information • Ms. Nancy Forman, President, Language Liaison, PO Box 1772, Pacific Palisades, CA 90272; *Phone:* 800-284-4448; *Fax:* 310-454-1706. *E-mail:* learn@languageliaison. com. *World Wide Web:* http://www.languageliaison.com/

RUTGERS, THE STATE UNIVERSITY OF NEW JERSEY
SUMMER INTERNSHIP IN BRAZIL

Held at Folha de São Paulo
Academic Focus • Journalism, Portuguese.
Program Information • Classes are held on the campus of Folha de São Paulo (São Paulo, Brazil). Faculty members are drawn from the sponsor's U.S. staff and local instructors hired by the sponsor. Field trips to Porto Seguro, Bahia. Students typically earn 6 semester credits per term.
Sessions • Jun–Aug (summer), Program runs every other year.
Eligibility Requirements • Open to sophomores, juniors, seniors; 2.5 GPA; 1 letter of recommendation; good academic standing at home school; official transcript from all tertiary schools attended; fluency in Portuguese.
Living Arrangements • Students live in hotels. Quarters are shared with host institution students. Meals are taken on one's own, in central dining facility.
Costs (2005) • $3093 for New Jersey residents; $4093 for nonresidents; includes tuition, housing, some meals, insurance, excursions, international airfare. $20 application fee. $500 nonrefundable deposit required. Financial aid available for students from sponsoring institution: scholarships, loans.
For More Information • Ms. Lindy Black, Regional Coordinator, Rutgers, The State University of New Jersey, 102 College Avenue, New Brunswick, NJ 08901-8543; *Phone:* 732-932-7787; *Fax:* 732-932-8659. *E-mail:* ru_abroad@email.rutgers.edu. *World Wide Web:* http://studyabroad.rutgers.edu/

UNIVERSITY AT ALBANY, STATE UNIVERSITY OF NEW YORK
LANGUAGE AND CULTURAL STUDIES AT MACKENZIE UNIVERSITY

Hosted by Mackenzie University
Academic Focus • Brazilian studies, Portuguese.
Program Information • Students attend classes at Mackenzie University (São Paulo, Brazil). Students typically earn 6 semester credits per term.
Sessions • Jun–Jul (summer).
Eligibility Requirements • Open to freshmen, sophomores, juniors, seniors, graduate students, adults; 1 letter of recommendation; good academic standing at home school; no foreign language proficiency required.
Living Arrangements • Students live in host family homes, hotels. Meals are taken on one's own, with host family, in residences, in restaurants.
Costs (2005) • Contact sponsor for cost. $150 nonrefundable deposit required. Financial aid available for students from sponsoring institution: all customary sources.
For More Information • University at Albany, State University of New York, Office of International Education, LI 66, Albany, NY 12222; *Phone:* 518-442-3525; *Fax:* 518-442-3338. *E-mail:* intled@ uamail.albany.edu. *World Wide Web:* http://www.albany.edu/studyabroad/

UNIVERSITY OF ILLINOIS AT URBANA-CHAMPAIGN
BRAZIL: AN EMERGING SOCIETY

Hosted by University of São Paulo

Academic Focus • Business administration/management, commerce, international business, Portuguese.

Program Information • Students attend classes at University of São Paulo (São Paulo, Brazil). Field trips to local businesses and companies; optional travel to Rio de Janeiro, Paraty at an extra cost. Students typically earn 6 semester credits per term.

Sessions • May–Jul (summer).

Eligibility Requirements • Open to sophomores, juniors, seniors, graduate students; 2.5 GPA; 2 letters of recommendation; good academic standing at home school; no foreign language proficiency required.

Living Arrangements • Students live in host family homes. Meals are taken with host family, in residences, in restaurants.

Costs (2005) • $3300; includes tuition, housing, some meals, insurance, student support services. $55 application fee. $500 nonrefundable deposit required. Financial aid available for students from sponsoring institution: scholarships, loans.

For More Information • Mr. Ian Keil, Assistant Director, University of Illinois at Urbana-Champaign, 115 International Studies Building, 910 South Fifth Street, Champaign, IL 61820; *Phone:* 217-333-6322; *Fax:* 217-244-0249. *E-mail:* iankeil@uiuc.edu. *World Wide Web:* http://www.ips.uiuc.edu/sao/index.shtml

VITÓRIA

UNIVERSITY OF KANSAS
PORTUGUESE LANGUAGE AND CULTURE IN VITÓRIA, BRAZIL

Hosted by Federal University of Espirito Santo

Academic Focus • Brazilian studies, Portuguese.

Program Information • Students attend classes at Federal University of Espirito Santo (Vitória, Brazil). Scheduled travel to Rio de Janeiro, Ouro Preto; field trips to Pedra Azul, Domingos Martins, Biriricas. Students typically earn 6 semester credits per term.

Sessions • Jun–Aug (summer).

Eligibility Requirements • Minimum age 18; open to sophomores, juniors, seniors, graduate students; 2.5 GPA; 2 letters of recommendation; good academic standing at home school; no foreign language proficiency required.

Living Arrangements • Students live in host family homes. Meals are taken on one's own, with host family, in residences, in restaurants.

Costs (2005) • $3200; includes tuition, some meals, excursions, student support services, medical evacuation and repatriation insurance. $38 application fee. $300 nonrefundable deposit required. Financial aid available for students from sponsoring institution: scholarships, loans.

For More Information • Ms. Angela Dittrich, Assistant Director, University of Kansas, Office of Study Abroad, Lippincott Hall, 1410 Jayhawk Boulevard, Room 108, Lawrence, KS 66045-7515; *Phone:* 785-864-3742; *Fax:* 785-864-5040. *E-mail:* osa@ku.edu. *World Wide Web:* http://www.ku.edu/~osa/

$\mathcal{B}$ULGARIA

SOFIA

RUTGERS, THE STATE UNIVERSITY OF NEW JERSEY
SUMMER STUDY IN BULGARIA

Academic Focus • Political science and government.
Program Information • Faculty members are drawn from the sponsor's U.S. staff and local instructors hired by the sponsor. Students typically earn 6 semester credits per term.
Sessions • Jul-Aug (summer).
Eligibility Requirements • Open to sophomores, juniors, seniors; 2.5 GPA; good academic standing at home school; official transcripts from all tertiary schools attended; references; no foreign language proficiency required.
Living Arrangements • Students live in host institution dormitories. Quarters are shared with host institution students. Meals are taken as a group, in residences.
Costs (2006) • $3250 New Jersey resident; $4250 nonresident; includes tuition, housing, insurance, excursions, student support services. $20 application fee. $500 nonrefundable deposit required. Financial aid available for students from sponsoring institution: scholarships, loans.
For More Information • Ms. Lindy Black, Regional Coordinator, Rutgers, The State University of New Jersey, 102 College Avenue, New Brunswick, NJ 08901; *Phone:* 732-932-7787; *Fax:* 732-932-8659. *E-mail:* ru_abroad@email.rutgers.edu. *World Wide Web:* http://studyabroad.rutgers.edu/

VÉLIKO TURNOVO

ST. JOHN'S UNIVERSITY
BULGARIA

Held at 'St. Cyril and St. Methodius' University of Véliko Turnovo
Academic Focus • Philosophy.
Program Information • Classes are held on the campus of 'St. Cyril and St. Methodius' University of Véliko Turnovo (Véliko Turnovo, Bulgaria). Faculty members are drawn from the sponsor's U.S. staff. Field trips; optional travel. Students typically earn 3 semester credits per term.
Sessions • Jul (summer).
Eligibility Requirements • Open to sophomores, juniors, seniors; 2.75 GPA; 2 letters of recommendation; interview; no foreign language proficiency required.
Living Arrangements • Students live in locally rented apartments, hotels. Meals are taken on one's own, in restaurants.
Costs (2005) • $3000; includes tuition, housing, some meals, excursions, international airfare. $30 application fee. $750 nonrefundable deposit required. Financial aid available for students from sponsoring institution: loans.
For More Information • Dr. Ruth De Paula, Director, Office of Study Abroad Programs, St. John's University, 8000 Utopia Parkway, Jamaica, NY 11439; *Phone:* 718-990-6105; *Fax:* 718-990-2321. *E-mail:* intled@stjohns.edu. *World Wide Web:* http://www.stjohns.edu/studyabroad/

$\mathscr{C}$AMBODIA

SIEM REAP

CIEE

CIEE STUDY CENTER AT THE CENTER FOR KHMER STUDIES, SIEM REAP, CAMBODIA

Hosted by The Center for Khmer Studies

Academic Focus • Asian studies, cultural studies, history, peace and conflict studies, political science and government.

Program Information • Students attend classes at The Center for Khmer Studies (Siem Reap, Cambodia). Field trips to Angkor Wat; Angkovean Temples, Choeung Ek, Khmer Villages; Tuol Sleng Museum of Genocide, National Museum, Royal Palace. Students typically earn 6 semester credits per term.

Sessions • Jun–Aug (summer).

Eligibility Requirements • Minimum age 18; open to sophomores, juniors, seniors; 2.75 GPA; 1 letter of recommendation; good academic standing at home school; no foreign language proficiency required.

Living Arrangements • Students live in guest house. Quarters are shared with host institution students. Meals are taken on one's own, in restaurants.

Costs (2007) • Contact sponsor for cost. $30 application fee. $300 nonrefundable deposit required. Financial aid available for all students: scholarships, minority student scholarship, travel grants.

For More Information • Information Center, CIEE, 7 Custom House Street, 3rd Floor, Portland, ME 04101; *Phone:* 800-40-STUDY; *Fax:* 207-553-7699. *E-mail:* studyinfo@ciee.org. *World Wide Web:* http://www.ciee.org/isp/

CANADA

CITY-TO-CITY

COOPERATIVE CENTER FOR STUDY ABROAD
CANADA

Academic Focus • Biological/life sciences.
Program Information • Faculty members are drawn from the sponsor's U.S. staff. Field trips. Students typically earn 3 semester credits per term.
Sessions • Aug (summer).
Eligibility Requirements • Minimum age 18; good academic standing at home school.
Living Arrangements • Students live in hotels. Quarters are shared with host institution students. Meals are taken as a group, on one's own, in central dining facility, in restaurants.
Costs (2007) • $2795; includes housing, some meals, insurance, excursions, international airfare, airport transfers. $200 nonrefundable deposit required. Financial aid available for students from sponsoring institution: scholarships, loans.
For More Information • Dr. Michael A. Klembara, Executive Director, Cooperative Center for Study Abroad, Northern Kentucky University, Nunn Drive, Founders Hall 301, Highland Heights, KY 41099; *Phone:* 859-572-6512; *Fax:* 859-572-6650. *E-mail:* ccsa@nku.edu. *World Wide Web:* http://www.ccsa.cc/

MICHIGAN STATE UNIVERSITY
NATURAL RESOURCES AND TOURISM MANAGEMENT

Academic Focus • Forestry, natural resources, parks and recreation.
Program Information • Faculty members are drawn from the sponsor's U.S. staff. Scheduled travel to Seward, Valdez, Skagway, Whitehorse; field trips to forests, wildlife preserves, national parks. Students typically earn 4 semester credits per term.
Sessions • Aug (summer).
Eligibility Requirements • Minimum age 18; open to juniors, seniors, graduate students; major in agriculture and natural resources; 2.0 GPA; good academic standing at home school; letter of intent; faculty approval.
Living Arrangements • Students live in motorhomes; campsites. Meals are taken as a group, in restaurants.
Costs (2004) • $2196 (estimated); includes housing, some meals, insurance, excursions, student support services. $100 application fee. $200 nonrefundable deposit required. Financial aid available for students from sponsoring institution: scholarships, loans.
For More Information • Ms. Yvonne Squiers, Secretary, Michigan State University, Office of Study Abroad, 109 International Center, East Lansing, MI 48824-1035; *Phone:* 517-353-8920; *Fax:* 517-432-2082. *E-mail:* squiers@msu.edu. *World Wide Web:* http://studyabroad.msu.edu/

MICHIGAN STATE UNIVERSITY
NATURAL SCIENCE IN THE CANADIAN ROCKIES

Academic Focus • Earth sciences, environmental science/studies.
Program Information • Faculty members are drawn from the sponsor's U.S. staff. Field trips to national parks, forests, rivers, glacial fields. Students typically earn 6 semester credits per term.
Sessions • Jul–Aug (2 sessions).
Eligibility Requirements • Minimum age 18; open to freshmen, sophomores, juniors, seniors; major in natural science; 2.0 GPA; good academic standing at home school; faculty approval; good physical condition; interview; essay.
Living Arrangements • Students live in hotels, campsites; chalets. Meals are taken as a group, in restaurants.
Costs (2005) • $1566 (estimated); includes housing, some meals, insurance, excursions, student support services, camping fees, transportation during program. $100 application fee. $200 nonrefundable deposit required. Financial aid available for students from sponsoring institution: scholarships, loans.
For More Information • Ms. Yvonne Squiers, Secretary, Michigan State University, Office of Study Abroad, 109 International Center, East Lansing, MI 48824-1035; *Phone:* 517-353-8920; *Fax:* 517-432-2082. *E-mail:* squiers@msu.edu. *World Wide Web:* http://studyabroad.msu.edu/

ROUND RIVER CONSERVATION STUDIES
BRITISH COLUMBIA: TAKU RIVER WILDLIFE CONSERVATION PROJECT

Academic Focus • Biological/life sciences, conservation studies, ecology, wildlife studies.
Program Information • Faculty members are drawn from the sponsor's U.S. staff and local instructors hired by the sponsor. Scheduled travel to different sacred locations of Taku River Tlingit; field trips to hiking traditional Taku River Tlingit trails. Students typically earn 9 semester credits per term.
Sessions • Jul–Aug (summer).

Eligibility Requirements • Minimum age 18; open to freshmen, sophomores, juniors, seniors; 3.0 GPA; 2 letters of recommendation; good academic standing at home school.

Living Arrangements • Students live in program-owned houses, a remote fieldcamp, a program cabin. Meals are taken as a group, in central dining facility.

Costs (2005) • $7500; includes tuition, housing, all meals, excursions, lab equipment, student support services. $50 application fee. $1000 nonrefundable deposit required. Financial aid available for all students: scholarships.

For More Information • Mr. Doug Milek, Student Program Director, Round River Conservation Studies, 284 West 400 North, Suite 105, Salt Lake City, UT 84103; *Phone:* 801-694-3321. *E-mail:* dougmilek@roundriver.org. *World Wide Web:* http://www.roundriver.org/

STERLING COLLEGE
JAMES BAY, QUEBEC

Academic Focus • Canadian studies, ecology, environmental science/studies, sociology.

Program Information • Faculty members are drawn from the sponsor's U.S. staff and local instructors hired by the sponsor. Scheduled travel; field trips. Students typically earn 3 semester credits per term.

Sessions • Sep (summer).

Eligibility Requirements • Minimum age 18; open to freshmen, sophomores, juniors, seniors, graduate students, adults; 2 letters of recommendation; good academic standing at home school.

Living Arrangements • Students live in host family homes, campsites. Meals are taken as a group, on one's own, with host family, in residences.

Costs (2004) • $1820; includes tuition, housing, all meals, excursions, transportation. $35 application fee. Financial aid available for all students: scholarships, loans.

For More Information • Mr. Erik Hansen, Director of Global Field Studies, Sterling College, PO Box 72, Craftsbury Common, VT 05827; *Phone:* 802-586-7711 Ext. 128; *Fax:* 802-586-2596. *E-mail:* admissions@sterlingcollege.edu. *World Wide Web:* http://www.sterlingcollege.edu/

STERLING COLLEGE
LABRADOR AND NEWFOUNDLAND

Academic Focus • Botany, Canadian studies, ecology, wildlife studies.

Program Information • Faculty members are drawn from the sponsor's U.S. staff and local instructors hired by the sponsor. Scheduled travel to alpine tundra, seaside terraces, the serpentine barrens of the table lands; field trips to Gros Morne National Park, L'anse aux Meadows World Heritage site. Students typically earn 3 semester credits per term.

Sessions • Sep (2 weeks).

Eligibility Requirements • Minimum age 18; open to freshmen, sophomores, juniors, seniors, graduate students, adults; 2 letters of recommendation; good academic standing at home school.

Living Arrangements • Students live in host family homes, hotels, campsites. Meals are taken as a group, with host family, in residences, in restaurants.

Costs (2005) • $2470; includes tuition, housing, some meals, excursions, transportation. Financial aid available for all students: scholarships, loans.

For More Information • Mr. Erik Hansen, Director of Global Field Studies, Sterling College, PO Box 72, Craftsbury Common, VT 05827; *Phone:* 802-586-7711 Ext. 128; *Fax:* 802-586-2596. *E-mail:* admissions@sterlingcollege.edu. *World Wide Web:* http://www.sterlingcollege.edu/

UNIVERSITY OF CALIFORNIA, SANTA BARBARA, WILDLANDS STUDIES
THE VANCOUVER ISLAND PROGRAM

Academic Focus • Ecology, environmental science/studies, geography, marine sciences.

Program Information • Faculty members are drawn from the sponsor's U.S. staff. Scheduled travel to wildland field locations. Students typically earn 5-10 quarter credits per term.

Sessions • Jul–Aug (summer).

Eligibility Requirements • Minimum age 18; open to freshmen, sophomores, juniors, seniors; course work in biology or environmental studies; good academic standing at home school; application essay.

Living Arrangements • Students live in field study sites. Meals are taken as a group.

Costs (2006) • $625–$1425; includes tuition. $75 application fee.

For More Information • Mr. Crandall Bay, Director, Wildlands Studies Program, University of California, Santa Barbara, Wildlands Studies, 3 Mosswood Circle, Cazadero, CA 95421; *Phone:* 707-632-5665; *Fax:* 707-632-5665. *E-mail:* wildlands@sonic.net. *World Wide Web:* http://www.wildlandsstudies.com/

MONTRÉAL

LANGUAGE LIAISON
FRENCH IN MONTRÉAL

Hosted by Language Liaison

Academic Focus • Canadian studies, French language and literature.

Program Information • Students attend classes at Language Liaison (Montreal, Canada). Field trips; optional travel at an extra cost. Students typically earn 5-15 semester credits per term.

Sessions • New programs begin weekly, year-round.

Eligibility Requirements • Minimum age 13; open to precollege students, freshmen, sophomores, juniors, seniors, graduate students, adults; no foreign language proficiency required.

Living Arrangements • Students live in locally rented apartments, host family homes, hotels, a residence center. Meals are taken as a group, on one's own, with host family, in residences, in central dining facility, in restaurants.

Costs (2005) • Contact sponsor for cost. $175 application fee. Financial aid available for all students: scholarship research service.

For More Information • Ms. Nancy Forman, President, Language Liaison, PO Box 1772, Pacific Palisades, CA 90272; *Phone:* 800-284-4448; *Fax:* 310-454-1706. *E-mail:* learn@languageliaison.com. *World Wide Web:* http://www.languageliaison.com/

LINGUA SERVICE WORLDWIDE
VACATION 'N LEARN FRENCH IN CANADA

Hosted by Language Studies Canada Montréal

Academic Focus • French language and literature, French studies.

Program Information • Students attend classes at Language Studies Canada Montréal (Montréal, Canada). Optional travel to Québec, Toronto, New York at an extra cost. Students typically earn 3 semester credits for 3 weeks, 6 semester credits for 5 weeks.

Sessions • Sessions of 2 or more weeks begin on Mondays, year-round.

Eligibility Requirements • Minimum age 16; open to precollege students, freshmen, sophomores, juniors, seniors, graduate students, adults; no foreign language proficiency required.

Living Arrangements • Students live in host institution dormitories, locally rented apartments, host family homes, hotels. Quarters are shared with host institution students. Meals are taken with host family.

Costs (2006–2007) • Contact sponsor for cost. $100 application fee.

For More Information • Assistant Director, Lingua Service Worldwide, 75 Prospect Street, Suite 4, Huntington, NY 11743; *Phone:* 800-394-5327; *Fax:* 631-271-3441. *E-mail:* linguaservice@att.net. *World Wide Web:* http://www.linguaserviceworldwide.com/

NUNAVUT

SYRACUSE UNIVERSITY
ARCTIC JOURNEY: THE INUIT AND THEIR LAND

Hosted by Arctic College

Academic Focus • Anthropology, social sciences, sociology.

Program Information • Students attend classes at Arctic College (Nunavut, Canada). Students typically earn 6 semester credits per term.

CANADA
Nunavut

Sessions • May–Jun (summer).
Eligibility Requirements • Open to freshmen, sophomores, juniors, seniors, graduate students; good academic standing at home school.
Living Arrangements • Students live in host institution dormitories, hotels. Quarters are shared with host institution students. Meals are taken as a group, in central dining facility.
Costs (2006) • $7000; includes tuition, housing, all meals, international student ID. $55 application fee. $350 nonrefundable deposit required. Financial aid available for all students: loans, need-based tuition grants.
For More Information • Mrs. Daisy Fried, Associate Director, Syracuse University, 106 Walnut Place, Syracuse, NY 13244-4170; *Phone:* 800-251-9674; *Fax:* 315-443-4593. *E-mail:* dsfried@syr.edu. *World Wide Web:* http://suabroad.syr.edu/

QUÉBEC

COLLEGE CONSORTIUM FOR INTERNATIONAL STUDIES–BROOKDALE COMMUNITY COLLEGE
FRENCH AND SNOW PROGRAM IN QUÉBEC, CANADA

Hosted by University of Québec at Chicoutimi
Academic Focus • Canadian studies, French language and literature.
Program Information • Students attend classes at University of Québec at Chicoutimi (Chicoutimi, Canada). Scheduled travel to Québec City; field trips to historic sites in Chicoutimi, Musée du Saguenay, Lac Saint Jean, skiing, skating, ice fishing, tobogganing, dog sledding. Students typically earn 4 semester credits per term.
Sessions • Jan (winter).
Eligibility Requirements • Minimum age 18; open to freshmen, sophomores, juniors, seniors, graduate students; 2.5 GPA; 2 letters of recommendation; essay; transcript; completion of 15 credits prior to application; no foreign language proficiency required.
Living Arrangements • Students live in host family homes. Meals are taken with host family, in residences, in central dining facility.
Costs (2006–2007) • $2175; includes tuition, housing, all meals, insurance, books and class materials, student support services, some excursions, fees, e-mail access. $35 application fee. Financial aid available for students from sponsoring institution: scholarships, loans.
For More Information • College Consortium for International Studies–Brookdale Community College, 2000 P Street, NW, Suite 503, Washington, DC 20036; *Phone:* 800-453-6956; *Fax:* 202-223-0999. *E-mail:* info@ccisabroad.org. *World Wide Web:* http://www.ccisabroad.org/. Students may also apply through Brookdale Community College, International Center, 765 Newman Springs Road, Lincroft, NJ 07738-1597.

COLLEGE CONSORTIUM FOR INTERNATIONAL STUDIES–BROOKDALE COMMUNITY COLLEGE
INTENSIVE FRENCH IMMERSION PROGRAM IN QUÉBEC, CANADA

Hosted by University of Québec at Chicoutimi
Academic Focus • Canadian studies, French language and literature.
Program Information • Students attend classes at University of Québec at Chicoutimi (Chicoutimi, Canada). Scheduled travel to Québec City; field trips to historic sites in Chicoutimi, Musée du Saguenay-Lac Saint Jean, whale watching in Tadoussac, Parc du Saguenay. Students typically earn 4–7 semester credits per term.
Sessions • May–Jun (summer), Jul–Jul (summer 2); Jul–Aug (summer 3).
Eligibility Requirements • Minimum age 18; open to freshmen, sophomores, juniors, seniors, graduate students; 2.5 GPA; 2 letters of recommendation; essay; transcript; completion of 15 credits prior to application; no foreign language proficiency required.
Living Arrangements • Students live in host institution dormitories, host family homes. Meals are taken as a group, with host family, in residences, in central dining facility.
Costs (2006–2007) • $2175 for 3 weeks; $2515 for 5 weeks; includes tuition, housing, some meals, insurance, books and class

materials, student support services, some excursions, fees, e-mail access, airport pick-up. $35 application fee. Financial aid available for students from sponsoring institution: scholarships, loans.
For More Information • College Consortium for International Studies–Brookdale Community College, 2000 P Street, NW, Suite 503, Washington, DC 20036; *Phone:* 800-453-6956; *Fax:* 202-223-0999. *E-mail:* info@ccisabroad.org. *World Wide Web:* http://www.ccisabroad.org/. Students may also apply through Brookdale Community College, International Center, 765 Newman Springs Road, Lincroft, NJ 07738-1597.

ILLINOIS STATE UNIVERSITY
QUÉBEC, CANADA

Hosted by Laval University
Academic Focus • French language and literature.
Program Information • Students attend classes at Laval University (Québec City, Canada). Students typically earn 6 semester credits per term.
Sessions • May–Jun (summer), Jul–Aug (summer 2).
Eligibility Requirements • Minimum age 18; open to sophomores, juniors, seniors, graduate students, adults; 2.5 GPA; 2 letters of recommendation; good academic standing at home school; essay in French; 1 year of college course work in French.
Living Arrangements • Students live in host institution dormitories, host family homes. Quarters are shared with host institution students, students from other programs. Meals are taken on one's own, with host family.
Costs (2005) • $3805–$3831; includes tuition, housing, some meals, insurance, international airfare, books and class materials, international student ID, student support services, personal expenses. $150 application fee. Financial aid available for students from sponsoring institution: scholarships, loans.
For More Information • Mr. Jim Reid, Professor, Illinois State University, 6120 International Studies Office, Normal, IL 61790-6120; *Phone:* 309-438-7894; *Fax:* 309-438-3987. *E-mail:* jhreid@ilstu.edu. *World Wide Web:* http://www.internationalstudies.ilstu.edu/

LINGUA SERVICE WORLDWIDE
VACATION 'N LEARN FRENCH IN CANADA

Hosted by Centre International Bouchereau
Academic Focus • French language and literature, French studies.
Program Information • Students attend classes at Centre International Bouchereau (Québec, Canada). Optional travel to Québec, Toronto, New York at an extra cost. Students typically earn 3 semester credits for 3 weeks, 6 semester credits for 5 weeks.
Sessions • Sessions of 2 or more weeks begin on Mondays, year-round.
Eligibility Requirements • Minimum age 16; open to precollege students, freshmen, sophomores, juniors, seniors, graduate students, adults; no foreign language proficiency required.
Living Arrangements • Students live in host institution dormitories, locally rented apartments, host family homes, hotels. Quarters are shared with host institution students. Meals are taken with host family.
Costs (2006–2007) • Contact sponsor for cost. $100 application fee.
For More Information • Assistant Director, Lingua Service Worldwide, 75 Prospect Street, Suite 4, Huntington, NY 11743; *Phone:* 800-394-5327; *Fax:* 631-271-3441. *E-mail:* linguaservice@att.net. *World Wide Web:* http://www.linguaserviceworldwide.com/

TROIS-PISTOLES

STATE UNIVERSITY OF NEW YORK COLLEGE AT BUFFALO
FRENCH IMMERSION PROGRAM

Hosted by Trois-Pistoles French Immersion School, University of Western Ontario
Academic Focus • French language and literature.
Program Information • Students attend classes at Trois-Pistoles French Immersion School, University of Western Ontario (Trois-

Pistoles, Canada). Field trips to Montréal; optional travel to Québec City at an extra cost. Students typically earn 6–10 semester credits per term.

Sessions • Jul (summer), Jul–Aug (summer 2).

Eligibility Requirements • Open to precollege students, freshmen, sophomores, juniors, seniors, graduate students, adults; 2.5 GPA; 1 letter of recommendation; 0.5 years of college course work in French.

Living Arrangements • Students live in host family homes. Quarters are shared with students from other programs. Meals are taken with host family, in residences.

Costs (2005) • $2178–$3318 for New York residents; $2838–$4725 for nonresidents; includes tuition, housing, all meals, insurance, excursions, books and class materials, student support services, train transportation. $10 application fee. $250 nonrefundable deposit required. Financial aid available for students from sponsoring institution: scholarships, loans.

For More Information • Dr. Lee Ann Grace, Assistant Dean, International and Exchange Programs, State University of New York College at Buffalo, 1300 Elmwood Avenue, Buffalo, NY 14222-1095; *Phone:* 716-878-4620; *Fax:* 716-878-3054. *E-mail:* intleduc@buffalostate.edu. *World Wide Web:* http://www.buffalostate.edu/studyabroad/

VICTORIA

UNIVERSITY OF ILLINOIS COLLEGE OF LAW
INTERNATIONAL AND COMPARATIVE INTELLECTUAL PROPERTY LAW PROGRAM

Hosted by University of Victoria

Academic Focus • Law and legal studies.

Program Information • Students attend classes at University of Victoria (Victoria, Canada). Field trips to Supreme Court and Legislature.

Sessions • Jun–Aug (summer).

Eligibility Requirements • Open to graduate students; good academic standing at home school; American J.D. candidates must complete one year of law study at American law school.

Living Arrangements • Students live in host institution dormitories. Meals are taken as a group, in central dining facility.

Costs (2005) • $5568; includes tuition, insurance, excursions, books and class materials. $400 refundable deposit required.

For More Information • Ms. Sherry Cibelli, Administrative Assistant, University of Illinois College of Law, 504 East Pennsylvania Avenue, Champaign, IL 61820; *Phone:* 217-244-1476; *Fax:* 217-244-1478. *E-mail:* summerip@law.uiuc.edu. *World Wide Web:* http://www.law.uiuc.edu/

CAYMAN ISLANDS

LITTLE CAYMAN

RUTGERS, THE STATE UNIVERSITY OF NEW JERSEY
SUMMER CORAL REEF INTERNSHIP IN THE ISLAND OF LITTLE CAYMAN

Academic Focus • Marine sciences.

Program Information • Faculty members are drawn from the sponsor's U.S. staff and local instructors hired by the sponsor. Optional travel. Students typically earn 4–6 semester credits per term.

Sessions • Jul–Aug (summer).

Eligibility Requirements • Open to sophomores, juniors, seniors, adults; course work in Marine Sciences; 2.5 GPA; 1 letter of recommendation; good academic standing at home school; official transcripts from all tertiary schools attended.

Living Arrangements • Students live in program-owned apartments. Quarters are shared with host institution students. Meals are taken as a group, on one's own, in residences, in central dining facility, in restaurants.

Costs (2006) • $4200 for New Jersey residents; $4800 for nonresidents; includes tuition, housing, some meals, insurance, excursions, student support services. $20 application fee. $500 nonrefundable deposit required. Financial aid available for students from sponsoring institution: scholarships, loans.

For More Information • Ms. Lindy Black, Regional Coordinator, Rutgers, The State University of New Jersey, 102 College Avenue, New Brunswick, NJ 08901; *Phone:* 732-932-7787; *Fax:* 732-932-8657. *E-mail:* ru_abroad@email.rutgers.edu. *World Wide Web:* http://studyabroad.rutgers.edu/

HILE

CITY-TO-CITY

UNIVERSITY OF CALIFORNIA, SANTA BARBARA, WILDLANDS STUDIES
WILDLIFE AND WILDLANDS IN CHILE

Academic Focus • Ecology, environmental science/studies, geography, wildlife studies.
Program Information • Faculty members are drawn from the sponsor's U.S. staff and local instructors hired by the sponsor. Scheduled travel to wildlands field locations. Students typically earn 15 quarter credits per term.
Sessions • Jan–Mar (winter).
Eligibility Requirements • Minimum age 18; open to freshmen, sophomores, juniors, seniors; course work in biology or environmental studies; good academic standing at home school; application essay; no foreign language proficiency required.
Living Arrangements • Students live in field study sites. Meals are taken as a group.
Costs (2007) • $1995; includes tuition. $75 application fee.
For More Information • Mr. Crandall Bay, Director, Wildlands Studies Program, University of California, Santa Barbara, Wildlands Studies, 3 Mosswood Circle, Cazadero, CA 95421; *Phone:* 707-632-5665; *Fax:* 707-632-5665. *E-mail:* wildlands@sonic.net. *World Wide Web:* http://www.wildlandsstudies.com/

SANTIAGO

ENFOREX–SPANISH IN THE SPANISH WORLD
SPANISH INTENSIVE COURSE SANTIAGO DE CHILE

Hosted by ENFOREX
Academic Focus • Dance, Spanish studies.
Program Information • Students attend classes at ENFOREX (Santiago, Chile). Field trips; optional travel to sky on the Sierra at an extra cost. Students typically earn 4 semester credits per term.
Sessions • Year-round.
Eligibility Requirements • Minimum age 18; open to precollege students, freshmen, sophomores, seniors, graduate students, adults; no foreign language proficiency required.
Living Arrangements • Students live in host family homes, hotels. Meals are taken with host family.
Costs (2006) • $1700 per month; includes tuition, housing, some meals, books and class materials. $100 application fee. $250 nonrefundable deposit required.
For More Information • Mr. Antonio Anadón, Director of Spanish Department, ENFOREX–Spanish in the Spanish World, Alberto Aguilera, 26, 28015 Madrid, Spain; *Phone:* +34 91-594-3776; *Fax:* +34 91-594-5159. *E-mail:* promotion@enforex.es. *World Wide Web:* http://www.enforex.com/

LANGUAGE LIAISON
SPANISH IN CHILE–SANTIAGO

Hosted by Language Liaison
Academic Focus • Spanish language and literature.
Program Information • Students attend classes at Language Liaison (Santiago, Chile). Field trips; optional travel at an extra cost. Students typically earn 3–15 semester credits per term.
Sessions • New programs begin weekly, year-round.
Eligibility Requirements • Minimum age 17; open to freshmen, sophomores, juniors, seniors, graduate students, adults; no foreign language proficiency required.
Living Arrangements • Students live in locally rented apartments, host family homes, hotels. Meals are taken on one's own, with host family, in residences, in restaurants.
Costs (2005) • Contact sponsor for cost. $175 application fee. Financial aid available for all students: scholarship research service.
For More Information • Ms. Nancy Forman, President, Language Liaison, PO Box 1772, Pacific Palisades, CA 90272; *Phone:* 800-284-4448; *Fax:* 310-454-1706. *E-mail:* learn@languageliaison.com. *World Wide Web:* http://www.languageliaison.com/

LANGUAGE LINK
ECELA OF SANTIAGO, CHILE

Hosted by ECELA of Santiago, Chile
Academic Focus • Spanish language and literature.

CHILE
Santiago

Program Information • Students attend classes at ECELA of Santiago, Chile (Santiago, Chile). Field trips to Viña del Mar, Valparaíso. Students typically earn 6-15 semester credits per term.
Sessions • Classes begin every Monday, year-round.
Eligibility Requirements • Minimum age 18; open to freshmen, sophomores, juniors, seniors, graduate students, adults; no foreign language proficiency required.
Living Arrangements • Students live in host family homes. Quarters are shared with host institution students. Meals are taken with host family, in residences.
Costs (2005) • $300; includes tuition, housing, some meals, books and class materials, student support services, cultural activities.
For More Information • Ms. Kay G, Rafool, Director, Language Link, PO Box 3006, Peoria, IL 61612-3006; *Phone:* 800-552-2051; *Fax:* 309-692-2926. *E-mail:* info@langlink.com. *World Wide Web:* http://www.langlink.com/

NEW YORK UNIVERSITY
SUMMER IN CHILE

Hosted by NYU at Santiago
Academic Focus • Chilean studies, political science and government.
Program Information • Students attend classes at NYU at Santiago (Santiago, Chile). Field trips. Students typically earn 4 semester credits per term.
Sessions • Jun (summer).
Eligibility Requirements • Minimum age 18; open to freshmen, sophomores, juniors, seniors; 3.0 GPA; good academic standing at home school.
Living Arrangements • Students live in host institution dormitories. Quarters are shared with host institution students. Meals are taken on one's own, in restaurants.
Costs (2007) • $5000; includes tuition, housing, some meals, excursions. $25 application fee. $300 nonrefundable deposit required.
For More Information • New York University, Office of Summer Sessions, 7 E. 12th Street, 6th Floor, New York, NY 10003; *Phone:* 212-992-2292; *Fax:* 212-995-4642. *E-mail:* summer.info@nyu.edu. *World Wide Web:* http://www.nyu.edu/global/studyabroad.html

SCHOOL FOR INTERNATIONAL TRAINING, SIT STUDY ABROAD
CHILE: EDUCATION, POLICY, AND SOCIAL CHANGE

Academic Focus • Education, Spanish language and literature, teaching.
Program Information • Faculty members are drawn from the sponsor's U.S. staff and local instructors hired by the sponsor. Scheduled travel to Buenos Aires, Argentina, rural Chile or Peru; field trips to cultural events. Students typically earn 8 semester credits per term.
Sessions • Jun-Jul (summer).
Eligibility Requirements • Open to freshmen, sophomores, juniors, seniors; course work in Latin American studies, education, or development; 2.5 GPA; 2 letters of recommendation; good academic standing at home school; 2 recent semesters of college-level Spanish.
Living Arrangements • Students live in hotels, guest houses. Meals are taken as a group, in residences, in restaurants.
Costs (2005–2006) • $6814; includes tuition, housing, all meals, insurance, excursions. $50 application fee. $400 nonrefundable deposit required. Financial aid available for all students: scholarships.
For More Information • SIT Study Abroad, School for International Training, SIT Study Abroad, PO Box 676, Kipling Road, Brattleboro, VT 05302-0676; *Phone:* 888-272-7881; *Fax:* 802-258-3296. *E-mail:* studyabroad@sit.edu. *World Wide Web:* http://www.sit.edu/studyabroad/

UNIVERSITY STUDIES ABROAD CONSORTIUM
SPANISH, ANTHROPOLOGICAL, AND LITERARY STUDIES: SANTIAGO, CHILE

Hosted by National University Andres Bello Santiago
Academic Focus • Anthropology, dance, history, Latin American studies, Spanish language and literature.

Program Information • Students attend classes at National University Andres Bello Santiago (Santiago, Chile). Field trips to Valparaíso, Anconcagua (pre-Andean mountains), Viña del Mar, Pomaire, Isla Negra, Parque Natural el Morado; optional travel to Calama, Moon Valley, Puritama, Atacama Plateau, Tocona, Cuyo, Fort Quitor, San Pedro, Pampa Union, Chacabuco at an extra cost. Students typically earn 5-10 semester credits per term.
Sessions • May-Jun (summer), Jun-Jul (summer 2).
Eligibility Requirements • Minimum age 18; open to freshmen, sophomores, juniors, seniors, graduate students, adults; 2.5 GPA; no foreign language proficiency required.
Living Arrangements • Students live in host institution dormitories, locally rented apartments, host family homes. Quarters are shared with host institution students, students from other programs. Meals are taken on one's own, with host family, in residences, in restaurants.
Costs (2007) • $2480 for 1 session; $4860 for 2 sessions; includes tuition, housing, some meals, insurance, excursions, student support services, transportation from airport to Santiago. $100 application fee. $200 refundable deposit required. Financial aid available for all students: scholarships, loans.
For More Information • University Studies Abroad Consortium, USAC/323, Reno, NV 89557-0093; *Phone:* 775-784-6569; *Fax:* 775-784-6010. *E-mail:* usac@unr.edu. *World Wide Web:* http://usac.unr.edu/

VALPARAÍSO

INTERNATIONAL STUDIES ABROAD
VALPARAÍSO, CHILE–SUMMER AND INTENSIVE MONTHS

Hosted by Catholic University of Valparaíso
Academic Focus • Chilean studies, Spanish language and literature.
Program Information • Students attend classes at Catholic University of Valparaíso (Valparaíso, Chile). Scheduled travel to Santiago; field trips to La Serena, Valle del Elqui, Isla Negra, Horcon; optional travel to Portillo at an extra cost. Students typically earn 6 semester credits per term.
Sessions • May-Jun (summer), May-Jun, Jun-Jul, Jan-Jan (intensive language months).
Eligibility Requirements • Minimum age 18; open to freshmen, sophomores, juniors, seniors, graduate students, adults; 2.5 GPA; good academic standing at home school; transcripts; no foreign language proficiency required.
Living Arrangements • Students live in locally rented apartments, host family homes. Meals are taken with host family, in residences.
Costs (2005) • Contact sponsor for cost. $200 deposit required. Financial aid available for all students: scholarships, loans, U.S. federal financial aid.
For More Information • Chile Site Specialist, International Studies Abroad, 901 West 24th Street, Austin, TX 78705; *Phone:* 800-580-8826; *Fax:* 512-480-8866. *E-mail:* isa@studiesabroad.com. *World Wide Web:* http://www.studiesabroad.com/

UNIVERSITY OF MIAMI
UNIVERSITY OF MIAMI IN CHILE

Held at Universidad de Playa Ancha
Academic Focus • International affairs, Latin American studies, Spanish studies.
Program Information • Classes are held on the campus of Universidad de Playa Ancha (Valparaíso, Chile). Faculty members are drawn from the sponsor's U.S. staff and local instructors hired by the sponsor. Field trips; optional travel. Students typically earn 6 semester credits per term.
Sessions • May-Jun (summer).
Eligibility Requirements • Minimum age 18; open to sophomores, juniors, seniors, graduate students; good academic standing at home school; 2 years of college course work in Spanish.
Living Arrangements • Students live in hotels. Quarters are shared with host institution students. Meals are taken as a group, in residences, in central dining facility.
Costs (2005) • $2961-$5872; includes tuition, housing, some meals, excursions, student support services. $40 application fee. $500 nonrefundable deposit required. Financial aid available for students from sponsoring institution: scholarships, loans.

For More Information • Ms. Glenda Hayley, Director, International Education and Exchange Programs, University of Miami, 5050 Brunson Drive, Allen Hall Room 212, PO Box 248005, Coral Gables, FL 33124-1610; *Phone:* 305-284-3434; *Fax:* 305-284-4235. *E-mail:* ieep@miami.edu. *World Wide Web:* http://www.studyabroad.miami.edu/

VILLANOVA UNIVERSITY
LATIN AMERICAN STUDIES
Hosted by Catholic University of Valparaíso
Academic Focus • Latin American studies.
Program Information • Students attend classes at Catholic University of Valparaíso (Valparaíso, Chile). Scheduled travel to La Serena; field trips to Santiago, Central Valley regions, Playa Zapallar. Students typically earn 6 semester credits per term.
Sessions • Jun–Aug (summer).

Eligibility Requirements • Minimum age 18; open to freshmen, sophomores, juniors, seniors; 2.5 GPA; 2 letters of recommendation; good academic standing at home school; 2 years of college course work in Spanish.
Living Arrangements • Students live in host family homes. Quarters are shared with host institution students. Meals are taken with host family, in residences.
Costs (2005) • $4250; includes tuition, housing, all meals, insurance, excursions. $450 nonrefundable deposit required. Financial aid available for students from sponsoring institution: scholarships, loans.
For More Information • Dr. Estrella Ogden, Professor of Spanish and Latin American Studies, Villanova University, Middleton Hall, 800 Lancaster Avenue, Villanova, PA 19085; *Phone:* 610-519-6412; *Fax:* 610-519-7649. *E-mail:* estrella.ogden@villanova.edu. *World Wide Web:* http://www.internationalstudies.villanova.edu/

CHINA

CITY-TO-CITY

AMERICAN INSTITUTE FOR FOREIGN STUDY (AIFS)
AIFS–VARIOUS CITIES IN CHINA–BEIJING LANGUAGE AND CULTURE UNIVERSITY, NANJING UNIVERSITY, SHANGHAI FINANCE UNIVERSITY

Academic Focus • Business administration/management, history, sociology.
Program Information • Field trips to Shanghai, Hangzhou, Xian, Great Wall of China, welcome dinners in Beijing and Nanjing, farewell dinner in Shanchai; specialist lectures; cultural activities. Students typically earn 6 semester credits per term.
Sessions • Jun–Jul (summer).
Eligibility Requirements • Minimum age 17; open to precollege students, freshmen, sophomores, juniors, seniors; 2.0 GPA; Visas must be obtained at student's expense; no foreign language proficiency required.
Living Arrangements • Students live in host institution dormitories, program-owned apartments, hotels. Quarters are shared with host institution students. Meals are taken as a group, in residences.
Costs (2007) • 4 weeks: $4499; includes tuition, housing, some meals, insurance, excursions, student support services, On-site Resident Director, Phone Card to call the U.S. $95 application fee. $350 nonrefundable deposit required. Financial aid available for all students: scholarships.
For More Information • Mr. David Mauro, Admissions Advisor, American Institute For Foreign Study (AIFS), 9 West Broad Street, Stamford, CT 06902-3788; *Phone:* 800-727-2437 Ext. 5163; *Fax:* 203-399-5597. *E-mail:* dmauro@aifs.com. *World Wide Web:* http://www.aifsabroad.com/

CITY COLLEGE OF SAN FRANCISCO
SUMMER IN CHINA

Academic Focus • Asian studies.
Program Information • Faculty members are drawn from the sponsor's U.S. staff. Scheduled travel to Yunnan province; field trips. Students typically earn 3 semester credits per term.
Sessions • Jun–Jul (summer).
Eligibility Requirements • Minimum age 18; open to freshmen, sophomores, juniors, seniors, adults; 2.0 GPA; no foreign language proficiency required.
Living Arrangements • Students live in hotels. Meals are taken as a group, in central dining facility, in restaurants.
Costs (2005) • $2925; includes housing, all meals, insurance, excursions, international airfare, international student ID, student support services. $300 nonrefundable deposit required. Financial aid available for students from sponsoring institution: scholarships, loans.
For More Information • Ms. Jill Heffron, Study Abroad Coordinator, City College of San Francisco, 50 Phelan Avenue, Box C212, San Francisco, CA 94112; *Phone:* 415-239-3778; *Fax:* 415-239-3804. *E-mail:* studyabroad@ccsf.edu. *World Wide Web:* http://www.ccsf.edu/studyabroad/

KENTUCKY INSTITUTE FOR INTERNATIONAL STUDIES
CHINA

Held at Yunnan Normal University
Academic Focus • Chinese studies, history.
Program Information • Classes are held on the campus of Yunnan Normal University (Kunming). Faculty members are drawn from the sponsor's U.S. staff. Field trips to sites of regional interest, Dali, Xi'an, Beijing. Students typically earn 6 semester credits per term.
Sessions • May–Jul (summer).
Eligibility Requirements • Minimum age 18; open to freshmen, sophomores, juniors, seniors, graduate students, adults; 2.0 GPA; 1 letter of recommendation; no foreign language proficiency required.
Living Arrangements • Students live in host institution dormitories. Quarters are shared with host institution students. Meals are taken as a group, in central dining facility.
Costs (2006) • $3760; includes housing, some meals, insurance, excursions, international airfare, international student ID, visas, instructional expenses. $150 application fee. Financial aid available for all students: scholarships.
For More Information • Ms. Nancy Martin, Coordinator, Kentucky Institute for International Studies, PO Box 9, Murray, KY 42071-0009; *Phone:* 270-762-3091; *Fax:* 270-762-3434. *E-mail:* kiismsu@murraystate.edu. *World Wide Web:* http://www.kiis.org/

NEW YORK UNIVERSITY
MEDIA AND GLOBALIZATION: THE ASIAN EXPERIENCE IN BEIJING AND HONG KONG

Held at New York University

Academic Focus • Communications, speech communication.

Program Information • Classes are held on the campus of New York University (Hong Kong). Faculty members are drawn from the sponsor's U.S. staff and local instructors hired by the sponsor. Field trips to Great Wall, Forbidden City, Tiananmen Square, Ming Tombs. Students typically earn 4-6 semester credits per term.

Sessions • May-Jun (summer).

Eligibility Requirements • Minimum age 18; open to juniors, seniors, graduate students; major in culture and communication; good academic standing at home school; essay; transcript; resume; no foreign language proficiency required.

Living Arrangements • Students live in hotels. Meals are taken on one's own, in restaurants.

Costs (2005) • $6532; includes tuition, housing, excursions, registration fees. $50 application fee.

For More Information • Mr. Daniel Young, Program Associate, New York University, 82 Washington Square East, 5th Floor, New York, NY 10003; *Phone:* 212-992-9380; *Fax:* 212-995-4923. *E-mail:* dy14@nyu.edu. *World Wide Web:* http://www.nyu.edu/global/studyabroad.html

STATE UNIVERSITY OF NEW YORK COLLEGE AT CORTLAND
CHINA SUMMER STUDY (HISTORY, CULTURE, AND THE ARTS)

Hosted by Shanghai University

Academic Focus • Ceramics and pottery, Chinese studies, cultural studies.

Program Information • Students attend classes at Shanghai University (Shanghai). Scheduled travel; field trips. Students typically earn 3 semester credits per term.

Sessions • May-Jun (summer).

Eligibility Requirements • Minimum age 18; open to freshmen, sophomores, juniors, seniors; 2.5 GPA; 2 letters of recommendation; good academic standing at home school; no foreign language proficiency required.

Living Arrangements • Students live in host institution dormitories, hotels. Meals are taken as a group, in restaurants.

Costs (2005) • $3664; includes tuition, housing, all meals, insurance, excursions, international airfare, books and class materials. $20 application fee. $200 nonrefundable deposit required. Financial aid available for students from sponsoring institution: scholarships, loans.

For More Information • Ms. Liz McCartney, Assistant Director, Office of International Programs, State University of New York College at Cortland, PO Box 2000, Cortland, NY 13045; *Phone:* 607-753-2209; *Fax:* 607-753-5989. *E-mail:* cortlandabroad@cortland.edu. *World Wide Web:* http://www.cortlandabroad.com/

SYRACUSE UNIVERSITY
ARCHITECTURE IN HONG KONG, BEIJING, AND SHANGHAI

Hosted by Syracuse University Hong Kong

Academic Focus • Architecture.

Program Information • Students attend classes at Syracuse University Hong Kong (Hong Kong). Scheduled travel; field trips. Students typically earn 6 semester credits per term.

Sessions • May-Jun (summer).

Eligibility Requirements • Open to juniors, seniors, graduate students, adults; course work in architecture (1 year); no foreign language proficiency required.

Living Arrangements • Students live in host institution dormitories. Quarters are shared with students from other programs. Meals are taken on one's own, in central dining facility.

Costs (2005) • $7210; includes tuition, housing, some meals, excursions, international student ID, student support services. $55 application fee. $350 nonrefundable deposit required. Financial aid available for all students: scholarships, loans, need-based tuition grants.

For More Information • Ms. Daisy Fried, Associate Director, Syracuse University, 106 Walnut Place, Syracuse, NY 13244-4170;

Phone: 800-251-9674; *Fax:* 315-443-4593. *E-mail:* dipasum@syr.edu. *World Wide Web:* http://suabroad.syr.edu/

UNIVERSITY OF CALIFORNIA, SANTA BARBARA, WILDLANDS STUDIES
MOUNTAIN ECOSYSTEMS OF CHINA

Academic Focus • Asian studies, ecology, environmental science/studies, geography, wildlife studies.

Program Information • Faculty members are drawn from the sponsor's U.S. staff and local instructors hired by the sponsor. Scheduled travel to wildland field locations. Students typically earn 15 quarter credits per term.

Sessions • Apr-Jun (spring).

Eligibility Requirements • Minimum age 18; open to freshmen, sophomores, juniors, seniors; course work in biology or environmental studies; good academic standing at home school; application essay; no foreign language proficiency required.

Living Arrangements • Students live in field study sites. Meals are taken as a group.

Costs (2007) • $1995; includes tuition. $75 application fee.

For More Information • Mr. Crandall Bay, Director, Wildlands Studies Program, University of California, Santa Barbara, Wildlands Studies, 3 Mosswood Circle, Cazadero, CA 95421; *Phone:* 707-632-5665; *Fax:* 707-632-5665. *E-mail:* wildlands@sonic.net. *World Wide Web:* http://www.wildlandsstudies.com/

BEIJING

AMERICAN INSTITUTE FOR FOREIGN STUDY (AIFS)
AIFS–BEIJING, CHINA–BEIJING LANGUAGE AND CULTURE UNIVERSITY

Hosted by Beijing Language and Culture University

Academic Focus • Chinese language and literature, history, sociology.

Program Information • Students attend classes at Beijing Language and Culture University (Beijing, China). Scheduled travel to 3-day orientation in Shanghai; field trips to Xi'an, activities based on cultural history course. Students typically earn 7 semester credits per term.

Sessions • Jun-Jul (5 weeks).

Eligibility Requirements • Minimum age 17; open to precollege students, freshmen, sophomores, juniors, seniors; 2.0 GPA; Students must take an intensive Mandarin Chinese language course for 5 credits.

Living Arrangements • Students live in host institution dormitories, program-owned apartments, hotels. Quarters are shared with host institution students. Meals are taken as a group, in residences.

Costs (2007) • $4299; includes tuition, housing, some meals, insurance, excursions, student support services, On-site Resident Director, Phone Card to call the U.S., Computer Facilities/Internet. $95 application fee. $395 nonrefundable deposit required. Financial aid available for all students: scholarships.

For More Information • Mr. David Mauro, Admissions Advisor, American Institute For Foreign Study (AIFS), 9 West Broad Street, Stamford, CT 06902-3788; *Phone:* 800-727-2437 Ext. 5163; *Fax:* 203-399-5597. *E-mail:* dmauro@aifs.com. *World Wide Web:* http://www.aifsabroad.com/

ASSOCIATED COLLEGES IN CHINA
ASSOCIATED COLLEGES IN CHINA

Held at Capital University of Economics and Business

Academic Focus • Chinese language and literature.

Program Information • Classes are held on the campus of Capital University of Economics and Business (Beijing, China). Faculty members are drawn from the sponsor's U.S. staff and local instructors hired by the sponsor. Field trips to Datong, Suzhou, Shanghai, Xi'an. Students typically earn 2 Hamilton units per term.

Sessions • Jun-Aug (summer).

Eligibility Requirements • Minimum age 18; open to sophomores, juniors, seniors, graduate students; course work in East Asian culture

CHINA
Beijing

(at least 1 course); 3.0 GPA; 2 letters of recommendation; good academic standing at home school; 1 year of college course work in Chinese.

Living Arrangements • Students live in host institution dormitories. Quarters are shared with host institution students. Meals are taken on one's own, in restaurants.

Costs (2006) • $4950; includes tuition, housing, excursions, books and class materials, lab equipment, student support services. $40 application fee. $300 nonrefundable deposit required. Financial aid available for all students: scholarships.

For More Information • Ms. Dana Hubbard, Program Coordinator, Associated Colleges in China, Hamilton College, 198 College Hill Road, Clinton, NY 13323; *Phone:* 315-859-4326; *Fax:* 315-859-4687. *E-mail:* acchina@hamilton.edu. *World Wide Web:* http://www.hamilton.edu/academics/acc/

BOSTON UNIVERSITY
BEIJING INTENSIVE CHINESE LANGUAGE PROGRAM

Hosted by CET Language Training Center

Academic Focus • Chinese language and literature.

Program Information • Students attend classes at CET Language Training Center (Beijing, China). Field trips to Qingdao, Datong. Students typically earn 8 semester credits per term.

Sessions • Jun–Aug (summer).

Eligibility Requirements • Open to freshmen, sophomores, juniors, seniors, adults; 1 letter of recommendation; good academic standing at home school; essay; approval of participation; transcript; minimum GPA of 3.0 in major and overall; no foreign language proficiency required.

Living Arrangements • Students live in host institution dormitories. Quarters are shared with host institution students, students from other programs. Meals are taken as a group, on one's own, in central dining facility, in restaurants.

Costs (2005) • $6300; includes tuition, housing, all meals, insurance, excursions, books and class materials, visa fees, limited reimbursement for cultural activities, host family program, emergency medical evacuation insurance. $50 application fee. $400 nonrefundable deposit required. Financial aid available for all students: scholarships, loans.

For More Information • Division of International Programs, Boston University, 232 Bay State Road, Boston, MA 02215; *Phone:* 617-353-9888; *Fax:* 617-353-5402. *E-mail:* abroad@bu.edu. *World Wide Web:* http://www.bu.edu/abroad/

CENTER FOR STUDY ABROAD (CSA)
BEIJING LANGUAGE AND CULTURE UNIVERSITY

Hosted by Beijing Language and Culture University

Academic Focus • Chinese language and literature, Chinese studies.

Program Information • Students attend classes at Beijing Language and Culture University (Beijing, China). Optional travel to Beijing tourist attractions, Datong, Tianjin, Chengde at an extra cost. Students typically earn 4–10 semester credits per term.

Sessions • Classes begin weekly, year-round.

Eligibility Requirements • Minimum age 17; open to freshmen, sophomores, juniors, seniors, graduate students, adults; good health; no foreign language proficiency required.

Living Arrangements • Students live in host institution dormitories, locally rented apartments. Quarters are shared with students from other programs. Meals are taken on one's own, in central dining facility.

Costs (2005) • Contact sponsor for cost. $45 application fee.

For More Information • Ms. Alima K. Virtue, Program Director, Center for Study Abroad (CSA), 325 Washington Avenue South #93, Kent, WA 98032; *Phone:* 206-726-1498; *Fax:* 253-850-0454. *E-mail:* info@centerforstudyabroad.com. *World Wide Web:* http://www.centerforstudyabroad.com/

CIEE
CIEE STUDY CENTER AT PEKING UNIVERSITY, BEIJING, CHINA

Hosted by Peking University

Academic Focus • Chinese language and literature.

Program Information • Students attend classes at Peking University (Beijing, China). Field trips to the Great Wall, Tiananmen Square, Ming Tombs, Temple of Heaven, other temples, Beijing Opera, music concerts, acrobatics show. Students typically earn 10 semester credits per term.

Sessions • Jun–Aug (summer).

Eligibility Requirements • Minimum age 18; open to sophomores, juniors, seniors; course work in one Chinese area studies course recommended; 2.75 GPA; 1 letter of recommendation; good academic standing at home school; evaluation should be from a language professor; 1 year of college course work in Mandarin Chinese.

Living Arrangements • Students live in host institution dormitories. Quarters are shared with host institution students. Meals are taken on one's own, in central dining facility, in restaurants.

Costs (2006) • $5100; includes tuition, housing, some meals, insurance, excursions, student support services, visa fees, predeparture advising, cultural activities, on-site pick-up, orientation. $30 application fee. $300 nonrefundable deposit required. Financial aid available for all students: scholarships, minority student scholarships, Department of Education grant, travel grants.

For More Information • Information Center, CIEE, 7 Custom House Street, 3rd Floor, Portland, ME 04101; *Phone:* 800-40-STUDY; *Fax:* 207-553-7699. *E-mail:* studyinfo@ciee.org. *World Wide Web:* http://www.ciee.org/isp/

COLUMBIA UNIVERSITY
SUMMER LANGUAGE PROGRAM IN BEIJING

Hosted by Peking University

Academic Focus • Chinese language and literature.

Program Information • Students attend classes at Peking University (Beijing, China). Field trips to the Great Wall, local temples, Ming tombs; optional travel at an extra cost. Students typically earn 10 semester credits per term.

Sessions • Jun–Aug (summer).

Eligibility Requirements • Minimum age 18; open to sophomores, juniors, seniors, graduate students, adults; 3.0 GPA; 1 letter of recommendation; good academic standing at home school; .5 years college course work in Chinese.

Living Arrangements • Students live in host institution dormitories, host family homes. Meals are taken on one's own, with host family, in residences, in central dining facility, in restaurants.

Costs (2005) • $4500; includes tuition, housing, some meals, books and class materials, student support services, some excursions, private tutoring. $50 application fee. $500 nonrefundable deposit required.

For More Information • Information Center, Columbia University, 2970 Broadway, MC 4110, 303 Lewisohn, New York, NY 10027-6902; *Phone:* 212-854-9699; *Fax:* 212-854-5841. *E-mail:* beijing@columbia.edu. *World Wide Web:* http://www.ce.columbia.edu/op/

EMORY UNIVERSITY
CHINESE STUDIES

Hosted by Beijing Normal University

Academic Focus • Chinese language and literature, Chinese studies, history.

Program Information • Students attend classes at Beijing Normal University (Beijing, China). Scheduled travel to Hong Kong, Xi'an; field trips to Chengde. Students typically earn 8 semester credits per term.

Sessions • May–Jun (summer).

Eligibility Requirements • Minimum age 18; open to freshmen, sophomores, juniors, seniors; 2.0 GPA; good academic standing at home school; no foreign language proficiency required.

Living Arrangements • Meals are taken as a group, in central dining facility.

Costs (2005) • $6800; includes tuition, housing, all meals, insurance, excursions. $350 nonrefundable deposit required. Financial aid available for students from sponsoring institution: scholarships, loans.

For More Information • Ms. Gail Scheu, Study Abroad Coordinator, Emory University, 1385 Oxford Road, Atlanta, GA 30322; *Phone:* 404-727-2240; *Fax:* 404-727-6724. *E-mail:* lscheu@emory.edu. *World Wide Web:* http://www.cipa.emory.edu/

JAMES MADISON UNIVERSITY
SUMMER IN CHINA

Academic Focus • Chinese language and literature, Chinese studies, international business.
Program Information • Faculty members are drawn from the sponsor's U.S. staff and local instructors hired by the sponsor. Field trips. Students typically earn 10 semester credits per term.
Sessions • Jun–Jul (summer).
Eligibility Requirements • Minimum age 18; open to sophomores, juniors, seniors; 2.0 GPA; 1 letter of recommendation; good academic standing at home school; no foreign language proficiency required.
Living Arrangements • Students live in host institution dormitories. Meals are taken as a group, on one's own, in central dining facility, in restaurants.
Costs (2005) • $4680 for Virginia residents; $7480 for nonresidents; includes tuition, housing, some meals, excursions, books and class materials, international student ID. $400 nonrefundable deposit required.
For More Information • Mr. Felix Wang, Director, James Madison University, Office of International Programs, MSC 5731, 1077 South Main Street, Harrisonburg, VA 22807; *Phone:* 540-568-6419; *Fax:* 540-568-3310. *E-mail:* studyabroad@jmu.edu. *World Wide Web:* http://www.jmu.edu/international/

KNOWLEDGE EXCHANGE INSTITUTE (KEI)
ASIAN BUSINESS, LAW, AND DIPLOMACY

Hosted by University of International Business and Economics Beijing
Academic Focus • Advertising and public relations, Asian studies, business administration/management, Chinese language and literature, Chinese studies, commerce, economics, entrepreneurship, finance, international business, law and legal studies, marketing, political science and government.
Program Information • Students attend classes at University of International Business and Economics Beijing (Beijing, China). Scheduled travel to Shanghai, Hong Kong, Hainan Island, Xian; Tibet; field trips to Beijing, Great Wall. Students typically earn 9 semester credits per term.
Sessions • Jun–Jul (summer).
Eligibility Requirements • Open to freshmen, sophomores, juniors, seniors, graduate students, adults; 2.2 GPA; good academic standing at home school; no foreign language proficiency required.
Living Arrangements • Students live in host institution dormitories. Meals are taken on one's own, in central dining facility, in restaurants.
Costs (2006) • $3985; includes tuition, housing, insurance, excursions, books and class materials, lab equipment, student support services, mobile telephone. $50 application fee. $500 nonrefundable deposit required. Financial aid available for all students: scholarships, loans.
For More Information • Mr. Eduard Izraylovsky, Director, Knowledge Exchange Institute (KEI), 111 John Street, Suite 800, New York, NY 10638; *Phone:* 800-831-5095; *Fax:* 212-528-2095. *E-mail:* info@knowledgeexchange.org. *World Wide Web:* http://www.knowledgeexchange.org/

KNOWLEDGE EXCHANGE INSTITUTE (KEI)
BEIJING INTERNSHIP PROGRAM

Hosted by University of International Business and Economics Beijing
Academic Focus • Accounting, actuarial science, advertising and public relations, brokerage, business administration/management, commerce, communication services, communications, community service, criminal justice, economics, entrepreneurship, finance, hospitality services, hotel and restaurant management, human resources, information science, international business, law and legal studies, management information systems, marketing, political science and government, public administration, social services, social work, tourism and travel.
Program Information • Students attend classes at University of International Business and Economics Beijing (Beijing, China). Field trips to Beijing, Great Wall. Students typically earn 6 semester credits per term.
Sessions • Jun–Aug (summer).

Eligibility Requirements • Open to freshmen, sophomores, juniors, seniors, graduate students, adults; 2.2 GPA; good academic standing at home school; no foreign language proficiency required.
Living Arrangements • Students live in host institution dormitories, program-owned apartments, host family homes. Quarters are shared with host institution students, students from other programs. Meals are taken on one's own, with host family, in residences, in restaurants.
Costs (2006) • $3450; includes tuition, housing, insurance, excursions, student support services, mobile telephone. $50 application fee. $500 nonrefundable deposit required. Financial aid available for all students: scholarships, loans.
For More Information • Mr. Eduard Izraylovsky, Director, Knowledge Exchange Institute (KEI), 111 John Street, Suite 800, New York, NY 10038; *Phone:* 800-831-5095; *Fax:* 212-528-2095. *E-mail:* info@knowledgeexchange.org. *World Wide Web:* http://www.knowledgeexchange.org/

KNOWLEDGE EXCHANGE INSTITUTE (KEI)
CHINESE LANGUAGE, CULTURE, AND HUMANITIES

Hosted by University of International Business and Economics Beijing
Academic Focus • Asian studies, Chinese language and literature, Chinese studies, economics, history, intercultural studies, political science and government.
Program Information • Students attend classes at University of International Business and Economics Beijing (Beijing, China). Scheduled travel to Shanghai, Hong Kong, Hainan Island, Xian; Tibet; field trips to Beijing, Great Wall. Students typically earn 9 semester credits per term.
Sessions • Jun–Jul (summer).
Eligibility Requirements • Open to freshmen, sophomores, juniors, seniors, graduate students, adults; 2.2 GPA; 2 letters of recommendation; good academic standing at home school; no foreign language proficiency required.
Living Arrangements • Students live in host institution dormitories. Meals are taken on one's own, in central dining facility, in restaurants.
Costs (2006) • $3985; includes tuition, housing, insurance, excursions, lab equipment, student support services, mobile telephone. $50 application fee. $500 nonrefundable deposit required. Financial aid available for all students: scholarships, loans.
For More Information • Mr. Eduard Izraylovsky, Director, Knowledge Exchange Institute (KEI), 111 John Street, Suite 800, New York, NY 10038; *Phone:* 800-831-5095; *Fax:* 212-528-2095. *E-mail:* info@knowledgeexchange.org. *World Wide Web:* http://www.knowledgeexchange.org/

LANGUAGE LIAISON
CHINESE IN BEIJING

Hosted by Language Liaison
Academic Focus • Chinese language and literature.
Program Information • Students attend classes at Language Liaison (Beijing, China). Field trips; optional travel at an extra cost. Students typically earn 3–15 semester credits per term.
Sessions • Classes begin weekly, year-round.
Eligibility Requirements • Minimum age 17; open to precollege students, freshmen, sophomores, juniors, seniors, graduate students, adults; no foreign language proficiency required.
Living Arrangements • Students live in locally rented apartments, host family homes, hotels. Meals are taken on one's own, with host family, in residences, in restaurants.
Costs (2005) • Contact sponsor for cost. $175 application fee. Financial aid available for all students: scholarship research service.
For More Information • Ms. Nancy Forman, President, Language Liaison, PO Box 1772, Pacific Palisades, CA 90272; *Phone:* 800-284-4448; *Fax:* 310-454-1706. *E-mail:* learn@languageliaison.com. *World Wide Web:* http://www.languageliaison.com/

MICHIGAN STATE UNIVERSITY
CHINA IN WORLD AFFAIRS

Held at People's University of China Beijing

CHINA
Beijing

Academic Focus • Chinese language and literature, Chinese studies, interdisciplinary studies, international affairs, political science and government.
Program Information • Classes are held on the campus of People's University of China Beijing (Beijing, China). Faculty members are drawn from the sponsor's U.S. staff and local instructors hired by the sponsor. Optional travel to sightseeing locations in and around Beijing at an extra cost. Students typically earn 8 semester credits per term.
Sessions • May–Jun (summer), Program runs every other year.
Eligibility Requirements • Minimum age 18; open to sophomores, juniors, seniors; 2.5 GPA; good academic standing at home school; no foreign language proficiency required.
Living Arrangements • Students live in host institution dormitories. Meals are taken on one's own, in central dining facility, in restaurants.
Costs (2004) • $1189; includes housing, some meals, insurance, student support services. $100 application fee. $200 nonrefundable deposit required. Financial aid available for students from sponsoring institution: scholarships, loans.
For More Information • Ms. Darla Conley, Office Assistant, Michigan State University, Office of Study Abroad, 109 International Center, East Lansing, MI 48824-1035; *Phone:* 517-355-4654; *Fax:* 517-353-8727. *E-mail:* conleyd@msu.edu. *World Wide Web:* http://studyabroad.msu.edu/

MICHIGAN STATE UNIVERSITY
INTERNATIONAL BUSINESS IN CHINA

Academic Focus • Chinese studies, marketing.
Program Information • Faculty members are drawn from the sponsor's U.S. staff. Field trips to Hong Kong, Shanghai.
Sessions • Jun (summer).
Eligibility Requirements • Minimum age 18; open to juniors, seniors; major in Eli Broad College of Business; 3.0 GPA; good academic standing at home school; essay; no foreign language proficiency required.
Living Arrangements • Students live in host institution dormitories. Meals are taken as a group, in restaurants.
Costs (2005) • $1149; includes housing, some meals, insurance, excursions, student support services. $100 application fee. $200 deposit required. Financial aid available for students from sponsoring institution: scholarships, loans.
For More Information • Ms. Darla Conley, Secretary, Michigan State University, Office of Study Abroad, 109 International Center, East Lansing, MI 48824-1035; *Phone:* 517-355-4654; *Fax:* 517-353-8727. *E-mail:* conleyd@msn.edu. *World Wide Web:* http://studyabroad.msu.edu/

MICHIGAN STATE UNIVERSITY
PREPARING RESOURCE AND ENVIRONMENTAL MANAGERS WITH INTERNATIONAL UNDERSTANDING AND MERIT

Academic Focus • Chinese studies, conservation studies, earth sciences, environmental science/studies, forestry, geography, geology, natural resources, parks and recreation, wildlife studies.
Program Information • Faculty members are drawn from the sponsor's U.S. staff and local instructors hired by the sponsor. Field trips to the Three Georges Dam Project, the Wolong Panda Reserve, the World Horticulture Garden. Students typically earn 6 semester credits per term.
Sessions • May–Jul (summer).
Eligibility Requirements • Minimum age 18; open to juniors, seniors; 3.0 GPA; 2 letters of recommendation; good academic standing at home school; program-specific application; essay; no foreign language proficiency required.
Living Arrangements • Students live in hotels. Meals are taken as a group, in restaurants.
Costs (2005) • Contact sponsor for cost. $100 application fee. $200 nonrefundable deposit required. Financial aid available for students from sponsoring institution: scholarships, loans.
For More Information • Ms. Darla Conley, Secretary, Michigan State University, Office of Study Abroad, 109 International Center, East Lansing, MI 48824-1035; *Phone:* 517-355-4654; *Fax:* 517-353-8727. *E-mail:* conleyd@msu.edu. *World Wide Web:* http://studyabroad.msu.edu/

STATE UNIVERSITY OF NEW YORK AT NEW PALTZ
POLITICAL SCIENCE STUDY MISSION–SUMMER PROGRAM

Academic Focus • Political science and government.
Program Information • Faculty members are drawn from the sponsor's U.S. staff and local instructors hired by the sponsor. Scheduled travel to Chongqing, Shanghai; field trips to Beijing, Xi'an. Students typically earn 6 semester credits per term.
Sessions • May–Jun (summer).
Eligibility Requirements • Minimum age 18; open to sophomores, juniors, seniors; 2.5 GPA; 1 letter of recommendation; no foreign language proficiency required.
Living Arrangements • Students live in hotels. Meals are taken on one's own, in restaurants.
Costs (2006) • $3000; includes tuition, housing, all meals, excursions. $25 application fee. $300 refundable deposit required. Financial aid available for all students: scholarships, loans.
For More Information • Marketing Coordinator, Study Abroad, State University of New York at New Paltz, 1 Hawk Drive, Suite 9, New Paltz, NY 12561; *Phone:* 845-257-3125; *Fax:* 845-257-3129. *E-mail:* studyabroad@newpaltz.edu. *World Wide Web:* http://www.newpaltz.edu/studyabroad/

UNIVERSITY OF DELAWARE
WINTER SESSION IN CHINA–EAST ASIAN STUDIES

Academic Focus • Chinese language and literature, Chinese studies, East Asian studies, history, music.
Program Information • Faculty members are drawn from the sponsor's U.S. staff and local instructors hired by the sponsor. Scheduled travel to Xi'an, Shanghai; field trips to cultural sites. Students typically earn 6–7 semester credits per term.
Sessions • Jan–Feb (winter).
Eligibility Requirements • Open to freshmen, sophomores, juniors, seniors, adults; 2.0 GPA; 1 letter of recommendation; no foreign language proficiency required.
Living Arrangements • Students live in host institution dormitories, hotels. Meals are taken as a group, in central dining facility, in restaurants.
Costs (2005) • Contact sponsor for cost. $200 nonrefundable deposit required. Financial aid available for all students: scholarships.
For More Information • Center for International Studies, University of Delaware, 186 South College Avenue, Newark, DE 19716-1450; *Phone:* 888-831-4685; *Fax:* 302-831-6042. *E-mail:* studyabroad@udel.edu. *World Wide Web:* http://www.udel.edu/studyabroad/

UNIVERSITY OF MINNESOTA
MADE IN CHINA

Academic Focus • Marketing.
Program Information • Faculty members are drawn from the sponsor's U.S. staff and local instructors hired by the sponsor. Scheduled travel; field trips. Students typically earn 3 semester credits per term.
Sessions • May–Jun (summer).
Eligibility Requirements • Minimum age 18; open to freshmen, sophomores, juniors, seniors, adults; 2.5 GPA; good academic standing at home school; no foreign language proficiency required.
Living Arrangements • Students live in host institution dormitories, hotels. Quarters are shared with students from other programs. Meals are taken as a group, on one's own, in central dining facility, in restaurants.
Costs (2006) • Contact sponsor for cost; includes tuition, housing, all meals, insurance, excursions, international airfare, student support services. Financial aid available for students from sponsoring institution: scholarships, loans.
For More Information • Learning Abroad Center, University of Minnesota, 230 Heller Hall, 271 19th Avenue South, Minneapolis, MN 55455; *Phone:* 800-700-UOFM; *Fax:* 612-626-8009. *E-mail:* umabroad@umn.edu. *World Wide Web:* http://www.umabroad.umn.edu/

CHENGDU

UNIVERSITY STUDIES ABROAD CONSORTIUM

CHINESE AND INTERNATIONAL RELATIONS STUDIES: CHENGDU, CHINA

Hosted by Southwest University for Nationalities

Academic Focus • Anthropology, art, Chinese language and literature, Chinese studies, culinary arts, cultural studies, economics, environmental health, political science and government.

Program Information • Students attend classes at Southwest University for Nationalities (Chengdu, China). Field trips to Leshan, Emei Shan, Chengdu, Yellow Dragon River, a panda research institute, San Xingdui Museum; optional travel to Beijing at an extra cost. Students typically earn 6–12 semester credits per term.

Sessions • May–Jun (summer), Jun–Aug (summer 2).

Eligibility Requirements • Minimum age 18; open to freshmen, sophomores, juniors, seniors, graduate students, adults; 2.5 GPA; no foreign language proficiency required.

Living Arrangements • Students live in host institution dormitories, locally rented apartments, host family homes. Quarters are shared with host institution students. Meals are taken on one's own, in central dining facility, in restaurants.

Costs (2007) • $2690 for 1 session; $5280 for 2 sessions; includes tuition, housing, insurance, excursions, student support services. $100 application fee. $200 refundable deposit required. Financial aid available for all students: scholarships, loans.

For More Information • University Studies Abroad Consortium, USAC/323, Reno, NV 89557-0093; *Phone:* 775-784-6569; *Fax:* 775-784-6010. *E-mail:* usac@unr.edu. *World Wide Web:* http://usac.unr.edu/

HONG KONG

THE CHINESE UNIVERSITY OF HONG KONG

IASP SUMMER SESSION

Hosted by The Chinese University of Hong Kong

Academic Focus • Asian studies, business administration/management, Chinese language and literature, classics and classical languages.

Program Information • Students attend classes at The Chinese University of Hong Kong (Hong Kong, China). Scheduled travel to major city in mainland China (e.g. Shanghai, Beijing); field trips to cultural sites, business organizations and government entities in Hong Kong; optional travel to Majro city in mainland China at an extra cost. Students typically earn 3–12 semester credits per term.

Sessions • Jun–Aug (summer).

Eligibility Requirements • Open to sophomores, juniors, seniors, graduate students, adults; 2 letters of recommendation; good academic standing at home school; statement of purpose; no foreign language proficiency required.

Living Arrangements • Students live in host institution dormitories. Quarters are shared with students from other programs. Meals are taken on one's own, in central dining facility.

Costs (2004–2005) • $3230; includes tuition, housing, excursions, student support services, basic medical care, language instruction, student union membership, bedding. $52 application fee.

For More Information • Mr. Louis Wang, Programme Associate, The Chinese University of Hong Kong, Office of Academic Links, Lady Ho Tung Hall, Shatin, N.T., Hong Kong SAR, China; *Phone:* +852 3163-4034; *Fax:* +852 2609-5045. *E-mail:* louiswong@cuhk.edu.hk. *World Wide Web:* http://www.cuhk.edu.hk/

CHINA
Hong Kong

COOPERATIVE CENTER FOR STUDY ABROAD
HONG KONG WINTER

Academic Focus • Music.

Program Information • Faculty members are drawn from the sponsor's U.S. staff. Students typically earn 3 semester credits per term.

Sessions • Dec–Jan (summer).

Eligibility Requirements • Minimum age 18; good academic standing at home school; no foreign language proficiency required.

Living Arrangements • Students live in hotels. Quarters are shared with host institution students. Meals are taken on one's own, in central dining facility, in restaurants.

Costs (2006–2007) • $3995; includes housing, some meals, insurance, excursions, international airfare, airport transfers. $200 nonrefundable deposit required. Financial aid available for students from sponsoring institution: scholarships, loans.

For More Information • Dr. Michael A. Klembara, Executive Director, Cooperative Center for Study Abroad, Northern Kentucky University, Nunn Drive, Founders Hall 301, Highland Heights, KY 41099; *Phone:* 859-572-6512; *Fax:* 859-572-6650. *E-mail:* ccsa@nku.edu. *World Wide Web:* http://www.ccsa.cc/

UNIVERSITY OF MIAMI
CHINESE UNIVERSITY OF HONG KONG SUMMER PROGRAM

Hosted by The Chinese University of Hong Kong

Academic Focus • Chinese language and literature, cultural studies, marketing.

Program Information • Students attend classes at The Chinese University of Hong Kong (Hong Kong, China). Optional travel to Shanghai at an extra cost. Students typically earn 6 semester credits per term.

Sessions • Jun–Jul (summer).

Eligibility Requirements • Minimum age 18; open to freshmen, sophomores, juniors, seniors; good academic standing at home school; no foreign language proficiency required.

Living Arrangements • Students live in host institution dormitories. Quarters are shared with students from other programs. Meals are taken as a group, in central dining facility.

Costs (2005) • $4320; includes tuition, student support services. $40 application fee. $500 nonrefundable deposit required. Financial aid available for students from sponsoring institution: scholarships, loans.

For More Information • International Education and Exchange Programs, University of Miami, 5050 Brunson Drive, Allen Hall Room 212, PO Box 248005, Coral Gables, FL 33124-1610; *Phone:* 305-284-3434; *Fax:* 305-284-4235. *E-mail:* ieep@miami.edu. *World Wide Web:* http://www.studyabroad.miami.edu/

KUNMING

SCHOOL FOR INTERNATIONAL TRAINING, SIT STUDY ABROAD
CHINA: PUBLIC HEALTH AND TRADITIONAL CHINESE MEDICINE

Hosted by Yunnan Provincial Hospital of Traditional Chinese Medicine

Academic Focus • Chinese language and literature, public health.

Program Information • Students attend classes at Yunnan Provincial Hospital of Traditional Chinese Medicine (Kunming, China). Scheduled travel to local sites, Dali, Lijiang; field trips to cultural events. Students typically earn 8 semester credits per term.

Sessions • Jun–Jul (summer).

Eligibility Requirements • Open to sophomores, juniors, seniors; 2.5 GPA; 2 letters of recommendation; good academic standing at home school; significant preparation in the health sciences; no foreign language proficiency required.

Living Arrangements • Students live in hotels, guest houses. Meals are taken in residences, in restaurants.

Costs (2005–2006) • $6589; includes tuition, housing, all meals, insurance, excursions. $50 application fee. $400 nonrefundable deposit required. Financial aid available for all students: scholarships.

For More Information • SIT Study Abroad, School for International Training, SIT Study Abroad, PO Box 676, Kipling Road, Brattleboro, VT 05302-0676; *Phone:* 888-272-7881; *Fax:* 802-258-3296. *E-mail:* studyabroad@sit.edu. *World Wide Web:* http://www.sit.edu/studyabroad/

WESTERN WASHINGTON UNIVERSITY
WWU IN KUNMING

Hosted by Yunnan Normal University

Academic Focus • Chinese language and literature, Chinese studies.

Program Information • Students attend classes at Yunnan Normal University (Kunming, China). Scheduled travel to Beijing; field trips to Beijing, Dali, Lijiang and other places in Yunnan province. Students typically earn 15 quarter credits per term.

Sessions • Jun–Aug (summer).

Eligibility Requirements • Open to sophomores, juniors, seniors, graduate students; 2.5 GPA; good academic standing at home school; 1 year of college course work in Chinese.

Living Arrangements • Students live in host institution dormitories. Quarters are shared with host institution students. Meals are taken as a group, in central dining facility.

Costs (2006) • $6006; includes tuition, housing, all meals, insurance, excursions, international airfare, books and class materials, student support services, resident director, personal expenses. $60 application fee. $400 refundable deposit required. Financial aid available for students from sponsoring institution: scholarships, loans, institutional grants and scholarships.

For More Information • Ms. Krista Mitchell, Program Coordinator, International Program and Exchange, Western Washington University, 516 High Street, Bellingham, WA 98225-9100; *Phone:* 360-650-7627; *Fax:* 360-650-6572. *E-mail:* krista.mitchell@wwu.edu. *World Wide Web:* http://wwu.edu/~ipewwu/

NANJING

NEW YORK UNIVERSITY
NYU IN NANJING

Hosted by Nanjing University

Academic Focus • Chinese language and literature, Chinese studies.

Program Information • Students attend classes at Nanjing University (Nanjing, China). Scheduled travel to Beijing, Xi'an, Wuxi; field trips to Fuzi Miao (Temple of Confucius), the Shili Qinhuai River, Zhonghua Gate, Jiming Temple. Students typically earn 8 semester credits per term.

Sessions • Jun–Jul (summer).

Eligibility Requirements • Minimum age 18; open to freshmen, sophomores, juniors, seniors; 3.0 GPA; good academic standing at home school; personal statement for non-New York University students; no foreign language proficiency required.

Living Arrangements • Students live in host institution dormitories. Quarters are shared with host institution students. Meals are taken on one's own, in central dining facility.

Costs (2006) • $6434; includes tuition, housing, some meals, excursions, student support services, program fee, one week of travel. $25 application fee. $300 nonrefundable deposit required. Financial aid available for students from sponsoring institution: loans.

For More Information • Summer Session Admission, New York University, 7 East 12th Street, 6th Floor, New York, NY 10003; *Phone:* 212-998-2292; *Fax:* 212-995-4642. *E-mail:* summer.info@nyu.edu. *World Wide Web:* http://www.nyu.edu/global/studyabroad.html

RUTGERS, THE STATE UNIVERSITY OF NEW JERSEY
SUMMER STUDY ABROAD IN CHINA

Held at Nanjing University

Academic Focus • Chinese language and literature.

Program Information • Classes are held on the campus of Nanjing University (Nanjing, China). Faculty members are drawn from the sponsor's U.S. staff and local instructors hired by the sponsor. Field trips to Shanghai, Suzhou, Hangzhou. Students typically earn 6–9 semester credits per term.

Sessions • May-Jul (summer).
Eligibility Requirements • Open to sophomores, juniors, seniors, graduate students; 2.5 GPA; 1 letter of recommendation; good academic standing at home school; official transcript from each tertiary school attended; 1 year of college course work in Chinese.
Living Arrangements • Students live in host institution dormitories. Quarters are shared with host institution students. Meals are taken on one's own, in restaurants.
Costs (2005) • $3304 for New Jersey residents; $4389 for nonresidents; includes tuition, housing, insurance, excursions, student support services. $20 application fee. $500 nonrefundable deposit required. Financial aid available for students from sponsoring institution: scholarships, loans.
For More Information • Ms. Lindy Black, Regional Coordinator, Rutgers, The State University of New Jersey, 102 College Avenue, New Brunswick, NJ 08901-8543; *Phone:* 732-932-7787; *Fax:* 732-932-8659. *E-mail:* ru_abroad@email.rutgers.edu. *World Wide Web:* http://studyabroad.rutgers.edu/

SHANGHAI

CENTER FOR STUDY ABROAD (CSA)
FUDAN UNIVERSITY

Hosted by Fudan University
Academic Focus • Art, Chinese language and literature, Chinese studies, history, philosophy.
Program Information • Students attend classes at Fudan University (Shanghai, China). Optional travel to Shanghai tourist sites, Beijing at an extra cost. Students typically earn 4-10 semester credits per term.
Sessions • Classes begin weekly, year-round.
Eligibility Requirements • Minimum age 17; open to precollege students, freshmen, sophomores, juniors, seniors, graduate students, adults; no foreign language proficiency required.
Living Arrangements • Students live in host institution dormitories, locally rented apartments. Quarters are shared with students from other programs. Meals are taken on one's own, in central dining facility.
Costs (2005) • Contact sponsor for cost. $45 application fee.
For More Information • Ms. Alima K. Virtue, Program Director, Center for Study Abroad (CSA), 325 Washington Avenue South #93, Kent, WA 98032; *Phone:* 206-726-1498; *Fax:* 253-850-0454. *E-mail:* info@centerforstudyabroad.com. *World Wide Web:* http://www.centerforstudyabroad.com/

CIEE
CIEE STUDY CENTER AT DONGHUA UNIVERSITY, SHANGHAI, CHINA

Hosted by Donghua University
Academic Focus • Chinese language and literature, Chinese studies.
Program Information • Students attend classes at Donghua University (Shanghai, China). Field trips to temples; the countryside; government agencies, Nanjing; Chinese companies and factories, media, traditional Chinese clinics, museums, acrobatic show, a river cruise, Pelang Opera, Chinese talent show. Students typically earn 9 semester credits per term.
Sessions • Jun-Aug (summer).
Eligibility Requirements • Minimum age 18; open to sophomores, juniors, seniors, adults; course work in Chinese area studies course recommended; 2.75 GPA; 1 letter of recommendation; good academic standing at home school; if more than 1 semester of Mandarin Chinese, evaluation should be from a language professor; 1 year of college course work in Mandarin Chinese.
Living Arrangements • Students live in locally rented apartments, host family homes. Quarters are shared with host institution students. Meals are taken on one's own, with host family, in residences, in restaurants.
Costs (2006) • $5200; includes tuition, housing, insurance, excursions, student support services, visa fees, cultural activities, pre-departure advising, optional on-site pick-up, orientation, resident director. $30 application fee. $300 nonrefundable deposit required. Financial aid available for all students: scholarships, minority student scholarships, Department of Education grant, travel grants.

For More Information • Information Center, CIEE, 7 Custom House Street, 3rd Floor, Portland, ME 04101; *Phone:* 800-40-STUDY; *Fax:* 207-553-7699. *E-mail:* studyinfo@ciee.org. *World Wide Web:* http://www.ciee.org/isp/

COLLEGE CONSORTIUM FOR INTERNATIONAL STUDIES–COLLEGE OF STATEN ISLAND/CITY UNIVERSITY OF NEW YORK
CUNY PROGRAM IN SHANGHAI, CHINA

Hosted by Shanghai University
Academic Focus • Chinese language and literature, international business.
Program Information • Students attend classes at Shanghai University (Shanghai, China). Field trips to the Jade Buddha Temple, Yu Yuan Garden, the Shanghai Museum, local businesses, Suzhow, Hanzhow. Students typically earn 6 semester credits per term.
Sessions • Jun-Jul (summer), Dec-Jan (January winter intersession).
Eligibility Requirements • Minimum age 18; open to freshmen, sophomores, juniors, seniors, graduate students, adults; 2.5 GPA; 1 letter of recommendation; essay; transcript; no foreign language proficiency required.
Living Arrangements • Students live in host institution dormitories. Quarters are shared with students from other programs. Meals are taken on one's own, in central dining facility, in restaurants.
Costs (2007) • $1510 for CCIS members; all others contact sponsor for cost; includes tuition, housing, some meals, insurance, excursions, books and class materials, student support services, fees, airport ground transfer. $330 nonrefundable deposit required. Financial aid available for students from sponsoring institution: loans, grants.
For More Information • College Consortium for International Studies–College of Staten Island/City University of New York, 2000 P Street, NW, Suite 503, Washington, DC 20036; *Phone:* 202-223-0330; *Fax:* 202-223-0999. *E-mail:* info@ccisabroad.org. *World Wide Web:* http://www.ccisabroad.org/. Students may also apply through College of Staten Island, The City University of New York, Center for International Service, Building 2A, Room 206, 2800 Victory Boulevard, Staten Island, NY 10314.

COLUMBIA UNIVERSITY
SUMMER BUSINESS CHINESE AND INTERNSHIP PROGRAM IN SHANGHAI

Hosted by Shanghai Jiaotong University
Academic Focus • Chinese language and literature.
Program Information • Students attend classes at Shanghai Jiaotong University (Shanghai, China). Field trips to the Great Wall, local temples, Ming tombs; optional travel to sites in China at an extra cost. Students typically earn 10 semester credits per term.
Sessions • Jun-Aug (summer).
Eligibility Requirements • Minimum age 18; open to sophomores, juniors, seniors, graduate students, adults; 3.0 GPA; 1 letter of recommendation; good academic standing at home school; no foreign language proficiency required.
Living Arrangements • Students live in host family homes, hotels. Meals are taken on one's own, with host family, in residences, in central dining facility, in restaurants.
Costs (2005) • $4800; includes tuition, housing, some meals, excursions, books and class materials, student support services, private tutoring. $35 application fee. $500 nonrefundable deposit required.
For More Information • Information Center, Columbia University, 2970 Broadway, MC 4110, 303 Lewisohn, New York, NY 10027-6902; *Phone:* 212-854-9699; *Fax:* 212-854-5841. *E-mail:* beijing@columbia.edu. *World Wide Web:* http://www.ce.columbia.edu/op/

LEXIA INTERNATIONAL
LEXIA SUMMER IN SHANGHAI

Hosted by Fudan University
Academic Focus • Anthropology, area studies, art history, Asian studies, Chinese language and literature, Chinese studies, civilization studies, comparative history, cultural studies, economics, ethnic

studies, geography, history, interdisciplinary studies, international affairs, liberal studies, literature, political science and government, social sciences, sociology.

Program Information • Students attend classes at Fudan University (Shanghai, China). Scheduled travel to Hong Kong, Shenzhen; field trips to the Pudong Economic Zone, nearby villages, Beijing. Students typically earn 8-10 semester credits per term.

Sessions • Jun-Aug (summer).

Eligibility Requirements • Minimum age 18; open to freshmen, sophomores, juniors, seniors, graduate students, adults; 2.5 GPA; 2 letters of recommendation; no foreign language proficiency required.

Living Arrangements • Students live in host institution dormitories. Quarters are shared with host institution students. Meals are taken on one's own, in residences, in central dining facility.

Costs (2006) • $6450; includes tuition, housing, some meals, insurance, excursions, international student ID, student support services, transcript, computer access. $40 application fee. $300 nonrefundable deposit required. Financial aid available for all students: scholarships, work study.

For More Information • Lexia International, 23 South Main Street, Hanover, NH 03755; *Phone:* 800-775-3942; *Fax:* 603-643-9899. *E-mail:* info@lexiaintl.org. *World Wide Web:* http://www.lexiaintl. org/

NEW YORK UNIVERSITY
COMPARATIVE APPROACH TO MULILINGUAL, MULTICULTURAL EDUCATION

Academic Focus • Bilingual education, teaching, teaching English as a second language.

Program Information • Faculty members are drawn from the sponsor's U.S. staff and local instructors hired by the sponsor. Field trips to Victoria Peak, Great Wall, Tiananmen Square, Macau. Students typically earn 6 semester credits per term.

Sessions • Jun-Jul (summer).

Eligibility Requirements • Minimum age 18; open to graduate students; major in teaching and learning; letter(s) of recommendation; good academic standing at home school; advisor approval; no foreign language proficiency required.

Living Arrangements • Students live in host institution dormitories. Meals are taken on one's own, in restaurants.

Costs (2005) • $5634; includes tuition, registration fees. $50 application fee.

For More Information • Mr. Daniel Young, Program Associate, New York University, 82 Washington Square East, New York, NY 10003; *Phone:* 212-992-9380. *E-mail:* dy14@nyu.edu. *World Wide Web:* http://www.nyu.edu/global/studyabroad.html

SYRACUSE UNIVERSITY
LAW AND BUSINESS IN CHINA

Academic Focus • Business administration/management, finance, law and legal studies.

Program Information • Faculty members are drawn from the sponsor's U.S. staff. Students typically earn 6 semester credits per term.

Sessions • May-Jun (summer).

Eligibility Requirements • Open to freshmen, sophomores, juniors, seniors, graduate students, adults; 1 letter of recommendation; good academic standing at home school; no foreign language proficiency required.

Living Arrangements • Students live in hotels. Meals are taken on one's own, in restaurants.

Costs (2005) • $6685; includes tuition, housing, some meals, excursions, international student ID, student support services. $55 application fee. $350 nonrefundable deposit required. Financial aid available for all students: loans, need-based tuition grants.

For More Information • Mrs. Daisy Fried, Associate Director, Syracuse University, 106 Walnut Place, Syracuse, NY 13244-4170; *Phone:* 800-251-9674; *Fax:* 315-443-4593. *E-mail:* dipasum@syr.edu. *World Wide Web:* http://suabroad.syr.edu/

VILLANOVA UNIVERSITY
STUDIES IN CHINESE BUSINESS, CULTURE, AND SOCIETY

Hosted by East China Normal University Shanghai

Academic Focus • International business.

Program Information • Students attend classes at East China Normal University Shanghai (Shanghai, China). Scheduled travel to Beijing; field trips to the Shanghai Museum, Buddha temple, local businesses, Great Wall. Students typically earn 3 semester credits per term.

Sessions • Jun-Aug (summer).

Eligibility Requirements • Minimum age 18; open to juniors, seniors, graduate students; major in business/commerce, finance; course work in business; 2.5 GPA; 2 letters of recommendation; good academic standing at home school; no foreign language proficiency required.

Living Arrangements • Students live in host institution dormitories. Quarters are shared with host institution students. Meals are taken on one's own, in restaurants.

Costs (2005) • $3750; includes tuition, housing, some meals, excursions, international airfare, international student ID. $450 deposit required. Financial aid available for students from sponsoring institution.

For More Information • Dr. Wen Mao, Professor, Villanova University, Bartley Hall, Room 346, 800 Lancaster Avenue, Villanova, PA 19085; *Phone:* 610-519-6429; *Fax:* 610-519-7649. *E-mail:* wen.mao@villanova.edu. *World Wide Web:* http://www. internationalstudies.villanova.edu/

SHENYANG

BEMIDJI STATE UNIVERSITY
SINOSUMMER

Hosted by Liaoning University

Academic Focus • Anthropology, economics, geography, history, international affairs, political science and government, sociology.

Program Information • Students attend classes at Liaoning University (Shenyang, China). Scheduled travel to Beijing, Shenyang, Xi'an, Guangzhou, Guilin, Hong Kong, Hawaii; field trips to Inner Mongolia, farms, factories, a zoo, a steel mill. Students typically earn 12 semester credits per term.

Sessions • May-Jun (summer).

Eligibility Requirements • Minimum age 18; open to sophomores, juniors, seniors, graduate students, adults; 2.0 GPA; good academic standing at home school; sophomore status; no foreign language proficiency required.

Living Arrangements • Students live in host institution dormitories, hotels. Meals are taken as a group, in central dining facility, in restaurants.

Costs (2005) • $4000; includes tuition, housing, all meals, excursions, international airfare, lab equipment, student support services, 2-week tour. $150 nonrefundable deposit required. Financial aid available for students from sponsoring institution: scholarships, loans, grants.

For More Information • Ms. LaMae Ritchie, Director, International Program Center, Bemidji State University, Deputy Hall 103, Box 13, 1500 Birchmont Drive, NE, Bemidji, MN 56601-2699; *Phone:* 218-755-4096; *Fax:* 218-755-2074. *E-mail:* lritchie@bemidjistate.edu. *World Wide Web:* http://www.bemidjistate.edu/international/ study_abroad.htm

SUZHOU

SOUTHERN METHODIST UNIVERSITY
SMU-IN-SUZHOU

Hosted by Suzhou University

Academic Focus • Cultural studies.

Program Information • Students attend classes at Suzhou University (Suzhou, China). Scheduled travel to Shanghai, Nanjing, Beijing, Xian; field trips. Students typically earn 3 semester credits per term.

Sessions • May-Jun (summer).

Eligibility Requirements • Open to sophomores, juniors, seniors; 2.5 GPA; 1 letter of recommendation; good academic standing at home school; interview; no foreign language proficiency required.
Living Arrangements • Students live in host institution dormitories. Quarters are shared with host institution students. Meals are taken as a group, in central dining facility.
Costs (2005) • $3530; includes tuition, housing, some meals, excursions, student support services. $40 application fee. $400 deposit required. Financial aid available for students from sponsoring institution: scholarships, loans.
For More Information • Ms. Nancy Simmons, Associate Director, Southern Methodist University, The International Center/Study Abroad, SMU PO Box 750391, Dallas, TX 75275-0391; *Phone:* 214-768-2338; *Fax:* 214-768-1051. *E-mail:* intlpro@mail.smu.edu. *World Wide Web:* http://www.smu.edu/studyabroad/

TAIPEI

LANGUAGE LIAISON
MANDARIN IN TAIWAN

Hosted by Language Liaison
Academic Focus • Chinese language and literature.
Program Information • Students attend classes at Language Liaison (Taipei, Taiwan). Students typically earn 3–15 semester credits per term.
Sessions • Classes begin weekly, year-round.
Eligibility Requirements • Minimum age 17; open to freshmen, sophomores, juniors, seniors, graduate students, adults; no foreign language proficiency required.
Living Arrangements • Students live in host institution dormitories, locally rented apartments, host family homes, hotels. Meals are taken on one's own, with host family, in residences, in restaurants.
Costs (2005) • Contact sponsor for cost. $175 application fee. Financial aid available for all students: scholarship research service.
For More Information • Ms. Nancy Forman, President, Language Liaison, PO Box 1772, Pacific Palisades, CA 90272; *Phone:* 800-284-4448; *Fax:* 310-454-1706. *E-mail:* learn@languageliaison.com. *World Wide Web:* http://www.languageliaison.com/

TIANJIN

MICHIGAN STATE UNIVERSITY
CHINESE LANGUAGE AND CULTURE

Held at Nankai University
Academic Focus • Chinese language and literature, Chinese studies.
Program Information • Classes are held on the campus of Nankai University (Tianjin, China). Faculty members are drawn from the sponsor's U.S. staff. Field trips to the Great Wall, the Forbidden City, the ancient city of Si'an. Students typically earn 8 semester credits per term.
Sessions • May–Jul (summer), Program runs every other year.
Eligibility Requirements • Minimum age 18; open to freshmen, sophomores, juniors, seniors, graduate students; major in Chinese, arts and letters; 2.5 GPA; good academic standing at home school; minimum 2.5 GPA overall; minimum 3.0 GPA in Chinese; 1 year of college course work in Chinese.
Living Arrangements • Students live in host institution dormitories. Meals are taken on one's own, in central dining facility.
Costs (2004) • $2268; includes housing, some meals, insurance, student support services, some field trips. $100 application fee. $200 nonrefundable deposit required. Financial aid available for students from sponsoring institution: scholarships, loans.
For More Information • Ms. Darla Conley, Secretary, Michigan State University, Office of Study Abroad, 109 International Center, East Lansing, MI 48824-1035; *Phone:* 517-355-4654; *Fax:* 517-353-8727. *E-mail:* conleyd@msu.edu. *World Wide Web:* http://studyabroad.msu.edu/

XI'AN

XI'AN JIAOTONG UNIVERSITY/SINO-AMERICAN FIELD SCHOOL OF ARCHAEOLOGY
SUMMER EXCAVATION PRACTICUM AND CHINESE CULTURE HISTORY STUDIES IN XI'AN, CHINA

Hosted by Sino-American Field School, Xi'an Jiaotong University/Sino-American Field School of Archaeology
Academic Focus • Archaeology, Chinese studies.
Program Information • Students attend classes at Sino-American Field School (Xi'an, China), Xi'an Jiaotong University/Sino-American Field School of Archaeology (Xi'an, China). Scheduled travel to Shanghai, Nanjing, Beijing (Great Wall and Ming Tombs); field trips to Xi'an, Beijing. Students typically earn 6 semester credits per term.
Sessions • Jul–Aug (summer).
Eligibility Requirements • Minimum age 17; open to juniors, seniors, graduate students; 1 letter of recommendation; good academic standing at home school; no foreign language proficiency required.
Living Arrangements • Students live in hotels. Meals are taken as a group.
Costs (2005) • $3795; includes tuition, housing, all meals, excursions, international airfare, books and class materials, lab equipment. $200 application fee.
For More Information • Dr. Alfonz Lengyel, Professor, Director, Xi'an Jiaotong University/Sino-American Field School of Archaeology, 4206-73rd Terrace East, Sarasota, FL 34273; *Phone:* 941-351-8208; *Fax:* 941-351-8208. *E-mail:* fmfsatsa@juno.com

 OLOMBIA

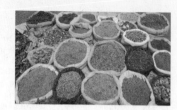

BOGOTÁ

NUEVA LENGUA
NUEVA LENGUA/UNIVERSIDAD DE LA SABANA INTERNATIONAL PROGRAMS

Hosted by Universidad de la Sabana
Academic Focus • Cultural studies, Latin American studies, Spanish language and literature.
Program Information • Students attend classes at Universidad de la Sabana (Bogotá, Colombia). Field trips to Villa de Leyva, Guatavita, Zipaquira, coffee region; optional travel to Cartagena at an extra cost. Students typically earn 5-12 semester credits per term.
Sessions • Jun-Jul (summer).
Eligibility Requirements • Minimum age 18; open to freshmen, sophomores, juniors, seniors, graduate students, adults; 2 letters of recommendation; good academic standing at home school; 1 year of college course work in Spanish.
Living Arrangements • Students live in host family homes. Meals are taken with host family.
Costs (2007) • $3500; includes tuition, housing, some meals, books and class materials, student support services. $40 application fee. $100 nonrefundable deposit required.
For More Information • Juan David Medina, Nueva Lengua, Edigicio G, Oficina G-109, Km 21 Autopista norte de Bogóta, Universidad de la Sabana, Departamento de Lenguas, Bogóta, Colombia; *Phone:* +1 202-4702555; *Fax:* +1 202-5210624. *E-mail:* summerterm@nuevalengua.com. *World Wide Web:* http://www.nuevalengua.com

COSTA RICA

CITY-TO-CITY

CENTER FOR CULTURAL INTERCHANGE
COSTA RICA LANGUAGE SCHOOL

Hosted by Cosí Language Institute
Academic Focus • Spanish language and literature.
Program Information • Students attend classes at Cosí Language Institute (Manuel Antonio), Cosí Language Institute (San José). Field trips to cultural activities, guided city tours, museum visits.
Sessions • 3, 4, or 6 week sessions begin every Monday, year-round.
Eligibility Requirements • Minimum age 14; open to precollege students, freshmen, sophomores, juniors, seniors, graduate students, adults; no foreign language proficiency required.
Living Arrangements • Students live in host family homes. Quarters are shared with host institution students. Meals are taken with host family, in residences.
Costs (2005) • $2700 for 4 weeks; includes tuition, housing, some meals, insurance, books and class materials, student support services, cultural activities. Financial aid available for students from sponsoring institution: scholarships.
For More Information • Ms. Juliet Jones, Outbound Programs Director, Center for Cultural Interchange, 325 West Huron, Suite 706, Chicago, IL 60610; *Phone:* 866-684-9675; *Fax:* 312-944-2644. *E-mail:* info@cci-exchange. com. *World Wide Web:* http://www.cci-exchange.com/

ESTUDIO SAMPERE
INTENSIVE SPANISH COURSES IN COSTA RICA

Hosted by Estudio Sampere
Academic Focus • Spanish language and literature, Spanish studies, translation.
Program Information • Students attend classes at Estudio Sampere (San José Coranado).
Sessions • 2 to 12 week sessions held year-round, classes begin on the first Monday of every month.
Eligibility Requirements • Minimum age 17; open to precollege students, freshmen, sophomores, seniors, graduate students, adults; no foreign language proficiency required.
Living Arrangements • Students live in host institution dormitories, program-owned apartments, host family homes. Quarters are shared with host institution students. Meals are taken on one's own, with host family.
Costs (2006) • $710 for 2 weeks; $5400 for 16 weeks; includes tuition, some meals, insurance, excursions, books and class materials, student support services, homestay housing. $150 application fee. $200 nonrefundable deposit required.
For More Information • Mr. Juan M. Sampere, Director, Estudio Sampere, Lagasca, 16, 28001 Madrid, Spain; *Phone:* +34 91-431 4366; *Fax:* +34 91-575 9509. *E-mail:* jmanuel@sampere.es. *World Wide Web·* http://www.sampere.es/. Students may also apply through Spanish Works, Inc., PO Box 1434, Healdsburg, CA 95448.

INTERCULTURA COSTA RICA
INTENSIVE SPANISH WITH CULTURAL ACTIVITIES

Hosted by Intercultura Costa Rica, Intercultura Samara Beach School
Academic Focus • Costa Rican studies, culinary arts, dance, intercultural studies, Spanish language and literature.
Program Information • Students attend classes at Intercultura Costa Rica (Heredia), Intercultura Samara Beach School (Samara Beach). Scheduled travel to Arenal Volcano and lake, Tortuguero National Park, Manuel Antonio National Park and beach, Monteverde National Park; field trips to Poás Volcano, Los Chorros waterfalls, coffee plantations, Cafe Britt, a San José museum tour, the National Institute of Biodiversity, Zoo-Ave, a local market; optional travel to Isla Tortuga, Monteverde Cloud Forest, Braulio Carillo, Tamarindo Beach, rafting on the Pacuarc River at an extra cost. Students typically earn 3–12 semester credits per term.
Sessions • Year-round, classes begin every Monday.
Eligibility Requirements • Minimum age 16; open to precollege students, freshmen, sophomores, juniors, seniors, graduate students, adults; genuine interest in learning the language and culture; no foreign language proficiency required.
Living Arrangements • Students live in locally rented apartments, host family homes, hotels. Meals are taken with host family, in residences, in restaurants.
Costs (2004–2005) • $1165 for the first 4 weeks; $280 per week thereafter; includes tuition, housing, some meals, excursions, books and class materials, lab equipment, international student ID, student support services, cultural lecture series, intercambio, daily Latin dance classes, cooking class, cultural activities. Financial aid available for all students: work-study English teacher exchange.

COSTA RICA
City-to-City

For More Information • Ms. Laura Ellington, Founding Director, Intercultura Costa Rica, Apartado 1952-3000, Heredia, Costa Rica; *Phone:* +50 6-260-8480; *Fax:* +50 6-260-9243. *E-mail:* info@ interculturacostarica.com. *World Wide Web:* http://www. interculturacostarica.com/. Students may also apply through Intercultura SJO, COD 364, PO Box 025369, Miami, FL 33102.

LANGUAGE LIAISON
ALAJUELA, COSTA RICA

Hosted by Language Liaison
Academic Focus • Spanish language and literature.
Program Information • Students attend classes at Language Liaison (Alajuela). Field trips; optional travel at an extra cost. Students typically earn 3–15 semester credits per term.
Sessions • Classes begin weekly, year-round.
Eligibility Requirements • Minimum age 16; open to precollege students, freshmen, sophomores, juniors, seniors, graduate students, adults; no foreign language proficiency required.
Living Arrangements • Students live in locally rented apartments, host family homes, hotels. Meals are taken on one's own, with host family, in residences, in restaurants.
Costs (2005) • Contact sponsor for cost. $175 application fee. Financial aid available for all students: scholarship research service.
For More Information • Ms. Nancy Forman, President, Language Liaison, PO Box 1772, Pacific Palisades, CA 90272; *Phone:* 800-284-4448; *Fax:* 310-454-1706. *E-mail:* learn@languageliaison. com. *World Wide Web:* http://www.languageliaison.com/

LANGUAGE LINK
INTERCULTURA

Hosted by Intercultura Costa Rica, Intercultura Costa Rica
Academic Focus • Spanish language and literature.
Program Information • Students attend classes at Intercultura Costa Rica (Samara), Intercultura Costa Rica (Heredia). Scheduled travel to Sámara Beach program; field trips to national parks, beaches. Students typically earn 6–15 semester credits per term.
Sessions • Year-round, start any Monday.
Eligibility Requirements • Minimum age 18; open to freshmen, sophomores, juniors, seniors, graduate students, adults; no foreign language proficiency required.
Living Arrangements • Students live in host family homes. Quarters are shared with host institution students. Meals are taken with host family, in residences.
Costs (2005) • $300 per week; includes tuition, housing, some meals, books and class materials, student support services, cultural activities, airport pick-up.
For More Information • Ms. Kay G. Rafool, Director, Language Link, PO Box 3006, Peoria, IL 61612-3006; *Phone:* 800-552-2051; *Fax:* 309-692-2926. *E-mail:* info@langlink.com. *World Wide Web:* http://www.langlink.com/

MICHIGAN STATE UNIVERSITY
ENVIRONMENTAL STUDIES IN COSTA RICA

Academic Focus • Environmental science/studies.
Program Information • Faculty members are drawn from the sponsor's U.S. staff. Field trips to national parks, mountain ranges, volcanoes. Students typically earn 6 semester credits per term.
Sessions • Dec–Jan (winter break).
Eligibility Requirements • Minimum age 18; open to freshmen, sophomores, juniors, seniors; 2.0 GPA; good academic standing at home school; faculty approval; good physical condition; no foreign language proficiency required.
Living Arrangements • Students live in hotels, a field station, a campsite. Meals are taken as a group, on one's own, in central dining facility, in restaurants.
Costs (2004–2005) • $2182 (estimated); includes housing, insurance, excursions, books and class materials, student support services, in-country transportation. $100 application fee. $200 nonrefundable deposit required. Financial aid available for students from sponsoring institution: scholarships, loans.
For More Information • Mr. Mark Davis, Coordinator, Michigan State University, Office of Study Abroad, 109 International Center,

East Lansing, MI 48824-1035; *Phone:* 517-432-1315; *Fax:* 517-432-2082. *E-mail:* mdavis@msu.edu. *World Wide Web:* http://studyabroad. msu.edu/

ORGANIZATION FOR TROPICAL STUDIES
OTS UNDERGRADUATE ETHNOBIOLOGY COURSE

Held at La Selva Biological Station, Las Cruces Biological Station
Academic Focus • Biological/life sciences, botany, conservation studies, pharmacology, Spanish language and literature.
Program Information • Classes are held on the campus of La Selva Biological Station (Puerto Viejo), Las Cruces Biological Station (San Vito). Faculty members are drawn from the sponsor's U.S. staff and local instructors hired by the sponsor. Scheduled travel to Guaymi Indian reservation, Guaitil, La Cruz; field trips to national parks, Indian reservations. Students typically earn 7 semester credits per term.
Sessions • Jul–Aug (summer).
Eligibility Requirements • Open to freshmen, sophomores, juniors, seniors; course work in biology; 1 letter of recommendation; good academic standing at home school; 1 year of college course work in Spanish.
Living Arrangements • Students live in host institution dormitories, host family homes, biological field stations. Quarters are shared with host institution students. Meals are taken as a group, in central dining facility.
Costs (2005–2006) • $5800; includes tuition, housing, all meals, excursions, books and class materials, lab equipment. $1000 refundable deposit required. Financial aid available for students: scholarships for minorities and under-represented groups in the sciences.
For More Information • Mr. Rodney J. Vargas, Undergraduate Program Officer, Organization for Tropical Studies, Box 90630, Durham, NC 27708-0630; *Phone:* 919-684-5774; *Fax:* 919-684-5661. *E-mail:* nao@duke.edu. *World Wide Web:* http://www.ots.duke.edu/

UNIVERSITY OF CALIFORNIA, SANTA BARBARA, WILDLANDS STUDIES
ENVIRONMENTS AND CULTURES OF COSTA RICA

Academic Focus • Ecology, environmental science/studies, geography, wildlife studies.
Program Information • Faculty members are drawn from the sponsor's U.S. staff. Scheduled travel to ecological field locations. Students typically earn 15 quarter credits per term.
Sessions • Jun–Aug (summer).
Eligibility Requirements • Minimum age 18; open to freshmen, sophomores, juniors, seniors; course work in biology or geography; good academic standing at home school; application essay; no foreign language proficiency required.
Living Arrangements • Students live in host family homes, tents. Meals are taken as a group.
Costs (2006) • $1995; includes tuition. $75 application fee.
For More Information • Mr. Crandall Bay, Director, Wildlands Studies Program, University of California, Santa Barbara, Wildlands Studies, 3 Mosswood Circle, Cazadero, CA 95421; *Phone:* 707-632-5665; *Fax:* 707-632-5665. *E-mail:* wildlands@sonic.net. *World Wide Web:* http://www.wildlandsstudies.com/

UNIVERSITY OF NORTH CAROLINA AT WILMINGTON
COSTA RICA SUMMER PROGRAM

Academic Focus • Biological/life sciences, psychology.
Program Information • Faculty members are drawn from the sponsor's U.S. staff. Scheduled travel; field trips to various jungle sites. Students typically earn 6 semester credits per term.
Sessions • May–Jun (summer).
Eligibility Requirements • Good academic standing at home school; college level course work in psychology or biology or consent of instructor; no foreign language proficiency required.
Living Arrangements • Students live in hotels. Meals are taken as a group, in central dining facility.
Costs (2005) • $3000 for North Carolina residents; $4000 for nonresidents; includes tuition, housing, all meals, insurance, international airfare, student support services. $200 nonrefundable

deposit required. Financial aid available for students from sponsoring institution: scholarships, loans.

For More Information • Ms. Elizabeth A. Adams, Director, Education Abroad, University of North Carolina at Wilmington, 601 South College Road, Wilmington, NC 28403-5965; *Phone:* 910-962-3685; *Fax:* 910-962-4053. *E-mail:* studyabroad@uncw.edu. *World Wide Web:* http://www.uncw.edu/intprogs/

ALAJUELA

LANGUAGE LIAISON
SPANISH IN ALAJUELA, COSTA RICA

Hosted by Language Liaison

Academic Focus • Spanish language and literature.

Program Information • Students attend classes at Language Liaison (Alajuela, Costa Rica). Field trips; optional travel at an extra cost. Students typically earn 3-15 semester credits per term.

Sessions • Classes begin weekly, year-round.

Eligibility Requirements • Minimum age 14; open to precollege students, freshmen, sophomores, juniors, seniors, graduate students, adults; no foreign language proficiency required.

Living Arrangements • Students live in locally rented apartments, host family homes, hotels. Meals are taken on one's own, with host family, in residences, in restaurants.

Costs (2005) • Contact sponsor for cost. $175 application fee. Financial aid available for all students: scholarship research service.

For More Information • Ms. Nancy Forman, President, Language Liaison, PO Box 1772, Pacific Palisades, CA 90272; *Phone:* 800-284-4448; *Fax:* 310-454-1706. *E-mail:* learn@languageliaison. com. *World Wide Web:* http://www.languageliaison.com/

ATENAS

THE SCHOOL FOR FIELD STUDIES
COSTA RICA: SUSTAINING TROPICAL ECOSYSTEMS: BIODIVERSITY, CONSERVATION, AND DEVELOPMENT

Hosted by Center for Sustainable Development

Academic Focus • Agriculture, biological/life sciences, conservation studies, Costa Rican studies, ecology, economics, environmental science/studies, forestry, Latin American studies, natural resources.

Program Information • Students attend classes at Center for Sustainable Development (Atenas, Costa Rica). Scheduled travel to the Pacific coastal region; field trips to the Carara Biological Reserve, Poás Volcano. Students typically earn 4 semester credits per term.

Sessions • Jun–Jul (summer), Jul–Aug (summer 2).

Eligibility Requirements • Minimum age 16; open to precollege students, freshmen, sophomores, juniors, seniors; 2.5 GPA; 2 letters of recommendation; personal statement; no foreign language proficiency required.

Living Arrangements • Students live in host institution dormitories. Quarters are shared with host institution students. Meals are taken as a group, in central dining facility.

Costs (2007) • $3665; includes tuition, housing, all meals, excursions, lab equipment. $45 application fee. $450 nonrefundable deposit required. Financial aid available for all students: scholarships, loans.

For More Information • Admissions Department, The School for Field Studies, 10 Federal Street, Suite 24, Salem, MA 01970-3876; *Phone:* 800-989-4418; *Fax:* 978-741-3551. *E-mail:* admissions@ fieldstudies.org. *World Wide Web:* http://www.fieldstudies.org/

CURRIDABAT

LANGUAGE LIAISON
LEARN SPANISH IN COSTA RICA

Hosted by Language Liaison

Academic Focus • Spanish language and literature.

Program Information • Students attend classes at Language Liaison (Curridabat, Costa Rica). Field trips; optional travel at an extra cost. Students typically earn 3-15 semester credits per term.

Sessions • New programs begin weekly, year-round.

Eligibility Requirements • Minimum age 16; open to precollege students, freshmen, sophomores, juniors, seniors, graduate students, adults; no foreign language proficiency required.

Living Arrangements • Students live in locally rented apartments, host family homes, hotels. Meals are taken on one's own, with host family, in residences, in restaurants.

Costs (2005) • Contact sponsor for cost. $175 application fee. Financial aid available for all students: scholarship research service.

For More Information • Ms. Nancy Forman, President, Language Liaison, PO Box 1772, Pacific Palisades, CA 90272; *Phone:* 800-284-4448; *Fax:* 310-454-1706. *E-mail:* learn@languageliaison. com. *World Wide Web:* http://www.languageliaison.com/

FLAMINGO BEACH

ENFOREX–SPANISH IN THE SPANISH WORLD
SPANISH INTENSIVE COURSE FLAMINGO BEACH

Hosted by ENFOREX

Academic Focus • Spanish language and literature, Spanish studies.

Program Information • Students attend classes at ENFOREX (Flamingo Beach, Costa Rica). Field trips to the Guanacaste region; optional travel to a rainforest, volcanoes at an extra cost. Students typically earn 4 semester credits per term.

Sessions • Year-round.

Eligibility Requirements • Minimum age 18; open to freshmen, juniors, seniors, graduate students, adults; no foreign language proficiency required.

Living Arrangements • Students live in host family homes, hotels. Meals are taken as a group, on one's own, with host family.

Costs (2005) • $1390 per month; includes tuition, housing, all meals, excursions, books and class materials, lab equipment, international student ID, student support services. $100 application fee. $250 nonrefundable deposit required.

For More Information • Mr. Antonio Anadón, Director of Spanish Department, ENFOREX-Spanish in the Spanish World, Alberto Aguilera, 26, 28015 Madrid, Spain; *Phone:* +34 91-594-3776; *Fax:* +34 91-594-5159. *E-mail:* promotion@enforex.es. *World Wide Web:* http://www.enforex.com/

HEREDIA

ENFOREX–SPANISH IN THE SPANISH WORLD
SPANISH INTENSIVE COURSE HEREDIA

Hosted by ENFOREX

Academic Focus • Spanish language and literature, Spanish studies.

Program Information • Students attend classes at ENFOREX (Heredia, Costa Rica). Field trips to colonial sites; optional travel to a rainforest at an extra cost. Students typically earn 4 semester credits per term.

Sessions • Year-round.

Eligibility Requirements • Minimum age 18; open to freshmen, juniors, seniors, graduate students, adults; no foreign language proficiency required.

Living Arrangements • Students live in host family homes, hotels. Meals are taken as a group, on one's own, with host family.

Costs (2005) • $1390 per month; includes tuition, housing, all meals, excursions, books and class materials, lab equipment, international student ID, student support services. $100 application fee. $250 nonrefundable deposit required.

For More Information • Mr. Antonio Anadón, Director of Spanish Department, ENFOREX-Spanish in the Spanish World, Alberto Aguilera, 26, 28015 Madrid, Spain; *Phone:* +34 91-594-3776; *Fax:* +34 91-594-5159. *E-mail:* promotion@enforex.es. *World Wide Web:* http://www.enforex.com/

COSTA RICA
Heredia

UNIVERSITY STUDIES ABROAD CONSORTIUM
SPANISH, ECOLOGICAL, AND LATIN AMERICAN STUDIES: HEREDIA, COSTA RICA

Hosted by National University

Academic Focus • Anthropology, bilingual education, biological/life sciences, dance, ecology, environmental science/studies, history, Latin American studies, Spanish language and literature.

Program Information • Students attend classes at National University (Heredia, Costa Rica). Field trips to INBio Parque, Arenal Volcano, Monteverde Cloud Forest, Fortuna, Café Britt, Poas Volcano; optional travel to southern Costa Rica, Playa Dominical, Drake's Bay, Corcovado National Park at an extra cost. Students typically earn 6–12 semester credits per term.

Sessions • May–Jun (summer), Jun–Aug (summer 2).

Eligibility Requirements • Minimum age 18; open to freshmen, sophomores, juniors, seniors, graduate students, adults; 2.5 GPA; no foreign language proficiency required.

Living Arrangements • Students live in host family homes. Meals are taken on one's own, with host family, in residences, in restaurants.

Costs (2007) • $2880 for 1 session; $5660 for 2 sessions; includes tuition, housing, some meals, insurance, excursions, student support services, transportation from airport to Heredia, entry to some museums and cultural events. $100 application fee. $200 refundable deposit required. Financial aid available for all students: scholarships, loans.

For More Information • University Studies Abroad Consortium, USAC/323, Reno, NV 89557-0093; *Phone:* 775-784-6569; *Fax:* 775-784-6010. *E-mail:* usac@unr.edu. *World Wide Web:* http://usac.unr.edu/

LIMÓN

RUTGERS, THE STATE UNIVERSITY OF NEW JERSEY
SUMMER STUDY AND SERVICE PROGRAM IN COSTA RICA

Academic Focus • Costa Rican studies, teaching English as a second language.

Program Information • Faculty members are drawn from the sponsor's U.S. staff and local instructors hired by the sponsor. Field trips to San José. Students typically earn 6 semester credits per term.

Sessions • May–Jun (summer).

Eligibility Requirements • Open to freshmen, sophomores, juniors, seniors; 2.5 GPA; 1 letter of recommendation; good academic standing at home school; official transcript from all tertiary schools attended; no foreign language proficiency required.

Living Arrangements • Students live in hotels. Meals are taken on one's own, in residences, in restaurants.

Costs (2005) • $2951 for New Jersey residents; $3951 for nonresidents; includes tuition, housing, insurance, excursions, student support services. $20 application fee. $500 nonrefundable deposit required. Financial aid available for students from sponsoring institution: scholarships, loans.

For More Information • Ms. Lindy Black, Regional Coordinator, Rutgers, The State University of New Jersey, 102 College Avenue, New Brunswick, NJ 08901-8543; *Phone:* 732-932-7787; *Fax:* 732-932-8659. *E-mail:* ru_abroad@email.rutgers.edu. *World Wide Web:* http://studyabroad.rutgers.edu/

MANUEL ANTONIO

LANGUAGE LIAISON
LEARN SPANISH AT MANUEL ANTONIO

Hosted by Language Liaison

Academic Focus • Spanish language and literature.

Program Information • Students attend classes at Language Liaison (Manuel Antonio, Costa Rica). Field trips; optional travel at an extra cost. Students typically earn 3–5 semester credits per term.

Sessions • Classes begin weekly, year-round.

Eligibility Requirements • Minimum age 16; open to precollege students, freshmen, sophomores, juniors, seniors, graduate students, adults; no foreign language proficiency required.

Living Arrangements • Students live in host institution dormitories, locally rented apartments, host family homes, hotels. Meals are taken as a group, on one's own, with host family, in residences.

Costs (2005) • Contact sponsor for cost. $175 application fee. Financial aid available for all students.

For More Information • Ms. Nancy Forman, President, Language Liaison, PO Box 1772, Pacific Palisades, CA 90272; *Phone:* 800-284-4448; *Fax:* 310-454-1706. *E-mail:* learn@languageliaison.com. *World Wide Web:* http://www.languageliaison.com/

LINGUA SERVICE WORLDWIDE
COSTA RICA SPANISH INSTITUTE

Hosted by Costa Rica Spanish Institute

Academic Focus • Spanish language and literature, Spanish studies.

Program Information • Students attend classes at Costa Rica Spanish Institute (Manuel Antonio, Costa Rica). Optional travel at an extra cost. Students typically earn 3 semester credits for 3 weeks, 6 semester credits for 5 weeks.

Sessions • Year-round sessions of 2 or more weeks.

Eligibility Requirements • Minimum age 16; open to precollege students, freshmen, sophomores, juniors, seniors, graduate students, adults; no foreign language proficiency required.

Living Arrangements • Students live in locally rented apartments, host family homes, hotels. Quarters are shared with host institution students. Meals are taken on one's own.

Costs (2006–2007) • Contact sponsor for cost. $100 application fee.

For More Information • Assistant Director, Lingua Service Worldwide, 75 Prospect Street, Suite 4, Huntington, NY 11743; *Phone:* 800-394-5327; *Fax:* 631-271-3441. *E-mail:* linguaservice@att.net. *World Wide Web:* http://www.linguaserviceworldwide.com/

MONTEVERDE

ASSOCIATED COLLEGES OF THE SOUTH
SUSTAINABLE DEVELOPMENT–COSTA RICA

Held at Costa Rica Conservation Foundation

Academic Focus • Anthropology, biological/life sciences, conservation studies, economics, environmental science/studies, forestry, history, political science and government.

Program Information • Classes are held on the campus of Costa Rica Conservation Foundation (Monteverde, Costa Rica). Faculty members are drawn from the sponsor's U.S. staff and local instructors hired by the sponsor. Scheduled travel to the lowlands, cloud forests, the foothills of the coast, rainforests; field trips to sustainable development projects, cheese factory, coffee farm, coffee processing plant, butterfly garden, amphibian exhibit. Students typically earn 8 semester credits per term.

Sessions • Jun–Jul (summer).

Eligibility Requirements • Open to sophomores, juniors, seniors; 1 letter of recommendation; good academic standing at home school; junior or senior status preferred.

Living Arrangements • Students live in host institution dormitories, hotels. Quarters are shared with host institution students. Meals are taken as a group, in central dining facility, in restaurants.

Costs (2005) • $3750; includes tuition, housing, all meals, excursions, books and class materials, student support services. $50 application fee. $500 refundable deposit required. Financial aid available for students from sponsoring institution.

For More Information • Dr. Barry Allen, Environmental Studies Department, Associated Colleges of the South, 1000 Holt Avenue, Winter Park, FL 32789; *Phone:* 407-646-2647; *Fax:* 407-646-2364. *E-mail:* ballen@rollins.edu. *World Wide Web:* http://www.colleges.org/~international/

CIEE
CIEE STUDY CENTER IN MONTEVERDE, COSTA RICA– TROPICAL ECOLOGY AND CONSERVATION

Hosted by Biological Station of Monteverde

Academic Focus • Agriculture, biological/life sciences, Spanish language and literature.
Program Information • Students attend classes at Biological Station of Monteverde (Monteverde, Costa Rica). Scheduled travel to Corcovado National Park, Santa Rosa National Park, Tortuguero National Park, La Selva Forest; field trips to San José, Carara National Park, San Gerardo, San Luis. Students typically earn 10 semester credits per term.
Sessions • Jun–Aug (summer).
Eligibility Requirements • Minimum age 18; open to sophomores, juniors, seniors; course work in 1 semester biology: 1 additional semester biology, ecology, or environmental; 2.75 GPA; 1 letter of recommendation; good academic standing at home school; some Spanish recommended.
Living Arrangements • Students live in host family homes, a biological station, hostels, tents. Quarters are shared with host institution students. Meals are taken as a group, in residences, in central dining facility, in restaurants.
Costs (2006) • $4900; includes tuition, housing, all meals, insurance, excursions, books and class materials, lab equipment, student support services, pre-departure advising, cultural activities, national park entry fees, camping equipment, field house lab access, resident director, on-site pick-up. $30 application fee. $300 nonrefundable deposit required. Financial aid available for all students: minority student scholarships, travel grants, 1 specific program scholarship.
For More Information • Information Center, CIEE, 7 Custom House Street, 3rd Floor, Portland, ME 04101; *Phone:* 800-40-STUDY; *Fax:* 207-553-7699. *E-mail:* studyinfo@ciee.org. *World Wide Web:* http://www.ciee.org/isp/

ENFOREX–SPANISH IN THE SPANISH WORLD
SPANISH INTENSIVE COURSE MONTE VERDE

Hosted by ENFOREX
Academic Focus • Spanish language and literature, Spanish studies.
Program Information • Students attend classes at ENFOREX (Monteverde, Costa Rica). Field trips to colonial sites; optional travel to a rainforest, a tropical forest at an extra cost. Students typically earn 4 semester credits per term.
Sessions • Year-round.
Eligibility Requirements • Minimum age 18; open to freshmen, juniors, seniors, graduate students, adults; no foreign language proficiency required.
Living Arrangements • Students live in host family homes. Meals are taken as a group, on one's own, with host family.
Costs (2005) • $1390 per month; includes tuition, housing, all meals, excursions, books and class materials, lab equipment, international student ID, student support services. $100 application fee. $250 nonrefundable deposit required.
For More Information • Mr. Antonio Anadón, Director of Spanish Department, ENFOREX-Spanish in the Spanish World, Alberto Aguilera, 26, 28015 Madrid, Spain; *Phone:* +34 91-594-3776; *Fax:* +34 91-594-5159. *E-mail:* promotion@enforex.es. *World Wide Web:* http://www.enforex.com/

PUERTO VIEJO DE TALAMANCA

UNIVERSITY OF KANSAS
FIELD METHODS IN APPLIED CULTURAL ANTHROPOLOGY

Academic Focus • Anthropology.
Program Information • Faculty members are drawn from the sponsor's U.S. staff and local instructors hired by the sponsor. Scheduled travel to San José, Cartago, Monteverde Cloud Forest. Students typically earn 3 semester credits per term.
Sessions • Jun (summer).
Eligibility Requirements • Minimum age 18; open to freshmen, sophomores, juniors, seniors, graduate students; 2.5 GPA; 2 letters of recommendation; good academic standing at home school; no foreign language proficiency required.
Living Arrangements • Students live in hotels. Meals are taken as a group, on one's own, in restaurants.

Costs (2005) • $2050; includes tuition, housing, some meals, excursions, student support services, emergency medical evacuation and repatriation services. $38 application fee. $300 nonrefundable deposit required. Financial aid available for students from sponsoring institution: scholarships, loans.
For More Information • Ms. Angela Dittrich, Assistant Director, University of Kansas, Office of Study Abroad, Lippincott Hall, 1410 Jayhawk Boulevard, Room 108, Lawrence, KS 66045-7515; *Phone:* 785-864-3742; *Fax:* 785-864-5040. *E-mail:* osa@ku.edu. *World Wide Web:* http://www.ku.edu/~osa/

PUNTARENAS

UNIVERSITY STUDIES ABROAD CONSORTIUM
SPANISH ECOLOGICAL AND LATIN AMERICAN STUDIES: PUNTARENAS, COSTA RICA

Hosted by National University
Academic Focus • Anthropology, biological/life sciences, dance, ecology, Latin American studies, Spanish language and literature, Spanish studies.
Program Information • Students attend classes at National University (Puntarenas, Costa Rica). Field trips to Montezuma beach, Curo wildlife refuge, Cloud Forest, national park, crocodile tour, Arenal volcano, waterfall tour; optional travel to Southern Costa Rica tour at an extra cost. Students typically earn 6 semester credits per term.
Sessions • May–Jun (summer), Jun–Aug (summer 2).
Eligibility Requirements • Minimum age 18; open to freshmen, sophomores, juniors, seniors, graduate students, adults; 2.5 GPA.
Living Arrangements • Students live in locally rented apartments, host family homes. Quarters are shared with host institution students. Meals are taken on one's own, with host family, in residences, in restaurants.
Costs (2007) • $3280 for 1 session; $6460 for 2 sessions; includes tuition, housing, insurance, excursions. $100 application fee. $200 refundable deposit required. Financial aid available for all students: scholarships, loans.
For More Information • University Studies Abroad Consortium, USAC/323, Reno, NV 89557-0093; *Phone:* 775-784-6569; *Fax:* 775-784-6010. *E-mail:* usac@unr.edu. *World Wide Web:* http://usac.unr.edu/

QUEPOS

LANGUAGE LIAISON
SPANISH IN COSTA RICA–QUEPOS

Hosted by Language Liaison
Academic Focus • Spanish language and literature.
Program Information • Students attend classes at Language Liaison (Quepos, Costa Rica). Field trips; optional travel at an extra cost. Students typically earn 3–15 semester credits per term.
Sessions • Classes begin weekly, year-round.
Eligibility Requirements • Minimum age 18; open to precollege students, freshmen, sophomores, juniors, seniors, graduate students, adults; no foreign language proficiency required.
Living Arrangements • Students live in locally rented apartments, host family homes, hotels. Meals are taken on one's own, with host family, in residences, in restaurants.
Costs (2005) • Contact sponsor for cost. $175 application fee. Financial aid available for all students: scholarship research service.
For More Information • Ms. Nancy Forman, President, Language Liaison, PO Box 1772, Pacific Palisades, CA 90272; *Phone:* 800-284-4448; *Fax:* 310-454-1706. *E-mail:* learn@languageliaison.com. *World Wide Web:* http://www.languageliaison.com/

SAN JOAQUIN DE FLORES

ACADEMIC PROGRAMS INTERNATIONAL (API)
(API)–SAN JOAQUIN DE FLORES (COSTA RICA)

Hosted by Instituto San Joaquin de Flores

COSTA RICA
San Joaquin de Flores

Academic Focus • Environmental science/studies, Latin American studies, Spanish language and literature, Spanish studies.
Program Information • Students attend classes at Instituto San Joaquin de Flores (San Joaquin de Flores, Costa Rica). Field trips to Tortuga Island, San Vase, Punta Uva and Puerto Viejo, Manuel Antonio; Playa Carillo. Students typically earn 6 semester credits per term.
Sessions • Jun–Jul (summer).
Eligibility Requirements • Minimum age 18; open to freshmen, sophomores, juniors, seniors; 2.75 GPA; 1 letter of recommendation; good academic standing at home school; official transcript from home university; no foreign language proficiency required.
Living Arrangements • Students live in host family homes. Quarters are shared with host institution students. Meals are taken on one's own, with host family.
Costs (2006–2007) • $4200; includes tuition, housing, all meals, insurance, excursions, student support services, airport reception, on-site director, online services. $150 nonrefundable deposit required. Financial aid available for all students: scholarships.
For More Information • Ms. Jennifer C. Allen, Director, Academic Programs International (API), 107 East Hoplins, San Marcos, TX 78666; *Phone:* 800-844-4124; *Fax:* 512-392-8420. *E-mail:* api@academicintl.com. *World Wide Web:* http://www.academicintl.com/

SAN JOSÉ

ACADEMIC PROGRAMS INTERNATIONAL (API)
(API)–SAN JOSÉ, COSTA RICA
Hosted by University of Costa Rica
Academic Focus • Earth sciences, geology, international business, Spanish language and literature, Spanish studies.
Program Information • Students attend classes at University of Costa Rica (San José, Costa Rica). Field trips to Manuel Antonio/Quepos-Puntarenas, Tortuga Island Cruise. Students typically earn 6 semester credits per term.
Sessions • July.
Eligibility Requirements • Minimum age 18; open to freshmen, sophomores, juniors, seniors; 2.75 GPA; 1 letter of recommendation; good academic standing at home school; official transcript from home university; no foreign language proficiency required.
Living Arrangements • Students live in host family homes. Quarters are shared with host institution students. Meals are taken on one's own, with host family.
Costs (2006) • $4200; includes tuition, housing, insurance, excursions, student support services, airport reception; online services; on-site director. $150 nonrefundable deposit required. Financial aid available for all students: scholarships.
For More Information • Ms. Jennifer C. Allen, Director, Academic Programs International (API), 107 East Hopkins, San Marcos, TX 78666; *Phone:* 800-844-4124; *Fax:* 512-392-8420. *E-mail:* api@academicintl.com. *World Wide Web:* http://www.academicintl.com/

CENTER FOR STUDY ABROAD (CSA)
UNIVERSITY OF VERITAS
Hosted by Veritas University
Academic Focus • Latin American studies, Spanish language and literature, Spanish studies.
Program Information • Students attend classes at Veritas University (San José, Costa Rica). Optional travel. Students typically earn 4–15 semester credits per term.
Sessions • 1 month sessions held year-round.
Eligibility Requirements • Minimum age 18; open to precollege students, freshmen, sophomores, juniors, seniors, graduate students, adults; no foreign language proficiency required.
Living Arrangements • Students live in host family homes. Meals are taken with host family.
Costs (2005–2006) • Contact sponsor for cost. $45 application fee.
For More Information • Ms. Alima K. Virtue, Program Director, Center for Study Abroad (CSA), 325 Washington Avenue South #93, Kent, WA 98032; *Phone:* 206-726-1498; *Fax:* 253-850-0454. *E-mail:* info@centerforstudyabroad.com. *World Wide Web:* http://www.centerforstudyabroad.com/

COLLEGE CONSORTIUM FOR INTERNATIONAL STUDIES–MIAMI DADE COLLEGE
INTENSIVE SPANISH IN COSTA RICA–SAN JOSÉ
Hosted by Centro Lingüístico CONVERSA
Academic Focus • Spanish language and literature.
Program Information • Students attend classes at Centro Lingüístico CONVERSA (San José, Costa Rica). Optional travel to the Pacific coast, national parks, volcanoes at an extra cost. Students typically earn 6 semester credits per term.
Sessions • 1 month cycles throughout the year.
Eligibility Requirements • Minimum age 18; open to freshmen, sophomores, juniors, seniors, graduate students, adults; 2.5 GPA; 2 letters of recommendation; good academic standing at home school; no foreign language proficiency required.
Living Arrangements • Students live in host family homes. Meals are taken with host family, in residences.
Costs (2006) • $2680 per 4 week session; includes tuition, housing, some meals, insurance, books and class materials, student support services. $30 application fee. $300 nonrefundable deposit required. Financial aid available for students from sponsoring institution: loans.
For More Information • Center for International Education, College Consortium for International Studies–Miami Dade College, 100 East Normal, Kirk Building 114, Kirksville, MO 63501; *Phone:* 660-785-4076; *Fax:* 660-785-7473. *E-mail:* ciea@truman.edu. *World Wide Web:* http://www.ccisabroad.org/. Students may also apply through Miami Dade College, Office of International Education, 300 NE 2nd Avenue, Suite 1450, Miami, FL 33132-2297.

COLLEGE CONSORTIUM FOR INTERNATIONAL STUDIES–MIAMI DADE COLLEGE
VERITAS SUMMER IN COSTA RICA (SAN JOSÉ)
Hosted by Veritas University
Academic Focus • Costa Rican studies, ecology, environmental science/studies, international business, Latin American literature, marine sciences, social sciences, Spanish language and literature.
Program Information • Students attend classes at Veritas University (San José, Costa Rica). Optional travel to volcanoes, national parks, the Pacific coast at an extra cost. Students typically earn 8 semester credits per term.
Sessions • Jul–Aug (summer).
Eligibility Requirements • Minimum age 18; open to freshmen, sophomores, juniors, seniors, adults; 2.5 GPA; 2 letters of recommendation; good academic standing at home school; no foreign language proficiency required.
Living Arrangements • Students live in locally rented apartments, host family homes. Quarters are shared with students from other programs. Meals are taken with host family, in residences.
Costs (2006) • $3400 for 5 weeks; $4400 for 8 weeks (estimated); includes tuition, housing, some meals, insurance. $30 application fee. $300 nonrefundable deposit required. Financial aid available for students from sponsoring institution: loans.
For More Information • Center for International Education, College Consortium for International Studies–Miami Dade College, 100 East Normal, Kirk Building 114, Kirksville, MO 63501; *Phone:* 660-785-4076; *Fax:* 660-785-7473. *E-mail:* ciea@truman.edu. *World Wide Web:* http://www.ccisabroad.org/. Students may also apply through Miami Dade College, Office of International Education, 300 NE 2nd Avenue, Suite 1450, Miami, FL 33132-2297.

COLLEGE CONSORTIUM FOR INTERNATIONAL STUDIES–TRUMAN STATE UNIVERSITY
INTENSIVE SPANISH IN COSTA RICA–SAN JOSÉ
Hosted by Centro Lingüístico CONVERSA
Academic Focus • Spanish language and literature.
Program Information • Students attend classes at Centro Lingüístico CONVERSA (San José, Costa Rica). Optional travel to the Pacific coast, national parks, volcanoes at an extra cost. Students typically earn 8 semester credits per term.
Sessions • 1 month sessions held year-round.

Eligibility Requirements • Minimum age 18; open to freshmen, sophomores, juniors, seniors, graduate students, adults; 2.5 GPA; 2 letters of recommendation; good academic standing at home school; no foreign language proficiency required.

Living Arrangements • Students live in host family homes. Meals are taken with host family, in residences.

Costs (2006–2007) • $2922 per 4 week session; includes tuition, housing, some meals, insurance, books and class materials, student support services. $300 nonrefundable deposit required. Financial aid available for students from sponsoring institution: loans.

For More Information • Center for International Education, College Consortium for International Studies–Truman State University, 100 East Normal, Kirk Building 114, Kirksville, MO 63501; *Phone:* 660-785-4076; *Fax:* 660-785-7473. *E-mail:* ciea@truman.edu. *World Wide Web:* http://www.ccisabroad.org/

COLLEGE CONSORTIUM FOR INTERNATIONAL STUDIES–TRUMAN STATE UNIVERSITY
VERITAS SUMMER IN COSTA RICA (SAN JOSÉ)

Hosted by Veritas University

Academic Focus • Costa Rican studies, ecology, environmental science/studies, international business, Latin American literature, marine sciences, social sciences, Spanish language and literature.

Program Information • Students attend classes at Veritas University (San José, Costa Rica). Optional travel to volcanoes, national parks, the Pacific coast at an extra cost. Students typically earn 8 semester credits per term.

Sessions • Jul–Aug (summer), Jul–Aug (5 weeks).

Eligibility Requirements • Minimum age 18; open to freshmen, sophomores, juniors, seniors, adults; 2.5 GPA; 2 letters of recommendation; good academic standing at home school; no foreign language proficiency required.

Living Arrangements • Students live in locally rented apartments, host family homes. Quarters are shared with students from other programs. Meals are taken with host family, in residences.

Costs (2007) • $3500 for 5 weeks; $4500 for 8 weeks; includes tuition, housing, some meals, insurance. $300 nonrefundable deposit required. Financial aid available for students from sponsoring institution: loans.

For More Information • Center for International Education, College Consortium for International Studies–Truman State University, 100 East Normal, Kirk Building 114, Kirksville, MO 63501; *Phone:* 660-785-4076; *Fax:* 660-785-7473. *E-mail:* ciea@truman.edu. *World Wide Web:* http://www.ccisabroad.org/. Students may also apply through Miami Dade College, Office of International Education, 300 NE 2nd Avenue, Miami, FL 33132-2297.

INTERNATIONAL STUDIES ABROAD
SAN JOSÉ, COSTA RICA: INTENSIVE MONTH

Hosted by Veritas University

Academic Focus • Spanish language and literature.

Program Information • Students attend classes at Veritas University (San José, Costa Rica). Optional travel at an extra cost. Students typically earn 4-5 semester credits per term.

Sessions • Intensive month periods begin during the first 10 days of each month: Jan–May, Aug–Dec.

Eligibility Requirements • Minimum age 18; open to freshmen, sophomores, juniors, seniors, graduate students, adults; 2.5 GPA; good academic standing at home school; 1 letter of recommendation if GPA is lower than 2.5; no foreign language proficiency required.

Living Arrangements • Students live in locally rented apartments, host family homes. Quarters are shared with host institution students, students from other programs. Meals are taken with host family, in residences.

Costs (2005–2006) • Contact sponsor for cost. $200 deposit required. Financial aid available for all students: scholarships, loans, U.S. federal financial aid.

For More Information • Costa Rica Site Specialist, International Studies Abroad, 901 West 24th Street, Austin, TX 78705; *Phone:* 800-580-8826; *Fax:* 512-480-8866. *E-mail:* isa@studiesabroad.com. *World Wide Web:* http://www.studiesabroad.com/

INTERNATIONAL STUDIES ABROAD
SAN JOSÉ, COSTA RICA–SUMMER LANGUAGE AND CULTURE

Hosted by Latin American University of Science and Technology

Academic Focus • Ecology, Spanish language and literature.

Program Information • Students attend classes at Latin American University of Science and Technology (San José, Costa Rica). Scheduled travel to Manuel Antonio National Park, Arenal Volcano, Puerto Viejo, Cahuita; field trips to Cartago, Irazu Volcano. Students typically earn 6 semester credits per term.

Sessions • May–Aug (summer).

Eligibility Requirements • Minimum age 18; open to freshmen, sophomores, juniors, seniors, graduate students, adults; 2.5 GPA; good academic standing at home school; 1 reference/letter of recommendation if GPA is under 2.5; 2 years of Spanish for regular college courses; 1 year college course work in Spanish for upper-division level courses.

Living Arrangements • Students live in locally rented apartments, host family homes. Quarters are shared with host institution students, students from other programs. Meals are taken with host family, in residences.

Costs (2005–2006) • Contact sponsor for cost. $200 deposit required. Financial aid available for all students: scholarships, loans, U.S. federal financial aid.

For More Information • Costa Rica Site Specialist, International Studies Abroad, 901 West 24th Street, Austin, TX 78705; *Phone:* 800-580-8826; *Fax:* 512-480-8866. *E-mail:* isa@studiesabroad.com. *World Wide Web:* http://www.studiesabroad.com/

INTERNATIONAL STUDIES ABROAD
SAN JOSÉ, COSTA RICA–SUMMER LANGUAGE, CULTURE, AND ECOLOGY

Hosted by Veritas University

Academic Focus • Spanish language and literature.

Program Information • Students attend classes at Veritas University (San José, Costa Rica). Scheduled travel to Arenal Volcano, Monteverde, Puerto Viejo and Cahuita; field trips to Cartago, Irazu Volcano. Students typically earn 4-5 semester credits per term.

Sessions • May–Aug (summer).

Eligibility Requirements • Minimum age 18; open to freshmen, sophomores, juniors, seniors, graduate students, adults; 2.5 GPA; good academic standing at home school; 1 reference/letter of recommendation if GPA is under 2.5; no foreign language proficiency required.

Living Arrangements • Students live in locally rented apartments, host family homes. Quarters are shared with host institution students, students from other programs. Meals are taken with host family, in residences.

Costs (2005) • Contact sponsor for cost. $200 deposit required. Financial aid available for all students: scholarships, loans, U.S. federal financial aid.

For More Information • Costa Rica Site Specialist, International Studies Abroad, 901 West 24th Street, Austin, TX 78705; *Phone:* 800-580-8826; *Fax:* 512-480-8866. *E-mail:* isa@studiesabroad.com. *World Wide Web:* http://www.studiesabroad.com/

LANGUAGE LIAISON
SPANISH IN COSTA RICA

Hosted by Language Liaison

Academic Focus • Spanish language and literature.

Program Information • Students attend classes at Language Liaison (San José, Costa Rica). Field trips; optional travel at an extra cost. Students typically earn 3-15 semester credits per term.

Sessions • New programs begin weekly, year-round.

Eligibility Requirements • Minimum age 16; open to precollege students, freshmen, sophomores, juniors, seniors, graduate students, adults; no foreign language proficiency required.

Living Arrangements • Students live in locally rented apartments, host family homes, hotels. Meals are taken on one's own, with host family, in residences, in restaurants.

Costs (2005) • Contact sponsor for cost. $175 application fee. Financial aid available for all students: scholarship research service.

For More Information • Ms. Nancy Forman, President, Language Liaison, PO Box 1772, Pacific Palisades, CA 90272; *Phone:*

COSTA RICA
San José

800-284-4448; *Fax:* 310-454-1706. *E-mail:* learn@languageliaison. com. *World Wide Web:* http://www.languageliaison.com/

LANGUAGE LINK
ILISA
Hosted by ILISA
Academic Focus • Spanish language and literature.
Program Information • Students attend classes at ILISA (San José, Costa Rica). Field trips to national parks, beaches. Students typically earn 6–15 semester credits per term.
Sessions • Year-round, start any Monday.
Eligibility Requirements • Minimum age 16; open to precollege students, freshmen, sophomores, juniors, seniors, graduate students, adults; no foreign language proficiency required.
Living Arrangements • Students live in locally rented apartments, host family homes, hotels, a guest house. Quarters are shared with host institution students. Meals are taken as a group, with host family, in residences, in central dining facility.
Costs (2005) • $345 per week, plus $200 registration fee; includes tuition, housing, some meals, insurance, books and class materials, lab equipment, student support services, cultural activities.
For More Information • Ms. Kay G. Rafool, Director, Language Link, PO Box 3006, Peoria, IL 61612-3006; *Phone:* 800-552-2051; *Fax:* 309-692-2926. *E-mail:* info@langlink.com. *World Wide Web:* http://www.langlink.com/

LINGUA SERVICE WORLDWIDE
COSTA RICA SPANISH INSTITUTE
Hosted by Costa Rica Spanish Institute
Academic Focus • Spanish language and literature, Spanish studies.
Program Information • Students attend classes at Costa Rica Spanish Institute (San José, Costa Rica). Optional travel at an extra cost. Students typically earn 3 semester credits for 3 weeks, 6 semester credits for 5 weeks.
Sessions • Year-round sessions of 2 or more weeks.
Eligibility Requirements • Minimum age 16; open to precollege students, freshmen, sophomores, juniors, seniors, graduate students, adults; no foreign language proficiency required.
Living Arrangements • Students live in locally rented apartments, host family homes, hotels. Quarters are shared with host institution students. Meals are taken on one's own.
Costs (2006–2007) • Contact sponsor for cost. $100 application fee.
For More Information • Assistant Director, Lingua Service Worldwide, 75 Prospect Street, Suite 4, Huntington, NY 11743; *Phone:* 800-394-5327; *Fax:* 631-271-3441. *E-mail:* linguaservice@att. net. *World Wide Web:* http://www.linguaserviceworldwide.com/

LINGUA SERVICE WORLDWIDE
VACATION 'N LEARN SPANISH IN COSTA RICA
Hosted by Forester International Institute
Academic Focus • Spanish language and literature, Spanish studies.
Program Information • Students attend classes at Forester International Institute (San José, Costa Rica). Optional travel to cultural sites throughout Costa Rica at an extra cost. Students typically earn 3 semester credits for 3 weeks, 6 semester credits for 5 weeks.
Sessions • Sessions of 2 or more weeks begin on Mondays, year-round.
Eligibility Requirements • Minimum age 16; open to precollege students, freshmen, sophomores, juniors, seniors, graduate students, adults; no foreign language proficiency required.
Living Arrangements • Students live in host family homes, hotels. Meals are taken with host family.
Costs (2006–2007) • Contact sponsor for cost. $100 application fee.
For More Information • Assistant Director, Lingua Service Worldwide, 75 Prospect Street, Suite 4, Huntington, NY 11743; *Phone:* 800-394-5327; *Fax:* 631-271-3441. *E-mail:* linguaservice@att. net. *World Wide Web:* http://www.linguaserviceworldwide.com/

MICHIGAN STATE UNIVERSITY
ETHICS AND HISTORY OF DEVELOPMENT AND HEALTH CARE IN COSTA RICA
Hosted by Costa Rica Spanish Institute
Academic Focus • Ethics, history, interdisciplinary studies, philosophy, Spanish language and literature.
Program Information • Students attend classes at Costa Rica Spanish Institute (San José, Costa Rica). Field trips to clinics, hospitals, national parks. Students typically earn 11 semester credits per term.
Sessions • May–Jul (summer).
Eligibility Requirements • Minimum age 18; open to sophomores, juniors, seniors; 2.5 GPA; good academic standing at home school; essay expressing interest in program; no foreign language proficiency required.
Living Arrangements • Students live in host family homes. Meals are taken with host family, in residences.
Costs (2005) • $2337 (estimated); includes housing, some meals, insurance, excursions, student support services. $100 application fee. $200 nonrefundable deposit required. Financial aid available for students from sponsoring institution: scholarships, loans.
For More Information • Mr. Mark Davis, Coordinator, Michigan State University, Office of Study Abroad, 109 International Center, East Lansing, MI 48824-1035; *Phone:* 517-432-1315; *Fax:* 517-432-2082. *E-mail:* mdavis@msu.edu. *World Wide Web:* http://studyabroad. msu.edu/

MODERN LANGUAGE STUDIES ABROAD
MLSA–CHRISTMAS PROGRAM AT UNIVERSIDAD DE COSTA RICA
Hosted by University of Costa Rica
Academic Focus • Civilization studies, Costa Rican studies, cultural studies, Latin American studies, linguistics, Spanish language and literature, Spanish studies, teaching.
Program Information • Students attend classes at University of Costa Rica (San José, Costa Rica). Field trips to Tortuga Island, museums of San José, Volcano Poas, Cartago. Students typically earn 3–9 semester credits per term.
Sessions • Jun–Jul (summer), Dec–Jan (winter).
Eligibility Requirements • Minimum age 17; open to freshmen, sophomores, juniors, seniors, graduate students, adults; Spanish: college level.
Living Arrangements • Students live in locally rented apartments, host family homes. Quarters are shared with host institution students. Meals are taken with host family, in residences.
Costs (2005) • $1985; includes tuition, housing, some meals, excursions, international airfare, books and class materials, student support services. $100 application fee.
For More Information • Dr. Celestino Ruiz, Professor of Spanish, Modern Language Studies Abroad, PO Box 548, Frankfort, IL 60423; *Phone:* 815-464-1800; *Fax:* 815-464-9458. *E-mail:* mlsa@sprintmail. com. *World Wide Web:* http://www.mlsa.com/

MODERN LANGUAGE STUDIES ABROAD
MLSA–INTERNSHIP PROGRAM IN COSTA RICA
Academic Focus • Communication services, computer science, ecology, education, health-care management, hospitality services, hotel and restaurant management, international business, labor and industrial relations, social work, wildlife studies.
Program Information • Faculty members are local instructors hired by the sponsor. Field trips; optional travel at an extra cost. Students typically earn 6 semester credits per term.
Sessions • May–Jun (summer), Jun–Jul (summer 2).
Eligibility Requirements • Minimum age 17; open to freshmen, sophomores, juniors, seniors, graduate students, adults; 2 letters of recommendation; curriculum vitae; 1 year of college course work in Spanish.
Living Arrangements • Students live in host family homes. Meals are taken with host family, in residences.
Costs (2006) • $1985; includes tuition, housing, some meals, international airfare, student support services. $100 application fee.
For More Information • Dr. Celestino Ruiz, Coordinator, Modern Language Studies Abroad, PO Box 548, Frankfort, IL 60423; *Phone:* 815-464-1800; *Fax:* 815-464-9458. *E-mail:* mlsa@sprintmail.com. *World Wide Web:* http://www.mlsa.com/

MODERN LANGUAGE STUDIES ABROAD
MLSA–SPANISH INTENSIVE ONE MONTH PROGRAMS IN COSTA RICA

Hosted by Veritas University

Academic Focus • Architecture, art, biological/life sciences, botany, business administration/management, communications, Costa Rican studies, drawing/painting, ecology, graphic design/illustration, international business, marine sciences, music, oceanography, philosophy, political science and government, Spanish language and literature.

Program Information • Students attend classes at Veritas University (San José, Costa Rica). Field trips to museums, San José, volcanoes, Rain Forest; beaches; optional travel at an extra cost.

Sessions • 4 week courses year-round.

Eligibility Requirements • Minimum age 17; open to freshmen, sophomores, juniors, seniors, graduate students, adults; no foreign language proficiency required.

Living Arrangements • Students live in locally rented apartments, host family homes. Quarters are shared with host institution students, students from other programs. Meals are taken with host family, in residences.

Costs (2007) • $1985; includes tuition, housing, some meals, international airfare, student support services. $100 application fee.

For More Information • Dr. Celestino Ruiz, Director, Study Abroad Programs, Modern Language Studies Abroad, MLSA-PO Box 548, Frankfort, IL 60423; *Phone:* 815-464-1800; *Fax:* 815-464-9458. *E-mail:* info@mlsa.com. *World Wide Web:* http://www.mlsa.com/

MODERN LANGUAGE STUDIES ABROAD
MLSA–SPANISH SEMESTER PROGRAMS IN COSTA RICA

Hosted by Veritas University

Academic Focus • Architecture, art, biological/life sciences, botany, business administration/management, communications, Costa Rican studies, drawing/painting, ecology, graphic design/illustration, international business, marine sciences, music, oceanography, philosophy, political science and government, Spanish language and literature.

Program Information • Students attend classes at Veritas University (San José, Costa Rica). Scheduled travel; field trips; optional travel to museums, volcanoes, beaches, rain forest at an extra cost.

Sessions • Fall: October-Dec; Winter: Jan-March; Spring: Apr-Jun.

Eligibility Requirements • Minimum age 17; open to freshmen, sophomores, juniors, seniors, graduate students, adults; no foreign language proficiency required.

Living Arrangements • Students live in host family homes. Quarters are shared with host institution students, students from other programs. Meals are taken with host family, in residences.

Costs (2007) • $1985; includes tuition, housing, some meals. $100 application fee.

For More Information • Dr. Celestino Ruiz, Professor of Spanish, Modern Language Studies Abroad, PO Box 548, Franfort, IL 60423; *Phone:* 815-464-1800; *Fax:* 815-464-9458. *E-mail:* info@mesa.com. *World Wide Web:* http://www.mlsa.com/

MODERN LANGUAGE STUDIES ABROAD
MLSA–SUMMER STUDY AT THE UNIVERSIDAD DE COSTA RICA–GRADUATE/UNDERGRADUATE

Hosted by University of Costa Rica

Academic Focus • Civilization studies, Costa Rican studies, cultural studies, drama/theater, education, Latin American studies, Spanish language and literature, Spanish studies, teaching.

Program Information • Students attend classes at University of Costa Rica (San José, Costa Rica). Field trips to Tortuga Island, museums of San José, Volcano Poas, Cartago. Students typically earn 6 semester credits per term.

Sessions • May–Jun (summer).

COSTA RICA
San José

Eligibility Requirements • Minimum age 17; open to freshmen, sophomores, juniors, seniors, graduate students, adults; no foreign language proficiency required.
Living Arrangements • Students live in host family homes. Meals are taken with host family, in residences.
Costs (2006) • $1985; includes tuition, housing, some meals, excursions, international airfare, books and class materials, international student ID, student support services. $100 application fee.
For More Information • Dr. Celestino Ruiz, Professor of Spanish, Modern Language Studies Abroad, PO Box 548, Frankfort, IL 60423; *Phone:* 815-464-1800; *Fax:* 815-464-9458. *E-mail:* mlsa@sprintmail.com. *World Wide Web:* http://www.mlsa.com/

NORTHERN ILLINOIS UNIVERSITY
INTERNATIONAL CAREER DEVELOPMENT AND SPANISH LANGUAGE IN COSTA RICA

Hosted by Asesoría Gerencial, S.A.
Academic Focus • Art conservation studies, Costa Rican studies, ecology, interdisciplinary studies, international business, performing arts, Spanish language and literature, urban/regional planning.
Program Information • Students attend classes at Asesoría Gerencial, S.A. (San José, Costa Rica). Scheduled travel; field trips to rainforests, coastal areas. Students typically earn 6–9 semester credits per term.
Sessions • Jun–Jul (summer).
Eligibility Requirements • Minimum age 18; open to juniors, seniors, adults; 2.5 GPA; good academic standing at home school; approval of NIU Chair of Department of Foreign Languages; 2 years of college course work in Spanish.
Living Arrangements • Students live in host family homes. Quarters are shared with host institution students. Meals are taken with host family, in residences.
Costs (2005) • $2750; includes tuition, housing, all meals, insurance, excursions, international student ID. $200 nonrefundable deposit required. Financial aid available for students from sponsoring institution: loans.
For More Information • Ms. Rita Withrow, Program Assistant, Northern Illinois University, Study Abroad Office, Williston Hall 417, DeKalb, IL 60115; *Phone:* 815-753-0700; *Fax:* 815-753-0825. *E-mail:* niuabroad@niu.edu. *World Wide Web:* http://www.niu.edu/niuabroad/

NORTHERN ILLINOIS UNIVERSITY
SPANISH LANGUAGE AND CULTURE IN COSTA RICA

Hosted by Asesoría Gerencial, S.A.
Academic Focus • Latin American studies, Spanish language and literature.
Program Information • Students attend classes at Asesoría Gerencial, S.A. (San José, Costa Rica). Scheduled travel; field trips to rainforests, coasts. Students typically earn 6 semester credits per term.
Sessions • May–Jul (summer).
Eligibility Requirements • Minimum age 18; open to juniors, seniors; 2.75 GPA; good academic standing at home school; approval of NIU Chair of Department of Foreign Languages; 2 years of college course work in Spanish.
Living Arrangements • Students live in host family homes. Quarters are shared with host institution students. Meals are taken with host family, in residences.
Costs (2005) • $3180; includes tuition, housing, all meals, insurance, excursions, international student ID, student support services. $200 nonrefundable deposit required. Financial aid available for students from sponsoring institution: loans.
For More Information • Ms. Rita Withrow, Program Assistant, Northern Illinois University, Study Abroad Office, Williston Hall 417, DeKalb, IL 60115; *Phone:* 815-753-0700; *Fax:* 815-753-0825. *E-mail:* niuabroad@niu.edu. *World Wide Web:* http://www.niu.edu/niuabroad/

ORGANIZATION FOR TROPICAL STUDIES
OTS UNDERGRADUATE SUMMER COURSES IN TROPICAL BIOLOGY

Held at La Selva Biological Station, Las Cruces Biological Station, Palo Verde Biological Station
Academic Focus • Conservation studies, ecology, environmental science/studies.
Program Information • Classes are held on the campus of Palo Verde Biological Station (Bagaces, Costa Rica), La Selva Biological Station (Puerto Viejo, Costa Rica), Las Cruces Biological Station (San Vito, Costa Rica). Faculty members are drawn from the sponsor's U.S. staff and local instructors hired by the sponsor. Scheduled travel to natural reserves, biological field stations, national parks; field trips to biological reserves, national parks. Students typically earn 4 semester credits per term.
Sessions • May–Jun (summer).
Eligibility Requirements • Open to freshmen, sophomores, juniors, seniors; course work in biology; 1 letter of recommendation; good academic standing at home school; no foreign language proficiency required.
Living Arrangements • Students live in biological field stations. Quarters are shared with host institution students. Meals are taken as a group, in central dining facility.
Costs (2005–2006) • $4824; includes tuition, housing, all meals, excursions, books and class materials, lab equipment. $1000 nonrefundable deposit required. Financial aid available for all students: scholarships for under-represented groups in the sciences.
For More Information • Mr. Rodney J. Vargas, Undergraduate Program Officer, Organization for Tropical Studies, Box 90630, Durham, NC 27708-0630; *Phone:* 919-684-5774; *Fax:* 919-684-5661. *E-mail:* nao@duke.edu. *World Wide Web:* http://www.ots.duke.edu/

PITZER COLLEGE
PITZER COLLEGE SUMMER HEALTH PROGRAM IN COSTA RICA

Hosted by Institute for Central American Development Studies
Academic Focus • Health, Spanish language and literature.
Program Information • Students attend classes at Institute for Central American Development Studies (San José, Costa Rica). Field trips. Students typically earn 8 semester credits per term.
Sessions • May–Jul (summer).
Eligibility Requirements • Open to sophomores, juniors, seniors; course work in health development; 2.5 GPA; 1 letter of recommendation; good academic standing at home school; 1 year of college course work in Spanish.
Living Arrangements • Students live in host family homes. Meals are taken with host family, in residences.
Costs (2005) • $7380; includes tuition, housing, all meals, excursions, international airfare, books and class materials, international student ID, student support services, evacuation insurance. $25 application fee. $500 nonrefundable deposit required. Financial aid available for students from sponsoring institution: scholarships, loans.
For More Information • Ms. Neva Barker, Director of External Studies Admissions, Pitzer College, 1050 North Mills Avenue, Claremont, CA 91711; *Phone:* 909-621-8104; *Fax:* 909-621-0518. *E-mail:* external_studies@pitzer.edu. *World Wide Web:* http://www.pitzer.edu/external_studies/

STATE UNIVERSITY OF NEW YORK COLLEGE AT BROCKPORT
COSTA RICA PROGRAM

Hosted by Escuela de Idiomas
Academic Focus • Accounting, business administration/management, communications, computer science, criminal justice, ecology, education, finance, full curriculum, health, health and physical education, history, hotel and restaurant management, international business, journalism, Latin American studies, nursing, parks and recreation, political science and government, psychology, sociology, Spanish language and literature, tourism and travel, zoology.
Program Information • Students attend classes at Escuela de Idiomas (San José, Costa Rica). Field trips to various city-sites in San José. Students typically earn 6–12 semester credits per term.
Sessions • Jul–Aug (summer).
Eligibility Requirements • Minimum age 18; open to sophomores, juniors, seniors, graduate students; course work in area of internship, if applicable; 2.5 GPA; 2 letters of recommendation; good academic standing at home school; ability to do upper-division

course work; résumé for internship option; must be at least a second semester sophomore; 1 year college course work in Spanish.
Living Arrangements • Students live in host family homes. Meals are taken with host family, in residences.
Costs (2005) • Contact sponsor for cost; includes tuition, housing, some meals, excursions, international student ID. $200 nonrefundable deposit required. Financial aid available for students from sponsoring institution: scholarships, loans, regular financial aid, grants.
For More Information • Dr. John J. Perry, Director, Office of International Education, State University of New York College at Brockport, 350 New Campus Drive, Brockport, NY 14420; *Phone:* 800-298-SUNY; *Fax:* 585-637-3218. *E-mail:* overseas@brockport.edu. *World Wide Web:* http://www.brockport.edu/studyabroad/

STATE UNIVERSITY OF NEW YORK COLLEGE AT CORTLAND
COSTA RICA SUMMER

Hosted by Veritas University
Academic Focus • Full curriculum.
Program Information • Students attend classes at Veritas University (San José, Costa Rica). Optional travel to Monte Verde Cloud Forest, beaches, rainforests, mountains. Students typically earn 4–16 semester credits per term.
Sessions • May–Aug (6 sessions).
Eligibility Requirements • Minimum age 18; open to freshmen, sophomores, juniors; 2.5 GPA; 2 letters of recommendation; good academic standing at home school; no foreign language proficiency required.
Living Arrangements • Students live in locally rented apartments, host family homes. Quarters are shared with host institution students, students from other programs. Meals are taken on one's own, in residences, in central dining facility.
Costs (2005) • $2722; includes tuition, housing, all meals, insurance, international airfare, books and class materials, international student ID, student support services. $20 application fee. $200 nonrefundable deposit required. Financial aid available for students from sponsoring institution: scholarships, loans.
For More Information • Ms. Liz McCartney, Assistant Director, Office of International Programs, State University of New York College at Cortland, PO Box 2000, Cortland, NY 13045; *Phone:* 607-753-2209; *Fax:* 607-753-5989. *E-mail:* cortlandabroad@cortland. edu. *World Wide Web:* http://www.cortlandabroad.com/

TEMPLE UNIVERSITY
TEMPLE IN COSTA RICA

Hosted by University of Costa Rica
Academic Focus • Health-care management.
Program Information • Students attend classes at University of Costa Rica (San José, Costa Rica). Field trips to a tropical rainforest, agricultural cooperatives, banana plantations. Students typically earn 6 semester credits per term.
Sessions • May–Jun (summer).
Eligibility Requirements • Open to sophomores, juniors, seniors, graduate students; 2.5 GPA; 1 letter of recommendation; good academic standing at home school; official transcripts; essay; no foreign language proficiency required.
Living Arrangements • Students live in host family homes, hotels. Quarters are shared with host institution students. Meals are taken on one's own, with host family, in residences.
Costs (2005) • $4200–$6000; includes tuition, housing, all meals, program fee, local travel. $30 application fee. $200 nonrefundable deposit required. Financial aid available for students from sponsoring institution: scholarships, loans.
For More Information • Ms. Erin Joslyn, Study Abroad Coordinator, Temple University, International Programs, 200 Tuttleman Learning Center, 1809 North 13th Street, Philadelphia, PA 19122; *Phone:* 215-204-0720; *Fax:* 215-204-0729. *E-mail:* study.abroad@temple.edu. *World Wide Web:* http://www.temple.edu/studyabroad/

UNIVERSITY OF DELAWARE
WINTER SESSION IN COSTA RICA

Academic Focus • Science, wildlife studies.
Program Information • Faculty members are drawn from the sponsor's U.S. staff. Scheduled travel to San José; field trips to national parks. Students typically earn 6 semester credits per term.
Sessions • Jan (winter).
Eligibility Requirements • Open to freshmen, sophomores, juniors, seniors, graduate students, adults; 2.0 GPA; 1 letter of recommendation; no foreign language proficiency required.
Living Arrangements • Students live in host institution dormitories, hotels. Meals are taken as a group, in central dining facility.
Costs (2005) • Contact sponsor for cost. $200 nonrefundable deposit required. Financial aid available for all students: scholarships.
For More Information • Center for International Studies, University of Delaware, 186 South College Avenue, Newark, DE 19716-1450; *Phone:* 888-831-4685; *Fax:* 302-831-6042. *World Wide Web:* http://www.udel.edu/studyabroad/

UNIVERSITY OF DELAWARE
WINTER SESSION IN COSTA RICA: DEPARTMENT OF PHILOSOPHY

Held at Tropical Youth Center
Academic Focus • Philosophy.
Program Information • Classes are held on the campus of Tropical Youth Center (San José, Costa Rica). Faculty members are drawn from the sponsor's U.S. staff. Field trips to cultural sites. Students typically earn 6 semester credits per term.
Sessions • Jan (winter).
Eligibility Requirements • Open to freshmen, sophomores, juniors, seniors, adults; 2.0 GPA; 1 letter of recommendation; no foreign language proficiency required.
Living Arrangements • Students live in host institution dormitories. Quarters are shared with host institution students. Meals are taken as a group, in central dining facility.
Costs (2005) • Contact sponsor for cost. $200 nonrefundable deposit required. Financial aid available for all students: scholarships.
For More Information • Center for International Studies, University of Delaware, 186 South College Avenue, Newark, DE 19716-1450; *Phone:* 888-831-4685; *Fax:* 302-831-6042. *E-mail:* studyabroad@udel. edu. *World Wide Web:* http://www.udel.edu/studyabroad/

UNIVERSITY OF DELAWARE
WINTER SESSION IN COSTA RICA: FOREIGN LANGUAGES AND LITERATURES

Held at Latin University of Costa Rica
Academic Focus • Costa Rican studies, Spanish language and literature.
Program Information • Classes are held on the campus of Latin University of Costa Rica (San José, Costa Rica). Faculty members are drawn from the sponsor's U.S. staff and local instructors hired by the sponsor. Scheduled travel to Tamarindo, Manuel Antonio National Park; field trips to a coffee plantation, Teatro Nacional, Arenal and Poas Volcanoes; optional travel to Latin America at an extra cost. Students typically earn 6–7 semester credits per term.
Sessions • Jan–Feb (winter).
Eligibility Requirements • Open to freshmen, sophomores, juniors, seniors, adults; 2.0 GPA; 1 letter of recommendation; 1 year of college course work in Spanish.
Living Arrangements • Students live in host family homes. Quarters are shared with host institution students. Meals are taken with host family, in residences.
Costs (2005) • Contact sponsor for cost. $200 nonrefundable deposit required. Financial aid available for all students: scholarships.
For More Information • Center for International Studies, University of Delaware, 186 South College Avenue, Newark, DE 19716-1450; *Phone:* 888-831-4685; *Fax:* 302-831-6042. *E-mail:* studyabroad@udel. edu. *World Wide Web:* http://www.udel.edu/studyabroad/

THE UNIVERSITY OF NORTH CAROLINA AT CHARLOTTE
SPANISH LANGUAGE AND CULTURE IN COSTA RICA

Hosted by Forester International Institute

COSTA RICA
San José

Academic Focus • Costa Rican studies, Spanish language and literature.
Program Information • Students attend classes at Forester International Institute (San José, Costa Rica). Field trips to various points of interest in and around San José. Students typically earn 6 semester credits per term.
Sessions • Jul–Aug (summer).
Eligibility Requirements • Minimum age 18; open to freshmen, sophomores, juniors, seniors, graduate students, adults; 2.5 GPA; 1 letter of recommendation; good academic standing at home school; no foreign language proficiency required.
Living Arrangements • Students live in host family homes. Meals are taken with host family, in residences.
Costs (2005) • $2900; includes tuition, housing, some meals, insurance, excursions, international airfare, student support services. $10 application fee. $300 refundable deposit required. Financial aid available for students from sponsoring institution: scholarships, loans.
For More Information • Mr. Brad Sekulich, Interim Director of Education Abroad, The University of North Carolina at Charlotte, 9201 University City Boulevard, Charlotte, NC 28223-0001; *Phone:* 704-687-2464; *Fax:* 704-687-3168. *E-mail:* edabroad@email.uncc.edu. *World Wide Web:* http://www.uncc.edu/edabroad/

SAN RAMÓN

UNIVERSITY OF NEW ORLEANS
UNO–COSTA RICA

Held at University of Costa Rica–San Ramon
Academic Focus • Anthropology, archaeology, biological/life sciences, civilization studies, comparative history, comparative literature, conservation studies, Costa Rican studies, ecology, environmental science/studies, geography, geology, history, natural resources, political science and government, social sciences, Spanish language and literature.
Program Information • Classes are held on the campus of University of Costa Rica–San Ramon (San Ramon, Costa Rica). Faculty members are drawn from the sponsor's U.S. staff and local instructors hired by the sponsor. Field trips to Quepos, San José, Monteverde, Arenal Volcano. Students typically earn 6 semester credits per term.
Sessions • May–Jun (summer).
Eligibility Requirements • Minimum age 18; open to freshmen, sophomores, juniors, seniors, graduate students, adults; 2.5 GPA; good academic standing at home school; no foreign language proficiency required.
Living Arrangements • Students live in host family homes. Meals are taken with host family, in residences, in restaurants.
Costs (2005) • $2595; includes tuition, housing, some meals, insurance, excursions, student support services. $150 application fee. $150 refundable deposit required. Financial aid available for students from sponsoring institution: scholarships, loans, need-based aid.
For More Information • Ms. Marie Kaposchyn, Program Director, University of New Orleans, PO Box 569, New Orleans, LA 70148; *Phone:* 504-280-7455; *Fax:* 504-280-7317. *E-mail:* mkaposch@uno.edu. *World Wide Web:* http://inst.uno.edu/

SANTA ANA

COLLEGE CONSORTIUM FOR INTERNATIONAL STUDIES–MIAMI DADE COLLEGE
INTENSIVE SPANISH IN COSTA RICA–SANTA ANA

Hosted by Centro Lingüístico CONVERSA
Academic Focus • Spanish language and literature.
Program Information • Students attend classes at Centro Lingüístico CONVERSA (Santa Ana, Costa Rica). Optional travel to national parks, Pacific coast resorts at an extra cost. Students typically earn 6 semester credits per term.
Sessions • 1 month cycles throughout the year.
Eligibility Requirements • Minimum age 18; open to freshmen, sophomores, juniors, seniors, graduate students, adults; 2.5 GPA; 2 letters of recommendation; good academic standing at home school; no foreign language proficiency required.
Living Arrangements • Students live in host family homes, lodges on the Santa Ana campus. Meals are taken with host family, in residences.
Costs (2006) • $3355 per 4 week session; includes tuition, housing, all meals, insurance, books and class materials, student support services. $300 nonrefundable deposit required. Financial aid available for students from sponsoring institution: loans.
For More Information • Center for International Education, College Consortium for International Studies–Miami Dade College, 100 East Normal, Kirk Building 114, Kirksville, MO 63501; *Phone:* 660-785-4076; *Fax:* 660-785-7473. *E-mail:* ciea@truman.edu. *World Wide Web:* http://www.ccisabroad.org/. Students may also apply through Miami Dade College, Office of International Education, 300 NE 2nd Avenue, Suite 1450, Miami, FL 33132.

COLLEGE CONSORTIUM FOR INTERNATIONAL STUDIES–TRUMAN STATE UNIVERSITY
INTENSIVE SPANISH IN COSTA RICA–SANTA ANA

Hosted by Centro Lingüístico CONVERSA
Academic Focus • Spanish language and literature.
Program Information • Students attend classes at Centro Lingüístico CONVERSA (Santa Ana, Costa Rica). Optional travel to national parks, Pacific coast resorts at an extra cost. Students typically earn 8 semester credits per term.
Sessions • 1 month sessions held year-round.
Eligibility Requirements • Minimum age 18; open to freshmen, sophomores, juniors, seniors, graduate students, adults; 2.5 GPA; 2 letters of recommendation; good academic standing at home school; no foreign language proficiency required.
Living Arrangements • Students live in host family homes, lodges on the Santa Ana campus. Meals are taken with host family, in residences.
Costs (2007) • $3555 per 4 week session; includes tuition, housing, all meals, insurance, books and class materials, student support services. $300 nonrefundable deposit required. Financial aid available for students from sponsoring institution: loans.
For More Information • Center for International Education, College Consortium for International Studies–Truman State University, 100 East Normal, Kirk Building 114, Kirksville, MO 63501; *Phone:* 660-785-4076; *Fax:* 660-785-7473. *E-mail:* ciea@truman.edu. *World Wide Web:* http://www.ccisabroad.org/

LANGUAGE LIAISON
SPANISH IN SANTA ANA, COSTA RICA

Hosted by Language Liaison
Academic Focus • Spanish language and literature.
Program Information • Students attend classes at Language Liaison (Santa Ana, Costa Rica). Field trips; optional travel at an extra cost. Students typically earn 3–15 semester credits per term.
Sessions • New programs begin weekly, year-round.
Eligibility Requirements • Minimum age 17; open to precollege students, freshmen, sophomores, juniors, seniors, graduate students, adults; no foreign language proficiency required.
Living Arrangements • Students live in program-owned apartments, host family homes, lodges. Meals are taken on one's own, with host family, in residences.
Costs (2005) • Contact sponsor for cost. $175 application fee. Financial aid available for all students: scholarship research service.
For More Information • Ms. Nancy Forman, President, Language Liaison, PO Box 1772, Pacific Palisades, CA 90272; *Phone:* 800-284-4448; *Fax:* 310-454-1706. *E-mail:* learn@languageliaison.com. *World Wide Web:* http://www.languageliaison.com/

SANTA CLARA

KENTUCKY INSTITUTE FOR INTERNATIONAL STUDIES
COSTA RICA

Held at Technological Institute of Costa Rica San Carlos Campus

Academic Focus • Education.

Program Information • Classes are held on the campus of Technological Institute of Costa Rica San Carlos Campus (San Carlos, Costa Rica). Faculty members are drawn from the sponsor's U.S. staff. Scheduled travel; field trips to a rainforest, Arenal Volcano, the Tabacon Thermal Water Complex. Students typically earn 3–6 semester credits per term.

Sessions • Jun (summer).

Eligibility Requirements • Minimum age 18; open to freshmen, sophomores, juniors, seniors, graduate students, adults; 3.0 GPA; 1 letter of recommendation; no foreign language proficiency required.

Living Arrangements • Students live in host institution dormitories. Quarters are shared with host institution students. Meals are taken as a group, in restaurants.

Costs (2006) • $2290; includes housing, some meals, insurance, excursions, international airfare, international student ID, instructional expenses. $150 application fee. Financial aid available for all students: scholarships.

For More Information • Ms. Nancy Martin, Coordinator, Kentucky Institute for International Studies, PO Box 9, Murray, KY 42071-0009; *Phone:* 270-762-3091; *Fax:* 270-762-3434. *E-mail:* kiismsu@murraystate.edu. *World Wide Web:* http://www.kiis.org/

TAMARINDO

EF INTERNATIONAL LANGUAGE SCHOOLS
SPANISH IN COSTA RICA

Hosted by EF Escuela Internacional de Español

Academic Focus • Spanish language and literature.

Program Information • Students attend classes at EF Escuela Internacional de Español (Tamarindo, Costa Rica). Scheduled travel; field trips to La Guácima, Monteverde, San José, Parque Nacional Chirripó; optional travel at an extra cost.

Sessions • Program length 2 to 52 weeks; year round.

Eligibility Requirements • Minimum age 16; open to precollege students, freshmen, sophomores, juniors, seniors, graduate students, adults; no foreign language proficiency required.

Living Arrangements • Students live in host family homes. Quarters are shared with host institution students. Meals are taken with host family, in residences.

Costs (2006–2007) • $790 for 2 weeks; includes tuition, housing, some meals, books and class materials, student support services. $145 application fee. Financial aid available for all students: scholarships.

For More Information • Ms. Varvara Kirakosyan, Director of Admissions, EF International Language Schools, One Education Street, Cambridge, MA 02141; *Phone:* 800-992-1892; *Fax:* 800-590-1125. *E-mail:* ils@ef.com. *World Wide Web:* http://www.ef.com/

LANGUAGE LIAISON
LEARN SPANISH IN PLAYA TAMARINDO

Hosted by Language Liaison

Academic Focus • Spanish language and literature.

Program Information • Students attend classes at Language Liaison (Tamarindo, Costa Rica). Field trips; optional travel at an extra cost. Students typically earn 3–15 semester credits per term.

Sessions • Classes begin weekly, year-round.

Eligibility Requirements • Minimum age 17; open to precollege students, freshmen, sophomores, juniors, seniors, graduate students, adults; no foreign language proficiency required.

Living Arrangements • Students live in locally rented apartments, host family homes, hotels. Meals are taken on one's own, with host family, in residences, in restaurants.

Costs (2005) • Contact sponsor for cost. $175 application fee. Financial aid available for all students: scholarship research service.

For More Information • Ms. Nancy Forman, President, Language Liaison, PO Box 1772, Pacific Palisades, CA 90272; *Phone:* 800-284-4448; *Fax:* 310-454-1706. *E-mail:* learn@languageliaison.com. *World Wide Web:* http://www.languageliaison.com/

CROATIA

CITY-TO-CITY

UNIVERSITY OF KANSAS
LANGUAGE AND CULTURE IN DUBROVNIK AND ZAGREB, CROATIA

Hosted by The Center for Foreign Languages, University of Zagreb
Academic Focus • Slavic languages.
Program Information • Students attend classes at The Center for Foreign Languages (Dubrovnik), University of Zagreb (Zagreb). Scheduled travel to Macedonia; field trips to Korcula, Hrvatsko Zagorje. Students typically earn 8 semester credits per term.
Sessions • Jul–Aug (summer).
Eligibility Requirements • Minimum age 18; open to freshmen, sophomores, juniors, seniors, graduate students, adults; 2.5 GPA; 2 letters of recommendation; good academic standing at home school; no foreign language proficiency required.
Living Arrangements • Students live in host institution dormitories. Quarters are shared with students from other programs. Meals are taken as a group, on one's own, in central dining facility, in restaurants.
Costs (2005) • $4600; includes tuition, housing, some meals, excursions, student support services, medical evacuation and repatriation services. $38 application fee. $300 nonrefundable deposit required. Financial aid available for students from sponsoring institution: scholarships, loans.
For More Information • Ms. Justine Hamilton, Program Coordinator, University of Kansas, Office of Study Abroad, Lippincott Hall, 1410 Jayhawk Boulevard, Room 108, Lawrence, KS 66045-7515; *Phone:* 785-864-3742; *Fax:* 785-864-5040. *E-mail:* osa@ku.edu. *World Wide Web:* http://www.ku.edu/~osa/

DUBROVNIK

ST. CLOUD STATE UNIVERSITY
CROATIA–CRIMINAL JUSTICE/VICTIMOLOGY

Academic Focus • Criminal justice.
Program Information • Faculty members are drawn from the sponsor's U.S. staff. Field trips to Italy; optional travel at an extra cost. Students typically earn 3 semester credits per term.
Sessions • May (summer).
Eligibility Requirements • Minimum age 18; open to sophomores, juniors, seniors; 2.0 GPA; no foreign language proficiency required.
Living Arrangements • Students live in host institution dormitories, hotels. Meals are taken as a group, on one's own, in restaurants.
Costs (2005) • $3950; includes housing, some meals, excursions, international airfare, international student ID, student support services. $75 application fee. Financial aid available for students from sponsoring institution: scholarships, work study, loans.
For More Information • Ms. Linda Raine, Study Abroad Coordinator, St. Cloud State University, Center for International Studies, 720 4th Avenue, South, St. Cloud, MN 56301; *Phone:* 320-308-4287; *Fax:* 320-308-4223. *E-mail:* study_abroad@stcloudstate.edu. *World Wide Web:* http://www.stcloudstate.edu/studyabroad

ZAGREB

RUTGERS, THE STATE UNIVERSITY OF NEW JERSEY
CROATIA

Academic Focus • Political science and government.
Program Information • Faculty members are drawn from the sponsor's U.S. staff and local instructors hired by the sponsor. Field trips. Students typically earn 6 semester credits per term.
Sessions • Jul (summer).
Eligibility Requirements • Open to sophomores, juniors, seniors; 2.5 GPA; 1 letter of recommendation; good academic standing at home school; official transcripts from all tertiary schools attended; no foreign language proficiency required.
Living Arrangements • Students live in host institution dormitories. Meals are taken on one's own.
Costs (2005) • $2847 for New Jersey residents; $3347 for nonresidents; includes tuition, housing, insurance, excursions, student support services. $20 application fee. $500 nonrefundable deposit required. Financial aid available for all students: scholarships, loans.
For More Information • Ms. Lindy Black, Regional Coordinator, Rutgers, The State University of New Jersey, 102 College Avenue, New Brunswick, NJ 08901-8543; *Phone:* 732-932-7787; *Fax:* 732-932-8659. *E-mail:* ru_abroad@email.rutgers.edu. *World Wide Web:* http://studyabroad.rutgers.edu/

CUBA

HAVANA

ENFOREX–SPANISH IN THE SPANISH WORLD
SPANISH INTENSIVE COURSE HABANA CUBA

Hosted by ENFOREX
Academic Focus • Dance, Spanish studies.
Program Information • Students attend classes at ENFOREX (Havana, Cuba). Field trips to Trinidad; optional travel at an extra cost. Students typically earn 4 semester credits per term.
Sessions • Year-round.
Eligibility Requirements • Minimum age 18; open to precollege students, freshmen, sophomores, seniors, graduate students, adults; no foreign language proficiency required.
Living Arrangements • Students live in host family homes, hotels. Meals are taken with host family, in residences, in restaurants.
Costs (2005) • $1525; includes tuition, housing, some meals, books and class materials. $100 application fee. $250 nonrefundable deposit required.
For More Information • Mr. Antonio Anadón, Director of Spanish Department, ENFOREX–Spanish in the Spanish World, Alberto Aguilera, 26, 28015 Madrid, Spain; *Phone:* +34 91-594-3776; *Fax:* +34 91-594-5159. *E-mail:* promotion@enforex.es. *World Wide Web:* http://www.enforex.com/

LEXIA INTERNATIONAL
LEXIA SUMMER IN HAVANA

Hosted by University of Havana
Academic Focus • Anthropology, area studies, art history, civilization studies, comparative history, cultural studies, economics, ethnic studies, geography, history, interdisciplinary studies, international affairs, Latin American literature, Latin American studies, liberal studies, literature, political science and government, social sciences, sociology, Spanish language and literature.
Program Information • Students attend classes at University of Havana (Havana, Cuba). Field trips to Pinar del Rio, Guantánamo provinces. Students typically earn 8-10 semester credits per term.
Sessions • Jun–Aug (summer).
Eligibility Requirements • Minimum age 18; open to freshmen, sophomores, juniors, seniors, graduate students, adults; 3.2 GPA; 2 letters of recommendation; 2 years college course work in Spanish.
Living Arrangements • Students live in hotels. Meals are taken on one's own, in residences.
Costs (2006) • $6450; includes tuition, housing, insurance, excursions, international student ID, student support services, transcript, computer access. $40 application fee. $300 nonrefundable deposit required. Financial aid available for all students: scholarships, work study.
For More Information • Lexia International, 23 South Main Street, Hanover, NH 03755; *Phone:* 800-775-3942; *Fax:* 603-643-9899. *E-mail:* info@lexiaintl.org. *World Wide Web:* http://www.lexiaintl.org/

SANTIAGO

ENFOREX–SPANISH IN THE SPANISH WORLD
SPANISH INTENSIVE COURSE SANTIAGO DE CUBA

Hosted by ENFOREX
Academic Focus • Dance, Spanish studies.
Program Information • Students attend classes at ENFOREX (Santiago, Cuba). Field trips to Guantanamo; optional travel at an extra cost. Students typically earn 4 semester credits per term.
Sessions • Year-round.
Eligibility Requirements • Minimum age 18; open to precollege students, freshmen, sophomores, seniors, graduate students, adults; no foreign language proficiency required.
Living Arrangements • Students live in host family homes, hotels. Meals are taken with host family, in residences, in restaurants.
Costs (2005) • $1365 per month; includes tuition, housing, some meals, books and class materials. $100 application fee. $250 nonrefundable deposit required.
For More Information • Mr. Antonio Anadón, Director of Spanish Department, ENFOREX–Spanish in the Spanish World, Alberto Aguilera, 26, 28015 Madrid, Spain; *Phone:* +34 91-594-3776; *Fax:* +34 91-594-5159. *E-mail:* promotion@enforex.es. *World Wide Web:* http://www.enforex.com/

*C*YPRUS

PAPHOS

UNIVERSITY OF DELAWARE
SUMMER SESSION IN CYPRUS: THEATER

Academic Focus • Drama/theater.

Program Information • Faculty members are drawn from the sponsor's U.S. staff. Field trips to cultural and historic sites. Students typically earn 6 semester credits per term.

Sessions • Jul–Aug (summer).

Eligibility Requirements • Open to freshmen, sophomores, juniors, seniors, graduate students, adults; 2.0 GPA; 1 letter of recommendation; no foreign language proficiency required.

Living Arrangements • Students live in locally rented apartments. Meals are taken as a group, in restaurants.

Costs (2005) • Contact sponsor for cost. $200 nonrefundable deposit required. Financial aid available for all students: scholarships.

For More Information • Center for International Studies, University of Delaware, 186 South College Avenue, Newark, DE 19716-1450; *Phone:* 888-831-4685; *Fax:* 302-831-6042. *E-mail:* studyabroad@udel.edu. *World Wide Web:* http://www.udel.edu/studyabroad/

CZECH REPUBLIC

PRAGUE

AMERICAN INSTITUTE FOR FOREIGN STUDY (AIFS)
AIFS–PRAGUE, CZECH REPUBLIC–CHARLES UNIVERSITY

Hosted by Charles University
Academic Focus • Art history, Czech, film and media studies, history, political science and government.
Program Information • Students attend classes at Charles University (Prague, Czech Republic). Scheduled travel to Moravia, Krakow and Auschwitz-Birkenau; field trips to walking tours of Prague, concerts, museums and palaces, wine tasting, historical site excursions, cultural activities; optional travel to 3-day visit to Vienna for a supplement of $249 at an extra cost. Students typically earn 6 semester credits per term.
Sessions • Jun–Jul (summer).
Eligibility Requirements • Minimum age 17; open to precollege students, freshmen, sophomores, juniors, seniors; 2.0 GPA; no foreign language proficiency required.
Living Arrangements • Students live in host institution dormitories, program-owned apartments, hotels. Quarters are shared with host institution students. Meals are taken as a group, in residences.
Costs (2007) • $4799; includes tuition, housing, some meals, insurance, excursions, student support services, On-site Resident Director, Transportation pass in Prague, Phone Card to call the U.S., Computer Facilities/Internet. $95 application fee. $395 nonrefundable deposit required. Financial aid available for all students: scholarships.
For More Information • Mr. David Mauro, Admissions Advisor, American Institute For Foreign Study (AIFS), 9 West Broad Street, Stamford, CT 06902-3788; *Phone:* 800-727-2437 Ext. 5163; *Fax:* 203-399-5597. *E-mail:* dmauro@aifs.com. *World Wide Web:* http://www.aifsabroad.com/

CENTRAL EUROPEAN EDUCATION AND CULTURAL EXCHANGE (CEECE)
CEECE IN PRAGUE, CZECH REPUBLIC

Hosted by Anglo-American College
Academic Focus • Art history, business administration/management, Central European studies, Czech, Eastern European studies, full curriculum, history, political science and government, social sciences.
Program Information • Students attend classes at Anglo-American College (Prague, Czech Republic). Field trips to southern Bohemia, western Bohemia; optional travel to Berlin, Vienna, Budapest, Krakow, Munich at an extra cost. Students typically earn 3–12 semester credits per term.
Sessions • Jun–Jul (summer), Jul (summer 2).
Eligibility Requirements • Minimum age 18; open to freshmen, sophomores, juniors, seniors, graduate students, adults; 2.0 GPA; good academic standing at home school; no foreign language proficiency required.
Living Arrangements • Students live in locally rented apartments. Meals are taken on one's own, in restaurants.
Costs (2006) • $2499–$2999 $3499–$3979; includes tuition, housing, excursions, books and class materials, student support services, local transportation pass, use of a pre-paid cellular phone. $300 refundable deposit required. Financial aid available for all students: home university financial aid.
For More Information • Mr. Eric Molengraf, Executive Director, Central European Education and Cultural Exchange (CEECE), 2956 Florence Drive, Grand Rapids, MI 49418; *Phone:* 800-352-9845. *E-mail:* info@ceece.org. *World Wide Web:* http://www.ceece.org/

CIEE
CIEE STUDY CENTER AT CHARLES UNIVERSITY–PRAGUE, CZECH REPUBLIC

Hosted by Charles University
Academic Focus • Art, art history, Czech, history, Jewish studies, literature, philosophy, political science and government, social sciences.
Program Information • Students attend classes at Charles University (Prague, Czech Republic). Field trips to cultural sites in and around Prague: Kutna Hora, Terezin, Litomerice, Plzen, Jachymov. Students typically earn 3 semester credits per term.
Sessions • Jun (summer), Jun–Jul (summer 2).
Eligibility Requirements • Minimum age 18; open to sophomores, juniors, seniors; 2.75 GPA; 1 letter of recommendation; good academic standing at home school; no foreign language proficiency required.
Living Arrangements • Students live in locally rented apartments. Quarters are shared with host institution students. Meals are taken as a group, on one's own, in residences, in restaurants.
Costs (2006) • $2500 for 1 session; $4900 for 2 sessions; includes tuition, housing, some meals, insurance, excursions, student support services, pre-departure advising, cultural activities, optional on-site pick-up, orientation, resident director. $30 application fee. $300 nonrefundable deposit required. Financial aid available for all students: scholarships, minority student scholarships, travel grants.

CZECH REPUBLIC
Prague

For More Information • Information Center, CIEE, 7 Custom House Street, 3rd Floor, Portland, ME 04101; *Phone:* 800-40-STUDY; *Fax:* 207-553-7699. *E-mail:* studyinfo@ciee.org. *World Wide Web:* http://www.ciee.org/isp/

LEXIA INTERNATIONAL
LEXIA SUMMER IN PRAGUE
Hosted by Charles University

Academic Focus • Anthropology, area studies, art history, civilization studies, comparative history, cultural studies, Czech, Eastern European studies, economics, ethnic studies, geography, history, interdisciplinary studies, international affairs, liberal studies, literature, political science and government, Slavic languages, social sciences, sociology.

Program Information • Students attend classes at Charles University (Prague, Czech Republic). Field trips to Znojmo, Kutna Hora, Brno, Cesky Krumlov. Students typically earn 8-10 semester credits per term.

Sessions • Jun–Aug (summer).

Eligibility Requirements • Minimum age 18; open to freshmen, sophomores, juniors, seniors, graduate students, adults; 2.5 GPA; 2 letters of recommendation; no foreign language proficiency required.

Living Arrangements • Students live in host institution dormitories, host family homes. Quarters are shared with host institution students, students from other programs. Meals are taken on one's own, with host family, in residences, in central dining facility, in restaurants.

Costs (2006) • $5950; includes tuition, housing, some meals, insurance, excursions, international student ID, student support services, computer access, transcript. $40 application fee. $300 nonrefundable deposit required.

For More Information • Lexia International, 23 South Main Street, Hanover, NH 03755; *Phone:* 800-775-3942; *Fax:* 603-643-9899. *E-mail:* info@lexiaintl.org. *World Wide Web:* http://www.lexiaintl.org/

NEW YORK UNIVERSITY
FILMMAKING IN PRAGUE: PRAGUE, CZECH REPUBLIC
Hosted by Academy of Performing Arts–FAMU

Academic Focus • Film and media studies.

Program Information • Students attend classes at Academy of Performing Arts–FAMU (Prague, Czech Republic). Students typically earn 8 semester credits per term.

Sessions • May–Jun (summer).

Eligibility Requirements • Minimum age 18; open to sophomores, juniors, seniors, graduate students, adults; course work in film production; no foreign language proficiency required.

Living Arrangements • Students live in university-owned housing. Quarters are shared with host institution students. Meals are taken on one's own, in central dining facility.

Costs (2005) • $5400; includes tuition. $50 application fee. Financial aid available for students from sponsoring institution: scholarships.

For More Information • Mr. Josh Murray, Assistant Director, New York University, 721 Broadway, 12th Floor, New York, NY 10003; *Phone:* 212-998-1500; *Fax:* 212-995-4578. *E-mail:* tisch.special.info@nyu.edu. *World Wide Web:* http://www.nyu.edu/global/studyabroad.html

NEW YORK UNIVERSITY
NYU IN PRAGUE
Hosted by NYU Center in Prague

Academic Focus • Architecture, art history, Central European studies, Czech, film and media studies, Jewish studies, literature, political science and government.

Program Information • Students attend classes at NYU Center in Prague (Prague, Czech Republic). Field trips to Cesky Krumlov, Terezin; optional travel to Auschwitz, Vienna at an extra cost. Students typically earn 8 semester credits per term.

Sessions • Jun–Aug (summer).

Eligibility Requirements • Minimum age 18; open to freshmen, sophomores, juniors, seniors, graduate students; 3.0 GPA; good

academic standing at home school; statement of purpose for non-New York University students; no foreign language proficiency required.

Living Arrangements • Students live in host institution dormitories. Quarters are shared with host institution students. Meals are taken on one's own, in restaurants.

Costs (2006) • $6670; includes tuition, housing, excursions, student support services, program fee. $25 application fee. $300 nonrefundable deposit required. Financial aid available for students from sponsoring institution: loans.

For More Information • Office of Summer Sessions, New York University, 7 East 12th Street, 6th Floor, New York, NY 10003; *Phone:* 212-998-2292; *Fax:* 212-995-4642. *E-mail:* summer.info@nyu.edu. *World Wide Web:* http://www.nyu.edu/global/studyabroad.html

NEW YORK UNIVERSITY
PRAGUE, CZECH REPUBLIC: HOSPITALITY, TOURISM, AND SPORTS MANAGEMENT
Hosted by NYU in Prague

Academic Focus • Sports management.

Program Information • Students attend classes at NYU in Prague (Prague, Czech Republic). Scheduled travel; field trips to Cesky Krumlov, Terizen, Klovany Vary. Students typically earn 3 semester credits per term.

Sessions • Summer-2 week intensive.

Eligibility Requirements • Minimum age 19; open to juniors, seniors, graduate students; major in HTTM or SMLS; course work in Hospitality, Tourism or Sports; good academic standing at home school; no foreign language proficiency required.

Living Arrangements • Students live in host institution dormitories. Quarters are shared with host institution students. Meals are taken on one's own, in restaurants.

Costs (2006) • $3200; includes tuition, housing, excursions. $25 application fee. $300 nonrefundable deposit required.

For More Information • Sharr Prohaska, Director, New York University, 10 Aetor Place, 502-B, New York City, NY 10003; *Phone:* 212-998-9109; *Fax:* 212-995-4676. *E-mail:* sp27@nyu.edu. *World Wide Web:* http://www.nyu.edu/global/studyabroad.html

STATE UNIVERSITY OF NEW YORK AT NEW PALTZ
SUMMER MODERN DANCE PROGRAM

Academic Focus • Dance.

Program Information • Faculty members are drawn from the sponsor's U.S. staff and local instructors hired by the sponsor. Field trips to dance and music concerts, southern Bohemia. Students typically earn 3 semester credits per term.

Sessions • Jul–Aug (summer).

Eligibility Requirements • Minimum age 18; open to freshmen, sophomores, juniors, seniors; 2.5 GPA; 1 letter of recommendation; good academic standing at home school; prior dance experience; no foreign language proficiency required.

Living Arrangements • Students live in hotels. Quarters are shared with students from other programs. Meals are taken as a group, in restaurants.

Costs (2006) • $2800 for New York residents; $3500 for nonresidents; includes tuition, housing, some meals, excursions, student support services, administrative fee. $25 application fee. $300 nonrefundable deposit required. Financial aid available for students from sponsoring institution: scholarships, loans.

For More Information • Center for International Programs, State University of New York at New Paltz, 1 Hawk Drive, New Paltz, NY 12561-2443; *Phone:* 845-257-3125; *Fax:* 845-257-3129. *E-mail:* studyabroad@newpaltz.edu. *World Wide Web:* http://www.newpaltz.edu/studyabroad/

UNIVERSITY OF MIAMI
PHOTOGRAPHY IN PRAGUE SUMMER PROGRAM

Academic Focus • Graphic design/illustration.

Program Information • Faculty members are drawn from the sponsor's U.S. staff. Field trips to Berlin, Vienna, Budapest. Students typically earn 6 semester credits per term.

Sessions • Jun–Aug (summer).

Eligibility Requirements • Minimum age 18; open to sophomores, juniors, seniors, graduate students; good academic standing at home school; no foreign language proficiency required.
Living Arrangements • Students live in locally rented apartments. Meals are taken as a group, on one's own, in restaurants.
Costs (2005) • $5022; includes tuition. $500 nonrefundable deposit required. Financial aid available for students from sponsoring institution: scholarships, loans.
For More Information • Ms. Amy Cosan, Coordinator, International Education and Exchange Programs, University of Miami, 5050 Brunson Drive, Allen Hall Room 212, PO Box 248005, Coral Gables, FL 33124-1610; *Phone:* 305-284-3434; *Fax:* 305-284-4235. *E-mail:* ieep@miami.edu. *World Wide Web:* http://www.studyabroad.miami.edu/

UNIVERSITY OF MIAMI
SUMMER FILM PROGRAM IN PRAGUE
Hosted by Academy of Performing Arts–FAMU
Academic Focus • Film and media studies.
Program Information • Students attend classes at Academy of Performing Arts–FAMU (Prague, Czech Republic). Field trips to Bohemia, Moravia; optional travel to Vienna, Berlin at an extra cost. Students typically earn 6 semester credits per term.
Sessions • Jul–Aug (summer).
Eligibility Requirements • Minimum age 18; open to sophomores, juniors, seniors, graduate students; major in film/theater; 3.0 GPA; 2 letters of recommendation; personal interview; no foreign language proficiency required.
Living Arrangements • Students live in a hostel. Quarters are shared with host institution students. Meals are taken on one's own, in restaurants.
Costs (2005–2006) • $5022; includes tuition. $500 nonrefundable deposit required. Financial aid available for students from sponsoring institution: scholarships, loans.
For More Information • Ms. Amy Cosan, Coordinator, University of Miami, International Education and Exchange Programs, 5050 Brunson Drive, Allen Hall 212, PO Box 248005, Coral Gables, FL 33124-1610; *Phone:* 305-284-3434; *Fax:* 305-284-4235. *E-mail:* ieep@miami.edu. *World Wide Web:* http://www.studyabroad.miami.edu/

UNIVERSITY OF NEW ORLEANS
PRAGUE SUMMER SEMINARS
Held at Charles University
Academic Focus • Architecture, art, art history, cinematography, communications, comparative literature, drama/theater, film and media studies, graphic design/illustration, history, literature, music, music history, performing arts, photography, political science and government, visual and performing arts.
Program Information • Classes are held on the campus of Charles University (Prague, Czech Republic). Faculty members are drawn from the sponsor's U.S. staff and local instructors hired by the sponsor. Field trips to local museums and towns; optional travel to the Karlovy Vary Film Festival at an extra cost. Students typically earn 6 semester credits per term.
Sessions • Jul (summer).
Eligibility Requirements • Minimum age 18; open to freshmen, sophomores, juniors, seniors, graduate students, adults; 2.5 GPA; good academic standing at home school; no foreign language proficiency required.
Living Arrangements • Students live in host institution dormitories, locally rented apartments. Quarters are shared with students from other programs. Meals are taken on one's own, in restaurants.

Costs (2005) • $3295; includes tuition, housing, some meals, insurance, excursions, books and class materials, lab equipment, student support services. $150 application fee. $150 refundable deposit required. Financial aid available for students from sponsoring institution: scholarships, loans.
For More Information • Dr. Irene B. Ziegler, Program Coordinator, University of New Orleans, PO Box 1097, New Orleans, LA 70148; *Phone:* 504-280-7318; *Fax:* 504-280-7317. *E-mail:* iziegler@uno.edu. *World Wide Web:* http://inst.uno.edu/

UNIVERSITY OF PENNSYLVANIA
PENN-IN-PRAGUE
Hosted by CERGE-EI
Academic Focus • Czech, European studies, Jewish studies, political science and government.
Program Information • Students attend classes at CERGE-EI (Prague, Czech Republic). Field trips to museums, churches, gardens in Prague. Students typically earn 2 course units per term.
Sessions • Jul–Aug (summer).
Eligibility Requirements • Open to freshmen, sophomores, juniors, seniors, graduate students; 1 letter of recommendation; good academic standing at home school; no foreign language proficiency required.
Living Arrangements • Students live in hotels. Meals are taken on one's own, in restaurants.
Costs (2005) • $5700; includes tuition, housing, insurance, excursions. $50 application fee. $300 nonrefundable deposit required. Financial aid available for students from sponsoring institution: scholarships, loans.
For More Information • Penn Summer Abroad, University of Pennsylvania, 3440 Market Street, Suite 100, Philadelphia, PA 19104-3335; *Phone:* 215-746-6900; *Fax:* 215-573-2053. *E-mail:* summerabroad@sas.upenn.edu. *World Wide Web:* http://www.sas.upenn.edu/summer/

UNIVERSITY STUDIES ABROAD CONSORTIUM
POLITICS, CULTURE, AND ART: PRAGUE, CZECH REPUBLIC
Hosted by Charles University
Academic Focus • Anthropology, art, Czech, film and media studies, history, Jewish studies, literature, political science and government.
Program Information • Students attend classes at Charles University (Prague, Czech Republic). Field trips to Kutna Hora, Terezin; optional travel to Vienna, Budapest at an extra cost. Students typically earn 8 semester credits per term.
Sessions • May–Jul (summer).
Eligibility Requirements • Minimum age 18; open to freshmen, sophomores, juniors, seniors, graduate students, adults; 2.5 GPA; no foreign language proficiency required.
Living Arrangements • Students live in host institution dormitories. Quarters are shared with host institution students. Meals are taken on one's own, in central dining facility, in restaurants.
Costs (2007) • $3480; includes tuition, housing, some meals, insurance, excursions, student support services. $100 application fee. $200 refundable deposit required. Financial aid available for all students: scholarships, loans.
For More Information • University Studies Abroad Consortium, USAC/323, Reno, NV 89557-0093; *Phone:* 775-784-6569; *Fax:* 775-784-6010. *E-mail:* usac@unr.edu. *World Wide Web:* http://usac.unr.edu/

$\mathcal{D}$ENMARK

COPENHAGEN

DIS, DENMARK'S INTERNATIONAL STUDY PROGRAM
DIS SUMMER PROGRAMS

Hosted by Denmark's Design School, DIS, Denmark's International Study Program
Academic Focus • Full curriculum.
Program Information • Students attend classes at Denmark's Design School (Copenhagen, Denmark), DIS, Denmark's International Study Program (Copenhagen, Denmark). Scheduled travel to Sweden, Finland, the Netherlands, Germany, Belgium, Poland, Luxembourg, London, Paris; field trips to Denmark. Students typically earn 6-9 semester credits per term.
Sessions • May-Jun (summer), Jun-Jul (summer 2), Jul-Aug (summer 3).
Eligibility Requirements • Open to sophomores, juniors, seniors, graduate students; 3.0 GPA; good academic standing at home school; major requirement is dependent on intended area of study; no foreign language proficiency required.
Living Arrangements • Students live in locally rented apartments, host family homes, a Danish Higher Education "Kollegium". Quarters are shared with host institution students. Meals are taken on one's own, with host family, in residences.
Costs (2005) • $6000-$8000; includes tuition, housing, some meals, insurance, excursions, books and class materials, lab equipment, student support services, local transportation. $500 nonrefundable deposit required. Financial aid available for all students: scholarships, work study.
For More Information • Mr. Brad Stepan, Field Director, DIS, Denmark's International Study Program, North American Office, 94 Blegen Hall, University of Minnesota, 269 19th Avenue South, Minneapolis, MN 55455; *Phone:* 800-247-3477; *Fax:* 612-626-8009. *E-mail:* dis@umn.edu. *World Wide Web:* http://www.discopenhagen.org/. Students may also apply through DIS Denmark's International Study Program, Vestergade 7, DK-1456, Copenhagen K, Denmark.

KENTUCKY INSTITUTE FOR INTERNATIONAL STUDIES
DENMARK

Academic Focus • Education.
Program Information • Faculty members are drawn from the sponsor's U.S. staff. Scheduled travel to Aarhus; field trips to Viborg, Odense. Students typically earn 3-6 semester credits per term.
Sessions • May-Jun (summer).
Eligibility Requirements • Minimum age 18; open to sophomores, juniors, seniors, graduate students, adults; 3.0 GPA; 1 letter of recommendation; no foreign language proficiency required.
Living Arrangements • Students live in host institution dormitories, host family homes, hotels. Meals are taken as a group, in residences, in restaurants.
Costs (2006) • $3240; includes housing, some meals, international airfare, international student ID, instructional expenses. $150 application fee. Financial aid available for all students: scholarships.
For More Information • Ms. Nancy Martin, Coordinator, Kentucky Institute for International Studies, PO Box 9, Murray, KY 42071-0009; *Phone:* 270-762-3091; *Fax:* 270-762-3434. *E-mail:* kiismsu@murraystate.edu. *World Wide Web:* http://www.kiis.org/

STATE UNIVERSITY OF NEW YORK AT NEW PALTZ
SUMMER STUDY ABROAD IN DENMARK–INTERNATIONAL SOCIAL WELFARE

Academic Focus • Social services.
Program Information • Faculty members are drawn from the sponsor's U.S. staff. Scheduled travel to Blue Lagoon. Students typically earn 3 semester credits per term.
Sessions • Jun (summer).
Eligibility Requirements • Minimum age 18; open to freshmen, sophomores, juniors, seniors, graduate students; 2.5 GPA; 1 letter of recommendation; good academic standing at home school; interview with program director; no foreign language proficiency required.
Living Arrangements • Students live in host family homes. Quarters are shared with students from other programs. Meals are taken on one's own, in restaurants.
Costs (2006) • $1000 for New York residents; $1800 for nonresidents; includes tuition, housing, some meals, excursions, administrative fee. $25 application fee. $300 nonrefundable deposit required. Financial aid available for students from sponsoring institution: scholarships, loans.
For More Information • Center for International Programs, State University of New York at New Paltz, 1 Hawk Drive, New Paltz, NY 12561-2443; *Phone:* 845-257-3125; *Fax:* 845-257-3129. *E-mail:* studyabroad@newpaltz.edu. *World Wide Web:* http://www.newpaltz.edu/studyabroad/

UNIVERSITY STUDIES ABROAD CONSORTIUM
INTERNATIONAL BUSINESS AND INTERCULTURAL COMMUNICATION STUDIES: COPENHAGEN, DENMARK

Hosted by Copenhagen Business School

Academic Focus • Accounting, business administration/management, communications, Danish, economics, entrepreneurship, international business, marketing, tourism and travel.

Program Information • Students attend classes at Copenhagen Business School (Copenhagen, Denmark). Students typically earn 6 semester credits per term.

Sessions • Jun–Aug (summer).

Eligibility Requirements • Minimum age 18; open to freshmen, sophomores, juniors, seniors, graduate students, adults; 3.0 GPA; no foreign language proficiency required.

Living Arrangements • Students live in host institution dormitories, locally rented apartments. Quarters are shared with host institution students. Meals are taken on one's own, in residences, in restaurants.

Costs (2007) • $2280; includes tuition, insurance, student support services. $100 application fee. $200 refundable deposit required. Financial aid available for all students: scholarships, loans.

For More Information • University Studies Abroad Consortium, USAC/323, Reno, NV 89557-0093; *Phone:* 775-784-6569; *Fax:* 775-784-6010. *E-mail:* usac@unr.edu. *World Wide Web:* http://usac.unr.edu/

DOMINICAN REPUBLIC

SANTIAGO

CIEE
CIEE STUDY CENTER AT PONTIFICIA UNIVERSIDAD CATOLICA MADRE Y MAESTRA, SANTIAGO, DOMINICAN REPUBLIC-COMMUNITY HEALTH

Hosted by Catholic University 'Madre y Maestra,' El Campus de Santiago de los Caballeros
Academic Focus • Premedical studies, public health, Spanish language and literature.
Program Information • Students attend classes at Catholic University 'Madre y Maestra,' El Campus de Santiago de los Caballeros (Santiago, Dominican Republic). Scheduled travel to Santo Domingo, Samaná, La Romana, Altos de Chavon, Higuey; field trips to Rio San Juan, Jarabacoa, La Vega Vieja, Bateyes. Students typically earn 9 semester credits per term.
Sessions • May–Jul (summer).
Eligibility Requirements • Minimum age 18; open to sophomores, juniors, seniors; course work in public health recommended; 2.75 GPA; 1 letter of recommendation; good academic standing at home school; 2 years of college course work in Spanish.
Living Arrangements • Students live in host family homes, a health clinic. Meals are taken with host family, in residences.
Costs (2006) • $4300; includes tuition, housing, all meals, insurance, excursions, books and class materials, student support services, computer and library access, pre-departure advising, orientation cultural activities, on-site pick-up. $30 application fee. $300 nonrefundable deposit required. Financial aid available for all students: minority student scholarships, travel grants.
For More Information • Information Center, CIEE, 7 Custom House Street, 3rd Floor, Portland, ME 04101; *Phone:* 800-40-STUDY; *Fax:* 207-553-7699. *E-mail:* studyinfo@ciee.org. *World Wide Web:* http://www.ciee.org/isp/

INTERNATIONAL STUDIES ABROAD
SANTIAGO, DOMINICAN REPUBLIC–SUMMER SPANISH LANGUAGE AND CULTURE

Hosted by Catholic University 'Madre y Maestra,' El Campus de Santiago de los Caballeros
Academic Focus • Spanish language and literature.
Program Information • Students attend classes at Catholic University 'Madre y Maestra,' El Campus de Santiago de los Caballeros (Santiago, Dominican Republic). Field trips to Santo Domingo, Jarabacoa, Puerto Plata. Students typically earn 6–8 semester credits per term.
Sessions • Jun–Jul (summer).
Eligibility Requirements • Minimum age 18; open to freshmen, sophomores, juniors, seniors, graduate students, adults; 2.5 GPA; 1 letter of recommendation; good academic standing at home school; transcripts; no foreign language proficiency required.
Living Arrangements • Students live in host family homes. Quarters are shared with host institution students, students from other programs. Meals are taken with host family.
Costs (2005–2006) • Contact sponsor for cost. $200 deposit required. Financial aid available for all students: scholarships, U.S. federal financial aid.
For More Information • Dominican Republic Site Specialist, International Studies Abroad, 901 West 24th Street, Austin, TX 78705; *Phone:* 800-580-8826; *Fax:* 512-480-8866. *E-mail:* isa@studiesabroad.com. *World Wide Web:* http://www.studiesabroad.com/

SANTO DOMINGO

COLLEGE CONSORTIUM FOR INTERNATIONAL STUDIES–FLORIDA AGRICULTURAL AND MECHANICAL UNIVERSITY
CCIS–DOMINICAN REPUBLIC SUMMER PROGRAM

Hosted by Catholic University 'Madre y Maestra'
Academic Focus • Full curriculum.
Program Information • Students attend classes at Catholic University 'Madre y Maestra' (Santo Domingo, Dominican Republic). Field trips to in-country tours and visits to cultural museums.
Sessions • May–Jul (summer).

Eligibility Requirements • Open to sophomores, juniors, seniors, graduate students, adults; 2.5 GPA; 2 letters of recommendation; good academic standing at home school; no foreign language proficiency required.

Living Arrangements • Students live in host family homes. Meals are taken with host family, in residences.

Costs (2007) • $3500; includes tuition, housing, some meals, insurance, excursions, books and class materials, student support services. $250 application fee.

For More Information • Ms. Cindy Peters, Education Abroad Coordinator, College Consortium for International Studies–Florida Agricultural and Mechanical University, Florida Agricultural & Mechanical University, Office of International Education & Development, Tallahassee, FL 32307; *Phone:* 850-599-3562; *Fax:* 850-561-2387. *E-mail:* famuabroad@famus.edu

MICHIGAN STATE UNIVERSITY
REGIONAL DEVELOPMENT IN THE CARIBBEAN: THE DOMINICAN REPUBLIC EXPERIENCE

Held at Catholic University 'Madre y Maestra'

Academic Focus • Geography, interdisciplinary studies, social sciences.

Program Information • Classes are held on the campus of Catholic University 'Madre y Maestra' (Santo Domingo, Dominican Republic). Faculty members are drawn from the sponsor's U.S. staff. Scheduled travel; field trips. Students typically earn 7 semester credits per term.

Sessions • May (summer).

Eligibility Requirements • Open to freshmen, sophomores, juniors, seniors, adults; 2.0 GPA; good academic standing at home school; no foreign language proficiency required.

Living Arrangements • Students live in hotels. Meals are taken on one's own, in restaurants.

Costs (2005) • $1825; includes housing, some meals, insurance, excursions, books and class materials, student support services. $100 application fee. $200 nonrefundable deposit required. Financial aid available for all students: scholarships, loans.

For More Information • Mr. Mark Davis, Coordinator, Michigan State University, Office of Study Abroad, 109 International Center, East Lansing, MI 48824-1035; *Phone:* 517-432-1315; *Fax:* 517-432-2082. *E-mail:* mdavis@msu.edu. *World Wide Web:* http://studyabroad.msu.edu/

UNIVERSITY AT ALBANY, STATE UNIVERSITY OF NEW YORK
DOMINICAN AND CARIBBEAN CULTURE STUDY TOUR WITH THE PUCMM

Hosted by Catholic University 'Madre y Maestra'

Academic Focus • African-American studies, intercultural studies, Latin American studies.

Program Information • Students attend classes at Catholic University 'Madre y Maestra' (Santo Domingo, Dominican Republic). Scheduled travel to Cibao, Santiago, San Juan de la Maguana, Jimani. Students typically earn 3 semester credits per term.

Sessions • Jan (winter).

Eligibility Requirements • Open to freshmen, sophomores, juniors, seniors, adults; 1 letter of recommendation; good academic standing at home school; no foreign language proficiency required.

Living Arrangements • Students live in hotels. Meals are taken as a group, on one's own, in restaurants.

Costs (2005) • Contact sponsor for cost. $150 nonrefundable deposit required. Financial aid available for students from sponsoring institution: all customary soruces.

For More Information • University at Albany, State University of New York, Office of International Education, LI 66, Albany, NY 12222; *Phone:* 518-442-3525; *Fax:* 518-442-3338. *E-mail:* intled@uamail.albany.edu. *World Wide Web:* http://www.albany.edu/studyabroad/

UNIVERSITY AT ALBANY, STATE UNIVERSITY OF NEW YORK
LANGUAGE AND CULTURAL STUDIES IN ENGLISH AT THE PUCMM

Hosted by Catholic University 'Madre y Maestra'

Academic Focus • African-American studies, cultural studies, Spanish language and literature.

Program Information • Students attend classes at Catholic University 'Madre y Maestra' (Santo Domingo, Dominican Republic). Field trips to cultural sites related to course syllabus. Students typically earn 9 semester credits per term.

Sessions • Jun–Jul (summer).

Eligibility Requirements • Open to sophomores, juniors, seniors, adults; 2 letters of recommendation; good academic standing at home school; no foreign language proficiency required.

Living Arrangements • Students live in host family homes. Meals are taken on one's own, with host family, in residences, in restaurants.

Costs (2005) • Contact sponsor for cost. $150 nonrefundable deposit required. Financial aid available for students from sponsoring institution: all customary sources.

For More Information • University at Albany, State University of New York, Office of International Education, LI 66, Albany, NY 12222; *Phone:* 518-442-3525; *Fax:* 518-442-3338. *E-mail:* intled@uamail.albany.edu. *World Wide Web:* http://www.albany.edu/studyabroad/

$\mathcal{E}$CUADOR

CITY-TO-CITY

SAINT MARY'S COLLEGE
ENVIRONMENTS OF ECUADOR

Academic Focus • Biological/life sciences, ecology, environmental science/studies, Galapagos area studies.
Program Information • Faculty members are drawn from the sponsor's U.S. staff. Scheduled travel to Quito, Galapagos Islands, Andes highlands, Otavalo, Quichua Village. Students typically earn 3 semester credits per term.
Sessions • May–Jun (summer), Program only runs in even-numbered years.
Eligibility Requirements • Minimum age 18; open to freshmen, sophomores, juniors, seniors; 2.5 GPA; 3 letters of recommendation; good academic standing at home school; no foreign language proficiency required.
Living Arrangements • Students live in hotels. Meals are taken as a group, in restaurants.
Costs (2004) • $3450; includes housing, some meals, excursions, student support services. $30 application fee.
For More Information • Dr. Thomas Fogle, Faculty Director, Saint Mary's College, Department of Biology, Notre Dame, IN 46556; *Phone:* 574-284-4675; *Fax:* 574-284-4141. *E-mail:* tfogle@saintmarys.edu. *World Wide Web:* http://www.saintmarys.edu/~cwil

CUENCA

CENTER FOR CULTURAL INTERCHANGE
ECUADOR LANGUAGE SCHOOL

Hosted by Estudio Sampere
Academic Focus • Spanish language and literature.
Program Information • Students attend classes at Estudio Sampere (Cuenca, Ecuador). Field trips to museums, cultural destinations, places of interest.
Sessions • 3, 4, or 6 week sessions begin every Monday, year-round.
Eligibility Requirements • Minimum age 18; open to precollege students, freshmen, sophomores, juniors, seniors, graduate students, adults; no foreign language proficiency required.
Living Arrangements • Students live in host family homes. Quarters are shared with students from other programs. Meals are taken with host family, in residences.
Costs (2005) • $2070 for 4 weeks; includes tuition, housing, some meals, insurance, books and class materials, student support services, activities. Financial aid available for students from sponsoring institution: scholarships.
For More Information • Ms. Juliet Jones, Outbound Programs Director, Center for Cultural Interchange, 325 West Huron, Suite 706, Chicago, IL 60610; *Phone:* 866-684-9675; *Fax:* 372-944-2644. *E-mail:* info@cci-exchange.com. *World Wide Web:* http://www.cci-exchange.com/

ESTUDIO SAMPERE
INTENSIVE SPANISH COURSES IN ECUADOR

Hosted by Estudio Sampere
Academic Focus • Art, crafts, Ecuadorian studies, Spanish language and literature.
Program Information • Students attend classes at Estudio Sampere (Cuenca, Ecuador). Field trips to Inga Pirca, Chordeleg; optional travel to the Galapagos Islands, a rainforest at an extra cost. Students typically earn 6 semester credits for 4 week session.
Sessions • 2 to 16 weeks, beginning the first Monday of each month.
Eligibility Requirements • Minimum age 18; open to freshmen, sophomores, juniors, seniors, graduate students, adults; 0.5 years of college course work in Spanish.
Living Arrangements • Students live in locally rented apartments, host family homes, hotels. Quarters are shared with host institution students. Meals are taken with host family, in restaurants.
Costs (2005) • $580 for 2 weeks; $4125 for 16 weeks; includes tuition, housing, all meals, excursions, books and class materials, student support services. $150 application fee. $200 nonrefundable deposit required.
For More Information • Mr. Juan M. Sampere, Director, Estudio Sampere, Lagasca, 16, 28001 Madrid, Spain; *Phone:* +34 91-4314366; *Fax:* +34 91-5759509. *E-mail:* jmanuel@sampere.es. *World Wide Web:* http://www.sampere.es/. Students may also apply through Spanish Works, Inc., PO Box 1434, Healdsburg, CA 95448.

LANGUAGE LIAISON
SPANISH IN ECUADOR–CUENCA

Hosted by Language Liaison
Academic Focus • Spanish language and literature.
Program Information • Students attend classes at Language Liaison (Cuenca, Ecuador). Field trips; optional travel at an extra cost. Students typically earn 3–15 semester credits per term.
Sessions • New programs begin weekly, year-round.
Eligibility Requirements • Minimum age 17; open to precollege students, freshmen, sophomores, juniors, seniors, graduate students, adults; no foreign language proficiency required.
Living Arrangements • Students live in locally rented apartments, host family homes, hotels. Meals are taken on one's own, with host family, in residences, in restaurants.
Costs (2005) • Contact sponsor for cost. $175 application fee. Financial aid available for all students: scholarship research service.
For More Information • Ms. Nancy Forman, President, Language Liaison, PO Box 1772, Pacific Palisades, CA 90272; *Phone:* 800-284-4448; *Fax:* 310-454-1706. *E-mail:* learn@languageliaison. com. *World Wide Web:* http://www.languageliaison.com/

LINGUA SERVICE WORLDWIDE
VACATION 'N LEARN SPANISH IN ECUADOR

Hosted by Estudio Sampere
Academic Focus • Spanish language and literature, Spanish studies.
Program Information • Students attend classes at Estudio Sampere (Cuenca, Ecuador). Optional travel to cultural sites thoughout Ecuador at an extra cost. Students typically earn 3 semester credits for 3 weeks, 6 semester credits for 5 weeks.
Sessions • Sessions of 2 or more weeks begin on Mondays, year-round.
Eligibility Requirements • Minimum age 16; open to precollege students, freshmen, sophomores, juniors, seniors, graduate students, adults; no foreign language proficiency required.
Living Arrangements • Students live in host family homes, hotels. Meals are taken with host family.
Costs (2006–2007) • Contact sponsor for cost. $100 application fee.
For More Information • Assistant Director, Lingua Service Worldwide, 75 Prospect Street, Suite 4, Huntington, NY 11743; *Phone:* 800-394-5327; *Fax:* 631-271-3441. *E-mail:* linguaservice@att. net. *World Wide Web:* http://www.linguaserviceworldwide.com/

LYCOMING COLLEGE
SUMMER LANGUAGE STUDY IN ECUADOR

Hosted by Estudio Sampere
Academic Focus • Spanish language and literature.
Program Information • Students attend classes at Estudio Sampere (Cuenca, Ecuador). Field trips; optional travel at an extra cost. Students typically earn 4 semester credits per term.
Sessions • 4 week sessions beginning in May.
Eligibility Requirements • Open to sophomores, juniors, seniors; 2.5 GPA; 2 letters of recommendation; good academic standing at home school; 1 year of college course work in Spanish.
Living Arrangements • Students live in host family homes. Quarters are shared with host institution students. Meals are taken with host family, in residences.
Costs (2005) • $1595 per 4 week session; includes tuition, housing, all meals, books and class materials.
For More Information • Dr. Barbara F. Buedel, Coordindator of Study Abroad, Lycoming College, Box 2, 700 College Place, Williamsport, PA 17701-5192; *Phone:* 570-321-4210; *Fax:* 570-321-4389. *E-mail:* buedel@lycoming.edu. *World Wide Web:* http://www. lycoming.edu/

GUAYAQUIL

COLLEGE CONSORTIUM FOR INTERNATIONAL STUDIES–COLLEGE OF STATEN ISLAND/CUNY AND BROOKDALE COMMUNITY COLLEGE
SUMMER PROGRAM IN GUAYAQUIL, ECUADOR

Hosted by Catholic University of Santiago of Guayaquil

Academic Focus • Ecuadorian studies, Spanish language and literature.
Program Information • Students attend classes at Catholic University of Santiago of Guayaquil (Guayaquil, Ecuador). Field trips to Isla de la Plata, Cuenca, Cerro Blanco, Manabi; optional travel to Cuenca, Baños, Salinas, Quito, Otavalo at an extra cost. Students typically earn 7 semester credits per term.
Sessions • Jul (summer), Dec–Jan (January term).
Eligibility Requirements • Minimum age 18; open to freshmen, sophomores, juniors, seniors, graduate students, adults; 2.5 GPA; 2 letters of recommendation; essay; transcript; no foreign language proficiency required.
Living Arrangements • Students live in host family homes. Meals are taken with host family, in residences.
Costs (2006–2007) • $2120; includes tuition, housing, some meals, insurance, excursions, student support services, fees, airport pick-up. Financial aid available for students from sponsoring institution: scholarships, loans.
For More Information • College Consortium for International Studies–College of Staten Island/CUNY and Brookdale Community College, 2000 P Street, NW, Suite 503, Washington, DC 20036; *Phone:* 800-453-6956; *Fax:* 202-223-0999. *E-mail:* info@ccisabroad. org. *World Wide Web:* http://www.ccisabroad.org/. Students may also apply through College of Staten Island, The City University of New York, Center for International Service, Building 2A, Room 206, 2800 Victory Boulevard, Staten Island, NY 10314; Brookdale Community College, International Center, 765 Newman Springs Road, Lincroft, NJ 07738-1597.

THE INTERNATIONAL PARTNERSHIP FOR SERVICE LEARNING AND LEADERSHIP
ECUADOR SERVICE–LEARNING (GUAYAQUIL)

Hosted by 'Espiritu Santo' University Guayaquil
Academic Focus • Community service, education, international affairs, Latin American studies, liberal studies, social sciences, Spanish language and literature.
Program Information • Students attend classes at 'Espiritu Santo' University Guayaquil (Guayaquil, Ecuador). Field trips to Quito, Cuenca; optional travel to the Galapagos Islands, the Amazon at an extra cost. Students typically earn 6 semester credits per term.
Sessions • May–Jul (summer), May–Jun (summer 2), Jun–Jul (summer 3).
Eligibility Requirements • Minimum age 18; open to freshmen, sophomores, juniors, seniors, graduate students, adults; 2 letters of recommendation; good academic standing at home school; evidence of maturity; 1 year of college course work in Spanish.
Living Arrangements • Students live in host family homes. Meals are taken with host family, in residences.
Costs (2005–2006) • $3900 per session; includes tuition, housing, some meals, student support services, internship placement. $50 application fee. $250 refundable deposit required. Financial aid available for all students: federal financial aid.
For More Information • Director of Student Programs, The International Partnership for Service Learning and Leadership, 815 Second Avenue, New York, NY 10017-4594; *Phone:* 212-986-0989; *Fax:* 212-986-5039. *E-mail:* info@ipsl.org. *World Wide Web:* http://www.ipsl.org/

STATE UNIVERSITY OF NEW YORK AT NEW PALTZ
SUMMER STUDY IN ECUADOR

Hosted by 'Espiritu Santo' University Guayaquil
Academic Focus • Business administration/management, education, Latin American studies, social services, Spanish language and literature.
Program Information • Students attend classes at 'Espiritu Santo' University Guayaquil (Guayaquil, Ecuador). Field trips to coastal Ecuador, Cuenca, local attractions, Quito; optional travel to the Galapagos Islands, the Amazon rainforest at an extra cost. Students typically earn 6 semester credits per term.
Sessions • Jun–Jul (summer), Jul–Aug (summer 2).
Eligibility Requirements • Minimum age 18; open to freshmen, sophomores, juniors, seniors; 2.5 GPA; 1 letter of recommendation; good academic standing at home school; 1 year of college course work in Spanish.

ECUADOR
Guayaquil

Living Arrangements • Students live in host family homes. Meals are taken with host family, in residences.
Costs (2006) • $2600 for New York residents; $4200 for nonresidents; includes tuition, housing, all meals, excursions, student support services, administrative fee. $25 application fee. $300 nonrefundable deposit required. Financial aid available for students from sponsoring institution: scholarships, loans.
For More Information • Center for International Programs, State University of New York at New Paltz, 1 Hawk Drive, New Paltz, NY 12561-2443; *Phone:* 845-257-3125; *Fax:* 845-257-3129. *E-mail:* studyabroad@newpaltz.edu. *World Wide Web:* http://www.newpaltz.edu/studyabroad/

QUITO

ALMA COLLEGE
SUMMER PROGRAM OF STUDIES IN QUITO, ECUADOR

Hosted by Academia Latinoamericana
Academic Focus • Cultural studies, Spanish language and literature.
Program Information • Students attend classes at Academia Latinoamericana (Quito, Ecuador). Field trips to the "Middle of the World" (Equator monument), a folk ballet; optional travel to a cloud forest, the Galapagos Islands at an extra cost. Students typically earn 3–12 semester credits per term.
Sessions • Apr–Aug (1 to 4 months).
Eligibility Requirements • Minimum age 18; open to sophomores, juniors, seniors, graduate students; 2.5 GPA; 2 letters of recommendation; good academic standing at home school; no foreign language proficiency required.
Living Arrangements • Students live in host family homes. Meals are taken with host family, in residences.
Costs (2005) • $2200–$6600; includes tuition, housing, some meals, insurance, excursions, books and class materials, international student ID, student support services, on-site orientation, airport pick-up. $50 application fee. $200 refundable deposit required.
For More Information • Ms. Julie Elenbaas, Office Associate, International Education, Alma College, 614 West Superior Street, Alma, MI 48801-1599; *Phone:* 989-463-7055; *Fax:* 989-463-7126. *E-mail:* intl_studies@alma.edu. *World Wide Web:* http://international.alma.edu/

COLLEGE CONSORTIUM FOR INTERNATIONAL STUDIES–COLLEGE OF STATEN ISLAND/CUNY AND BROOKDALE COMMUNITY COLLEGE
SUMMER PROGRAM IN QUITO, ECUADOR

Hosted by Universidad San Francisco Quito
Academic Focus • Andean studies, anthropology, ecology, Ecuadorian studies, Latin American studies, Spanish language and literature.
Program Information • Students attend classes at Universidad San Francisco Quito (Quito, Ecuador). Field trips to Otavalo, Baños; optional travel to Esmeraldas at an extra cost. Students typically earn 9 semester credits per term.
Sessions • Jun–Jul (summer).
Eligibility Requirements • Minimum age 18; open to freshmen, sophomores, juniors, seniors, graduate students, adults; 2.5 GPA; 1 letter of recommendation; essay; transcript; 2 years of college course work in Spanish.
Living Arrangements • Students live in host family homes. Meals are taken with host family, in residences.
Costs (2006) • $4465; includes tuition, housing, some meals, insurance, excursions, student support services, fees, airport pick-up. $135 deposit required. Financial aid available for students from sponsoring institution: loans, grants.
For More Information • College Consortium for International Studies–College of Staten Island/CUNY and Brookdale Community College, 2000 P Street, NW, Suite 503, Washington, DC 20036; *Phone:* 800-453-6956; *Fax:* 202-223-0999. *E-mail:* info@ccisabroad.org. *World Wide Web:* http://www.ccisabroad.org/. Students may also apply through College of Staten Island, The City University of New York, Center for International Service, Building 2A, Room 206, 2800 Victory Boulevard, Staten Island, NY 10314; Brookdale Community College, International Center, 765 Newman Springs Road, Lincroft, NJ 07738-1597.

EF INTERNATIONAL LANGUAGE SCHOOLS
SPANISH IN QUITO, ECUADOR

Hosted by EF Escuela Internacional de Español
Academic Focus • Spanish language and literature.
Program Information • Students attend classes at EF Escuela Internacional de Español (Quito, Ecuador). Field trips to the Otavalo Market, Baños, Santo Domingo; optional travel to the Galapagos Islands, Cuenca, Esmeraldas, Isla de la Plata at an extra cost. Students typically earn 15–18 quarter credits per term.
Sessions • Program length 2 to 52 weeks, year-round.
Eligibility Requirements • Minimum age 16; open to precollege students, freshmen, sophomores, juniors, seniors, graduate students, adults; no foreign language proficiency required.
Living Arrangements • Students live in host institution dormitories, host family homes. Quarters are shared with host institution students. Meals are taken with host family, in residences.
Costs (2006–2007) • $790 for 2 weeks; includes tuition, housing, some meals, books and class materials. $145 application fee. Financial aid available for all students: scholarships.
For More Information • Ms. Varvara Kirakosyan, Director of Admissions, EF International Language Schools, One Education Street, Cambridge, MA 02141; *Phone:* 800-992-1892; *Fax:* 800-590-1125. *E-mail:* ils@ef.com. *World Wide Web:* http://www.ef.com/

ENFOREX–SPANISH IN THE SPANISH WORLD
SPANISH INTENSIVE COURSE QUITO

Hosted by ENFOREX
Academic Focus • Spanish language and literature, Spanish studies.
Program Information • Students attend classes at ENFOREX (Quito, Ecuador). Field trips to Quito Colonial; optional travel to the Galapagos Islands, Amazonas, Sierra Azul at an extra cost. Students typically earn 4 semester credits per term.
Sessions • Year-round.
Eligibility Requirements • Minimum age 18; open to freshmen, sophomores, juniors, seniors, graduate students, adults; no foreign language proficiency required.
Living Arrangements • Students live in host family homes, hotels. Meals are taken as a group, on one's own, with host family.
Costs (2005) • $1100 per month; includes tuition, housing, all meals, excursions, books and class materials, lab equipment, international student ID, student support services. $100 application fee. $250 nonrefundable deposit required.
For More Information • Mr. Antonio Anadón, Director of Spanish Department, ENFOREX–Spanish in the Spanish World, Alberto Aguilera, 26, 28015 Madrid, Spain; *Phone:* +34 91-594-3776; *Fax:* +34 91-594-5159. *E-mail:* promotion@enforex.es. *World Wide Web:* http://www.enforex.com/

KENTUCKY INSTITUTE FOR INTERNATIONAL STUDIES
ECUADOR

Academic Focus • Biological/life sciences, ecology.
Program Information • Faculty members are drawn from the sponsor's U.S. staff. Scheduled travel to the Galapagos Islands, Rio Napo; field trips to areas of regional interest. Students typically earn 3–6 semester credits per term.
Sessions • May–Jun (summer).
Eligibility Requirements • Minimum age 18; open to freshmen, sophomores, juniors, seniors, graduate students, adults; 2.0 GPA; 1 letter of recommendation; no foreign language proficiency required.
Living Arrangements • Students live in hotels. Meals are taken as a group, in restaurants.
Costs (2006) • $3490; includes housing, some meals, insurance, excursions, international airfare, international student ID, instructional expenses. $150 application fee. Financial aid available for all students: scholarships.
For More Information • Ms. Nancy Martin, Coordinator, Kentucky Institute for International Studies, PO Box 9, Murray, KY 42071-0009; *Phone:* 270-762-3091; *Fax:* 270-762-3434. *E-mail:* kiismsu@murraystate.edu. *World Wide Web:* http://www.kiis.org/

LANGUAGE LIAISON
SPANISH IN ECUADOR–QUITO

Hosted by Language Liaison

Academic Focus • Spanish language and literature.

Program Information • Students attend classes at Language Liaison (Quito, Ecuador). Field trips; optional travel at an extra cost. Students typically earn 3–15 semester credits per term.

Sessions • New programs begin weekly, year-round.

Eligibility Requirements • Minimum age 17; open to precollege students, freshmen, sophomores, juniors, seniors, graduate students, adults; no foreign language proficiency required.

Living Arrangements • Students live in host family homes, hotels. Meals are taken with host family, in residences.

Costs (2005) • Contact sponsor for cost. $175 application fee. Financial aid available for all students: scholarship research service.

For More Information • Ms. Nancy Forman, President, Language Liaison, PO Box 1772, Pacific Palisades, CA 90272; *Phone:* 800-284-4448; *Fax:* 310-454-1706. *E-mail:* learn@languageliaison.com. *World Wide Web:* http://www.languageliaison.com/

LANGUAGE LINK
ACADEMIA DE ESPAÑOL–QUITO

Hosted by Academia de Español, Quito

Academic Focus • Spanish language and literature.

Program Information • Students attend classes at Academia de Español, Quito (Quito, Ecuador). Scheduled travel to the Amazon region; field trips to Otavalo, Saquisilí; optional travel to the Galapagos Islands at an extra cost. Students typically earn 6–12 semester credits per term.

Sessions • Classes begin every Monday, year-round.

Eligibility Requirements • Minimum age 14; open to precollege students, freshmen, sophomores, juniors, seniors, graduate students, adults; no foreign language proficiency required.

Living Arrangements • Students live in host family homes. Quarters are shared with host institution students. Meals are taken with host family, in residences.

Costs (2005) • $294 per week; includes tuition, housing, some meals, books and class materials, student support services, cultural activities, airport pick-up.

For More Information • Ms. Kay G. Rafool, Director, Language Link, PO Box 3006, Peoria, IL 61612-3006; *Phone:* 800-552-2051; *Fax:* 309-692-2926. *E-mail:* info@langlink.com. *World Wide Web:* http://www.langlink.com/

LINGUA SERVICE WORLDWIDE
VACATION 'N LEARN SPANISH IN ECUADOR

Hosted by Academia de Español, Quito

Academic Focus • Spanish language and literature, Spanish studies.

Program Information • Students attend classes at Academia de Español, Quito (Quito, Ecuador). Optional travel to cultural sites throughout Ecuador at an extra cost. Students typically earn 3 semester credits for 3 weeks, 6 semester credits for 5 weeks.

Sessions • Sessions of 2 or more weeks begin on Mondays, year-round.

Eligibility Requirements • Minimum age 16; open to precollege students, freshmen, sophomores, juniors, seniors, graduate students, adults; no foreign language proficiency required.

Living Arrangements • Students live in host family homes, hotels. Meals are taken with host family.

Costs (2006–2007) • Contact sponsor for cost. $100 application fee.

For More Information • Assistant Director, Lingua Service Worldwide, 75 Prospect Street, Suite 4, Huntington, NY 11743; *Phone:* 800-394-5327; *Fax:* 631-271-3441. *E-mail:* linguaservice@att.net. *World Wide Web:* http://www.linguaserviceworldwide.com/

UNIVERSITY OF DELAWARE
WINTER SESSION IN ECUADOR AND THE GALAPAGOS

Academic Focus • Botany, Spanish language and literature.

Program Information • Faculty members are drawn from the sponsor's U.S. staff and local instructors hired by the sponsor. Scheduled travel to the Galapagos Islands, national parks; field trips to cultural sites. Students typically earn 6 semester credits per term.

Sessions • Jan–Feb (winter).

Eligibility Requirements • Open to freshmen, sophomores, juniors, seniors, adults; 2.0 GPA; 1 letter of recommendation; no foreign language proficiency required.

Living Arrangements • Students live in host institution dormitories, host family homes. Meals are taken as a group, with host family, in central dining facility.

Costs (2005) • Contact sponsor for cost. $200 nonrefundable deposit required. Financial aid available for all students: scholarships.

For More Information • Center for International Studies, University of Delaware, 186 South College Avenue, Newark, DE 19716-1450; *Phone:* 888-831-4685; *Fax:* 302-831-6042. *E-mail:* studyabroad@udel.edu. *World Wide Web:* http://www.udel.edu/studyabroad/

UNIVERSITY OF NORTH CAROLINA AT WILMINGTON
SUMMER IN QUITO, ECUADOR

Hosted by Universidad San Francisco Quito

Academic Focus • Full curriculum.

Program Information • Students attend classes at Universidad San Francisco Quito (Quito, Ecuador). Scheduled travel to Tiputini, Puerto Lopez; field trips to the Otavalo Indian market, attractions around Quito, the "Middle of the World" (Equator monument); optional travel to the Galapagos Islands at an extra cost. Students typically earn 9 semester credits per term.

Sessions • May–Jul (summer).

Eligibility Requirements • Minimum age 18; open to sophomores, juniors, seniors, graduate students, adults; 2.5 GPA; 2 letters of recommendation; good academic standing at home school; 1 year of college course work in Spanish.

Living Arrangements • Students live in host family homes. Meals are taken with host family, in residences.

Costs (2005) • $4150; includes tuition, housing, some meals, insurance, excursions, student support services, laundry service. $200 nonrefundable deposit required. Financial aid available for students from sponsoring institution: scholarships, loans.

For More Information • Ms. Elizabeth A. Adams, Director, Education Abroad, University of North Carolina at Wilmington, 601 South College Road, Wilmington, NC 28403-5965; *Phone:* 910-962-3685; *Fax:* 910-962-4053. *E-mail:* adamse@uncw.edu. *World Wide Web:* http://www.uncw.edu/intprogs/

EGYPT

CAIRO

AMERICAN UNIVERSITY IN CAIRO
INTENSIVE ARABIC LANGUAGE PROGRAM

Hosted by American University in Cairo
Academic Focus • Arabic, Fusha.
Program Information • Students attend classes at American University in Cairo (Cairo, Egypt). Scheduled travel to upper Egypt, Sharm El Sheikh; field trips to the Citadel, Sakkara, mosques, churches; optional travel to Siwa, Dahab, Sinai at an extra cost. Students typically earn 12–15 semester credits per term.
Sessions • Jun–Jul (summer).
Eligibility Requirements • Minimum age 15; open to precollege students, freshmen, sophomores, juniors, seniors, graduate students, adults; 1 letter of recommendation; interest in Arabic language; no foreign language proficiency required.
Living Arrangements • Students live in host institution dormitories, locally rented apartments. Quarters are shared with host institution students, students from other programs. Meals are taken on one's own, in residences, in central dining facility, in restaurants.
Costs (2006) • $3625; includes tuition, insurance, student support services, medical services and insurance. $250 refundable deposit required.
For More Information • Ms. Dina Iskaros, Senior Student Affairs Officer, American University in Cairo, 420 Fifth Avenue, 3rd Floor, New York, NY 10018-2729; *Phone:* 212-730-8800; *Fax:* 212-730-1600. *E-mail:* diskaros@aucnyo.edu. *World Wide Web:* http://www.aucegypt.edu/catalog03/undergrad/studabroad/studabroad. html. Students may also apply through Arabic Language Institute, PO Box 2511, Cairo 11511, Egypt.

More About the Program
The Arabic Language Institute at the American University in Cairo offers contemporary Arabic language training in Egyptian colloquial and modern standard Arabic for students, businesspeople, diplomats, and scholars. Students may concentrate their studies of 20 hours per week in spoken (Egyptian) or literary Arabic or take a combination of both (10 hours of each). An equivalent amount of time is spent on assignments. The summer program runs from early June to early August and includes course-related travel around Egypt. Enrollment is limited to 100. Applications for the summer Intensive Arabic Program are due by March 1.

AMERICAN UNIVERSITY IN CAIRO
SUMMER STUDY ABROAD PROGRAM

Hosted by American University in Cairo
Academic Focus • Full curriculum.
Program Information • Students attend classes at American University in Cairo (Cairo, Egypt). Scheduled travel to Abu Simbel, Aswan, Luxor; field trips to pyramids, Alexandria, Memphis, Sharm El Sheikh, Hurghada; optional travel to Mt. Sinai, Sharm El Sheikh, Hurghada at an extra cost. Students typically earn 3–6 semester credits per term.
Sessions • Jun–Jul (summer).
Eligibility Requirements • Open to sophomores, juniors, graduate students; 2.5 GPA; 2 letters of recommendation; good academic standing at home school; English language proficiency; no foreign language proficiency required.
Living Arrangements • Students live in host institution dormitories, locally rented apartments. Quarters are shared with students from other programs. Meals are taken on one's own, in residences, in central dining facility, in restaurants.
Costs (2006) • $3625; includes tuition, student support services, medical services and insurance.
For More Information • Ms. Dina Iskaros, Senior Student Affairs Officer, American University in Cairo, 420 Fifth Avenue, 3rd Floor, New York, NY 10018-2729; *Phone:* 212-730-8800 Ext. 223; *Fax:* 212-730-1600. *E-mail:* diskaros@aucnyo.edu. *World Wide Web:* http://www.aucegypt.edu/catalog03/undergrad/studabroad/studabroad. html

More About the Program
The American University in Cairo (AUC) offers visiting students an opportunity to select courses from its undergraduate summer offerings. Areas of interest have been Egyptian, Arab, and Middle East history; politics; Middle East society; and Arabic. The language of instruction is English. Opportunities are available

for travel in Egypt. AUC is accredited by the Middle States Association of Colleges and Schools; the Accreditation Board for Engineering and Technology, Inc. (ABET); and the Computer Sciences Accreditation Board (CSAB).

AMERICAN UNIVERSITY IN CAIRO
WINTER PROGRAM

Hosted by American University in Cairo

Academic Focus • Arabic, art, Middle Eastern studies.

Program Information • Students attend classes at American University in Cairo (Cairo, Egypt). Scheduled travel to Sharm El Sheikh, Hurghada; field trips to Sharm El Sheikh, Hurghada. Students typically earn 3 semester credits per term.

Sessions • Jan (winter).

Eligibility Requirements • Open to freshmen, sophomores, juniors, seniors, adults; 2.0 GPA; English language proficiency; no foreign language proficiency required.

Living Arrangements • Students live in host institution dormitories, locally rented apartments. Quarters are shared with host institution students, students from other programs. Meals are taken on one's own, in residences, in central dining facility, in restaurants.

Costs (2006) • $563 per credit hour; includes tuition.

For More Information • Ms. Dina Iskaros, Senior Student Affairs Officer, American University in Cairo, 420 Fifth Avenue, 3rd Floor, New York, NY 10018-2729; *Phone:* 212-730-8800; *Fax:* 212-730-1600. *E-mail:* diskaros@aucnyo.edu. *World Wide Web:* http://www.aucegypt.edu/catalog03/undergrad/studabroad/studabroad.html. Students may also apply through American University in Cairo, Admission Office, PO Box 2511, Cairo 11511, Egypt.

More About the Program

In January, the American University in Cairo holds a three-week winter session that allows visiting students either to take concentrated study in beginning Modern Standard Arabic or elect to take one of a variety of subjects that change annually. Visiting students study in English with AUC's regular student body. In the past, courses have included subjects in environmental biology and Middle East studies. Planned cultural activities and travel to important sites near Cairo and within Egypt are an important part of the winter session. A comprehensive fee covers tuition, academic fees, and housing. Applications are due October 15.

STATE UNIVERSITY OF NEW YORK COLLEGE AT CORTLAND
AMERICAN UNIVERSITY CAIRO (SUMMER)

Hosted by American University in Cairo

Academic Focus • Arabic.

Program Information • Students attend classes at American University in Cairo (Cairo, Egypt). Field trips to the Red Sea, Alexandria; optional travel to Luxor, Aswan, Red Sea, Mount Sinai, Petra, Istanbul, Jerusalem at an extra cost. Students typically earn 6 semester credits per term.

Sessions • Jun–Aug (summer).

Eligibility Requirements • Minimum age 18; open to sophomores, juniors, seniors; 2.5 GPA; 2 letters of recommendation; good academic standing at home school; no foreign language proficiency required.

Living Arrangements • Students live in host institution dormitories, locally rented apartments. Quarters are shared with host institution students. Meals are taken on one's own, in central dining facility, in restaurants.

Costs (2005) • $6603; includes tuition, housing, all meals, insurance, excursions, international airfare, books and class materials, international student ID, student support services, passport and visa fees. $20 application fee. $200 nonrefundable deposit required. Financial aid available for students from sponsoring institution: scholarships, loans.

For More Information • Ms. Liz McCartney, Assistant Director, Office of International Programs, State University of New York College at Cortland, PO Box 2000, Cortland, NY 13045; *Phone:* 607-753-2209; *Fax:* 607-753-5989. *E-mail:* cortlandabroad@cortland.edu. *World Wide Web:* http://www.cortlandabroad.com/

ENGLAND

See also Ireland, Northern Ireland, Scotland, and Wales.

CITY-TO-CITY

UNIVERSITY OF KANSAS
BRITISH SUMMER INSTITUTE IN THE HUMANITIES

Academic Focus • Art history, British studies, English literature, history.
Program Information • Faculty members are drawn from the sponsor's U.S. staff. Scheduled travel to London, Edinburgh, York, the Lake District; field trips to Salisbury, Oxford, St. Andrews or the Borders, Glasgow. Students typically earn 9 semester credits per term.
Sessions • Jun–Jul (summer).
Eligibility Requirements • Minimum age 18; open to freshmen, sophomores, juniors, seniors; 2.5 GPA; 2 letters of recommendation; good academic standing at home school.
Living Arrangements • Students live in host institution dormitories, locally rented apartments, hotels. Meals are taken as a group, on one's own, in central dining facility, in restaurants.
Costs (2005) • $6000; includes tuition, housing, some meals, excursions, student support services, ground transportation within Great Britain, British Heritage Pass, medical evacuation and repatriation services. $38 application fee. $300 nonrefundable deposit required. Financial aid available for students from sponsoring institution: scholarships, loans.
For More Information • Mr. David Wiley, Program Coordinator, University of Kansas, Office of Study Abroad, Lippincott Hall, 1410 Jayhawk Boulevard, Room 108, Lawrence, KS 66045-7515; *Phone:* 785-864-3742; *Fax:* 785-864-5040. *E-mail:* osa@ku.edu. *World Wide Web:* http://www.ku.edu/~osa/

ALNWICK

ST. CLOUD STATE UNIVERSITY
ALNWICK CASTLE PROGRAM

Held at Alnwick Castle
Academic Focus • History, marketing, photography, social sciences.
Program Information • Classes are held on the campus of Alnwick Castle (Alnwick, England). Faculty members are drawn from the sponsor's U.S. staff and local instructors hired by the sponsor. Scheduled travel to London; field trips to local historic/cultural sites, Edinburgh; optional travel to Africa, Europe at an extra cost. Students typically earn 12 semester credits per term.
Sessions • May–Aug (summer).
Eligibility Requirements • Minimum age 18; open to freshmen, sophomores, juniors, seniors; 2.5 GPA.
Living Arrangements • Students live in a modernized 12th-century castle. Quarters are shared with host institution students. Meals are taken as a group, in central dining facility.
Costs (2005–2006) • $4395; includes housing, some meals, excursions, international airfare, international student ID, student support services. $75 application fee. Financial aid available for students from sponsoring institution: scholarships, work study, loans.
For More Information • Ms. Linda Raine, Study Abroad Coordinator, St. Cloud State University, Center for International Studies, 720 4th Avenue, South, St. Cloud, MN 56301; *Phone:* 320-308-4287; *Fax:* 320-308-4223. *E-mail:* study_abroad@stcloudstate.edu. *World Wide Web:* http://www.stcloudstate.edu/studyabroad

BATH

UNIVERSITY OF MINNESOTA
STONEHENGE TO STEAM

Academic Focus • British studies, costume design, engineering.
Program Information • Faculty members are drawn from the sponsor's U.S. staff and local instructors hired by the sponsor. Field trips to London, Bristol. Students typically earn 3 semester credits per term.
Sessions • May–Jun (summer).
Eligibility Requirements • Minimum age 18; open to freshmen, sophomores, juniors, seniors; 2.5 GPA.
Living Arrangements • Students live in YMCA. Quarters are shared with host institution students. Meals are taken as a group, on one's own, in central dining facility, in restaurants.
Costs (2007) • $4500; includes tuition, housing, some meals, insurance, excursions, international airfare, student support services. $50 application fee. $400 nonrefundable deposit required. Financial aid available for students from sponsoring institution: scholarships, loans.

For More Information • Learning Abroad Center, University of Minnesota, 230 Heller Hall, 271 19th Avenue South, Minneapolis, MN 55455; *Phone:* 612-626-9000; *Fax:* 612-626-8009. *E-mail:* umabroad@umn.edu. *World Wide Web:* http://www.umabroad.umn.edu/

BRIGHTON

INSTITUTE FOR STUDY ABROAD, BUTLER UNIVERSITY
UNIVERSITY OF SUSSEX–SUMMER STUDY

Hosted by University of Sussex
Academic Focus • American studies, architecture, art, creative writing, drama/theater, engineering, English literature, film and media studies, music, science, social sciences.
Program Information • Students attend classes at University of Sussex (Brighton, England). Optional travel to Oxford, London, Bath at an extra cost. Students typically earn 5-9 semester credits per term.
Sessions • Jun–Jul (summer), Jul–Aug (summer 2).
Eligibility Requirements • Open to sophomores, juniors, seniors; 2.5 GPA; good academic standing at home school; enrollment at an accredited American college or university.
Living Arrangements • Students live in host institution dormitories, program-owned apartments, program-owned houses. Quarters are shared with host institution students. Meals are taken on one's own, in residences.
Costs (2005) • $3775 for 1 session; $5875 for 2 sessions; includes tuition, housing, student support services, pre-departure advising. $40 application fee. $500 nonrefundable deposit required. Financial aid available for all students: scholarships.
For More Information • Institute for Study Abroad, Butler University, 1100 West 42nd Street, Suite 305, Indianapolis, IN 46208-3345; *Phone:* 800-858-0229; *Fax:* 317-940-9704. *E-mail:* study-abroad@butler.edu. *World Wide Web:* http://www.ifsa-butler.org/

MICHIGAN STATE UNIVERSITY
BUSINESS STUDY ABROAD IN BRIGHTON

Held at University of Brighton
Academic Focus • Accounting, business administration/management.
Program Information • Classes are held on the campus of University of Brighton (Brighton, England). Faculty members are drawn from the sponsor's U.S. staff. Scheduled travel to France, Belgium, Netherlands.
Sessions • Jul–Aug (summer).
Eligibility Requirements • Minimum age 18; open to freshmen, sophomores, juniors, seniors; major in business; course work in business; 2.0 GPA.
Living Arrangements • Students live in host institution dormitories. Quarters are shared with students from other programs. Meals are taken on one's own, in residences.
Costs (2005) • $3264; includes housing, some meals, insurance, excursions, student support services. $100 application fee. $200 nonrefundable deposit required. Financial aid available for students from sponsoring institution: scholarships, loans.
For More Information • Mrs. Meghan Hock, Educational Programs Coordinator, Michigan State University, Office of Study Abroad, 109 International Center, East Lansing, MI 48824; *Phone:* 517-353-8920; *Fax:* 517-432-2082. *E-mail:* hock@msu.edu. *World Wide Web:* http://studyabroad.msu.edu/

UNIVERSITY OF SUSSEX
INTERNATIONAL SUMMER SCHOOL

Hosted by University of Sussex
Academic Focus • Full curriculum.
Program Information • Students attend classes at University of Sussex (Brighton, England). Field trips to local area sites, the Imperial War Museum, Globe Theatre, Kent, Essex, France. Students typically earn 18 Sussex credits per term.
Sessions • Jun–Jul (summer), Jul–Aug (summer 2).

ENGLAND
Brighton

Eligibility Requirements • Minimum age 17; open to precollege students, freshmen, sophomores, juniors, seniors, graduate students, adults; good academic standing at home school; prerequisites for some courses.
Living Arrangements • Students live in host institution dormitories, locally rented apartments, program-owned apartments, program-owned houses. Meals are taken as a group, on one's own, in residences, in central dining facility, in restaurants.
Costs (2005) • £980 for 4 weeks; £1850 for 8 weeks; includes tuition, lab equipment, student support services, computer, library, and sports facility access, class-related excursions. £100 deposit required. Financial aid available for students: scholarships, scholarships and work-study opportunities for students from developing countries.
For More Information • Dr. Penny Chaloner, Director, International Summer School, University of Sussex, International and Study Abroad Office, Arts B, Falmer, Brighton BN1 9QN, England; *Phone:* +44 1273-678314; *Fax:* +44 1273-678640. *E-mail:* summer@sussex.ac.uk. *World Wide Web:* http://www.sussex.ac.uk/international

BRISTOL

ILLINOIS STATE UNIVERSITY
SUMMER PROGRAM IN BRISTOL, ENGLAND

Hosted by University of the West of England
Academic Focus • British studies, international business.
Program Information • Students attend classes at University of the West of England (Bristol, England). Scheduled travel to Brussels, Belgium; field trips to London, Roman Baths, Berkley Castle. Students typically earn 6 semester credits per term.
Sessions • May–Jun (summer).
Eligibility Requirements • Open to sophomores, juniors, seniors; course work in economics, international business; 2.5 GPA; 2 letters of recommendation; good academic standing at home school; essay.
Living Arrangements • Students live in host family homes, hotels. Quarters are shared with host institution students, students from other programs. Meals are taken on one's own, in restaurants.
Costs (2005) • $5619; includes tuition, housing, all meals, insurance, excursions, international airfare, books and class materials, international student ID, student support services, personal expenses. $150 application fee. Financial aid available for students from sponsoring institution: scholarships, loans.
For More Information • Office of International Studies and Programs, Illinois State University, Campus Box 6120, Normal, IL 61790-6120; *Phone:* 309-438-5276; *Fax:* 309-438-3987. *E-mail:* oisp@ilstu.edu. *World Wide Web:* http://www.internationalstudies.ilstu.edu/

CAMBRIDGE

MICHIGAN STATE UNIVERSITY
BUSINESS SUMMER PROGRAM IN CAMBRIDGE

Held at Cambridge University Center
Academic Focus • Business administration/management.
Program Information • Classes are held on the campus of Cambridge University Center (Cambridge, England). Faculty members are drawn from the sponsor's U.S. staff and local instructors hired by the sponsor. Students typically earn 6 semester credits per term.
Sessions • Jul–Aug (summer).
Eligibility Requirements • Minimum age 18; open to sophomores, juniors, seniors; major in business; 2.0 GPA; good academic standing at home school.
Living Arrangements • Students live in host institution dormitories. Quarters are shared with host institution students. Meals are taken on one's own, in residences.
Costs (2005) • $2900; includes housing, some meals, insurance, excursions. $100 application fee. $200 nonrefundable deposit required. Financial aid available for students from sponsoring institution: scholarships, loans.
For More Information • Mrs. Meghan Hock, Educational Programs Coordinator, Michigan State University, Office of Study Abroad, 109

International Center, East Lansing, MI 48824-1035; *Phone:* 517-353-8920; *Fax:* 517-432-2082. *E-mail:* hock@msu.edu. *World Wide Web:* http://studyabroad.msu.edu/

MICHIGAN STATE UNIVERSITY
PUBLIC AFFAIRS IN CAMBRIDGE

Hosted by University of Cambridge
Academic Focus • International affairs, urban studies.
Program Information • Students attend classes at University of Cambridge (Cambridge, England). Students typically earn 8 semester credits per term.
Sessions • Jul–Aug (summer).
Eligibility Requirements • Minimum age 18; open to freshmen, sophomores, juniors, seniors; good academic standing at home school; faculty approval; minimum 3.0 GPA for freshmen, minimum 2.4 GPA for all others.
Living Arrangements • Students live in host institution dormitories. Quarters are shared with host institution students, students from other programs. Meals are taken as a group, on one's own, in central dining facility, in restaurants.
Costs (2005) • $3500; includes housing, some meals, insurance, excursions, student support services. $100 application fee. $200 nonrefundable deposit required. Financial aid available for students from sponsoring institution: scholarships, loans.
For More Information • Mrs. Meghan Hock, Educational Programs Coordinator, Michigan State University, Office of Study Abroad, 109 International Center, East Lansing, MI 48824-1035; *Phone:* 517-353-8920; *Fax:* 517-432-2082. *E-mail:* hock@msu.edu. *World Wide Web:* http://studyabroad.msu.edu/

ROCKLAND COMMUNITY COLLEGE
UNIVERSITY OF CAMBRIDGE SUMMER HONORS SCHOOL

Hosted by University of Cambridge
Academic Focus • Art history, English literature, history, science.
Program Information • Students attend classes at University of Cambridge (Cambridge, England). Optional travel to Stratford-upon-Avon, London, Warwick, Sandringham, Norwich at an extra cost. Students typically earn 4 semester credits per term.
Sessions • Jun–Jul (summer), Jul–Aug (summer 2).
Eligibility Requirements • Minimum age 18; open to freshmen, sophomores, juniors, seniors; 3.3 GPA; completion of 24 college credits; 2 honors courses.
Living Arrangements • Students live in host institution dormitories. Meals are taken as a group, in central dining facility.
Costs (2005) • $4250 (estimated); includes tuition, housing, some meals, insurance, international student ID. $200 nonrefundable deposit required. Financial aid available for students from sponsoring institution: scholarships, loans.
For More Information • Ms. Fran Rodríguez, Coordinator, Study Abroad, Rockland Community College, 145 College Road, Suffern, NY 10901; *Phone:* 845-574-4205; *Fax:* 845-574-4423. *E-mail:* study-abroad@sunyrockland.edu. *World Wide Web:* http://www.rocklandabroad.com/

UNIVERSITY OF CAMBRIDGE
ART HISTORY SUMMER SCHOOL

Hosted by University of Cambridge
Academic Focus • Art, art history.
Program Information • Students attend classes at University of Cambridge (Cambridge, England). Field trips to museums, galleries, theatres. Students typically earn 4 semester credits per term.
Sessions • Jul (summer).
Eligibility Requirements • Minimum age 18; open to freshmen, sophomores, juniors, seniors, graduate students, adults.
Living Arrangements • Students live in program-owned apartments, college single-study bedrooms. Quarters are shared with students from other programs. Meals are taken as a group, in residences, in central dining facility.
Costs (2007) • Contact sponsor for cost. £400 application fee. Financial aid available for students: scholarships available to nominated individuals.
For More Information • Mrs. Zoe Burton, Student Relations Officer, University of Cambridge, International Programmes, Greenwich House, Madingley Rise, Madingley Road, Cambridge CB3 0TX,

England; *Phone:* +44 1223-760850; *Fax:* +44 1223-760848. *E-mail:* intenq@cont-ed.cam.ac.uk. *World Wide Web:* http://www.cont-ed.cam.ac.uk/IntSummer/

UNIVERSITY OF CAMBRIDGE
HISTORY SUMMER SCHOOL

Hosted by University of Cambridge

Academic Focus • Ancient history, civilization studies, history, Renaissance studies.

Program Information • Students attend classes at University of Cambridge (Cambridge, England). Field trips to museums, galleries, theatres. Students typically earn 4 semester credits per term.

Sessions • Jul (summer), half program also available.

Eligibility Requirements • Minimum age 18; open to freshmen, sophomores, juniors, seniors, graduate students, adults.

Living Arrangements • Students live in program-owned apartments, college single-study bedrooms. Quarters are shared with students from other programs. Meals are taken as a group, in residences, in central dining facility.

Costs (2007) • Contact sponsor for cost. £400 application fee. Financial aid available for students: scholarships available to nominated individuals.

For More Information • Mrs. Zoe Burton, Student Relations Officer, University of Cambridge, International Programmes, Greenwich House, Madingley Rise, Madingley Road, Cambridge CB3 0TX, England; *Phone:* +44 1223-760850; *Fax:* +44 1223-760848. *E-mail:* intenq@cont-ed.cam.ac.uk. *World Wide Web:* http://www.cont-ed.cam.ac.uk/IntSummer/

UNIVERSITY OF CAMBRIDGE
LITERATURE SUMMER SCHOOL

Hosted by University of Cambridge

Academic Focus • English literature, literature.

Program Information • Students attend classes at University of Cambridge (Cambridge, England). Field trips to museums, galleries, theatres. Students typically earn 4 semester credits per term.

Sessions • Jul (summer), half program also available.

Eligibility Requirements • Minimum age 18; open to freshmen, sophomores, juniors, seniors, graduate students, adults.

Living Arrangements • Students live in program-owned apartments, college single-study bedrooms. Quarters are shared with host institution students. Meals are taken as a group, in residences, in central dining facility.

Costs (2007) • Contact sponsor for cost. £400 application fee. Financial aid available for students: scholarships available to nominated individuals.

For More Information • Mrs. Zoe Burton, Student Relations Officer, University of Cambridge, International Programmes, Greenwich House, Madingley Rise, Madingley Road, Cambridge CB3 0TX, England; *Phone:* +44 1223-760850; *Fax:* +44 1954-760848. *E-mail:* intenq@cont-ed.cam.ac.uk. *World Wide Web:* http://www.cont-ed.cam.ac.uk/IntSummer/

UNIVERSITY OF CAMBRIDGE
MEDIEVAL STUDIES SUMMER SCHOOL

Hosted by University of Cambridge

Academic Focus • Area studies, European studies, history, interdisciplinary studies, literature, philosophy, religious studies, Renaissance studies.

Program Information • Students attend classes at University of Cambridge (Cambridge, England). Field trips. Students typically earn 4 semester credits per term.

Sessions • Jul–Aug (summer).

Eligibility Requirements • Minimum age 18; open to freshmen, sophomores, juniors, seniors, graduate students, adults.

Living Arrangements • Students live in program-owned apartments, college single-study bedrooms. Quarters are shared with students from other programs. Meals are taken as a group, in residences, in central dining facility.

Costs (2007) • Contact sponsor for cost. £400 application fee.

For More Information • Mrs. Zoe Burton, Student Relations Officer, University of Cambridge, International Programmes, Greenwich House, Madingley Rise, Madingley Road, Cambridge CB3 0TX,

England; *Phone:* +44 1223-760850; *Fax:* +44 1223-760848. *E-mail:* intenq@cont-ed.cam.ac.uk. *World Wide Web:* http://www.cont-ed.cam.ac.uk/IntSummer/

UNIVERSITY OF CAMBRIDGE
SCIENCE SUMMER SCHOOL

Hosted by University of Cambridge

Academic Focus • Biological/life sciences, botany, chemical sciences, earth sciences, psychology, science.

Program Information • Students attend classes at University of Cambridge (Cambridge, England). Field trips to museums, galleries, theatres. Students typically earn 4 semester credits per term.

Sessions • Jul–Aug (summer).

Eligibility Requirements • Minimum age 18; open to freshmen, sophomores, juniors, seniors, graduate students, adults.

Living Arrangements • Students live in program-owned apartments, college single-study bedrooms. Quarters are shared with students from other programs. Meals are taken as a group, in residences, in central dining facility.

Costs (2007) • Contact sponsor for cost. £400 application fee. Financial aid available for students: scholarships available to nominated individuals.

For More Information • Mrs. Zoe Burton, Student Relations Officer, University of Cambridge, International Programmes, Greenwich House, Madingley Rise, Madingley Road, Cambridge CB3 0TX, England; *Phone:* +44 1223-760850; *Fax:* +44 1223-760848. *E-mail:* intenq@cont-ed.cam.ac.uk. *World Wide Web:* http://www.cont-ed.cam.ac.uk/IntSummer/

UNIVERSITY OF CAMBRIDGE
SHAKESPEARE SUMMER SCHOOL

Hosted by University of Cambridge

Academic Focus • British studies, English literature, history, interdisciplinary studies, literature, performing arts.

Program Information • Students attend classes at University of Cambridge (Cambridge, England). Field trips to museums, galleries, theatres. Students typically earn 4 semester credits per term.

Sessions • Jul–Aug (summer).

Eligibility Requirements • Minimum age 18; open to freshmen, sophomores, juniors, seniors, graduate students, adults.

Living Arrangements • Students live in program-owned apartments, college single-study bedrooms. Quarters are shared with students from other programs. Meals are taken as a group, in residences, in central dining facility.

Costs (2007) • Contact sponsor for cost. £400 application fee.

For More Information • Mrs. Zoe Burton, Student Relations Officer, University of Cambridge, International Programmes, Greenwich House, Madingley Rise, Madingley Road, Cambridge CB3 0TX, England; *Phone:* +44 1223-760850; *Fax:* +44 1223-760848. *E-mail:* intenq@cont-ed.cam.ac.uk. *World Wide Web:* http://www.cont-ed.cam.ac.uk/IntSummer/

UNIVERSITY OF CAMBRIDGE
UNIVERSITY OF CAMBRIDGE INTERNATIONAL SUMMER SCHOOLS PROGRAMME

Hosted by University of Cambridge

Academic Focus • Art history, cultural studies, English literature, history, interdisciplinary studies, literature, psychology, Renaissance studies, science, social sciences.

Program Information • Students attend classes at University of Cambridge (Cambridge, England). Field trips to museums, galleries, buildings of architectural interest. Students typically earn 4 semester credits per term.

Sessions • Jul–Aug (summer), Aug (summer 2).

Eligibility Requirements • Minimum age 18; open to freshmen, sophomores, juniors, seniors, graduate students, adults.

Living Arrangements • Students live in program-owned apartments, hotels, college single-study bedrooms. Quarters are shared with students from other programs. Meals are taken as a group, in residences, in central dining facility.

Costs (2007) • Contact sponsor for cost. £400 application fee. Financial aid available for students: scholarships available to nominated individuals.

ENGLAND
Cambridge

For More Information • Mrs. Zoe Burton, Student Relations Officer, University of Cambridge, International Programmes, Greenwich House, Madingley Rise, Madingley Road, Cambridge CB3 0TX, England; *Phone:* +44 1223-760850; *Fax:* +44 1223-760848. *E-mail:* intenq@cont-ed.cam.ac.uk. *World Wide Web:* http://www.cont-ed.cam.ac.uk/IntSummer/

More About the Program
Every summer, the University of Cambridge opens its doors to an international community of students, aged from 18 to more than 80, from all over the world. International Summer Schools have been held at the University for more than eighty years and offer plenary lectures and seminars as well as a chance to participate in extracurricular events and excursions. All programs take place in historic Cambridge, staying within college accommodations. In addition to the specialist subject programs—art history, history, literature, medieval studies, science, and Shakespeare—there are two interdisciplinary Summer Schools. For more information, students may contact the program (phone: +44-1223-760850; fax: +44-1223-760848; e-mail: intenq@cont-ed.cam.ac.uk; Web site: http://www.cont-ed.cam.ac.uk/IntSummer).

UNIVERSITY OF KANSAS
LEGAL HISTORY, POLITICS, AND CULTURE IN CAMBRIDGE, ENGLAND

Held at University of Cambridge–Newnham College
Academic Focus • History, law and legal studies.
Program Information • Classes are held on the campus of University of Cambridge–Newnham College (Cambridge, England). Faculty members are drawn from the sponsor's U.S. staff and local instructors hired by the sponsor. Scheduled travel to Edinburgh; field trips to London, Oxford. Students typically earn 6 semester credits per term.
Sessions • Jun-Jul (summer).
Eligibility Requirements • Minimum age 18; open to freshmen, sophomores, juniors, seniors, adults; 2.5 GPA; 2 letters of recommendation; good academic standing at home school; preference given to students planning a career in law.
Living Arrangements • Students live in host institution dormitories. Meals are taken as a group, on one's own, in central dining facility, in restaurants.
Costs (2005) • $4650; includes tuition, housing, some meals, excursions, student support services, medical evacuation and repatriation services. $38 application fee. $300 nonrefundable deposit required. Financial aid available for students from sponsoring institution: scholarships, loans.
For More Information • Mr. David Wiley, Program Coordinator, University of Kansas, Office of Study Abroad, Lippincott Hall, 1410 Jayhawk Boulevard, Room 108, Lawrence, KS 66045-7515; *Phone:* 785-864-3742; *Fax:* 785-864-5040. *E-mail:* osa@ku.edu. *World Wide Web:* http://www.ku.edu/~osa/

UNIVERSITY OF NEW HAMPSHIRE
CAMBRIDGE SUMMER PROGRAM

Hosted by University of Cambridge–Gonville and Caius College
Academic Focus • Creative writing, English literature, history.
Program Information • Students attend classes at University of Cambridge–Gonville and Caius College (Cambridge, England). Field trips to London, Avebury, Bath, Dover, Canterbury, Coventry, Stratford-upon-Avon; optional travel to Edinburgh, Wales at an extra cost. Students typically earn 8 semester credits per term.
Sessions • Jul-Aug (summer).
Eligibility Requirements • Open to sophomores, juniors, seniors, graduate students, adults; 1 letter of recommendation; good academic standing at home school; transcripts of all prior college work.
Living Arrangements • Students live in host institution dormitories. Meals are taken as a group, in central dining facility.

Costs (2006) • $6475; includes tuition, housing, some meals, excursions. $35 application fee. $300 nonrefundable deposit required. Financial aid available for students from sponsoring institution: loans.
For More Information • Mr. Andrew Merton, Director, University of New Hampshire, Hamilton Smith Hall, 95 Main Street, Durham, NH 03824-3574; *Phone:* 603-862-3962; *Fax:* 603-862-3962. *E-mail:* cambridge.program@unh.edu. *World Wide Web:* http://www.unh.edu/cie/index.html

EASTBOURNE

ILLINOIS STATE UNIVERSITY
NURSING IN ENGLAND

Hosted by University of Brighton
Academic Focus • Nursing.
Program Information • Students attend classes at University of Brighton (Eastbourne, England). Students typically earn 3 semester credits per term.
Sessions • May (summer).
Eligibility Requirements • Open to juniors, seniors; major in nursing; 2.5 GPA; 2 letters of recommendation; good academic standing at home school; essay.
Living Arrangements • Students live in host institution dormitories. Quarters are shared with host institution students, students from other programs. Meals are taken on one's own, in residences, in restaurants.
Costs (2005) • $2773; includes tuition, housing, all meals, insurance, international airfare, international student ID, student support services, personal expenses. $150 application fee. Financial aid available for students from sponsoring institution: scholarships, loans.
For More Information • Transcultural Program Coordinator, Illinois State University, 5810 Mennonite College of Nursing, Edwards Hall, Normal, IL 61790-5810; *Phone:* 309-438-7400; *Fax:* 309-438-2620. *E-mail:* meninfo@ilstu.edu. *World Wide Web:* http://www.internationalstudies.ilstu.edu/

ILLINOIS STATE UNIVERSITY
UNIVERSITY OF BRIGHTON'S SUMMER SCHOOL PROGRAM IN ENGLAND

Hosted by University of Brighton
Academic Focus • Education.
Program Information • Students attend classes at University of Brighton (Eastbourne, England). Field trips to Brighton, London; optional travel to Bath, Stonehenge, Paris at an extra cost. Students typically earn 6 semester credits per term.
Sessions • Jul-Aug (summer).
Eligibility Requirements • Open to sophomores, juniors, seniors, graduate students; major in education; 2.5 GPA; 1 letter of recommendation; good academic standing at home school.
Living Arrangements • Students live in host institution dormitories. Quarters are shared with host institution students, students from other programs. Meals are taken on one's own, in residences.
Costs (2005) • $5300; includes tuition, housing, insurance, international airfare, books and class materials, international student ID, student support services, personal expenses and food. $150 application fee. Financial aid available for students from sponsoring institution: scholarships, loans.
For More Information • Office of International Studies and Programs, Illinois State University, Campus Box 6120, Normal, IL 61790-6120; *Phone:* 309-438-5276; *Fax:* 309-438-3987. *E-mail:* oisp@ilstu.edu. *World Wide Web:* http://www.internationalstudies.ilstu.edu/

GRANTHAM

UNIVERSITY OF EVANSVILLE
HARLAXTON COLLEGE

Hosted by University of Evansville–Harlaxton College

Academic Focus • Business administration/management, cultural studies, drama/theater, education, English literature, European studies, health-care management, music, nursing, political science and government.

Program Information • Students attend classes at University of Evansville–Harlaxton College (Grantham, England). Field trips to London, York, Coventry, Stratford-upon-Avon, Cambridge; optional travel to Ireland, Paris, Edinburgh, London at an extra cost. Students typically earn 3–6 semester credits per term.

Sessions • May–Jun (summer).

Eligibility Requirements • Minimum age 19; open to sophomores, juniors, seniors, graduate students; 2.5 GPA; 1 letter of recommendation; good academic standing at home school; consent of advisor.

Living Arrangements • Students live in a Victorian manor house and carriage house. Quarters are shared with host institution students, students from other programs. Meals are taken as a group, in central dining facility.

Costs (2005) • $2395 for 3 credits; $3355 for 6 credits; includes tuition, housing, all meals, student support services, registration, transport fee, health fee, activity fee. $250 nonrefundable deposit required.

For More Information • Mr. Earl Kirk, Director of Study Abroad, University of Evansville, 1800 Lincoln Avenue, Union 208, Evansville, IN 47722; *Phone:* 812-488-1040; *Fax:* 812-488-6389. *E-mail:* ek43@evansville.edu. *World Wide Web:* http://www.ueharlax.ac.uk/

KINGSTON UPON THAMES

KINGSTON UNIVERSITY
KINGSTON SUMMER SCHOOL

Hosted by Kingston University

Academic Focus • Art history, British studies, English literature, international business.

Program Information • Students attend classes at Kingston University (Kingston upon Thames, England). Field trips to Oxford, Stonehenge, Bath, Greenwich; theatre; House of Parliament; optional travel to Paris, Amsterdam, Dublin, Edinburgh at an extra cost. Students typically earn 3–6 semester credits per term.

Sessions • Jun–Jul (summer).

Eligibility Requirements • Minimum age 18; open to freshmen, sophomores, juniors, seniors, graduate students, adults; 2.5 GPA; 1 letter of recommendation; good academic standing at home school.

Living Arrangements • Students live in host institution dormitories. Quarters are shared with students from other programs. Meals are taken on one's own, in restaurants.

Costs (2005) • £1650 for 1 course; $1975 for 2 courses; includes tuition, housing, some meals, excursions, books and class materials, student support services, 1 month all London Travelcard, airport pick-up and return, welcome reception, farewell dinner. Financial aid available for all students: loans, home university financial aid.

For More Information • Ms. Allison Cooper, Study Abroad Manager, Kingston University, Millennium House, 21 Eden Street, Kingston upon Thames KT1 1BL, England; *Phone:* +44 208-547-7784; *Fax:* +44 208-547-7789. *E-mail:* amcooper@kingston.ac.uk. *World Wide Web:* http://www.kingston.ac.uk/avsp/

LANCASTER

LANCASTER UNIVERSITY
CHANGING PLACES–LANCASTER AND THE LAKE DISTRICT: HISTORICAL, GEOGRAPHICAL, AND CULTURAL PERSPECTIVES

Hosted by Lancaster University

Academic Focus • British studies, English literature, environmental science/studies, interdisciplinary studies, parks and recreation.

Program Information • Students attend classes at Lancaster University (Lancaster, England). Field trips to the Lake District, Hadrian's Wall, sites of historic and cultural interest. Students typically earn 4 semester credits per term.

Sessions • Aug–Sep (summer).

Eligibility Requirements • Minimum age 18; open to sophomores, juniors, seniors; 2.8 GPA; 2 letters of recommendation; good academic standing at home school; personal statement; academic transcript.

Living Arrangements • Students live in on-campus single rooms. Meals are taken on one's own, in residences.

Costs (2006) • $2500 (estimated); includes tuition, housing, insurance, excursions, student support services, class materials. $500 nonrefundable deposit required.

For More Information • Ms. Jane Atkinson, Director, Study Abroad Program, Lancaster University, University House, Lancaster LA1 4YW, England; *Phone:* +44 1524-592035; *Fax:* +44 1524-593907. *E-mail:* nao@lancaster.ac.uk. *World Wide Web:* http://www.lancaster.ac.uk/users/international/overseas/indx.htm. Students may also apply through Arcadia University, Center for Education Abroad, 450 South Easton Road, Glenside, PA 19038-3295; Butler University, Institute for Study Abroad, 1100 West 42nd Street, Suite 305, Indianapolis, IN 46208-3345.

More About the Program

Lancaster University offers 3 presession programs that are 4 weeks long and run from mid-August to mid-September. Each course is worth 4 upper-division semester credits.

This Scepter'd Isle: Aspects of British History and Culture explores the origins of the Church of England, the Industrial Revolution and the development of democracy, the poetry of Wordsworth, and British politics since 1945.

Changing Places—Lancaster and the Lake District offers historical, cultural, and geographical perspectives on northwest England, looking at the Roman occupation, the interpretation of the landscape, the Lake District's cultural heritage, and tourism, society, and the environment.

The World About Us: Explorations in the History, Principles, and Applications of Science looks at the history of medicine from ancient Greece to the early modern period, physics for nonmathematicians, ecology, and geology.

Additional information can be found at http://www.lancs.ac.uk/depts/conted/presession/index.htm.

LANCASTER UNIVERSITY
THIS SCEPTER'D ISLE: ASPECTS OF BRITISH HISTORY AND CULTURE

Hosted by Lancaster University

Academic Focus • British studies, English literature, history, interdisciplinary studies, political science and government.

Program Information • Students attend classes at Lancaster University (Lancaster, England). Field trips to the Lake District, industrial heritage sites, sites of literary, religious, and historic interest. Students typically earn 4 semester credits per term.

Sessions • Aug–Sep (summer).

Eligibility Requirements • Minimum age 18; open to sophomores, juniors, seniors; 2.7 GPA; 2 letters of recommendation; good academic standing at home school; personal statement; academic transcript.

Living Arrangements • Students live in on-campus single rooms. Quarters are shared with students from other programs. Meals are taken on one's own, in residences.

Costs (2006) • $2500 (estimated); includes tuition, housing, insurance, excursions, student support services, class materials. $500 nonrefundable deposit required.

For More Information • Ms. Jane Atkinson, Director, Study Abroad Program, Lancaster University, University House, Lancaster LA1 4YW, England; *Phone:* +44 1524-592035; *Fax:* +44 1524-593907. *E-mail:* nao@lancaster.ac.uk. *World Wide Web:* http://www.lancaster.ac.uk/users/international/overseas/indx.htm. Students may also apply through Arcadia University, Center for Education Abroad, 450 South Easton Road, Glenside, PA 19038-3295; Butler University, Institute for Study Abroad, 1100 West 42nd Street, Suite 305, Indianapolis, IN 46208-3345.

ENGLAND
Lancaster

LANCASTER UNIVERSITY
THE WORLD ABOUT US: EXPLORATIONS IN THE HISTORY, PRINCIPLES, AND APPLICATIONS OF SCIENCE

Hosted by Lancaster University
Academic Focus • Ecology, geology, physics, science.
Program Information • Students attend classes at Lancaster University (Lancaster, England). Field trips to the Lake District, sites of historic and scientific interest. Students typically earn 4 semester credits per term.
Sessions • Aug–Sep (summer).
Eligibility Requirements • Minimum age 18; open to sophomores, juniors, seniors; 2.8 GPA; 2 letters of recommendation; good academic standing at home school; personal statement; academic transcript.
Living Arrangements • Students live in on-campus single rooms. Meals are taken on one's own, in residences.
Costs (2006) • $2500 (estimated); includes tuition, housing, insurance, excursions, student support services, class materials. $500 nonrefundable deposit required.
For More Information • Ms. Jane Atkinson, Director, Study Abroad Program, Lancaster University, University House, Lancaster LA1 4YW, England; *Phone:* +44 1524-592035; *Fax:* +44 1524-593807. *E-mail:* nao@lancaster.ac.uk. *World Wide Web:* http://www.lancaster.ac.uk/users/international/overseas/indx.htm. Students may also apply through Arcadia University, Center for Education Abroad, 450 South Easton Road, Glenside, PA 19038-3295; Butler University, Institute for Study Abroad, 1100 West 42nd Street, Suite 305, Indianapolis, IN 46208-3345.

LONDON

ACADEMIC PROGRAMS INTERNATIONAL (API)
(API)–LONDON LIBERAL ARTS AND HUMANITIES

Hosted by London Metropolitan University
Academic Focus • Art history, drama/theater, English literature, history.
Program Information • Students attend classes at London Metropolitan University (London, England). Field trips to Brighton, Nottingham, Oxford, York; Stratford-upon-Avon. Students typically earn 6 semester credits per term.
Sessions • Jun–Jul (summer).
Eligibility Requirements • Minimum age 18; open to sophomores, juniors, seniors; 2.75 GPA; 1 letter of recommendation; good academic standing at home school; official transcript from home university; personal essay.
Living Arrangements • Students live in locally rented apartments. Quarters are shared with host institution students. Meals are taken on one's own, in restaurants.
Costs (2006) • $16,600; includes tuition, housing, insurance, excursions, student support services. $150 nonrefundable deposit required. Financial aid available for all students: scholarships.
For More Information • Ms. Jennifer C. Allen, Director, Academic Programs International (API), 107 East Hopkins, San Marcos, TX 78666; *Phone:* 800-844-4124; *Fax:* 512-392-8420. *E-mail:* api@academicintl.com. *World Wide Web:* http://www.academicintl.com/

ACADEMIC STUDIES ABROAD
ACADEMIC STUDIES ABROAD–LONDON, ENGLAND

Hosted by Regent's College
Academic Focus • Full curriculum.
Program Information • Students attend classes at Regent's College (London, England). Field trips to Cambridge, Bath. Students typically earn 3–6 semester credits per term.
Sessions • May–Jun (summer).
Eligibility Requirements • Minimum age 18; open to sophomores, juniors, seniors; 2.5 GPA; college transcript.
Living Arrangements • Students live in host institution dormitories. Quarters are shared with host institution students. Meals are taken as a group, in central dining facility.
Costs (2006) • $4200; includes tuition, housing, all meals, insurance, excursions, international student ID, student support services, cell phone. $150 refundable deposit required. Financial aid available for all students: scholarships.

For More Information • Mr. Lee Frankel, Director, Academic Studies Abroad, 434 Massachusetts Avenue, Suite 501, Boston, MA 02118; *Phone:* 617-437-9388; *Fax:* 617-437-9390. *E-mail:* lee@academicstudies.com. *World Wide Web:* http://www.academicstudies.com

ACCENT INTERNATIONAL CONSORTIUM FOR ACADEMIC PROGRAMS ABROAD
SUMMER IN LONDON

Academic Focus • History, visual and performing arts.
Program Information • Faculty members are drawn from the sponsor's U.S. staff. Field trips to Stonehenge, Salisbury, Bath, Oxford. Students typically earn 6 semester credits per term.
Sessions • Jul–Aug (summer).
Eligibility Requirements • Minimum age 18; open to freshmen, sophomores, juniors, seniors, graduate students, adults.
Living Arrangements • Students live in locally rented apartments. Quarters are shared with students from other programs. Meals are taken on one's own, in residences.
Costs (2005) • $3550; includes housing, excursions, international student ID, student support services. $250 nonrefundable deposit required.
For More Information • ACCENT International Consortium for Academic Programs Abroad, 870 Market Street, Suite 1026, San Francisco, CA 94102; *Phone:* 800-869-9291; *Fax:* 415-835-3749. *E-mail:* info@accentintl.com. *World Wide Web:* http://www.accentintl.com/

AMERICAN INSTITUTE FOR FOREIGN STUDY (AIFS)
AIFS–LONDON, ENGLAND–RICHMOND, THE AMERICAN INTERNATIONAL UNIVERSITY IN LONDON

Hosted by Richmond–The American International University in London
Academic Focus • Business administration/management, communications, film and media studies, marketing, music, political science and government, public policy, sociology.
Program Information • Students attend classes at Richmond–The American International University in London (London, England). Field trips to Stonehenge, Salisbury, Greenwich, Cambridge, Oxford, Hampton Court, Windsor and Brighton; Cultural Activities; optional travel to Weekend excursion to Paris for a supplement of $499 at an extra cost. Students typically earn up to 9 credits.
Sessions • May–Jul (3, 6, or 9 week programs).
Eligibility Requirements • Minimum age 18; open to freshmen, sophomores, juniors, seniors; 2.0 GPA; good academic standing at home school.
Living Arrangements • Students live in host institution dormitories, program-owned apartments, hotels. Quarters are shared with host institution students. Meals are taken as a group, in residences.
Costs (2007) • 3 weeks: $4799, 6 weeks; $6899, 9 weeks: $8999; includes tuition, housing, some meals, insurance, excursions, student support services, On-site Resident Director, Phone Card to call the U.S., Computer Facilities/Internet. $95 application fee. $395 nonrefundable deposit required. Financial aid available for all students: scholarships.
For More Information • Mr. David Mauro, Admissions Advisor, American Institute For Foreign Study (AIFS), 9 West Broad Street, Stamford, CT 06902-3788; *Phone:* 800-727-2437 Ext. 5163; *Fax:* 203-399-5597. *E-mail:* dmauro@aifs.com. *World Wide Web:* http://www.aifsabroad.com/

AMERICAN INSTITUTE FOR FOREIGN STUDY (AIFS)
AIFS–LONDON, ENGLAND–RICHMOND, THE AMERICAN INTERNATIONAL UNIVERSITY IN LONDON, INTERNSHIP

Hosted by Richmond–The American International University in London
Academic Focus • Anthropology, business administration/management, communications, economics, fine/studio arts, history, literature, marketing, music, photography, political science and government, sociology.

Program Information • Students attend classes at Richmond-The American International University in London (London, England). Field trips to cultural activities, Stonehenge, Salisbury, Greenwich, Cambridge, Oxford, Hampton Court, Windsor, Brighton; optional travel to weekend excursion to Paris for a supplement of $499 at an extra cost. Students typically earn 9 semester credits per term.
Sessions • May–Aug (summer).
Eligibility Requirements • Minimum age 20; open to juniors, seniors; 2.75 GPA; 2 letters of recommendation; Students applying for this program must also complete a separate internship application.
Living Arrangements • Students live in host institution dormitories, program-owned apartments, hotels. Quarters are shared with host institution students. Meals are taken as a group, in residences.
Costs (2007) • $8999; includes tuition, housing, some meals, insurance, excursions, student support services, On-site Resident Director, Phone Card to call the U.S. $95 application fee. $395 nonrefundable deposit required. Financial aid available for all students: scholarships.
For More Information • Mr. David Mauro, Admissions Advisor, American Institute For Foreign Study (AIFS), 9 West Broad Street, Stamford, CT 06902-3788; *Phone:* 800-727-2437 Ext. 5163; *Fax:* 203-399-5597. *E-mail:* dmauro@aifs.com. *World Wide Web:* http://www.aifsabroad.com/

AMERICAN INTERCONTINENTAL UNIVERSITY
LONDON PROGRAM

Hosted by American InterContinental University–London
Academic Focus • Advertising and public relations, art, British studies, business administration/management, commercial art, communications, computer science, design and applied arts, fashion design, fashion merchandising, film and media studies, fine/studio arts, intercultural studies, interior design, international business, liberal studies, management information systems, marketing, photography, textiles.
Program Information • Students attend classes at American InterContinental University-London (London, England). Field trips to other areas of the United Kingdom, Europe; optional travel to Paris, Prague, Barcelona, Rome, Bruges, Wales, Ireland at an extra cost. Students typically earn 10 quarter credits per term.
Sessions • Jun–Aug (summer).
Eligibility Requirements • Open to freshmen, sophomores, juniors, seniors, graduate students, adults; 2.0 GPA; good academic standing at home school; approval of advisor, dean or department chair, and study abroad office; college transcripts.
Living Arrangements • Students live in locally rented apartments. Quarters are shared with host institution students. Meals are taken on one's own, in residences, in central dining facility, in restaurants.
Costs (2005) • $2490 for 1 class for 5 weeks; $9400 for 4 classes for 11 weeks; includes tuition, student support services. $75 application fee.
For More Information • American InterContinental University, Study Abroad Programs, 3150 West Higgins Road, Suite 105, Hoffman Estates, IL 60195; *Phone:* 800-255-6839; *Fax:* 847-885-8422. *E-mail:* studyabroad@aiuniv.edu. *World Wide Web:* http://www.studyabroad.aiuniv.edu/

ARCADIA UNIVERSITY
LONDON SUMMER INTERNSHIP

Academic Focus • Business administration/management, communications, public policy, social services.
Program Information • Faculty members are local instructors hired by the sponsor. Optional travel at an extra cost. Students typically earn 6 semester credits per term.
Sessions • Jun–Jul (summer).
Eligibility Requirements • Open to sophomores, juniors, seniors, graduate students, adults; 3.0 GPA; 2 letters of recommendation; résumé.
Living Arrangements • Students live in locally rented apartments, program-owned houses. Meals are taken on one's own, in residences, in restaurants.

Costs (2005) • $4595; includes tuition, housing, insurance, international student ID, student support services, transcript, pre-departure guide, orientation. $35 application fee. $500 nonrefundable deposit required.
For More Information • Arcadia University, Center for Education Abroad, 450 South Easton Road, Glenside, PA 19038-3295; *Phone:* 866-927-2234; *Fax:* 215-572-2174. *E-mail:* cea@arcadia.edu. *World Wide Web:* http://www.arcadia.edu/cea/

ARCADIA UNIVERSITY
SUMMER IN LONDON

Hosted by City University
Academic Focus • Art history, English literature, political science and government.
Program Information • Students attend classes at City University (London, England). Field trips; optional travel to Brussels, Paris, Wales at an extra cost. Students typically earn 3–6 semester credits per term.
Sessions • Jun–Jul (summer).
Eligibility Requirements • Open to freshmen, sophomores, juniors, seniors, graduate students, adults; 3.0 GPA; 1 letter of recommendation.
Living Arrangements • Students live in program-owned apartments, program-owned houses, Thoresby House. Quarters are shared with host institution students. Meals are taken on one's own, in residences, in restaurants.
Costs (2005) • $3690 for 1 course; $4475 for 2 courses; includes tuition, housing, insurance, international student ID, student support services, transcript, pre-departure guide, orientation. $35 application fee. $500 nonrefundable deposit required. Financial aid available for all students: loans.
For More Information • Arcadia University, Center for Education Abroad, 450 South Easton Road, Glenside, PA 19038-3295; *Phone:* 866-927-2234; *Fax:* 215-572-2174. *E-mail:* cea@arcadia.edu. *World Wide Web:* http://www.arcadia.edu/cea/

BOSTON UNIVERSITY
LONDON GRADUATE MASS COMMUNICATIONS PROGRAM

Held at Boston University–London Centre
Academic Focus • Communications.
Program Information • Classes are held on the campus of Boston University-London Centre (London, England). Faculty members are drawn from the sponsor's U.S. staff and local instructors hired by the sponsor. Students typically earn 16 semester credits per term.
Sessions • May–Aug (summer).
Eligibility Requirements • Open to seniors, graduate students; 1 letter of recommendation; good academic standing at home school; essay; transcript; approval of participation; minimum GPA of 3.0 in major and overall.
Living Arrangements • Students live in locally rented apartments, program-owned apartments. Quarters are shared with host institution students. Meals are taken as a group, on one's own, in residences, in restaurants.
Costs (2005) • $17,000; includes tuition, housing, insurance, international airfare, internship placement, communications fee. $50 application fee. $400 nonrefundable deposit required. Financial aid available for all students: scholarships, loans.
For More Information • Division of International Programs, Boston University, 232 Bay State Road, Boston, MA 02215; *Phone:* 617-353-9888; *Fax:* 617-353-5402. *E-mail:* abroad@bu.edu. *World Wide Web:* http://www.bu.edu/abroad/

BOSTON UNIVERSITY
LONDON INTERNSHIP PROGRAM

Held at Boston University–London Centre
Academic Focus • Advertising and public relations, art history, business administration/management, communications, drama/theater, economics, film and media studies, health, international affairs, journalism, law and legal studies, liberal studies, political science and government, psychology, social sciences.
Program Information • Classes are held on the campus of Boston University-London Centre (London, England). Faculty members are drawn from the sponsor's U.S. staff and local instructors hired by the sponsor. Field trips to the House of Commons, art museums,

theaters; optional travel to Oxford, Wales, Stonehenge at an extra cost. Students typically earn 16 semester credits per term.

Sessions • May–Aug (summer).

Eligibility Requirements • Open to sophomores, juniors, seniors, adults; 3.0 GPA; 1 letter of recommendation; good academic standing at home school; essay; approval of participation; transcript.

Living Arrangements • Students live in locally rented apartments, program-owned apartments. Meals are taken on one's own, in residences, in restaurants.

Costs (2005) • $12,700; includes tuition, housing, insurance, internship placement, communications fee. $50 application fee. $400 nonrefundable deposit required. Financial aid available for all students: scholarships, loans, resident and program assistant positions.

For More Information • Division of International Programs, Boston University, 232 Bay State Road, Boston, MA 02215; *Phone:* 617-353-9888; *Fax:* 617-353-5402. *E-mail:* abroad@bu.edu. *World Wide Web:* http://www.bu.edu/abroad/

BOSTON UNIVERSITY
LONDON SUMMER TERM I AND II

Held at Boston University–London Centre

Academic Focus • Advertising and public relations, art history, British studies, business administration/management, communications, economics, journalism, law and legal studies, liberal studies, political science and government, psychology, sociology.

Program Information • Classes are held on the campus of Boston University–London Centre (London, England). Faculty members are drawn from the sponsor's U.S. staff and local instructors hired by the sponsor. Field trips to the House of Commons, theaters, art museums, Greenwich; optional travel to Oxford, Bath, Wales at an extra cost. Students typically earn 8 semester credits per term.

Sessions • May–Jun (summer), Jul–Aug (summer 2).

Eligibility Requirements • Open to sophomores, juniors, seniors, graduate students, adults; 3.0 GPA; 1 letter of recommendation; good academic standing at home school; essay; transcript; approval of participation.

Living Arrangements • Students live in locally rented apartments, program-owned apartments. Meals are taken as a group, on one's own, in residences, in restaurants.

Costs (2005) • $6250; includes tuition, housing, insurance, excursions. $50 application fee. $400 nonrefundable deposit required. Financial aid available for all students: scholarships, loans.

For More Information • Division of International Programs, Boston University, 232 Bay State Road, Boston, MA 02215; *Phone:* 617-353-9888; *Fax:* 617-353-5402. *E-mail:* abroad@bu.edu. *World Wide Web:* http://www.bu.edu/abroad/

CENTRAL SAINT MARTINS COLLEGE OF ART AND DESIGN
SUMMER STUDY ABROAD PROGRAM

Hosted by Central Saint Martins College of Art and Design

Academic Focus • Art, commercial art, design and applied arts, fashion design, textiles.

Program Information • Students attend classes at Central Saint Martins College of Art and Design (London, England). Scheduled travel to cultural sites throughout London; field trips to galleries, areas of London. Students typically earn 3 credit hours per term.

Sessions • Jul (summer).

Eligibility Requirements • Minimum age 18; open to freshmen, sophomores, juniors, seniors, graduate students; major in art, design; 2.8 GPA; 1 letter of recommendation; good academic standing at home school; slide portfolio for review for Fine Art or Design programs.

Living Arrangements • Students live in host institution dormitories. Quarters are shared with students from other programs. Meals are taken on one's own, in residences.

Costs (2006) • £995; includes tuition, lab equipment. £350 nonrefundable deposit required.

For More Information • Mr. Ashley Palmer, Study Abroad Coordinator, Central Saint Martins College of Art and Design, Southampton Row, London WC1B 4AP, England; *Phone:* +44 020-7514-7285; *Fax:* +44 020-7514-7016. *E-mail:* studyabroad@csm.arts.ac.uk. *World Wide Web:* http://www.csm.arts.ac.uk/

COLLEGE CONSORTIUM FOR INTERNATIONAL STUDIES–SUNY ROCKLAND COMMUNITY COLLEGE AND MONTANA STATE UNIVERSITY
SUMMER SESSION AT KINGSTON UNIVERSITY, LONDON, ENGLAND

Hosted by Kingston University

Academic Focus • Architecture, art history, British studies, environmental science/studies, history, international business, literature.

Program Information • Students attend classes at Kingston University (Kingston upon Thames, England). Field trips to Bath, Stonehenge, Oxford, Cambridge. Students typically earn 3–6 semester credits per term.

Sessions • Jul–Aug (summer).

Eligibility Requirements • Minimum age 18; open to sophomores, juniors, seniors; 2.5 GPA; 2 letters of recommendation; good academic standing at home school.

Living Arrangements • Students live in host institution dormitories. Quarters are shared with host institution students. Meals are taken on one's own, in residences, in restaurants.

Costs (2005–2006) • $3730 for 3 credits; $4470 for 6 credits; includes tuition, housing, some meals, insurance, excursions, international student ID, student support services, one-month travel card. $400 nonrefundable deposit required. Financial aid available for all students: scholarships, loans, Pell, TAP.

For More Information • Ms. Melissa Gluckmann, Coordinator of Study Abroad, College Consortium for International Studies–SUNY Rockland Community College and Montana State University, 145 College Road, Suffern, NY 10901; *Phone:* 845-574-4205; *Fax:* 845-574-4423. *E-mail:* study-abroad@sunyrockland.edu. *World Wide Web:* http://www.ccisabroad.org/. Students may also apply through Montana State University, Office of International Programs, 400 Culbertson Hall, Bozeman, MT 59717.

COOPERATIVE CENTER FOR STUDY ABROAD
INTERNSHIPS IN LONDON

Academic Focus • Full curriculum.

Sessions • Year-round.

Eligibility Requirements • Minimum age 18; open to freshmen, sophomores, juniors, seniors, graduate students, adults; 2 letters of recommendation; good academic standing at home school.

Living Arrangements • Students live in host family homes. Quarters are shared with students from other programs. Meals are taken on one's own, with host family, in residences, in restaurants.

Costs (2007) • $4995–$5295; includes housing, some meals, insurance, international student ID, student support services, internship placement. $200 nonrefundable deposit required. Financial aid available for students from sponsoring institution: scholarships, loans.

For More Information • Dr. Michael A. Klembara, Executive Director, Cooperative Center for Study Abroad, Northern Kentucky University, Nunn Drive, Founders Hall 316, Highland Heights, KY 41099; *Phone:* 800-319-6015; *Fax:* 859-572-6650. *E-mail:* ccsa@nku.edu. *World Wide Web:* http://www.ccsa.cc/

COOPERATIVE CENTER FOR STUDY ABROAD
LONDON–SUMMER

Held at King's College London, University of London

Academic Focus • Art, biological/life sciences, communications, cultural studies, drama/theater, English, environmental health, geography, history, hospitality services, interior design, journalism, literature, music, political science and government, psychology, social work.

Program Information • Classes are held on the campus of King's College London, University of London (London, England). Faculty members are drawn from the sponsor's U.S. staff. Field trips to Salisbury, London; optional travel to Edinburgh, Paris at an extra cost. Students typically earn 3–6 semester credits per term.

Sessions • Jul–Aug (summer).

Eligibility Requirements • Minimum age 18; open to freshmen, sophomores, juniors, seniors, graduate students, adults; good academic standing at home school.

Living Arrangements • Students live in host institution dormitories. Quarters are shared with host institution students. Meals are taken as a group, on one's own, in central dining facility, in restaurants.

Costs (2007) • $4795; includes housing, some meals, insurance, excursions, international airfare, student support services, BritRail Pass, London Travelcard, airport transfers. $200 nonrefundable deposit required. Financial aid available for students from sponsoring institution: scholarships, loans.

For More Information • Dr. Michael A. Klembara, Executive Director, Cooperative Center for Study Abroad, Northern Kentucky University, Nunn Drive, Founders Hall 301, Highland Heights, KY 41099; *Phone:* 800-319-6015; *Fax:* 859-572-6650. *E-mail:* ccsa@nku. edu. *World Wide Web:* http://www.ccsa.cc/

COOPERATIVE CENTER FOR STUDY ABROAD
LONDON WINTER

Academic Focus • Art, business administration/management, drama/theater, drawing/painting, history, journalism, literature, mathematics, philosophy, political science and government, psychology, religious studies, sports management.

Program Information • Faculty members are drawn from the sponsor's U.S. staff. Field trips to Stonehenge, Dover, Canterbury, Bath, Stratford-upon-Avon, London. Students typically earn 3 semester credits per term.

Sessions • Dec–Jan (winter).

Eligibility Requirements • Minimum age 18; open to freshmen, sophomores, juniors, seniors, graduate students, adults; good academic standing at home school.

Living Arrangements • Students live in hotels. Quarters are shared with host institution students. Meals are taken as a group, on one's own, in central dining facility, in restaurants.

Costs (2006–2007) • $3195; includes housing, some meals, insurance, excursions, international airfare, student support services, airport transfers. $200 nonrefundable deposit required. Financial aid available for students from sponsoring institution: scholarships, loans.

For More Information • Dr. Michael A. Klembara, Executive Director, Cooperative Center for Study Abroad, Northern Kentucky University, Nunn Drive, Founders Hall 301, Highland Heights, KY 41099; *Phone:* 800-319-6015; *Fax:* 859-572-6650. *E-mail:* ccsa@nku. edu. *World Wide Web:* http://www.ccsa.cc/

EASTERN CONNECTICUT STATE UNIVERSITY
INTERNATIONAL SUMMER SCHOOL IN LONDON

Hosted by London Metropolitan University

Academic Focus • Art history, drama/theater, performing arts, visual and performing arts.

Program Information • Students attend classes at London Metropolitan University (London, England). Field trips to Stonehenge, Stratford, Brighton; optional travel to European cities at an extra cost. Students typically earn 6 semester credits per term.

Sessions • Jun–Jul (summer).

Eligibility Requirements • Minimum age 16; open to freshmen, sophomores, juniors, seniors, graduate students, adults; 2 letters of recommendation; good academic standing at home school.

Living Arrangements • Students live in host institution dormitories. Meals are taken as a group, on one's own, in residences, in restaurants.

Costs (2005–2006) • $4500; includes tuition, housing, some meals, excursions, international airfare, books and class materials, international student ID, student support services, shows, concerts, museums, transport to and from airport, month-long travel card. $200 nonrefundable deposit required. Financial aid available for students from sponsoring institution: scholarships, loans.

For More Information • Ms. Ellen Brodie, Director of Theatre, Eastern Connecticut State University, Shafer 13, Willimantic, CT 06226; *Phone:* 860-465-5122; *Fax:* 860-465-5764. *E-mail:* brodice@ easternct.edu. *World Wide Web:* http://www.easternct.edu/

EMORY UNIVERSITY
PSYCHOLOGY–CHILD DEVELOPMENT

Held at University College London

Academic Focus • Psychology.

Program Information • Classes are held on the campus of University College London (London, England). Faculty members are drawn from the sponsor's U.S. staff. Scheduled travel to Dundee, Scotland, Galway, Ireland, Canterbury, England. Students typically earn 8 semester credits per term.

Sessions • Jun–Jul (summer).

Eligibility Requirements • Minimum age 18; open to sophomores, juniors, seniors; 2.0 GPA; good academic standing at home school; introductory course in psychology.

Living Arrangements • Students live in host institution dormitories. Meals are taken as a group, on one's own, in restaurants.

Costs (2005) • $7700; includes tuition, housing, some meals, insurance, excursions. $350 nonrefundable deposit required. Financial aid available for students from sponsoring institution: scholarships, loans.

For More Information • Ms. Gail Scheu, Study Abroad Coordinator, Emory University, 1385 Oxford Road, Atlanta, GA 30322; *Phone:* 404-727-2240; *Fax:* 404-727-6724. *E-mail:* lscheu@emory.edu. *World Wide Web:* http://www.cipa.emory.edu/

FOUNDATION FOR INTERNATIONAL EDUCATION
LONDON INTERNSHIP PROGRAM

Hosted by Foundation for International Education

Academic Focus • British studies, design and applied arts, English literature, intercultural studies.

Program Information • Students attend classes at Foundation for International Education (London, England). Field trips to Cambridge, Oxford, Bath; optional travel to a Wales Adventure Weekend. Students typically earn 9 quarter credits per term.

Sessions • May–Aug (summer).

Eligibility Requirements • Open to sophomores, juniors, seniors; 2.75 GPA; advisor's approval.

Living Arrangements • Students live in host institution dormitories, program-owned apartments. Quarters are shared with students from other programs. Meals are taken on one's own, in residences, in restaurants.

Costs (2006) • $7580 ($7955 with optional transcript fee); includes tuition, housing, insurance, excursions, student support services, membership of Imperial College Student Union, co- and extracurricular program and internship placement, preparation and ongoing support. $500 deposit required.

For More Information • Ms. Erika Richards, Director of Program Development, Foundation for International Education, PMB 326, 5 Bessom Street, Marblehead, MA 01945; *Phone:* 781-631-6153. *E-mail:* studyabroad@fie.org.uk. *World Wide Web:* http://www.fie. org.uk/

FOUNDATION FOR INTERNATIONAL EDUCATION
LONDON STUDY PROGRAM

Hosted by Foundation for International Education

Academic Focus • British studies, design and applied arts, English literature, intercultural studies.

Program Information • Students attend classes at Foundation for International Education (London, England). Field trips to Cambridge, Oxford, Bath; optional travel to a Wales Adventure Weekend. Students typically earn 9 quarter credits per term.

Sessions • May–Jul (summer).

Eligibility Requirements • Open to sophomores, juniors, seniors; 2.75 GPA; advisor's approval.

Living Arrangements • Students live in host institution dormitories, program-owned apartments. Quarters are shared with students from other programs. Meals are taken on one's own, in residences, in restaurants.

Costs (2006) • $5430 ($5805 with optional transcript fee); includes tuition, housing, insurance, excursions, student support services, membership of Imperial College Student Union, co- and extracurricular program. $500 deposit required.

ENGLAND
London

For More Information • Ms. Erika Richards, Director of Program Development, Foundation for International Education, PMB 326, 5 Bessom Street, Marblehead, MA 01945; *Phone:* 781-631-6153. *E-mail:* studyabroad@fie.org.uk. *World Wide Web:* http://www.fie.org.uk/

GONZAGA UNIVERSITY
GONZAGA UNIVERSITY–LITERARY LONDON

Hosted by Gonzaga at The London Center
Academic Focus • English literature.
Program Information • Students attend classes at Gonzaga at The London Center (London, England). Scheduled travel to Stratford, The Lake District; field trips. Students typically earn 6 semester credits per term.
Sessions • May–Jun (summer).
Eligibility Requirements • Open to sophomores, juniors, seniors; 2.5 GPA; 1 letter of recommendation; Dean of Students approval.
Living Arrangements • Students live in host institution dormitories. Quarters are shared with host institution students, students from other programs. Meals are taken on one's own, in restaurants.
Costs (2005) • $4600; includes tuition, housing, some meals, international student ID. $50 application fee. $500 deposit required. Financial aid available for all students: loans.
For More Information • Ms. Wanda Reynolds, Director, Study Abroad, Gonzaga University, East 502 Boone Avenue, Spokane, WA 99258; *Phone:* 800-440-5391; *Fax:* 509-323-5987. *E-mail:* reynolds@gu.gonzaga.edu. *World Wide Web:* http://www.gonzaga.edu/studyabroad/

ILLINOIS STATE UNIVERSITY
GEOGRAPHY IN LONDON, ENGLAND

Academic Focus • Geography.
Program Information • Faculty members are drawn from the sponsor's U.S. staff. Field trips to the Tower of London, Westminster Abbey, St. Paul's Cathedral. Students typically earn 3 semester credits per term.
Sessions • Jun (summer).
Eligibility Requirements • Minimum age 18; open to sophomores, juniors, seniors, graduate students, adults; 2.5 GPA; 2 letters of recommendation; good academic standing at home school; essay.
Living Arrangements • Students live in host institution dormitories. Meals are taken as a group, in restaurants.
Costs (2004) • $3051; includes tuition, housing, some meals, insurance, excursions, international airfare, books and class materials, international student ID, student support services, personal expenses. $150 application fee. Financial aid available for students from sponsoring institution: scholarships, loans.
For More Information • Mr. Daniel Hammel, Professor, Illinois State University, Campus Box 6120, Normal, IL 61790-6120; *Phone:* 309-438-8112; *Fax:* 309-438-3987. *E-mail:* dhammel@ilstu.edu. *World Wide Web:* http://www.internationalstudies.ilstu.edu/

INSTITUTE FOR STUDY ABROAD, BUTLER UNIVERSITY
MIDDLESEX UNIVERSITY SUMMER STUDY

Hosted by Middlesex University
Academic Focus • Accounting, art, biological/life sciences, business administration/management, computer science, cultural studies, design and applied arts, education, environmental science/studies, film and media studies, French language and literature, history, human resources, information science, law and legal studies, marketing, performing arts, political science and government, psychology, social sciences, Spanish language and literature.
Program Information • Students attend classes at Middlesex University (London, England). Field trips to London theater, Bath, Stratford-on-Avon; optional travel to Paris at an extra cost. Students typically earn 2–10 semester credits per term.
Sessions • Jun–Aug (summer).
Eligibility Requirements • Open to freshmen, sophomores, juniors, seniors; 2.5 GPA; enrollment at an accredited American college or university.
Living Arrangements • Students live in host institution dormitories. Quarters are shared with host institution students, students from other programs. Meals are taken on one's own, in residences.

Costs (2005) • $5475 for 1 course; $5995 for 2 courses; includes tuition, housing, some meals, excursions, student support services, pre-departure advising. $40 application fee. $500 nonrefundable deposit required. Financial aid available for all students: scholarships.
For More Information • Institute for Study Abroad, Butler University, 1100 West 42nd Street, Suite 305, Indianapolis, IN 46208-3345; *Phone:* 800-858-0229; *Fax:* 317-940-9704. *E-mail:* study-abroad@butler.edu. *World Wide Web:* http://www.ifsa-butler.org/

INSTITUTE FOR STUDY ABROAD, BUTLER UNIVERSITY
UNIVERSITY OF WESTMINSTER–SUMMER STUDY

Hosted by University of Westminster
Academic Focus • Art, creative writing, drama/theater, English literature, history, international affairs, journalism, law and legal studies.
Program Information • Students attend classes at University of Westminster (London, England). Optional travel to Oxford, Stonehenge, Bath at an extra cost. Students typically earn 4 semester credits per term.
Sessions • Jul–Aug (summer).
Eligibility Requirements • Open to sophomores, juniors, seniors; 2.5 GPA; 1 letter of recommendation; good academic standing at home school; enrollment at an accredited American college or university.
Living Arrangements • Students live in host institution dormitories. Quarters are shared with host institution students. Meals are taken on one's own, in residences.
Costs (2005) • $2975; includes tuition, housing, student support services, pre-departure advising. $40 application fee. $500 nonrefundable deposit required. Financial aid available for all students: scholarships.
For More Information • Institute for Study Abroad, Butler University, 1100 West 42nd Street, Suite 305, Indianapolis, IN 46208-3345; *Phone:* 800-858-0229; *Fax:* 317-940-9704. *E-mail:* study-abroad@butler.edu. *World Wide Web:* http://www.ifsa-butler.org/

INTERNATIONAL STUDIES ABROAD
LONDON, ENGLAND–SUMMER UNIVERSITY OF WESTMINSTER

Hosted by University of Westminster
Academic Focus • Art, art history, English, history.
Program Information • Students attend classes at University of Westminster (London, England). Optional travel at an extra cost. Students typically earn 4 semester credits per term.
Sessions • Jul–Aug (summer).
Eligibility Requirements • Minimum age 18; open to sophomores, juniors, seniors, graduate students, adults; 3.0 GPA; good academic standing at home school; transcripts.
Living Arrangements • Students live in host institution dormitories. Quarters are shared with host institution students, students from other programs. Meals are taken as a group, on one's own, in residences, in restaurants.
Costs (2005–2006) • Contact sponsor for cost. $200 deposit required. Financial aid available for all students: scholarships, loans, US federal financial aid.
For More Information • England Site Specialist, International Studies Abroad, 901 West 24th Street, Austin, TX 78705; *Phone:* 800-580-8826; *Fax:* 512-480-8866. *E-mail:* isa@studiesabroad.com. *World Wide Web:* http://www.studiesabroad.com/

ITHACA COLLEGE
ITHACA COLLEGE-LONDON CENTER (SUMMER)

Hosted by Ithaca College–London Center
Academic Focus • Art history, British studies, Celtic studies, communications, drama/theater, English literature, film and media studies, history, interdisciplinary studies, international affairs, international business, Irish literature, literature, music, political science and government, psychology, sociology.
Program Information • Students attend classes at Ithaca College-London Center (London, England). Scheduled travel to Dublin,

Edinburgh; field trips to Stratford-upon-Avon, Bath; optional travel to Edinburgh, Dublin, Paris at an extra cost. Students typically earn 12–18 semester credits per term.

Sessions • May–Jun (summer).

Eligibility Requirements • Open to sophomores, juniors, seniors; 2.5 GPA; 2 letters of recommendation; good academic standing at home school; judicial review.

Living Arrangements • Students live in host institution dormitories, locally rented apartments, host family homes. Quarters are shared with host institution students, students from other programs. Meals are taken on one's own, in residences.

Costs (2005–2006) • $6500; includes tuition, housing, insurance, excursions, international airfare, books and class materials, student support services. $50 application fee. $500 nonrefundable deposit required. Financial aid available for students from sponsoring institution: scholarships, work study, loans.

For More Information • Ms. Rachel Cullenen, Associate Director for Study Abroad, Ithaca College, Office of International Programs, 214-2 Center for Health Sciences, Ithaca, NY 14850-7150; *Phone:* 607-274-3306; *Fax:* 607-274-1515. *E-mail:* rcullenen@ithaca.edu. *World Wide Web:* http://www.ithaca.edu/oip/

JAMES MADISON UNIVERSITY
SUMMER PROGRAM IN LONDON

Hosted by James Madison University–London

Academic Focus • Art history, drama/theater, English, history, literature.

Program Information • Students attend classes at James Madison University–London (London, England). Scheduled travel to Stratford-upon-Avon, Wales, Bath; field trips to Cambridge. Students typically earn 9 semester credits per term.

Sessions • Jun–Jul (summer).

Eligibility Requirements • Minimum age 18; open to sophomores, juniors, seniors; 2.0 GPA; 1 letter of recommendation; good academic standing at home school.

Living Arrangements • Students live in the Madison House (hostel). Quarters are shared with host institution students. Meals are taken as a group, on one's own, in central dining facility, in restaurants.

Costs (2005) • $4862 for Virginia residents; $7382 for nonresidents; includes tuition, housing, some meals, excursions, books and class materials, international student ID. $400 nonrefundable deposit required. Financial aid available for students from sponsoring institution: scholarships, work study.

For More Information • Mr. Felix Wang, Director, James Madison University, Office of International Programs, MSC 5731, 1077 South Main Street, Harrisonburg, VA 22807; *Phone:* 540-568-6419; *Fax:* 540-568-3310. *E-mail:* studyabroad@jmu.edu. *World Wide Web:* http://www.jmu.edu/international/

LEXIA INTERNATIONAL
LEXIA SUMMER IN LONDON

Hosted by Academic Solutions

Academic Focus • Anthropology, area studies, art history, British studies, civilization studies, classics and classical languages, comparative history, cultural studies, economics, ethnic studies, geography, history, intercultural studies, interdisciplinary studies, international affairs, liberal studies, literature, political science and government, social sciences, sociology.

Program Information • Students attend classes at Academic Solutions (London, England). Field trips to Stratford-upon-Avon, Stonehenge, Bath, Cambridge, Oxford. Students typically earn 8–10 semester credits per term.

Sessions • Jun–Aug (summer).

Eligibility Requirements • Minimum age 18; open to freshmen, sophomores, juniors, seniors, graduate students, adults; 2.5 GPA; 2 letters of recommendation.

Living Arrangements • Students live in locally rented apartments. Quarters are shared with host institution students. Meals are taken on one's own, in residences.

Costs (2006) • $6850; includes tuition, housing, insurance, excursions, international student ID, student support services, transcript, computer access. $40 application fee. $300 nonrefundable deposit required. Financial aid available for all students: scholarships, work study.

For More Information • Lexia International, 23 South Main Street, Hanover, NH 03755; *Phone:* 800-775-3942; *Fax:* 603-643-9899. *E-mail:* info@lexiaintl.org. *World Wide Web:* http://www.lexiaintl.org/

LONDON COLLEGE OF FASHION
STUDY ABROAD SUMMER PROGRAM

Hosted by London College of Fashion

Academic Focus • Design and applied arts, fashion design, fashion merchandising.

Program Information • Students attend classes at London College of Fashion (London, England). Scheduled travel to Paris; field trips to museums, fashion-related visits, art galleries, fashion shows; optional travel to Paris at an extra cost. Students typically earn 1–6 semester credits per course.

Sessions • Summer.

Eligibility Requirements • Open to freshmen, sophomores, juniors, seniors, graduate students, adults; major in fashion design, merchandising, or a related field; 2.8 GPA; 1 letter of recommendation; good academic standing at home school; application essay or examples of work.

Living Arrangements • Students live in host institution dormitories, locally rented apartments. Quarters are shared with host institution students, students from other programs. Meals are taken on one's own, in residences.

Costs (2005) • Contact sponsor for cost. £300 deposit required.

For More Information • Ms. Basia Szkutnicka, Director of Study Abroad, London College of Fashion, 20 John Princes Street, London W1M 0BJ, England; *Phone:* +44 207-514-7540; *Fax:* +44 207-514-7490. *E-mail:* studyabroad@lcf.linst.ac.uk. *World Wide Web:* http://www.fashion.arts.ac.uk/

LOYOLA UNIVERSITY NEW ORLEANS
SUMMER SESSION IN LONDON

Academic Focus • Communications, history.

Program Information • Faculty members are drawn from the sponsor's U.S. staff. Field trips to Blenheim, Oxford, Bath, Stonehenge, Warwick, Stratford, Windsor; optional travel to Paris or other European cities at an extra cost. Students typically earn 6 semester credits per term.

Sessions • Jul–Aug (summer).

Eligibility Requirements • Minimum age 18; open to freshmen, sophomores, juniors, seniors, graduate students; 2.0 GPA; good academic standing at home school.

Living Arrangements • Students live in locally rented apartments, program-owned apartments. Meals are taken on one's own, in residences.

Costs (2005) • $3950; includes tuition, housing, some meals, insurance, excursions, student support services. $300 deposit required. Financial aid available for students from sponsoring institution: loans.

For More Information • Dr. William Hammel, Department of Communications, Loyola University New Orleans, 6363 Saint Charles Avenue, New Orleans, LA 70118; *Phone:* 504-865-3288; *Fax:* 504-865-2666. *E-mail:* wmhammel@loyno.edu. *World Wide Web:* http://www.loyno.edu/cie/

MICHIGAN STATE UNIVERSITY
ARTS AND HUMANITIES: TRENDS IN BRITISH AND AMERICAN CREATIVE ARTS

Held at University of Glasgow, University of London

Academic Focus • British studies, literature.

Program Information • Classes are held on the campus of University of London (London, England), University of Glasgow (Glasgow, Scotland). Faculty members are drawn from the sponsor's U.S. staff. Scheduled travel to Glasgow; field trips to surrounding areas. Students typically earn 7 semester credits per term.

Sessions • Jun–Aug (summer).

Eligibility Requirements • Minimum age 18; open to freshmen, sophomores, juniors, seniors; 2.0 GPA; good academic standing at home school; faculty approval.

Living Arrangements • Students live in host institution dormitories. Quarters are shared with host institution students. Meals are taken as a group, on one's own, in central dining facility, in restaurants.

Costs (2005) • $4200; includes housing, some meals, insurance, excursions, student support services. $100 application fee. $200 nonrefundable deposit required. Financial aid available for students from sponsoring institution: scholarships, loans.

For More Information • Mrs. Meghan Hock, Educational Programs Coordinator, Michigan State University, Office of Study Abroad, 109 International Center, East Lansing, MI 48824-1035; *Phone:* 517-353-8920; *Fax:* 517-432-2082. *E-mail:* hock@msu.edu. *World Wide Web:* http://studyabroad.msu.edu/

MICHIGAN STATE UNIVERSITY
COMPARATIVE CRIMINAL JUSTICE

Hosted by Thames Valley Police Academy
Academic Focus • Criminal justice.
Program Information • Students attend classes at Thames Valley Police Academy (Oxfordshire, England). Classes are also held on the campus of Birkbeck, University of London (London, England). Scheduled travel to Cambridge; field trips to courts, correctional facilities, police departments. Students typically earn 6 semester credits per term.
Sessions • Jul–Aug (summer), Program runs every other year.
Eligibility Requirements • Minimum age 18; open to freshmen, sophomores, juniors, seniors, graduate students; 2.0 GPA; good academic standing at home school; faculty approval.
Living Arrangements • Students live in host institution dormitories. Meals are taken on one's own, in central dining facility, in restaurants.
Costs (2004) • $3568; includes housing, some meals, insurance, excursions, student support services. $100 application fee. $200 nonrefundable deposit required. Financial aid available for students from sponsoring institution: scholarships, loans.
For More Information • Mrs. Meghan Hock, Educational Programs Coordinator, Michigan State University, Office of Study Abroad, 109 International Center, East Lansing, MI 48824-1035; *Phone:* 517-353-8920; *Fax:* 517-432-2082. *E-mail:* hock@msu.edu. *World Wide Web:* http://studyabroad.msu.edu/

MICHIGAN STATE UNIVERSITY
ECONOMICS OF LAW AND PUBLIC POLICY

Held at University of London
Academic Focus • Economics.
Program Information • Classes are held on the campus of University of London (London, England). Faculty members are drawn from the sponsor's U.S. staff. Students typically earn 6 semester credits per term.
Sessions • Jul–Aug (summer).
Eligibility Requirements • Minimum age 18; open to freshmen, sophomores, juniors, seniors; course work in Introduction to Microeconomics; 2.5 GPA.
Living Arrangements • Students live in host institution dormitories. Quarters are shared with students from other programs. Meals are taken on one's own, in residences, in central dining facility, in restaurants.
Costs (2005) • $3338; includes housing, some meals, insurance, excursions, student support services. $100 application fee. $200 nonrefundable deposit required. Financial aid available for students from sponsoring institution: scholarships, loans.
For More Information • Mrs. Meghan Hock, Educational Programs Coordinator, Michigan State University, Office of Study Abroad, 109 International Center, East Lansing, MI 48824-1035; *Phone:* 517-353-8920; *Fax:* 517-432-2082. *E-mail:* hock@msu.edu. *World Wide Web:* http://studyabroad.msu.edu/

MICHIGAN STATE UNIVERSITY
ENGLISH LITERATURE IN LONDON

Held at University of London
Academic Focus • English literature.
Program Information • Classes are held on the campus of University of London (London, England). Faculty members are

drawn from the sponsor's U.S. staff. Field trips to York. Students typically earn 8–10 semester credits per term.
Sessions • Jun–Aug (summer).
Eligibility Requirements • Minimum age 18; open to freshmen, sophomores, juniors, seniors; 2.0 GPA; good academic standing at home school; faculty approval.
Living Arrangements • Students live in host institution dormitories. Quarters are shared with students from other programs. Meals are taken as a group, on one's own, in residences, in central dining facility, in restaurants.
Costs (2005) • $4335 (estimated); includes housing, some meals, insurance, excursions, student support services. $100 application fee. $200 nonrefundable deposit required. Financial aid available for students from sponsoring institution: scholarships, loans.
For More Information • Mrs. Meghan Hock, Educational Programs Coordinator, Michigan State University, Office of Study Abroad, 109 International Center, East Lansing, MI 48824-1035; *Phone:* 517-353-8920; *Fax:* 517-432-2082. *E-mail:* hock@msu.edu. *World Wide Web:* http://studyabroad.msu.edu/

MICHIGAN STATE UNIVERSITY
FILM IN BRITAIN

Held at British Film Institute, University of London
Academic Focus • Film and media studies.
Program Information • Classes are held on the campus of University of London (London, England), British Film Institute (London, England). Faculty members are drawn from the sponsor's U.S. staff. Students typically earn 7–13 semester credits per term.
Sessions • Jul–Aug (summer).
Eligibility Requirements • Minimum age 18; open to freshmen, sophomores, juniors, seniors; 2.0 GPA; good academic standing at home school; faculty approval.
Living Arrangements • Students live in host institution dormitories. Quarters are shared with students from other programs. Meals are taken on one's own, in residences, in central dining facility, in restaurants.
Costs (2005) • $4000 (estimated); includes housing, some meals, insurance, excursions, student support services. $100 application fee. $200 nonrefundable deposit required. Financial aid available for students from sponsoring institution: scholarships, loans.
For More Information • Mrs. Meghan Hock, Office Assistant, Michigan State University, Office of Study Abroad, 109 International Center, East Lansing, MI 48824-1035; *Phone:* 517-353-8920; *Fax:* 517-432-2082. *E-mail:* hock@msu.edu. *World Wide Web:* http://studyabroad.msu.edu/

MICHIGAN STATE UNIVERSITY
FORENSIC ANTHROPOLOGY AND HUMAN IDENTIFICATION

Held at University of London
Academic Focus • Anthropology.
Program Information • Classes are held on the campus of University of London (London, England). Faculty members are drawn from the sponsor's U.S. staff. Field trips to Cambridge, museums, the London Zoo, hospitals. Students typically earn 4–6 semester credits per term.
Sessions • Jul–Aug (summer), Program runs every other year.
Eligibility Requirements • Minimum age 18; open to freshmen, sophomores, juniors, seniors, graduate students; 2.5 GPA; good academic standing at home school; faculty approval.
Living Arrangements • Students live in host institution dormitories. Meals are taken as a group, on one's own, in central dining facility, in restaurants.
Costs (2004) • $3068 (estimated); includes housing, some meals, insurance, excursions, student support services. $100 application fee. $200 nonrefundable deposit required. Financial aid available for students from sponsoring institution: scholarships, loans.
For More Information • Mrs. Meghan Hock, Educational Programs Coordinator, Michigan State University, Office of Study Abroad, 109 International Center, East Lansing, MI 48824-1035; *Phone:* 517-353-8920; *Fax:* 517-432-2082. *E-mail:* hock@msu.edu. *World Wide Web:* http://studyabroad.msu.edu/

MICHIGAN STATE UNIVERSITY
HISTORY, ARTS, AND HUMANITIES IN THE UNITED KINGDOM

Held at University of London

Academic Focus • British studies, history.

Program Information • Classes are held on the campus of University of London (London, England). Faculty members are drawn from the sponsor's U.S. staff. Scheduled travel to Edinburgh, Bath, York, Liverpool; field trips to museums, art galleries, historic sites. Students typically earn 8 semester credits per term.

Sessions • Jun–Aug (summer).

Eligibility Requirements • Minimum age 18; open to freshmen, sophomores, juniors, seniors, graduate students; 2.0 GPA; good academic standing at home school; faculty approval.

Living Arrangements • Students live in host institution dormitories, hotels. Quarters are shared with students from other programs. Meals are taken as a group, on one's own, in central dining facility, in restaurants.

Costs (2005) • $3995; includes housing, some meals, insurance, excursions, student support services. $100 application fee. $200 nonrefundable deposit required. Financial aid available for students from sponsoring institution: scholarships, loans.

For More Information • Mrs. Meghan Hock, Educational Programs Coordinator, Michigan State University, Office of Study Abroad, 109 International Center, East Lansing, MI 48824-1035; *Phone:* 517-353-8920; *Fax:* 517-432-2082. *E-mail:* hock@msu.edu. *World Wide Web:* http://studyabroad.msu.edu/

MICHIGAN STATE UNIVERSITY
MEDICAL ETHICS AND THE HISTORY OF HEALTH CARE

Held at University College London

Academic Focus • History, premedical studies.

Program Information • Classes are held on the campus of University College London (London, England). Faculty members are drawn from the sponsor's U.S. staff. Field trips to hospitals, clinics, museums. Students typically earn 7 semester credits per term.

Sessions • Jun–Jul (summer).

Eligibility Requirements • Minimum age 18; open to sophomores, juniors, seniors, graduate students; 2.0 GPA; good academic standing at home school; faculty approval.

Living Arrangements • Students live in host institution dormitories. Quarters are shared with host institution students. Meals are taken as a group, on one's own, in central dining facility, in restaurants.

Costs (2005) • $2874; includes housing, insurance, excursions, student support services. $100 application fee. $200 nonrefundable deposit required. Financial aid available for students from sponsoring institution: scholarships, loans.

For More Information • Mrs. Meghan Hock, Educational Programs Coordinator, Michigan State University, Office of Study Abroad, 109 International Center, East Lansing, MI 48824-1035; *Phone:* 517-353-8920; *Fax:* 517-432-2082. *E-mail:* hock@msu.edu. *World Wide Web:* http://studyabroad.msu.edu/

MICHIGAN STATE UNIVERSITY
NURSING IN LONDON

Academic Focus • Nursing.

Program Information • Faculty members are drawn from the sponsor's U.S. staff. Field trips to hospitals, museums, Parliament. Students typically earn 5 semester credits per term.

Sessions • Jun–Jul (summer).

Eligibility Requirements • Minimum age 18; open to juniors, seniors, graduate students; major in nursing; course work in clinical nursing; 2.5 GPA; good academic standing at home school; faculty approval.

Living Arrangements • Students live in host institution dormitories. Meals are taken as a group, on one's own, in central dining facility, in restaurants.

Costs (2005) • $2993; includes housing, some meals, insurance, excursions, student support services. $100 application fee. $200 nonrefundable deposit required. Financial aid available for students from sponsoring institution: scholarships, loans.

For More Information • Mrs. Meghan Hock, Educational Programs Coordinator, Michigan State University, Office of Study Abroad, 109 International Center, East Lansing, MI 48824-1035; *Phone:* 517-353-8920; *Fax:* 517-432-2082. *E-mail:* hock@msu.edu. *World Wide Web:* http://studyabroad.msu.edu/

MICHIGAN STATE UNIVERSITY
PACKAGING IN ENGLAND

Held at Birkbeck, University of London

Academic Focus • Packaging.

Program Information • Classes are held on the campus of Birkbeck, University of London (London, England). Faculty members are drawn from the sponsor's U.S. staff and local instructors hired by the sponsor. Field trips to companies, industrial visits, the University of Nottingham. Students typically earn 4 semester credits per term.

Sessions • Jun–Jul (summer).

Eligibility Requirements • Minimum age 18; open to freshmen, sophomores, juniors, seniors; major in packaging; course work in packaging (at least an introductory course); 2.0 GPA; good academic standing at home school; faculty approval.

Living Arrangements • Students live in host institution dormitories. Quarters are shared with students from other programs. Meals are taken as a group, on one's own, in residences, in central dining facility, in restaurants.

Costs (2005) • $4093; includes housing, some meals, insurance, excursions, student support services. $100 application fee. $200 nonrefundable deposit required. Financial aid available for students from sponsoring institution: scholarships, loans.

For More Information • Mrs. Meghan Hock, Office Assistant, Michigan State University, Office of Study Abroad, 109 International Center, East Lansing, MI 48824-1035; *Phone:* 517-353-8920; *Fax:* 517-432-2082. *E-mail:* hock@msu.edu. *World Wide Web:* http://studyabroad.msu.edu/

MICHIGAN STATE UNIVERSITY
PHILOSOPHY OF LOVE AND ART IN LONDON

Held at Birkbeck, University of London

Academic Focus • Philosophy.

Program Information • Classes are held on the campus of Birkbeck, University of London (London, England). Faculty members are drawn from the sponsor's U.S. staff. Students typically earn 8 semester credits per term.

Sessions • Jun–Aug (summer).

Eligibility Requirements • Minimum age 18; open to freshmen, sophomores, juniors, seniors; 2.0 GPA; good academic standing at home school; faculty approval.

Living Arrangements • Students live in host institution dormitories. Quarters are shared with students from other programs. Meals are taken on one's own, in residences, in central dining facility, in restaurants.

Costs (2005) • $3820; includes housing, some meals, insurance, excursions, student support services. $100 application fee. $200 nonrefundable deposit required. Financial aid available for students from sponsoring institution: scholarships, loans.

For More Information • Mrs. Meghan Hock, Educational Programs Coordinator, Michigan State University, Office of Study Abroad, 109 International Center, East Lansing, MI 48824-1035; *Phone:* 517-353-8920; *Fax:* 517-432-2082. *E-mail:* hock@msu.edu. *World Wide Web:* http://studyabroad.msu.edu/

MICHIGAN STATE UNIVERSITY
POLITICAL SCIENCE IN THE U.K.

Held at University of London

Academic Focus • Political science and government.

Program Information • Classes are held on the campus of University of London (London, England). Faculty members are drawn from the sponsor's U.S. staff. Field trips to Parliament, Churchill war rooms, the Tower of London, the Old Bailey. Students typically earn 6-12 semester credits per term.

Sessions • Jun–Aug (summer).

Eligibility Requirements • Minimum age 18; open to freshmen, sophomores, juniors, seniors; 2.0 GPA; good academic standing at home school; faculty approval.

Living Arrangements • Students live in host institution dormitories. Quarters are shared with students from other programs. Meals are taken as a group, on one's own, in residences, in central dining facility, in restaurants.

Costs (2005) • $3416; includes housing, some meals, insurance, excursions, student support services. $100 application fee. $200 nonrefundable deposit required. Financial aid available for students from sponsoring institution: scholarships, loans.

For More Information • Mrs. Meghan Hock, Educational Programs Coordinator, Michigan State University, Office of Study Abroad, 109 International Center, East Lansing, MI 48824-1035; *Phone:* 517-353-8920; *Fax:* 517-432-2082. *E-mail:* hock@msu.edu. *World Wide Web:* http://studyabroad.msu.edu/

MICHIGAN STATE UNIVERSITY
THEATRE IN LONDON

Academic Focus • Drama/theater.

Program Information • Faculty members are drawn from the sponsor's U.S. staff. Field trips to Stratford. Students typically earn 6 semester credits per term.

Sessions • Jun–Aug (summer).

Eligibility Requirements • Minimum age 18; open to sophomores, juniors, seniors; 2.5 GPA; good academic standing at home school; faculty approval.

Living Arrangements • Students live in a Victorian townhouse. Meals are taken on one's own, in residences, in restaurants.

Costs (2005) • $3685 (estimated); includes housing, insurance, excursions, student support services. $100 application fee. $200 nonrefundable deposit required. Financial aid available for students from sponsoring institution: scholarships, loans.

For More Information • Mrs. Meghan Hock, Educational Program/Coordinator, Michigan State University, Office of Study Abroad, 109 International Center, East Lansing, MI 48824-1035; *Phone:* 517-353-8920; *Fax:* 517-432-2082. *E-mail:* hock@msu.edu. *World Wide Web:* http://studyabroad.msu.edu/

MICHIGAN STATE UNIVERSITY
WOMEN'S STUDIES IN LONDON

Held at University of London

Academic Focus • Women's studies.

Program Information • Classes are held on the campus of University of London (London, England). Faculty members are drawn from the sponsor's U.S. staff. Field trips to the London Women's Resource Center, museums, the theater, galleries. Students typically earn 6–8 semester credits per term.

Sessions • Jun–Aug (summer).

Eligibility Requirements • Minimum age 18; open to freshmen, sophomores, juniors, seniors; 2.0 GPA; good academic standing at home school; faculty approval.

Living Arrangements • Students live in host institution dormitories. Quarters are shared with students from other programs. Meals are taken on one's own, in residences, in central dining facility, in restaurants.

Costs (2005) • $3834; includes housing, some meals, insurance, excursions, student support services. $100 application fee. $200 nonrefundable deposit required. Financial aid available for students from sponsoring institution: scholarships, loans.

For More Information • Mrs. Meghan Hock, Educational Programs Coordinator, Michigan State University, Office of Study Abroad, 109 International Center, East Lansing, MI 48824-1035; *Phone:* 517-353-8920; *Fax:* 517-432-2082. *E-mail:* hock@msu.edu. *World Wide Web:* http://studyabroad.msu.edu/

NEW YORK UNIVERSITY
THE ARTS IN LONDON

Hosted by Institute of Contemporary Arts

Academic Focus • Visual and performing arts.

Program Information • Students attend classes at Institute of Contemporary Arts (London, England). Students typically earn 8 semester credits per term.

Sessions • Jun–Aug (summer).

Eligibility Requirements • Minimum age 18; open to freshmen, sophomores, juniors, seniors, graduate students, adults.

Living Arrangements • Students live in program-owned apartments. Quarters are shared with host institution students. Meals are taken on one's own, in central dining facility.

Costs (2005) • $5400; includes tuition. $50 application fee. Financial aid available for students from sponsoring institution: scholarships.

For More Information • Mr. Josh Murray, Assistant Director, New York University, 721 Broadway, 12th Floor, New York, NY 10003; *Phone:* 212-998-1500; *Fax:* 212-995-4578. *E-mail:* tisch.special.info@nyu.edu. *World Wide Web:* http://www.nyu.edu/global/studyabroad.html

NEW YORK UNIVERSITY
BROADENING HORIZONS IN SPEECH AND LANGUAGE: LONDON, ENGLAND

Hosted by New York University

Academic Focus • Speech pathology.

Program Information • Students attend classes at New York University (London, England). Field trips to Oxford, Bath, Stratford-Upon-Avon. Students typically earn 6 semester credits per term.

Sessions • Jul (summer).

Eligibility Requirements • Minimum age 18; open to juniors, seniors, graduate students; major in speech pathology and audiology; good academic standing at home school; essay; transcript; resume.

Living Arrangements • Students live in host institution dormitories. Meals are taken on one's own, in residences, in restaurants.

Costs (2005) • $6482; includes tuition, housing, excursions. $50 application fee.

For More Information • Ms. Daniel Young, Program Associate, New York University, 82 Washington Square East, 5th Floor, New York, NY 10003; *Phone:* 212-992-9380; *Fax:* 212-995-4923. *E-mail:* dy14@nyu.edu. *World Wide Web:* http://www.nyu.edu/global/studyabroad.html

NEW YORK UNIVERSITY
JOURNALISM IN LONDON

Hosted by NYU Center in London

Academic Focus • Art history, creative writing, drama/theater, English literature, journalism, political science and government.

Program Information • Students attend classes at NYU Center in London (London, England). Field trips to the London area, Stratford-upon-Avon. Students typically earn 8 semester credits per term.

Sessions • Jun–Aug (summer).

Eligibility Requirements • Minimum age 18; open to freshmen, sophomores, juniors, seniors; 3.0 GPA; good academic standing at home school.

Living Arrangements • Students live in host institution dormitories. Quarters are shared with host institution students. Meals are taken on one's own, in residences, in restaurants.

Costs (2006) • $7919; includes tuition, housing, excursions, student support services, program and activities fee. $25 application fee. $300 nonrefundable deposit required. Financial aid available for students from sponsoring institution: loans.

For More Information • Office of Summer Sessions, New York University, 7 East 12th Street, 6th Floor, New York, NY 10003; *Phone:* 212-998-2292; *Fax:* 212-995-4642. *E-mail:* summer.info@nyu.edu. *World Wide Web:* http://www.nyu.edu/global/studyabroad.html

NEW YORK UNIVERSITY
NYU IN LONDON

Hosted by NYU in London

Academic Focus • Art history, creative writing, drama/theater, English literature, political science and government.

Program Information • Students attend classes at NYU in London (London, England). Field trips to Canterbury, Bath, Stonehenge. Students typically earn 8 semester credits per term.

Sessions • Jun–Aug (summer).

Eligibility Requirements • Minimum age 18; open to freshmen, sophomores, juniors, seniors, graduate students; 3.0 GPA; good academic standing at home school; personal statement for non-New York University students.

Living Arrangements • Students live in host institution dormitories. Quarters are shared with host institution students. Meals are taken on one's own, in residences, in restaurants.
Costs (2006) • $7919; includes tuition, housing, excursions, student support services, program fee. $25 application fee. $300 nonrefundable deposit required. Financial aid available for students from sponsoring institution: scholarships, loans.
For More Information • Office of Summer Sessions, New York University, 7 East 12th Street, 6th Floor, New York, NY 10003; *Phone:* 212-998-2292; *Fax:* 212-995-4642. *E-mail:* summer.info@nyu. edu. *World Wide Web:* http://www.nyu.edu/global/studyabroad. html

NEW YORK UNIVERSITY
URBAN DESIGN IN LONDON

Academic Focus • Architecture, art administration, art history, urban/regional planning.
Program Information • Faculty members are drawn from the sponsor's U.S. staff and local instructors hired by the sponsor. Field trips to Stonehenge, the Midlands, Oxford. Students typically earn 8 semester credits per term.
Sessions • Jul (summer).
Eligibility Requirements • Minimum age 18; open to freshmen, sophomores, juniors, seniors, adults; 3.0 GPA; good academic standing at home school.
Living Arrangements • Students live in host institution dormitories. Quarters are shared with students from other programs. Meals are taken as a group, in residences, in restaurants.
Costs (2006) • $4150; includes tuition, housing, excursions, student support services, program fee. $25 application fee. $300 nonrefundable deposit required. Financial aid available for students from sponsoring institution: loans.
For More Information • Summer Session Admission, New York University, 7 East 12th Street, 6th Floor, New York, NY 10003; *Phone:* 212-998-2292; *Fax:* 212-998-4642. *E-mail:* summer.info@nyu. edu. *World Wide Web:* http://www.nyu.edu/global/studyabroad. html

NORTHERN ILLINOIS UNIVERSITY
ACADEMIC INTERNSHIPS IN ENGLAND

Held at Educational Programmes Abroad
Academic Focus • Full curriculum.
Program Information • Classes are held on the campus of Educational Programmes Abroad (London, England). Faculty members are local instructors hired by the sponsor. Optional travel at an extra cost. Students typically earn 6 semester credits per term.
Sessions • Jun-Jul (summer), Jun-Aug (summer 2).
Eligibility Requirements • Open to juniors, seniors; 3.0 GPA; 2 letters of recommendation; good academic standing at home school; essay.
Living Arrangements • Students live in locally rented apartments, host family homes. Quarters are shared with host institution students. Meals are taken as a group, on one's own, with host family, in residences, in restaurants.
Costs (2005) • $6290; includes tuition, housing, some meals, insurance, international student ID, student support services, internship placement. $45 application fee. $500 nonrefundable deposit required. Financial aid available for students from sponsoring institution: regular financial aid.
For More Information • Ms. Emily Gorlewski, Program Assistant, Northern Illinois University, Study Abroad Office, Williston Hall 417, DeKalb, IL 60115; *Phone:* 815-753-0420; *Fax:* 815-753-0825. *E-mail:* niuabroad@niu.edu. *World Wide Web:* http://www.niu.edu/ niuabroad/

OKLAHOMA STATE UNIVERSITY
SUMMER IN LONDON

Held at Regent's College
Academic Focus • Accounting, finance, international business, marketing.
Program Information • Classes are held on the campus of Regent's College (London, England). Faculty members are drawn from the sponsor's U.S. staff. Field trips to the Houses of Parliament, the Drury Lane Theatre (backstage); optional travel to Cambridge,

Hampton Court, Bath and Stonehenge at an extra cost. Students typically earn 6 semester credits per term.
Sessions • Jun-Jul (summer).
Eligibility Requirements • Open to sophomores, juniors, seniors, graduate students, adults; ability to take 4000-level courses.
Living Arrangements • Students live in host institution dormitories. Quarters are shared with host institution students, students from other programs. Meals are taken as a group, in central dining facility.
Costs (2006) • $3950; includes tuition, housing, some meals, lab equipment, student support services, Tube pass, Houses of Parliament. $400 nonrefundable deposit required. Financial aid available for students from sponsoring institution: scholarships, loans.
For More Information • Ms. Vickie Karns, Program Manager, Oklahoma State University, 215 Spears School of Business, Stillwater, OK 74078; *Phone:* 866-678-3933; *Fax:* 405-744-6143. *E-mail:* vickie.karns@okstate.edu. *World Wide Web:* http://spears.okstate. edu/cepd.content/study_travel.php

ROCKLAND COMMUNITY COLLEGE
WINTER SESSION IN LONDON

Academic Focus • Communications, criminal justice, education, English literature, international business, nursing, social sciences, visual and performing arts.
Program Information • Faculty members are drawn from the sponsor's U.S. staff. Field trips to Cambridge, Stratford-upon-Avon, Bath, Canterbury, Stonehenge. Students typically earn 3 semester credits per term.
Sessions • Jan (winter).
Eligibility Requirements • Minimum age 18; open to freshmen, sophomores, juniors, seniors, adults; good academic standing at home school.
Living Arrangements • Students live in hotels. Meals are taken on one's own, in restaurants.
Costs (2005) • $2450; includes tuition, housing, some meals, excursions, international airfare, student support services. $400 nonrefundable deposit required. Financial aid available for students from sponsoring institution: scholarships, loans.
For More Information • Ms. Fran Rodríguez, Coordinator, Study Abroad, Rockland Community College, 145 College Road, Suffern, NY 10901; *Phone:* 845-574-4205; *Fax:* 845-574-4423. *E-mail:* study-abroad@sunyrockland.edu. *World Wide Web:* http://www. rocklandabroad.com/

SOUTHERN METHODIST UNIVERSITY
LONDON: COMMUNICATIONS

Held at Regent's College
Academic Focus • Advertising and public relations, communications, journalism.
Program Information • Classes are held on the campus of Regent's College (London, England). Faculty members are drawn from the sponsor's U.S. staff and local instructors hired by the sponsor. Scheduled travel to Scotland; field trips to Bath, Cambridge, Oxford. Students typically earn 6 semester credits per term.
Sessions • Jun-Jul (summer).
Eligibility Requirements • Open to sophomores, juniors, seniors; 2.5 GPA; 1 letter of recommendation; good academic standing at home school; interview; essay.
Living Arrangements • Students live in host institution dormitories. Quarters are shared with host institution students. Meals are taken as a group, in central dining facility.
Costs (2005) • $5610; includes tuition, housing, some meals, excursions, student support services, Underground rail passes, tickets for some group theater events. $40 application fee. $400 nonrefundable deposit required. Financial aid available for students from sponsoring institution: scholarships, loans.
For More Information • Ms. Nancy Simmons, Associate Director, Southern Methodist University, The International Center/Study Abroad, SMU PO Box 750391, Dallas, TX 75275-0391; *Phone:* 214-768-2338; *Fax:* 214-768-1051. *E-mail:* intlpro@mail.smu.edu. *World Wide Web:* http://www.smu.edu/studyabroad/

ENGLAND
London

STATE UNIVERSITY OF NEW YORK AT NEW PALTZ
LONDON ART SEMINAR

Academic Focus • Art, art history, fine/studio arts.
Program Information • Faculty members are drawn from the sponsor's U.S. staff. Field trips to Greenwich, Bath, Windsor. Students typically earn 3 semester credits per term.
Sessions • Jan (winter).
Eligibility Requirements • Minimum age 18; open to freshmen, sophomores, juniors, seniors; 2.5 GPA; 1 letter of recommendation; good academic standing at home school.
Living Arrangements • Students live in hotels. Quarters are shared with host institution students. Meals are taken on one's own, in restaurants.
Costs (2006) • $2110 for New York residents; $3000 for nonresidents; includes tuition, housing, insurance, excursions, international airfare, attendance at plays, administrative fee, museum fees. $25 application fee. $300 nonrefundable deposit required. Financial aid available for students from sponsoring institution: scholarships, loans.
For More Information • Marketing Coordinator, State University of New York at New Paltz, 1 Hawk Drive, New Paltz, NY 12561; *Phone:* 845-257-3125; *Fax:* 845-257-3129. *E-mail:* studyabroad@newpaltz.edu. *World Wide Web:* http://www.newpaltz.edu/studyabroad/

STATE UNIVERSITY OF NEW YORK AT NEW PALTZ
LONDON THEATER SEMINAR

Academic Focus • Drama/theater.
Program Information • Faculty members are drawn from the sponsor's U.S. staff and local instructors hired by the sponsor. Field trips to Greenwich, Stratford-upon-Avon, Windsor, Bath. Students typically earn 3 semester credits per term.
Sessions • Jan (winter).
Eligibility Requirements • Minimum age 18; open to freshmen, sophomores, juniors, seniors, adults; 2.5 GPA; 1 letter of recommendation; good academic standing at home school.
Living Arrangements • Students live in hotels. Meals are taken on one's own, in restaurants.
Costs (2005) • $2900 for New York residents; $3000 for nonresidents; includes tuition, housing, insurance, excursions, international airfare, attendance at plays, administrative fee. $25 application fee. $300 nonrefundable deposit required. Financial aid available for students from sponsoring institution: scholarships, loans.
For More Information • Center for International Programs, State University of New York at New Paltz, 1 Hawk Drive, New Paltz, NY 12561; *Phone:* 845-257-3125; *Fax:* 845-257-3129. *E-mail:* studyabroad@newpaltz.edu. *World Wide Web:* http://www.newpaltz.edu/studyabroad/

STATE UNIVERSITY OF NEW YORK AT NEW PALTZ
SUMMER STUDIES AT KINGSTON UNIVERSITY, LONDON

Hosted by Kingston University
Academic Focus • Full curriculum.
Program Information • Students attend classes at Kingston University (Kingston upon Thames, England). Field trips to Stonehenge, Brighton, Bath. Students typically earn 6 semester credits per term.
Sessions • Jun–Jul (summer).
Eligibility Requirements • Minimum age 18; open to sophomores, juniors, seniors; 2.75 GPA; 1 letter of recommendation.
Living Arrangements • Students live in host institution dormitories. Quarters are shared with host institution students, students from other programs. Meals are taken on one's own, in residences, in central dining facility, in restaurants.
Costs (2006) • $5366 for New York residents; $6932 for nonresidents; includes tuition, housing, some meals, social package. $25 application fee. $300 nonrefundable deposit required. Financial aid available for students from sponsoring institution: scholarships, loans.

For More Information • Marketing Coordinator, Study Abroad, State University of New York at New Paltz, Center for International Programs, 1 Hawk Drive, New Paltz, NY 12561; *Phone:* 845-257-3125; *Fax:* 845-257-3129. *E-mail:* studyabroad@newpaltz.edu. *World Wide Web:* http://www.newpaltz.edu/studyabroad/

STATE UNIVERSITY OF NEW YORK AT NEW PALTZ
SUMMER STUDIES AT MIDDLESEX UNIVERSITY, LONDON

Hosted by Middlesex University
Academic Focus • Full curriculum.
Program Information • Students attend classes at Middlesex University (London, England). Field trips to Bath, Stratford-upon-Avon, Hampton Court Palace, Brighton. Students typically earn 6 semester credits per term.
Sessions • Jul–Aug (summer).
Eligibility Requirements • Minimum age 18; open to freshmen, sophomores, juniors, seniors; 2.5 GPA; 1 letter of recommendation; good academic standing at home school.
Living Arrangements • Students live in host institution dormitories. Quarters are shared with host institution students, students from other programs. Meals are taken on one's own, in residences, in central dining facility, in restaurants.
Costs (2006) • $5400 for New York residents; $6900 for nonresidents; includes tuition, housing, some meals, excursions, administrative fee. $25 application fee. $300 nonrefundable deposit required. Financial aid available for students from sponsoring institution: scholarships, loans.
For More Information • Center for International Programs, State University of New York at New Paltz, 1 Hawk Drive, New Paltz, NY 12561-2443; *Phone:* 845-257-3125; *Fax:* 845-257-3129. *E-mail:* studyabroad@newpaltz.edu. *World Wide Web:* http://www.newpaltz.edu/studyabroad/

STATE UNIVERSITY OF NEW YORK AT OSWEGO
LONDON INTERNSHIP PROGRAM

Hosted by Centre for Academic Programmes Abroad
Academic Focus • Business administration/management.
Program Information • Students attend classes at Centre for Academic Programmes Abroad (London, England). Field trips to Bath. Students typically earn 6 semester credits per term.
Sessions • May–Jul (summer).
Eligibility Requirements • Open to freshmen, sophomores, juniors, seniors; 2.5 GPA; 1 letter of recommendation; good academic standing at home school; program of study statement.
Living Arrangements • Students live in host institution dormitories, locally rented apartments. Quarters are shared with students from other programs. Meals are taken on one's own, in restaurants.
Costs (2005) • $4550 (estimated); includes tuition, housing, some meals, insurance, excursions, international airfare, books and class materials, student support services, weekly food stipend, Tube pass, cultural events. $250 nonrefundable deposit required. Financial aid available for students: home university financial aid; loan processing and scholarships for Oswego students.
For More Information • Ms. Mary Kerr, Program Specialist, State University of New York at Oswego, 122A Swetman Hall, Oswego, NY 13126-3599; *Phone:* 888-4-OSWEGO; *Fax:* 315-312-2477. *E-mail:* intled@oswego.edu. *World Wide Web:* http://www.oswego.edu/intled/

STATE UNIVERSITY OF NEW YORK AT OSWEGO
LONDON SUMMER ACADEMIC PROGRAM

Hosted by Huron University USA in London
Academic Focus • Art, business administration/management, commerce, communications, finance, international business, marketing.
Program Information • Students attend classes at Huron University USA in London (London, England). Optional travel at an extra cost. Students typically earn 6 semester credits per term.
Sessions • May–Jun (summer).

Eligibility Requirements • Open to freshmen, sophomores, juniors, seniors; 2.5 GPA; 1 letter of recommendation; good academic standing at home school.

Living Arrangements • Students live in host institution dormitories. Quarters are shared with host institution students. Meals are taken on one's own, in residences, in restaurants.

Costs (2005) • $4850; includes tuition, housing, insurance, books and class materials, student support services. $250 nonrefundable deposit required. Financial aid available for students: home university financial aid; loan processing and scholarships for Oswego students.

For More Information • Ms. Mary Kerr, Program Specialist, State University of New York at Oswego, 122A Swetman Hall, Oswego, NY 13126-3599; *Phone:* 888-4-OSWEGO; *Fax:* 315-312-2477. *E-mail:* intled@oswego.edu. *World Wide Web:* http://www.oswego.edu/intled/

STATE UNIVERSITY OF NEW YORK COLLEGE AT BROCKPORT
THE AMERICAN REVOLUTION FROM A BRITISH PERSPECTIVE

Academic Focus • History.

Program Information • Faculty members are drawn from the sponsor's U.S. staff. Field trips. Students typically earn 3 credits per term.

Sessions • Jul (summer).

Eligibility Requirements • Minimum age 18; open to juniors, seniors, graduate students; 2.75 GPA; 2 letters of recommendation; good academic standing at home school.

Living Arrangements • Students live in host institution dormitories, University of Westminster's residence hall. Quarters are shared with host institution students. Meals are taken on one's own, in restaurants.

Costs (2006–2007) • $3800; includes tuition, housing, some meals, excursions, international student ID, student support services. $200 nonrefundable deposit required. Financial aid available for all students: scholarships, loans, regular financial aid, grants.

For More Information • Dr. John Perry, Director, International Education, State University of New York College at Brockport, 350 New Campus Drive, Brockport, NY 14420; *Phone:* 800-298-SUNY; *Fax:* 585-637-3218. *E-mail:* overseas@brockport.edu. *World Wide Web:* http://www.brockport.edu/studyabroad/

STATE UNIVERSITY OF NEW YORK COLLEGE AT BROCKPORT
LONDON INTERNSHIP PROGRAM

Academic Focus • Accounting, advertising and public relations, art administration, business administration/management, communications, criminal justice, ecology, film and media studies, full curriculum, health and physical education, history, international business, journalism, law and legal studies, marketing, nursing, parks and recreation, political science and government, radio, social work.

Program Information • Field trips to sites around London. Students typically earn 12 semester credits per term.

Sessions • May-Aug (summer).

Eligibility Requirements • Minimum age 18; open to juniors, seniors, graduate students; course work in area of internship; 2.5 GPA; 2 letters of recommendation; good academic standing at home school; résumé.

Living Arrangements • Students live in locally rented apartments. Meals are taken on one's own, in residences.

Costs (2005) • Contact sponsor for cost; includes tuition, international student ID. $200 nonrefundable deposit required. Financial aid available for students from sponsoring institution: scholarships, loans, grants.

For More Information • Dr. John J. Perry, Director, Office of International Education, State University of New York College at Brockport, 350 New Campus Drive, Brockport, NY 14420; *Phone:* 800-298-SUNY; *Fax:* 585-637-3218. *E-mail:* overseas@brockport.edu. *World Wide Web:* http://www.brockport.edu/studyabroad/

STATE UNIVERSITY OF NEW YORK COLLEGE AT BROCKPORT
UNIVERSITY OF WESTMINSTER–SUMMER SCHOOL PROGRAM

Hosted by University of Westminster

Academic Focus • Full curriculum, liberal studies, social sciences.

Program Information • Students attend classes at University of Westminster (London, England). Field trips to sites throughout London. Students typically earn 4 semester credits per term.

Sessions • Jul-Aug (summer), Jun-Jul.

Eligibility Requirements • Minimum age 18; open to freshmen, sophomores, juniors, seniors; 3.0 GPA; 2 letters of recommendation; good academic standing at home school; must be at least a second semester freshman.

Living Arrangements • Students live in host institution dormitories. Quarters are shared with host institution students. Meals are taken on one's own, in residences.

Costs (2005) • $3250; includes tuition, housing, excursions, international airfare, international student ID, student support services, airport pick-up upon arrival in London. $200 nonrefundable deposit required. Financial aid available for students: scholarships, loans.

For More Information • Dr. John J. Perry, Director, Office of International Education, State University of New York College at Brockport, 350 New Campus Drive, Brockport, NY 14420; *Phone:* 800-298-SUNY; *Fax:* 585-637-3218. *E-mail:* overseas@brockport.edu. *World Wide Web:* http://www.brockport.edu/studyabroad/

SYRACUSE UNIVERSITY
FASHION PHOTOGRAPHY IN LONDON

Hosted by Syracuse University–London

Academic Focus • Photography.

Program Information • Students attend classes at Syracuse University–London (London, England). Scheduled travel to Scotland; field trips. Students typically earn 6 semester credits per term.

Sessions • May-Jul (summer).

Eligibility Requirements • Open to seniors, graduate students, adults; major in photography or equivalent experience; 2.5 GPA; 1 letter of recommendation; good academic standing at home school.

Living Arrangements • Quarters are shared with students from other programs. Meals are taken on one's own, in residences.

Costs (2005) • $6200; includes tuition, some meals, excursions, international student ID, student support services. $55 application fee. $350 nonrefundable deposit required. Financial aid available for all students: loans, need-based tuition grants.

For More Information • Ms. Daisy Fried, Associate Director, Syracuse University, 106 Walnut Place, Syracuse, NY 13244-4170; *Phone:* 800-251-9674; *Fax:* 315-443-4593. *E-mail:* dipasum@syr.edu. *World Wide Web:* http://suabroad.syr.edu/

SYRACUSE UNIVERSITY
GRADUATE INTERNSHIPS AND RESEARCH IN NEWS, POLITICS, AND PUBLIC POLICY

Hosted by Syracuse University–London

Academic Focus • Communications, journalism, political science and government, public administration.

Program Information • Students attend classes at Syracuse University–London (London, England). Field trips to Oxford. Students typically earn 6 semester credits per term.

Sessions • May-Jul (summer).

Eligibility Requirements • Open to graduate students; 1 letter of recommendation; good academic standing at home school.

Living Arrangements • Students live in locally rented apartments. Meals are taken on one's own, in residences.

Costs (2005) • $6292; includes tuition, some meals, excursions, international student ID, student support services. $55 application fee. $350 nonrefundable deposit required. Financial aid available for all students: loans, need-based tuition grants.

For More Information • Ms. Daisy Fried, Associate Director, Syracuse University, 106 Walnut Place, Syracuse, NY 13244-4170; *Phone:* 315-443-9420; *Fax:* 315-443-4593. *E-mail:* dipasum@syr.edu. *World Wide Web:* http://suabroad.syr.edu/

ENGLAND
London

SYRACUSE UNIVERSITY
LAW IN LONDON

Hosted by Syracuse University–London
Academic Focus • Law and legal studies.
Program Information • Students attend classes at Syracuse University–London (London, England). Students typically earn 6 semester credits per term.
Sessions • May–Jul (summer).
Eligibility Requirements • Open to graduate students; major in law; good academic standing at home school; must be a second-year law student.
Living Arrangements • Students live in locally rented apartments. Meals are taken on one's own, in residences.
Costs (2005) • $6352; includes tuition, some meals, international student ID, student support services. $55 application fee. $350 nonrefundable deposit required. Financial aid available for all students: loans, need-based tuition grants.
For More Information • Ms. Daisy Fried, Associate Director, Syracuse University, 106 Walnut Place, Syracuse, NY 13244-4170; *Phone:* 800-251-9674; *Fax:* 315-443-4593. *E-mail:* dipasum@syr.edu. *World Wide Web:* http://suabroad.syr.edu/

SYRACUSE UNIVERSITY
LONDON THROUGH THE LENS: VIDEO AND PHOTOGRAPHY EXPERIENCE

Hosted by Syracuse University–London
Academic Focus • Film and media studies, photography.
Program Information • Students attend classes at Syracuse University–London (London, England). Students typically earn 6 semester credits per term.
Sessions • May–Jul (summer).
Eligibility Requirements • Open to freshmen, sophomores, juniors, seniors, graduate students, adults; major in photography, video; 1 letter of recommendation; good academic standing at home school.
Living Arrangements • Meals are taken on one's own, in residences.
Costs (2005) • $5785; includes tuition, some meals, excursions, lab equipment, international student ID, student support services. $55 application fee. $350 nonrefundable deposit required. Financial aid available for all students: loans, need-based tuition grants.
For More Information • Ms. Daisy Fried, Associate Director, Syracuse University, 106 Walnut Place, Syracuse, NY 13244-4170; *Phone:* 315-443-9420; *Fax:* 315-443-4593. *E-mail:* dipasum@syr.edu. *World Wide Web:* http://suabroad.syr.edu/

SYRACUSE UNIVERSITY
MANAGEMENT INTERNSHIPS IN LONDON

Hosted by Syracuse University–London
Academic Focus • Business administration/management.
Program Information • Students attend classes at Syracuse University–London (London, England). Students typically earn 6 semester credits per term.
Sessions • May–Jul (summer).
Eligibility Requirements • Open to sophomores, juniors, seniors, graduate students; 1 letter of recommendation; good academic standing at home school.
Living Arrangements • Students live in locally rented apartments. Meals are taken on one's own, in residences.
Costs (2005) • $5325; includes tuition, some meals, international student ID, student support services. $55 application fee. $350 nonrefundable deposit required. Financial aid available for all students: loans, need-based tuition grants.
For More Information • Ms. Daisy Fried, Associate Director, Syracuse University, 106 Walnut Place, Syracuse, NY 13244-4170; *Phone:* 800-251-9674; *Fax:* 315-443-4593. *E-mail:* dipasum@syr.edu. *World Wide Web:* http://suabroad.syr.edu/

SYRACUSE UNIVERSITY
POLITICS AND MEDIA IN ENGLAND

Hosted by Syracuse University–London
Academic Focus • Advertising and public relations, communications, film and media studies, journalism, political science and government.

Program Information • Students attend classes at Syracuse University–London (London, England). Students typically earn 6 semester credits per term.
Sessions • May–Jul (summer), Jul–Aug (optional internship).
Eligibility Requirements • Open to freshmen, sophomores, juniors, seniors; 1 letter of recommendation; good academic standing at home school.
Living Arrangements • Students live in locally rented apartments. Meals are taken on one's own, in residences.
Costs (2005) • $5410 ($7585 with 3 credit internship); includes tuition, some meals, excursions, international student ID, student support services. $55 application fee. $350 nonrefundable deposit required. Financial aid available for all students: loans, need-based tuition grants.
For More Information • Ms. Daisy Fried, Associate Director, Syracuse University, 106 Walnut Place, Syracuse, NY 13244-4170; *Phone:* 800-251-9674; *Fax:* 315-443-4593. *E-mail:* dipasum@syr.edu. *World Wide Web:* http://suabroad.syr.edu/

SYRACUSE UNIVERSITY
RELIGION'S ROLE IN BRITISH SOCIETY

Held at Syracuse University–London
Academic Focus • Religious studies.
Program Information • Classes are held on the campus of Syracuse University–London (London, England). Faculty members are drawn from the sponsor's U.S. staff. Field trips to Stonehenge, Canterbury, Edinburgh. Students typically earn 3 semester credits per term.
Sessions • Jun–Jul (summer).
Eligibility Requirements • Open to freshmen, sophomores, juniors, seniors, graduate students; good academic standing at home school.
Living Arrangements • Students live in locally rented apartments. Quarters are shared with host institution students. Meals are taken on one's own, in restaurants.
Costs (2006) • $4000; includes tuition, housing, some meals, international student ID. $55 application fee. $350 refundable deposit required. Financial aid available for all students: loans.
For More Information • Ms. Daisy Fried, Associate Director, Syracuse University, 106 Walnut Place, Syracuse, NY 13244-4170; *Phone:* 800-251-9674; *Fax:* 315-443-4593. *E-mail:* dsfried@syr.edu. *World Wide Web:* http://suabroad.syr.edu/

UNIVERSITY OF DELAWARE
SUMMER SESSION IN LONDON, ENGLAND

Hosted by University of Delaware London Centre
Academic Focus • Design and applied arts, English, photography, political science and government.
Program Information • Students attend classes at University of Delaware London Centre (London, England). Scheduled travel to Scotland or Ireland; field trips to local and regional cultural sites; optional travel to other areas of the United Kingdom at an extra cost. Students typically earn 6 semester credits per term.
Sessions • Jun–Jul (summer).
Eligibility Requirements • Open to freshmen, sophomores, juniors, seniors, adults; 2.0 GPA; 1 letter of recommendation.
Living Arrangements • Students live in locally rented apartments. Quarters are shared with host institution students. Meals are taken on one's own, in residences.
Costs (2005) • Contact sponsor for cost. $200 nonrefundable deposit required. Financial aid available for all students: scholarships.
For More Information • Center for International Studies, University of Delaware, 186 South College Avenue, Newark, DE 19716-1450; *Phone:* 888-831-4685; *Fax:* 302-831-6042. *E-mail:* studyabroad@udel.edu. *World Wide Web:* http://www.udel.edu/studyabroad/

UNIVERSITY OF DELAWARE
WINTER SESSION IN LONDON: COMPARATIVE LITERATURE AND ART HISTORY

Held at University of Delaware London Centre
Academic Focus • Art history, comparative literature.
Program Information • Classes are held on the campus of University of Delaware London Centre (London, England). Faculty members are drawn from the sponsor's U.S. staff and local instructors hired by the sponsor. Field trips to Stratford-upon-Avon,

the BBC, the Museum of the Moving Image, Hampton Court, Bath; optional travel to Europe at an extra cost. Students typically earn 6 semester credits per term.
Sessions • Jan–Feb (winter).
Eligibility Requirements • Open to freshmen, sophomores, juniors, seniors, adults; 2.0 GPA; 1 letter of recommendation.
Living Arrangements • Students live in locally rented apartments. Quarters are shared with host institution students. Meals are taken on one's own, in restaurants.
Costs (2005) • Contact sponsor for cost. $200 deposit required. Financial aid available for all students: scholarships.
For More Information • Center for International Studies, University of Delaware, 186 South College Avenue, Newark, DE 19716-1450; *Phone:* 888-831-4685; *Fax:* 302-831-6042. *E-mail:* studyabroad@udel.edu. *World Wide Web:* http://www.udel.edu/studyabroad/

UNIVERSITY OF DELAWARE
WINTER SESSION IN LONDON–ENGLISH

Held at University of Delaware London Centre
Academic Focus • English literature.
Program Information • Classes are held on the campus of University of Delaware London Centre (London, England). Faculty members are drawn from the sponsor's U.S. staff. Field trips to Stratford-upon-Avon; optional travel to Europe at an extra cost. Students typically earn 6 semester credits per term.
Sessions • Jan–Feb (winter).
Eligibility Requirements • Open to freshmen, sophomores, juniors, seniors; 2.0 GPA; 1 letter of recommendation.
Living Arrangements • Students live in locally rented apartments, hotels. Meals are taken on one's own, in residences, in restaurants.
Costs (2005) • Contact sponsor for cost. $200 nonrefundable deposit required. Financial aid available for all students: scholarships.
For More Information • Center for International Studies, University of Delaware, 186 South College Avenue, Newark, DE 19716-1450; *Phone:* 888-831-4685; *Fax:* 302-831-6042. *E-mail:* studyabroad@udel.edu. *World Wide Web:* http://www.udel.edu/studyabroad/

UNIVERSITY OF DELAWARE
WINTER SESSION IN LONDON: MUSIC

Held at University of Delaware London Centre
Academic Focus • Music.
Program Information • Classes are held on the campus of University of Delaware London Centre (London, England). Faculty members are drawn from the sponsor's U.S. staff. Field trips to historic and cultural sites; optional travel to Europe at an extra cost. Students typically earn 6 semester credits per term.
Sessions • Jan–Feb (winter).
Eligibility Requirements • Open to freshmen, sophomores, juniors, seniors, adults; 2.0 GPA; 1 letter of recommendation.
Living Arrangements • Students live in locally rented apartments. Quarters are shared with host institution students. Meals are taken on one's own, in residences.
Costs (2005) • Contact sponsor for cost. $200 nonrefundable deposit required. Financial aid available for all students: scholarships.
For More Information • Center for International Studies, University of Delaware, 186 South College Avenue, Newark, DE 19716-1450; *Phone:* 888-831-4685; *Fax:* 302-831-6042. *E-mail:* studyabroad@udel.edu. *World Wide Web:* http://www.udel.edu/studyabroad/

UNIVERSITY OF DELAWARE
WINTER SESSION IN LONDON: THEATER AND COSTUME

Held at University of Delaware London Centre
Academic Focus • Costume design.
Program Information • Classes are held on the campus of University of Delaware London Centre (London, England). Faculty members are drawn from the sponsor's U.S. staff. Field trips to cultural sites; optional travel to Europe at an extra cost. Students typically earn 6 semester credits per term.
Sessions • Jan–Feb (winter).
Eligibility Requirements • Open to freshmen, sophomores, juniors, seniors, adults; 2.0 GPA; 1 letter of recommendation.

Living Arrangements • Students live in locally rented apartments. Meals are taken on one's own, in residences.
Costs (2005) • Contact sponsor for cost. $200 nonrefundable deposit required. Financial aid available for all students: scholarships.
For More Information • Center for International Studies, University of Delaware, 186 South College Avenue, Newark, DE 19716-1450; *Phone:* 888-831-4685; *Fax:* 302-831-6042. *E-mail:* studyabroad@udel.edu. *World Wide Web:* http://www.udel.edu/studyabroad/

UNIVERSITY OF DELAWARE
WINTER SESSION LONDON CENTRE PROGRAM

Hosted by University of Delaware London Centre
Academic Focus • Art history, history, political science and government.
Program Information • Students attend classes at University of Delaware London Centre (London, England). Field trips to Hampton Court, Bath, Stonehenge, Oxford; optional travel to Europe at an extra cost. Students typically earn 6 semester credits per term.
Sessions • Jan–Feb (winter).
Eligibility Requirements • Open to freshmen, sophomores, juniors, seniors, adults; 2.0 GPA; 1 letter of recommendation.
Living Arrangements • Students live in locally rented apartments. Quarters are shared with host institution students. Meals are taken on one's own, in residences.
Costs (2005) • Contact sponsor for cost. $200 nonrefundable deposit required. Financial aid available for all students: scholarships.
For More Information • Center for International Studies, University of Delaware, 186 South College Avenue, Newark, DE 19716-1450; *Phone:* 888-831-4685; *Fax:* 302-831-6042. *E-mail:* studyabroad@udel.edu. *World Wide Web:* http://www.udel.edu/studyabroad/

UNIVERSITY OF MIAMI
HISTORY OF ENGLISH CINEMA SUMMER PROGRAM

Hosted by University of Westminster
Academic Focus • Film and media studies.
Program Information • Students attend classes at University of Westminster (London, England). Students typically earn 6 semester credits per term.
Sessions • Jun–Aug (summer).
Eligibility Requirements • Minimum age 18; open to sophomores, juniors, seniors, graduate students; good academic standing at home school.
Living Arrangements • Students live in locally rented apartments. Quarters are shared with host institution students. Meals are taken as a group, on one's own, in residences, in restaurants.
Costs (2005) • $5022; includes tuition. $500 nonrefundable deposit required. Financial aid available for students from sponsoring institution: scholarships, loans.
For More Information • Ms. Amy Cosan, Coordinator, International Education and Exchange Programs, University of Miami, 5050 Brunson Drive, Allen Hall Room 212, PO Box 248005, Coral Gables, FL 33124-1610; *Phone:* 305-284-3434; *Fax:* 305-284-4235. *E-mail:* ieep@miami.edu. *World Wide Web:* http://www.studyabroad.miami.edu/

UNIVERSITY OF MIAMI
LONDON SCHOOL OF ECONOMICS

Hosted by London School of Economics and Political Science
Academic Focus • Accounting, business administration/management, economics, finance, international affairs.
Program Information • Students attend classes at London School of Economics and Political Science (London, England). Students typically earn 3–6 semester credits per term.
Sessions • Jul–Aug (summer).
Eligibility Requirements • Minimum age 18; open to sophomores, juniors, seniors; 3.0 GPA; 2 letters of recommendation; good academic standing at home school; transcripts, essay.
Living Arrangements • Students live in host institution dormitories. Quarters are shared with host institution students, students from other programs. Meals are taken on one's own, in restaurants.

ENGLAND
London

Costs (2005–2006) • $5011–$9122; includes tuition, housing, some meals, student support services. $40 application fee. $500 deposit required. Financial aid available for students from sponsoring institution: loans.

For More Information • Ms. Elyse Resnick, Assistant Director, International Education and Exchange Programs, University of Miami, 5050 Brunson Drive, Allen Hall Room 212, PO Box 248005, Coral Gables, FL 33124-1610; *Phone:* 305-284-3434; *Fax:* 305-284-4235. *E-mail:* eresnick@miami.edu. *World Wide Web:* http://www.studyabroad.miami.edu/

UNIVERSITY OF MINNESOTA
FREEDOM OF THE PRESS IN THE UNITED KINGDOM

Academic Focus • Film and media studies.

Program Information • Faculty members are drawn from the sponsor's U.S. staff and local instructors hired by the sponsor. Scheduled travel to Glasgow, Scotland; field trips; optional travel at an extra cost. Students typically earn 3 semester credits per term.

Sessions • May–Jun (summer).

Eligibility Requirements • Minimum age 18; open to freshmen, sophomores, juniors, seniors, adults; 2.5 GPA; good academic standing at home school.

Living Arrangements • Students live in host institution dormitories, program-owned apartments, hotels. Meals are taken as a group, on one's own, in central dining facility, in restaurants.

Costs (2006) • Contact sponsor for cost; includes tuition, housing, some meals, insurance, international airfare, student support services. $50 application fee. $400 nonrefundable deposit required. Financial aid available for students from sponsoring institution: scholarships, loans.

For More Information • Learning Abroad Center, University of Minnesota, 230 Heller Hall, 271 19th Avenue South, Minneapolis, MN 55455; *Phone:* 800-700-UOFM; *Fax:* 612-626-8009. *E-mail:* umabroad@umn.edu. *World Wide Web:* http://www.umabroad.umn.edu/

UNIVERSITY OF MINNESOTA
A HISTORY OF ENGLISH GARDENS

Academic Focus • Horticulture.

Program Information • Faculty members are drawn from the sponsor's U.S. staff and local instructors hired by the sponsor. Optional travel at an extra cost. Students typically earn 3 semester credits per term.

Sessions • May–Jun (summer).

Eligibility Requirements • Minimum age 18; open to freshmen, sophomores, juniors, seniors, adults; 2.5 GPA; good academic standing at home school.

Living Arrangements • Students live in host institution dormitories, hotels. Meals are taken as a group, on one's own, in central dining facility, in restaurants.

Costs (2006) • Contact sponsor for cost; includes tuition, housing, some meals, insurance, international airfare, student support services. $50 application fee. $400 nonrefundable deposit required. Financial aid available for students from sponsoring institution: scholarships, loans.

For More Information • Learning Abroad Center, University of Minnesota, 230 Heller Hall, 271 19th Avenue South, Minneapolis, MN 55455; *Phone:* 800-700-UOFM; *Fax:* 612-626-8009. *E-mail:* umabroad@umn.edu. *World Wide Web:* http://www.umabroad.umn.edu/

UNIVERSITY OF MINNESOTA
STUDY AND INTERNSHIPS IN LONDON

Hosted by Centre for Academic Programmes Abroad

Academic Focus • British studies, drama/theater, international business.

Program Information • Students attend classes at Centre for Academic Programmes Abroad (London, England). Field trips to London, Bath, Stonehenge; optional travel to Paris, Amsterdam at an extra cost. Students typically earn 6 semester credits per term.

Sessions • Jun–Jul (summer).

Eligibility Requirements • Minimum age 18; open to freshmen, sophomores, juniors, seniors, graduate students, adults; 2.5 GPA;

good academic standing at home school; 1 letter of recommendation for regular session; 2 for internship.

Living Arrangements • Students live in locally rented apartments. Quarters are shared with host institution students, students from other programs. Meals are taken on one's own, in residences, in restaurants.

Costs (2006) • Contact sponsor for cost; includes tuition, housing, some meals, insurance, excursions. Financial aid available for students from sponsoring institution: scholarships, loans.

For More Information • Learning Abroad Center, University of Minnesota, 230 Heller Hall, 271 19th Avenue South, Minneapolis, MN 55455; *Phone:* 888-700-UOFM; *Fax:* 612-626-8009. *E-mail:* umabroad@umn.edu. *World Wide Web:* http://www.umabroad.umn.edu/

THE UNIVERSITY OF NORTH CAROLINA AT CHARLOTTE
PUBLIC RELATIONS SEMINAR IN THE U.K.

Held at Regent's College

Academic Focus • Communications.

Program Information • Classes are held on the campus of Regent's College (London, England). Faculty members are drawn from the sponsor's U.S. staff and local instructors hired by the sponsor. Field trips to The Hague, Amsterdam, Belgium. Students typically earn 8 semester credits per term.

Sessions • May (summer).

Eligibility Requirements • Minimum age 18; open to sophomores, juniors, seniors, graduate students, adults; 2.5 GPA; good academic standing at home school; 'Principles of Public Relations' course or instructor permission.

Living Arrangements • Students live in hotels. Meals are taken on one's own, in restaurants.

Costs (2005) • $3020; includes tuition, housing, some meals, insurance, excursions, student support services. $500 nonrefundable deposit required. Financial aid available for students from sponsoring institution: scholarships, loans.

For More Information • Mr. Brad Sekulich, Interim Director of Education Abroad, The University of North Carolina at Charlotte, 9201 University City Boulevard, Charlotte, NC 28223-0001; *Phone:* 704-687-2464; *Fax:* 704-687-3168. *E-mail:* edabroad@email.uncc.edu. *World Wide Web:* http://www.uncc.edu/edabroad/

UNIVERSITY OF PENNSYLVANIA
PENN-IN-LONDON

Academic Focus • Drama/theater, literature.

Program Information • Faculty members are drawn from the sponsor's U.S. staff and local instructors hired by the sponsor. Field trips to museums, castles. Students typically earn 2 course units per term.

Sessions • Jun–Jul (summer).

Eligibility Requirements • Open to freshmen, sophomores, juniors, seniors, graduate students; 1 letter of recommendation; good academic standing at home school.

Living Arrangements • Students live in host institution dormitories, locally rented apartments. Meals are taken on one's own, in restaurants.

Costs (2005) • $6350; includes tuition, housing, insurance, excursions. $50 application fee. $300 nonrefundable deposit required. Financial aid available for students from sponsoring institution: loans.

For More Information • Penn Summer Abroad, University of Pennsylvania, 3440 Market Street, Suite 100, Philadelphia, PA 19104-3335; *Phone:* 215-746-6900; *Fax:* 215-573-2053. *E-mail:* summerabroad@sas.upenn.edu. *World Wide Web:* http://www.sas.upenn.edu/summer/

UNIVERSITY OF ROCHESTER
INTERNSHIPS IN EUROPE–ENGLAND

Academic Focus • Advertising and public relations, art administration, art history, biomedical sciences, business administration/management, drama/theater, health-care management, history, international affairs, law and legal studies, marketing, political science and government, psychology, public policy.

Program Information • Field trips to London. Students typically earn 8 semester credits per term.
Sessions • May–Jul (summer), Jun–Aug (summer 2).
Eligibility Requirements • Open to sophomores, juniors, seniors; 3.0 GPA; 2 letters of recommendation; good academic standing at home school.
Living Arrangements • Students live in locally rented apartments, host family homes. Meals are taken on one's own, with host family, in residences, in restaurants.
Costs (2005) • $6450; includes tuition, housing, student support services, some meals if homestay option chosen. $30 application fee. $300 nonrefundable deposit required. Financial aid available for students from sponsoring institution: loans.
For More Information • Ms. Jacqueline Levine, Study Abroad Director, University of Rochester, Center for Study Abroad, PO Box 270376, Lattimore 206, Rochester, NY 14627-0376; *Phone:* 585-275-7532; *Fax:* 585-461-5131. *E-mail:* abroad@mail.rochester.edu. *World Wide Web:* http://www.rochester.edu/college/study-abroad/

UNIVERSITY OF SOUTHERN MISSISSIPPI
BRITISH STUDIES PROGRAM

Held at King's College
Academic Focus • Full curriculum.
Program Information • Classes are held on the campus of King's College (London, England). Faculty members are drawn from the sponsor's U.S. staff and local instructors hired by the sponsor. Scheduled travel; field trips; optional travel at an extra cost. Students typically earn 6 semester credits per term.
Sessions • Jul–Aug (summer).
Eligibility Requirements • Minimum age 18; open to sophomores, juniors, seniors, graduate students, adults; 2.0 GPA; good academic standing at home school.
Living Arrangements • Students live in host institution dormitories, locally rented apartments. Quarters are shared with host institution students. Meals are taken as a group, on one's own, in residences, in restaurants.
Costs (2005) • $4999 for undergraduate students; $5299 for graduate students; includes tuition, housing, international airfare, student support services, some excursions. $250 nonrefundable deposit required. Financial aid available for students from sponsoring institution: scholarships, loans.
For More Information • Director, British Studies Program, University of Southern Mississippi, 118 College Drive #10047, Hattiesburg, MS 39406-0001; *Phone:* 601-266-4344; *Fax:* 601-266-5699 *E-mail:* frances.sudduth@usm.edu. *World Wide Web:* http://www.usm.edu/internationaledu/

UNIVERSITY OF WISCONSIN–PLATTEVILLE
SUMMER SESSION IN LONDON

Hosted by Thames Valley University
Academic Focus • Art history, drama/theater, history, psychology.
Program Information • Students attend classes at Thames Valley University (London, England). Field trips to Windsor Castle, Hampton Court, Oxford, Blenheim Palace, Stonehenge, Salisbury. Students typically earn 6 semester credits per term.
Sessions • Jun–Jul (summer).
Eligibility Requirements • Minimum age 18; open to freshmen, sophomores, juniors, seniors; 2.0 GPA; 2 letters of recommendation; good academic standing at home school.
Living Arrangements • Students live in host family homes. Meals are taken on one's own, with host family, in residences, in restaurants.
Costs (2005) • $4395 for Wisconsin and Minnesota residents; $4695 for nonresidents; includes tuition, housing, some meals, insurance, excursions, books and class materials, international student ID, student support services. $25 application fee. $400 nonrefundable deposit required. Financial aid available for students from sponsoring institution: scholarships, loans, federal and state grants.
For More Information • Ms. Donna Anderson, Director, Study Abroad Programs, University of Wisconsin–Platteville, Institute for Study Abroad Programs, 111 Royce Hall, 1 University Plaza, Platteville, WI 53818-3099; *Phone:* 800-342-1725; *Fax:* 608-342-1736. *E-mail:* studyabroad@uwplatt.edu. *World Wide Web:* http://www.uwplatt.edu/studyabroad/

UNIVERSITY STUDIES ABROAD CONSORTIUM
THEATER AND ARTS STUDIES: LONDON, ENGLAND

Hosted by London Metropolitan University
Academic Focus • Art, British studies, history, literature, theater management.
Program Information • Students attend classes at London Metropolitan University (London, England). Field trips to Brighton-by-the-Sea, London; optional travel to Scotland at an extra cost. Students typically earn 6 semester credits per term.
Sessions • Jun–Jul (summer).
Eligibility Requirements • Minimum age 18; open to freshmen, sophomores, juniors, seniors, graduate students, adults; 2.5 GPA.
Living Arrangements • Students live in host institution dormitories. Quarters are shared with host institution students. Meals are taken on one's own, in residences, in restaurants.
Costs (2007) • $4680; includes tuition, housing, insurance, excursions, student support services. $100 application fee. $200 refundable deposit required. Financial aid available for all students: scholarships, loans.
For More Information • University Studies Abroad Consortium, USAC/323, Reno, NV 89557-0093; *Phone:* 775-784-6569; *Fax:* 775-784-6010. *E-mail:* usac@unr.edu. *World Wide Web:* http://usac.unr.edu/

VILLANOVA UNIVERSITY
STUDIES AND INTERNSHIP IN INTERNATIONAL BUSINESS: LONDON

Hosted by London School of Economics and Political Science
Academic Focus • Business administration/management, international business.
Program Information • Students attend classes at London School of Economics and Political Science (London, England). Field trips to Buckingham Palace, Windsor Castle, West End musical; optional travel to Oxford University, Brighton at an extra cost. Students typically earn 6 semester credits per term.
Sessions • 8, 9, and 10 weeks.
Eligibility Requirements • Minimum age 18; open to sophomores, juniors, seniors; course work in business; 3.3 GPA; 2 letters of recommendation; good academic standing at home school.
Living Arrangements • Students live in host institution dormitories. Quarters are shared with host institution students. Meals are taken on one's own, in restaurants.
Costs (2005) • $8500–$9850; includes tuition, housing, excursions, student support services, cell phone rental, Metro pass. $450 nonrefundable deposit required. Financial aid available for students from sponsoring institution.
For More Information • Dr. Peggy Chaudry, Professor, Villanova University, 800 Lancaster Avenue, Middleton Hall, Villanova, PA 19085; *Phone:* 610-519-6412; *Fax:* 610-519-7649. *E-mail:* peggy.chaudry@villanova.edu. *World Wide Web:* http://www.internationalstudies.villanova.edu/

OXFORD

INSTITUTE FOR STUDY ABROAD, BUTLER UNIVERSITY
ST. PETER'S COLLEGE, OXFORD UNIVERSITY SUMMER STUDY

Hosted by University of Oxford–Saint Peter's College
Academic Focus • Cultural studies, English literature, environmental science/studies.
Program Information • Students attend classes at University of Oxford–Saint Peter's College (Oxford, England). Field trips to London; Bath; Hampshire; Stratford-upon-Avon. Students typically earn 6 semester credits per term.
Sessions • Jun–Aug (summer).
Eligibility Requirements • Open to freshmen, sophomores, juniors, seniors; 3.0 GPA; 1 letter of recommendation; good academic standing at home school; enrollment at an accredited American college or university; writing sample.

ENGLAND
Oxford

Living Arrangements • Students live in host institution dormitories, program-owned apartments. Quarters are shared with students from other programs. Meals are taken on one's own, in residences, in central dining facility.

Costs (2005) • $6975; includes tuition, housing, some meals, excursions, student support services, pre-departure advising. $40 application fee. $500 nonrefundable deposit required. Financial aid available for all students: scholarships.

For More Information • Institute for Study Abroad, Butler University, 1100 West 42nd Street, Suite 305, Indianapolis, IN 46208-3345; *Phone:* 800-858-0229; *Fax:* 317-940-9704. *E-mail:* study-abroad@butler.edu. *World Wide Web:* http://www.ifsa-butler.org/

NORTHERN ILLINOIS UNIVERSITY
NIU AT OXFORD

Hosted by University of Oxford–Oriel College

Academic Focus • Botany, British studies, English literature, political science and government.

Program Information • Students attend classes at University of Oxford–Oriel College (Oxford, England). Field trips to Kew Gardens, Stratford-upon-Avon, London, theatres. Students typically earn 3–6 semester credits per term.

Sessions • Jun–Aug (summer).

Eligibility Requirements • Minimum age 18; open to sophomores, juniors, seniors, graduate students, adults; 2.5 GPA; good academic standing at home school.

Living Arrangements • Students live in host institution dormitories. Quarters are shared with host institution students. Meals are taken as a group, in central dining facility.

Costs (2005) • $6420; includes tuition, housing, some meals, insurance, excursions, international student ID, student support services. $200 nonrefundable deposit required. Financial aid available for students from sponsoring institution: loans.

For More Information • Ms. Rita Withrow, Program Assistant, Northern Illinois University, Study Abroad Office, Williston Hall 417, DeKalb, IL 60115; *Phone:* 815-753-0700; *Fax:* 815-753-0825. *E-mail:* niuabroad@niu.edu. *World Wide Web:* http://www.niu.edu/niuabroad/

OXFORD NETWORK SERVICES
OXFORD VACATION PROGRAMMES

Hosted by College of International Education, Oxford International College

Academic Focus • Full curriculum.

Program Information • Students attend classes at College of International Education (Oxford, England), Oxford International College (Oxford, England). Field trips to Stratford, Warwick, Bath; optional travel to Paris, Amsterdam, Dublin at an extra cost.

Sessions • Jul–Aug (summer), Jun–Sep (summer 2), Mar–Apr (Easter).

Eligibility Requirements • Minimum age 11; open to precollege students, freshmen, sophomores, juniors, seniors, graduate students, adults; 1 letter of recommendation.

Living Arrangements • Students live in host institution dormitories, host family homes, hotels. Quarters are shared with host institution students. Meals are taken on one's own, with host family, in residences, in central dining facility.

Costs (2005–2006) • £315 per week; includes tuition. £50 application fee.

For More Information • Ms. Heather Buck, Director, Oxford Network Services, 53 Blenheim Drive, Oxford OX2 8DL, England; *Phone:* +44 1865-553144; *Fax:* +44 1865-553144. *E-mail:* info@oxnetservices.co.uk. *World Wide Web:* http://www.oxnetservices.co.uk/

SOUTHERN METHODIST UNIVERSITY
SMU IN OXFORD

Hosted by University of Oxford–University College

Academic Focus • Business administration/management, drama/theater, English literature, history, political science and government, religious studies.

Program Information • Students attend classes at University of Oxford–University College (Oxford, England). Field trips to London, Stratford-upon-Avon, Bath, Stonehenge, a cruise on the Thames. Students typically earn 6 semester credits per term.

Sessions • Jul–Aug (summer).

Eligibility Requirements • Open to sophomores, juniors, seniors; 2.5 GPA; 1 letter of recommendation; good academic standing at home school; personal interview; essay.

Living Arrangements • Students live in host institution dormitories. Quarters are shared with host institution students. Meals are taken as a group, in central dining facility.

Costs (2005) • $6950; includes tuition, housing, some meals, excursions, student support services. $40 application fee. $400 nonrefundable deposit required. Financial aid available for students from sponsoring institution: scholarships, loans.

For More Information • Ms. Nancy Simmons, Associate Director, Southern Methodist University, The International Center/Study Abroad, SMU PO Box 750391, Dallas, TX 75275-0391; *Phone:* 214-768-2338; *Fax:* 214-768-1051. *E-mail:* intlpro@mail.smu.edu. *World Wide Web:* http://www.smu.edu/studyabroad/

UNIVERSITY OF ALABAMA
ALABAMA AT OXFORD

Held at Oxford University–Wadham College

Academic Focus • Comparative literature, English literature, fine/studio arts, history, political science and government, religious studies.

Program Information • Classes are held on the campus of Oxford University–Wadham College (Oxford, England). Faculty members are drawn from the sponsor's U.S. staff and local instructors hired by the sponsor. Field trips to Edinburgh, the Lake District; optional travel to Paris at an extra cost. Students typically earn 6 semester credits per term.

Sessions • Jul–Aug (summer).

Eligibility Requirements • Open to freshmen, sophomores, juniors, seniors, graduate students, adults; 2.5 GPA; good academic standing at home school.

Living Arrangements • Students live in host institution dormitories. Quarters are shared with host institution students. Meals are taken as a group, in central dining facility.

Costs (2005) • $6350; includes tuition, housing, some meals, insurance, international airfare, international student ID, student support services, BritRail pass, Heritage pass. $100 application fee. $500 nonrefundable deposit required. Financial aid available for all students: scholarships, loans.

For More Information • Ms. Angela L. Channell, Director of Overseas Study, University of Alabama, Box 870254, Tuscaloosa, AL 35487-0254; *Phone:* 205-348-7024; *Fax:* 205-348-5298. *E-mail:* achannel@aalan.ua.edu. *World Wide Web:* http://www.overseas-study.ua.edu/

UNIVERSITY OF MIAMI
ENGLISH LITERATURE, HISTORY, POLITICS, AND SOCIETY PROGRAM IN ENGLAND

Hosted by University of Oxford

Academic Focus • British studies, English literature, history, political science and government.

Program Information • Students attend classes at University of Oxford (Oxford, England). Field trips to Stratford-upon-Avon. Students typically earn 3–6 semester credits per term.

Sessions • Jul (summer), Jul–Aug (summer 2).

Eligibility Requirements • Minimum age 18; open to seniors; course work in literature, history, or political science; 3.0 GPA; 2 letters of recommendation.

Living Arrangements • Students live in host institution dormitories. Quarters are shared with students from other programs. Meals are taken as a group, in central dining facility.

Costs (2005) • $4541–$8080; includes tuition, housing, some meals. $40 application fee. $500 deposit required. Financial aid available for students from sponsoring institution: loans.

For More Information • Ms. Elyse Resnick, Assistant Director, University of Miami, International Education and Exchange Programs, 5050 Brunson Drive, Allen Hall 212, PO Box 248005, Coral Gables, FL 33124-1610; *Phone:* 305-284-3434; *Fax:* 305-284-4235. *E-mail:* ieep@miami.edu. *World Wide Web:* http://www.studyabroad.miami.edu/

WASHINGTON INTERNATIONAL STUDIES COUNCIL

WISC OXFORD COLLEGES PROGRAM

Held at University of Oxford–New College, University of Oxford–Trinity College

Academic Focus • Full curriculum.

Program Information • Classes are held on the campus of University of Oxford–Trinity College (Oxford, England), University of Oxford–New College (Oxford, England). Faculty members are local instructors hired by the sponsor. Field trips to London, Stratford-upon-Avon, Bath, Stonehenge. Students typically earn 14–18 semester credits per term.

Sessions • Intervals from May–Sep, 4 week minimum stay.

Eligibility Requirements • Minimum age 18; open to sophomores, juniors, seniors, graduate students, adults; 3.2 GPA; 1 letter of recommendation; good academic standing at home school; minimum GPA of 3.2 in major.

Living Arrangements • Students live in host institution dormitories, locally rented apartments, program-owned apartments, program-owned houses. Quarters are shared with host institution students. Meals are taken as a group, on one's own, in residences, in central dining facility.

Costs (2005) • $4600 for 4 weeks; $6100 for 6 weeks; $7400 for 8 weeks; $9800 for 10 weeks; $11,100 for 12 weeks; includes tuition, housing, excursions, student support services. $300 refundable deposit required. Financial aid available for all students: scholarships.

For More Information • Ms. Danielle Roe, Associate Director, Washington International Studies Council, 214 Massachusetts Avenue, NE, Suite 370, Washington, DC 20002; *Phone:* 800-323-WISC; *Fax:* 202-547-1470. *E-mail:* wisc@erols.com. *World Wide Web:* http://www.wiscabroad.com/. Students may also apply through WISC, 21-27 George Street, 3rd Floor Chester House, Oxford OX1 2AY, England.

STRATFORD-UPON-AVON

UNIVERSITY OF KANSAS

SHAKESPEARE IN PERFORMANCE

Academic Focus • Drama/theater.

Program Information • Faculty members are drawn from the sponsor's U.S. staff and local instructors hired by the sponsor. Field trips to London, Hampton Court, Oxford, Blenheim Palace. Students typically earn 6 semester credits per term.

Sessions • Jun–Jul (summer).

Eligibility Requirements • Minimum age 18; open to freshmen, sophomores, juniors, seniors; 2.5 GPA; 2 letters of recommendation; good academic standing at home school.

Living Arrangements • Students live in hotels. Meals are taken as a group, on one's own, in restaurants.

Costs (2005) • $5140; includes tuition, housing, some meals, excursions, student support services, emergency medical evacuation and repatriation services, entrance fee to seven shows. $38 application fee. $300 nonrefundable deposit required. Financial aid available for students from sponsoring institution: scholarships, loans.

For More Information • Mr. David Wiley, Program Coordinator, University of Kansas, Office of Study Abroad, Lippincott Hall, 1410 Jayhawk Boulevard, Room 108, Lawrence, KS 66045-7515; *Phone:* 785-864-3742; *Fax:* 785-864-5040. *E-mail:* osa@ku.edu. *World Wide Web:* http://www.ku.edu/~osa/

THE UNIVERSITY OF NORTH CAROLINA AT CHARLOTTE

SHAKESPEARE IN PERFORMANCE SUMMER INSTITUTE

Academic Focus • Drama/theater, English literature.

Program Information • Faculty members are drawn from the sponsor's U.S. staff and local instructors hired by the sponsor. Field trips to the Globe Theatre, the National Theatre in London, Shakespeare's birthplace, other Shakespeare sites, Warwick Castle, Blenheim Palace, Oxford. Students typically earn 6 semester credits per term.

Sessions • Jul (summer).

Eligibility Requirements • Minimum age 18; open to freshmen, sophomores, juniors, seniors, graduate students, adults; 2.5 GPA; good academic standing at home school; high school diploma.

Living Arrangements • Students live in host institution dormitories, locally rented apartments, hotels. Meals are taken as a group, in residences, in restaurants.

Costs (2005) • $3850; includes tuition, housing, some meals, insurance, excursions, international airfare, student support services, ground transport in England, tickets to 7 plays. $10 application fee. $500 nonrefundable deposit required. Financial aid available for students from sponsoring institution: scholarships, loans.

For More Information • Mr. Brad Sekulich, Interim Director of Education Abroad, The University of North Carolina at Charlotte, 9201 University City Boulevard, Charlotte, NC 28223-0001; *Phone:* 704-687-2464; *Fax:* 704-687-3168. *E-mail:* edabroad@email.uncc.edu. *World Wide Web:* http://www.uncc.edu/edabroad/

ESTONIA

CITY-TO-CITY

UNIVERSITY OF TARTU
INTERNATIONAL SUMMER UNIVERSITY

Hosted by University of Tartu
Academic Focus • Eastern European studies, European studies, international affairs, political science and government, social sciences.
Program Information • Students attend classes at University of Tartu (Tartu). Field trips to Narva, Viljandi, Saaremha. Students typically earn 18 ECTS per term.
Sessions • Jul–Aug (summer).
Eligibility Requirements • Minimum age 18; open to sophomores, juniors, seniors, graduate students; good academic standing at home school; no foreign language proficiency required.
Living Arrangements • Students live in host institution dormitories. Quarters are shared with host institution students, students from other programs. Meals are taken on one's own, in residences, in restaurants.
Costs (2006) • €1500; includes tuition, housing, excursions, books and class materials, student support services, transportation between cities where program is conducted. €100 application fee.
For More Information • Mr. Mart Susi, International Summer University, University of Tartu, Office in Tallinn, Kahrli Pst. 3, 10119 Tallinn, Estonia; *Phone:* +372 737-6109; *Fax:* +372 737-5153. *E-mail:* mart.susi@ut.ee. *World Wide Web:* http://www.ut.ee/studentoffice/

NARVA

UNIVERSITY OF TARTU
PRACTICAL RUSSIAN LANGUAGE SUMMER COURSE

Hosted by University of Tartu
Academic Focus • Russian language and literature.
Program Information • Students attend classes at University of Tartu (Tartu, Estonia). Field trips to northeast Estonia. Students typically earn 5 ECTS per term.
Sessions • Jul–Aug (summer).
Eligibility Requirements • Minimum age 18; open to freshmen, sophomores, juniors, seniors, graduate students, adults; good academic standing at home school; pre-intermediate level of Russian.
Living Arrangements • Students live in host institution dormitories. Quarters are shared with host institution students, students from other programs. Meals are taken on one's own, in residences, in restaurants.
Costs (2006) • €255; includes tuition, housing, excursions, books and class materials, student support services.
For More Information • Ms. Anneli Roose, Narva College, University of Tartu, Kerese 14, 20304 Narva, Estonia; *Phone:* +372 356-0608; *Fax:* +372 356-1911. *E-mail:* anneli.roose@ut.ee. *World Wide Web:* http://www.ut.ee/studentoffice/

TARTU

UNIVERSITY OF TARTU
ESTONIAN LANGUAGE SUMMER COURSE

Hosted by University of Tartu
Academic Focus • Language studies.
Program Information • Students attend classes at University of Tartu (Tartu, Estonia). Optional travel to Tallinn at an extra cost. Students typically earn 5–9 ECTS per term.
Sessions • Jul–Aug (summer).
Eligibility Requirements • Minimum age 18; open to freshmen, sophomores, juniors, seniors, graduate students, adults; good academic standing at home school; no foreign language proficiency required.
Living Arrangements • Students live in host institution dormitories. Quarters are shared with host institution students, students from other programs. Meals are taken on one's own, in residences, in restaurants.
Costs (2006) • €320–€640; includes tuition, books and class materials, student support services, museum visits.
For More Information • Ms. Kersti Reinson, Language Center, University of Tartu, Näituse 2, 50409 Tartu, Estonia; *Phone:* +372 737-5357; *Fax:* +372 737-5357. *E-mail:* kersti.reinson@ut.ee. *World Wide Web:* http://www.ut.ee/studentoffice/

CITY-TO-CITY

UNIVERSITY OF CALIFORNIA, SANTA BARBARA, WILDLANDS STUDIES
ENVIRONMENTS AND CULTURES OF FIJI

Academic Focus • Ecology, environmental science/studies, geography, Pacific studies, wildlife studies.

Program Information • Faculty members are drawn from the sponsor's U.S. staff. Scheduled travel to ecological field locations. Students typically earn 15 quarter credits per term.

Sessions • Oct–Dec (fall).

Eligibility Requirements • Minimum age 18; open to freshmen, sophomores, juniors, seniors; course work in geography, environmental studies; good academic standing at home school; application essay.

Living Arrangements • Students live in host family homes, tents. Meals are taken as a group.

Costs (2006) • $1995; includes tuition. $75 application fee.

For More Information • Mr. Crandall Bay, Director, Wildlands Studies Program, University of California, Santa Barbara, Wildlands Studies, 3 Mosswood Circle, Cazadero, CA 95421; *Phone:* 707-632-5665; *Fax:* 707-632-5665. *E-mail:* wildlands@sonic.net. *World Wide Web:* http://www.wildlandsstudies.com/

SUVA

AMERICAN UNIVERSITIES INTERNATIONAL PROGRAMS (AUIP)
FIJI: HUMANS AND THE ENVIRONMENT

Hosted by University of the South Pacific

Academic Focus • Anthropology, conservation studies, ecology, forestry, geography, natural resources, parks and recreation.

Program Information • Students attend classes at University of the South Pacific (Suva, Fiji). Scheduled travel to Suva, Nadi, Yasawa Islands, Coral Coast, Lautoka; field trips. Students typically earn 3 semester credits per term.

Sessions • Jun (summer), Jul–Jul (summer 2), Dec–Dec (winter).

Eligibility Requirements • Minimum age 18; open to sophomores, juniors, seniors, graduate students, adults; 2.0 GPA; 2 letters of recommendation; good academic standing at home school; essay; official transcript.

Living Arrangements • Students live in host family homes, hotels, hostels. Meals are taken as a group, with host family, in residences, in restaurants.

Costs (2006) • $950; includes housing, some meals, insurance, excursions, student support services, all in-country travel and activities. $300 application fee.

For More Information • Dr. Michael Tarrant, Program Director, American Universities International Programs (AUIP), 108 South Main Street, Winterville, GA 30683; *Phone:* 706-742-9285. *E-mail:* info@auip.com. *World Wide Web:* http://www.auip.com/

# FRANCE

CITY-TO-CITY

CENTER FOR STUDY ABROAD (CSA)
UNIVERSITY OF PARIS–SORBONNE (FRENCH STUDIES)

Hosted by University Paris-Sorbonne (Paris IV)
Academic Focus • French language and literature.
Program Information • Students attend classes at University Paris-Sorbonne (Paris IV) (Paris). Students typically earn 4–10 semester credits per term.
Sessions • Summer.
Eligibility Requirements • Minimum age 18; open to precollege students, freshmen, sophomores, juniors, seniors, graduate students, adults.
Living Arrangements • Students live in host institution dormitories, foyers.
Costs (2005) • Contact sponsor for cost. $45 application fee.
For More Information • Ms. Alima K. Virtue, Program Director, Center for Study Abroad (CSA), 325 Washington Avenue South #93, Kent, WA 98032; *Phone:* 206-726-1498; *Fax:* 253-850-0454. *E-mail:* info@centerforstudyabroad.com. *World Wide Web:* http://www.centerforstudyabroad.com/

MICHIGAN STATE UNIVERSITY
INTERIOR DESIGN AND ARCHITECTURE

Academic Focus • Interior design.
Program Information • Faculty members are drawn from the sponsor's U.S. staff and local instructors hired by the sponsor. Scheduled travel to various European sites of interest; field trips to museums, historic villas, showrooms. Students typically earn 6 semester credits per term.
Sessions • May–Jun (summer).
Eligibility Requirements • Minimum age 18; open to freshmen, sophomores, juniors, seniors, graduate students; 2.0 GPA; good academic standing at home school; faculty approval; no foreign language proficiency required.
Living Arrangements • Students live in hotels. Meals are taken as a group, on one's own, in restaurants.
Costs (2005) • $3407 (estimated); includes housing, some meals, insurance, excursions, student support services. $100 application fee. $200 nonrefundable deposit required. Financial aid available for students from sponsoring institution: scholarships, loans.
For More Information • Ms. Yvonne Squiers, Secretary, Michigan State University, Office of Study Abroad, 109 International Center, East Lansing, MI 48824-1035; *Phone:* 517-353-8920; *Fax:* 517-432-2082. *E-mail:* squiers@msu.edu. *World Wide Web:* http://studyabroad.msu.edu/

AGEN

NORTHERN ILLINOIS UNIVERSITY
COMPARATIVE AND EUROPEAN UNION LAW IN AGEN, FRANCE

Hosted by University Montesquieu–Bordeaux IV
Academic Focus • Law and legal studies.
Program Information • Students attend classes at University Montesquieu–Bordeaux IV (Pessac, France). Field trips. Students typically earn 6 semester credits per term.
Sessions • May–Jul (summer).
Eligibility Requirements • Minimum age 18; open to graduate students, adults; major in law or a law-related field; course work in Law; 2.75 GPA; good academic standing at home school; no foreign language proficiency required.
Living Arrangements • Students live in host institution dormitories. Quarters are shared with host institution students. Meals are taken as a group, in central dining facility.
Costs (2005) • $5935; includes tuition, housing, some meals, insurance, excursions, international student ID. $200 nonrefundable deposit required. Financial aid available for students from sponsoring institution: loans.
For More Information • Ms. Rita Withrow, Program Assistant, Northern Illinois University, Study Abroad Office, Williston Hall 417, DeKalb, IL 60115; *Phone:* 815-753-0700; *Fax:* 815-753-0825. *E-mail:* niuabroad@niu.edu. *World Wide Web:* http://www.niu.edu/niuabroad/

AIX-EN-PROVENCE

ACADEMIC STUDIES ABROAD
ACADEMIC STUDIES ABROAD–AIX-EN-PROVENCE, FRANCE

Hosted by Le Centre d'Aix
Academic Focus • Full curriculum.
Program Information • Students attend classes at Le Centre d'Aix (Aix-en-Provence, France). Field trips to Luberon Valley, Cote d'Azur. Students typically earn 6 semester credits per term.
Sessions • Jun–Jul (summer).
Eligibility Requirements • Minimum age 18; open to freshmen, sophomores, juniors, seniors; 2.5 GPA; college transcript; no foreign language proficiency required.
Living Arrangements • Students live in host family homes. Quarters are shared with host institution students. Meals are taken with host family, in residences.
Costs (2006) • $4450; includes tuition, housing, some meals, insurance, excursions, international student ID, student support services, cell phone. $150 refundable deposit required. Financial aid available for all students: scholarships.
For More Information • Mr. Lee Frankel, Director, Academic Studies Abroad, 434 Massachusetts Avenue, Suite 501, Boston, MA 02118; *Phone:* 617-437-9388; *Fax:* 617-437-9390. *E-mail:* lee@academicstudies.com. *World Wide Web:* http://www.academicstudies.com

COLLEGE CONSORTIUM FOR INTERNATIONAL STUDIES–MIAMI DADE COLLEGE
SUMMER IN FRANCE (AIX-EN-PROVENCE)

Hosted by Institute for American Universities (IAU)–Aix-en-Provence
Academic Focus • Art history, French language and literature, international affairs, international business.

Program Information • Students attend classes at Institute for American Universities (IAU)–Aix-en-Provence (Aix-en-Provence, France), Institute for American Universities (IAU)–Aix-en-Provence (Aix-en-Provence, France). Field trips to Côte d'Azur, Roman/Medieval Provence. Students typically earn 6 semester credits per term.
Sessions • Jun–Jul (summer).
Eligibility Requirements • Minimum age 18; open to freshmen, sophomores, juniors, seniors, graduate students, adults; 2.5 GPA; 2 letters of recommendation; good academic standing at home school; no foreign language proficiency required.
Living Arrangements • Students live in host family homes. Quarters are shared with students from other programs. Meals are taken with host family.
Costs (2006) • $4935; includes tuition, housing, insurance, excursions, books and class materials, international student ID, student support services. $30 application fee. $300 nonrefundable deposit required. Financial aid available for students from sponsoring institution: loans.
For More Information • Center for International Education, College Consortium for International Studies–Miami Dade College, Truman State University, 114 Kirk Building, Kirksville, MO 63501; *Phone:* 660-785-4076; *Fax:* 660-785-7473. *E-mail:* ciea@truman.edu. *World Wide Web:* http://www.ccisabroad.org/. Students may also apply through Miami Dade College, Office of International Education, 300 NE 2nd Avenue, Suite 1450, Miami, FL 33132.

COLLEGE CONSORTIUM FOR INTERNATIONAL STUDIES–MIAMI DADE COLLEGE
SUMMER STUDIO ART IN PROVENCE

Hosted by Institute for American Universities (IAU)–Marchutz School of Painting and Drawing
Academic Focus • Drawing/painting, fine/studio arts.

FRANCE
Aix-en-Provence

Program Information • Students attend classes at Institute for American Universities (IAU)–Marchutz School of Painting and Drawing (Aix-en-Provence, France). Students typically earn 6 semester credits per term.
Sessions • Jun–Jul (summer).
Eligibility Requirements • Minimum age 18; open to freshmen, sophomores, juniors, seniors, graduate students, adults; 2.5 GPA; 2 letters of recommendation; good academic standing at home school; no foreign language proficiency required.
Living Arrangements • Students live in locally rented apartments, host family homes, hotels. Meals are taken with host family, in restaurants.
Costs (2006) • $4935; includes tuition, housing, some meals, insurance, international student ID, student support services. $30 application fee. $300 nonrefundable deposit required. Financial aid available for students from sponsoring institution: loans.
For More Information • Center for International Education, College Consortium for International Studies–Miami Dade College, Truman State University, 114 Kirk Building, Kirksville, MO 63501; *Phone:* 660-785-4076; *Fax:* 660-785-7473. *E-mail:* ciea@truman.edu. *World Wide Web:* http://www.ccisabroad.org/. Students may also apply through Miami Dade College, Office of International Education, 300 NE 2nd Avenue, Suite 1450, Miami, FL 33132.

COLLEGE CONSORTIUM FOR INTERNATIONAL STUDIES–TRUMAN STATE UNIVERSITY
SUMMER IN FRANCE (AIX-EN-PROVENCE)

Hosted by Institute for American Universities (IAU)–Aix-en-Provence
Academic Focus • Art history, art history, French language and literature, French language and literature, international affairs, international affairs, international business, international business.
Program Information • Students attend classes at Institute for American Universities (IAU)–Aix-en-Provence (Aix-en-Provence, France), Institute for American Universities (IAU)–Aix-en-Provence (Aix-en-Provence, France). Field trips to Côte d'Azur, Roman/Medieval Provence. Students typically earn 6 semester credits per term.
Sessions • Jun–Jul (summer).
Eligibility Requirements • Minimum age 18; open to freshmen, sophomores, juniors, seniors, graduate students, adults; 2.5 GPA; 2 letters of recommendation; good academic standing at home school; no foreign language proficiency required.
Living Arrangements • Students live in host family homes. Quarters are shared with students from other programs. Meals are taken with host family.
Costs (2007) • $5027; includes tuition, housing, some meals, insurance, excursions, books and class materials, international student ID, student support services. $300 nonrefundable deposit required. Financial aid available for students from sponsoring institution: loans.
For More Information • Center for International Education, College Consortium for International Studies–Truman State University, Truman State University, 114 Kirk Building, Kirksville, MO 63501; *Phone:* 660-785-4076; *Fax:* 660-785-7473. *E-mail:* ciea@truman.edu. *World Wide Web:* http://www.ccisabroad.org/. Students may also apply through Miami Dade College, Office of International Education, 300 NE 2nd Avenue, Suite 1450, Miami, FL 33132-2297; Truman State University, Center for International Education Abroad, 100 East Normal, Kirksville, MO 63501.

COLLEGE CONSORTIUM FOR INTERNATIONAL STUDIES–TRUMAN STATE UNIVERSITY
SUMMER STUDIO ART IN PROVENCE

Hosted by Institute for American Universities (IAU)–Marchutz School of Painting and Drawing
Academic Focus • Drawing/painting, drawing/painting, fine/studio arts, fine/studio arts.
Program Information • Students attend classes at Institute for American Universities (IAU)–Marchutz School of Painting and Drawing (Aix-en-Provence, France), Institute for American Universi-

ties (IAU)–Marchutz School of Painting and Drawing (Aix-en-Provence, France). Students typically earn 6 semester credits per term.
Sessions • Jun–Jul (summer).
Eligibility Requirements • Minimum age 18; open to freshmen, sophomores, juniors, seniors, graduate students, adults; 2.5 GPA; 2 letters of recommendation; good academic standing at home school; no foreign language proficiency required.
Living Arrangements • Students live in locally rented apartments, host family homes, hotels. Meals are taken with host family, in restaurants.
Costs (2007) • $5187; includes tuition, housing, some meals, insurance, international student ID, student support services. $300 nonrefundable deposit required. Financial aid available for students from sponsoring institution: loans.
For More Information • Center for International Education, College Consortium for International Studies–Truman State University, Truman State University, 114 Kirk Building, Kirksville, MO 63501; *Phone:* 660-785-4076; *Fax:* 660-785-7473. *E-mail:* ciea@truman.edu. *World Wide Web:* http://www.ccisabroad.org/. Students may also apply through Truman State University, Center for International Education Abroad, 100 East Normal, Kirksville, MO 63501.

FRENCH-AMERICAN EXCHANGE
SUMMER STUDY ABROAD IN AIX-EN-PROVENCE

Hosted by University of Law, Economics and Science (Aix-Marseilles III)
Academic Focus • Art history, civilization studies, communications, drama/theater, film and media studies, French language and literature, French studies, history, linguistics, music, political science and government.
Program Information • Students attend classes at University of Law, Economics and Science (Aix-Marseilles III) (Aix-en-Provence, France). Field trips to villages of Provence, the French Riviera; optional travel to the French Riviera, Spain, Italy, Germany, Paris at an extra cost. Students typically earn 6 semester credits per term.
Sessions • 4 week sessions in Jun, Jul, and Sep.
Eligibility Requirements • Minimum age 19; open to sophomores, juniors, seniors, graduate students, adults; good academic standing at home school; no foreign language proficiency required.
Living Arrangements • Students live in locally rented apartments, host family homes. Meals are taken on one's own, with host family, in residences, in restaurants.
Costs (2005) • $2470; includes tuition, housing, some meals, books and class materials, lab equipment, student support services. $50 application fee. $500 refundable deposit required.
For More Information • Mr. James Pondolfino, Executive Director, French-American Exchange, 3213 Duke Street, #620, Alexandria, VA 22314; *Phone:* 800-995-5087; *Fax:* 703-823-4447. *E-mail:* info@frenchamericanexchange.com. *World Wide Web:* http://www.frenchamericanexchange.com/

INSTITUTE FOR AMERICAN UNIVERSITIES (IAU)
ART IN PROVENCE–THE MARCHUTZ SCHOOL

Hosted by Institute for American Universities (IAU)–Marchutz School of Painting and Drawing
Academic Focus • Aesthetics, art history, drawing/painting.
Program Information • Students attend classes at Institute for American Universities (IAU)–Marchutz School of Painting and Drawing (Aix-en-Provence, France). Field trips to Arles, Vaucluse, St. Remy, Aix countryside. Students typically earn 6 semester credits per term.
Sessions • Jun–Jul (summer).
Eligibility Requirements • Minimum age 18; open to freshmen, sophomores, juniors, seniors, graduate students, adults; 2.5 GPA; good academic standing at home school; interest in and commitment to art or art history; no foreign language proficiency required.
Living Arrangements • Students live in locally rented apartments, host family homes. Quarters are shared with host institution students, students from other programs. Meals are taken with host family.
Costs (2005) • $4520; includes tuition, housing, some meals, insurance, excursions, books and class materials, international

Looking to study abroad this summer?

Consider a **CIEE Study Center** in one of sixteen countries around the world. Go for ten days to eight weeks and study business, language, or film, among many other offerings.

Have more than a suntan to show for your summer.

summer

www.ciee.org   1.800.40.STUDY   studyinfo@ciee.org

SMILE! YOU ARE IN SPAIN

ESPAÑA

Learn and hone your languages
Make new friends. Smile! You are in Spain

www.spain.info

student ID, student support services, art supplies. $30 application fee. $500 nonrefundable deposit required.

For More Information • Mr. Kurt Schick, Director of Enrollment Management, Institute for American Universities (IAU), I.A.U. U.S. Office, 1830 Sherman Avenue at University Place, Evanston, IL 60204; *Phone:* 800-221-2051; *Fax:* 847-864-6897. *E-mail:* usa@ iaufrance.org. *World Wide Web:* http://www.iaufrance.org/. Students may also apply through College Consortium for International Studies, c/o Miami-Dade Community College, Department of Foreign Languages, South Campus, 11011 SW 104th Street, Miami, FL 33176; Northern Illinois University, Study Abroad Office, Williston Hall 417, DeKalb, IL 60115-2854; Eckerd College, International Education and Off-Campus Programs, 4200 54th Avenue South, St. Petersburg, FL 33711.

INSTITUTE FOR AMERICAN UNIVERSITIES (IAU)
LE CENTRE D'AIX

Hosted by Institute for American Universities (IAU)–Aix-en-Provence

Academic Focus • Archaeology, art history, French language and literature, international affairs, international business, political science and government.

Program Information • Students attend classes at Institute for American Universities (IAU)–Aix-en-Provence (Aix-en-Provence, France). Field trips to Côte d'Azur, Lubéron Valley, Arles, St. Remy. Students typically earn 6 semester credits per term.

Sessions • Jun–Jul (summer).

Eligibility Requirements • Minimum age 18; open to freshmen, sophomores, juniors, seniors, adults; 2.5 GPA; 1 letter of recommendation; good academic standing at home school; no foreign language proficiency required.

Living Arrangements • Students live in host family homes. Quarters are shared with host institution students, students from other programs. Meals are taken with host family.

Costs (2005) • $4200; includes tuition, housing, some meals, insurance, excursions, books and class materials, student support services. $30 application fee. $500 nonrefundable deposit required. Financial aid available for all students: scholarships.

For More Information • Mr. Kurt Schick, Director of Enrollment Management, Institute for American Universities (IAU), I.A.U. U.S. Office, 1830 Sherman Avenue at University Place, Evanston, IL 60204; *Phone:* 800-221-2051; *Fax:* 847-864-6897. *E-mail:* usa@ iaufrance.org. *World Wide Web:* http://www.iaufrance.org/. Students may also apply through College Consortium for International Studies, c/o Miami-Dade Community College, Department of Foreign Languages, South Campus, 11011 SW 104th Street, Miami, FL 33176; Northern Illinois University, Study Abroad Office, Williston Hall 417, DeKalb, IL 60115-2854; Eckerd College, International Education and Off-Campus Programs, 4200 54th Avenue South, St. Petersburg, FL 33711.

LANGUAGE LIAISON
LEARN FRENCH IN AIX-EN-PROVENCE

Hosted by Language Liaison

Academic Focus • French language and literature.

Program Information • Students attend classes at Language Liaison (Aix-en-Provence, France). Field trips; optional travel at an extra cost. Students typically earn 3–15 semester credits per term.

Sessions • Classes begin weekly, year-round.

Eligibility Requirements • Minimum age 16; open to precollege students, freshmen, sophomores, juniors, seniors, graduate students, adults; no foreign language proficiency required.

Living Arrangements • Students live in locally rented apartments, host family homes, hotels. Meals are taken on one's own, with host family, in residences, in restaurants.

Costs (2005) • Contact sponsor for cost. $175 application fee. Financial aid available for all students: scholarship research service.

For More Information • Ms. Nancy Forman, President, Language Liaison, PO Box 1772, Pacific Palisades, CA 90272; *Phone:* 800-284-4448; *Fax:* 310-454-1706. *E-mail:* learn@languageliaison. com. *World Wide Web:* http://www.languageliaison.com/

LINGUA SERVICE WORLDWIDE
VACATION 'N LEARN FRENCH IN FRANCE

Hosted by Institut Scandinave Aix-en-Provence

Academic Focus • French language and literature, French studies.

Program Information • Students attend classes at Institut Scandinave Aix-en-Provence (Aix-en-Provence, France). Optional travel to cultural sites throughout France at an extra cost. Students typically earn 3 semester credits for 3 weeks, 6 semester credits for 5 weeks.

Sessions • Sessions of 2 or more weeks begin on Mondays, year-round.

Eligibility Requirements • Minimum age 16; open to precollege students, freshmen, sophomores, juniors, seniors, graduate students, adults; no foreign language proficiency required.

Living Arrangements • Students live in host institution dormitories, locally rented apartments, host family homes, hotels. Quarters are shared with host institution students. Meals are taken with host family.

Costs (2006–2007) • Contact sponsor for cost. $100 application fee.

For More Information • Assistant Director, Lingua Service Worldwide, 75 Prospect Street, Suite 4, Huntington, NY 11743; *Phone:* 800-394-5327; *Fax:* 631-271-3441. *E-mail:* linguaservice@att. net. *World Wide Web:* http://www.linguaserviceworldwide.com/

NORTHERN ILLINOIS UNIVERSITY
FRENCH STUDIES AT LE CENTRE D'AIX

Hosted by Institute for American Universities (IAU)–Aix-en-Provence

Academic Focus • Art history, business administration/management, economics, fine/studio arts, French language and literature, geography, history, philosophy, political science and government, psychology.

Program Information • Students attend classes at Institute for American Universities (IAU)–Aix-en-Provence (Aix-en-Provence, France). Field trips to southern France; optional travel to Vienna, Paris, Venice, Switzerland at an extra cost. Students typically earn 6 semester credits per term.

Sessions • Jun–Jul (summer).

Eligibility Requirements • Open to sophomores, juniors, seniors; 2.75 GPA; 2 letters of recommendation; good academic standing at home school; application essay; no foreign language proficiency required.

Living Arrangements • Students live in host family homes. Quarters are shared with host institution students. Meals are taken with host family, in residences.

Costs (2005) • $4600; includes tuition, housing, some meals, insurance, books and class materials, international student ID, student support services, advisory services, activity fee, computer lab access. $45 application fee. $200 refundable deposit required. Financial aid available for students from sponsoring institution: regular financial aid.

For More Information • Ms. Clare Foust, Program Assistant, Northern Illinois University, Study Abroad Office, Williston Hall 417, DeKalb, IL 60115; *Phone:* 815-753-0420; *Fax:* 815-753-0825. *E-mail:* niuabroad@niu.edu. *World Wide Web:* http://www.niu.edu/niuabroad/

NORTHERN ILLINOIS UNIVERSITY
PAINTING AND DRAWING

Hosted by Institute for American Universities (IAU)–Marchutz School of Painting and Drawing

Academic Focus • Art, drawing/painting.

Program Information • Students attend classes at Institute for American Universities (IAU)–Marchutz School of Painting and Drawing (Aix-en-Provence, France). Optional travel to Venice, Paris at an extra cost. Students typically earn 6 semester credits per term.

Sessions • Jun–Jul (summer).

Eligibility Requirements • Open to juniors, seniors; major in art; 2.75 GPA; 2 letters of recommendation; good academic standing at home school; application essay; portfolio; no foreign language proficiency required.

Living Arrangements • Students live in host family homes. Quarters are shared with host institution students. Meals are taken on one's own.

FRANCE
Aix-en-Provence

Costs (2005) • $4920; includes tuition, housing, some meals, insurance, excursions, books and class materials, international student ID, student support services, cultural activities. $45 application fee. $500 refundable deposit required. Financial aid available for students from sponsoring institution: regular financial aid.

For More Information • Ms. Emily Gorlewski, Program Assistant, Northern Illinois University, Study Abroad Office, Williston Hall 417, DeKalb, IL 60115; *Phone:* 815-753-0420; *Fax:* 815-753-0825. *E-mail:* niuabroad@niu.edu. *World Wide Web:* http://www.niu.edu/niuabroad/

ANGERS

AHA INTERNATIONAL AN ACADEMIC PROGRAM OF THE UNIVERSITY OF OREGON
ANGERS, FRANCE: NORTHWEST COUNCIL ON STUDY ABROAD (NCSA)

Hosted by Catholic University of the West, Angers
Academic Focus • French language and literature, French studies, history.
Program Information • Students attend classes at Catholic University of the West, Angers (Angers, France). Field trips to Saint-Malo, Mont-Saint-Michel, châteaux of the Loire, Normandy. Students typically earn 6–12 quarter credits per term.
Sessions • 4 week sessions in Jul, Aug, and Sep.
Eligibility Requirements • Open to sophomores, juniors, seniors; 2 letters of recommendation; good academic standing at home school; official transcripts; no foreign language proficiency required.
Living Arrangements • Students live in host institution dormitories, host family homes. Quarters are shared with host institution students, students from other programs. Meals are taken on one's own, with host family, in central dining facility, in restaurants.
Costs (2005–2006) • $3376–$3729; includes tuition, housing, all meals, insurance, excursions, international student ID, student support services, on-site orientation. $50 application fee. $200 deposit required. Financial aid available for all students: scholarships, loans, home institution financial aid.
For More Information • Mr. Edward Helgeson, Associate Director for University Programs, AHA International An Academic Program of the University of Oregon, 221 NW 2nd Avenue, Suite 200, Portland, OR 97209; *Phone:* 503-295-7730; *Fax:* 503-295-5969. *E-mail:* mail@aha-intl.org. *World Wide Web:* http://www.aha-intl.org/

ILLINOIS STATE UNIVERSITY
SUMMER BUSINESS STUDY AT ESSCA

Hosted by Ecole Supérieure des Sciences Commerciales d'Angers ESSCA
Academic Focus • French studies, international business.
Program Information • Students attend classes at Ecole Supérieure des Sciences Commerciales d'Angers ESSCA (Angers, France). Scheduled travel to Paris, Brussels; field trips to Normandy beaches, Loire castles. Students typically earn 6 semester credits per term.
Sessions • Jun–Jul (summer).
Eligibility Requirements • Open to juniors, seniors; course work in business; 2.5 GPA; 2 letters of recommendation; good academic standing at home school; essay; no foreign language proficiency required.
Living Arrangements • Students live in hotels. Quarters are shared with host institution students, students from other programs. Meals are taken as a group, in restaurants.
Costs (2005) • $5225; includes tuition, housing, all meals, insurance, excursions, international airfare, international student ID, student support services, personal expenses. $150 application fee. Financial aid available for students from sponsoring institution: scholarships, loans.
For More Information • Dr. Iris Varner, Director of International Business, Illinois State University, Williams Hall 351, Campus Box 5590, Normal, IL 61790-5590; *Phone:* 309-438-7843; *Fax:* 309-438-3987. *E-mail:* izvarner@ilstu.edu. *World Wide Web:* http://www.internationalstudies.ilstu.edu/

ILLINOIS STATE UNIVERSITY
SUMMER STUDY IN INTERNATIONAL AGRICULTURE AND AGRIBUSINESS

Hosted by Ecole Supérieure d'Agriculture d'Angers
Academic Focus • Agriculture, business administration/management, French studies.
Program Information • Students attend classes at Ecole Supérieure d'Agriculture d'Angers (Angers, France). Scheduled travel to Belgium, Paris, Chartres, Loire River Valley; field trips to local farms, local businesses. Students typically earn 6 semester credits per term.
Sessions • May–Jun (summer).
Eligibility Requirements • Open to sophomores, juniors, seniors; 2.5 GPA; good academic standing at home school; no foreign language proficiency required.
Living Arrangements • Students live in host institution dormitories, locally rented apartments, host family homes. Meals are taken as a group.
Costs (2005) • $4554; includes tuition, housing, all meals, insurance, excursions, international airfare, international student ID, student support services, personal expenses. $150 application fee. Financial aid available for students from sponsoring institution: scholarships, loans.
For More Information • Office of International Studies and Programs, Illinois State University, Campus Box 6120, Normal, IL 61790-6120; *Phone:* 309-438-5276; *Fax:* 309-438-3987. *E-mail:* oisp@ilstu.edu. *World Wide Web:* http://www.internationalstudies.ilstu.edu/

ANNECY

COLLEGE CONSORTIUM FOR INTERNATIONAL STUDIES–TRUMAN STATE UNIVERSITY
SUMMER IN FRANCE: INTENSIVE FRENCH

Academic Focus • French language and literature, French studies.
Program Information • Faculty members are local instructors hired by the sponsor. Optional travel at an extra cost. Students typically earn 4 semester credits per term.
Sessions • Jun (summer), Jul -Aug (summer 2), Jul-Aug (summer 3).
Eligibility Requirements • Minimum age 18; open to freshmen, sophomores, juniors, seniors, adults; 2.5 GPA; 2 letters of recommendation; good academic standing at home school; no foreign language proficiency required.
Living Arrangements • Students live in host institution dormitories, locally rented apartments, host family homes. Quarters are shared with host institution students. Meals are taken on one's own, with host family.
Costs (2007) • $2037; includes tuition, insurance, books and class materials, international student ID, student support services, housing deposit. $300 nonrefundable deposit required. Financial aid available for students from sponsoring institution: scholarships, loans.
For More Information • Center for International Education, College Consortium for International Studies–Truman State University, 100 East Normal, Kirk Building 114, Kirksville, MO 63501; *Phone:* 660-785-4076; *Fax:* 660-785-7473. *E-mail:* ciea@truman.edu. *World Wide Web:* http://www.ccisabroad.org/. Students may also apply through Miami Dade College, Office of International Education, 300 NE 2nd Avenue, Suite 1450, Miami, FL 33132-2297.

NORTHERN ARIZONA UNIVERSITY
SUMMER STUDY ABROAD IN FRANCE

Hosted by Institut Français des Alpes
Academic Focus • French studies.
Program Information • Students attend classes at Institut Français des Alpes (Annecy, France). Field trips to local sites; optional travel to Paris at an extra cost. Students typically earn 7 semester credits per term.
Sessions • May–Jul (summer).
Eligibility Requirements • Minimum age 18; open to freshmen, sophomores, juniors, seniors, adults; 2.5 GPA; good academic standing at home school; no foreign language proficiency required.

Living Arrangements • Students live in host institution dormitories, host family homes. Meals are taken on one's own, with host family, in residences, in central dining facility.
Costs (2005) • $2800; includes tuition, housing, all meals, excursions, international student ID, student support services. $125 application fee. Financial aid available for all students: scholarships, loans.
For More Information • International Office, Northern Arizona University, NAU Box 5598, Flagstaff, AZ 86011-5598; *Phone:* 928-523-2409; *Fax:* 928-523-9489. *E-mail:* international.office@nau.edu. *World Wide Web:* http://internationaloffice.nau.edu/

TUFTS UNIVERSITY
TUFTS IN ANNECY (FRANCE)
Hosted by Institut Français d'Annecy
Academic Focus • French language and literature.
Program Information • Students attend classes at Institut Français d'Annecy (Annecy, France). Field trips to Chamonix, Avignon, Lyon; optional travel to Paris, Lyon, Avignon at an extra cost. Students typically earn 1 semester credit per term.
Sessions • Jun–Jul (summer).
Eligibility Requirements • Minimum age 18; open to freshmen, sophomores, juniors, seniors, graduate students, adults; 2.0 GPA; no foreign language proficiency required.
Living Arrangements • Students live in host family homes. Quarters are shared with host institution students. Meals are taken with host family, in residences.
Costs (2006) • $3635; includes tuition, housing, all meals, student support services. $40 application fee. $500 nonrefundable deposit required. Financial aid available for students from sponsoring institution: scholarships.
For More Information • Ms. Maura Leary, Coordinator, Tufts University, Tufts European Center, 108 Packard Avenue, Medford, MA 02155; *Phone:* 617-627-3290; *Fax:* 617-627-3457. *E-mail:* france@tufts.edu. *World Wide Web:* http://ase.tufts.edu/studyabroad/. Students may also apply through Tufts University, Le Prieure, 74290, Talloires, France.

UNIVERSITY OF COLORADO AT BOULDER
SUMMER INTENSIVE FRENCH PROGRAM
Hosted by Institut Français des Alpes
Academic Focus • French language and literature, French studies.
Program Information • Students attend classes at Institut Français des Alpes (Annecy, France). Field trips to a local cheese factory; optional travel to Geneva, Lyon, Chamonix, Provence at an extra cost. Students typically earn 4–8 semester credits per term.
Sessions • Jun (summer).
Eligibility Requirements • Open to freshmen, sophomores, juniors, seniors, graduate students, adults; 2.75 GPA; 2 letters of recommendation; good academic standing at home school; no foreign language proficiency required.
Living Arrangements • Students live in host institution dormitories, host family homes. Meals are taken on one's own, with host family, in central dining facility, in restaurants.
Costs (2005) • $4095; includes tuition, housing, some meals, insurance, excursions, international airfare, books and class materials, student support services. $400 nonrefundable deposit required. Financial aid available for students from sponsoring institution: scholarships, loans.
For More Information • Study Abroad Programs, University of Colorado at Boulder, International Education, 123 UCB, Boulder, CO 80309-0123; *Phone:* 303-492-7741; *Fax:* 303-492-5185. *E-mail:* studyabr@colorado.edu. *World Wide Web:* http://www.colorado.edu/OIE/

ANTIBES

CENTER FOR CULTURAL INTERCHANGE
ANTIBES, FRANCE LANGUAGE SCHOOL
Hosted by Centre International d'Antibes
Academic Focus • French language and literature.

Program Information • Students attend classes at Centre International d'Antibes (Antibes, France). Field trips to cultural activities, guided tours, museum visits.
Sessions • 3, 4, or 6 week sessions begin every Monday, year-round.
Eligibility Requirements • Minimum age 14; open to precollege students, freshmen, sophomores, juniors, seniors, graduate students, adults; no foreign language proficiency required.
Living Arrangements • Students live in host family homes. Quarters are shared with host institution students. Meals are taken with host family, in residences.
Costs (2005) • $3290 for 4 weeks; includes tuition, housing, some meals, insurance, books and class materials, student support services, activities. Financial aid available for students from sponsoring institution: scholarships.
For More Information • Ms. Juliet Jones, Outbound Programs Director, Center for Cultural Interchange, 325 West Huron, Suite 706, Chicago, IL 60610; *Phone:* 866-684-9675; *Fax:* 872-944-2644. *E-mail:* info@cci-exchange.com. *World Wide Web:* http://www.cci-exchange.com/

LANGUAGE LIAISON
LEARN FRENCH IN ANTIBES
Hosted by Language Liaison
Academic Focus • French language and literature.
Program Information • Students attend classes at Language Liaison (Antibes, France). Field trips; optional travel at an extra cost. Students typically earn 3–15 semester credits per term.
Sessions • Classes begin weekly, year-round.
Eligibility Requirements • Minimum age 14; open to precollege students, freshmen, sophomores, juniors, seniors, graduate students, adults; no foreign language proficiency required.
Living Arrangements • Students live in host institution dormitories, locally rented apartments, host family homes, hotels. Meals are taken as a group, on one's own, with host family, in residences, in central dining facility, in restaurants.
Costs (2005) • Contact sponsor for cost. $175 application fee. Financial aid available for all students: scholarship research service.
For More Information • Ms. Nancy Forman, President, Language Liaison, PO Box 1772, Pacific Palisades, CA 90272; *Phone:* 800-284-4448; *Fax:* 310-454-1706. *E-mail:* learn@languageliaison.com. *World Wide Web:* http://www.languageliaison.com/

LINGUA SERVICE WORLDWIDE
VACATION 'N LEARN FRENCH IN FRANCE
Hosted by Centre International d'Antibes
Academic Focus • French language and literature, French studies.
Program Information • Students attend classes at Centre International d'Antibes (Antibes, France). Optional travel to cultural sites throughout France at an extra cost. Students typically earn 3 semester credits for 3 weeks, 6 semester credits for 5 weeks.
Sessions • Sessions of 2 or more weeks begin on Mondays, year-round.
Eligibility Requirements • Minimum age 16; open to precollege students, freshmen, sophomores, juniors, seniors, graduate students, adults; no foreign language proficiency required.
Living Arrangements • Students live in host institution dormitories, locally rented apartments, host family homes, hotels. Quarters are shared with host institution students. Meals are taken with host family.
Costs (2006–2007) • Contact sponsor for cost. $100 application fee.
For More Information • Assistant Director, Lingua Service Worldwide, 75 Prospect Street, Suite 4, Huntington, NY 11743; *Phone:* 800-394-5327; *Fax:* 631-271-3441. *E-mail:* linguaservice@att.net. *World Wide Web:* http://www.linguaserviceworldwide.com/

AVIGNON

COLLEGE CONSORTIUM FOR INTERNATIONAL STUDIES–MIAMI DADE COLLEGE
AVIGNON SUMMER PROGRAM
Hosted by Institute for American Universities (IAU)–Avignon
Academic Focus • Art history, French language and literature.

FRANCE
Avignon

Program Information • Students attend classes at Institute for American Universities (IAU)-Avignon (Avignon, France). Students typically earn 6 semester credits per term.
Sessions • Jun-Jul (summer).
Eligibility Requirements • Minimum age 18; open to freshmen, sophomores, juniors, seniors, graduate students, adults; 2.5 GPA; 2 letters of recommendation; good academic standing at home school; statement of purpose in French; 2 years of college course work in French.
Living Arrangements • Students live in host family homes. Quarters are shared with students from other programs. Meals are taken with host family.
Costs (2006) • $4935; includes tuition, housing, some meals, insurance, books and class materials, international student ID. $30 application fee. $300 nonrefundable deposit required. Financial aid available for students from sponsoring institution: loans.
For More Information • Center for International Education, College Consortium for International Studies–Miami Dade College, Truman State University, 114 Kirk Building, Kirksville, MO 63501; *Phone:* 660-785-4076; *Fax:* 660-785-7473. *E-mail:* ciea@truman.edu. *World Wide Web:* http://www.ccisabroad.org/. Students may also apply through Miami Dade College, Office of International Education, 300 NE 2nd Avenue, Suite 1450, Miami, FL 33132.

COLLEGE CONSORTIUM FOR INTERNATIONAL STUDIES–TRUMAN STATE UNIVERSITY
AVIGNON SUMMER PROGRAM

Hosted by Institute for American Universities (IAU)–Avignon
Academic Focus • Art history, art history, French language and literature, French language and literature.
Program Information • Students attend classes at Institute for American Universities (IAU)-Avignon (Avignon, France), Institute for American Universities (IAU)-Avignon (Avignon, France). Students typically earn 6 semester credits per term.
Sessions • Jun-Jul (summer).
Eligibility Requirements • Minimum age 18; open to freshmen, sophomores, juniors, seniors, graduate students, adults; 2.5 GPA; 2 letters of recommendation; good academic standing at home school; statement of purpose in French; 2 years of college course work in French.
Living Arrangements • Students live in host family homes. Quarters are shared with students from other programs. Meals are taken with host family.
Costs (2007) • $5000; includes tuition, housing, some meals, insurance, books and class materials, international student ID. $300 nonrefundable deposit required. Financial aid available for students from sponsoring institution: loans.
For More Information • Center for International Education, College Consortium for International Studies–Truman State University, Truman State University, 114 Kirk Building, Kirksville, MO 63501; *Phone:* 660-785-4076; *Fax:* 660-785-7473. *E-mail:* ciea@truman.edu. *World Wide Web:* http://www.ccisabroad.org/. Students may also apply through Truman State University, Center for International Education Abroad, 100 East Normal, Kirksville, MO 63501.

INSTITUTE FOR AMERICAN UNIVERSITIES (IAU)
LE CENTRE D'AVIGNON

Hosted by Institute for American Universities (IAU)–Avignon
Academic Focus • Art history, drama/theater, French language and literature, history.
Program Information • Students attend classes at Institute for American Universities (IAU)-Avignon (Avignon, France). Field trips to Côte d'Azur, Lubéron Valley. Students typically earn 6 semester credits per term.
Sessions • Jun-Jul (summer).
Eligibility Requirements • Minimum age 18; open to juniors, seniors, graduate students, adults; 3.0 GPA; 1 letter of recommendation; good academic standing at home school; French professor recommendation; 2 years of college course work in French.
Living Arrangements • Students live in host family homes. Meals are taken with host family, in residences.

Costs (2005) • $4200; includes tuition, housing, some meals, insurance, excursions, books and class materials, international student ID, student support services. $30 application fee. $500 nonrefundable deposit required.
For More Information • Mr. Kurt Schick, Director of Enrollment Management, Institute for American Universities (IAU), I.A.U. U.S. Office, 1830 Sherman Avenue at University Place, Evanston, IL 60204; *Phone:* 800-221-2051; *Fax:* 847-864-6897. *E-mail:* usa@iaufrance.org. *World Wide Web:* http://www.iaufrance.org/. Students may also apply through College Consortium for International Studies, c/o Miami-Dade Community College, Department of Foreign Languages, South Campus, 11011 SW 104th Street, Miami, FL 33176; Northern Illinois University, Study Abroad Office, Williston Hall 417, DeKalb, IL 60115-2854; Eckerd College, International Education and Off-Campus Programs, 4200 54th Avenue South, St. Petersburg, FL 33711.

LANGUAGE LIAISON
LEARN FRENCH IN AVIGNON

Hosted by Language Liaison
Academic Focus • French language and literature.
Program Information • Students attend classes at Language Liaison (Avignon, France). Field trips; optional travel at an extra cost. Students typically earn 3-15 semester credits per term.
Sessions • Classes begin weekly, year-round.
Eligibility Requirements • Minimum age 17; open to freshmen, sophomores, juniors, seniors, graduate students, adults; no foreign language proficiency required.
Living Arrangements • Students live in locally rented apartments, host family homes, hotels. Meals are taken on one's own, with host family, in residences, in restaurants.
Costs (2005) • Contact sponsor for cost. $175 application fee. Financial aid available for all students: scholarship research service.
For More Information • Ms. Nancy Forman, President, Language Liaison, PO Box 1772, Pacific Palisades, CA 90272; *Phone:* 800-284-4448; *Fax:* 310-454-1706. *E-mail:* learn@languageliaison.com. *World Wide Web:* http://www.languageliaison.com/

LINGUA SERVICE WORLDWIDE
VACATION 'N LEARN FRENCH IN FRANCE

Hosted by Centre d'Etudes Linguistiques de Avignon
Academic Focus • French language and literature, French studies.
Program Information • Students attend classes at Centre d'Etudes Linguistiques de Avignon (Avignon, France). Optional travel to cultural sites throughout France at an extra cost. Students typically earn 3 semester credits for 3 weeks, 6 semester credits for 5 weeks.
Sessions • Sessions of 2 or more weeks begin on Mondays, year-round.
Eligibility Requirements • Minimum age 16; open to precollege students, freshmen, sophomores, juniors, seniors, graduate students, adults; no foreign language proficiency required.
Living Arrangements • Students live in host institution dormitories, locally rented apartments, host family homes, hotels. Quarters are shared with host institution students. Meals are taken with host family.
Costs (2006–2007) • Contact sponsor for cost. $100 application fee.
For More Information • Assistant Director, Lingua Service Worldwide, 75 Prospect Street, Suite 4, Huntington, NY 11743; *Phone:* 800-394-5327; *Fax:* 631-271-3441. *E-mail:* linguaservice@att.net. *World Wide Web:* http://www.linguaserviceworldwide.com/

NORTHERN ILLINOIS UNIVERSITY
FRENCH LANGUAGE AND LITERATURE IN AVIGNON

Hosted by Institute for American Universities (IAU)–Avignon
Academic Focus • Art history, French language and literature, French studies.
Program Information • Students attend classes at Institute for American Universities (IAU)-Avignon (Avignon, France). Field trips to Lubéron, Marseille, St. Remy, Tarascon. Students typically earn 3-6 semester credits per term.
Sessions • Jun-Jul (summer).
Eligibility Requirements • Minimum age 18; open to juniors, seniors; 2 letters of recommendation; good academic standing at

home school; minimum GPA of 3.0 in French courses; minimum 2.75 GPA overall; 2 years of college course work in French.

Living Arrangements • Students live in host family homes. Quarters are shared with host institution students. Meals are taken with host family, in residences, in restaurants.

Costs (2005) • $4600; includes tuition, housing, some meals, insurance, excursions, international student ID, student support services. $45 application fee. $200 refundable deposit required. Financial aid available for students from sponsoring institution: regular financial aid.

For More Information • Ms. Emily Gorlewski, Program Assistant, Northern Illinois University, Study Abroad Office, Williston Hall 417, DeKalb, IL 60115; *Phone:* 815-753-0420; *Fax:* 815-753-0825. *E-mail:* cfoust@niu.edu. *World Wide Web:* http://www.niu.edu/niuabroad/

UNIVERSITY OF ILLINOIS AT URBANA-CHAMPAIGN
SUMMER IN AVIGNON

Hosted by Institute for American Universities (IAU)–Avignon
Academic Focus • French language and literature.
Program Information • Students attend classes at Institute for American Universities (IAU)–Avignon (Avignon, France). Field trips to Pont du Gard, Les Baux, Arles, Cassis. Students typically earn 4 semester credits per term.
Sessions • May–Jun (summer).
Eligibility Requirements • Minimum age 18; open to freshmen, sophomores, juniors, seniors, graduate students, adults; good academic standing at home school; 1 year of college course work in French.
Living Arrangements • Students live in host family homes. Meals are taken with host family, in residences.
Costs (2005) • $3365; includes tuition, housing, some meals, insurance, excursions, student support services. $250 nonrefundable deposit required. Financial aid available for all students: loans.
For More Information • Ms. Brenna Ross, Program Assistant, University of Illinois at Urbana-Champaign, Department of French, 2090 FLB MC-158, 707 South Mathews Avenue, Urbana, IL 61801; *Phone:* 217-333-2020; *Fax:* 217-244-2223. *E-mail:* bkross@uiuc.edu. *World Wide Web:* http://www.ips.uiuc.edu/sao/index.shtml

BIARRITZ

LANGUAGE LIAISON
LEARN FRENCH IN BIARRITZ

Hosted by Language Liaison
Academic Focus • French language and literature.
Program Information • Students attend classes at Language Liaison (Biarritz, France). Field trips; optional travel. Students typically earn 3-15 semester credits per term.
Sessions • Classes begin every week, year-round.
Eligibility Requirements • Minimum age 16; open to precollege students, freshmen, sophomores, juniors, seniors, graduate students, adults; no foreign language proficiency required.
Living Arrangements • Students live in locally rented apartments, host family homes, hotels. Meals are taken on one's own, in residences.
Costs (2005) • Contact sponsor for cost. $175 application fee.
For More Information • Ms. Nancy Forman, President, Language Liaison, PO Box 1772, Pacific Palisades, CA 90272; *Phone:* 800-284-4448; *Fax:* 310-454-1706. *World Wide Web:* http://www.languageliaison.com/

BORDEAUX

LANGUAGE LIAISON
FRENCH IN BORDEAUX

Hosted by Language Liaison
Academic Focus • French language and literature.
Program Information • Students attend classes at Language Liaison (Bordeaux, France). Field trips; optional travel at an extra cost. Students typically earn 3-15 semester credits per term.
Sessions • New programs begin weekly, year-round.

Eligibility Requirements • Minimum age 16; open to precollege students, freshmen, sophomores, juniors, seniors, graduate students, adults; no foreign language proficiency required.
Living Arrangements • Students live in host family homes, hotels. Meals are taken on one's own, with host family, in residences, in restaurants.
Costs (2005) • Contact sponsor for cost. $175 application fee. Financial aid available for all students: scholarship research service.
For More Information • Ms. Nancy Forman, President, Language Liaison, PO Box 1772, Pacific Palisades, CA 90272; *Phone:* 800-284-4448; *Fax:* 310-454-1706. *E-mail:* learn@languageliaison.com. *World Wide Web:* http://www.languageliaison.com/

LINGUA SERVICE WORLDWIDE
VACATION 'N LEARN FRENCH IN FRANCE

Hosted by Bordeaux Language Studies
Academic Focus • French language and literature, French studies.
Program Information • Students attend classes at Bordeaux Language Studies (Bordeaux, France). Optional travel to cultural sites throughout France at an extra cost. Students typically earn 3 semester credits for 3 weeks, 6 semester credits for 5 weeks.
Sessions • Sessions of 2 or more weeks begin on Mondays, year-round.
Eligibility Requirements • Minimum age 16; open to precollege students, freshmen, sophomores, juniors, seniors, graduate students, adults; no foreign language proficiency required.
Living Arrangements • Students live in host institution dormitories, locally rented apartments, host family homes, hotels. Quarters are shared with host institution students. Meals are taken with host family.
Costs (2006–2007) • Contact sponsor for cost. $100 application fee.
For More Information • Assistant Director, Lingua Service Worldwide, 75 Prospect Street, Suite 4, Huntington, NY 11743; *Phone:* 800-394-5327; *Fax:* 631-271-3441. *E-mail:* linguaservice@att.net. *World Wide Web:* http://www.linguaserviceworldwide.com/

BOURBONNAIS

COLUMBIA UNIVERSITY
SUMMER FIELD STUDY IN FRANCE

Academic Focus • Architecture, art history.
Program Information • Faculty members are drawn from the sponsor's U.S. staff. Field trips to the Bourbonnais region. Students typically earn 4 semester credits per term.
Sessions • Jun–Jul (summer).
Eligibility Requirements • Minimum age 18; open to freshmen, sophomores, juniors, seniors, graduate students, adults; 3.0 GPA; 1 letter of recommendation; good academic standing at home school; no foreign language proficiency required.
Living Arrangements • Students live in châteaus. Meals are taken as a group, on one's own, in central dining facility.
Costs (2004) • $5000; includes tuition, housing, some meals, excursions, lab equipment, student support services. $50 application fee. $500 nonrefundable deposit required.
For More Information • Information Center, Columbia University, 2970 Broadway, MC 4110, 303 Lewisohn, New York, NY 10027-6902; *Phone:* 212-854-9699; *Fax:* 212-854-5861. *E-mail:* studyabroad@columbia.edu. *World Wide Web:* http://www.ce.columbia.edu/op/

BREST

LANGUAGE LIAISON
LEARN FRENCH IN BREST

Hosted by Language Liaison
Academic Focus • French language and literature.
Program Information • Students attend classes at Language Liaison (Brest, France). Field trips; optional travel. Students typically earn 3-15 semester credits per term.
Sessions • Classes begin every week, year-round.

FRANCE
Brest

Eligibility Requirements • Minimum age 16; open to precollege students, freshmen, sophomores, juniors, seniors, graduate students, adults; no foreign language proficiency required.
Living Arrangements • Students live in locally rented apartments, host family homes, hotels. Meals are taken on one's own, in residences.
Costs (2005) • Contact sponsor for cost. $175 application fee.
For More Information • Ms. Nancy Forman, President, Language Liaison, PO Box 1772, Pacific Palisades, CA 90272; *Phone:* 800-284-4448; *Fax:* 310-454-1706. *World Wide Web:* http://www.languageliaison.com/

LINGUA SERVICE WORLDWIDE
VACATION 'N LEARN FRENCH IN FRANCE

Hosted by Centre International d'Etudes des Langues
Academic Focus • French language and literature, French studies.
Program Information • Students attend classes at Centre International d'Etudes des Langues (Brest, France). Optional travel to cultural sites thoughout France at an extra cost. Students typically earn 3 semester credits for 3 weeks, 6 semester credits for 5 weeks.
Sessions • Sessions of 2 or more weeks begin on Mondays, year-round.
Eligibility Requirements • Minimum age 16; open to precollege students, freshmen, sophomores, juniors, seniors, graduate students, adults; no foreign language proficiency required.
Living Arrangements • Students live in host institution dormitories, locally rented apartments, host family homes, hotels. Quarters are shared with host institution students. Meals are taken with host family.
Costs (2006–2007) • Contact sponsor for cost. $100 application fee.
For More Information • Assistant Director, Lingua Service Worldwide, 75 Prospect Street, Suite 4, Huntington, NY 11743; *Phone:* 800-394-5327; *Fax:* 631-271-3441. *E-mail:* linguaservice@att.net. *World Wide Web:* http://www.linguaserviceworldwide.com/

BRITTANY

LANGUAGE LIAISON
FRENCH IN BRITTANY

Hosted by Language Liaison
Academic Focus • French language and literature.
Program Information • Students attend classes at Language Liaison (Brittany, France). Field trips; optional travel at an extra cost. Students typically earn 3-15 semester credits per term.
Sessions • Classes begin weekly, year-round.
Eligibility Requirements • Minimum age 16; open to precollege students, freshmen, sophomores, juniors, seniors, graduate students, adults; no foreign language proficiency required.
Living Arrangements • Students live in locally rented apartments, program-owned apartments, host family homes, hotels. Meals are taken on one's own, with host family, in residences, in restaurants.
Costs (2005) • Contact sponsor for cost. $175 application fee. Financial aid available for all students: scholarship research service.
For More Information • Ms. Nancy Forman, President, Language Liaison, PO Box 1772, Pacific Palisades, CA 90272; *Phone:* 800-284-4448; *Fax:* 310-454-1706. *E-mail:* learn@languageliaison.com. *World Wide Web:* http://www.languageliaison.com/

CAEN

UNIVERSITY OF DELAWARE
WINTER SESSION IN CAEN, FRANCE

Hosted by University of Caen
Academic Focus • French language and literature, French studies.
Program Information • Students attend classes at University of Caen (Caen, France). Scheduled travel to Paris; field trips to Bayeux, Mont-Saint-Michel, Rouen, Versailles; optional travel to Europe at an extra cost. Students typically earn 6-7 semester credits per term.
Sessions • Jan–Feb (winter).

Eligibility Requirements • Open to freshmen, sophomores, juniors, seniors, adults; 2.0 GPA; 1 letter of recommendation; 1 year of college course work in French.
Living Arrangements • Students live in host family homes. Quarters are shared with host institution students. Meals are taken with host family, in residences, in central dining facility.
Costs (2005) • Contact sponsor for cost. $200 nonrefundable deposit required. Financial aid available for all students: scholarships.
For More Information • Center for International Studies, University of Delaware, 186 South College Avenue, Newark, DE 19716-1450; *Phone:* 888-831-4685; *Fax:* 302-831-6042. *E-mail:* studyabroad@udel.edu. *World Wide Web:* http://www.udel.edu/studyabroad/

CANNES

AMERICAN INSTITUTE FOR FOREIGN STUDY (AIFS)
AIFS–CANNES, FRANCE–COLLÈGE INTERNATIONAL DE CANNES

Hosted by College International de Cannes
Academic Focus • French language and literature.
Program Information • Students attend classes at College International de Cannes (Cannes, France). Field trips to Provence visit, local walking tours, sports, excursions to resorts, museums, art galleries, wine tasting, Cultural Activities; optional travel to Optional 3 day excursion to Paris for a supplement of $399. Students typically earn 8 semester credits per term.
Sessions • Jun-Jul (summer), Jun-Aug.
Eligibility Requirements • Minimum age 17; open to precollege students, freshmen, sophomores, juniors, seniors; 2.0 GPA.
Living Arrangements • Students live in host institution dormitories, program-owned apartments, hotels. Quarters are shared with host institution students. Meals are taken as a group, in residences.
Costs (2007) • 4 weeks: $5499, 6 weeks: $6999; includes tuition, housing, all meals, some meals, insurance, excursions, student support services, On-site Resident Director, Phone Card to call the U.S. $95 application fee. $395 nonrefundable deposit required. Financial aid available for all students: scholarships.
For More Information • Mr. David Mauro, Admissions Advisor, American Institute For Foreign Study (AIFS), 9 West Broad Street, Stamford, CT 06902-3788; *Phone:* 800-727-2437 Ext. 5163; *Fax:* 203-399-5597. *E-mail:* dmauro@aifs.com. *World Wide Web:* http://www.aifsabroad.com/

LINGUA SERVICE WORLDWIDE
VACATION 'N LEARN FRENCH IN FRANCE

Hosted by Collège International de Cannes
Academic Focus • French language and literature, French studies.
Program Information • Students attend classes at Collège International de Cannes (Cannes, France). Optional travel to cultural sites throughout France at an extra cost. Students typically earn 3 semester credits for 3 weeks, 6 semester credits for 5 weeks.
Sessions • Sessions of 2 or more weeks begin on Mondays, year-round.
Eligibility Requirements • Minimum age 16; open to precollege students, freshmen, sophomores, juniors, seniors, graduate students, adults; no foreign language proficiency required.
Living Arrangements • Students live in host institution dormitories, locally rented apartments, host family homes, hotels. Quarters are shared with host institution students. Meals are taken with host family.
Costs (2006–2007) • Contact sponsor for cost. $100 application fee.
For More Information • Assistant Director, Lingua Service Worldwide, 75 Prospect Street, Suite 4, Huntington, NY 11743; *Phone:* 800-394-5327; *Fax:* 631-271-3441. *E-mail:* linguaservice@att.net. *World Wide Web:* http://www.linguaserviceworldwide.com/

SOUTHERN METHODIST UNIVERSITY
SMU IN THE SOUTH OF FRANCE

Held at Cannes Complex
Academic Focus • French language and literature, French studies.

Program Information • Classes are held on the campus of Cannes Complex (Cannes, France). Faculty members are drawn from the sponsor's U.S. staff and local instructors hired by the sponsor. Field trips to Monaco, Nice, Provence, Arles, Avignon. Students typically earn 6 semester credits per term.
Sessions • May–Jun (summer).
Eligibility Requirements • Open to sophomores, juniors, seniors; 2.5 GPA; 1 letter of recommendation; good academic standing at home school; interview; no foreign language proficiency required.
Living Arrangements • Students live in program-leased apartments. Quarters are shared with host institution students. Meals are taken as a group, in central dining facility.
Costs (2005) • $5950; includes tuition, housing, some meals, excursions, student support services. $40 application fee. $400 nonrefundable deposit required. Financial aid available for students from sponsoring institution: scholarships, loans.
For More Information • Ms. Nancy Simmons, Associate Director, Southern Methodist University, The International Center/Study Abroad, SMU PO Box 750391, Dallas, TX 75275-0391; *Phone:* 214-768-2338; *Fax:* 214-768-1051. *E-mail:* intlpro@mail.smu.edu. *World Wide Web:* http://www.smu.edu/studyabroad/

UNIVERSITY OF PENNSYLVANIA
PENN-IN-CANNES

Academic Focus • Film and media studies.
Program Information • Faculty members are drawn from the sponsor's U.S. staff. Students typically earn 1 course units per term.
Sessions • May (summer).
Eligibility Requirements • Open to freshmen, sophomores, juniors, seniors, graduate students, adults; 1 letter of recommendation; good academic standing at home school; no foreign language proficiency required.
Living Arrangements • Students live in host family homes. Meals are taken on one's own, in restaurants.
Costs (2005) • $2800; includes tuition, housing, insurance. $50 application fee. $300 nonrefundable deposit required. Financial aid available for students from sponsoring institution: loans.
For More Information • Penn Summer Abroad, University of Pennsylvania, 3440 Market Street, Suite 100, Philadelphia, PA 19104-3335; *Phone:* 215-746-6900; *Fax:* 215-573-2053. *E-mail:* summerabroad@sas.upenn.edu. *World Wide Web:* http://www.sas.upenn.edu/summer/

CAP D'AIL

LINGUA SERVICE WORLDWIDE
VACATION 'N LEARN FRENCH IN FRANCE

Hosted by Centre Mediterranean Françiases
Academic Focus • French language and literature, French studies.
Program Information • Students attend classes at Centre Mediterranean Françiases (Cap d'Ail, France). Optional travel to cultural sites throughout France at an extra cost. Students typically earn 3 semester credits for 3 weeks, 6 semester credits for 5 weeks.
Sessions • Sessions of 2 or more weeks begin on Mondays, year-round.
Eligibility Requirements • Minimum age 16; open to precollege students, freshmen, sophomores, juniors, seniors, graduate students, adults; no foreign language proficiency required.
Living Arrangements • Students live in host institution dormitories, locally rented apartments, host family homes, hotels. Quarters are shared with host institution students. Meals are taken with host family.
Costs (2006–2007) • Contact sponsor for cost. $100 application fee.
For More Information • Assistant Director, Lingua Service Worldwide, 75 Prospect Street, Suite 4, Huntington, NY 11743; *Phone:* 800-394-5327; *Fax:* 631-271-3441. *E-mail:* linguaservice@att.net. *World Wide Web:* http://www.linguaserviceworldwide.com/

CHAMBÉRY

COLLEGE CONSORTIUM FOR INTERNATIONAL STUDIES–TRUMAN STATE UNIVERSITY
INTENSIVE FRENCH SUMMER

Academic Focus • French language and literature, French studies.
Program Information • Faculty members are local instructors hired by the sponsor. Optional travel to Lyon, Beaujolais, the Alps, Geneva; Avignon at an extra cost. Students typically earn 4 semester credits per term.
Sessions • Jun (summer), Jul-Jul (summer 2), July-Aug (summer 3).
Eligibility Requirements • Minimum age 18; open to freshmen, sophomores, juniors, seniors, adults; 2.5 GPA; 2 letters of recommendation; good academic standing at home school; no foreign language proficiency required.
Living Arrangements • Students live in host institution dormitories, locally rented apartments, host family homes. Quarters are shared with students from other programs. Meals are taken on one's own, with host family.
Costs (2007) • $2037; includes tuition, books and class materials, student support services, housing deposit. $300 nonrefundable deposit required. Financial aid available for students from sponsoring institution: scholarships, loans.
For More Information • Center for International Education, College Consortium for International Studies–Truman State University, 100 East Normal, Kirk Building 114, Kirksville, MO 63501; *Phone:* 660-785-4076; *Fax:* 660-785-7473. *E-mail:* ciea@truman.edu. *World Wide Web:* http://www.ccisabroad.org/. Students may also apply through Miami Dade College, Office of International Education, 300 NE 2nd Avenue, Suite 1450, Miami, FL 33132-2297.

UNIVERSITY OF IDAHO
FRENCH BUSINESS AND CULTURE

Hosted by Ecole Supérieure de Commerce de Chambery
Academic Focus • Business administration/management, French language and literature, French studies.
Program Information • Students attend classes at Ecole Supérieure de Commerce de Chambery (Chambery, France). Field trips to Grenoble, Hautecombe Abbey, Routin factory and laboratories. Students typically earn 6 semester credits per term.
Sessions • Jun–Jul (summer).
Eligibility Requirements • Open to freshmen, sophomores, juniors, seniors, graduate students, adults; 2.5 GPA; good academic standing at home school; no foreign language proficiency required.
Living Arrangements • Students live in locally rented apartments. Quarters are shared with host institution students, students from other programs. Meals are taken on one's own, in residences.
Costs (2006) • $2350; includes tuition, housing, excursions, student support services. $150 application fee. $200 refundable deposit required. Financial aid available for students from sponsoring institution: scholarships, loans.
For More Information • Ms. Kate Peterson, Program Advisor, University of Idaho, 901 Paradise Creek Street, LLC 3, Ground Floor, Moscow, ID 83844-1250; *Phone:* 208-885-4075; *Fax:* 208-885-2859. *E-mail:* abroad@uidaho.edu. *World Wide Web:* http://www.webs.uidaho.edu/ipo/abroad/

CLEMONT-FERRAND

EU STUDY ABROAD
INTENSIVE FRENCH

Hosted by University Blaise Pascal (Clermont-Ferrand II)
Academic Focus • French language and literature, French studies.
Program Information • Students attend classes at University Blaise Pascal (Clermont-Ferrand II) (Clermont-Ferrand, France). Scheduled travel to other areas of France and Europe; field trips to Loire Valley, Paris, Nice; optional travel to France or Europe at an extra cost. Students typically earn 3-6 semester credits per term.
Sessions • 1 month sessions held year-round.
Eligibility Requirements • Minimum age 12; open to precollege students, freshmen, sophomores, juniors, seniors, graduate students, adults; no foreign language proficiency required.

Living Arrangements • Students live in host institution dormitories, host family homes. Quarters are shared with host institution students, students from other programs. Meals are taken with host family, in residences.
Costs (2005–2006) • Contact sponsor for cost. $40 application fee. $200 refundable deposit required. Financial aid available for all students: scholarships, loans.
For More Information • Mr. Alexis Minkala, Program Director, EU Study Abroad, Box 333, 2020 Pennsylvania Avenue, Washington, DC 20006-1811; *Phone:* 202-492-7481. *E-mail:* info@eustudyabroad. com. *World Wide Web:* http://www.eustudyabroad.com/

COMPIÈGNE

UNIVERSITY OF PENNSYLVANIA
PENN-IN-COMPIÈGNE

Hosted by L'Université de Technologie de Compiègne
Academic Focus • French language and literature, sociology.
Program Information • Students attend classes at L'Université de Technologie de Compiègne (Compiègne, France). Students typically earn 2 course units per term.
Sessions • May–Jul (summer).
Eligibility Requirements • Open to freshmen, sophomores, juniors, seniors, graduate students; 1 letter of recommendation; good academic standing at home school; 2 years of college course work in French.
Living Arrangements • Students live in host family homes. Meals are taken with host family, in residences.
Costs (2005) • $5300–$6100; includes tuition, housing, all meals, insurance, books and class materials. $50 application fee. $300 nonrefundable deposit required. Financial aid available for students from sponsoring institution: loans.
For More Information • Penn Summer Abroad, University of Pennsylvania, 3440 Market Street, Suite 100, Philadelphia, PA 19104-3335; *Phone:* 215-746-6900; *Fax:* 215-573-2053. *E-mail:* summerabroad@sas.upenn.edu. *World Wide Web:* http://www.sas.upenn.edu/summer/

COTES D'AZUR

LANGUAGE LIAISON
LEARN FRENCH ON THE COTE D'AZUR

Hosted by Language Liaison
Academic Focus • French language and literature.
Program Information • Students attend classes at Language Liaison (Cotes d'Azur, France). Field trips; optional travel. Students typically earn 3–15 semester credits per term.
Sessions • Classes begin every week, year-round.
Eligibility Requirements • Minimum age 16; open to precollege students, freshmen, sophomores, juniors, seniors, graduate students, adults; no foreign language proficiency required.
Living Arrangements • Students live in host family homes. Meals are taken on one's own, in residences.
Costs (2005) • Contact sponsor for cost. $175 application fee.
For More Information • Ms. Nancy Forman, President, Language Liaison, PO Box 1772, Pacific Palisades, CA 90272; *Phone:* 800-284-4448; *Fax:* 310-454-1706. *E-mail:* learn@languageliaison. com. *World Wide Web:* http://www.languageliaison.com/

DIJON

CENTER FOR STUDY ABROAD (CSA)
UNIVERSITY OF BURGUNDY (DIJON)

Hosted by University of Burgundy Dijon
Academic Focus • Art history, drama/theater, French language and literature, French studies, history, music, philosophy.
Program Information • Students attend classes at University of Burgundy Dijon (Dijon, France). Optional travel at an extra cost. Students typically earn 4–10 semester credits per term.
Sessions • Classes begin weekly, year-round.

Eligibility Requirements • Minimum age 18; open to precollege students, freshmen, sophomores, juniors, seniors, graduate students, adults; students age 15 to 17 may apply with parental permission; no foreign language proficiency required.
Living Arrangements • Students live in host institution dormitories, locally rented apartments. Quarters are shared with students from other programs. Meals are taken on one's own, in central dining facility.
Costs (2005) • Contact sponsor for cost. $45 application fee.
For More Information • Ms. Alima K. Virtue, Program Director, Center for Study Abroad (CSA), 325 Washington Avenue South #93, Kent, WA 98032; *Phone:* 206-726-1498; *Fax:* 253-850-0454. *E-mail:* info@centerforstudyabroad.com. *World Wide Web:* http://www.centerforstudyabroad.com/

OKLAHOMA STATE UNIVERSITY
SUMMER IN FRANCE

Held at Burgundy School of Business ESC Dijon Bourqogne
Academic Focus • International business, marketing.
Program Information • Classes are held on the campus of Burgundy School of Business ESC Dijon Bourqogne (Dijon, France). Faculty members are drawn from the sponsor's U.S. staff. Scheduled travel to Paris; field trips to Dijon area day trips; optional travel to Italy at an extra cost. Students typically earn 6 semester credits per term.
Sessions • May–Jun (summer).
Eligibility Requirements • Open to sophomores, juniors, seniors, graduate students, adults; no foreign language proficiency required.
Living Arrangements • Students live in host institution dormitories, hotels. Quarters are shared with host institution students. Meals are taken as a group, in central dining facility, in restaurants.
Costs (2006) • $3500; includes tuition, housing, some meals, excursions, books and class materials, Eurail pass. $40 application fee. $400 nonrefundable deposit required.
For More Information • Ms. Karen Ward, Assistant Director, Oklahoma State University, Center for Executive and Professional Development, 215 Spears School of Business, Stillwater, OK 74078; *Phone:* 866-678-3933; *Fax:* 405-744-6143. *E-mail:* cepd@okstate.edu. *World Wide Web:* http://spears.okstate.edu/cepd.content/study_travel. php/

GRENOBLE

ACADEMIC PROGRAMS INTERNATIONAL (API)
(API)–GRENOBLE, FRANCE AT UNIVERSITY STENDHALL, GRENOBLE III

Hosted by University Stendhal Grenoble III
Academic Focus • Art history, civilization studies, French language and literature, French studies, history, political science and government, teaching.
Program Information • Students attend classes at University Stendhal Grenoble III (Grenoble, France). Scheduled travel to Paris, Versailles; field trips to Chamonix, Chartreuse, Lyon, Chambery, Geneva, Aix-en-Provence, Burgundy, Strasbourg, Avignon, Arles, Annecy. Students typically earn 5–6 semester credits per term.
Sessions • Jun–Jul (summer).
Eligibility Requirements • Minimum age 18; open to freshmen, sophomores, juniors, seniors, graduate students, adults; 2.75 GPA; 1 letter of recommendation; good academic standing at home school; official transcript from home university; no foreign language proficiency required.
Living Arrangements • Students live in host institution dormitories, host family homes. Quarters are shared with host institution students. Meals are taken on one's own, with host family, in residences, in central dining facility.
Costs (2006–2007) • $4700–$4800; includes tuition, housing, some meals, insurance, excursions, student support services, airport pick-up, ground transportation, monthly transit pass, mobile phone, on-line services, on-site director; wireless access in API office. $150 nonrefundable deposit required. Financial aid available for all students: scholarships.
For More Information • Ms. Jennifer C. Allen, Director, Academic Programs International (API), 107 East Hopkins, San Marcos, TX

78666; *Phone:* 800-844-4124; *Fax:* 512-392-8420. *E-mail:* api@academicintl.com. *World Wide Web:* http://www.academicintl.com/

ACADEMIC PROGRAMS INTERNATIONAL (API)
(API)–GRENOBLE, FRANCE–GRENOBLE ECOLE DE MANAGEMENT

Hosted by Grenoble Ecole de Management
Academic Focus • Business administration/management, European studies.
Program Information • Students attend classes at Grenoble Ecole de Management (Grenoble, France). Field trips to Chambourg, Chamonix, La Bourgogne, Paris; Versailles. Students typically earn 6 semester credits per term.
Sessions • June.
Eligibility Requirements • Minimum age 18; open to freshmen, sophomores, juniors, seniors; 2.75 GPA; 1 letter of recommendation; good academic standing at home school; resume; 6 passport-sized photos; official transcript from home university; no foreign language proficiency required.
Living Arrangements • Students live in host institution dormitories, locally rented apartments, host family homes. Quarters are shared with host institution students. Meals are taken as a group, on one's own, with host family, in residences, in central dining facility, in restaurants.
Costs (2006–2007) • Contact sponsor for cost. $150 nonrefundable deposit required. Financial aid available for all students: scholarships.
For More Information • Ms. Jennifer C. Allen, Director, Academic Programs International (API), 107 East Hopkins, San Marcos, TX 78666; *Phone:* 800-844-4124; *Fax:* 512-392-8420. *E-mail:* api@academicintl.com. *World Wide Web:* http://www.academicintl.com/

BOSTON UNIVERSITY
GRENOBLE LANGUAGE AND LIBERAL ARTS PROGRAM

Hosted by Centre Universitaire d'Etudes Francaises CUEF
Academic Focus • French language and literature, French studies.
Program Information • Students attend classes at Centre Universitaire d'Etudes Francaises CUEF (Grenoble, France). Field trips to Arles, Vienna, Chartreuse. Students typically earn 8 semester credits per term.
Sessions • Jun–Jul (summer).
Eligibility Requirements • Open to freshmen, sophomores, juniors, seniors, graduate students, adults; 1 letter of recommendation; good academic standing at home school; essay; approval of participation; transcript; minimum 3.0 GPA in major and overall; 1 year of college course work in French.
Living Arrangements • Students live in host family homes. Meals are taken on one's own, with host family, in residences, in central dining facility, in restaurants.
Costs (2005) • $6000; includes tuition, housing, all meals, insurance, excursions. $50 application fee. $400 nonrefundable deposit required. Financial aid available for all students: scholarships, loans.
For More Information • Division of International Programs, Boston University, 232 Bay State Road, Boston, MA 02215; *Phone:* 617-353-9888; *Fax:* 617-353-5402. *E-mail:* abroad@bu.edu. *World Wide Web:* http://www.bu.edu/abroad/

EU STUDY ABROAD
INTENSIVE FRENCH PROGRAM

Hosted by University of Grenoble
Academic Focus • French language and literature, French studies.
Program Information • Students attend classes at University of Grenoble (Grenoble, France). Scheduled travel; field trips; optional travel to France or Europe at an extra cost. Students typically earn 3-6 semester credits per term.
Sessions • 1 month sessions held year-round.
Eligibility Requirements • Minimum age 17; open to precollege students, freshmen, sophomores, juniors, seniors, graduate students, adults; 2.5 GPA; 1 letter of recommendation; good academic standing at home school; no foreign language proficiency required.

Living Arrangements • Students live in host institution dormitories, locally rented apartments, host family homes. Quarters are shared with host institution students. Meals are taken on one's own, with host family.
Costs (2005–2006) • $2850 for 1 month; $5595 for 2 months; includes tuition, housing, some meals, insurance, excursions, lab equipment, student support services, cell phone, student ID, sports activities, unlimited bus pass. $40 application fee. $200 refundable deposit required. Financial aid available for all students: scholarships, loans.
For More Information • Mr. Alexis Minkala, Program Director, EU Study Abroad, Box 333, 2020 Pennsylvania Avenue, Washington, DC 20006-1811; *Phone:* 202-492-7481. *E-mail:* info@eustudyabroad.com. *World Wide Web:* http://www.eustudyabroad.com/

EU STUDY ABROAD
INTERNATIONAL BUSINESS PROGRAM

Hosted by Grenoble Graduate School of Business
Academic Focus • Business administration/management, international business, marketing.
Program Information • Students attend classes at Grenoble Graduate School of Business (Grenoble, France). Scheduled travel to Paris, Nice, Monaco; field trips to sites throughout France and Europe; optional travel to Locations in France and Europe at an extra cost. Students typically earn 3 semester credits per term.
Sessions • Jun–Jul (summer).
Eligibility Requirements • Minimum age 17; open to freshmen, sophomores, juniors, seniors, graduate students, adults; 2.5 GPA; 2 letters of recommendation; 2 essays.
Living Arrangements • Students live in host institution dormitories, locally rented apartments, host family homes. Quarters are shared with host institution students. Meals are taken as a group, with host family, in residences, in central dining facility.
Costs (2005–2006) • $3220; includes tuition, housing, some meals, insurance, excursions, lab equipment, student support services, cell phone, student ID, sports actiivities, and unlimited bus pass. $40 application fee. $200 refundable deposit required. Financial aid available for all students: scholarships, loans.
For More Information • Mr. Alexis Minkala, Program Director, EU Study Abroad, Box 333, 2020 Pennsylvania Avenue, Washington, Washington, DC 20006-1811; *Phone:* 202-492-7481. *E-mail:* info@eustudyabroad.com. *World Wide Web:* http://www.eustudyabroad.com/

ILLINOIS STATE UNIVERSITY
SUMMER PROGRAM AT THE UNIVERSITÉ STENDHAL GRENOBLE

Hosted by University Stendhal Grenoble III
Academic Focus • French language and literature.
Program Information • Students attend classes at University Stendhal Grenoble III (Grenoble, France). Scheduled travel to Paris, Versailles; field trips to Chamonix, Mont Blanc, Avignon, the French Riviera. Students typically earn 6 semester credits per term.
Sessions • Jun–Aug (summer).
Eligibility Requirements • Open to sophomores, juniors, seniors, graduate students, adults; 2.5 GPA; 1 letter of recommendation; good academic standing at home school; essay in French; 1 year of college course work in French.
Living Arrangements • Students live in host institution dormitories, hotels. Quarters are shared with host institution students. Meals are taken as a group, in central dining facility.
Costs (2004) • $6400; includes tuition, housing, all meals, insurance, excursions, international airfare, books and class materials, international student ID, student support services, instructional costs at Grenoble, personal expenses. $150 application fee. Financial aid available for students from sponsoring institution: scholarships, loans.
For More Information • Office of International Studies and Programs, Illinois State University, Campus Box 6120, Normal, IL 61790-6120; *Phone:* 309-438-5276; *Fax:* 309-438-3987. *E-mail:* oisp@ilstu.edu. *World Wide Web:* http://www.internationalstudies.ilstu.edu/

FRANCE
Grenoble

LYCOMING COLLEGE
SUMMER LANGUAGE STUDY IN FRANCE

Hosted by University of Grenoble

Academic Focus • French language and literature.

Program Information • Students attend classes at University of Grenoble (Grenoble, France). Optional travel at an extra cost. Students typically earn 4–12 semester credits per term.

Sessions • 4 to 12 week sessions begin in Jun.

Eligibility Requirements • Open to sophomores, juniors, seniors; 2.5 GPA; 2 letters of recommendation; good academic standing at home school; 1 year of college course work in French.

Living Arrangements • Students live in host institution dormitories, locally rented apartments, host family homes. Quarters are shared with host institution students, students from other programs. Meals are taken on one's own, with host family, in residences, in restaurants.

Costs (2004) • $1400 for 4 weeks; includes tuition, housing, some meals, student support services. $300 refundable deposit required.

For More Information • Dr. Garett Heysel, Coordinator of Grenoble Program, Lycoming College, Campus Box 2, 700 College Place, Williamsport, PA 17701-5192; *Phone:* 570-321-4211; *Fax:* 570-321-4389. *E-mail:* heysel@lycoming.edu. *World Wide Web:* http://www.lycoming.edu/

HYÈRES

LANGUAGE LIAISON
LEARN FRENCH IN HYÈRES

Hosted by Language Liaison

Academic Focus • French language and literature.

Program Information • Students attend classes at Language Liaison (Hyères, France). Field trips; optional travel. Students typically earn 3–15 semester credits per term.

Sessions • New programs begin weekly, year-round.

Eligibility Requirements • Minimum age 16; open to precollege students, freshmen, sophomores, juniors, seniors, graduate students, adults; no foreign language proficiency required.

Living Arrangements • Students live in host family homes, hotels. Meals are taken on one's own, with host family, in restaurants.

Costs (2005) • Contact sponsor for cost. $175 application fee. Financial aid available for all students: scholarship research service.

For More Information • Ms. Nancy Forman, President, Language Liaison, PO Box 1772, Pacific Palisades, CA 90272; *Phone:* 800-284-4448; *Fax:* 310-454-1706. *E-mail:* learn@languageliaison.com. *World Wide Web:* http://www.languageliaison.com/

LA ROCHELLE

MINNESOTA STATE UNIVERSITY MANKATO
SUMMER STUDY IN FRANCE PROGRAM

Hosted by Institut d'Etudes Françaises

Academic Focus • French language and literature, French studies, teaching.

Program Information • Students attend classes at Institut d'Etudes Françaises (La Rochelle, France). Scheduled travel to Paris and surrounding region and Normandy (12 days); field trips to the Loire River Valley, Normandy, Cognac. Students typically earn 9 semester credits per term.

Sessions • Jun–Jul (summer).

Eligibility Requirements • Minimum age 16; open to precollege students, freshmen, sophomores, juniors, seniors, graduate students, adults; 1 letter of recommendation; good academic standing at home school; 1 year course work in French.

Living Arrangements • Students live in host family homes, hotels. Quarters are shared with host institution students. Meals are taken with host family, in residences, in central dining facility.

Costs (2006) • $5300; includes tuition, housing, some meals, excursions, books and class materials, student support services, all transportation in France. $75 application fee.

For More Information • Dr. John J. Janc, Director, Summer Study in France Program, Minnesota State University Mankato, 227 AH, Mankato, MN 56001; *Phone:* 507-389-1817; *Fax:* 507-389-5887. *E-mail:* john.janc@mnsu.edu. *World Wide Web:* http://www.mankato.msus.edu/dept/modernlang/

STATE UNIVERSITY OF NEW YORK COLLEGE AT CORTLAND
UNIVERSITY OF LA ROCHELLE (SUMMER)

Hosted by University of La Rochelle

Academic Focus • French language and literature.

Program Information • Students attend classes at University of La Rochelle (La Rochelle, France). Field trips to Cognac, Saintes, Ile de Ré. Students typically earn 4 semester credits per term.

Sessions • Jul (summer).

Eligibility Requirements • Minimum age 18; open to freshmen, sophomores, juniors, seniors, graduate students, adults; 2.5 GPA; 2 letters of recommendation; good academic standing at home school; 1 year of college course work in French.

Living Arrangements • Students live in host institution dormitories, locally rented apartments, host family homes. Quarters are shared with students from other programs. Meals are taken on one's own, in restaurants.

Costs (2005) • $2755; includes tuition, housing, all meals, international airfare, books and class materials, student support services, passport fees. $20 application fee. $200 nonrefundable deposit required. Financial aid available for students from sponsoring institution: scholarships, loans.

For More Information • Ms. Liz McCartney, Assistant Director, Office of International Programs, State University of New York College at Cortland, PO Box 2000, Cortland, NY 13045; *Phone:* 607-753-2209; *Fax:* 607-753-5989. *E-mail:* cortlandabroad@cortland.edu. *World Wide Web:* http://www.cortlandabroad.com/

MARSEILLE

CENTER FOR STUDY ABROAD (CSA)
UNIVERSITY OF AIX-MARSEILLES III

Hosted by University of Law, Economics and Science (Aix-Marseilles III)

Academic Focus • French language and literature, French studies.

Program Information • Students attend classes at University of Law, Economics and Science (Aix-Marseilles III) (Aix-en-Provence, France). Optional travel. Students typically earn 3–4 semester credits per term.

Sessions • Summer.

Eligibility Requirements • Minimum age 18; open to precollege students, freshmen, sophomores, juniors, seniors, graduate students, adults; no foreign language proficiency required.

Living Arrangements • Quarters are shared with students from other programs. Meals are taken on one's own, in residences, in central dining facility, in restaurants.

Costs (2005–2006) • Contact sponsor for cost. $45 application fee.

For More Information • Ms. Alima K. Virtue, Program Director, Center for Study Abroad (CSA), 325 Washington Avenue South #93, Kent, WA 98032; *Phone:* 206-226-1498; *Fax:* 253-850-0454. *E-mail:* info@centerforstudyabroad.com. *World Wide Web:* http://www.centerforstudyabroad.com/

UNIVERSITY OF NORTH CAROLINA AT WILMINGTON
SUMMER STUDY IN MARSEILLE, FRANCE

Hosted by CESEM Mediterrance

Academic Focus • European studies, French language and literature, international business.

Program Information • Students attend classes at CESEM Mediterrance (Marseille, France). Field trips to Camargue, a winery, Provence; optional travel to Spain, Italy, Nice, Paris at an extra cost. Students typically earn 9–12 semester credits per term.

Sessions • Jun–Jul (summer), Jun–Jul (summer 2).

Eligibility Requirements • Minimum age 18; open to sophomores, juniors, seniors; 2.75 GPA; good academic standing at home school; 1 year of college course work in French.

Living Arrangements • Students live in hotels. Meals are taken on one's own, in restaurants.

Costs (2005) • $3640 for 9 credit hours; $5210 for 12 credit hours; includes tuition, housing, all meals, insurance, excursions, student support services. $200 nonrefundable deposit required. Financial aid available for students from sponsoring institution: scholarships, loans.

For More Information • Ms. Elizabeth A. Adams, Director, Education Abroad, University of North Carolina at Wilmington, 601 South College Road, Wilmington, NC 28403; *Phone:* 910-962-3685; *Fax:* 910-962-4053. *E-mail:* adamse@uncw.edu. *World Wide Web:* http://www.uncw.edu/intprogs/

METZ

ILLINOIS STATE UNIVERSITY
SUMMER PROGRAM–METZ, FRANCE

Hosted by Ecole Supérieure Internationale de Commerce
Academic Focus • French studies, international business.
Program Information • Students attend classes at Ecole Supérieure Internationale de Commerce (Metz, France). Scheduled travel to Brussels, Normandy, Paris; field trips to French businesses. Students typically earn 6 semester credits per term.
Sessions • May–Jun (summer).
Eligibility Requirements • Open to sophomores, juniors, seniors; course work in business; 2.5 GPA; 2 letters of recommendation; good academic standing at home school; no foreign language proficiency required.
Living Arrangements • Students live in host institution dormitories, host family homes. Quarters are shared with host institution students. Meals are taken as a group, on one's own, with host family, in residences, in central dining facility, in restaurants.
Costs (2005) • $4621; includes tuition, housing, all meals, insurance, excursions, international airfare, international student ID, student support services, personal expenses. $150 application fee. Financial aid available for students from sponsoring institution: scholarships, loans.
For More Information • Study Abroad Coordinator, Illinois State University, Office of International Studies and Programs, Campus Box 6120, Normal, IL 61790-6120; *Phone:* 309-438-5276; *Fax:* 309-438-3987. *E-mail:* oisp@ilstu.edu. *World Wide Web:* http://www.internationalstudies.ilstu.edu/

MONTPELLIER

FRENCH-AMERICAN EXCHANGE
SUMMER STUDY ABROAD IN MONTPELLIER

Hosted by University of Montpellier–ILP Institute
Academic Focus • Civilization studies, French language and literature, French studies.
Program Information • Students attend classes at University of Montpellier–ILP Institute (Montpellier, France). Field trips to Palavas Beach, the Roman Coliseum at Nîmes, the medieval city of Aigue Morte, Avignon's Pope Palace; optional travel to Spain, the French Riviera, Italy, Paris at an extra cost. Students typically earn 6 semester credits per term.
Sessions • Jun–Sep (4 weeks).
Eligibility Requirements • Minimum age 19; open to sophomores, juniors, seniors, graduate students, adults; good academic standing at home school; no foreign language proficiency required.
Living Arrangements • Students live in host institution dormitories, locally rented apartments, host family homes. Meals are taken on one's own, with host family, in central dining facility, in restaurants.
Costs (2005) • $2275; includes tuition, housing, some meals, books and class materials, lab equipment, student support services. $50 application fee. $500 refundable deposit required.
For More Information • Mr. James Pondolfino, Executive Director, French-American Exchange, 3213 Duke Street, #620, Alexandria, VA 22314; *Phone:* 800-995-5087; *Fax:* 703-823-4447. *E-mail:* info@frenchamericanexchange.com. *World Wide Web:* http://www.frenchamericanexchange.com/

THE INTERNATIONAL PARTNERSHIP FOR SERVICE LEARNING AND LEADERSHIP
FRANCE SERVICE–LEARNING

Hosted by University of Montpellier III
Academic Focus • Community service, French language and literature, French studies, international affairs, liberal studies, social sciences.
Program Information • Students attend classes at University of Montpellier III (Montpellier, France). Field trips to southern France; optional travel to Spain, Switzerland at an extra cost. Students typically earn 9 semester credits per term.
Sessions • Jun–Aug (summer).
Eligibility Requirements • Minimum age 18; open to freshmen, sophomores, juniors, seniors, graduate students, adults; 2 letters of recommendation; good academic standing at home school; evidence of maturity; 1 year of college course work in French.
Living Arrangements • Students live in host family homes. Meals are taken with host family, in residences.
Costs (2005–2006) • $7200; includes tuition, housing, some meals, student support services, community service placement. $50 application fee. $250 refundable deposit required. Financial aid available for all students: federal financial aid.
For More Information • Director of Student Programs, The International Partnership for Service Learning and Leadership, 815 Second Avenue, New York, NY 10017-4594; *Phone:* 212-986-0989; *Fax:* 212-986-5039. *E-mail:* info@ipsl.org. *World Wide Web:* http://www.ipsl.org/

MICHIGAN STATE UNIVERSITY
INTERNATIONAL FOOD LAWS

Hosted by CIS-SYAL
Academic Focus • Agriculture, environmental science/studies, natural resources, parks and recreation, sociology.
Program Information • Students attend classes at CIS-SYAL (Montpellier, France). Scheduled travel to Cevennes-Causses regions, Camargues. Students typically earn 6 semester credits per term.
Sessions • May–Jun (summer).
Eligibility Requirements • Open to sophomores, juniors, seniors; 2.75 GPA; good academic standing at home school; good physical condition; no foreign language proficiency required.
Living Arrangements • Students live in host institution dormitories, hotels. Meals are taken as a group, on one's own, in central dining facility.
Costs (2005) • Contact sponsor for cost. $100 application fee. $200 nonrefundable deposit required. Financial aid available for students from sponsoring institution: scholarships, loans.
For More Information • Ms. Yvonne Squiers, Secretary, Michigan State University, Office of Study Abroad, 109 International Center, East Lansing, MI 48824-1035; *Phone:* 517-353-8920; *Fax:* 517-432-2082. *E-mail:* squiers@msu.edu. *World Wide Web:* http://studyabroad.msu.edu/

UNIVERSITY AT ALBANY, STATE UNIVERSITY OF NEW YORK
LANGUAGE AND CULTURAL STUDIES IN MONTPELLIER III

Hosted by University of Montpellier I
Academic Focus • French language and literature.
Program Information • Students attend classes at University of Montpellier I (Montpellier, France). Field trips. Students typically earn 6 semester credits per term.
Sessions • Jul–Aug (summer).
Eligibility Requirements • Open to sophomores, juniors, seniors; 2 letters of recommendation; good academic standing at home school; previous course work in French.
Living Arrangements • Students live in host family homes. Meals are taken on one's own, with host family, in residences, in restaurants.
Costs (2005) • Contact sponsor for cost. $150 nonrefundable deposit required. Financial aid available for students from sponsoring institution: all customary sources.
For More Information • University at Albany, State University of New York, Office of International Education, LI 66, Albany, NY

FRANCE
Montpellier

12222; *Phone:* 518-442-3525; *Fax:* 518-442-3338. *E-mail:* intled@ uamail.albany.edu. *World Wide Web:* http://www.albany.edu/ studyabroad/

UNIVERSITY OF MINNESOTA
STUDY ABROAD IN MONTPELLIER

Hosted by University Paul Valéry (Montpellier III)
Academic Focus • French language and literature.
Program Information • Students attend classes at University Paul Valéry (Montpellier III) (Montpellier, France). Field trips to local travel in and around Montpellier. Students typically earn 4–10 semester credits per term.
Sessions • Jul and Aug.
Eligibility Requirements • Open to sophomores, juniors, seniors, graduate students; 2.5 GPA; no foreign language proficiency required.
Living Arrangements • Students live in host institution dormitories. Quarters are shared with host institution students. Meals are taken on one's own, in central dining facility, in restaurants.
Costs (2006) • Contact sponsor for cost; includes tuition, housing, insurance, student support services. $50 application fee. $400 nonrefundable deposit required. Financial aid available for students from sponsoring institution: scholarships, loans.
For More Information • Learning Abroad Center, University of Minnesota, 230 Heller Hall, 271 19th Avenue South, Minneapolis, MN 55455; *Phone:* 800-700-UOFM; *Fax:* 612-626-8009. *E-mail:* umabroad@umn.edu. *World Wide Web:* http://www.umabroad.umn. edu/

UNIVERSITY OF MINNESOTA
TRAVELING AUTHORS IN SOUTHWEST FRANCE

Academic Focus • Comparative literature, French studies.
Program Information • Faculty members are drawn from the sponsor's U.S. staff. Field trips to Marseilles, Nime. Students typically earn 3 semester credits per term.
Sessions • May–Jun (summer).
Eligibility Requirements • Minimum age 18; open to freshmen, sophomores, juniors, seniors; 2.5 GPA; no foreign language proficiency required.
Living Arrangements • Students live in hotels. Quarters are shared with host institution students. Meals are taken on one's own, in residences, in restaurants.
Costs (2007) • $4000; includes tuition, housing, some meals, insurance, excursions, international airfare, student support services. $50 application fee. $400 nonrefundable deposit required. Financial aid available for students from sponsoring institution: scholarships, loans.
For More Information • Learning Abroad Center, University of Minnesota, 230 Heller Hall, 271 19th Avenue South, Minneapolis, MN 55455; *Phone:* 612-626-9000; *Fax:* 612-626-8009. *E-mail:* umabroad@umn.edu. *World Wide Web:* http://www.umabroad.umn. edu/

UNIVERSITY OF NEW ORLEANS
THE GLORIES OF FRANCE

Hosted by Cours Intensif de Français
Academic Focus • Anthropology, art, art history, civilization studies, communications, comparative literature, creative writing, English, French language and literature, French studies, history, music, music history.
Program Information • Students attend classes at Cours Intensif de Français (Montpellier, France). Scheduled travel to Paris; field trips to southern France; optional travel to Barcelona, other parts of France at an extra cost. Students typically earn 6 semester credits per term.
Sessions • Jul–Aug (summer).
Eligibility Requirements • Minimum age 18; open to freshmen, sophomores, juniors, seniors, graduate students; 2.5 GPA; good academic standing at home school; no foreign language proficiency required.
Living Arrangements • Students live in host institution dormitories, locally rented apartments. Quarters are shared with students from other programs. Meals are taken as a group, in central dining facility.

Costs (2005) • $3495; includes tuition, housing, some meals, insurance, excursions, student support services. $150 application fee. $150 refundable deposit required. Financial aid available for students from sponsoring institution: scholarships, loans, need-based aid.
For More Information • Ms. Marie Kaposchyn, Program Director, University of New Orleans, PO Box 569, New Orleans, LA 70148; *Phone:* 504-280-7455; *Fax:* 504-280-7317. *E-mail:* mkaposch@uno. edu. *World Wide Web:* http://inst.uno.edu/

NICE

ALMA COLLEGE
SUMMER PROGRAM OF STUDIES IN NICE

Hosted by Alliance Française
Academic Focus • French language and literature.
Program Information • Students attend classes at Alliance Française (Nice, France). Field trips to Mont-Saint-Michel, Loire Valley. Students typically earn 3–12 semester credits per term.
Sessions • May–Jul (1 to 3 months).
Eligibility Requirements • Minimum age 18; open to freshmen, sophomores, juniors, seniors, graduate students; 2.5 GPA; 2 letters of recommendation; good academic standing at home school; no foreign language proficiency required.
Living Arrangements • Students live in locally rented apartments, host family homes. Meals are taken with host family, in residences.
Costs (2005) • $4150–$9285; includes tuition, housing, some meals, insurance, excursions, international student ID, student support services, Metro pass, e-mail access, airport greeting. $50 application fee. $200 nonrefundable deposit required.
For More Information • Ms. Julie Elenbaas, Office Associate, International Education, Alma College, 614 West Superior Street, Alma, MI 48801-1599; *Phone:* 989-463-7055; *Fax:* 989-463-7126. *World Wide Web:* http://international.alma.edu/

EF INTERNATIONAL LANGUAGE SCHOOLS
FRENCH IN NICE

Hosted by EF Ecole Internationale de Français
Academic Focus • French language and literature.
Program Information • Students attend classes at EF Ecole Internationale de Français (Nice, France). Field trips to Cannes, Monaco; optional travel to Paris, the Alps, Florence, Venice at an extra cost. Students typically earn 15–18 quarter credits per term.
Sessions • Program length 2 to 52 weeks, year-round.
Eligibility Requirements • Minimum age 16; open to precollege students, freshmen, sophomores, juniors, seniors, graduate students, adults; no foreign language proficiency required.
Living Arrangements • Students live in host institution dormitories, host family homes. Quarters are shared with host institution students. Meals are taken with host family, in residences.
Costs (2006–2007) • $1130 for 2 weeks; includes tuition, housing, some meals, books and class materials, student support services. $145 application fee. Financial aid available for all students: scholarships.
For More Information • Ms. Varvara Kirakosyan, Director of Admissions, EF International Language Schools, One Education Street, Cambridge, MA 02141; *Phone:* 800-992-1892; *Fax:* 800-590-1125. *E-mail:* ils@ef.com. *World Wide Web:* http://www.ef.com/

FRENCH-AMERICAN EXCHANGE
SUMMER STUDY ABROAD IN NICE

Hosted by Ecole France Langue
Academic Focus • Civilization studies, French language and literature, French studies.
Program Information • Students attend classes at Ecole France Langue (Nice, France). Field trips to the French Riviera, art exhibits, villages of Provence; optional travel to France, Italy, Spain, Paris at an extra cost. Students typically earn 6 semester credits per term.
Sessions • Jun–Sep (4 weeks).
Eligibility Requirements • Minimum age 19; open to sophomores, juniors, seniors, graduate students, adults; good academic standing at home school; no foreign language proficiency required.

Living Arrangements • Students live in locally rented apartments, host family homes. Meals are taken on one's own, with host family, in residences, in restaurants.
Costs (2005) • $2630; includes tuition, housing, some meals, lab equipment, student support services. $50 application fee. $500 refundable deposit required.
For More Information • Mr. James Pondolfino, Executive Director, French-American Exchange, 3213 Duke Street, #620, Alexandria, VA 22314; *Phone:* 800-995-5087; *Fax:* 703-823-4447. *E-mail:* info@ frenchamericanexchange.com. *World Wide Web:* http://www. frenchamericanexchange.com/

LANGUAGE LIAISON
FRENCH IN NICE

Hosted by Language Liaison
Academic Focus • French language and literature.
Program Information • Students attend classes at Language Liaison (Nice, France). Field trips; optional travel at an extra cost. Students typically earn 3-15 semester credits per term.
Sessions • New programs begin weekly, year-round.
Eligibility Requirements • Minimum age 16; open to precollege students, freshmen, sophomores, juniors, seniors, graduate students, adults; no foreign language proficiency required.
Living Arrangements • Students live in host family homes, hotels. Meals are taken on one's own, with host family, in residences, in restaurants.
Costs (2005) • Contact sponsor for cost. $175 application fee. Financial aid available for all students: scholarship research service.
For More Information • Ms. Nancy Forman, President, Language Liaison, PO Box 1772, Pacific Palisades, CA 90272; *Phone:* 800-284-4448; *Fax:* 310-454-1706. *E-mail:* learn@languageliaison. com. *World Wide Web:* http://www.languageliaison.com/

LINGUA SERVICE WORLDWIDE
VACATION 'N LEARN FRENCH IN FRANCE

Hosted by Ecole France Langue
Academic Focus • French language and literature, French studies.
Program Information • Students attend classes at Ecole France Langue (Nice, France). Optional travel to cultural sites throughout France at an extra cost. Students typically earn 3 semester credits for 3 weeks, 6 semester credits for 5 weeks.
Sessions • Sessions of 2 or more weeks begin on Mondays, year-round.
Eligibility Requirements • Minimum age 16; open to precollege students, freshmen, sophomores, juniors, seniors, graduate students, adults; no foreign language proficiency required.
Living Arrangements • Students live in host institution dormitories, locally rented apartments, host family homes, hotels. Quarters are shared with host institution students. Meals are taken with host family.
Costs (2006–2007) • Contact sponsor for cost. $100 application fee.
For More Information • Assistant Director, Lingua Service Worldwide, 75 Prospect Street, Suite 4, Huntington, NY 11743; *Phone:* 800-394-5327; *Fax:* 631-271-3441. *E-mail:* linguaservice@att. net. *World Wide Web:* http://www.linguaserviceworldwide.com/

LINGUA SERVICE WORLDWIDE
VACATION 'N LEARN FRENCH IN FRANCE

Hosted by Azurlingua
Academic Focus • French language and literature, French studies.
Program Information • Students attend classes at Azurlingua (Nice, France). Optional travel to cultural sites throughout France at an extra cost. Students typically earn 3 semester credits for 3 weeks, 6 semester credits for 5 weeks.
Sessions • Sessions of 2 or more weeks begin on Mondays, year-round.
Eligibility Requirements • Minimum age 16; open to precollege students, freshmen, sophomores, juniors, seniors, graduate students, adults; no foreign language proficiency required.
Living Arrangements • Students live in host institution dormitories, locally rented apartments, host family homes, hotels. Quarters are shared with host institution students. Meals are taken with host family.

Costs (2006–2007) • Contact sponsor for cost. $100 application fee.
For More Information • Assistant Director, Lingua Service Worldwide, 75 Prospect Street, Suite 4, Huntington, NY 11743; *Phone:* 800-394-5327; *Fax:* 631-271-3441. *E-mail:* linguaservice@att. net. *World Wide Web:* http://www.linguaserviceworldwide.com/

NEW YORK UNIVERSITY
NICE, FRANCE: A CITY IN MOTION–EXPERIMENTAL VIDEO AND 3-D ANIMATION

Held at Villa Arson
Academic Focus • Film and media studies.
Program Information • Classes are held on the campus of Villa Arson (Nice, France). Faculty members are drawn from the sponsor's U.S. staff. Students typically earn 8 semester credits per term.
Sessions • Jun–Jul (summer).
Eligibility Requirements • Minimum age 18; open to freshmen, sophomores, juniors, seniors, graduate students, adults; course work in film production; no foreign language proficiency required.
Living Arrangements • Students live in locally rented apartments. Quarters are shared with host institution students. Meals are taken on one's own, in restaurants.
Costs (2005) • $5400; includes tuition. $50 application fee. Financial aid available for students from sponsoring institution: scholarships.
For More Information • Mr. Josh Murray, Assistant Director, New York University, 721 Broadway, 12th Floor, New York, NY 10003; *Phone:* 212-998-1500; *Fax:* 212-995-4578. *E-mail:* tisch.special.info@ nyu.edu. *World Wide Web:* http://www.nyu.edu/global/studyabroad. html

STATE UNIVERSITY OF NEW YORK AT OSWEGO
SUMMER IN THE SOUTH OF FRANCE

Hosted by University of Nice–Sophia Antipolis
Academic Focus • Business administration/management, film and media studies, French language and literature, international affairs, tourism and travel.
Program Information • Students attend classes at University of Nice–Sophia Antipolis (Nice, France). Field trips to Nice and nearby sites. Students typically earn 6 semester credits per term.
Sessions • Jun–Jul (summer).
Eligibility Requirements • Minimum age 18; open to freshmen, sophomores, juniors, seniors; 2.5 GPA; 1 letter of recommendation; good academic standing at home school; no foreign language proficiency required.
Living Arrangements • Students live in host institution dormitories, locally rented apartments. Quarters are shared with students from other programs. Meals are taken on one's own, in residences, in restaurants.
Costs (2005) • $3600–$5100; includes tuition, housing, some meals, insurance, excursions, books and class materials, student support services. $250 nonrefundable deposit required. Financial aid available for students: home university financial aid; loan processing and scholarships for Oswego students.
For More Information • Mr. Joshua McKeown, Associate Director, State University of New York at Oswego, 122A Swetman Hall, Oswego, NY 13126-3599; *Phone:* 888-4-OSWEGO; *Fax:* 315-312-2477. *E-mail:* intled@oswego.edu. *World Wide Web:* http://www. oswego.edu/intled/

NIMES

MICHIGAN STATE UNIVERSITY
FRENCH AND CLASSICAL STUDIES IN SOUTHERN FRANCE

Held at The Agora
Academic Focus • French language and literature.
Program Information • Classes are held on the campus of The Agora (Nimes, France). Faculty members are drawn from the sponsor's U.S. staff and local instructors hired by the sponsor. Field trips to nearby areas. Students typically earn 9 semester credits per term.

Sessions • May–Jul (summer).
Eligibility Requirements • Open to sophomores, juniors, seniors; 2.0 GPA; good academic standing at home school; no foreign language proficiency required.
Living Arrangements • Students live in host institution dormitories. Meals are taken as a group, on one's own, in central dining facility, in restaurants.
Costs (2005) • $2728; includes housing, some meals, insurance, excursions. $100 application fee. $200 nonrefundable deposit required. Financial aid available for students from sponsoring institution: scholarships, loans.
For More Information • Ms. Yvonne Squiers, Secretary, Michigan State University, Office of Study Abroad, 109 International Center, East Lansing, MI 48824-1035; *Phone:* 517-353-8920; *Fax:* 517-432-2082. *E-mail:* squiers@msu.edu. *World Wide Web:* http://studyabroad.msu.edu/

ORLÉANS

UNIVERSITY OF MIAMI
SUMMER PROGRAM IN INTENSIVE FRENCH AT UNIVERSITÉ D'ORLÉANS

Hosted by University of Orléans
Academic Focus • French language and literature.
Program Information • Students attend classes at University of Orléans (Orléans, France). Students typically earn 6 semester credits per term.
Sessions • Jun–Jul (summer).
Eligibility Requirements • Minimum age 18; open to sophomores, juniors, seniors; 2.7 GPA; 2 letters of recommendation; no foreign language proficiency required.
Living Arrangements • Students live in host institution dormitories, program-owned apartments, host family homes. Quarters are shared with host institution students. Meals are taken on one's own, with host family, in central dining facility, in restaurants.
Costs (2005) • $2511; includes tuition, student support services. $40 application fee. $500 nonrefundable deposit required. Financial aid available for students from sponsoring institution: scholarships, loans.
For More Information • University of Miami, International Education and Exchange Programs, 5050 Brunson Drive, Allen Hall 212, PO Box 248005, Coral Gables, FL 33124-1610; *Phone:* 305-284-3434; *Fax:* 305-284-4235. *E-mail:* ieep@miami.edu. *World Wide Web:* http://www.studyabroad.miami.edu/

PARIS

ACADEMIC PROGRAMS INTERNATIONAL (API)
(API)–UNIVERSITY OF MASSACHUSETTS AMHERST AND BOSTON IN PARIS, FRANCE

Hosted by University Paris-Sorbonne (Paris IV)
Academic Focus • French language and literature, French studies.
Program Information • Students attend classes at University Paris-Sorbonne (Paris IV) (Paris, France). Field trips to Chartres, Giverny and Normandy, Loire Valley, Champagne. Students typically earn 3–8 semester credits per term.
Sessions • May–Aug (summer), Jun–Aug (summer 2).
Eligibility Requirements • Minimum age 18; open to freshmen, sophomores, juniors, seniors; 2.75 GPA; 1 letter of recommendation; good academic standing at home school; official transcript from home university; no foreign language proficiency required.
Living Arrangements • Students live in host institution dormitories, locally rented apartments, host family homes. Quarters are shared with host institution students. Meals are taken on one's own, in residences, in central dining facility, in restaurants.
Costs (2006–2007) • $4500–$5500; includes tuition, housing, insurance, excursions, student support services, mobile phone, on-site director and offices, online services. $150 nonrefundable deposit required. Financial aid available for all students: scholarships.
For More Information • Ms. Jennifer C. Allen, Director, Academic Programs International (API), 107 East Hopkins, San Marcos, TX

78666; *Phone:* 800-844-4124; *Fax:* 512-392-8420. *E-mail:* api@academicintl.com. *World Wide Web:* http://www.academicintl.com/

ACCENT INTERNATIONAL CONSORTIUM FOR ACADEMIC PROGRAMS ABROAD
SUMMER IN PARIS

Hosted by University Paris-Sorbonne (Paris IV)
Academic Focus • Art history, French language and literature, French studies.
Program Information • Students attend classes at University Paris-Sorbonne (Paris IV) (Paris, France). Field trips to Amiens, the Loire Valley; optional travel to Normandy, Brittany at an extra cost. Students typically earn 6 semester credits per term.
Sessions • Jul–Aug (summer).
Eligibility Requirements • Minimum age 18; open to precollege students, freshmen, sophomores, juniors, seniors, adults; no foreign language proficiency required.
Living Arrangements • Students live in host institution dormitories, host family homes. Quarters are shared with students from other programs. Meals are taken on one's own, in central dining facility, in restaurants.
Costs (2005) • $3000; includes tuition, housing, some meals, insurance, excursions, international student ID, student support services, extracurricular activities, Paris transit pass. $250 nonrefundable deposit required.
For More Information • ACCENT International Consortium for Academic Programs Abroad, 870 Market Street, Suite 1026, San Francisco, CA 94102; *Phone:* 800-869-9291; *Fax:* 415-835-3749. *E-mail:* info@accentintl.com. *World Wide Web:* http://www.accentintl.com/

ALMA COLLEGE
SUMMER PROGRAM OF STUDIES IN PARIS

Hosted by Alliance Française
Academic Focus • Art history, French language and literature.
Program Information • Students attend classes at Alliance Française (Paris, France). Field trips to Mont-Saint-Michel, Loire valley. Students typically earn 3–12 semester credits per term.
Sessions • Jun (summer), Jul (summer 2).
Eligibility Requirements • Minimum age 18; open to freshmen, sophomores, juniors, seniors, graduate students; 2.5 GPA; 2 letters of recommendation; good academic standing at home school; no foreign language proficiency required.
Living Arrangements • Students live in locally rented apartments, host family homes. Meals are taken with host family, in residences.
Costs (2005) • $4150–$9285; includes tuition, housing, some meals, insurance, excursions, international student ID, student support services, Metro pass, e-mail access, airport greeting. $50 application fee. $200 nonrefundable deposit required.
For More Information • Ms. Julie Elenbaas, Office Associate, International Education, Alma College, 614 West Superior Street, Alma, MI 48801-1599; *Phone:* 989-463-7055; *Fax:* 989-463-7126. *E-mail:* intl_studies@alma.edu. *World Wide Web:* http://international.alma.edu/

AMERICAN INSTITUTE FOR FOREIGN STUDY (AIFS)
AIFS–PARIS, FRANCE–UNIVERSITY OF PARIS IV, COURS DE CIVILISATION FRANCAISE DE LA SORBONNE

Hosted by University Paris-Sorbonne (Paris IV)
Academic Focus • Art history, French language and literature.
Program Information • Students attend classes at University Paris-Sorbonne (Paris IV) (Paris, France). Scheduled travel to 3-day London stopover; field trips to cultural activities, walking tours, museums; optional travel to 3-day excursion to St. Malo and Mont St. Michel for a supplement of $299, 3-day excursion to Chateaux of the Loire Valley for a supplement of $299 at an extra cost. Students typically earn 4-week students take up to 6 credits, 6-week students take up to 8 credits.
Sessions • Jun–Jul (summer).
Eligibility Requirements • Minimum age 17; open to precollege students, freshmen, sophomores, juniors, seniors; 2.0 GPA.

Living Arrangements • Students live in host institution dormitories, program-owned apartments, hotels. Quarters are shared with host institution students. Meals are taken as a group, in residences.
Costs (2007) • 4-weeks: $5599, 6-weeks: $6999; includes tuition, housing, some meals, insurance, excursions, student support services, On-site Resident Director, Phone Card to call the U.S., Metro Pass. $95 application fee. $395 nonrefundable deposit required. Financial aid available for all students: scholarships.
For More Information • Mr. David Mauro, Admissions Advisor, American Institute For Foreign Study (AIFS), 9 West Broad Street, Stamford, CT 06902-3788; *Phone:* 800-727-2437 Ext. 5163; *Fax:* 203-399-5597. *E-mail:* dmauro@aifs.com. *World Wide Web:* http://www.aifsabroad.com/

AMERICAN INTERCONTINENTAL UNIVERSITY
PARIS PROGRAM

Academic Focus • Art, history.
Program Information • Faculty members are local instructors hired by the sponsor. Students typically earn 10 quarter credits per term.
Sessions • Jul–Aug (summer).
Eligibility Requirements • Open to freshmen, sophomores, juniors, seniors, graduate students, adults; 2.0 GPA; good academic standing at home school; approval of advisor, dean or department chair, and study abroad office; college transcripts; no foreign language proficiency required.
Living Arrangements • Students live in hotels. Meals are taken on one's own, in residences, in central dining facility, in restaurants.
Costs (2005) • $5990; includes tuition, housing, student support services. $75 application fee. $250 nonrefundable deposit required. Financial aid available for all students: scholarships, loans, financial aid where applicable.
For More Information • American InterContinental University, Study Abroad Programs, 3150 West Higgins Road, Suite 105, Hoffman Estates, IL 60195; *Phone:* 800-255-6839; *Fax:* 847-885-8422. *E-mail:* studyabroad@aiuniv.edu. *World Wide Web:* http://www.studyabroad.aiuniv.edu/

THE AMERICAN UNIVERSITY OF PARIS
FAST TRACK COURSES

Hosted by The American University of Paris
Academic Focus • Comparative literature, French studies, history, international affairs.
Program Information • Students attend classes at The American University of Paris (Paris, France). Optional travel to châteaux, Burgundy, the French Riviera, Brittany; Mont-Saint-Michel; Champagne region; Loire Valley at an extra cost. Students typically earn 3 semester credits per term.
Sessions • Jun–Aug (2 weeks).
Eligibility Requirements • Minimum age 18; open to precollege students, freshmen, sophomores, juniors, seniors, graduate students, adults; no foreign language proficiency required.
Living Arrangements • Students live in host family homes, French student residences. Quarters are shared with host institution students, students from other programs. Meals are taken as a group, in residences, in central dining facility, in restaurants.
Costs (2005) • Contact sponsor for cost. €40 application fee. Financial aid available for all students: scholarships.
For More Information • Ms. Holly de Montmarin, Summer Programs Coordinator, The American University of Paris, 6, Rue du Colonel Combes, 75007 Paris, France; *Phone:* +33 1-40-62-0720; *Fax:* +33 1-47-05-3432. *E-mail:* summer@aup.fr. *World Wide Web:* http://www.aup.edu/. Students may also apply through The American University of Paris/United States Office, 950 South Cherry Street, Suite 210, Denver, CO 80246.

THE AMERICAN UNIVERSITY OF PARIS
FRENCH IMMERSION PROGRAM

Hosted by The American University of Paris
Academic Focus • French language and literature, French studies.
Program Information • Students attend classes at The American University of Paris (Paris, France). Field trips to Paris museums, neighborhood walks, the theatre; optional travel to châteaux,

Burgundy, the French Riviera, Brittany, Mont-Saint-Michel, Champagne region, Loire Valley at an extra cost. Students typically earn 5 semester credits per term.
Sessions • Jun (summer), Jul–Aug (summer 2).
Eligibility Requirements • Minimum age 18; open to precollege students, freshmen, sophomores, juniors, seniors, graduate students, adults; no foreign language proficiency required.
Living Arrangements • Students live in host family homes, French student residences. Quarters are shared with host institution students, students from other programs. Meals are taken as a group, in residences, in central dining facility, in restaurants.
Costs (2005) • €3425; includes tuition, some meals, excursions, international student ID, student support services. €40 application fee. Financial aid available for all students: scholarships.
For More Information • Ms. Holly de Montmarin, Summer Programs Coordinator, The American University of Paris, 6, Rue du Colonel Combes, 75007 Paris, France; *Phone:* +33 1-40-62-0720; *Fax:* +33 1-47-05-3432. *E-mail:* summer@aup.fr. *World Wide Web:* http://www.aup.edu/. Students may also apply through The American University of Paris/United States Office, 950 South Cherry Street, Suite 210, Denver, CO 80246.

THE AMERICAN UNIVERSITY OF PARIS
SUMMER SESSIONS

Hosted by The American University of Paris
Academic Focus • Art history, communications, comparative literature, computer science, economics, English literature, European studies, film and media studies, fine/studio arts, French studies, history, international affairs, international business, philosophy, photography, political science and government, psychology, social sciences.
Program Information • Students attend classes at The American University of Paris (Paris, France). Field trips to Paris museums, Normandy, Mont-Saint-Michel, Loire Valley châteaux, Burgundy, Champagne Region. Students typically earn 6 semester credits per session.
Sessions • Jun–Jul (summer), Jul–Aug (summer 2).
Eligibility Requirements • Minimum age 18; open to precollege students, freshmen, sophomores, juniors, seniors, graduate students, adults; good academic standing at home school; no foreign language proficiency required.
Living Arrangements • Students live in host institution dormitories, host family homes. Meals are taken as a group, on one's own, with host family, in residences, in central dining facility, in restaurants.
Costs (2005) • $1920–$5120; includes tuition, international student ID, student support services. $45 application fee. Financial aid available for all students: scholarships.
For More Information • Ms. Holly de Montmarin, Summer Programs Coordinator, The American University of Paris, 6, Rue du Colonel Combes, 75007 Paris, France; *Phone:* +33 1-40-62-0720; *Fax:* +33 1-47-05-3432. *E-mail:* summer@aup.fr. *World Wide Web:* http://www.aup.edu/. Students may also apply through The American University of Paris/United States Office, 950 South Cherry Street, Suite 210, Denver, CO 80246.

BILINGUAL ACTING WORKSHOP
BILINGUAL ACTING WORKSHOP IN PARIS, FRANCE

Hosted by Bilingual Acting Workshop
Academic Focus • Cinematography, drama/theater, French language and literature, performing arts.
Program Information • Students attend classes at Bilingual Acting Workshop. Field trips to the Avignon Film Festival.
Sessions • Jun–Jul (summer), Semester and year-long terms also available.
Eligibility Requirements • Minimum age 18; open to precollege students, freshmen, sophomores, juniors, seniors, graduate students, adults; no foreign language proficiency required.
Living Arrangements • Students live in host institution dormitories. Quarters are shared with host institution students. Meals are taken on one's own, in central dining facility.
Costs (2004–2005) • $2200; includes tuition, housing, books and class materials. $700 application fee. Financial aid available for students: work study.

For More Information • Ms. Amy Werba, Artistic Director, Bilingual Acting Workshop, 24, rue de l'Esperance, 75013 Paris, France; *Phone:* +33 1-45 89 63 11. *E-mail:* info@bilingualacting.com. *World Wide Web:* http://www.bilingualacting.com/

BOSTON UNIVERSITY
PARIS LANGUAGE, LIBERAL ARTS, AND INTERNSHIP PROGRAM

Academic Focus • French language and literature, French studies.
Program Information • Faculty members are local instructors hired by the sponsor. Field trips to Versailles, Fontainebleau, cultural sites. Students typically earn 8 semester credits per term.
Sessions • May–Jul (summer).
Eligibility Requirements • Open to sophomores, juniors, seniors; 3.0 GPA; 1 letter of recommendation; good academic standing at home school; essay; transcript; approval of participation; no foreign language proficiency required.
Living Arrangements • Students live in host institution dormitories, host family homes. Meals are taken on one's own, with host family, in residences, in restaurants.
Costs (2005) • $6000; includes tuition, housing, insurance, excursions, books and class materials, internship placement when applicable. $50 application fee. $400 nonrefundable deposit required. Financial aid available for all students: scholarships, loans.
For More Information • Division of International Programs, Boston University, 232 Bay State Road, Boston, MA 02215; *Phone:* 617-353-9888; *Fax:* 617-353-5402. *E-mail:* abroad@bu.edu. *World Wide Web:* http://www.bu.edu/abroad/

CENTER FOR CULTURAL INTERCHANGE
PARIS, FRANCE LANGUAGE SCHOOL

Hosted by SILC International Education Services
Academic Focus • French language and literature.

Program Information • Students attend classes at SILC International Education Services (Paris, France). Field trips to cultural activities, guided city tours, museums.
Sessions • 3, 4, or 6 week sessions begin every Monday, year-round.
Eligibility Requirements • Minimum age 13; open to precollege students, freshmen, sophomores, juniors, seniors, graduate students, adults; no foreign language proficiency required.
Living Arrangements • Students live in host family homes. Quarters are shared with host institution students. Meals are taken with host family, in residences.
Costs (2005) • $3190 for 4 weeks; includes tuition, housing, some meals, insurance, books and class materials, student support services, activities. Financial aid available for students from sponsoring institution: scholarships.
For More Information • Ms. Juliet Jones, Outbound Programs Director, Center for Cultural Interchange, 325 West Huron, Suite 706, Chicago, IL 60610; *Phone:* 866-684-9675; *Fax:* 872-944-2644. *E-mail:* info@cci-exchange.com. *World Wide Web:* http://www.cci-exchange.com/

CIEE
CIEE STUDY CENTER AT THE PARIS CENTER FOR CRITICAL STUDIES, PARIS, FRANCE

Hosted by Paris Center for Critical Studies
Academic Focus • Anthropology, cultural studies, French language and literature, French studies, philosophy, visual and performing arts.
Program Information • Students attend classes at Paris Center for Critical Studies (Paris, France). Field trips to Marseille, Toulouse. Students typically earn 3 semester credits per term.
Sessions • Jun–Jul (summer), Jun–Jul (session 2).

Eligibility Requirements • Minimum age 18; open to sophomores, juniors, seniors; 2.75 GPA; 1 letter of recommendation; good academic standing at home school; no foreign language proficiency required.

Living Arrangements • Students live in host institution dormitories, host family homes. Quarters are shared with host institution students. Meals are taken as a group, on one's own, with host family, in residences, in central dining facility, in restaurants.

Costs (2006) • $2600 for 1 session; $4900 for 2 sessions; includes tuition, housing, insurance, excursions, student support services, pre-departure advising, orientation, resident director, airport pick-up, cultural activities. $30 application fee. $300 nonrefundable deposit required. Financial aid available for all students: scholarships, minority student scholarships.

For More Information • Information Center, CIEE, 7 Custom House Street, 3rd Floor, Portland, ME 04101; *Phone:* 800-40-STUDY; *Fax:* 207-553-7699. *E-mail:* studyinfo@ciee.org. *World Wide Web:* http://www.ciee.org/isp/

COLUMBIA UNIVERSITY
SUMMER PROGRAMS IN PARIS AT REID HALL

Hosted by Reid Hall

Academic Focus • Art history, French language and literature, French studies, history.

Program Information • Students attend classes at Reid Hall (Paris, France). Field trips to Champagne, Valence, Besançon, Château de la Loire, Reims; optional travel to independent travel in France at an extra cost. Students typically earn 3-6 semester credits per term.

Sessions • Jun–Jul (summer).

Eligibility Requirements • Open to freshmen, sophomores, juniors, seniors, graduate students, adults; good academic standing at home school; completion of 1 semester of college; 1 year course work in French for language courses.

Living Arrangements • Students live in host institution dormitories, locally rented apartments, host family homes. Meals are taken on one's own, with host family, in residences, in restaurants.

Costs (2005) • $2556–$5112; includes tuition, student support services, computer lab access. $50 application fee. $500 nonrefundable deposit required.

For More Information • Information Center, Columbia University, 2970 Broadway, MC 4110, 303 Lewisohn, New York, NY 10027-6902; *Phone:* 212-854-9699; *Fax:* 212-854-5861. *E-mail:* reidhall@columbia.edu. *World Wide Web:* http://www.ce.columbia.edu/op/

EMORY UNIVERSITY
FRENCH STUDIES

Held at Reid Hall

Academic Focus • Business administration/management, drama/theater, French language and literature.

Program Information • Classes are held on the campus of Reid Hall (Paris, France). Faculty members are drawn from the sponsor's U.S. staff and local instructors hired by the sponsor. Scheduled travel to Chartres, Loire Valley; field trips to Giverny, Versailles, Reims. Students typically earn 8-12 semester credits per term.

Sessions • Jun–Jul (summer).

Eligibility Requirements • Minimum age 18; open to freshmen, sophomores, juniors, seniors; 2.0 GPA; good academic standing at home school; 1 year of college course work in French.

Living Arrangements • Students live in host family homes. Meals are taken on one's own.

Costs (2005) • $7692; includes tuition, housing, some meals, insurance, excursions. $350 nonrefundable deposit required. Financial aid available for students from sponsoring institution: scholarships, loans.

For More Information • Ms. Gail Scheu, Study Abroad Coordinator, Emory University, 1385 Oxford Road, Atlanta, GA 30322; *Phone:* 404-727-2240; *Fax:* 404-727-6724. *E-mail:* lscheu@emory.edu. *World Wide Web:* http://www.cipa.emory.edu/

EUROPEAN HERITAGE INSTITUTE
ART, FASHION, AND INTERIOR DESIGN IN PARIS

Hosted by Paris American Academy

Academic Focus • Art, creative writing, design and applied arts, drawing/painting, fashion design, fine/studio arts, interior design.

Program Information • Students attend classes at Paris American Academy (Paris, France). Field trips to Versailles, Giverny, locations in and around Paris; optional travel to the Loire Valley, Mont-Saint-Michel, Normandy, the Provence area at an extra cost. Students typically earn 6 semester credits per term.

Sessions • Jul (summer).

Eligibility Requirements • Minimum age 18; open to freshmen, sophomores, juniors, seniors, graduate students, adults; 2.2 GPA; 2 letters of recommendation; no foreign language proficiency required.

Living Arrangements • Students live in locally rented apartments. Quarters are shared with host institution students, students from other programs. Meals are taken on one's own, in residences, in restaurants.

Costs (2006) • $3700; includes tuition, housing, excursions, student support services. $300 refundable deposit required.

For More Information • Dr. Antonio Masullo, Professor, European Heritage Institute, 2708 East Franklin Street, Richmond, VA 23223; *Phone:* 804-643-0661; *Fax:* 804-648-0826. *E-mail:* info@europeabroad.org. *World Wide Web:* http://www.europeabroad.org/

EUROPEAN HERITAGE INSTITUTE
SUMMER IN PARIS AT LA SORBONNE–FRANCE

Hosted by University Paris-Sorbonne (Paris IV)

Academic Focus • Civilization studies, French language and literature, French studies, history.

Program Information • Students attend classes at University Paris-Sorbonne (Paris IV) (Paris, France). Students typically earn 3-12 semester credits per term.

Sessions • Jun–Oct (short-term sessions).

Eligibility Requirements • Minimum age 18; open to freshmen, sophomores, juniors, seniors, graduate students, adults; 2.2 GPA; 2 letters of recommendation; no foreign language proficiency required.

Living Arrangements • Students live in host institution dormitories, locally rented apartments. Quarters are shared with host institution students, students from other programs. Meals are taken on one's own, in residences, in restaurants.

Costs (2006) • $1150–$3300; includes tuition, student support services, administrative fees. $300 refundable deposit required.

For More Information • Dr. Antonio Masullo, Professor, European Heritage Institute, 2708 East Franklin Street, Richmond, VA 23223; *Phone:* 804-643-0661; *Fax:* 804-648-0826. *E-mail:* info@europeabroad.org. *World Wide Web:* http://www.europeabroad.org/

FRENCH-AMERICAN EXCHANGE
SUMMER STUDY ABROAD IN PARIS

Hosted by Ecole France Langue

Academic Focus • Civilization studies, French language and literature, French studies.

Program Information • Students attend classes at Ecole France Langue (Paris, France). Field trips to museums, monuments, Versailles, Fontainebleau, Chartres, Vaux-le-Vicomte; optional travel to the Loire Valley, Brittany, Normandy, Europe at an extra cost. Students typically earn 6 semester credits per term.

Sessions • Jun–Sep (4 weeks).

Eligibility Requirements • Minimum age 19; open to sophomores, juniors, seniors, graduate students, adults; good academic standing at home school; no foreign language proficiency required.

Living Arrangements • Students live in locally rented apartments, host family homes. Meals are taken on one's own, with host family, in residences, in restaurants.

Costs (2005) • $2865; includes tuition, housing, some meals, lab equipment, student support services. $50 application fee. $500 refundable deposit required.

For More Information • Mr. James Pondolfino, Executive Director, French-American Exchange, 3213 Duke Street, #620, Alexandria, VA 22314; *Phone:* 800-995-5087; *Fax:* 703-823-4447. *E-mail:* info@frenchamericanexchange.com. *World Wide Web:* http://www.frenchamericanexchange.com/

FRANCE
Paris

ILLINOIS STATE UNIVERSITY
SUMMER PROGRAM–PARIS, FRANCE

Hosted by NEGOCIA

Academic Focus • Communications.

Program Information • Students attend classes at NEGOCIA (Paris, France). Field trips to course-related site visits, cultural activities. Students typically earn 6 semester credits per term.

Sessions • Jun–Jul (summer).

Eligibility Requirements • Open to sophomores, juniors, seniors, graduate students; major in communication; 2.5 GPA; 2 letters of recommendation; good academic standing at home school; essay; no foreign language proficiency required.

Living Arrangements • Students live in program-owned apartments. Quarters are shared with host institution students. Meals are taken on one's own, in residences.

Costs (2005) • $6058; includes tuition, housing, all meals, insurance, excursions, international airfare, international student ID, student support services, personal expenses. $150 application fee. Financial aid available for students from sponsoring institution: scholarships, loans.

For More Information • Study Abroad Coordinator, Illinois State University, Office of International Studies and Programs, Campus Box 6120, Normal, IL 61790-6120; *Phone:* 309-438-5276; *Fax:* 309-438-3987. *E-mail:* oisp@ilstu.edu. *World Wide Web:* http://www.internationalstudies.ilstu.edu/

INTERNATIONAL STUDIES ABROAD
PARIS, FRANCE FINE ARTS

Academic Focus • Drawing/painting, fine/studio arts, French language and literature, photography.

Program Information • Faculty members are local instructors hired by the sponsor. Field trips to Versailles, the Loire Valley, Mont-Saint-Michel, Normandy. Students typically earn 6–8 semester credits per term.

Sessions • May–Jun (summer).

Eligibility Requirements • Minimum age 18; open to freshmen, sophomores, juniors, seniors, adults; 2.5 GPA; good academic standing at home school; transcripts; JU Abroad Transient Credit Form; no foreign language proficiency required.

Living Arrangements • Students live in host institution dormitories, host family homes. Quarters are shared with students from other programs. Meals are taken with host family, in residences.

Costs (2006) • $4200; includes tuition, housing, some meals, insurance, excursions, student support services, laundry (for students with host family), tutorials, transportation for excursions, airport transfers. $200 deposit required. Financial aid available for all students: scholarships, loans, U.S. federal financial aid.

For More Information • France Site Specialist, International Studies Abroad, 901 West 24th Street, Austin, TX 78705; *Phone:* 800-580-8826; *Fax:* 512-480-8866. *E-mail:* isa@studiesabroad.com. *World Wide Web:* http://www.studiesabroad.com/

INTERNATIONAL STUDIES ABROAD
PARIS, FRANCE, FRENCH LANGUAGE

Hosted by Catholic University of Paris

Academic Focus • Business administration/management, French language and literature.

Program Information • Students attend classes at Catholic University of Paris (Paris, France). Field trips to Versailles, Chartres, Mont-Saint-Michel, Normandy. Students typically earn 5 semester credits per term.

Sessions • Jun–Jul (summer).

Eligibility Requirements • Minimum age 18; open to freshmen, sophomores, juniors, seniors, adults; 2.5 GPA; good academic standing at home school; transcripts; no foreign language proficiency required.

Living Arrangements • Students live in host institution dormitories, host family homes. Quarters are shared with host institution students, students from other programs. Meals are taken with host family, in residences.

Costs (2006–2007) • $4150; includes tuition, housing, some meals, insurance, excursions, student support services, laundry (for students with host families only), tutorials, Internet access, airport transfer. $200 deposit required. Financial aid available for all students: scholarships, loans, U.S. federal financial aid.

For More Information • France Site Specialist, International Studies Abroad, 901 West 24th Street, Austin, TX 78705; *Phone:* 800-580-8826; *Fax:* 512-480-8866. *E-mail:* isa@studiesabroad.com. *World Wide Web:* http://www.studiesabroad.com/

JAMES MADISON UNIVERSITY
SUMMER IN PARIS

Academic Focus • Art, French language and literature.

Program Information • Faculty members are drawn from the sponsor's U.S. staff. Students typically earn 9 semester credits per term.

Sessions • Jun–Jul (summer).

Eligibility Requirements • Minimum age 18; open to sophomores, juniors, seniors; 2.0 GPA; 1 letter of recommendation; good academic standing at home school; no foreign language proficiency required.

Living Arrangements • Students live in locally rented apartments. Meals are taken as a group, on one's own, in central dining facility, in restaurants.

Costs (2005) • $3362 for Virginia residents; $5882 for nonresidents; includes tuition, housing, some meals, books and class materials, international student ID. $400 nonrefundable deposit required. Financial aid available for students from sponsoring institution: work study.

For More Information • Mr. Felix Wang, Director, James Madison University, Office of International Programs, MSC 5731, 1077 South Main Street, Harrisonburg, VA 22087; *Phone:* 540-568-6419; *Fax:* 540-568-3310. *E-mail:* studyabroad@jmu.edu. *World Wide Web:* http://www.jmu.edu/international/

KENTUCKY INSTITUTE FOR INTERNATIONAL STUDIES
FRANCE

Academic Focus • French language and literature, French studies.

Program Information • Faculty members are drawn from the sponsor's U.S. staff. Field trips to local points of interest; optional travel to other European capitals at an extra cost. Students typically earn 6 semester credits per term.

Sessions • May–Jun (summer).

Eligibility Requirements • Minimum age 18; open to freshmen, sophomores, juniors, seniors, graduate students; 2.0 GPA; 1 letter of recommendation; no foreign language proficiency required.

Living Arrangements • Students live in host institution dormitories, hotels. Meals are taken as a group, in central dining facility.

Costs (2006) • $3610; includes housing, some meals, insurance, excursions, international airfare, international student ID, instructional expenses. $150 application fee. Financial aid available for all students: scholarships.

For More Information • Ms. Nancy Martin, Coordinator, Kentucky Institute for International Studies, PO Box 9, Murray, KY 42071-0009; *Phone:* 270-762-3091; *Fax:* 270-762-3434. *E-mail:* kiismsu@murraystate.edu. *World Wide Web:* http://www.kiis.org/

LANGUAGE LIAISON
LEARN FRENCH IN PARIS

Hosted by Language Liaison

Academic Focus • French language and literature.

Program Information • Students attend classes at Language Liaison (Paris, France). Field trips; optional travel at an extra cost. Students typically earn 3–15 semester credits per term.

Sessions • Classes begin weekly, year-round.

Eligibility Requirements • Minimum age 16; open to precollege students, freshmen, sophomores, juniors, seniors, graduate students, adults; no foreign language proficiency required.

Living Arrangements • Students live in locally rented apartments, host family homes, hotels. Meals are taken on one's own, with host family, in residences, in restaurants.

Costs (2005) • Contact sponsor for cost. $175 application fee. Financial aid available for all students: scholarship research service.

For More Information • Ms. Nancy Forman, President, Language Liaison, PO Box 1772, Pacific Palisades, CA 90272; *Phone:* 800-284-4448; *Fax:* 310-454-1706. *E-mail:* learn@languageliaison.com. *World Wide Web:* http://www.languageliaison.com/

LEXIA INTERNATIONAL
LEXIA SUMMER IN PARIS

Hosted by University Paris-Sorbonne (Paris IV)

Academic Focus • Anthropology, area studies, art history, civilization studies, classics and classical languages, comparative history, cultural studies, economics, ethnic studies, French language and literature, French studies, geography, history, interdisciplinary studies, international affairs, liberal studies, literature, political science and government, social sciences, sociology.

Program Information • Students attend classes at University Paris-Sorbonne (Paris IV) (Paris, France). Field trips to sites in and around the city of Paris, Normandy, Brittany. Students typically earn 8–10 semester credits per term.

Sessions • Jun–Aug (summer).

Eligibility Requirements • Minimum age 18; open to freshmen, sophomores, juniors, seniors, graduate students, adults; 2.5 GPA; 2 letters of recommendation; no foreign language proficiency required.

Living Arrangements • Students live in host family homes. Meals are taken on one's own, with host family, in residences.

Costs (2006) • $6850; includes tuition, housing, some meals, insurance, excursions, international student ID, student support services, transcript, computer access. $40 application fee. $300 nonrefundable deposit required. Financial aid available for all students: scholarships, work study.

For More Information • Lexia International, 23 South Main Street, Hanover, NH 03755; *Phone:* 800-775-3942; *Fax:* 603-643-9899. *E-mail:* info@lexiaintl.org. *World Wide Web:* http://www.lexiaintl.org/

LINGUA SERVICE WORLDWIDE
VACATION 'N LEARN FRENCH IN FRANCE

Hosted by Ecole France Langue

Academic Focus • French language and literature, French studies.

Program Information • Students attend classes at Ecole France Langue (Paris, France). Optional travel to cultural sites throughout France at an extra cost. Students typically earn 3 semester credits for 3 weeks, 6 semester credits for 5 weeks.

Sessions • Sessions of 2 or more weeks begin on Mondays, year-round.

Eligibility Requirements • Minimum age 16; open to precollege students, freshmen, sophomores, juniors, seniors, graduate students, adults; no foreign language proficiency required.

Living Arrangements • Students live in host institution dormitories, locally rented apartments, host family homes, hotels. Quarters are shared with host institution students. Meals are taken with host family.

Costs (2006–2007) • Contact sponsor for cost. $100 application fee.

For More Information • Assistant Director, Lingua Service Worldwide, 75 Prospect Street, Suite 4, Huntington, NY 11743; *Phone:* 800-394-5327; *Fax:* 631-271-3441. *E-mail:* linguaservice@att.net. *World Wide Web:* http://www.linguaserviceworldwide.com/

LINGUA SERVICE WORLDWIDE
VACATION 'N LEARN FRENCH IN FRANCE

Hosted by Ecole de Langue Française pour Etrangers

Academic Focus • French language and literature, French studies.

Program Information • Students attend classes at Ecole de Langue Française pour Etrangers (Paris, France). Optional travel to cultural sites throughout France at an extra cost. Students typically earn 3 semester credits for 3 weeks, 6 semester credits for 5 weeks.

Sessions • Sessions of 2 or more weeks begin on Mondays, year-round.

Eligibility Requirements • Minimum age 16; open to precollege students, freshmen, sophomores, juniors, seniors, graduate students, adults; no foreign language proficiency required.

Living Arrangements • Students live in host institution dormitories, locally rented apartments, host family homes, hotels. Quarters are shared with host institution students. Meals are taken with host family.

Costs (2006–2007) • Contact sponsor for cost. $100 application fee.

For More Information • Assistant Director, Lingua Service Worldwide, 75 Prospect Street, Suite 4, Huntington, NY 11743;

Phone: 800-394-5327; *Fax:* 631-271-3441. *E-mail:* linguaservice@att.net. *World Wide Web:* http://www.linguaserviceworldwide.com/

LOYOLA UNIVERSITY NEW ORLEANS
SUMMER STUDY IN PARIS

Held at FIAP Jean Monnet

Academic Focus • French language and literature, French studies, literature.

Program Information • Classes are held on the campus of FIAP Jean Monnet (Paris, France). Faculty members are drawn from the sponsor's U.S. staff. Field trips to Chartres, Giverny, Rheims, Versailles; optional travel to various European cities at an extra cost. Students typically earn 6 semester credits per term.

Sessions • May–Jun (summer).

Eligibility Requirements • Minimum age 18; open to freshmen, sophomores, juniors, seniors; 2.0 GPA; good academic standing at home school; no foreign language proficiency required.

Living Arrangements • Students live in host institution dormitories. Quarters are shared with students from other programs. Meals are taken as a group, in central dining facility.

Costs (2006) • $3800; includes tuition, housing, some meals, insurance, excursions, student support services. $380 deposit required. Financial aid available for students from sponsoring institution: scholarships, loans.

For More Information • Dr. Mary McCay, Professor of English, Loyola University New Orleans, 6363 Saint Charles Avenue, New Orleans, LA 70118; *Phone:* 504-865-3389; *Fax:* 504-865-2294. *E-mail:* mccay@loyno.edu. *World Wide Web:* http://www.loyno.edu/cie/

MICHIGAN STATE UNIVERSITY
ORGANIZATIONAL AND INTERNATIONAL COMMUNICATION IN PARIS

Held at Cité Universitaire

Academic Focus • Communications.

Program Information • Classes are held on the campus of Cité Universitaire (Paris, France). Faculty members are drawn from the sponsor's U.S. staff. Field trips to Belgium. Students typically earn 7 semester credits per term.

Sessions • Jul–Aug (summer).

Eligibility Requirements • Open to juniors, seniors; 2.5 GPA; good academic standing at home school; no foreign language proficiency required.

Living Arrangements • Students live in host institution dormitories. Meals are taken on one's own, in central dining facility, in restaurants.

Costs (2005) • $3138; includes housing, insurance, excursions. $100 application fee. $200 nonrefundable deposit required. Financial aid available for students from sponsoring institution: scholarships, loans.

For More Information • Ms. Yvonne Squiers, Secretary, Michigan State University, Office of Study Abroad, 109 International Center, East Lansing, MI 48824-1035; *Phone:* 517-353-8920; *Fax:* 517-432-2082. *E-mail:* squiers@msu.edu. *World Wide Web:* http://studyabroad.msu.edu/

NEW YORK UNIVERSITY
NYU IN PARIS

Hosted by NYU Center in France

Academic Focus • Art history, civilization studies, cultural studies, film and media studies, French language and literature, history.

Program Information • Students attend classes at NYU Center in France (Paris, France). Scheduled travel to the Loire Valley, Avignon, Provence; field trips to Chartres, Reims, Versailles. Students typically earn 8 semester credits per term.

Sessions • Jun–Aug (summer).

Eligibility Requirements • Minimum age 18; open to freshmen, sophomores, juniors, seniors, graduate students; 3.0 GPA; good academic standing at home school; some college course work in French required for French courses.

Living Arrangements • Students live in host institution dormitories, locally rented apartments. Quarters are shared with host institution students. Meals are taken as a group, on one's own, in residences, in restaurants.

FRANCE
Paris

Costs (2006) • $7434; includes tuition, housing, some meals, excursions, student support services, program fee. $25 application fee. $300 nonrefundable deposit required. Financial aid available for students from sponsoring institution: loans.
For More Information • Office of Summer Sessions, New York University, 7 East 12th Street, 6th Floor, New York, NY 10003; *Phone:* 212-998-2292; *Fax:* 212-995-4642. *E-mail:* summer.info@nyu.edu. *World Wide Web:* http://www.nyu.edu/global/studyabroad.html

NEW YORK UNIVERSITY
PARIS, FRANCE: THE ARTS IN PARIS

Held at Le Conservatoire Européen d'Ecriture Audiovisuelle
Academic Focus • Film and media studies.
Program Information • Classes are held on the campus of Le Conservatoire Européen d'Ecriture Audiovisuelle (Paris, France). Faculty members are drawn from the sponsor's U.S. staff. Students typically earn 8 semester credits per term.
Sessions • Jun–Aug (summer).
Eligibility Requirements • Minimum age 18; open to freshmen, sophomores, juniors, seniors, graduate students, adults; course work in video production experience; no foreign language proficiency required.
Living Arrangements • Students live in locally rented apartments. Quarters are shared with host institution students. Meals are taken on one's own, in restaurants.
Costs (2005) • $5400; includes tuition. $50 application fee. Financial aid available for students from sponsoring institution: scholarships.
For More Information • Mr. Josh Murray, Assistant Director, New York University, 721 Broadway, 12th Floor, New York, NY 10003; *Phone:* 212-998-1500; *Fax:* 212-995-4578. *E-mail:* tisch.special.info@nyu.edu. *World Wide Web:* http://www.nyu.edu/global/studyabroad.html

ROCKLAND COMMUNITY COLLEGE
ART IN PARIS: CRUCIBLE OF MODERNISM

Academic Focus • Art, art history.
Program Information • Faculty members are drawn from the sponsor's U.S. staff. Field trips to the Louvre, Musée d'Orsay, the Picasso Museum, Beaubourg. Students typically earn 3 semester credits per term.
Sessions • Jun (summer).
Eligibility Requirements • Minimum age 18; open to freshmen, sophomores, juniors, seniors, adults; good academic standing at home school; no foreign language proficiency required.
Living Arrangements • Students live in hotels. Meals are taken on one's own, in restaurants.
Costs (2005) • $2785 (estimated); includes tuition, housing, some meals, insurance, international airfare, international student ID. $400 nonrefundable deposit required. Financial aid available for students from sponsoring institution: scholarships, loans.
For More Information • Ms. Fran Rodríguez, Coordinator, Study Abroad, Rockland Community College, 145 College Road, Suffern, NY 10901; *Phone:* 845-574-4205; *Fax:* 845-574-4423. *E-mail:* study-abroad@sunyrockland.edu. *World Wide Web:* http://www.rocklandabroad.com/

ROCKLAND COMMUNITY COLLEGE
HISTORY IN PARIS: MONUMENTS OF FRENCH HISTORY

Academic Focus • History.
Program Information • Faculty members are drawn from the sponsor's U.S. staff. Field trips to the Louvre, Musée d'Orsay, the Picasso Museum, Beaubourg. Students typically earn 3 semester credits per term.
Sessions • Jun (summer).
Eligibility Requirements • Minimum age 18; open to freshmen, sophomores, juniors, seniors, adults; good academic standing at home school; no foreign language proficiency required.
Living Arrangements • Students live in hotels. Meals are taken on one's own, in restaurants.

Costs (2005) • $2785; includes tuition, housing, some meals, international airfare. $250 nonrefundable deposit required. Financial aid available for students from sponsoring institution: scholarships, loans.
For More Information • Ms. Fran Rodríguez, Coordinator, Study Abroad, Rockland Community College, 145 College Road, Suffern, NY 10901; *Phone:* 845-574-4205; *Fax:* 845-574-4423. *E-mail:* study-abroad@sunyrockland.edu. *World Wide Web:* http://www.rocklandabroad.com/

RUTGERS, THE STATE UNIVERSITY OF NEW JERSEY
SUMMER INSTITUTE IN ART HISTORY IN PARIS

Academic Focus • Art history.
Program Information • Faculty members are drawn from the sponsor's U.S. staff. Students typically earn 6 semester credits per term.
Sessions • Jun–Jul (summer).
Eligibility Requirements • Open to freshmen, sophomores, juniors, seniors; course work in art history; 2.5 GPA; 1 letter of recommendation; good academic standing at home school; official transcripts from all tertiary schools attended; no foreign language proficiency required.
Living Arrangements • Students live in hotels. Meals are taken as a group, in residences, in restaurants.
Costs (2005) • $4587 for New Jersey residents; $5672 for nonresidents; includes tuition, housing, insurance, excursions, student support services. $20 application fee. $500 nonrefundable deposit required. Financial aid available for students from sponsoring institution: scholarships, loans.
For More Information • Ms. Lindy Black, Regional Coordinator, Rutgers, The State University of New Jersey, 102 College Avenue, New Brunswick, NJ 08901-8543; *Phone:* 732-932-7787; *Fax:* 732-932-8659. *E-mail:* ru_abroad@email.rutgers.edu. *World Wide Web:* http://studyabroad.rutgers.edu/

ST. JOHN'S UNIVERSITY
FRANCE PROGRAM–PARIS AND THE SOUTH OF FRANCE

Held at Drome Provençale
Academic Focus • Art, cultural studies, French language and literature.
Program Information • Classes are held on the campus of Drome Provençale (Paris, France). Faculty members are drawn from the sponsor's U.S. staff. Scheduled travel; field trips to Versailles, castles of the Loire Valley, the Louvre, the south of France, a cruise on the Seine; optional travel to London, Provence at an extra cost. Students typically earn 3-6 semester credits per term.
Sessions • Jun–Jul (summer).
Eligibility Requirements • Minimum age 18; open to freshmen, sophomores, juniors, seniors; 2.75 GPA; 2 letters of recommendation; good academic standing at home school; interview; no foreign language proficiency required.
Living Arrangements • Students live in host institution dormitories, locally rented apartments, hotels. Quarters are shared with host institution students. Meals are taken as a group, on one's own, in residences, in central dining facility, in restaurants.
Costs (2004) • $2995; includes housing, some meals, excursions, international airfare, student support services, unlimited bus/metro pass in Paris, some museum admissions. $30 application fee. $750 nonrefundable deposit required. Financial aid available for students from sponsoring institution: scholarships, loans, students must be enrolled for 6 credits to receive aid.
For More Information • Dr. Ruth De Paula, Director, Office of Study Abroad Programs, St. John's University, 8000 Utopia Parkway, Jamaica, NY 11439; *Phone:* 718-990-6105; *Fax:* 718-990-2321. *E-mail:* intled@stjohns.edu. *World Wide Web:* http://www.stjohns.edu/studyabroad/

SAN FRANCISCO STATE UNIVERSITY/ EUROPEAN STUDIES ASSOCIATION
SUMMER STUDY IN PARIS

Hosted by Catholic University of Paris
Academic Focus • French language and literature, French studies.

Program Information • Students attend classes at Catholic University of Paris (Paris, France). Scheduled travel to Mont-Saint-Michel, Bayeux, Saint-Malo, Rouen; Fontainebleau; field trips to Brittany, Normandy; optional travel to Belgium at an extra cost. Students typically earn 4 semester units per term.
Sessions • Jul (summer).
Eligibility Requirements • Minimum age 17; open to precollege students, freshmen, sophomores, juniors, seniors, graduate students, adults; no foreign language proficiency required.
Living Arrangements • Students live in host institution dormitories, locally rented apartments, host family homes. Meals are taken on one's own, with host family, in residences.
Costs (2006) • $2550; includes tuition, housing, some meals, excursions, books and class materials, international student ID, student support services, transit pass. Financial aid available for all students: scholarships.
For More Information • Dr. Thomas Blair, Director, San Francisco State University/European Studies Association, European Studies Association, 424 Dorado Terrace, San Francisco, CA 94112-1753; *Phone:* 415-334-4222; *Fax:* 415-334-4222. *E-mail:* tblair@ccsf.edu. *World Wide Web:* http://www.esaparis.org/

SIENA SOJOURN
(PARIS SOJOURN OF) SOJOURNS ABROAD

Academic Focus • French language and literature.
Program Information • Faculty members are drawn from the sponsor's U.S. staff and local instructors hired by the sponsor. Scheduled travel to Reims, Strasbourg, Nice, St. Paul de Vence; field trips to Bayeux, Normandy, Loire Valley, Brussels.
Sessions • Jun-Jul (summer).
Eligibility Requirements • Minimum age 18; open to freshmen, sophomores, juniors, seniors, graduate students; 1 letter of recommendation; application/personal statement; no foreign language proficiency required.
Living Arrangements • Students live in host family homes. Meals are taken with host family, in residences.
Costs (2007) • $8500; includes tuition, housing, some meals, excursions, books and class materials, museum entry fees, concerts, sporting events, cultural activities. $250 application fee. Financial aid available for all students: scholarships.
For More Information • Mr. John Nissen, Director, Siena Sojourn, Box 1171, Manchester, VT 05254; *Phone:* 802-362-5855; *Fax:* 802-332-6205. *E-mail:* info@sojournsabroad.org. *World Wide Web:* http://www.sojournsabroad.org

SOUTHERN METHODIST UNIVERSITY
SUMMER IN PARIS

Held at Reid Hall
Academic Focus • Cultural studies, history.
Program Information • Classes are held on the campus of Reid Hall (Paris, France). Faculty members are drawn from the sponsor's U.S. staff and local instructors hired by the sponsor. Field trips to Versailles, Fontainebleau, the Loire Valley. Students typically earn 6 semester credits per term.
Sessions • May-Jun (summer).
Eligibility Requirements • Open to sophomores, juniors, seniors; 2.5 GPA; 1 letter of recommendation; good academic standing at home school; essay; personal interview; no foreign language proficiency required.
Living Arrangements • Students live in host institution dormitories. Quarters are shared with students from other programs. Meals are taken as a group, in central dining facility.
Costs (2005) • $5650; includes tuition, housing, some meals, excursions. $40 application fee. $400 nonrefundable deposit required. Financial aid available for students from sponsoring institution: scholarships, loans.
For More Information • Ms. Nancy Simmons, Associate Director, Southern Methodist University, The International Center/Study Abroad, SMU PO Box 750391, Dallas, TX 75275-0391; *Phone:* 214-768-2338; *Fax:* 214-768-1051. *E-mail:* intlpro@mail.smu.edu. *World Wide Web:* http://www.smu.edu/studyabroad/

STATE UNIVERSITY OF NEW YORK AT NEW PALTZ
ON-SITE ART HISTORY SUMMER ABROAD PROGRAM

Academic Focus • Art history.
Program Information • Faculty members are drawn from the sponsor's U.S. staff. Scheduled travel to Córdoba, Seville, Granada. Students typically earn 3 semester credits per term.
Sessions • Jul (summer).
Eligibility Requirements • Minimum age 18; open to freshmen, sophomores, juniors, seniors, graduate students; 2.5 GPA; 1 letter of recommendation; good academic standing at home school; no foreign language proficiency required.
Living Arrangements • Students live in hotels. Meals are taken on one's own, in restaurants.
Costs (2006) • $2700 for New York residents; $3500 for nonresidents; includes tuition, housing, some meals, excursions, student support services, administrative fee. $25 application fee. $300 nonrefundable deposit required. Financial aid available for students from sponsoring institution: scholarships, loans.
For More Information • Center for International Programs, State University of New York at New Paltz, 1 Hawk Drive, New Paltz, NY 12561-2443; *Phone:* 845-257-3125; *Fax:* 845-257-3129. *E-mail:* studyabroad@newpaltz.edu. *World Wide Web:* http://www.newpaltz.edu/studyabroad/

STATE UNIVERSITY OF NEW YORK AT NEW PALTZ
SUMMER FRENCH LANGUAGE STUDIES

Academic Focus • French language and literature.
Program Information • Faculty members are drawn from the sponsor's U.S. staff and local instructors hired by the sponsor. Field trips to Giverny, châteaux of the Loire, Normandy, Versailles, Chartres, Reims, Mercier Champagne visit. Students typically earn 6 semester credits per term.
Sessions • Jul (summer).
Eligibility Requirements • Minimum age 18; open to precollege students, freshmen, sophomores, juniors, seniors, graduate students; 2.5 GPA; 1 letter of recommendation; good academic standing at home school; 1 year of college course work in French.
Living Arrangements • Students live in host institution dormitories. Quarters are shared with students from other programs. Meals are taken on one's own, in residences, in central dining facility.
Costs (2006) • $3900 for New York residents; $5500 for nonresidents; includes tuition, housing, all meals, insurance, excursions, student support services, administrative fee, subway transportation, entrance fees. $25 application fee. $300 nonrefundable deposit required. Financial aid available for students from sponsoring institution: scholarships, loans.
For More Information • Center for International Programs, State University of New York at New Paltz, 1 Hawk Drive, New Paltz, NY 12561-2443; *Phone:* 845-257-3125; *Fax:* 845-257-3129. *E-mail:* studyabroad@newpaltz.edu. *World Wide Web:* http://www.newpaltz.edu/studyabroad/

SWEET BRIAR COLLEGE
SUMMER PROGRAM IN FRANCE

Held at Sweet Briar College
Academic Focus • French language and literature.
Program Information • Classes are held on the campus of Sweet Briar College (Paris, France). Faculty members are local instructors hired by the sponsor. Field trips; optional travel at an extra cost. Students typically earn 4-6 semester credits per term.
Sessions • Jun-Jul (summer).
Eligibility Requirements • Open to sophomores, juniors, seniors; 3.0 GPA; 1 letter of recommendation; good academic standing at home school; intermediate French.
Living Arrangements • Students live in host family homes. Meals are taken with host family.
Costs (2006) • Contact sponsor for cost. $50 application fee. $250 nonrefundable deposit required. Financial aid available for all students: scholarships.
For More Information • Dr. Margaret Scouten, Director, Junior Year in France, Sweet Briar College, Sweet Briar, VA 24595; *Phone:* 434-381-6109; *Fax:* 434-381-6283. *E-mail:* jyf@sbc.edu

FRANCE
Paris

SYRACUSE UNIVERSITY
PARIS NOIR: LITERATURE, ART, AND CONTEMPORARY LIFE IN DIASPORA

Academic Focus • African-American studies, cultural studies, literature, women's studies.
Program Information • Faculty members are drawn from the sponsor's U.S. staff. Field trips to museums, performances, guest lectures. Students typically earn 6 semester credits per term.
Sessions • May–Jul (summer).
Eligibility Requirements • Minimum age 18; open to sophomores, juniors, seniors, graduate students; 1 letter of recommendation; good academic standing at home school; no foreign language proficiency required.
Living Arrangements • Students live in hotels. Meals are taken on one's own, in restaurants.
Costs (2005) • $7770; includes tuition, housing, some meals, excursions, international student ID. $55 application fee. $350 nonrefundable deposit required. Financial aid available for all students: loans, need-based tuition grants.
For More Information • Mrs. Daisy Fried, Associate Director, Syracuse University, 106 Walnut Place, Syracuse, NY 13244-4170; *Phone:* 800-251-9674; *Fax:* 315-443-4593. *E-mail:* dipasum@syr.edu. *World Wide Web:* http://suabroad.syr.edu/

TEMPLE UNIVERSITY
SORBONNE STUDY PROGRAM

Hosted by University Paris-Sorbonne (Paris IV)
Academic Focus • French language and literature.
Program Information • Students attend classes at University Paris-Sorbonne (Paris IV) (Paris, France). Field trips to Chartres, Reims. Students typically earn 4–6 semester credits per term.
Sessions • Jun–Aug (summer).
Eligibility Requirements • Open to precollege students, freshmen, sophomores, juniors, seniors, graduate students, adults; 2.5 GPA; 1 letter of recommendation; good academic standing at home school; official transcripts; no foreign language proficiency required.
Living Arrangements • Students live in host institution dormitories, locally rented apartments, host family homes. Quarters are shared with host institution students, students from other programs. Meals are taken on one's own, in residences.
Costs (2005) • $2800–$5500; includes tuition, housing, excursions. $30 application fee. $200 nonrefundable deposit required. Financial aid available for students from sponsoring institution: scholarships, loans.
For More Information • Ms. Erin Joslyn, Study Abroad Coordinator, Temple University, International Programs, 200 Tuttleman Learning Center, 1809 North 13th Street, Philadelphia, PA 19122; *Phone:* 215-204-0720; *Fax:* 215-204-0729. *E-mail:* study.abroad@temple.edu. *World Wide Web:* http://www.temple.edu/studyabroad/

UNIVERSITY OF DELAWARE
SUMMER SESSION IN PARIS, FRANCE

Held at Reid Hall
Academic Focus • Art history, French language and literature, music.
Program Information • Classes are held on the campus of Reid Hall (Paris, France). Faculty members are drawn from the sponsor's U.S. staff and local instructors hired by the sponsor. Field trips to Normandy, Versailles, several concerts; optional travel to other areas of Europe at an extra cost. Students typically earn 6 semester credits per term.
Sessions • Jun–Jul (summer).
Eligibility Requirements • Open to freshmen, sophomores, juniors, seniors, adults; 2.0 GPA; 1 letter of recommendation; no foreign language proficiency required.
Living Arrangements • Students live in host family homes. Meals are taken with host family, in residences.
Costs (2005) • Contact sponsor for cost. $200 nonrefundable deposit required. Financial aid available for all students: scholarships.
For More Information • Center for International Studies, University of Delaware, 186 South College Avenue, Newark, DE 19716-1450; *Phone:* 888-831-4685; *Fax:* 302-831-6042. *E-mail:* studyabroad@udel. edu. *World Wide Web:* http://www.udel.edu/studyabroad/

UNIVERSITY OF DELAWARE
WINTER SESSION IN PARIS, FRANCE: CONSUMER STUDIES

Academic Focus • Commerce, fashion design.
Program Information • Faculty members are drawn from the sponsor's U.S. staff. Field trips to cultural sites in Paris; optional travel to Europe at an extra cost. Students typically earn 6 semester credits per term.
Sessions • Jan–Feb (winter).
Eligibility Requirements • Open to freshmen, sophomores, juniors, seniors, adults; 2.0 GPA; 1 letter of recommendation; no foreign language proficiency required.
Living Arrangements • Students live in hotels. Meals are taken as a group, on one's own, in restaurants.
Costs (2005) • Contact sponsor for cost. $200 nonrefundable deposit required. Financial aid available for all students: scholarships.
For More Information • Center for International Studies, University of Delaware, 186 South College Avenue, Newark, DE 19716-1450; *Phone:* 888-831-4685; *Fax:* 302-831-6042. *E-mail:* studyabroad@udel. edu. *World Wide Web:* http://www.udel.edu/studyabroad/

UNIVERSITY OF DELAWARE
WINTER SESSION IN PARIS, HISTORY

Academic Focus • History.
Program Information • Faculty members are drawn from the sponsor's U.S. staff. Field trips to Normandy. Students typically earn 6 semester credits per term.
Sessions • Jan–Feb (winter).
Eligibility Requirements • Open to freshmen, sophomores, juniors, seniors, adults; 2.0 GPA; 1 letter of recommendation; no foreign language proficiency required.
Living Arrangements • Students live in hotels. Meals are taken on one's own, in restaurants.
Costs (2005) • Contact sponsor for cost. $200 nonrefundable deposit required. Financial aid available for all students: scholarships.
For More Information • Center for International Studies, University of Delaware, 186 South College Avenue, Newark, DE 19716-1450; *Phone:* 888-831-4685; *Fax:* 302-831-6042. *E-mail:* studyabroad@udel. edu. *World Wide Web:* http://www.udel.edu/studyabroad/

UNIVERSITY OF KANSAS
EUROPEAN BUSINESS STUDIES IN PARIS, FRANCE

Hosted by NEGOCIA
Academic Focus • Business administration/management, international business, marketing.
Program Information • Students attend classes at NEGOCIA (Paris, France). Field trips to Brussels, site visits to companies in Paris. Students typically earn 6 semester credits per term.
Sessions • Jun (summer).
Eligibility Requirements • Minimum age 18; open to juniors, seniors, graduate students; major in business, European studies; 2.8 GPA; 2 letters of recommendation; good academic standing at home school; .5 years course work in French.
Living Arrangements • Students live in host institution dormitories. Meals are taken as a group, on one's own, in central dining facility.
Costs (2005) • $4470; includes tuition, housing, some meals, excursions, student support services, medical evacuation and repatriation services. $38 application fee. $300 nonrefundable deposit required. Financial aid available for students from sponsoring institution: scholarships, loans.
For More Information • Ms. Ingrid Horton, Program Coordinator, University of Kansas, Office of Study Abroad, Lippincott Hall, 1410 Jayhawk Boulevard, Room 108, Lawrence, KS 66045-7515; *Phone:* 785-864-3742; *Fax:* 785-864-5040. *E-mail:* osa@ku.edu. *World Wide Web:* http://www.ku.edu/~osa/

UNIVERSITY OF KANSAS
FRENCH LANGUAGE AND CULTURE IN PARIS, FRANCE

Hosted by L'Étoile: Centre de Langue et Vie Françaises
Academic Focus • French language and literature, French studies.

Program Information • Students attend classes at L'Étoile: Centre de Langue et Vie Françaises (Paris, France). Scheduled travel to Normandy, Touraine, Brittany. Students typically earn 6 semester credits per term.
Sessions • Jun–Jul (summer).
Eligibility Requirements • Minimum age 18; open to freshmen, sophomores, juniors, seniors; 2.5 GPA; 2 letters of recommendation; good academic standing at home school; 1 year of college course work in French.
Living Arrangements • Students live in host institution dormitories, hotels. Quarters are shared with host institution students. Meals are taken as a group, on one's own, in central dining facility, in restaurants.
Costs (2005) • $5930; includes tuition, housing, some meals, excursions, student support services, cultural events in Paris, emergency medical evacuation and repatriation service, carte orange in Paris. $38 application fee. $300 nonrefundable deposit required. Financial aid available for students from sponsoring institution: scholarships, loans.
For More Information • Ms. Ingird Horton, Senior Program Coordinator, University of Kansas, Office of Study Abroad, Lippincott Hall, 1410 Jayhawk Boulevard, Room 108, Lawrence, KS 66045-7515; *Phone:* 785-864-3742; *Fax:* 785-864-5040. *E-mail:* osa@ku.edu. *World Wide Web:* http://www.ku.edu/~osa/

UNIVERSITY OF MIAMI
AMERICAN UNIVERSITY OF PARIS SUMMER PROGRAM

Hosted by The American University of Paris
Academic Focus • Business administration/management, communications, French language and literature, psychology.
Program Information • Students attend classes at The American University of Paris (Paris, France). Optional travel to Loire Valley, French Riviera, Versailles, Champagne region at an extra cost. Students typically earn 3–9 semester credits per term.
Sessions • Jun–Jul (summer), Jul–Aug (summer 2).
Eligibility Requirements • Open to freshmen, sophomores, juniors, seniors; 2.5 GPA; no foreign language proficiency required.
Living Arrangements • Students live in host institution dormitories, host family homes. Quarters are shared with students from other programs. Meals are taken on one's own, in residences, in restaurants.
Costs (2005) • $837 per credit hour; includes tuition. $40 application fee. $500 nonrefundable deposit required. Financial aid available for students from sponsoring institution: scholarships, loans.
For More Information • International Education and Exchange Programs, University of Miami, 5050 Brunson Drive, Allen Hall Room 212, PO Box 248005, Coral Gables, FL 33124-1610; *Phone:* 305-284-3434; *Fax:* 305-284-4235. *E-mail:* ieep@miami.edu. *World Wide Web:* http://www.studyabroad.miami.edu/

UNIVERSITY OF MINNESOTA
MODERN PARIS FROM THE FRENCH REVOLUTION TO THE PRESENT

Academic Focus • French studies, history.
Program Information • Faculty members are drawn from the sponsor's U.S. staff. Field trips to Verdun, Paris museums. Students typically earn 3 semester credits per term.
Sessions • Dec–Jan (summer).
Eligibility Requirements • Minimum age 18; open to freshmen, sophomores, juniors, seniors, adults; 2.5 GPA; good academic standing at home school; no foreign language proficiency required.
Living Arrangements • Students live in hotels. Quarters are shared with students from other programs. Meals are taken as a group, on one's own, in residences, in restaurants.
Costs (2006) • Contact sponsor for cost; includes tuition, housing, all meals, insurance, excursions, international airfare, student support services. Financial aid available for students from sponsoring institution: scholarships, loans.
For More Information • Learning Abroad Center, University of Minnesota, 230 Heller Hall, 271 19th Avenue South, Minneapolis, MN 55455; *Phone:* 800-700-UOFM; *Fax:* 612-626-8009. *E-mail:* umabroad@umn.edu. *World Wide Web:* http://www.umabroad.umn.edu/

THE UNIVERSITY OF NORTH CAROLINA AT CHARLOTTE
MARKETING RESEARCH IN PARIS

Academic Focus • Marketing.
Program Information • Faculty members are drawn from the sponsor's U.S. staff. Students typically earn 3 semester credits per term.
Sessions • Jun (summer).
Eligibility Requirements • Minimum age 18; open to sophomores, juniors, seniors; 2.5 GPA; 2 letters of recommendation; no foreign language proficiency required.
Living Arrangements • Students live in locally rented apartments. Meals are taken as a group, in restaurants.
Costs (2005) • $2990; includes tuition, housing, some meals, insurance, student support services. $10 application fee. $300 nonrefundable deposit required. Financial aid available for students from sponsoring institution: scholarships, loans.
For More Information • Mr. Brad Sekulich, Interim Director of Education Abroad, The University of North Carolina at Charlotte, 9201 University City Boulevard, Charlotte, NC 28223-0001; *Phone:* 704-687-2464; *Fax:* 704-687-3168. *E-mail:* edabroad@email.uncc.edu. *World Wide Web:* http://www.uncc.edu/edabroad/

PAU

UNIVERSITY STUDIES ABROAD CONSORTIUM
FRENCH STUDIES: PAU, FRANCE

Hosted by University of Pau
Academic Focus • Anthropology, art history, Basque studies, French language and literature, French studies, history, music, photography.
Program Information • Students attend classes at University of Pau (Pau, France). Field trips to Toulouse, St Jean-Pied-de-Port, Basque country, the Pyrenees Mountains; optional travel to Paris at an extra cost. Students typically earn 5–11 semester credits per term.
Sessions • May–Jun (summer), Jun–Jul (summer 2).
Eligibility Requirements • Minimum age 18; open to freshmen, sophomores, juniors, seniors, graduate students, adults; 2.5 GPA; no foreign language proficiency required.
Living Arrangements • Students live in host institution dormitories, host family homes. Quarters are shared with host institution students. Meals are taken on one's own, with host family, in residences, in central dining facility, in restaurants.
Costs (2007) • $3580–$3760 for 1 session; $7240 for 2 sessions; includes tuition, housing, some meals, insurance, excursions, student support services, some entries to museum and cultural events. $100 application fee. $200 refundable deposit required. Financial aid available for all students: scholarships, loans.
For More Information • University Studies Abroad Consortium, USAC/323, Reno, NV 89557-0093; *Phone:* 775-784-6569; *Fax:* 775-784-6010. *E-mail:* usac@unr.edu. *World Wide Web:* http://usac.unr.edu/

RENNES

UNIVERSITY OF ROCHESTER
FRENCH IN FRANCE

Held at Institut Franco-Americain
Academic Focus • French language and literature.
Program Information • Classes are held on the campus of Institut Franco-Americain (Rennes, France). Faculty members are drawn from the sponsor's U.S. staff. Field trips to Mont-Saint-Michel, Saint-Malo, Normandy beaches. Students typically earn 6 semester credits per term.
Sessions • May–Jun (summer).
Eligibility Requirements • Minimum age 18; open to freshmen, sophomores, juniors, seniors; 1 letter of recommendation; good academic standing at home school; 1 year of college course work in French.
Living Arrangements • Students live in host family homes. Meals are taken with host family, in residences.

Costs (2005) • $3400; includes tuition, housing, some meals, excursions, books and class materials, student support services. $250 refundable deposit required. Financial aid available for students from sponsoring institution: scholarships, loans.
For More Information • Ms. Anne Lutkus, Language Coordinator, University of Rochester, Department of Modern Languages and Cultures, PO Box 270082, Rochester, NY 14627-0082; *Phone:* 585-275-2235; *Fax:* 585-273-1097. *E-mail:* adlt@mail.rochester.edu. *World Wide Web:* http://www.rochester.edu/college/study-abroad/

VILLANOVA UNIVERSITY
INTENSIVE FRENCH LANGUAGE AND LITERATURE
Hosted by University of Burgundy Dijon, University of Rennes II–Haute-Bretagne
Academic Focus • French language and literature.
Program Information • Students attend classes at University of Burgundy Dijon (Dijon, France), University of Rennes II–Haute-Bretagne (Rennes, France). Scheduled travel to Saint Malo; field trips to Le Mont St. Michel, Brocéliande. Students typically earn 6 semester credits per term.
Sessions • Jul–Aug (summer).
Eligibility Requirements • Minimum age 18; open to freshmen, sophomores, juniors, seniors; 2.75 GPA; 2 letters of recommendation; good academic standing at home school; 1 year college course work in French.
Living Arrangements • Students live in host institution dormitories, locally rented apartments, host family homes. Quarters are shared with students from other programs. Meals are taken on one's own, with host family, in residences, in central dining facility.
Costs (2005) • $3850; includes tuition, housing, all meals, excursions. $450 nonrefundable deposit required. Financial aid available for students from sponsoring institution: loans.
For More Information • Dr. Jan Rigaud, Assistant Professor, Villanova University, 800 Lancaster Avenue, Department of Classical Modern Languages and Literature, Villanova, PA 19085; *Phone:* 610-519-6412; *Fax:* 610-519-7649. *E-mail:* jan.rigaud@villanova.edu. *World Wide Web:* http://www.internationalstudies.villanova.edu/

ROANNE

LANGUAGE LIAISON
LEARN FRENCH IN A CHATEAU, ROANNE
Hosted by Language Liaison
Academic Focus • French language and literature.
Program Information • Students attend classes at Language Liaison (Roanne, France). Students typically earn 3–15 semester credits per term.
Sessions • Classes begin weekly, year-round.
Eligibility Requirements • Minimum age 17; open to freshmen, sophomores, juniors, seniors, graduate students, adults; no foreign language proficiency required.
Living Arrangements • Students live in a château. Meals are taken as a group, in central dining facility.
Costs (2005) • Contact sponsor for cost. $175 application fee. Financial aid available for all students: scholarship research service.
For More Information • Ms. Nancy Forman, President, Language Liaison, PO Box 1772, Pacific Palisades, CA 90272; *Phone:* 800-284-4448; *Fax:* 310-454-1706. *E-mail:* learn@languageliaison.com. *World Wide Web:* http://www.languageliaison.com/

SAINT MALO

LINGUA SERVICE WORLDWIDE
VACATION 'N LEARN FRENCH IN FRANCE
Hosted by Centre d'Etudes des Langues
Academic Focus • French language and literature, French studies.
Program Information • Students attend classes at Centre d'Etudes des Langues (Saint Malo, France). Optional travel to cultural sites throughout France at an extra cost. Students typically earn 3 semester credits for 3 weeks, 6 semester credits for 5 weeks.
Sessions • Sessions of 2 or more weeks begin on Mondays, year-round.

Eligibility Requirements • Minimum age 16; open to precollege students, freshmen, sophomores, juniors, seniors, graduate students, adults; no foreign language proficiency required.
Living Arrangements • Students live in host institution dormitories, locally rented apartments, host family homes, hotels. Quarters are shared with host institution students. Meals are taken with host family.
Costs (2006–2007) • Contact sponsor for cost. $100 application fee.
For More Information • Assistant Director, Lingua Service Worldwide, 75 Prospect Street, Suite 4, Huntington, NY 11743; *Phone:* 800-394-5327; *Fax:* 631-271-3441. *E-mail:* linguaservice@att.net. *World Wide Web:* http://www.linguaserviceworldwide.com/

STRASBOURG

MARQUETTE UNIVERSITY
MARQUETTE SUMMER PROGRAM AT IECS–STRASBOURG, FRANCE
Hosted by Robert Schuman University Strasbourg
Academic Focus • French language and literature, marketing, political science and government.
Program Information • Students attend classes at Robert Schuman University Strasbourg (Strasbourg, France). Field trips to Frankfurt, Germany, Basel, Switzerland. Students typically earn 7 semester credits per term.
Sessions • Jun (summer).
Eligibility Requirements • Open to sophomores, juniors, seniors; major in business, economics, political science, international affairs; course work in business/economics; 2.5 GPA; intermediate French.
Living Arrangements • Students live in locally rented apartments, hotels. Quarters are shared with students from other programs. Meals are taken on one's own, in residences, in restaurants.
Costs (2006–2007) • $2700; includes tuition, housing, excursions, books and class materials, student support services. $500 refundable deposit required. Financial aid available for students from sponsoring institution: scholarships, loans.
For More Information • Dr. Jamshid Hosseini, Director of International Business Studies and Study Abroad, Marquette University, College of Business Administration, 606 North 13th Street, David Strat, Jr. Building, Milwaukee, WI 53233; *Phone:* 414-288-3433; *Fax:* 414-288-7440. *E-mail:* jamshid.hosseini@marquette.edu. *World Wide Web:* http://www.marquette.edu/studyabroad/

SYRACUSE UNIVERSITY
ENGINEERING INTERNSHIPS AND RESEARCH PROJECTS IN STRASBOURG
Hosted by Syracuse University–Strasbourg
Academic Focus • Electrical engineering, engineering, mechanical engineering.
Program Information • Students attend classes at Syracuse University–Strasbourg (Strasbourg, France). Students typically earn 3–7 semester credits per term.
Sessions • May–Jul (summer).
Eligibility Requirements • Open to sophomores, juniors, seniors, graduate students; 1 letter of recommendation; good academic standing at home school; no foreign language proficiency required.
Living Arrangements • Students live in host family homes. Meals are taken with host family, in residences.
Costs (2005) • $4000 for 3 credits; $7000 for 7 credits; includes tuition, housing, some meals, international student ID, student support services. $55 application fee. $350 nonrefundable deposit required. Financial aid available for all students: loans, need-based tuition grants.
For More Information • Ms. Daisy Fried, Associate Director, Syracuse University, 106 Walnut Place, Syracuse, NY 13244-4170; *Phone:* 800-251-9674; *Fax:* 315-443-4593. *E-mail:* dipasum@syr.edu. *World Wide Web:* http://suabroad.syr.edu/

SYRACUSE UNIVERSITY
HUMAN RIGHTS AND CONFLICT RESOLUTION IN EUROPE
Hosted by Syracuse University–Strasbourg
Academic Focus • Political science and government.

Program Information • Students attend classes at Syracuse University–Strasbourg (Strasbourg, France). Scheduled travel; field trips to Geneva, Colmar. Students typically earn 6 semester credits per term.
Sessions • May–Jul (summer).
Eligibility Requirements • Open to freshmen, sophomores, juniors, seniors, graduate students; 2.5 GPA; 1 letter of recommendation; good academic standing at home school; no foreign language proficiency required.
Living Arrangements • Students live in host family homes. Meals are taken with host family, in residences.
Costs (2005) • $6400; includes tuition, housing, some meals, excursions, international student ID, student support services. $55 application fee. $350 nonrefundable deposit required. Financial aid available for all students: scholarships, loans, need-based tuition grants.
For More Information • Mrs. Daisy Fried, Associate Director, Syracuse University, 106 Walnut Place, Syracuse, NY 13244-4170; *Phone:* 800-251-9674; *Fax:* 315-443-4593. *E-mail:* dipasum@syr.edu. *World Wide Web:* http://suabroad.syr.edu/

SYRACUSE UNIVERSITY
SUMMER INTERNSHIPS IN STRASBOURG

Hosted by Syracuse University–Strasbourg
Academic Focus • Full curriculum.
Program Information • Students attend classes at Syracuse University–Strasbourg (Strasbourg, France). Students typically earn 6 semester credits per term.
Sessions • May–Jul (summer).
Eligibility Requirements • Open to juniors, seniors, adults; 1 letter of recommendation; good academic standing at home school; basic knowledge of French.
Living Arrangements • Students live in host family homes. Meals are taken with host family, in residences.
Costs (2005) • $6140; includes tuition, some meals, international student ID, student support services. $55 application fee. $350 nonrefundable deposit required. Financial aid available for all students: loans, need-based tuition grants.
For More Information • Ms. Daisy Fried, Associate Director, Syracuse University, 106 Walnut Place, Syracuse, NY 13244-4170; *Phone:* 800-251-9674; *Fax:* 315-443-4593. *E-mail:* dipasum@syr.edu. *World Wide Web:* http://suabroad.syr.edu/

UNIVERSITY OF IDAHO
FRENCH STUDIES PROGRAM

Hosted by Institut International d'Etudes Francaises IIEF
Academic Focus • Art history, creative writing, French language and literature.
Program Information • Students attend classes at Institut International d'Etudes Francaises IIEF (Strasbourg, France). Field trips to local attractions. Students typically earn 3–4 semester credits per term.
Sessions • Jun–Jul (summer).
Eligibility Requirements • Open to freshmen, sophomores, juniors, seniors, graduate students, adults; 2.5 GPA; good academic standing at home school; no foreign language proficiency required.
Living Arrangements • Students live in locally rented apartments, program-owned apartments. Quarters are shared with host institution students, students from other programs. Meals are taken on one's own, in residences.
Costs (2006) • $900–$1200; includes tuition, student support services. $150 application fee. $200 refundable deposit required. Financial aid available for students from sponsoring institution: scholarships, loans.
For More Information • Ms. Kate Peterson, Program Advisor, University of Idaho, 901 Paradise Creek Street, LLC 3, Ground Floor, Moscow, ID 83844-1250; *Phone:* 208-885-4075; *Fax:* 208-885-2859. *E-mail:* abroad@uidaho.edu. *World Wide Web:* http://www.webs.uidaho.edu/ipo/abroad/

UNIVERSITY OF KANSAS
ADVANCED FRENCH STUDIES IN STRASBOURG, FRANCE

Hosted by Marc Bloch University (Strasbourg II)

Academic Focus • European studies, French language and literature, French studies.
Program Information • Students attend classes at Marc Bloch University (Strasbourg II) (Strasbourg, France). Scheduled travel to Paris; optional travel to Route du Vin, Colmar, the Vosges at an extra cost. Students typically earn 6 semester credits per term.
Sessions • Jun–Jul (summer).
Eligibility Requirements • Minimum age 18; open to sophomores, juniors, seniors, graduate students; 2.5 GPA; 2 letters of recommendation; good academic standing at home school; 3 years of college course work in French.
Living Arrangements • Students live in host institution dormitories. Quarters are shared with host institution students. Meals are taken as a group, on one's own, in central dining facility, in restaurants.
Costs (2005) • $5300; includes tuition, housing, some meals, student support services, medical evacuation and repatriation services, most excursions. $38 application fee. $300 nonrefundable deposit required. Financial aid available for students from sponsoring institution: scholarships, loans.
For More Information • Ms. Ingrid Horton, Program Coordinator, University of Kansas, Office of Study Abroad, Lippincott Hall, 1410 Jayhawk Boulevard, Room 108, Lawrence, KS 66045-7515; *Phone:* 785-864-3742; *Fax:* 785-864-5040. *E-mail:* osa@ku.edu. *World Wide Web:* http://www.ku.edu/~osa/

TALLOIRES

TUFTS UNIVERSITY
TUFTS IN TALLOIRES (FRANCE)

Hosted by Tufts University
Academic Focus • Art history, botany, French language and literature.
Program Information • Students attend classes at Tufts University (Talloires, France). Scheduled travel to Paris, Provence; field trips to Chamonix, Geneva, Lyon; optional travel to Provence, Paris at an extra cost. Students typically earn 2 semester credits per term.
Sessions • May–Jun (summer).
Eligibility Requirements • Minimum age 18; open to freshmen, sophomores, juniors, seniors; 2.5 GPA; no foreign language proficiency required.
Living Arrangements • Students live in host family homes. Quarters are shared with host institution students. Meals are taken with host family, in residences.
Costs (2006) • $5049; includes tuition, housing, all meals, excursions, student support services. $40 application fee. $500 nonrefundable deposit required. Financial aid available for students from sponsoring institution: scholarships.
For More Information • Ms. Melissa Nicolls, Coordinator, Tufts University, Tufts European Center, 108 Packard Avenue, Medford, MA 02155; *Phone:* 617-627-3290; *Fax:* 617-627-3457. *E-mail:* france@tufts.edu. *World Wide Web:* http://ase.tufts.edu/studyabroad/. Students may also apply through Tufts University, Le Prieure, 74290, Talloires, France.

TOURS

DAVIDSON COLLEGE
DAVIDSON SUMMER PROGRAM IN TOURS, FRANCE

Hosted by Institut de Touraine
Academic Focus • French language and literature.
Program Information • Students attend classes at Institut de Touraine (Tours, France). Scheduled travel to Paris; field trips to La Rochelle, the Loire Valley, Mont-Saint Michel, Saint-Malo. Students typically earn 4 semester credits per term.
Sessions • May–Jun (summer).
Eligibility Requirements • Minimum age 18; open to sophomores, juniors; 2.75 GPA; 1 letter of recommendation; good academic standing at home school; 1 year of college course work in French.
Living Arrangements • Students live in host family homes. Quarters are shared with host institution students. Meals are taken with host family, in residences.

FRANCE
Tours

Costs (2005) • $4500; includes tuition, housing, all meals, excursions, international airfare, international student ID, student support services. $100 application fee. $100 nonrefundable deposit required.

For More Information • Ms. Carolyn Ortmayer, Study Abroad Coordinator, Davidson College, Box 7155, Davidson, NC 28035-7155; *Phone:* 704-894-2250; *Fax:* 704-894-2120. *E-mail:* abroad@davidson.edu. *World Wide Web:* http://www.davidson.edu/international/

FRENCH-AMERICAN EXCHANGE
SUMMER STUDY ABROAD IN TOURS

Hosted by University François Rabelais of Tours
Academic Focus • Art history, civilization studies, French language and literature, French studies, linguistics.
Program Information • Students attend classes at University François Rabelais of Tours (Tours, France). Field trips to the Loire River Valley, vineyards, châteaux; optional travel to Normandy, Brittany, Paris, Riviera, Europe at an extra cost. Students typically earn 6 semester credits per term.
Sessions • Jun–Sep (4 weeks).
Eligibility Requirements • Minimum age 19; open to sophomores, juniors, seniors, graduate students, adults; good academic standing at home school; no foreign language proficiency required.
Living Arrangements • Students live in host institution dormitories, locally rented apartments, host family homes. Quarters are shared with host institution students. Meals are taken on one's own, with host family, in central dining facility, in restaurants.
Costs (2005) • $2695; includes tuition, housing, some meals, books and class materials, lab equipment, student support services. $50 application fee. $500 refundable deposit required.
For More Information • Mr. James Pondolfino, Executive Director, French-American Exchange, 3213 Duke Street, #620, Alexandria, VA 22314; *Phone:* 800-995-5087; *Fax:* 703-823-4447. *E-mail:* info@frenchamericanexchange.com. *World Wide Web:* http://www.frenchamericanexchange.com/

LINGUA SERVICE WORLDWIDE
VACATION 'N LEARN FRENCH IN FRANCE

Hosted by Centre Linguistique pour Etrangeres
Academic Focus • French language and literature, French studies.
Program Information • Students attend classes at Centre Linguistique pour Etrangeres (Tours, France). Optional travel to cultural sites throughout France at an extra cost. Students typically earn 3 semester credits for 3 weeks, 6 semester credits for 5 weeks.
Sessions • Sessions of 2 or more weeks begin on Mondays, year-round.
Eligibility Requirements • Minimum age 16; open to precollege students, freshmen, sophomores, juniors, seniors, graduate students, adults; no foreign language proficiency required.
Living Arrangements • Students live in host institution dormitories, locally rented apartments, host family homes, hotels. Quarters are shared with host institution students. Meals are taken with host family.
Costs (2006–2007) • Contact sponsor for cost. $100 application fee.
For More Information • Assistant Director, Lingua Service Worldwide, 75 Prospect Street, Suite 4, Huntington, NY 11743; *Phone:* 800-394-5327; *Fax:* 631-271-3441. *E-mail:* linguaservice@att.net. *World Wide Web:* http://www.linguaserviceworldwide.com/

MICHIGAN STATE UNIVERSITY
FRENCH LANGUAGE, LITERATURE, AND CULTURE IN TOURS

Hosted by Institut de Touraine
Academic Focus • French language and literature.
Program Information • Students attend classes at Institut de Touraine (Tours, France). Field trips to neighboring cities, castles. Students typically earn 12 semester credits per term.
Sessions • Jun–Jul (summer).
Eligibility Requirements • Minimum age 18; open to freshmen, sophomores, juniors, seniors; 2.5 GPA; good academic standing at home school; faculty approval; 2 years of college course work in French.

Living Arrangements • Students live in host family homes. Meals are taken with host family, in residences.
Costs (2005) • $2865 (estimated); includes housing, some meals, insurance, excursions, student support services. $100 application fee. $200 nonrefundable deposit required. Financial aid available for students from sponsoring institution: scholarships, loans.
For More Information • Ms. Yvonne Squiers, Secretary, Michigan State University, Office of Study Abroad, 109 International Center, East Lansing, MI 48824-1035; *Phone:* 517-353-8920; *Fax:* 517-432-2082. *E-mail:* squiers@msu.edu. *World Wide Web:* http://studyabroad.msu.edu/

RUTGERS, THE STATE UNIVERSITY OF NEW JERSEY
SUMMER INSTITUTE IN EUROPEAN STUDIES IN TOURS, FRANCE

Academic Focus • European studies, political science and government.
Program Information • Faculty members are local instructors hired by the sponsor. Field trips to the Loire Valley. Students typically earn 6 semester credits per term.
Sessions • Jun–Jul (summer).
Eligibility Requirements • Open to freshmen, sophomores, juniors, seniors; 2.5 GPA; 1 letter of recommendation; good academic standing at home school; official transcripts from all tertiary schools attended; no foreign language proficiency required.
Living Arrangements • Students live in locally rented apartments. Meals are taken on one's own, in residences.
Costs (2005) • $3287 for New Jersey residents; $4420 for nonresidents; includes tuition, housing, insurance, excursions, student support services, seminar in French culture. $20 application fee. $500 nonrefundable deposit required. Financial aid available for students from sponsoring institution: scholarships, loans.
For More Information • Ms. Lindy Black, Regional Coordinator, Rutgers, The State University of New Jersey, 102 College Avenue, New Brunswick, NJ 08901-8543; *Phone:* 732-932-7787; *Fax:* 732-932-8659. *E-mail:* ru_abroad@email.rutgers.edu. *World Wide Web:* http://studyabroad.rutgers.edu/

UNIVERSITY OF ALABAMA
ALABAMA IN FRANCE

Hosted by Institut de Touraine
Academic Focus • French language and literature, French studies.
Program Information • Students attend classes at Institut de Touraine (Tours, France). Scheduled travel to Paris; field trips; optional travel to the Loire Valley, the coast of Brittany at an extra cost. Students typically earn 6 semester credits per term.
Sessions • May–Jun (summer).
Eligibility Requirements • Open to freshmen, sophomores, juniors, seniors, graduate students, adults; 2.5 GPA; good academic standing at home school; 1 year of college course work in French.
Living Arrangements • Students live in host family homes. Quarters are shared with host institution students. Meals are taken with host family, in residences.
Costs (2005) • $4390; includes tuition, housing, some meals, excursions, international airfare, international student ID, student support services. $100 application fee. $500 nonrefundable deposit required. Financial aid available for all students: scholarships, loans.
For More Information • Ms. Angela L. Channell, Director of Overseas Study, University of Alabama, Capstone International Center, Box 870254, Tuscaloosa, AL 35487-0254; *Phone:* 205-348-7024; *Fax:* 205-348-5298. *E-mail:* achannel@aalan.ua.edu. *World Wide Web:* http://www.overseas-study.ua.edu/

UNIVERSITY OF PENNSYLVANIA
PENN-IN-TOURS

Held at University of Tours
Academic Focus • Art history, European studies, French language and literature.
Program Information • Classes are held on the campus of University of Tours (Tours, France). Faculty members are drawn from the sponsor's U.S. staff and local instructors hired by the sponsor. Field trips to historic places around Tours. Students typically earn 2 course units per term.

Sessions • May–Jul (summer).

Eligibility Requirements • Open to freshmen, sophomores, juniors, seniors, graduate students, adults; 1 letter of recommendation; good academic standing at home school; language proficiency requirement is dependent on course chosen.

Living Arrangements • Students live in host family homes. Meals are taken with host family.

Costs (2005) • $6200; includes tuition, housing, some meals, insurance, excursions. $50 application fee. $300 nonrefundable deposit required. Financial aid available for students from sponsoring institution: loans.

For More Information • Penn Summer Abroad, University of Pennsylvania, 3440 Market Street, Suite 100, Philadelphia, PA 19104-3335; *Phone:* 215-746-6900; *Fax:* 215-573-2053. *E-mail:* summerabroad@sas.upenn.edu. *World Wide Web:* http://www.sas.upenn.edu/summer/

VILLEFRANCHE

LANGUAGE LIAISON
LEARN FRENCH IN VILLEFRANCHE

Hosted by Language Liaison

Academic Focus • French language and literature.

Program Information • Students attend classes at Language Liaison (Villefranche, France). Field trips; optional travel. Students typically earn 3–9 semester credits per term.

Sessions • Classes begin every week, year-round.

Eligibility Requirements • Minimum age 16; open to precollege students, freshmen, sophomores, juniors, seniors, graduate students, adults; no foreign language proficiency required.

Living Arrangements • Students live in host family homes. Meals are taken on one's own.

Costs (2005) • Contact sponsor for cost. $175 application fee.

For More Information • Ms. Nancy Forman, President, Language Liaison, PO Box 1772, Pacific Palisades, CA 90272; *Phone:* 800-284-4448; *Fax:* 310-454-1706. *E-mail:* learn@languageliaison.com. *World Wide Web:* http://www.languageliaison.com/

LANGUAGE LIAISON
LEARN FRENCH ON THE RIVIERA

Hosted by Language Liaison

Academic Focus • French language and literature.

Program Information • Students attend classes at Language Liaison (Villefranche, France). Field trips; optional travel. Students typically earn 3–15 semester credits per term.

Sessions • New programs begin weekly, year-round.

Eligibility Requirements • Minimum age 16; open to precollege students, freshmen, sophomores, juniors, seniors, graduate students, adults; no foreign language proficiency required.

Living Arrangements • Students live in host family homes, hotels. Meals are taken on one's own, with host family, in residences, in restaurants.

Costs (2005) • Contact sponsor for cost. $175 application fee. Financial aid available for all students: scholarship research service.

For More Information • Ms. Nancy Forman, President, Language Liaison, PO Box 1772, Pacific Palisades, CA 90272; *Phone:* 800-284-4448; *Fax:* 310-454-1706. *E-mail:* learn@languageliaison.com. *World Wide Web:* http://www.languageliaison.com/

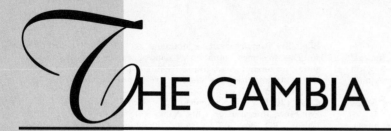HE GAMBIA

SERREKUNDA

ST. JOHN'S UNIVERSITY
THE GAMBIA SUMMER PROGRAM

Held at University of the Gambia

Academic Focus • History.

Program Information • Classes are held on the campus of University of the Gambia (Serrekunda, The Gambia). Faculty members are drawn from the sponsor's U.S. staff. Field trips. Students typically earn 3 semester credits per term.

Sessions • May (summer).

Eligibility Requirements • Minimum age 18; open to freshmen, sophomores, juniors, seniors; 2.75 GPA; 2 letters of recommendation; interview; no foreign language proficiency required.

Living Arrangements • Students live in locally rented apartments. Quarters are shared with host institution students. Meals are taken as a group, in central dining facility.

Costs (2005) • $2700–$3000; includes tuition, housing, some meals, excursions, international airfare, lab equipment. $30 application fee. $750 nonrefundable deposit required. Financial aid available for students from sponsoring institution: scholarships, loans.

For More Information • Dr. Ruth De Paula, Director, Office of Study Abroad Programs, St. John's University, 8000 Utopia Parkway, Jamaica, NY 11439; *Phone:* 718-990-6105; *Fax:* 718-990-2321. *E-mail:* intled@stjohns.edu. *World Wide Web:* http://www.stjohns.edu/studyabroad/

GERMANY

CITY-TO-CITY

CENTER FOR CULTURAL INTERCHANGE
MUNICH, GERMANY LANGUAGE SCHOOL

Hosted by did Language Institute
Academic Focus • German language and literature.
Program Information • Students attend classes at did Language Institute (Berlin), did Language Institute (Munich). Field trips to cultural activities, guided city tours, museum visits.
Sessions • 3, 4, or 6 week sessions begin every Monday, year-round.
Eligibility Requirements • Minimum age 17; open to precollege students, freshmen, sophomores, juniors, seniors, graduate students, adults; no foreign language proficiency required.
Living Arrangements • Students live in host family homes. Quarters are shared with host institution students. Meals are taken with host family, in residences.
Costs (2005) • $2730 for 4 weeks; includes tuition, housing, some meals, insurance, books and class materials, student support services, cultural activities. Financial aid available for students from sponsoring institution: scholarships.
For More Information • Ms. Juliet Jones, Outbound Programs Director, Center for Cultural Interchange, 325 West Huron, Suite 706, Chicago, IL 60610; *Phone:* 866-684-9675; *Fax:* 312-944-2644. *E-mail:* info@cci-exchange. com. *World Wide Web:* http://www.cci-exchange.com/

NORTHERN ILLINOIS UNIVERSITY
ACADEMIC INTERNSHIPS IN GERMANY

Held at Educational Programmes Abroad
Academic Focus • Social services.
Program Information • Classes are held on the campus of Educational Programmes Abroad (Bonn), Educational Programmes Abroad (Cologne). Faculty members are local instructors hired by the sponsor. Optional travel at an extra cost. Students typically earn 6 semester credits per term.
Sessions • Jun–Jul (summer).
Eligibility Requirements • Open to juniors, seniors; 3.0 GPA; 2 letters of recommendation; good academic standing at home school; application essay; résumé; 3 years of college course work in German.
Living Arrangements • Students live in host family homes. Quarters are shared with students from other programs. Meals are taken on one's own, with host family, in residences, in restaurants.
Costs (2005) • $6165; includes tuition, housing, some meals, insurance, international student ID, internship placement. $45 application fee. $500 refundable deposit required. Financial aid available for students from sponsoring institution: regular financial aid.
For More Information • Ms. Emily Gorlewski, Program Assistant, Northern Illinois University, Study Abroad Office, Williston Hall 417, DeKalb, IL 60115; *Phone:* 815-753-0420; *Fax:* 815-753-0825. *E-mail:* niuabroad@niu. edu. *World Wide Web:* http://www.niu.edu/niuabroad/

BAYREUTH

UNIVERSITY OF DELAWARE
WINTER SESSION IN BAYREUTH, GERMANY

Hosted by University of Bayreuth
Academic Focus • German language and literature, German studies.
Program Information • Students attend classes at University of Bayreuth (Bayreuth, Germany). Scheduled travel to Berlin, Munich; field trips to Bamberg, Nuremberg; optional travel to Europe at an extra cost. Students typically earn 6–7 semester credits per term.
Sessions • Jan–Feb (winter).
Eligibility Requirements • Open to freshmen, sophomores, juniors, seniors, adults; 2.0 GPA; 1 letter of recommendation; 1 year of college course work in German.
Living Arrangements • Students live in host family homes. Quarters are shared with host institution students. Meals are taken on one's own, in central dining facility, in restaurants.
Costs (2005) • Contact sponsor for cost. $200 nonrefundable deposit required. Financial aid available for all students: scholarships.
For More Information • Center for International Studies, University of Delaware, 186 South College Avenue, Newark, DE 19716-1450; *Phone:* 888-831-4685; *Fax:* 302-831-6042. *E-mail:* studyabroad@udel.edu. *World Wide Web:* http://www.udel.edu/studyabroad/

BERLIN

LANGUAGE LIAISON
BERLIN–LEARN GERMAN IN BERLIN

Hosted by Language Liaison

Academic Focus • German language and literature.

Program Information • Students attend classes at Language Liaison (Berlin, Germany). Field trips; optional travel at an extra cost. Students typically earn 3–15 semester credits per term.

Sessions • Classes begin weekly, year-round.

Eligibility Requirements • Minimum age 16; open to precollege students, freshmen, sophomores, juniors, seniors, graduate students, adults; no foreign language proficiency required.

Living Arrangements • Students live in host institution dormitories, locally rented apartments, host family homes, hotels. Meals are taken as a group, with host family, in residences, in central dining facility, in restaurants.

Costs (2005) • Contact sponsor for cost. $175 application fee. Financial aid available for all students: scholarship research service.

For More Information • Ms. Nancy Forman, President, Language Liaison, PO Box 1772, Pacific Palisades, CA 90272; *Phone:* 800-284-4448; *Fax:* 310-454-1706. *E-mail:* learn@languageliaison.com. *World Wide Web:* http://www.languageliaison.com/

LEXIA INTERNATIONAL
LEXIA INTERNATIONAL–SUMMER ARCHITECTURE IN BERLIN

Hosted by DAZ–German Architecture Center, Die Neue Schule

Academic Focus • Architecture, art history, drawing/painting, German language and literature, interior design, urban/regional planning, visual and performing arts.

Program Information • Students attend classes at DAZ–German Architecture Center (Berlin, Germany), Die Neue Schule (Berlin, Germany). Field trips to Berlin, Potsdam, Weimar, Dresden; Poland.

Sessions • Jan–Aug (summer).

Eligibility Requirements • Minimum age 18; open to sophomores, juniors, seniors, graduate students, adults; 2.5 GPA; 2 letters of recommendation; good academic standing at home school; no foreign language proficiency required.

Living Arrangements • Students live in locally rented apartments, host family homes. Quarters are shared with host institution students. Meals are taken on one's own, in residences, in central dining facility, in restaurants.

Costs (2006) • $6850; includes tuition, housing, insurance, excursions, international student ID, student support services, transcript. $40 application fee. $300 nonrefundable deposit required. Financial aid available for all students: scholarships, work study.

For More Information • Lexia International, 23 South Main Street, Hanover, NH 03755; *Phone:* 800-775-3942; *Fax:* 603-643-9898. *E-mail:* info@lexiaintl.org. *World Wide Web:* http://www.lexiaintl.org/

LEXIA INTERNATIONAL
LEXIA INTERNATIONAL–THE SUMMER VISUAL CULTURE PROGRAM IN BERLIN

Hosted by Die Neue Schule

Academic Focus • Art history, drawing/painting, film and media studies, fine/studio arts, German language and literature, interior design, photography, visual and performing arts.

Program Information • Students attend classes at Die Neue Schule (Berlin, Germany). Field trips to Berlin, Dresden, Potsdam, Weimar; Poland.

Sessions • Jun–Aug (summer).

Eligibility Requirements • Minimum age 18; open to freshmen, sophomores, juniors, seniors, graduate students, adults; 2.5 GPA; 2 letters of recommendation; good academic standing at home school; no foreign language proficiency required.

Living Arrangements • Students live in locally rented apartments, host family homes. Quarters are shared with host institution students. Meals are taken on one's own, in residences, in central dining facility, in restaurants.

Costs (2006) • $6850; includes tuition, housing, insurance, excursions, international student ID, student support services. $40 application fee. $300 nonrefundable deposit required. Financial aid available for all students: scholarships, work study.

For More Information • Lexia International, 23 South Main Street, Hanover, NH 03755; *Phone:* 800-775-3942; *Fax:* 603-643-9899. *E-mail:* info@lexiaintl.org. *World Wide Web:* http://www.lexiaintl.org/

LEXIA INTERNATIONAL
LEXIA SUMMER IN BERLIN

Hosted by Die Neue Schule

Academic Focus • Anthropology, architecture, area studies, art, art history, civilization studies, comparative history, cultural studies, economics, ethnic studies, geography, German language and literature, German studies, history, interdisciplinary studies, international affairs, liberal studies, literature, photography, political science and government, social sciences, sociology, visual and performing arts.

Program Information • Students attend classes at Die Neue Schule (Berlin, Germany). Field trips to Potsdam, Poland, Weimar, Dresden. Students typically earn 8–10 semester credits per term.

Sessions • Jun–Aug (summer).

Eligibility Requirements • Minimum age 18; open to freshmen, sophomores, juniors, seniors, graduate students, adults; 2.5 GPA; 2 letters of recommendation; no foreign language proficiency required.

Living Arrangements • Students live in locally rented apartments, host family homes. Quarters are shared with host institution students. Meals are taken on one's own, with host family, in residences, in restaurants.

Costs (2006) • $6850; includes tuition, housing, some meals, insurance, excursions, international student ID, student support services, transcript. $40 application fee. $300 nonrefundable deposit required. Financial aid available for all students: scholarships, work study.

For More Information • Lexia International, 23 South Main Street, Hanover, NH 03755; *Phone:* 800-775-3942; *Fax:* 603-643-9899. *E-mail:* info@lexiaintl.org. *World Wide Web:* http://www.lexiaintl.org/

LINGUA SERVICE WORLDWIDE
VACATION 'N LEARN GERMAN IN GERMANY

Hosted by Deutsche in Deutschland

Academic Focus • German language and literature, German studies.

Program Information • Students attend classes at Deutsche in Deutschland (Berlin, Germany). Field trips; optional travel at an extra cost. Students typically earn 3 semester credits for 3 weeks, 6 semester credits for 5 weeks.

Sessions • Sessions of 2 or more weeks year-round; start of each month for beginners, every other Monday for all others.

Eligibility Requirements • Minimum age 16; open to precollege students, freshmen, sophomores, juniors, seniors, graduate students, adults; no foreign language proficiency required.

Living Arrangements • Students live in host institution dormitories, locally rented apartments, host family homes, hotels. Quarters are shared with host institution students. Meals are taken with host family.

Costs (2006–2007) • Contact sponsor for cost. $100 application fee.

For More Information • Assistant Director, Lingua Service Worldwide, 75 Prospect Street, Suite 4, Huntington, NY 11743; *Phone:* 800-394-5327; *Fax:* 631-271-3441. *E-mail:* linguaservice@att.net. *World Wide Web:* http://www.linguaserviceworldwide.com/

LINGUA SERVICE WORLDWIDE
VACATION 'N LEARN GERMAN IN GERMANY

Hosted by GLS Sprachenzentrum

Academic Focus • German language and literature, German studies.

Program Information • Students attend classes at GLS Sprachenzentrum (Berlin, Germany). Field trips; optional travel at an extra cost. Students typically earn 3 semester credits for 3 weeks, 6 semester credits for 5 weeks.

Sessions • Sessions of 2 or more weeks year-round; start of each month for beginners, every other Monday for all others.

Eligibility Requirements • Minimum age 16; open to precollege students, freshmen, sophomores, juniors, seniors, graduate students, adults; no foreign language proficiency required.

Living Arrangements • Students live in host institution dormitories, locally rented apartments, host family homes, hotels. Quarters are shared with host institution students. Meals are taken with host family.

Costs (2006–2007) • Contact sponsor for cost. $100 application fee.

For More Information • Assistant Director, Lingua Service Worldwide, 75 Prospect Street, Suite 4, Huntington, NY 11743; *Phone:* 800-394-5327; *Fax:* 631-271-3441. *E-mail:* linguaservice@att.net. *World Wide Web:* http://www.linguaserviceworldwide.com/

MICHIGAN STATE UNIVERSITY
GERMAN EMPLOYMENT RELATIONS: BERLIN STUDY ABROAD

Academic Focus • Labor and industrial relations.

Program Information • Faculty members are drawn from the sponsor's U.S. staff. Field trips to employers, labor unions, German Labor Ministry. Students typically earn 3 semester credits per term.

Sessions • May (summer).

Eligibility Requirements • Minimum age 18; open to graduate students; course work in collective bargaining; 3.0 GPA; good academic standing at home school; graduate students only; faculty approval; no foreign language proficiency required.

Living Arrangements • Students live in hotels. Meals are taken on one's own, in restaurants.

Costs (2005) • $859 (estimated); includes housing, some meals, insurance, student support services, S-Bahn rail pass. $100 application fee. $200 nonrefundable deposit required. Financial aid available for students from sponsoring institution: scholarships, loans.

For More Information • Ms. Yvonne Squiers, Secretary, Michigan State University, Office of Study Abroad, 109 International Center, East Lansing, MI 48824-1035; *Phone:* 517-353-8920; *Fax:* 517-432-2082. *E-mail:* squiers@msu.edu. *World Wide Web:* http://studyabroad.msu.edu/

NEW YORK UNIVERSITY
NYU IN BERLIN

Held at Humboldt University of Berlin

Academic Focus • Architecture, art history, German language and literature, German studies, history.

Program Information • Classes are held on the campus of Humboldt University of Berlin (Berlin, Germany). Faculty members are drawn from the sponsor's U.S. staff and local instructors hired by the sponsor. Scheduled travel to Dresden; field trips to Potsdam, places of cultural interest. Students typically earn 8 semester credits per term.

Sessions • Jun–Jul (summer).

Eligibility Requirements • Minimum age 18; open to freshmen, sophomores, juniors, seniors; 3.0 GPA; good academic standing at home school; personal statement for non-New York University students; no foreign language proficiency required.

Living Arrangements • Students live in locally rented apartments. Meals are taken on one's own, in restaurants.

Costs (2006) • $6834; includes tuition, housing, excursions, student support services, program fee. $25 application fee. $300 nonrefundable deposit required. Financial aid available for students from sponsoring institution: loans.

For More Information • Office of Summer Sessions, New York University, 7 East 12th Street, 6th Floor, New York, NY 10003; *Phone:* 212-998-2292; *Fax:* 212-995-4642. *E-mail:* summer.info@nyu.edu. *World Wide Web:* http://www.nyu.edu/global/studyabroad.html

UNIVERSITY OF MINNESOTA
METROPOLIS ON FILM: EXPLORING GERMAN FILM/HISTORY IN BERLIN

Academic Focus • Film and media studies, history.

Program Information • Faculty members are drawn from the sponsor's U.S. staff and local instructors hired by the sponsor. Field trips to Sachsunhausen, Potsdam, Dresden, Sprewald. Students typically earn 3 semester credits per term.

Sessions • May–Jun (summer).

Eligibility Requirements • Minimum age 18; open to freshmen, sophomores, juniors, seniors, adults; 2.5 GPA; good academic standing at home school; no foreign language proficiency required.

Living Arrangements • Students live in host institution dormitories, hotels. Quarters are shared with students from other programs. Meals are taken as a group, on one's own, in central dining facility, in restaurants.

Costs (2006) • Contact sponsor for cost; includes tuition, housing, some meals, insurance, excursions, international airfare, student support services. Financial aid available for students from sponsoring institution: scholarships, loans.

For More Information • Learning Abroad Center, University of Minnesota, 230 Heller Hall, 271 19th Avenue South, Minneapolis, MN 55455; *Phone:* 800-700-UOFM; *Fax:* 612-626-8009. *E-mail:* umabroad@umn.edu. *World Wide Web:* http://www.umabroad.umn.edu/

UNIVERSITY OF ROCHESTER
GERMAN IN GERMANY

Hosted by Studienforum Berlin

Academic Focus • German language and literature, German studies.

Program Information • Students attend classes at Studienforum Berlin (Berlin, Germany). Field trips to Dresden, Potsdam, Erfurt. Students typically earn 8 semester credits per term.

Sessions • May–Jul (summer).

Eligibility Requirements • Minimum age 18; open to freshmen, sophomores, juniors, seniors; 1 letter of recommendation; good academic standing at home school; 1 year of college course work in German.

Living Arrangements • Students live in host family homes. Meals are taken with host family, in residences.

Costs (2005) • $4240; includes tuition, housing, some meals, excursions, books and class materials, student support services. $250 refundable deposit required. Financial aid available for students from sponsoring institution: scholarships, loans.

For More Information • Ms. Anne Lutkus, Language Coordinator, University of Rochester, Department of Modern Languages and Cultures, PO Box 270082, Rochester, NY 14627-0082; *Phone:* 585-275-2235; *Fax:* 585-273-1097. *E-mail:* adlt@mail.rochester.edu. *World Wide Web:* http://www.rochester.edu/college/study-abroad/

BONN

UNIVERSITY OF ROCHESTER
INTERNSHIPS IN EUROPE–GERMANY

Academic Focus • Advertising and public relations, art administration, business administration/management, computer science, drama/theater, history, journalism, law and legal studies, political science and government, psychology, social sciences.

Program Information • Field trips to Cologne, Bonn (introductory tour); optional travel to Heidelberg, Koblenz, Limburg an der Lahn at an extra cost. Students typically earn 8 semester credits per term.

Sessions • May–Jul (summer).

Eligibility Requirements • Open to juniors, seniors; 3.0 GPA; 2 letters of recommendation; good academic standing at home school; 2 years of college course work in German.

Living Arrangements • Students live in locally rented apartments, host family homes. Meals are taken on one's own, with host family, in residences.

Costs (2005) • $6450; includes tuition, housing, student support services, some meals if living in a homestay. $30 application fee. $300 nonrefundable deposit required. Financial aid available for students from sponsoring institution: loans.

For More Information • Ms. Jacqueline Levine, Study Abroad Director, University of Rochester, Center for Study Abroad, PO Box 270376, Lattimore 206, Rochester, NY 14627-0376; *Phone:* 585-275-7532; *Fax:* 585-461-5131. *E-mail:* abroad@mail.rochester.edu. *World Wide Web:* http://www.rochester.edu/college/study-abroad/

BRAUNSCHWEIG

UNIVERSITY AT ALBANY, STATE UNIVERSITY OF NEW YORK
LANGUAGE AND CULTURE STUDIES AT BRAUNSCHWEIG UNIVERSITY

Hosted by Technische University Carolo Wilhelmina
Academic Focus • German language and literature, German studies.
Program Information • Students attend classes at Technische University Carolo Wilhelmina (Braunschweig, Germany). Scheduled travel to Berlin; field trips to local sites, Hanover, Harz Mountains. Students typically earn 6 semester credits per term.
Sessions • Jul–Aug (summer).
Eligibility Requirements • Open to precollege students, freshmen, sophomores, juniors, seniors, adults; 1 letter of recommendation; good academic standing at home school; 1 year of college course work in German.
Living Arrangements • Students live in host institution dormitories, locally rented apartments, host family homes. Quarters are shared with host institution students, students from other programs. Meals are taken on one's own, in residences, in central dining facility, in restaurants.
Costs (2005–2006) • Contact sponsor for cost. $150 nonrefundable deposit required. Financial aid available for students from sponsoring institution: all customary sources.
For More Information • University at Albany, State University of New York, Office of International Education, LI 66, Albany, NY 12222; *Phone:* 518-442-3525; *Fax:* 518-442-3338. *E-mail:* intled@uamail.albany.edu. *World Wide Web:* http://www.albany.edu/studyabroad/

BREMEN

UNIVERSITY OF DELAWARE
WINTER SESSION IN BREMEN: ENGINEERING

Hosted by University of Bremen
Academic Focus • Engineering, history.
Program Information • Students attend classes at University of Bremen (Bremen, Germany). Scheduled travel to Berlin; field trips to historic sites, engineering institutes. Students typically earn 6 semester credits per term.
Sessions • Jan–Feb (winter).
Eligibility Requirements • Open to freshmen, sophomores, juniors, seniors, adults; 2.0 GPA; 1 letter of recommendation; no foreign language proficiency required.
Living Arrangements • Students live in locally rented apartments. Quarters are shared with host institution students. Meals are taken on one's own, in residences.
Costs (2005) • Contact sponsor for cost. $200 nonrefundable deposit required. Financial aid available for all students: scholarships.
For More Information • Center for International Studies, University of Delaware, 186 South College Avenue, Newark, DE 19716-1450; *Phone:* 888-831-4685; *Fax:* 302-831-6042. *E-mail:* studyabroad@udel.edu. *World Wide Web:* http://www.udel.edu/studyabroad/

UNIVERSITY OF NORTH CAROLINA AT WILMINGTON
GERMANY SUMMER PROGRAM–BUSINESS

Hosted by Hochschule Bremen
Academic Focus • Business administration/management, German language and literature.
Program Information • Students attend classes at Hochschule Bremen (Bremen, Germany). Field trips to various sites in Germany; optional travel to Berlin, Munich, Poland, Prague at an extra cost. Students typically earn 6 semester credits per term.
Sessions • Jul–Aug (summer).
Eligibility Requirements • Open to juniors; good academic standing at home school; no foreign language proficiency required.
Living Arrangements • Students live in hotels. Quarters are shared with students from other programs. Meals are taken on one's own, in restaurants.

Costs (2005) • $3659; includes tuition, housing, insurance, international airfare, books and class materials. $200 nonrefundable deposit required.
For More Information • Ms. Elizabeth A. Adams, Director, Education Abroad, University of North Carolina at Wilmington, 601 South College Road, Wilmington, NC 28403-5965; *Phone:* 910-962-3685; *Fax:* 910-962-4053. *E-mail:* studyabroad@uncw.edu. *World Wide Web:* http://www.uncw.edu/intprogs/

UNIVERSITY OF NORTH CAROLINA AT WILMINGTON
SUMMER PROGRAM IN GERMANY (LANGUAGE)

Hosted by Hochschule Bremen
Academic Focus • German language and literature.
Program Information • Students attend classes at Hochschule Bremen (Bremen, Germany). Scheduled travel to Bonn or Berlin; field trips to various sites in Germany; optional travel to Berlin, Munich, Poland, Prague at an extra cost. Students typically earn 6 semester credits per term.
Sessions • Jul–Aug (summer).
Eligibility Requirements • Minimum age 19; good academic standing at home school; no foreign language proficiency required.
Living Arrangements • Students live in host family homes. Quarters are shared with students from other programs. Meals are taken on one's own, in residences.
Costs (2005) • $2032 for North Carolina residents; $3632 for nonresidents; includes tuition, housing, insurance, excursions, student support services. $200 nonrefundable deposit required. Financial aid available for students from sponsoring institution: scholarships, loans.
For More Information • Ms. Elizabeth A. Adams, Director, Education Abroad, University of North Carolina at Wilmington, 601 South College Road, Wilmington, NC 28403-5965; *Phone:* 910-962-3685; *Fax:* 910-962-4053. *E-mail:* studyabroad@uncw.edu. *World Wide Web:* http://www.uncw.edu/intprogs/

COLOGNE

LINGUA SERVICE WORLDWIDE
VACATION 'N LEARN GERMAN IN GERMANY

Hosted by Carl Duisberg Center
Academic Focus • German language and literature, German studies.
Program Information • Students attend classes at Carl Duisberg Center (Cologne, Germany). Field trips; optional travel at an extra cost. Students typically earn 3 semester credits for 3 weeks, 6 semester credits for 5 weeks.
Sessions • Sessions of 2 or more weeks year-round; start of each month for beginners, every other Monday for all others.
Eligibility Requirements • Minimum age 16; open to precollege students, freshmen, sophomores, juniors, seniors, graduate students, adults; no foreign language proficiency required.
Living Arrangements • Students live in host institution dormitories, locally rented apartments, host family homes, hotels. Quarters are shared with host institution students. Meals are taken with host family.
Costs (2006–2007) • Contact sponsor for cost. $100 application fee.
For More Information • Assistant Director, Lingua Service Worldwide, 75 Prospect Street, Suite 4, Huntington, NY 11743; *Phone:* 800-394-5327; *Fax:* 631-271-3441. *E-mail:* linguaservice@att.net. *World Wide Web:* http://www.linguaserviceworldwide.com/

STATE UNIVERSITY OF NEW YORK COLLEGE AT CORTLAND
GERMAN SPORT UNIVERSITY OF COLOGNE–COLOGNE, GERMANY

Hosted by German Sport University of Cologne
Academic Focus • Health and physical education, sports management.
Program Information • Students attend classes at German Sport University of Cologne (Cologne, Germany). Scheduled travel to Berlin; field trips to local and regional institutions and exhibits;

optional travel to continental European cities at an extra cost. Students typically earn 12–16 semester credits per term.

Sessions • May–Jul (summer).

Eligibility Requirements • Minimum age 19; open to sophomores, juniors, seniors; major in physical education, sports management, coaching, rehabilitation; 2.5 GPA; 2 letters of recommendation; good academic standing at home school; 1 year of college course work in German.

Living Arrangements • Students live in host institution dormitories. Quarters are shared with students from other programs. Meals are taken on one's own, in central dining facility.

Costs (2006) • $5622; includes tuition, housing, all meals, insurance, excursions, international airfare, books and class materials, international student ID, student support services, residence permit. $20 application fee. $250 nonrefundable deposit required. Financial aid available for students from sponsoring institution: scholarships, loans.

For More Information • Ms. Liz McCartney, Assistant Director, Office of International Programs, State University of New York College at Cortland, PO Box 2000, Cortland, NY 13045; *Phone:* 607-753-2209; *Fax:* 607-753-5989. *E-mail:* cortlandabroad@cortland. edu. *World Wide Web:* http://www.cortlandabroad.com/

EUTIN

UNIVERSITY OF KANSAS
INTERMEDIATE GERMAN LANGUAGE AND CULTURE IN EUTIN, GERMANY

Academic Focus • German language and literature, German studies.

Program Information • Faculty members are drawn from the sponsor's U.S. staff and local instructors hired by the sponsor. Scheduled travel to Vienna, Munich, Badenheim, Mainz, Berlin, Salzburg; field trips to Lübeck, Kiel, Schwerin, Hamburg, Schleswig, Flensburg, the North Sea coast. Students typically earn 9 semester credits per term.

Sessions • May–Jul (summer).

Eligibility Requirements • Minimum age 18; open to freshmen, sophomores, juniors, seniors; 2.5 GPA; 2 letters of recommendation; good academic standing at home school; 1 year of college course work in German.

Living Arrangements • Students live in host family homes, hotels. Meals are taken as a group, on one's own, with host family, in residences, in restaurants.

Costs (2005) • $4700; includes tuition, housing, all meals, excursions, student support services, medical evacuation and repatriation services. $38 application fee. $300 nonrefundable deposit required. Financial aid available for students from sponsoring institution: scholarships, loans.

For More Information • Ms. Justine Hamilton, Program Coordinator, University of Kansas, Office of Study Abroad, Lippincott Hall, 1410 Jayhawk Boulevard, Room 108, Lawrence, KS 66045-7515; *Phone:* 785-864-3742; *Fax:* 785-864-5040. *E-mail:* osa@ku.edu. *World Wide Web:* http://www.ku.edu/~osa/

FRANKFURT

LINGUA SERVICE WORLDWIDE
VACATION 'N LEARN GERMAN IN GERMANY

Hosted by Deutsche in Deutschland

Academic Focus • German language and literature, German studies.

Program Information • Students attend classes at Deutsche in Deutschland (Frankfurt, Germany). Optional travel at an extra cost. Students typically earn 3 semester credits for 3 weeks, 6 semester credits for 5 weeks.

Sessions • Sessions of 2 or more weeks year-round; start of each month for beginners, every other Monday for all others.

Eligibility Requirements • Minimum age 16; open to precollege students, freshmen, sophomores, juniors, seniors, graduate students, adults; no foreign language proficiency required.

Living Arrangements • Students live in host institution dormitories, locally rented apartments, host family homes, hotels. Quarters are shared with host institution students. Meals are taken with host family.

Costs (2006–2007) • Contact sponsor for cost. $100 application fee.

For More Information • Assistant Director, Lingua Service Worldwide, 75 Prospect Street, Suite 4, Huntington, NY 11743; *Phone:* 800-394-5327; *Fax:* 631-271-3441. *E-mail:* linguaservice@att. net. *World Wide Web:* http://www.linguaserviceworldwide.com/

HAMBURG

LANGUAGE LIAISON
LEARN GERMAN IN GERMANY–HAMBURG

Hosted by Language Liaison

Academic Focus • German language and literature.

Program Information • Students attend classes at Language Liaison (Hamburg, Germany). Field trips; optional travel at an extra cost. Students typically earn 3–15 semester credits per term.

Sessions • Classes begin weekly, year-round.

Eligibility Requirements • Minimum age 17; open to freshmen, sophomores, juniors, seniors, graduate students, adults; no foreign language proficiency required.

Living Arrangements • Students live in host family homes, hotels. Meals are taken with host family, in residences, in restaurants.

Costs (2005) • Contact sponsor for cost. $175 application fee. Financial aid available for all students: scholarship research service.

For More Information • Ms. Nancy Forman, President, Language Liaison, PO Box 1772, Pacific Palisades, CA 90272; *Phone:* 800-284-4448; *Fax:* 310-454-1706. *E-mail:* learn@languageliaison. com. *World Wide Web:* http://www.languageliaison.com/

LINGUA SERVICE WORLDWIDE
VACATION 'N LEARN GERMAN IN GERMANY

Hosted by German Language Centre

Academic Focus • German language and literature, German studies.

Program Information • Students attend classes at German Language Centre (Hamburg, Germany). Field trips; optional travel at an extra cost. Students typically earn 3 semester credits for 3 weeks, 6 semester credits for 5 weeks.

Sessions • Sessions of 2 or more weeks year-round; start of each month for beginners, every other Monday for all others.

Eligibility Requirements • Minimum age 16; open to precollege students, freshmen, sophomores, juniors, seniors, graduate students, adults; no foreign language proficiency required.

Living Arrangements • Students live in host institution dormitories, locally rented apartments, host family homes, hotels. Quarters are shared with host institution students. Meals are taken with host family.

Costs (2006–2007) • Contact sponsor for cost. $100 application fee.

For More Information • Assistant Director, Lingua Service Worldwide, 75 Prospect Street, Suite 4, Huntington, NY 11743; *Phone:* 800-394-5327; *Fax:* 631-271-3441. *E-mail:* linguaservice@att. net. *World Wide Web:* http://www.linguaserviceworldwide.com/

HEIDELBERG

COLLEGE CONSORTIUM FOR INTERNATIONAL STUDIES–OCEAN COUNTY COLLEGE AND ST. AMBROSE UNIVERSITY
INTENSIVE GERMAN LANGUAGE

Hosted by Collegium Palatinum

Academic Focus • German language and literature.

Program Information • Students attend classes at Collegium Palatinum (Heidelberg, Germany). Field trips to Michelstadt, Frankfurt, Speyer, Stuttgart; optional travel to other countries in Europe at an extra cost. Students typically earn 12 semester credits per term.

Sessions • 8 week sessions, year-round.

Eligibility Requirements • Minimum age 18; open to freshmen, sophomores, juniors, seniors, graduate students, adults; 2.5 GPA; 2 letters of recommendation; no foreign language proficiency required.

Living Arrangements • Students live in host institution dormitories, locally rented apartments, host family homes. Quarters are shared with host institution students, students from other programs. Meals are taken on one's own, with host family, in residences, in central dining facility, in restaurants.

Costs (2006) • $3695; includes tuition, housing, insurance, student support services, cultural activity, CCIS and administrative fees, some student support services. $20 application fee. $200 nonrefundable deposit required. Financial aid available for students from sponsoring institution: scholarships, loans, federal financial aid.

For More Information • College Consortium for International Studies–Ocean County College and St. Ambrose University, 2000 P Street, NW, Suite 503, Washington, DC 20036; *Phone:* 800-453-6956; *Fax:* 202-223-0999. *E-mail:* info@ccisabroad.org. *World Wide Web:* http://www.ccisabroad.org/. Students may also apply through Ocean County College, International Education, PO Box 2001, Toms River, NJ 08754-2001; St. Ambrose University, Study Abroad Office, 518 West Locust Street, Davenport, IA 52803.

HEIDELBERG COLLEGE
HEIDELBERG@HEIDELBERG

Hosted by Heidelberg University–American Junior Year Center

Academic Focus • German language and literature, German studies.

Program Information • Students attend classes at Heidelberg University–American Junior Year Center (Heidelberg, Germany). Scheduled travel to Berlin (4-day seminar); field trips to Strassburg, the Black Forest, the Rhine River. Students typically earn 6-8 semester credits per term.

Sessions • May-Jul (summer).

Eligibility Requirements • Open to freshmen, sophomores; 2.8 GPA; 2 letters of recommendation; good academic standing at home school; 1 year college course work in German.

Living Arrangements • Students live in host institution dormitories, locally rented apartments. Quarters are shared with host institution students. Meals are taken on one's own, in residences, in central dining facility, in restaurants.

Costs (2006) • $4210; includes tuition, housing, some meals, insurance, excursions, books and class materials, student support services, German Rail Pass. $20 application fee.

For More Information • Ms. Peggy George, Administrative Assistant, Heidelberg College, 310 East Market Street, Tiffin, OH 44883; *Phone:* 419-448-2062; *Fax:* 419-448-2217. *E-mail:* ajy@heidelberg.edu. *World Wide Web:* http://www.heidelberg.edu/offices/global-ed/study-abroad/ajy/

HOLZKIRCHEN

UNIVERSITY OF KANSAS
ADVANCED GERMAN LANGUAGE AND CULTURE IN HOLZKIRCHEN, GERMANY

Hosted by Volkshochschule Holzkirchen

Academic Focus • German language and literature, German studies.

Program Information • Students attend classes at Volkshochschule Holzkirchen (Holzkirchen, Germany). Scheduled travel to Cologne, Wurzburg, Bonn, Weimar, Dresden, Eisenach, Rothenburg ob der Tauber, Nuremberg, Berlin; field trips to Salzburg, Chiemsee, Landkreis Miesbach, Berchtesgaden, Neuschwanstein, Dachau. Students typically earn 9 semester credits per term.

Sessions • Jun-Aug (summer).

Eligibility Requirements • Minimum age 18; open to freshmen, sophomores, juniors, seniors, graduate students; 2.5 GPA; 2 letters of recommendation; good academic standing at home school; 2 years of college course work in German.

Living Arrangements • Students live in host family homes, hotels. Quarters are shared with host institution students. Meals are taken as a group, on one's own, with host family, in residences, in restaurants.

Costs (2005) • $4800; includes tuition, housing, all meals, excursions, student support services, commuter pass for metropolitan Munich, medical evacuation and repatriation services. $38 application fee. $300 nonrefundable deposit required. Financial aid available for students from sponsoring institution: scholarships, loans.

For More Information • Ms. Justine Hamilton, Program Coordinator, University of Kansas, Office of Study Abroad, Lippincott Hall, 1410 Jayhawk Boulevard, Room 108, Lawrence, KS 66045-7515; *Phone:* 785-864-3742; *Fax:* 785-864-5040. *E-mail:* osa@ku.edu. *World Wide Web:* http://www.ku.edu/~osa/

KAISERSLAUTERN

MICHIGAN STATE UNIVERSITY
ELECTRICAL AND COMPUTER ENGINEERING IN KAISERSLAUTERN

Hosted by University of Kaiserslautern

Academic Focus • Electrical engineering, German language and literature.

Program Information • Students attend classes at University of Kaiserslautern (Kaiserlautern, Germany). Students typically earn 7 semester credits per term.

Sessions • May-Jul (summer).

Eligibility Requirements • Minimum age 18; open to juniors, seniors; major in electrical or computer engineering; 3.0 GPA; good academic standing at home school; faculty approval; no foreign language proficiency required.

Living Arrangements • Students live in host institution dormitories, locally rented apartments. Quarters are shared with host institution students. Meals are taken on one's own, in central dining facility.

Costs (2005) • $1687 (estimated); includes housing, insurance, student support services. $100 application fee. $200 nonrefundable deposit required. Financial aid available for students from sponsoring institution: scholarships, loans.

For More Information • Ms. Yvonne Squiers, Secretary, Michigan State University, Office of Study Abroad, 109 International Center, East Lansing, MI 48824-1035; *Phone:* 517-353-8920; *Fax:* 517-432-2082. *E-mail:* squiers@msu.edu. *World Wide Web:* http://studyabroad.msu.edu/

KASSEL

ALMA COLLEGE
SUMMER PROGRAM OF STUDIES IN GERMANY

Hosted by Europa Kolleg

Academic Focus • German language and literature.

Program Information • Students attend classes at Europa Kolleg (Kassel, Germany). Field trips to the cathedral at Fulda, Weimar, Hannoversch, Moudon; optional travel at an extra cost. Students typically earn 3-12 semester credits per term.

Sessions • Jun-Aug (3 to 11 weeks).

Eligibility Requirements • Minimum age 18; open to freshmen, sophomores, juniors, seniors, graduate students; 2.5 GPA; 2 letters of recommendation; good academic standing at home school; no foreign language proficiency required.

Living Arrangements • Students live in host family homes. Meals are taken with host family, in residences.

Costs (2005) • $2320–$6540; includes tuition, housing, some meals, insurance, excursions, international student ID, student support services. $50 application fee. $200 refundable deposit required.

For More Information • Ms. Julie Elenbaas, Office Associate, International Education, Alma College, 614 West Superior Street, Alma, MI 48801-1599; *Phone:* 989-463-7055; *Fax:* 989-463-7126. *E-mail:* intl_studies@alma.edu. *World Wide Web:* http://international.alma.edu/

UNIVERSITY OF COLORADO AT BOULDER
SUMMER INTENSIVE GERMAN PROGRAM

Hosted by Europa Kolleg

Academic Focus • German language and literature, German studies.

Program Information • Students attend classes at Europa Kolleg (Kassel, Germany). Optional travel to Marburg, Goslar, Fulda at an extra cost. Students typically earn 3-6 semester credits per term.

Sessions • Jun-Jul (summer).

Eligibility Requirements • Open to freshmen, sophomores, juniors, seniors; 2.75 GPA; 2 letters of recommendation; good academic standing at home school; no foreign language proficiency required.
Living Arrangements • Students live in host family homes. Meals are taken with host family.
Costs (2005) • $3518 for 3 weeks; $8673 for 11 weeks; includes tuition, housing, all meals, insurance, excursions, books and class materials, student support services. $400 nonrefundable deposit required. Financial aid available for students from sponsoring institution: scholarships, loans.
For More Information • Study Abroad Programs, University of Colorado at Boulder, International Education, 123 UCB, Boulder, CO 80309-0123; *Phone:* 303-492-7741; *Fax:* 303-492-5185. *E-mail:* studyabr@colorado.edu. *World Wide Web:* http://www.colorado.edu/OIE/

LEIPZIG

TEMPLE UNIVERSITY
TEMPLE IN GERMANY

Hosted by University of Leipzig
Academic Focus • German language and literature, German studies.
Program Information • Students attend classes at University of Leipzig (Leipzig, Germany). Field trips to Berlin. Students typically earn 4 semester credits per term.
Sessions • Jun–Jul (summer).
Eligibility Requirements • Minimum age 19; open to sophomores, juniors, seniors; 2.5 GPA; 1 letter of recommendation; good academic standing at home school; official transcripts; 0.5 years of college course work in German.
Living Arrangements • Students live in host institution dormitories. Quarters are shared with host institution students. Meals are taken on one's own, in residences.
Costs (2005) • $2100–$3000; includes tuition, housing, excursions, program fee. $30 application fee. $200 nonrefundable deposit required. Financial aid available for students from sponsoring institution: scholarships, loans.
For More Information • Ms. Erin Joslyn, Study Abroad Coordinator, Temple University, International Programs, 200 Tuttleman Learning Center, 1809 North 13th Street, Philadelphia, PA 19122; *Phone:* 215-204-0720; *Fax:* 215-204-0729. *E-mail:* study.abroad@temple.edu. *World Wide Web:* http://www.temple.edu/studyabroad/

LÜNEBURG

UNIVERSITY STUDIES ABROAD CONSORTIUM
GERMAN AND EUROPEAN STUDIES: LÜNEBURG, GERMANY

Hosted by University of Lüneburg
Academic Focus • Anthropology, art history, cultural studies, film and media studies, German language and literature, history, literature, political science and government, speech communication.
Program Information • Students attend classes at University of Lüneburg (Lüneburg, Germany). Field trips to Hamburg, Lübeck, Travemünde, Lüneburg; Bremen; optional travel to Berlin at an extra cost. Students typically earn 6–12 semester credits per term.
Sessions • May–Jun (summer), Jun–Aug (summer 2).
Eligibility Requirements • Minimum age 18; open to freshmen, sophomores, juniors, seniors, graduate students, adults; 2.5 GPA; no foreign language proficiency required.
Living Arrangements • Students live in host institution dormitories, locally rented apartments, host family homes. Quarters are shared with host institution students. Meals are taken on one's own, with host family, in residences, in central dining facility.
Costs (2007) • $3280 for 1 session; $6460 for 2 sessions; includes tuition, housing, some meals, insurance, excursions, student support services. $100 application fee. $200 refundable deposit required. Financial aid available for all students: scholarships, loans.
For More Information • University Studies Abroad Consortium, USAC/323, Reno, NV 89557-0093; *Phone:* 775-784-6569; *Fax:* 775-784-6010. *E-mail:* usac@unr.edu. *World Wide Web:* http://usac.unr.edu/

MAYEN

MICHIGAN STATE UNIVERSITY
GERMAN LANGUAGE AND CULTURE

Academic Focus • German language and literature.
Program Information • Faculty members are drawn from the sponsor's U.S. staff and local instructors hired by the sponsor. Scheduled travel to Berlin; field trips to Cologne, Trier, Bonn. Students typically earn 6 semester credits per term.
Sessions • May–Jul (summer).
Eligibility Requirements • Minimum age 18; open to freshmen, sophomores, juniors, seniors; major in arts and letters; 2.0 GPA; good academic standing at home school; faculty approval; interview; 2 years of college course work in German.
Living Arrangements • Students live in host family homes, hotels, hostels. Meals are taken on one's own, with host family, in residences, in restaurants.
Costs (2005) • $1734 (estimated); includes housing, some meals, insurance, excursions, student support services. $100 application fee. $200 nonrefundable deposit required. Financial aid available for students from sponsoring institution: scholarships, loans.
For More Information • Ms. Yvonne Squiers, Secretary, Michigan State University, Office of Study Abroad, 109 International Center, East Lansing, MI 48824-1035; *Phone:* 517-353-8920; *Fax:* 517-432-2082. *E-mail:* squiers@msu.edu. *World Wide Web:* http://studyabroad.msu.edu/

MUNICH

EF INTERNATIONAL LANGUAGE SCHOOLS
GERMAN IN MUNICH, GERMANY

Hosted by EF Internationale Sprachshule
Academic Focus • German language and literature.
Program Information • Students attend classes at EF Internationale Sprachshule (Munich, Germany). Field trips to Dachau, Château Schlei Bheim; optional travel to Innsbruck, Prague, Nuremberg, King's Castle, Salzburg at an extra cost. Students typically earn 15–18 quarter credits per term.
Sessions • Program length 2 to 52 weeks, year-round.
Eligibility Requirements • Minimum age 16; open to precollege students, freshmen, sophomores, juniors, seniors, graduate students, adults; no foreign language proficiency required.
Living Arrangements • Students live in host family homes. Quarters are shared with host institution students. Meals are taken with host family.
Costs (2006–2007) • $1110 for 2 weeks; includes tuition, housing, some meals, books and class materials, student support services. $145 application fee. Financial aid available for all students: scholarships.
For More Information • Ms. Varvara Kirakosyan, Director of Admissions, EF International Language Schools, One Education Street, Cambridge, MA 02141; *Phone:* 800-992-1892; *Fax:* 800-590-1125. *E-mail:* ils@ef.com. *World Wide Web:* http://www.ef.com/

KENTUCKY INSTITUTE FOR INTERNATIONAL STUDIES
GERMANY

Academic Focus • German language and literature, German studies.
Program Information • Faculty members are drawn from the sponsor's U.S. staff. Scheduled travel to Berlin; field trips to Neuschwanstein; optional travel to other European capitals at an extra cost. Students typically earn 3-6 semester credits per term.
Sessions • Jun–Jul (summer).
Eligibility Requirements • Minimum age 18; open to freshmen, sophomores, juniors, seniors, graduate students, adults; 2.0 GPA; 1 letter of recommendation; 1 year of college course work in German.
Living Arrangements • Students live in host family homes. Meals are taken with host family, in residences.
Costs (2006) • $2840; includes housing, some meals, insurance, excursions, international airfare, international student ID, instructional expenses. $150 application fee. Financial aid available for all students: scholarships.

GERMANY
Munich

For More Information • Ms. Nancy Martin, Coordinator, Kentucky Institute for International Studies, PO Box 9, Murray, KY 42071-0009; *Phone:* 270-762-3091; *Fax:* 270-762-3434. *E-mail:* kiismsu@murraystate.edu. *World Wide Web:* http://www.kiis.org/

LANGUAGE LIAISON
GERMAN IN MUNICH

Hosted by Language Liaison
Academic Focus • German language and literature.
Program Information • Students attend classes at Language Liaison (Munich, Germany). Field trips; optional travel at an extra cost. Students typically earn 3–15 semester credits per term.
Sessions • Classes begin weekly, year-round.
Eligibility Requirements • Minimum age 17; open to precollege students, freshmen, sophomores, juniors, seniors, graduate students, adults; no foreign language proficiency required.
Living Arrangements • Students live in locally rented apartments, host family homes, hotels. Meals are taken on one's own, with host family, in residences, in restaurants.
Costs (2005) • Contact sponsor for cost. $175 application fee. Financial aid available for all students: scholarship research service.
For More Information • Ms. Nancy Forman, President, Language Liaison, PO Box 1772, Pacific Palisades, CA 90272; *Phone:* 800-284-4448; *Fax:* 310-454-1706. *E-mail:* learn@languageliaison.com. *World Wide Web:* http://www.languageliaison.com/

LINGUA SERVICE WORLDWIDE
VACATION 'N LEARN GERMAN IN GERMANY

Hosted by Deutsche in Deutschland
Academic Focus • German language and literature, German studies.
Program Information • Students attend classes at Deutsche in Deutschland (Munich, Germany). Field trips; optional travel at an extra cost. Students typically earn 3 semester credits for 3 weeks, 6 semester credits for 5 weeks.
Sessions • Sessions of 2 or more weeks year-round; start of each month for beginners, every other Monday for all others.
Eligibility Requirements • Minimum age 16; open to precollege students, freshmen, sophomores, juniors, seniors, graduate students, adults; no foreign language proficiency required.
Living Arrangements • Students live in host institution dormitories, locally rented apartments, host family homes, hotels. Quarters are shared with host institution students. Meals are taken with host family.
Costs (2006–2007) • Contact sponsor for cost. $100 application fee.
For More Information • Assistant Director, Lingua Service Worldwide, 75 Prospect Street, Suite 4, Huntington, NY 11743; *Phone:* 800-394-5327; *Fax:* 631-271-3441. *E-mail:* linguaservice@att.net. *World Wide Web:* http://www.linguaserviceworldwide.com/

RUTGERS, THE STATE UNIVERSITY OF NEW JERSEY
SUMMER STUDY IN MUNICH IN LANDSCAPE ARCHITECTURE

Academic Focus • Landscape architecture.
Program Information • Faculty members are drawn from the sponsor's U.S. staff. Field trips to sites around Berlin, Potsdam, the Alps. Students typically earn 5 semester credits per term.
Sessions • May–Jul (summer).
Eligibility Requirements • Open to freshmen, sophomores, juniors, seniors; 2.5 GPA; 1 letter of recommendation; good academic standing at home school; official transcripts from all tertiary schools attended; no foreign language proficiency required.
Living Arrangements • Students live in locally rented apartments, hotels. Meals are taken on one's own, in residences, in restaurants.
Costs (2005) • $3500 for New Jersey residents; $4500 for nonresidents; includes tuition, housing, insurance, excursions, student support services. $20 application fee. $500 nonrefundable deposit required. Financial aid available for students from sponsoring institution: scholarships, loans.
For More Information • Ms. Lindy Black, Regional Coordinator, Rutgers, The State University of New Jersey, 102 College Avenue, New Brunswick, NJ 08901-8543; *Phone:* 732-932-7787; *Fax:* 732-932-8659. *E-mail:* ru_abroad@email.rutgers.edu. *World Wide Web:* http://studyabroad.rutgers.edu/

STUTTGART

CENTER FOR STUDY ABROAD (CSA)
GERMAN IN STUTTGART

Hosted by AGI Language Institute
Academic Focus • German language and literature, German studies.
Program Information • Students attend classes at AGI Language Institute (Stuttgart, Germany). Field trips; optional travel. Students typically earn 4–10 semester credits per term.
Sessions • Typically 4 week sessions, classes begin weekly, year-round.
Eligibility Requirements • Minimum age 17; open to precollege students, freshmen, sophomores, juniors, seniors, graduate students, adults; no foreign language proficiency required.
Living Arrangements • Students live in host family homes. Meals are taken with host family.
Costs (2005) • Contact sponsor for cost. $45 application fee.
For More Information • Ms. Alima K. Virtue, Program Director, Center for Study Abroad (CSA), 325 Washington Avenue South #93, Kent, WA 98032; *Phone:* 206-726-1498; *Fax:* 253-850-0454. *E-mail:* info@centerforstudyabroad.com. *World Wide Web:* http://www.centerforstudyabroad.com/

LANGUAGE LIAISON
LEARN GERMAN IN GERMANY–STUTTGART

Hosted by Language Liaison
Academic Focus • German language and literature.
Program Information • Students attend classes at Language Liaison (Stuttgart, Germany). Field trips; optional travel at an extra cost. Students typically earn 3–15 semester credits per term.
Sessions • Classes begin weekly, year-round.
Eligibility Requirements • Minimum age 16; open to precollege students, freshmen, sophomores, juniors, seniors, graduate students, adults; no foreign language proficiency required.
Living Arrangements • Students live in host institution dormitories, locally rented apartments, host family homes, hotels. Meals are taken on one's own, with host family, in residences, in restaurants.
Costs (2005) • Contact sponsor for cost. $175 application fee. Financial aid available for all students: scholarship research service.
For More Information • Ms. Nancy Forman, President, Language Liaison, PO Box 1772, Pacific Palisades, CA 90272; *Phone:* 800-284-4448; *Fax:* 310-454-1706. *E-mail:* learn@languageliaison.com. *World Wide Web:* http://www.languageliaison.com/

LINGUA SERVICE WORLDWIDE
VACATION 'N LEARN GERMAN IN GERMANY

Hosted by Anglo-German Institute
Academic Focus • German language and literature, German studies.
Program Information • Students attend classes at Anglo-German Institute (Stuttgart, Germany). Field trips; optional travel at an extra cost. Students typically earn 3 semester credits for 3 weeks, 6 semester credits for 5 weeks.
Sessions • Sessions of 2 or more weeks year-round; start of each month for beginners, every other Monday for all others.
Eligibility Requirements • Minimum age 16; open to precollege students, freshmen, sophomores, juniors, seniors, graduate students, adults; no foreign language proficiency required.
Living Arrangements • Students live in host institution dormitories, locally rented apartments, host family homes, hotels. Quarters are shared with host institution students. Meals are taken with host family.
Costs (2006–2007) • Contact sponsor for cost. $100 application fee.
For More Information • Assistant Director, Lingua Service Worldwide, 75 Prospect Street, Suite 4, Huntington, NY 11743; *Phone:* 800-394-5327; *Fax:* 631-271-3441. *E-mail:* linguaservice@att.net. *World Wide Web:* http://www.linguaserviceworldwide.com/

WEIMAR

SOUTHERN METHODIST UNIVERSITY
SMU-IN-GERMANY

Held at Bauhaus University of Weimar
Academic Focus • German language and literature, music history.
Program Information • Classes are held on the campus of Bauhaus University of Weimar (Weimar, Germany). Faculty members are drawn from the sponsor's U.S. staff. Field trips to Dresden, Leipzig, Berlin, Potsdam. Students typically earn 6 semester credits per term.
Sessions • May–Jun (summer).
Eligibility Requirements • Open to sophomores, juniors, seniors; 2.5 GPA; good academic standing at home school; personal interview; essay; no foreign language proficiency required.
Living Arrangements • Students live in host institution dormitories. Quarters are shared with host institution students. Meals are taken as a group, on one's own, in central dining facility.
Costs (2005) • $5020; includes tuition, housing, some meals, excursions, student support services, transportation from the Frankfurt Airport to Weimar for students on the group flight. $40 application fee. $400 nonrefundable deposit required. Financial aid available for students from sponsoring institution: scholarships, loans.
For More Information • Ms. Nancy Simmons, Associate Director, Southern Methodist University, The International Center/Study Abroad, SMU PO Box 750391, Dallas, TX 75205-0391; *Phone:* 214-768-2338; *Fax:* 214-768-1051. *E-mail:* intlpro@mail.smu.edu. *World Wide Web:* http://www.smu.edu/studyabroad/

WÜRZBURG

UNIVERSITY AT ALBANY, STATE UNIVERSITY OF NEW YORK
LANGUAGE AND CULTURAL STUDIES AT THE UNIVERSITY OF WÜRZBURG

Hosted by University of Würzburg
Academic Focus • German language and literature, German studies.
Program Information • Students attend classes at University of Würzburg (Würzburg, Germany). Scheduled travel to Berlin; field trips to local sites. Students typically earn 10 semester credits per term.
Sessions • May–Jul (summer).
Eligibility Requirements • Minimum age 18; open to freshmen, sophomores, juniors, seniors, graduate students, adults; 2.5 GPA; 1 letter of recommendation; 1 year of college course work in German.
Living Arrangements • Students live in host institution dormitories, locally rented apartments. Quarters are shared with students from other programs. Meals are taken on one's own, in central dining facility, in restaurants.
Costs (2005) • Contact sponsor for cost. $150 nonrefundable deposit required. Financial aid available for students from sponsoring institution: all customary sources.
For More Information • University at Albany, State University of New York, Office of International Education, LI 66, Albany, NY 12222; *Phone:* 518-442-3525; *Fax:* 518-442-3338. *E-mail:* intled@uamail.albany.edu. *World Wide Web:* http://www.albany.edu/studyabroad/

HANA

CITY-TO-CITY

COOPERATIVE CENTER FOR STUDY ABROAD
GHANA

Academic Focus • History.
Program Information • Faculty members are drawn from the sponsor's U.S. staff. Field trips to Accra, Cape Coast, Kumasi. Students typically earn 3 semester credits per term.
Sessions • Jun (summer).
Eligibility Requirements • Minimum age 18; open to freshmen, sophomores, juniors, seniors, graduate students, adults; good academic standing at home school.
Living Arrangements • Students live in hotels. Quarters are shared with host institution students. Meals are taken as a group, on one's own, in central dining facility, in restaurants.
Costs (2007) • $4595; includes housing, some meals, excursions, international airfare, airport transfers. $200 nonrefundable deposit required. Financial aid available for students from sponsoring institution: scholarships, loans.
For More Information • Dr. Michael A. Klembara, Executive Director, Cooperative Center for Study Abroad, Northern Kentucky University, Nunn Drive, Founders Hall 301, Highland Heights, KY 41099; *Phone:* 859-572-6512; *Fax:* 859-572-6650. *E-mail:* ccsa@nku.edu. *World Wide Web:* http://www.ccsa.cc/

UNIVERSITY OF MINNESOTA
SOCIAL WORK IN GHANA

Academic Focus • African studies, social sciences, social work.
Program Information • Faculty members are drawn from the sponsor's U.S. staff. Field trips to Accra, Cape Cost, Elimina, Kumasi. Students typically earn 3 semester credits per term.
Sessions • May–Jun (summer).
Eligibility Requirements • Minimum age 18; open to freshmen, sophomores, juniors, seniors, adults; 2.5 GPA; good academic standing at home school; no foreign language proficiency required.
Living Arrangements • Students live in host institution dormitories, host family homes, hotels. Quarters are shared with students from other programs. Meals are taken as a group, on one's own, with host family, in residences, in restaurants.
Costs (2006) • Contact sponsor for cost; includes tuition, housing, all meals, insurance, excursions, student support services. Financial aid available for students from sponsoring institution: scholarships, loans.
For More Information • Learning Abroad Center, University of Minnesota, 230 Heller Hall, 271 19th Avenue South, Minneapolis, MN 55455; *Phone:* 888-700-UOFM; *Fax:* 612-626-8009. *E-mail:* umabroad@umn.edu. *World Wide Web:* http://www.umabroad.umn.edu/

ACCRA

COLLEGE CONSORTIUM FOR INTERNATIONAL STUDIES–UNIVERSITY OF MEMPHIS
GHANA SUMMER PROGRAM

Hosted by University of Ghana
Academic Focus • Aesthetics, history.
Program Information • Students attend classes at University of Ghana (Accra, Ghana). Field trips to Kumasi, Cape Coast, Elmina, Ho, Ada. Students typically earn 3 semester credits per term.
Sessions • Jul–Aug (summer).
Eligibility Requirements • Minimum age 18; open to freshmen, sophomores, juniors, seniors, graduate students, adults; 2.5 GPA; 2 letters of recommendation; good academic standing at home school; no foreign language proficiency required.
Living Arrangements • Students live in the Institute of African Studies chalets. Quarters are shared with host institution students. Meals are taken as a group, in residences.
Costs (2005) • $3500; includes tuition, housing, all meals, insurance, excursions, international student ID, student support services. $350 application fee. Financial aid available for all students: loans.
For More Information • Ms. Rebecca Laumann, Study Abroad Director, College Consortium for International Studies–University of Memphis, Center for International Programs, Brister Hall, Room 102, Memphis, TN 38152; *Phone:* 901-678-2814; *Fax:* 901-678-4949. *E-mail:* rlaumann@memphis.edu. *World Wide Web:* http://www.ccisabroad.org/

ILLINOIS STATE UNIVERSITY
HISTORY AND CULTURE OF GHANA

Held at University of Ghana
Academic Focus • African studies.
Program Information • Classes are held on the campus of University of Ghana (Accra, Ghana). Faculty members are drawn from the sponsor's U.S. staff. Field trips to the Wli Waterfalls, Mount Afadjato, Lake Bosomtwi, Cape Coast, Elmna Castle, home of W.E.B. DuBois. Students typically earn 3-6 semester credits per term.
Sessions • May-Jun (summer).
Eligibility Requirements • Open to sophomores, juniors, seniors, graduate students, adults; 2.5 GPA; good academic standing at home school; no foreign language proficiency required.
Living Arrangements • Students live in host institution dormitories. Quarters are shared with host institution students, students from other programs. Meals are taken as a group, in central dining facility.
Costs (2005) • $4700; includes tuition, housing, all meals, insurance, excursions, international airfare, international student ID, student support services, personal expenses. $150 nonrefundable deposit required. Financial aid available for students from sponsoring institution: scholarships, loans.
For More Information • Study Abroad Coordinator, Illinois State University, Office of International Studies and Programs, Campus Box 6120, Normal, IL 61790-6120; *Phone:* 309-438-5276; *Fax:* 309-438-3987. *E-mail:* oisp@ilstu.edu. *World Wide Web:* http://www.internationalstudies.ilstu.edu/

JAMES MADISON UNIVERSITY
SUMMER IN GHANA

Hosted by University of Ghana
Academic Focus • African studies, liberal studies.
Program Information • Students attend classes at University of Ghana (Accra, Ghana). Field trips to Kumasi, Aburi Botanical Gardens, Elmina and Cape Coast castles. Students typically earn 6 semester credits per term.
Sessions • Jun-Jul (summer).
Eligibility Requirements • Minimum age 18; open to sophomores, juniors, seniors; 2.0 GPA; 1 letter of recommendation; good academic standing at home school; no foreign language proficiency required.
Living Arrangements • Students live in hotels. Meals are taken as a group, on one's own, in central dining facility, in restaurants.
Costs (2005) • $3158 for Virginia residents; $4838 for nonresidents; includes tuition, housing, some meals, excursions, books and class materials, international student ID. $400 nonrefundable deposit required. Financial aid available for students from sponsoring institution: scholarships.
For More Information • Mr. Felix Wang, Director, James Madison University, Office of International Programs, MSC 5731, 1077 South Main Street, Harrisonburg, VA 22807; *Phone:* 540-568-6419; *Fax:* 540-568-3310. *E-mail:* studyabroad@jmu.edu. *World Wide Web:* http://www.jmu.edu/international/

MICHIGAN STATE UNIVERSITY
GHANA: A MULTIDISCIPLINARY PERSPECTIVE

Hosted by University of Ghana
Academic Focus • African studies, health-care management, interdisciplinary studies, journalism, nursing, social sciences.
Program Information • Students attend classes at University of Ghana (Accra, Ghana). Field trips to Elmina Castle, Rumast market, Bonwire, Volta Lake, Akosombo Dam. Students typically earn 6 semester credits per term.
Sessions • May-Jun (summer).
Eligibility Requirements • Minimum age 18; open to sophomores, juniors, seniors, graduate students; 2.0 GPA; good academic standing at home school; no foreign language proficiency required.
Living Arrangements • Students live in hotels. Meals are taken as a group, on one's own, in central dining facility.
Costs (2005) • $2253; includes housing, some meals, insurance, excursions, student support services. $100 application fee. $200 nonrefundable deposit required. Financial aid available for all students: scholarships, loans.
For More Information • Ms. Cindy Felbeck Chalou, Assistant Director, Michigan State University, Office of Study Abroad, 109 International Center, East Lansing, MI 48824-1035; *Phone:* 517-432-4345; *Fax:* 517-432-2082. *E-mail:* chalouc@msu.edu. *World Wide Web:* http://studyabroad.msu.edu/

NEW YORK UNIVERSITY
THE ARTS IN GHANA

Held at National Film and Television Institute, National Theatre, University of Ghana
Academic Focus • Drama/theater, film and media studies, photography.
Program Information • Classes are held on the campus of University of Ghana (Accra, Ghana), National Film and Television Institute (Accra, Ghana), National Theatre (Accra, Ghana). Faculty members are drawn from the sponsor's U.S. staff and local instructors hired by the sponsor. Students typically earn 8 semester credits per term.
Sessions • May-Jun (summer).
Eligibility Requirements • Open to freshmen, sophomores, juniors, seniors; 3.0 GPA; good academic standing at home school; no foreign language proficiency required.
Living Arrangements • Students live in host institution dormitories. Quarters are shared with host institution students. Meals are taken on one's own, in residences, in restaurants.
Costs (2006) • $6710; includes tuition, housing, some meals, lab equipment. $50 application fee. Financial aid available for students from sponsoring institution: scholarships.
For More Information • Mr. Josh Murray, Assistant Director, New York University, 721 Broadway, 12th Floor, New York, NY 10003; *Phone:* 212-998-1517; *Fax:* 212-995-4578. *E-mail:* josh.murray@nyu.edu. *World Wide Web:* http://www.nyu.edu/global/studyabroad.html

TEMPLE UNIVERSITY
TEMPLE IN WEST AFRICA: GHANA

Hosted by University of Ghana
Academic Focus • Aesthetics, African studies.
Program Information • Students attend classes at University of Ghana (Accra, Ghana). Field trips to ancient slave castles, Akosmbo, Bosumtwi, the W.E.B. DuBois Memorial, Kwame Nkrumah Memorial, national cultural centers, residences of Ghanaian kings. Students typically earn 6 semester credits per term.
Sessions • Jul-Aug (summer).
Eligibility Requirements • Minimum age 19; open to sophomores, juniors, seniors, graduate students; 2.5 GPA; 1 letter of recommendation; good academic standing at home school; official transcript; no foreign language proficiency required.
Living Arrangements • Students live in host institution dormitories, locally rented apartments. Quarters are shared with host institution students. Meals are taken on one's own, in residences.
Costs (2005) • $3500–$5400; includes tuition, housing, all meals, excursions, program fee, local travel. $30 application fee. $200 nonrefundable deposit required. Financial aid available for students from sponsoring institution: scholarships, loans.
For More Information • Ms. Erin Joslyn, Study Abroad Coordinator, Temple University, International Programs, 200 Tuttleman Learning Center, 1809 North 13th Street, Philadelphia, PA 19122; *Phone:* 215-204-0720; *Fax:* 215-204-0729. *E-mail:* study.abroad@temple.edu. *World Wide Web:* http://www.temple.edu/studyabroad/

UNIVERSITY OF ALABAMA
ALABAMA IN GHANA

Held at University of Ghana
Academic Focus • Geography.
Program Information • Classes are held on the campus of University of Ghana (Accra, Ghana). Faculty members are drawn from the sponsor's U.S. staff. Students typically earn 6 semester credits per term.
Sessions • Jun-Jul (summer).
Eligibility Requirements • Minimum age 18; open to sophomores, juniors, seniors, graduate students; course work in geography; 2.5 GPA; good academic standing at home school; no foreign language proficiency required.

GHANA
Accra

Living Arrangements • Students live in hotels. Quarters are shared with host institution students. Meals are taken as a group, in central dining facility, in restaurants.
Costs (2005) • $4200; includes tuition, housing, all meals, insurance, international airfare, books and class materials, international student ID, student support services. $100 application fee. $500 nonrefundable deposit required. Financial aid available for all students: scholarships, work study, loans.
For More Information • Ms. Angela L. Channell, Director of Overseas Study, University of Alabama, Box 870254, Tuscaloosa, AL 35487-0254; *Phone:* 205-348-5256; *Fax:* 205-348-5298. *E-mail:* achannell@aalan.ua.edu. *World Wide Web:* http://www.overseas-study. ua.edu/

UNIVERSITY OF MIAMI
UNIVERSITY OF MIAMI IN GHANA

Held at University of Miami
Academic Focus • African studies, history.
Program Information • Classes are held on the campus of University of Miami (Accra, Ghana). Faculty members are drawn from the sponsor's U.S. staff. Scheduled travel; field trips. Students typically earn 3 semester credits per term.
Sessions • May–Jun (summer).
Eligibility Requirements • Minimum age 18; open to sophomores, juniors, seniors; 1 letter of recommendation; good academic standing at home school; no foreign language proficiency required.
Living Arrangements • Students live in hotels. Quarters are shared with students from other programs. Meals are taken as a group, in residences, in restaurants.
Costs (2005) • $3711; includes tuition, housing, some meals, excursions, student support services. $40 application fee. $500 nonrefundable deposit required. Financial aid available for students from sponsoring institution: scholarships, loans.
For More Information • Ms. Amy Cosan, Coordinator, International Education and Exchange Programs, University of Miami, 5050 Brunson Drive, Allen Hall Room 212, PO Box 248005, Coral Gables, FL 33124-1610; *Phone:* 305-284-3434; *Fax:* 305-284-4235. *E-mail:* ieep@miami.edu. *World Wide Web:* http://www.studyabroad.miami. edu/

UNIVERSITY STUDIES ABROAD CONSORTIUM
AFRICAN STUDIES–ACCRA, GHANA

Hosted by University of Ghana
Academic Focus • African languages and literature, African studies, dance, music, political science and government.
Program Information • Students attend classes at University of Ghana (Accra, Ghana). Field trips to Cape Coast, Lake Volta, Kakum National Forest; optional travel to Kumasi, Benin/Togo at an extra cost. Students typically earn 7 semester credits per term.
Sessions • Jun–Jul (summer).
Eligibility Requirements • Minimum age 18; open to freshmen, sophomores, juniors, seniors, graduate students, adults; 2.5 GPA; no foreign language proficiency required.
Living Arrangements • Students live in host institution dormitories. Quarters are shared with host institution students. Meals are taken on one's own, in central dining facility.
Costs (2007) • $2980; includes tuition, housing, insurance, excursions. $100 application fee. $200 refundable deposit required. Financial aid available for all students: scholarships, loans.

For More Information • University Studies Abroad Consortium, USAC/323, Reno, NV 89557-0093; *Phone:* 775-784-6569; *Fax:* 775-784-6010. *E-mail:* usac@unr.edu. *World Wide Web:* http://usac. unr.edu/

CAPE COAST

DAVIDSON COLLEGE
DAVIDSON SUMMER PROGRAM IN CAPE COAST, GHANA

Hosted by University of Cape Coast
Academic Focus • Anthropology, sociology.
Program Information • Students attend classes at University of Cape Coast (Cape Coast, Ghana). Field trips to a Cacun rainforest, Kumasi, the Volta region. Students typically earn 4 semester credits per term.
Sessions • May–Jul (summer).
Eligibility Requirements • Minimum age 18; open to freshmen, sophomores, juniors, seniors; 2.5 GPA; 2 letters of recommendation; good academic standing at home school; no foreign language proficiency required.
Living Arrangements • Students live in a local guest house. Meals are taken as a group, in central dining facility.
Costs (2004) • $3900; includes tuition, housing, some meals, excursions, international airfare, student support services. $1500 nonrefundable deposit required.
For More Information • Ms. Carolyn Ortmayer, Study Abroad Coordinator, Davidson College, Box 7155, Davidson, NC 28035-7155; *Phone:* 704-894-2250; *Fax:* 704-894-2120. *E-mail:* abroad@ davidson.edu. *World Wide Web:* http://www.davidson.edu/ international/

WINNEBA

NORTHERN ILLINOIS UNIVERSITY
NIU IN GHANA, WEST AFRICA

Held at University College of Education of Winneba
Academic Focus • African studies.
Program Information • Classes are held on the campus of University College of Education of Winneba (Winneba, Ghana). Faculty members are drawn from the sponsor's U.S. staff. Students typically earn 3–6 semester credits per term.
Sessions • May–Jun (summer).
Eligibility Requirements • Minimum age 18; open to sophomores, juniors, seniors, graduate students; 2.5 GPA; good academic standing at home school; no foreign language proficiency required.
Living Arrangements • Students live in host family homes. Quarters are shared with host institution students. Meals are taken with host family, in residences.
Costs (2005) • $4235; includes tuition, housing, some meals, insurance, excursions, international student ID, student support services. $200 nonrefundable deposit required. Financial aid available for students from sponsoring institution: loans.
For More Information • Ms. Rita Withrow, Program Assistant, Northern Illinois University, Study Abroad Office, Williston Hall 417, De Kalb, IL 60115; *Phone:* 815-753-0700; *Fax:* 815-753-0825. *E-mail:* niuabroad@niu.edu. *World Wide Web:* http://www.niu.edu/ niuabroad/

GREECE

CITY-TO-CITY

COLLEGE YEAR IN ATHENS
COLLEGE YEAR IN ATHENS–SUMMER COURSES

Hosted by College Year in Athens
Academic Focus • Anthropology, archaeology, art history, Greek studies, history.
Program Information • Students attend classes at College Year in Athens (Athens). Field trips to Delphi, Attica. Students typically earn 3-4 semester credits per term.
Sessions • May–Jul (summer).
Eligibility Requirements • Minimum age 18; open to freshmen, sophomores, juniors, seniors, graduate students, adults; 2 letters of recommendation; good academic standing at home school; high school diploma; no foreign language proficiency required.
Living Arrangements • Students live in locally rented apartments, hotels. Quarters are shared with host institution students. Meals are taken on one's own, in restaurants.
Costs (2006) • $1800–$2900 per course; includes tuition, housing, books and class materials, student support services. $30 application fee. $300 refundable deposit required.
For More Information • Ms. Erica Huffman, Campus and Student Relations, College Year in Athens, PO Box 390890, Cambridge, MA 02139; *Phone:* 617-868-8200; *Fax:* 617-828-8207. *E-mail:* info@cyathens.org. *World Wide Web:* http://www.cyathens.org/

SAINT MARY'S COLLEGE
GREECE STUDY TOUR

Academic Focus • Ancient history, civilization studies, Greek studies, religious studies.
Program Information • Faculty members are drawn from the sponsor's U.S. staff. Scheduled travel to Athens, Nauplion, Corinth, Mycenae; Olympia; Aafpaktos; Delphi; Island of Aegina. Students typically earn 3 semester credits per term.
Sessions • May–Jun (summer).
Eligibility Requirements • Minimum age 18; open to freshmen, sophomores, juniors, seniors; 2.0 GPA; 3 letters of recommendation; good academic standing at home school; no foreign language proficiency required.
Living Arrangements • Students live in hotels. Meals are taken as a group, in restaurants.
Costs (2005) • $2619; includes housing, some meals, excursions, international airfare, student support services. $30 application fee.
For More Information • Dr. John Fotopoulos, Faculty Director, Saint Mary's College, Department of Religious Studies, Notre Dame, IN 46556; *Phone:* 574-284-4071; *Fax:* 574-284-4141. *E-mail:* jfotopoulos@saintmarys.edu. *World Wide Web:* http://www.saintmarys.edu/~cwil

UNIVERSITY OF KANSAS
ANCIENT GREECE: AN ARCHAEOLOGICAL TOUR

Academic Focus • Anthropology, archaeology, art history, Greek studies.
Program Information • Faculty members are drawn from the sponsor's U.S. staff. Scheduled travel to Athens, Nafplion, Sparta, Pylos, Olympia, Delphi, Crete, Lasithi, Siteia, Heraklian. Students typically earn 3-6 semester credits per term.
Sessions • May–Jun (summer).
Eligibility Requirements • Minimum age 18; open to freshmen, sophomores, juniors, seniors, graduate students; 2.5 GPA; 2 letters of recommendation; good academic standing at home school; no foreign language proficiency required.
Living Arrangements • Students live in hotels. Meals are taken as a group, on one's own, in restaurants.
Costs (2005) • $5200 for 3 credits; $5616 for 6 credits; includes tuition, housing, some meals, excursions, student support services, medical evacuation and repatriation services. $38 application fee. $300 nonrefundable deposit required. Financial aid available for students from sponsoring institution: scholarships, loans.
For More Information • Ms. Justine Hamilton, Program Coordinator, University of Kansas, Office of Study Abroad, Lippincott Hall, 1410 Jayhawk Boulevard, Room 108, Lawrence, KS 66045-7515; *Phone:* 785-864-3742; *Fax:* 785-864-5040. *E-mail:* osa@ku.edu. *World Wide Web:* http://www.ku.edu/~osa/

UNIVERSITY OF NEW ORLEANS
HONORS TOUR TO GREECE

Academic Focus • Classics and classical languages, Greek studies, interdisciplinary studies, philosophy.

GREECE
City-to-City

Program Information • Faculty members are drawn from the sponsor's U.S. staff and local instructors hired by the sponsor. Scheduled travel to sailing; field trips to Greek Islands, Mount Olympus, Delphi. Students typically earn 6 semester credits per term.
Sessions • May–Jun (summer).
Eligibility Requirements • Minimum age 18; open to freshmen, sophomores, juniors, seniors; 2.5 GPA; 1 letter of recommendation; good academic standing at home school; must be an honors student; no foreign language proficiency required.
Living Arrangements • Students live in hotels. Meals are taken as a group, in restaurants.
Costs (2005) • $3095; includes tuition, housing, some meals, insurance, excursions, student support services. $150 application fee. $150 refundable deposit required. Financial aid available for students from sponsoring institution: scholarships, loans.
For More Information • Mr. Peter Alongia, Coordinator, University of New Orleans, PO Box 1315, New Orleans, LA 70148; *Phone:* 504-280-7116; *Fax:* 504-280-7317. *E-mail:* palongia@uno.edu. *World Wide Web:* http://inst.uno.edu/

THE UNIVERSITY OF NORTH CAROLINA AT CHARLOTTE
MAY IN GREECE

Academic Focus • Greek studies, liberal studies.
Program Information • Faculty members are drawn from the sponsor's U.S. staff. Scheduled travel to Athens, Thebes, Delphi, Olympia, Pylos, Sparta. Students typically earn 3 semester credits per term.
Sessions • May (summer).
Eligibility Requirements • Minimum age 18; open to sophomores, juniors, seniors, graduate students, adults; 2.5 GPA; good academic standing at home school; no foreign language proficiency required.
Living Arrangements • Students live in hotels. Meals are taken as a group, in restaurants.
Costs (2005) • $1950; includes tuition, housing, some meals, insurance, excursions, student support services, in-country transportation. $500 nonrefundable deposit required. Financial aid available for students from sponsoring institution: scholarships, loans.
For More Information • Mr. Brad Sekulich, Interim Director of Education Abroad, The University of North Carolina at Charlotte, 9201 University City Boulevard, Charlotte, NC 28223-0001; *Phone:* 704-687-2464; *Fax:* 704-687-3168. *E-mail:* edabroad@email.uncc.edu. *World Wide Web:* http://www.uncc.edu/edabroad/

VILLANOVA UNIVERSITY
RHETORIC AND PERFORMANCE IN ANCIENT GREECE

Academic Focus • Ancient history, communications.
Program Information • Faculty members are drawn from the sponsor's U.S. staff. Scheduled travel to Delphi, Olympia; field trips to Epidaurus, Nafplion, Mycenae. Students typically earn 6 semester credits per term.
Sessions • Jun–Aug (summer).
Eligibility Requirements • Minimum age 18; open to freshmen, sophomores, juniors, seniors; 2.5 GPA; 2 letters of recommendation; good academic standing at home school; no foreign language proficiency required.
Living Arrangements • Students live in hotels. Meals are taken as a group, in restaurants.
Costs (2005) • $4250; includes tuition, housing, all meals, insurance, excursions, student support services, all land transport between sites. $450 nonrefundable deposit required. Financial aid available for students from sponsoring institution.
For More Information • Dr. Susan Mackey-Kallis, Professor, Villanova University, 800 Lancaster Avenue, Middleton Hall, Villanova, PA 19085; *Phone:* 610-519-6412; *Fax:* 610-519-7649. *E-mail:* susan.mackeykallis@villanova.edu. *World Wide Web:* http://www.internationalstudies.villanova.edu/

ATHENS

AHA INTERNATIONAL AN ACADEMIC PROGRAM OF THE UNIVERSITY OF OREGON
ATHENS, GREECE: NORTHWEST COUNCIL ON STUDY ABROAD (NCSA)

Hosted by Athens Centre
Academic Focus • Art, creative writing, drama/theater, Greek.
Program Information • Students attend classes at Athens Centre (Athens, Greece). Field trips to Island of Spetses. Students typically earn 6–12 semester credits per term.
Sessions • Jun–Jul (summer).
Eligibility Requirements • Minimum age 17; open to freshmen, sophomores, juniors, seniors, adults; 2 letters of recommendation; good academic standing at home school; official transcripts; no foreign language proficiency required.
Living Arrangements • Students live in locally rented apartments. Quarters are shared with host institution students. Meals are taken on one's own, in residences, in central dining facility, in restaurants.
Costs (2005–2006) • $2860–$3650; includes tuition, housing, some meals, insurance, excursions, books and class materials, international student ID, student support services, on-site orientation. $50 application fee. $200 refundable deposit required. Financial aid available for all students: scholarships, loans, home institution financial aid.
For More Information • Mr. Edward Helgeson, Associate Director for University Programs, AHA International An Academic Program of the University of Oregon, 221 NW 2nd Avenue, Suite 200, Portland, OR 97209; *Phone:* 503-295-7730; *Fax:* 503-295-5969. *E-mail:* mail@aha-intl.org. *World Wide Web:* http://www.aha-intl.org/

ARCADIA UNIVERSITY
OF GODS AND THE CITY

Hosted by Arcadia Center for Hellenic, Mediterranean and Balkan Studies and Research
Academic Focus • Archaeology, art history, classics and classical languages, Greek studies, history.
Program Information • Students attend classes at Arcadia Center for Hellenic, Mediterranean and Balkan Studies and Research (Athens, Greece). Scheduled travel to Sparta, Delphi; field trips to field excursions. Students typically earn 3 semester credits per term.
Sessions • May–Jun (summer).
Eligibility Requirements • Open to sophomores, juniors, seniors, graduate students, adults; 3.0 GPA; 1 letter of recommendation; no foreign language proficiency required.
Living Arrangements • Students live in locally rented apartments, hotels. Quarters are shared with host institution students. Meals are taken as a group, on one's own, in residences, in restaurants.
Costs (2005) • $3120; includes tuition, housing, some meals, insurance, excursions, books and class materials, international student ID, student support services, transcript, pre-departure guide, orientation. $35 application fee. $500 nonrefundable deposit required. Financial aid available for all students: scholarships, loans.
For More Information • Arcadia University, Center for Education Abroad, 450 South Easton Road, Glenside, PA 19038-3295; *Phone:* 866-927-2234; *Fax:* 215-572-2174. *E-mail:* cea@arcadia.edu. *World Wide Web:* http://www.arcadia.edu/cea/

ARCADIA UNIVERSITY
ON THE TRAIL OF ALEXANDER THE GREAT

Hosted by Arcadia Center for Hellenic, Mediterranean and Balkan Studies and Research
Academic Focus • Archaeology, art history, classics and classical languages, Greek studies, history.
Program Information • Students attend classes at Arcadia Center for Hellenic, Mediterranean and Balkan Studies and Research (Athens, Greece). Scheduled travel to Samos, Priene, Miletos; field trips to field excursions. Students typically earn 3 semester credits per term.
Sessions • Jun–Jul (summer).
Eligibility Requirements • Open to sophomores, juniors, seniors, graduate students, adults; 3.0 GPA; 1 letter of recommendation; no foreign language proficiency required.

Living Arrangements • Students live in locally rented apartments, hotels. Quarters are shared with host institution students. Meals are taken as a group, on one's own, in residences, in restaurants.
Costs (2005) • $3440; includes tuition, housing, some meals, insurance, excursions, books and class materials, international student ID, student support services, transcript, pre-departure guide, orientation. $35 application fee. $500 nonrefundable deposit required. Financial aid available for all students: scholarships, loans.
For More Information • Arcadia University, Center for Education Abroad, 450 South Easton Road, Glenside, PA 19038-3295; *Phone:* 866-927-2234; *Fax:* 215-572-2174. *E-mail:* cea@arcadia.edu. *World Wide Web:* http://www.arcadia.edu/cea/

CITY UNIVERSITY, ATHENS
CITY UNIVERSITY ATHENS SUMMER PROGRAM

Hosted by City University, Athens
Academic Focus • Full curriculum.
Program Information • Students attend classes at City University, Athens (Athens, Greece). Scheduled travel to Delphi, Ancient Corinth, Ancient Olympia, Mycenean, Meteora; field trips to Acropolis, museums, Parthenon, Sounion; optional travel to Greek Islands at an extra cost. Students typically earn 15-21 quarter credits per term.
Sessions • Jun-Jul (summer).
Eligibility Requirements • Minimum age 17; open to freshmen, sophomores, juniors, seniors, graduate students, adults; 2.3 GPA; 2 letters of recommendation.
Living Arrangements • Students live in locally rented apartments, hotels. Quarters are shared with students from other programs. Meals are taken in residences, in restaurants.
Costs (2006) • $7900; includes tuition, housing, insurance, excursions, books and class materials, lab equipment, international student ID, student support services. $80 application fee. $800 refundable deposit required. Financial aid available for students from sponsoring institution: scholarships.
For More Information • Ms. Georgia Berlemi, Student Abroad Program, City University, Athens, Karitsi 1 and Kolokotroni, Syntagma, Athens 10561, Greece; *Phone:* +30 210-3243222; *Fax:* +30 210-3225253. *World Wide Web:* http://www.cityu.gr/

COLLEGE YEAR IN ATHENS
COLLEGE YEAR IN ATHENS–INTENSIVE MODERN GREEK

Hosted by College Year in Athens, College Year in Athens
Academic Focus • Greek.
Program Information • Students attend classes at College Year in Athens (Athens, Greece), College Year in Athens (Paros, Greece). Students typically earn 4-8 semester credits per term.
Sessions • May-Jun (summer).
Eligibility Requirements • Minimum age 18; open to freshmen, sophomores, juniors, seniors, graduate students, adults; 2 letters of recommendation; good academic standing at home school; high school diploma; no foreign language proficiency required.
Living Arrangements • Students live in locally rented apartments, hotels. Quarters are shared with host institution students. Meals are taken on one's own, in restaurants.
Costs (2006) • $1700 (Athens); $2100 (Paros); includes tuition, housing, books and class materials, student support services. $30 application fee. $300 refundable deposit required.
For More Information • Ms. Erica Huffman, Campus and Student Relations, College Year in Athens, PO Box 390890, Cambridge, MA 02139; *Phone:* 617-868-8200; *Fax:* 617-828-8207. *E-mail:* info@cyathens.org. *World Wide Web:* http://www.cyathens.org/

LANGUAGE LIAISON
LEARN GREEK IN GREECE–ATHENS

Hosted by Language Liaison
Academic Focus • Greek.
Program Information • Students attend classes at Language Liaison (Athens, Greece). Field trips; optional travel at an extra cost. Students typically earn 3-15 semester credits per term.
Sessions • Classes begin weekly, year-round.
Eligibility Requirements • Minimum age 17; open to freshmen, sophomores, juniors, seniors, graduate students, adults; no foreign language proficiency required.

Living Arrangements • Students live in host family homes, hotels. Meals are taken with host family, in residences, in restaurants.
Costs (2005) • Contact sponsor for cost. $175 application fee. Financial aid available for all students: scholarship research service.
For More Information • Ms. Nancy Forman, President, Language Liaison, PO Box 1772, Pacific Palisades, CA 90272; *Phone:* 800-284-4448; *Fax:* 310-454-1706. *E-mail:* learn@languageliaison.com. *World Wide Web:* http://www.languageliaison.com/

LINGUA SERVICE WORLDWIDE
VACATION 'N LEARN GREEK IN GREECE

Hosted by Alexander the Great Hellenic Language School
Academic Focus • Greek, Greek studies.
Program Information • Students attend classes at Alexander the Great Hellenic Language School (Athens, Greece). Optional travel to cultural sites thoughout Greece at an extra cost. Students typically earn 3 semester credits for 3 weeks, 6 semester credits for 5 weeks.
Sessions • 2 to 15 week sessions, year-round.
Eligibility Requirements • Minimum age 18; open to freshmen, sophomores, juniors, seniors, graduate students, adults; no foreign language proficiency required.
Living Arrangements • Students live in host family homes, hotels. Meals are taken with host family.
Costs (2006–2007) • Contact sponsor for cost. $100 application fee.
For More Information • Assistant Director, Lingua Service Worldwide, 75 Prospect Street, Suite 4, Huntington, NY 11743; *Phone:* 800-394-5327; *Fax:* 631-271-3441. *E-mail:* linguaservice@att.net. *World Wide Web:* http://www.linguaserviceworldwide.com/

NEW YORK UNIVERSITY
NYU IN ATHENS

Held at Al Andar
Academic Focus • Archaeology, Greek, Greek studies, literature, social sciences.
Program Information • Classes are held on the campus of Al Andar (Athens, Greece). Faculty members are drawn from the sponsor's U.S. staff and local instructors hired by the sponsor. Scheduled travel to Greek islands, sites of historic and cultural importance; field trips to archaeological sites, theatrical and musical performances, sites of historic and cultural importance, Greek landscape. Students typically earn 8 semester credits per term.
Sessions • Jun-Aug (summer).
Eligibility Requirements • Minimum age 18; open to freshmen, sophomores, juniors, seniors, graduate students; 3.0 GPA; 1 letter of recommendation; good academic standing at home school; statement of purpose for visiting students; no foreign language proficiency required.
Living Arrangements • Students live in hotels. Quarters are shared with host institution students. Meals are taken on one's own, in restaurants.
Costs (2006) • $8164; includes tuition, housing, some meals, excursions, student support services. $25 application fee. $300 nonrefundable deposit required. Financial aid available for students from sponsoring institution: loans.
For More Information • Office of Summer Sessions, New York University, 7 East 12th Street, 6th Floor, New York, NY 10003; *Phone:* 212-998-2292; *Fax:* 212-995-4642. *E-mail:* summer.info@nyu.edu. *World Wide Web:* http://www.nyu.edu/global/studyabroad.html

RUTGERS, THE STATE UNIVERSITY OF NEW JERSEY
SUMMER STUDY ABROAD IN GREECE

Academic Focus • Classics and classical languages.
Program Information • Faculty members are drawn from the sponsor's U.S. staff. Scheduled travel to Crete, Macedonia, Athens, Peloponnese; field trips to Thessaloniki. Students typically earn 6 semester credits per term.
Sessions • May-Jun (summer).
Eligibility Requirements • Open to sophomores, juniors, seniors; 2.5 GPA; 1 letter of recommendation; good academic standing at home school; official transcripts from all tertiary schools attended; no foreign language proficiency required.

Why is this globe upside down?

?right to left read Why

Why drive on the
right-hand side of the road?

It's all a matter of perspective.

Studying abroad changes your perspective and gives you new insight into how the world looks to different people and cultures.

See for yourself in one of our 40 programs worldwide. Enjoy your crossing...

732.932.7787
RU_Abroad@email.rutgers.edu
http://studyabroad.rutgers.edu

Rutgers Study Abroad

Living Arrangements • Students live in hotels. Meals are taken on one's own, in restaurants.
Costs (2005) • $3995 for New Jersey residents; $4995 for nonresidents; includes tuition, housing, some meals, insurance, excursions. $20 application fee. $500 nonrefundable deposit required. Financial aid available for students from sponsoring institution: scholarships, loans.
For More Information • Ms. Lindy Black, Regional Coordinator, Rutgers, The State University of New Jersey, 102 College Avenue, New Brunswick, NJ 08901-8543; *Phone:* 732-932-7787; *Fax:* 732-932-8659. *E-mail:* ru_abroad@email.rutgers.edu. *World Wide Web:* http://studyabroad.rutgers.edu/

STATE UNIVERSITY OF NEW YORK COLLEGE AT BROCKPORT
STUDY TOUR OF GREECE

Academic Focus • Greek studies, literature.
Program Information • Faculty members are drawn from the sponsor's U.S. staff. Scheduled travel to Crete, Santorini, Mykonos, the Island of Delos; field trips to Athens, Olympia, Mycenae. Students typically earn 3 semester credits per term.
Sessions • Jun-Jul (summer).
Eligibility Requirements • Minimum age 18; open to freshmen, sophomores, juniors, seniors, graduate students, adults; 2.5 GPA; 2 letters of recommendation; good academic standing at home school; no foreign language proficiency required.
Living Arrangements • Students live in hotels. Meals are taken as a group, on one's own, in restaurants.
Costs (2005) • Contact sponsor for cost; includes housing, some meals, excursions. $200 nonrefundable deposit required. Financial aid available for students: scholarships, loans.
For More Information • Dr. John J. Perry, Director, Office of International Education, State University of New York College at Brockport, 350 New Campus Drive, Brockport, NY 14420; *Phone:* 800-298-SUNY; *Fax:* 585-637-3218. *E-mail:* overseas@brockport.edu. *World Wide Web:* http://www.brockport.edu/studyabroad/

UNIVERSITY OF ALABAMA
ALABAMA IN GREECE

Academic Focus • Classics and classical languages, Greek studies.
Program Information • Faculty members are drawn from the sponsor's U.S. staff. Field trips to Corinth, Mycenae, Olympia, Delphi; Dion; Thessaloniki. Students typically earn 6 semester credits per term.
Sessions • May-Jun (summer).
Eligibility Requirements • Open to freshmen, sophomores, juniors, seniors, graduate students, adults; course work in classics; 2.5 GPA; good academic standing at home school; no foreign language proficiency required.
Living Arrangements • Students live in locally rented apartments, hotels. Meals are taken as a group, in restaurants.
Costs (2005) • $3300; includes tuition, housing, excursions, international airfare, international student ID, student support services. $100 application fee. $500 nonrefundable deposit required. Financial aid available for all students: scholarships, loans.
For More Information • Ms. Angela L. Channell, Director of Overseas Study, University of Alabama, Capstone International Center, Box 870254, Tuscaloosa, AL 35487-0254; *Phone:* 205-348-7024; *Fax:* 205-348-5298. *E-mail:* achannel@aalan.ua.edu. *World Wide Web:* http://www.overseas-study.ua.edu/

UNIVERSITY OF DELAWARE
SUMMER SESSION IN ATHENS

Hosted by Athens Centre
Academic Focus • Art history, Greek, Greek studies, history.
Program Information • Students attend classes at Athens Centre (Athens, Greece). Field trips to cultural and historic sites. Students typically earn 7 semester credits per term.
Sessions • Jun-Jul (summer).
Eligibility Requirements • Open to freshmen, sophomores, juniors, seniors, adults; 2.0 GPA; 1 letter of recommendation; no foreign language proficiency required.

Living Arrangements • Students live in locally rented apartments. Quarters are shared with host institution students. Meals are taken on one's own, in residences.
Costs (2005) • Contact sponsor for cost. $200 nonrefundable deposit required. Financial aid available for all students: scholarships.
For More Information • Center for International Studies, University of Delaware, 186 South College Avenue, Newark, DE 19716-1450; *Phone:* 888-831-4685; *Fax:* 302-831-6042. *E-mail:* studyabroad@udel.edu. *World Wide Web:* http://www.udel.edu/studyabroad/

UNIVERSITY OF INDIANAPOLIS–ATHENS CAMPUS
SUMMER ODYSSEY IN ATHENS

Hosted by University of Indianapolis–Athens Campus
Academic Focus • Full curriculum.
Program Information • Students attend classes at University of Indianapolis–Athens Campus (Athens, Greece). Field trips to Delphi, the Saronic Gulf islands, Mycenae, Epidaurus, Olympia; optional travel at an extra cost.
Sessions • Jun-Jul (summer).
Eligibility Requirements • Minimum age 17; open to freshmen, sophomores, juniors, seniors, graduate students; good academic standing at home school; potential to benefit from experience; no foreign language proficiency required.
Living Arrangements • Students live in locally rented apartments. Quarters are shared with host institution students. Meals are taken on one's own, in residences, in restaurants.
Costs (2005) • $2500; includes tuition, housing, excursions, student support services. $100 application fee. $950 deposit required. Financial aid available for all students: scholarships.
For More Information • Ms. Dina Skias, Director, Student Affairs, Odyssey in Athens, University of Indianapolis–Athens Campus, 9 Ipitou Street, Athens 10557, Greece; *Phone:* +30 210-32-37-077; *Fax:* +30 210-32-48-502. *E-mail:* skiasd@uindy.gr. *World Wide Web:* http://www.uindy.gr

CRETE

ARIADNE INSTITUTE
GODDESS PILGRIMAGE TO CRETE

Academic Focus • Archaeology, history, religious studies, women's studies.
Program Information • Faculty members are drawn from the sponsor's U.S. staff. Scheduled travel to sites around Crete; field trips to sites around Crete. Students typically earn 3 semester credits per term.
Sessions • May-Jun (summer), Sep-Oct (summer 2).
Eligibility Requirements • Open to precollege students, freshmen, sophomores, juniors, seniors, graduate students, adults; no foreign language proficiency required.
Living Arrangements • Students live in hotels. Meals are taken as a group, in restaurants.
Costs (2004–2005) • $2850; includes tuition, housing, some meals, excursions, student support services. $500 nonrefundable deposit required. Financial aid available for all students: scholarships, loans.
For More Information • Ms. Susan Glassow, Co-Director, Ariadne Institute, PO Box 303, Blue River, OR 97413; *Phone:* 541-822-3201; *Fax:* 541-822-8190. *E-mail:* institute@goddessariadne.org. *World Wide Web:* http://www.goddessariadne.org/

LINGUA SERVICE WORLDWIDE
VACATION 'N LEARN GREEK IN GREECE

Hosted by Alexander the Great Hellenic Language School
Academic Focus • Greek, Greek studies.
Program Information • Students attend classes at Alexander the Great Hellenic Language School (Crete, Greece). Optional travel to cultural sites throughout Greece at an extra cost. Students typically earn 3 semester credits for 3 weeks, 6 semester credits for 5 weeks.
Sessions • Minimum 2 week sessions.
Eligibility Requirements • Minimum age 18; open to freshmen, sophomores, juniors, seniors, graduate students, adults; no foreign language proficiency required.

Living Arrangements • Students live in host family homes, hotels. Meals are taken with host family.
Costs (2006–2007) • Contact sponsor for cost. $100 application fee.
For More Information • Assistant Director, Lingua Service Worldwide, 75 Prospect Street, Suite 4, Huntington, NY 11743; *Phone:* 800-394-5327; *Fax:* 631-271-3441. *E-mail:* linguaservice@att. net. *World Wide Web:* http://www.linguaserviceworldwide.com/

KATOHI

UNIVERSITY OF KANSAS
THEATRE IN GREECE

Academic Focus • Drama/theater, Greek studies.
Program Information • Faculty members are drawn from the sponsor's U.S. staff and local instructors hired by the sponsor. Scheduled travel to Epidaurus, Mycenae, Corinth; field trips to Delphi, Oiniades. Students typically earn 6 semester credits per term.
Sessions • Jun–Jul (summer), Program runs every other year.
Eligibility Requirements • Minimum age 18; open to freshmen, sophomores, juniors, seniors, graduate students, adults; 2.5 GPA; 2 letters of recommendation; good academic standing at home school; no foreign language proficiency required.
Living Arrangements • Students live in host institution dormitories, hotels. Meals are taken as a group, on one's own, in central dining facility, in restaurants.
Costs (2004) • $3850; includes tuition, housing, some meals, excursions, student support services, medical evacuation and repatriation services. $38 application fee. $300 nonrefundable deposit required. Financial aid available for students from sponsoring institution: scholarships, loans.
For More Information • Ms. Justine Hamilton, Program Coordinator, University of Kansas, Office of Study Abroad, Lippincott Hall, 1410 Jayhawk Boulevard, Room 108, Lawrence, KS 66045-7515; *Phone:* 785-864-3742; *Fax:* 785-864-5040. *E-mail:* osa@ku.edu. *World Wide Web:* http://www.ku.edu/~osa/

MYTILENE

MICHIGAN STATE UNIVERSITY
SOCIAL SCIENCE IN THE EASTERN MEDITERRANEAN
Hosted by University of the Aegean

Academic Focus • Interdisciplinary studies, Mediterranean studies, social sciences, sociology.
Program Information • Students attend classes at University of the Aegean (Mytilene, Greece). Scheduled travel to Pergamos, Turkey, Petra, Greece. Students typically earn 7 semester credits per term.
Sessions • May–Jun (summer), Jun–Jul (summer 2).
Eligibility Requirements • Minimum age 18; open to juniors, seniors; 2.0 GPA; good academic standing at home school; essay; no foreign language proficiency required.
Living Arrangements • Students live in host institution dormitories, locally rented apartments. Meals are taken on one's own, in restaurants.
Costs (2005) • $2952; includes housing, some meals, insurance, excursions, student support services. $100 application fee. $200 nonrefundable deposit required. Financial aid available for all students: scholarships, loans.
For More Information • Ms. Cindy Felbeck Chalou, Assistant Director, Michigan State University, Office of Study Abroad, 109 International Center, East Lansing, MI 48824-1053; *Phone:* 517-432-4345; *Fax:* 517-432-2082. *E-mail:* chalouc@msu.edu. *World Wide Web:* http://studyabroad.msu.edu/

SYROS

SAINT JOSEPH'S UNIVERSITY
SUMMER IN GREECE

Academic Focus • Political science and government, psychology, religious studies.
Program Information • Faculty members are drawn from the sponsor's U.S. staff. Scheduled travel to Santorini; field trips to Athens. Students typically earn 3 semester credits per term.
Sessions • May–Jun (summer).
Eligibility Requirements • Minimum age 18; open to sophomores, juniors, seniors; 2.5 GPA; good academic standing at home school; no foreign language proficiency required.
Living Arrangements • Students live in host institution dormitories. Meals are taken on one's own, in residences, in restaurants.
Costs (2005–2006) • Contact sponsor for cost. $300 nonrefundable deposit required. Financial aid available for students from sponsoring institution: loans.
For More Information • Ms. Susan Jacobs, Assistant Director for Study Abroad, Saint Joseph's University, 5600 City Avenue, Philadelphia, PA 19131-1395; *Phone:* 610-660-1835; *Fax:* 610-660-1697. *E-mail:* cip@sju.edu. *World Wide Web:* http://www.sju.edu/cip/

$\mathcal{G}$UATEMALA

CITY-TO-CITY
LANGUAGE LIAISON
SPANISH IN GUATEMALA (QUETZALTENAGO)

Hosted by Language Liaison
Academic Focus • Spanish language and literature.
Program Information • Students attend classes at Language Liaison (Quetzaltenago). Field trips; optional travel at an extra cost. Students typically earn 3–15 semester credits per term.
Sessions • Classes begin weekly, year-round.
Eligibility Requirements • Open to precollege students, freshmen, sophomores, juniors, seniors, graduate students, adults; no foreign language proficiency required.
Living Arrangements • Students live in locally rented apartments, host family homes, hotels. Meals are taken on one's own, with host family, in residences, in restaurants.
Costs (2005) • Contact sponsor for cost. $175 application fee. Financial aid available for all students: scholarship research service.
For More Information • Ms. Nancy Forman, President, Language Liaison, PO Box 1772, Pacific Palisades, CA 90272; *Phone:* 800-284-4448; *Fax:* 310-454-1706. *E-mail:* learn@languageliaison.com. *World Wide Web:* http://www.languageliaison.com/

ANTIGUA
ENFOREX–SPANISH IN THE SPANISH WORLD
SPANISH INTENSIVE COURSE ANTIGUA

Hosted by ENFOREX
Academic Focus • Spanish language and literature, Spanish studies.
Program Information • Students attend classes at ENFOREX (Antigua, Guatemala). Field trips to Antiqua Colonial; optional travel to Noye Civilization sites at an extra cost. Students typically earn 4 semester credits per term.
Sessions • Year-round.
Eligibility Requirements • Minimum age 18; open to freshmen, juniors, seniors, graduate students, adults; no foreign language proficiency required.
Living Arrangements • Students live in host family homes, hotels. Meals are taken as a group, on one's own, with host family.
Costs (2005) • $845 per month; includes tuition, housing, all meals, excursions, books and class materials, lab equipment, international student ID, student support services. $100 application fee. $250 nonrefundable deposit required.
For More Information • Mr. Antonio Anadón, Director of Spanish Department, ENFOREX–Spanish in the Spanish World, Alberto Aguilera, 26, 28015 Madrid, Spain; *Phone:* +34 91-594-3776; *Fax:* +34 91-594-5159. *E-mail:* promotion@enforex.es. *World Wide Web:* http://www.enforex.com/

LANGUAGE LIAISON
SPANISH IN GUATEMALA (ANTIGUA)

Hosted by Language Liaison
Academic Focus • Spanish language and literature.
Program Information • Students attend classes at Language Liaison (Antigua, Guatemala). Field trips; optional travel at an extra cost. Students typically earn 3–15 semester credits per term.
Sessions • Classes begin weekly, year-round.
Eligibility Requirements • Minimum age 17; open to freshmen, sophomores, juniors, seniors, graduate students, adults; no foreign language proficiency required.
Living Arrangements • Students live in locally rented apartments, host family homes, hotels. Meals are taken with host family, in residences, in restaurants.
Costs (2005) • Contact sponsor for cost. $175 application fee. Financial aid available for all students: scholarship research service.
For More Information • Ms. Nancy Forman, President, Language Liaison, PO Box 1772, Pacific Palisades, CA 90272; *Phone:* 800-284-4448; *Fax:* 310-454-1706. *E-mail:* learn@languageliaison.com. *World Wide Web:* http://www.languageliaison.com/

LANGUAGE LINK
PROJECTO LINGUISTICO FRANCISCO MARROQUIN OF ANTIGUA, GUATEMALA

Hosted by Projecto Linguisto Francisco Marroquin
Academic Focus • Mayan studies, Spanish language and literature.

GUATEMALA
Antigua

Program Information • Students attend classes at Projecto Linguisto Francisco Marroquin (Antigua, Guatemala). Field trips to Chichicastenango, Lake Atitlán. Students typically earn 6–15 semester credits per term.

Sessions • Classes begin every Monday, year-round.

Eligibility Requirements • Minimum age 7; open to precollege students, freshmen, sophomores, juniors, seniors, graduate students, adults; no foreign language proficiency required.

Living Arrangements • Students live in host family homes, hotels. Quarters are shared with host institution students. Meals are taken with host family, in residences, in restaurants.

Costs (2005) • $210 per week; includes tuition, housing, some meals, books and class materials, student support services. $50 deposit required.

For More Information • Ms. Kay G. Rafool, Director, Language Link, PO Box 3006, Peoria, IL 61612-3006; *Phone:* 800-552-2051; *Fax:* 309-692-2926. *E-mail:* info@langlink.com. *World Wide Web:* http://www.langlink.com/

HONDURAS

CITY-TO-CITY

SAINT MARY'S COLLEGE
HONDURAS: POVERTY AND DEVELOPMENT SUMMER SERVICE–LEARNING PROJECT

Academic Focus • Latin American studies, peace and conflict studies, political science and government.

Program Information • Faculty members are drawn from the sponsor's U.S. staff. Scheduled travel to Teguciagalpa, Copan. Students typically earn 3 semester credits per term.

Sessions • May–Jun (summer).

Eligibility Requirements • Open to freshmen, sophomores, juniors, seniors; 2.5 GPA; 3 letters of recommendation; good academic standing at home school; no foreign language proficiency required.

Living Arrangements • Meals are taken as a group, in central dining facility.

Costs (2005) • $2000; includes tuition, housing, all meals, excursions, student support services. $30 application fee.

For More Information • Mr. Marc Belanger, Faculty Director of Honduras Program, Saint Mary's College, Department of Political Science, Notre Dame, IN 46556; *Phone:* 574-284-4470; *Fax:* 574-284-4141. *E-mail:* belanger@saintmarys.edu. *World Wide Web:* http://www.saintmarys.edu/~cwil

UNIVERSITY OF SOUTHERN MISSISSIPPI
HONDURAN STUDIES

Academic Focus • Geography, psychology.

Program Information • Faculty members are drawn from the sponsor's U.S. staff. Scheduled travel; field trips. Students typically earn 4 semester credits per term.

Sessions • May–Jun (summer).

Eligibility Requirements • Minimum age 18; open to sophomores, juniors, seniors, graduate students, adults; 2.0 GPA; good academic standing at home school; no foreign language proficiency required.

Living Arrangements • Students live in hotels. Meals are taken as a group, on one's own.

Costs (2005) • $1899 for undergraduate students; $2099 for graduate students; includes tuition, housing, excursions, international airfare. $200 nonrefundable deposit required. Financial aid available for students from sponsoring institution: scholarships, loans.

For More Information • Director, Honduran Studies, University of Southern Mississippi, 118 College Drive #10047, Hattiesburg, MS 39406-0001; *Phone:* 601-266-5009; *Fax:* 601-266-5699. *E-mail:* holly.buckner@usm.edu. *World Wide Web:* http://www.usm.edu/internationaledu/

TEGUCIGALPA

CENTRO DE DISEÑO ARQUITECTURA Y CONSTRUCCIÓN
STUDENT INTERNSHIPS IN HONDURAS

Hosted by Centro de Diseño Arquitectura y Construcción

Academic Focus • Architecture, design and applied arts, graphic design/illustration, historic preservation, interior design, urban/regional planning.

Program Information • Students attend classes at Centro de Diseño Arquitectura y Construcción (Tegucigalpa, Honduras). Scheduled travel to Copan ruins; field trips to national parks, local sites; optional travel to eco-tours at an extra cost. Students typically earn 12 semester credits per term.

Sessions • Classes held year-round, start dates in Jan, May, Sep.

Eligibility Requirements • Minimum age 17; open to freshmen, sophomores, juniors, seniors; major in architecture, graphic design, interior design; 2 letters of recommendation; intermediate Spanish.

Living Arrangements • Students live in locally rented apartments, host family homes. Meals are taken on one's own, with host family, in residences, in restaurants.

Costs (2005) • $2000 for 3.5 months; includes tuition, housing, some meals, student support services, some excursions. $500 deposit required. Financial aid available for students from sponsoring institution.

For More Information • Ms. Lorette Pellettiere Calix, Administrative Vice Rector, Centro de Diseño Arquitectura y Construcción, Apartado Postal 3900, Tegucigalpa, Honduras; *Phone:* 504-232-4195; *Fax:* 504-231-0729. *E-mail:* administracion@cedac.edu.hn. *World Wide Web:* http://www.cedac.edu.hn/

 UNGARY

BUDAPEST

ACADEMIC PROGRAMS INTERNATIONAL (API)
(API)–BUDAPEST, HUNGARY

Hosted by Corvinus University of Budapest
Academic Focus • Business administration/management, economics, European studies, marketing.
Program Information • Students attend classes at Corvinus University of Budapest (Budapest, Hungary). Scheduled travel to Translyania, Romania; field trips to Buda Hills, Lake Balaton, Szentendre. Students typically earn 6 semester credits per term.
Sessions • June.
Eligibility Requirements • Minimum age 18; open to freshmen, sophomores, juniors, seniors; 2.75 GPA; 1 letter of recommendation; good academic standing at home school; official transcript from home university; no foreign language proficiency required.
Living Arrangements • Students live in locally rented apartments. Quarters are shared with host institution students. Meals are taken on one's own, in restaurants.
Costs (2006–2007) • $3400–$3500; includes tuition, housing, insurance, excursions, student support services, mobile phone, on-site director, online services. $150 nonrefundable deposit required. Financial aid available for all students: scholarships.
For More Information • Ms. Jennifer C. Allen, Director, Academic Programs International (API), 107 East Hopkins, San Marcos, TX 78666; *Phone:* 800-844-4124; *Fax:* 512-392-8420. *E-mail:* api@academicintl.com. *World Wide Web:* http://www.academicintl.com/

AMERICAN INSTITUTE FOR FOREIGN STUDY (AIFS)
AIFS–BUDAPEST, HUNGARY–CORVINUS UNIVERSITY OF BUDAPEST

Hosted by Corvinus University of Budapest
Academic Focus • Art history, economics, film and media studies, history, marketing.
Program Information • Students attend classes at Corvinus University of Budapest (Budapest, Hungary). Scheduled travel to 3-day London stopover; field trips to visit Szentendre, Visegrad, Estergom, Jewish Budapest, Hungarian Parliament, cultural activities; optional travel to 3-day excursion to Vienna for a supplement of $229 at an extra cost. Students typically earn 3-6 semester credits per term.
Sessions • Jun-Jul (summer).
Eligibility Requirements • Minimum age 17; open to precollege students, freshmen, sophomores, juniors, seniors; 2.5 GPA; no foreign language proficiency required.
Living Arrangements • Students live in host institution dormitories, program-owned apartments, hotels. Quarters are shared with host institution students. Meals are taken as a group, in residences.
Costs (2007) • 4-weeks: $4499; includes tuition, housing, some meals, insurance, excursions, student support services, On-site Resident Director, Phone Card to call the U.S., 1 month Transportation Pass, Computer Facilities. $95 application fee. $395 nonrefundable deposit required. Financial aid available for all students: scholarships.
For More Information • Mr. David Mauro, Admissions Advisor, American Institute For Foreign Study (AIFS), 9 West Broad Street, Stamford, CT 06902-3788; *Phone:* 800-727-2437 Ext. 5163; *Fax:* 203-399-5597. *E-mail:* dmauro@aifs.com. *World Wide Web:* http://www.aifsabroad.com/

CENTRAL EUROPEAN EDUCATION AND CULTURAL EXCHANGE (CEECE)
CEECE IN BUDAPEST, HUNGARY

Hosted by Corvinus University of Budapest
Academic Focus • Business administration/management.
Program Information • Students attend classes at Corvinus University of Budapest (Budapest, Hungary). Students typically earn 3 semester credits per term.
Sessions • Jun (summer).
Eligibility Requirements • Minimum age 18; open to freshmen, sophomores, juniors, seniors, graduate students, adults; 2.0 GPA; good academic standing at home school; no foreign language proficiency required.
Living Arrangements • Students live in host institution dormitories. Quarters are shared with host institution students. Meals are taken on one's own, in central dining facility, in restaurants.
Costs (2006) • $2499; includes tuition, housing. $300 refundable deposit required. Financial aid available for all students: home university financial aid.
For More Information • Mr. Eric Molengraf, Executive Director, Central European Education and Cultural Exchange (CEECE), 2956 Florence Drive, Grand Rapids, MI 49418; *Phone:* 800-352-9845. *E-mail:* info@ceece.org. *World Wide Web:* http://www.ceece.org/

LEXIA INTERNATIONAL
LEXIA SUMMER IN BUDAPEST

Hosted by Eötvös Collegium Budapest, Pázmány Péter Catholic University

Academic Focus • Anthropology, area studies, art history, civilization studies, comparative history, cultural studies, Eastern European studies, economics, ethnic studies, geography, history, Hungarian, Hungarian studies, interdisciplinary studies, international affairs, liberal studies, literature, political science and government, Slavic languages, social sciences, sociology.

Program Information • Students attend classes at Eötvös Collegium Budapest (Budapest, Hungary), Pázmány Péter Catholic University (Budapest, Hungary). Field trips to Szeged, Eger, Transylvania. Students typically earn 8–10 semester credits per term.

Sessions • Jun–Aug (summer).

Eligibility Requirements • Minimum age 18; open to freshmen, sophomores, juniors, seniors, graduate students, adults; 2.5 GPA; 2 letters of recommendation; no foreign language proficiency required.

Living Arrangements • Students live in host institution dormitories. Quarters are shared with host institution students. Meals are taken on one's own, in residences, in central dining facility, in restaurants.

Costs (2006) • $5950; includes tuition, housing, insurance, excursions, student support services, computer access, transcript. $40 application fee. $300 refundable deposit required. Financial aid available for all students: scholarships, work study.

For More Information • Lexia International, 23 South Main Street, Hanover, NH 03755; *Phone:* 800-775-3942; *Fax:* 603-643-9899. *E-mail:* info@lexiaintl.org. *World Wide Web:* http://www.lexiaintl.org/

INDIA

CITY-TO-CITY

COOPERATIVE CENTER FOR STUDY ABROAD
INDIA WINTER

Academic Focus • Art, literature.
Program Information • Faculty members are drawn from the sponsor's U.S. staff. Field trips. Students typically earn 3 semester credits per term.
Sessions • Dec-Jan (summer).
Eligibility Requirements • Minimum age 18; good academic standing at home school; no foreign language proficiency required.
Living Arrangements • Quarters are shared with host institution students. Meals are taken as a group, on one's own, in central dining facility, in restaurants.
Costs (2006–2007) • $4295; includes housing, some meals, insurance, excursions, international airfare, airport transfers. $200 nonrefundable deposit required. Financial aid available for students from sponsoring institution: scholarships, loans.
For More Information • Dr. Michael A. Klembara, Executive Director, Cooperative Center for Study Abroad, Northern Kentucky University, Nunn Drive, Founders Hall 301, Highland Heights, KY 41099; *Phone:* 859-572-6512; *Fax:* 859-572-6650. *E-mail:* ccsa@nku.edu. *World Wide Web:* http://www.ccsa.cc/

JAMES MADISON UNIVERSITY
SUMMER IN INDIA

Academic Focus • Comparative literature, international business, religious studies.
Program Information • Faculty members are drawn from the sponsor's U.S. staff. Scheduled travel. Students typically earn 6 semester credits per term.
Sessions • Jun-Jul (summer).
Eligibility Requirements • Minimum age 18; open to sophomores, juniors, seniors; 2.0 GPA; 1 letter of recommendation; good academic standing at home school; no foreign language proficiency required.
Living Arrangements • Students live in hotels. Meals are taken as a group, in restaurants.
Costs (2005) • $3208 for Virginia residents; $4888 for nonresidents; includes tuition, housing, some meals, excursions, books and class materials, international student ID. $400 deposit required.
For More Information • Mr. Felix Wang, Director, James Madison University, Office of International Programs, MSC 5731, 1077 South Main Street, Harrisonburg, VA 22807; *Phone:* 540-568-6419; *Fax:* 540-568-3310. *E-mail:* studyabroad@jmu.edu. *World Wide Web:* http://www.jmu.edu/international/

NEW YORK UNIVERSITY
SUMMER IN INDIA

Academic Focus • Cultural studies, Indian studies.
Program Information • Faculty members are drawn from the sponsor's U.S. staff and local instructors hired by the sponsor. Scheduled travel; field trips; optional travel. Students typically earn 4 semester credits per term.
Sessions • Jun (summer).
Eligibility Requirements • Minimum age 18; open to freshmen, sophomores, juniors, seniors; 3.0 GPA; good academic standing at home school.
Living Arrangements • Students live in hotels. Meals are taken on one's own, in restaurants.
Costs (2007) • $4500; includes tuition, housing, some meals, excursions. $25 application fee. $300 nonrefundable deposit required.
For More Information • Office of Summer Sessions, New York University, 7 E. 12th Street, 6th Floor, New York, NY 10003; *Phone:* 212-998-2292; *Fax:* 212-995-4642. *E-mail:* summer.info@nyu.edu. *World Wide Web:* http://www.nyu.edu/global/studyabroad.html

NORTHERN ILLINOIS UNIVERSITY
HEALTH STUDIES IN INDIA

Academic Focus • Health-care management.
Program Information • Faculty members are drawn from the sponsor's U.S. staff. Students typically earn 3 semester credits per term.
Sessions • Dec-Jan (summer).
Eligibility Requirements • Minimum age 18; open to juniors, seniors, graduate students, adults; 2.5 GPA; good academic standing at home school; no foreign language proficiency required.
Living Arrangements • Students live in hotels. Meals are taken as a group, in central dining facility.
Costs (2005) • Contact sponsor for cost. $200 nonrefundable deposit required. Financial aid available for students from sponsoring institution: loans.

For More Information • Ms. Rita Withrow, Program Assistant, Northern Illinois University, Study Abroad Office, Williston Hall 417, DeKalb, IL 60115-2854; *Phone:* 815-753-0700; *Fax:* 815-753-0825. *E-mail:* niuabroad@niu.edu. *World Wide Web:* http://www.niu.edu/niuabroad/

CALCUTTA

THE INTERNATIONAL PARTNERSHIP FOR SERVICE LEARNING AND LEADERSHIP
INDIA SERVICE–LEARNING
Hosted by Loreto College

Academic Focus • Community service, history, Indian studies, international affairs, social sciences.

Program Information • Students attend classes at Loreto College (Calcutta, India). Scheduled travel to Delhi, Agra, the Taj Mahal; field trips to Calcutta and surrounding villages, archaeological sites; optional travel to sites in India at an extra cost. Students typically earn 6 semester credits per term.

Sessions • Aug–Sep (summer), Dec–Jan (January term).

Eligibility Requirements • Minimum age 18; open to freshmen, sophomores, juniors, seniors, graduate students, adults; 2 letters of recommendation; good academic standing at home school; evidence of maturity; no foreign language proficiency required.

Living Arrangements • Students live in host family homes, hotels, guest houses. Meals are taken on one's own, with host family, in residences.

Costs (2005–2006) • $7600; includes tuition, housing, some meals, excursions, international airfare, books and class materials, student support services, service placement and supervision. $50 application fee. $250 refundable deposit required. Financial aid available for all students: federal student aid.

For More Information • Director of Student Programs, The International Partnership for Service Learning and Leadership, 815 Second Avenue, New York, NY 10017-4594; *Phone:* 212-986-0989; *Fax:* 212-986-5039. *E-mail:* info@ipsl.org. *World Wide Web:* http://www.ipsl.org/

CHENNAI

ILLINOIS STATE UNIVERSITY
CRIMINAL JUSTICE IN INDIA
Hosted by University of Madras

Academic Focus • Criminal justice.

Program Information • Students attend classes at University of Madras (Chennai, India). Field trips to the Taj Mahal. Students typically earn 3 semester credits per term.

Sessions • Jul–Aug (summer).

Eligibility Requirements • Minimum age 18; open to sophomores, juniors, seniors, graduate students, adults; major in criminal justice (preferred); 2.5 GPA; good academic standing at home school; no foreign language proficiency required.

Living Arrangements • Students live in hotels. Quarters are shared with host institution students. Meals are taken as a group, in restaurants.

Costs (2004) • $3952 (estimated); includes tuition, housing, all meals, insurance, excursions, international airfare, international student ID, student support services, personal expenses. $150 application fee. Financial aid available for students from sponsoring institution: scholarships, loans.

For More Information • Dr. Sesha Kethineni, Professor, Illinois State University, Campus Box 6120, Normal, IL 61790-6120; *Phone:* 309-438-5566; *Fax:* 309-438-3987. *E-mail:* skethine@ilstu.edu. *World Wide Web:* http://www.internationalstudies.ilstu.edu/

DHRANGADHRA

TEMPLE UNIVERSITY
TEMPLE IN INDIA

Academic Focus • Anthropology, Asian studies.

Program Information • Faculty members are drawn from the sponsor's U.S. staff and local instructors hired by the sponsor. Field trips to medieval castles, temples, villages, fairs; festivals. Students typically earn 6 semester credits per term.

Sessions • Jul–Aug (summer).

Eligibility Requirements • Minimum age 19; open to sophomores, juniors, seniors, graduate students; 2.5 GPA; 1 letter of recommendation; good academic standing at home school; official transcripts; essay; no foreign language proficiency required.

Living Arrangements • Students live in hotels. Meals are taken on one's own, in residences.

Costs (2005) • $3200–$5000; includes tuition, housing, all meals, program fee, local travel. $30 application fee. $200 nonrefundable deposit required. Financial aid available for students from sponsoring institution: scholarships, loans.

For More Information • Ms. Erin Joslyn, Study Abroad Coordinator, Temple University, International Programs, 200 Tuttleman Learning Center, 1809 North 13th Street, Philadelphia, PA 19122; *Phone:* 215-204-0720; *Fax:* 215-204-0720. *E-mail:* study.abroad@temple.edu. *World Wide Web:* http://www.temple.edu/studyabroad/

PUNE

UNIVERSITY OF PENNSYLVANIA
PENN-IN-INDIA

Academic Focus • Economics, Indian studies, medicine, performing arts, religious studies.

Program Information • Faculty members are drawn from the sponsor's U.S. staff and local instructors hired by the sponsor. Field trips to cultural sites throughout Pune. Students typically earn 2 course units per term.

Sessions • Jun–Jul (summer).

Eligibility Requirements • Open to freshmen, sophomores, juniors, seniors, graduate students; 2 letters of recommendation; good academic standing at home school; no foreign language proficiency required.

Living Arrangements • Students live in host family homes. Meals are taken with host family.

Costs (2005) • $6400; includes tuition, housing, all meals, insurance, excursions, international airfare. $50 application fee. $300 nonrefundable deposit required. Financial aid available for students from sponsoring institution: scholarships, loans.

For More Information • Penn Summer Abroad, University of Pennsylvania, 3440 Market Street, Suite 100, Philadelphia, PA 19104-3335; *Phone:* 215-746-6900; *Fax:* 215-573-2053. *E-mail:* summerabroad@sas.upenn.edu. *World Wide Web:* http://www.sas.upenn.edu/summer/

RAJASTHAN

MICHIGAN STATE UNIVERSITY
INTERNATIONAL LODGING DEVELOPMENT AND MANAGEMENT

Academic Focus • Hospitality services, international business.

Program Information • Faculty members are drawn from the sponsor's U.S. staff and local instructors hired by the sponsor. Scheduled travel to Dubai; field trips to forts, palaces, ancient villas. Students typically earn 6 semester credits per term.

Sessions • Jul–Aug (summer).

Eligibility Requirements • Minimum age 18; open to juniors, seniors, graduate students; 2.0 GPA; good academic standing at home school; no foreign language proficiency required.

Living Arrangements • Students live in hotels. Meals are taken as a group, in central dining facility.

Costs (2005) • $2279 (estimated); includes housing, all meals, insurance, excursions, student support services. $100 application fee. $200 nonrefundable deposit required. Financial aid available for students from sponsoring institution: scholarships, loans.

For More Information • Ms. Yvonne Squiers, Secretary, Michigan State University, Office of Study Abroad, 109 International Center, East Lansing, MI 48824-1035; *Phone:* 517-353-8920; *Fax:* 517-432-2082. *E-mail:* squiers@msu.edu. *World Wide Web:* http://studyabroad.msu.edu/

 NDONESIA

BALI

ARTIS ART RESEARCH TOURS AND INTERNATIONAL STUDIOS
THE ARTS IN PARADISE

Hosted by ARTIS/private studios
Academic Focus • Crafts, drawing/painting, textiles.
Program Information • Students attend classes at ARTIS/private studios (Ubud, Indonesia). Field trips to Ulu Danu, Tenganan, the beach at Jimbaran. Students typically earn 6 semester credits per term.
Sessions • Jul (summer), Jul–Aug (summer 2).
Eligibility Requirements • Minimum age 18; open to freshmen, sophomores, juniors, seniors, graduate students, adults; applicants must be in good physical and mental health; no foreign language proficiency required.
Living Arrangements • Students live in hotels. Quarters are shared with host institution students. Meals are taken on one's own, in restaurants.
Costs (2005) • $3600; includes housing, some meals, insurance, excursions, international airfare, books and class materials, student support services, class instruction, lectures. $400 nonrefundable deposit required. Financial aid available for students from sponsoring institution: scholarships, loans.
For More Information • Mr. David Renfrow, Program Director, ARTIS Art Research Tours and International Studios, 1709 Apache Drive, Medford, OR 97501; *Phone:* 800-232-6893; *Fax:* 541-535-8604. *E-mail:* david@artis.info. *World Wide Web:* http://www.artis-tours.org/

 # IRELAND

See also England, Northern Ireland, Scotland, and Wales.

CITY-TO-CITY

CENTER FOR INTERNATIONAL STUDIES
IRELAND AND THE IRISH

Academic Focus • History, Irish literature, Irish studies, political science and government.

Program Information • Faculty members are drawn from the sponsor's U.S. staff and local instructors hired by the sponsor. Scheduled travel to Ballyvaughan, Dublin, Limerick, Galway, Drogheda; field trips to Dublin, Galway, Limerick, Drogheda, Ballyvaughan. Students typically earn 3 semester credits per term.

Sessions • Jun (summer), Jan (winter).

Eligibility Requirements • Minimum age 18; open to freshmen, sophomores, juniors, seniors, graduate students, adults; 2.5 GPA; good academic standing at home school; personal statement.

Living Arrangements • Students live in hotels, cottages. Meals are taken as a group, in residences, in restaurants.

Costs (2005) • $3100–$3300 for summer term; $3100 for winter term; includes tuition, housing, some meals, excursions, international airfare, international student ID, student support services, airport reception. $50 application fee. $500 nonrefundable deposit required. Financial aid available for all students: scholarships.

For More Information • Mr. Jeff Palm, Program Director, Center for International Studies, 25 New South Street, #105, Northampton, MA 01060; *Phone:* 413-582-0407; *Fax:* 413-582-0327. *E-mail:* jpalm@cisabroad.com. *World Wide Web:* http://www.cisabroad.com/

COOPERATIVE CENTER FOR STUDY ABROAD
IRELAND PROGRAM

Held at Marino Institute of Education

Academic Focus • Archaeology, cultural studies, education, history, journalism, literature, nursing, political science and government.

Program Information • Classes are held on the campus of Marino Institute of Education (Dublin). Faculty members are drawn from the sponsor's U.S. staff. Scheduled travel to Galway; field trips to the Aran Islands, Boyne Valley, Wicklow County. Students typically earn 3 semester credits per term.

Sessions • May–Jun (summer), Jul (summer 2).

Eligibility Requirements • Minimum age 18; open to freshmen, sophomores, juniors, seniors, graduate students, adults; good academic standing at home school.

Living Arrangements • Students live in host institution dormitories, host family homes, hotels. Quarters are shared with host institution students. Meals are taken as a group, on one's own, in central dining facility, in restaurants.

Costs (2007) • $3795–$3995; includes housing, some meals, insurance, excursions, international airfare, student support services, Dublin bus/city rail pass, airport transfers. $200 nonrefundable deposit required. Financial aid available for students from sponsoring institution: scholarships, loans.

For More Information • Dr. Michael A. Klembara, Executive Director, Cooperative Center for Study Abroad, Northern Kentucky University, Nunn Drive, Founders Hall 301, Highland Heights, KY 41099; *Phone:* 800-319-6015; *Fax:* 859-572-6650. *E-mail:* ccsa@nku.edu. *World Wide Web:* http://www.ccsa.cc/

UNIVERSITY OF DELAWARE
WINTER SESSION IN IRELAND: EDUCATION

Academic Focus • Education.

Program Information • Faculty members are drawn from the sponsor's U.S. staff. Field trips to cultural and historic sites. Students typically earn 6 semester credits per term.

Sessions • Jan–Feb (winter).

Eligibility Requirements • Open to freshmen, sophomores, juniors, seniors, adults; 2.0 GPA; 1 letter of recommendation.

Living Arrangements • Students live in hotels. Meals are taken on one's own, in restaurants.

Costs (2005) • Contact sponsor for cost. $200 nonrefundable deposit required. Financial aid available for all students: scholarships.

For More Information • Center for International Studies, University of Delaware, 186 South College Avenue, Newark, DE 19716-1450; *Phone:* 888-831-4685; *Fax:* 302-831-6042. *E-mail:* studyabroad@udel.edu. *World Wide Web:* http://www.udel.edu/studyabroad/

CORK

ACADEMIC PROGRAMS INTERNATIONAL (API)
(API)–CORK, IRELAND
Hosted by University College Cork
Academic Focus • History, Irish studies.
Program Information • Students attend classes at University College Cork (Cork, Ireland). Scheduled travel to Dublin; field trips to Blarney Castle; Bunratty Castle, The Burren; Kinsale;, Connemara; Cliffs of Moher; Ring of Kerry, Mountshannon. Students typically earn 6 semester credits per term.
Sessions • Jun–Jul (summer).
Eligibility Requirements • Minimum age 18; open to freshmen, sophomores, juniors, seniors; 2.85 GPA; 1 letter of recommendation; good academic standing at home school; official transcript from home university.
Living Arrangements • Students live in host institution dormitories, locally rented apartments. Quarters are shared with host institution students, students from other programs. Meals are taken on one's own, in residences, in restaurants.
Costs (2006–2007) • $4900; includes tuition, housing, insurance, excursions, student support services, airport reception, ground transportation, mobile phone, on-line service, on-site director. $150 nonrefundable deposit required. Financial aid available for all students: scholarships.
For More Information • Ms. Jennifer C. Allen, Director, Academic Programs International (API), 107 East. Hopkins, San Marcos, TX 78666; *Phone:* 800-844-4124; *Fax:* 512-392-8420. *E-mail:* api@academicintl.com. *World Wide Web:* http://www.academicintl.com/

INSTITUTE FOR STUDY ABROAD, BUTLER UNIVERSITY
UNIVERSITY COLLEGE CORK–SUMMER STUDY
Hosted by University College Cork
Academic Focus • Irish studies.
Program Information • Students attend classes at University College Cork (Cork, Ireland). Field trips to literary and historic tours of Cork and Munster. Students typically earn 6 semester credits per term.
Sessions • Jun–Jul (summer).
Eligibility Requirements • Open to sophomores, juniors, seniors; 2.5 GPA; good academic standing at home school; enrollment at an accredited American college or university.
Living Arrangements • Students live in program-owned apartments. Quarters are shared with host institution students. Meals are taken on one's own, in residences, in restaurants.
Costs (2005) • $3375; includes tuition, housing, excursions, student support services, pre-departure advising. $40 application fee. $500 nonrefundable deposit required. Financial aid available for all students: scholarships.
For More Information • Institute for Study Abroad, Butler University, 1100 West 42nd Street, Suite 305, Indianapolis, IN 46208-3345; *Phone:* 800-858-0229; *Fax:* 317-940-9704. *E-mail:* study-abroad@butler.edu. *World Wide Web:* http://www.ifsa-butler.org/

STATE UNIVERSITY OF NEW YORK COLLEGE AT CORTLAND
UNIVERSITY COLLEGE CORK, IRELAND–SUMMER
Hosted by University College Cork
Academic Focus • History, Irish literature, Irish studies.
Program Information • Students attend classes at University College Cork (Cork, Ireland). Scheduled travel to Kilkenny, other sites of historic, cultural, and artistic significance; field trips to Blarney Castle, archaeological sites, historic sites; optional travel at an extra cost. Students typically earn 4–6 semester credits per term.
Sessions • Jun–Jul (summer).
Eligibility Requirements • Minimum age 18; open to freshmen, sophomores, juniors, seniors; 2.5 GPA; 2 letters of recommendation; good academic standing at home school.

Living Arrangements • Students live in locally rented apartments. Quarters are shared with students from other programs. Meals are taken on one's own, in residences.
Costs (2005) • $4785; includes tuition, housing, all meals, insurance, excursions, international airfare, books and class materials, international student ID, student support services, passport fees. $20 application fee. $250 nonrefundable deposit required. Financial aid available for students from sponsoring institution: scholarships, loans.
For More Information • Ms. Liz McCartney, Assistant Director, Office of International Programs, State University of New York College at Cortland, PO Box 2000, Cortland, NY 13045; *Phone:* 607-753-2209; *Fax:* 607-753-5989. *E-mail:* cortlandabroad@cortland.edu. *World Wide Web:* http://www.cortlandabroad.com/

DINGLE

STATE UNIVERSITY OF NEW YORK COLLEGE AT CORTLAND
ART IN IRELAND–DINGLE, IRELAND
Academic Focus • Drawing/painting, fine/studio arts.
Program Information • Faculty members are drawn from the sponsor's U.S. staff. Optional travel to Dublin, Shannon, Cork, Galway, Ring of Kerry at an extra cost. Students typically earn 6 semester credits per term.
Sessions • May–Jun (summer).
Eligibility Requirements • Minimum age 18; open to freshmen, sophomores, juniors, seniors, graduate students, adults; 2.5 GPA; 2 letters of recommendation; good academic standing at home school; college course work in painting or drawing or permission of instructor.
Living Arrangements • Students live in locally rented apartments, hostels. Quarters are shared with students from other programs. Meals are taken on one's own, in central dining facility, in restaurants.
Costs (2005) • $4531; includes tuition, housing, all meals, insurance, excursions, international airfare, books and class materials, international student ID, student support services, passport fees, transfers. $20 application fee. $200 nonrefundable deposit required. Financial aid available for students from sponsoring institution: scholarships, loans.
For More Information • Ms. Liz McCartney, Assistant Director, Office of International Programs, State University of New York College at Cortland, PO Box 2000, Cortland, NY 13045; *Phone:* 607-753-2209; *Fax:* 607-753-5989. *E-mail:* cortlandabroad@cortland.edu. *World Wide Web:* http://www.cortlandabroad.com/

DUBLIN

AHA INTERNATIONAL AN ACADEMIC PROGRAM OF THE UNIVERSITY OF OREGON
DUBLIN, IRELAND: MIDWEST CONSORTIUM FOR STUDY ABROAD (MCSA) AND NORTHWEST COUNCIL ON STUDY ABROAD (NCSA)
Held at AHA Dublin Centre
Academic Focus • Drama/theater, film and media studies, history, Irish literature, Irish studies.
Program Information • Classes are held on the campus of AHA Dublin Centre (Dublin, Ireland). Faculty members are drawn from the sponsor's U.S. staff and local instructors hired by the sponsor. Field trips to local areas of academic interest. Students typically earn 6–12 semester credits per term.
Sessions • Jul–Aug (summer).
Eligibility Requirements • Open to sophomores, juniors, seniors; 2.5 GPA; 2 letters of recommendation; good academic standing at home school; official transcripts.
Living Arrangements • Students live in host family homes. Quarters are shared with host institution students. Meals are taken with host family, in residences, in restaurants.
Costs (2005) • $3215; includes tuition, housing, some meals, insurance, excursions, books and class materials, international student ID, student support services, local transportation pass, VCD library, computer lab access, on-site orientation. $50 application fee.

$200 refundable deposit required. Financial aid available for all students: scholarships, loans, home institution financial aid.
For More Information • Ms. Gail Lavin, Associate Director for University Programs, AHA International An Academic Program of the University of Oregon, 221 NW 2nd Avenue, Suite 200, Portland, OR 97209; *Phone:* 503-295-7730; *Fax:* 503-295-5969. *E-mail:* mail@aha-intl.org. *World Wide Web:* http://www.aha-intl.org/

AMERICAN COLLEGE DUBLIN
AMERICAN COLLEGE DUBLIN (SUMMER)
Hosted by American College Dublin
Academic Focus • Art history, history, hospitality services, hotel and restaurant management, human resources, international business, Irish literature, Irish studies.
Program Information • Students attend classes at American College Dublin (Dublin, Ireland). Optional travel to Italy, Ireland (Irish Commerce Study Tour) at an extra cost. Students typically earn 6-9 semester credits per term.
Sessions • Jun–Jul (summer).
Eligibility Requirements • Minimum age 18; open to freshmen, sophomores, juniors, seniors; 2.5 GPA; good academic standing at home school; must be at least a second semester freshman.
Living Arrangements • Students live in host institution dormitories. Quarters are shared with host institution students. Meals are taken as a group, in central dining facility.
Costs (2005) • $3450 for 4 weeks; $4900 for 6 weeks (optional study tour is an additional $1950); includes tuition, housing, some meals, student support services. $35 application fee. $500 nonrefundable deposit required.
For More Information • Mr. Rich Wehmeyer, Director, American College Dublin Study Abroad Program, American College Dublin, 3001 Philadelphia Pike, Claymont, DE 19703; *Phone:* 302-793-1106; *Fax:* 302-793-1140. *E-mail:* richw@acdireland.edu. *World Wide Web:* http://www.acdireland.edu/

ARCADIA UNIVERSITY
CONTEMPORARY IRISH STUDIES
Hosted by Institute of Public Administration
Academic Focus • History, Irish literature, Irish studies, political science and government.
Program Information • Students attend classes at Institute of Public Administration (Dublin, Ireland). Field trips to the theater, Irish Parliament, areas outside Dublin. Students typically earn 6 semester credits per term.
Sessions • Jun–Aug (summer).
Eligibility Requirements • Open to sophomores, juniors, seniors, graduate students, adults; 3.0 GPA; 1 letter of recommendation; 3 semesters of college-level work.
Living Arrangements • Students live in locally rented apartments. Quarters are shared with host institution students. Meals are taken on one's own, in residences, in restaurants.
Costs (2005–2006) • $3875; includes tuition, housing, insurance, international student ID, student support services, transcript, pre-departure guide, orientation. $35 application fee. $500 nonrefundable deposit required. Financial aid available for all students: loans.
For More Information • Arcadia University, Center for Education Abroad, 450 South Easton Road, Glenside, PA 19038-3295; *Phone:* 866-927-2234; *Fax:* 215-572-2174. *E-mail:* cea@arcadia.edu. *World Wide Web:* http://www.arcadia.edu/cea/

BOSTON UNIVERSITY
DUBLIN LIBERAL ARTS AND INTERNSHIP PROGRAM
Held at Dublin City University
Academic Focus • Advertising and public relations, art history, communications, economics, film and media studies, history, international affairs, Irish literature, Irish studies, journalism, law and legal studies, political science and government, visual and performing arts.
Program Information • Classes are held on the campus of Dublin City University (Dublin, Ireland). Faculty members are local instructors hired by the sponsor. Students typically earn 8 semester credits per term.
Sessions • May–Jul (summer).

Eligibility Requirements • Open to sophomores, juniors, seniors; 1 letter of recommendation; good academic standing at home school; essay; approval of participation; transcript; minimum GPA of 3.0 in major and overall.
Living Arrangements • Students live in program-owned apartments. Meals are taken on one's own, in residences, in restaurants.
Costs (2005) • $6000; includes tuition, housing, insurance, excursions, academic fees. $50 application fee. $400 nonrefundable deposit required. Financial aid available for all students: scholarships, loans.
For More Information • Division of International Programs, Boston University, 232 Bay State Street, Boston, MA 02215; *Phone:* 617-353-9888; *Fax:* 617-353-5402. *E-mail:* abroad@bu.edu. *World Wide Web:* http://www.bu.edu/abroad/

CIEE
CIEE STUDY CENTER AT DUBLIN CITY UNIVERSITY, DUBLIN, IRELAND
Hosted by Dublin City University
Academic Focus • Irish studies.
Program Information • Students attend classes at Dublin City University (Dublin, Ireland). Field trips to Galway, Derry, museums, cathedrals, galleries, historic sites. Students typically earn 3 semester credits per term.
Sessions • Jun–May (summer).
Eligibility Requirements • Minimum age 18; open to sophomores, juniors, seniors; 2.75 GPA; 1 letter of recommendation; good academic standing at home school.
Living Arrangements • Students live in host institution dormitories, host family homes. Quarters are shared with host institution students. Meals are taken on one's own, with host family, in residences, in central dining facility, in restaurants.
Costs (2007) • Contact sponsor for cost. $30 application fee. $300 nonrefundable deposit required. Financial aid available for all students: scholarships, minority student scholarships.
For More Information • Information Center, CIEE, 7 Custom House Street, 3rd Floor, Portland, ME 04101; *Phone:* 800-40-STUDY; *Fax:* 207-553-7699. *E-mail:* studyinfo@ciee.org. *World Wide Web:* http://www.ciee.org/isp/

COOPERATIVE CENTER FOR STUDY ABROAD
INTERNSHIPS IN DUBLIN
Academic Focus • Full curriculum.
Sessions • Year-round.
Eligibility Requirements • Minimum age 18; open to freshmen, sophomores, juniors, seniors, graduate students, adults; 2 letters of recommendation; good academic standing at home school.
Living Arrangements • Students live in host family homes. Quarters are shared with students from other programs. Meals are taken on one's own, with host family, in residences, in restaurants.
Costs (2007) • $3995-$4295; includes housing, some meals, insurance, international student ID, student support services, internship placement. $200 nonrefundable deposit required. Financial aid available for students from sponsoring institution: scholarships, loans.
For More Information • Dr. Michael A. Klembara, Executive Director, Cooperative Center for Study Abroad, Northern Kentucky University, Nunn Drive, Founders Hall 301, Highland Heights, KY 41099; *Phone:* 800-319-6015; *Fax:* 859-572-6650. *E-mail:* ccsa@nku.edu. *World Wide Web:* http://www.ccsa.cc/

GRIFFITH COLLEGE DUBLIN
SUMMER STUDY ABROAD
Hosted by Griffith College Dublin
Academic Focus • Full curriculum.
Program Information • Students attend classes at Griffith College Dublin (Dublin, Ireland). Optional travel to Galway, Killarney at an extra cost. Students typically earn 3-6 semester credits per term.
Sessions • Jul–Aug (summer).
Eligibility Requirements • Minimum age 17; open to precollege students, freshmen, sophomores, juniors, seniors, graduate students, adults; 2.5 GPA; 2 letters of recommendation; good academic standing at home school.

IRELAND
Dublin

Living Arrangements • Students live in host institution dormitories, locally rented apartments, host family homes. Quarters are shared with host institution students. Meals are taken on one's own, in residences.
Costs (2005) • €2500; includes tuition, student support services. €100 application fee. €600 nonrefundable deposit required. Financial aid available for all students: scholarships, loans.
For More Information • Ms. Laura Scott, Field Director, North America, Griffith College Dublin, 804 122nd Street Ct NW, Gig Harbor, WA 98332; *Phone:* 253-853-1524; *Fax:* 253-858-9741. *E-mail:* gcdlaurascott@yahoo.com. *World Wide Web:* http://www.gcdinternational.ie/

JAMES MADISON UNIVERSITY
SUMMER IN IRELAND

Academic Focus • Creative writing, film and media studies, Irish literature.
Program Information • Faculty members are drawn from the sponsor's U.S. staff. Scheduled travel to Dublin, Cork, Galway. Students typically earn 6 semester credits per term.
Sessions • Jun–Jul (summer).
Eligibility Requirements • Minimum age 18; open to juniors, seniors; 2.0 GPA; good academic standing at home school.
Living Arrangements • Students live in host institution dormitories, hotels. Meals are taken as a group, on one's own, in central dining facility, in restaurants.
Costs (2005) • $4188 for Virginia residents; $5868 for nonresidents; includes tuition, housing, some meals, excursions, books and class materials, international student ID. $400 nonrefundable deposit required. Financial aid available for students from sponsoring institution: work study.
For More Information • Mr. Felix Wang, Director, James Madison University, Office of International Programs, MSC 5731, 1077 South Main Street, Harrisonburg, VA 22807; *Phone:* 540-568-6419; *Fax:* 540-568-3310. *E-mail:* studyabroad@jmu.edu. *World Wide Web:* http://www.jmu.edu/international/

KNOWLEDGE EXCHANGE INSTITUTE (KEI)
BUSINESS LAW AND DIPLOMACY

Hosted by Griffith College Dublin
Academic Focus • Accounting, advertising and public relations, business administration/management, Celtic studies, commerce, communications, community service, criminal justice, economics, entrepreneurship, European studies, finance, hospitality services, hotel and restaurant management, human resources, information science, intercultural studies, interdisciplinary studies, international affairs, Irish studies, labor and industrial relations, law and legal studies, liberal studies, management information systems, marketing, political science and government, public administration, public policy, sports management, statistics, tourism and travel.
Program Information • Students attend classes at Griffith College Dublin (Dublin, Ireland). Scheduled travel to Northern Ireland, Great Britain; field trips to Limerick, Galway, Cork. Students typically earn 12 semester credits per term.
Sessions • Jun–Aug (summer).
Eligibility Requirements • Open to freshmen, sophomores, juniors, seniors, graduate students, adults; 2.2 GPA; 2 letters of recommendation; good academic standing at home school.
Living Arrangements • Students live in host institution dormitories. Quarters are shared with host institution students, students from other programs. Meals are taken on one's own, in residences, in central dining facility, in restaurants.
Costs (2006) • $5970; includes tuition, housing, insurance, excursions, lab equipment, student support services, mobile phone and internet access. $50 application fee. $500 nonrefundable deposit required. Financial aid available for all students: scholarships, loans.
For More Information • Mr. Eduard Izraylovsky, Director, Knowledge Exchange Institute (KEI), 111 John Street, Suite 800, New York, NY 10038; *Phone:* 800-831-5095; *Fax:* 212-528-2095. *E-mail:* info@knowledgeexchange.org. *World Wide Web:* http://www.knowledgeexchange.org/

KNOWLEDGE EXCHANGE INSTITUTE (KEI)
COMPUTER SCIENCE AND SOFTWARE ENGINEERING

Hosted by Griffith College Dublin
Academic Focus • Celtic studies, communication services, communications, computer science, cultural studies, economics, graphic design/illustration, information science, intercultural studies, international business, Irish studies, telecommunications.
Program Information • Students attend classes at Griffith College Dublin (Dublin, Ireland). Scheduled travel to Northern Ireland, Great Britain; field trips to Galway, Cork, Limerick. Students typically earn 12 semester credits per term.
Sessions • Jun–Aug (summer).
Eligibility Requirements • Open to freshmen, sophomores, juniors, seniors, graduate students, adults; 2.2 GPA; 2 letters of recommendation; good academic standing at home school.
Living Arrangements • Students live in host institution dormitories. Quarters are shared with host institution students, students from other programs. Meals are taken on one's own, in central dining facility, in restaurants.
Costs (2006) • $5970; includes tuition, housing, insurance, excursions, lab equipment, student support services, mobile phone, internet access. $50 application fee. $500 nonrefundable deposit required. Financial aid available for all students: scholarships, loans.
For More Information • Mr. Eduard Izraylovsky, Director, Knowledge Exchange Institute (KEI), 111 John Street, Suite 800, New York, NY 10038; *Phone:* 800-831-5095; *Fax:* 212-528-2095. *E-mail:* info@knowledgeexchange.org. *World Wide Web:* http://www.knowledgeexchange.org/

KNOWLEDGE EXCHANGE INSTITUTE (KEI)
DUBLIN INTERNSHIP PROGRAM

Held at Griffith College Dublin
Academic Focus • Accounting, actuarial science, advertising and public relations, art administration, business administration/management, Celtic studies, cinematography, commerce, commercial art, communication services, communications, community service, computer science, criminal justice, drama/theater, economics, entrepreneurship, fashion design, film and media studies, finance, hospitality services, human resources, information science, interior design, international affairs, international business, Irish literature, journalism, law and legal studies, management information systems, marketing, music, music performance, peace and conflict studies, performing arts, photography, political science and government, psychology, public administration, radio, social services, social work, sports management, telecommunications, theater management, tourism and travel, visual and performing arts.
Program Information • Classes are held on the campus of Griffith College Dublin (Dublin, Ireland). Field trips to Dublin, Cork, Galway. Students typically earn 6 semester credits per term.
Sessions • Jun–Aug (summer).
Eligibility Requirements • Open to freshmen, sophomores, juniors, seniors, graduate students, adults; 2.2 GPA; 2 letters of recommendation; good academic standing at home school.
Living Arrangements • Students live in host institution dormitories, program-owned apartments, host family homes. Quarters are shared with host institution students, students from other programs. Meals are taken on one's own, with host family, in residences, in restaurants.
Costs (2006) • $4965; includes tuition, housing, insurance, excursions, student support services, mobile phone. $50 application fee. $500 nonrefundable deposit required. Financial aid available for all students: scholarships.
For More Information • Mr. Eduard Izraylovsky, Director, Knowledge Exchange Institute (KEI), 111 John Street, Suite 800, New York, NY 10038; *Phone:* 800-831-5095; *Fax:* 212-528-2095. *E-mail:* info@knowledgeexchange.org. *World Wide Web:* http://www.knowledgeexchange.org/

KNOWLEDGE EXCHANGE INSTITUTE (KEI)
INTERIOR DESIGN

Hosted by Griffith College Dublin
Academic Focus • Aesthetics, architecture, art, Celtic studies, cultural studies, interdisciplinary studies, interior design, Irish studies, liberal studies.

Program Information • Students attend classes at Griffith College Dublin (Dublin, Ireland). Scheduled travel to Northern Ireland, Great Britain; field trips to Galway, Cork, Limerick, Dublin. Students typically earn 12 semester credits per term.
Sessions • Jun–Aug (summer).
Eligibility Requirements • Open to freshmen, sophomores, juniors, seniors, graduate students, adults; 2.2 GPA; 2 letters of recommendation; good academic standing at home school.
Living Arrangements • Students live in host institution dormitories. Quarters are shared with host institution students, students from other programs. Meals are taken on one's own, in central dining facility, in restaurants.
Costs (2006) • $5970; includes tuition, housing, insurance, excursions, lab equipment, student support services, mobile phone, internet access. $50 application fee. $500 nonrefundable deposit required. Financial aid available for all students: scholarships, loans.
For More Information • Mr. Eduard Izraylovsky, Director, Knowledge Exchange Institute (KEI), 111 John Street, Suite 800, New York, NY 10038; *Phone:* 800-831-5095; *Fax:* 212-528-2095. *E-mail:* info@knowledgeexchange.org. *World Wide Web:* http://www.knowledgeexchange.org/

KNOWLEDGE EXCHANGE INSTITUTE (KEI)
IRISH CULTURE AND HUMANITIES

Hosted by Griffith College Dublin
Academic Focus • Art, Celtic studies, communications, community service, comparative history, comparative literature, creative writing, criminal justice, economics, English, English literature, ethics, ethnic studies, history, intercultural studies, interdisciplinary studies, Irish literature, Irish studies, law and legal studies, liberal studies, literature, mathematics, philosophy, political science and government, psychology, public policy, Serbian, social sciences, social work, sociology.
Program Information • Students attend classes at Griffith College Dublin (Dublin, Ireland). Scheduled travel to Nmorthern Ireland, Great Britain; field trips to Galway, Cork, Limerick. Students typically earn 12 semester credits per term.
Sessions • Jun–Aug (summer).
Eligibility Requirements • Open to freshmen, sophomores, juniors, seniors, graduate students, adults; 2.2 GPA; 2 letters of recommendation; good academic standing at home school.
Living Arrangements • Students live in host institution dormitories. Quarters are shared with host institution students, students from other programs. Meals are taken on one's own, in central dining facility, in restaurants.
Costs (2006) • $5970; includes tuition, housing, insurance, excursions, lab equipment, student support services, mobile phone, internet access. $50 application fee. $500 nonrefundable deposit required. Financial aid available for all students: scholarships, loans.
For More Information • Mr. Eduard Izraylovsky, Director, Knowledge Exchange Institute (KEI), 111 John Street, Suite 800, New York, NY 10038; *Phone:* 800-831-5095; *Fax:* 212-528-2095. *E-mail:* info@knowledgeexchange.org. *World Wide Web:* http://www.knowledgeexchange.org/

KNOWLEDGE EXCHANGE INSTITUTE (KEI)
JOURNALISM AND MASS MEDIA

Hosted by Griffith College Dublin
Academic Focus • Celtic studies, communication services, communications, comparative literature, creative writing, cultural studies, English, English literature, European studies, film and media studies, information science, intercultural studies, interdisciplinary studies, international affairs, Irish literature, Irish studies, journalism, liberal studies, literature, photography, radio, speech communication, speech pathology, telecommunications.
Program Information • Students attend classes at Griffith College Dublin (Dublin, Ireland). Scheduled travel to Northern Ireland, Great Britain; field trips to Galway, Cork, Limerick. Students typically earn 12 semester credits per term.
Sessions • Jun–Aug (summer).
Eligibility Requirements • Open to freshmen, sophomores, juniors, seniors, graduate students, adults; 2.2 GPA; 2 letters of recommendation; good academic standing at home school.
Living Arrangements • Students live in host institution dormitories. Quarters are shared with host institution students, students

from other programs. Meals are taken on one's own, in residences, in central dining facility, in restaurants.
Costs (2006) • $5970; includes tuition, housing, insurance, excursions, lab equipment, student support services, mobile phone, internet access. $50 application fee. $500 nonrefundable deposit required. Financial aid available for all students: scholarships, loans.
For More Information • Mr. Eduard Izraylovsky, Director, Knowledge Exchange Institute (KEI), 111 John Street, Suite 800, New York, NY 10038; *Phone:* 800-831-5095; *Fax:* 212-528-2095. *E-mail:* info@knowledgeexchange.org. *World Wide Web:* http://www.knowledgeexchange.org/

KNOWLEDGE EXCHANGE INSTITUTE (KEI)
MUSIC AND DRAMA

Hosted by Griffith College Dublin
Academic Focus • Celtic studies, cultural studies, drama/theater, graphic design/illustration, interdisciplinary studies, liberal studies, music, music theory, performing arts, speech communication, theater management, visual and performing arts.
Program Information • Students attend classes at Griffith College Dublin (Dublin, Ireland). Scheduled travel to Northern Ireland, Great Britain; field trips to Galway, Cork, Limerick. Students typically earn 12 semester credits per term.
Sessions • Jun–Aug (summer).
Eligibility Requirements • Open to freshmen, sophomores, juniors, seniors, graduate students, adults; 2.2 GPA; 2 letters of recommendation; good academic standing at home school.
Living Arrangements • Students live in host institution dormitories. Quarters are shared with host institution students, students from other programs. Meals are taken on one's own, in central dining facility, in restaurants.
Costs (2006) • $5970; includes tuition, housing, insurance, excursions, lab equipment, student support services, mobile phone, internet access. $50 application fee. $500 nonrefundable deposit required. Financial aid available for all students: scholarships, loans.
For More Information • Mr. Eduard Izraylovsky, Director, Knowledge Exchange Institute (KEI), 111 John Street, Suite 800, New York, NY 10038; *Phone:* 800-831-5095; *Fax:* 212-528-2095. *E-mail:* info@knowledgeexchange.org. *World Wide Web:* http://www.knowledgeexchange.org/

LOYOLA UNIVERSITY NEW ORLEANS
IRISH STUDIES SUMMER PROGRAM

Held at University of Dublin–Trinity College
Academic Focus • English literature, philosophy, religious studies.
Program Information • Classes are held on the campus of University of Dublin–Trinity College (Dublin, Ireland). Faculty members are drawn from the sponsor's U.S. staff. Field trips to Sligo, Belfast; optional travel to England, France at an extra cost. Students typically earn 6 semester credits per term.
Sessions • Jul (summer).
Eligibility Requirements • Minimum age 18; open to freshmen, sophomores, juniors, seniors; 2.0 GPA; good academic standing at home school.
Living Arrangements • Students live in host institution dormitories. Quarters are shared with host institution students. Meals are taken on one's own, in restaurants.
Costs (2006) • $3800; includes tuition, housing, some meals, insurance, excursions, student support services. $380 nonrefundable deposit required. Financial aid available for students from sponsoring institution: scholarships, loans.
For More Information • Dr. Mary McCay, Professor of English, Loyola University New Orleans, 6363 Saint Charles Avenue, New Orleans, LA 70018; *Phone:* 504-865-3389; *Fax:* 504-865-2294. *E-mail:* mccay@loyno.edu. *World Wide Web:* http://www.loyno.edu/cie/

LYNN UNIVERSITY
ACADEMIC ADVENTURE ABROAD–IRELAND

Hosted by American College Dublin
Academic Focus • Art history, business administration/management, communications, economics, English, history, hospitality services, hotel and restaurant management, international affairs, international business, Irish literature, Irish studies, literature, marketing, psychology, sociology, tourism and travel.

IRELAND
Dublin

Program Information • Students attend classes at American College Dublin (Dublin, Ireland). Field trips; optional travel to Ireland (10-day tour), Italy (10-day arts and humanities tour) at an extra cost. Students typically earn 6–9 semester credits per term.
Sessions • May-June (4-weeks); May-July (6 weeks); June-July (4 weeks).
Eligibility Requirements • Open to freshmen, sophomores, juniors, seniors, graduate students, adults; 2.0 GPA; good academic standing at home school; essay and separate application required for internship program.
Living Arrangements • Students live in host institution dormitories. Quarters are shared with host institution students. Meals are taken as a group, on one's own, in residences, in restaurants.
Costs (2006) • $3635 for 4 weeks; $5120 for 6 weeks (estimated); includes tuition, housing, some meals, insurance, student support services. $35 application fee. $500 nonrefundable deposit required. Financial aid available for all students: scholarships, work study, loans, consortium agreements for non-Lynn University students.
For More Information • Study Abroad Advisor-Ireland Programs, Lynn University, 3601 North Military Trail, Boca Raton, FL 33431-5598; *Phone:* 800-453-8306; *Fax:* 561-237-7095. *E-mail:* studyabroad@lynn.edu. *World Wide Web:* http://www.lynn.edu/studyabroad/

MICHIGAN STATE UNIVERSITY
ENGLISH DEPARTMENT SUMMER PROGRAM IN DUBLIN

Held at Irish Film Centre, Irish Writer's Centre
Academic Focus • Comparative literature, creative writing, English literature, Irish literature.
Program Information • Classes are held on the campus of Irish Film Centre (Dublin, Ireland), Irish Writer's Centre (Dublin, Ireland). Faculty members are drawn from the sponsor's U.S. staff and local instructors hired by the sponsor. Field trips to historic sites in Galway and Sligo. Students typically earn 8 semester credits per term.
Sessions • Jul–Aug (summer).
Eligibility Requirements • Minimum age 18; open to freshmen, sophomores, juniors, seniors, graduate students; 2.0 GPA; 2 letters of recommendation; good academic standing at home school; faculty approval.
Living Arrangements • Students live in host institution dormitories, locally rented apartments. Quarters are shared with host institution students, students from other programs. Meals are taken on one's own, in residences, in restaurants.
Costs (2005) • $4150; includes housing, some meals, insurance, excursions, student support services. $100 application fee. $200 nonrefundable deposit required. Financial aid available for students from sponsoring institution: scholarships, loans.
For More Information • Mrs. Meghan Hock, Educational Programs Coordinator, Michigan State University, Office of Study Abroad, 109 International Center, East Lansing, MI 48824-1035; *Phone:* 517-353-8920; *Fax:* 517-432-2082. *E-mail:* hock@msu.edu. *World Wide Web:* http://studyabroad.msu.edu/

NEW YORK UNIVERSITY
NYU IN DUBLIN

Hosted by University of Dublin–Trinity College
Academic Focus • Celtic studies, drama/theater, Gaelic, history, Irish literature, Irish studies, political science and government.
Program Information • Students attend classes at University of Dublin–Trinity College (Dublin, Ireland). Scheduled travel to Donegal, Wicklow, Galway; field trips to Wicklow, Donegal, Galway. Students typically earn 8 semester credits per term.
Sessions • Jun–Aug (summer).

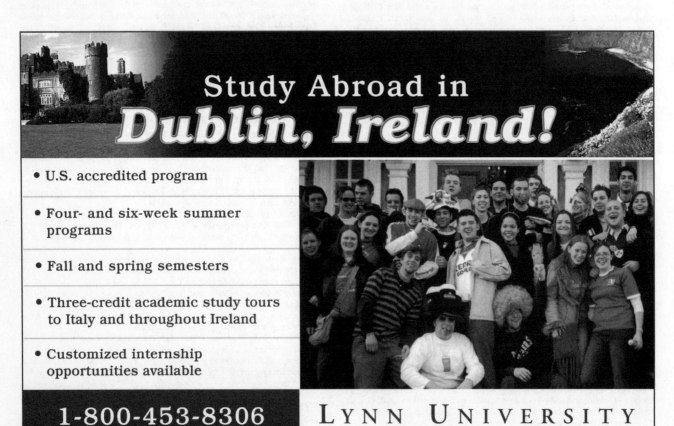

Study Abroad in Dublin, Ireland!

- U.S. accredited program
- Four- and six-week summer programs
- Fall and spring semesters
- Three-credit academic study tours to Italy and throughout Ireland
- Customized internship opportunities available

1-800-453-8306
studyabroad@lynn.edu
www.lynn.edu/studyabroad

LYNN UNIVERSITY
Study Abroad

Eligibility Requirements • Minimum age 18; open to freshmen, sophomores, juniors, seniors, graduate students; 3.0 GPA; good academic standing at home school; personal statement for non-New York University students.

Living Arrangements • Students live in host institution dormitories, locally rented apartments. Quarters are shared with host institution students. Meals are taken on one's own, in residences.

Costs (2006) • $8059; includes tuition, housing, excursions, student support services, program fee. $25 application fee. $300 nonrefundable deposit required. Financial aid available for students from sponsoring institution: loans.

For More Information • Office of Summer Sessions, New York University, 7 East 12th Street, 6th Floor, New York, NY 10003; *Phone:* 212-998-2292; *Fax:* 212-995-4642. *E-mail:* summer.info@nyu.edu. *World Wide Web:* http://www.nyu.edu/global/studyabroad.html

NORTHERN ILLINOIS UNIVERSITY
MEDIA AND CULTURE IN IRELAND

Held at Dublin City University

Academic Focus • Communications, film and media studies, Irish literature, Irish studies.

Program Information • Classes are held on the campus of Dublin City University (Dublin, Ireland). Faculty members are drawn from the sponsor's U.S. staff. Scheduled travel to Galway Film Festival; field trips. Students typically earn 3-6 semester credits per term.

Sessions • Jun-Jul (summer).

Eligibility Requirements • Minimum age 18; open to sophomores, juniors, seniors, graduate students, adults; 2.5 GPA; good academic standing at home school.

Living Arrangements • Students live in host family homes. Quarters are shared with host institution students. Meals are taken with host family, in residences.

Costs (2005) • $3275; includes tuition, housing, some meals, insurance, excursions, international student ID, student support services. $200 nonrefundable deposit required. Financial aid available for students from sponsoring institution: loans.

For More Information • Ms. Rita Withrow, Program Assistant, Northern Illinois University, Study Abroad Office, Williston Hall 417, DeKalb, IL 60115; *Phone:* 815-753-0700; *Fax:* 815-753-0825. *E-mail:* niuabroad@niu.edu. *World Wide Web:* http://www.niu.edu/niuabroad/

STATE UNIVERSITY OF NEW YORK AT OSWEGO
SUMMER INTERNSHIPS IN DUBLIN, IRELAND

Hosted by University College Dublin–National University of Ireland, Dublin

Academic Focus • Business administration/management, Irish studies.

Program Information • Students attend classes at University College Dublin–National University of Ireland, Dublin (Dublin, Ireland). Field trips; optional travel at an extra cost. Students typically earn 6 semester credits per term.

Sessions • Jun-Jul (summer).

Eligibility Requirements • Minimum age 18; open to freshmen, sophomores, juniors, seniors; 3.0 GPA; 1 letter of recommendation; good academic standing at home school.

Living Arrangements • Students live in host institution dormitories, locally rented apartments. Quarters are shared with students from other programs. Meals are taken on one's own, in restaurants.

Costs (2005) • $5100; includes tuition, insurance, excursions, books and class materials, student support services, internship placement. $250 nonrefundable deposit required. Financial aid available for students: home institution financial aid; loan processing and scholarships for Oswego students.

For More Information • Ms. Mary Kerr, Program Specialist, State University of New York at Oswego, 122A Swetman Hall, Oswego, NY 13126-3599; *Phone:* 888-4-OSWEGO; *Fax:* 315-312-2477. *E-mail:* intled@oswego.edu. *World Wide Web:* http://www.oswego.edu/intled/

STATE UNIVERSITY OF NEW YORK COLLEGE AT BROCKPORT
GRIFFITH COLLEGE, DUBLIN, IRELAND

Hosted by Griffith College Dublin

Academic Focus • Business administration/management, communications, hospitality services, information science, Irish studies, tourism and travel.

Program Information • Students attend classes at Griffith College Dublin (Dublin, Ireland). Field trips. Students typically earn 6-12 credits per term.

Sessions • May-Aug (summer).

Eligibility Requirements • Minimum age 18; open to juniors, seniors; 2.5 GPA; 2 letters of recommendation; good academic standing at home school; resume for internship.

Living Arrangements • Students live in host institution dormitories. Quarters are shared with host institution students. Meals are taken on one's own, in residences, in restaurants.

Costs (2006–2007) • $9150; includes tuition, housing, excursions, international student ID, student support services. $200 nonrefundable deposit required. Financial aid available for all students: scholarships, loans, regular financial aid, grants.

For More Information • Dr. John Perry, Director, International Education, State University of New York College at Brockport, 350 New Campus Drive, Brockport, NY 14420; *Phone:* 800-298-SUNY; *Fax:* 585-637-3218. *E-mail:* overseas@brockport.edu. *World Wide Web:* http://www.brockport.edu/studyabroad/

STATE UNIVERSITY OF NEW YORK COLLEGE AT BROCKPORT
SPECIAL EDUCATION PROGRAM, IRELAND

Held at St. Patrick's College

Academic Focus • Education.

Program Information • Classes are held on the campus of St. Patrick's College (Dublin, Ireland). Faculty members are drawn from the sponsor's U.S. staff. Students typically earn 3 semester credits per term.

Sessions • Jun (summer).

Eligibility Requirements • Minimum age 18; open to sophomores, juniors, seniors, graduate students, adults; course work in education; 2.5 GPA; 2 letters of recommendation; good academic standing at home school.

Living Arrangements • Students live in host institution dormitories. Meals are taken as a group, on one's own, in central dining facility, in restaurants.

Costs (2005) • Contact sponsor for cost; includes tuition, housing, some meals, international student ID. $300 nonrefundable deposit required. Financial aid available for students: scholarships.

For More Information • Dr. John J. Perry, Director, Office of International Education, State University of New York College at Brockport, 350 New Campus Drive, Brockport, NY 14420; *Phone:* 800-298-SUNY; *Fax:* 585-637-3218. *E-mail:* overseas@brockport.edu. *World Wide Web:* http://www.brockport.edu/studyabroad/

STATE UNIVERSITY OF NEW YORK COLLEGE AT CORTLAND
DUBLIN INTERNSHIP–SUMMER

Academic Focus • Full curriculum.

Program Information • Optional travel to London, sites of historic and cultural significance within Ireland at an extra cost. Students typically earn 8 semester credits per term.

Sessions • Jun-Aug (summer), Jun-Aug (summer 2).

Eligibility Requirements • Minimum age 19; open to juniors, seniors; 2.5 GPA; 2 letters of recommendation; good academic standing at home school.

Living Arrangements • Students live in locally rented apartments, host family homes. Meals are taken with host family, in residences.

Costs (2005) • $5077; includes tuition, housing, all meals, insurance, international airfare, international student ID, student support services, passport and visa fees. $20 application fee. $200 nonrefundable deposit required. Financial aid available for students from sponsoring institution: scholarships, loans.

For More Information • Ms. Liz McCartney, Assistant Director, Office of International Programs, State University of New York College at Cortland, PO Box 2000, Cortland, NY 13045; *Phone:*

IRELAND
Dublin

607-753-2209; *Fax:* 607-753-5989. *E-mail:* cortlandabroad@cortland.edu. *World Wide Web:* http://www.cortlandabroad.com/

SYRACUSE UNIVERSITY
IRISH DRAMA: POLITICS AND WAR

Academic Focus • Drama/theater, English, history, Irish literature, Irish studies.

Program Information • Faculty members are drawn from the sponsor's U.S. staff. Scheduled travel to Galway; field trips to Glendalough, Newgrange, Tara. Students typically earn 6 semester credits per term.

Sessions • Jun–Jul (summer).

Eligibility Requirements • Open to freshmen, sophomores, juniors, seniors, graduate students; 1 letter of recommendation; good academic standing at home school.

Living Arrangements • Students live in host institution dormitories. Meals are taken on one's own, in restaurants.

Costs (2005) • $7125; includes tuition, housing, some meals, excursions, international student ID, student support services. $55 application fee. $350 nonrefundable deposit required. Financial aid available for all students: loans, need-based tuition grants.

For More Information • Mrs. Daisy Fried, Associate Director, Syracuse University, 106 Walnut Place, Syracuse, NY 13244-4170; *Phone:* 800-251-9674; *Fax:* 315-443-4593. *E-mail:* dipasum@syr.edu. *World Wide Web:* http://suabroad.syr.edu/

UNIVERSITY OF ALABAMA
ALABAMA IN IRELAND

Held at National University of Ireland, Galway, University of Dublin–Trinity College

Academic Focus • Drama/theater, English literature, history, Irish studies.

Program Information • Classes are held on the campus of National University of Ireland, Galway (Galway, Ireland), University of Dublin–Trinity College (Dublin, Ireland). Faculty members are drawn from the sponsor's U.S. staff. Students typically earn 6 semester credits per term.

Sessions • Jul–Aug (summer).

Eligibility Requirements • Minimum age 18; open to freshmen, sophomores, juniors, seniors, graduate students; 3.0 GPA; good academic standing at home school.

Living Arrangements • Students live in host institution dormitories. Quarters are shared with host institution students. Meals are taken on one's own, in restaurants.

Costs (2005) • $3400; includes tuition, housing, insurance, international student ID, student support services. $100 application fee. $500 nonrefundable deposit required. Financial aid available for all students: scholarships, work study, loans.

For More Information • Ms. Angela L. Channell, Director of Overseas Study, University of Alabama, Box 870254, Tuscaloosa, AL 35487-0254; *Phone:* 205-348-5256; *Fax:* 205-348-5298. *E-mail:* achannel@aalan.ua.edu. *World Wide Web:* http://www.overseas-study.ua.edu/

UNIVERSITY OF DELAWARE
SUMMER SESSION IN DUBLIN

Held at University College Dublin–National University of Ireland, Dublin

Academic Focus • History, Irish literature.

Program Information • Classes are held on the campus of University College Dublin–National University of Ireland, Dublin (Dublin, Ireland). Faculty members are drawn from the sponsor's U.S. staff. Field trips to historic/cultural sights around Dublin; optional travel to Ireland. Students typically earn 6 semester credits per term.

Sessions • Jun–Jul (summer).

Eligibility Requirements • Open to freshmen, sophomores, juniors, seniors, adults; 2.0 GPA; 1 letter of recommendation.

Living Arrangements • Students live in host institution dormitories. Meals are taken as a group, in central dining facility.

Costs (2005) • Contact sponsor for cost. $200 nonrefundable deposit required. Financial aid available for all students: scholarships.

For More Information • Center for International Studies, University of Delaware, 186 South College Avenue, Newark, DE 19716-1450; *Phone:* 888-831-4685; *Fax:* 302-831-6042. *E-mail:* studyabroad@udel.edu. *World Wide Web:* http://www.udel.edu/studyabroad/

UNIVERSITY OF NOTRE DAME
DUBLIN SUMMER PROGRAM

Hosted by Queen's University, University of Dublin–Trinity College

Academic Focus • Irish studies.

Program Information • Students attend classes at Queen's University (Belfast, Ireland), University of Dublin–Trinity College (Dublin, Ireland). Scheduled travel to Belfast; field trips to Boyne Valley, County Wicklow. Students typically earn 6 semester credits per term.

Sessions • Jun–Aug (summer).

Eligibility Requirements • Open to sophomores, juniors, seniors; good academic standing at home school.

Living Arrangements • Students live in host institution dormitories, host family homes. Quarters are shared with students from other programs. Meals are taken on one's own, with host family, in residences.

Costs (2004–2005) • €5740–€6635; includes tuition, housing, some meals, excursions, transportation pass for homestay students. €200 nonrefundable deposit required. Financial aid available for students from sponsoring institution: scholarships, loans.

For More Information • Dr. Claudia Kselman, Associate Director, University of Notre Dame, 158 Hurley Building, Notre Dame, IN 46556; *Phone:* 574-631-5882; *Fax:* 574-631-5711. *E-mail:* kselman.2@nd.edu. *World Wide Web:* http://www.nd.edu/~intlstud/

GALWAY

ACADEMIC PROGRAMS INTERNATIONAL (API)
(API)–GALWAY, IRELAND

Hosted by National University of Ireland, Galway

Academic Focus • Archaeology, film and media studies, Gaelic, history, Irish studies, social sciences.

Program Information • Students attend classes at National University of Ireland, Galway (Galway, Ireland). Scheduled travel to Dublin, other European cities; field trips to the Cliffs of Moher, Cork, Blarney Castle, Bunratty Castle and Folk Park, Connemara, the Burren Dublin, Glendalough, County Wicklow, Kinsale, Mountshannon, Ring of Kerry, Waterford. Students typically earn 6 semester credits per term.

Sessions • Jun–Jul (summer).

Eligibility Requirements • Minimum age 18; open to freshmen, sophomores, juniors, seniors; 2.75 GPA; 1 letter of recommendation; good academic standing at home school; official transcript from home university.

Living Arrangements • Students live in host institution dormitories, locally rented apartments. Quarters are shared with host institution students. Meals are taken on one's own, in residences, in restaurants.

Costs (2006) • $4950; includes tuition, housing, insurance, excursions, student support services, ground transportation, airport pick-up, mobile phone, on-line services, on-site director. $150 nonrefundable deposit required. Financial aid available for all students: scholarships.

For More Information • Ms. Jennifer C. Allen, Director, Academic Programs International (API), 107 East Hopkins, San Marcos, TX 78666; *Phone:* 800-844-4124; *Fax:* 512-392-8420. *E-mail:* api@academicintl.com. *World Wide Web:* http://www.academicintl.com/

COLLEGE CONSORTIUM FOR INTERNATIONAL STUDIES–ST. BONAVENTURE UNIVERSITY AND TRUMAN STATE UNIVERSITY
NATIONAL UNIVERSITY OF IRELAND, GALWAY

Hosted by National University of Ireland, Galway

Academic Focus • Creative writing, Gaelic, Irish literature, Irish studies.

Program Information • Students attend classes at National University of Ireland, Galway (Galway, Ireland). Optional travel to Aran Islands, Dublin at an extra cost. Students typically earn 6 semester credits per term.

Sessions • Jun-Jul (summer).

Eligibility Requirements • Minimum age 18; open to freshmen, sophomores, juniors, seniors, graduate students, adults; 3.0 GPA; 2 letters of recommendation; statement of purpose.

Living Arrangements • Students live in host institution dormitories, locally rented apartments, host family homes. Quarters are shared with host institution students, students from other programs. Meals are taken as a group, on one's own, with host family, in residences.

Costs (2006) • $2990; includes tuition, insurance, fees. $30 application fee. $300 nonrefundable deposit required. Financial aid available for students from sponsoring institution: scholarships, loans.

For More Information • Center for International Education, College Consortium for International Studies–St. Bonaventure University and Truman State University, 100 East Normal, Kirk Building 114, Kirksville, MO 63501; *Phone:* 660-785-4076; *Fax:* 660-785-7476. *E-mail:* ciea@truman.edu. *World Wide Web:* http://www.ccisabroad.org/. Students may also apply through St. Bonaventure University, St. Bonaventure, NY 14778.

FAIRFIELD UNIVERSITY
AN IRISH EXPERIENCE IN GALWAY

Hosted by National University of Ireland, Galway

Academic Focus • Irish literature.

Program Information • Students attend classes at National University of Ireland, Galway (Galway, Ireland). Field trips to the Aran Islands, Cliffs of Moher. Students typically earn 3 semester credits per term.

Sessions • May-Jun (summer).

Eligibility Requirements • Minimum age 18; open to freshmen, sophomores, juniors, seniors, adults; 2.8 GPA; 2 letters of recommendation; good academic standing at home school.

Living Arrangements • Students live in a hostel. Quarters are shared with host institution students. Meals are taken on one's own, in restaurants.

Costs (2005) • $2625; includes tuition, housing, some meals, insurance, excursions, international student ID, student support services. $300 refundable deposit required.

For More Information • Office of International Education, Fairfield University, Dolan House, 1073 North Benson Road, Fairfield, CT 06824; *Phone:* 203-254-4332; *Fax:* 203-254-4261. *E-mail:* studyabroadoffice@mail.fairfield.edu. *World Wide Web:* http://www.fairfield.edu/studyabroad.xml/

INSTITUTE FOR STUDY ABROAD, BUTLER UNIVERSITY
NATIONAL UNIVERSITY OF IRELAND, GALWAY–SUMMER STUDY

Hosted by National University of Ireland, Galway

Academic Focus • Irish studies.

Program Information • Students attend classes at National University of Ireland, Galway (Galway, Ireland). Field trips to locations in the Irish-speaking area (Gaeltacht). Students typically earn 6 semester credits per term.

Sessions • Jun-Jul (summer).

Eligibility Requirements • Open to sophomores, juniors, seniors; 3.0 GPA; good academic standing at home school; enrollment at an accredited American college or university.

Living Arrangements • Students live in locally rented apartments, program-owned apartments. Quarters are shared with host institution students. Meals are taken on one's own, in residences.

Costs (2005) • $4275; includes tuition, housing, excursions, student support services, pre-departure advising. $40 application fee. $500 nonrefundable deposit required. Financial aid available for all students: scholarships.

For More Information • Institute for Study Abroad, Butler University, 1100 West 42nd Street, Suite 305, Indianapolis, IN 46208-3345; *Phone:* 800-858-0229; *Fax:* 317-940-9704. *E-mail:* study-abroad@butler.edu. *World Wide Web:* http://www.ifsa-butler.org/

UNIVERSITY AT ALBANY, STATE UNIVERSITY OF NEW YORK
IRISH STUDIES PROGRAM: EDUCATION, IRISH LANGUAGE

Hosted by National University of Ireland, Galway

Academic Focus • Architecture, film and media studies, Gaelic, Irish literature, Irish studies, music history.

Program Information • Students attend classes at National University of Ireland, Galway (Galway, Ireland). Field trips to local museums and historic sites. Students typically earn 3–8 semester credits per term.

Sessions • Jun-Jul (summer), Jul-Aug (summer 2).

Eligibility Requirements • Open to freshmen, sophomores, juniors, seniors; 2.5 GPA; 2 letters of recommendation; good academic standing at home school.

Living Arrangements • Students live in locally rented apartments. Quarters are shared with students from other programs. Meals are taken on one's own, in residences, in restaurants.

Costs (2005) • Contact sponsor for cost. $150 nonrefundable deposit required. Financial aid available for students from sponsoring institution: all customary sources.

For More Information • University at Albany, State University of New York, Office of International Education, LI 66, Albany, NY 12222; *Phone:* 518-442-3525; *Fax:* 518-442-3338. *E-mail:* intled@uamail.albany.edu. *World Wide Web:* http://www.albany.edu/studyabroad/

UNIVERSITY STUDIES ABROAD CONSORTIUM
IRISH STUDIES: GALWAY, IRELAND

Hosted by National University of Ireland, Galway

Academic Focus • Irish studies, literature, music history.

Program Information • Students attend classes at National University of Ireland, Galway (Galway, Ireland). Field trips to Gaelic Aran Islands; optional travel to Dublin Tour at an extra cost. Students typically earn 6 semester credits per term.

Sessions • Jul-Aug (summer).

Eligibility Requirements • Minimum age 18; open to freshmen, sophomores, juniors, seniors, graduate students, adults; 2.5 GPA.

Living Arrangements • Students live in program-owned apartments. Quarters are shared with host institution students. Meals are taken on one's own, in residences, in restaurants.

Costs (2007) • $3980; includes tuition, housing, insurance, excursions, student support services. $100 application fee. $200 refundable deposit required. Financial aid available for all students: scholarships, loans.

For More Information • University Studies Abroad Consortium, USAC 323, Reno, NV 89557-0093; *Phone:* 775-784-6569; *Fax:* 775-784-6010. *E-mail:* usac@unr.edu. *World Wide Web:* http://usac.unr.edu/

VILLANOVA UNIVERSITY
IRISH STUDIES

Hosted by National University of Ireland, Galway

Academic Focus • Irish studies.

Program Information • Students attend classes at National University of Ireland, Galway (Galway, Ireland). Scheduled travel to Aran Islands, Dublin. Students typically earn 6 semester credits per term.

Sessions • Jun-Aug (summer).

Eligibility Requirements • Minimum age 18; open to freshmen, sophomores, juniors, seniors; 2.75 GPA; 2 letters of recommendation; good academic standing at home school.

Living Arrangements • Students live in host family homes. Quarters are shared with host institution students. Meals are taken with host family, in residences.

Costs (2005) • $4250; includes tuition, housing, some meals, excursions. $450 nonrefundable deposit required. Financial aid available for students from sponsoring institution: loans.

For More Information • Dr. James J. Murphy, Director of Irish Studies, Villanova University, 800 Lancaster Avenue, Middleton Hall,

Villanova, PA 19085; *Phone:* 610-519-6412; *Fax:* 610-519-7649. *E-mail:* james.murphy@villanova.edu. *World Wide Web:* http://www. internationalstudies.villanova.edu/

LIMERICK

ACADEMIC PROGRAMS INTERNATIONAL (API)

(API)–LIMERICK, IRELAND

Hosted by University of Limerick

Academic Focus • Irish literature, Irish studies.

Program Information • Students attend classes at University of Limerick (Limerick, Ireland). Scheduled travel to Dublin; field trips to the Cliffs of Moher; Cork, Blarney Castle; the Burren; Dublin;, Bunratty Castle and Folk Park; Connemara, Glendalough; Kinsale, Mountshannon; Ring of Kerry; Waterford. Students typically earn 3 semester credits per term.

Sessions • Jun–Jul (summer).

Eligibility Requirements • Minimum age 18; open to freshmen, sophomores, juniors, seniors, graduate students, adults; 2.5 GPA; 1 letter of recommendation; good academic standing at home school; official transcript from home university.

Living Arrangements • Students live in host institution dormitories, locally rented apartments. Quarters are shared with host institution students. Meals are taken on one's own, in residences, in restaurants.

Costs (2006) • $4500; includes tuition, housing, insurance, excursions, student support services, ground transportation, airport pick-up, mobile phone, on-line services, on-site director. $150 nonrefundable deposit required. Financial aid available for all students: scholarships.

For More Information • Ms. Jennifer C. Allen, Director, Academic Programs International (API), 107 East Hopkins, San Marcos, TX 78666; *Phone:* 800-844-4124; *Fax:* 512-392-8420. *E-mail:* api@ academicintl.com. *World Wide Web:* http://www.academicintl.com/

AMERICAN INSTITUTE FOR FOREIGN STUDY (AIFS)

AIFS–LIMERICK, IRELAND–UNIVERSITY OF LIMERICK
SUMMER SCHOOL IN IRISH STUDIES

Hosted by University of Limerick

Academic Focus • Art history, business administration/ management, economics, history, literature, sociology, telecommunications.

Program Information • Students attend classes at University of Limerick (Limerick, Ireland). Scheduled travel to 3-day London stopover; field trips to Excursions to Limerick City, Dublin and Lahinch, cultural activities, sporting events. Students typically earn 3 semester credits per term.

Sessions • Jun–Jul (summer).

Eligibility Requirements • Minimum age 17; open to precollege students, freshmen, sophomores, juniors, seniors; 2.5 GPA.

Living Arrangements • Students live in host institution dormitories. Quarters are shared with host institution students. Meals are taken as a group, in residences.

Costs (2007) • 4-week: $5599; includes tuition, housing, some meals, insurance, excursions, international airfare, student support services, On-site Resident Director, Phone Card to call the U.S. Computer Facilities/Internet, Membership to the new University Sports Arena/Olympic-sized pool. $95 application fee. $395 nonrefundable deposit required. Financial aid available for all students: scholarships.

For More Information • Mr. David Mauro, Admissions Advisor, American Institute For Foreign Study (AIFS), 9 West Broad Street, Stamford, CT 06902-3788; *Phone:* 800-727-2437 Ext. 5163; *Fax:* 203-399-5597. *E-mail:* dmauro@aifs.com. *World Wide Web:* http:// www.aifsabroad.com/

COLLEGE CONSORTIUM FOR INTERNATIONAL STUDIES–ST. BONAVENTURE UNIVERSITY AND TRUMAN STATE UNIVERSITY

SUMMER LIMERICK

Hosted by University of Limerick

Academic Focus • Irish studies.

Program Information • Students attend classes at University of Limerick (Limerick, Ireland). Field trips to Dublin, Kilfinane, the Burren; optional travel at an extra cost. Students typically earn 3 semester credits per term.

Sessions • May–Jun (summer).

Eligibility Requirements • Minimum age 18; open to precollege students, freshmen, sophomores, juniors, seniors, graduate students, adults; 2.5 GPA; 2 letters of recommendation; good academic standing at home school; statement of purpose.

Living Arrangements • Students live in host institution dormitories. Quarters are shared with host institution students, students from other programs. Meals are taken as a group, on one's own, in residences, in restaurants.

Costs (2006) • $4300; includes tuition, housing, insurance, excursions, instructional and administrative fees. $30 application fee. $300 nonrefundable deposit required. Financial aid available for students from sponsoring institution: scholarships, loans.

For More Information • Ms. Alice Sayegh, Director, International Studies, College Consortium for International Studies–St. Bonaventure University and Truman State University, St. Bonaventure, NY 14778; *Phone:* 716-377-2574; *Fax:* 716-375-7882. *E-mail:* asayegh@sbu.edu. *World Wide Web:* http://www.ccisabroad.org/. Students may also apply through Truman State University, Center for International Education, 100 East Normal, Kirk Building #114, Kirksville, MO 63501.

ILLINOIS STATE UNIVERSITY

SUMMER PROGRAM AT THE UNIVERSITY OF LIMERICK

Hosted by University of Limerick

Academic Focus • Irish studies.

Program Information • Students attend classes at University of Limerick (Limerick, Ireland). Field trips to Limerick, Dublin, Dingle. Students typically earn 3 semester credits per term.

Sessions • Jun (summer).

Eligibility Requirements • Open to sophomores, juniors, seniors; 2.5 GPA; 2 letters of recommendation; good academic standing at home school; essay.

Living Arrangements • Students live in host institution dormitories. Quarters are shared with host institution students, students from other programs. Meals are taken on one's own, in residences, in central dining facility.

Costs (2005) • $6420; includes tuition, housing, all meals, insurance, excursions, international airfare, international student ID, student support services, personal expenses. $150 application fee. Financial aid available for students from sponsoring institution: scholarships, loans.

For More Information • Study Abroad Coordinator, Illinois State University, Office of International Studies and Programs, Campus Box 6120, Normal, IL 61790-6120; *Phone:* 309-438-5276; *Fax:* 309-438-3987. *E-mail:* oisp@ilstu.edu. *World Wide Web:* http://www. internationalstudies.ilstu.edu/

STATE UNIVERSITY OF NEW YORK AT NEW PALTZ

SUMMER IRISH STUDIES IN IRELAND

Hosted by University of Limerick

Academic Focus • Art history, Irish literature, Irish studies, political science and government, sociology.

Program Information • Students attend classes at University of Limerick (Limerick, Ireland). Field trips to Dublin, Dingle. Students typically earn 6 semester credits per term.

Sessions • Jun (summer).

Eligibility Requirements • Minimum age 18; open to sophomores, juniors, seniors; 2.5 GPA; 1 letter of recommendation.

Living Arrangements • Students live in host institution dormitories. Quarters are shared with students from other programs. Meals are taken on one's own, in central dining facility.

Costs (2006) • $4302 for New York residents; $5095 for nonresidents; includes tuition, housing, some meals, insurance, excursions, receptions. $25 application fee. $300 nonrefundable deposit required. Financial aid available for students from sponsoring institution: scholarships, loans.

For More Information • Marketing Coordinator, Study Abroad, State University of New York at New Paltz, 1 Hawk Drive, Suite 9, New Paltz, NY 12561; *Phone:* 845-257-3125; *Fax:* 845-257-3129. *E-mail:* studyabroad@newpaltz.edu. *World Wide Web:* http://www.newpaltz.edu/studyabroad/

UNIVERSITY OF KANSAS
LAW IN LIMERICK

Hosted by University of Limerick
Academic Focus • Law and legal studies.
Program Information • Students attend classes at University of Limerick (Limerick, Ireland). Scheduled travel to Dublin. Students typically earn 5 semester credits per term.
Sessions • Jul (summer).
Eligibility Requirements • Minimum age 18; open to graduate students; good academic standing at home school; must be a second-year law student.
Living Arrangements • Students live in host institution dormitories, locally rented apartments. Meals are taken on one's own, in restaurants.
Costs (2005) • $2800; includes tuition, student support services, emergency medical evacuation and repatriation services. $30 application fee. $300 deposit required. Financial aid available for students from sponsoring institution: scholarships, loans.
For More Information • Mr. David Wiley, Program Coordinator, University of Kansas, Office of Study Abroad, Lippincott Hall, 1410 Jayhawk Boulevard, Room 108, Lawrence, KS 66045-7515; *Phone:* 785-864-3742; *Fax:* 785-864-5040. *E-mail:* osa@ku.edu. *World Wide Web:* http://www.ku.edu/~osa/

RIVERSTOWN

ILLINOIS STATE UNIVERSITY
RIVERSTOWN, COUNTY SLIGO, IRELAND SUMMER

Academic Focus • Archaeology.
Program Information • Faculty members are drawn from the sponsor's U.S. staff. Students typically earn 3–6 semester credits per term.
Sessions • Jun–Jul (summer).
Eligibility Requirements • Open to sophomores, juniors, seniors, graduate students; course work in anthropology; 2.5 GPA; good academic standing at home school.

Living Arrangements • Students live in locally rented apartments. Meals are taken as a group, in restaurants.
Costs (2005) • $3500–$5500; includes tuition, housing, some meals, insurance, international airfare, international student ID, student support services, personal expenses. $150 application fee. Financial aid available for students from sponsoring institution: scholarships, loans.
For More Information • Dr. Charles Orser, Department of Sociology and Anthropology, Illinois State University, Campus Box 4640, Normal, IL 61790-4640; *Phone:* 309-438-2271; *Fax:* 309-438-3987. *E-mail:* ceorser@ilstu.edu. *World Wide Web:* http://www.internationalstudies.ilstu.edu/

WATERFORD

STATE UNIVERSITY OF NEW YORK COLLEGE AT BROCKPORT
THE IRISH LEGAL OR IRISH SOCIAL SERVICE SYSTEMS

Hosted by Waterford Institute of Technology
Academic Focus • Criminal justice, cultural studies, education, international affairs, Irish studies, language studies, literature, music, political science and government, religious studies, social work, women's studies.
Program Information • Students attend classes at Waterford Institute of Technology (Waterford, Ireland). Scheduled travel to the west of Ireland; field trips to Dublin, Kilkenny, Cork, Cobh, Tramore, Cashel. Students typically earn 6 semester credits per term.
Sessions • Jun–Jul (summer).
Eligibility Requirements • Minimum age 18; open to sophomores, juniors, seniors; 2.5 GPA; 2 letters of recommendation; good academic standing at home school; second-semester sophomore or higher.
Living Arrangements • Students live in host institution dormitories. Meals are taken as a group, on one's own, in residences, in central dining facility, in restaurants.
Costs (2005) • $3995; includes tuition, housing, some meals, excursions, international airfare, international student ID, student support services, evening group activities, all program-related travel in Ireland, orientation, welcome party upon arrival. $200 nonrefundable deposit required. Financial aid available for students from sponsoring institution: scholarships, loans, regular financial aid, grants.
For More Information • Dr. John J. Perry, Director, Office of International Education, State University of New York College at Brockport, 350 New Campus Drive, Brockport, NY 14420; *Phone:* 800-298-SUNY; *Fax:* 585-637-3218. *E-mail:* overseas@brockport.edu. *World Wide Web:* http://www.brockport.edu/studyabroad/

ISRAEL

HAIFA

UNIVERSITY OF HAIFA
OVERSEAS STUDENT STUDIES PROGRAM

Hosted by University of Haifa
Academic Focus • Hebrew.
Program Information • Students attend classes at University of Haifa (Haifa, Israel). Field trips to various sites in Israel; optional travel to various sites in Israel at an extra cost. Students typically earn 5 semester credits per term.
Sessions • Jul–Aug (summer), Jan–Feb (winter).
Eligibility Requirements • Minimum age 18; open to freshmen, sophomores, juniors, seniors, graduate students, adults; no foreign language proficiency required.
Living Arrangements • Students live in host institution dormitories. Quarters are shared with host institution students. Meals are taken on one's own, in residences.
Costs (2004) • $970–$1810; includes tuition, housing, student support services. $50 application fee. $200 refundable deposit required. Financial aid available for all students: scholarships.
For More Information • Ms. Lisa Berman, Admissions Coordinator, University of Haifa, Department of Overseas Studies, Haifa 31905, Israel; *Phone:* +972 4-824-0766; *Fax:* +972 4-824-0391. *E-mail:* info@mail.uhaifa.org. *World Wide Web:* http://www.uhaifa.org/

JERUSALEM

HEBREW UNIVERSITY OF JERUSALEM
SUMMER COURSES IN JERUSALEM

Hosted by Hebrew University of Jerusalem
Academic Focus • Ancient history, Arabic, archaeology, Biblical studies, Hebrew, international affairs, Islamic studies, Israeli studies, Jewish studies, Middle Eastern studies, peace and conflict studies, religious studies, Yiddish.
Program Information • Students attend classes at Hebrew University of Jerusalem (Jerusalem, Israel). Scheduled travel to Golan Heights, Galilee, Negev; field trips to Golan Heights, Negev, Galilee, local sites in the vicinity of Jerusalem. Students typically earn 3–8 semester credits per term.
Sessions • Jun–Aug (summer).
Eligibility Requirements • Minimum age 17; open to precollege students, freshmen, sophomores, juniors, seniors, graduate students, adults; 1 letter of recommendation; good academic standing at home school; most recent transcript; no foreign language proficiency required.
Living Arrangements • Students live in host institution dormitories, locally rented apartments. Quarters are shared with host institution students. Meals are taken on one's own, in residences, in central dining facility, in restaurants.
Costs (2006) • $2500; includes tuition, housing, insurance, excursions, international airfare, books and class materials, student support services. $60 application fee. $75 nonrefundable deposit required. Financial aid available for all students: scholarships, need-based aid.
For More Information • Ms. Jo Ann Panzella, Admissions Officer, Hebrew University of Jerusalem, Office of Academic Affairs, One Battery Park Plaza, 25th Floor, New York, NY 10004; *Phone:* 800-404-8622; *Fax:* 212-809-4183. *E-mail:* hebrewu@hebrewu.com. *World Wide Web:* http://overseas.huji.ac.il/

HEBREW UNIVERSITY OF JERUSALEM
SUMMER LANGUAGE PROGRAM

Hosted by Hebrew University of Jerusalem
Academic Focus • Arabic, Hebrew, Yiddish.
Program Information • Students attend classes at Hebrew University of Jerusalem (Jerusalem, Israel). Scheduled travel to Negev, Galilee, Golan Heights, the Dead Sea; field trips to historic, religious, and cultural sites in the vicinity of Jerusalem. Students typically earn 6–10 semester credits per term.
Sessions • Jul–Sep (summer).
Eligibility Requirements • Open to freshmen, sophomores, juniors, seniors, graduate students, adults; 1 letter of recommendation; good academic standing at home school; no foreign language proficiency required.
Living Arrangements • Students live in host institution dormitories, locally rented apartments. Quarters are shared with host institution students, students from other programs. Meals are taken on one's own, in residences, in central dining facility, in restaurants.

Costs (2006) • $2500; includes tuition, housing, insurance, international airfare, student support services. $60 application fee. $75 nonrefundable deposit required. Financial aid available for all students: scholarships, loans, need and merit-based aid.
For More Information • Ms. Jo Ann Panzella, Admissions Officer, Hebrew University of Jerusalem, Office of Academic Affairs, One Battery Park Plaza, 25th Floor, New York, NY 10004; *Phone:* 800-404-8622; *Fax:* 212-809-4183. *E-mail:* hebrewu@hebrewu.com. *World Wide Web:* http://overseas.huji.ac.il/

JERUSALEM UNIVERSITY COLLEGE
TWO OR THREE WEEK HISTORICAL GEOGRAPHY AND ISRAEL STUDY TOURS

Hosted by Jerusalem University College
Academic Focus • Ancient history, archaeology, Biblical studies, geography, Middle Eastern studies, religious studies.
Program Information • Students attend classes at Jerusalem University College (Jerusalem, Israel). Scheduled travel to Galilee, Negev, Jordan; field trips to the surrounding area of Jerusalem; optional travel to Jordan, Egypt at an extra cost. Students typically earn 4 semester credits per term.
Sessions • May (summer), Jun (summer 2), Jul (summer 3), Jan (winter).
Eligibility Requirements • Minimum age 18; open to freshmen, sophomores, juniors, seniors, graduate students, adults; 2.0 GPA; 3 letters of recommendation; good academic standing at home school; excellent physical conditioning; no foreign language proficiency required.
Living Arrangements • Students live in host institution dormitories, hotels. Quarters are shared with host institution students, students from other programs. Meals are taken as a group, in central dining facility, in restaurants.
Costs (2005) • $1960; includes tuition, housing, all meals, excursions. $50 application fee. $100 refundable deposit required.
For More Information • Ms. Amelia Nakai, Program Coordinator, Jerusalem University College, 4249 East State Street, Suite 203, Rockford, IL 61108; *Phone:* 815-229-5900; *Fax:* 815-229-5901. *E-mail:* admissions@juc.edu. *World Wide Web:* http://www.juc.edu/

ITALY

CITY-TO-CITY

AMERICAN INSTITUTE FOR FOREIGN STUDY (AIFS)
AIFS–ITALIAN INFLUENCE ON WESTERN CIVILIZATION, THE AMERICAN INTERNATIONAL UNIVERSITY IN LONDON

Academic Focus • History.
Program Information • Scheduled travel to Rome (5 nights), Sorrento (4 nights), Florence (6 nights), Venice (5 nights); Milan (4 nights); field trips to London (2 nights), Siena (1 night), day visits to Pompeii, Capri, Amalfi. Students typically earn 4 semester credits per term.
Sessions • Jun–Jul (summer).
Eligibility Requirements • Minimum age 18; open to freshmen, sophomores, juniors, seniors, adults; 2.0 GPA.
Living Arrangements • Students live in hotels. Quarters are shared with host institution students. Meals are taken as a group, in residences.
Costs (2007) • $6199; includes tuition, housing, some meals, insurance, excursions, student support services, Entrance/transfers, accompanying faculty and travel manager, Phone Card to call the U.S. $95 application fee. $395 nonrefundable deposit required. Financial aid available for all students: scholarships.
For More Information • Mr. David Mauro, Admissions Advisor, American Institute For Foreign Study (AIFS), 9 West Broad Street, Stamford, CT 06902-3788; *Phone:* 800-727-2437 Ext. 5163; *Fax:* 203-399-5597. *E-mail:* dmauro@aifs.com. *World Wide Web:* http://www.aifsabroad.com/

CENTER FOR STUDY ABROAD (CSA)
ITALIAN LANGUAGE CENTER–ROME, FLORENCE, SIENA

Hosted by Italian Language Center
Academic Focus • Italian language and literature, Italian studies.
Program Information • Students attend classes at Italian Language Center (Florence), Italian Language Center (Rome), Italian Language Center (Siena). Optional travel. Students typically earn 4-10 semester credits per term.
Sessions • Typically 4 week sessions, classes begin weekly, year-round.
Eligibility Requirements • Minimum age 17; open to precollege students, freshmen, sophomores, juniors, seniors, graduate students, adults; no foreign language proficiency required.
Living Arrangements • Students live in locally rented apartments, host family homes. Meals are taken with host family, in residences, in restaurants.
Costs (2005) • Contact sponsor for cost. $45 application fee.
For More Information • Ms. Alima K. Virtue, Program Director, Center for Study Abroad (CSA), 325 Washington Avenue South #93, Kent, WA 98032; *Phone:* 206-726-1498; *Fax:* 253-850-0454. *E-mail:* info@centerforstudyabroad.com. *World Wide Web:* http://www.centerforstudyabroad.com/

KENTUCKY INSTITUTE FOR INTERNATIONAL STUDIES
ITALY

Academic Focus • Art, art history, Italian studies.
Program Information • Faculty members are drawn from the sponsor's U.S. staff. Field trips to sites of local interest. Students typically earn 3-6 semester credits per term.
Sessions • Jun–Jul (summer).
Eligibility Requirements • Minimum age 18; open to freshmen, sophomores, juniors, seniors, graduate students, adults; 2.0 GPA; 1 letter of recommendation; no foreign language proficiency required.
Living Arrangements • Students live in hotels. Meals are taken as a group, in central dining facility.
Costs (2006) • $3700; includes housing, some meals, insurance, excursions, international airfare, international student ID, instructional expenses. $150 application fee. Financial aid available for all students: scholarships.
For More Information • Ms. Nancy Martin, Coordinator, Kentucky Institute for International Studies, PO Box 9, Murray, KY 42071-0009; *Phone:* 270-762-3091; *Fax:* 270-762-3434. *E-mail:* kiismsu@murraystate.edu. *World Wide Web:* http://www.kiis.org/

LANGUAGE LIAISON
LEARN ITALIAN IN FLORENCE, LUCCA, CORTONA, ORBETELLO, AND BOLOGNA

Hosted by Language Liaison
Academic Focus • Italian language and literature.
Program Information • Students attend classes at Language Liaison (Bologna), Language Liaison (Cortona), Language Liaison (Florence), Language Liaison (Lucca), Language Liaison (Orbetello). Field trips; optional travel at an extra cost. Students typically earn 3-15 semester credits per term.

Sessions • New programs begin weekly, year-round.
Eligibility Requirements • Minimum age 16; open to precollege students, freshmen, sophomores, juniors, seniors, graduate students, adults; no foreign language proficiency required.
Living Arrangements • Students live in locally rented apartments, host family homes, hotels. Meals are taken on one's own, with host family, in residences, in restaurants.
Costs (2005) • Contact sponsor for cost. $175 application fee. Financial aid available for all students: scholarship research service.
For More Information • Ms. Nancy Forman, President, Language Liaison, PO Box 1772, Pacific Palisades, CA 90272; *Phone:* 800-284-4448; *Fax:* 310-454-1706. *E-mail:* learn@languageliaison. com. *World Wide Web:* http://www.languageliaison.com/

NORTHERN ILLINOIS UNIVERSITY
ITALIAN FASHION: MILAN AND ROME

Academic Focus • Fashion design, fashion merchandising, textiles.
Program Information • Faculty members are drawn from the sponsor's U.S. staff. Field trips. Students typically earn 3 semester credits per term.
Sessions • May (summer).
Eligibility Requirements • Minimum age 18; open to juniors, seniors, graduate students, adults; 2.5 GPA; good academic standing at home school; no foreign language proficiency required.
Living Arrangements • Students live in hotels. Meals are taken on one's own, in restaurants.
Costs (2005) • Contact sponsor for cost. $200 nonrefundable deposit required. Financial aid available for students from sponsoring institution: loans.
For More Information • Ms. Rita Withrow, Program Assistant, Northern Illinois University, Study Abroad Office, Williston Hall 417, DeKalb, IL 60015-2854; *Phone:* 815-753-0700; *Fax:* 815-753-0825. *E-mail:* niuabroad@niu.edu. *World Wide Web:* http://www.niu.edu/niuabroad/

ROCKLAND COMMUNITY COLLEGE
ITALIAN RENAISSANCE: PRESENCE OF THE PAST

Academic Focus • Architecture, art history, Italian studies, literature.
Program Information • Faculty members are drawn from the sponsor's U.S. staff. Field trips to sites in and around Rome and Florence; optional travel at an extra cost. Students typically earn 3 semester credits per term.
Sessions • May–Jun (summer).
Eligibility Requirements • Minimum age 18; open to freshmen, sophomores, juniors, seniors, adults; good academic standing at home school; no foreign language proficiency required.
Living Arrangements • Students live in hotels. Meals are taken on one's own, in restaurants.
Costs (2005) • $3785; includes tuition, housing, some meals, insurance, excursions, international airfare. $400 nonrefundable deposit required. Financial aid available for students from sponsoring institution: scholarships, loans.
For More Information • Ms. Fran Rodríguez, Coordinator, Study Abroad, Rockland Community College, 145 College Road, Suffern, NY 10901; *Phone:* 845-574-4205; *Fax:* 845-574-4423. *E-mail:* study-abroad@sunyrockland.edu. *World Wide Web:* http://www.rocklandabroad.com/

SYRACUSE UNIVERSITY
HUMANISM AND THE ARTS IN RENAISSANCE ITALY

Hosted by Syracuse University Center–Florence
Academic Focus • Aesthetics, art history, philosophy.
Program Information • Students attend classes at Syracuse University Center–Florence (Florence). Scheduled travel to Venice, Vicenza, Rome, Florence; field trips to Siena, Padua, San Gimignano. Students typically earn 6 semester credits per term.
Sessions • Jun–Jul (summer).
Eligibility Requirements • Open to freshmen, sophomores, juniors, seniors, graduate students, adults; 1 letter of recommendation; good academic standing at home school; no foreign language proficiency required.

Living Arrangements • Students live in hotels. Quarters are shared with host institution students. Meals are taken on one's own, in restaurants.
Costs (2005) • $7690; includes tuition, housing, some meals, excursions, international student ID, student support services. $55 application fee. $350 nonrefundable deposit required. Financial aid available for all students: loans, need-based tuition grants.
For More Information • Mrs. Daisy Fried, Associate Director, Syracuse University, 106 Walnut Place, Syracuse, NY 13244-4170; *Phone:* 800-251-9674; *Fax:* 315-443-4593. *E-mail:* dipasum@syr.edu. *World Wide Web:* http://suabroad.syr.edu/

UNIVERSITY OF COLORADO AT BOULDER
ART HISTORY IN ITALY

Academic Focus • Art history.
Program Information • Faculty members are drawn from the sponsor's U.S. staff. Field trips to Fiesole, Pompeii, Siena. Students typically earn 6 semester credits per term.
Sessions • Jun–Jul (summer), Program runs every other year.
Eligibility Requirements • Open to sophomores, juniors, seniors, graduate students, adults; course work in fine arts/humanities; 2.75 GPA; 1 letter of recommendation; good academic standing at home school; no foreign language proficiency required.
Living Arrangements • Students live in hotels. Meals are taken on one's own, in restaurants.
Costs (2004) • $7475; includes tuition, housing, some meals, insurance, excursions, international airfare, books and class materials, student support services. $400 nonrefundable deposit required. Financial aid available for students from sponsoring institution: scholarships, loans.
For More Information • Study Abroad Programs, University of Colorado at Boulder, International Education, 123 UCB, Boulder, CO 80309-0123; *Phone:* 303-492-7741; *Fax:* 303-492-5185. *E-mail:* studyabr@colorado.edu. *World Wide Web:* http://www.colorado.edu/OIE/

UNIVERSITY OF SOUTHERN MISSISSIPPI
ART IN ITALY

Academic Focus • Art history.
Program Information • Faculty members are drawn from the sponsor's U.S. staff. Scheduled travel; field trips; optional travel. Students typically earn 4 semester credits per term.
Sessions • May–Jun (summer).
Eligibility Requirements • Minimum age 18; open to sophomores, juniors, seniors, graduate students, adults; 2.0 GPA; good academic standing at home school; no foreign language proficiency required.
Living Arrangements • Students live in host institution dormitories, locally rented apartments, host family homes. Meals are taken as a group, on one's own, with host family, in restaurants.
Costs (2005) • $3799; includes tuition, housing, excursions, international airfare, student support services. $200 nonrefundable deposit required. Financial aid available for students from sponsoring institution: scholarships, loans.
For More Information • Director, Art in Italy, University of Southern Mississippi, 118 College Drive #10047, Hattiesburg, MS 39406-0001; *Phone:* 601-266-4344; *Fax:* 601-266-5009. *E-mail:* holly.buckner@usm.edu. *World Wide Web:* http://www.usm.edu/internationaledu/

VILLANOVA UNIVERSITY
INTENSIVE ITALIAN LANGUAGE AND LITERATURE–FLORENCE

Hosted by Lorenzo de Medici School, University of Urbino
Academic Focus • Italian language and literature.
Program Information • Students attend classes at Lorenzo de Medici School (Florence), University of Urbino (Urbino). Field trips to Rome, Venice, Perugia, Pompei; Capri; Ravenna; Sorrento. Students typically earn 6-9 semester credits per term.
Sessions • Jun–Aug (summer).
Eligibility Requirements • Minimum age 18; open to freshmen, sophomores, juniors, seniors; 2.75 GPA; 2 letters of recommendation; good academic standing at home school; no foreign language proficiency required.

Living Arrangements • Students live in host institution dormitories, locally rented apartments. Quarters are shared with students from other programs. Meals are taken as a group, in central dining facility.

Costs (2005) • $3900; includes tuition, housing, some meals, excursions, student support services. $450 nonrefundable deposit required. Financial aid available for students from sponsoring institution.

For More Information • Dr. Gaetano Pastore, Director, International Studies, Villanova University, Middleton Hall, 800 Lancaster Avenue, Villanova, PA 19085; *Phone:* 610-519-6412; *Fax:* 610-519-7649. *E-mail:* gaetano.pastore@villanova.edu. *World Wide Web:* http://www.internationalstudies.villanova.edu/

ALTAMURA

JAMES MADISON UNIVERSITY
SUMMER IN ALTAMURA

Academic Focus • Anthropology, art, art history.

Program Information • Faculty members are drawn from the sponsor's U.S. staff. Students typically earn 3 semester credits per term.

Sessions • Jun (summer).

Eligibility Requirements • Minimum age 18; open to sophomores, juniors, seniors; 2.0 GPA; 1 letter of recommendation; good academic standing at home school; no foreign language proficiency required.

Living Arrangements • Students live in hotels. Meals are taken as a group, on one's own, in central dining facility, in restaurants.

Costs (2005) • $1854 for Virginia residents; $2694 for nonresidents; includes tuition, housing, some meals, excursions, books and class materials, international student ID. $400 nonrefundable deposit required.

For More Information • Mr. Felix Wang, Director, James Madison University, Office of International Programs, MSC 5731, 1077 South Main Street, Harrisonburg, VA 22807; *Phone:* 540-568-6419; *Fax:* 540-568-3310. *E-mail:* studyabroad@jmu.edu. *World Wide Web:* http://www.jmu.edu/international/

ALTOMONTE

STATE UNIVERSITY OF NEW YORK AT OSWEGO
ROME AND ALTOMONTE, ITALY

Academic Focus • Italian language and literature, Italian studies.

Program Information • Faculty members are drawn from the sponsor's U.S. staff. Scheduled travel to Rome; field trips to Calabria. Students typically earn 6 semester credits per term.

Sessions • Jul–Aug (summer).

Eligibility Requirements • Minimum age 17; open to precollege students, freshmen, sophomores, juniors, seniors, adults; 2.5 GPA; 1 letter of recommendation; good academic standing at home school; personal statement; no foreign language proficiency required.

Living Arrangements • Students live in locally rented apartments, hotels. Meals are taken as a group, in central dining facility, in restaurants.

Costs (2005) • $3100; includes tuition, housing, all meals, insurance, excursions, books and class materials, student support services. $250 nonrefundable deposit required. Financial aid available for students: home university financial aid; loan processing and scholarships for Oswego students.

For More Information • Ms. Lizette Alvarado, Program Specialist, State University of New York at Oswego, 122A Swetman Hall, Oswego, NY 13126-3599; *Phone:* 888-4-OSWEGO; *Fax:* 315-312-2477. *E-mail:* intled@oswego.edu. *World Wide Web:* http://www.oswego.edu/intled/

AREZZO

THE UNIVERSITY OF NORTH CAROLINA AT CHARLOTTE
ARCHITECTURAL DESIGN STUDIO AND FIELD STUDY IN ITALY

Academic Focus • Architecture.

Program Information • Faculty members are drawn from the sponsor's U.S. staff and local instructors hired by the sponsor. Field trips to sites in the surrounding areas. Students typically earn 6–8 semester credits per term.

Sessions • May–Jul (summer).

Eligibility Requirements • Minimum age 18; open to juniors, seniors, graduate students; course work in architecture (3 years); 2.5 GPA; 2 letters of recommendation; good academic standing at home school; no foreign language proficiency required.

Living Arrangements • Students live in locally rented apartments, hotels. Meals are taken on one's own, in restaurants.

Costs (2005) • $4000; includes tuition, housing, insurance, excursions, student support services. $500 refundable deposit required. Financial aid available for students from sponsoring institution: scholarships, loans.

For More Information • Ms. Ann Bennett, College of Architecture, The University of North Carolina at Charlotte, 9201 University City Boulevard, Charlotte, NC 28223-0001; *Phone:* 704-687-2358; *Fax:* 704-687-3353. *E-mail:* abennett@email.uncc.edu. *World Wide Web:* http://www.uncc.edu/edabroad/

UNIVERSITY OF ROCHESTER
ARCHAEOLOGY IN AREZZO, ITALY

Academic Focus • Archaeology.

Program Information • Faculty members are drawn from the sponsor's U.S. staff and local instructors hired by the sponsor. Field trips to Cortona, Florence, Siena, Rome. Students typically earn 8 semester credits per term.

Sessions • Jul (summer).

Eligibility Requirements • Open to sophomores, juniors, seniors; 1 letter of recommendation; good academic standing at home school; no foreign language proficiency required.

Living Arrangements • Students live in host institution dormitories. Quarters are shared with students from other programs. Meals are taken as a group, in central dining facility.

Costs (2005) • $4500; includes tuition, housing, all meals, excursions. $500 nonrefundable deposit required.

For More Information • Ms. Julie Nowak Piccirillo, Administrator, University of Rochester, Center for Judaic Studies, Lattimore 317, Rochester, NY 14627; *Phone:* 585-273-5001. *E-mail:* jano@mail.rochester.edu. *World Wide Web:* http://www.rochester.edu/college/study-abroad/

ASSISI

EUROPEAN HERITAGE INSTITUTE
YEAR-ROUND PROGRAMS IN ASSISI

Hosted by Academia Lingua Italiana

Academic Focus • Italian language and literature.

Program Information • Students attend classes at Academia Lingua Italiana (Assisi, Italy). Field trips to the Umbria Region; optional travel to Rome at an extra cost. Students typically earn 3–6 semester credits per term.

Sessions • 2 to 4 week sessions, year-round.

Eligibility Requirements • Minimum age 18; open to freshmen, sophomores, juniors, seniors, graduate students, adults; 2.5 GPA; 2 letters of recommendation; no foreign language proficiency required.

Living Arrangements • Students live in locally rented apartments, host family homes. Quarters are shared with host institution students, students from other programs. Meals are taken on one's own, with host family, in residences, in restaurants.

Costs (2005) • $1575 for 4 weeks; $3000 for 8 weeks; includes tuition, housing, excursions, books and class materials, student support services. $300 refundable deposit required.

For More Information • Dr. Antonio Masullo, Professor, European Heritage Institute, 2708 East Franklin Street, Richmond, VA 23223; *Phone:* 804-643-0661; *Fax:* 804-648-0826. *E-mail:* info@europeabroad. org. *World Wide Web:* http://www.europeabroad.org/

FLORENCE

ACADEMIC PROGRAMS INTERNATIONAL (API)
(API) AT APICIUS, THE CULINARY INSTITUTE OF FLORENCE
Hosted by Apicius, The Culinary Institute of Florence
Academic Focus • Culinary arts, food service, hospitality services, hotel and restaurant management.
Program Information • Students attend classes at Apicius, The Culinary Institute of Florence (Florence, Italy). Scheduled travel to Rome, Venice; field trips to Cinque Terre, Perugia, Lucca, Versilia, Lake Garda, Verona, Rome, Bologna and Modena, Portovenere, Venice, Assisi, Cortona, Orvieto, Pierza, Pisa, Siena, San Giginignamo. Students typically earn 12–16 semester credits per term.
Sessions • May–Jul (summer).
Eligibility Requirements • Minimum age 18; open to freshmen, sophomores, juniors, seniors, graduate students, adults; 2.75 GPA; 1 letter of recommendation; good academic standing at home school; official transcript from home university; no foreign language proficiency required.
Living Arrangements • Students live in locally rented apartments. Quarters are shared with host institution students. Meals are taken on one's own, in residences, in restaurants.
Costs (2006) • Contact sponsor for cost. $150 nonrefundable deposit required. Financial aid available for all students: scholarships.
For More Information • Ms. Jennifer C. Allen, Director, Academic Programs International (API), 107 East Hopkins, San Marcos, TX 78666; *Phone:* 800-844-4124; *Fax:* 512-392-8420. *E-mail:* api@academicintl.com. *World Wide Web:* http://www.academicintl.com/

ACADEMIC PROGRAMS INTERNATIONAL (API)
(API)–LORENZO DE MEDICI IN FLORENCE, ITALY
Hosted by Lorenzo de Medici School
Academic Focus • Full curriculum.
Program Information • Students attend classes at Lorenzo de Medici School (Florence, Italy). Scheduled travel to Rome; field trips to Venice, Bologna and Modena, Cinque Terre and Portovanere, Cortona; Umbria; Orivieto; Perugia. Students typically earn 3–6 semester credits per term.
Sessions • May–Jun (summer), Jun–Jul (summer 2).
Eligibility Requirements • Minimum age 18; open to freshmen, sophomores, juniors, seniors, graduate students, adults; 2.75 GPA; 1 letter of recommendation; good academic standing at home school; official transcript from home university; no foreign language proficiency required.
Living Arrangements • Students live in locally rented apartments. Quarters are shared with students from other programs. Meals are taken on one's own, in residences, in restaurants.
Costs (2006) • Contact sponsor for cost. $150 nonrefundable deposit required. Financial aid available for all students: scholarships.
For More Information • Ms. Jennifer C. Allen, Director, Academic Programs International (API), 107 East Hopkins, San Marcos, TX 78666; *Phone:* 800-844-4124; *Fax:* 512-392-8420. *E-mail:* api@academicintl.com. *World Wide Web:* http://www.academicintl.com/

ACADEMIC STUDIES ABROAD
ACADEMIC STUDIES ABROAD–FLORENCE, ITALY
Hosted by Instituto Europeo, Florence Italy
Academic Focus • Art, Italian language and literature, Italian studies.
Program Information • Students attend classes at Instituto Europeo, Florence Italy (Florence, Italy). Field trips to Siena, Via Riggio. Students typically earn 6 semester credits per term.
Sessions • May–Jun (summer), Jun–Jul (summer 2).

Eligibility Requirements • Minimum age 18; open to freshmen, sophomores, juniors, seniors; 2.5 GPA; college transcript; no foreign language proficiency required.
Living Arrangements • Students live in locally rented apartments, host family homes. Quarters are shared with host institution students. Meals are taken on one's own, with host family, in residences.
Costs (2006) • $4500; includes tuition, housing, some meals, insurance, excursions, international student ID, student support services, cell phone. $150 refundable deposit required. Financial aid available for all students: scholarships.
For More Information • Mr. Lee Frankel, Director, Academic Studies Abroad, 434 Massachusetts Avenue, Suite 501, Boston, MA 02118; *Phone:* 617-437-9388; *Fax:* 617-437-9390. *E-mail:* lee@academicstudies.com. *World Wide Web:* http://www.academicstudies.com

ACCADEMIA RIACI
ACCADEMIA RIACI PRE-COLLEGE SUMMER CREDIT PROGRAM IN ART, DESIGN, LANGUAGE, AND CUISINE
Hosted by Accademia Riaci
Academic Focus • Art, art conservation studies, art history, ceramics and pottery, commercial art, crafts, culinary arts, drawing/painting, fashion design, fine/studio arts, graphic design/illustration, interior design, Italian studies, leather working, textiles.
Program Information • Students attend classes at Accademia Riaci (Florence, Italy). Field trips to Boboli Garden, Pitti Palace, Ruins, Museums, Gucci Bag Factory, Ceramics Village, Textile Factory; optional travel to Venice, Winery, Mediterranean Sea. Students typically earn 3–12 semester credits per term.
Sessions • Jun–Aug (summer).
Eligibility Requirements • Minimum age 16; open to precollege students; no foreign language proficiency required.
Living Arrangements • Students live in locally rented apartments, program-owned apartments, host family homes, hotels. Quarters are shared with host institution students. Meals are taken on one's own, in residences, in restaurants.
Costs (2006–2007) • €1900–€2700 for 4 weeks; €2700–€5300 for 8 weeks; includes tuition, housing, some meals, excursions, lab equipment, international student ID, student support services, Language assistance by interpreters (English and Japanese), Italian language courses. €100 application fee.
For More Information • Ms. Emanuela Gucci, Secretary, Accademia Riaci, Via dé Conti 4, 50123 Florence, Italy; *Phone:* +39 055-289831; *Fax:* +39 055-212791. *E-mail:* accademiariaci@accademiariaci.info. *World Wide Web:* http://www.accademiariaci.info/english/index_e. html. Students may also apply through Accademia Riaci Tokyo Office, Nishiazabu 4-10-1 MF Bldg. 2F, Minato-Ku, Tokyo 106-0031, Japan.

ACCADEMIA RIACI
SHORT ART/DESIGN/COOKING PROGRAMS IN FLORENCE, ITALY
Hosted by Accademia Riaci
Academic Focus • Art, art conservation studies, ceramics and pottery, commercial art, crafts, design and applied arts, drawing/painting, fashion design, fine/studio arts, graphic design/illustration, interior design, Italian studies, leather working, textiles.
Program Information • Students attend classes at Accademia Riaci (Florence, Italy). Field trips to Boboli Garden, Pitti Palace, Gucci Bag Factory, Ruins, Museums, Textile Factory; optional travel to Rome, Venice, Milan, Winery (Chianti), Medditerranean Sea.
Sessions • 1 week to 3 months. Courses begin every Monday.
Eligibility Requirements • Minimum age 16; open to precollege students, freshmen, sophomores, juniors, seniors, graduate students, adults; no foreign language proficiency required.
Living Arrangements • Students live in locally rented apartments, program-owned apartments, host family homes, hotels. Quarters are shared with host institution students, students from other programs. Meals are taken on one's own, in residences, in restaurants.
Costs (2006–2007) • Contact sponsor for cost; includes tuition, some meals, lab equipment, international student ID, student support services, application/enrollment fee. €100 application fee.
For More Information • Ms. Emanuela Gucci, Secretary, Accademia Riaci, Via dé Conti 4, 50123 Florence, Italy; *Phone:* +39 055-289831;

Fax: +39 055-212791. *E-mail:* accademiariaci@accademiariaci.info. *World Wide Web:* http://www.accademiariaci.info/english/index_e.html. Students may also apply through Accademia Riaci Tokyo Office, Nishiazabu 4-10-1 MF Bldg. 2F, Minato-Ku, Tokyo 106-0031, Japan.

ACCADEMIA RIACI
SUMMER ART PROGRAM IN FLORENCE AT ACCADEMIA RIACI

Hosted by Accademia Riaci

Academic Focus • Art, art conservation studies, ceramics and pottery, commercial art, crafts, culinary arts, drawing/painting, fashion design, fine/studio arts, graphic design/illustration, interior design, Italian studies, leather working, textiles.

Program Information • Students attend classes at Accademia Riaci (Florence, Italy). Field trips to the Boboli garden, the Gucci Bag Factory, textile factory, Pitti Palace, ruins and museums; optional travel to Rome, Venice, a winery, the Mediterranean Sea at an extra cost. Students typically earn 3-12 semester credits per term.

Sessions • May-Jun (summer), Jun-Jul (summer 2); May-Jul (summer 3).

Eligibility Requirements • Minimum age 16; open to precollege students, freshmen, sophomores, juniors, seniors, graduate students, adults; no foreign language proficiency required.

Living Arrangements • Students live in locally rented apartments, program-owned apartments, host family homes, hotels. Quarters are shared with host institution students, students from other programs. Meals are taken on one's own, in residences, in restaurants.

Costs (2006–2007) • €1900–€2700 for 4 weeks; €2700–€5300 for 8 weeks; includes tuition, excursions, lab equipment, international student ID, student support services, language assistance by interpreters (English and Japanese).

For More Information • Ms. Emanuela Gucci, Secretary, Accademia Riaci, Via de'Conti 4, 50123 Florence, Italy; *Phone:* +39 055-289831; *Fax:* +39 055-212791. *E-mail:* accademiariaci@accademiariaci.info. *World Wide Web:* http://www.accademiariaci.info/english/index_e.html. Students may also apply through Accademia Riaci Tokyo Office, Nishiababu 4-10-1 MF Bldg. 2F, Minato-Ku, Tokyo 106-0031, Japan.

ACCENT INTERNATIONAL CONSORTIUM FOR ACADEMIC PROGRAMS ABROAD
ART, MUSIC, AND CULTURE IN FLORENCE

Held at Scuola Leonardo daVinci

Academic Focus • Art history, Italian studies, music history, music theory.

Program Information • Classes are held on the campus of Scuola Leonardo daVinci (Florence, Italy). Faculty members are drawn from the sponsor's U.S. staff and local instructors hired by the sponsor. Scheduled travel to Venice, Rome; field trips to Siena, Verona, San Gimignano, Pisa, Lucca, Torre del Lago. Students typically earn 6 semester credits per term.

Sessions • Jun-Jul (summer).

Eligibility Requirements • Minimum age 18; open to precollege students, freshmen, sophomores, juniors, seniors, graduate students, adults; no foreign language proficiency required.

Living Arrangements • Students live in locally rented apartments, hotels. Quarters are shared with students from other programs. Meals are taken on one's own, in residences, in restaurants.

Costs (2005) • $3600; includes housing, excursions, books and class materials, international student ID, student support services, extracurricular activities. $250 nonrefundable deposit required.

For More Information • ACCENT International Consortium for Academic Programs Abroad, 870 Market Street, Suite 1026, San Francisco, CA 94102; *Phone:* 800-869-9291; *Fax:* 415-835-3749. *E-mail:* info@accentintl.com. *World Wide Web:* http://www.accentintl.com/

ACCENT INTERNATIONAL CONSORTIUM FOR ACADEMIC PROGRAMS ABROAD
SUMMER IN FLORENCE

Hosted by Scuola Leonardo daVinci

Academic Focus • Art history, Italian language and literature, Italian studies.

Program Information • Students attend classes at Scuola Leonardo daVinci (Florence, Italy). Scheduled travel to Venice or Rome; field trips to Siena, Pisa, San Gimignano, Lucca. Students typically earn 4 semester credits per term.

Sessions • Jun-Jul (summer).

Eligibility Requirements • Minimum age 18; open to precollege students, freshmen, sophomores, juniors, seniors, adults; no foreign language proficiency required.

Living Arrangements • Students live in locally rented apartments. Quarters are shared with students from other programs. Meals are taken on one's own, in residences, in restaurants.

Costs (2005) • $3400; includes tuition, housing, excursions, international student ID, student support services, extracurricular activities. $250 nonrefundable deposit required.

For More Information • ACCENT International Consortium for Academic Programs Abroad, 870 Market Street, Suite 1026, San Francisco, CA 94102; *Phone:* 800-869-9291; *Fax:* 415-835-3749. *E-mail:* info@accentintl.com. *World Wide Web:* http://www.accentintl.com/

ACCENT INTERNATIONAL CONSORTIUM FOR ACADEMIC PROGRAMS ABROAD
WINTER SESSION IN FLORENCE

Hosted by Scuola Leonardo daVinci

Academic Focus • Art, Italian language and literature.

Program Information • Students attend classes at Scuola Leonardo daVinci (Florence, Italy). Scheduled travel to Venice, Rome; field trips to Siena, Pisa, San Gimignano, Lucca. Students typically earn 8 semester credits per term.

Sessions • Jan (winter).

Eligibility Requirements • Minimum age 18; open to freshmen, sophomores, juniors, seniors, graduate students, adults; no foreign language proficiency required.

Living Arrangements • Students live in locally rented apartments. Quarters are shared with students from other programs. Meals are taken on one's own, in residences.

Costs (2006) • $3425; includes housing, excursions, international student ID, student support services. $250 nonrefundable deposit required.

For More Information • ACCENT International Consortium for Academic Programs Abroad, 870 Market Street, Suite 1026, San Francisco, CA 94102; *Phone:* 800-869-9291; *Fax:* 415-835-3749. *E-mail:* info@accentintl.com. *World Wide Web:* http://www.accentintl.com/

AMERICAN INSTITUTE FOR FOREIGN STUDY (AIFS)
AIFS–FLORENCE, ITALY–RICHMOND IN FLORENCE

Hosted by Richmond College International Study Center, Richmond in Florence

Academic Focus • Art history, fine/studio arts, history, Italian language and literature, literature, music, photography, sociology.

Program Information • Students attend classes at Richmond College International Study Center (Florence, Italy), Richmond in Florence (Florence, Italy). Scheduled travel to 3-day stopover in London; field trips to cultural activities, museums, art galleries, monuments; optional travel to 3-day excursion to Venice for a supplement of $329, 3-day excursion to Rome for a supplement of $379. Students typically earn 6 semester credits per term.

Sessions • May-Jul (summer).

Eligibility Requirements • Minimum age 17; open to precollege students, freshmen, sophomores, juniors, seniors; 2.0 GPA; good academic standing at home school; no foreign language proficiency required.

Living Arrangements • Students live in host institution dormitories, program-owned apartments, hotels, as a paying guest in private home. Quarters are shared with host institution students. Meals are taken as a group, in restaurants.

Costs (2007) • $5499; includes tuition, housing, some meals, insurance, excursions, student support services, On-site Resident Director, Phone Card to call the U.S., Computer Facilities/Internet. $95 application fee. $395 nonrefundable deposit required. Financial aid available for all students: scholarships.

For More Information • Mr. David Mauro, Admissions Advisor, American Institute For Foreign Study (AIFS), 9 West Broad Street,

Stamford, CT 06902-3788; *Phone:* 800-727-2437 Ext. 5163; *Fax:* 203-399-5597. *E-mail:* dmauro@aifs.com. *World Wide Web:* http://www.aifsabroad.com/

AMERICAN INTERCONTINENTAL UNIVERSITY
FLORENCE PROGRAM

Academic Focus • Art, communications.
Program Information • Faculty members are local instructors hired by the sponsor. Students typically earn 10 quarter credits per term.
Sessions • Jun–Aug (summer).
Eligibility Requirements • Open to freshmen, sophomores, juniors, seniors, graduate students, adults; 2.0 GPA; good academic standing at home school; approval of advisor, dean or department chair, and study abroad office; college transcripts; no foreign language proficiency required.
Living Arrangements • Students live in hotels. Meals are taken on one's own, in residences, in central dining facility, in restaurants.
Costs (2005) • $5990 for 2 classes; includes tuition, housing, student support services. $75 application fee. $250 nonrefundable deposit required. Financial aid available for all students: scholarships, loans, financial aid where applicable.
For More Information • American InterContinental University, Study Abroad Programs, 3150 West Higgins Road, Suite 105, Hoffman Estates, IL 60195; *Phone:* 800-255-6839; *Fax:* 847-885-8422. *E-mail:* studyabroad@aiuniv.edu. *World Wide Web:* http://www.studyabroad.aiuniv.edu/

ARCADIA UNIVERSITY
SUMMER IN FLORENCE

Hosted by Accademia Italiana
Academic Focus • Italian language and literature, Italian studies, photography, social sciences.

Program Information • Students attend classes at Accademia Italiana (Florence, Italy). Field trips to Rome; optional travel. Students typically earn 3–6 semester credits per term.
Sessions • Jun–Jul (summer).
Eligibility Requirements • Minimum age 18; open to sophomores, juniors, seniors, adults; 3.0 GPA; 1 letter of recommendation; no foreign language proficiency required.
Living Arrangements • Students live in locally rented apartments. Quarters are shared with host institution students. Meals are taken on one's own, in residences.
Costs (2005–2006) • $3050–$3950; includes tuition, housing, insurance, international student ID, student support services, transcript, pre-departure guide, orientation. $35 application fee. $500 nonrefundable deposit required.
For More Information • Arcadia University, Center for Education Abroad, 450 South Easton Road, Glenside, PA 19038-3295; *Phone:* 866-927-2234; *Fax:* 215-572-2174. *E-mail:* cea@arcadia.edu. *World Wide Web:* http://www.arcadia.edu/cea/

ARTIS ART RESEARCH TOURS AND INTERNATIONAL STUDIOS
BIRTH OF THE RENAISSANCE

Held at ARTIS/Studio Fuji
Academic Focus • Art history, drawing/painting, fashion design, photography.
Program Information • Classes are held on the campus of ARTIS/Studio Fuji (Florence, Italy). Faculty members are drawn from the sponsor's U.S. staff and local instructors hired by the sponsor. Scheduled travel to Rome; field trips to Venice, Pisa, Siena; optional travel to locations in Italy at an extra cost. Students typically earn 3–6 semester credits per term.
Sessions • May–Jun (summer), Jun–Jul (summer 2).

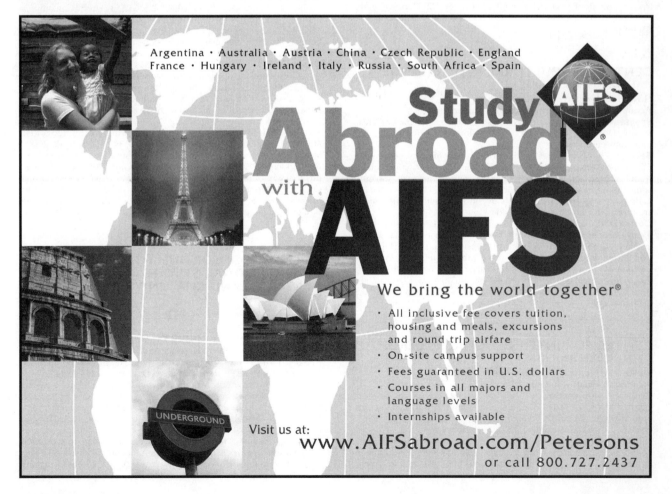

Eligibility Requirements • Minimum age 18; open to freshmen, sophomores, juniors, seniors, graduate students, adults; good physical and mental health; no foreign language proficiency required.

Living Arrangements • Students live in locally rented apartments. Quarters are shared with host institution students. Meals are taken on one's own, in residences.

Costs (2005) • $4200; includes housing, insurance, excursions, international airfare, student support services, some books, class instruction, history lectures. $400 nonrefundable deposit required. Financial aid available for students: loans for college students.

For More Information • Mr. David Renfrow, Program Director, ARTIS Art Research Tours and International Studios, 1709 Apache Drive, Medford, OR 97501; *Phone:* 800-232-6893; *Fax:* 541-535-8604. *E-mail:* david@artis.info. *World Wide Web:* http://www.artis-tours.org/

ART UNDER ONE ROOF
ART UNDER ONE ROOF

Academic Focus • Ceramics and pottery, drawing/painting, fine/studio arts, Italian language and literature, music performance, photography.

Program Information • Faculty members are local instructors hired by the sponsor. Field trips to Siena, Lucca, Pisa; optional travel at an extra cost. Students typically earn 6-9 semester credits per term.

Sessions • Jun-Jul (summer).

Eligibility Requirements • Minimum age 18; open to freshmen, sophomores, juniors, seniors, adults; 2.5 GPA; good academic standing at home school; no foreign language proficiency required.

Living Arrangements • Students live in locally rented apartments, host family homes. Meals are taken on one's own, with host family.

Costs (2006) • €1500 with language option; includes tuition, books and class materials. €750 refundable deposit required.

For More Information • Mrs. Kirste Milligan, School Secretary, Art Under One Roof, Via dei Pandofini 46R, 50122 Florence, Italy; *Phone:* +39 055-247-8867; *Fax:* +39 055-247-8867. *E-mail:* arte1@arteurope.it

CENTER FOR CULTURAL INTERCHANGE
ITALY LANGUAGE SCHOOL

Hosted by Linguaviva Italian School

Academic Focus • Italian language and literature.

Program Information • Students attend classes at Linguaviva Italian School (Florence, Italy). Field trips to cultural activities, guided city tours, museum visits.

Sessions • 3, 4, or 6 week sessions begin every Monday, year-round.

Eligibility Requirements • Minimum age 17; open to precollege students, freshmen, sophomores, juniors, seniors, graduate students, adults; no foreign language proficiency required.

Living Arrangements • Students live in host family homes. Meals are taken with host family, in residences.

Costs (2005) • $2590 for 4 weeks; includes tuition, housing, some meals, insurance, student support services, activities. Financial aid available for students from sponsoring institution: scholarships.

For More Information • Ms. Juliet Jones, Outbound Programs Director, Center for Cultural Interchange, 325 West Huron, Suite 706, Chicago, IL 60610; *Phone:* 866-684-9675; *Fax:* 372-944-2644. *E-mail:* info@cci-exchange.com. *World Wide Web:* http://www.cci-exchange.com/

CENTER FOR INTERNATIONAL STUDIES
CIS FLORENCE PROGRAM

Hosted by Instituto Europeo, Florence Italy

Academic Focus • Full curriculum.

Program Information • Students attend classes at Instituto Europeo, Florence Italy (Florence, Italy). Field trips to Italian cities. Students typically earn 6 semester credits per term.

Sessions • Jun-Jul (summer), Jul-Aug (summer 2).

Eligibility Requirements • Minimum age 18; open to freshmen, sophomores, juniors, seniors, adults; 2.5 GPA; 1 letter of recommendation; good academic standing at home school; personal statement; no foreign language proficiency required.

Living Arrangements • Students live in locally rented apartments, host family homes. Quarters are shared with host institution students. Meals are taken as a group, on one's own, with host family, in residences, in restaurants.

Costs (2005) • $4500-$4900; includes tuition, housing, some meals, insurance, excursions, international student ID, student support services, airport reception, pay-as-you-go cell phone. $50 application fee. $800 nonrefundable deposit required. Financial aid available for all students: scholarships.

For More Information • Mr. Jeff Palm, Director, Center for International Studies, 25 New South Street, Suite 105, Northampton, MA 01060; *Phone:* 413-582-0407; *Fax:* 413-582-0327. *E-mail:* jpalm@cisabroad.com. *World Wide Web:* http://www.cisabroad.com/

COLLEGE CONSORTIUM FOR INTERNATIONAL STUDIES–COLLEGE OF STATEN ISLAND/CITY UNIVERSITY OF NEW YORK
SUMMER PROGRAM IN FLORENCE, ITALY: LIBERAL ARTS AND STUDIO ART

Hosted by Lorenzo de' Medici–The Art Institute of Florence

Academic Focus • Art conservation studies, art history, culinary arts, drawing/painting, fine/studio arts, Italian language and literature, Italian studies, photography.

Program Information • Students attend classes at Lorenzo de' Medici–The Art Institute of Florence (Florence, Italy). Field trips to Florence and environs; optional travel to Venice, Siena, San Gimignano, Verona, Lake Garda, Portofino, Cinque Terre at an extra cost. Students typically earn 3-6 semester credits per term.

Sessions • May-Jun (summer), Jun-Jul (summer 2); Jul-Aug (summer 3).

Eligibility Requirements • Minimum age 18; open to freshmen, sophomores, juniors, seniors, adults; 2.5 GPA; 1 letter of recommendation; essay; transcript; no foreign language proficiency required.

Living Arrangements • Students live in locally rented apartments, hotels. Quarters are shared with students from other programs. Meals are taken on one's own, in residences, in restaurants.

Costs (2007) • $2845 for 6 credits; $1995 for 3 credits for New York residents and CCIS member students. All others contact the College of Staten Island; includes tuition, insurance, excursions, student support services, fees. $135 nonrefundable deposit required. Financial aid available for students from sponsoring institution: loans, grants.

For More Information • College Consortium for International Studies–College of Staten Island/City University of New York, 2000 P Street, NW, Suite 503, Washington, DC 20036; *Phone:* 800-453-6956; *Fax:* 202-233-0999. *E-mail:* info@ccisabroad.org. *World Wide Web:* http://www.ccisabroad.org/. Students may also apply through College of Staten Island, The City University of New York, Center for International Service, Building 2A, Room 206, 2800 Victory Boulevard, Staten Island, NY 10314.

COLLEGE CONSORTIUM FOR INTERNATIONAL STUDIES–COLLEGE OF STATEN ISLAND/CITY UNIVERSITY OF NEW YORK
SUMMER PROGRAM IN FLORENCE, ITALY: SUPER-INTENSIVE ITALIAN

Hosted by Lorenzo de' Medici–The Art Institute of Florence

Academic Focus • Italian language and literature.

Program Information • Students attend classes at Lorenzo de' Medici–The Art Institute of Florence (Florence, Italy). Field trips to Florence and environs; optional travel to Verona, Lake Garda, Venice, Siena, San Gimignano, Portofino, Cinque Terre at an extra cost. Students typically earn 6 semester credits per term.

Sessions • May-Jun (summer), Jun-Jul (summer 2); Jul-Aug (summer 3).

Eligibility Requirements • Minimum age 18; open to freshmen, sophomores, juniors, seniors, graduate students, adults; 2.5 GPA; 1 letter of recommendation; essay; transcript; no foreign language proficiency required.

Living Arrangements • Students live in locally rented apartments, hotels. Quarters are shared with students from other programs. Meals are taken on one's own, in residences, in restaurants.

Costs (2006) • $1845 for New York residents and CCIS member students; all others contact the College of Staten Island; includes tuition, insurance, excursions, student support services, fees. $135 nonrefundable deposit required. Financial aid available for students from sponsoring institution: loans, grants.

For More Information • College Consortium for International Studies–College of Staten Island/City University of New York, 2000 P Street, NW, Suite 503, Washington, DC 20036; *Phone:* 800-453-6956; *Fax:* 202-233-0999. *E-mail:* info@ccisabroad.org. *World Wide Web:* http://www.ccisabroad.org/. Students may also apply through College of Staten Island, The City University of New York, Center for International Service, Building 2A, Room 206, 2800 Victory Boulevard, Staten Island, NY 10314.

DRAKE UNIVERSITY
INSTITUTE OF ITALIAN STUDIES–FLORENCE SUMMER

Hosted by Institute of Italian Studies–Florence, Lorenzo de Medici School, Lorenzo de' Medici–The Art Institute of Florence

Academic Focus • Architecture, art, art history, communications, culinary arts, film and media studies, Italian language and literature, Italian studies, liberal studies.

Program Information • Students attend classes at Institute of Italian Studies–Florence (Florence, Italy), Lorenzo de Medici School (Florence, Italy), Lorenzo de' Medici–The Art Institute of Florence (Florence, Italy). Optional travel to Venice at an extra cost. Students typically earn 6 semester credits per term.

Sessions • May–Aug (summer).

Eligibility Requirements • Minimum age 19; open to sophomores, juniors, seniors; 2.75 GPA; no foreign language proficiency required.

Living Arrangements • Students live in locally rented apartments. Quarters are shared with host institution students, students from other programs. Meals are taken on one's own, in residences.

Costs (2006) • $2600; includes tuition. $35 application fee. Financial aid available for students: most forms of aid are transferable.

For More Information • Mr. Rick Soria, Director, Drake University, PO Box 27077, West Des Moines, IA 50265; *Phone:* 800-443-7253 Ext. 3984; *Fax:* 515-225-0196. *E-mail:* drakeiis@drake.edu. *World Wide Web:* http://www.italy.drake.edu/iis/

EUROPEAN HERITAGE INSTITUTE
MUSIC AND ART IN FLORENCE (YEAR-ROUND)

Hosted by Istituto Europeo

Academic Focus • Art, art history, civilization studies, drawing/painting, fine/studio arts, history, Italian language and literature, Italian studies, music, music history, music performance, photography, visual and performing arts.

Program Information • Students attend classes at Istituto Europeo (Florence, Italy). Field trips; optional travel to Rome, Venice, Verona at an extra cost. Students typically earn 3–6 semester credits per term.

Sessions • Minimum 2 week sessions held year-round; month-long sessions held May–Aug.

Eligibility Requirements • Minimum age 18; open to freshmen, sophomores, juniors, seniors, adults; 2.25 GPA; 2 letters of recommendation; good academic standing at home school; no foreign language proficiency required.

Living Arrangements • Students live in locally rented apartments, host family homes. Quarters are shared with host institution students, students from other programs. Meals are taken on one's own, with host family, in residences, in restaurants.

Costs (2006) • $2600; includes tuition, excursions, student support services. $300 refundable deposit required.

For More Information • Dr. Antonio Masullo, Professor, European Heritage Institute, 2708 East Franklin Street, Richmond, VA 23223; *Phone:* 804-643-0661; *Fax:* 804-648-0826. *E-mail:* info@europeabroad.org. *World Wide Web:* http://www.europeabroad.org/

EUROPEAN HERITAGE INSTITUTE
STUDY ABROAD IN FLORENCE

Hosted by Lorenzo de Medici School

Academic Focus • Full curriculum.

Program Information • Students attend classes at Lorenzo de Medici School (Florence, Italy). Field trips to Florence, Tuscany, Rome, Venice and the Lake Country. Students typically earn 3–6 semester credits per term.

Sessions • Minimum 2 week sessions held year-round; month-long sessions held May–Aug and in Jan.

Eligibility Requirements • Minimum age 18; open to freshmen, sophomores, juniors, seniors, graduate students, adults; 2.25 GPA; 2 letters of recommendation; no foreign language proficiency required.

Living Arrangements • Students live in host institution dormitories, locally rented apartments, host family homes, hotels. Quarters are shared with host institution students, students from other programs. Meals are taken on one's own, with host family, in residences, in restaurants.

Costs (2006) • $1100–$3150; includes tuition, insurance, excursions, student support services. $300 refundable deposit required.

For More Information • Dr. Antonio Masullo, Professor, European Heritage Institute, 2708 East Franklin Street, Richmond, VA 23223; *Phone:* 804-643-0661; *Fax:* 804-648-0826. *E-mail:* info@europeabroad.org. *World Wide Web:* http://www.europeabroad.org/

FAIRFIELD UNIVERSITY
FAIRFIELD UNIVERSITY SUMMER PROGRAM IN FLORENCE

Hosted by Lorenzo de' Medici–The Art Institute of Florence

Academic Focus • Art, art history, history, Italian language and literature, marketing, social sciences.

Program Information • Students attend classes at Lorenzo de' Medici–The Art Institute of Florence (Florence, Italy). Field trips to Medici villas, museums, gardens, cultural events; optional travel to Venice, Verona, Cinque Terra at an extra cost. Students typically earn 6 semester credits per term.

Sessions • May–Jun (summer), Jun–Jul (summer 2).

Eligibility Requirements • Minimum age 18; open to precollege students, freshmen, sophomores, juniors, seniors, adults; 2.8 GPA; 2 letters of recommendation; good academic standing at home school; transcripts; no foreign language proficiency required.

Living Arrangements • Students live in locally rented apartments. Quarters are shared with host institution students. Meals are taken as a group, on one's own, in residences, in restaurants.

Costs (2005) • $4400; includes tuition, housing, some meals, insurance, international student ID, student support services, weekly activities. $1000 refundable deposit required.

For More Information • Office of International Education, Fairfield University, Dolan House, 1073 North Benson Road, Fairfield, CT 06824; *Phone:* 203-254-4332; *Fax:* 203-254-4261. *E-mail:* studyabroadoffice@mail.fairfield.edu. *World Wide Web:* http://www.fairfield.edu/studyabroad.xml/

FAIRFIELD UNIVERSITY
JANUARY EXPERIENCE IN FLORENCE

Academic Focus • Art history, history.

Program Information • Faculty members are drawn from the sponsor's U.S. staff and local instructors hired by the sponsor. Field trips to museums, villas, towns. Students typically earn 3 semester credits per term.

Sessions • Jan (winter).

Eligibility Requirements • Minimum age 18; open to freshmen, sophomores, juniors, seniors, adults; 2.8 GPA; 1 letter of recommendation; good academic standing at home school; no foreign language proficiency required.

Living Arrangements • Students live in locally rented apartments. Meals are taken on one's own, in residences.

Costs (2006) • $2400; includes tuition, housing, some meals, insurance, excursions, international student ID, student support services. $1000 refundable deposit required.

For More Information • Office of International Education, Fairfield University, Dolan House, 1073 North Benson Road, Fairfield, CT 06824; *Phone:* 203-254-4332; *Fax:* 203-254-4261. *E-mail:* studyabroadoffice@mail.fairfield.edu. *World Wide Web:* http://www.fairfield.edu/studyabroad.xml/

ITALY
Florence

FIRENZE ARTI VISIVE
FIRENZE ARTI VISIVE

Hosted by Firenze Arti Visive
Academic Focus • Art, art history, film and media studies, photography, visual and performing arts.
Program Information • Students attend classes at Firenze Arti Visive (Florence, Italy). Field trips to Venice, Rome, Siena, Pisa, Luca; optional travel to Paris, Berlin at an extra cost. Students typically earn 6 semester credits per term.
Sessions • Jun–Jul (summer).
Eligibility Requirements • Minimum age 18; open to freshmen, sophomores, juniors, seniors; 2.0 GPA; 2 letters of recommendation; good academic standing at home school; no foreign language proficiency required.
Living Arrangements • Quarters are shared with host institution students, students from other programs. Meals are taken on one's own, in residences.
Costs (2005) • $3200; includes tuition. $50 application fee. $500 nonrefundable deposit required. Financial aid available for all students: scholarships.
For More Information • Mr. Carlo Conti, Studio Arts Director, Firenze Arti Visive, Palazzo Antinori Corsini, Borgo Santa Crose, Florence, 50122, Italy; *Phone:* +001 39-340 3168477; *Fax:* +001 39-005 702849. *E-mail:* info@firenze_artivisive.org. *World Wide Web:* http://www.firenze_artivisive.org/

GONZAGA UNIVERSITY
GONZAGA IN FLORENCE

Hosted by Gonzaga in Florence
Academic Focus • Art, art history, business administration/management, history, Italian language and literature, philosophy, religious studies.
Program Information • Students attend classes at Gonzaga in Florence (Florence, Italy). Scheduled travel to Rome, Greece, Germany, Austria; optional travel to Capri, Amalfi Coast, Munich, Barcelona, France, Switzerland, Cinque Terra, Sicily at an extra cost. Students typically earn 6 semester credits per term.
Sessions • May–Jun (summer).
Eligibility Requirements • Open to sophomores, juniors, seniors, adults; 2.5 GPA; 1 letter of recommendation; Dean of Students approval; no foreign language proficiency required.
Living Arrangements • Students live in hotels. Quarters are shared with host institution students. Meals are taken as a group, in residences.
Costs (2005) • $6250; includes tuition, housing, some meals, international student ID, 6-day opening tour of Italy. $50 application fee. $500 deposit required. Financial aid available for all students: loans.
For More Information • Ms. Wanda Reynolds, Director, Study Abroad, Gonzaga University, East 502 Boone Avenue, Spokane, WA 99258; *Phone:* 800-440-5391; *Fax:* 509-323-5987. *E-mail:* reynolds@gu.gonzaga.edu. *World Wide Web:* http://www.gonzaga.edu/studyabroad/

ILLINOIS STATE UNIVERSITY
ITALY SUMMER PROGRAM

Hosted by Lorenzo de Medici School
Academic Focus • Art, art history, ceramics and pottery, fashion design, Italian language and literature, Italian studies.
Program Information • Students attend classes at Lorenzo de Medici School (Florence, Italy). Field trips to course-based destinations; optional travel to Venice, Siena at an extra cost. Students typically earn 3–9 semester credits per term.
Sessions • May–Jun (summer).
Eligibility Requirements • Minimum age 18; open to sophomores, juniors, seniors, graduate students, adults; 2.5 GPA; 2 letters of recommendation; essay; no foreign language proficiency required.
Living Arrangements • Students live in locally rented apartments, hotels. Quarters are shared with host institution students, students from other programs. Meals are taken on one's own, in residences, in restaurants.
Costs (2005) • $5367–$6417; includes tuition, housing, all meals, insurance, international airfare, international student ID, student support services, personal expenses, personal travel. $150 application fee. Financial aid available for students from sponsoring institution: scholarships, loans.
For More Information • Study Abroad Coordinator, Illinois State University, Campus Box 6120, International Studies, Normal, IL 61790-6120; *Phone:* 309-438-5276; *Fax:* 309-438-3987. *E-mail:* oisp@ilstu.edu. *World Wide Web:* http://www.internationalstudies.ilstu.edu/

JAMES MADISON UNIVERSITY
SUMMER PROGRAM IN FLORENCE

Hosted by The British Institute
Academic Focus • Art history, film and media studies, Italian language and literature, Italian studies, literature.
Program Information • Students attend classes at The British Institute (Florence, Italy). Scheduled travel to Rome; field trips to Venice, Pisa, Siena. Students typically earn 9 semester credits per term.
Sessions • May–Jul (summer).
Eligibility Requirements • Minimum age 18; open to sophomores, juniors, seniors; 2.0 GPA; good academic standing at home school; no foreign language proficiency required.
Living Arrangements • Students live in host family homes. Quarters are shared with host institution students. Meals are taken on one's own, with host family, in residences, in restaurants.
Costs (2005) • $4662 for Virginia residents; $7182 for nonresidents; includes tuition, housing, some meals, excursions, books and class materials, international student ID. $400 nonrefundable deposit required. Financial aid available for students from sponsoring institution: scholarships, work study.
For More Information • Mr. Felix Wang, Director, James Madison University, Office of International Programs, MSC 5731, 1077 South Main Street, Harrisonburg, VA 22807; *Phone:* 540-568-6419; *Fax:* 540-568-3310. *E-mail:* studyabroad@jmu.edu. *World Wide Web:* http://www.jmu.edu/international/

LANGUAGE LIAISON
ART STUDIES IN FLORENCE

Hosted by Language Liaison
Academic Focus • American studies, art history, fine/studio arts.
Program Information • Students attend classes at Language Liaison (Florence, Italy). Optional travel at an extra cost. Students typically earn 3–18 semester credits per term.
Sessions • New programs begin weekly, year-round.
Eligibility Requirements • Minimum age 18; open to freshmen, sophomores, juniors, seniors, graduate students, adults; no foreign language proficiency required.
Living Arrangements • Students live in locally rented apartments, host family homes. Meals are taken on one's own, with host family, in residences, in restaurants.
Costs (2005) • Contact sponsor for cost. $175 application fee. Financial aid available for all students: scholarship research service.
For More Information • Ms. Nancy Forman, President, Language Liaison, PO Box 1772, Pacific Palisades, CA 90272; *Phone:* 800-284-4448; *Fax:* 310-454-1706. *E-mail:* learn@languageliaison.com. *World Wide Web:* http://www.languageliaison.com/

LANGUAGE LIAISON
LEARN ITALIAN IN FLORENCE

Hosted by Language Liaison
Academic Focus • Italian language and literature.
Program Information • Students attend classes at Language Liaison (Florence, Italy). Field trips; optional travel at an extra cost. Students typically earn 3–15 semester credits per term.
Sessions • New programs begin weekly, year-round.
Eligibility Requirements • Minimum age 17; open to precollege students, freshmen, sophomores, juniors, seniors, graduate students, adults; no foreign language proficiency required.
Living Arrangements • Students live in locally rented apartments, host family homes, hotels. Meals are taken on one's own, with host family, in residences, in restaurants.
Costs (2005) • Contact sponsor for cost. $175 application fee. Financial aid available for all students: scholarship research service.

For More Information • Ms. Nancy Forman, President, Language Liaison, PO Box 1772, Pacific Palisades, CA 90272; *Phone:* 800-284-4448; *Fax:* 310-454-1706. *E-mail:* learn@languageliaison. com. *World Wide Web:* http://www.languageliaison.com/

LINGUA SERVICE WORLDWIDE
VACATION 'N LEARN ITALIAN IN ITALY

Hosted by Scuola Leonardo daVinci
Academic Focus • Italian language and literature, Italian studies.
Program Information • Students attend classes at Scuola Leonardo daVinci (Florence, Italy). Optional travel to cultural sites thoughout Italy at an extra cost. Students typically earn 3 semester credits for 3 weeks, 6 semester credits for 5 weeks.
Sessions • Sessions of 2 or more weeks begin on Mondays, year-round.
Eligibility Requirements • Minimum age 16; open to freshmen, sophomores, juniors, seniors, graduate students, adults; no foreign language proficiency required.
Living Arrangements • Students live in host institution dormitories, locally rented apartments, host family homes, hotels. Quarters are shared with host institution students. Meals are taken with host family.
Costs (2006–2007) • Contact sponsor for cost. $100 application fee.
For More Information • Assistant Director, Lingua Service Worldwide, 75 Prospect Street, Suite 4, Huntington, NY 11743; *Phone:* 800-394-5327; *Fax:* 631-271-3441. *E-mail:* linguaservice@att. net. *World Wide Web:* http://www.linguaserviceworldwide.com/

LINGUA SERVICE WORLDWIDE
VACATION 'N LEARN ITALIAN IN ITALY

Hosted by Instituto Michelangelo
Academic Focus • Italian language and literature, Italian studies.
Program Information • Students attend classes at Instituto Michelangelo (Florence, Italy). Optional travel to cultural sites throughout Italy at an extra cost. Students typically earn 3 semester credits for 3 weeks, 6 semester credits for 5 weeks.
Sessions • Sessions of 2 or more weeks begin on Mondays, year-round.
Eligibility Requirements • Minimum age 16; open to freshmen, sophomores, juniors, seniors, graduate students, adults; no foreign language proficiency required.
Living Arrangements • Students live in host institution dormitories, locally rented apartments, host family homes, hotels. Quarters are shared with host institution students. Meals are taken with host family.
Costs (2006–2007) • Contact sponsor for cost. $100 application fee.
For More Information • Assistant Director, Lingua Service Worldwide, 75 Prospect Street, Suite 4, Huntington, NY 11743; *Phone:* 800-394-5327; *Fax:* 631-271-3441. *E-mail:* linguaservice@att. net. *World Wide Web:* http://www.linguaserviceworldwide.com/

MICHIGAN STATE UNIVERSITY
ITALIAN LANGUAGE, LITERATURE, AND CULTURE IN FLORENCE

Hosted by Centro Linguistico Italiano Dante Alighieri
Academic Focus • Italian language and literature, Italian studies.
Program Information • Students attend classes at Centro Linguistico Italiano Dante Alighieri (Florence, Italy). Field trips to galleries, churches, museums, the theatre, Siena, Cinque Terre. Students typically earn 7 semester credits per term.
Sessions • May–Jun (summer).
Eligibility Requirements • Minimum age 18; open to freshmen, sophomores, juniors, seniors, graduate students; 2.0 GPA; good academic standing at home school; faculty approval; no foreign language proficiency required.
Living Arrangements • Students live in host family homes. Meals are taken as a group, with host family, in residences, in central dining facility.
Costs (2005) • $3802 (estimated); includes housing, some meals, insurance, excursions, student support services. $100 application fee. $200 nonrefundable deposit required. Financial aid available for students from sponsoring institution: scholarships, loans.

For More Information • Ms. Maggie Matice, Secretary, Michigan State University, Office of Study Abroad, 109 International Center, East Lansing, MI 48824-1035; *Phone:* 517-353-8920; *Fax:* 517-432-2082. *E-mail:* matice@msu.edu. *World Wide Web:* http://studyabroad. msu.edu/

NECA–NEW ETRURIA COLLEGE ASSOCIATION
NECA PROGRAMS

Hosted by NECA–New Etruria College Association
Academic Focus • Full curriculum.
Program Information • Students attend classes at NECA–New Etruria College Association (Florence, Italy). Field trips to Pisa, Florentine Hills; optional travel to Siena, Rome, other excursions off the beaten path at an extra cost. Students typically earn 3–6 semester credits per term.
Sessions • Jun (summer).
Eligibility Requirements • Minimum age 18; open to freshmen, sophomores, juniors, seniors, graduate students, adults; two semesters of college or equivalent; no foreign language proficiency required.
Living Arrangements • Students live in locally rented apartments, host family homes, student residence. Quarters are shared with host institution students, students from other programs. Meals are taken on one's own.
Costs (2007) • $3350–$3850; includes tuition, housing, excursions, student support services, orientation program. $300 nonrefundable deposit required. Financial aid available for all students: scholarships.
For More Information • Dr. Francesco Convertini, Director, NECA–New Etruria College Association, Via Scipione Ammirato 98, 50136 Florence, Italy; *Phone:* +39 340-356-7661; *Fax:* +39 055-677-503. *E-mail:* neca@necaflorence.com. *World Wide Web:* http://www.necaflorence.com

NEW YORK UNIVERSITY
THE 30-SECOND COMMERCIAL REEL: FLORENCE, ITALY

Hosted by New York University in Florence
Academic Focus • Film and media studies.
Program Information • Students attend classes at New York University in Florence (Florence, Italy). Students typically earn 8 semester credits per term.
Sessions • May–Jun (summer).
Eligibility Requirements • Minimum age 18; open to freshmen, sophomores, juniors, seniors, adults; course work in film production.
Living Arrangements • Students live in La Pietra. Quarters are shared with host institution students. Meals are taken on one's own, in central dining facility.
Costs (2005) • $5400; includes tuition. $50 application fee. Financial aid available for students from sponsoring institution: scholarships.
For More Information • Mr. Josh Murray, Assistant Director, New York University, 721 Broadway, 12th Floor, New York, NY 10003; *Phone:* 212-998-1500; *Fax:* 212-995-4578. *E-mail:* tisch.special.info@ nyu.edu. *World Wide Web:* http://www.nyu.edu/global/studyabroad. html

NEW YORK UNIVERSITY
COMMEDIA DELL'ARTE: THE ACTOR AS CREATOR, CLOWN, AND POET–FLORENCE, ITALY

Academic Focus • Drama/theater.
Program Information • Faculty members are drawn from the sponsor's U.S. staff. Students typically earn 8 semester credits per term.
Sessions • May–Jun (summer).
Eligibility Requirements • Minimum age 18; open to freshmen, sophomores, juniors, seniors, graduate students, adults; course work in acting; no foreign language proficiency required.
Living Arrangements • Students live in program-owned houses. Meals are taken on one's own, in central dining facility.
Costs (2005) • $5400; includes tuition. $50 application fee. Financial aid available for students from sponsoring institution: scholarships.

ITALY
Florence

For More Information • Mr. Josh Murray, Assistant Director, New York University, 721 Broadway, 12th Floor, New York, NY 10003; *Phone:* 212-998-1500; *Fax:* 212-995-4578. *E-mail:* tisch.special.info@nyu.edu. *World Wide Web:* http://www.nyu.edu/global/studyabroad.html

NEW YORK UNIVERSITY
HUMANITIES SEMINAR: FLORENCE, ITALY
Held at New York University in Florence

Academic Focus • Art history, literature, philosophy.

Program Information • Classes are held on the campus of New York University in Florence (Florence, Italy). Faculty members are drawn from the sponsor's U.S. staff and local instructors hired by the sponsor. Field trips to Siena, San Giminjano; optional travel to Tuscany at an extra cost. Students typically earn 4 semester credits per term.

Sessions • Jun (summer).

Eligibility Requirements • Open to freshmen, sophomores, juniors, seniors, graduate students, adults; 3.0 GPA; 1 letter of recommendation; one-page essay; no foreign language proficiency required.

Living Arrangements • Students live in host institution dormitories. Quarters are shared with host institution students. Meals are taken as a group, on one's own, in central dining facility, in restaurants.

Costs (2005) • $3500; includes tuition, housing, some meals, insurance, excursions. $300 nonrefundable deposit required. Financial aid available for students from sponsoring institution: scholarships.

For More Information • Ms. Vanessa Manko, Academic Adviser, New York University, 719 Broadway, Room 529B, New York, NY 10003; *Phone:* 212-998-7365; *Fax:* 212-995-4002. *E-mail:* vkm201@nyu.edu. *World Wide Web:* http://www.nyu.edu/global/studyabroad.html

NEW YORK UNIVERSITY
NYU IN FLORENCE
Hosted by NYU at La Pietra

Academic Focus • Art history, civilization studies, comparative literature, film and media studies, Italian language and literature, Italian studies.

Program Information • Students attend classes at NYU at La Pietra (Florence, Italy). Scheduled travel to Rome; field trips to San Gimignano, Siena, Pisa, Fiesole, Pienza, Multepulciano, Lucca, Perugia, Assisi, Ravenna. Students typically earn 8-10 semester credits per term.

Sessions • Jun–Aug (summer).

Eligibility Requirements • Minimum age 18; open to freshmen, sophomores, juniors, seniors; 3.0 GPA; good academic standing at home school; personal statement for non-New York University students; no foreign language proficiency required.

Living Arrangements • Students live in host institution dormitories. Quarters are shared with host institution students. Meals are taken as a group, in central dining facility.

Costs (2006) • $7367; includes tuition, housing, some meals, excursions, student support services, program fee. $25 application fee. $300 nonrefundable deposit required. Financial aid available for students from sponsoring institution: loans.

For More Information • Office of Summer Sessions, New York University, 7 East 12th Street, 6th Floor, New York, NY 10003; *Phone:* 212-998-2292; *Fax:* 212-995-4642. *E-mail:* summer.info@nyu.edu. *World Wide Web:* http://www.nyu.edu/global/studyabroad.html

NEW YORK UNIVERSITY
WRITING FLORENCE: FLORENCE, ITALY

Academic Focus • Creative writing.

Program Information • Faculty members are drawn from the sponsor's U.S. staff. Students typically earn 8 semester credits per term.

Sessions • May–Jun (summer).

Eligibility Requirements • Minimum age 18; open to freshmen, sophomores, juniors, seniors, adults; no foreign language proficiency required.

Living Arrangements • Students live in program-owned houses. Meals are taken on one's own, in central dining facility.

Costs (2005) • $5400; includes tuition. $50 application fee. Financial aid available for students from sponsoring institution: scholarships.

For More Information • Mr. Josh Murray, Assistant Director, New York University, 721 Broadway, 12th Floor, New York, NY 10003; *Phone:* 212-998-1500; *Fax:* 212-995-4578. *E-mail:* tisch.special.info@nyu.edu. *World Wide Web:* http://www.nyu.edu/global/studyabroad.html

SKIDMORE COLLEGE
SKIDMORE SUMMER SESSION AT SACI
Hosted by Studio Art Centers International

Academic Focus • Art history, fine/studio arts, Italian language and literature.

Program Information • Students attend classes at Studio Art Centers International (Florence, Italy). Field trips to Pisa, Lucca, Siena. Students typically earn 6-8 semester credits per term.

Sessions • May–Jul (summer).

Eligibility Requirements • Minimum age 18; open to sophomores, juniors, seniors; 3.0 GPA; 1 letter of recommendation; good academic standing at home school; no foreign language proficiency required.

Living Arrangements • Students live in locally rented apartments, program-owned apartments. Quarters are shared with host institution students, students from other programs. Meals are taken on one's own, in residences.

Costs (2005) • Contact sponsor for cost. $80 application fee. $300 refundable deposit required.

For More Information • Mr. James Chansky, Director, Summer Special Programs and Summer Sessions, Skidmore College, Office of the Dean of Special Programs, Saratoga Springs, NY 12866; *Phone:* 518-580-5590; *Fax:* 518-580-5548. *E-mail:* jchansky@skidmore.edu. *World Wide Web:* http://www.skidmore.edu/internationalprograms/

STATE UNIVERSITY OF NEW YORK COLLEGE AT BROCKPORT
INTERNSHIPS IN ITALY

Academic Focus • Art, health and physical education, Italian studies.

Program Information • Field trips. Students typically earn 12 credits per term.

Sessions • May–Aug (summer).

Eligibility Requirements • Minimum age 18; open to juniors, seniors; 2.75 GPA; 2 letters of recommendation; good academic standing at home school; some Italian helpful.

Living Arrangements • Students live in program-owned apartments. Quarters are shared with host institution students. Meals are taken on one's own, in residences, in restaurants.

Costs (2006–2007) • $7350; includes tuition, excursions, international student ID, student support services. $200 nonrefundable deposit required. Financial aid available for all students: scholarships, loans, regular financial aid, grants.

For More Information • Dr. John Perry, Director, International Education, State University of New York College at Brockport, 350 New Campus Drive, Brockport, NY 14420; *Phone:* 800-298-SUNY; *Fax:* 585-637-3218. *E-mail:* overseas@brockport.edu. *World Wide Web:* http://www.brockport.edu/studyabroad/

STUDIO ART CENTERS INTERNATIONAL (SACI)
SUMMER STUDIES
Hosted by Studio Art Centers International

Academic Focus • Archaeology, architecture, art, art conservation studies, art history, ceramics and pottery, cinematography, crafts, creative writing, design and applied arts, drawing/painting, film and media studies, fine/studio arts, graphic design/illustration, interior design, Italian language and literature, Italian studies, music history, photography, textiles, visual and performing arts.

Program Information • Students attend classes at Studio Art Centers International (Florence, Italy). Field trips to Siena, Pisa, Arezzo, Bologna, Lucca, San Gimignano, Fiesole. Students typically earn 6 semester credits per term.

Sessions • May–Jun (summer), Jun–Jul (summer 2).

Eligibility Requirements • Minimum age 18; open to freshmen, sophomores, juniors, seniors, graduate students, adults; 2.75 GPA; 2 letters of recommendation; statement of intent; official transcript; completed application; no foreign language proficiency required.

Living Arrangements • Students live in locally rented apartments. Quarters are shared with host institution students. Meals are taken on one's own, in residences.

Costs (2005) • $3510; includes tuition. $50 application fee. $400 refundable deposit required.

For More Information • SACI Coordinator, Studio Art Centers International (SACI), Institute of International Education, 809 United Nations Plaza, New York, NY 10017; *Phone:* 212-984-5548; *Fax:* 212-984-5325. *E-mail:* saci@iie.org. *World Wide Web:* http://www.saci-florence.org/

STUDY ABROAD ITALY
APICIUS–THE CULINARY INSTITUTE OF FLORENCE

Hosted by Apicius The Culinary Institute of Florence

Academic Focus • Communication services, culinary arts, graphic design/illustration, hotel and restaurant management.

Program Information • Students attend classes at Apicius The Culinary Institute of Florence (Florence, Italy). Students typically earn 3–15 semester credits per term.

Sessions • Classes held weekly and monthly, year-round.

Eligibility Requirements • Minimum age 18; open to freshmen, sophomores, juniors, seniors, graduate students, adults; no foreign language proficiency required.

Living Arrangements • Students live in locally rented apartments, host family homes, hotels. Quarters are shared with host institution students, students from other programs. Meals are taken on one's own, in residences, in central dining facility, in restaurants.

Costs (2005) • $1400–$2800; includes tuition, housing, books and class materials, student support services, basic emergency travel assistance insurance. $75 application fee.

For More Information • Ms. Marilyn Etchell, Admissions Officer, Study Abroad Italy, 7151 Wilton Avenue, Suite 202, Sebastopol, CA 95472; *Phone:* 800-655-8965; *Fax:* 707-824-0198. *E-mail:* mae@studyabroad-italy.com. *World Wide Web:* http://www.studyabroad-italy.com/

STUDY ABROAD ITALY
FLORENCE UNIVERSITY OF THE ARTS

Hosted by Florence University of the Arts

Academic Focus • Full curriculum.

Program Information • Students attend classes at Florence University of the Arts (Florence, Italy). Scheduled travel to Rome, Milan, Sicily, Venice; field trips to Rome, Milan, Sicily; optional travel to Rome, Milan, Sicily, Venice at an extra cost. Students typically earn 9 semester credits per term.

Sessions • May–Jun (session 1), Jun–Jul (session 2).

Eligibility Requirements • Minimum age 18; open to freshmen, sophomores, juniors, seniors, graduate students, adults; no foreign language proficiency required.

Living Arrangements • Students live in locally rented apartments, host family homes. Quarters are shared with host institution students. Meals are taken on one's own, in residences.

Costs (2005) • $2700–$4800; includes tuition, housing, insurance, excursions, student support services. $75 application fee. $1000 refundable deposit required. Financial aid available for all students: scholarships, work study, loans.

For More Information • Ms. Annie Pisanic, Admissions Officer, Study Abroad Italy, 7151 Wilton Avenue, Suite 201, Sebastopol, CA 95472; *Phone:* 800-655-8965; *Fax:* 707-824-0198. *E-mail:* aep@studyabroaditaly.com. *World Wide Web:* http://www.studyabroad-italy.com/

SYRACUSE UNIVERSITY
ARCHITECTURE IN FLORENCE

Hosted by Syracuse University Center–Florence

Academic Focus • Architecture.

Program Information • Students attend classes at Syracuse University Center-Florence (Florence, Italy). Field trips. Students typically earn 9 semester credits per term.

Sessions • May–Jul (summer).

Eligibility Requirements • Open to juniors, seniors, graduate students; major in architecture; 1 letter of recommendation; good academic standing at home school; no foreign language proficiency required.

Living Arrangements • Students live in locally rented apartments. Meals are taken on one's own, in residences, in restaurants.

Costs (2005) • $10,470; includes tuition, housing, some meals, excursions, international student ID, student support services. $55 application fee. $350 nonrefundable deposit required. Financial aid available for all students: loans, need-based tuition.

For More Information • Mrs. Daisy Fried, Associate Director, Syracuse University, 106 Walnut Place, Syracuse, NY 13244-4170; *Phone:* 800-251-9674; *Fax:* 315-443-4593. *E-mail:* dipasum@syr.edu. *World Wide Web:* http://suabroad.syr.edu/

SYRACUSE UNIVERSITY
DISABILITY STUDIES AND EDUCATIONAL PRACTICE: FOCUS ON FLORENCE

Hosted by Syracuse University Center–Florence

Academic Focus • Education.

Program Information • Students attend classes at Syracuse University Center-Florence (Florence, Italy). Field trips to Parma, Siena. Students typically earn 6 semester credits per term.

Sessions • May–Jun (summer).

Eligibility Requirements • Minimum age 18; open to freshmen, sophomores, juniors, seniors, graduate students, adults; 1 letter of recommendation; good academic standing at home school; no foreign language proficiency required.

Living Arrangements • Students live in locally rented apartments. Quarters are shared with host institution students. Meals are taken on one's own, in residences.

Costs (2006) • $8200; includes tuition, housing, some meals, excursions, international student ID, student support services. $55 application fee. $350 nonrefundable deposit required. Financial aid available for all students: loans, need-based tuition grants.

For More Information • Ms. Daisy Fried, Associate Director, Syracuse University, 106 Walnut Place, Syracuse, NY 13244-4170; *Phone:* 800-251-9674; *Fax:* 315-443-4593. *E-mail:* dsfried@syr.edu. *World Wide Web:* http://suabroad.syr.edu/

SYRACUSE UNIVERSITY
DISCOVERING ITALY: THE LANGUAGE, THE CULTURE

Hosted by Syracuse University Center–Florence

Academic Focus • Art history, Italian language and literature, Italian studies.

Program Information • Students attend classes at Syracuse University Center-Florence (Florence, Italy). Field trips to Rome, Venice, Tuscany. Students typically earn 6–7 semester credits per term.

Sessions • May–Jul (summer).

Eligibility Requirements • Open to freshmen, sophomores, juniors, seniors, adults; 1 letter of recommendation; good academic standing at home school; no foreign language proficiency required.

Living Arrangements • Students live in host family homes. Meals are taken with host family, in residences.

Costs (2005) • $7500 for 6 credits; $8225 for 7 credits; includes tuition, housing, some meals, excursions, international student ID, student support services. $55 application fee. $350 nonrefundable deposit required. Financial aid available for all students: loans, need-based tuition grants.

For More Information • Mrs. Daisy Fried, Associate Director, Syracuse University, 106 Walnut Place, Syracuse, NY 13244-4170; *Phone:* 800-251-9674; *Fax:* 315-443-4593. *E-mail:* dipasum@syr.edu. *World Wide Web:* http://suabroad.syr.edu/

SYRACUSE UNIVERSITY
PRE-ARCHITECTURE IN FLORENCE

Hosted by Syracuse University Center–Florence

Academic Focus • Architecture.

Program Information • Students attend classes at Syracuse University Center-Florence (Florence, Italy). Field trips to Rome, Siena, Venice, Assisi; optional travel to Verona, Mantua, Pompeii at an extra cost. Students typically earn 6 semester credits per term.

ITALY
Florence

Sessions • May–Jul (summer).

Eligibility Requirements • Open to freshmen, sophomores, juniors, seniors, graduate students; 1 letter of recommendation; good academic standing at home school; no foreign language proficiency required.

Living Arrangements • Students live in locally rented apartments. Meals are taken on one's own, in residences.

Costs (2005) • $8295; includes tuition, housing, some meals, excursions, international student ID, student support services. $55 application fee. $350 nonrefundable deposit required. Financial aid available for all students: scholarships, loans, need-based tuition grants.

For More Information • Mrs. Daisy Fried, Associate Director, Syracuse University, 106 Walnut Place, Syracuse, NY 13244-4170; *Phone:* 800-251-9674; *Fax:* 315-443-4593. *E-mail:* dipasum@syr.edu. *World Wide Web:* http://suabroad.syr.edu/

SYRACUSE UNIVERSITY
VISUAL ARTS IN FLORENCE

Hosted by Syracuse University Center–Florence

Academic Focus • Art history, drawing/painting, fine/studio arts, photography, textiles.

Program Information • Students attend classes at Syracuse University Center-Florence (Florence, Italy). Field trips to Rome, Venice, Siena, San Gimignano. Students typically earn 6 semester credits per term.

Sessions • May–Jul (summer).

Eligibility Requirements • Open to freshmen, sophomores, juniors, seniors, graduate students, adults; 1 letter of recommendation; good academic standing at home school; no foreign language proficiency required.

Living Arrangements • Students live in host family homes. Meals are taken with host family, in residences.

Costs (2005) • $7475; includes tuition, housing, some meals, excursions, international student ID, student support services. $55 application fee. $350 nonrefundable deposit required. Financial aid available for all students: loans, need-based tuition grants.

For More Information • Mrs. Daisy Fried, Associate Director, Syracuse University, 106 Walnut Place, Syracuse, NY 13244-4170; *Phone:* 800-251-9674; *Fax:* 315-443-4593. *E-mail:* dipasum@syr.edu. *World Wide Web:* http://suabroad.syr.edu/

UNIVERSITY OF ALABAMA
ALABAMA IN ITALY

Hosted by Centro Linguistico Italiano Dante Alighieri

Academic Focus • Art, comparative literature, drama/theater, Italian language and literature, literature.

Program Information • Students attend classes at Centro Linguistico Italiano Dante Alighieri (Florence, Italy). Scheduled travel to Rome, Venice; field trips to Rome, Venice; optional travel to Pisa, Siena, San Gimignano at an extra cost. Students typically earn 6 semester credits per term.

Sessions • May–Jun (summer).

Eligibility Requirements • Open to freshmen, sophomores, juniors, seniors, graduate students, adults; 2.5 GPA; 1 letter of recommendation; good academic standing at home school; no foreign language proficiency required.

Living Arrangements • Students live in host family homes. Quarters are shared with host institution students. Meals are taken with host family, in residences, in restaurants.

Costs (2005) • $4550; includes tuition, housing, some meals, excursions, international airfare, books and class materials, international student ID, student support services. $100 application fee. $500 nonrefundable deposit required. Financial aid available for all students: scholarships, loans.

For More Information • Ms. Angela L. Channell, Director of Overseas Study, University of Alabama, Box 870254, Tuscaloosa, AL 35487-0254; *Phone:* 205-348-5256; *Fax:* 205-348-5298. *E-mail:* achannell@aalan.ua.edu. *World Wide Web:* http://www.overseas-study.ua.edu/

UNIVERSITY OF DELAWARE
SUMMER SESSION IN FLORENCE

Academic Focus • Art, drawing/painting, fine/studio arts.

Program Information • Faculty members are drawn from the sponsor's U.S. staff and local instructors hired by the sponsor. Scheduled travel to Tuscany, Rome, the Vatican; field trips to historic/cultural sites around Florence. Students typically earn 6 semester credits per term.

Sessions • Jun–Jul (summer).

Eligibility Requirements • Open to freshmen, sophomores, juniors, seniors, adults; 2.0 GPA; 1 letter of recommendation; no foreign language proficiency required.

Living Arrangements • Students live in locally rented apartments. Meals are taken on one's own, in restaurants.

Costs (2005) • Contact sponsor for cost. $200 nonrefundable deposit required. Financial aid available for all students: scholarships.

For More Information • Center for International Studies, University of Delaware, 186 South College Avenue, Newark, DE 19716-1450; *Phone:* 888-831-4685; *Fax:* 302-831-6042. *E-mail:* studyabroad@udel.edu. *World Wide Web:* http://www.udel.edu/studyabroad/

UNIVERSITY OF KANSAS
ITALIAN LANGUAGE AND CULTURE IN FLORENCE, ITALY

Hosted by Centro Linguistico Italiano Dante Alighieri

Academic Focus • Italian language and literature, Italian studies.

Program Information • Students attend classes at Centro Linguistico Italiano Dante Alighieri (Florence, Italy). Optional travel to Piza, Luca, Cinque Terra at an extra cost. Students typically earn 6–10 semester credits per term.

Sessions • May–Jun (summer), Jun–Jul (summer 2).

Eligibility Requirements • Minimum age 18; open to freshmen, sophomores, juniors, seniors; 2.5 GPA; 2 letters of recommendation; good academic standing at home school; 1 year course work in Italian.

Living Arrangements • Students live in host family homes. Meals are taken on one's own, with host family, in residences, in restaurants.

Costs (2005) • $4070 for 1 session; $6730 for 2 sessions; includes tuition, housing, some meals, excursions, books and class materials, student support services, emergency medical evacuation and repatriation service, cooking classes. $38 application fee. $300 nonrefundable deposit required. Financial aid available for students from sponsoring institution: scholarships, loans.

For More Information • Ms. Ingrid Horton, Senior Program Coordinator, University of Kansas, Office of Study Abroad, Lippincott Hall, 1410 Jayhawk Boulevard, Room 108, Lawrence, KS 66045-7515; *Phone:* 785-864-3742; *Fax:* 785-864-5040. *E-mail:* osa@ku.edu. *World Wide Web:* http://www.ku.edu/~osa/

UNIVERSITY OF MINNESOTA
GREAT MINDS OF THE RENAISSANCE

Academic Focus • Art history, cultural studies, history.

Program Information • Faculty members are drawn from the sponsor's U.S. staff. Field trips to Rome, Pisa, Siena; Lucca; San Gimignano; optional travel at an extra cost. Students typically earn 3 semester credits per term.

Sessions • May–Jun (summer).

Eligibility Requirements • Minimum age 18; open to freshmen, sophomores, juniors, seniors, adults; 2.5 GPA; good academic standing at home school; no foreign language proficiency required.

Living Arrangements • Students live in locally rented apartments. Meals are taken on one's own, in residences, in restaurants.

Costs (2006) • Contact sponsor for cost; includes tuition, housing, insurance, international airfare, student support services. $50 application fee. $400 nonrefundable deposit required. Financial aid available for students from sponsoring institution: scholarships, loans.

For More Information • Learning Abroad Center, University of Minnesota, 230 Heller Hall, 271 19th Avenue South, Minneapolis, MN 55455; *Phone:* 888-700-UOFM; *Fax:* 612-626-8009. *E-mail:* umabroad@umn.edu. *World Wide Web:* http://www.umabroad.umn.edu/

UNIVERSITY OF MINNESOTA
SUSTAINABLE FOOD SYSTEMS OF ITALY: A CULTURE OF FOOD AND CITIZENSHIP

Academic Focus • Ethics, food science.

Program Information • Faculty members are drawn from the sponsor's U.S. staff and local instructors hired by the sponsor. Field trips to markets, farms; optional travel at an extra cost. Students typically earn 3 semester credits per term.

Sessions • May–Jun (summer).

Eligibility Requirements • Minimum age 18; open to freshmen, sophomores, juniors, seniors, adults; 2.5 GPA; good academic standing at home school; no foreign language proficiency required.

Living Arrangements • Students live in host institution dormitories, locally rented apartments, hotels. Meals are taken as a group, on one's own, in central dining facility, in restaurants.

Costs (2006) • Contact sponsor for cost; includes tuition, housing, some meals, insurance, international airfare, student support services. $50 application fee. $400 nonrefundable deposit required. Financial aid available for students from sponsoring institution: scholarships, loans.

For More Information • Learning Abroad Center, University of Minnesota, 230 Heller Hall, 271 19th Avenue South, Minneapolis, MN 55455; *Phone:* 800-700-UOFM; *Fax:* 612-626-8009. *E-mail:* umabroad@umn.edu. *World Wide Web:* http://www.umabroad.umn.edu/

UNIVERSITY OF PENNSYLVANIA
PENN-IN-FLORENCE

Academic Focus • Art history, Italian language and literature, Italian studies.

Program Information • Faculty members are drawn from the sponsor's U.S. staff and local instructors hired by the sponsor. Field trips to San Gimignano, Siena, Rome, Venice. Students typically earn 2 course units per term.

Sessions • Jun–Jul (summer).

Eligibility Requirements • Open to freshmen, sophomores, juniors, seniors, graduate students; 1 letter of recommendation; good academic standing at home school; language proficiency requirement is dependent on course chosen.

Living Arrangements • Students live in host family homes, hotels. Meals are taken on one's own, in residences, in restaurants.

Costs (2005) • $7100 with family stay; $7620 with hotel stay; includes tuition, housing, insurance, excursions. $50 application fee. $200 nonrefundable deposit required. Financial aid available for all students: scholarships.

For More Information • Penn Summer Abroad, University of Pennsylvania, 3440 Market Street, Suite 100, Philadelphia, PA 19104-3335; *Phone:* 215-746-6900; *Fax:* 215-573-2053. *E-mail:* summerabroad@sas.upenn.edu. *World Wide Web:* http://www.sas.upenn.edu/summer/

GENOA

NEW YORK UNIVERSITY
NEW MUSIC, EXPERIMENTAL DANCE, AND INTERACTIVE TECHNOLOGY IN GENOA, ITALY

Held at New York University

Academic Focus • Dance, music.

Program Information • Classes are held on the campus of New York University (Genoa, Italy). Faculty members are drawn from the sponsor's U.S. staff and local instructors hired by the sponsor. Students typically earn 6 semester credits per term.

Sessions • Jul (summer).

Eligibility Requirements • Minimum age 18; open to juniors, seniors, graduate students; major in music/dance; good academic standing at home school; essay; transcript; resume; no foreign language proficiency required.

Living Arrangements • Students live in host institution dormitories. Quarters are shared with host institution students. Meals are taken on one's own, in restaurants.

Costs (2005) • $5232; includes tuition, registration fees. $50 application fee.

For More Information • Mr. Daniel Young, Program Associate, New York University, 82 Washington Square East, Room 62, New

York, NY 10003; *Phone:* 212-992-9380; *Fax:* 212-995-4923. *E-mail:* dy14@nyu.edu. *World Wide Web:* http://www.nyu.edu/global/studyabroad.html

L'AQUILA

UNIVERSITY OF MIAMI
ITALIAN LANGUAGE AND HUMANITIES PROGRAM IN L'AQUILA

Hosted by University of L'Aquila

Academic Focus • Drama/theater, Italian language and literature, Italian studies.

Program Information • Students attend classes at University of L'Aquila (L'Aquila, Italy). Students typically earn 3–6 semester credits per term.

Sessions • Jun–Jul (summer).

Eligibility Requirements • Minimum age 18; open to sophomores, juniors, seniors; 2 letters of recommendation; good academic standing at home school; no foreign language proficiency required.

Living Arrangements • Students live in locally rented apartments. Quarters are shared with host institution students, students from other programs. Meals are taken on one's own, in residences, in restaurants.

Costs (2005–2006) • $2835–$4920; includes tuition, housing, student support services. $40 application fee. $500 nonrefundable deposit required. Financial aid available for students from sponsoring institution: loans.

For More Information • Ms. Elyse Resnick, Assistant Director, University of Miami, International Education and Exchange Programs, 5050 Brunson Drive, Allen Hall 212, PO Box 248005, Coral Gables, FL 33124-1610; *Phone:* 305-284-3434; *Fax:* 305-284-4235. *E-mail:* ieep@miami.edu. *World Wide Web:* http://www.studyabroad.miami.edu/

MERANO

UNIVERSITY OF NEW ORLEANS
EZRA POUND CENTER FOR LITERATURE

Held at Brunnenburg Castle

Academic Focus • English literature.

Program Information • Classes are held on the campus of Brunnenburg Castle (Merano, Italy). Faculty members are drawn from the sponsor's U.S. staff. Scheduled travel to Venice, Italy; field trips to northern Italy, Austria. Students typically earn 6 semester credits per term.

Sessions • Jun–Jul (summer).

Eligibility Requirements • Minimum age 18; open to freshmen, sophomores, juniors, seniors, graduate students, adults; 2.5 GPA; 2 letters of recommendation; good academic standing at home school; essay; no foreign language proficiency required.

Living Arrangements • Students live in Brunnenburg Castle. Quarters are shared with host institution students. Meals are taken as a group, in residences, in restaurants.

Costs (2005) • $2695; includes tuition, housing, some meals, insurance, excursions, books and class materials, student support services. $150 application fee. $150 refundable deposit required. Financial aid available for students from sponsoring institution: scholarships, loans.

For More Information • Mr. William Lavender, Coordinator, University of New Orleans, PO Box 1315, New Orleans, LA 70148; *Phone:* 504-280-7457; *Fax:* 504-280-7317. *E-mail:* wlavende@uno.edu. *World Wide Web:* http://inst.uno.edu/

MILAN

LANGUAGE LIAISON
ITALIAN IN MILAN, ITALY

Hosted by Language Liaison

Academic Focus • Italian language and literature.

ITALY
Milan

Program Information • Students attend classes at Language Liaison (Milan, Italy). Field trips; optional travel at an extra cost. Students typically earn 3–15 semester credits per term.
Sessions • New programs begin weekly, year-round.
Eligibility Requirements • Minimum age 17; open to precollege students, freshmen, sophomores, juniors, seniors, graduate students, adults; no foreign language proficiency required.
Living Arrangements • Students live in locally rented apartments, host family homes, hotels. Meals are taken on one's own, with host family, in residences, in restaurants.
Costs (2005) • Contact sponsor for cost. $175 application fee. Financial aid available for all students: scholarship research service.
For More Information • Ms. Nancy Forman, President, Language Liaison, PO Box 1772, Pacific Palisades, CA 90272; *Phone:* 800-284-4448; *Fax:* 310-454-1706. *E-mail:* learn@languageliaison. com. *World Wide Web:* http://www.languageliaison.com/

NORTHERN ILLINOIS UNIVERSITY
DESIGN AND ARCHITECTURE IN NORTHERN ITALY

Academic Focus • Architecture, art, design and applied arts.
Program Information • Faculty members are drawn from the sponsor's U.S. staff. Scheduled travel to Florence, Sorrento; field trips to Florence, Venice. Students typically earn 3–6 semester credits per term.
Sessions • May–Jun (summer).
Eligibility Requirements • Minimum age 18; open to sophomores, juniors, seniors, graduate students, adults; 2.5 GPA; good academic standing at home school; no foreign language proficiency required.
Living Arrangements • Students live in hotels. Meals are taken as a group, in restaurants.
Costs (2005) • $3585; includes tuition, housing, some meals, insurance, excursions, international student ID. $200 nonrefundable deposit required. Financial aid available for students from sponsoring institution: loans.

For More Information • Ms. Rita Withrow, Program Assistant, Northern Illinois University, Study Abroad Office, Williston Hall 417, DeKalb, IL 60115; *Phone:* 815-753-0700; *Fax:* 815-753-0825. *E-mail:* niuabroad@niu.edu. *World Wide Web:* http://www.niu.edu/ niuabroad/

NUOVA ACCADEMIA DI BELLE ARTI, MILANO
SUMMER STUDY ABROAD
Hosted by Nuova Accademia di Belle Arti, Milano
Academic Focus • Design and applied arts, fashion design, graphic design/illustration, interior design, visual and performing arts.
Program Information • Students attend classes at Nuova Accademia di Belle Arti, Milano (Milan, Italy). Scheduled travel to Venice, Florence, Rome; field trips to Venice, Florence, Rome; optional travel to Italy at an extra cost. Students typically earn 6 semester credits per term.
Sessions • Three sessions in July.
Eligibility Requirements • Open to freshmen, sophomores, juniors, seniors, graduate students, adults; good academic standing at home school; application form; basic knowledge of Italian recommended.
Living Arrangements • Students live in program-owned apartments, program-owned houses, hotels. Quarters are shared with host institution students. Meals are taken as a group, in residences, in restaurants.
Costs (2007) • From 1250,00 to 2560,00; includes tuition, housing, lab equipment, student support services.
For More Information • Ms. Marzia Muscato, International Relations, Nuova Accademia di Belle Arti, Milano, Via Darwin 20, 20143 Milan, Italy; *Phone:* +0039 02-973721; *Fax:* +0039 02-97372280. *E-mail:* int.info@naba.it. *World Wide Web:* http://www. naba.it/

MONTECASTELLO DI VIBIO

INTERNATIONAL SCHOOL OF PAINTING, DRAWING, AND SCULPTURE
INTERNATIONAL SCHOOL OF PAINTING, DRAWING, AND SCULPTURE

Hosted by International School of Painting, Drawing, and Sculpture

Academic Focus • Art, art history, fine/studio arts.

Program Information • Students attend classes at International School of Painting, Drawing, and Sculpture (Montecastello di Vibio, Italy). Field trips to Rome, Florence, Siena, Assisi, Perugia, Arezzo, Bologna; optional travel at an extra cost. Students typically earn 6–18 semester credits per term.

Sessions • Jun–Sep (summer), two 6 week sessions: Jun–Jul and Jul–Sep.

Eligibility Requirements • 2 letters of recommendation; portfolio; no foreign language proficiency required.

Living Arrangements • Students live in host institution dormitories. Quarters are shared with host institution students. Meals are taken as a group, in central dining facility.

Costs (2006) • €4900 for 6 weeks; $10,000 for 13 weeks; includes tuition, housing, all meals, excursions. €40 application fee.

For More Information • Mr. Marc Sevin, Director, International School of Painting, Drawing, and Sculpture, Via Regina Margherita 6, 06057 Montecatello di Vibio (PG), Italy; *Phone:* 866-449-3604; *Fax:* +39 075-8780-072. *E-mail:* info@giotto.us. *World Wide Web:* http://www.giotto.us/

NAPLES

LANGUAGE LIAISON
LEARN ITALIAN IN NAPLES

Hosted by Language Liaison

Academic Focus • Italian language and literature.

Program Information • Students attend classes at Language Liaison (Naples, Italy). Field trips; optional travel at an extra cost. Students typically earn 3–15 semester credits per term.

Sessions • Classes begin weekly, year-round.

Eligibility Requirements • Minimum age 17; open to precollege students, freshmen, sophomores, juniors, seniors, graduate students, adults; no foreign language proficiency required.

Living Arrangements • Students live in locally rented apartments, host family homes, hotels. Meals are taken on one's own, with host family, in residences, in restaurants.

Costs (2005) • Contact sponsor for cost. $175 application fee. Financial aid available for all students: scholarship research service.

For More Information • Ms. Nancy Forman, President, Language Liaison, PO Box 1772, Pacific Palisades, CA 90272; *Phone:* 800-284-4448; *Fax:* 310-454-1706. *E-mail:* learn@languageliaison.com. *World Wide Web:* http://www.languageliaison.com/

OIRA

UNIVERSITY OF OREGON
HISTORIC PRESERVATION SUMMER FIELD SCHOOL IN OIRA

Academic Focus • Architecture, historic preservation, history.

Program Information • Faculty members are drawn from the sponsor's U.S. staff and local instructors hired by the sponsor. Field trips to nearby towns and natural settings, local quarries. Students typically earn 9 quarter credits per term.

Sessions • Jun–Jul (summer).

Eligibility Requirements • Minimum age 18; open to freshmen, sophomores, juniors, seniors, graduate students, adults; 2.5 GPA; good academic standing at home school; no foreign language proficiency required.

Living Arrangements • Students live in locally rented apartments. Meals are taken as a group, in central dining facility.

Costs (2005) • $3500–$3700; includes tuition, housing, all meals, student support services. $50 application fee. $1750 nonrefundable deposit required. Financial aid available for students from sponsoring institution: scholarships, loans, grants.

For More Information • Michael Cockram, Assistant Professor of Architecture, University of Oregon, Eugene, OR 97403-1206; *Phone:* 541-346-0512; *Fax:* 541-346-3626. *E-mail:* cockram@uoregon.edu. *World Wide Web:* http://studyabroad.uoregon.edu

ORVIETO

SOUTHERN METHODIST UNIVERSITY
SMU IN ITALY

Academic Focus • Art, art history, drama/theater, drawing/painting.

Program Information • Faculty members are drawn from the sponsor's U.S. staff. Field trips to Rome, Florence, Ostia Antica, Siena. Students typically earn 6 semester credits per term.

Sessions • May–Jun (summer).

Eligibility Requirements • Open to sophomores, juniors, seniors; 2.5 GPA; interview; essay; no foreign language proficiency required.

Living Arrangements • Students live in hotels. Meals are taken as a group, in central dining facility.

Costs (2005) • $5195; includes tuition, housing, some meals, excursions, transportation passes in Rome, welcome dinner, farewell reception. $40 application fee. $400 nonrefundable deposit required. Financial aid available for students from sponsoring institution: scholarships, loans.

For More Information • Ms. Nancy Simmons, Associate Director, Southern Methodist University, The International Center/Study Abroad, SMU PO Box 750391, Dallas, TX 75275-0391; *Phone:* 214-768-2338; *Fax:* 214-768-1051. *E-mail:* intlpro@mail.smu.edu. *World Wide Web:* http://www.smu.edu/studyabroad/

PADUA

BOSTON UNIVERSITY
PADOVA LANGUAGE AND LIBERAL ARTS PROGRAM

Held at Centro Studi

Academic Focus • Art history, history, Italian language and literature.

Program Information • Classes are held on the campus of Centro Studi (Padua, Italy). Faculty members are drawn from the sponsor's U.S. staff and local instructors hired by the sponsor. Field trips to Venice, Ravenna, Euganean Hills. Students typically earn 8 semester credits per term.

Sessions • May–Jul (summer).

Eligibility Requirements • Open to freshmen, sophomores, juniors, seniors, graduate students, adults; 1 letter of recommendation; good academic standing at home school; essay; approval of participation; transcript; minimum GPA of 3.0 in major and overall; no foreign language proficiency required.

Living Arrangements • Students live in host family homes. Meals are taken on one's own, with host family, in residences, in central dining facility, in restaurants.

Costs (2005) • $6000; includes tuition, housing, all meals, insurance, excursions. $50 application fee. $400 nonrefundable deposit required. Financial aid available for all students: scholarships, loans.

For More Information • Division of International Programs, Boston University, 232 Bay State Road, Boston, MA 02215; *Phone:* 617-353-9888; *Fax:* 617-353-5402. *E-mail:* abroad@bu.edu. *World Wide Web:* http://www.bu.edu/abroad/

FAIRFIELD UNIVERSITY
SUMMER IN PADOVA FOR NURSING STUDENTS

Held at CERFF, The Institute of Research and Advanced Education

Academic Focus • Nursing.

Program Information • Classes are held on the campus of CERFF, The Institute of Research and Advanced Education (Padua, Italy). Faculty members are drawn from the sponsor's U.S. staff. Field trips to hospitals; optional travel to Venice, Florence at an extra cost. Students typically earn 3 semester credits per term.

Sessions • Jun (summer).

ITALY
Padua

Eligibility Requirements • Minimum age 18; open to juniors, graduate students; major in nursing; course work in nursing; 2.8 GPA; 1 letter of recommendation; good academic standing at home school; transcripts; no foreign language proficiency required.

Living Arrangements • Students live in hotels. Quarters are shared with host institution students. Meals are taken on one's own, in restaurants.

Costs (2006) • $3750; includes tuition, housing, some meals, insurance, international student ID, student support services. $300 refundable deposit required. Financial aid available for students from sponsoring institution.

For More Information • Assistant Director, Study Abroad Programs, Fairfield University, Dolan House, 1073 North Benson Road, Fairfield, CT 06824; *Phone:* 203-254-4332; *Fax:* 203-254-4261. *E-mail:* studyabroadoffice@mail.fairfield.edu. *World Wide Web:* http://www.fairfield.edu/studyabroad.xml/

UNIVERSITY OF ROCHESTER
ITALIAN IN ITALY

Academic Focus • Italian language and literature.

Program Information • Faculty members are drawn from the sponsor's U.S. staff. Field trips to Florence, Venice, Rome. Students typically earn 6 semester credits per term.

Sessions • May–Jun (summer).

Eligibility Requirements • Minimum age 18; open to freshmen, sophomores, juniors, seniors, adults; 1 letter of recommendation; good academic standing at home school; 1 year of college course work in Italian.

Living Arrangements • Students live in host family homes. Meals are taken with host family, in residences.

Costs (2005) • $3350; includes tuition, housing, some meals, excursions, books and class materials, student support services. $250 deposit required. Financial aid available for students from sponsoring institution: scholarships, loans.

For More Information • Ms. Anne Lutkus, Language Coordinator, University of Rochester, Department of Modern Languages and Cultures, PO Box 270082, Rochester, NY 14627-0082; *Phone:* 585-275-2235; *Fax:* 585-273-1097. *E-mail:* adlt@mail.rochester.edu. *World Wide Web:* http://www.rochester.edu/college/study-abroad/

PERUGIA

ARCADIA UNIVERSITY
SUMMER IN PERUGIA

Hosted by The Umbra Institute

Academic Focus • Art history, Italian language and literature, Italian studies, social sciences.

Program Information • Students attend classes at The Umbra Institute (Perugia, Italy). Field trips to Umbria; optional travel to Rome, Florence at an extra cost. Students typically earn 3-6 semester credits per term.

Sessions • May–Jun (summer).

Eligibility Requirements • Minimum age 18; open to sophomores, juniors, seniors, adults; 2.7 GPA; 1 letter of recommendation; no foreign language proficiency required.

Living Arrangements • Students live in locally rented apartments. Quarters are shared with host institution students. Meals are taken on one's own, in residences.

Costs (2005–2006) • $3200–$3950; includes tuition, housing, insurance, international student ID, student support services, transcript, pre-departure guide. $35 application fee. $500 nonrefundable deposit required.

For More Information • Arcadia University, Center for Education Abroad, 450 South Easton Road, Glenside, PA 19038-3295; *Phone:* 866-927-2234; *Fax:* 215-572-2174. *E-mail:* cea@arcadia.edu. *World Wide Web:* http://www.arcadia.edu/cea/

EUROPEAN HERITAGE INSTITUTE
SUMMER AND ONE-MONTH PROGRAMS IN PERUGIA

Hosted by University for Foreigners Perugia

Academic Focus • Civilization studies, commerce, history, Italian language and literature, Italian studies.

Program Information • Students attend classes at University for Foreigners Perugia (Perugia, Italy). Field trips to Umbria, Siena, Rome, Florence; Naples; Venice; optional travel to Tuscany, Venice, southern Italy at an extra cost. Students typically earn 3-6 semester credits per term.

Sessions • 1 month sessions held year-round.

Eligibility Requirements • Minimum age 18; open to freshmen, sophomores, juniors, seniors, graduate students, adults; 2.2 GPA; 2 letters of recommendation; no foreign language proficiency required.

Living Arrangements • Students live in locally rented apartments, host family homes. Quarters are shared with host institution students, students from other programs. Meals are taken on one's own, in residences, in central dining facility, in restaurants.

Costs (2006) • $1575 for the first month; $1875 for 2 months; $2300 for 3 months; includes tuition, housing, insurance, student support services. $300 refundable deposit required.

For More Information • Dr. Antonio Masullo, Professor, European Heritage Institute, 2708 East Franklin Street, Richmond, VA 23223; *Phone:* 804-643-0661; *Fax:* 804-648-0826. *E-mail:* info@europeabroad. org. *World Wide Web:* http://www.europeabroad.org/

JAMES MADISON UNIVERSITY
SUMMER IN PERUGIA

Academic Focus • Psychology.

Program Information • Faculty members are drawn from the sponsor's U.S. staff. Field trips to Assisi, Florence, Pisa, Siena. Students typically earn 3 semester credits per term.

Sessions • May–Jun (summer).

Eligibility Requirements • Minimum age 18; open to sophomores, juniors, seniors; 2.0 GPA; 1 letter of recommendation; good academic standing at home school; no foreign language proficiency required.

Living Arrangements • Students live in hotels. Meals are taken as a group, on one's own, in central dining facility, in restaurants.

Costs (2005) • $2654 for Virginia residents; $3494 for non residents; includes tuition, housing, some meals, excursions, books and class materials, international student ID. $400 deposit required.

For More Information • Mr. Felix Wang, Director, James Madison University, Office of International Programs, MSC 5731, 1077 South Main Street, Harrisonburg, VA 22807; *Phone:* 540-568-6419; *Fax:* 540-568-3310. *E-mail:* studyabroad@jmu.edu. *World Wide Web:* http://www.jmu.edu/international/

UNIVERSITY OF OREGON
TWO-MONTH INTENSIVE ITALIAN LANGUAGE PROGRAM IN PERUGIA

Hosted by University for Foreigners Perugia

Academic Focus • Italian language and literature.

Program Information • Students attend classes at University for Foreigners Perugia (Perugia, Italy). Optional travel to Siena, Florence, Rome, smaller towns near Penigia at an extra cost. Students typically earn 12 quarter credits per term.

Sessions • Jun–Aug (summer).

Eligibility Requirements • Minimum age 18; open to freshmen, sophomores, juniors, seniors, graduate students; 2.5 GPA; 2 letters of recommendation; good academic standing at home school; no foreign language proficiency required.

Living Arrangements • Students live in locally rented apartments. Quarters are shared with host institution students. Meals are taken on one's own, in residences, in central dining facility.

Costs (2005) • $6565–$6970; includes tuition, housing, all meals, insurance, international airfare, books and class materials, student support services, personal expenses. $50 application fee. $200 nonrefundable deposit required. Financial aid available for students from sponsoring institution: scholarships, loans, grants.

For More Information • Mr. Roger Adkins, Overseas Program Coordinator, University of Oregon, Overseas Programs, Eugene, OR 97403-5209; *Phone:* 541-346-1204; *Fax:* 541-346-1232. *E-mail:* radkins@uoregon.edu. *World Wide Web:* http://studyabroad.uoregon. edu

POGGIO COLLA

SOUTHERN METHODIST UNIVERSITY
ARCHAEOLOGY IN ITALY

Hosted by Poggio Colla Field School
Academic Focus • Archaeology, art history.
Program Information • Students attend classes at Poggio Colla Field School (Poggio Colla, Italy). Students typically earn 6 semester credits per term.
Sessions • Jun–Aug (summer).
Eligibility Requirements • Open to sophomores, juniors, seniors, graduate students; 2.5 GPA; 1 letter of recommendation; good academic standing at home school; personal interview; essay; no foreign language proficiency required.
Living Arrangements • Students live in a local farmhouse. Quarters are shared with students from other programs. Meals are taken as a group, in central dining facility.
Costs (2005) • $5020; includes tuition, housing, some meals, lab equipment, student support services. $40 application fee. $400 nonrefundable deposit required. Financial aid available for students from sponsoring institution: scholarships, loans.
For More Information • Ms. Nancy Simmons, Associate Director, Southern Methodist University, The International Center/Study Abroad, SMU PO Box 750391, Dallas, TX 75275-0391; *Phone:* 214-768-2338; *Fax:* 214-768-1051. *E-mail:* intlpro@mail.smu.edu. *World Wide Web:* http://www.smu.edu/studyabroad/

REGGELLO

UNIVERSITY OF NEW ORLEANS
A COUNSELOR'S VIEW OF ITALY

Academic Focus • Education.
Program Information • Faculty members are drawn from the sponsor's U.S. staff and local instructors hired by the sponsor. Field trips to Florence, Siena, Lucca, Pisa; Assisi. Students typically earn 3 semester credits per term.
Sessions • May–Jun (summer).
Eligibility Requirements • Minimum age 18; open to freshmen, sophomores, juniors, seniors, graduate students, adults; 2.5 GPA; good academic standing at home school; no foreign language proficiency required.
Living Arrangements • Students live in host institution dormitories, locally rented apartments. Quarters are shared with students from other programs. Meals are taken as a group, in central dining facility.
Costs (2005) • $1995; includes tuition, housing, some meals, insurance, excursions, student support services. $150 application fee. $150 refundable deposit required. Financial aid available for students from sponsoring institution: scholarships, loans.
For More Information • Mr. Peter Alongia, Coordinator, University of New Orleans, PO Box 1315, New Orleans, LA 70148; *Phone:* 504-280-7116; *Fax:* 504-280-7317. *E-mail:* palongia@uno.edu. *World Wide Web:* http://inst.uno.edu/

RIMINI

LANGUAGE LIAISON
ITALIAN IN RIMINI

Hosted by Language Liaison
Academic Focus • Italian language and literature.
Program Information • Students attend classes at Language Liaison (Rimini, Italy). Field trips; optional travel at an extra cost. Students typically earn 3–15 semester credits per term.
Sessions • New programs begin weekly, year-round.
Eligibility Requirements • Minimum age 16; open to precollege students, freshmen, sophomores, juniors, seniors, graduate students, adults; no foreign language proficiency required.
Living Arrangements • Students live in locally rented apartments, host family homes, hotels. Meals are taken with host family, in residences, in restaurants.
Costs (2005) • Contact sponsor for cost. $175 application fee. Financial aid available for all students: scholarship research service.

For More Information • Ms. Nancy Forman, President, Language Liaison, PO Box 1772, Pacific Palisades, CA 90272; *Phone:* 800-284-4448; *Fax:* 310-454-1706. *E-mail:* learn@languageliaison.com. *World Wide Web:* http://www.languageliaison.com/

LINGUA SERVICE WORLDWIDE
VACATION 'N LEARN ITALIAN IN ITALY

Hosted by I Malatesta
Academic Focus • Italian language and literature, Italian studies.
Program Information • Students attend classes at I Malatesta (Rimini, Italy). Optional travel to cultural sites throughout Italy at an extra cost. Students typically earn 3 semester credits for 3 weeks, 6 semester credits for 5 weeks.
Sessions • Sessions of 2 or more weeks begin on Mondays, year-round.
Eligibility Requirements • Minimum age 16; open to freshmen, sophomores, juniors, seniors, graduate students, adults; no foreign language proficiency required.
Living Arrangements • Students live in host institution dormitories, locally rented apartments, host family homes, hotels. Quarters are shared with host institution students. Meals are taken with host family.
Costs (2006–2007) • Contact sponsor for cost. $100 application fee.
For More Information • Assistant Director, Lingua Service Worldwide, 75 Prospect Street, Suite 4, Huntington, NY 11743; *Phone:* 800-394-5327; *Fax:* 631-271-3441. *E-mail:* linguaservice@att.net. *World Wide Web:* http://www.linguaserviceworldwide.com/

ROME

ACADEMIC PROGRAMS INTERNATIONAL (API)
(API)–JOHN CABOT UNIVERSITY IN ROME, ITALY

Hosted by John Cabot University
Academic Focus • Full curriculum.
Program Information • Students attend classes at John Cabot University (Rome, Italy). Field trips to Florence, Perugia, Capri, Ponza, Naples, Amalfi Coast, Pompeii, Sorrento,, Luua, Pienza, Pisa, Siena, San Gimignano. Students typically earn 3–7 semester credits per term.
Sessions • May–Jun (summer), Jun–Aug (summer 2); May–Aug (summer 3).
Eligibility Requirements • Minimum age 18; open to freshmen, sophomores, juniors, seniors, graduate students, adults; 2.75 GPA; 1 letter of recommendation; good academic standing at home school; official transcript from home university; no foreign language proficiency required.
Living Arrangements • Students live in locally rented apartments. Quarters are shared with host institution students, students from other programs. Meals are taken on one's own, in residences, in restaurants.
Costs (2006) • Contact sponsor for cost. $150 nonrefundable deposit required. Financial aid available for all students: scholarships.
For More Information • Ms. Jennifer C. Allen, Director, Academic Programs International (API), 107 East Hopkins, San Marcos, TX 78666; *Phone:* 800-844-4124; *Fax:* 512-392-8420. *E-mail:* api@academicintl.com. *World Wide Web:* http://www.academicintl.com/

ACADEMIC PROGRAMS INTERNATIONAL (API)
(API)–ROME–LORENZO DE MEDICI SCHOOL

Hosted by The Lorenzo de Medici School
Academic Focus • Full curriculum.
Program Information • Students attend classes at The Lorenzo de Medici School (Rome, Italy). Field trips to Florence, Cinque Terre, Venice, Tuscany. Students typically earn 6 semester credits per term.
Sessions • Jun–Jul (summer).
Eligibility Requirements • Minimum age 18; open to freshmen, sophomores, juniors, seniors; 2.75 GPA; 1 letter of recommendation; good academic standing at home school; official transcript from home university.

Living Arrangements • Students live in locally rented apartments. Quarters are shared with host institution students. Meals are taken on one's own, in residences, in restaurants.

Costs (2007–2008) • Contact sponsor for cost. $150 nonrefundable deposit required. Financial aid available for all students: scholarships.

For More Information • Ms. Jennifer C. Allen, Director, Academic Programs International (API), 107 East Hopkins, San Marcos, TX 78666; *Phone:* 800-844-4124; *Fax:* 512-392-8420. *E-mail:* api@academicintl.com. *World Wide Web:* http://www.academicintl.com/

AMERICAN INSTITUTE FOR FOREIGN STUDY (AIFS)
AIFS–ROME, ITALY–RICHMOND IN ROME

Hosted by Richmond in Rome

Academic Focus • Art history, communications, fine/studio arts, history, Italian language and literature, music, photography.

Program Information • Students attend classes at Richmond in Rome (Rome, Italy). Scheduled travel to 3-day stopover in London; field trips to overnight visit in Florence, cultural activities, museums, art galleries, monuments, opera, jazz concerts, cooking and wine tasting classes; optional travel to 3-day excursion to Venice for a supplement of $329, 3-day excursion to Pompeii, Vesuvius, Naples, Capri for a supplement of $379. Students typically earn 6 semester credits per term.

Sessions • Jun–Jul (summer).

Eligibility Requirements • Minimum age 17; open to precollege students, freshmen, sophomores, juniors, seniors; 2.0 GPA; no foreign language proficiency required.

Living Arrangements • Students live in host institution dormitories, program-owned apartments, hotels. Quarters are shared with host institution students. Meals are taken as a group, in restaurants.

Costs (2007) • $5499; includes tuition, housing, some meals, insurance, excursions, student support services, On-site Resident Director, Phone Card to call the U.S., Computer Facilities/Internet. $95 application fee. $395 nonrefundable deposit required. Financial aid available for all students: scholarships.

For More Information • Mr. David Mauro, Admissions Advisor, American Institute For Foreign Study (AIFS), 9 West Broad Street, Stamford, CT 06902-3788; *Phone:* 800-727-2437 Ext. 5163; *Fax:* 203-399-5597. *E-mail:* dmauro@aifs.com. *World Wide Web:* http://www.aifsabroad.com/

ARCADIA UNIVERSITY
SUMMER IN ROME

Hosted by Accademia Italiana

Academic Focus • Italian language and literature, Italian studies, photography, social sciences.

Program Information • Students attend classes at Accademia Italiana (Rome, Italy). Field trips to Florence; optional travel. Students typically earn 3–6 semester credits per term.

Sessions • Jun–Jul (summer).

Eligibility Requirements • Minimum age 18; open to sophomores, juniors, seniors, adults; 3.0 GPA; no foreign language proficiency required.

Living Arrangements • Students live in locally rented apartments. Quarters are shared with host institution students. Meals are taken on one's own, in residences.

Costs (2005–2006) • $3360–$4200; includes tuition, housing, insurance, international student ID, student support services, transcript, pre-departure guide, orientation. $35 application fee. $500 nonrefundable deposit required.

For More Information • Arcadia University, Center for Education Abroad, 450 South Easton Road, Glenside, PA 19038; *Phone:* 866-927-2234; *Fax:* 215-572-2174. *E-mail:* cea@arcadia.edu. *World Wide Web:* http://www.arcadia.edu/cea/

COLLEGE CONSORTIUM FOR INTERNATIONAL STUDIES–COLLEGE OF STATEN ISLAND/CITY UNIVERSITY OF NEW YORK
SUMMER PROGRAM IN ROME, ITALY

Hosted by The American University of Rome

Academic Focus • Art history, business administration/management, communications, economics, film and media studies, international business, Italian language and literature, Italian studies, marketing, photography, religious studies.

Program Information • Students attend classes at The American University of Rome (Rome, Italy). Optional travel to Florence, Pompeii; Paestum at an extra cost. Students typically earn 6 semester credits per term.

Sessions • May–Jun (summer).

Eligibility Requirements • Minimum age 18; open to freshmen, sophomores, juniors, seniors; 2.5 GPA; 1 letter of recommendation; essay; transcript; no foreign language proficiency required.

Living Arrangements • Students live in locally rented apartments. Quarters are shared with host institution students, students from other programs. Meals are taken on one's own, in residences, in restaurants.

Costs (2007) • $3145; includes tuition, insurance, student support services, fees. $135 nonrefundable deposit required. Financial aid available for students from sponsoring institution: loans, grants.

For More Information • College Consortium for International Studies–College of Staten Island/City University of New York, 2000 P Street, NW, Suite 503, Washington, DC 20036; *Phone:* 800-453-6956; *Fax:* 202-223-0999. *E-mail:* info@ccisabroad.org. *World Wide Web:* http://www.ccisabroad.org/. Students may also apply through College of Staten Island, The City University of New York, Center for International Service, Building 2A, Room 206, 2800 Victory Boulevard, Staten Island, NY 10314.

EF INTERNATIONAL LANGUAGE SCHOOLS
ITALIAN IN ROME

Hosted by DILIT

Academic Focus • Italian language and literature.

Program Information • Students attend classes at DILIT (Rome, Italy). Field trips to Fiesole, Siena, the Uffizi Gallery; optional travel to Rome, Sicily, Pisa, Perugia at an extra cost. Students typically earn 15–18 quarter credits per term.

Sessions • Program length 2 to 52 weeks, year-round.

Eligibility Requirements • Minimum age 16; open to precollege students, freshmen, sophomores, juniors, seniors, graduate students, adults; no foreign language proficiency required.

Living Arrangements • Students live in program-owned apartments, host family homes. Quarters are shared with host institution students. Meals are taken on one's own, with host family.

Costs (2006–2007) • $990 for 2 weeks; includes tuition, housing, some meals, books and class materials, student support services. $145 application fee. Financial aid available for students from sponsoring institution: scholarships.

For More Information • Ms. Varvara Kirakosyan, Director of Admissions, EF International Language Schools, One Education Street, Cambridge, MA 02141; *Phone:* 800-992-1892; *Fax:* 800-590-4835. *E-mail:* ils@ef.com. *World Wide Web:* http://www.ef.com/

INTERNATIONAL STUDIES ABROAD
ROME, ITALY–SUMMER AT THE AMERICAN UNIVERSITY OF ROME

Hosted by The American University of Rome

Academic Focus • Art history, international business, Italian studies.

Program Information • Students attend classes at The American University of Rome (Rome, Italy). Field trips to Florence, Capri, Sorrento, Pompeii; Ostia. Students typically earn 6 semester credits per term.

Sessions • May–Jun (summer), Jul–Aug (summer 2).

Eligibility Requirements • Minimum age 18; open to freshmen, sophomores, juniors, seniors, adults; 2.75 GPA; no foreign language proficiency required.

Living Arrangements • Students live in locally rented apartments. Quarters are shared with host institution students. Meals are taken on one's own, in restaurants.

Costs (2005–2006) • Contact sponsor for cost. $200 deposit required. Financial aid available for all students: scholarships, loans, US federal financial aid.

For More Information • Italy Site Specialist, International Studies Abroad, 901 West 24th Street, Austin, TX 78705; *Phone:* 800-580-

8826; *Fax:* 512-480-8866. *E-mail:* isa@studiesabroad.com. *World Wide Web:* http://www.studiesabroad.com/

ITALIAIDEA
ITALIAIDEA

Hosted by Italiaidea
Academic Focus • Italian language and literature, Italian studies.
Program Information • Students attend classes at Italiaidea (Rome, Italy). Field trips to Pompeii, Siena, Florence, Naples. Students typically earn 3 semester credits for 4 weeks.
Sessions • 4 week sessions begin on Mondays, year-round.
Eligibility Requirements • Minimum age 16; open to freshmen, sophomores, juniors, seniors, graduate students, adults; no foreign language proficiency required.
Living Arrangements • Students live in locally rented apartments, host family homes, hotels. Quarters are shared with host institution students. Meals are taken on one's own, with host family, in central dining facility, in restaurants.
Costs (2005) • Contact sponsor for cost. €35 application fee.
For More Information • Ms. Katharina Hembus, Secretary, Italiaidea, Via dei Due Macelli 47, 00186 Rome, Italy; *Phone:* +39 06-69941314; *Fax:* +39 06-69202174. *E-mail:* k.hembus@italiaidea. com. *World Wide Web:* http://www.italiaidea.com/

JAMES MADISON UNIVERSITY
SUMMER STUDY IN ROME

Held at Marymount International School
Academic Focus • Education.
Program Information • Classes are held on the campus of Marymount International School (Rome, Italy). Faculty members are drawn from the sponsor's U.S. staff. Field trips to Florence, Venice. Students typically earn 3 semester credits per term.
Sessions • May–Jun (summer).
Eligibility Requirements • Minimum age 18; open to juniors, seniors; major in education; 2.0 GPA; good academic standing at home school; no foreign language proficiency required.
Living Arrangements • Students live in host institution dormitories. Quarters are shared with host institution students. Meals are taken as a group, on one's own, in central dining facility, in restaurants.
Costs (2005) • $3554 for Virginia residents; $4394 for nonresidents; includes tuition, housing, some meals, excursions, international student ID. $400 nonrefundable deposit required.
For More Information • Mr. Felix Wang, Director, James Madison University, Office of International Programs, MSC 5731, 1077 South Main Street, Harrisonburg, VA 22807; *Phone:* 540-568-6419; *Fax:* 540-568-3310. *E-mail:* studyabroad@jmu.edu. *World Wide Web:* http://www.jmu.edu/international/

LANGUAGE LIAISON
LEARN ITALIAN IN ROME

Hosted by Language Liaison
Academic Focus • Italian language and literature.
Program Information • Students attend classes at Language Liaison (Rome, Italy). Field trips; optional travel at an extra cost. Students typically earn 3-15 semester credits per term.
Sessions • New programs begin weekly, year-round.
Eligibility Requirements • Minimum age 17; open to freshmen, sophomores, juniors, seniors, graduate students, adults; no foreign language proficiency required.
Living Arrangements • Students live in locally rented apartments, host family homes, hotels. Meals are taken on one's own, with host family, in residences, in restaurants.
Costs (2005) • Contact sponsor for cost. $175 application fee. Financial aid available for all students: scholarship research service.
For More Information • Ms. Nancy Forman, President, Language Liaison, PO Box 1772, Pacific Palisades, CA 90272; *Phone:* 800-284-4448; *Fax:* 310-454-1706. *E-mail:* learn@languageliaison. com. *World Wide Web:* http://www.languageliaison.com/

LEXIA INTERNATIONAL
LEXIA SUMMER IN ROME

Hosted by Instituto Italiano

Academic Focus • Anthropology, area studies, art history, civilization studies, classics and classical languages, comparative history, cultural studies, economics, ethnic studies, geography, history, interdisciplinary studies, international affairs, Italian language and literature, Italian studies, liberal studies, literature, political science and government, social sciences, sociology.
Program Information • Students attend classes at Instituto Italiano (Rome, Italy). Field trips to sites in and around the city of Rome, Florence, Sorrento. Students typically earn 8–10 semester credits per term.
Sessions • Jun–Aug (summer).
Eligibility Requirements • Minimum age 18; open to freshmen, sophomores, juniors, seniors, graduate students, adults; 2.5 GPA; 2 letters of recommendation; no foreign language proficiency required.
Living Arrangements • Students live in locally rented apartments, host family homes. Meals are taken on one's own, with host family, in residences.
Costs (2006) • $6850; includes tuition, housing, insurance, excursions, international student ID, student support services, transcript, computer access. $40 application fee. $300 nonrefundable deposit required. Financial aid available for all students: scholarships, work study.
For More Information • Lexia International, 23 South Main Street, Hanover, NH 03755; *Phone:* 800-775-3942; *Fax:* 603-643-9899. *E-mail:* info@lexiaintl.org. *World Wide Web:* http://www.lexiaintl. org/

LINGUA SERVICE WORLDWIDE
VACATION 'N LEARN ITALIAN IN ITALY

Hosted by Instituto Italiano
Academic Focus • Italian language and literature, Italian studies.
Program Information • Students attend classes at Instituto Italiano (Rome, Italy). Optional travel to cultural sites throughout Italy at an extra cost. Students typically earn 3 semester credits for 3 weeks, 6 semester credits for 5 weeks.
Sessions • Sessions of 2 or more weeks begin on Mondays, year-round.
Eligibility Requirements • Minimum age 16; open to freshmen, sophomores, juniors, seniors, graduate students, adults; no foreign language proficiency required.
Living Arrangements • Students live in host institution dormitories, locally rented apartments, host family homes, hotels. Quarters are shared with host institution students. Meals are taken with host family.
Costs (2006–2007) • Contact sponsor for cost. $100 application fee.
For More Information • Assistant Director, Lingua Service Worldwide, 75 Prospect Street, Suite 4, Huntington, NY 11743; *Phone:* 800-394-5327; *Fax:* 631-271-3441. *E-mail:* linguaservice@att. net. *World Wide Web:* http://www.linguaserviceworldwide.com/

LINGUA SERVICE WORLDWIDE
VACATION 'N LEARN ITALIAN IN ITALY

Hosted by Scuola Leonardo daVinci
Academic Focus • Italian language and literature, Italian studies.
Program Information • Students attend classes at Scuola Leonardo daVinci (Rome, Italy). Optional travel to cultural sites throughout Italy at an extra cost. Students typically earn 3 semester credits for 3 weeks, 6 semester credits for 5 weeks.
Sessions • Sessions of 2 or more weeks begin on Mondays, year-round.
Eligibility Requirements • Minimum age 16; open to freshmen, sophomores, juniors, seniors, graduate students, adults; no foreign language proficiency required.
Living Arrangements • Students live in host institution dormitories, locally rented apartments, host family homes, hotels. Quarters are shared with host institution students. Meals are taken with host family.
Costs (2006–2007) • Contact sponsor for cost. $100 application fee.
For More Information • Assistant Director, Lingua Service Worldwide, 75 Prospect Street, Suite 4, Huntington, NY 11743; *Phone:* 800-394-5327; *Fax:* 631-271-3441. *E-mail:* linguaservice@att. net. *World Wide Web:* http://www.linguaserviceworldwide.com/

ITALY
Rome

MARQUETTE UNIVERSITY
SUMMER PROGRAM AT JOHN CABOT UNIVERSITY

Hosted by John Cabot University

Academic Focus • Art history, communications, drama/theater, economics, English literature, ethics, European studies, fine/studio arts, history, language studies, literature, marketing, mathematics, philosophy, political science and government, religious studies, social sciences.

Program Information • Students attend classes at John Cabot University (Rome, Italy). Students typically earn 6 semester credits per session.

Sessions • May–Jun (summer), Jul–Aug (summer 2).

Eligibility Requirements • Open to sophomores, juniors, seniors; 2.5 GPA; no foreign language proficiency required.

Living Arrangements • Students live in locally rented apartments. Quarters are shared with host institution students. Meals are taken on one's own, in residences, in restaurants.

Costs (2006–2007) • $4580 per session; includes tuition, housing, books and class materials, student support services. $500 refundable deposit required. Financial aid available for students from sponsoring institution: scholarships, loans.

For More Information • Dr. Jamshid Hosseini, Director of International Business Studies and Study Abroad, Marquette University, College of Business Administration, 606 North 13th Street, David Strat, Jr. Building, Milwaukee, WI 53233; *Phone:* 414-288-3433; *Fax:* 414-288-7440. *E-mail:* jamshid.hosseini@marquette.edu. *World Wide Web:* http://www.marquette.edu/studyabroad/

MICHIGAN STATE UNIVERSITY
SOCIAL SCIENCE IN ROME

Held at Italiaidea

Academic Focus • Geography, social sciences.

Program Information • Classes are held on the campus of Italiaidea (Rome, Italy). Faculty members are drawn from the sponsor's U.S. staff and local instructors hired by the sponsor. Field trips to the surrounding area. Students typically earn 7 semester credits per term.

Sessions • Jun–Jul (summer).

Eligibility Requirements • Minimum age 18; open to sophomores, juniors, seniors; 2.0 GPA; good academic standing at home school; faculty approval; no foreign language proficiency required.

Living Arrangements • Students live in hotels. Meals are taken as a group, on one's own, in residences, in restaurants.

Costs (2005) • $3905 (estimated); includes housing, insurance, excursions, student support services. $100 application fee. $200 nonrefundable deposit required. Financial aid available for students from sponsoring institution: scholarships, loans.

For More Information • Ms. Maggie Matice, Secretary, Michigan State University, Office of Study Abroad, 109 International Center, East Lansing, MI 48824-1035; *Phone:* 517-353-8920; *Fax:* 517-432-2082. *E-mail:* matice@msu.edu. *World Wide Web:* http://studyabroad.msu.edu/

NORTHERN ILLINOIS UNIVERSITY
ROME ETERNAL: AN UNFORGETTABLE EXPERIENCE

Academic Focus • Art history.

Program Information • Faculty members are drawn from the sponsor's U.S. staff. Field trips to Naples, Pompeii, Herculaneum. Students typically earn 3–6 semester credits per term.

Sessions • May–Jun (summer).

Eligibility Requirements • Minimum age 18; open to juniors, seniors, graduate students, adults; 2.5 GPA; good academic standing at home school; no foreign language proficiency required.

Living Arrangements • Students live in hotels. Meals are taken on one's own, in restaurants.

Costs (2005) • Contact sponsor for cost. $200 nonrefundable deposit required. Financial aid available for students from sponsoring institution: loans.

For More Information • Ms. Rita Withrow, Program Assistant, Northern Illinois University, Study Abroad Office, Williston Hall 417, DeKalb, IL 60115-2854; *Phone:* 815-753-0700; *Fax:* 815-753-0825. *E-mail:* niuabroad@niu.edu. *World Wide Web:* http://www.niu.edu/niuabroad/

RUTGERS, THE STATE UNIVERSITY OF NEW JERSEY
SUMMER STUDY IN ART HISTORY IN ROME

Academic Focus • Art history.

Program Information • Faculty members are drawn from the sponsor's U.S. staff and local instructors hired by the sponsor. Students typically earn 6 semester credits per term.

Sessions • Jul–Aug (summer).

Eligibility Requirements • Open to freshmen, sophomores, juniors, seniors; course work in art history; 2.5 GPA; good academic standing at home school; official transcripts from all tertiary schools attended; no foreign language proficiency required.

Living Arrangements • Students live in locally rented apartments. Quarters are shared with host institution students. Meals are taken as a group, in residences.

Costs (2006) • $4250 for New Jersey residents; $5250 for nonresidents; includes tuition, housing, insurance, excursions, student support services. $20 application fee. $500 nonrefundable deposit required. Financial aid available for students from sponsoring institution: scholarships, loans.

For More Information • Ms. Lindy Black, Regional Coordinator, Rutgers, The State University of New Jersey, 102 College Avenue, New Brunswick, NJ 08901-8543; *Phone:* 732-932-7787; *Fax:* 732-932-8659. *E-mail:* ru_abroad@email.rutgers.edu. *World Wide Web:* http://studyabroad.rutgers.edu/

ST. JOHN'S UNIVERSITY
ITALY SUMMER PROGRAM

Hosted by Saint John's University Rome Campus

Academic Focus • Art history, cultural studies, design and applied arts, drawing/painting, Italian language and literature.

Program Information • Students attend classes at Saint John's University Rome Campus (Rome, Italy). Field trips to Florence, Pompeii, Paestum, Venice, Naples. Students typically earn 3–6 semester credits per term.

Sessions • May–Jun (summer), Jul–Aug (summer 2).

Eligibility Requirements • Minimum age 18; open to freshmen, sophomores, juniors, seniors, graduate students, adults; 2.75 GPA; 2 letters of recommendation; good academic standing at home school; interview; no foreign language proficiency required.

Living Arrangements • Students live in locally rented apartments, hotels. Quarters are shared with host institution students. Meals are taken as a group, on one's own, in residences, in restaurants.

Costs (2005) • $2600–$2895; includes housing, some meals, excursions, international airfare, student support services, unlimited monthly metro/bus pass in Rome, transportation to and from airport in Rome and between cities. $30 application fee. $750 nonrefundable deposit required. Financial aid available for students from sponsoring institution: scholarships, loans, students must be enrolled for 6 credits to receive aid.

For More Information • Dr. Ruth De Paula, Director, Office of Study Abroad Programs, St. John's University, 8000 Utopia Parkway, Jamaica, NY 11439; *Phone:* 718-990-6105; *Fax:* 718-990-2321. *E-mail:* intled@stjohns.edu. *World Wide Web:* http://www.stjohns.edu/studyabroad/

SOUTHERN METHODIST UNIVERSITY
SMU-IN-ROME AND BOLOGNA

Held at The Rome Center

Academic Focus • Italian language and literature.

Program Information • Classes are held on the campus of The Rome Center (Rome, Italy). Faculty members are drawn from the sponsor's U.S. staff and local instructors hired by the sponsor. Scheduled travel to Voltrona; field trips. Students typically earn 6 semester credits per term.

Sessions • Jun–Jul (summer).

Eligibility Requirements • Open to sophomores, juniors, seniors; 2.5 GPA; 1 letter of recommendation; good academic standing at home school; personal interview; essay; no foreign language proficiency required.

Living Arrangements • Students live in host institution dormitories, hotels. Quarters are shared with host institution students, students from other programs. Meals are taken as a group, in central dining facility.

Costs (2005) • $5020; includes tuition, housing, some meals, excursions, student support services, airport transfers for students on the group flight. $40 application fee. $400 nonrefundable deposit required. Financial aid available for students from sponsoring institution: scholarships, loans.

For More Information • Ms. Nancy Simmons, Associate Director, Southern Methodist University, The International Center/Study Abroad, SMU PO Box 750391, Dallas, TX 75275-0391; *Phone:* 214-768-2338; *Fax:* 214-768-1051. *E-mail:* intlpro@mail.smu.edu. *World Wide Web:* http://www.smu.edu/studyabroad/

STUDY ABROAD ITALY
STUDY ABROAD ROME–JOHN CABOT UNIVERSITY

Hosted by John Cabot University

Academic Focus • Arabic, art history, business administration/management, classics and classical languages, computer science, creative writing, economics, English, English literature, fine/studio arts, history, Italian language and literature, mathematics, philosophy, political science and government, psychology, religious studies, science, Spanish language and literature.

Program Information • Students attend classes at John Cabot University (Rome, Italy). Field trips to Florence, Amalfi Coast; optional travel to Venice, Amalfi Coast, Pompeii, Naples, Florence, Capri, the Italian Alps at an extra cost. Students typically earn 3-6 semester credits per term.

Sessions • May–Jun (summer), Jun–Aug (summer 2).

Eligibility Requirements • Minimum age 18; open to freshmen, sophomores, juniors, seniors, adults; 2.75 GPA; good academic standing at home school; no foreign language proficiency required.

Living Arrangements • Students live in locally rented apartments, host family homes. Quarters are shared with host institution students. Meals are taken on one's own, in residences.

Costs (2005) • $2900 for 1 course; $3900 for 2 courses; includes tuition, housing, insurance, student support services. $50 application fee. $1000 deposit required. Financial aid available for students from sponsoring institution: scholarships, work study, loans, federal financial aid; veterans benefits.

For More Information • Mr. Rod Harris, Admissions Officer, Study Abroad Italy, 7151 Wilton Avenue, Suite 202, Sebastopol, CA 95472; *Phone:* 800-655-8965; *Fax:* 707-824-0198. *E-mail:* rsh@studyabroad-italy.com. *World Wide Web:* http://www.studyabroad-italy.com/

TEMPLE UNIVERSITY
TEMPLE UNIVERSITY ROME: ART AND CULTURE SEMINAR

Hosted by Temple University Rome

Academic Focus • Aesthetics, art, literature.

Program Information • Students attend classes at Temple University Rome (Rome, Italy). Field trips to Florence, Pompeii. Students typically earn 6 semester credits per term.

Sessions • May–Jun (summer).

Eligibility Requirements • Open to seniors, graduate students; good academic standing at home school; no foreign language proficiency required.

Living Arrangements • Students live in locally rented apartments. Quarters are shared with host institution students. Meals are taken on one's own, in residences.

Costs (2005) • $4000–$5200; includes tuition, housing, activity fee. $30 application fee. $200 nonrefundable deposit required. Financial aid available for students from sponsoring institution: scholarships, loans.

For More Information • Ms. Erin Joslyn, Study Abroad Coordinator, Temple University, International Programs, 200 Tuttleman Learning Center, 1809 North 13th Street, Philadelphia, PA 19122; *Phone:* 215-204-0720; *Fax:* 215-204-0729. *E-mail:* study.abroad@temple.edu. *World Wide Web:* http://www.temple.edu/studyabroad/

TEMPLE UNIVERSITY
TEMPLE UNIVERSITY ROME: SUMMER SESSION

Hosted by Temple University Rome

Academic Focus • Anthropology, art, art history, business administration/management, drawing/painting, finance, human resources, Italian language and literature, liberal studies, marketing.

Program Information • Students attend classes at Temple University Rome (Rome, Italy). Field trips to Todi, Tarquinia, Cerveteri, Tivoli. Students typically earn 6 semester credits per term.

Sessions • May–Jul (summer).

Eligibility Requirements • Minimum age 19; open to sophomores, juniors, seniors, graduate students; 2.5 GPA; 1 letter of recommendation; good academic standing at home school; official transcripts; no foreign language proficiency required.

Living Arrangements • Students live in locally rented apartments. Quarters are shared with host institution students. Meals are taken on one's own, in residences.

Costs (2005) • $3600–$5800; includes tuition, housing, activity fee. $30 application fee. $200 nonrefundable deposit required. Financial aid available for students from sponsoring institution: scholarships, work study, loans.

For More Information • Ms. Erin Joslyn, Study Abroad Coordinator, Temple University, International Programs, 200 Tuttleman Learning Center, 1809 North 13th Street, Philadelphia, PA 19122; *Phone:* 215-204-0720; *Fax:* 215-204-0729. *E-mail:* study.abroad@temple.edu. *World Wide Web:* http://www.temple.edu/studyabroad/

TRINITY COLLEGE
TRINITY COLLEGE/ROME CAMPUS

Hosted by Trinity College–Rome Campus

Academic Focus • Art history, history, Italian language and literature.

Program Information • Students attend classes at Trinity College-Rome Campus (Rome, Italy). Scheduled travel to Capri, Pompeii, Herculaneum; field trips to the city. Students typically earn 6-7 semester credits per term.

Sessions • May–Jul (summer).

Eligibility Requirements • Minimum age 18; open to freshmen, sophomores, juniors, seniors; 2.67 GPA; 1 letter of recommendation; good academic standing at home school; no foreign language proficiency required.

Living Arrangements • Students live in hotels. Quarters are shared with host institution students. Meals are taken as a group, in central dining facility.

Costs (2005) • $5800; includes tuition, housing, some meals, excursions, student support services. $50 application fee. $500 deposit required. Financial aid available for students from sponsoring institution: scholarships.

For More Information • Ms. Jane Decatur, Assistant Director of International Programs, Trinity College, 300 Summit Street, Hartford, CT 06106-3100; *Phone:* 860-297-2364; *Fax:* 860-297-5218. *E-mail:* jane.decatur@trincoll.edu. *World Wide Web:* http://www.trincoll.edu/depts/rome/

UNIVERSITY OF DELAWARE
WINTER AND SUMMER SESSIONS IN ITALY: LINGUISTICS

Academic Focus • English, linguistics.

Program Information • Faculty members are drawn from the sponsor's U.S. staff. Scheduled travel to Rome, Naples, Florence; field trips to local schools, cultural events; optional travel to sites within Italy at an extra cost. Students typically earn 6 semester credits per term.

Sessions • Jun–Jul (summer), Jan–Feb (winter).

Eligibility Requirements • Open to freshmen, sophomores, juniors, seniors, adults; 2.0 GPA; 1 letter of recommendation; no foreign language proficiency required.

Living Arrangements • Students live in hotels. Meals are taken on one's own, in restaurants.

Costs (2005) • Contact sponsor for cost. $200 nonrefundable deposit required. Financial aid available for all students: scholarships.

For More Information • Center for International Studies, University of Delaware, 186 South College Avenue, Newark, DE 19716-1450; *Phone:* 888-831-4685; *Fax:* 302-831-6042. *E-mail:* studyabroad@udel.edu. *World Wide Web:* http://www.udel.edu/studyabroad/

UNIVERSITY OF NEW ORLEANS
UNO–ROME AND ITALY

Academic Focus • Art, art history.

ITALY
Rome

Program Information • Faculty members are drawn from the sponsor's U.S. staff and local instructors hired by the sponsor. Students typically earn 6 semester credits per term.
Sessions • Jul (summer).
Eligibility Requirements • Minimum age 18; open to freshmen, sophomores, juniors, seniors, graduate students, adults; 2.5 GPA; good academic standing at home school; no foreign language proficiency required.
Living Arrangements • Students live in host institution dormitories, hotels. Quarters are shared with students from other programs. Meals are taken as a group, in central dining facility.
Costs (2004) • $3395; includes tuition, housing, some meals, insurance, excursions, student support services. $150 application fee. $150 refundable deposit required. Financial aid available for students from sponsoring institution: scholarships, loans.
For More Information • Ms. Marie Kaposchyn, Program Director, University of New Orleans, PO Box 569, New Orleans, LA 70148; *Phone:* 504-280-7455; *Fax:* 504-280-7317. *E-mail:* mkaposch@uno. edu. *World Wide Web:* http://inst.uno.edu/

VILLANOVA UNIVERSITY
STUDIES IN INTERNATIONAL BUSINESS, ROME

Hosted by John Cabot University
Academic Focus • International business.
Program Information • Students attend classes at John Cabot University (Rome, Italy). Field trips to local businesses. Students typically earn 6 semester credits per term.
Sessions • Jun–Aug (summer).
Eligibility Requirements • Minimum age 18; open to freshmen, sophomores, juniors, seniors; course work in business; 2.5 GPA; 2 letters of recommendation; good academic standing at home school; no foreign language proficiency required.
Living Arrangements • Students live in program-owned apartments. Quarters are shared with students from other programs. Meals are taken on one's own, in residences.
Costs (2005) • $4250; includes tuition, housing, some meals, excursions, international student ID, transfers. $450 nonrefundable deposit required. Financial aid available for students from sponsoring institution.
For More Information • Dr. Robert LeClair, Faculty Coordinator, Villanova University, 336 Bartley Hall, 800 Lancaster Avenue, Villanova, PA 19085; *Phone:* 610-519-6412; *Fax:* 610-519-7649. *E-mail:* robert.leclair@villanova.edu. *World Wide Web:* http://www. internationalstudies.villanova.edu/

SICILY

LANGUAGE LIAISON
LEARN ITALIAN IN SICILY

Hosted by Language Liaison
Academic Focus • Italian language and literature.
Program Information • Students attend classes at Language Liaison (Sicily, Italy). Field trips; optional travel at an extra cost. Students typically earn 3–15 semester credits per term.
Sessions • Classes begin weekly, year-round.
Eligibility Requirements • Minimum age 17; open to precollege students, freshmen, sophomores, juniors, seniors, graduate students, adults; no foreign language proficiency required.
Living Arrangements • Students live in locally rented apartments, host family homes, hotels. Meals are taken on one's own, with host family, in residences, in restaurants.
Costs (2005) • Contact sponsor for cost. $175 application fee. Financial aid available for all students: scholarship research service.
For More Information • Ms. Nancy Forman, President, Language Liaison, PO Box 1772, Pacific Palisades, CA 90272; *Phone:* 800-284-4448; *Fax:* 310-454-1706. *E-mail:* learn@languageliaison. com. *World Wide Web:* http://www.languageliaison.com/

NEW YORK UNIVERSITY
SOUTHERN ITALY

Hosted by NYU at Sicily
Academic Focus • Cultural studies, religious studies.

Program Information • Students attend classes at NYU at Sicily (Sicily, Italy). Scheduled travel to Amalfi Coast, Rome, Sicily; field trips to Amalfi Coast, Rome, Sicily. Students typically earn 4 semester credits per term.
Sessions • Jun (summer).
Eligibility Requirements • Minimum age 18; open to freshmen, sophomores, juniors, seniors; 3.0 GPA; good academic standing at home school; no foreign language proficiency required.
Living Arrangements • Students live in hotels. Quarters are shared with host institution students. Meals are taken on one's own, in restaurants.
Costs (2007) • $5500; includes tuition, housing, some meals, excursions. $25 application fee. $300 nonrefundable deposit required.
For More Information • Office of Summer Sessions, New York University, 7 E. 12th Street, 6th Floor, New York, NY 10003; *Phone:* 212-998-2292; *Fax:* 212-995-4642. *E-mail:* summer.info@nyu.edu. *World Wide Web:* http://www.nyu.edu/global/studyabroad.html

SIENA

AHA INTERNATIONAL AN ACADEMIC PROGRAM OF THE UNIVERSITY OF OREGON
SIENA, ITALY: NORTHWEST COUNCIL ON STUDY ABROAD

Hosted by AHA Siena Center, University for Foreigners Siena
Academic Focus • Italian language and literature.
Program Information • Students attend classes at AHA Siena Center (Siena, Italy), University for Foreigners Siena (Siena, Italy). Students typically earn 6–12 quarter credits per term.
Sessions • Sep (fall intensive).
Eligibility Requirements • Open to sophomores, juniors, seniors; 2 letters of recommendation; good academic standing at home school; official transcript.
Living Arrangements • Students live in locally rented apartments, host family homes. Quarters are shared with host institution students, students from other programs. Meals are taken on one's own, in residences, in central dining facility.
Costs (2005–2006) • $1965; includes tuition, housing, insurance, international student ID, student support services, local transportation pass, orientation. $50 application fee. $200 refundable deposit required. Financial aid available for all students: scholarships, loans, home institution financial aid.
For More Information • Mr. Edward Helgeson, Associate Director for University Programs, AHA International An Academic Program of the University of Oregon, 221 NW 2nd Avenue, Suite 200, Portland, OR 97209; *Phone:* 503-295-7730; *Fax:* 503-295-5969. *E-mail:* mail@aha-intl.org. *World Wide Web:* http://www.aha-intl.org/

EMORY UNIVERSITY
CHEMISTRY STUDIES

Hosted by University of Siena
Academic Focus • Chemical sciences.
Program Information • Students attend classes at University of Siena (Siena, Italy). Field trips to Florence, Cinque Terre. Students typically earn 8 semester credits per term.
Sessions • May–Jul (summer).
Eligibility Requirements • Minimum age 18; open to freshmen, sophomores, juniors, seniors; 3.0 GPA; good academic standing at home school; organic chemistry; no foreign language proficiency required.
Living Arrangements • Students live in hotels. Meals are taken as a group, in restaurants.
Costs (2005) • $7950; includes tuition, housing, some meals, insurance, excursions, lab equipment. $350 nonrefundable deposit required. Financial aid available for students from sponsoring institution: scholarships, loans.
For More Information • Ms. Gail Scheu, Study Abroad Coordinator, Emory University, 1385 Oxford Road, Atlanta, GA 30322; *Phone:* 404-727-2240; *Fax:* 404-727-6724. *E-mail:* lscheu@emory.edu. *World Wide Web:* http://www.cipa.emory.edu/

LANGUAGE LIAISON
LEARN ITALIAN IN SIENA

Hosted by Language Liaison
Academic Focus • Italian language and literature.
Program Information • Students attend classes at Language Liaison (Siena, Italy). Field trips; optional travel at an extra cost. Students typically earn 3-15 semester credits per term.
Sessions • New programs begin weekly, year-round.
Eligibility Requirements • Minimum age 17; open to precollege students, freshmen, sophomores, juniors, seniors, graduate students, adults; no foreign language proficiency required.
Living Arrangements • Students live in locally rented apartments, host family homes, hotels. Meals are taken on one's own, with host family, in residences, in restaurants.
Costs (2005) • Contact sponsor for cost. $175 application fee. Financial aid available for all students: scholarship research service.
For More Information • Ms. Nancy Forman, President, Language Liaison, PO Box 1772, Pacific Palisades, CA 90272; *Phone:* 800-284-4448; *Fax:* 310-454-1706. *E-mail:* learn@languageliaison. com. *World Wide Web:* http://www.languageliaison.com/

LINGUA SERVICE WORLDWIDE
VACATION 'N LEARN ITALIAN IN ITALY

Hosted by Scuola Leonardo daVinci
Academic Focus • Italian language and literature, Italian studies.
Program Information • Students attend classes at Scuola Leonardo daVinci (Siena, Italy). Optional travel to cultural sites throughout Italy at an extra cost. Students typically earn 3 semester credits for 3 weeks, 6 semester credits for 5 weeks.
Sessions • Sessions of 2 weeks or more, beginning on Mondays, year-round.
Eligibility Requirements • Minimum age 16; open to freshmen, sophomores, juniors, seniors, graduate students, adults; no foreign language proficiency required.
Living Arrangements • Students live in host institution dormitories, locally rented apartments, host family homes, hotels. Quarters are shared with host institution students. Meals are taken with host family.
Costs (2006–2007) • Contact sponsor for cost. $100 application fee.
For More Information • Assistant Director, Lingua Service Worldwide, 75 Prospect Street, Suite 4, Huntington, NY 11743; *Phone:* 800-394-5327; *Fax:* 631-271-3441. *E-mail:* linguaservice@att. net. *World Wide Web:* http://www.linguaserviceworldwide.com/

LINGUA SERVICE WORLDWIDE
VACATION 'N LEARN ITALIAN IN ITALY

Hosted by Centro Internazionale Dante Alighieri
Academic Focus • Italian language and literature, Italian studies.
Program Information • Students attend classes at Centro Internazionale Dante Alighieri (Siena, Italy). Optional travel to cultural sites thoughout Italy at an extra cost. Students typically earn 3 semester credits for 3 weeks, 6 semester credits for 5 weeks.
Sessions • Sessions of 2 or more weeks begin on Mondays, year-round.
Eligibility Requirements • Minimum age 16; open to freshmen, sophomores, juniors, seniors, graduate students, adults; no foreign language proficiency required.
Living Arrangements • Students live in host institution dormitories, locally rented apartments, host family homes, hotels. Quarters are shared with host institution students. Meals are taken with host family.
Costs (2006–2007) • Contact sponsor for cost. $100 application fee.
For More Information • Assistant Director, Lingua Service Worldwide, 75 Prospect Street, Suite 4, Huntington, NY 11743; *Phone:* 800-394-5327; *Fax:* 631-271-3441. *E-mail:* linguaservice@att. net. *World Wide Web:* http://www.linguaserviceworldwide.com/

SIENA SOJOURN
(SIENA SOJOURN OF) SOJOURNS ABROAD

Academic Focus • Italian language and literature.

Program Information • Faculty members are drawn from the sponsor's U.S. staff and local instructors hired by the sponsor. Scheduled travel to Rome, Venice, Cinqua Terra; field trips to Assisi, museums, countryside.
Sessions • Jun-Jul (summer).
Eligibility Requirements • Minimum age 18; open to precollege students, freshmen, sophomores, juniors, seniors, graduate students, adults; 1 letter of recommendation; application/personal statement; no foreign language proficiency required.
Living Arrangements • Students live in locally rented apartments, host family homes. Meals are taken with host family, in residences.
Costs (2007) • $8500; includes tuition, housing, some meals, excursions, books and class materials, museum entry fees, concerts, sporting events, cultural activities. $250 application fee. Financial aid available for all students: scholarships.
For More Information • Mr. John Nissen, Director, Siena Sojourn, Box 1171, Manchester, VT 05254; *Phone:* 802-362-5855. *E-mail:* info@sojournsabroad.org. *World Wide Web:* http://www. sojournsabroad.org

UNIVERSITY OF DELAWARE
WINTER SESSION IN SIENA, ITALY

Hosted by University for Foreigners Siena
Academic Focus • Italian language and literature, Italian studies.
Program Information • Students attend classes at University for Foreigners Siena (Siena, Italy). Scheduled travel to Rome; field trips to Naples, Florence, Assisi; optional travel to Europe at an extra cost. Students typically earn 6-7 semester credits per term.
Sessions • Jan-Feb (winter).
Eligibility Requirements • Open to freshmen, sophomores, juniors, seniors, adults; 2.0 GPA; 1 letter of recommendation; no foreign language proficiency required.
Living Arrangements • Students live in hotels. Quarters are shared with host institution students. Meals are taken on one's own, in restaurants.
Costs (2005) • Contact sponsor for cost. $200 nonrefundable deposit required. Financial aid available for all students: scholarships.
For More Information • Center for International Studies, University of Delaware, 186 South College Avenue, Newark, DE 19716-1450; *Phone:* 888-831-4685; *Fax:* 302-831-6042. *E-mail:* studyabroad@udel. edu. *World Wide Web:* http://www.udel.edu/studyabroad/

SYRACUSE

ACADEMIC PROGRAMS INTERNATIONAL (API)
(API)–SYRACUSE, ITALY

Hosted by Mediterranean Center for Arts and Sciences
Academic Focus • Anthropology, archaeology, art, art history, geology, Islamic studies, Italian language and literature, Jewish studies, Middle Eastern studies, physical sciences.
Program Information • Students attend classes at Mediterranean Center for Arts and Sciences (Syracuse, Italy). Scheduled travel to Rome; field trips to Aeolian Islands, Agrigento and Roman Villa at Casale, Cava Grande; Fonte Ciane, Palermo Pantalica, Piraimito; Noto; Ragusa; Modica; Taormina. Students typically earn 3-7 semester credits per term.
Sessions • May-Jun (summer), Jul-Aug (summer 2).
Eligibility Requirements • Minimum age 18; open to freshmen, sophomores, juniors, seniors, graduate students, adults; 2.75 GPA; 1 letter of recommendation; good academic standing at home school; official transcript from home university; no foreign language proficiency required.
Living Arrangements • Students live in locally rented apartments, host family homes. Quarters are shared with students from other programs. Meals are taken on one's own, with host family, in residences, in restaurants.
Costs (2006) • Contact sponsor for cost. $150 nonrefundable deposit required. Financial aid available for all students: scholarships.
For More Information • Ms. Jennifer C. Allen, Director, Academic Programs International (API), 107 East Hopkins, San Marcos, TX

ITALY

Syracuse

78666; *Phone:* 800-844-4124; *Fax:* 512-392-8420. *E-mail:* api@academicintl.com. *World Wide Web:* http://www.academicintl.com/

STUDY ABROAD ITALY
THE MEDITERRANEAN CENTER FOR ARTS AND SCIENCES

Hosted by Mediterranean Center for Arts and Sciences
Academic Focus • Classics and classical languages, environmental science/studies, fine/studio arts, geology, history, international affairs, Italian language and literature, Mediterranean studies, political science and government.
Program Information • Students attend classes at Mediterranean Center for Arts and Sciences (Syracuse, Italy). Field trips to Agrigento, the Aeolian Islands, Taormina, Etna. Students typically earn 6 semester credits per term.
Sessions • May–Jun (summer), Jun–Aug (summer 2).
Eligibility Requirements • Minimum age 18; open to precollege students, freshmen, sophomores, juniors, seniors, graduate students, adults; 2.5 GPA; good academic standing at home school; no foreign language proficiency required.
Living Arrangements • Students live in locally rented apartments, host family homes. Quarters are shared with host institution students. Meals are taken on one's own, in residences, in restaurants.
Costs (2005–2006) • $3675 for 1 course; $4375 for 2 courses; includes tuition, housing, insurance, excursions, international student ID, student support services, emergency medical and repatriation insurance; 50 hours of internet use. $75 application fee. $1000 deposit required. Financial aid available for all students: scholarships, loans.
For More Information • Ms. Chelsea Brand, Admissions Officer, Study Abroad Italy, 7151 Wilton Avenue, Suite 202, Sebastopol, CA 95472; *Phone:* 800-655-8965; *Fax:* 707-824-0198. *E-mail:* cab@studyabroad-italy.com. *World Wide Web:* http://www.studyabroad-italy.com/

TAORMINA

BABILONIA CENTRO DI LINGUA E CULTURA ITALIANA
ITALIAN LANGUAGE AND CULTURE COURSES

Hosted by Babilonia Centro di Lingua e Cultura Italiana
Academic Focus • Art history, history, Italian language and literature, Italian studies.
Program Information • Students attend classes at Babilonia Centro di Lingua e Cultura Italiana (Taormina, Italy). Field trips to archaeological and historic areas, naturalistic areas; optional travel to Sicily at an extra cost. Students typically earn 3-6 semester credits per term.
Sessions • Classes begin every other Monday.
Eligibility Requirements • Open to precollege students, freshmen, sophomores, juniors, seniors, graduate students, adults; no foreign language proficiency required.
Living Arrangements • Students live in locally rented apartments, host family homes, hotels. Quarters are shared with host institution students, students from other programs. Meals are taken on one's own, with host family, in residences, in restaurants.
Costs (2005) • €145–€500 per week; includes insurance, books and class materials, internet access, discount card, activities, some excursions, film seminars.
For More Information • Mr. Alessandro Adorno, Director, Babilonia Centro di Lingua e Cultura Italiana, Via del Ginnasio 20, 98039 Taormina, Italy; *Phone:* +39 0942-23441; *Fax:* +39 0942-23441. *E-mail:* director@babilonia.it. *World Wide Web:* http://www.babilonia.it/

TURIN

UNIVERSITY STUDIES ABROAD CONSORTIUM
INTERNATIONAL BUSINESS, ART AND ARCHITECTURE, AND ITALIAN STUDIES: TORINO, ITALY

Hosted by University of Turin
Academic Focus • Architecture, art history, business administration/management, culinary arts, interior design, international business, Italian language and literature, Italian studies, marketing, political science and government, speech communication.
Program Information • Students attend classes at University of Turin (Turin, Italy). Field trips to the Italian Riviera, Piedmont, the Lake Region, mountains; optional travel to Pisa, Florence, Siena, Lucca, Viareggio, San Gimignano at an extra cost. Students typically earn 6-12 semester credits per term.
Sessions • May–Jun (summer), Jun–Aug (summer 2).
Eligibility Requirements • Minimum age 18; open to freshmen, sophomores, juniors, seniors, graduate students, adults; 2.5 GPA; no foreign language proficiency required.
Living Arrangements • Students live in locally rented apartments. Quarters are shared with host institution students. Meals are taken on one's own, in residences, in central dining facility, in restaurants.
Costs (2007) • $3540 for 1 session; $6980 for 2 sessions; includes tuition, housing, insurance, excursions, student support services. $100 application fee. $200 refundable deposit required. Financial aid available for all students: scholarships, loans.
For More Information • University Studies Abroad Consortium, USAC/323, Reno, NV 89557-0093; *Phone:* 775-784-6569; *Fax:* 775-784-6010. *E-mail:* usac@unr.edu. *World Wide Web:* http://usac.unr.edu/

TUSCANY

ACADEMIC PROGRAMS INTERNATIONAL (API)
(API)–TUSCANIA, ITALY

Hosted by Lorenzo de Medici
Academic Focus • Full curriculum.
Program Information • Students attend classes at Lorenzo de Medici (Tuscania, Italy). Field trips to Rome, Tuscany, Lazio, Cinque Terre, Florence, Venice. Students typically earn 6 semester credits per term.
Sessions • Jun–Jul (summer), Jul–Aug (summer 2).
Eligibility Requirements • Minimum age 18; open to freshmen, sophomores, juniors, seniors; 2.75 GPA; 1 letter of recommendation; good academic standing at home school; official transcript from home university; no foreign language proficiency required.
Living Arrangements • Students live in host institution dormitories, locally rented apartments, host family homes. Quarters are shared with host institution students. Meals are taken as a group, on one's own, with host family, in residences, in central dining facility, in restaurants.
Costs (2007–2008) • Contact sponsor for cost. $150 nonrefundable deposit required. Financial aid available for all students: scholarships.
For More Information • Ms. Jennifer C. Allen, Director, Academic Programs International (API), 107 East Hopkins, San Marcos, TX 78666; *Phone:* 800-844-4124; *Fax:* 512-392-8420. *E-mail:* api@academicintl.com. *World Wide Web:* http://www.academicintl.com/

COLLEGE CONSORTIUM FOR INTERNATIONAL STUDIES–COLLEGE OF STATEN ISLAND/CITY UNIVERSITY OF NEW YORK
SUMMER PROGRAM IN TUSCANIA, ITALY

Hosted by Lorenzo de Medici School
Academic Focus • Archaeology, art history, culinary arts, drawing/painting, film and media studies, history, Italian language and literature, philosophy, photography.
Program Information • Students attend classes at Lorenzo de Medici School (Florence, Italy). Optional travel to Tarquinia, Rome, Siena, Assisi; Sardinia at an extra cost. Students typically earn 6 semester credits per term.
Sessions • May–Jun (summer), Jun–Jul (summer 2).
Eligibility Requirements • Minimum age 18; open to freshmen, sophomores, juniors, seniors; 2.5 GPA; 1 letter of recommendation; essay; transcript; no foreign language proficiency required.
Living Arrangements • Students live in locally rented apartments, hotels. Quarters are shared with host institution students, students

from other programs. Meals are taken on one's own, in residences, in central dining facility, in restaurants.

Costs (2007) • $2180; includes tuition, insurance, student support services, fees. $135 nonrefundable deposit required. Financial aid available for students from sponsoring institution: loans, grants.

For More Information • College Consortium for International Studies–College of Staten Island/City University of New York, 2000 P Street, NW, Suite 503, Washington, DC 20036; *Phone:* 800-453-6956; *Fax:* 202-223-0999. *E-mail:* info@ccisabroad.org. *World Wide Web:* http://www.ccisabroad.org/. Students may also apply through College of Staten Island, The City University of New York, Center for International Service, Building 2A, Room 206, 2800 Victory Boulevard, Staten Island, NY 10314.

EUROPEAN HERITAGE INSTITUTE
TUSCANIA: SUMMER STUDIES IN FILMMAKING, ART, AND MORE

Hosted by Lorenzo de Medici

Academic Focus • Archaeology, art, art history, drawing/painting, film and media studies, history, Italian language and literature, Italian studies, performing arts.

Program Information • Students attend classes at Lorenzo de Medici (Tuscania, Italy). Field trips to Rome, Florence, Venice, Tuscany. Students typically earn 3–6 semester credits per term.

Sessions • Classes begin monthly, year-round.

Eligibility Requirements • Minimum age 18; open to freshmen, sophomores, juniors, seniors, graduate students, adults; 2.25 GPA; 2 letters of recommendation; no foreign language proficiency required.

Living Arrangements • Students live in host institution dormitories, locally rented apartments, host family homes, hotels. Quarters are shared with students from other programs. Meals are taken on one's own, in residences, in central dining facility, in restaurants.

Costs (2006) • $2000; includes tuition, excursions, fees. $300 refundable deposit required.

For More Information • Dr. Antonio Masullo, Professor, European Heritage Institute, 2708 East Franklin Street, Richmond, VA 23223; *Phone:* 804-643-0661; *Fax:* 804-648-0826. *E-mail:* info@europeabroad.org. *World Wide Web:* http://www.europeabroad.org/

LANGUAGE LIAISON
LEARN ITALIAN IN TUSCANY

Hosted by Language Liaison

Academic Focus • Italian language and literature.

Program Information • Students attend classes at Language Liaison (Tuscany, Italy). Field trips; optional travel. Students typically earn 3–9 semester credits per term.

Sessions • Classes begin weekly, year-round.

Eligibility Requirements • Minimum age 16; open to precollege students, freshmen, sophomores, juniors, seniors, graduate students, adults; no foreign language proficiency required.

Living Arrangements • Students live in host institution dormitories, locally rented apartments, host family homes, hotels. Meals are taken as a group, on one's own, with host family, in central dining facility, in restaurants.

Costs (2005) • Contact sponsor for cost. $175 application fee.

For More Information • Ms. Nancy Forman, President, Language Liaison, PO Box 1772, Pacific Palisades, CA 90272; *Phone:* 800-284-4448; *Fax:* 310-454-1706. *E-mail:* learn@languageliaison.com. *World Wide Web:* http://www.languageliaison.com/

LANGUAGE LIAISON
LEARN ITALIAN IN VIAREGGIO

Hosted by Language Liaison

Academic Focus • Italian language and literature.

ITALY
Tuscany

Program Information • Students attend classes at Language Liaison (Viaveggio, Italy). Field trips; optional travel. Students typically earn 3–9 semester credits per term.
Sessions • Classes begin every week, year-round.
Eligibility Requirements • Minimum age 16; open to precollege students, freshmen, sophomores, juniors, seniors, graduate students, adults; no foreign language proficiency required.
Living Arrangements • Students live in host institution dormitories, locally rented apartments, host family homes, hotels. Meals are taken as a group, on one's own, with host family, in central dining facility, in restaurants.
Costs (2005) • Contact sponsor for cost. $175 application fee.
For More Information • Ms. Nancy Forman, President, Language Liaison, PO Box 1772, Pacific Palisades, CA 90272; *Phone:* 800-284-4448; *Fax:* 310-454-1706. *E-mail:* learn@languageliaison. com. *World Wide Web:* http://www.languageliaison.com/

URBINO

SOUTHERN CONNECTICUT STATE UNIVERSITY
SOUTHERN CONNECTICUT STATE UNIVERSITY IN URBINO, ITALY

Hosted by University of Urbino
Academic Focus • Art, art history, Italian language and literature.
Program Information • Students attend classes at University of Urbino (Urbino, Italy). Scheduled travel to Venice, Florence, Rome; field trips to Ravenna; optional travel at an extra cost. Students typically earn 3 semester credits per term.
Sessions • Jul–Aug (summer).
Eligibility Requirements • Minimum age 18; open to precollege students, freshmen, sophomores, juniors, seniors; major in humanities, arts; course work in history, art; 2.5 GPA; 1 letter of recommendation; 1 year of college course work in Italian.
Living Arrangements • Students live in host institution dormitories, locally rented apartments. Quarters are shared with host institution students, students from other programs. Meals are taken as a group, in central dining facility.
Costs (2005) • $2400; includes housing, all meals, excursions. $300 application fee. $500 deposit required. Financial aid available for students from sponsoring institution: federal and state loans.
For More Information • Dr. Michael Vena, Professor of Foreign Language, Southern Connecticut State University, 501 Crescent Street, New Haven, CT 06515; *Phone:* 203-392-6766; *Fax:* 203-392-6136.

STATE UNIVERSITY OF NEW YORK AT NEW PALTZ
SUMMER ITALIAN LANGUAGE STUDIES

Hosted by University of Urbino
Academic Focus • Italian language and literature.
Program Information • Students attend classes at University of Urbino (Urbino, Italy). Scheduled travel to Rome, Florence; field trips to Assisi, Gubbio, Arezzo, Bologna. Students typically earn 6 semester credits per term.
Sessions • Jul–Aug (summer).
Eligibility Requirements • Minimum age 18; open to freshmen, sophomores, juniors, seniors, adults; 2.5 GPA; 1 letter of recommendation; good academic standing at home school; 1 semester college course work in Italian.
Living Arrangements • Students live in host institution dormitories. Quarters are shared with host institution students, students from other programs. Meals are taken on one's own, in central dining facility.
Costs (2006) • $1900 for New York residents; $3300 for nonresidents; includes tuition, housing, some meals, student support services, administrative fee. $25 application fee. $300 nonrefundable deposit required. Financial aid available for students from sponsoring institution: scholarships, loans.
For More Information • Center for International Programs, State University of New York at New Paltz, 1 Hawk Drive, New Paltz, NY 12561-2443; *Phone:* 845-257-3125; *Fax:* 845-257-3129. *E-mail:* studyabroad@newpaltz.edu. *World Wide Web:* http://www.newpaltz.edu/studyabroad/

VENICE

COLLEGE CONSORTIUM FOR INTERNATIONAL STUDIES–COLLEGE OF STATEN ISLAND/CITY UNIVERSITY OF NEW YORK
SUMMER PROGRAM IN VENICE, ITALY: SUPER-INTENSIVE ITALIAN

Hosted by Instituto Venezia–The Venice Institute
Academic Focus • Italian language and literature.
Program Information • Students attend classes at Instituto Venezia–The Venice Institute (Venice, Italy). Students typically earn 6 semester credits per term.
Sessions • May–Jun (summer), Jun–Jul (summer 2); Jul–Aug (summer 3).
Eligibility Requirements • Minimum age 18; open to freshmen, sophomores, juniors, seniors; 2.5 GPA; 1 letter of recommendation; essay; transcript; no foreign language proficiency required.
Living Arrangements • Students live in locally rented apartments. Quarters are shared with host institution students, students from other programs. Meals are taken on one's own, in residences, in restaurants.
Costs (2007) • $1400 for New York residents and CCIS member students; all others contact the College of Staten Island; includes tuition, insurance, excursions, student support services, fees. $135 nonrefundable deposit required. Financial aid available for students from sponsoring institution: loans, grants.
For More Information • College Consortium for International Studies–College of Staten Island/City University of New York, 2000 P Street, NW, Suite 503, Washington, DC 20036; *Phone:* 800-453-6956; *Fax:* 202-233-0999. *E-mail:* info@ccisabroad.org. *World Wide Web:* http://www.ccisabroad.org/. Students may also apply through College of Staten Island, The City University of New York, Center for International Service, Building 2A, Room 206, 2800 Victory Boulevard, Staten Island, NY 10314.

COLUMBIA UNIVERSITY
SUMMER ART AND ARCHITECTURE IN VENICE

Academic Focus • Architecture, art history.
Program Information • Faculty members are drawn from the sponsor's U.S. staff. Scheduled travel to Padua, Vicenza, Veneto; field trips. Students typically earn 4 semester credits per term.
Sessions • Jul (summer).
Eligibility Requirements • Minimum age 18; open to freshmen, sophomores, juniors, seniors, graduate students, adults; course work in art history (1 course); 3.0 GPA; 1 letter of recommendation; good academic standing at home school; no foreign language proficiency required.
Living Arrangements • Students live in locally rented apartments. Meals are taken as a group, on one's own, in residences, in restaurants.
Costs (2005) • $6000; includes tuition, housing, some meals, excursions, books and class materials, student support services. $50 application fee. $500 nonrefundable deposit required.
For More Information • Information Center, Columbia University, 2970 Broadway, MC4110, 303 Lewisohn, New York, NY 10027-6902; *Phone:* 212-854-9699; *Fax:* 212-854-5841. *E-mail:* studyabroad@columbia.edu. *World Wide Web:* http://www.ce.columbia.edu/op/

EUROPEAN HERITAGE INSTITUTE
YEAR-ROUND PROGRAMS IN VENICE

Hosted by The Venice Institute
Academic Focus • Italian language and literature, Italian studies.
Program Information • Students attend classes at The Venice Institute (Venice, Italy). Field trips to cultural sites throughout Venice. Students typically earn 3–6 semester credits per month.
Sessions • Minimum 2 week sessions held year-round; month-long sessions held May–Aug.
Eligibility Requirements • Minimum age 18; open to freshmen, sophomores, juniors, seniors, graduate students, adults; 2.25 GPA; 2 letters of recommendation; no foreign language proficiency required.

Living Arrangements • Students live in locally rented apartments, host family homes. Quarters are shared with host institution students, students from other programs. Meals are taken on one's own, with host family, in residences, in restaurants.

Costs (2006) • $1800 per month; includes tuition, housing, excursions, student support services. $300 refundable deposit required.

For More Information • Dr. Antonio Masullo, Professor, European Heritage Institute, 2708 East Franklin Street, Richmond, VA 23223; *Phone:* 804-643-0661; *Fax:* 804-648-0826. *E-mail:* info@europeabroad. org. *World Wide Web:* http://www.europeabroad.org/

KNOWLEDGE EXCHANGE INSTITUTE (KEI)
GRADUATE DIPLOMA IN VISUAL ARTS AND GRAPHIC DESIGN

Hosted by Scoula Internazionale di Grafica

Academic Focus • Art, art history, drawing/painting, fine/studio arts, Italian language and literature, photography, visual and performing arts.

Program Information • Students attend classes at Scoula Internazionale di Grafica (Venice, Italy). Scheduled travel to Rome; field trips to Veneto, Milan, Florence. Students typically earn 6 semester credits per term.

Sessions • May–Jun (summer), Jun–Jul (summer 2).

Eligibility Requirements • Open to seniors, graduate students, adults; 2.2 GPA; 2 letters of recommendation; good academic standing at home school.

Living Arrangements • Students live in program-owned apartments. Quarters are shared with host institution students, students from other programs. Meals are taken on one's own, in residences, in central dining facility, in restaurants.

Costs (2006) • $5850; includes tuition, housing, insurance, excursions, books and class materials, lab equipment, student support services, mobile telephone. $50 application fee. $500 nonrefundable deposit required. Financial aid available for all students: scholarships, loans.

For More Information • Mr. Eduard Izraylovsky, Director, Knowledge Exchange Institute (KEI), 111 John Street, Suite 800, New York, NY 10038; *Phone:* 800-831-5095; *Fax:* 212-528-2095. *E-mail:* info@knowledgeexchange.org. *World Wide Web:* http://www. knowledgeexchange.org/

KNOWLEDGE EXCHANGE INSTITUTE (KEI)
VISUAL ARTS AND GRAPHIC DESIGN

Hosted by Scoula Internazionale di Grafica

Academic Focus • Art, art history, drawing/painting, fine/studio arts, Italian language and literature, photography, visual and performing arts.

Program Information • Students attend classes at Scoula Internazionale di Grafica (Venice, Italy). Scheduled travel to Rome; field trips to Veneto, Milan, Florence. Students typically earn 6 semester credits per term.

Sessions • May–Jun (summer), Jun–Jul (summer 2).

Eligibility Requirements • Open to freshmen, sophomores, juniors, seniors, graduate students, adults; 2.2 GPA; 2 letters of recommendation; good academic standing at home school; no foreign language proficiency required.

Living Arrangements • Students live in program-owned apartments. Quarters are shared with host institution students, students from other programs. Meals are taken on one's own, in residences, in central dining facility, in restaurants.

Costs (2006) • $5850; includes tuition, housing, insurance, excursions, lab equipment, student support services, mobile telephone. $50 application fee. $500 nonrefundable deposit required. Financial aid available for all students: scholarships, loans.

For More Information • Mr. Eduard Izraylovsky, Director, Knowledge Exchange Institute (KEI), 111 John Street, Suite 800, New York, NY 10038; *Phone:* 800-831-5095; *Fax:* 212-528-2095. *E-mail:* info@knowledgeexchange.org. *World Wide Web:* http://www. knowledgeexchange.org/

LANGUAGE LIAISON
LEARN ITALIAN IN VENICE

Hosted by Language Liaison

Academic Focus • Italian language and literature.

Program Information • Students attend classes at Language Liaison (Venice, Italy). Field trips; optional travel at an extra cost. Students typically earn 3–15 semester credits per term.

Sessions • Classes begin weekly, year-round.

Eligibility Requirements • Minimum age 17; open to precollege students, freshmen, sophomores, juniors, seniors, graduate students, adults; no foreign language proficiency required.

Living Arrangements • Students live in locally rented apartments, host family homes, hotels. Meals are taken on one's own, with host family, in residences, in restaurants.

Costs (2005) • Contact sponsor for cost. $175 application fee. Financial aid available for all students: scholarship research service.

For More Information • Ms. Nancy Forman, President, Language Liaison, PO Box 1772, Pacific Palisades, CA 90272; *Phone:* 800-284-4448; *Fax:* 310-454-1706. *E-mail:* learn@languageliaison. com. *World Wide Web:* http://www.languageliaison.com/

LEXIA INTERNATIONAL
LEXIA SUMMER IN VENICE

Hosted by The Venice Institute

Academic Focus • Anthropology, area studies, art history, civilization studies, classics and classical languages, comparative history, cultural studies, economics, ethnic studies, geography, history, interdisciplinary studies, international affairs, Italian language and literature, Italian studies, liberal studies, literature, political science and government, social sciences, sociology.

Program Information • Students attend classes at The Venice Institute (Venice, Italy). Field trips to a Palladian Villa tour, Verona, Florence, Urbino, Padua. Students typically earn 8–10 semester credits per term.

Sessions • Jun–Aug (summer).

Eligibility Requirements • Minimum age 18; open to freshmen, sophomores, juniors, seniors, graduate students, adults; 2.5 GPA; 2 letters of recommendation; no foreign language proficiency required.

Living Arrangements • Students live in locally rented apartments, host family homes. Quarters are shared with host institution students. Meals are taken on one's own, with host family, in residences, in central dining facility, in restaurants.

Costs (2006) • $6850; includes tuition, housing, insurance, excursions, student support services, computer access, transcript. $40 application fee. $300 nonrefundable deposit required. Financial aid available for all students: scholarships, work study.

For More Information • Lexia International, 23 South Main Street, Hanover, NH 03755; *Phone:* 800-775-3942; *Fax:* 603-643-9899. *E-mail:* info@lexiaintl.org. *World Wide Web:* http://www.lexiaintl. org/

NEW YORK UNIVERSITY
STUDIO ART IN VENICE, ITALY

Hosted by NYU at Venice

Academic Focus • Art, art history, fine/studio arts.

Program Information • Students attend classes at NYU at Venice (Venice, Italy). Field trips to visits to museum and art exhibits, Rome, Padua, Verona. Students typically earn 6 semester credits per term.

Sessions • Jul–Aug (summer).

Eligibility Requirements • Open to graduate students; major in studio art; good academic standing at home school; advisor approval; no foreign language proficiency required.

Living Arrangements • Students live in locally rented apartments. Quarters are shared with host institution students. Meals are taken on one's own, in restaurants.

Costs (2005) • $11,268; includes tuition, registration fees. $50 application fee. Financial aid available for students from sponsoring institution: scholarships.

For More Information • Mr. Daniel Young, Program Associate, New York University, 82 Washington Square East, New York, NY 10003; *Phone:* 212-992-9380. *E-mail:* dy14@nyu.edu. *World Wide Web:* http://www.nyu.edu/global/studyabroad.html

SYRACUSE UNIVERSITY
VENICE BY DESIGN

Academic Focus • Design and applied arts, engineering.
Program Information • Faculty members are drawn from the sponsor's U.S. staff. Field trips to Vicenza, Verona.
Sessions • May–Jun (summer).
Eligibility Requirements • Open to freshmen, sophomores, juniors, seniors, graduate students, adults; 1 letter of recommendation; good academic standing at home school; no foreign language proficiency required.
Living Arrangements • Students live in hotels. Meals are taken on one's own, in restaurants.
Costs (2006) • $6000; includes tuition, housing, excursions, international student ID. $55 application fee. $350 nonrefundable deposit required. Financial aid available for all students: loans.
For More Information • Ms. Daisy Fried, Associate Director, Syracuse University, 106 Walnut Place, Syracuse, NY 13244-4170; *Phone:* 800-251-9674; *Fax:* 315-443-4593. *E-mail:* dsfried@syr.edu. *World Wide Web:* http://suabroad.syr.edu/

WIDENER UNIVERSITY SCHOOL OF LAW
VENICE SUMMER INTERNATIONAL LAW INSTITUTE

Hosted by University of Venice
Academic Focus • Law and legal studies.
Program Information • Students attend classes at University of Venice (Venice, Italy). Field trips to various legal institutions, wineries, tourist sites; optional travel at an extra cost. Students typically earn 6 semester credits per term.
Sessions • May–Jun (summer).
Eligibility Requirements • Open to graduate students; good academic standing at home school; no foreign language proficiency required.
Living Arrangements • Students live in host institution dormitories, locally rented apartments. Quarters are shared with students from other programs. Meals are taken on one's own, in residences, in restaurants.
Costs (2005) • $8300; includes tuition, housing, some meals, excursions, international airfare, books and class materials, student support services. $100 application fee. Financial aid available for all students: loans.
For More Information • Ms. Peggie Wyant, Coordinator, International Programs, Widener University School of Law, 4601 Concord Pike, Room 418 Law Building, Wilmington, DE 19803; *Phone:* 302-477-2248; *Fax:* 302-477-2257. *E-mail:* mawyant@mail.widener.edu. *World Wide Web:* http://www.law.widener.edu/go/summer/

VIAREGGIO

SANTA BARBARA CITY COLLEGE
ITALIAN LANGUAGE AND CULTURE SUMMER PROGRAM IN VIAREGGIO, ITALY

Hosted by Centro Culturale Giacomo Puccini
Academic Focus • Italian studies.

Program Information • Students attend classes at Centro Culturale Giacomo Puccini (Viareggio, Italy). Scheduled travel to Cinque Terre, Rome; field trips to Lucca, Pisa. Students typically earn 4–6 semester credits per term.
Sessions • Jun–Jul (summer).
Eligibility Requirements • Minimum age 18; open to precollege students, freshmen, sophomores, juniors, seniors, graduate students, adults; good academic standing at home school; no foreign language proficiency required.
Living Arrangements • Students live in locally rented apartments, host family homes. Meals are taken with host family, in restaurants.
Costs (2006) • $2500; includes housing, excursions, international student ID, student support services. $200 refundable deposit required. Financial aid available for all students: scholarships, loans.
For More Information • Ms. Naomi Sullwold, Program Assistant, Santa Barbara City College, 721 Cliff Drive, Santa Barbara, CA 93109; *Phone:* 805-965-0581 Ext. 2494; *Fax:* 805-963-7222. *E-mail:* sullwold@sbcc.edu. *World Wide Web:* http://www.sbcc.edu/studyabroad/

VITERBO

UNIVERSITY STUDIES ABROAD CONSORTIUM
ART HISTORY AND ITALIAN STUDIES: VITERBO, ITALY

Hosted by Università de Tuscia
Academic Focus • Architecture, art, art history, geography, history, Italian language and literature.
Program Information • Students attend classes at Università de Tuscia (Viterbo, Italy). Field trips to Umbria; Rome, Mountain Region, Ostia Antica, Lake Region; optional travel to Heart of Italy tour: Tuscany, Florence, Lucca, Naples and Viareggio at an extra cost. Students typically earn 6 semester credits per term.
Sessions • May–Jun (session 1); Jun–Aug (session 2).
Eligibility Requirements • Minimum age 18; open to freshmen, sophomores, juniors, seniors, graduate students, adults; 2.5 GPA; no foreign language proficiency required.
Living Arrangements • Students live in locally rented apartments. Quarters are shared with host institution students. Meals are taken on one's own, in residences, in restaurants.
Costs (2007) • $3540 for 1 session; $6980 for 2 sessions; includes tuition, housing, insurance, excursions, student support services. $100 application fee. $200 refundable deposit required. Financial aid available for all students: scholarships, loans.
For More Information • Coordinator, College, University Studies Abroad Consortium, USAC/323, Reno, NV 89557-0093; *Phone:* 775-784-6569; *Fax:* 775-784-6010. *E-mail:* usac@unr.edu. *World Wide Web:* http://usac.unr.edu/

JAMAICA

CITY-TO-CITY

SAINT MARY'S COLLEGE
JAMAICAN FIELD STUDY

Academic Focus • Biological/life sciences, ecology, environmental science/studies.
Program Information • Faculty members are drawn from the sponsor's U.S. staff. Students typically earn 3 semester credits per term.
Sessions • Mar (summer), Program only runs in even-numbered years.
Eligibility Requirements • Minimum age 18; open to sophomores, juniors, seniors; 3 letters of recommendation; good academic standing at home school.
Living Arrangements • Students live in hotels. Meals are taken as a group, in restaurants.
Costs (2004) • $1779; includes tuition, housing, some meals, excursions, lab equipment, student support services. $30 application fee.
For More Information • Dr. Thomas Platt, Faculty Director, Saint Mary's College, Department of Biology, Notre Dame, IN 46556; *Phone:* 574-284-4669; *Fax:* 574-284-4141. *E-mail:* tplatt@saintmarys.edu. *World Wide Web:* http://www.saintmarys.edu/~cwil

FALMOUTH

COOPERATIVE CENTER FOR STUDY ABROAD
JAMAICA

Academic Focus • Archaeology.
Program Information • Faculty members are drawn from the sponsor's U.S. staff. Field trips. Students typically earn 4-5 semester credits per term.
Sessions • Jul–Aug (summer).
Eligibility Requirements • Minimum age 18; open to juniors, seniors, graduate students, adults; good academic standing at home school.
Living Arrangements • Students live in hotels. Quarters are shared with host institution students. Meals are taken as a group, on one's own, in central dining facility, in restaurants.
Costs (2007) • $3295; includes housing, some meals, insurance, excursions, international airfare, airport transfers. $200 nonrefundable deposit required. Financial aid available for students from sponsoring institution: scholarships, loans.
For More Information • Dr. Michael A. Klembara, Executive Director, Cooperative Center for Study Abroad, Northern Kentucky University, Nunn Drive, Founders Hall 301, Highland Heights, KY 41099; *Phone:* 800-319-6015; *Fax:* 859-572-6650. *E-mail:* ccsa@nku.edu. *World Wide Web:* http://www.ccsa.cc/

KINGSTON

THE INTERNATIONAL PARTNERSHIP FOR SERVICE LEARNING AND LEADERSHIP
JAMAICA SERVICE–LEARNING

Hosted by University of Technology
Academic Focus • Community service, education, intercultural studies, international affairs, liberal studies, social sciences.
Program Information • Students attend classes at University of Technology (Kingston, Jamaica). Field trips to Ocho Rios, Mandeville; optional travel to Montego Bay at an extra cost. Students typically earn 6 semester credits per term.
Sessions • Jun–Aug (summer), Jun–Aug (summer 2).
Eligibility Requirements • Minimum age 18; open to freshmen, sophomores, juniors, seniors, graduate students, adults; 2 letters of recommendation; good academic standing at home school; evidence of maturity.
Living Arrangements • Students live in host family homes. Meals are taken with host family, in residences.
Costs (2005–2006) • $5500; includes tuition, housing, some meals, excursions, student support services, community service placement. $50 application fee. $250 refundable deposit required. Financial aid available for all students: federal financial aid.
For More Information • Director of Student Programs, The International Partnership for Service Learning and Leadership, 815 Second Avenue, New York, NY 10017-4594; *Phone:* 212-986-0989; *Fax:* 212-986-5039. *E-mail:* info@ipsl.org. *World Wide Web:* http://www.ipsl.org/

MONA

MICHIGAN STATE UNIVERSITY
HISTORY, MUSIC, AND CULTURE OF AFRICA, THE CARIBBEAN, AND THE AMERICAS

Held at University of the West Indies

Academic Focus • African studies, history, music.

Program Information • Classes are held on the campus of University of the West Indies (Kingston, Jamaica). Faculty members are drawn from the sponsor's U.S. staff and local instructors hired by the sponsor. Field trips. Students typically earn 7 semester credits per term.

Sessions • Jul–Aug (summer).

Eligibility Requirements • Minimum age 18; open to freshmen, sophomores, juniors, seniors; 2.0 GPA; good academic standing at home school; faculty approval.

Living Arrangements • Students live in host institution dormitories. Quarters are shared with host institution students. Meals are taken as a group, in restaurants.

Costs (2005) • $2041 (estimated); includes housing, some meals, insurance. $100 application fee. $200 nonrefundable deposit required. Financial aid available for students from sponsoring institution: scholarships, loans.

For More Information • Mr. Mark Davis, Coordinator, Michigan State University, Office of Study Abroad, 109 International Center, East Lansing, MI 48824-1035; *Phone:* 517-432-1315; *Fax:* 517-432-2082. *E-mail:* mdavis@msu.edu. *World Wide Web:* http://studyabroad.msu.edu/

OCHO RIOS

UNIVERSITY OF SOUTHERN MISSISSIPPI
CARIBBEAN STUDIES PROGRAM

Academic Focus • Anthropology, archaeology, criminal justice, literature, music history, nursing, social work, sociology.

Program Information • Faculty members are drawn from the sponsor's U.S. staff and local instructors hired by the sponsor. Scheduled travel; field trips. Students typically earn 4 semester credits per term.

Sessions • May (summer).

Eligibility Requirements • Minimum age 18; open to sophomores, juniors, seniors, graduate students, adults; 2.0 GPA; good academic standing at home school.

Living Arrangements • Students live in hotels. Meals are taken as a group, on one's own, in residences, in restaurants.

Costs (2005) • $2599 for undergraduate students; $2799 for graduate students; includes tuition, housing, excursions, international airfare, student support services. $200 nonrefundable deposit required. Financial aid available for students from sponsoring institution: scholarships, loans.

For More Information • Director, Caribbean Studies Program, University of Southern Mississippi, 118 College Drive #10047, Hattiesburg, MS 39406-0001; *Phone:* 601-266-4344; *Fax:* 601-266-5699. *E-mail:* sylvia.mcnabb@usm.edu. *World Wide Web:* http://www.usm.edu/internationaledu/

JAPAN

CITY-TO-CITY

KENTUCKY INSTITUTE FOR INTERNATIONAL STUDIES
JAPAN

Academic Focus • Japanese, Japanese studies.
Program Information • Faculty members are drawn from the sponsor's U.S. staff. Field trips; optional travel at an extra cost. Students typically earn 3–6 semester credits per term.
Sessions • Jun–Jul (summer).
Eligibility Requirements • Minimum age 18; open to freshmen, sophomores, juniors, seniors, graduate students, adults; 2.0 GPA; 1 letter of recommendation; no foreign language proficiency required.
Living Arrangements • Students live in hotels. Meals are taken as a group, on one's own, in central dining facility, in restaurants.
Costs (2006) • $3430; includes housing, some meals, insurance, excursions, international airfare, international student ID, instructional expenses. $150 application fee. Financial aid available for all students: scholarships.
For More Information • Ms. Nancy Martin, Coordinator, Kentucky Institute for International Studies, PO Box 9, Murray, KY 42071-0009; *Phone:* 270-762-3091; *Fax:* 270-762-3434. *E-mail:* kiismsu@murraystate.edu. *World Wide Web:* http://www.kiis.org/

STERLING COLLEGE
SUSTAINABLE JAPANESE SYSTEMS

Academic Focus • Agriculture, conservation studies, forestry, Japanese studies.
Program Information • Faculty members are drawn from the sponsor's U.S. staff and local instructors hired by the sponsor. Scheduled travel to managed forests, organic farms, zen gardens, Hokkaido University; field trips. Students typically earn 3 semester credits per term.
Sessions • Sep (2 weeks).
Eligibility Requirements • Minimum age 18; open to freshmen, sophomores, juniors, seniors, graduate students, adults; 2 letters of recommendation; good academic standing at home school; no foreign language proficiency required.
Living Arrangements • Students live in host family homes, hotels. Meals are taken as a group, with host family, in residences, in restaurants.
Costs (2005) • $3470; includes tuition, housing, all meals, excursions, international airfare, in-country transportation. $35 application fee. Financial aid available for all students: scholarships, loans.
For More Information • Mr. Erik Hansen, Director of Global Field Studies, Sterling College, PO Box 72, Craftsbury Common, VT 05827; *Phone:* 802-586-7711 Ext. 128; *Fax:* 802-586-2596. *E-mail:* admissions@ sterlingcollege.edu. *World Wide Web:* http://www.sterlingcollege.edu/

ASAHIKAWA

ILLINOIS STATE UNIVERSITY
ASAHIKAWA, JAPAN SUMMER PROGRAM

Hosted by Hokkaido University
Academic Focus • Education, Japanese studies.
Program Information • Students attend classes at Hokkaido University (Asahikawa, Japan). Field trips to local schools, cultural centers. Students typically earn 6 semester credits per term.
Sessions • May–Jun (summer).
Eligibility Requirements • Open to sophomores, juniors, seniors, graduate students; major in education preferred; 2.5 GPA; 2 letters of recommendation; good academic standing at home school; essay; no foreign language proficiency required.
Living Arrangements • Students live in host family homes. Quarters are shared with host institution students. Meals are taken with host family, in residences.
Costs (2005) • $3650; includes tuition, housing, all meals, insurance, excursions, international airfare, books and class materials, international student ID, student support services, personal expenses. $150 application fee. Financial aid available for students from sponsoring institution: scholarships, loans.
For More Information • Office of International Studies and Programs, Illinois State University, Campus Box 6120, Normal, IL 61790-6120; *Phone:* 309-438-5276; *Fax:* 309-438-3987. *E-mail:* oisp@ilstu.edu. *World Wide Web:* http://www.internationalstudies.ilstu.edu/

HIKONE

MICHIGAN STATE UNIVERSITY
MARKETING AND CULTURAL STUDIES IN JAPAN

Academic Focus • Interdisciplinary studies, Japanese studies, marketing.

Program Information • Faculty members are drawn from the sponsor's U.S. staff. Field trips to Kyoto, Osaka. Students typically earn 6 semester credits per term.

Sessions • May–Jun (summer).

Eligibility Requirements • Minimum age 18; open to juniors, seniors; major in business; 3.0 GPA; good academic standing at home school; essay; no foreign language proficiency required.

Living Arrangements • Students live in host institution dormitories, host family homes. Meals are taken on one's own, in restaurants.

Costs (2005) • $1862; includes housing, some meals, insurance, excursions, student support services. $100 application fee. $200 nonrefundable deposit required. Financial aid available for students from sponsoring institution: scholarships, loans.

For More Information • Ms. Darla Conley, Secretary, Michigan State University, Office of Study Abroad, 109 International Center, East Lansing, MI 48824-1035; *Phone:* 517-355-4654; *Fax:* 517-353-8727. *E-mail:* conleyd@msn.edu. *World Wide Web:* http://studyabroad.msu.edu/

HIRAKATA

UNIVERSITY OF ALABAMA
ALABAMA IN JAPAN

Held at Kansai Gaidai University

Academic Focus • Japanese, Japanese studies.

Program Information • Classes are held on the campus of Kansai Gaidai University (Hirakata City, Japan). Faculty members are drawn from the sponsor's U.S. staff and local instructors hired by the sponsor. Field trips to Osaka, Kyoto. Students typically earn 6 semester credits per term.

Sessions • Jun–Jul (summer).

Eligibility Requirements • Minimum age 18; open to freshmen, sophomores, juniors, seniors, graduate students; 2.5 GPA; good academic standing at home school; no foreign language proficiency required.

Living Arrangements • Students live in host institution dormitories. Meals are taken as a group, in restaurants.

Costs (2005) • $3000; includes tuition, housing, insurance, excursions, international airfare, international student ID, student support services. $100 application fee. $500 nonrefundable deposit required. Financial aid available for students from sponsoring institution: scholarships, work study, loans.

For More Information • Ms. Angela L. Channell, Director of Overseas Study, University of Alabama, Box 870254, Tuscaloosa, AL 35487-0254; *Phone:* 205-348-5256; *Fax:* 205-348-5298. *E-mail:* achannel@aalan.ua.edu. *World Wide Web:* http://www.overseas-study.ua.edu/

HIRATSUKA

UNIVERSITY OF KANSAS
EXPLORING CONTEMPORARY JAPAN

Hosted by Kanagawa University–Shonan Hiratsuka Campus

Academic Focus • Japanese, Japanese studies.

Program Information • Students attend classes at Kanagawa University–Shonan Hiratsuka Campus (Hiratsuka, Japan). Scheduled travel to Kyoto; field trips to Tokyo, local businesses and civic institutions, Kamakura. Students typically earn 6 semester credits per term.

Sessions • Jun–Jul (summer).

Eligibility Requirements • Minimum age 18; open to freshmen, sophomores, juniors, seniors, graduate students, adults; 2.5 GPA; 2 letters of recommendation; good academic standing at home school; no foreign language proficiency required.

Living Arrangements • Students live in host institution dormitories, host family homes. Quarters are shared with host institution students. Meals are taken as a group, on one's own, with host family, in residences, in central dining facility, in restaurants.

Costs (2005) • $4400; includes tuition, housing, some meals, excursions, student support services, emergency medical evacuation and repatriation service. $38 application fee. $300 nonrefundable deposit required. Financial aid available for students from sponsoring institution: scholarships, loans.

For More Information • Ms. Renée Frias, Program Coordinator, University of Kansas, Office of Study Abroad, Lippincott Hall, 1410 Jayhawk Boulevard, Room 108, Lawrence, KS 66045-7515; *Phone:* 785-864-3742; *Fax:* 785-864-5040. *E-mail:* osa@ku.edu. *World Wide Web:* http://www.ku.edu/~osa/

KOBE

CENTER FOR STUDY ABROAD (CSA)
SUMMER IN KOBE, JAPAN

Held at Kobe YMCA

Academic Focus • Japanese, Japanese studies.

Program Information • Classes are held on the campus of Kobe YMCA (Kobe, Japan). Faculty members are local instructors hired by the sponsor. Field trips to Kyoto, Nara, Osaka; optional travel. Students typically earn 4–10 semester credits per term.

Sessions • Classes begin weekly, year-round.

Eligibility Requirements • Minimum age 17; open to precollege students, freshmen, sophomores, juniors, seniors, graduate students, adults; no foreign language proficiency required.

Living Arrangements • Students live in host family homes. Meals are taken with host family.

Costs (2005) • Contact sponsor for cost. $45 application fee.

For More Information • Ms. Alima K. Virtue, Program Director, Center for Study Abroad (CSA), 325 Washington Avenue South #93, Kent, WA 98032; *Phone:* 206-726-1498; *Fax:* 253-850-0454. *E-mail:* info@centerforstudyabroad.com. *World Wide Web:* http://www.centerforstudyabroad.com/

UNIVERSITY OF DELAWARE
SUMMER SESSION IN KOBE, JAPAN

Held at Shoin University

Academic Focus • Japanese, Japanese studies.

Program Information • Classes are held on the campus of Shoin University (Kobe, Japan). Faculty members are drawn from the sponsor's U.S. staff and local instructors hired by the sponsor. Field trips to Kyoto, Mt. Rokko National Park, Nara, Osaka. Students typically earn 6–7 semester credits per term.

Sessions • May–Jul (summer).

Eligibility Requirements • Open to freshmen, sophomores, juniors, seniors, adults; 2.0 GPA; 1 letter of recommendation; no foreign language proficiency required.

Living Arrangements • Students live in host institution dormitories. Quarters are shared with host institution students. Meals are taken on one's own, in restaurants.

Costs (2005) • Contact sponsor for cost. $200 nonrefundable deposit required. Financial aid available for all students: scholarships.

For More Information • Center for International Studies, University of Delaware, 186 South College Avenue, Newark, DE 19716-1450; *Phone:* 888-831-4685; *Fax:* 302-831-6042. *E-mail:* studyabroad@udel.edu. *World Wide Web:* http://www.udel.edu/studyabroad/

SETO

BOWLING GREEN STATE UNIVERSITY
SUMMER STUDY IN JAPAN

Hosted by Nagoya Gakuin University

Academic Focus • Conservation studies, Japanese studies.

Program Information • Students attend classes at Nagoya Gakuin University (Seto, Japan). Scheduled travel to Kyoto, Nara, Hiroshima;

field trips to Kyoto, Nara, Nagoya, the Seto and Hiroshima areas; optional travel to Tokyo at an extra cost. Students typically earn 6 semester credits per term.
Sessions • Jul (summer).
Eligibility Requirements • Minimum age 18; open to freshmen, sophomores, juniors, seniors, graduate students; 2 letters of recommendation; 1 year college course work in Japanese or the equivalent.
Living Arrangements • Students live in host institution dormitories. Quarters are shared with host institution students. Meals are taken as a group, in central dining facility.
Costs (2005) • Contact sponsor for cost. Financial aid available for students from sponsoring institution: scholarships, loans.
For More Information • Akiko Kawano Jones, Lecturer and Director of the Program, Bowling Green State University, Department of German, Russian, and East Asian Languages, 103 Shatzel Hall, Bowling Green, OH 43403; *Phone:* 419-372-7136; *Fax:* 419-372-2571. *E-mail:* jakiko@bgnet.bgsu.edu. *World Wide Web:* http://www.bgsu.edu/

TOKYO

CIEE
CIEE STUDY CENTER AT SOPHIA UNIVERSITY, TOKYO, JAPAN
Hosted by Sophia University
Academic Focus • Art, art history, business administration/management, drama/theater, economics, history, Japanese, literature, political science and government, religious studies, sociology.
Program Information • Students attend classes at Sophia University (Tokyo, Japan). Field trips to local shrines, museums, traditional theater, Meiji shrine, Edo-Tokyo Museum, Noh; Kabuki. Students typically earn 6 semester credits per term.
Sessions • Jul–Aug (summer).
Eligibility Requirements • Minimum age 18; open to sophomores, juniors, seniors; 2.75 GPA; 1 letter of recommendation; good academic standing at home school; no foreign language proficiency required.
Living Arrangements • Students live in hotels. Meals are taken on one's own, in restaurants.
Costs (2006) • $4900; includes tuition, housing, insurance, excursions, student support services, on-site pick-up, resident director, orientation, local commuter pass, cultural activities, pre-departure advising. $30 application fee. $300 nonrefundable deposit required. Financial aid available for all students: scholarships, minority student scholarships, travel grants.
For More Information • Information Center, CIEE, 7 Customs House Street, 3rd Floor, Portland, ME 04101; *Phone:* 800-40-STUDY; *Fax:* 207-553-7699. *E-mail:* studyinfo@ciee.org. *World Wide Web:* http://www.ciee.org/isp/

COLLEGE CONSORTIUM FOR INTERNATIONAL STUDIES–LINCOLN UNIVERSITY OF PENNSYLVANIA
KCP INTERNATIONAL LANGUAGE INSTITUTE
Hosted by KCP International Language Institute
Academic Focus • Cultural studies, Japanese, Japanese studies.
Program Information • Students attend classes at KCP International Language Institute (Tokyo, Japan). Field trips; optional travel to Osaka (in-country), Korea, Thailand at an extra cost. Students typically earn 10-14 semester credits per term.
Sessions • Jul–Sep (summer), Jun–Aug (summer short).
Eligibility Requirements • Minimum age 18; open to freshmen, sophomores, juniors, seniors; 2.5 GPA; 1 letter of recommendation; transcript; some exposure to Hiragana.
Living Arrangements • Students live in host institution dormitories, host family homes. Quarters are shared with host institution students. Meals are taken on one's own, with host family, in residences, in central dining facility, in restaurants.
Costs (2006) • $6320–$6530 summer short-term: $5375–$5705; includes tuition, housing, insurance, excursions, books and class materials, on-site orientation, administration fees, airport pick-up,

half board for homestay, local transportation. $400 application fee. Financial aid available for students from sponsoring institution: scholarships, loans, grants.
For More Information • Ms. Myrtis Gray, Program Assistant/International Advisor, College Consortium for International Studies–Lincoln University of Pennsylvania, PO Box 179, MSC 50, Lincoln University, PA 19352; *Phone:* 610-932-8300 Ext. 3786; *Fax:* 610-998-6022. *E-mail:* mgray@lincoln.edu. *World Wide Web:* http://www.ccisabroad.org/

ILLINOIS STATE UNIVERSITY
SUMMER PROGRAM–TOKYO, JAPAN
Hosted by Chuo University
Academic Focus • International business, Japanese studies.
Program Information • Students attend classes at Chuo University (Tokyo, Japan). Field trips to cultural excursions and company visits. Students typically earn 6 semester credits per term.
Sessions • Jun–Jul (summer).
Eligibility Requirements • Open to sophomores, juniors, seniors; course work in business; 2.5 GPA; 2 letters of recommendation; good academic standing at home school; essay; no foreign language proficiency required.
Living Arrangements • Students live in host family homes. Quarters are shared with host institution students. Meals are taken as a group, with host family, in residences, in central dining facility.
Costs (2005) • $3978; includes tuition, housing, all meals, insurance, excursions, international airfare, international student ID, student support services, personal expenses. $150 application fee. Financial aid available for students from sponsoring institution: scholarships, loans.
For More Information • Study Abroad Coordinator, Illinois State University, Office of International Studies and Programs, Campus Box 6120, Normal, IL 61790-6120; *Phone:* 309-438-5276; *Fax:* 309-438-3987. *E-mail:* oisp@ilstu.edu. *World Wide Web:* http://www.internationalstudies.ilstu.edu/

KCP INTERNATIONAL LANGUAGE INSTITUTE
KCP INTERNATIONAL LANGUAGE INSTITUTE
Hosted by KCP International Language Institute
Academic Focus • Japanese, Japanese studies.
Program Information • Students attend classes at KCP International Language Institute (Tokyo, Japan). Scheduled travel to Kamakura, Hakone; field trips to a Sumo beya, museums, temples. Students typically earn 14 semester credits per term.
Sessions • Jul–Sep (summer), Jun–Aug (summer 2).
Eligibility Requirements • Minimum age 18; open to freshmen, sophomores, juniors, seniors, graduate students, adults; 2.5 GPA; 1 letter of recommendation; no foreign language proficiency required.
Living Arrangements • Students live in host institution dormitories, locally rented apartments, host family homes, hotels. Quarters are shared with host institution students, students from other programs. Meals are taken as a group, on one's own, with host family, in residences.
Costs (2003–2004) • $1800–$5500; includes tuition, housing, some meals, insurance, excursions, books and class materials, student support services. $350 application fee. Financial aid available for students: scholarships and loans for U.S. citizens.
For More Information • Mr. Mike Anderson, Director, KCP International Language Institute, PO Box 28028, Bellingham, WA 98228-0028; *Phone:* 360-441-1800; *Fax:* 360-647-0736. *E-mail:* mike@kcp-usa.com. *World Wide Web:* http://www.Lincoln-japan.com/

LANGUAGE LIAISON
LEARN JAPANESE IN JAPAN
Hosted by Language Liaison
Academic Focus • Japanese.
Program Information • Students attend classes at Language Liaison (Tokyo, Japan). Field trips; optional travel at an extra cost. Students typically earn 3-15 semester credits per term.
Sessions • New programs begin weekly, year-round.

Eligibility Requirements • Minimum age 18; open to precollege students, freshmen, sophomores, juniors, seniors, graduate students, adults; no foreign language proficiency required.

Living Arrangements • Students live in locally rented apartments, host family homes, hotels. Meals are taken on one's own, with host family, in residences, in restaurants.

Costs (2005) • Contact sponsor for cost. $175 application fee. Financial aid available for all students: scholarship research service.

For More Information • Ms. Nancy Forman, President, Language Liaison, PO Box 1772, Pacific Palisades, CA 90272; *Phone:* 800-284-4448; *Fax:* 310-454-1706. *E-mail:* learn@languageliaison. com. *World Wide Web:* http://www.languageliaison.com/

LINGUA SERVICE WORLDWIDE
VACATION 'N LEARN JAPANESE IN JAPAN

Hosted by L.I.C. Kokusai Gakuin

Academic Focus • Japanese, Japanese studies.

Program Information • Students attend classes at L.I.C. Kokusai Gakuin (Tokyo, Japan). Optional travel to cultural sites throughout Japan at an extra cost. Students typically earn 3 semester credits for 3 weeks, 6 semester credits for 5 weeks.

Sessions • Year-round.

Eligibility Requirements • Minimum age 18; open to freshmen, sophomores, juniors, seniors, graduate students, adults; no foreign language proficiency required.

Living Arrangements • Students live in host institution dormitories, locally rented apartments, host family homes, hotels. Meals are taken with host family.

Costs (2006–2007) • Contact sponsor for cost. $100 application fee.

For More Information • Assistant Director, Lingua Service Worldwide, 75 Prospect Street, Suite 4, Huntington, NY 11743; *Phone:* 800-394-5327; *Fax:* 631-271-3441. *E-mail:* linguaservice@att. net. *World Wide Web:* http://www.linguaserviceworldwide.com/

MICHIGAN STATE UNIVERSITY
PACKAGING IN JAPAN

Academic Focus • Packaging.

Program Information • Faculty members are drawn from the sponsor's U.S. staff. Field trips to company tours. Students typically earn 3 semester credits per term.

Sessions • Jun (summer), Program runs every other year.

Eligibility Requirements • Minimum age 18; open to sophomores, juniors, seniors, graduate students; course work in packaging; 2.35 GPA; good academic standing at home school; faculty approval; no foreign language proficiency required.

Living Arrangements • Students live in host institution dormitories. Meals are taken as a group, on one's own, in central dining facility, in restaurants.

Costs (2004) • $1906; includes housing, some meals, insurance, excursions, student support services. $100 application fee. $200 nonrefundable deposit required. Financial aid available for students from sponsoring institution: scholarships, loans.

For More Information • Ms. Darla Conley, Office Assistant, Michigan State University, Office of Study Abroad, 109 International Center, East Lansing, MI 48824-1035; *Phone:* 517-355-4654; *Fax:* 517-353-8727. *E-mail:* stackma1@msu.edu. *World Wide Web:* http:// studyabroad.msu.edu/

TEMPLE UNIVERSITY
TEMPLE UNIVERSITY JAPAN: ASIAN STUDIES SUMMER SESSION

Hosted by Temple University Japan

Academic Focus • Art history, Asian studies, Chinese language and literature, communications, history, Japanese, political science and government, religious studies.

Program Information • Students attend classes at Temple University Japan (Tokyo, Japan). Field trips to a visit to a Japanese high school and traditional castle in Odawara; optional travel to Kyoto, other Asian destinations at an extra cost. Students typically earn 6–12 semester credits per term.

Sessions • May–Aug (summer).

Eligibility Requirements • Minimum age 19; open to sophomores, juniors, seniors; 2.5 GPA; 1 letter of recommendation; good academic standing at home school; official transcripts; no foreign language proficiency required.

Living Arrangements • Students live in locally rented apartments, program-owned apartments. Quarters are shared with host institution students. Meals are taken on one's own, in residences.

Costs (2005) • $6100–$8400; includes tuition, housing. $30 application fee. $200 refundable deposit required. Financial aid available for students from sponsoring institution: scholarships, loans.

For More Information • Ms. Erin Joslyn, Study Abroad Coordinator, Temple University, International Programs, 200 Tuttleman Learning Center, 1809 North 13th Street, Philadelphia, PA 19122; *Phone:* 215-204-0720; *Fax:* 215-204-0729. *E-mail:* study.abroad@temple.edu. *World Wide Web:* http://www.temple.edu/studyabroad/

TEMPLE UNIVERSITY
TEMPLE UNIVERSITY JAPAN: CONTEMPORARY URBAN CULTURE WORKSHOP

Hosted by Temple University Japan

Academic Focus • Advertising and public relations, journalism.

Program Information • Students attend classes at Temple University Japan (Tokyo, Japan). Field trips to Tokyo. Students typically earn 6 semester credits per term.

Sessions • Jul–Aug (summer).

Eligibility Requirements • Open to sophomores, juniors, seniors, graduate students; 2.5 GPA; 1 letter of recommendation; good academic standing at home school; official transcript; no foreign language proficiency required.

Living Arrangements • Students live in program-owned apartments. Quarters are shared with host institution students. Meals are taken on one's own, in residences.

Costs (2005) • $3400–$5000; includes tuition, housing, program fee. $30 application fee. $200 nonrefundable deposit required. Financial aid available for students from sponsoring institution: scholarships, loans.

For More Information • Ms. Erin Joslyn, Study Abroad Coordinator, Temple University, International Programs, 200 Tuttleman Learning Center, 1809 North 13th Street, Philadelphia, PA 19122; *Phone:* 215-204-0720; *Fax:* 215-204-0729. *E-mail:* study.abroad@temple.edu. *World Wide Web:* http://www.temple.edu/studyabroad/

TEMPLE UNIVERSITY
TEMPLE UNIVERSITY JAPAN: GRAPHIC DESIGN AND DIGITAL PHOTOGRAPHY WORKSHOP

Hosted by Temple University Japan

Academic Focus • Architecture, art, art history, film and media studies.

Program Information • Students attend classes at Temple University Japan (Tokyo, Japan). Field trips to Tokyo, Kyoto. Students typically earn 6 semester credits per term.

Sessions • May–Jun (summer).

Eligibility Requirements • Open to sophomores, juniors, seniors, graduate students; major in art-related fields, design, media, architecture, critical studies; 2.5 GPA; 1 letter of recommendation; good academic standing at home school; official transcripts; no foreign language proficiency required.

Living Arrangements • Students live in program-owned apartments. Quarters are shared with host institution students. Meals are taken on one's own, in residences.

Costs (2005) • $3700–$5300; includes tuition, housing, excursions, program fee. $30 application fee. $200 nonrefundable deposit required. Financial aid available for students from sponsoring institution: scholarships, loans.

For More Information • Ms. Erin Joslyn, Study Abroad Coordinator, Temple University, International Programs, 200 Tuttleman Learning Center, 1809 North 13th Street, Philadelphia, PA 19122; *Phone:* 215-204-0720; *Fax:* 215-204-0729. *E-mail:* study.abroad@temple.edu. *World Wide Web:* http://www.temple.edu/studyabroad/

TEMPLE UNIVERSITY
TEMPLE UNIVERSITY JAPAN: VISUAL ANTHROPOLOGY

Hosted by Temple University Japan

Academic Focus • Anthropology, Asian studies.

Program Information • Students attend classes at Temple University Japan (Tokyo, Japan). Field trips. Students typically earn 6 semester credits per term.

Sessions • May–Jun (summer).

Eligibility Requirements • Minimum age 19; open to sophomores, juniors, seniors, graduate students; 2.5 GPA; 1 letter of recommendation; good academic standing at home school; official transcripts; no foreign language proficiency required.

Living Arrangements • Students live in locally rented apartments, program-owned apartments. Quarters are shared with host institution students. Meals are taken on one's own, in residences.

Costs (2005) • $3400–$5500; includes tuition, housing, program fee. $30 application fee. $200 nonrefundable deposit required. Financial aid available for students from sponsoring institution: scholarships, loans.

For More Information • Ms. Erin Joslyn, Study Abroad Coordinator, Temple University, International Programs, 200 Tuttleman Learning Center, 1809 North 13th Street, Philadelphia, PA 19122; *Phone:* 215-204-0720; *Fax:* 215-204-0729. *E-mail:* study.abroad@temple.edu. *World Wide Web:* http://www.temple.edu/studyabroad/

UNIVERSITY OF IDAHO
KCP INTERNATIONAL LANGUAGE INSTITUTE

Hosted by KCP International Language Institute

Academic Focus • Japanese, Japanese studies.

Program Information • Students attend classes at KCP International Language Institute (Tokyo, Japan). Field trips to Kamakura, the Edo-Tokyo Museum, Nikko, Asakusa Temple, the Imperial Palace, NHK Broadcasting Company, a Sumo beya, Kabuki and Bunraku theaters; optional travel to other cities in Japan at an extra cost. Students typically earn 12 semester credits per term.

Sessions • Jul–Sep (summer), Jun–Aug (summer 2).

Eligibility Requirements • Minimum age 18; open to freshmen, sophomores, juniors, seniors, graduate students, adults; 2.5 GPA; 1 letter of recommendation; good academic standing at home school; completion of 20 semester hours; no foreign language proficiency required.

Living Arrangements • Students live in host institution dormitories, host family homes. Quarters are shared with host institution students, students from other programs. Meals are taken on one's own, with host family, in residences, in central dining facility.

Costs (2006) • $5990–$6200 for regular term; $5375 for short term; includes tuition, housing, some meals, insurance, excursions, books and class materials, student support services, local transportation pass, airport pickup. $150 application fee. $325 nonrefundable deposit required. Financial aid available for all students: scholarships, loans.

For More Information • Ms. Kate Peterson, Program Advisor, University of Idaho, 901 Paradise Creek Street, LLC 3, Ground Floor, Moscow, ID 83844-1250; *Phone:* 208-885-4075; *Fax:* 208-885-2859. *E-mail:* abroad@uidaho.edu. *World Wide Web:* http://www.webs.uidaho.edu/ipo/abroad/

UNIVERSITY OF MIAMI
ASIAN STUDIES AT SOPHIA UNIVERSITY

Hosted by Sophia University

Academic Focus • Asian studies.

Program Information • Students attend classes at Sophia University (Tokyo, Japan). Field trips to a Meiji Shrine, the Nissan Motor Factory, the Supreme Court of Justice, the Edo-Tokyo Museum, Noh play, Kabuki theater. Students typically earn 6 semester credits per term.

Sessions • Jul–Aug (summer).

Eligibility Requirements • Minimum age 17; open to freshmen, sophomores, juniors, seniors; 3.0 GPA; 2 letters of recommendation; no foreign language proficiency required.

Living Arrangements • Students live in host institution dormitories, locally rented apartments, hotels. Quarters are shared with host institution students, students from other programs. Meals are taken on one's own, in restaurants.

Costs (2005) • $4320; includes tuition, excursions, student support services. $40 application fee. $500 nonrefundable deposit required. Financial aid available for students from sponsoring institution: loans.

For More Information • University of Miami, International Education and Exchange Programs, 5050 Brunson Drive, Allen Hall 212, PO Box 248005, Coral Gables, FL 33124-1610; *Phone:* 305-284-3434; *Fax:* 305-284-4235. *E-mail:* ieep@miami.edu. *World Wide Web:* http://www.studyabroad.miami.edu/

WESTERN WASHINGTON UNIVERSITY
KCP INTERNATIONAL LANGUAGE INSTITUTE

Held at KCP International Language Institute

Academic Focus • Japanese, Japanese studies.

Program Information • Classes are held on the campus of KCP International Language Institute (Tokyo, Japan). Faculty members are local instructors hired by the sponsor. Field trips to Kamakura, the Edo-Tokyo Museum, Nikko, Asakusa Temple, the Imperial Palace, NHK Broadcasting Company, a Sumo beya, Kabuki and Bunraku theaters; optional travel to historic sites outside Tokyo, Mount Fuji at an extra cost. Students typically earn 15–18 quarter credits per term.

Sessions • Jul–Sep (summer), Jun–Aug (summer 2).

Eligibility Requirements • Minimum age 18; open to freshmen, sophomores, juniors, seniors, graduate students, adults; 2.5 GPA; 1 letter of recommendation; good academic standing at home school; .5 years of Japanese or a knowledge of Hiragana and Katakana.

Living Arrangements • Students live in host institution dormitories, host family homes. Quarters are shared with host institution students, students from other programs. Meals are taken on one's own, with host family, in residences, in central dining facility.

Costs (2005) • $5251 summer short-term; $6076 summer with homestay; includes tuition, housing, some meals, insurance, excursions, books and class materials, lab equipment, student support services, train pass between the school and housing. $105 application fee. $200 refundable deposit required. Financial aid available for students from sponsoring institution: scholarships, loans.

For More Information • Mr. Mike P. Anderson, Director, KCP International U.S.A., Inc., Western Washington University, PO Box 28028, Bellingham, WA 98228-0028; *Phone:* 360-647-0072; *Fax:* 360-647-0736. *E-mail:* kcp@kcp-usa.com. *World Wide Web:* http://wwu.edu/~ipewwu/. Students may also apply through Western Washington University, Bellingham, WA 98225-9100.

ENYA

CITY-TO-CITY

MICHIGAN STATE UNIVERSITY
SOCIETY AND ECOLOGY IN KENYA

Academic Focus • African studies, biological/life sciences, geography, interdisciplinary studies, social sciences, zoology.

Program Information • Faculty members are drawn from the sponsor's U.S. staff and local instructors hired by the sponsor. Scheduled travel to Swara Plains Estate, Amboseli National Park, Watanu. Students typically earn 6 semester credits per term.

Sessions • May–Jun (summer).

Eligibility Requirements • Minimum age 18; open to sophomores, juniors, seniors, graduate students; 2.0 GPA; no foreign language proficiency required.

Living Arrangements • Students live in hotels, cabins; campsites. Meals are taken as a group, in central dining facility.

Costs (2005) • $3771; includes housing, all meals, insurance, excursions, student support services. $100 application fee. $200 nonrefundable deposit required. Financial aid available for all students: scholarships, loans.

For More Information • Ms. Cindy Felbeck Chalou, Assistant Director, Michigan State University, Office of Study Abroad, 109 International Center, East Lansing, MI 48824-1035; *Phone:* 517-432-4345; *Fax:* 517-432-2082. *E-mail:* chalouc@msu.edu. *World Wide Web:* http://studyabroad.msu.edu/

THE SCHOOL FOR FIELD STUDIES
KENYA: COMMUNITY WILDLIFE MANAGEMENT

Hosted by Center for Wildlife Management Studies

Academic Focus • African studies, biological/life sciences, conservation studies, ecology, economics, environmental science/studies, natural resources, wildlife studies.

Program Information • Students attend classes at Center for Wildlife Management Studies (Kilimanjaro Bush Camp), Center for Wildlife Management Studies (Nairobi National Park). Scheduled travel to the Masai Mara Wildlife Area; field trips to Amboseli and Tsavo National Park. Students typically earn 4 semester credits per term.

Sessions • Jun–Jul (summer), Jul–Aug (summer 2).

Eligibility Requirements • Minimum age 16; open to precollege students, freshmen, sophomores, juniors, seniors; 2.5 GPA; 2 letters of recommendation; personal statement; no foreign language proficiency required.

Living Arrangements • Students live in thatched-roof bandas. Quarters are shared with host institution students. Meals are taken as a group, in central dining facility.

Costs (2007) • $4115; includes tuition, housing, all meals, excursions. $45 application fee. $450 nonrefundable deposit required. Financial aid available for all students: scholarships, loans.

For More Information • Admissions Department, The School for Field Studies, 10 Federal Street, Suite 24, Salem, MA 01970-3876; *Phone:* 800-989-4418; *Fax:* 978-741-3551. *E-mail:* admissions@fieldstudies.org. *World Wide Web:* http://www.fieldstudies.org/

UNIVERSITY OF CALIFORNIA, SANTA BARBARA, WILDLANDS STUDIES
WILDLIFE AND CULTURES OF KENYA

Academic Focus • Ecology, environmental science/studies, geography, wildlife studies.

Program Information • Faculty members are drawn from the sponsor's U.S. staff. Scheduled travel to ecological field locations; field trips to ecological field locations. Students typically earn 15 quarter credits per term.

Sessions • Jun–Aug (summer).

Eligibility Requirements • Minimum age 18; open to freshmen, sophomores, juniors, seniors; course work in biology or geography; good academic standing at home school; application essay; no foreign language proficiency required.

Living Arrangements • Students live in host institution dormitories, host family homes, tents. Meals are taken as a group.

Costs (2006) • $1995; includes tuition. $75 application fee.

For More Information • Mr. Crandall Bay, Director, Wildlands Studies Program, University of California, Santa Barbara, Wildlands Studies, 3 Mosswood Circle, Cazadero, CA 95421; *Phone:* 707-632-5665; *Fax:* 707-632-5665. *E-mail:* wildlands@sonic.net. *World Wide Web:* http://www.wildlandsstudies.com/

MASAI MARA

MICHIGAN STATE UNIVERSITY
BEHAVIORAL ECOLOGY OF AFRICAN MAMMALS

Academic Focus • Zoology.

Program Information • Faculty members are drawn from the sponsor's U.S. staff. Students typically earn 6 semester credits per term.

Sessions • May–Jun (summer), Program runs every other year.

Eligibility Requirements • Minimum age 18; open to freshmen, sophomores, juniors, seniors, graduate students; major in biological studies; course work in zoology; 2.5 GPA; 1 letter of recommendation; good academic standing at home school; faculty approval; no foreign language proficiency required.

Living Arrangements • Students live in lodges; campsites. Meals are taken as a group, on one's own, in restaurants.

Costs (2005) • $3667; includes housing, some meals, insurance, excursions, student support services. $100 application fee. $200 nonrefundable deposit required. Financial aid available for all students: scholarships, loans.

For More Information • Ms. Cindy Felbeck Chalou, Assistant Director, Michigan State University, Office of Study Abroad, 109 International Center, East Lansing, MI 48824-1035; *Phone:* 517-432-4345; *Fax:* 517-432-2082. *E-mail:* chalouc@msu.edu. *World Wide Web:* http://studyabroad.msu.edu/

MOMBASA

RUTGERS, THE STATE UNIVERSITY OF NEW JERSEY
SUMMER STUDY IN KENYA–SWAHILI FIELD SCHOOL

Academic Focus • African studies, Swahili.

Program Information • Faculty members are drawn from the sponsor's U.S. staff and local instructors hired by the sponsor. Scheduled travel to Nairobi, Mombara, Malinidi, Lamu; field trips to Nairobi, Mombosa, Malinidi, Lamu. Students typically earn 6 semester credits per term.

Sessions • Jul–Aug (summer).

Eligibility Requirements • Open to freshmen, sophomores, juniors, seniors; 2.5 GPA; 1 letter of recommendation; good academic standing at home school; official transcripts from all tertiary schools attended; no foreign language proficiency required.

Living Arrangements • Students live in host institution dormitories, host family homes, hotels. Quarters are shared with host institution students. Meals are taken as a group, in residences.

Costs (2006) • $3750 for New Jersey residents; $4250 for nonresidents; includes tuition, housing, insurance, excursions, student support services. $20 application fee. $500 nonrefundable deposit required. Financial aid available for students from sponsoring institution: scholarships, loans.

For More Information • Ms. Lindy Black, Regional Coordinator, Rutgers, The State University of New Jersey, 102 College Avenue, New Brunswick, NJ 08901; *Phone:* 732-932-7787; *Fax:* 732-932-8659. *E-mail:* ru_abroad@email.rutgers.edu. *World Wide Web:* http://studyabroad.rutgers.edu/

NAIROBI

JAMES MADISON UNIVERSITY
SUMMER IN KENYA

Academic Focus • Anthropology.

Program Information • Faculty members are drawn from the sponsor's U.S. staff. Scheduled travel; field trips. Students typically earn 6 semester credits per term.

Sessions • May–Jun (summer).

Eligibility Requirements • Minimum age 18; open to sophomores, juniors, seniors, graduate students, adults; 2.0 GPA; good academic standing at home school; no foreign language proficiency required.

Living Arrangements • Students live in a camp. Meals are taken as a group, on one's own, in central dining facility, in restaurants.

Costs (2005) • $3608 for Virginia residents; $5288 for nonresidents; includes tuition, housing, all meals, excursions, books and class materials, international student ID, student support services. $400 nonrefundable deposit required.

For More Information • Mr. Felix Wang, Director, James Madison University, Office of International Programs, MSC 5731, 1077 South Main Street, Harrisonburg, VA 22807; *Phone:* 540-568-6419; *Fax:* 540-568-3310. *E-mail:* studyabroad@jmu.edu. *World Wide Web:* http://www.jmu.edu/international/

KNOWLEDGE EXCHANGE INSTITUTE (KEI)
AFRICAN BUSINESS, LAW, AND DIPLOMACY

Hosted by United States International University–Nairobi

Academic Focus • Accounting, advertising and public relations, African languages and literature, African studies, business administration/management, commerce, communication services, communications, economics, entrepreneurship, finance, human resources, information science, international affairs, international business, labor and industrial relations, law and legal studies, liberal studies, management information systems, marketing, peace and conflict studies, political science and government, public administration, public policy, Swahili.

Program Information • Students attend classes at United States International University–Nairobi (Nairobi, Kenya). Scheduled travel to Mombassa, Mt. Kilimanjaro, safaris in Kenya; field trips to Nairobi City, Nairobi National Park. Students typically earn 15 semester credits per term.

Sessions • May–Aug (summer).

Eligibility Requirements • Open to freshmen, sophomores, juniors, seniors, graduate students, adults; 2.2 GPA; 2 letters of recommendation; good academic standing at home school; no foreign language proficiency required.

Living Arrangements • Students live in host institution dormitories. Quarters are shared with host institution students, students from other programs. Meals are taken on one's own, in central dining facility, in restaurants.

Costs (2006) • $5977; includes tuition, housing, insurance, excursions, books and class materials, lab equipment, student support services, mobile telephone, internet access. $50 application fee. $500 nonrefundable deposit required. Financial aid available for all students: scholarships, loans.

For More Information • Mr. Eduard Izraylovsky, Director, Knowledge Exchange Institute (KEI), 111 John Street, Suite 800, New York, NY 10038; *Phone:* 800-831-5095; *Fax:* 212-528-2095. *E-mail:* info@knowledgeexchange.org. *World Wide Web:* http://www.knowledgeexchange.org/

KNOWLEDGE EXCHANGE INSTITUTE (KEI)
AFRICAN STUDIES AND SWAHILI LANGUAGE

Hosted by United States International University–Nairobi

Academic Focus • African languages and literature, African studies, anthropology, archaeology, biological/life sciences, business administration/management, civilization studies, communications, community service, comparative literature, computer science, conservation studies, creative writing, cultural studies, earth sciences, ecology, economics, English, English literature, environmental health, environmental science/studies, ethics, health and physical education, history, information science, intercultural studies, interdisciplinary studies, international affairs, liberal studies, literature, natural resources, parks and recreation, peace and conflict studies, philosophy, political science and government, popular culture, science, social sciences, social work, sociology, statistics, Swahili, Turkish, wildlife studies.

Program Information • Students attend classes at United States International University–Nairobi (Nairobi, Kenya). Scheduled travel to Mombassa, Mt. Kilimanjaro, safaris in Kenya; field trips to Nairobi City, Nairobi National Park. Students typically earn 15 semester credits per term.

Sessions • May–Aug (summer).

Eligibility Requirements • Open to freshmen, sophomores, juniors, seniors, graduate students, adults; 2.2 GPA; 2 letters of recommendation; good academic standing at home school; no foreign language proficiency required.

KENYA
Nairobi

Living Arrangements • Students live in host institution dormitories. Quarters are shared with host institution students, students from other programs. Meals are taken on one's own, in central dining facility, in restaurants.

Costs (2006) • $5977; includes tuition, housing, insurance, excursions, books and class materials, lab equipment, student support services, mobile telephone, internet access. $50 application fee. $500 nonrefundable deposit required. Financial aid available for all students: scholarships, loans.

For More Information • Mr. Eduard Izraylovsky, Director, Knowledge Exchange Institute (KEI), 111 John Street, Suite 800, New York, NY 10038; *Phone:* 800-831-5095; *Fax:* 212-528-2095. *E-mail:* info@knowledgeexchange.org. *World Wide Web:* http://www.knowledgeexchange.org/

KNOWLEDGE EXCHANGE INSTITUTE (KEI)
AFRICAN TOURISM AND HOSPITALITY

Hosted by United States International University–Nairobi

Academic Focus • Advertising and public relations, African languages and literature, African studies, business administration/management, commerce, cultural studies, economics, finance, hospitality services, hotel and restaurant management, intercultural studies, interdisciplinary studies, international business, liberal studies, marketing, Swahili, tourism and travel.

Program Information • Students attend classes at United States International University-Nairobi (Nairobi, Kenya). Scheduled travel to Mombassa, Mt. Kilimanjaro, safaris in Kenya; field trips to Nairobi City, Nairobi National Park. Students typically earn 15 semester credits per term.

Sessions • May–Aug (summer).

Eligibility Requirements • Open to freshmen, sophomores, juniors, seniors, adults; 2.2 GPA; 2 letters of recommendation; good academic standing at home school; no foreign language proficiency required.

Living Arrangements • Students live in host institution dormitories. Quarters are shared with host institution students, students from other programs. Meals are taken on one's own, in central dining facility, in restaurants.

Costs (2006) • $5977; includes tuition, housing, insurance, excursions, books and class materials, lab equipment, student support services, mobile telephone, internet access. $50 application fee. $500 nonrefundable deposit required. Financial aid available for all students: scholarships, loans.

For More Information • Mr. Eduard Izraylovsky, Director, Knowledge Exchange Institute (KEI), 111 John Street, Suite 800, New York, NY 10038; *Phone:* 800-831-5095; *Fax:* 212-528-2095. *E-mail:* info@knowledgeexchange.org. *World Wide Web:* http://www.knowledgeexchange.org/

KNOWLEDGE EXCHANGE INSTITUTE (KEI)
JOURNALISM AND MASS MEDIA

Hosted by United States International University–Nairobi

Academic Focus • African languages and literature, African studies, cinematography, communication services, communications, comparative literature, creative writing, cultural studies, English, English literature, intercultural studies, interdisciplinary studies, journalism, liberal studies, literature, photography, radio, speech communication, Swahili, telecommunications.

Program Information • Students attend classes at United States International University-Nairobi (Nairobi, Kenya). Scheduled travel to Mombassa, Mt. Kilimanjaro, safaris in Kenya; field trips to Nairobi City, Nairobi National Park. Students typically earn 15 semester credits per term.

Sessions • May–Aug (summer).

Eligibility Requirements • Open to freshmen, sophomores, juniors, seniors, graduate students, adults; 2.2 GPA; 2 letters of recommendation; good academic standing at home school; no foreign language proficiency required.

Living Arrangements • Students live in host institution dormitories. Quarters are shared with host institution students, students from other programs. Meals are taken on one's own, in residences, in central dining facility, in restaurants.

Costs (2006) • $5977; includes tuition, housing, insurance, excursions, books and class materials, lab equipment, student

support services, mobile telephone, internet access. $50 application fee. $500 nonrefundable deposit required. Financial aid available for all students: scholarships, loans.

For More Information • Mr. Eduard Izraylovsky, Director, Knowledge Exchange Institute (KEI), 111 John Street, Suite 800, New York, NY 10038; *Phone:* 800-831-5095; *Fax:* 212-528-2095. *E-mail:* info@knowledgeexchange.org. *World Wide Web:* http://www.knowledgeexchange.org/

KNOWLEDGE EXCHANGE INSTITUTE (KEI)
NAIROBI INTERNSHIP PROGRAM

Hosted by United States International University–Nairobi

Academic Focus • Accounting, actuarial science, advertising and public relations, African studies, anthropology, brokerage, business administration/management, commerce, communication services, communications, community service, computer science, conservation studies, criminal justice, cultural studies, economics, entrepreneurship, environmental health, environmental science/studies, ethnic studies, finance, health-care management, hospitality services, hotel and restaurant management, human resources, information science, intercultural studies, interdisciplinary studies, international affairs, international business, journalism, law and legal studies, management information systems, medicine, natural resources, nutrition, parks and recreation, peace and conflict studies, political science and government, premedical studies, public administration, public health, radio, social services, social work, Swahili, tourism and travel, veterinary science.

Program Information • Students attend classes at United States International University-Nairobi (Nairobi, Kenya). Scheduled travel to Mombassa, safari; field trips to Nairobi. Students typically earn 6 semester credits per term.

Sessions • Jun–Aug (summer).

Eligibility Requirements • Open to freshmen, sophomores, juniors, seniors, graduate students, adults; 2.2 GPA; 2 letters of recommendation; good academic standing at home school; no foreign language proficiency required.

Living Arrangements • Students live in host institution dormitories, program-owned apartments, host family homes. Quarters are shared with host institution students, students from other programs. Meals are taken on one's own, with host family, in residences, in restaurants.

Costs (2006) • $4350; includes tuition, housing, insurance, excursions, student support services, mobile telephone. $50 application fee. $500 nonrefundable deposit required. Financial aid available for students: scholarships, loans.

For More Information • Mr. Eduard Izraylovsky, Director, Knowledge Exchange Institute (KEI), 111 John Street, Suite 800, New York, NY 10038; *Phone:* 800-831-5095; *Fax:* 212-528-2095. *E-mail:* info@knowledgeexchange.org. *World Wide Web:* http://www.knowledgeexchange.org/

KNOWLEDGE EXCHANGE INSTITUTE (KEI)
PSYCHOLOGY, SOCIOLOGY, AND HUMAN BEHAVIOR

Hosted by United States International University–Nairobi

Academic Focus • African languages and literature, African studies, community service, cultural studies, health-care management, intercultural studies, interdisciplinary studies, liberal studies, premedical studies, psychology, public health, science, social sciences, social services, social work, sociology, statistics, Swahili.

Program Information • Students attend classes at United States International University-Nairobi (Nairobi, Kenya). Scheduled travel to Mombassa, Mt. Kilimanjaro, safaris in Kenya; field trips to Nairobi City, Nairobi National Park. Students typically earn 15 semester credits per term.

Sessions • May–Aug (summer).

Eligibility Requirements • Open to freshmen, sophomores, juniors, seniors, graduate students, adults; 2.2 GPA; 2 letters of recommendation; good academic standing at home school; no foreign language proficiency required.

Living Arrangements • Students live in host institution dormitories. Quarters are shared with host institution students, students from other programs. Meals are taken on one's own, in central dining facility, in restaurants.

Costs (2006) • $5977; includes tuition, housing, insurance, excursions, books and class materials, lab equipment, student support services, mobile telephone, internet access. $50 application fee. $500 nonrefundable deposit required. Financial aid available for all students: scholarships, loans.

For More Information • Mr. Eduard Izraylovsky, Director, Knowledge Exchange Institute (KEI), 111 John Street, Suite 800, New York, NY 10038; *Phone:* 800-831-5095; *Fax:* 212-528-2095. *E-mail:* info@knowledgeexchange.org. *World Wide Web:* http://www.knowledgeexchange.org/

RUTGERS, THE STATE UNIVERSITY OF NEW JERSEY
SUMMER STUDY PROGRAM AT KOOBI FORA FIELD SCHOOL IN KENYA

Academic Focus • Anthropology, archaeology.

Program Information • Faculty members are drawn from the sponsor's U.S. staff. Students typically earn 8 semester credits per term.

Sessions • Jun–Jul (summer).

Eligibility Requirements • Open to freshmen, sophomores, juniors, seniors, graduate students; 2.5 GPA; 1 letter of recommendation; good academic standing at home school; official transcript from all tertiary schools attended; no foreign language proficiency required.

Living Arrangements • Students live in campsites. Meals are taken as a group, in central dining facility.

Costs (2005) • $4590 for New Jersey residents; $5130 for nonresidents; includes tuition, housing, all meals, insurance, student support services. $20 application fee. $500 nonrefundable deposit required. Financial aid available for students from sponsoring institution: scholarships, loans.

For More Information • Ms. Lindy Black, Regional Coordinator, Rutgers, The State University of New Jersey, 102 College Avenue, New Brunswick, NJ 08901-8543; *Phone:* 732-932-7787; *Fax:* 732-932-8659. *E-mail:* ru_abroad@email.rutgers.edu. *World Wide Web:* http://studyabroad.rutgers.edu/

WIDENER UNIVERSITY SCHOOL OF LAW
NAIROBI, KENYA SUMMER LAW INSTITUTE

Hosted by University of Nairobi

Academic Focus • Law and legal studies.

Program Information • Students attend classes at University of Nairobi (Nairobi, Kenya). Field trips to safaris; optional travel at an extra cost. Students typically earn 6 semester credits per term.

Sessions • Jun–Jul (summer).

Eligibility Requirements • Open to graduate students; good academic standing at home school; students must be enrolled in an accredited law school or be a law school graduate; no foreign language proficiency required.

Living Arrangements • Students live in locally rented apartments. Quarters are shared with students from other programs. Meals are taken on one's own, in residences, in restaurants.

Costs (2005) • $7800; includes tuition, housing, some meals, international airfare, books and class materials, student support services. $100 application fee. Financial aid available for all students: loans.

For More Information • Ms. Peggie Wyant, Coordinator, International Programs, Widener University School of Law, 4601 Concord Pike, Room 418 Law Building, Wilmington, DE 19803; *Phone:* 302-477-2248; *Fax:* 302-477-2257. *E-mail:* mawyant@mail.widener.edu. *World Wide Web:* http://www.law.widener.edu/go/summer/

KOREA

BUCHEON CITY

SAINT MARY'S COLLEGE
SOUTH KOREA CULTURAL STUDY

Hosted by Catholic University
Academic Focus • Korean, Korean Studies.
Program Information • Students attend classes at Catholic University (Bucheon City, Korea). Field trips to Seoul. Students typically earn 3 semester credits per term.
Sessions • May–Jun (summer).
Eligibility Requirements • Minimum age 18; open to freshmen, sophomores, juniors, seniors; 2.5 GPA; 3 letters of recommendation; good academic standing at home school; no foreign language proficiency required.
Living Arrangements • Students live in host institution dormitories, host family homes. Quarters are shared with students from other programs. Meals are taken in central dining facility, in restaurants.
Costs (2005) • $3000; includes tuition, housing, all meals, excursions, student support services. $30 application fee.
For More Information • Dr. Insook Chung, Faculty Coordinator, Saint Mary's College, Department of Education, Notre Dame, IN 46556; *Phone:* 574-284-4467; *Fax:* 574-284-4141. *E-mail:* ichung@saintmarys.edu. *World Wide Web:* http://www.saintmarys.edu/~cwil

SEOUL

NORTHERN ARIZONA UNIVERSITY
SUMMER STUDY ABROAD IN KOREA

Hosted by Seoul Women's University
Academic Focus • Korean Studies.
Program Information • Students attend classes at Seoul Women's University (Seoul, Korea). Scheduled travel to a host family weekend stay; field trips to Gyeongbok Palace, Insadong, Dongdaemun, Myong dong, Cheon, Gyeong, Panmonjeon. Students typically earn 6 semester credits per term.
Sessions • Jul (summer).
Eligibility Requirements • Minimum age 18; open to sophomores, juniors, seniors, graduate students, adults; 2.5 GPA; 2 letters of recommendation; good academic standing at home school; no foreign language proficiency required.
Living Arrangements • Students live in host institution dormitories. Quarters are shared with host institution students. Meals are taken as a group, in central dining facility.
Costs (2005) • $1022; includes tuition, housing, all meals, excursions, books and class materials, international student ID, student support services. $125 application fee. Financial aid available for all students: loans.
For More Information • Mr. Matthew Geisler, International Office, Northern Arizona University, NAU Box 5598, Flagstaff, AZ 86011-5598; *Phone:* 928-523-2409; *Fax:* 928-523-9489. *E-mail:* international.office@nau.edu. *World Wide Web:* http://internationaloffice.nau.edu/

UNIVERSITY AT ALBANY, STATE UNIVERSITY OF NEW YORK
LANGUAGE AND CULTURAL STUDIES IN ENGLISH AT YONSEI UNIVERSITY

Hosted by Yonsei University Seoul
Academic Focus • Business administration/management, communications, economics, Korean, Korean Studies, philosophy, sociology.
Program Information • Students attend classes at Yonsei University Seoul (Seoul, Korea). Optional travel at an extra cost. Students typically earn 6–9 semester credits per term.
Sessions • Jun–Aug (summer).
Eligibility Requirements • Open to sophomores, juniors, seniors; 2.5 GPA; 2 letters of recommendation; no foreign language proficiency required.
Living Arrangements • Students live in host institution dormitories. Meals are taken on one's own, in central dining facility, in restaurants.
Costs (2005) • Contact sponsor for cost. $150 nonrefundable deposit required. Financial aid available for students from sponsoring institution: all customary sources.
For More Information • University at Albany, State University of New York, Office of International Education, LI 66, Albany, NY 12222; *Phone:* 518-442-3525; *Fax:* 518-442-3338. *E-mail:* intled@uamail.albany.edu. *World Wide Web:* http://www.albany.edu/studyabroad/

UNIVERSITY OF PENNSYLVANIA
PENN-IN-SEOUL

Hosted by Kyung Hee University

Academic Focus • Economics, social sciences.

Program Information • Students attend classes at Kyung Hee University (Seoul, Korea). Field trips to cultural sites throughout Seoul. Students typically earn 2 course units per term.

Sessions • Jun–Jul (summer).

Eligibility Requirements • Open to freshmen, sophomores, juniors, seniors, graduate students; 1 letter of recommendation; good academic standing at home school; no foreign language proficiency required.

Living Arrangements • Students live in host institution dormitories, locally rented apartments. Meals are taken as a group, in central dining facility.

Costs (2005) • $5000; includes tuition, some meals, insurance, housing during academic portion. $50 application fee. $300 nonrefundable deposit required. Financial aid available for students from sponsoring institution: scholarships, loans.

For More Information • Penn Summer Abroad, University of Pennsylvania, 3440 Market Street, Suite 100, Philadelphia, PA 19104-3335; *Phone:* 215-746-6900; *Fax:* 215-573-2053. *E-mail:* summerabroad@sas.upenn.edu. *World Wide Web:* http://www.sas.upenn.edu/summer/

UNIVERSITY STUDIES ABROAD CONSORTIUM
INTERNATIONAL BUSINESS AND EAST ASIAN STUDIES: SEOUL, KOREA

Hosted by Yonsei University Seoul

Academic Focus • East Asian studies, international affairs, international business, Korean.

Program Information • Students attend classes at Yonsei University Seoul (Seoul, Korea). Optional travel to Seoul and surrounding areas at an extra cost. Students typically earn 6 semester credits per term.

Sessions • Jun–Aug (summer).

Eligibility Requirements • Minimum age 18; open to juniors, seniors, graduate students, adults; 2.7 GPA; no foreign language proficiency required.

Living Arrangements • Students live in host institution dormitories, locally rented apartments. Quarters are shared with host institution students. Meals are taken on one's own, in central dining facility.

Costs (2007) • $3450; includes tuition, insurance, 5-week internship. $100 application fee. $200 refundable deposit required. Financial aid available for all students: scholarships, loans.

For More Information • University Studies Abroad Consortium, USAC/323, Reno, NV 89557-0093; *Phone:* 775-784-6569; *Fax:* 775-784-6010. *E-mail:* usac@unr.edu. *World Wide Web:* http://usac.unr.edu/

TAEJON

NORTHERN ARIZONA UNIVERSITY
SUMMER STUDY ABROAD IN KOREA

Hosted by Woosong University

Academic Focus • Korean Studies.

Program Information • Students attend classes at Woosong University (Taejon, Korea). Scheduled travel to Paechon Beach, Kyeongju, a homestay with a Korean family; field trips to Independence Hall, Donghakas Temple, Poolee Park, Buyeo National Museum. Students typically earn 4 semester credits per term.

Sessions • Jul (summer).

Eligibility Requirements • Minimum age 18; open to sophomores, juniors, seniors, graduate students, adults; 2.5 GPA; 2 letters of recommendation; good academic standing at home school; no foreign language proficiency required.

Living Arrangements • Students live in host institution dormitories, host family homes. Quarters are shared with host institution students. Meals are taken as a group, in central dining facility.

Costs (2005) • $1132; includes tuition, housing, all meals, excursions, books and class materials, international student ID, student support services. $125 application fee. Financial aid available for all students: loans.

For More Information • Mr. Matthew Geisler, International Office, Northern Arizona University, NAU Box 5598, Flagstaff, AZ 86011-5598; *Phone:* 928-523-2409; *Fax:* 928-523-9489. *E-mail:* international.office@nau.edu. *World Wide Web:* http://internationaloffice.nau.edu/

MALAYSIA

KUALA LUMPUR

BEMIDJI STATE UNIVERSITY
SEMESTER BREAK IN MALAYSIA

Hosted by HELP Institute

Academic Focus • Anthropology, economics, geography, history, international affairs, political science and government.

Program Information • Students attend classes at HELP Institute (Kuala Lumpur, Malaysia). Scheduled travel to the Taman Negara Rain Forest, Bangkok, Thailand; field trips to the Klang Valley, north Malaysia, Malacca, Kuala Lumpur, University of Putra, Genting Highlands, Singapore. Students typically earn 6 semester credits per term.

Sessions • Dec–Jan (winter).

Eligibility Requirements • Minimum age 18; open to sophomores, juniors, seniors, graduate students, adults; 2.0 GPA; good academic standing at home school; sophomore status; no foreign language proficiency required.

Living Arrangements • Students live in locally rented apartments, host family homes, hotels. Meals are taken as a group, in restaurants.

Costs (2005–2006) • $3500; includes housing, all meals, excursions, international airfare, student support services. $150 nonrefundable deposit required. Financial aid available for students from sponsoring institution: scholarships, loans, grants.

For More Information • Ms. LaMae Ritchie, Director, International Program Center, Bemidji State University, Deputy Hall 103, Box 13, 1500 Birchmont Drive, NE, Bemidji, MN 56601-2699; *Phone:* 218-755-4096; *Fax:* 218-755-2074. *E-mail:* lritchie@bemidjistate.edu. *World Wide Web:* http://www.bemidjistate.edu/international/study_abroad.htm

$\mathcal{M}$ALI

BAMAKO

DREW UNIVERSITY
DREW IN WEST AFRICA

Academic Focus • Anthropology, art.
Program Information • Faculty members are drawn from the sponsor's U.S. staff and local instructors hired by the sponsor. Scheduled travel to Mopti, Timbuctu, Segou. Students typically earn 8 semester credits per term.
Sessions • Jul–Aug (summer).
Eligibility Requirements • Open to freshmen, sophomores, juniors, seniors, graduate students, adults; 1 letter of recommendation; good academic standing at home school; no foreign language proficiency required.
Living Arrangements • Students live in hotels. Meals are taken on one's own, in restaurants.
Costs (2004–2005) • $5250; includes tuition, housing, some meals, excursions, international airfare. $25 application fee. $300 nonrefundable deposit required. Financial aid available for all students: scholarships.
For More Information • Mr. Carlo Colecchia, Director, Drew University, International and Off-Campus Programs, 36 Madison Avenue, Madison, NJ 07940; *Phone:* 973-408-3438; *Fax:* 973-408-3768. *E-mail:* intiprog@drew.edu. *World Wide Web:* http://www.depts.drew.edu/offcamp/

MICHIGAN STATE UNIVERSITY
ETHICS AND DEVELOPMENT IN MALI

Academic Focus • Agriculture, ethics, interdisciplinary studies, philosophy, social sciences.
Program Information • Faculty members are drawn from the sponsor's U.S. staff and local instructors hired by the sponsor. Scheduled travel to cities, villages, scenic attractions; field trips to cultural destinations. Students typically earn 6 semester credits per term.
Sessions • Jul–Aug (summer), Program only runs in even-numbered years.
Eligibility Requirements • Minimum age 18; open to sophomores, juniors, seniors, graduate students; 2.0 GPA; no foreign language proficiency required.
Living Arrangements • Students live in host institution dormitories, hotels. Meals are taken as a group, in central dining facility, in restaurants.
Costs (2004) • $2377; includes housing, some meals, insurance, excursions, student support services. $100 application fee. $200 nonrefundable deposit required. Financial aid available for all students: scholarships, loans.
For More Information • Ms. Cindy Felbeck Chalou, Assistant Director, Michigan State University, Office of Study Abroad, 109 International Center, East Lansing, MI 48824-1035; *Phone:* 517-432-4345; *Fax:* 517-432-2082. *E-mail:* chalouc@msu.edu. *World Wide Web:* http://studyabroad.msu.edu/

 # MALTA

CITY-TO-CITY

JAMES MADISON UNIVERSITY
SUMMER IN MALTA

Hosted by University of Malta

Academic Focus • Engineering, environmental science/studies.

Program Information • Students attend classes at University of Malta (Msida). Field trips to Maltese villages. Students typically earn 4 semester credits per term.

Sessions • May–Jun (summer).

Eligibility Requirements • Minimum age 18; open to sophomores, juniors, seniors; major in energy technology (environmental engineering); 2.0 GPA; 1 letter of recommendation; good academic standing at home school; no foreign language proficiency required.

Living Arrangements • Students live in host institution dormitories. Quarters are shared with host institution students. Meals are taken as a group, on one's own, in central dining facility, in restaurants.

Costs (2005) • $2772 for Virginia residents; $3892 for nonresidents; includes tuition, housing, some meals, excursions, international student ID. $400 nonrefundable deposit required.

For More Information • Mr. Felix Wang, Director, James Madison University, Office of International Programs, MSC 5731, 1077 South Main Street, Harrisonburg, VA 22807; *Phone:* 540-568-6419; *Fax:* 540-568-3310. *E-mail:* studyabroad@jmu.edu. *World Wide Web:* http://www.jmu.edu/international/

 ARTINIQUE

CITY-TO-CITY

UNIVERSITY OF DELAWARE
WINTER SESSION IN MARTINIQUE

Held at University of the Antilles and Guyane

Academic Focus • French language and literature.

Program Information • Classes are held on the campus of University of the Antilles and Guyane (Fort-de-France). Faculty members are drawn from the sponsor's U.S. staff and local instructors hired by the sponsor. Field trips to La Caravelle, Sainte-Anne, Mont-Pele, a sugar plantation. Students typically earn 6–7 semester credits per term.

Sessions • Jan–Feb (winter).

Eligibility Requirements • Open to freshmen, sophomores, juniors, seniors, adults; 2.0 GPA; 1 letter of recommendation; no foreign language proficiency required.

Living Arrangements • Students live in host family homes. Quarters are shared with host institution students. Meals are taken with host family, in residences.

Costs (2005) • Contact sponsor for cost. $200 nonrefundable deposit required. Financial aid available for all students: scholarships.

For More Information • Center for International Studies, University of Delaware, 186 South College Avenue, Newark, DE 19716-1450; *Phone:* 888-831-4685; *Fax:* 302-831-6042. *E-mail:* studyabroad@udel.edu. *World Wide Web:* http://www.udel.edu/studyabroad/

$\mathcal{M}$EXICO

CITY-TO-CITY

LANGUAGE LIAISON
SPANISH IN MEXICO–CUERNAVACA

Hosted by Language Liaison
Academic Focus • Full curriculum.
Program Information • Students attend classes at Language Liaison (Cuernavaca). Field trips; optional travel at an extra cost. Students typically earn 3-15 semester credits per term.
Sessions • New programs begin weekly, year-round.
Eligibility Requirements • Minimum age 13; open to precollege students, freshmen, sophomores, juniors, seniors, graduate students, adults; no foreign language proficiency required.
Living Arrangements • Students live in locally rented apartments, program-owned apartments, program-owned houses, host family homes, hotels. Meals are taken on one's own, with host family, in residences, in restaurants.
Costs (2005) • Contact sponsor for cost. $175 application fee. Financial aid available for all students: scholarship research service.
For More Information • Ms. Nancy Forman, President, Language Liaison, PO Box 1772, Pacific Palisades, CA 90272; *Phone:* 800-284-4448; *Fax:* 310-454-1706. *E-mail:* learn@languageliaison.com. *World Wide Web:* http://www.languageliaison.com/

LIVING ROUTES–STUDY ABROAD IN ECOVILLAGES
LIVING ROUTES–MEXICO: LEADERSHIP FOR SOCIAL JUSTICE AT HUEHUECOYOTL

Hosted by Huehuecoyotl Ecovillage
Academic Focus • Agriculture, communications, community service, conservation studies, ecology, environmental health, environmental science/studies, interdisciplinary studies, peace and conflict studies, social sciences, urban/regional planning.
Program Information • Students attend classes at Huehuecoyotl Ecovillage (Mexico City). Field trips to Aztec ruins, Mexican Revolutionary sites, Indigenous villages. Students typically earn 4 semester credits per term.
Sessions • Jan (winter).
Eligibility Requirements • Minimum age 17; open to precollege students, freshmen, sophomores, juniors, seniors, graduate students, adults; 2.5 GPA; good academic standing at home school; no foreign language proficiency required.
Living Arrangements • Students live in host institution dormitories. Quarters are shared with host institution students. Meals are taken as a group, in central dining facility.
Costs (2006) • $2250; includes tuition, housing, all meals, excursions, student support services. $25 application fee. $300 nonrefundable deposit required. Financial aid available for all students: scholarships.
For More Information • Mr. Gregg Orifici, Director of Admissions, Living Routes–Study Abroad in Ecovillages, 79 South Pleasant Street, Suite A5, Amherst, MA 01002; *Phone:* 888-515-7333; *Fax:* 413-259-9355. *E-mail:* programs@livingroutes.org. *World Wide Web:* http://www.LivingRoutes.org/

STATE UNIVERSITY OF NEW YORK AT OSWEGO
SUMMER PROGRAMS IN MEXICO

Hosted by Instituto Tecnológico y de Estudios Superiores de Monterrey–Guaymas Campus, Instituto Tecnológico y de Estudios Superiores de Monterrey–Monterrey Campus, Instituto Tecnológico y de Estudios Superiores de Monterrey–Morelos Campus
Academic Focus • Anthropology, archaeology, Mexican studies, Spanish language and literature, Spanish studies.
Program Information • Students attend classes at Instituto Tecnológico y de Estudios Superiores de Monterrey–Guaymas Campus (Guaymas), Instituto Tecnológico y de Estudios Superiores de Monterrey–Monterrey Campus (Monterrey), Instituto Tecnológico y de Estudios Superiores de Monterrey–Morelos Campus (Cuernavaca). Optional travel at an extra cost. Students typically earn 6-12 semester credits per term.
Sessions • May-Jul (summer).
Eligibility Requirements • Open to freshmen, sophomores, juniors, seniors; 2.5 GPA; 1 letter of recommendation; good academic standing at home school; personal statement; no foreign language proficiency required.
Living Arrangements • Students live in host institution dormitories, host family homes, hotels. Quarters are shared with students from other programs. Meals are taken on one's own, with host family, in residences, in central dining facility, in restaurants.
Costs (2005) • $2000 (estimated); includes tuition, insurance, excursions, books and class materials, student support services. $250 nonrefundable deposit required. Financial aid available for students: home university financial aid; loan processing and scholarships for Oswego students.

For More Information • Ms. Lizette Alvarado, Program Specialist, State University of New York at Oswego, 122A Swetman Hall, Oswego, NY 13126-3599; *Phone:* 888-4-OSWEGO; *Fax:* 315-312-2477. *E-mail:* intled@oswego.edu. *World Wide Web:* http://www.oswego.edu/intled/

UNIVERSITY OF DELAWARE
WINTER SESSION IN MÉRIDA, MEXICO

Held at Instituto Tecnológico de Merida

Academic Focus • Art history, political science and government, Spanish language and literature.

Program Information • Classes are held on the campus of Instituto Tecnológico de Merida (Mérida). Faculty members are drawn from the sponsor's U.S. staff and local instructors hired by the sponsor. Scheduled travel to Chichen Itzá, Cobá, Playa del Carmen; field trips to Celestún, Labná, Progreso, an archaeological museum; optional travel to Mexico at an extra cost. Students typically earn 6 semester credits per term.

Sessions • Jan–Feb (winter).

Eligibility Requirements • Open to freshmen, sophomores, juniors, seniors, adults; 2.0 GPA; 1 letter of recommendation; no foreign language proficiency required.

Living Arrangements • Students live in host family homes. Quarters are shared with host institution students. Meals are taken with host family, in residences.

Costs (2005) • Contact sponsor for cost. $200 nonrefundable deposit required. Financial aid available for all students: scholarships.

For More Information • Center for International Studies, University of Delaware, 186 South College Avenue, Newark, DE 19716-1450; *Phone:* 888-831-4685; *Fax:* 302-831-6042. *E-mail:* studyabroad@udel.edu. *World Wide Web:* http://www.udel.edu/studyabroad/

UNIVERSITY OF IDAHO
SPANISH AND LATIN AMERICAN STUDIES

Hosted by Instituto Tecnológico y de Estudios Superiores de Monterrey–Cuernavaca Campus, Instituto Tecnológico y de Estudios Superiores de Monterrey–Estado de México Campus, Instituto Tecnológico y de Estudios Superiores de Monterrey–Guadalajara Campus, Instituto Tecnológico y de Estudios Superiores de Monterrey–Matzatlan Campus, Instituto Tecnológico y de Estudios Superiores de Monterrey–Mexico City Campus, Instituto Tecnológico y de Estudios Superiores de Monterrey–Monterrey Campus, Instituto Tecnológico y de Estudios Superiores de Monterrey–Querétaro Campus, Instituto Tecnológico y de Estudios Superiores de Monterrey–Toluca Campus

Academic Focus • Business administration/management, hotel and restaurant management, Latin American studies, Mexican studies, Spanish language and literature, tourism and travel.

Program Information • Students attend classes at Instituto Tecnológico y de Estudios Superiores de Monterrey-Cuernavaca Campus (Temixco), Instituto Tecnológico y de Estudios Superiores de Monterrey-Estado de México Campus (Estado de Mexico), Instituto Tecnológico y de Estudios Superiores de Monterrey-Guadalajara Campus (Zapopan), Instituto Tecnológico y de Estudios Superiores de Monterrey-Matzatlan Campus (Mazatlán), Instituto Tecnológico y de Estudios Superiores de Monterrey-Mexico City Campus (Mexico City), Instituto Tecnológico y de Estudios Superiores de Monterrey–Monterrey Campus (Monterrey), Instituto Tecnológico y de Estudios Superiores de Monterrey–Querétaro Campus (Querétaro), Instituto Tecnológico y de Estudios Superiores de Monterrey-Toluca Campus (Toluca). Field trips to La Silla Mountain, Garcia Caves; optional travel to Guanajuato, Mexico City, Zacatecas at an extra cost. Students typically earn 6 semester credits per term.

Sessions • Jun–Jul (summer), May–Jun (inter-campus program).

Eligibility Requirements • Open to freshmen, sophomores, juniors, seniors, graduate students, adults; 2.5 GPA; good academic standing at home school; no foreign language proficiency required.

Living Arrangements • Students live in host institution dormitories, locally rented apartments, host family homes. Quarters are shared with host institution students, students from other programs. Meals are taken on one's own, with host family, in residences, in central dining facility.

Costs (2006) • $1310–$4620; includes tuition, excursions, student support services, some meals and in-country air transport are included for the inter-campus program. $150 application fee. $200 refundable deposit required. Financial aid available for students from sponsoring institution: scholarships, loans.

For More Information • Ms. Kate Peterson, Program Advisor, University of Idaho, 901 Paradise Creek Street, LLC 3, Ground Floor, Moscow, ID 83844-1250; *Phone:* 208-885-4075; *Fax:* 208-885-2859. *E-mail:* abroad@uidaho.edu. *World Wide Web:* http://www.webs.uidaho.edu/ipo/abroad/

CANCÚN

LANGUAGE LIAISON
SPANISH IN CANCÚN

Hosted by Language Liaison

Academic Focus • Spanish language and literature.

Program Information • Students attend classes at Language Liaison (Cancún, Mexico). Field trips; optional travel at an extra cost. Students typically earn 3–15 semester credits per term.

Sessions • Classes begin weekly, year-round.

Eligibility Requirements • Minimum age 17; open to precollege students, freshmen, sophomores, juniors, seniors, graduate students, adults; no foreign language proficiency required.

Living Arrangements • Students live in locally rented apartments, host family homes, hotels. Meals are taken as a group, with host family, in residences, in restaurants.

Costs (2005) • Contact sponsor for cost. $175 application fee. Financial aid available for all students: scholarship research service.

For More Information • Ms. Nancy Forman, President, Language Liaison, PO Box 1772, Pacific Palisades, CA 90272; *Phone:* 800-284-4448; *Fax:* 310-454-1706. *E-mail:* learn@languageliaison.com. *World Wide Web:* http://www.languageliaison.com/

LANGUAGE LINK
EL BOSQUE DEL CARIBE

Hosted by El Bosque del Caribe

Academic Focus • Spanish language and literature.

Program Information • Students attend classes at El Bosque del Caribe (Cancún, Mexico). Field trips to Mayan archaeological sites, Isla Mujeres. Students typically earn 6–15 semester credits per term.

Sessions • Classes begin every Monday, year-round.

Eligibility Requirements • Minimum age 18; open to freshmen, sophomores, juniors, seniors, graduate students, adults; no foreign language proficiency required.

Living Arrangements • Students live in program-owned apartments, host family homes. Quarters are shared with host institution students. Meals are taken on one's own, with host family, in residences, in restaurants.

Costs (2005) • $335 per week; includes tuition, housing, all meals, student support services.

For More Information • Ms. Kay G. Rafool, Director, Language Link, PO Box 3006, Peoria, IL 61612-3006; *Phone:* 800-552-2051; *Fax:* 309-692-2926. *E-mail:* info@langlink.com. *World Wide Web:* http://www.langlink.com/

CUERNAVACA

CENTER FOR CULTURAL INTERCHANGE
MEXICO LANGUAGE SCHOOL

Hosted by The Center for Bilingual Multicultural Studies Universidad Internacional

Academic Focus • Spanish language and literature.

Program Information • Students attend classes at The Center for Bilingual Multicultural Studies Universidad Internacional (Cuernavaca, Mexico). Field trips to museums, guided city tours, cultural activities.

Sessions • 3, 4, or 6 week sessions begin every Monday, year-round.

Eligibility Requirements • Minimum age 13; open to precollege students, freshmen, sophomores, juniors, seniors, graduate students, adults; no foreign language proficiency required.

MEXICO
Cuernavaca

Living Arrangements • Students live in host family homes. Quarters are shared with host institution students. Meals are taken with host family, in residences.
Costs (2005) • $2050 for 4 weeks; includes tuition, housing, all meals, insurance, books and class materials, student support services, cultural activities. Financial aid available for students from sponsoring institution: scholarships.
For More Information • Ms. Juliet Jones, Outbound Programs Director, Center for Cultural Interchange, 325 West Huron, Suite 706, Chicago, IL 60610; *Phone:* 866-684-9675; *Fax:* 312-944-2644. *E-mail:* info@cci-exchange.com. *World Wide Web:* http://www.cci-exchange.com/

LANGUAGE LIAISON
LEARN SPANISH IN MEXICO–CENTRAL CUERNAVACA
Hosted by Language Liaison
Academic Focus • Spanish language and literature.
Program Information • Students attend classes at Language Liaison (Cuernavaca, Mexico). Field trips; optional travel at an extra cost. Students typically earn 3-15 semester credits per term.
Sessions • New programs begin weekly, year-round.
Eligibility Requirements • Minimum age 16; open to precollege students, freshmen, sophomores, juniors, seniors, graduate students, adults; no foreign language proficiency required.
Living Arrangements • Students live in host institution dormitories, locally rented apartments, host family homes. Meals are taken on one's own, with host family, in residences, in restaurants.
Costs (2005) • Contact sponsor for cost. $175 application fee. Financial aid available for all students: scholarship research service.
For More Information • Ms. Nancy Forman, President, Language Liaison, PO Box 1772, Pacific Palisades, CA 90272; *Phone:* 800-284-4448; *Fax:* 310-454-1706. *E-mail:* learn@languageliaison.com. *World Wide Web:* http://www.languageliaison.com/

LANGUAGE LINK
SPANISH LANGUAGE INSTITUTE
Hosted by Spanish Language Institute
Academic Focus • Spanish language and literature.
Program Information • Students attend classes at Spanish Language Institute (Cuernavaca, Mexico). Field trips to Teotihuacán, Taxco, Tepoztlán; optional travel to Acapulco, Puebla at an extra cost. Students typically earn 6-12 semester credits per term.
Sessions • Classes begin every Monday, year-round.
Eligibility Requirements • Minimum age 12; open to precollege students, freshmen, sophomores, juniors, seniors, graduate students, adults; no foreign language proficiency required.
Living Arrangements • Students live in host family homes. Quarters are shared with host institution students. Meals are taken with host family, in residences.
Costs (2005) • $280 per week; includes tuition, housing, all meals, student support services, cultural activities. $100 nonrefundable deposit required.
For More Information • Ms. Kay G. Rafool, Director, Language Link, PO Box 3006, Peoria, IL 61612-3006; *Phone:* 800-552-2051; *Fax:* 309-692-2926. *E-mail:* info@langlink.com. *World Wide Web:* http://www.langlink.com/

LINGUA SERVICE WORLDWIDE
VACATION 'N LEARN SPANISH IN MEXICO
Hosted by The Center for Bilingual Multicultural Studies Universidad Internacional
Academic Focus • Spanish language and literature, Spanish studies.
Program Information • Students attend classes at The Center for Bilingual Multicultural Studies Universidad Internacional (Cuernavaca, Mexico). Optional travel to beach sites, Mayan and Aztec ruins at an extra cost. Students typically earn 3 semester credits for 3 weeks, 6 semester credits for 5 weeks.
Sessions • Year-round sessions of 1 week or more, beginning on Mondays.
Eligibility Requirements • Minimum age 16; open to precollege students, freshmen, sophomores, juniors, seniors, graduate students, adults; no foreign language proficiency required.

Living Arrangements • Students live in host institution dormitories, locally rented apartments, host family homes, hotels. Meals are taken with host family.
Costs (2006–2007) • Contact sponsor for cost. $100 application fee.
For More Information • Assistant Director, Lingua Service Worldwide, 75 Prospect Street, Suite 4, Huntington, NY 11743; *Phone:* 800-394-5327; *Fax:* 631-271-3441. *E-mail:* linguaservice@att.net. *World Wide Web:* http://www.linguaserviceworldwide.com/

STATE UNIVERSITY OF NEW YORK COLLEGE AT BROCKPORT
SPANISH LANGUAGE IMMERSION PROGRAM, CUERNAVACA
Hosted by The Center for Bilingual Multicultural Studies Universidad Internacional
Academic Focus • Cultural studies, Latin American studies, Mexican studies, Spanish language and literature.
Program Information • Students attend classes at The Center for Bilingual Multicultural Studies Universidad Internacional (Cuernavaca, Mexico). Field trips to Mexico City, Teotihuacán; optional travel. Students typically earn 6 semester credits per term.
Sessions • Jul-Aug (summer).
Eligibility Requirements • Minimum age 18; open to sophomores, juniors, seniors; course work in area of internship, if applicable; 2.5 GPA; 2 letters of recommendation; good academic standing at home school; résumé required for internship; must be at least a second semester sophomore; 1 year college course work in Spanish.
Living Arrangements • Students live in host family homes. Meals are taken with host family, in residences.
Costs (2005) • Contact sponsor for cost; includes housing, some meals, international student ID. $200 nonrefundable deposit required. Financial aid available for all students: scholarships, loans, regular financial aid.
For More Information • Dr. John J. Perry, Director, Office of International Education, State University of New York College at Brockport, 350 New Campus Drive, Brockport, NY 14420; *Phone:* 800-298-SUNY; *Fax:* 585-637-3218. *E-mail:* overseas@brockport.edu. *World Wide Web:* http://www.brockport.edu/studyabroad/

STATE UNIVERSITY OF NEW YORK COLLEGE AT CORTLAND
WINTER SESSION IN CUERNAVACA, MEXICO
Hosted by The Spanish Language Institute
Academic Focus • Latin American studies, Spanish language and literature.
Program Information • Students attend classes at The Spanish Language Institute (Cuernavaca, Mexico). Field trips to archaeological ruins of Teotihuacan, Mexico City, the Museum of Anthropology; optional travel to Acapulco, Xochicalco, Taxco, Puebla; Tepóztlan at an extra cost. Students typically earn 3 semester credits per term.
Sessions • Dec-Jan (winter).
Eligibility Requirements • Minimum age 18; open to freshmen, sophomores, juniors, seniors, graduate students; 2.5 GPA; 2 letters of recommendation; good academic standing at home school; no foreign language proficiency required.
Living Arrangements • Students live in host family homes. Quarters are shared with host institution students. Meals are taken with host family, in residences.
Costs (2005–2006) • $2510; includes tuition, housing, all meals, insurance, excursions, international airfare, books and class materials, international student ID, student support services. $20 application fee. $200 nonrefundable deposit required. Financial aid available for students from sponsoring institution: scholarships, loans.
For More Information • Ms. Liz McCartney, Assistant Director, Office of International Programs, State University of New York College at Cortland, PO Box 2000, Cortland, NY 13045; *Phone:* 607-753-2209; *Fax:* 607-753-5989. *E-mail:* cortlandabroad@cortland.edu. *World Wide Web:* http://www.cortlandabroad.com/

UNIVERSITY OF MINNESOTA
LANGUAGE AND CULTURE IN MEXICO
Hosted by Cemanahuac Educational Community
Academic Focus • Spanish language and literature.

Program Information • Students attend classes at Cemanahuac Educational Community (Cuernavaca, Mexico). Field trips to Teotihuacán. Students typically earn 5 semester credits per term.

Sessions • Classes held in May, Jun, Jul and Aug.

Eligibility Requirements • Minimum age 18; open to precollege students, freshmen, sophomores, juniors, seniors, graduate students, adults; 2.5 GPA; good academic standing at home school; no foreign language proficiency required.

Living Arrangements • Students live in host family homes. Quarters are shared with host institution students. Meals are taken with host family, in residences.

Costs (2006) • Contact sponsor for cost. $50 application fee. $400 nonrefundable deposit required. Financial aid available for students from sponsoring institution: scholarships, loans.

For More Information • Learning Abroad Center, University of Minnesota, 230 Heller Hall, 271 19th Avenue South, Minneapolis, MN 55455; *Phone:* 888-700-UOFM; *Fax:* 612-626-8009. *E-mail:* umabroad@umn.edu. *World Wide Web:* http://www.umabroad.umn.edu/

ENSENADA

UNIVERSITY OF CALIFORNIA SAN DIEGO EXTENSION
SPANISH IMMERSION PROGRAM: ENSENADA, MEXICO

Hosted by Center of Languages

Academic Focus • Mexican studies, Spanish language and literature.

Program Information • Students attend classes at Center of Languages (Ensenada, Mexico). Field trips to La Bufadora, a local winery, downtown center. Students typically earn 1-3 quarter credits per term.

Sessions • Week-long and weekend sessions available.

Eligibility Requirements • Minimum age 18; open to freshmen, sophomores, juniors, seniors, graduate students, adults; no foreign language proficiency required.

Living Arrangements • Students live in host family homes, hotels. Quarters are shared with host institution students, students from other programs. Meals are taken with host family, in residences.

Costs (2005) • $495 per week; $265 per weekend; includes tuition, housing, all meals, books and class materials, student support services. $125 application fee. Financial aid available for all students: loans.

For More Information • Ms. Natalie Bruce, Travel Study Coordinator, University of California San Diego Extension, Department of Arts, Humanities and Languages, 0170A, 9500 Gilman Drive, San Diego, CA 92093-0170; *Phone:* 858-964-1050; *Fax:* 858-964-1099. *E-mail:* travelstudy@ucsd.edu. *World Wide Web:* http://www.extension.ucsd.edu/travelstudy/

GUADALAJARA

COLLEGE CONSORTIUM FOR INTERNATIONAL STUDIES–CENTRAL WASHINGTON UNIVERSITY
PROGRAM IN GUADALAJARA, MEXICO

Hosted by Autonomous University of Guadalajara

Academic Focus • Spanish language and literature.

Program Information • Students attend classes at Autonomous University of Guadalajara (Guadalajara, Mexico). Field trips to the city center of Guadalajara, markets, Tequila, Mexico City; optional travel to Mexico City, Puerto Vallarta, Guanajuato at an extra cost. Students typically earn 6 quarter credits per term.

Sessions • 4 week sessions, from May to Oct.

Eligibility Requirements • Minimum age 18; open to sophomores, juniors, seniors, graduate students, adults; 2.5 GPA; 2 letters of recommendation; good academic standing at home school; good disciplinary standing at home school; some Spanish recommended.

Living Arrangements • Students live in host family homes. Quarters are shared with host institution students, students from other programs. Meals are taken with host family, in residences.

Costs (2006) • $800 for the first cycle; $675 for each additional cycle; includes tuition, excursions, student support services, health insurance. $50 application fee. $300 nonrefundable deposit required. Financial aid available for students from sponsoring institution: scholarships, loans.

For More Information • Ms. Katie McCarthy, Study Abroad Advisor, College Consortium for International Studies–Central Washington University, 400 East University Way, Ellensburg, WA 98926-7408; *Phone:* 509-963-3612; *Fax:* 509-963-1558. *E-mail:* goabroad@cwu.edu. *World Wide Web:* http://www.ccisabroad.org/

THE INTERNATIONAL PARTNERSHIP FOR SERVICE LEARNING AND LEADERSHIP
MEXICO SERVICE–LEARNING

Hosted by Autonomous University of Guadalajara

Academic Focus • Community service, education, international affairs, liberal studies, Mexican studies, social sciences, Spanish language and literature.

Program Information • Students attend classes at Autonomous University of Guadalajara (Guadalajara, Mexico). Field trips to sites around Guadalajara and neighboring villages; optional travel to Mexico City, Guanajuato, Puerto Vallarta at an extra cost. Students typically earn 6-9 semester credits per term.

Sessions • Jun-Aug (summer), Jun-Aug (summer 2).

Eligibility Requirements • Minimum age 18; open to freshmen, sophomores, juniors, seniors, graduate students, adults; 2 letters of recommendation; good academic standing at home school; evidence of maturity; 1 year of college course work in Spanish.

Living Arrangements • Students live in host family homes. Meals are taken with host family, in residences.

Costs (2005–2006) • $5900; includes tuition, housing, some meals, student support services, community service placement. $50 application fee. $250 refundable deposit required. Financial aid available for all students: federal financial aid.

For More Information • Director of Student Programs, The International Partnership for Service Learning and Leadership, 815 Second Avenue, New York, NY 10017-4594; *Phone:* 212-986-0989; *Fax:* 212-986-5039. *E-mail:* info@ipsl.org. *World Wide Web:* http://www.ipsl.org/

UNIVERSITY OF CALIFORNIA SAN DIEGO EXTENSION
SPANISH IMMERSION PROGRAM: GUADALAJARA, MEXICO

Hosted by University of Guadalajara

Academic Focus • Mexican studies, Spanish language and literature.

Program Information • Students attend classes at University of Guadalajara (Guadalajara, Mexico). Field trips to Tequila, Chapala, Tlaquepaque (for five-week program participants only); optional travel to Puerto Vallarta, Mexico City, Oaxaca (for five-week program participants only) at an extra cost. Students typically earn 4.5 quarter credits for 2 weeks, 9 quarter credits for 5 weeks.

Sessions • 2 or 5 week sessions held year-round.

Eligibility Requirements • Minimum age 18; open to freshmen, sophomores, juniors, seniors, graduate students, adults; no foreign language proficiency required.

Living Arrangements • Students live in host family homes, hotels, a university guest house. Quarters are shared with host institution students, students from other programs. Meals are taken with host family, in residences.

Costs (2005) • $1031 for 2 weeks; $1952 for 5 weeks; includes tuition, housing, all meals, student support services, registration/application fee. $125 application fee. Financial aid available for all students: loans.

For More Information • Ms. Natalie Bruce, Travel Study Coordinator, University of California San Diego Extension, Department of Arts, Humanities and Languages, 0170A, 9500 Gilman Drive, San Diego, CA 92093-0170; *Phone:* 858-964-1050; *Fax:* 858-964-1099. *E-mail:* travelstudy@ucsd.edu. *World Wide Web:* http://www.extension.ucsd.edu/travelstudy/

UNIVERSITY OF COLORADO AT BOULDER
GUADALAJARA SUMMER LANGUAGE PROGRAM

Hosted by University of Guadalajara

Academic Focus • Mexican studies, Spanish language and literature.

MEXICO
Guadalajara

Program Information • Students attend classes at University of Guadalajara (Guadalajara, Mexico). Optional travel to Mexico City, Oaxaca at an extra cost. Students typically earn 3-6 semester credits per term.
Sessions • Jun-Jul (summer), Jul-Aug (summer 2).
Eligibility Requirements • Open to sophomores, juniors, seniors, adults; 2.5 GPA; 2 letters of recommendation; good academic standing at home school; teacher evaluation or Spanish placement test results; 1.5 years college course work in Spanish.
Living Arrangements • Students live in host family homes. Quarters are shared with students from other programs. Meals are taken with host family.
Costs (2005) • $2086; includes tuition, housing, all meals, insurance, excursions, international airfare, books and class materials, student support services. $400 nonrefundable deposit required. Financial aid available for students from sponsoring institution: scholarships, loans.
For More Information • Study Abroad Programs, University of Colorado at Boulder, International Education, 123 UCB, Boulder, CO 80309-0123; *Phone:* 303-492-7741; *Fax:* 303-492-5185. *E-mail:* studyabr@colorado.edu. *World Wide Web:* http://www.colorado.edu/OIE/

UNIVERSITY OF IDAHO
SPANISH AND LATIN AMERICAN STUDIES

Hosted by Autonomous University of Guadalajara
Academic Focus • Mexican studies, Spanish language and literature.
Program Information • Students attend classes at Autonomous University of Guadalajara (Guadalajara, Mexico). Field trips to Lake Chapala, Tequila, Tlaquepaque; optional travel to Mexico City, Guanajuato, Michoacán at an extra cost. Students typically earn 7 semester credits per term.
Sessions • May-Jun (summer), Jun-Jul (summer 2); Jul-Aug (summer 3).
Eligibility Requirements • Open to freshmen, sophomores, juniors, seniors, graduate students, adults; 2.5 GPA; good academic standing at home school; no foreign language proficiency required.
Living Arrangements • Students live in locally rented apartments, host family homes. Quarters are shared with host institution students, students from other programs. Meals are taken on one's own, with host family, in residences.
Costs (2006) • $815-$1800; includes tuition, excursions, student support services. $150 application fee. $200 refundable deposit required. Financial aid available for students from sponsoring institution: scholarships, loans.
For More Information • Ms. Kate Peterson, Program Advisor, University of Idaho, 901 Paradise Creek Street, LLC 3, Ground Floor, Moscow, ID 83844-1250; *Phone:* 208-885-4075; *Fax:* 208-885-2859. *E-mail:* abroad@uidaho.edu. *World Wide Web:* http://www.webs.uidaho.edu/ipo/abroad/

THE UNIVERSITY OF NORTH CAROLINA AT CHARLOTTE
SUMMER INTERNSHIP IN GUADALAJARA

Hosted by University of Guadalajara
Academic Focus • Civilization studies, international business, Spanish language and literature, Spanish studies.
Program Information • Students attend classes at University of Guadalajara (Guadalajara, Mexico). Scheduled travel to Puerto Vallarta, Guanajuato; optional travel at an extra cost. Students typically earn 6 semester credits per term.
Sessions • Jul-Aug (summer).
Eligibility Requirements • Minimum age 18; open to sophomores, juniors, seniors, graduate students; 2.5 GPA; 2 letters of recommendation; good academic standing at home school; 1 year of college course work in Spanish.
Living Arrangements • Students live in host family homes. Quarters are shared with students from other programs. Meals are taken with host family, in residences.
Costs (2005) • $3440; includes tuition, housing, some meals, insurance, excursions, international airfare, student support services. $10 application fee. $500 nonrefundable deposit required. Financial aid available for students from sponsoring institution: scholarships, loans.

For More Information • Mr. Brad Sekulich, Interim Director of Education Abroad, The University of North Carolina at Charlotte, 9201 University City Boulevard, Charlotte, NC 28223-0001; *Phone:* 704-687-2464; *Fax:* 704-687-3168. *E-mail:* edabroad@email.uncc.edu. *World Wide Web:* http://www.uncc.edu/edabroad/

VANCOUVER LANGUAGE CENTRE
SPANISH LANGUAGE PROGRAMS IN MEXICO

Hosted by Vancouver Language Centre
Academic Focus • Spanish language and literature.
Program Information • Students attend classes at Vancouver Language Centre (Guadalajara, Mexico).
Sessions • 4 week sessions, year-round.
Eligibility Requirements • No foreign language proficiency required.
Living Arrangements • Students live in host family homes.
Costs (2005) • $250-$550 per 4 week session; includes tuition. $75 application fee.
For More Information • Ms. Patricia J. Moir, Director, Vancouver Language Centre, Av. Vallarta 1151, Col. Americana, Guadalajara, Jalisco CP 44100, Mexico; *Phone:* +52 33-3826-0944; *Fax:* +52 33-3828-2051. *E-mail:* vlc@vec.bc.ca. *World Wide Web:* http://www.study-mexico.com/

GUANAJUATO

ACADEMIA FALCON A.C.
INTENSIVE SPANISH LANGUAGE PROGRAM

Hosted by Academia Falcon A.C.
Academic Focus • Mexican studies.
Program Information • Students attend classes at Academia Falcon A.C. (Guanajuato, Mexico). Field trips to hot springs, local historic sites, volcano hikes, sporting events, cinema, restaurants. Students typically earn 9-18 semester credits per term.
Sessions • Classes begin every Monday.
Eligibility Requirements • Minimum age 6; open to precollege students, freshmen, sophomores, juniors, seniors, graduate students, adults; no foreign language proficiency required.
Living Arrangements • Students live in host institution dormitories, locally rented apartments, host family homes, hotels. Quarters are shared with host institution students, students from other programs. Meals are taken on one's own, with host family, in residences, in central dining facility, in restaurants.
Costs (2005-2006) • $65-$120 per week; includes tuition. $75 application fee. $50 nonrefundable deposit required. Financial aid available for all students: scholarships, work study.
For More Information • Ms. Eri Takami, Office Manager, Academia Falcon A.C., 158 Callejon de la Mora, Guanajuato 36000, Mexico; *Phone:* +52 473-731-07-45; *Fax:* +52 473-731-07-45. *E-mail:* academiafalcon@int.com.mx. *World Wide Web:* http://www.academiafalcon.com/

CIEE
CIEE STUDY CENTER AT THE UNIVERSITY OF GUANAJUATO, MEXICO

Hosted by University of Guanajuato
Academic Focus • Art, art history, Spanish language and literature.
Program Information • Students attend classes at University of Guanajuato (Guanajuato, Mexico). Field trips to Michoacán, San Miguel de Allende, Dolores Hidalgo, Zacatecar. Students typically earn 3 semester credits per term.
Sessions • Jun-Jul (summer), Jun-Jul (summer 2).
Eligibility Requirements • Minimum age 18; open to sophomores, juniors, seniors; 2.75 GPA; 1 letter of recommendation; good academic standing at home school; evaluation should be from a language professor; 1 year of college course work in Spanish.
Living Arrangements • Students live in host family homes. Meals are taken with host family, in residences.
Costs (2006) • $2100 for 1 term; $4200 for 2 terms; includes tuition, housing, all meals, insurance, excursions, student support services, resident director, orientation, cultural activities, on-site pick-up, predeparture advice. $30 application fee. $300 nonrefund-

able deposit required. Financial aid available for all students: scholarships, minority student scholarships, travel grants.
For More Information • Information Center, CIEE, 7 Custom House Street, 3rd Floor, Portland, ME 04101; *Phone:* 800-40-STUDY; *Fax:* 207-553-7699. *E-mail:* studyinfo@ciee.org. *World Wide Web:* http://www.ciee.org/isp/

CIEE
CIEE STUDY CENTER AT THE UNIVERSITY OF GUANAJUATO, MEXICO–JANUARY PROGRAM

Hosted by University of Guanajuato
Academic Focus • Spanish language and literature.
Program Information • Students attend classes at University of Guanajuato (Guanajuato, Mexico). Field trips to Mexico City, art musems; pyramids, Michoácan craft workshops, cooking seminars. Students typically earn 3 semester credits per term.
Sessions • Jan (winter).
Eligibility Requirements • Minimum age 18; open to sophomores, juniors, seniors; 2.75 GPA; 1 letter of recommendation; good academic standing at home school; recommendation; evaluation must be by a language professor; 1 year of college course work in Spanish.
Living Arrangements • Students live in host family homes. Meals are taken with host family, in residences.
Costs (2007) • Contact sponsor for cost. $30 application fee. $300 nonrefundable deposit required. Financial aid available for all students: scholarships, minority student scholarships, travel grants.
For More Information • Information Center, CIEE, 7 Custom House Street, 3rd Floor, Portland, ME 04101; *Phone:* 800-40-STUDY; *Fax:* 207-553-7699. *E-mail:* studyinfo@ciee.org. *World Wide Web:* http://www.ciee.org/isp/

DON QUIJOTE
MEDICAL SPANISH

Hosted by Don Quijote
Academic Focus • Medicine, nursing, Romance languages, Spanish language and literature, Spanish studies.
Program Information • Students attend classes at Don Quijote (Guanajuato, Mexico). Field trips to historic sites, cultural attractions. Students typically earn 4 semester credits per term.
Sessions • Jul (summer), Aug–Sep (summer 2).
Eligibility Requirements • Minimum age 18; open to freshmen, sophomores, juniors, seniors, graduate students, adults; intermediate Spanish.
Living Arrangements • Students live in host institution dormitories, program-owned apartments, host family homes. Quarters are shared with host institution students, students from other programs. Meals are taken on one's own, in residences.
Costs (2006) • $613; includes tuition, books and class materials, lab equipment, student support services, guided cultural tour, welcome dinner, student discount card, level test, tutor, end-of-course certificate. $65 application fee. $500 nonrefundable deposit required. Financial aid available for all students: scholarships.
For More Information • Ms. Carmen Cantarino, USA Director, Don Quijote, Plaza San Marcos 7, 37002 Salamanca, Spain; *Phone:* +34 923-268874; *Fax:* +34 923-260674. *E-mail:* usa@donquijote.org. *World Wide Web:* http://www.donquijote.org/

DON QUIJOTE
GUANAJUATO, MEXICO

Hosted by Don Quijote
Academic Focus • Romance languages, Spanish language and literature, Spanish studies.
Program Information • Students attend classes at Don Quijote (Guanajuato, Mexico). Students typically earn 4 semester credits per term.
Sessions • 1 week minimum sessions start every Monday year-round.
Eligibility Requirements • Minimum age 18; open to freshmen, sophomores, juniors, seniors, graduate students, adults; no foreign language proficiency required.
Living Arrangements • Students live in host institution dormitories, host family homes. Quarters are shared with host institution students, students from other programs. Meals are taken on one's own, with host family, in residences.

Costs (2006) • €229 for the first week; $146 for each additional week; includes tuition, books and class materials, lab equipment, student support services, welcome dinner, guided cultural tour, student discount card, level test, tutor, end-of-course certificate. €65 application fee. €500 nonrefundable deposit required. Financial aid available for all students: scholarships.
For More Information • Ms. Carmen Cantarino, USA Director, Don Quijote, Plaza San Marcos 7, 37002 Salamanca, Spain; *Phone:* +34 923-268874; *Fax:* +34 923-260674. *E-mail:* usa@donquijote.org. *World Wide Web:* http://www.donquijote.org/

DON QUIJOTE
SUPER INTENSIVE SPANISH COURSE–GUANAJUATO, MEXICO

Hosted by Don Quijote
Academic Focus • Romance languages, Spanish language and literature, Spanish studies.
Program Information • Students attend classes at Don Quijote (Guanajuato, Mexico). Field trips to historic sites, cultural attractions. Students typically earn 4 semester credits per term.
Sessions • 1 week minimum, classes start every Monday.
Eligibility Requirements • Minimum age 18; open to freshmen, sophomores, juniors, seniors, graduate students, adults.
Living Arrangements • Students live in host institution dormitories, host family homes. Quarters are shared with host institution students, students from other programs. Meals are taken on one's own, with host family, in residences.
Costs (2006) • €344 for the first week; $219 for each additional week; includes tuition, books and class materials, lab equipment, student support services, guided cultural tour, welcome dinner, student discount card, level test, tutor, end-of-course certificate. €65 application fee. €500 nonrefundable deposit required. Financial aid available for all students: scholarships.
For More Information • Ms. Carmen Cantarino, USA Director, Don Quijote, Plaza San Marcos 7, 37002 Salamanca, Spain; *Phone:* +34 923-268874; *Fax:* +34 923-260674. *E-mail:* usa@donquijote.org. *World Wide Web:* http://www.donquijote.org/

INTERNATIONAL STUDIES ABROAD
GUANAJUATO, MEXICO SUMMER

Hosted by University of Guanajuato
Academic Focus • Latin American literature, Mexican studies, Spanish language and literature.
Program Information • Students attend classes at University of Guanajuato (Guanajuato, Mexico). Scheduled travel to Puerto Vallarta; field trips to San Miguel de Allende, Querétaro; optional travel to Michoacán at an extra cost. Students typically earn 6-8 semester credits per term.
Sessions • May-Jul (summer), Jul-Aug (summer 2).
Eligibility Requirements • Minimum age 18; open to freshmen, sophomores, juniors, seniors, graduate students, adults; 2.5 GPA; 1 letter of recommendation; good academic standing at home school; transcripts.
Living Arrangements • Students live in locally rented apartments, host family homes. Quarters are shared with host institution students, students from other programs. Meals are taken with host family.
Costs (2005) • Contact sponsor for cost. $200 deposit required. Financial aid available for all students: scholarships, loans, U.S. federal financial aid.
For More Information • Mexico Site Specialist, International Studies Abroad, 901 West 24th Street, Austin, TX 78705; *Phone:* 800-580-8826; *Fax:* 512-480-8866. *E-mail:* isa@studiesabroad.com. *World Wide Web:* http://www.studiesabroad.com/

LA PAZ

LANGUAGE LIAISON
LEARN SPANISH IN MEXICO

Hosted by Language Liaison
Academic Focus • Spanish language and literature.
Program Information • Students attend classes at Language Liaison (La Paz, Mexico). Students typically earn 3-9 semester credits per term.

MEXICO
La Paz

Sessions • Classes begin every week, year-round.
Eligibility Requirements • Minimum age 16; open to precollege students, freshmen, sophomores, juniors, seniors, graduate students, adults; no foreign language proficiency required.
Living Arrangements • Students live in locally rented apartments, program-owned apartments, host family homes, hotels. Meals are taken on one's own, in residences.
Costs (2005) • Contact sponsor for cost. $175 application fee.
For More Information • Ms. Nancy Forman, President, Language Liaison, PO Box 1772, Pacific Palisades, CA 90272; *Phone:* 800-284-448; *Fax:* 310-454-1706. *E-mail:* learn@languageliaison.com. *World Wide Web:* http://www.languageliaison.com/

LEÓN

MICHIGAN STATE UNIVERSITY
VETERINARY MEDICINE IN MEXICO

Hosted by University de La Salle Bajilo
Academic Focus • Spanish language and literature, veterinary science.
Program Information • Students attend classes at University de La Salle Bajilo (León, Mexico). Field trips to Guanajuato. Students typically earn 6 semester credits per term.
Sessions • Jul–Aug (summer).
Eligibility Requirements • Minimum age 18; open to sophomores, juniors, seniors; major in veterinary medicine; course work in second-year pre-veterinary students; 2.5 GPA; good academic standing at home school; statement of purpose at application; proficiency in Spanish.
Living Arrangements • Students live in host family homes. Meals are taken with host family, in residences.
Costs (2005) • $1885 (estimated); includes housing, all meals, insurance, student support services. $100 application fee. $200 nonrefundable deposit required. Financial aid available for students from sponsoring institution: scholarships, loans.
For More Information • Mr. Mark Davis, Coordinator, Michigan State University, Office of Study Abroad, 109 International Center, East Lansing, MI 48824-1035; *Phone:* 517-432-1315; *Fax:* 517-432-2082. *E-mail:* mdavis@msu.edu. *World Wide Web:* http://studyabroad.msu.edu/

MÉRIDA

INSTITUTE FOR STUDY ABROAD, BUTLER UNIVERSITY
SUMMER ARCHAELOGY AND ANTHROPOLOGY PROGRAM IN MEXICO

Hosted by Autonomous University of Yucatán
Academic Focus • Mayan studies, Mexican studies, Spanish language and literature.
Program Information • Students attend classes at Autonomous University of Yucatán (Mérida, Mexico). Scheduled travel; field trips to archaeological sites, historic towns, nature preserves. Students typically earn 6–9 semester credits per term.
Sessions • Jun–Jul (summer).
Eligibility Requirements • Open to sophomores, juniors, seniors; 3.0 GPA; 1 letter of recommendation; good academic standing at home school; enrollment at an American college or university; 1–2 years of college course work in Spanish.
Living Arrangements • Students live in host family homes. Meals are taken with host family, in residences.
Costs (2005) • $3200; includes tuition, housing, all meals, excursions, student support services, pre-departure advising; cultural and sporting events. $40 application fee. $500 nonrefundable deposit required. Financial aid available for all students: scholarships.
For More Information • Institute for Study Abroad, Butler University, 1100 West 42nd Street, Suite 305, Indianapolis, IN 46208-3345; *Phone:* 800-858-0229; *Fax:* 317-940-9704. *E-mail:* pilas@butler.edu. *World Wide Web:* http://www.ifsa-butler.org/

INSTITUTO BENJAMIN FRANKLIN DE YUCATAN
SPANISH IN YUCATAN

Hosted by Instituto Benjamin Franklin de Yucatan
Academic Focus • Full curriculum.
Program Information • Students attend classes at Instituto Benjamin Franklin de Yucatan (Mérida, Mexico). Field trips to beaches, archaeological sites, city tours; optional travel to Cancún, Palenque, Mexico City, Central America, Chichen Itza, Uxmal, Gulf of Mexico beaches, Cozumel, Playa del Carmen at an extra cost. Students typically earn 3–12 quarter credits per term.
Sessions • Classes begin every Monday, year-round.
Eligibility Requirements • Minimum age 15; open to precollege students, freshmen, sophomores, juniors, seniors, graduate students, adults; no foreign language proficiency required.
Living Arrangements • Students live in locally rented apartments, host family homes, hotels. Quarters are shared with host institution students. Meals are taken with host family.
Costs (2005–2006) • $10 per hour; includes tuition, books and class materials, student support services.
For More Information • Mr. Guillermo Vales, Director, Instituto Benjamin Franklin de Yucatan, Calle 57 474-A Centro, Merída 97000, Mexico; *Phone:* +52 999-9286005; *Fax:* +52 999-9280097. *E-mail:* franklin@finred.com.mx. *World Wide Web:* http://www.benjaminfranklin.com.mx/

LEXIA INTERNATIONAL
LEXIA SUMMER IN MÉRIDA

Hosted by Autonomous University of Yucatán
Academic Focus • Anthropology, archaeology, architecture, area studies, art, business administration/management, cultural studies, economics, film and media studies, geography, history, international affairs, Latin American studies, political science and government, sociology, Spanish language and literature, visual and performing arts.
Program Information • Students attend classes at Autonomous University of Yucatán (Mérida, Mexico). Field trips. Students typically earn 8–10 semester credits per term.
Sessions • Jun–Aug (summer).
Eligibility Requirements • Minimum age 18; open to freshmen, sophomores, juniors, seniors, graduate students, adults; 2.5 GPA; 2 letters of recommendation; good academic standing at home school; no foreign language proficiency required.
Living Arrangements • Students live in host family homes, hotels. Quarters are shared with host institution students. Meals are taken on one's own, in residences, in central dining facility, in restaurants.
Costs (2006) • $5950; includes tuition, housing, some meals, insurance, excursions, international student ID, student support services, computer access, transcript. $40 application fee. $300 nonrefundable deposit required. Financial aid available for all students: scholarships, work study.
For More Information • Lexia International, 23 South Main Street, Hanover, NH 03755; *Phone:* 800-775-3942; *Fax:* 603-643-9899. *E-mail:* info@lexiaintl.org. *World Wide Web:* http://www.lexiaintl.org/

LINGUA SERVICE WORLDWIDE
VACATION 'N LEARN SPANISH IN MEXICO

Hosted by Centro de Idiomas del Sureste (CIS)
Academic Focus • Spanish language and literature, Spanish studies.
Program Information • Students attend classes at Centro de Idiomas del Sureste (CIS) (Mérida, Mexico). Optional travel to beach sites, Mayan and Aztec ruins at an extra cost. Students typically earn 3 semester credits for 3 weeks, 6 semester credits for 5 weeks.
Sessions • Year-round sessions of 1 week or more, beginning on Mondays.
Eligibility Requirements • Minimum age 16; open to precollege students, freshmen, sophomores, juniors, seniors, graduate students, adults; no foreign language proficiency required.
Living Arrangements • Students live in host institution dormitories, locally rented apartments, host family homes, hotels. Meals are taken with host family.
Costs (2006–2007) • Contact sponsor for cost. $100 application fee.

For More Information • Assistant Director, Lingua Service Worldwide, 75 Prospect Street, Suite 4, Huntington, NY 11743; *Phone:* 800-394-5327; *Fax:* 631-271-3441. *E-mail:* linguaservice@att. net. *World Wide Web:* http://www.linguaserviceworldwide.com/

MICHIGAN STATE UNIVERSITY
HONORS BUSINESS PROGRAM IN MÉRIDA, MEXICO

Held at Centro de Idiomas del Sureste (CIS)

Academic Focus • International business.

Program Information • Classes are held on the campus of Centro de Idiomas del Sureste (CIS) (Mérida, Mexico). Faculty members are drawn from the sponsor's U.S. staff and local instructors hired by the sponsor. Field trips to the Yucatán area, Mérida. Students typically earn 3 semester credits per term.

Sessions • Jun (summer).

Eligibility Requirements • Open to freshmen, sophomores, juniors, seniors, graduate students; 3.3 GPA; good academic standing at home school; must be an honors student; interview and statement of purpose; no foreign language proficiency required.

Living Arrangements • Students live in hotels. Meals are taken as a group, on one's own, in restaurants.

Costs (2005) • $1311 (estimated); includes housing, some meals, insurance, excursions. $100 application fee. $200 nonrefundable deposit required. Financial aid available for students from sponsoring institution: scholarships, loans.

For More Information • Mr. Mark Davis, Coordinator, Michigan State University, Office of Study Abroad, 109 International Center, East Lansing, MI 48824-1035; *Phone:* 517-432-1315; *Fax:* 517-432-2082. *E-mail:* mdavis@msu.edu. *World Wide Web:* http://studyabroad. msu.edu/

MICHIGAN STATE UNIVERSITY
REGIONAL DEVELOPMENT AND CONTEMPORARY ISSUES IN MEXICO

Academic Focus • Agriculture, environmental science/studies, social sciences.

Program Information • Faculty members are drawn from the sponsor's U.S. staff. Field trips to sites in the surrounding area. Students typically earn 6 semester credits per term.

Sessions • Dec–Jan (winter break).

Eligibility Requirements • Minimum age 18; open to freshmen, sophomores, juniors, seniors; 2.0 GPA; good academic standing at home school; faculty approval; no foreign language proficiency required.

Living Arrangements • Students live in host family homes. Meals are taken with host family, in residences.

Costs (2004–2005) • $1316 (estimated); includes housing, some meals, insurance, excursions, student support services. $100 application fee. $200 nonrefundable deposit required. Financial aid available for students from sponsoring institution: scholarships, loans.

For More Information • Mr. Mark Davis, Coordinator, Michigan State University, Office of Study Abroad, 109 International Center, East Lansing, MI 48824-1035; *Phone:* 517-432-1315; *Fax:* 517-432-2082. *E-mail:* mdavis@msu.edu. *World Wide Web:* http://studyabroad. msu.edu/

MEXICO CITY

CITY COLLEGE OF SAN FRANCISCO
DIEGO RIVERA AND THE MURALISTS

Academic Focus • Latin American studies, music.

Program Information • Faculty members are drawn from the sponsor's U.S. staff. Scheduled travel to Mexico City; field trips to Oaxaca, Cuernavaca, Xalapa. Students typically earn 6 semester credits per term.

Sessions • Dec–Jan (winter break).

Eligibility Requirements • Minimum age 18; open to freshmen, sophomores, juniors, seniors, graduate students, adults; 2.0 GPA; good academic standing at home school; no foreign language proficiency required.

Living Arrangements • Students live in hotels. Meals are taken as a group, in restaurants.

Costs (2005–2006) • $2719; includes housing, some meals, insurance, excursions, international airfare, student support services. $395 nonrefundable deposit required. Financial aid available for students from sponsoring institution: scholarships, loans.

For More Information • Ms. Jill Heffron, Study Abroad Coordinator, City College of San Francisco, 50 Phelan Avenue, Box C212, San Francisco, CA 94112; *Phone:* 415-239-3778; *Fax:* 415-239-3804. *E-mail:* jheffron@ccsf.edu. *World Wide Web:* http://www.ccsf.edu/ studyabroad/. Students may also apply through eTrav, One Education Street, Cambridge, MA 02141.

KNOWLEDGE EXCHANGE INSTITUTE (KEI)
LATIN AMERICAN BUSINESS, LAW, AND DIPLOMACY

Hosted by Alliant International University–Mexico

Academic Focus • Accounting, advertising and public relations, business administration/management, commerce, communication services, cultural studies, economics, entrepreneurship, finance, human resources, information science, intercultural studies, interdisciplinary studies, international affairs, international business, labor and industrial relations, Latin American studies, law and legal studies, liberal studies, management information systems, marketing, Mexican studies, peace and conflict studies, political science and government, public administration, public policy, social sciences, Spanish language and literature.

Program Information • Students attend classes at Alliant International University–Mexico (Mexico D.F., Mexico). Scheduled travel to Puebla, San Miguel; field trips to pyramids of Teotihuacan, Mexico City. Students typically earn 6 semester credits per term.

Sessions • Jun–Jul (summer), Jul–Aug (summer 2).

Eligibility Requirements • Open to freshmen, sophomores, juniors, seniors, graduate students, adults; 2.2 GPA; 2 letters of recommendation; good academic standing at home school; no foreign language proficiency required.

Living Arrangements • Students live in locally rented apartments, program-owned apartments, host family homes. Quarters are shared with host institution students, students from other programs. Meals are taken on one's own, in residences, in restaurants.

Costs (2006) • $4970; includes tuition, housing, insurance, excursions, student support services, mobile telephone. $50 application fee. $500 nonrefundable deposit required. Financial aid available for all students: scholarships, loans.

For More Information • Mr. Eduard Izraylovsky, Director, Knowledge Exchange Institute (KEI), 111 John Street, Suite 800, New York, NY 10038; *Phone:* 800-831-5095; *Fax:* 212-528-2095. *E-mail:* info@knowledgeexchange.org. *World Wide Web:* http://www. knowledgeexchange.org/

KNOWLEDGE EXCHANGE INSTITUTE (KEI)
LATIN AMERICAN STUDIES AND SPANISH LANGUAGE

Hosted by Alliant International University–Mexico

Academic Focus • Ancient history, anthropology, civilization studies, communication services, communications, community service, comparative history, conservation studies, cultural studies, economics, environmental science/studies, ethics, ethnic studies, history, intercultural studies, interdisciplinary studies, international affairs, Latin American studies, liberal studies, mathematics, Mayan studies, Mexican studies, natural resources, peace and conflict studies, philosophy, political science and government, popular culture, public policy, science, social sciences, social services, social work, sociology, Spanish language and literature, urban studies.

Program Information • Students attend classes at Alliant International University–Mexico (Mexico D.F., Mexico). Scheduled travel to Puebla, San Miguel; field trips to pyramids of Teotihuacan; optional travel at an extra cost. Students typically earn 6 semester credits per term.

Sessions • Jun–Jul (summer), Jul–Aug (summer 2).

Eligibility Requirements • Open to freshmen, sophomores, juniors, seniors, graduate students, adults; 2.2 GPA; 2 letters of recommendation; good academic standing at home school; no foreign language proficiency required.

Living Arrangements • Students live in locally rented apartments, program-owned apartments, host family homes. Quarters are shared with host institution students, students from other programs. Meals are taken on one's own, in residences, in restaurants.

MEXICO
Mexico City

Costs (2006) • $4970; includes tuition, housing, insurance, excursions, books and class materials, lab equipment, student support services, mobile telephone. $50 application fee. $500 nonrefundable deposit required. Financial aid available for all students: scholarships, loans.
For More Information • Mr. Eduard Izraylovsky, Director, Knowledge Exchange Institute (KEI), 111 John Street, Suite 800, New York, NY 10038; *Phone:* 800-831-5095; *Fax:* 212-528-2095. *E-mail:* info@knowledgeexchange.org. *World Wide Web:* http://www.knowledgeexchange.org/

KNOWLEDGE EXCHANGE INSTITUTE (KEI)
LATIN AMERICAN TOURISM AND HOSPITALITY MANAGEMENT

Hosted by Alliant International University–Mexico
Academic Focus • Advertising and public relations, business administration/management, commerce, cultural studies, economics, finance, food service, hotel and restaurant management, intercultural studies, interdisciplinary studies, international business, Latin American studies, liberal studies, marketing, Mexican studies, parks and recreation, Spanish language and literature, Spanish studies, tourism and travel.
Program Information • Students attend classes at Alliant International University-Mexico (Mexico D.F., Mexico). Scheduled travel to Puebla, San Miguel; field trips to pyramids of Teotihuacan, Mexico City. Students typically earn 6 semester credits per term.
Sessions • Jun–Jul (summer), Jul–Aug (summer 2).
Eligibility Requirements • Open to freshmen, sophomores, juniors, seniors, graduate students, adults; 2.2 GPA; 2 letters of recommendation; good academic standing at home school; no foreign language proficiency required.
Living Arrangements • Students live in locally rented apartments, program-owned apartments, host family homes. Quarters are shared with host institution students, students from other programs. Meals are taken on one's own, in residences, in restaurants.
Costs (2006) • $4970; includes tuition, housing, insurance, excursions, student support services, mobile telephone. $50 application fee. $500 nonrefundable deposit required. Financial aid available for all students: scholarships, loans.
For More Information • Mr. Eduard Izraylovsky, Director, Knowledge Exchange Institute (KEI), 111 John Street, Suite 800, New York, NY 10038; *Phone:* 800-831-5095; *Fax:* 212-528-2095. *E-mail:* info@knowledgeexchange.org. *World Wide Web:* http://www.knowledgeexchange.org/

KNOWLEDGE EXCHANGE INSTITUTE (KEI)
MEXICO CITY INTERNSHIP PROGRAM

Hosted by Alliant International University–Mexico
Academic Focus • Accounting, actuarial science, advertising and public relations, brokerage, business administration/management, commerce, communication services, communications, community service, criminal justice, economics, entrepreneurship, environmental health, finance, health-care management, hospitality services, hotel and restaurant management, human resources, information science, international affairs, international business, Latin American studies, law and legal studies, management information systems, marketing, Mexican studies, peace and conflict studies, political science and government, psychology, public administration, social sciences, social services, social work, sociology, Spanish language and literature, tourism and travel.
Program Information • Students attend classes at Alliant International University-Mexico (Mexico D.F., Mexico). Field trips to Mexico City, Teotihuacan. Students typically earn 6 semester credits per term.
Sessions • Jun–Aug (summer).
Eligibility Requirements • Open to freshmen, sophomores, juniors, seniors, graduate students, adults; 2.2 GPA; 2 letters of recommendation; good academic standing at home school; no foreign language proficiency required.
Living Arrangements • Students live in host institution dormitories, program-owned apartments, host family homes. Quarters are shared with host institution students, students from other programs. Meals are taken on one's own, with host family, in residences, in restaurants.

Costs (2006) • $4975; includes tuition, housing, insurance, excursions, student support services, mobile telephone. $50 application fee. $500 nonrefundable deposit required. Financial aid available for all students: scholarships, loans.
For More Information • Mr. Eduard Izraylovsky, Director, Knowledge Exchange Institute (KEI), 111 John Street, Suite 800, New York, NY 10038; *Phone:* 800-831-5095; *Fax:* 212-528-2095. *E-mail:* info@knowledgeexchange.org. *World Wide Web:* http://www.knowledgeexchange.org/

KNOWLEDGE EXCHANGE INSTITUTE (KEI)
PSYCHOLOGY, SOCIOLOGY, AND HUMAN BEHAVIOR

Hosted by Alliant International University–Mexico
Academic Focus • Communications, community service, cultural studies, health-care management, intercultural studies, interdisciplinary studies, Latin American studies, liberal studies, Mexican studies, philosophy, psychology, public health, public policy, social sciences, social services, social work, sociology, Spanish language and literature, Spanish studies, statistics.
Program Information • Students attend classes at Alliant International University-Mexico (Mexico D.F., Mexico). Scheduled travel to Puebla, San Miguel; field trips to pyramids of Teotihuacan, Mexico City. Students typically earn 6 semester credits per term.
Sessions • Jun–Jul (summer), Jul–Aug (summer 2).
Eligibility Requirements • Open to freshmen, sophomores, juniors, seniors, graduate students, adults; 2.2 GPA; 2 letters of recommendation; good academic standing at home school; no foreign language proficiency required.
Living Arrangements • Students live in locally rented apartments, program-owned apartments, host family homes. Quarters are shared with host institution students, students from other programs. Meals are taken on one's own, in residences, in restaurants.
Costs (2006) • $4970; includes tuition, housing, insurance, excursions, lab equipment, student support services, mobile telephone. $50 application fee. $500 nonrefundable deposit required. Financial aid available for all students: scholarships, loans.
For More Information • Mr. Eduard Izraylovsky, Director, Knowledge Exchange Institute (KEI), 111 John Street, Suite 800, New York, NY 10038; *Phone:* 800-831-5095; *Fax:* 212-528-2095. *E-mail:* info@knowledgeexchange.org. *World Wide Web:* http://www.knowledgeexchange.org/

KNOWLEDGE EXCHANGE INSTITUTE (KEI)
SPANISH ON THE ROAD IN MEXICO

Hosted by Alliant International University–Mexico
Academic Focus • Anthropology, archaeology, area studies, art history, comparative history, conservation studies, cultural studies, environmental science/studies, ethnic studies, history, interdisciplinary studies, Latin American studies, natural resources, Spanish language and literature, Spanish studies.
Program Information • Students attend classes at Alliant International University-Mexico (Mexico D.F., Mexico). Scheduled travel to Guadalajara, Playa Azul, Pericutin, Metepec; Chalma; field trips to Mexico City, Teotihuacan, Tula, San Miguel; Morella. Students typically earn 6 semester credits per term.
Sessions • Jun–Jul (summer).
Eligibility Requirements • Open to precollege students, freshmen, sophomores, juniors, seniors; 2.2 GPA; 2 letters of recommendation; good academic standing at home school; no foreign language proficiency required.
Living Arrangements • Students live in host institution dormitories, program-owned apartments, host family homes, hotels. Quarters are shared with host institution students, students from other programs. Meals are taken as a group, with host family, in residences, in restaurants.
Costs (2006) • $5995; includes tuition, housing, all meals, insurance, excursions, books and class materials, student support services, mobile telephone. $50 application fee. $500 nonrefundable deposit required. Financial aid available for all students: scholarships, loans.
For More Information • Mr. Eduard Izraylovsky, Director, Knowledge Exchange Institute (KEI), 111 John Street, Suite 800, New York, NY 10038; *Phone:* 800-831-5095; *Fax:* 212-528-2095. *E-mail:* info@knowledgeexchange.org. *World Wide Web:* http://www.knowledgeexchange.org/

LOYOLA UNIVERSITY NEW ORLEANS
SUMMER SESSION IN MEXICO CITY

Hosted by Universidad Iberoamericana

Academic Focus • Communications, education, history, international affairs, Latin American studies, Mexican studies, music, political science and government, sociology, Spanish language and literature, visual and performing arts.

Program Information • Students attend classes at Universidad Iberoamericana (Mexico City, Mexico). Scheduled travel to Mexico City, Cuernavaca, Teotihuacán, Taxco; field trips to Mexico City, Cuernavaca, Teotihuacán, Taxco; optional travel to Acapulco, Cancún, Dayaca, Guanajuato at an extra cost. Students typically earn 6–10 semester credits per term.

Sessions • Jun–Jul (summer).

Eligibility Requirements • Minimum age 17; open to freshmen, sophomores, juniors, seniors, graduate students, adults; good academic standing at home school; interview; no foreign language proficiency required.

Living Arrangements • Students live in host family homes. Meals are taken with host family, in residences.

Costs (2006) • $3500; includes tuition, housing, some meals, insurance, excursions, student support services. $25 application fee. Financial aid available for all students: scholarships, loans.

For More Information • Dr. Maurice Brungardt, Director, Mexico Program, Loyola University New Orleans, 6363 Saint Charles Avenue, New Orleans, LA 70118; *Phone:* 504-865-3537; *Fax:* 504-865-2010. *E-mail:* brungard@loyno.edu. *World Wide Web:* http://www.loyno.edu/cie/

NEW YORK UNIVERSITY
MEXICO CITY AND THE URBAN EXPERIENCE IN LATIN AMERICA

Academic Focus • Latin American studies, urban studies, urban/regional planning.

Program Information • Faculty members are drawn from the sponsor's U.S. staff and local instructors hired by the sponsor. Field trips. Students typically earn 4 semester credits per term.

Sessions • Jun–Jul (summer).

Eligibility Requirements • Minimum age 18; open to freshmen, sophomores, juniors, seniors; no foreign language proficiency required.

Living Arrangements • Students live in hotels. Quarters are shared with host institution students. Meals are taken as a group, on one's own, in central dining facility, in restaurants.

Costs (2005) • $3500; includes tuition, housing, some meals, excursions, student support services. $300 nonrefundable deposit required. Financial aid available for students from sponsoring institution: scholarships.

For More Information • Ms. Vanessa Manko, Academic Adviser, New York University, 719 Broadway, 529B, New York, NY 10003; *Phone:* 212-998-7365; *Fax:* 212-995-4002. *E-mail:* vkm201@nyu.edu. *World Wide Web:* http://www.nyu.edu/global/studyabroad.html

SAINT MARY'S COLLEGE
BUSINESS IN MEXICO CITY

Academic Focus • Economics, international business, labor and industrial relations.

Program Information • Faculty members are drawn from the sponsor's U.S. staff. Field trips. Students typically earn 1 semester credit per term.

Sessions • May (summer).

Eligibility Requirements • Minimum age 18; open to freshmen, sophomores, juniors, seniors; 2.5 GPA; 3 letters of recommendation; good academic standing at home school; no foreign language proficiency required.

Living Arrangements • Students live in hotels. Quarters are shared with students from other programs. Meals are taken as a group, in restaurants.

Costs (2005) • $1195; includes all meals, insurance, excursions, international airfare, student support services. $30 application fee.

For More Information • Dr. Pablo Hernandez, Faculty Coordinator for Mexico Program, Saint Mary's College, Department of Business and Economics, Notre Dame, IN 46556; *Phone:* 574-284-4263; *Fax:* 574-284-4141. *E-mail:* phernand@saintmarys.edu. *World Wide Web:* http://www.saintmarys.edu/~cwil

UNIVERSIDAD IBEROAMERICANA
INTENSIVE SPANISH SIX-WEEK SUMMER SESSION

Hosted by Universidad Iberoamericana

Academic Focus • Spanish language and literature.

Program Information • Students attend classes at Universidad Iberoamericana (Mexico City, Mexico). Field trips to Mexico City. Students typically earn 16 UIA credits per term.

Sessions • Jun–Jul (summer).

Eligibility Requirements • Minimum age 18; open to juniors, seniors, graduate students, adults; 2.5 GPA; no foreign language proficiency required.

Living Arrangements • Students live in host family homes. Quarters are shared with host institution students. Meals are taken with host family, in residences, in central dining facility, in restaurants.

Costs (2006) • $2500 for 2 courses; $3150 for 3 courses; includes tuition, housing, all meals, excursions, international student ID, student support services, ID card for library, infirmary, discounts at museums. $50 application fee.

For More Information • Ms. Catherine Fanning, Assistant Director, Student Exchange Program, Universidad Iberoamericana, Prol. Paseo de la Reforma 880, Col. Lomas de Santa Fe, D.F. 01210, Mexico; *Phone:* +52 55-5950-4243; *Fax:* +52 55-5950-4241. *E-mail:* international@uia.mx. *World Wide Web:* http://www.uia.mx/. Students may also apply through Alma College, Alma, MI 48801-1599; Loyola University New Orleans, 6363 St. Charles Avenue, New Orleans, LA 70118; Pomona College, 333 North College Way, Claremont, CA 91711-6334.

MONTERREY

MICHIGAN STATE UNIVERSITY
DOING BUSINESS IN MEXICO

Held at Instituto Tecnológico y de Estudios Superiores de Monterrey–Monterrey Campus

Academic Focus • Business administration/management, human resources, international business.

Program Information • Classes are held on the campus of Instituto Tecnológico y de Estudios Superiores de Monterrey–Monterrey Campus (Monterrey, Mexico). Faculty members are drawn from the sponsor's U.S. staff. Field trips to Mexican companies. Students typically earn 3 semester credits per term.

Sessions • May (summer).

Eligibility Requirements • Open to graduate students; 3.0 GPA; good academic standing at home school; MBA students only; no foreign language proficiency required.

Living Arrangements • Students live in hotels. Meals are taken as a group, on one's own, in restaurants.

Costs (2005) • $1307 (estimated); includes housing, all meals, insurance, excursions. $100 application fee. $200 nonrefundable deposit required. Financial aid available for students from sponsoring institution: scholarships, loans.

For More Information • Mr. Mark Davis, Coordinator, Michigan State University, Office of Study Abroad, 109 International Center, East Lansing, MI 48824-1035; *Phone:* 517-432-1315; *Fax:* 517-432-2082. *E-mail:* mdavis@msu.edu. *World Wide Web:* http://studyabroad.msu.edu/

MORELIA

AHA INTERNATIONAL AN ACADEMIC PROGRAM OF THE UNIVERSITY OF OREGON
MORELIA, MEXICO: MIDWEST CONSORTIUM FOR STUDY ABROAD (MCSA) AND NORTHWEST COUNCIL ON STUDY ABROAD (NCSA)

Hosted by Latin University of America

Academic Focus • Education, history, Spanish language and literature.

Program Information • Students attend classes at Latin University of America (Morelia, Mexico). Field trips to local course-related sites. Students typically earn 6–12 quarter credits per term.

Sessions • Jul (summer), Jul–Aug (language and culture).

MEXICO
Morelia

Eligibility Requirements • Open to freshmen, sophomores, juniors, seniors, graduate students, adults; 2 letters of recommendation; good academic standing at home school; no foreign language proficiency required.

Living Arrangements • Students live in host family homes. Quarters are shared with host institution students. Meals are taken with host family, in residences.

Costs (2005–2006) • $1905–$2685; includes tuition, housing, all meals, insurance, excursions, books and class materials, international student ID, student support services, on-site orientation. $50 application fee. $200 refundable deposit required. Financial aid available for all students: scholarships, loans, home institution financial aid.

For More Information • Mr. Richard Browning, Associate Director for University Programs, AHA International An Academic Program of the University of Oregon, 221 NW 2nd Avenue, Suite 200, Portland, OR 97209; *Phone:* 503-295-7730; *Fax:* 503-295-5969. *E-mail:* mail@aha-intl.org. *World Wide Web:* http://www.aha-intl.org/

KENTUCKY INSTITUTE FOR INTERNATIONAL STUDIES
MEXICO

Academic Focus • Mexican studies, Spanish language and literature.

Program Information • Faculty members are drawn from the sponsor's U.S. staff. Field trips to Santa Clara del Cobre, Guanajuato, Pátzcuaro, Janitzio. Students typically earn 3–6 semester credits per term.

Sessions • May–Jun (summer).

Eligibility Requirements • Minimum age 18; open to freshmen, sophomores, juniors, seniors, graduate students, adults; 2.0 GPA; 1 letter of recommendation; no foreign language proficiency required.

Living Arrangements • Students live in host family homes. Meals are taken with host family, in residences.

Costs (2006) • $2290; includes housing, some meals, insurance, excursions, international airfare, international student ID, instructional expenses. $150 application fee. Financial aid available for all students: scholarships.

For More Information • Ms. Nancy Martin, Coordinator, Kentucky Institute for International Studies, PO Box 9, Murray, KY 42071-0009; *Phone:* 270-762-3091; *Fax:* 270-762-3434. *E-mail:* kiismsu@murraystate.edu. *World Wide Web:* http://www.kiis.org/

KENTUCKY INSTITUTE FOR INTERNATIONAL STUDIES
MEXICO–PRE-PROFESSIONAL

Academic Focus • Spanish language and literature, Spanish studies.

Program Information • Faculty members are drawn from the sponsor's U.S. staff. Field trips to local points of interest; optional travel at an extra cost. Students typically earn 3–6 semester credits per term.

Sessions • Jul–Aug (summer).

Eligibility Requirements • Minimum age 18; open to freshmen, sophomores, juniors, seniors, graduate students; 2.0 GPA; 1 letter of recommendation; years of college course work in Spanish.

Living Arrangements • Students live in host institution dormitories, host family homes, hotels. Meals are taken as a group, with host family, in residences, in central dining facility.

Costs (2006) • $2290; includes housing, some meals, insurance, excursions, international airfare, international student ID, instructional costs. $150 application fee. Financial aid available for all students: scholarships.

For More Information • Ms. Nancy Martin, Coordinator, Kentucky Institute for International Studies, PO Box 9, Murray, KY 42071-0009; *Phone:* 270-762-3091; *Fax:* 270-762-3434. *E-mail:* kiismsu@murraystate.edu. *World Wide Web:* http://www.kiis.org/

OAXACA

ACADEMIC PROGRAMS INTERNATIONAL (API)
(API)–OAXACA, MEXICO

Hosted by La Universidad Regional del Sureste
Academic Focus • Art history, cultural studies, history, Latin American studies, Mayan studies, Mexican studies, Spanish language and literature.
Program Information • Students attend classes at La Universidad Regional del Sureste (Oaxaca, Mexico). Field trips to Dainzu, Heirue el Agua, Mitla, Monte Alban, Teotitlan de Valle, Tlacolula, Yagul, Pacific coast of Oaxaca. Students typically earn 6 semester credits per term.
Sessions • May–Jul (summer).
Eligibility Requirements • Minimum age 18; open to freshmen, sophomores, juniors, seniors; 2.75 GPA; 1 letter of recommendation; good academic standing at home school; official transcript from home university; no foreign language proficiency required.
Living Arrangements • Students live in host family homes. Quarters are shared with students from other programs. Meals are taken on one's own, with host family, in residences, in restaurants.
Costs (2006–2007) • $2950–$3050; includes tuition, housing, all meals, insurance, excursions, student support services, airport reception, ground transportation, mobile phone, on-line service, on-site director. $150 nonrefundable deposit required. Financial aid available for all students: scholarships.
For More Information • Ms. Jennifer C. Allen, Director, Academic Programs International (API), 107 East Hopkins, San Marcos, TX 78666; *Phone:* 800-844-4124; *Fax:* 512-392-8420. *E-mail:* api@academicintl.com. *World Wide Web:* http://www.academicintl.com/

CITY COLLEGE OF SAN FRANCISCO
SUMMER IN OAXACA

Hosted by Instituto Cultural Oaxaca
Academic Focus • Spanish studies.
Program Information • Students attend classes at Instituto Cultural Oaxaca (Oaxaca, Mexico). Field trips to Monte Alban, Teotitlán del Valle, Mitla. Students typically earn 3 semester credits per term.
Sessions • Jun–Jul (summer).
Eligibility Requirements • Minimum age 18; open to freshmen, sophomores, juniors, seniors, graduate students, adults; 2.0 GPA; good academic standing at home school; no foreign language proficiency required.
Living Arrangements • Students live in host family homes, hotels. Meals are taken on one's own, with host family, in residences, in restaurants.
Costs (2005) • $2108; includes tuition, housing, some meals, insurance, international airfare, international student ID, student support services. $250 refundable deposit required. Financial aid available for students from sponsoring institution: scholarships, loans.
For More Information • Ms. Jill Heffron, Study Abroad Coordinator, City College of San Francisco, 50 Phelan Avenue, Box C212, San Francisco, CA 94112; *Phone:* 415-239-3778; *Fax:* 415-239-3804. *E-mail:* studyabroad@ccsf.edu. *World Wide Web:* http://www.ccsf.edu/studyabroad/

LANGUAGE LIAISON
LEARN SPANISH IN OAXACA

Hosted by Language Liaison
Academic Focus • Spanish language and literature.
Program Information • Students attend classes at Language Liaison (Oaxaca, Mexico). Field trips; optional travel at an extra cost. Students typically earn 3–15 semester credits per term.
Sessions • Classes begin weekly, year-round.
Eligibility Requirements • Minimum age 17; open to freshmen, sophomores, juniors, seniors, graduate students, adults; no foreign language proficiency required.
Living Arrangements • Students live in locally rented apartments, host family homes, hotels. Meals are taken with host family, in residences, in restaurants.
Costs (2005) • Contact sponsor for cost. $175 application fee. Financial aid available for all students: scholarship research service.
For More Information • Ms. Nancy Forman, President, Language Liaison, PO Box 1772, Pacific Palisades, CA 90272; *Phone:* 800-284-4448; *Fax:* 310-454-1706. *E-mail:* learn@languageliaison.com. *World Wide Web:* http://www.languageliaison.com/

LANGUAGE LIAISON
SPANISH IN OAXACA

Hosted by Language Liaison
Academic Focus • Spanish language and literature.
Program Information • Students attend classes at Language Liaison (Oaxaca, Mexico). Field trips; optional travel at an extra cost. Students typically earn 3–15 semester credits per term.
Sessions • Classes begin weekly, year-round.
Eligibility Requirements • Minimum age 17; open to precollege students, freshmen, sophomores, juniors, seniors, graduate students, adults; no foreign language proficiency required.
Living Arrangements • Students live in locally rented apartments, host family homes, hotels. Meals are taken on one's own, with host family, in residences, in restaurants.
Costs (2005) • Contact sponsor for cost. $175 application fee. Financial aid available for all students: scholarship research service.
For More Information • Ms. Nancy Forman, President, Language Liaison, PO Box 1772, Pacific Palisades, CA 90272; *Phone:* 800-284-4448; *Fax:* 310-454-1706. *E-mail:* learn@languageliaison.com. *World Wide Web:* http://www.languageliaison.com/

LANGUAGE LINK
BECARI OF OAXACA

Hosted by Becari Language School
Academic Focus • Spanish language and literature.
Program Information • Students attend classes at Becari Language School (Oaxaca, Mexico). Field trips to archaeological sites, artisan workshops. Students typically earn 6–15 semester credits per term.
Sessions • Year-round, start any Monday.
Eligibility Requirements • Minimum age 18; open to freshmen, sophomores, juniors, seniors, graduate students, adults; no foreign language proficiency required.
Living Arrangements • Students live in host family homes. Quarters are shared with host institution students. Meals are taken on one's own, with host family, in residences, in restaurants.
Costs (2005) • $210 per week; includes tuition, housing, some meals, books and class materials, student support services, cultural activities, airport pick-up.
For More Information • Ms. Kay G. Rafool, Director, Language Link, PO Box 3006, Peoria, IL 61612-3006; *Phone:* 800-552-2051; *Fax:* 309-692-2926. *E-mail:* info@langlink.com. *World Wide Web:* http://www.langlink.com/

LINGUA SERVICE WORLDWIDE
VACATION 'N LEARN SPANISH IN MEXICO

Hosted by Instituto Cultural Oaxaca
Academic Focus • Spanish language and literature, Spanish studies.
Program Information • Students attend classes at Instituto Cultural Oaxaca (Oaxaca, Mexico). Optional travel to beach sites, Mayan and Aztec ruins at an extra cost. Students typically earn 3 semester credits for 3 weeks, 6 semester credits for 5 weeks.
Sessions • Year-round sessions of 1 week or more, beginning on Mondays.
Eligibility Requirements • Minimum age 16; open to precollege students, freshmen, sophomores, juniors, seniors, graduate students, adults; no foreign language proficiency required.
Living Arrangements • Students live in host institution dormitories, locally rented apartments, host family homes, hotels. Meals are taken with host family.
Costs (2006–2007) • Contact sponsor for cost. $100 application fee.
For More Information • Assistant Director, Lingua Service Worldwide, 75 Prospect Street, Suite 4, Huntington, NY 11743; *Phone:* 800-394-5327; *Fax:* 631-271-3441. *E-mail:* linguaservice@att.net. *World Wide Web:* http://www.linguaserviceworldwide.com/

MEXICO
Oaxaca

PROWORLD SERVICE CORPS
PROWORLD SERVICE CORPS

Academic Focus • Community service, cultural studies, environmental science/studies, Latin American studies, Mayan studies, Mexican studies, public policy, social sciences, social work, Spanish language and literature.

Program Information • Faculty members are drawn from the sponsor's U.S. staff and local instructors hired by the sponsor. Field trips to ancient ruins, outdoor adventures, cultural activities; optional travel to beaches, remote communities at an extra cost. Students typically earn 3 semester credits per term.

Sessions • 4 week sessions begin every month, year-round.

Eligibility Requirements • Minimum age 18; open to freshmen, sophomores, juniors, seniors, graduate students, adults; good academic standing at home school; desire to learn and help others; no foreign language proficiency required.

Living Arrangements • Students live in host family homes. Meals are taken with host family, in residences.

Costs (2005) • $1950 for 4 weeks; $300 for each additional week; includes tuition, housing, all meals, insurance, excursions, books and class materials, lab equipment, international student ID, student support services. $200 nonrefundable deposit required. Financial aid available for all students: scholarships.

For More Information • Ms. Anne Connolly, Marketing and Placement Advisor, ProWorld Service Corps, PO Box 21121, Billings, MT 59104-1121; *Phone:* 877-429-6753; *Fax:* 406-252-3973. *E-mail:* info@proworldsc.org. *World Wide Web:* http://www.proworldsc. org

UNIVERSITY OF ROCHESTER
SPANISH IN MEXICO

Hosted by Instituto Cultural Oaxaca

Academic Focus • Spanish language and literature, Spanish studies.

Program Information • Students attend classes at Instituto Cultural Oaxaca (Oaxaca, Mexico). Field trips to archaeological and tourist sites near Oaxaca. Students typically earn 6 semester credits per term.

Sessions • May–Jun (summer).

Eligibility Requirements • Minimum age 18; open to freshmen, sophomores, juniors, seniors; 1 letter of recommendation; good academic standing at home school; 1 year of college course work in Spanish.

Living Arrangements • Students live in host family homes. Meals are taken with host family, in residences.

Costs (2005) • $2890; includes tuition, housing, some meals, excursions, books and class materials, student support services, in-country airfare. $250 refundable deposit required. Financial aid available for students from sponsoring institution: scholarships, loans.

For More Information • Ms. Anne Lutkus, Language Coordinator, University of Rochester, Department of Modern Languages and Cultures, PO Box 270082, Rochester, NY 14627-0082; *Phone:* 585-275-2235; *Fax:* 585-273-1097. *E-mail:* adlt@mail.rochester.edu. *World Wide Web:* http://www.rochester.edu/college/study-abroad/

PLAYA DEL CARMEN

LANGUAGE LINK
IH RIVIERA MAYA

Hosted by IH Riviera Maya

Academic Focus • Spanish language and literature.

Program Information • Students attend classes at IH Riviera Maya (Playa del Carmen, Mexico). Field trips to Cozumel, Chichen Itzá. Students typically earn 6-15 semester credits per term.

Sessions • Classes begin every Monday, year-round.

Eligibility Requirements • Minimum age 17; open to precollege students, freshmen, sophomores, juniors, seniors, graduate students, adults; no foreign language proficiency required.

Living Arrangements • Students live in host family homes, residence center. Quarters are shared with host institution students. Meals are taken as a group, with host family, in residences, in central dining facility.

Costs (2005) • $360 per week; includes tuition, housing, some meals, student support services, cultural activities.

For More Information • Ms. Kay G. Rafool, Director, Language Link, PO Box 3006, Peoria, IL 61612-3006; *Phone:* 800-552-2051; *Fax:* 309-692-2926. *E-mail:* info@langlink.com. *World Wide Web:* http://www.langlink.com/

LINGUA SERVICE WORLDWIDE
SOLÉXICO

Hosted by Soléxico Language and Cultural Centers

Academic Focus • Spanish language and literature, Spanish studies.

Program Information • Students attend classes at Soléxico Language and Cultural Centers (Playa del Carmen, Mexico). Optional travel to cultural sites throughout Mexico at an extra cost. Students typically earn 3 semester credits for 3 weeks, 6 semester credits for 5 weeks.

Sessions • Sessions of 2 or more weeks begin on Mondays, year-round.

Eligibility Requirements • Minimum age 16; open to precollege students, freshmen, sophomores, juniors, seniors, graduate students, adults; no foreign language proficiency required.

Living Arrangements • Students live in host family homes, hotels. Meals are taken with host family.

Costs (2006–2007) • Contact sponsor for cost. $100 application fee.

For More Information • Assistant Director, Lingua Service Worldwide, 75 Prospect Street, Suite 4, Huntington, NY 11743; *Phone:* 800-394-5327; *Fax:* 631-271-3441. *E-mail:* linguaservice@att. net. *World Wide Web:* http://www.linguaserviceworldwide.com/

PUEBLA

ACADEMIC PROGRAMS INTERNATIONAL (API)
(API)–PUEBLA, MEXICO

Hosted by University of the Americas–Puebla

Academic Focus • Business administration/management, Latin American studies, Mayan studies, medicine, Mexican studies, nursing, political science and government, public health, Spanish language and literature.

Program Information • Students attend classes at University of the Americas–Puebla (Puebla, Mexico). Scheduled travel to Mexico City; field trips to Acapulco, Cuernavaca, Michoacan, Oaxaca, Taxco, Tlaxcala Tepoztlan. Students typically earn 6 semester credits per term.

Sessions • May–Jul (summer).

Eligibility Requirements • Minimum age 18; open to freshmen, sophomores, juniors, seniors; 2.75 GPA; 1 letter of recommendation; good academic standing at home school; official transcript from home university; no foreign language proficiency required.

Living Arrangements • Students live in host institution dormitories, host family homes. Quarters are shared with students from other programs. Meals are taken on one's own, with host family, in residences, in restaurants.

Costs (2006–2007) • $4400–$4450; includes tuition, housing, insurance, excursions, student support services, mobile phone, airport reception; ground transportation; online services; on-site director. $150 nonrefundable deposit required. Financial aid available for all students: scholarships.

For More Information • Ms. Jennifer C. Allen, Director, Academic Programs International (API), 107 East Hopkins, San Marcos, TX 78666; *Phone:* 800-844-4124; *Fax:* 512-392-8420. *E-mail:* api@ academicintl.com. *World Wide Web:* http://www.academicintl.com/

UNIVERSITY OF KANSAS
SUMMER LANGUAGE AND CULTURE IN PUEBLA, MEXICO

Hosted by University of the Americas–Puebla

Academic Focus • Mexican studies, Spanish language and literature.

Program Information • Students attend classes at University of the Americas–Puebla (Puebla, Mexico). Field trips to downtown Puebla, Cholula, Amparo museum, Tonanzintla and San Francisco Acatepec churches; optional travel to Mexico City, Acapulco, Veracruz, Teotihuacán, Oaxaca, Cuetzalan, Tlaxcala, and Cacaxtla at an extra cost. Students typically earn 7 semester credits per term.

Sessions • May-Jul (summer).

Eligibility Requirements • Minimum age 18; open to freshmen, sophomores, juniors, seniors; 2.5 GPA; 2 letters of recommendation; good academic standing at home school; minimum 2.5 GPA overall and in Spanish; 2 years of college course work in Spanish.

Living Arrangements • Students live in host family homes. Meals are taken with host family, in residences.

Costs (2005) • $3850; includes tuition, housing, all meals, excursions, student support services, medical evacuation and repatriation insurance. $38 application fee. $300 nonrefundable deposit required. Financial aid available for students from sponsoring institution: scholarships, loans.

For More Information • Ms. Angela Dittrich, Assistant Director, University of Kansas, Office of Study Abroad, Lippincott Hall, 1410 Jayhawk Boulevard, Room 108, Lawrence, KS 66045-7515; *Phone:* 785-864-3742; *Fax:* 785-864-5040. *E-mail:* osa@ku.edu. *World Wide Web:* http://www.ku.edu/~osa/

UNIVERSITY OF NOTRE DAME
PUEBLA SUMMER PROGRAM

Hosted by University of the Americas–Puebla

Academic Focus • Engineering, Latin American studies, Spanish language and literature.

Program Information • Students attend classes at University of the Americas–Puebla (Puebla, Mexico). Optional travel at an extra cost. Students typically earn 6 semester credits per term.

Sessions • May-Jul (summer).

Eligibility Requirements • Open to sophomores, juniors, seniors; good academic standing at home school; no foreign language proficiency required.

Living Arrangements • Students live in host institution dormitories. Quarters are shared with students from other programs. Meals are taken in central dining facility, in restaurants.

Costs (2004–2005) • $3600; includes tuition, housing, all meals, cultural workshops. Financial aid available for students from sponsoring institution: scholarships, loans.

For More Information • Dr. Claudia Kselman, Associate Director, University of Notre Dame, 158 Hurley Building, Notre Dame, IN 46556; *Phone:* 574-631-5882; *Fax:* 574-631-5711. *E-mail:* kselman.2@nd.edu. *World Wide Web:* http://www.nd.edu/~intlstud/

UNIVERSITY OF SOUTHERN MISSISSIPPI
SPANISH IN MEXICO

Hosted by University of the Americas–Puebla

Academic Focus • Spanish language and literature.

Program Information • Students attend classes at University of the Americas–Puebla (Puebla, Mexico). Scheduled travel; field trips; optional travel at an extra cost. Students typically earn 6 semester credits per term.

Sessions • May-Jun (summer).

Eligibility Requirements • Minimum age 18; open to sophomores, juniors, seniors, graduate students, adults; 2.0 GPA; good academic standing at home school; previous experience in Spanish.

Living Arrangements • Students live in host institution dormitories. Quarters are shared with host institution students.

Costs (2005) • $3599; includes tuition, housing, some meals, excursions, international airfare. $200 nonrefundable deposit required. Financial aid available for students from sponsoring institution: scholarships, loans.

For More Information • Director, Spanish in Mexico, University of Southern Mississippi, 118 College Drive #10047, Hattiesburg, MS 39406-0001; *Phone:* 601-266-4344; *Fax:* 601-266-5699. *E-mail:* holly.buckner@usm.edu. *World Wide Web:* http://www.usm.edu/internationaledu/

UNIVERSITY STUDIES ABROAD CONSORTIUM
SPANISH SOCIOLOGY/HEALTH STUDIES, AND LATIN AMERICAN STUDIES: PUEBLA, MEXICO

Hosted by Universidad Iberoamericana Puebla

Academic Focus • Anthropology, dance, history, Latin American studies, political science and government, sociology, Spanish language and literature.

Program Information • Students attend classes at Universidad Iberoamericana Puebla (Puebla, Mexico). Field trips to Teotihuacán pyramids, a coffee-growing hacienda, Oaxtepec Aquatic Park; optional travel to the Gulf of Mexico, Campeche Bay, Veracruz at an extra cost. Students typically earn 5-10 semester credits per term.

Sessions • May-Jun (summer), Jun-Jul (summer 2).

Eligibility Requirements • Minimum age 18; open to freshmen, sophomores, juniors, seniors, graduate students, adults; 2.5 GPA; no foreign language proficiency required.

Living Arrangements • Students live in host institution dormitories, host family homes. Quarters are shared with host institution students. Meals are taken with host family, in residences, in restaurants.

Costs (2007) • $2480 for 1 session; $4860 for 2 sessions; includes tuition, housing, insurance, excursions. $100 application fee. $200 refundable deposit required. Financial aid available for all students: scholarships, loans.

For More Information • University Studies Abroad Consortium, USAC/323, Reno, NV 89557-0093; *Phone:* 775-784-6569; *Fax:* 775-784-6010. *E-mail:* usac@unr.edu. *World Wide Web:* http://usac.unr.edu/

PUERTO SAN CARLOS

THE SCHOOL FOR FIELD STUDIES
MEXICO: PRESERVING COASTAL DIVERSITY: SEA TURTLES AND BAY RESOURCES

Hosted by Center for Coastal Studies

Academic Focus • Biological/life sciences, conservation studies, ecology, economics, environmental science/studies, Latin American studies, marine sciences, Mexican studies, natural resources.

Program Information • Students attend classes at Center for Coastal Studies (Puerto San Carlos, Mexico). Field trips to local communities, Isla Magdalena. Students typically earn 4 semester credits per term.

Sessions • Jun-Jul (summer), Jul-Aug (summer 2).

Eligibility Requirements • Minimum age 16; open to precollege students, freshmen, sophomores, juniors, seniors; 2.5 GPA; 2 letters of recommendation; personal statement; no foreign language proficiency required.

Living Arrangements • Students live in cabins on the waterfront. Quarters are shared with host institution students. Meals are taken as a group, in central dining facility.

Costs (2007) • $3480; includes tuition, housing, all meals, excursions, lab equipment. $45 application fee. $450 nonrefundable deposit required. Financial aid available for all students: scholarships, loans.

For More Information • Admissions Department, The School for Field Studies, 10 Federal Street, Suite 24, Salem, MA 01970-3876; *Phone:* 800-989-4418; *Fax:* 978-741-3551. *E-mail:* admissions@fieldstudies.org. *World Wide Web:* http://www.fieldstudies.org/

PUERTO VALLARTA

CENTER FOR STUDY ABROAD (CSA)
UNIVERSITY OF GUADALAJARA, PUERTO VALLARTA

Hosted by University of Guadalajara

Academic Focus • Mexican studies, Spanish language and literature, Spanish studies.

Program Information • Students attend classes at University of Guadalajara (Puerto Vallarta, Mexico). Optional travel. Students typically earn 4-10 semester credits per term.

Sessions • Classes begin weekly, year-round.

Eligibility Requirements • Minimum age 18; open to precollege students, freshmen, sophomores, juniors, seniors, graduate students, adults; no foreign language proficiency required.

Living Arrangements • Students live in host family homes. Meals are taken with host family.

Costs (2005) • Contact sponsor for cost. $45 application fee.

For More Information • Ms. Alima K. Virtue, Program Director, Center for Study Abroad (CSA), 325 Washington Avenue South #93, Kent, WA 98032; *Phone:* 206-726-1498; *Fax:* 253-850-0454. *E-mail:* info@ccnterforstudyabroad.com. *World Wide Web:* http://www.centerforstudyabroad.com/

MEXICO
Puerto Vallarta

LANGUAGE LIAISON
LEARN SPANISH IN PUERTO VALLARTA

Hosted by Language Liaison
Academic Focus • Spanish language and literature.
Program Information • Students attend classes at Language Liaison (Puerto Vallarta, Mexico). Field trips; optional travel at an extra cost. Students typically earn 3–15 semester credits per term.
Sessions • Classes begin weekly, year-round.
Eligibility Requirements • Minimum age 17; open to freshmen, sophomores, juniors, seniors, graduate students, adults; no foreign language proficiency required.
Living Arrangements • Students live in host institution dormitories, host family homes, hotels. Meals are taken with host family, in residences, in restaurants.
Costs (2005) • Contact sponsor for cost. $175 application fee. Financial aid available for all students: scholarship research service.
For More Information • Ms. Nancy Forman, President, Language Liaison, PO Box 1772, Pacific Palisades, CA 90272; *Phone:* 800-284-4448; *Fax:* 310-454-1706. *E-mail:* learn@languageliaison. com. *World Wide Web:* http://www.languageliaison.com/

QUERÉTARO
ILLINOIS STATE UNIVERSITY
SUMMER STUDY IN MEXICO

Hosted by Instituto Tecnológico y de Estudios Superiores de Monterrey–Querétaro Campus
Academic Focus • International business, Mexican studies.
Program Information • Students attend classes at Instituto Tecnológico y de Estudios Superiores de Monterrey–Querétaro Campus (Querétaro, Mexico). Field trips to Aztec pyramids, Guanajuato, San Miguel de Allende; optional travel to Puerto Vallarta or Acapulco at an extra cost. Students typically earn 6 semester credits per term.

Sessions • Jun–Jul (summer).
Eligibility Requirements • Open to sophomores, juniors, seniors; course work in business; 2.5 GPA; 2 letters of recommendation; good academic standing at home school; essay; no foreign language proficiency required.
Living Arrangements • Students live in host family homes. Quarters are shared with host institution students, students from other programs. Meals are taken with host family, in residences.
Costs (2005) • $4740; includes tuition, housing, all meals, insurance, excursions, international airfare, books and class materials, international student ID, student support services, personal expenses. $150 application fee. Financial aid available for students from sponsoring institution: scholarships, loans.
For More Information • Office of International Studies and Programs, Illinois State University, Campus Box 6120, Normal, IL 61790-6120; *Phone:* 309-438-5276; *Fax:* 309-438-3987. *E-mail:* oisp@ilstu.edu. *World Wide Web:* http://www.internationalstudies. ilstu.edu/

INTERAMERICAN UNIVERSITY STUDIES INSTITUTE
SUMMER SPANISH

Hosted by Interamerican University Studies Institute
Academic Focus • Mexican studies, Spanish language and literature.
Program Information • Students attend classes at Interamerican University Studies Institute (Querétaro, Mexico). Field trips to Mexico City, Michoacán. Students typically earn 8–12 quarter credits per term.
Sessions • Jun–Jul and Jul–Sep (6 week sessions), Jul–Aug (5 week session).
Eligibility Requirements • Minimum age 18; open to freshmen, sophomores, juniors, seniors, graduate students; course work in

Latin America Social Sciences; 2.75 GPA; 2 letters of recommendation; good academic standing at home school; 1 year of college course work in Spanish.
Living Arrangements • Students live in host family homes. Meals are taken with host family.
Costs (2005) • $2817 for 5 weeks; $3140 for 6 weeks; includes tuition, housing, all meals, excursions, student support services, University of Oregon accreditation fee. $50 application fee. $200 nonrefundable deposit required.
For More Information • Ms. Jennifer Jewett, Program Coordinator, Interamerican University Studies Institute, PO Box 10958, Eugene, OR 97440; *Phone:* 800-345-4874; *Fax:* 541-686-5947. *E-mail:* office@iusi.org. *World Wide Web:* http://www.iusi.org/

MICHIGAN STATE UNIVERSITY
INTENSIVE FIRST AND SECOND YEAR SPANISH
Hosted by Autonomous University of Querétaro
Academic Focus • Spanish language and literature.
Program Information • Students attend classes at Autonomous University of Querétaro (Querétaro, Mexico). Students typically earn 8 semester credits per term.
Sessions • May-Jul (summer).
Eligibility Requirements • Minimum age 18; open to freshmen, sophomores, juniors, seniors; 2.5 GPA; good academic standing at home school; faculty approval; no foreign language proficiency required.
Living Arrangements • Students live in host family homes. Meals are taken on one's own, with host family, in residences.
Costs (2005) • $1700 (estimated); includes housing, all meals, insurance, excursions, student support services. $100 application fee. $200 nonrefundable deposit required. Financial aid available for students from sponsoring institution: scholarships, loans.
For More Information • Mr. Mark Davis, Coordinator, Michigan State University, Office of Study Abroad, 109 International Center, East Lansing, MI 48824-1035; *Phone:* 517-432-1315; *Fax:* 517-432-2082. *E-mail:* mdavis@msu.edu. *World Wide Web:* http://studyabroad.msu.edu/

SAN MIGUEL DE ALLENDE

ACADEMIA HISPANO AMERICANA
INTENSIVE, SEMI-INTENSIVE, AND ONE-TO-ONE SPANISH
Hosted by Academia Hispano Americana
Academic Focus • Spanish language and literature, Spanish studies.
Program Information • Students attend classes at Academia Hispano Americana (San Miguel de Allende, Mexico). Field trips to Guanajuato, Querétaro, Dolores Hidalgo. Students typically earn 7 semester credits for 4 weeks.
Sessions • 12 four-week sessions per year.
Eligibility Requirements • Minimum age 16; open to precollege students, freshmen, sophomores, juniors, seniors, graduate students, adults; no foreign language proficiency required.
Living Arrangements • Students live in host family homes. Quarters are shared with students from other programs. Meals are taken with host family, in residences.
Costs (2006) • $1302; includes tuition, housing, all meals, excursions, books and class materials, enrollment fee. $50 application fee.
For More Information • Ms. Paulina Hawkins, Director, Academia Hispano Americana, Academic Hispano Americana, Mesones #4, San Miguel de Allende, Guanajuato, C.P. 37900, Mexico; *Phone:* +52 (415)-152-0349; *Fax:* +52 (415)-152-2333. *E-mail:* info@ahaspeakspanish.com. *World Wide Web:* http://www.ahaspeakspanish.com/

LANGUAGE LIAISON
SPANISH IN MEXICO–SAN MIGUEL DE ALLENDE
Hosted by Language Liaison
Academic Focus • Spanish language and literature.
Program Information • Students attend classes at Language Liaison (San Miguel de Allende, Mexico). Field trips; optional travel at an extra cost. Students typically earn 3-15 semester credits per term.
Sessions • New programs begin weekly, year-round.

Eligibility Requirements • Minimum age 17; open to precollege students, freshmen, sophomores, juniors, seniors, graduate students, adults; no foreign language proficiency required.
Living Arrangements • Students live in locally rented apartments, host family homes, hotels. Meals are taken on one's own, with host family, in residences, in restaurants.
Costs (2005) • Contact sponsor for cost. $175 application fee. Financial aid available for all students: scholarship research service.
For More Information • Ms. Nancy Forman, President, Language Liaison, PO Box 1772, Pacific Palisades, CA 90272; *Phone:* 800-284-4448; *Fax:* 310-454-1706. *E-mail:* learn@languageliaison.com. *World Wide Web:* http://www.languageliaison.com/

TAXCO

ILLINOIS STATE UNIVERSITY
SUMMER PROGRAM IN TAXCO, MEXICO
Hosted by National Autonomous University of Mexico (UNAM)–Taxco Branch
Academic Focus • Spanish language and literature.
Program Information • Students attend classes at National Autonomous University of Mexico (UNAM)-Taxco Branch (Taxco, Mexico). Field trips to Mexico City, Teotihuacán. Students typically earn 6 semester credits per term.
Sessions • Jun-Jul (summer).
Eligibility Requirements • Open to sophomores, juniors, seniors, graduate students, adults; 2.7 GPA; 2 letters of recommendation; good academic standing at home school; 1 year of college course work in Spanish.
Living Arrangements • Students live in host family homes. Quarters are shared with host institution students. Meals are taken with host family.
Costs (2005) • $4117; includes tuition, housing, all meals, insurance, excursions, international airfare, books and class materials, international student ID, student support services, instructional costs at UNAM, personal expenses. $150 application fee. Financial aid available for students from sponsoring institution: scholarships, loans.
For More Information • Mr. James J. Alstrum, Foreign Languages Department, Illinois State University, 4300 Foreign Language, Normal, IL 61790-4300; *Phone:* 309-438-7620; *Fax:* 309-438-3987. *E-mail:* jjalstrum@ilstu.edu. *World Wide Web:* http://www.internationalstudies.ilstu.edu/

XALAPA

SOUTHERN METHODIST UNIVERSITY
SMU IN XALAPA, MEXICO
Hosted by University of Veracruz
Academic Focus • Spanish language and literature.
Program Information • Students attend classes at University of Veracruz (Xalapa, Mexico). Field trips to Coatepec, Xico, El Tajín. Students typically earn 6 semester credits per term.
Sessions • Jun-Jul (summer).
Eligibility Requirements • Open to freshmen, sophomores, juniors, seniors; 2.5 GPA; 1 letter of recommendation; good academic standing at home school; personal interview; essay; 1 year of college course work in Spanish.
Living Arrangements • Students live in host family homes. Quarters are shared with host institution students, students from other programs. Meals are taken with host family, in residences.
Costs (2005) • $5020; includes tuition, housing, all meals, excursions, student support services. $40 application fee. $400 nonrefundable deposit required. Financial aid available for students from sponsoring institution: scholarships, loans.
For More Information • Ms. Nancy Simmons, Associate Director, Southern Methodist University, The International Center/Study Abroad, SMU PO Box 750391, Dallas, TX 75275-0391; *Phone:* 214-768-2338; *Fax:* 214-768-1051. *E-mail:* intlpro@mail.smu.edu. *World Wide Web:* http://www.smu.edu/studyabroad/

MOROCCO

IFRANE

COLLEGE CONSORTIUM FOR INTERNATIONAL STUDIES–MONTANA STATE UNIVERSITY
SUMMER IN MOROCCO PROGRAM

Hosted by Al Akhawayn University
Academic Focus • African studies, Arabic, architecture, Islamic studies, literature.
Program Information • Students attend classes at Al Akhawayn University (Ifrane, Morocco). Field trips to Marrakesh, the Tafilalt area (Errachida, Erfoud, and Merzouga); optional travel to Volubilis, Fez, Meknes at an extra cost. Students typically earn 6-11 semester credits per term.
Sessions • Jun–Aug (summer).
Eligibility Requirements • Open to sophomores, juniors, seniors, graduate students; 2.5 GPA; 2 letters of recommendation; no foreign language proficiency required.
Living Arrangements • Students live in host institution dormitories. Quarters are shared with host institution students. Meals are taken on one's own, in central dining facility, in restaurants.
Costs (2006) • $3175-$4730; includes tuition, housing, all meals, insurance, excursions, international student ID, student support services, airport pick-up. $400 nonrefundable deposit required. Financial aid available for students from sponsoring institution: scholarships, loans.
For More Information • Ms. Hilary Papendick, Study Abroad Adviser/Outreach Coordinator, College Consortium for International Studies–Montana State University, 400 Culbertson Hall, Montana State University, Bozeman, MT 59717; *Phone:* 406-994-7151; *Fax:* 406-994-1619. *E-mail:* morocco@montana.edu. *World Wide Web:* http://www.ccisabroad.org/

COLLEGE CONSORTIUM FOR INTERNATIONAL STUDIES–SUNY ROCKLAND COMMUNITY COLLEGE AND MONTANA STATE UNIVERSITY
CCIS MOROCCO SUMMER PROGRAM

Hosted by Al Akhawayn University
Academic Focus • African studies, Arabic, architecture, cultural studies, Islamic studies.
Program Information • Students attend classes at Al Akhawayn University (Ifrane, Morocco). Field trips to Marrakesh, Taf Ilalt Areas (Grrachida, Erfoud and Merzouga); optional travel to Fez, Meknes, Volubilis at an extra cost. Students typically earn 6-12 semester credits credits.
Sessions • May–Aug (summer), 4-8 weeks.
Eligibility Requirements • Open to sophomores, juniors, seniors, adults; 2.5 GPA; 2 letters of recommendation; sophomore status; no foreign language proficiency required.
Living Arrangements • Students live in host institution dormitories. Quarters are shared with host institution students. Meals are taken on one's own, in central dining facility.
Costs (2006) • $3170-$4730; includes tuition, housing, all meals, insurance, excursions, student support services. $400 nonrefundable deposit required.
For More Information • Ms. Hilary Papendick, Study Abroad Advisor/Outreach Coordinator, College Consortium for International Studies–SUNY Rockland Community College and Montana State University, 400 Culbertson Hall, Bozeman, MT 59717; *Phone:* 406-994-7151; *Fax:* 406-994-1619. *E-mail:* hilaryp@montana.edu. *World Wide Web:* http://www.ccisabroad.org/. Students may also apply through CCIS Abroad, 2000 P Street, NW, Suite 503, Washington, DC 20036.

UNIVERSITY OF IDAHO
SHORT-TERM SUMMER IN MOROCCO

Hosted by Al Akhawayn University
Academic Focus • Arabic, biological/life sciences, business administration/management, engineering, French language and literature, political science and government, science, social sciences, sociology.
Program Information • Students attend classes at Al Akhawayn University (Ifrane, Morocco). Students typically earn 6 semester credits per term.
Sessions • Jul (summer).
Eligibility Requirements • Open to sophomores, juniors, seniors, graduate students, adults; 2.5 GPA; no foreign language proficiency required.
Living Arrangements • Students live in host institution dormitories. Meals are taken as a group, in residences, in central dining facility.
Costs (2006–2007) • $3150 summer term; includes tuition, housing, some meals, student support services. $150 application fee. $200 nonrefundable deposit required. Financial aid available for students from sponsoring institution: scholarships, loans.

For More Information • Ms. Kate Peterson, Program Advisor, University of Idaho, 901 Paradise Creek Street, LLC #3, Ground Floor, Moscow, ID 83844-4075; *Phone:* 208-885-4075; *Fax:* 208-885-2859. *E-mail:* abroad@uidaho.edu. *World Wide Web:* http://www.webs.uidaho.edu/ipo/abroad/

UNIVERSITY OF KANSAS
ARABIC STUDIES AT AL-AKHAWAYN UNIVERSITY IN IFRANE, MOROCCO

Hosted by Al Akhawayn University
Academic Focus • Arabic, area studies, Islamic studies.
Program Information • Students attend classes at Al Akhawayn University (Ifrane, Morocco). Field trips to Tafilalt area, Marrakesh; optional travel to Fez, Meknes at an extra cost. Students typically earn 6–13 semester credits per term.
Sessions • May–Jul (summer).
Eligibility Requirements • Minimum age 18; open to freshmen, sophomores, juniors, seniors, graduate students; 2.5 GPA; 2 letters of recommendation; good academic standing at home school; 0.5 years of college course work in Arabic.
Living Arrangements • Students live in host institution dormitories. Meals are taken as a group, on one's own, in central dining facility.
Costs (2005) • $5120–$5620; includes tuition, housing, all meals, excursions, books and class materials, student support services, medical evacuation and repatriation services. $38 application fee. $300 nonrefundable deposit required. Financial aid available for students from sponsoring institution: scholarships, loans.
For More Information • Ms. Ingrid Horton, Program Coordinator, University of Kansas, Office of Study Abroad, Lippincott Hall, 1410

Jayhawk Boulevard, Room 108, Lawrence, KS 66045-7515; *Phone:* 785-864-3742; *Fax:* 785-864-5040. *E-mail:* osa@ku.edu. *World Wide Web:* http://www.ku.edu/~osa/

RABAT

SCHOOL FOR INTERNATIONAL TRAINING, SIT STUDY ABROAD
MOROCCO: INTENSIVE ARABIC LANGUAGE AND MOROCCAN CULTURE

Hosted by Center for Cross-Cultural Learning
Academic Focus • Arabic, Middle Eastern studies.
Program Information • Students attend classes at Center for Cross-Cultural Learning (Rabat, Morocco). Scheduled travel to Asilah, Tangier, Chefchaoven, Quazzane; Fes; Beni Mellani; Ouzoud; field trips to cultural events. Students typically earn 9 semester credits per term.
Sessions • Jun–Jul (summer).
Eligibility Requirements • Open to freshmen, sophomores, juniors, seniors; 2.5 GPA; 2 letters of recommendation; good academic standing at home school; no foreign language proficiency required.
Living Arrangements • Students live in host family homes, hotels, guest houses. Meals are taken as a group, with host family, in residences, in restaurants.
Costs (2005) • $7564; includes tuition, housing, all meals, insurance. $50 application fee. $400 nonrefundable deposit required. Financial aid available for all students: scholarships.
For More Information • SIT Study Abroad, School for International Training, SIT Study Abroad, PO Box 676, Kipling Road, Brattleboro, VT 05302-0676; *Phone:* 888-272-7881; *Fax:* 802-258-3296. *E-mail:* studyabroad@sit.edu. *World Wide Web:* http://www.sit.edu/studyabroad/

NEPAL

KATHMANDU

SANN RESEARCH INSTITUTE
ANTHROPOLOGICAL STUDIES IN NEPAL

Held at Sann Research Institute
Academic Focus • Anthropology.
Program Information • Classes are held on the campus of Sann Research Institute (Kathmandu, Nepal). Faculty members are local instructors hired by the sponsor. Scheduled travel to trekking in the Himalayas; field trips to Patan, Bhaktapur; optional travel to Bangkok at an extra cost. Students typically earn 3 semester credits per term.
Sessions • May–Jun (summer).
Eligibility Requirements • Minimum age 18; open to freshmen, sophomores, juniors, seniors; 2.5 GPA; good health; no foreign language proficiency required.
Living Arrangements • Students live in host family homes. Meals are taken with host family, in residences.
Costs (2005–2006) • $3200; includes tuition, housing, all meals, international airfare. $275 application fee. $500 deposit required.
For More Information • Narayan Shrestha, President, Sann Research Institute, 948 Pearl Street, Boulder, CO 80302; *Phone:* 303-449-4279; *Fax:* 303-440-7328. *E-mail:* info@sannr.com. *World Wide Web:* http://www.sannr.com/

SANN RESEARCH INSTITUTE
ECOTOURISM IN NEPAL

Held at Sann Research Institute
Academic Focus • Tourism and travel.
Program Information • Classes are held on the campus of Sann Research Institute (Kathmandu, Nepal). Faculty members are local instructors hired by the sponsor. Scheduled travel to trekking in the Himalayas; optional travel to Bangkok at an extra cost. Students typically earn 3 semester credits per term.
Sessions • Sep (summer).
Eligibility Requirements • Minimum age 18; open to freshmen, sophomores, juniors, seniors; 2.5 GPA; good health; no foreign language proficiency required.
Living Arrangements • Students live in host family homes, hotels. Quarters are shared with host institution students. Meals are taken as a group, with host family, in residences, in central dining facility.
Costs (2005–2006) • $3350; includes tuition, housing, all meals, international airfare. $275 application fee. $500 deposit required.
For More Information • Narayan Shrestha, President, Sann Research Institute, 948 Pearl Street, Boulder, CO 80302; *Phone:* 303-449-4279; *Fax:* 303-440-7328. *E-mail:* info@sannr.com. *World Wide Web:* http://www.sannr.com/

SANN RESEARCH INSTITUTE
FOOD AND NUTRITION STUDIES IN NEPAL

Held at Sann Research Institute
Academic Focus • Nutrition.
Program Information • Classes are held on the campus of Sann Research Institute (Kathmandu, Nepal). Faculty members are local instructors hired by the sponsor. Scheduled travel to Himalayan trekking; field trips to Bhaktapur; optional travel to Bangkok at an extra cost. Students typically earn 3 semester credits per term.
Sessions • Dec–Jan (winter).
Eligibility Requirements • Minimum age 18; open to freshmen, sophomores, juniors, seniors; 2.5 GPA; good health; no foreign language proficiency required.
Living Arrangements • Students live in host family homes. Meals are taken with host family, in residences.
Costs (2005–2006) • $3350; includes tuition, housing, all meals, international airfare. $275 application fee. $500 deposit required.
For More Information • Narayan Shrestha, President, Sann Research Institute, 948 Pearl Street, Boulder, CO 80302; *Phone:* 303-449-4279; *Fax:* 303-440-7328. *E-mail:* info@sannr.com. *World Wide Web:* http://www.sannr.com/

SANN RESEARCH INSTITUTE
PHOTOGRAPHY STUDIES IN NEPAL

Hosted by Sann International College
Academic Focus • Photography.

Program Information • Students attend classes at Sann International College (Kathmandu, Nepal). Scheduled travel to trekking to the Himalayas; field trips to study-related field sites; optional travel to Bangkok at an extra cost. Students typically earn 3 semester credits per term.

Sessions • Dec–Jan (winter).

Eligibility Requirements • Minimum age 18; open to freshmen, sophomores, juniors, seniors; 2.5 GPA; good health; no foreign language proficiency required.

Living Arrangements • Students live in host family homes, hotels. Meals are taken as a group, with host family, in residences, in central dining facility.

Costs (2005–2006) • $3600; includes tuition, housing, all meals, international airfare. $275 application fee. $500 deposit required.

For More Information • Narayan Shrestha, President, Sann Research Institute, 948 Pearl Street, Boulder, CO 80302; *Phone:* 303-449-4279; *Fax:* 303-440-7328. *E-mail:* info@sannr.com. *World Wide Web:* http://www.sannr.com/

SANN RESEARCH INSTITUTE
PHOTOJOURNALISM IN NEPAL

Hosted by Sann International College

Academic Focus • Journalism, photography.

Program Information • Students attend classes at Sann International College (Kathmandu, Nepal). Scheduled travel to Annapurna Base Camp; field trips to the Himalayas, a temple and other photography sites; optional travel to Bangkok, India at an extra cost. Students typically earn 3 semester credits per term.

Sessions • May–Jun (summer), Dec–Jan (winter).

Eligibility Requirements • Minimum age 18; open to freshmen, sophomores, juniors, seniors; 2.5 GPA; 2 letters of recommendation; good academic standing at home school; good health; no foreign language proficiency required.

Living Arrangements • Students live in host family homes. Quarters are shared with host institution students. Meals are taken as a group, with host family, in residences.

Costs (2005–2006) • $3500; includes tuition, housing, all meals, excursions, international airfare, lab equipment, student support services, visa fee, program related transportation and communications. $225 application fee. $500 nonrefundable deposit required.

For More Information • Narayan Shrestha, President, Sann Research Institute, 948 Pearl Street, Boulder, CO 80302; *Phone:* 303-449-4279; *Fax:* 303-440-7328. *E-mail:* info@sannr.com. *World Wide Web:* http://www.sannr.com/

SANN RESEARCH INSTITUTE
RELIGIOUS STUDY IN NEPAL

Hosted by Sann International College

Academic Focus • Philosophy, religious studies.

Program Information • Students attend classes at Sann International College (Kathmandu, Nepal). Scheduled travel to Annapurna Base Camp trekking; field trips to various religious sites in Nepal; optional travel to Thailand, India at an extra cost. Students typically earn 3 semester credits per term.

Sessions • May–Jun (summer), Oct–Jan (winter).

Eligibility Requirements • Minimum age 18; open to freshmen, sophomores, juniors, seniors; 2.5 GPA; 2 letters of recommendation; good academic standing at home school; good health; no foreign language proficiency required.

Living Arrangements • Students live in host family homes. Quarters are shared with host institution students. Meals are taken with host family, in residences.

Costs (2005–2006) • $3550; includes tuition, housing, all meals, excursions, international airfare, student support services, visa fee, in-transit hotel stay. $225 application fee. $500 nonrefundable deposit required.

For More Information • Narayan Shrestha, President, Sann Research Institute, 948 Pearl Street, Boulder, CO 80302; *Phone:* 303-449-4279; *Fax:* 303-440-7328. *E-mail:* info@sannr.com. *World Wide Web:* http://www.sannr.com/

SANN RESEARCH INSTITUTE
THE STUDY OF CULTURE AND PEOPLE OF NEPAL

Held at Sann Research Institute

Academic Focus • Cultural studies.

Program Information • Classes are held on the campus of Sann Research Institute (Kathmandu, Nepal). Faculty members are local instructors hired by the sponsor. Scheduled travel to Chitwan; field trips to Bhaktapur, Patan; optional travel to Bangkok at an extra cost. Students typically earn 6 semester credits per term.

Sessions • Dec–Jan (winter).

Eligibility Requirements • Minimum age 18; open to freshmen, sophomores, juniors, seniors; 2.5 GPA; good health; no foreign language proficiency required.

Living Arrangements • Students live in host family homes. Meals are taken with host family, in residences.

Costs (2005–2006) • $3480; includes tuition, housing, all meals, international airfare. $275 application fee. $500 nonrefundable deposit required.

For More Information • Narayan Shrestha, President, Sann Research Institute, 948 Pearl Street, Boulder, CO 80302; *Phone:* 303-449-4279; *Fax:* 303-440-7328. *E-mail:* info@sannr.com. *World Wide Web:* http://www.sannr.com/

SANN RESEARCH INSTITUTE
STUDY ON VIOLENCE AGAINST WOMEN AND CHILDREN IN NEPAL

Hosted by Sann International College

Academic Focus • Area studies, cultural studies, ethnic studies.

Program Information • Students attend classes at Sann International College (Kathmandu, Nepal). Scheduled travel to trekking in Annaparna Base Camp; field trips to a village in Nepal; optional travel to Thailand, India at an extra cost. Students typically earn 3 semester credits per term.

Sessions • May–Jun (summer), Dec–Jan (winter).

Eligibility Requirements • Minimum age 18; open to freshmen, sophomores, juniors, seniors; 2.5 GPA; 2 letters of recommendation; good academic standing at home school; good health; no foreign language proficiency required.

Living Arrangements • Students live in host family homes. Quarters are shared with host institution students. Meals are taken with host family, in residences.

Costs (2005–2006) • $3550; includes tuition, housing, all meals, excursions, international airfare, student support services, visa fee, in-transit hotel stay. $225 application fee. $500 nonrefundable deposit required.

For More Information • Narayan Shrestha, President, Sann Research Institute, 948 Pearl Street, Boulder, CO 80302; *Phone:* 303-449-4279; *Fax:* 303-440-7328. *E-mail:* info@sannr.com. *World Wide Web:* http://www.sannr.com/

SANN RESEARCH INSTITUTE
SUMMER HIGH ALTITUDE STUDIES IN NEPAL AND TIBET

Held at Sann Research Institute

Academic Focus • Science.

Program Information • Classes are held on the campus of Sann Research Institute (Kathmandu, Nepal). Faculty members are drawn from the sponsor's U.S. staff. Scheduled travel to Lhasa in Tibet; optional travel to Bangkok at an extra cost. Students typically earn 3–6 semester credits per term.

Sessions • May–Jun (summer).

Eligibility Requirements • Minimum age 18; open to freshmen, sophomores, juniors, seniors; 2.5 GPA; good health; no foreign language proficiency required.

Living Arrangements • Students live in host family homes, hotels. Meals are taken as a group, with host family, in residences, in central dining facility.

Costs (2005–2006) • $4695; includes tuition, housing, all meals, international airfare. $275 application fee. $500 deposit required.

For More Information • Narayan Shrestha, President, Sann Research Institute, 948 Pearl Street, Boulder, CO 80302; *Phone:* 303-449-4279; *Fax:* 303-460-7328. *E-mail:* info@sannr.com. *World Wide Web:* http://www.sannr.com/

NEPAL
Kathmandu

SANN RESEARCH INSTITUTE
SUMMER IN NEPAL

Hosted by Sann Research Institute

Academic Focus • Nepali, photography, political science and government, religious studies.

Program Information • Students attend classes at Sann Research Institute (Kathmandu, Nepal). Scheduled travel to Tibet, Nepali villages, a safari; field trips to study-related sites; optional travel to Bangkok, nearby Asian countries at an extra cost. Students typically earn 9 semester credits per term.

Sessions • May–Aug (summer).

Eligibility Requirements • Minimum age 18; open to freshmen, sophomores, juniors, seniors, adults; 2.5 GPA; good health; no foreign language proficiency required.

Living Arrangements • Students live in host family homes. Meals are taken with host family, in residences, in central dining facility.

Costs (2005–2006) • $7000; includes tuition, housing, all meals, excursions, international airfare, student support services, visa fee, in-transit hotel stay. $500 refundable deposit required.

For More Information • Narayan Shrestha, President, Sann Research Institute, 948 Pearl Street, Boulder, CO 80302; *Phone:* 303-449-4279; *Fax:* 303-440-7328. *E-mail:* info@sannr.com. *World Wide Web:* http://www.sannr.com/

SANN RESEARCH INSTITUTE
WINTER HIGH ALTITUDE STUDIES IN NEPAL

Held at Sann Research Institute

Academic Focus • Science.

Program Information • Classes are held on the campus of Sann Research Institute (Kathmandu, Nepal). Faculty members are drawn from the sponsor's U.S. staff. Scheduled travel to trekking in the Annapurna region; optional travel to Bangkok at an extra cost. Students typically earn 3–6 semester credits per term.

Sessions • Dec–Jan (winter).

Eligibility Requirements • Minimum age 18; open to freshmen, sophomores, juniors, seniors; 2.5 GPA; good health; no foreign language proficiency required.

Living Arrangements • Students live in host family homes, hotels. Meals are taken as a group, with host family, in residences, in central dining facility, in restaurants.

Costs (2005–2006) • $3900; includes tuition, housing, all meals, international airfare. $275 application fee. $500 deposit required.

For More Information • Narayan Shrestha, President, Sann Research Institute, 948 Pearl Street, Boulder, CO 80302; *Phone:* 303-449-4279; *Fax:* 303-440-7328. *E-mail:* info@sannr.com. *World Wide Web:* http://www.sannr.com/

UNIVERSITY OF IDAHO
SUMMER NEPAL PROGRAM

Hosted by Sann Research Institute

Academic Focus • Nepali, philosophy, photography, religious studies.

Program Information • Students attend classes at Sann Research Institute (Kathmandu, Nepal). Scheduled travel to trekking in the Himalayas; field trips to Bandipur, Swayambunath, Patan, Bhaktapur. Students typically earn 9 semester credits per term.

Sessions • Jun–Aug (summer).

Eligibility Requirements • Open to freshmen, sophomores, juniors, seniors, graduate students, adults; 2.5 GPA; good academic standing at home school; no foreign language proficiency required.

Living Arrangements • Students live in host family homes. Quarters are shared with host institution students. Meals are taken with host family, in residences.

Costs (2005) • $3800; includes tuition, housing, all meals, excursions, student support services. $150 application fee. $200 refundable deposit required. Financial aid available for students from sponsoring institution: scholarships, loans.

For More Information • Ms. Kate Peterson, Program Advisor, University of Idaho, 901 Paradise Creek Street, LLC 3, Ground Floor, Moscow, ID 83844-1250; *Phone:* 208-885-4075; *Fax:* 208-885-2859. *E-mail:* abroad@uidaho.edu. *World Wide Web:* http://www.webs.uidaho.edu/ipo/abroad/

NETHERLANDS

AMSTERDAM

CIEE
CIEE STUDY CENTER IN AMSTERDAM, THE NETHERLANDS

Hosted by CIEE Study Center
Academic Focus • Cultural studies, European studies, social sciences.
Program Information • Students attend classes at CIEE Study Center (Amsterdam, Netherlands). Field trips to Zeeland, coastal Dutch fishing villages. Students typically earn 3 semester credits per term.
Sessions • Jun (summer).
Eligibility Requirements • Minimum age 18; open to sophomores, juniors, seniors; 2.75 GPA; 1 letter of recommendation; good academic standing at home school; no foreign language proficiency required.
Living Arrangements • Students live in host institution dormitories. Quarters are shared with host institution students. Meals are taken on one's own, in residences, in central dining facility, in restaurants.
Costs (2007) • Contact sponsor for cost. $30 application fee. $300 nonrefundable deposit required. Financial aid available for all students: scholarships, minority student scholarships.
For More Information • Information Center, CIEE, 7 Custom House Street, 3rd Floor, Portland, ME 04101; *Phone:* 800-40-STUDY; *Fax:* 207-553-7699. *E-mail:* studyinfo@ciee.org. *World Wide Web:* http://www.ciee.org/isp/

NEW YORK UNIVERSITY
INTERNATIONAL THEATRE WORKSHOP: AMSTERDAM, THE NETHERLANDS

Academic Focus • Drama/theater.
Program Information • Faculty members are drawn from the sponsor's U.S. staff. Students typically earn 8 semester credits per term.
Sessions • Jun–Aug (summer).
Eligibility Requirements • Open to freshmen, sophomores, juniors, seniors, adults; 3.0 GPA; good academic standing at home school; prior acting training; no foreign language proficiency required.
Living Arrangements • Students live in locally rented apartments. Meals are taken on one's own, in restaurants.
Costs (2005) • $8696; includes tuition, housing. $50 application fee. Financial aid available for students from sponsoring institution: scholarships.
For More Information • Mr. Scott Loane, Department of Drama, New York University, 721 Broadway, 3rd Floor, New York, NY 10003; *Phone:* 212-998-1872. *E-mail:* scott.loane@nyu.edu. *World Wide Web:* http://www.nyu.edu/global/studyabroad.html

UNIVERSITY OF MINNESOTA
ETHICAL TOLERANCE IN AMSTERDAM

Academic Focus • Ethics.
Program Information • Faculty members are drawn from the sponsor's U.S. staff. Field trips; optional travel at an extra cost. Students typically earn 3 semester credits per term.
Sessions • May–Jun (summer).
Eligibility Requirements • Minimum age 18; open to freshmen, sophomores, juniors, seniors, adults; 2.5 GPA; good academic standing at home school; no foreign language proficiency required.
Living Arrangements • Students live in host institution dormitories, hotels. Quarters are shared with host institution students. Meals are taken as a group, on one's own, in central dining facility, in restaurants.
Costs (2006) • Contact sponsor for cost; includes tuition, housing, some meals, insurance, international airfare, student support services. $50 application fee. $400 nonrefundable deposit required. Financial aid available for students from sponsoring institution: scholarships, loans.
For More Information • Learning Abroad Center, University of Minnesota, 230 Heller Hall, 271 19th Avenue South, Minneapolis, MN 55455; *Phone:* 800-700-UOFM; *Fax:* 612-626-8009. *E-mail:* umabroad@umn.edu. *World Wide Web:* http://www.umabroad.umn.edu/

MAASTRICHT

THE UNIVERSITY OF NORTH CAROLINA AT CHARLOTTE
SUMMER INSTITUTE IN EUROPE: HEALTH CARE SYSTEMS IN THE NETHERLANDS

Academic Focus • Nursing.

NETHERLANDS
Maastricht

Program Information • Faculty members are drawn from the sponsor's U.S. staff and local instructors hired by the sponsor. Field trips to surrounding areas. Students typically earn 3 semester credits per term.
Sessions • May (summer).
Eligibility Requirements • Minimum age 18; open to freshmen, sophomores, juniors, seniors, graduate students, adults; 2.5 GPA; good academic standing at home school; no foreign language proficiency required.
Living Arrangements • Students live in hotels. Meals are taken on one's own, in restaurants.

Costs (2005) • $2190; includes tuition, housing, some meals, insurance, excursions, books and class materials, student support services. $10 application fee. $500 nonrefundable deposit required. Financial aid available for students from sponsoring institution: scholarships, loans.
For More Information • Mr. Brad Sekulich, Interim Director of Education Abroad, The University of North Carolina at Charlotte, 9201 University City Boulevard, Charlotte, NC 28223-0001; *Phone:* 704-687-2464; *Fax:* 704-687-3168. *E-mail:* edabroad@email.uncc. edu. *World Wide Web:* http://www.uncc.edu/edabroad/

$\mathscr{N}$ETHERLANDS ANTILLES

BONAIRE

CIEE
CIEE STUDY CENTER IN BONAIRE, SOUTHERN CARIBBEAN–TROPICAL MARINE ECOLOGY AND CONSERVATION

Hosted by CIEE Study Center

Academic Focus • Biological/life sciences, ecology, marine sciences.

Program Information • Students attend classes at CIEE Study Center (Bonaire, Netherlands Antilles). Field trips to Washington Slagbaai Park; Klein; Lac Bay; Mangrove Center. Students typically earn 3 semester credits per term.

Sessions • May–Jun (summer).

Eligibility Requirements • Minimum age 18; open to sophomores, juniors, seniors; course work in biology or environmental science (1 semester); 2.75 GPA; 1 letter of recommendation; scuba certification or PADI referral.

Living Arrangements • Students live in program-owned houses. Quarters are shared with host institution students. Meals are taken as a group, in central dining facility.

Costs (2006) • $2700; includes tuition, housing, all meals, insurance, excursions, student support services, resident director, orientation, cultural activities, on-site pick-up, pre-departure advice. $30 application fee. $300 nonrefundable deposit required. Financial aid available for all students: scholarships, minority student scholarships, travel grants.

For More Information • Information Center, CIEE, 7 Custom House Street, 3rd Floor, Portland, ME 04101; *Phone:* 800-40-STUDY; *Fax:* 207-553-7699. *E-mail:* studyinfo@ciee.org. *World Wide Web:* http://www.ciee.org/isp/

NEW ZEALAND

CITY-TO-CITY

MICHIGAN STATE UNIVERSITY
ENVIRONMENTAL SCIENCE AND POLICY IN NEW ZEALAND

Academic Focus • Agriculture, environmental science/studies, natural resources.
Program Information • Faculty members are drawn from the sponsor's U.S. staff. Scheduled travel to Christchurch, Auckland; field trips to Te Anau, Rotura, Wellington, Abel Tasman, Queenstown. Students typically earn 6 semester credits per term.
Sessions • Dec–Jan (winter break).
Eligibility Requirements • Minimum age 18; open to sophomores, juniors, seniors; 2.5 GPA; good academic standing at home school.
Living Arrangements • Students live in hotels. Meals are taken as a group, on one's own, in restaurants.
Costs (2005–2006) • $2960; includes housing, some meals, insurance, excursions, student support services. $100 application fee. $200 nonrefundable deposit required. Financial aid available for students from sponsoring institution: scholarships, loans.
For More Information • Ms. Sandy Tupper, Educational Programs Coordinator, Michigan State University, Office of Study Abroad, 109 International Center, East Lansing, MI 48824-1035; *Phone:* 517-353-8920; *Fax:* 517-432-2082. *E-mail:* tuppers@msu.edu. *World Wide Web:* http://studyabroad.msu.edu/

UNIVERSITY OF CALIFORNIA, SANTA BARBARA, WILDLANDS STUDIES
ECOSYSTEMS AND CULTURES OF NEW ZEALAND

Academic Focus • Ecology, environmental science/studies, geography, Pacific studies, wildlife studies.
Program Information • Faculty members are drawn from the sponsor's U.S. staff. Scheduled travel to wildlife field locations. Students typically earn 15 quarter credits per term.
Sessions • Jan–Mar (winter).
Eligibility Requirements • Minimum age 18; open to freshmen, sophomores, juniors, seniors; course work in biology or environmental studies; good academic standing at home school; application essay.
Living Arrangements • Students live in field study sites. Meals are taken as a group.
Costs (2007) • $1995; includes tuition. $75 application fee.
For More Information • Mr. Crandall Bay, Director, Wildlands Studies Program, University of California, Santa Barbara, Wildlands Studies, 3 Mosswood Circle, Cazadero, CA 95421; *Phone:* 707-632-5665; *Fax:* 707-632-5665. *E-mail:* wildlands@sonic.net. *World Wide Web:* http://www.wildlandsstudies.com/

UNIVERSITY OF DELAWARE
WINTER SESSION IN NEW ZEALAND: ART

Academic Focus • Photography.
Program Information • Faculty members are drawn from the sponsor's U.S. staff. Scheduled travel; field trips to cultural sites. Students typically earn 6 semester credits per term.
Sessions • Jan–Feb (winter).
Eligibility Requirements • Open to freshmen, sophomores, juniors, seniors, adults; 2.0 GPA; 1 letter of recommendation.
Living Arrangements • Students live in host institution dormitories, hotels, campsites; hostels. Meals are taken as a group, on one's own, in central dining facility.
Costs (2005) • Contact sponsor for cost. $200 nonrefundable deposit required. Financial aid available for all students: scholarships.
For More Information • Center for International Studies, University of Delaware, 186 South College Avenue, Newark, DE 19716-1450; *Phone:* 888-831-4685; *Fax:* 302-831-6042. *E-mail:* studyabroad@udel.edu. *World Wide Web:* http://www.udel.edu/studyabroad/

CHRISTCHURCH

AMERICAN UNIVERSITIES INTERNATIONAL PROGRAMS (AUIP)
NEW ZEALAND: HUMANS AND THE ENVIRONMENT

Academic Focus • Anthropology, conservation studies, ecology, forestry, geography, natural resources, parks and recreation.
Program Information • Faculty members are drawn from the sponsor's U.S. staff and local instructors hired by the sponsor. Scheduled travel to Mt. Cook, Fiordland, West Coast, Fox Glacier, Queenstown, Punakaiki, Nelson

Lakes, Abel Tasman, Kaikoura; field trips to Mt. Cook, Fiordland, West Coast, Fox Glacier, Queenstown, Punakaiki, Nelson Lakes, Abel Tasman, Kaikoura; optional travel at an extra cost. Students typically earn 6 semester credits per term.

Sessions • May–Jun (summer), Dec–Jan (winter).

Eligibility Requirements • Minimum age 18; open to sophomores, juniors, seniors, graduate students, adults; 2.0 GPA; 2 letters of recommendation; good academic standing at home school; essay; transcript.

Living Arrangements • Students live in hotels, hostels. Meals are taken as a group, on one's own, in residences, in restaurants.

Costs (2006) • $2450; includes tuition, housing, some meals, insurance, excursions, student support services, all in-country travel and activities. $300 application fee.

For More Information • Dr. Michael Tarrant, Program Director, American Universities International Programs (AUIP), 108 South Main Street, Winterville, GA 30683; *Phone:* 706-742-9285. *E-mail:* info@auip.com. *World Wide Web:* http://www.auip.com/

# NICARAGUA

CITY-TO-CITY

MICHIGAN STATE UNIVERSITY
RAINFORESTS AND REALITY

Academic Focus • Biological/life sciences, ecology, interdisciplinary studies.
Program Information • Faculty members are drawn from the sponsor's U.S. staff. Field trips to Bluefields, Miskitu coast. Students typically earn 2 semester credits per term.
Sessions • Mar (spring break).
Eligibility Requirements • Open to freshmen, sophomores, juniors, seniors, adults; 2.5 GPA; good academic standing at home school; rigorous hiking; physical activity; no foreign language proficiency required.
Living Arrangements • Students live in host institution dormitories, hotels. Meals are taken as a group, in restaurants.
Costs (2004) • $749; includes housing, some meals, insurance, excursions, books and class materials, student support services. $100 application fee. $200 nonrefundable deposit required. Financial aid available for all students: scholarships, loans.
For More Information • Mr. Mark Davis, Coordinator, Michigan State University, Office of Study Abroad, 109 International Center, East Lansing, MI 48824-1035; *Phone:* 517-432-1315; *Fax:* 517-432-2082. *E-mail:* mdavis@msu.edu. *World Wide Web:* http://studyabroad.msu.edu/

MANAGUA

FAIRFIELD UNIVERSITY
SUMMER IN MANAGUA

Hosted by Central American University, Managua
Academic Focus • Latin American studies, sociology, Spanish language and literature.
Program Information • Students attend classes at Central American University, Managua (Managua, Nicaragua). Field trips to beaches, villages; optional travel at an extra cost. Students typically earn 6 semester credits per term.
Sessions • May–Jun (summer).
Eligibility Requirements • Minimum age 18; open to freshmen, sophomores, juniors, seniors; 2.8 GPA; 1 letter of recommendation; good academic standing at home school; good social standing; 3 years of college course work in Spanish.
Living Arrangements • Students live in host family homes. Quarters are shared with host institution students. Meals are taken with host family.
Costs (2006) • $3600; includes tuition, housing, some meals, insurance, excursions, international student ID, student support services, language partner. $300 refundable deposit required.
For More Information • Study Abroad Programs, Fairfield University, Dolan House, 1073 North Benson Road, Fairfield, CT 06824; *Phone:* 203-254-4332; *Fax:* 203-254-4261. *E-mail:* studyabroadoffice@mail.fairfield.edu. *World Wide Web:* http://www.fairfield.edu/studyabroad.xml/

NORTHERN IRELAND

See also England, Ireland, Scotland, and Wales.

BELFAST

INSTITUTE FOR STUDY ABROAD, BUTLER UNIVERSITY
QUEEN'S UNIVERSITY BELFAST SUMMER STUDY

Hosted by Queen's University Belfast

Academic Focus • Irish studies.

Program Information • Students attend classes at Queen's University Belfast (Belfast, Northern Ireland). Field trips to Barony of Lecale, Strangford Lough. Students typically earn 3 semester credits per term.

Sessions • Jul–Aug (summer).

Eligibility Requirements • Open to sophomores, juniors, seniors; 2.5 GPA; good academic standing at home school; enrollment at an accredited American college or university.

Living Arrangements • Students live in locally rented apartments. Quarters are shared with host institution students. Meals are taken on one's own, in residences.

Costs (2005) • $2675; includes tuition, housing, some meals, excursions, student support services, pre-departure advising. $40 application fee. $500 nonrefundable deposit required. Financial aid available for all students: scholarships.

For More Information • Institute for Study Abroad, Butler University, 1100 West 42nd Street, Suite 305, Indianapolis, IN 46208-3345; *Phone:* 800-858-0229; *Fax:* 317-940-9704. *E-mail:* study-abroad@butler.edu. *World Wide Web:* http://www.ifsa-butler.org/

 NORWAY

BODO

BODO UNIVERSITY COLLEGE
BODO INTERNATIONAL SUMMER UNIVERSITY

Hosted by Bodo University College
Academic Focus • Peace and conflict studies.
Program Information • Students attend classes at Bodo University College (Bodo, Norway). Field trips to the Arctic outdoors of Norway; optional travel to Lofoten Islands at an extra cost. Students typically earn 10 ECTS credits per term.
Sessions • Jun–Jul (summer), Jun–Aug (summer 2).
Eligibility Requirements • Minimum age 18; open to freshmen, sophomores, juniors, seniors, graduate students, adults; good academic standing at home school; no foreign language proficiency required.
Living Arrangements • Students live in host institution dormitories, program-owned apartments. Quarters are shared with host institution students. Meals are taken on one's own, in residences.
Costs (2005) • NKr8000; includes tuition, housing, student support services. Financial aid available for all students: scholarships.
For More Information • Mr. Espen Arnoy, BISU Coordinator, Bodo University College, 8049 Bodo, Norway; *Phone:* +47-7551 7846; *Fax:* +47-7551 7545. *E-mail:* bisu@hibo.no. *World Wide Web:* http://www.hibo.no/

MOSS

UNIVERSITY OF NORTH DAKOTA
UND-AMERICAN UNIVERSITY OF NORWAY–STUDY IN NORWAY

Hosted by American College of Norway
Academic Focus • Area studies, communications, history, international business, Norwegian, political science and government, sociology.
Program Information • Students attend classes at American College of Norway (Moss, Norway). Field trips to Oslo. Students typically earn 3–7 semester credits per term.
Sessions • May–Jun (summer).
Eligibility Requirements • Minimum age 18; open to freshmen, sophomores, juniors, seniors; 2.5 GPA; 1 letter of recommendation; good academic standing at home school; no foreign language proficiency required.
Living Arrangements • Students live in host institution dormitories. Quarters are shared with host institution students. Meals are taken as a group, in residences, in central dining facility.
Costs (2005–2006) • Contact sponsor for cost. $25 application fee. $100 nonrefundable deposit required. Financial aid available for all students: scholarships, loans.
For More Information • Mr. Raymond Lagasse, Assistant Director for Education Abroad, University of North Dakota, Box 7901, Grand Forks, ND 58202-7109; *Phone:* 701-777-2938; *Fax:* 701-777-4773. *E-mail:* raymond.lagasse@mail.und.nodak.edu. *World Wide Web:* http://www.und.nodak.edu/dept/oip/. Students may also apply through American College of Norway, Henrik Gerners Gt. 14, 1530 Moss, Norway.

PANAMA

CITY-TO-CITY

MICHIGAN STATE UNIVERSITY
TROPICAL BIODIVERSITY AND CONSERVATION IN PANAMA

Held at Autonomous University of Chiriqui, Smithsonian Tropical Research Institute
Academic Focus • Science.
Program Information • Classes are held on the campus of Autonomous University of Chiriqui (David), Smithsonian Tropical Research Institute (Panama City). Faculty members are drawn from the sponsor's U.S. staff and local instructors hired by the sponsor. Scheduled travel to various natural preserves, national parks; field trips to various natural preserves, national parks. Students typically earn 5 semester credits per term.
Sessions • Jun (summer).
Eligibility Requirements • Minimum age 18; open to freshmen, sophomores, juniors, seniors, graduate students; major in science; 2.5 GPA; good physical condition; no foreign language proficiency required.
Living Arrangements • Students live in field stations. Meals are taken as a group, in central dining facility.
Costs (2005) • $1753 (estimated); includes housing, some meals, insurance, excursions, books and class materials. $100 application fee. $200 nonrefundable deposit required. Financial aid available for students from sponsoring institution: scholarships, loans.
For More Information • Mr. Mark Davis, Coordinator, Michigan State University, Office of Study Abroad, 109 International Center, East Lansing, MI 48824-1035; *Phone:* 517-432-1315; *Fax:* 517-423-2082. *E-mail:* mdavis@msu.edu. *World Wide Web:* http://studyabroad.msu.edu/

PANAMA CITY

LANGUAGE LINK
ILISA PANAMA

Hosted by ILISA Panama
Academic Focus • Spanish language and literature.
Program Information • Students attend classes at ILISA Panama (Panama City, Panama). Field trips to cultural areas. Students typically earn 6–15 semester credits per term.
Sessions • Classes begin every Monday, year-round.
Eligibility Requirements • Minimum age 17; open to freshmen, sophomores, juniors, seniors, graduate students, adults; no foreign language proficiency required.
Living Arrangements • Students live in program-owned apartments, host family homes. Quarters are shared with host institution students. Meals are taken with host family, in residences.
Costs (2005) • $345 per week, plus $200 registration fee; includes tuition, housing, all meals, books and class materials, student support services, cultural activities.
For More Information • Ms. Kay G. Rafool, Director, Language Link, PO Box 3006, Peoria, IL 61612-3006; *Phone:* 800-552-2051; *Fax:* 309-692-2926. *World Wide Web:* http://www.langlink.com/

PERU

CITY-TO-CITY

BOSTON UNIVERSITY
LIMA AND AYACUCHO: UNDERSTANDING CONTEMPORARY PERU

Held at National University of 'San Cristóbal de Huamanga', Pontifical Catholic University of Peru
Academic Focus • History, political science and government, Spanish language and literature.
Program Information • Classes are held on the campus of Pontifical Catholic University of Peru (Lima), National University of 'San Cristóbal de Huamanga' (Ayacucho). Faculty members are drawn from the sponsor's U.S. staff. Scheduled travel to Cuzco, Machu Picchu; field trips to Wari, Quinua. Students typically earn 10 semester credits per term.
Sessions • Jul–Aug (summer).
Eligibility Requirements • Open to juniors, seniors; 3.0 GPA; 1 letter of recommendation; good academic standing at home school; advisor approval; transcript; essay; writing sample in Spanish; 2 years of college course work in Spanish.
Living Arrangements • Students live in host family homes, hotels. Meals are taken on one's own, with host family, in residences, in central dining facility.
Costs (2005) • $6250; includes tuition, housing, all meals, excursions, emergency medical evacuation insurance. $50 application fee. $400 nonrefundable deposit required. Financial aid available for all students: scholarships, loans.
For More Information • Division of International Programs, Boston University, 232 Bay State Road, Boston, MA 02215; *Phone:* 617-353-9888; *Fax:* 617-353-5402. *E-mail:* abroad@bu.edu. *World Wide Web:* http://www.bu.edu/abroad/

CUSCO

ALMA COLLEGE
ALMA IN PERU (CUSCO)

Hosted by Academia Latinoamericana
Academic Focus • Cultural studies, Spanish language and literature.
Program Information • Students attend classes at Academia Latinoamericana (Cusco, Peru). Field trips to Pipon, Pisac, Chinchero; optional travel to Machu Picchu, the Temple of the Sun at an extra cost. Students typically earn 3–12 semester credits per term.
Sessions • Apr–Aug (1 to 4 months).
Eligibility Requirements • Minimum age 18; open to sophomores, juniors, seniors, graduate students, adults; 2.5 GPA; 2 letters of recommendation; good academic standing at home school; no foreign language proficiency required.
Living Arrangements • Students live in host family homes. Quarters are shared with students from other programs. Meals are taken with host family, in residences.
Costs (2005) • $2200–$6600; includes tuition, housing, some meals, insurance, excursions, books and class materials, international student ID, student support services, on-site orientation, airport pick-up. $50 application fee. $200 refundable deposit required.
For More Information • Ms. Julie Elenbaas, Office Associate, International Education, Alma College, 614 West Superior Street, Alma, MI 48801-1599; *Phone:* 989-463-7055; *Fax:* 989-463-7126. *E-mail:* intl_studies@alma.edu. *World Wide Web:* http://international.alma.edu/

CENTER FOR CULTURAL INTERCHANGE
PERU LANGUAGE SCHOOL

Hosted by Don Quijote
Academic Focus • Spanish language and literature.
Program Information • Students attend classes at Don Quijote (Cusco, Peru). Field trips to museums, cultural destinations, places of interest.
Sessions • 1 to 12 week programs begin every Monday, year-round.
Eligibility Requirements • Minimum age 18; open to precollege students, freshmen, sophomores, juniors, seniors, graduate students, adults; no foreign language proficiency required.
Living Arrangements • Students live in host family homes. Quarters are shared with students from other programs. Meals are taken with host family, in residences.
Costs (2005) • $2050 for 4 weeks; includes tuition, housing, some meals, insurance, books and class materials, student support services, activities. Financial aid available for students from sponsoring institution: scholarships.

For More Information • Ms. Juliet Jones, Outbound Programs Director, Center for Cultural Interchange, 325 West Huron, Suite 706, Chicago, IL 60610; *Phone:* 866-684-9675; *Fax:* 872-944-2644. *E-mail:* info@cci-exchange.com. *World Wide Web:* http://www.cci-exchange.com/

ENFOREX–SPANISH IN THE SPANISH WORLD
SPANISH INTENSIVE COURSE CUZCO

Hosted by ENFOREX

Academic Focus • Spanish language and literature, Spanish studies.
Program Information • Students attend classes at ENFOREX (Cusco, Peru). Field trips to Machu Picchu; optional travel to Luce Roule at an extra cost. Students typically earn 4 semester credits per term.
Sessions • Year-round.
Eligibility Requirements • Minimum age 18; open to freshmen, juniors, seniors, graduate students, adults; no foreign language proficiency required.
Living Arrangements • Students live in host family homes, hotels. Meals are taken as a group, on one's own, with host family.
Costs (2005) • $825 per month; includes tuition, housing, all meals, excursions, books and class materials, lab equipment, international student ID, student support services. $100 application fee. $250 nonrefundable deposit required.
For More Information • Mr. Antonio Anadón, Director of Spanish Department, ENFOREX–Spanish in the Spanish World, Alberto Aguilera, 26, 28015 Madrid, Spain; *Phone:* +34 91-594-3776; *Fax:* +34 91-594-5159. *E-mail:* promotion@enforex.es. *World Wide Web:* http://www.enforex.com/

LANGUAGE LINK
AMAUTA OF CUSCO, PERU

Hosted by Amauta

Academic Focus • Spanish language and literature.
Program Information • Students attend classes at Amauta (Cusco, Peru). Scheduled travel to the Manu rainforest, Inca Trail, the Sacred Valley; field trips to Machu Picchu, the Sacred Valley. Students typically earn 6-15 semester credits per term.
Sessions • Year-round, classes begin every Monday.
Eligibility Requirements • Minimum age 18; open to freshmen, sophomores, juniors, seniors, graduate students, adults; no foreign language proficiency required.
Living Arrangements • Students live in host institution dormitories, host family homes. Quarters are shared with host institution students. Meals are taken as a group, with host family, in residences, in central dining facility.
Costs (2005) • $220 per week; includes tuition, housing, all meals, student support services, airport pick-up.
For More Information • Ms. Kay G. Rafool, Director, Language Link, PO Box 3006, Peoria, IL 61612-3006; *Phone:* 800-552-2051; *Fax:* 309-692-2926. *E-mail:* info@langlink.com. *World Wide Web:* http://www.langlink.com/

PROWORLD SERVICE CORPS
PROWORLD SERVICE CORPS

Academic Focus • Andean studies, community service, cultural studies, environmental science/studies, Latin American literature, Latin American studies, Mapuche/Aymara studies, public health, public policy, Quechua, social sciences, social work, Spanish language and literature.
Program Information • Faculty members are drawn from the sponsor's U.S. staff and local instructors hired by the sponsor. Field trips to cultural events, Incan ruins, Glacier Lakes; optional travel to a rainforest, Peruvian coast, Machu Picchu at an extra cost. Students typically earn 3 semester credits per term.
Sessions • 4 week sessions begin every month, year-round.

Eligibility Requirements • Minimum age 18; open to freshmen, sophomores, juniors, seniors, graduate students, adults; good academic standing at home school; desire to learn and help others; no foreign language proficiency required.
Living Arrangements • Students live in host family homes. Meals are taken with host family, in residences.
Costs (2005) • $1950 for 4 weeks; $300 for each additional week; includes tuition, housing, all meals, insurance, excursions, books and class materials, lab equipment, international student ID, student support services. $200 nonrefundable deposit required. Financial aid available for all students: scholarships.
For More Information • Ms. Anne Connolly, Marketing and Placement Advisor, ProWorld Service Corps, PO Box 21121, Billings, MT 59104-1121; *Phone:* 877-429-6753; *Fax:* 406-252-3973. *E-mail:* info@proworldsc.org. *World Wide Web:* http://www.proworldsc.org

UNIVERSITY OF DELAWARE
WINTER SESSION IN PERU

Academic Focus • Business administration/management, international business.
Program Information • Faculty members are drawn from the sponsor's U.S. staff. Field trips to Barranco; optional travel to the Amazon River, the Andes Mountains, Machu Picchu. Students typically earn 6 semester credits per term.
Sessions • Jan–Feb (winter).
Eligibility Requirements • Open to freshmen, sophomores, juniors, seniors; 2.0 GPA; 1 letter of recommendation; no foreign language proficiency required.
Living Arrangements • Students live in hotels. Meals are taken on one's own, in restaurants.
Costs (2005) • Contact sponsor for cost. $200 nonrefundable deposit required. Financial aid available for all students: scholarships.
For More Information • Center for International Studies, University of Delaware, 186 South College Avenue, Newark, DE 19716-1450; *Phone:* 888-831-4685; *Fax:* 302-831-6042. *E-mail:* studyabroad@udel.edu. *World Wide Web:* http://www.udel.edu/studyabroad/

URUBAMBA

PROWORLD SERVICE CORPS
PROWORLD SERVICE CORPS

Academic Focus • Andean studies, community service, cultural studies, environmental science/studies, Latin American studies, Mapuche/Aymara studies, public health, public policy, Quechua, social sciences, social work, Spanish language and literature.
Program Information • Faculty members are drawn from the sponsor's U.S. staff and local instructors hired by the sponsor. Field trips to Incan ruins, Glacier Lakes, cultural events; optional travel to rainforest, Peruvian coast, Manchu Picchu at an extra cost. Students typically earn 3 semester credits per term.
Sessions • 4 week sessions begin every month, year-round.
Eligibility Requirements • Minimum age 18; open to freshmen, sophomores, juniors, seniors, graduate students, adults; good academic standing at home school; desire to learn and help others; no foreign language proficiency required.
Living Arrangements • Students live in host family homes. Meals are taken with host family, in residences.
Costs (2005) • $1950 for 4 weeks; $300 for each additional week; includes tuition, housing, all meals, insurance, excursions, books and class materials, lab equipment, international student ID, student support services. $200 nonrefundable deposit required. Financial aid available for all students: scholarships.
For More Information • Ms. Anne Connolly, Marketing and Placement Advisor, ProWorld Service Corps, PO Box 21121, Billings, MT 59104-1121; *Phone:* 877-429-6753; *Fax:* 406-252-3973. *E-mail:* info@proworldsc.org. *World Wide Web:* http://www.proworldsc.org

PHILIPPINES

MANILA

THE INTERNATIONAL PARTNERSHIP FOR SERVICE LEARNING AND LEADERSHIP
PHILIPPINES SERVICE–LEARNING

Hosted by Trinity College
Academic Focus • Asian studies, community service, international affairs, liberal studies, Pacific studies, social sciences.
Program Information • Students attend classes at Trinity College (Quezon City, Philippines). Field trips to sites around Manila, Baguio; optional travel to other areas of the Philippines at an extra cost. Students typically earn 6–9 semester credits per term.
Sessions • Jun–Aug (summer).
Eligibility Requirements • Minimum age 18; open to freshmen, sophomores, juniors, seniors, graduate students, adults; 2 letters of recommendation; good academic standing at home school; evidence of maturity; no foreign language proficiency required.
Living Arrangements • Students live in host institution dormitories, locally rented apartments. Quarters are shared with host institution students. Meals are taken in central dining facility.
Costs (2006) • $6300; includes tuition, housing, some meals, excursions, student support services, community service placement and supervision. $50 application fee. $250 refundable deposit required. Financial aid available for all students: scholarships, federal financial aid.
For More Information • Director of Student Programs, The International Partnership for Service Learning and Leadership, 815 Second Avenue, New York, NY 10017-4594; *Phone:* 212-986-0989; *Fax:* 212-986-5039. *E-mail:* info@ipsl.org. *World Wide Web:* http://www.ipsl.org/

POLAND

KRAKOW

ACADEMIC PROGRAMS INTERNATIONAL (API)
(API)–KRAKOW, POLAND

Hosted by Jagiellonian University
Academic Focus • European studies, history, Polish, Polish studies, religious studies.
Program Information • Students attend classes at Jagiellonian University (Krakow, Poland). Scheduled travel to Budapest; field trips to Gdansk, Auschwitz, Warsaw, the Wieliczka Salt Mine, Zakopane. Students typically earn 6-8 semester credits per term.
Sessions • Jul–Aug (summer).
Eligibility Requirements • Minimum age 18; open to freshmen, sophomores, juniors, seniors, graduate students, adults; 2.75 GPA; 1 letter of recommendation; good academic standing at home school; official transcript from home university; no foreign language proficiency required.
Living Arrangements • Students live in host institution dormitories, locally rented apartments, host family homes. Quarters are shared with host institution students. Meals are taken on one's own, with host family, in residences, in central dining facility, in restaurants.
Costs (2006) • $4500; includes tuition, housing, some meals, insurance, excursions, student support services, airport pick-up, ground transportation, mobile phone, on-line services, on-site director. $150 nonrefundable deposit required. Financial aid available for all students: scholarships.
For More Information • Ms. Jennifer C. Allen, Director, Academic Programs International (API), 107 East Hopkins, San Marcos, TX 78666; *Phone:* 800-844-4124; *Fax:* 512-392-8420. *E-mail:* api@academicintl.com. *World Wide Web:* http://www.academicintl.com/

CENTRAL EUROPEAN EDUCATION AND CULTURAL EXCHANGE (CEECE)
CEECE IN KRAKOW, POLAND

Hosted by Jagiellonian University
Academic Focus • Agriculture, Central European studies, Eastern European studies, history, Jewish studies, Polish, Polish studies.
Program Information • Students attend classes at Jagiellonian University (Krakow, Poland). Field trips to the Tatra Mountains, Zakopane, Auschwitz, Birkenau; optional travel to Berlin, Vienna, Budapest, Prague, Munich at an extra cost. Students typically earn 6-9 semester credits per term.
Sessions • Jul (summer), Jul-Aug (summer 2).
Eligibility Requirements • Minimum age 18; open to freshmen, sophomores, juniors, seniors, graduate students, adults; 2.0 GPA; good academic standing at home school; no foreign language proficiency required.
Living Arrangements • Students live in host institution dormitories. Quarters are shared with host institution students. Meals are taken on one's own, in central dining facility, in restaurants.
Costs (2006) • $2499-$3999; includes tuition, housing, all meals, excursions, student support services. $300 refundable deposit required. Financial aid available for all students: home university financial aid.
For More Information • Mr. Eric Molengraf, Executive Director, Central European Education and Cultural Exchange (CEECE), 2956 Florence Drive, Grand Rapids, MI 49418; *Phone:* 800-352-9845. *E-mail:* info@ceece.org. *World Wide Web:* http://www.ceece.org/

LEXIA INTERNATIONAL
LEXIA SUMMER IN KRAKOW

Hosted by Jagiellonian University
Academic Focus • Anthropology, area studies, art history, civilization studies, comparative history, cultural studies, Eastern European studies, economics, ethnic studies, geography, history, interdisciplinary studies, international affairs, liberal studies, literature, Polish, Polish studies, political science and government, Slavic languages, social sciences, sociology.
Program Information • Students attend classes at Jagiellonian University (Krakow, Poland). Field trips to Warsaw, Auschwitz, Gdansk, Birkenau. Students typically earn 8-10 semester credits per term.
Sessions • Jun–Aug (summer).
Eligibility Requirements • Minimum age 18; open to freshmen, sophomores, juniors, seniors, adults; 2.5 GPA; 2 letters of recommendation; no foreign language proficiency required.
Living Arrangements • Students live in host institution dormitories, host family homes. Quarters are shared with host institution students. Meals are taken on one's own, with host family, in residences, in central dining facility, in restaurants.
Costs (2006) • $5950; includes tuition, housing, insurance, excursions, student support services, computer access, transcript. $40 application fee. $300 nonrefundable deposit required. Financial aid available for all students: scholarships, work study.

For More Information • Lexia International, 23 South Main Street, Hanover, NH 03755; *Phone:* 800-775-3942; *Fax:* 603-643-9899. *E-mail:* info@lexiaintl.org. *World Wide Web:* http://www.lexiaintl.org/

MICHIGAN STATE UNIVERSITY
EASTERN EUROPEAN JEWRY IN POLAND

Hosted by Jagiellonian University
Academic Focus • History, Polish, political science and government, Yiddish.
Program Information • Students attend classes at Jagiellonian University (Krakow, Poland). Field trips to Warsaw. Students typically earn 7 semester credits per term.
Sessions • Jun–Jul (summer).
Eligibility Requirements • Open to sophomores, juniors, seniors, graduate students; 2.3 GPA; good academic standing at home school; no foreign language proficiency required.
Living Arrangements • Students live in host institution dormitories. Meals are taken as a group, on one's own, in central dining facility.
Costs (2005) • $2252; includes housing, all meals, insurance, excursions. $100 application fee. $200 nonrefundable deposit required. Financial aid available for students from sponsoring institution: scholarships, loans.
For More Information • Ms. Yvonne Squiers, Secretary, Michigan State University, Office of Study Abroad, 109 International Center, East Lansing, MI 48824-1035; *Phone:* 517-353-8920; *Fax:* 517-432-2082. *E-mail:* squiers@msu.edu. *World Wide Web:* http://studyabroad.msu.edu/

UNIVERSITY OF KANSAS
SUMMER LANGUAGE AND CULTURE INSTITUTE IN KRAKOW, POLAND

Hosted by Jagiellonian University
Academic Focus • Art, cultural studies, film and media studies, history, music, Polish, Polish studies, political science and government.
Program Information • Students attend classes at Jagiellonian University (Krakow, Poland). Field trips to the Martyrdom Museum Auschwitz-Birkenau, the Wieliczka Salt Mines, Pieskowa Skala Castle, Pieniny Montains, Zakopane. Students typically earn 8 semester credits per term.
Sessions • Jul–Aug (summer).
Eligibility Requirements • Minimum age 18; open to freshmen, sophomores, juniors, seniors, graduate students, adults; 2.5 GPA; 2 letters of recommendation; good academic standing at home school; no foreign language proficiency required.
Living Arrangements • Students live in host institution dormitories. Meals are taken as a group, on one's own, in central dining facility.
Costs (2005) • $2510; includes tuition, housing, all meals, excursions, student support services, medical evacuation and repatriation services. $38 application fee. $300 nonrefundable deposit required. Financial aid available for students from sponsoring institution: scholarships, loans.
For More Information • Ms. Justine Hamilton, Program Coordinator, University of Kansas, Office of Study Abroad, Lippincott Hall, 1410 Jayhawk Boulevard, Room 108, Lawrence, KS 66045-7515; *Phone:* 785-864-3742; *Fax:* 785-864-5040. *E-mail:* osa@ku.edu. *World Wide Web:* http://www.ku.edu/~osa/

LODZ

ST. CLOUD STATE UNIVERSITY
POLAND–MASS MEDIA/HOLOCAUST STUDIES

Held at University of Lodz
Academic Focus • Advertising and public relations, Jewish studies.
Program Information • Classes are held on the campus of University of Lodz (Lodz, Poland). Faculty members are drawn from the sponsor's U.S. staff. Field trips to Krakow, Warsaw. Students typically earn 3 semester credits per term.
Sessions • May (summer).
Eligibility Requirements • Minimum age 18; open to juniors, seniors, graduate students; 2.0 GPA; good academic standing at home school; no foreign language proficiency required.
Living Arrangements • Students live in host institution dormitories. Meals are taken as a group, in central dining facility.
Costs (2004–2005) • $2975; includes housing, some meals, excursions, international airfare, international student ID. $75 application fee.
For More Information • Ms. Linda Raine, Study Abroad Coordinator, St. Cloud State University, Center for International Studies, 720 4th Avenue, South, St. Cloud, MN 56301; *Phone:* 320-308-4287; *Fax:* 320-308-4223. *E-mail:* study_abroad@stcloudstate.edu. *World Wide Web:* http://www.stcloudstate.edu/studyabroad

LUBLIN

UNIVERSITY OF WISCONSIN–MILWAUKEE
SUMMER SCHOOL OF POLISH LANGUAGE AND CULTURE

Hosted by Catholic University of Lublin
Academic Focus • Cultural studies, history, literature, Polish.
Program Information • Students attend classes at Catholic University of Lublin (Lublin, Poland). Field trips to Warsaw, Kazimierz; optional travel to Krakow, Bialowieza at an extra cost. Students typically earn 5 semester credits per term.
Sessions • Jul–Aug (summer), Aug (2 to 5 week sessions).
Eligibility Requirements • Minimum age 18; open to freshmen, sophomores, juniors, seniors, graduate students, adults; no foreign language proficiency required.
Living Arrangements • Students live in host institution dormitories, locally rented apartments, program-owned houses. Quarters are shared with host institution students. Meals are taken as a group, in central dining facility.
Costs (2005) • $3375; includes tuition, housing, all meals, insurance, excursions, international airfare, books and class materials, lab equipment, international student ID, student support services. $250 refundable deposit required. Financial aid available for students from sponsoring institution: scholarships.
For More Information • Mr. Michael J. Mikos, Professor, University of Wisconsin–Milwaukee, Department of Slavic Languages, Milwaukee, WI 53201; *Phone:* 414-229-4313; *Fax:* 414-229-2741. *E-mail:* mikos@uwm.edu. *World Wide Web:* http://www.lrc.uwm.edu/tour/

WROCLAW

STATE UNIVERSITY OF NEW YORK COLLEGE AT BROCKPORT
UNIVERSITY OF LOWER SILESIA, WROCLAW, POLAND

Hosted by University of Lower Silesia
Academic Focus • Anthropology, history, urban studies.
Program Information • Students attend classes at University of Lower Silesia (Wroclaw, Poland). Field trips. Students typically earn 6 credits per term.
Sessions • Jun–Jul (summer).
Eligibility Requirements • Minimum age 18; open to juniors, seniors; 2.75 GPA; 2 letters of recommendation; good academic standing at home school; no foreign language proficiency required.
Living Arrangements • Students live in hotels. Meals are taken in restaurants.
Costs (2006–2007) • $3800; includes tuition, housing, some meals, international student ID, student support services. $200 nonrefundable deposit required. Financial aid available for all students: scholarships, loans, regular financial aid, grants.
For More Information • Dr. John Perry, Director, International Education, State University of New York College at Brockport, 350 New Campus Drive, Brockport, NY 14420; *Phone:* 800-298-7869; *Fax:* 585-637-3218. *E-mail:* overseas@brockport.edu. *World Wide Web:* http://www.brockport.edu/studyabroad/

PORTUGAL

CITY-TO-CITY

LANGUAGE LIAISON
STUDY PORTUGUESE IN PORTUGAL–PORTO, FARO, LISBOA

Hosted by Language Liaison
Academic Focus • Portuguese.
Program Information • Students attend classes at Language Liaison (Faro), Language Liaison (Lisboa), Language Liaison (Porto). Field trips; optional travel at an extra cost. Students typically earn 3–15 semester credits per term.
Sessions • New programs begin weekly, year-round.
Eligibility Requirements • Minimum age 17; open to precollege students, freshmen, sophomores, juniors, seniors, graduate students, adults; no foreign language proficiency required.
Living Arrangements • Students live in locally rented apartments, host family homes, hotels. Meals are taken on one's own, with host family, in residences, in restaurants.
Costs (2005) • Contact sponsor for cost. $175 application fee. Financial aid available for all students: scholarship research service.
For More Information • Ms. Nancy Forman, President, Language Liaison, PO Box 1772, Pacific Palisades, CA 90272; *Phone:* 800-384-4448; *Fax:* 310-454-1706. *E-mail:* learn@languageliaison.com. *World Wide Web:* http://www.languageliaison.com/

FARO

LINGUA SERVICE WORLDWIDE
VACATION 'N LEARN PORTUGUESE IN PORTUGAL

Hosted by CIAL Centro de Linguas
Academic Focus • Portuguese, Portuguese studies.
Program Information • Students attend classes at CIAL Centro de Linguas (Faro, Portugal). Optional travel to cultural sites throughout Portugal at an extra cost. Students typically earn 3 semester credits for 3 weeks, 6 semester credits for 5 weeks.
Sessions • Sessions of 2 or more weeks begin once a month, year-round.
Eligibility Requirements • Minimum age 18; open to freshmen, sophomores, juniors, seniors, graduate students, adults; no foreign language proficiency required.
Living Arrangements • Students live in host family homes, hotels. Quarters are shared with host institution students. Meals are taken with host family.
Costs (2006–2007) • Contact sponsor for cost. $100 application fee.
For More Information • Assistant Director, Lingua Service Worldwide, 75 Prospect Street, Suite 4, Huntington, NY 11743; *Phone:* 800-394-5327; *Fax:* 631-271-3441. *E-mail:* linguaservice@att.net. *World Wide Web:* http://www.linguaserviceworldwide.com/

LISBON

COLLEGE CONSORTIUM FOR INTERNATIONAL STUDIES–ST. AMBROSE UNIVERSITY
STUDY IN PORTUGAL

Hosted by CIAL Centro de Linguas, CIAL Centro de Linguas
Academic Focus • Brazilian studies, Portuguese, Portuguese studies.
Program Information • Students attend classes at CIAL Centro de Linguas (Faro, Portugal), CIAL Centro de Linguas (Lisbon, Portugal). Field trips to museums, castles, factories and businesses; optional travel to Nazare, Fatima, Estoril at an extra cost. Students typically earn 3–5 semester credits for 4 weeks.
Sessions • 4 week sessions begin on the first Monday of the month, year-round.
Eligibility Requirements • Minimum age 18; open to freshmen, sophomores, juniors, seniors, graduate students, adults; 2.5 GPA; 2 letters of recommendation; no foreign language proficiency required.
Living Arrangements • Students live in locally rented apartments, host family homes, hotels. Meals are taken on one's own, with host family, in residences, in restaurants.
Costs (2005–2006) • $2500 per month; $6000 for 3 months; includes tuition, housing, some meals, books and class materials, fees. $25 application fee. Financial aid available for students from sponsoring institution: scholarships, loans, Pell grants and government loans.

PORTUGAL
Lisbon

For More Information • College Consortium for International Studies–St. Ambrose University, 2000 P Street, NW, Suite 503, Washington, DC 20036; *Phone:* 800-453-6956; *Fax:* 202-223-0999. *E-mail:* info@ccisabroad.org. *World Wide Web:* http://www. ccisabroad.org/. Students may also apply through St. Ambrose University, Study Abroad Office, 518 West Locust Street, Davenport, IA 52803.

LINGUA SERVICE WORLDWIDE
VACATION 'N LEARN PORTUGUESE IN PORTUGAL

Hosted by CIAL Centro de Linguas
Academic Focus • Portuguese, Portuguese studies.
Program Information • Students attend classes at CIAL Centro de Linguas (Lisbon, Portugal). Optional travel to cultural sites throughout Portugal at an extra cost. Students typically earn 3 semester credits for 3 weeks, 6 semester credits for 5 weeks.
Sessions • Sessions of 2 or more weeks begin once a month, year-round.
Eligibility Requirements • Minimum age 18; open to freshmen, sophomores, juniors, seniors, graduate students, adults; no foreign language proficiency required.
Living Arrangements • Students live in host family homes, hotels. Quarters are shared with host institution students. Meals are taken with host family.
Costs (2006–2007) • Contact sponsor for cost. $100 application fee.
For More Information • Assistant Director, Lingua Service Worldwide, 75 Prospect Street, Suite 4, Huntington, NY 11743; *Phone:* 800-394-5327; *Fax:* 631-271-3441. *E-mail:* linguaservice@att. net. *World Wide Web:* http://www.linguaserviceworldwide.com/

PORTO

LINGUA SERVICE WORLDWIDE
VACATION 'N LEARN PORTUGUESE IN PORTUGAL

Hosted by Fast Forward Institute
Academic Focus • Portuguese, Portuguese studies.
Program Information • Students attend classes at Fast Forward Institute (Porto, Portugal). Optional travel to cultural sites throughout Portugal at an extra cost. Students typically earn 3 semester credits for 3 weeks, 6 semester credits for 5 weeks.
Sessions • Sessions of 2 or more weeks begin once a month, year-round.
Eligibility Requirements • Minimum age 18; open to freshmen, sophomores, juniors, seniors, graduate students, adults; no foreign language proficiency required.
Living Arrangements • Students live in host family homes, hotels. Quarters are shared with host institution students. Meals are taken with host family.
Costs (2006–2007) • Contact sponsor for cost. $100 application fee.
For More Information • Assistant Director, Lingua Service Worldwide, 75 Prospect Street, Suite 4, Huntington, NY 11743; *Phone:* 800-394-5327; *Fax:* 631-271-3441. *E-mail:* linguaservice@att. net. *World Wide Web:* http://www.linguaserviceworldwide.com/

PUERTO RICO

SAN JUAN

LANGUAGE LIAISON
SPANISH IN PUERTO RICO

Hosted by Language Liaison
Academic Focus • Spanish language and literature.
Program Information • Students attend classes at Language Liaison (San Juan, Puerto Rico). Field trips; optional travel at an extra cost. Students typically earn 3–15 semester credits per term.
Sessions • Classes begin weekly, year-round.
Eligibility Requirements • Minimum age 17; open to precollege students, freshmen, sophomores, juniors, seniors, graduate students, adults; no foreign language proficiency required.
Living Arrangements • Students live in locally rented apartments, host family homes, hotels. Meals are taken on one's own, with host family, in residences, in restaurants.
Costs (2005) • Contact sponsor for cost. $175 application fee. Financial aid available for all students: scholarship research service.
For More Information • Ms. Nancy Forman, President, Language Liaison, PO Box 1772, Pacific Palisades, CA 90272; *Phone:* 800-284-4448; *Fax:* 310-454-1706. *E-mail:* learn@languageliaison.com. *World Wide Web:* http://www.languageliaison.com/

STATE UNIVERSITY OF NEW YORK COLLEGE AT BROCKPORT
UNIVERSITY OF PUERTO RICO, RIO PIEDRAS CAMPUS

Hosted by University of Puerto Rico Rio Piedras
Academic Focus • Spanish studies.
Program Information • Students attend classes at University of Puerto Rico Rio Piedras (Rio Piedras, Puerto Rico). Field trips. Students typically earn 3–6 credits per term.
Sessions • Jun–Jul (summer).
Eligibility Requirements • Minimum age 18; open to juniors, seniors, graduate students; 2.5 GPA; 2 letters of recommendation; good academic standing at home school; 2 years college course work and fluency in Spanish.
Living Arrangements • Students live in host institution dormitories. Meals are taken as a group, on one's own, in central dining facility, in restaurants.
Costs (2006–2007) • $3500; includes tuition, housing, excursions, international student ID, student support services. $200 nonrefundable deposit required. Financial aid available for all students: scholarships, loans, regular financial aid, grants.
For More Information • Dr. John Perry, Director, International Education, State University of New York College at Brockport, 350 New Campus Drive, Brockport, NY 14420; *Phone:* 800-298-SUNY; *Fax:* 585-637-3218. *E-mail:* overseas@brockport.edu. *World Wide Web:* http://www.brockport.edu/studyabroad/

RUSSIA

KAMCHATKA

MICHIGAN STATE UNIVERSITY
FISH, WILDLIFE, AND ENVIRONMENTAL ISSUES IN RUSSIA

Academic Focus • Fisheries studies, natural resources.
Program Information • Faculty members are drawn from the sponsor's U.S. staff. Field trips to Moscow, St. Petersburg. Students typically earn 6 semester credits per term.
Sessions • May (summer).
Eligibility Requirements • Open to sophomores, juniors, seniors; 2.0 GPA; good academic standing at home school; essay; no foreign language proficiency required.
Living Arrangements • Students live in locally rented apartments, hotels. Meals are taken as a group, on one's own, in central dining facility, in restaurants.
Costs (2005) • Contact sponsor for cost. $100 application fee. $200 nonrefundable deposit required. Financial aid available for students from sponsoring institution: scholarships, loans.
For More Information • Ms. Yvonne Squiers, Secretary, Michigan State University, Office of Study Abroad, 109 International Center, East Lansing, MI 48824-1035; *Phone:* 517-353-8920; *Fax:* 517-432-2082. *E-mail:* squiers@msu.edu. *World Wide Web:* http://studyabroad.msu.edu/

MOSCOW

COLLEGE CONSORTIUM FOR INTERNATIONAL STUDIES–TRUMAN STATE UNIVERSITY
TRUMAN IN MOSCOW

Hosted by Moscow Academy for the Humanities and Social Sciences
Academic Focus • Russian language and literature, Russian studies.
Program Information • Students attend classes at Moscow Academy for the Humanities and Social Sciences (Moscow, Russia). Field trips to Moscow, Golden Ring; optional travel to Saint Petersburg at an extra cost. Students typically earn 6-9 semester credits per term.
Sessions • May-Jun (summer), May-Jul (summer 2).
Eligibility Requirements • Minimum age 18; open to freshmen, sophomores, juniors, seniors, graduate students, adults; 2.5 GPA; 3 letters of recommendation; no foreign language proficiency required.
Living Arrangements • Students live in host institution dormitories, host family homes. Quarters are shared with students from other programs. Meals are taken as a group, in residences.
Costs (2007) • $2725-$4894; includes tuition, housing, all meals, excursions, books and class materials, international student ID, student support services. $300 nonrefundable deposit required. Financial aid available for students from sponsoring institution: scholarships, loans.
For More Information • Center for International Education, College Consortium for International Studies–Truman State University, 100 East Normal, Kirk Building 114, Kirksville, MO 63501; *Phone:* 660-785-4076; *Fax:* 660-785-7473. *E-mail:* ciea@truman.edu. *World Wide Web:* http://www.ccisabroad.org/

THE INTERNATIONAL PARTNERSHIP FOR SERVICE LEARNING AND LEADERSHIP
RUSSIA SERVICE–LEARNING

Hosted by GRINT Centre for Education
Academic Focus • Community service, Russian language and literature, Russian studies, social sciences, social work.
Program Information • Students attend classes at GRINT Centre for Education (Moscow, Russia). Scheduled travel to St. Petersburg, Tver (a provincial Russian town), Golden Ring towns; field trips to weekly theater, music, or circus performances; optional travel at an extra cost. Students typically earn 4-8 semester credits per term.
Sessions • May-Jul (summer).
Eligibility Requirements • Minimum age 18; open to freshmen, sophomores, juniors, seniors, graduate students, adults; 2 letters of recommendation; good academic standing at home school; evidence of maturity; no foreign language proficiency required.
Living Arrangements • Students live in host family homes, hostels or Institute of Youth. Quarters are shared with host institution students, students from other programs. Meals are taken on one's own, with host family, in residences.

Costs (2005–2006) • $5800; includes tuition, housing, some meals, service placement and supervision. $50 application fee. $250 refundable deposit required. Financial aid available for all students: federal financial aid.

For More Information • Director of Student Programs, The International Partnership for Service Learning and Leadership, 815 Second Avenue, New York, NY 10017-4594; *Phone:* 212-986-0989; *Fax:* 212-986-5039. *E-mail:* info@ipsl.org. *World Wide Web:* http://www.ipsl.org/

KNOWLEDGE EXCHANGE INSTITUTE (KEI)
EAST EUROPEAN BUSINESS, LAW, AND DIPLOMACY

Hosted by Moscow State University

Academic Focus • Accounting, advertising and public relations, business administration/management, commerce, communication services, communications, Eastern European studies, economics, entrepreneurship, finance, history, information science, intercultural studies, interdisciplinary studies, international affairs, international business, law and legal studies, liberal studies, management information systems, marketing, political science and government, public administration, public policy, Russian language and literature, Russian studies, social sciences.

Program Information • Students attend classes at Moscow State University (Moscow, Russia). Scheduled travel to St. Petersburg; field trips to Moscow, Serpukhov, Vladimir, Suzdal. Students typically earn 6 semester credits per term.

Sessions • Jun–Jul (summer), Jul–Aug (summer 2).

Eligibility Requirements • Open to freshmen, sophomores, juniors, seniors, graduate students, adults; 2.2 GPA; 2 letters of recommendation; good academic standing at home school; no foreign language proficiency required.

Living Arrangements • Students live in host institution dormitories. Quarters are shared with host institution students, students from other programs. Meals are taken on one's own, in residences, in central dining facility, in restaurants.

Costs (2006) • $4655; includes tuition, housing, insurance, books and class materials, lab equipment, student support services, mobile telephone, internet access. $50 application fee. $500 nonrefundable deposit required. Financial aid available for all students: scholarships, loans.

For More Information • Mr. Eduard Izraylovsky, Director, Knowledge Exchange Institute (KEI), 111 John Street, Suite 800, New York, NY 10038; *Phone:* 800-831-5095; *Fax:* 212-528-2095. *E-mail:* info@knowledgeexchange.org. *World Wide Web:* http://www.knowledgeexchange.org/

KNOWLEDGE EXCHANGE INSTITUTE (KEI)
MEDICINE, HEALTH, AND BIOMEDICAL SCIENCE

Hosted by Moscow State University

Academic Focus • Anatomy, biochemistry, biological/life sciences, biomedical sciences, chemical sciences, health-care management, liberal studies, mathematics, medicine, nursing, nutrition, pharmacology, physical sciences, physics, pre-dentistry, premedical studies, psychology, public health, Russian language and literature, Russian studies, science, statistics.

Program Information • Students attend classes at Moscow State University (Moscow, Russia). Scheduled travel to St. Petersburg; field trips to Moscow, Serpukhov, Vladimir, Suzdal. Students typically earn 6 semester credits per term.

Sessions • Jun–Jul (summer), Jul–Aug (summer 2).

Eligibility Requirements • Open to freshmen, sophomores, juniors, seniors, graduate students, adults; 2.2 GPA; 2 letters of recommendation; good academic standing at home school; no foreign language proficiency required.

Living Arrangements • Students live in host institution dormitories. Quarters are shared with host institution students, students from other programs. Meals are taken on one's own, in residences, in central dining facility, in restaurants.

Costs (2006) • $4655; includes tuition, housing, insurance, excursions, books and class materials, lab equipment, student support services, mobile telephone and internet access. $50 application fee. $500 nonrefundable deposit required. Financial aid available for all students: scholarships, loans.

For More Information • Mr. Eduard Izraylovsky, Director, Knowledge Exchange Institute (KEI), 111 John Street, Suite 800,

New York, NY 10038; *Phone:* 800-831-5095; *Fax:* 212-528-2095. *E-mail:* info@knowledgeexchange.org. *World Wide Web:* http://www.knowledgeexchange.org/

KNOWLEDGE EXCHANGE INSTITUTE (KEI)
MOSCOW INTERNSHIP PROGRAM

Hosted by Moscow State University

Academic Focus • Accounting, actuarial science, advertising and public relations, biochemistry, biological/life sciences, biomedical sciences, botany, brokerage, business administration/management, chemical sciences, commerce, communication services, communications, community service, criminal justice, Eastern European studies, economics, entrepreneurship, ethnic studies, finance, health-care management, hospitality services, hotel and restaurant management, human resources, information science, international affairs, international business, law and legal studies, management information systems, marketing, medicine, nursing, nutrition, physical sciences, physics, political science and government, premedical studies, psychology, public administration, Russian language and literature, Russian studies, science, social services, social work, tourism and travel, veterinary science.

Program Information • Students attend classes at Moscow State University (Moscow, Russia). Scheduled travel to St. Petersburg; field trips to Moscow, Vladimir, Suzdal. Students typically earn 6 semester credits per term.

Sessions • Jun–Aug (summer).

Eligibility Requirements • Open to freshmen, sophomores, juniors, seniors, graduate students, adults; 2.2 GPA; 2 letters of recommendation; good academic standing at home school; no foreign language proficiency required.

Living Arrangements • Students live in host institution dormitories, program-owned apartments, host family homes. Quarters are shared with host institution students, students from other programs. Meals are taken on one's own, with host family, in residences, in restaurants.

Costs (2006) • $4550; includes tuition, housing, insurance, excursions, student support services, mobile telephone. $50 application fee. $500 nonrefundable deposit required. Financial aid available for all students: scholarships, loans.

For More Information • Mr. Eduard Izraylovsky, Director, Knowledge Exchange Institute (KEI), 111 John Street, Suite 800, New York, NY 10038; *Phone:* 800-831-5095; *Fax:* 212-528-2095. *E-mail:* info@knowledgeexchange.org. *World Wide Web:* http://www.knowledgeexchange.org/

KNOWLEDGE EXCHANGE INSTITUTE (KEI)
RUSSIAN LANGUAGE, CULTURE, AND HUMANITIES

Hosted by Moscow State University

Academic Focus • Art, art history, civilization studies, communications, community service, comparative history, cultural studies, Eastern European studies, economics, geography, intercultural studies, interdisciplinary studies, international affairs, liberal studies, peace and conflict studies, philosophy, psychology, public policy, Russian language and literature, Russian studies, science, social sciences, social work.

Program Information • Students attend classes at Moscow State University (Moscow, Russia). Scheduled travel to St. Petersburg; field trips to Moscow, Serpukhov, Vladimir, Suzdal. Students typically earn 6 semester credits per term.

Sessions • Jun–Jul (summer), Jul–Aug (summer 2).

Eligibility Requirements • Open to freshmen, sophomores, juniors, seniors, graduate students, adults; 2.2 GPA; 2 letters of recommendation; good academic standing at home school; no foreign language proficiency required.

Living Arrangements • Students live in host institution dormitories. Quarters are shared with host institution students, students from other programs. Meals are taken on one's own, in residences, in central dining facility, in restaurants.

Costs (2006) • $4655; includes tuition, housing, insurance, excursions, books and class materials, lab equipment, student support services, mobile telephone and internet access. $50 application fee. $500 nonrefundable deposit required. Financial aid available for all students: scholarships, loans.

For More Information • Mr. Eduard Izraylovsky, Director, Knowledge Exchange Institute (KEI), 111 John Street, Suite 800,

RUSSIA
Moscow

New York, NY 10038; *Phone:* 800-831-5095; *Fax:* 212-528-2095. *E-mail:* info@knowledgeexchange.org. *World Wide Web:* http://www. knowledgeexchange.org/

KNOWLEDGE EXCHANGE INSTITUTE (KEI)
SCIENCE, MATH, AND ENGINEERING
Hosted by Moscow State University
Academic Focus • Anatomy, biochemistry, biological/life sciences, biomedical sciences, botany, chemical sciences, computer science, earth sciences, ecology, electrical engineering, engineering, environmental science/studies, geology, interdisciplinary studies, liberal studies, mechanical engineering, meteorology, music history, physical sciences, physics, premedical studies, psychology, Russian language and literature, Russian studies, science, statistics, veterinary science, zoology.
Program Information • Students attend classes at Moscow State University (Moscow, Russia). Scheduled travel to St. Petersburg; field trips to Moscow, Serpukhov, Vladimir, Suzdal. Students typically earn 6 semester credits per term.
Sessions • Jun–Jul (summer), Jul–Aug (summer 2).
Eligibility Requirements • Open to freshmen, sophomores, juniors, seniors, graduate students, adults; 2.2 GPA; 2 letters of recommendation; good academic standing at home school; no foreign language proficiency required.
Living Arrangements • Students live in host institution dormitories. Quarters are shared with host institution students, students from other programs. Meals are taken on one's own, in residences, in central dining facility, in restaurants.
Costs (2006) • $4655; includes tuition, housing, insurance, excursions, books and class materials, lab equipment, student support services, mobile telephone and internet access. $50 application fee. $500 nonrefundable deposit required. Financial aid available for all students: scholarships, loans.
For More Information • Mr. Eduard Izraylovsky, Director, Knowledge Exchange Institute (KEI), 111 John Street, Suite 800, New York, NY 10038; *Phone:* 800-831-5095; *Fax:* 212-528-2095. *E-mail:* info@knowledgeexchange.org. *World Wide Web:* http://www. knowledgeexchange.org/

LINGUA SERVICE WORLDWIDE
VACATION 'N LEARN RUSSIAN IN RUSSIA
Hosted by Iporex
Academic Focus • Russian language and literature, Russian studies.
Program Information • Students attend classes at Iporex (Moscow, Russia). Optional travel to cultural sites throughout Russia at an extra cost. Students typically earn 3 semester credits for 3 weeks, 6 semester credits for 5 weeks.
Sessions • Sessions of 2 or more weeks begin on Mondays, year-round.
Eligibility Requirements • Minimum age 18; open to freshmen, sophomores, juniors, seniors, graduate students, adults; no foreign language proficiency required.
Living Arrangements • Students live in host institution dormitories, locally rented apartments, host family homes, hotels. Meals are taken with host family.
Costs (2006–2007) • Contact sponsor for cost. $100 application fee.
For More Information • Assistant Director, Lingua Service Worldwide, 75 Prospect Street, Suite 4, Huntington, NY 11743; *Phone:* 800-394-5327; *Fax:* 631-271-3441. *E-mail:* linguaservice@att. net. *World Wide Web:* http://www.linguaserviceworldwide.com/

LINGUA SERVICE WORLDWIDE
VACATION 'N LEARN RUSSIAN IN RUSSIA
Hosted by Liden and Denz Language Center
Academic Focus • Russian language and literature, Russian studies.
Program Information • Students attend classes at Liden and Denz Language Center (Moscow, Russia). Optional travel to cultural sites throughout Russia at an extra cost. Students typically earn 3 semester credits for 3 weeks, 6 semester credits for 5 weeks.
Sessions • Sessions of 2 or more weeks begin on Mondays, year-round.

Eligibility Requirements • Minimum age 18; open to freshmen, sophomores, juniors, seniors, graduate students, adults; no foreign language proficiency required.
Living Arrangements • Students live in host institution dormitories, locally rented apartments, host family homes, hotels. Meals are taken with host family.
Costs (2006–2007) • Contact sponsor for cost. $100 application fee.
For More Information • Assistant Director, Lingua Service Worldwide, 75 Prospect Street, Suite 4, Huntington, NY 11743; *Phone:* 800-394-5327; *Fax:* 631-271-3441. *E-mail:* linguaservice@att. net. *World Wide Web:* http://www.linguaserviceworldwide.com/

UNIVERSITY AT ALBANY, STATE UNIVERSITY OF NEW YORK
LANGUAGE AND CULTURAL STUDIES AT MOSCOW STATE UNIVERSITY
Hosted by Moscow State University
Academic Focus • Russian language and literature.
Program Information • Students attend classes at Moscow State University (Moscow, Russia). Scheduled travel to St. Petersburg; field trips to local sites, theaters, museums. Students typically earn 6 semester credits per term.
Sessions • May–Jun (summer).
Eligibility Requirements • Minimum age 18; open to freshmen, sophomores, juniors, seniors; 2.5 GPA; no foreign language proficiency required.
Living Arrangements • Students live in host institution dormitories. Quarters are shared with students from other programs. Meals are taken on one's own, in residences, in restaurants.
Costs (2005) • Contact sponsor for cost. $150 nonrefundable deposit required. Financial aid available for students from sponsoring institution: all customary sources.
For More Information • University at Albany, State University of New York, Office of International Education, LI 66, Albany, NY 12222; *Phone:* 518-442-3525; *Fax:* 518-442-3338. *E-mail:* intled@ uamail.albany.edu. *World Wide Web:* http://www.albany.edu/ studyabroad/

NOVGOROD
STATE UNIVERSITY OF NEW YORK COLLEGE AT BROCKPORT
INTERNSHIPS: RUSSIA
Held at Novgorod State University
Academic Focus • Archaeology, art, education, history, liberal studies, photography, Russian language and literature, Russian studies, social sciences, sociology, tourism and travel.
Program Information • Classes are held on the campus of Novgorod State University (Novgorod, Russia). Faculty members are drawn from the sponsor's U.S. staff. Scheduled travel to St. Petersburg; field trips to Pskov, Starraya. Students typically earn 6–12 semester credits per term.
Sessions • May–Aug (summer).
Eligibility Requirements • Minimum age 18; open to juniors, seniors; course work in area of internship if applicable; 2.5 GPA; 2 letters of recommendation; good academic standing at home school; résumé required for internship; basic knowledge of Russian.
Living Arrangements • Students live in host family homes. Meals are taken with host family, in residences.
Costs (2005) • $4000; includes tuition, housing, some meals, insurance, excursions, international airfare, international student ID, student support services, internship supervisor (if applicable), program-related travel, orientation. $200 nonrefundable deposit required. Financial aid available for students from sponsoring institution: scholarships, loans, grants, regular financial aid.
For More Information • Dr. John J. Perry, Director, Office of International Education, State University of New York College at Brockport, 350 New Campus Drive, Brockport, NY 14420; *Phone:* 800-298-SUNY; *Fax:* 585-637-3218. *E-mail:* overseas@brockport.edu. *World Wide Web:* http://www.brockport.edu/studyabroad/

STATE UNIVERSITY OF NEW YORK COLLEGE AT BROCKPORT
RUSSIAN LANGUAGE IMMERSION PROGRAM

Hosted by Novgorod State University

Academic Focus • International affairs, Russian language and literature, Russian studies.

Program Information • Students attend classes at Novgorod State University (Novgorod, Russia). Scheduled travel to St. Petersburg; field trips to sites of interest in and around Novgorod the Great. Students typically earn 6 semester credits per term.

Sessions • Jun–Aug (summer).

Eligibility Requirements • Minimum age 18; open to juniors, seniors, graduate students; course work in area of internship, if applicable; 2.5 GPA; 2 letters of recommendation; good academic standing at home school; résumé required for internship; 1 year college course work in Russian for internships.

Living Arrangements • Students live in host institution dormitories, host family homes. Meals are taken with host family, in residences.

Costs (2005) • $4000 (estimated); includes tuition, housing, some meals, insurance, excursions, international airfare, international student ID, student support services, local travel. $200 nonrefundable deposit required. Financial aid available for all students: scholarships, loans, regular financial aid.

For More Information • Dr. John J. Perry, Director, Office of International Education, State University of New York College at Brockport, 350 New Campus Drive, Brockport, NY 14420; *Phone:* 800-298-SUNY; *Fax:* 585-637-3218. *E-mail:* overseas@brockport.edu. *World Wide Web:* http://www.brockport.edu/studyabroad/

PETROZAVODSK

COLLEGE OF ST. SCHOLASTICA
RUSSIAN LANGUAGE CAMP

Hosted by Karelian State Pedagogical University

Academic Focus • Cultural studies, Russian language and literature.

Program Information • Students attend classes at Karelian State Pedagogical University (Petrozavodsk, Russia). Scheduled travel to St. Petersburg, Moscow; field trips to museums and points of interest in Karelia, summer cabins for weekend stays with families; optional travel to sites chosen by student at an extra cost. Students typically earn 4 semester credits per term.

Sessions • Jun–Jul (summer).

Eligibility Requirements • Minimum age 17; open to precollege students, freshmen, sophomores, juniors, seniors, graduate students, adults; good academic standing at home school; no foreign language proficiency required.

Living Arrangements • Students live in host institution dormitories. Quarters are shared with host institution students. Meals are taken as a group, in central dining facility.

Costs (2006) • $3895; includes tuition, housing, all meals, insurance, excursions, international airfare, books and class materials, student support services. $50 refundable deposit required. Financial aid available for students from sponsoring institution: scholarships, loans.

For More Information • Dr. Thomas Morgan, Associate Professor, College of St. Scholastica, 1200 Kenwood Avenue, Duluth, MN 55811; *Phone:* 218-723-6442; *Fax:* 218-723-6290. *E-mail:* tmorgan@css.edu. *World Wide Web:* http://www.css.edu/study_abroad/

PUSCHINO

KNOWLEDGE EXCHANGE INSTITUTE (KEI)
SCIENCE, MATHEMATICS, AND ENGINEERING RESEARCH

Hosted by Puschino Science Center

Academic Focus • Anatomy, biochemistry, biological/life sciences, biomedical sciences, botany, chemical sciences, computer science, earth sciences, ecology, electrical engineering, engineering, environmental science/studies, fisheries studies, forestry, industrial management, marine sciences, mechanical engineering, medicine, meteorology, natural resources, oceanography, pharmacology, physical sciences, physics, premedical studies, psychology, science, veterinary science, wildlife studies, zoology.

Program Information • Students attend classes at Puschino Science Center (Puschino, Russia). Scheduled travel to St. Petersburg; field trips to Moscow, Serpukhov, Vladimir. Students typically earn 9 semester credits per term.

Sessions • Jun–Jul (summer), Dec–Jan (summer 2).

Eligibility Requirements • Open to freshmen, sophomores, juniors, seniors, graduate students, adults; 2.5 GPA; 2 letters of recommendation; good academic standing at home school; no foreign language proficiency required.

Living Arrangements • Students live in host institution dormitories, host family homes. Quarters are shared with host institution students, students from other programs. Meals are taken as a group, in central dining facility, in restaurants.

Costs (2006) • $5705; includes tuition, housing, all meals, insurance, excursions, books and class materials, lab equipment, student support services, mobile telephones, internet access. $50 application fee. $500 nonrefundable deposit required. Financial aid available for all students: scholarships, loans.

For More Information • Mr. Eduard Izraylovsky, Director, Knowledge Exchange Institute (KEI), 111 John Street, Suite 800, New York, NY 10038; *Phone:* 800-831-5095; *Fax:* 212-528-2095. *E-mail:* info@knowledgeexchange.org. *World Wide Web:* http://www.knowledgeexchange.org/

ST. PETERSBURG

AMERICAN INSTITUTE FOR FOREIGN STUDY (AIFS)
AIFS–ST. PETERSBURG, RUSSIA–ST. PETERSBURG STATE POLYTECHNIC UNIVERSITY

Hosted by Saint Petersburg State Polytechnic University

Academic Focus • Art history, history, political science and government, Russian language and literature, sociology.

Program Information • Students attend classes at Saint Petersburg State Polytechnic University (St. Petersburg, Russia). Scheduled travel to 3-day London stopover, 3-day Moscow visit; field trips to cultural activities, museums, palaces, concerts. Students typically earn 7 semester credits per term.

Sessions • Jun–Jul (summer).

Eligibility Requirements • Minimum age 17; open to precollege students, freshmen, sophomores, juniors, seniors; 2.0 GPA; Students must travel with the AIFS group due to group visa dates; VISA is required; no foreign language proficiency required.

Living Arrangements • Students live in host institution dormitories, program-owned apartments, host family homes, hotels. Quarters are shared with host institution students. Meals are taken as a group, in residences.

Costs (2007) • $5299; includes tuition, housing, some meals, excursions, international student ID, student support services, On-site Resident Director, Phone Card to call the U.S., Visa. $95 application fee. $395 nonrefundable deposit required. Financial aid available for all students: scholarships.

For More Information • Mr. David Mauro, Admissions Advisor, American Institute For Foreign Study (AIFS), 9 West Broad Street, Stamford, CT 06902-3788; *Phone:* 800-727-2437 Ext. 5163; *Fax:* 203-399-5597. *E-mail:* dmauro@aifs.com. *World Wide Web:* http://www.aifsabroad.com/

BOWLING GREEN STATE UNIVERSITY
ST. PETERSBURG (RUSSIA) STUDY ABROAD PROGRAM

Hosted by Saint Petersburg State University

Academic Focus • Russian language and literature, Russian studies.

Program Information • Students attend classes at Saint Petersburg State University (St. Petersburg, Russia). Field trips to Novgorod, Moscow, museums, the summer palaces; optional travel to Novgorod, Moscow at an extra cost. Students typically earn 6-9 semester credits per term.

Sessions • May–Jun (summer).

Eligibility Requirements • Minimum age 18; open to freshmen, sophomores, juniors, seniors, graduate students, adults; 2.8 GPA; 3 letters of recommendation; no foreign language proficiency required.

RUSSIA
St. Petersburg

Living Arrangements • Students live in host institution dormitories, host family homes. Meals are taken with host family, in residences.
Costs (2005) • $3452–$4328; includes tuition, housing, some meals, excursions, international airfare, books and class materials, student support services. $100 nonrefundable deposit required. Financial aid available for students from sponsoring institution: loans.
For More Information • Dr. Irina Stakhanova, Director, Bowling Green State University, 124 Shatzel Hall, Bowling Green, OH 43403; *Phone:* 419-372-2268; *Fax:* 419-372-2571. *E-mail:* irina@bgnet.bgsu.edu. *World Wide Web:* http://www.bgsu.edu/

CIEE
CIEE STUDY CENTER AT ST. PETERSBURG STATE UNIVERSITY, RUSSIA–RUSSIAN LANGUAGE PROGRAM

Hosted by Saint Petersburg State University
Academic Focus • Russian language and literature, Russian studies.
Program Information • Students attend classes at Saint Petersburg State University (St. Petersburg, Russia). Field trips to cultural interest sites in St. Petersburg, Valaam, Pskov; Tallinn, Novgorod; Moscow. Students typically earn 8 semester credits per term.
Sessions • Jun–Aug (summer).
Eligibility Requirements • Minimum age 18; open to sophomores, juniors, seniors; 2.75 GPA; 1 letter of recommendation; good academic standing at home school; oral language exam; evaluation from language professor; 2 years of college course work in Russian.
Living Arrangements • Students live in host family homes. Meals are taken as a group, with host family, in residences, in central dining facility, in restaurants.
Costs (2006) • $5100; includes tuition, housing, all meals, insurance, excursions, books and class materials, student support services, visa fees, optional on-site pick-up, pre-departure advising, orientation, resident director, cultural activities. $30 application fee. $300 nonrefundable deposit required. Financial aid available for all students: minority student scholarships, travel grants.
For More Information • Information Center, CIEE, 7 Custom House Street, 3rd Floor, Portland, ME 04101; *Phone:* 800-40-STUDY; *Fax:* 207-553-7699. *E-mail:* studyinfo@ciee.org. *World Wide Web:* http://www.ciee.org/isp/

EMORY UNIVERSITY
RUSSIAN STUDIES

Held at Saint Petersburg University
Academic Focus • Russian language and literature, Russian studies.
Program Information • Classes are held on the campus of Saint Petersburg University (St. Petersburg, Russia). Faculty members are drawn from the sponsor's U.S. staff and local instructors hired by the sponsor. Scheduled travel to Moscow. Students typically earn 8–12 semester credits per term.
Sessions • Jun–Aug (summer).
Eligibility Requirements • Minimum age 18; open to freshmen, sophomores, juniors, seniors; 2.0 GPA; good academic standing at home school; no foreign language proficiency required.
Living Arrangements • Students live in host institution dormitories. Meals are taken on one's own, in central dining facility.
Costs (2005) • $7058; includes tuition, housing, some meals, insurance, excursions. $350 nonrefundable deposit required. Financial aid available for students from sponsoring institution: scholarships, loans.
For More Information • Ms. Gail Scheu, Study Abroad Coordinator, Emory University, 1385 Oxford Road, Atlanta, GA 30322; *Phone:* 404-727-2240; *Fax:* 404-727-6724. *E-mail:* lscheu@emory.edu. *World Wide Web:* http://www.cipa.emory.edu/

LINGUA SERVICE WORLDWIDE
VACATION 'N LEARN RUSSIAN IN RUSSIA

Hosted by Liden and Denz Language Center
Academic Focus • Russian language and literature, Russian studies.
Program Information • Students attend classes at Liden and Denz Language Center (St. Petersburg, Russia). Optional travel to cultural sites throughout Russia at an extra cost. Students typically earn 3 semester credits for 3 weeks, 6 semester credits for 5 weeks.
Sessions • Sessions of 2 or more weeks begin on Mondays, year-round.

Eligibility Requirements • Minimum age 18; open to freshmen, sophomores, juniors, seniors, graduate students, adults; no foreign language proficiency required.
Living Arrangements • Students live in host institution dormitories, locally rented apartments, host family homes, hotels. Meals are taken with host family.
Costs (2006–2007) • Contact sponsor for cost. $100 application fee.
For More Information • Assistant Director, Lingua Service Worldwide, 75 Prospect Street, Suite 4, Huntington, NY 11743; *Phone:* 800-394-5327; *Fax:* 631-271-3441. *E-mail:* linguaservice@att.net. *World Wide Web:* http://www.linguaserviceworldwide.com/

UNIVERSITY OF KANSAS
SUMMER LANGUAGE INSTITUTE IN ST. PETERSBURG, RUSSIA

Hosted by Saint Petersburg University
Academic Focus • Russian language and literature, Russian studies.
Program Information • Students attend classes at Saint Petersburg University (St. Petersburg, Russia). Scheduled travel to Moscow; field trips to Peter the Great's summer palace, Tsar's Village. Students typically earn 6 semester credits per term.
Sessions • May–Jul (summer).
Eligibility Requirements • Minimum age 18; open to sophomores, juniors, seniors, graduate students; 2.5 GPA; 2 letters of recommendation; good academic standing at home school; 2 years of college course work in Russian.
Living Arrangements • Students live in host family homes. Meals are taken as a group, on one's own, with host family, in residences, in central dining facility, in restaurants.
Costs (2005) • $3300; includes tuition, housing, some meals, excursions, student support services, medical evacuation and repatriation services. $38 application fee. $300 nonrefundable deposit required. Financial aid available for students from sponsoring institution: scholarships, loans.
For More Information • Ms. Justine Hamilton, Program Coordinator, University of Kansas, Office of Study Abroad, Lippincott Hall, 1410 Jayhawk Boulevard, Room 108, Lawrence, KS 66045-7515; *Phone:* 785-864-3742; *Fax:* 785-864-5040. *E-mail:* osa@ku.edu. *World Wide Web:* http://www.ku.edu/~osa/

UNIVERSITY OF ROCHESTER
RUSSIAN IN RUSSIA

Hosted by Saint Petersburg University
Academic Focus • Russian language and literature.
Program Information • Students attend classes at Saint Petersburg University (St. Petersburg, Russia). Field trips to Moscow, Novgorod. Students typically earn 6 semester credits per term.
Sessions • May–Jun (summer).
Eligibility Requirements • Minimum age 18; open to freshmen, sophomores, juniors, seniors, adults; 1 letter of recommendation; good academic standing at home school; 1 year of college course work in Russian.
Living Arrangements • Students live in host family homes. Meals are taken with host family, in residences.
Costs (2005) • $3120; includes tuition, housing, some meals, excursions, books and class materials, student support services. $250 deposit required. Financial aid available for students from sponsoring institution: scholarships, loans.
For More Information • Ms. Anne Lutkus, Language Coordinator, University of Rochester, Department of Modern Languages and Cultures, PO Box 270082, Rochester, NY 14627-0082; *Phone:* 585-275-2235; *Fax:* 585-273-1097. *E-mail:* adlt@mail.rochester.edu. *World Wide Web:* http://www.rochester.edu/college/study-abroad/

VLADIMIR

ILLINOIS STATE UNIVERSITY
CRIME AND CRIMINAL JUSTICE IN RUSSIA/POLITICS IN RUSSIA

Academic Focus • Criminal justice, political science and government.
Program Information • Faculty members are drawn from the sponsor's U.S. staff. Scheduled travel to Moscow, Murom; field trips

to various police stations, training centers, courtrooms, prisons; optional travel to St. Petersburg at an extra cost. Students typically earn 3-6 semester credits per term.

Sessions • May (summer).

Eligibility Requirements • Open to sophomores, juniors, seniors, graduate students, adults; major in criminal justice sciences, politics and government; 2.5 GPA; good academic standing at home school; no foreign language proficiency required.

Living Arrangements • Students live in host family homes, hotels. Meals are taken as a group, with host family, in residences, in restaurants.

Costs (2005) • $3630; includes tuition, housing, all meals, insurance, excursions, international airfare, international student ID, student support services, personal expenses. $150 application fee. Financial aid available for students from sponsoring institution: scholarships, loans.

For More Information • Dr. Frank Morn, ISU Criminal Justice Sciences, Illinois State University, Campus Box 5250, Normal, IL 61790-5250; *Phone:* 309-438-7853; *Fax:* 309-438-3987. *E-mail:* ftmorn@ilstu.edu. *World Wide Web:* http://www.internationalstudies.ilstu.edu/

# SCOTLAND

See also England, Ireland, Northern Ireland, and Wales.

CITY-TO-CITY

COOPERATIVE CENTER FOR STUDY ABROAD
SCOTLAND

Held at University of Edinburgh, University of Strathclyde
Academic Focus • Anthropology, creative writing, English, history, journalism, literature, photography, social work.
Program Information • Classes are held on the campus of University of Edinburgh (Edinburgh), University of Strathclyde (Glasgow). Faculty members are drawn from the sponsor's U.S. staff. Field trips to Glasgow, Edinburgh. Students typically earn 3 semester credits per term.
Sessions • Jun (summer).
Eligibility Requirements • Minimum age 18; open to freshmen, sophomores, juniors, seniors, graduate students, adults; good academic standing at home school.
Living Arrangements • Students live in host institution dormitories, hotels. Quarters are shared with host institution students. Meals are taken as a group, on one's own, in central dining facility, in restaurants.
Costs (2007) • $3995; includes housing, some meals, insurance, excursions, international airfare, student support services, airport transfers. $200 nonrefundable deposit required. Financial aid available for students from sponsoring institution: scholarships, loans.
For More Information • Dr. Michael A. Klembara, Executive Director, Cooperative Center for Study Abroad, Northern Kentucky University, Nunn Drive, Founders Hall 301, Highland Heights, KY 41099; *Phone:* 800-319-6015; *Fax:* 859-572-6650. *E-mail:* ccsa@nku.edu. *World Wide Web:* http://www.ccsa.cc/

JAMES MADISON UNIVERSITY
CULTURAL HISTORY OF SCOTLAND

Held at University of St. Andrews
Academic Focus • Art history, English, history.
Program Information • Classes are held on the campus of University of St. Andrews (St. Andrews). Faculty members are drawn from the sponsor's U.S. staff. Scheduled travel to St. Andrews, Edinburgh, Glasgow, Aberdeen, Stirling Castle, Loch Ness, Bannockburn, Culloden, the Highlands, Ben Neus, Isle of Sky. Students typically earn 3 semester credits per term.
Sessions • May–Jun (summer).
Eligibility Requirements • Minimum age 18; open to sophomores, juniors, seniors, graduate students, adults; 2.0 GPA; good academic standing at home school.
Living Arrangements • Students live in host institution dormitories, hotels. Quarters are shared with host institution students. Meals are taken as a group, on one's own, in central dining facility, in restaurants.
Costs (2005) • $3154 for Virginia residents; $3994 for nonresidents; includes tuition, housing, some meals, excursions, books and class materials, international student ID. $400 nonrefundable deposit required.
For More Information • Mr. Felix Wang, Director, James Madison University, Office of International Programs, MSC 5731, 1077 South Main Street, Harrisonburg, VA 22807; *Phone:* 540-568-6419; *Fax:* 540-568-3310. *E-mail:* studyabroad@jmu.edu. *World Wide Web:* http://www.jmu.edu/international/

EDINBURGH

ARCADIA UNIVERSITY
SCOTTISH UNIVERSITIES INTERNATIONAL SUMMER SCHOOL–LITERATURE AND CREATIVE WRITING IN SCOTLAND

Hosted by University of Edinburgh
Academic Focus • British studies, English literature.
Program Information • Students attend classes at University of Edinburgh (Edinburgh, Scotland). Field trips to an evening cultural program, ceilids. Students typically earn 3–6 semester credits per term.
Sessions • Jul (summer), Jul–Aug (summer 2).
Eligibility Requirements • Open to sophomores, juniors, seniors; 3.0 GPA; 1 letter of recommendation; 3 semesters of college-level work.
Living Arrangements • Students live in host institution dormitories. Quarters are shared with host institution students, students from other programs. Meals are taken as a group, in central dining facility.
Costs (2005) • $2950–$5190; includes tuition, housing, some meals, insurance, international student ID, student support services, pre-departure guide, transcripts, orientation. $35 application fee. $500 nonrefundable deposit required. Financial aid available for all students: loans.

For More Information • Arcadia University, Center for Education Abroad, 450 South Easton Road, Glenside, PA 19038-3295; *Phone:* 866-927-2234; *Fax:* 215-572-2174. *E-mail:* cea@arcadia.edu. *World Wide Web:* http://www.arcadia.edu/cea/

NORTHERN ILLINOIS UNIVERSITY
ACADEMIC INTERNSHIPS IN SCOTLAND
Held at Educational Programmes Abroad
Academic Focus • Full curriculum.
Program Information • Classes are held on the campus of Educational Programmes Abroad (Edinburgh, Scotland). Faculty members are local instructors hired by the sponsor. Optional travel to London at an extra cost. Students typically earn 6 semester credits per term.
Sessions • Jun (summer).
Eligibility Requirements • Open to juniors, seniors; 3.0 GPA; 2 letters of recommendation; good academic standing at home school; essay; résumé.
Living Arrangements • Students live in locally rented apartments, host family homes. Quarters are shared with students from other programs. Meals are taken on one's own, in restaurants.
Costs (2005) • $5915; includes tuition, housing, some meals, insurance, international student ID, student support services, internship placement. $45 application fee. $500 refundable deposit required. Financial aid available for students from sponsoring institution: loans.
For More Information • Ms. Emily Gorlewski, Program Assistant, Northern Illinois University, Study Abroad Office, Williston Hall 417, DeKalb, IL 60115; *Phone:* 815-753-0420; *Fax:* 815-753-0825. *E-mail:* niuabroad@niu.edu. *World Wide Web:* http://www.niu.edu/niuabroad/

GLASGOW

TEMPLE UNIVERSITY
TEMPLE IN SCOTLAND
Hosted by Glasgow School of Art
Academic Focus • Crafts, fine/studio arts.
Program Information • Students attend classes at Glasgow School of Art (Glasgow, Scotland). Scheduled travel to London; field trips to the Scottish Highlands. Students typically earn 6 semester credits per term.
Sessions • Jun–Jul (summer).
Eligibility Requirements • Open to sophomores, juniors, seniors, graduate students; course work in studio art (sophomore level); 2.5 GPA; 1 letter of recommendation; good academic standing at home school; official transcripts.
Living Arrangements • Students live in hotels. Quarters are shared with host institution students. Meals are taken as a group, on one's own, in residences.
Costs (2005) • $4400–$5700; includes tuition, housing, some meals, excursions, some art materials, local travel. $30 application fee. $200 nonrefundable deposit required. Financial aid available for students from sponsoring institution: scholarships, loans.
For More Information • Mr. Nicholas Kripal, Faculty, Temple University, Tyler School of Art, 7725 Penrose Avenue, Elkins Park, PA 19027; *Phone:* 215-782-2790; *Fax:* 215-782-2799. *E-mail:* nkripal@temple.edu. *World Wide Web:* http://www.temple.edu/studyabroad/

GREENOCK

COLLEGE CONSORTIUM FOR INTERNATIONAL STUDIES–BROOKDALE COMMUNITY COLLEGE
SUMMER PROGRAM IN SCOTLAND
Hosted by James Watt College
Academic Focus • Scottish studies.
Program Information • Students attend classes at James Watt College (Greenock, Scotland). Scheduled travel to the Highlands; field trips to Largs, Edinburgh, Loch Lomond, Glasgow, Stirling. Students typically earn 6 semester credits per term.
Sessions • Jun–Jul (summer).
Eligibility Requirements • Minimum age 18; open to freshmen, sophomores, juniors, seniors, graduate students; 2.5 GPA; 2 letters of recommendation; essay; transcript; completion of 15 credits prior to application; application for internship.
Living Arrangements • Students live in host institution dormitories. Quarters are shared with host institution students, students from other programs. Meals are taken on one's own, in residences, in central dining facility.
Costs (2006–2007) • $3005; includes tuition, housing, insurance, excursions, student support services, e-mail access, airport pick-up, fees. $35 application fee. Financial aid available for students from sponsoring institution: scholarships, loans.
For More Information • College Consortium for International Studies–Brookdale Community College, 2000 P Street, NW, Suite 503, Washington, DC 20036; *Phone:* 202-223-0330; *Fax:* 202-223-0999. *E-mail:* info@ccisabroad.org. *World Wide Web:* http://www.ccisabroad.org/. Students may also apply through Brookdale Community College, International Center, 765 Newman Springs Road, Lincroft, NJ 07738-1597.

STIRLING

ARCADIA UNIVERSITY
UNIVERSITY OF STIRLING SUMMER ACADEMIC PROGRAM
Hosted by University of Stirling
Academic Focus • Full curriculum.
Program Information • Students attend classes at University of Stirling (Stirling, Scotland). Students typically earn 5–10 semester credits per term.
Sessions • Jun–Aug (summer).
Eligibility Requirements • Open to sophomores, juniors, seniors; 3.0 GPA; 1 letter of recommendation; 3 semesters of college-level work.
Living Arrangements • Students live in host institution dormitories. Quarters are shared with students from other programs. Meals are taken on one's own, in residences, in central dining facility, in restaurants.
Costs (2005) • $3490–$5390; includes tuition, housing, insurance, international student ID, student support services, pre-departure guide, transcript, orientation. $35 application fee. $500 nonrefundable deposit required. Financial aid available for all students: loans.
For More Information • Arcadia University, Center for Education Abroad, 450 South Easton Road, Glenside, PA 19038-3295; *Phone:* 866-927-2234; *Fax:* 215-572-2174. *E-mail:* cea@arcadia.edu. *World Wide Web:* http://www.arcadia.edu/cea/

ILLINOIS STATE UNIVERSITY
STIRLING, SCOTLAND SUMMER PROGRAM
Hosted by University of Stirling
Academic Focus • Full curriculum.
Program Information • Students attend classes at University of Stirling (Stirling, Scotland). Students typically earn 7 semester credits per term.
Sessions • Jun–Aug (summer).
Eligibility Requirements • Open to sophomores, juniors, seniors; 3.0 GPA; 2 letters of recommendation; good academic standing at home school; essay.
Living Arrangements • Students live in host institution dormitories. Quarters are shared with host institution students, students from other programs. Meals are taken on one's own, in residences.
Costs (2005) • $7077 for 5 credit hours; $8361 for 7.5 credit hours; includes tuition, housing, all meals, insurance, international airfare, books and class materials, international student ID, student support services, $800 spending money. $150 application fee. Financial aid available for students from sponsoring institution: scholarships, loans.
For More Information • Office of International Studies and Programs, Illinois State University, Campus Box 6120, Normal, IL 61790-6120; *Phone:* 309-438-5276; *Fax:* 309-438-3987. *E-mail:* oisp@ilstu.edu. *World Wide Web:* http://www.internationalstudies.ilstu.edu/

INSTITUTE FOR STUDY ABROAD, BUTLER UNIVERSITY
UNIVERSITY OF STIRLING SUMMER STUDY

Hosted by University of Stirling

Academic Focus • Art history, business administration/ management, education, English literature, film and media studies, history, political science and government, science.

Program Information • Students attend classes at University of Stirling (Stirling, Scotland). Students typically earn 5–8 semester credits per term.

Sessions • Jun–Aug (summer).

Eligibility Requirements • Open to sophomores, juniors, seniors; 3.0 GPA; 1 letter of recommendation; good academic standing at home school; enrollment at an accredited American college or university.

Living Arrangements • Students live in host institution dormitories. Quarters are shared with host institution students, students from other programs. Meals are taken on one's own, in residences, in restaurants.

Costs (2005) • $3875 for 1 course; $4475 for 2 courses; includes tuition, housing, student support services, pre-departure advising. $40 application fee. $500 nonrefundable deposit required. Financial aid available for all students: scholarships.

For More Information • Institute for Study Abroad, Butler University, 1100 West 42nd Street, Suite 305, Indianapolis, IN 46208-3345; *Phone:* 800-858-0229; *Fax:* 317-940-9704. *E-mail:* study-abroad@butler.edu. *World Wide Web:* http://www.ifsa-butler.org/

ꙅENEGAL

CITY-TO-CITY

INTERCULTURAL DIMENSIONS, INC.
CROSSING CULTURES

Academic Focus • Art, business administration/management, computer science, dance, drama/theater, French language and literature, health and physical education, information science, medicine, music, nursing, philosophy, premedical studies, public health, religious studies, teaching, teaching English as a second language, Wolof.
Program Information • Faculty members are drawn from the sponsor's U.S. staff. Scheduled travel to small villages, other cities; field trips to hospitals, NGOs, small villages, cultural centers, schools, health centers; optional travel to volunteer work sites, field study sites at an extra cost.
Sessions • Jun–Jul (summer).
Eligibility Requirements • Minimum age 18; open to freshmen, sophomores, juniors, seniors, graduate students, adults; 3 letters of recommendation; interview with general director; intermediate French.
Living Arrangements • Students live in host family homes, hotels. Meals are taken as a group, with host family, in residences.
Costs (2005) • $1770; includes tuition, housing, all meals, excursions. $400 nonrefundable deposit required. Financial aid available for all students: scholarships.
For More Information • Ms. Janet L. Ghattas, General Director, Intercultural Dimensions, Inc., PO Box 391437, Cambridge, MA 02139; *Phone:* 617-864-8442. *E-mail:* janetid@aol.com. *World Wide Web:* http://www.interculturaldimensions.org/

DAKAR

LIVING ROUTES–STUDY ABROAD IN ECOVILLAGES
LIVING ROUTES–SENEGAL: SUSTAINABLE DEVELOPMENT AT ECOYOFF

Hosted by EcoYoff
Academic Focus • Agriculture, community service, conservation studies, cultural studies, ecology, environmental health, environmental science/studies, natural resources, peace and conflict studies, urban/regional planning, women's studies.
Program Information • Students attend classes at EcoYoff. Field trips to a cloth-dying cooperative, a fish-drying cooperative, a permaculture garden site, monkey preserves. Students typically earn 4 semester credits per term.
Sessions • Dec–Jan (winter).
Eligibility Requirements • Minimum age 18; open to precollege students, freshmen, sophomores, juniors, seniors, graduate students, adults; 2.5 GPA; good academic standing at home school; intermediate French.
Living Arrangements • Students live in host family homes. Quarters are shared with host institution students. Meals are taken as a group, with host family, in residences, in central dining facility.
Costs (2005–2006) • $2250; includes tuition, housing, all meals, excursions, student support services. $25 application fee. $300 nonrefundable deposit required. Financial aid available for all students: scholarships.
For More Information • Mr. Gregg Orifici, Director of Admissions, Living Routes–Study Abroad in Ecovillages, 79 South Pleasant Street, Suite A5, Amherst, MA 01002; *Phone:* 888-515-7333; *Fax:* 413-259-9355. *E-mail:* programs@livingroutes.org. *World Wide Web:* http://www.LivingRoutes.org/

SINGAPORE

CITY-TO-CITY

SYRACUSE UNIVERSITY
MANAGEMENT INTERNSHIPS IN SINGAPORE

Academic Focus • Business administration/management, finance, marketing.

Program Information • Faculty members are drawn from the sponsor's U.S. staff. Scheduled travel to Malaysia. Students typically earn 6 semester credits per term.

Sessions • Jun–Aug (summer).

Eligibility Requirements • Open to juniors, seniors, graduate students, adults; 1 letter of recommendation; good academic standing at home school; no foreign language proficiency required.

Living Arrangements • Students live in host institution dormitories, hotels. Meals are taken on one's own, in restaurants.

Costs (2004) • $6100; includes tuition, housing, some meals, excursions, international student ID, student support services. $55 application fee. $350 nonrefundable deposit required. Financial aid available for all students: loans, need-based tuition grants.

For More Information • Mrs. Daisy Fried, Associate Director, Syracuse University, 106 Walnut Place, Syracuse, NY 13244-4170; *Phone:* 800-251-9674; *Fax:* 315-443-4593. *E-mail:* dipasum@syr.edu. *World Wide Web:* http://suabroad.syr.edu/

LOVENIA

LJUBLJANA

UNIVERSITY OF MIAMI
UNIVERSITY OF LJUBLJANA

Hosted by University of Ljubljana
Academic Focus • Language studies, peace and conflict studies.
Program Information • Students attend classes at University of Ljubljana (Ljubljana, Slovenia). Students typically earn 6 semester credits per term.
Sessions • Jun–Aug (summer).
Eligibility Requirements • Minimum age 18; open to sophomores, juniors, seniors; 3.0 GPA; 2 letters of recommendation; good academic standing at home school; essay; transcript; no foreign language proficiency required.
Living Arrangements • Students live in locally rented apartments. Quarters are shared with host institution students. Meals are taken on one's own, in residences, in restaurants.
Costs (2005–2006) • $4950; includes tuition, housing, excursions, student support services. $40 application fee. $500 nonrefundable deposit required. Financial aid available for students from sponsoring institution: loans.
For More Information • Ms. Elyse Resnick, Assistant Director, International Education and Exchange Programs, University of Miami, 5050 Brunson Drive, Allen Hall Room 212, PO Box 248005, Coral Gables, FL 33124-1610; *Phone:* 305-284-3434; *Fax:* 305-284-4235. *E-mail:* ieep@miami.edu. *World Wide Web:* http://www.studyabroad.miami.edu/

$\mathcal{S}$OUTH AFRICA

CITY-TO-CITY

MICHIGAN STATE UNIVERSITY
CONSERVATION AND BIODIVERSITY IN SOUTH AFRICAN PARKS AND RESERVES

Academic Focus • Biological/life sciences, marine sciences, wildlife studies, zoology.
Program Information • Faculty members are drawn from the sponsor's U.S. staff and local instructors hired by the sponsor. Scheduled travel to parks and game reserves. Students typically earn 6 semester credits per term.
Sessions • May–Jun (summer).
Eligibility Requirements • Minimum age 18; open to juniors, seniors, graduate students; major in biological sciences; course work in biology/ecology; 2.0 GPA; good academic standing at home school.
Living Arrangements • Students live in hotels, cabins; camping. Meals are taken as a group, in central dining facility, in restaurants.
Costs (2005) • $3317; includes housing, all meals, insurance, excursions, student support services. $100 application fee. $200 nonrefundable deposit required. Financial aid available for all students: scholarships, loans.
For More Information • Ms. Cindy Felbeck Chalou, Assistant Director, Michigan State University, Office of Study Abroad, 109 International Center, East Lansing, MI 48824-1035; *Phone:* 517-432-4345; *Fax:* 517-432-2082. *E-mail:* chalouc@msu.edu. *World Wide Web:* http://studyabroad.msu.edu/

MICHIGAN STATE UNIVERSITY
CULTURAL HERITAGE OF THE NEW SOUTH AFRICA

Academic Focus • African studies, art, art history, historic preservation, interdisciplinary studies, literature, music, visual and performing arts.
Program Information • Faculty members are drawn from the sponsor's U.S. staff and local instructors hired by the sponsor. Scheduled travel to Cape Town, Durban, Johannesburg; field trips to museums, art galleries, gardens, parks. Students typically earn 7 semester credits per term.
Sessions • Jul (summer).
Eligibility Requirements • Minimum age 18; open to sophomores, juniors, seniors, graduate students; 2.0 GPA; good academic standing at home school.
Living Arrangements • Students live in hotels. Meals are taken as a group, in restaurants.
Costs (2005) • $2864; includes housing, some meals, insurance, excursions, student support services. $100 application fee. $200 nonrefundable deposit required. Financial aid available for all students: scholarships, loans.
For More Information • Ms. Cindy Felbeck Chalou, Assistant Director, Michigan State University, Office of Study Abroad, 109 International Center, East Lansing, MI 48824-1035; *Phone:* 517-432-4345; *Fax:* 517-432-2082. *E-mail:* chalouc@msu.edu. *World Wide Web:* http://studyabroad.msu.edu/

MICHIGAN STATE UNIVERSITY
EDUCATION, SOCIETY, AND LEARNING IN SOUTH AFRICA

Academic Focus • African studies, anthropology, education, English, geography, history, political science and government, sociology, teaching.
Program Information • Faculty members are drawn from the sponsor's U.S. staff and local instructors hired by the sponsor. Scheduled travel to Cape Town, Durban; field trips to schools, historic sites, colleges, surrounding communities. Students typically earn 6 semester credits per term.
Sessions • May–Jun (summer).
Eligibility Requirements • Minimum age 18; open to sophomores, juniors, seniors, graduate students; 2.5 GPA; good academic standing at home school; faculty approval.
Living Arrangements • Students live in host family homes, hotels. Meals are taken as a group, on one's own, with host family, in residences, in restaurants.
Costs (2005) • $2743; includes housing, all meals, insurance, excursions, student support services. $100 application fee. $200 nonrefundable deposit required. Financial aid available for all students: scholarships, loans.
For More Information • Ms. Cindy Felbeck Chalou, Assistant Director, Michigan State University, Office of Study Abroad, 109 International Center, East Lansing, MI 48824-1035; *Phone:* 517-432-4345; *Fax:* 517-432-2082. *E-mail:* chalouc@msu.edu. *World Wide Web:* http://studyabroad.msu.edu/

MICHIGAN STATE UNIVERSITY
RACE RELATIONS

Academic Focus • African studies, ethnic studies, history, interdisciplinary studies, sociology.
Program Information • Faculty members are drawn from the sponsor's U.S. staff and local instructors hired by the sponsor. Scheduled travel to Johannesburg, Durban, Grahamstown. Students typically earn 6 semester credits per term.

Sessions • May–Jul (summer).

Eligibility Requirements • Minimum age 18; open to freshmen, sophomores, juniors, seniors, graduate students; 2.0 GPA; good academic standing at home school; faculty approval.

Living Arrangements • Students live in host institution dormitories, hotels. Meals are taken as a group, in central dining facility, in restaurants.

Costs (2005) • $3790; includes housing, some meals, insurance, excursions, student support services. $100 application fee. $200 nonrefundable deposit required. Financial aid available for all students: scholarships, loans.

For More Information • Ms. Cindy Felbeck Chalou, Assistant Director, Michigan State University, Office of Study Abroad, 109 International Center, East Lansing, MI 48824-1035; *Phone:* 517-432-4345; *Fax:* 517-432-2082. *E-mail:* chalouc@msu.edu. *World Wide Web:* http://studyabroad.msu.edu/

CAPE TOWN

BEMIDJI STATE UNIVERSITY
SEMESTER BREAK IN SOUTH AFRICA

Hosted by University of Western Cape

Academic Focus • Anthropology, economics, geography, history, international affairs, political science and government.

Program Information • Students attend classes at University of Western Cape (Cape Town, South Africa). Scheduled travel to Johannesburg to Cape Town; field trips. Students typically earn 6 semester credits per term.

Sessions • Dec–Jan (semester break).

Eligibility Requirements • Minimum age 18; open to sophomores, juniors, seniors, graduate students, adults; 2.0 GPA; good academic standing at home school; sophomore status.

Living Arrangements • Students live in hotels. Meals are taken as a group, in central dining facility.

Costs (2004–2005) • $5150; includes housing, all meals, excursions, international airfare, student support services. $150 nonrefundable deposit required. Financial aid available for students from sponsoring institution: scholarships, loans, grants.

For More Information • Ms. LaMae Ritchie, Director, International Program Center, Bemidji State University, Deputy Hall 103, Box 13, 1500 Birchmont Drive, NE, Bemidji, MN 56601-2699; *Phone:* 218-755-4096; *Fax:* 218-755-2074. *E-mail:* lritchie@bemidjistate.edu. *World Wide Web:* http://www.bemidjistate.edu/international/study_abroad.htm

LEXIA INTERNATIONAL
LEXIA SUMMER IN CAPE TOWN

Hosted by University of Western Cape

Academic Focus • African languages and literature, African studies, anthropology, area studies, art history, civilization studies, comparative history, cultural studies, economics, ethnic studies, geography, history, interdisciplinary studies, international affairs, liberal studies, literature, political science and government, social sciences, sociology, Xhosa.

Program Information • Students attend classes at University of Western Cape (Cape Town, South Africa). Field trips to the Cape of Good Hope, a peninsula tour, the wine route, game parks, wildlife reserves. Students typically earn 8–10 semester credits per term.

Sessions • Jun–Aug (summer).

Eligibility Requirements • Minimum age 18; open to freshmen, sophomores, juniors, seniors, graduate students, adults; 2.5 GPA; 2 letters of recommendation; no foreign language proficiency required.

Living Arrangements • Students live in host institution dormitories, host family homes. Quarters are shared with host institution students. Meals are taken on one's own, with host family, in residences, in central dining facility.

Costs (2006) • $6450; includes tuition, housing, some meals, insurance, excursions, international student ID, student support services, computer access, transcript. $40 application fee. $300 nonrefundable deposit required. Financial aid available for all students: scholarships, work study.

For More Information • Lexia International, 23 South Main Street, Hanover, NH 03755; *Phone:* 800-775-3942; *Fax:* 603-643-9899. *E-mail:* info@lexiaintl.org. *World Wide Web:* http://www.lexiaintl.org/

MICHIGAN STATE UNIVERSITY
DOING BUSINESS IN SOUTH AFRICA

Academic Focus • Business administration/management, international business, marketing.

Program Information • Faculty members are drawn from the sponsor's U.S. staff and local instructors hired by the sponsor. Scheduled travel to Johannesburg; field trips to businesses. Students typically earn 3 semester credits per term.

Sessions • May–Jun (summer).

Eligibility Requirements • Minimum age 18; open to seniors, graduate students; major in business; 3.0 GPA; good academic standing at home school.

Living Arrangements • Students live in hotels. Meals are taken as a group, in restaurants.

Costs (2005) • $3486; includes housing, some meals, insurance, excursions, student support services. $100 application fee. $200 nonrefundable deposit required. Financial aid available for all students: scholarships, loans.

For More Information • Ms. Cindy Felbeck Chalou, Assistant Director, Michigan State University, Office of Study Abroad, 109 International Center, East Lansing, MI 48824-1035; *Phone:* 517-432-4345; *Fax:* 517-432-2082. *E-mail:* chalouc@msu.edu. *World Wide Web:* http://studyabroad.msu.edu/

NEW YORK UNIVERSITY
SUMMER IN SOUTH AFRICA

Hosted by NYU at Cape Town

Academic Focus • African studies, history, political science and government.

Program Information • Students attend classes at NYU at Cape Town (Cape Town, South Africa). Field trips. Students typically earn 4 semester credits per term.

Sessions • June.

Eligibility Requirements • Minimum age 18; open to freshmen, sophomores, juniors, seniors; 3.0 GPA; good academic standing at home school.

Living Arrangements • Students live in host institution dormitories. Meals are taken on one's own, in restaurants.

Costs (2007) • $4500; includes tuition, housing, excursions. $25 application fee. $300 nonrefundable deposit required.

For More Information • Office of Summer Sessions, New York University, 7 E. 12th Street, 6th Floor, New York, NY 10003; *Phone:* 212-998-2292; *Fax:* 212-995-4642. *E-mail:* summer.info@nyu.edu. *World Wide Web:* http://www.nyu.edu/global/studyabroad.html

DURBAN

SCHOOL FOR INTERNATIONAL TRAINING, SIT STUDY ABROAD
SOUTH AFRICA: EDUCATION AND SOCIAL CHANGE

Academic Focus • Education, teaching.

Program Information • Faculty members are drawn from the sponsor's U.S. staff and local instructors hired by the sponsor. Scheduled travel to Northern and Southern Kwa-Zulu Natal, Johannesburg, Pretoria; field trips to cultural events. Students typically earn 8 semester credits per term.

Sessions • Jun–Jul (summer).

Eligibility Requirements • Open to freshmen, sophomores, juniors, seniors; 2.5 GPA; 2 letters of recommendation; good academic standing at home school.

Living Arrangements • Students live in host family homes, hotels. Meals are taken as a group, in residences, in restaurants.

Costs (2005–2006) • $7222; includes tuition, housing, all meals, insurance, excursions. $50 application fee. $400 nonrefundable deposit required. Financial aid available for all students: scholarships.

For More Information • SIT Study Abroad, School for International Training, SIT Study Abroad, PO Box 676, Kipling Road, Brattleboro,

SOUTH AFRICA
Durban

VT 05302-0676; *Phone:* 888-272-7881; *Fax:* 802-258-3296. *E-mail:* studyabroad@sit.edu. *World Wide Web:* http://www.sit.edu/studyabroad/

UNIVERSITY AT ALBANY, STATE UNIVERSITY OF NEW YORK
LANGUAGE AND CULTURAL STUDIES AT THE UNIVERSITY OF KWAZULU-NATAL–DURBAN OR PIETERMARITZBURG

Hosted by University of Kwazulu-Natal, University of Kwazulu-Natal

Academic Focus • African studies, community service, literature, political science and government, Zulu.

Program Information • Students attend classes at University of Kwazulu-Natal (Pietermaritzburg, South Africa), University of Kwazulu-Natal (Durban, South Africa). Field trips to battle sites, a game park. Students typically earn 15 semester credits per term.

Sessions • Jun–Jul (summer).

Eligibility Requirements • Open to sophomores, juniors, seniors; 3.0 GPA; 2 letters of recommendation; good academic standing at home school.

Living Arrangements • Students live in host institution dormitories. Quarters are shared with students from other programs. Meals are taken on one's own, in central dining facility.

Costs (2005) • Contact sponsor for cost. $150 nonrefundable deposit required. Financial aid available for students from sponsoring institution: all customary sources.

For More Information • University at Albany, State University of New York, Office of International Education, LI 66, Albany, NY 12222; *Phone:* 518-442-3525; *Fax:* 518-442-3338. *E-mail:* intled@uamail.albany.edu. *World Wide Web:* http://www.albany.edu/studyabroad/

GRAHAMSTOWN

RUTGERS, THE STATE UNIVERSITY OF NEW JERSEY
SUMMER STUDY IN GRAHAMSTOWN, SOUTH AFRICA

Academic Focus • Political science and government.

Program Information • Faculty members are drawn from the sponsor's U.S. staff and local instructors hired by the sponsor. Field trips to Capetown. Students typically earn 6 semester credits per term.

Sessions • Jun–Jul (summer).

Eligibility Requirements • Open to sophomores, juniors, seniors; 2.5 GPA; 1 letter of recommendation; good academic standing at home school; official transcripts from all tertiary schools attended.

Living Arrangements • Students live in host institution dormitories. Quarters are shared with host institution students. Meals are taken as a group, on one's own, in residences, in central dining facility, in restaurants.

Costs (2006) • $3650 for New Jersey residents; $3950 for nonresidents; includes tuition, housing, insurance, excursions, student support services. $20 application fee. $500 nonrefundable deposit required. Financial aid available for students from sponsoring institution: scholarships, loans.

For More Information • Ms. Lindy Black, Regional Coordinator, Rutgers, The State University of New Jersey, 102 College Avenue, New Brunswick, NJ 08901; *Phone:* 732-932-7787; *Fax:* 732-932-8659. *E-mail:* ru_abroad@email.rutgers.edu. *World Wide Web:* http://studyabroad.rutgers.edu/

JOHANNESBURG

UNIVERSITY OF DELAWARE
WINTER SESSION IN SOUTH AFRICA

Academic Focus • Education, history, teaching.

Program Information • Faculty members are drawn from the sponsor's U.S. staff and local instructors hired by the sponsor. Field trips to Kruger National Park, Cape Town. Students typically earn 6 semester credits per term.

Sessions • Jan (winter).

Eligibility Requirements • Open to freshmen, sophomores, juniors, seniors, adults; 2.0 GPA; 1 letter of recommendation.

Living Arrangements • Students live in hotels. Meals are taken as a group, in central dining facility, in restaurants.

Costs (2005) • Contact sponsor for cost. $200 nonrefundable deposit required. Financial aid available for all students: scholarships.

For More Information • Center for International Studies, University of Delaware, 186 South College Avenue, Newark, DE 19716-1450; *Phone:* 888-831-4685; *Fax:* 302-831-6042. *E-mail:* studyabroad@udel.edu. *World Wide Web:* http://www.udel.edu/studyabroad/

PRETORIA

AMERICAN UNIVERSITIES INTERNATIONAL PROGRAMS (AUIP)
SOUTH AFRICA VETS IN THE WILD

Hosted by EcoLife Expeditions

Academic Focus • African studies, conservation studies, veterinary science, wildlife studies.

Program Information • Students attend classes at EcoLife Expeditions (Pretoria, South Africa). Classes are also held on the campus of University of Pretoria (Pretoria, South Africa). Scheduled travel to Kruger National Park, Sondelz Nahre Reserve Game Capture School; field trips to local game parks, Zulu villages, capture and care course. Students typically earn 4 semester credits per term.

Sessions • Jun (summer), Jul–Jul (summer 2), Aug–Aug (summer 3).

Eligibility Requirements • Minimum age 18; open to freshmen, sophomores, juniors, seniors, graduate students, adults; 2.0 GPA; 2 letters of recommendation; good academic standing at home school; essay; official transcript; must be veterinary or pre-veterinary student or qualified professional.

Living Arrangements • Students live in campgrounds; park lodges; hostels. Quarters are shared with host institution students. Meals are taken as a group, in central dining facility.

Costs (2006) • $3350; includes tuition, housing, all meals, insurance, lab equipment, student support services, guides, safari vehicles, in-country travel. $300 application fee.

For More Information • Dr. Michael Tarrant, Program Director, American Universities International Programs (AUIP), 108 South Main Street, Winterville, GA 30683; *Phone:* 706-742-9285. *E-mail:* info@auip.com. *World Wide Web:* http://www.auip.com/

AMERICAN UNIVERSITIES INTERNATIONAL PROGRAMS (AUIP)
SOUTH AFRICA WILLDLIFE MANAGEMENT FIELD STUDIES PROGRAM

Hosted by EcoLife Expeditions

Academic Focus • African studies, conservation studies, natural resources, parks and recreation, tourism and travel, wildlife studies.

Program Information • Students attend classes at EcoLife Expeditions (Pretoria, South Africa). Classes are also held on the campus of University of Pretoria (Pretoria, South Africa). Scheduled travel to South Africa, Kruger National Park, St. Lucia World Heritage Area, Zulu villages, Ndumo Game Reserve, Swaziland, Blyde Canyon, elephant reserves, private protected areas and guest ranches, the Indian Ocean; field trips to the field program, local game parks, tribal villages, rock art sites, Zulu villages. Students typically earn 8 semester credits per term.

Sessions • May–Jun (summer), Dec–Jan (winter).

Eligibility Requirements • Minimum age 18; open to freshmen, sophomores, juniors, seniors, graduate students, adults; 2.0 GPA; 2 letters of recommendation; good academic standing at home school; essay; original transcript.

Living Arrangements • Students live in program-rented tent camps; park housing; lodges. Quarters are shared with host institution students. Meals are taken as a group, in central dining facility.

Costs (2006) • $2795; includes tuition, housing, all meals, insurance, books and class materials, lab equipment, student support services, guides, safari vehicles, in-country travel. $300 application fee.

For More Information • Dr. Michael Tarrant, Program Director, American Universities International Programs (AUIP), 108 South

Main Street, Winterville, GA 30683; *Phone:* 706-742-9285. *E-mail:* info@auip.com. *World Wide Web:* http://www.auip.com/

KWA MADWALA GAP YEAR EXPERIENCE
KWA MADWALA GAP YEAR EXPERIENCE

Hosted by University of Pretoria

Academic Focus • Conservation studies, environmental science/studies.

Program Information • Students attend classes at University of Pretoria (Pretoria, South Africa). Scheduled travel to elephant-back safaris, camping trips; field trips to Kruger National Park, wildlife rehabilitation centres; optional travel to Mozambique, Swaziland, Cape Town at an extra cost.

Sessions • Jun–Aug (summer).

Eligibility Requirements • Minimum age 17; open to precollege students, freshmen, sophomores, juniors, seniors, adults; a love of wildlife.

Living Arrangements • Students live in program-owned apartments, game lodges and camps. Quarters are shared with students from other programs. Meals are taken as a group, in central dining facility.

Costs (2006–2007) • Contact sponsor for cost.

For More Information • Mr. Conrad Van Eyssen, Kwa Madwala GAP Year Experience, PO Box 192, Hectorspruit 1330, South Africa; *Phone:* +27 13-792-4219; *Fax:* +27 13-792-4219. *E-mail:* gm@kwamadwala.co.za. *World Wide Web:* http://www.kwamadwalagapyear.com/

RICHARDS BAY

MICHIGAN STATE UNIVERSITY
PRE-INTERNSHIP TEACHING IN SOUTH AFRICA

Academic Focus • African studies, education, teaching.

Program Information • Faculty members are drawn from the sponsor's U.S. staff and local instructors hired by the sponsor. Field trips to Durban, wildlife parks. Students typically earn 6 semester credits per term.

Sessions • Jul–Aug (summer).

Eligibility Requirements • Minimum age 18; open to graduate students; major in education; course work in education; 2.5 GPA; faculty approval.

Living Arrangements • Students live in host family homes. Meals are taken with host family, in residences.

Costs (2005) • $2610; includes housing, some meals, insurance, excursions, student support services. $100 application fee. $200 nonrefundable deposit required. Financial aid available for all students: scholarships, loans.

For More Information • Ms. Cindy Felbeck Chalou, Assistant Director, Michigan State University, Office of Study Abroad, 109 International Center, East Lansing, MI 48824-1035; *Phone:* 517-432-4345; *Fax:* 517-432-2082. *E-mail:* chalouc@msu.edu. *World Wide Web:* http://studyabroad.msu.edu/

STELLENBOSCH

AMERICAN INSTITUTE FOR FOREIGN STUDY (AIFS)
AIFS–STELLENBOSCH, SOUTH AFRICA–UNIVERSITY OF STELLENBOSCH

Hosted by University of Stellenbosch

Academic Focus • Art history, business administration/management, community service, economics, geography, history, literature, political science and government, sociology.

Program Information • Students attend classes at University of Stellenbosch (Stellenbosch, South Africa). Scheduled travel to 3-day London stopover, 6-day tour of the Garden Route, Cape Town, Robben Island, Karoo Desert, Cape of Good Hope, Table Mountain; field trips to visit to township of Kayamandi, cultural activities, vineyard tours, sports events, hiking. Students typically earn 6 semester credits per term.

Sessions • Jun–Jul (summer).

Eligibility Requirements • Minimum age 17; open to precollege students, freshmen, sophomores, juniors, seniors; 2.0 GPA; good academic standing at home school.

Living Arrangements • Students live in host institution dormitories, program-owned apartments, host family homes, hotels. Quarters are shared with host institution students. Meals are taken as a group, in residences.

Costs (2007) • $5799; includes tuition, housing, some meals, insurance, excursions, student support services, On-site Resident Director, Phone Card to call the U.S., Computer Facilities/Internet. $95 application fee. $395 nonrefundable deposit required. Financial aid available for all students: scholarships.

For More Information • Mr. David Mauro, Admissions Advisor, American Institute For Foreign Study (AIFS), 9 West Broad Street, Stamford, CT 06902-3788; *Phone:* 800-727-2437 Ext. 5163; *Fax:* 203-399-5597. *E-mail:* dmauro@aifs.com. *World Wide Web:* http://www.aifsabroad.com/

 PAIN

CITY-TO-CITY

CENTER FOR CULTURAL INTERCHANGE
SPAIN LANGUAGE SCHOOL

Hosted by Don Quijote, Estudio Sampere, Estudio Sampere, Estudio Sampere, Estudio Sampere
Academic Focus • Spanish language and literature.
Program Information • Students attend classes at Don Quijote (Barcelona), Don Quijote (Canary Islands), Don Quijote (Granada), Estudio Sampere (Alicante), Estudio Sampere (El Puerto de Santa Maria), Estudio Sampere (Salamanca), Estudio Sampere (Madrid). Classes are also held on the campus of CCI Spain (Valencia). Field trips to cultural excursions, guided city tours, museum visits.
Sessions • 3, 4, or 6 week sessions begin every Monday, year-round.
Eligibility Requirements • Minimum age 17; open to precollege students, freshmen, sophomores, juniors, seniors, graduate students, adults; no foreign language proficiency required.
Living Arrangements • Students live in host family homes. Quarters are shared with host institution students. Meals are taken with host family, in residences.
Costs (2005) • $2500 for 4 weeks; includes tuition, housing, all meals, insurance, books and class materials, student support services, cultural activities. Financial aid available for students from sponsoring institution: scholarships.
For More Information • Ms. Juliet Jones, Outbound Programs Director, Center for Cultural Interchange, 325 West Huron, Suite 706, Chicago, IL 60610; *Phone:* 866-684-9675; *Fax:* 312-944-2644. *E-mail:* info@cci-exchange. com. *World Wide Web:* http://www.cci-exchange.com/

CENTER FOR STUDY ABROAD (CSA)
INTENSIVE SPANISH

Hosted by Don Quijote, Don Quijote
Academic Focus • Spanish language and literature, Spanish studies.
Program Information • Students attend classes at Don Quijote (Barcelona), Don Quijote (Granada), Don Quijote (Salamanca), Don Quijote (Málaga). Optional travel. Students typically earn 4–10 semester credits per term.
Sessions • Typically 4 week sessions, classes begin weekly, year-round.
Eligibility Requirements • Minimum age 17; open to precollege students, freshmen, sophomores, juniors, seniors, graduate students, adults; no foreign language proficiency required.
Living Arrangements • Students live in locally rented apartments, host family homes. Quarters are shared with students from other programs. Meals are taken with host family, in residences, in restaurants.
Costs (2005) • Contact sponsor for cost. $45 application fee.
For More Information • Ms. Alima K. Virtue, Program Director, Center for Study Abroad (CSA), 325 Washington Avenue South #93, Kent, WA 98032; *Phone:* 206-726-1498; *Fax:* 253-850-0454. *E-mail:* info@centerforstudyabroad.com. *World Wide Web:* http://www.centerforstudyabroad.com/

CENTER FOR STUDY ABROAD
SPANISH IN SEVILLE

Hosted by Lenguaviva
Academic Focus • Spanish language and literature, Spanish studies.
Program Information • Students attend classes at Lenguaviva (Seville). Optional travel. Students typically earn 4–6 semester credits per term.
Sessions • Typically 4 week sessions, classes begin weekly, year-round.
Eligibility Requirements • Minimum age 17; open to precollege students, freshmen, sophomores, juniors, seniors, graduate students, adults; no foreign language proficiency required.
Living Arrangements • Students live in locally rented apartments, host family homes. Meals are taken with host family, in residences, in restaurants.
Costs (2005) • Contact sponsor for cost. $45 application fee.
For More Information • Ms. Alima K. Virtue, Program Director, Center for Study Abroad (CSA), 325 Washington Avenue South #93, Kent, WA 98032; *Phone:* 206-726-1498; *Fax:* 253-850-0454. *E-mail:* info@centerforstudyabroad.com. *World Wide Web:* http://www.centerforstudyabroad.com/

DON QUIJOTE
DELE PREPARATION COURSES IN BARCELONA, GRANADA, MADRID, SALAMANCA, SEVILLA, VALENCIA, TENERIFE

Hosted by Don Quijote

Academic Focus • Spanish language and literature, Spanish studies.

Program Information • Students attend classes at Don Quijote (Barcelona), Don Quijote (Granada), Don Quijote (Madrid), Don Quijote (Salamanca), Don Quijote (Seville), Don Quijote (Tenerife), Don Quijote (Valencia). Field trips to historic sites. Students typically earn 4 semester credits per term.

Sessions • 2, 3, or 4 weeks in Nov or May.

Eligibility Requirements • Minimum age 18; open to freshmen, sophomores, juniors, seniors, graduate students, adults; intermediate Spanish.

Living Arrangements • Students live in host institution dormitories, program-owned apartments, host family homes. Quarters are shared with host institution students, students from other programs. Meals are taken on one's own, with host family, in residences.

Costs (2006) • €406 (depending on level of DELE and length of course); includes tuition, housing, books and class materials, lab equipment, student support services. €65 application fee. €500 nonrefundable deposit required. Financial aid available for all students: scholarships.

For More Information • Ms. Carmen Cantarino, USA Director, Don Quijote, Plaza San Marcos 7, 37002 Salamanca, Spain; *Phone:* +34 923-268874; *Fax:* +34 923-260674. *E-mail:* usa@donquijote.org. *World Wide Web:* http://www.donquijote.org/

DON QUIJOTE
MULTI-CITY TRAVEL PROGRAM–BARCELONA, MADRID, SALAMANCA, SEVILLE, TENERIFE, GRANADA, VALENCIA

Hosted by Don Quijote

Academic Focus • Romance languages, Spanish language and literature, Spanish studies.

Program Information • Students attend classes at Don Quijote (Barcelona), Don Quijote (Granada), Don Quijote (Madrid), Don Quijote (Salamanca), Don Quijote (Seville), Don Quijote (Tenerife), Don Quijote (Valencia). Field trips to historic sites, cultural attractions; optional travel to Morocco at an extra cost. Students typically earn 4 semester credits per term.

Sessions • 1 week minimum, classes start every Monday, year-round.

Eligibility Requirements • Minimum age 18; open to freshmen, sophomores, juniors, seniors, graduate students, adults; no foreign language proficiency required.

Living Arrangements • Students live in host institution dormitories, program-owned apartments, host family homes. Quarters are shared with host institution students, students from other programs. Meals are taken on one's own, with host family, in residences.

Costs (2006) • €229 for the first week; €146 for each additional week; includes tuition, books and class materials, lab equipment, student support services, guided cultural tour, welcome dinner, student discount card, level test, tutor, end-of-course certificate. €65 application fee. €500 nonrefundable deposit required. Financial aid available for all students: scholarships.

For More Information • Ms. Carmen Cantarino, USA Director, Don Quijote, Plaza San Marcos 7, 37002 Salamanca, Spain; *Phone:* +34 923-268874; *Fax:* +34 923-260674. *E-mail:* usa@donquijote.org. *World Wide Web:* http://www.donquijote.org/

DON QUIJOTE
SUPER INTENSIVE SPANISH COURSE–BARCELONA, GRANADA, MADRID, SALAMANCA, SEVILLE, TENERIFE, VALENCIA

Hosted by Don Quijote

Academic Focus • Romance languages, Spanish language and literature, Spanish studies.

Program Information • Students attend classes at Don Quijote (Barcelona), Don Quijote (Granada), Don Quijote (Madrid), Don

Quijote (Salamanca), Don Quijote (Seville), Don Quijote (Tenerife), Don Quijote (Valencia). Field trips to historic sites, cultural attractions. Students typically earn 4 semester credits per term.
Sessions • 1 week minimum, classes start every Monday.
Eligibility Requirements • Minimum age 18; open to freshmen, sophomores, juniors, seniors, graduate students, adults; no foreign language proficiency required.
Living Arrangements • Students live in host institution dormitories, program-owned apartments, host family homes. Quarters are shared with host institution students, students from other programs. Meals are taken on one's own, with host family, in residences.
Costs (2006) • €344 for the first week; $219 for each additional week; includes tuition, books and class materials, lab equipment, student support services, guided cultural tour, welcome dinner, student discount card, level test, tutor, end-of-course certificate. €65 application fee. €500 nonrefundable deposit required. Financial aid available for all students: scholarships.
For More Information • Ms. Carmen Cantarino, USA Director, Don Quijote, Plaza San Marcos 7, 37002 Salamanca, Spain; *Phone:* +34 923-268874; *Fax:* +34 923-260674. *E-mail:* usa@donquijote.org. *World Wide Web:* http://www.donquijote.org/

ESTUDIO SAMPERE
SPANISH INTENSIVE COURSES IN SPAIN

Hosted by Estudio Sampere, Estudio Sampere, Estudio Sampere, Estudio Sampere
Academic Focus • Spanish language and literature, Spanish studies, translation.
Program Information • Students attend classes at Estudio Sampere (Alicante), Estudio Sampere (El Puerto de Santa Maria), Estudio Sampere (Salamanca), Estudio Sampere (Madrid). Field trips to Toledo, Sevilla, Salamanca, Ibiza; optional travel to Andalucía, Barcelona at an extra cost. Students typically earn 6 semester credits for 4 week session.

Sessions • Typically 2 to 12 week sessions, classes begin on the first Monday of every month, year-round.
Eligibility Requirements • Minimum age 17; open to precollege students, freshmen, sophomores, seniors, graduate students, adults; no foreign language proficiency required.
Living Arrangements • Students live in host institution dormitories, program-owned apartments, host family homes. Quarters are shared with host institution students. Meals are taken on one's own, with host family.
Costs (2006) • $710 for 2 weeks; $5400 for 16 weeks; includes tuition, some meals, insurance, excursions, books and class materials, student support services, homestay housing. $150 application fee. $200 nonrefundable deposit required.
For More Information • Mr. Juan M. Sampere, Director, Estudio Sampere, Lagasca, 16, 28001 Madrid, Spain; *Phone:* +34 91-4314366; *Fax:* +34 91-5759509. *E-mail:* jmanuel@sampere.es. *World Wide Web:* http://www.sampere.es/. Students may also apply through Spanish Works, Inc., PO Box 1434, Healdsburg, CA 95448.

LANGUAGE LIAISON
LEARN SPANISH IN SPAIN–BARCELONA, GRANADA, SALAMANCA

Hosted by Language Liaison
Academic Focus • Spanish language and literature.
Program Information • Students attend classes at Language Liaison (Barcelona), Language Liaison (Granada), Language Liaison (Salamanca). Field trips; optional travel at an extra cost. Students typically earn 3–15 semester credits per term.
Sessions • New programs begin weekly, year-round.
Eligibility Requirements • Minimum age 16; open to precollege students, freshmen, sophomores, juniors, seniors, graduate students, adults; no foreign language proficiency required.
Living Arrangements • Students live in locally rented apartments, host family homes, hotels.

Costs (2005) • Contact sponsor for cost. $175 application fee. Financial aid available for all students: scholarship research service.

For More Information • Ms. Nancy Forman, President, Language Liaison, PO Box 1772, Pacific Palisades, CA 90272; *Phone:* 800-284-4448; *Fax:* 310-454-1706. *E-mail:* learn@languageliaison. com. *World Wide Web:* http://www.languageliaison.com/

LANGUAGE LIAISON
SPANISH IN MADRID

Hosted by Language Liaison

Academic Focus • Spanish language and literature.

Program Information • Students attend classes at Language Liaison (Madrid), Language Liaison (Marbella). Field trips. Students typically earn 3–15 semester credits per term.

Sessions • Classes begin weekly, year-round.

Eligibility Requirements • Minimum age 10; open to precollege students, freshmen, sophomores, juniors, seniors, graduate students, adults; no foreign language proficiency required.

Living Arrangements • Students live in host institution dormitories, locally rented apartments, host family homes, hotels, a residence center. Meals are taken as a group, on one's own, with host family, in residences, in central dining facility, in restaurants.

Costs (2005) • Contact sponsor for cost. $175 application fee. Financial aid available for all students: scholarship research service.

For More Information • Ms. Nancy Forman, President, Language Liaison, PO Box 1772, Pacific Palisades, CA 90272; *Phone:* 800-284-4448; *Fax:* 310-454-1706. *E-mail:* learn@languageliaison. com. *World Wide Web:* http://www.languageliaison.com/

LANGUAGE LIAISON
SPANISH IN SPAIN–MADRID, SALAMANCA, EL PUERTO

Hosted by Language Liaison

Academic Focus • Spanish language and literature.

Program Information • Students attend classes at Language Liaison (El Puerto de Santa Maria), Language Liaison (Madrid), Language Liaison (Salamanca). Field trips to Segovia, Portugal; optional travel at an extra cost. Students typically earn 3–15 semester credits per term.

Sessions • New programs begin weekly, year-round.

Eligibility Requirements • Minimum age 17; open to precollege students, freshmen, sophomores, juniors, seniors, graduate students, adults; no foreign language proficiency required.

Living Arrangements • Students live in host institution dormitories, locally rented apartments, host family homes, hotels. Meals are taken on one's own, with host family, in residences, in restaurants.

Costs (2005) • Contact sponsor for cost. $175 application fee. Financial aid available for all students: scholarship research service.

For More Information • Ms. Nancy Forman, President, Language Liaison, PO Box 1772, Pacific Palisades, CA 90272; *Phone:* 800-284-4448; *Fax:* 310-454-1706. *E-mail:* learn@languageliaison. com. *World Wide Web:* http://www.languageliaison.com/

LANGUAGE LIAISON
SPANISH IN SPAIN–SEVILLE

Hosted by Language Liaison

Academic Focus • Spanish language and literature.

Program Information • Students attend classes at Language Liaison (Isla Cristina), Language Liaison (Seville). Field trips; optional travel at an extra cost. Students typically earn 3–15 semester credits per term.

Sessions • New programs begin weekly, year-round.

Eligibility Requirements • Minimum age 17; open to precollege students, freshmen, sophomores, juniors, seniors, graduate students, adults; no foreign language proficiency required.

Living Arrangements • Students live in host institution dormitories, locally rented apartments, program-owned apartments, host

family homes, hotels. Meals are taken on one's own, with host family, in residences, in restaurants.
Costs (2005) • Contact sponsor for cost. $175 application fee. Financial aid available for all students: scholarship research service.
For More Information • Ms. Nancy Forman, President, Language Liaison, PO Box 1772, Pacific Palisades, CA 90272; *Phone:* 800-284-4448; *Fax:* 310-454-1706. *E-mail:* learn@languageliaison. com. *World Wide Web:* http://www.languageliaison.com/

MICHIGAN STATE UNIVERSITY
PACKAGING IN SPAIN

Held at Instituto Agroquímica y Tecnología de Alimentos
Academic Focus • Packaging.
Program Information • Classes are held on the campus of Instituto Agroquímica y Tecnología de Alimentos (Valencia). Faculty members are drawn from the sponsor's U.S. staff and local instructors hired by the sponsor. Scheduled travel to Barcelona; field trips to manufacturing sites. Students typically earn 3 semester credits per term.
Sessions • May–Jun (summer), Program only runs in odd-numbered years.
Eligibility Requirements • Minimum age 18; open to freshmen, sophomores, juniors, seniors; 2.0 GPA; good academic standing at home school; faculty approval; no foreign language proficiency required.
Living Arrangements • Students live in hotels. Meals are taken as a group, on one's own, in restaurants.
Costs (2005) • $1872 (estimated); includes housing, some meals, insurance, excursions, student support services. $100 application fee. $200 nonrefundable deposit required. Financial aid available for students from sponsoring institution: scholarships, loans.
For More Information • Mr. Mark Davis, Coordinator, Michigan State University, Office of Study Abroad, 109 International Center, East Lansing, MI 48824-1035; *Phone:* 517-432-1315; *Fax:* 517-432-2082. *E-mail:* mdavis@msu.edu. *World Wide Web:* http://studyabroad.msu.edu/

ST. JOHN'S UNIVERSITY
SPAIN PROGRAM

Held at Colegio San Juan Evangelista, University of Cádiz
Academic Focus • Spanish language and literature.
Program Information • Classes are held on the campus of University of Cádiz (Cádiz), Colegio San Juan Evangelista (Madrid). Faculty members are drawn from the sponsor's U.S. staff. Scheduled travel to Madrid, Seville; field trips to El Escorial, Valley of the Fallen, Segovia; optional travel at an extra cost. Students typically earn 3-6 semester credits per term.
Sessions • Jul–Aug (summer).
Eligibility Requirements • Open to freshmen, sophomores, juniors, seniors, graduate students, adults; 2.75 GPA; 2 letters of recommendation; good academic standing at home school; interview; 1 year of college course work in Spanish.
Living Arrangements • Students live in host institution dormitories, locally rented apartments, hotels. Quarters are shared with host institution students. Meals are taken as a group, on one's own, in residences, in central dining facility, in restaurants.
Costs (2004) • $2750; includes housing, some meals, international airfare, student support services. $30 application fee. $750 nonrefundable deposit required. Financial aid available for students from sponsoring institution: scholarships, loans, students must be enrolled in 2 classes to receive aid.
For More Information • Dr. Ruth De Paula, Director, Office of Study Abroad Programs, St. John's University, 8000 Utopia Parkway, Jamaica, NY 11439; *Phone:* 718-990-6105; *Fax:* 718-990-2321. *E-mail:* intled@stjohns.edu. *World Wide Web:* http://www.stjohns.edu/studyabroad/

UNIVERSITY OF MARYLAND, COLLEGE PARK
SUMMER IN SPAIN

Hosted by El Colegio Hispano Continental, International House Barcelona
Academic Focus • Spanish language and literature, Spanish studies.
Program Information • Students attend classes at El Colegio Hispano Continental (Salamanca), International House Barcelona (Barcelona). Field trips to Segovia, Los Arribes, Toledo, Costa Brava. Students typically earn 6 semester credits per term.
Sessions • Jun–Jul (summer).
Eligibility Requirements • Open to sophomores, juniors, seniors; 2.5 GPA; 1 letter of recommendation; good academic standing at home school; 2 years of college course work in Spanish.
Living Arrangements • Students live in host institution dormitories, host family homes. Quarters are shared with host institution students. Meals are taken on one's own, with host family, in residences, in restaurants.
Costs (2006) • $3985; includes tuition, housing, some meals, excursions. $300 nonrefundable deposit required. Financial aid available for students from sponsoring institution: scholarships.
For More Information • Ms. Leah Howell, Coordinator, University of Maryland, College Park, 1101 Halzapfel, College Park, MD 20742; *Phone:* 301-314-7746; *Fax:* 301-314-9135. *E-mail:* studyabr@deans.umd.edu. *World Wide Web:* http://www.umd.edu/studyabroad/

UNIVERSITY OF SOUTHERN MISSISSIPPI
SPANISH IN SPAIN

Academic Focus • Spanish language and literature.
Program Information • Faculty members are drawn from the sponsor's U.S. staff and local instructors hired by the sponsor. Scheduled travel; field trips; optional travel at an extra cost. Students typically earn 6 semester credits per term.
Sessions • May–Jun (summer).
Eligibility Requirements • Minimum age 18; open to sophomores, juniors, seniors, graduate students, adults; 2.0 GPA; good academic standing at home school; previous experience in Spanish.
Living Arrangements • Students live in host family homes. Meals are taken with host family, in residences.
Costs (2005) • $3899 for undergraduate students; $4099 for graduate students; includes tuition, housing, some meals, excursions, international airfare, international student ID. $200 nonrefundable deposit required. Financial aid available for students from sponsoring institution: scholarships, loans.
For More Information • Director, Spanish in Spain, University of Southern Mississippi, 118 College Drive #10047, Hattiesburg, MS 39406-0001; *Phone:* 601-266-4344; *Fax:* 601-266-5699. *E-mail:* holly.buckner@usm.edu. *World Wide Web:* http://www.usm.edu/internationaledu/

ALCALÁ DE HENARES

BOWLING GREEN STATE UNIVERSITY
SUMMER PROGRAMS IN SPAIN

Hosted by University of Alcalá de Henares
Academic Focus • Spanish language and literature, Spanish studies.
Program Information • Students attend classes at University of Alcalá de Henares (Madrid, Spain). Scheduled travel to Barcelona-Sitges, Burgos, Santillana del Mar, Santander; field trips to Madrid, Toledo, Granada, Córdoba, Segovia. Students typically earn 12-14 semester credits per term.
Sessions • May–Jul (summer).
Eligibility Requirements • Open to freshmen, sophomores, juniors, seniors, graduate students, adults; good academic standing at home school; minimum 2.5 GPA overall; minimum 3.0 GPA in Spanish (if applicable); no foreign language proficiency required.
Living Arrangements • Students live in host family homes. Quarters are shared with host institution students. Meals are taken with host family, in residences.
Costs (2004) • $5522 for Ohio residents; $9002 for nonresidents; includes tuition, housing, all meals, insurance, excursions, books and class materials, application and program fees. $170 nonrefundable deposit required. Financial aid available for students from sponsoring institution: scholarships, loans.
For More Information • Ms. Cynthia Whipple, AYA Spain Director, Bowling Green State University, Department of Romance Languages, 102 Shatzel Hall, Bowling Green, OH 43403; *Phone:* 419-372-8053; *Fax:* 419-372-7332. *E-mail:* ayaspain@bgsu.edu. *World Wide Web:* http://www.bgsu.edu/

UNIVERSITY OF ALABAMA
ALABAMA IN SPAIN

Hosted by University of Alcalá de Henares
Academic Focus • Art, art history, drama/theater, Spanish language and literature, Spanish studies.
Program Information • Students attend classes at University of Alcalá de Henares (Madrid, Spain). Field trips to Madrid, Seville, Segovia, El Escorial, Toledo, Córdoba. Students typically earn 6-12 semester credits per term.
Sessions • May-Jul (summer), May-Aug (summer 2).
Eligibility Requirements • Open to freshmen, sophomores, juniors, seniors, graduate students, adults; 2.5 GPA; good academic standing at home school; 2 years of college course work in Spanish.
Living Arrangements • Students live in host family homes. Quarters are shared with host institution students. Meals are taken with host family, in residences.
Costs (2005) • $5100 for 1 term; $7100 for 2 terms; includes tuition, housing, all meals, insurance, excursions, international airfare, international student ID, student support services. $100 application fee. $1000 nonrefundable deposit required. Financial aid available for all students: scholarships, loans.
For More Information • Ms. Angela L. Channell, Director of Overseas Study, University of Alabama, Box 870254, Tuscaloosa, AL 35487-0254; *Phone:* 205-348-5256; *Fax:* 205-348-5298. *E-mail:* achannel@aalan.ua.edu. *World Wide Web:* http://www.overseas-study.ua.edu/

ALICANTE

CENTER FOR STUDY ABROAD (CSA)
SPANISH LANGUAGE AND CULTURE, ALICANTE–UNIVERSITY OF ALICANTE

Hosted by University of Alicante
Academic Focus • Spanish language and literature, Spanish studies.
Program Information • Students attend classes at University of Alicante (Alicante, Spain). Optional travel to Barcelona, Valencia, Granada. Students typically earn 4-10 semester credits per term.
Sessions • Classes begin weekly, year-round.
Eligibility Requirements • Minimum age 18; open to precollege students, freshmen, sophomores, juniors, seniors, graduate students, adults; no foreign language proficiency required.
Living Arrangements • Students live in host institution dormitories, locally rented apartments, host family homes. Quarters are shared with host institution students. Meals are taken on one's own, with host family, in residences.
Costs (2005) • Contact sponsor for cost. $45 application fee.
For More Information • Ms. Alima K. Virtue, Program Director, Center for Study Abroad (CSA), 325 Washington Avenue South #93, Kent, WA 98032; *Phone:* 206-726-1498; *Fax:* 253-850-0454. *E-mail:* info@centerforstudyabroad.com. *World Wide Web:* http://www.centerforstudyabroad.com/

CIEE
CIEE STUDY CENTER AT THE UNIVERSIDAD DE ALICANTE, SPAIN

Hosted by University of Alicante
Academic Focus • Art, art history, economics, film and media studies, political science and government, Spanish language and literature, Spanish studies.
Program Information • Students attend classes at University of Alicante (Alicante, Spain). Field trips to Valencia, Granada. Students typically earn 6 semester credits per term.
Sessions • Jun-Jul (summer).
Eligibility Requirements • Minimum age 18; open to sophomores, juniors, seniors; 2.75 GPA; 1 letter of recommendation; good academic standing at home school; personal essay; intermediate Spanish recommended.
Living Arrangements • Students live in host family homes. Meals are taken with host family, in residences.
Costs (2006) • $5100; includes tuition, housing, all meals, insurance, excursions, student support services, e-mail access, resident director, orientation, optional onsite pick-up, cultural activities, pre-departure advice. $30 application fee. $300 nonrefund-

able deposit required. Financial aid available for all students: scholarships, minority student scholarships.
For More Information • Information Center, CIEE, 7 Custom House Street, 3rd Floor, Portland, ME 04101; *Phone:* 800-40-STUDY; *Fax:* 207-553-7699. *E-mail:* studyinfo@ciee.org. *World Wide Web:* http://www.ciee.org/isp/

ENFOREX–SPANISH IN THE SPANISH WORLD
SPANISH INTENSIVE COURSE ALICANTE

Hosted by ENFOREX
Academic Focus • Dance, Spanish language and literature, Spanish studies.
Program Information • Students attend classes at ENFOREX (Alicante, Spain). Field trips to Valencia; optional travel to Ibiza at an extra cost. Students typically earn 4 quarter credits per term.
Sessions • Year-round.
Eligibility Requirements • Minimum age 14; open to precollege students, freshmen, sophomores, juniors, seniors, graduate students, adults; no foreign language proficiency required.
Living Arrangements • Students live in program-owned apartments, host family homes, hotels. Quarters are shared with host institution students. Meals are taken as a group, on one's own, with host family.
Costs (2005) • €1280 per month; includes tuition, housing, all meals, books and class materials, international student ID, student support services. €65 application fee. €250 nonrefundable deposit required.
For More Information • Mr. Antonio Anadón, Director of Spanish Department, ENFOREX–Spanish in the Spanish World, Alberto Aguilera, 26, 28015 Madrid, Spain; *Phone:* +34 91-594-3776; *Fax:* +34 91-594-5159. *E-mail:* promotion@enforex.es. *World Wide Web:* http://www.enforex.com/

LANGUAGE LIAISON
LEARN SPANISH IN ALICANTE

Hosted by Language Liaison
Academic Focus • Spanish language and literature.
Program Information • Students attend classes at Language Liaison (Alicante, Spain). Field trips; optional travel at an extra cost. Students typically earn 3-15 semester credits per term.
Sessions • Classes begin weekly, year-round.
Eligibility Requirements • Minimum age 17; open to precollege students, freshmen, sophomores, juniors, seniors, graduate students, adults; no foreign language proficiency required.
Living Arrangements • Students live in locally rented apartments, host family homes, hotels. Meals are taken on one's own, with host family, in residences, in restaurants.
Costs (2005) • Contact sponsor for cost. $175 application fee. Financial aid available for all students: scholarship research service.
For More Information • Ms. Nancy Forman, President, Language Liaison, PO Box 1772, Pacific Palisades, CA 90272; *Phone:* 800-284-4448; *Fax:* 310-454-1706. *E-mail:* learn@languageliaison.com. *World Wide Web:* http://www.languageliaison.com/

LINGUA SERVICE WORLDWIDE
ESTUDIO INTERNACIONAL SAMPERE–ALICANTE

Hosted by Estudio Sampere
Academic Focus • Spanish language and literature, Spanish studies.
Program Information • Students attend classes at Estudio Sampere (Alicante, Spain). Optional travel to cultural sites throughout Spain at an extra cost. Students typically earn 3 semester credits for 3 weeks, 6 semester credits for 5 weeks.
Sessions • Sessions of 2 or more weeks begin on Mondays, year-round.
Eligibility Requirements • Minimum age 18; open to freshmen, sophomores, juniors, seniors, graduate students, adults; no foreign language proficiency required.
Living Arrangements • Students live in host institution dormitories, locally rented apartments, host family homes, hotels. Quarters are shared with host institution students. Meals are taken with host family.
Costs (2006–2007) • Contact sponsor for cost. $100 application fee.

SPAIN
Alicante

For More Information • Assistant Director, Lingua Service Worldwide, 75 Prospect Street, Suite 4, Huntington, NY 11743; *Phone:* 800-394-5327; *Fax:* 631-271-3441. *E-mail:* linguaservice@att. net. *World Wide Web:* http://www.linguaserviceworldwide.com/

LINGUA SERVICE WORLDWIDE
VACATION 'N LEARN SPANISH IN SPAIN

Hosted by Colegio de España
Academic Focus • Spanish language and literature, Spanish studies.
Program Information • Students attend classes at Colegio de España (Alicante, Spain). Optional travel to cultural sites around Spain at an extra cost. Students typically earn 3 semester credits for 3 weeks, 6 semester credits for 5 weeks.
Sessions • Classes held year-round, beginning on Mondays, minimum session length is 2 weeks.
Eligibility Requirements • Minimum age 16; open to precollege students, freshmen, sophomores, juniors, seniors, graduate students, adults; no foreign language proficiency required.
Living Arrangements • Students live in host institution dormitories, locally rented apartments, host family homes, hotels. Quarters are shared with host institution students. Meals are taken with host family.
Costs (2006–2007) • Contact sponsor for cost. $100 application fee.
For More Information • Assistant Director, Lingua Service Worldwide, 75 Prospect Street, Suite 4, Huntington, NY 11743; *Phone:* 800-394-5327; *Fax:* 631-271-3441. *E-mail:* linguaservice@att. net. *World Wide Web:* http://www.linguaserviceworldwide.com/

UNIVERSITY OF PENNSYLVANIA
PENN-IN-ALICANTE, SPAIN

Hosted by University of Alicante
Academic Focus • Spanish language and literature, Spanish studies.
Program Information • Students attend classes at University of Alicante (Alicante, Spain). Scheduled travel; field trips to Granada and Toledo (pre-session). Students typically earn 2 course units per term.
Sessions • Jun–Jul (summer).
Eligibility Requirements • Open to freshmen, sophomores, juniors, seniors, graduate students, adults; 1 letter of recommendation; good academic standing at home school; language proficiency requirement is dependent on course chosen.
Living Arrangements • Students live in host family homes. Meals are taken with host family.
Costs (2005) • $7000; includes tuition, housing, all meals, insurance, excursions. $50 application fee. $300 nonrefundable deposit required. Financial aid available for students from sponsoring institution: loans.
For More Information • Penn Summer Abroad, University of Pennsylvania, 3440 Market Street, Suite 100, Philadelphia, PA 19104-3335; *Phone:* 215-746-6900; *Fax:* 215-573-2053. *E-mail:* summerabroad@sas.upenn.edu. *World Wide Web:* http://www.sas. upenn.edu/summer/

UNIVERSITY STUDIES ABROAD CONSORTIUM
SPANISH STUDIES: ALICANTE, SPAIN

Hosted by University of Alicante
Academic Focus • Art, film and media studies, history, social sciences, Spanish language and literature, Spanish studies, tourism and travel.
Program Information • Students attend classes at University of Alicante (Alicante, Spain). Field trips to Guadalest, Calpe, Altea, Fuentes de Algar, Benidorm, Santa Pola-Isla de Tabarca, Cabo San Antonio, Jávea-Denia, Valencia; optional travel to Madrid, Toledo at an extra cost. Students typically earn 6–12 semester credits per term.
Sessions • May–Jun (summer), Jun–Aug (summer 2).
Eligibility Requirements • Minimum age 18; open to freshmen, sophomores, juniors, seniors, graduate students, adults; 2.5 GPA; no foreign language proficiency required.
Living Arrangements • Students live in locally rented apartments, host family homes. Quarters are shared with host institution students. Meals are taken on one's own, with host family, in residences, in restaurants.

Costs (2007) • $3090–$3740 for 1 session; $6730 for 2 sessions; includes tuition, housing, some meals, insurance, excursions, student support services. $100 application fee. $200 refundable deposit required. Financial aid available for all students: scholarships, loans.
For More Information • University Studies Abroad Consortium, USAC/323, Reno, NV 89557-0093; *Phone:* 775-784-6569; *Fax:* 775-784-6010. *E-mail:* usac@unr.edu. *World Wide Web:* http://usac. unr.edu/

ALMUÑÉCAR

ENFOREX–SPANISH IN THE SPANISH WORLD
SPANISH INTENSIVE COURSE ALMUÑÉCAR

Hosted by ENFOREX
Academic Focus • Spanish studies.
Program Information • Students attend classes at ENFOREX (Almuñécar, Spain). Field trips to Granada, Córdoba, Málaga; optional travel to Barcelona, Seville, Madrid at an extra cost. Students typically earn 4 semester credits per term.
Sessions • Short term courses held year-round.
Eligibility Requirements • Minimum age 14; open to precollege students, freshmen, sophomores, juniors, seniors, graduate students, adults; no foreign language proficiency required.
Living Arrangements • Students live in host institution dormitories, program-owned apartments, host family homes, hotels. Quarters are shared with host institution students, students from other programs. Meals are taken as a group, on one's own, with host family.
Costs (2005) • €1280 per month; includes tuition, housing, all meals, excursions, books and class materials, lab equipment, international student ID, student support services. €65 application fee. €250 deposit required.
For More Information • Mr. Domenico Oppizzio, Marketing and Promotion, ENFOREX–Spanish in the Spanish World, Alberto Aguilera, 26, 28015 Madrid, Spain; *Phone:* +34 91-594-3776; *Fax:* +34 91-594-5159. *E-mail:* promotion@enforex.es. *World Wide Web:* http://www.enforex.com/

ANDALUCÍA

LANGUAGE LIAISON
LEARN SPANISH IN ANDALUCÍA

Hosted by Language Liaison
Academic Focus • Spanish language and literature.
Program Information • Students attend classes at Language Liaison (Andalucía, Spain). Field trips; optional travel at an extra cost. Students typically earn 3–15 semester credits per term.
Sessions • Classes begin weekly, year-round.
Eligibility Requirements • Minimum age 17; open to precollege students, freshmen, sophomores, juniors, seniors, graduate students, adults; no foreign language proficiency required.
Living Arrangements • Students live in locally rented apartments, host family homes, hotels. Meals are taken on one's own, with host family, in residences, in restaurants.
Costs (2005) • Contact sponsor for cost. $175 application fee. Financial aid available for all students: scholarship research service.
For More Information • Ms. Nancy Forman, President, Language Liaison, PO Box 1772, Pacific Palisades, CA 90272; *Phone:* 800-284-4448; *Fax:* 310-454-1706. *World Wide Web:* http://www. languageliaison.com/

AVILA

INSTITUTO ESPAÑOL "MURALLAS DE AVILA"
INTENSIVE COURSE IN SPANISH LANGUAGE AND CIVILIZATION

Hosted by Instituto Español "Murallas de Avila"

Academic Focus • Art history, cinematography, cultural studies, dance, Latin American literature, law and legal studies, music history, Spanish language and literature, Spanish studies.
Program Information • Students attend classes at Instituto Español "Murallas de Avila" (Avila, Spain). Optional travel to Madrid, Segovia, Salamanca, Toledo at an extra cost. Students typically earn 3–18 semester credits per term.
Sessions • Classes begin every Monday Feb–Nov, beginners start on the first Monday of each month.
Eligibility Requirements • Minimum age 16; open to precollege students, freshmen, sophomores, juniors, seniors, graduate students, adults; no foreign language proficiency required.
Living Arrangements • Students live in locally rented apartments, host family homes, hotels. Quarters are shared with host institution students, students from other programs. Meals are taken on one's own, with host family.
Costs (2004–2005) • $200 per week; includes tuition, housing, all meals, books and class materials, all school facilities.
For More Information • Dr. Rainer Rutkowski, Director, Instituto Español "Murallas de Avila", c/Martin Carramolino 6, E-05001 Avila, Spain; *Phone:* +34 920-222-773; *Fax:* +34 920-252-955. *E-mail:* iema@iema.com. *World Wide Web:* http://www.iema.com/

LOYOLA UNIVERSITY NEW ORLEANS
LOYOLA SUMMER PROGRAM IN SPAIN

Hosted by Catholic University of Avila Santa Teresa de Jesus
Academic Focus • Spanish language and literature, Spanish studies.
Program Information • Students attend classes at Catholic University of Avila Santa Teresa de Jesus (Avila, Spain). Field trips to Salamanca, Segovia, El Escorial, Madrid (Prado Museum). Students typically earn 6 semester credits per term.
Sessions • Jul (summer).
Eligibility Requirements • Minimum age 18; open to freshmen, sophomores, juniors, seniors, adults; good academic standing at home school; .5 years college course work in Spanish.
Living Arrangements • Quarters are shared with host institution students, students from other programs. Meals are taken as a group, in residences.
Costs (2005) • $3200; includes tuition, housing, all meals, insurance, excursions, books and class materials, international student ID, student support services. $300 nonrefundable deposit required. Financial aid available for students from sponsoring institution: scholarships, loans.
For More Information • Dr. Eileen J. Doll, Program Director/Associate Professor of Spanish, Loyola University New Orleans, Modern Foreign Languages and Literatures, Box 60, New Orleans, LA 70118; *Phone:* 504-865-3845; *Fax:* 504-865-2348. *E-mail:* edoll@loyno.edu. *World Wide Web:* http://www.loyno.edu/cie/

BARCELONA

ACADEMIC PROGRAMS INTERNATIONAL (API)
(API)–UNIVERSITY OF BARCELONA, SPAIN

Hosted by University of Barcelona
Academic Focus • Spanish language and literature.
Program Information • Students attend classes at University of Barcelona (Barcelona, Spain). Scheduled travel to Madrid; field trips to Toledo, El Escorial; Girona; Figueres; Madrid;, Bilbao; Mallorca, Cordoba, Granada; Jerez and Cadiz; Seville. Students typically earn 5-8 semester credits per term.
Sessions • Jun-Jul (summer), Jun-Jul (summer 2).
Eligibility Requirements • Minimum age 18; open to freshmen, sophomores, juniors, seniors, graduate students, adults; 2.75 GPA; 1 letter of recommendation; good academic standing at home school; official transcript from home university; no foreign language proficiency required.
Living Arrangements • Students live in host institution dormitories, locally rented apartments, host family homes. Quarters are shared with host institution students. Meals are taken on one's own, with host family, in residences, in restaurants.
Costs (2006–2007) • $4000-$4975; includes tuition, housing, all meals, insurance, excursions, student support services, group transportation, airport pick-up, mobile phone, on-line services,

on-site director; wireless access in API office. $150 nonrefundable deposit required. Financial aid available for all students: scholarships.
For More Information • Ms. Jennifer C. Allen, Director, Academic Programs International (API), 107 East Hopkins, San Marcos, TX 78666; *Phone:* 800-844-4124; *Fax:* 512-392-8420. *E-mail:* api@academicintl.com. *World Wide Web:* http://www.academicintl.com/

ACADEMIC STUDIES ABROAD
ACADEMIC STUDIES ABROAD–BARCELONA, SPAIN

Hosted by University Autonoma of Barcelona
Academic Focus • Spanish language and literature, Spanish studies.
Program Information • Students attend classes at University Autonoma of Barcelona (Barcelona, Spain). Scheduled travel to Figueres, Montserrat; field trips to Madrid, Mallora. Students typically earn 6 semester credits per term.
Sessions • May-Jul (summer).
Eligibility Requirements • Minimum age 18; open to freshmen, sophomores, juniors, seniors; 2.5 GPA; college transcript; no foreign language proficiency required.
Living Arrangements • Students live in host family homes. Quarters are shared with host institution students. Meals are taken with host family, in residences.
Costs (2006) • $4095; includes tuition, housing, all meals, insurance, excursions, international student ID, student support services, cell phone, laundry. $150 refundable deposit required. Financial aid available for all students: scholarships.
For More Information • Mr. Lee Frankel, Director, Academic Studies Abroad, 434 Massachusetts Avenue, Suite 501, Boston, MA 02118; *Phone:* 617-437-9388; *Fax:* 617-437-9390. *E-mail:* lee@academicstudies.com. *World Wide Web:* http://www.academicstudies.com

ALMA COLLEGE
SUMMER PROGRAM OF STUDIES IN BARCELONA, SPAIN

Hosted by ENFOREX
Academic Focus • Cultural studies, Spanish language and literature.
Program Information • Students attend classes at ENFOREX (Barcelona, Spain). Field trips to local sites. Students typically earn 3-9 semester credits per term.
Sessions • Apr-Aug (4 to 14 weeks).
Eligibility Requirements • Minimum age 18; open to freshmen, sophomores, juniors, seniors, graduate students, adults; 2.5 GPA; 2 letters of recommendation; good academic standing at home school; no foreign language proficiency required.
Living Arrangements • Students live in host family homes. Quarters are shared with students from other programs. Meals are taken on one's own, with host family, in residences, in restaurants.
Costs (2005) • $3200-$7700; includes tuition, housing, all meals, excursions, books and class materials, international student ID, student support services, e-mail access, on-site orientation, airport pick-up. $50 application fee. $200 refundable deposit required.
For More Information • Ms. Julie Elenbaas, Office Associate, International Education, Alma College, 614 West Superior Street, Alma, MI 48801-1599; *Phone:* 989-463-7055; *Fax:* 989-463-7128. *E-mail:* intl_studies@alma.edu. *World Wide Web:* http://international.alma.edu/

AMERICAN INSTITUTE FOR FOREIGN STUDY (AIFS)
AIFS–BARCELONA, SPAIN–POMPEU FABRA UNIVERSITY

Hosted by Pompeu Fabra University
Academic Focus • Art history, literature, Spanish language and literature.
Program Information • Students attend classes at Pompeu Fabra University (Barcelona, Spain). Scheduled travel to 3-day London stopover; field trips to cultural activities, walking tours, Figueras and Cadaques, Sitges, Gerona, Montserrat; optional travel to 4-day optional tour of Spain including Madrid, Toledo, Segovia and Valley of the Fallen for a supplemental fee of $599. Students typically earn 7-9 semester credits per term.
Sessions • Jun-Jul (summer), (Summer 2) 6 weeks Jun-Jul.

SPAIN
Barcelona

Eligibility Requirements • Minimum age 17; open to precollege students, freshmen, sophomores, juniors, seniors; 2.7 GPA; no foreign language proficiency required.

Living Arrangements • Students live in host institution dormitories, program-owned apartments, hotels. Quarters are shared with host institution students. Meals are taken as a group, in residences.

Costs (2007) • 4 weeks: $5199, 6 weeks: $6299; includes tuition, housing, some meals, insurance, excursions, student support services, On-site Resident Director, Phone Card to call the U.S., Computer Facilities/Internet. $95 application fee. $395 nonrefundable deposit required. Financial aid available for all students: scholarships.

For More Information • Mr. David Mauro, Admissions Advisor, American Institute For Foreign Study (AIFS), 9 West Broad Street, Stamford, CT 06902-3788; *Phone:* 800-727-2437 Ext. 5163; *Fax:* 203-399-5597. *E-mail:* dmauro@aifs.com. *World Wide Web:* http://www.aifsabroad.com/

ARCADIA UNIVERSITY
SUMMER IN BARCELONA, SPAIN

Hosted by Barcelona Center for Education Abroad

Academic Focus • Art history, fine/studio arts, Spanish language and literature.

Program Information • Students attend classes at Barcelona Center for Education Abroad (Barcelona, Spain). Field trips; optional travel. Students typically earn 3–6 semester credits per term.

Sessions • May–Jun (summer).

Eligibility Requirements • Open to freshmen, sophomores, juniors, seniors; 3.0 GPA; 1 letter of recommendation; no foreign language proficiency required.

Living Arrangements • Students live in locally rented apartments, host family homes. Quarters are shared with host institution students, students from other programs. Meals are taken on one's own, with host family, in residences, in restaurants.

Costs (2005) • Contact sponsor for cost. $35 application fee. $500 nonrefundable deposit required. Financial aid available for all students: scholarships, loans.

For More Information • Arcadia University, Center for Education Abroad, 450 South Easton Road, Glenside, PA 19038; *Phone:* 866-927-2234; *Fax:* 215-572-2174. *E-mail:* cea@arcadia.edu. *World Wide Web:* http://www.arcadia.edu/cea/

CIEE
CIEE STUDY CENTER AT ESCOLA SUPERIOR DE COMERÇ INTERNACIONAL–BARCELONA, SPAIN

Hosted by College of International Business

Academic Focus • Art history, business administration/management, economics, European studies, history, marketing, social sciences, Spanish language and literature.

Program Information • Students attend classes at College of International Business (Barcelona, Spain). Field trips to Figueras; Ampurias; Cadaques; Girona; Penedes. Students typically earn 6 semester credits per term.

Sessions • Jun–Jul (summer).

Eligibility Requirements • Minimum age 18; open to sophomores, juniors, seniors; course work in business; 3.0 GPA; 1 letter of recommendation; for ESCI courses, minimum of 3 courses in business-related subjects; for business course in Spanish, 5 semesters of college-level Spanish or equivalent.

Living Arrangements • Students live in host family homes. Meals are taken with host family, in residences.

Costs (2006) • $5100; includes tuition, housing, some meals, insurance, excursions, student support services, resident staff, orientation, on-site pick-up, cultural activities, pre-departure advice. $30 application fee. $300 nonrefundable deposit required. Financial aid available for all students: scholarships, minority student scholarships.

For More Information • Information Center, CIEE, 7 Custom House Street, 3rd Floor, Portland, ME 04101; *Phone:* 800-40-STUDY; *Fax:* 207-553-7699. *E-mail:* studyinfo@ciee.org. *World Wide Web:* http://www.ciee.org/isp/

DON QUIJOTE
INTENSIVE BUSINESS–BARCELONA

Hosted by Don Quijote

Academic Focus • International business, Romance languages, Spanish language and literature, Spanish studies.

Program Information • Students attend classes at Don Quijote (Barcelona, Spain). Field trips to historic sites, cultural attractions. Students typically earn 4 semester credits per term.

Sessions • 4 week courses start every Monday.

Eligibility Requirements • Minimum age 18; open to freshmen, sophomores, juniors, seniors, graduate students, adults; intermediate Spanish.

Living Arrangements • Students live in host institution dormitories, program-owned apartments, host family homes. Quarters are shared with host institution students, students from other programs. Meals are taken on one's own, in residences.

Costs (2006) • €1001; includes tuition, books and class materials, lab equipment, student support services, guided cultural tour, welcome dinner, student discount card, level test, tutor, end-of-course certificate. €65 application fee. €500 nonrefundable deposit required. Financial aid available for all students: scholarships.

For More Information • Ms. Carmen Cantarino, USA Director, Don Quijote, Plaza San Marcos 7, 37002 Salamanca, Spain; *Phone:* +34 923-268874; *Fax:* +34 923-260674. *E-mail:* usa@donquijote.org. *World Wide Web:* http://www.donquijote.org/

DON QUIJOTE
INTENSIVE SPANISH COURSE IN BARCELONA

Hosted by Don Quijote

Academic Focus • Romance languages, Spanish language and literature, Spanish studies.

Program Information • Students attend classes at Don Quijote (Barcelona, Spain). Field trips to historic sites, important cities in Spain. Students typically earn 4 semester credits per term.

Sessions • Minimum 1 week sessions begin every Monday.

Eligibility Requirements • Minimum age 18; open to freshmen, sophomores, juniors, seniors, graduate students, adults; no foreign language proficiency required.

Living Arrangements • Students live in host institution dormitories, program-owned apartments, host family homes. Quarters are shared with host institution students, students from other programs. Meals are taken on one's own, with host family, in residences.

Costs (2006) • Contact sponsor for cost. €65 application fee. €500 deposit required. Financial aid available for all students: scholarships.

For More Information • Ms. Carmen Cantarino, USA Director, Don Quijote, Plaza San Marcos 7, 37002 Salamanca, Spain; *Phone:* +34 923-268874; *Fax:* +34 923-260674. *E-mail:* usa@donquijote.org. *World Wide Web:* http://www.donquijote.org/

EF INTERNATIONAL LANGUAGE SCHOOLS
SPANISH IN BARCELONA

Hosted by EF Escuela Internacional de Español

Academic Focus • Spanish language and literature.

Program Information • Students attend classes at EF Escuela Internacional de Español (Barcelona, Spain). Field trips to the Picasso Museum, the Dali Museum, Sagrada Familia Cathedral; optional travel to Madrid, Seville, Costa Brava, the Pyrenees at an extra cost. Students typically earn 15–18 quarter credits per term.

Sessions • Program length 2 to 52 weeks, year-round.

Eligibility Requirements • Minimum age 16; open to precollege students, freshmen, sophomores, juniors, seniors, graduate students, adults; no foreign language proficiency required.

Living Arrangements • Students live in host institution dormitories, host family homes. Quarters are shared with host institution students. Meals are taken with host family, in residences.

Costs (2006–2007) • $970 for 2 weeks; includes tuition, housing, some meals, books and class materials, student support services. $145 application fee. Financial aid available for all students: scholarships.

For More Information • Ms. Varvara Kirakosyan, Director of Admissions, EF International Language Schools, One Education Street, Cambridge, MA 02141; *Phone:* 800-992-1892; *Fax:* 800-590-1125. *E-mail:* ils@ef.com. *World Wide Web:* http://www.ef.com/

ENFOREX–SPANISH IN THE SPANISH WORLD
SPANISH INTENSIVE COURSE BARCELONA

Hosted by ENFOREX

Academic Focus • Dance, Spanish language and literature, Spanish studies, teaching.

Program Information • Students attend classes at ENFOREX (Barcelona, Spain). Field trips to Sagrada Familia, Montserrat, Sitges; optional travel to Seville, Granada, Salamanca at an extra cost. Students typically earn 4 semester credits per term.

Sessions • Year-round.

Eligibility Requirements • Minimum age 14; open to precollege students, freshmen, sophomores, juniors, seniors, graduate students, adults; no foreign language proficiency required.

Living Arrangements • Students live in host institution dormitories, program-owned apartments, host family homes, hotels. Quarters are shared with host institution students. Meals are taken as a group, on one's own, with host family, in residences.

Costs (2005) • €1280 per month; includes tuition, housing, all meals, excursions, books and class materials, lab equipment, international student ID, student support services. €65 application fee. €250 nonrefundable deposit required.

For More Information • Mr. Antonio Anadón, Director of Spanish Department, ENFOREX–Spanish in the Spanish World, Alberto Aguilera, 26, 28015 Madrid, Spain; *Phone:* +34 91-594-3776; *Fax:* +34 91-594-5159. *E-mail:* promotion@enforex.es. *World Wide Web:* http://www.enforex.com/

EUROPEAN HERITAGE INSTITUTE
YEAR-ROUND PROGRAMS IN BARCELONA

Hosted by Don Quijote

Academic Focus • Business administration/management, commerce, Spanish language and literature, Spanish studies.

Program Information • Students attend classes at Don Quijote (Barcelona, Spain). Field trips to areas around Barcelona. Students typically earn 3–6 semester credits per term.

Sessions • 1 to 15 week sessions begin every Monday, year-round; 12 week internships held monthly.

Eligibility Requirements • Minimum age 18; open to freshmen, sophomores, juniors, seniors, graduate students, adults; 2.25 GPA; 2 letters of recommendation; no foreign language proficiency required.

Living Arrangements • Students live in host institution dormitories, locally rented apartments, host family homes, hotels, a residence center. Quarters are shared with host institution students. Meals are taken on one's own, with host family, in residences, in restaurants.

Costs (2006) • $1800 for 4 weeks; $3220 for 8 weeks; $4732 for 12 weeks; includes tuition, housing, some meals, excursions, books and class materials, student support services, cultural and other activities. $300 refundable deposit required.

For More Information • Dr. Antonio Masullo, Professor, European Heritage Institute, 2708 East Franklin Street, Richmond, VA 23223; *Phone:* 804-643-0661; *Fax:* 804-648-0826. *E-mail:* info@europeabroad.org. *World Wide Web:* http://www.europeabroad.org/

INTERNATIONAL HOUSE BARCELONA
INTENSIVE SPANISH COURSE

Hosted by International House Barcelona

Academic Focus • Spanish language and literature, Spanish studies.

Program Information • Students attend classes at International House Barcelona (Barcelona, Spain). Field trips to the Gothic Quarter, Gaudi's Sagrada Familia, Picasso Museum and full-day excursions to Tarragona (Roman ruins), or Figueras (Dali's museum), Cadaques by the sea, Montserrat, Gerona; optional travel to Valencia, Madrid, Mallorca at an extra cost. Students typically earn 3–8 semester credits per term.

SPAIN
Barcelona

Sessions • Courses begin every Monday, year-round.
Eligibility Requirements • Minimum age 16; open to precollege students, freshmen, sophomores, juniors, seniors, graduate students, adults; no foreign language proficiency required.
Living Arrangements • Students live in host institution dormitories, locally rented apartments, host family homes, hotels. Quarters are shared with host institution students, students from other programs. Meals are taken on one's own, with host family, in residences, in central dining facility, in restaurants.
Costs (2006) • €670 for 2 weeks; €1340 for 4 weeks; €2560 for 8 weeks; includes tuition, housing, some meals, excursions, books and class materials, student support services. €200 refundable deposit required.
For More Information • Ms. Carmen Sánchez, Marketing Manager, International House Barcelona, Trafalgar, 14, Barcelona 08010, Spain; *Phone:* +34 93-268-45-11; *Fax:* +34 93-268-02-39. *E-mail:* spanish@bcn.ihes.com. *World Wide Web:* http://www.ihes.com/bcn/

INTERNATIONAL STUDIES ABROAD
BARCELONA, SPAIN: SUMMER LANGUAGE AND CULTURE 1

Hosted by University Pompeu Fabra, Barcelona
Academic Focus • Art history, communications, Spanish language and literature.
Program Information • Students attend classes at University Pompeu Fabra, Barcelona (Barcelona, Spain). Scheduled travel to Madrid; field trips to El Escorial, Figueres, Girona, Madrid; San Sebastian; Sitges. Students typically earn 6–9 semester credits per term.
Sessions • May–Jul (summer).
Eligibility Requirements • Minimum age 18; open to freshmen, sophomores, juniors, seniors, graduate students, adults; 3.0 GPA; good academic standing at home school; no foreign language proficiency required.
Living Arrangements • Students live in host family homes. Meals are taken with host family, in residences.
Costs (2005–2006) • Contact sponsor for cost. $200 deposit required. Financial aid available for all students: scholarships, loans, US federal financial aid.
For More Information • Spain Site Specialist, International Studies Abroad, 901 West 24th Street, Austin, TX 78705; *Phone:* 800-580-8826; *Fax:* 512-480-8866. *E-mail:* isa@studiesabroad.com. *World Wide Web:* http://www.studiesabroad.com/

INTERNATIONAL STUDIES ABROAD
BARCELONA, SPAIN: SUMMER LANGUAGE AND CULTURE 2

Hosted by Menendez Pelayo International University
Academic Focus • Geography, history, Spanish language and literature.
Program Information • Students attend classes at Menendez Pelayo International University (Barcelona, Spain). Scheduled travel to Madrid; field trips to Sitges, Valencia, El Escorial, Girona, Toledo, Figueres; optional travel to San Sebastián at an extra cost. Students typically earn 5–6 semester credits per term.
Sessions • Jun–Jul (summer).
Eligibility Requirements • Minimum age 18; open to freshmen, sophomores, juniors, seniors, graduate students, adults; 2.5 GPA; 1 letter of recommendation; good academic standing at home school; transcripts; no foreign language proficiency required.
Living Arrangements • Students live in host family homes. Meals are taken with host family, in residences.
Costs (2005) • Contact sponsor for cost. $200 deposit required. Financial aid available for all students: scholarships, loans, U.S. federal financial aid.
For More Information • Spain Site Specialist, International Studies Abroad, 901 West 24th Street, Austin, TX 78705; *Phone:* 800-580-8826; *Fax:* 512-480-8866. *E-mail:* isa@studiesabroad.com. *World Wide Web:* http://www.studiesabroad.com/

KNOWLEDGE EXCHANGE INSTITUTE (KEI)
BARCELONA INTERNSHIP PROGRAM

Hosted by Barcelona Business School
Academic Focus • Accounting, actuarial science, advertising and public relations, brokerage, business administration/management, commerce, communication services, communications, community service, criminal justice, economics, entrepreneurship, finance, hospitality services, hotel and restaurant management, human resources, information science, international business, law and legal studies, management information systems, marketing, political science and government, public administration, social services, social work, tourism and travel.
Program Information • Students attend classes at Barcelona Business School (Barcelona, Spain). Field trips to Barcelona and surrounding areas. Students typically earn 6 semester credits per term.
Sessions • Jun–Aug (summer).
Eligibility Requirements • Open to freshmen, sophomores, juniors, seniors, graduate students, adults; 2.2 GPA; 2 letters of recommendation; good academic standing at home school; no foreign language proficiency required.
Living Arrangements • Students live in host institution dormitories, program-owned apartments, host family homes. Quarters are shared with host institution students, students from other programs. Meals are taken on one's own, with host family, in residences, in restaurants.
Costs (2006) • $4890; includes tuition, housing, insurance, excursions, student support services, mobile telephone. $50 application fee. $500 nonrefundable deposit required. Financial aid available for all students: scholarships, loans.
For More Information • Mr. Eduard Izraylovsky, Director, Knowledge Exchange Institute (KEI), 111 John Street, Suite 800, New York, NY 10038; *Phone:* 800-831-5095; *Fax:* 212-528-2095. *E-mail:* info@knowledgeexchange.org. *World Wide Web:* http://www.knowledgeexchange.org/

KNOWLEDGE EXCHANGE INSTITUTE (KEI)
SPANISH BUSINESS, LAW, AND DIPLOMACY

Hosted by Barcelona Business School
Academic Focus • Accounting, business administration/management, commerce, community service, cultural studies, Dutch, economics, entrepreneurship, European studies, finance, French language and literature, French studies, German language and literature, historic preservation, intercultural studies, interdisciplinary studies, international affairs, international business, labor and industrial relations, management information systems, marketing, political science and government, public administration, public policy, statistics, telecommunications.
Program Information • Students attend classes at Barcelona Business School (Barcelona, Spain). Scheduled travel to Madrid, Salamanca, Toledo, Valencia, Granada; field trips to Barcelona. Students typically earn 12 semester credits per term.
Sessions • Jun–Aug (summer).
Eligibility Requirements • Open to freshmen, sophomores, juniors, seniors, graduate students, adults; 2.2 GPA; 2 letters of recommendation; good academic standing at home school; no foreign language proficiency required.
Living Arrangements • Students live in program-owned houses. Quarters are shared with host institution students, students from other programs. Meals are taken on one's own, in residences, in restaurants.
Costs (2006) • $5870; includes tuition, housing, insurance, excursions, books and class materials, student support services, mobile phone, internet access. $50 application fee. $500 nonrefundable deposit required. Financial aid available for all students: scholarships, loans.
For More Information • Mr. Eduard Izraylovsky, Director, Knowledge Exchange Institute (KEI), 111 John Street, Suite 800, New York, NY 10038; *Phone:* 800-831-5095; *Fax:* 212-528-2095. *E-mail:* info@knowledgeexchange.org. *World Wide Web:* http://www.knowledgeexchange.org/

KNOWLEDGE EXCHANGE INSTITUTE (KEI)
SPANISH TOURISM AND HOSPITALITY

Hosted by Barcelona Business School
Academic Focus • Business administration/management, communications, cultural studies, Dutch, economics, European studies, French language and literature, French studies, German language

and literature, hospitality services, hotel and restaurant management, intercultural studies, interdisciplinary studies, international business, tourism and travel.

Program Information • Students attend classes at Barcelona Business School (Barcelona, Spain). Scheduled travel to Madrid, Salamanca, Toledo, Valencia; field trips to Barcelona. Students typically earn 12 semester credits per term.

Sessions • Jun–Aug (summer).

Eligibility Requirements • Open to freshmen, sophomores, juniors, seniors, graduate students, adults; 2.2 GPA; 2 letters of recommendation; good academic standing at home school; no foreign language proficiency required.

Living Arrangements • Students live in program-owned houses. Quarters are shared with host institution students, students from other programs. Meals are taken on one's own, in residences, in restaurants.

Costs (2006) • $5870; includes tuition, housing, insurance, excursions, books and class materials, lab equipment, student support services, mobile telephone and intenet access. $50 application fee. $500 nonrefundable deposit required. Financial aid available for all students: scholarships, loans.

For More Information • Mr. Eduard Izraylovsky, Director, Knowledge Exchange Institute (KEI), 111 John Street, Suite 800, New York, NY 10038; *Phone:* 800-831-5095; *Fax:* 212-528-2095. *E-mail:* info@knowledgeexchange.org. *World Wide Web:* http://www.knowledgeexchange.org/

LANGUAGE LIAISON
LEARN SPANISH IN BARCELONA

Hosted by Language Liaison

Academic Focus • Spanish language and literature.

Program Information • Students attend classes at Language Liaison (Barcelona, Spain). Field trips; optional travel at an extra cost. Students typically earn 3-15 semester credits per term.

Sessions • New programs begin weekly, year-round.

Eligibility Requirements • Minimum age 16; open to precollege students, freshmen, sophomores, juniors, seniors, graduate students, adults; no foreign language proficiency required.

Living Arrangements • Students live in host family homes, hotels. Meals are taken on one's own, with host family, in residences, in restaurants.

Costs (2005) • Contact sponsor for cost. $175 application fee. Financial aid available for all students: scholarship research service.

For More Information • Ms. Nancy Forman, President, Language Liaison, PO Box 1772, Pacific Palisades, CA 90272; *Phone:* 800-284-4448; *Fax:* 310-454-1706. *E-mail:* learn@languageliaison.com. *World Wide Web:* http://www.languageliaison.com/

LANGUAGE LINK
INTERNATIONAL HOUSE (IH) OF BARCELONA, SPAIN

Hosted by International House Barcelona

Academic Focus • Spanish language and literature.

Program Information • Students attend classes at International House Barcelona (Barcelona, Spain). Field trips to points of interest in Barcelona. Students typically earn 6-15 semester credits per term.

Sessions • Year-round, start dates every other Monday for beginners.

Eligibility Requirements • Minimum age 13; open to precollege students, freshmen, sophomores, juniors, seniors, graduate students, adults; no foreign language proficiency required.

Living Arrangements • Students live in locally rented apartments, host family homes. Quarters are shared with host institution students. Meals are taken on one's own, with host family, in residences, in restaurants.

Costs (2005) • $432 per week; includes tuition, housing, some meals, books and class materials, student support services, cultural activities.

For More Information • Ms. Kay G. Rafool, Director, Language Link, PO Box 3006, Peoria, IL 61612-3006; *Phone:* 800-552-2051; *Fax:* 309-692-2926. *E-mail:* info@langlink.com. *World Wide Web:* http://www.langlink.com/

LEXIA INTERNATIONAL
LEXIA SUMMER IN BARCELONA

Hosted by University of Barcelona

Academic Focus • Anthropology, architecture, area studies, art, art history, business administration/management, comparative history, economics, film and media studies, geography, intercultural studies, international affairs, literature, political science and government, sociology, Spanish language and literature, visual and performing arts.

Program Information • Students attend classes at University of Barcelona (Barcelona, Spain). Field trips. Students typically earn 8-10 semester credits per term.

Sessions • Jun–Aug (summer).

Eligibility Requirements • Minimum age 18; open to freshmen, sophomores, juniors, seniors, graduate students, adults; 2.5 GPA; 2 letters of recommendation; good academic standing at home school; no foreign language proficiency required.

Living Arrangements • Students live in locally rented apartments, host family homes. Quarters are shared with host institution students. Meals are taken on one's own, in residences, in central dining facility, in restaurants.

Costs (2006) • $6450; includes tuition, housing, all meals, insurance, excursions, international student ID, student support services, computer access, transcript. $40 application fee. $300 nonrefundable deposit required. Financial aid available for all students: scholarships, work study.

For More Information • Lexia International, 23 South Main Street, Hanover, NH 03755; *Phone:* 800-775-3942; *Fax:* 603-643-9899. *E-mail:* info@lexiaintl.org. *World Wide Web:* http://www.lexiaintl.org/

LINGUA SERVICE WORLDWIDE
INTERNATIONAL HOUSE BARCELONA

Hosted by International House Barcelona

Academic Focus • Spanish language and literature, Spanish studies.

Program Information • Students attend classes at International House Barcelona (Barcelona, Spain). Optional travel to cultural sites throughout Spain at an extra cost. Students typically earn 3 semester credits for 3 weeks, 6 semester credits for 5 weeks.

Sessions • Sessions of 2 or more weeks begin on Mondays, year-round.

Eligibility Requirements • Minimum age 16; open to precollege students, freshmen, sophomores, juniors, seniors, graduate students, adults; no foreign language proficiency required.

Living Arrangements • Students live in locally rented apartments, host family homes, hotels. Meals are taken with host family.

Costs (2006–2007) • Contact sponsor for cost. $100 application fee.

For More Information • Assistant Director, Lingua Service Worldwide, 75 Prospect Street, Suite 4, Huntington, NY 11743; *Phone:* 800-394-5327; *Fax:* 631-271-3441. *E-mail:* linguaservice@att.net. *World Wide Web:* http://www.linguaserviceworldwide.com/

LINGUA SERVICE WORLDWIDE
VACATION 'N LEARN SPANISH IN SPAIN

Hosted by Don Quijote

Academic Focus • Spanish language and literature, Spanish studies.

Program Information • Students attend classes at Don Quijote (Barcelona, Spain). Optional travel to cultural sites around Spain at an extra cost. Students typically earn 3 semester credits for 3 weeks, 6 semester credits for 5 weeks.

Sessions • Classes held year-round, beginning on Mondays, minimum session length is 2 weeks.

Eligibility Requirements • Minimum age 16; open to precollege students, freshmen, sophomores, juniors, seniors, graduate students, adults; no foreign language proficiency required.

Living Arrangements • Students live in host institution dormitories, locally rented apartments, host family homes, hotels. Quarters are shared with host institution students. Meals are taken with host family.

Costs (2006–2007) • Contact sponsor for cost. $100 application fee.

For More Information • Assistant Director, Lingua Service Worldwide, 75 Prospect Street, Suite 4, Huntington, NY 11743; *Phone:* 800-394-5327; *Fax:* 631-271-3441. *E-mail:* linguaservice@att.net. *World Wide Web:* http://www.linguaserviceworldwide.com/

SPAIN
Barcelona

SIENA SOJOURN
(BARCELONA SOJOURN OF) SOJOURNS ABROAD

Academic Focus • Spanish language and literature.
Program Information • Faculty members are drawn from the sponsor's U.S. staff and local instructors hired by the sponsor. Scheduled travel to Madrid, Salamanca, Seville; field trips to Bilbao, Valencia, Montserrat.
Sessions • Jun-Jul (summer).
Eligibility Requirements • Minimum age 18; open to freshmen, sophomores, juniors, seniors, graduate students; 1 letter of recommendation; application/personal statement; no foreign language proficiency required.
Living Arrangements • Students live in host family homes. Meals are taken with host family, in residences.
Costs (2007) • $8500; includes tuition, some meals, excursions, books and class materials, museum entry fees, concerts, sporting events, cultural activities. $250 application fee. Financial aid available for all students: scholarships.
For More Information • Mr. John Nissen, Director, Siena Sojourn, Box 1171, Manchester, VT 05254; *Phone:* 802-362-5855; *Fax:* 802-332-6205. *E-mail:* info@sojournsabroad.org. *World Wide Web:* http://www.sojournsabroad.org

STATE UNIVERSITY OF NEW YORK AT OSWEGO
BARCELONA, SPAIN SUMMER PROGRAM

Hosted by University of Barcelona
Academic Focus • Spanish language and literature.
Program Information • Students attend classes at University of Barcelona (Barcelona, Spain). Field trips to sites in and around Barcelona. Students typically earn 6 semester credits per term.
Sessions • Jun-Jul (summer).
Eligibility Requirements • Open to freshmen, sophomores, juniors, seniors; 2.5 GPA; 2 letters of recommendation; good academic standing at home school; personal statement; no foreign language proficiency required.
Living Arrangements • Students live in locally rented apartments, host family homes. Meals are taken on one's own, with host family, in residences.
Costs (2005) • $3300; includes tuition, housing, all meals, insurance, excursions, books and class materials, student support services. $250 nonrefundable deposit required. Financial aid available for students: home university financial aid; loan processing and scholarships for Oswego students.
For More Information • Ms. Lizette Alvarado, Program Specialist, State University of New York at Oswego, 122A Swetman Hall, Oswego, NY 13126-3599; *Phone:* 888-4-OSWEGO; *Fax:* 315-312-2477. *E-mail:* intled@oswego.edu. *World Wide Web:* http://www.oswego.edu/intled/

SYRACUSE UNIVERSITY
VISUAL ARTS IN BARCELONA

Hosted by Fundacio Center del Vidre de Barcelona
Academic Focus • Art history, ceramics and pottery, fine/studio arts.
Program Information • Students attend classes at Fundacio Center del Vidre de Barcelona (Barcelona, Spain). Field trips to Bilbao, Comillas. Students typically earn 6 semester credits per term.
Sessions • May-Jul (summer).
Eligibility Requirements • Minimum age 18; open to freshmen, sophomores, juniors, seniors, graduate students, adults; 2.8 GPA; 1 letter of recommendation; good academic standing at home school; no foreign language proficiency required.
Living Arrangements • Students live in host institution dormitories. Quarters are shared with host institution students. Meals are taken on one's own, in restaurants.
Costs (2005) • $7470; includes tuition, housing, some meals, excursions, international student ID, student support services. $55 application fee. $350 nonrefundable deposit required. Financial aid available for all students: loans, need-based tuition grants.
For More Information • Mrs. Daisy Fried, Associate Director, Syracuse University, 106 Walnut Place, Syracuse, NY 13244-4170; *Phone:* 800-251-9674; *Fax:* 315-443-4593. *E-mail:* dipasum@syr.edu. *World Wide Web:* http://suabroad.syr.edu/

UNIVERSITY OF KANSAS
LANGUAGE AND CULTURE IN BARCELONA, CATALONIA, SPAIN

Academic Focus • Spanish language and literature, Spanish studies.
Program Information • Faculty members are drawn from the sponsor's U.S. staff. Scheduled travel to Segovia, El Escorial, Silos, Burgos, Bilbao, San Sebastian, Pamplona; field trips to Dali Museum in Costa Brava, Valle de Boi, Zaragoza. Students typically earn 7 semester credits per term.
Sessions • Jun-Aug (summer).
Eligibility Requirements • Open to sophomores, juniors, seniors; 2.5 GPA; 2 letters of recommendation; good academic standing at home school; 1 year of college course work in Spanish.
Living Arrangements • Students live in host institution dormitories, hotels. Meals are taken on one's own, in central dining facility, in restaurants.
Costs (2005) • $5600; includes tuition, housing, some meals, excursions, student support services, emergency medical evacuation and repatriation insurance. $38 application fee. $300 nonrefundable deposit required. Financial aid available for students from sponsoring institution: scholarships.
For More Information • Ms. Angela Dittrich, Assistant Director, University of Kansas, Office of Study Abroad, Lippincott Hall, 1410 Jayhawk Boulevard, Room 108, Lawrence, KS 66045-7515; *Phone:* 785-864-3742; *Fax:* 785-864-5040. *E-mail:* osa@ku.edu. *World Wide Web:* http://www.ku.edu/~osa/

BENALMADENA

LANGUAGE LIAISON
SPANISH IN MÁLAGA, SPAIN

Hosted by Language Liaison
Academic Focus • Spanish language and literature.
Program Information • Students attend classes at Language Liaison (Benalmadena, Spain). Field trips; optional travel at an extra cost. Students typically earn 3-15 semester credits per term.
Sessions • New programs begin weekly, year-round.
Eligibility Requirements • Minimum age 14; open to precollege students, freshmen, sophomores, juniors, seniors, graduate students, adults; no foreign language proficiency required.
Living Arrangements • Students live in locally rented apartments, program-owned apartments, host family homes, hotels. Meals are taken on one's own, with host family, in residences, in restaurants.
Costs (2005) • Contact sponsor for cost. $175 application fee. Financial aid available for all students: scholarship research service.
For More Information • Ms. Nancy Forman, President, Language Liaison, PO Box 1772, Pacific Palisades, CA 90272; *Phone:* 800-284-4448; *Fax:* 310-454-1706. *E-mail:* learn@languageliaison.com. *World Wide Web:* http://www.languageliaison.com/

BILBAO

ACADEMIC PROGRAMS INTERNATIONAL (API)
(API)–BILBAO, SPAIN

Hosted by University of the Basque Country
Academic Focus • Art, art history, graphic design/illustration.
Program Information • Students attend classes at University of the Basque Country (Bilbao, Spain). Scheduled travel to Madria; field trips to El Escorial, Toledo, Burgus, Barcelona, Figueres, San Sebastian, Vitoria. Students typically earn 6 semester credits per term.
Sessions • Jun-Jul (summer).
Eligibility Requirements • Minimum age 18; open to freshmen, sophomores, juniors, seniors; 2.75 GPA; 1 letter of recommendation; good academic standing at home school; official transcript from home university; no foreign language proficiency required.
Living Arrangements • Students live in host institution dormitories, host family homes. Quarters are shared with students from other programs. Meals are taken on one's own, with host family, in residences, in restaurants.

Costs (2006–2007) • $4200–$4300; includes tuition, housing, all meals, insurance, excursions, student support services, airport reception, ground transportation, mobile phone, on-line services, on-site orientation; wireless access in API office. $150 nonrefundable deposit required. Financial aid available for all students: scholarships.

For More Information • Ms. Jennifer C. Allen, Director, Academic Programs International (API), 107 East Hopkins, San Marcos, TX 78666; *Phone:* 800-844-4124; *Fax:* 512-392-8420. *E-mail:* api@academicintl.com. *World Wide Web:* http://www.academicintl.com/

UNIVERSITY STUDIES ABROAD CONSORTIUM
INTERNATIONAL BUSINESS AND SPANISH STUDIES: BILBAO/GETXO, SPAIN

Hosted by University of the Basque Country
Academic Focus • Art, film and media studies, finance, management information systems, sociology, Spanish language and literature.
Program Information • Students attend classes at University of the Basque Country (Bilbao, Spain). Scheduled travel; field trips to Urdaibai and Province Bizkaia, San Sebastian; France; Iparralde; optional travel to Madrid at an extra cost. Students typically earn 6 semester credits per term.
Sessions • May 15 to June 15 (June Session); June 15 to July 15 (July Session).
Eligibility Requirements • Minimum age 18; open to freshmen, sophomores, juniors, seniors, graduate students, adults; 2.5 GPA; no foreign language proficiency required.
Living Arrangements • Students live in locally rented apartments, host family homes. Quarters are shared with host institution students. Meals are taken on one's own, with host family, in residences, in restaurants.
Costs (2006–2007) • $2180; includes tuition, some meals, insurance, excursions, student support services. $100 application fee. $200 refundable deposit required. Financial aid available for all students: scholarships, loans.
For More Information • University Studies Abroad Consortium, USAC/323, Reno, NV 89557-0093; *Phone:* 775-784-6569; *Fax:* 775-784-6010. *World Wide Web:* http://usac.unr.edu/

BURGOS
MODERN LANGUAGE STUDIES ABROAD
MLSA–BURGOS–MASTER IN SPANISH

Hosted by University of Burgos
Academic Focus • Civilization studies, cultural studies, Latin American studies, linguistics, Spanish language and literature, teaching.
Program Information • Students attend classes at University of Burgos (Burgos, Spain). Scheduled travel; field trips; optional travel at an extra cost. Students typically earn 6-9 semester credits per term.
Sessions • Jul–Aug (summer).
Eligibility Requirements • Open to graduate students, adults; Bachelor's degree in Spanish.
Living Arrangements • Students live in host institution dormitories, host family homes. Quarters are shared with host institution students, students from other programs. Meals are taken as a group, with host family, in residences, in central dining facility.
Costs (2006) • $3985; includes tuition, housing, all meals, international airfare, lab equipment, student support services. $100 application fee.
For More Information • Dr. Celestino Ruiz, Director, Modern Language Studies Abroad, PO Box 548, Frankfort, IL 60423; *Phone:* 815-464-1800; *Fax:* 815-464-9458. *E-mail:* mlsa@sprintmail.com. *World Wide Web:* http://www.mlsa.com/

CÁDIZ
ACADEMIC PROGRAMS INTERNATIONAL (API)
(API)–CÁDIZ, SPAIN

Hosted by University of Cádiz
Academic Focus • Communications, international business, Spanish language and literature, Spanish studies.
Program Information • Students attend classes at University of Cádiz (Cádiz, Spain). Scheduled travel to Madrid; field trips to Toledo, Granada, El Escorial, Sevilla, Córdoba, Jerez, Madrid. Students typically earn 6 semester credits per term.
Sessions • Jun–Jul (summer).
Eligibility Requirements • Minimum age 18; open to sophomores, juniors, seniors, adults; 2.75 GPA; 1 letter of recommendation; good academic standing at home school; official transcript from home university; 1 year of college course work in Spanish.
Living Arrangements • Students live in host institution dormitories, host family homes. Quarters are shared with host institution students, students from other programs. Meals are taken on one's own, with host family, in residences, in restaurants.
Costs (2006–2007) • $3800–$3900; includes tuition, housing, all meals, insurance, excursions, student support services, airport pick-up, ground transportation, mobile phone, on-line services, on-site director; wireless access in API office. $150 nonrefundable deposit required. Financial aid available for all students: scholarships.
For More Information • Ms. Jennifer C. Allen, Director, Academic Programs International (API), 107 East Hopkins, San Marcos, TX 78666; *Phone:* 800-844-4124; *Fax:* 512-392-8420. *E-mail:* api@academicintl.com. *World Wide Web:* http://www.academicintl.com/

DAVIDSON COLLEGE
DAVIDSON SUMMER PROGRAM IN CÁDIZ, SPAIN

Hosted by El Instituto San Fernando, University of Cádiz
Academic Focus • Spanish language and literature, Spanish studies.
Program Information • Students attend classes at El Instituto San Fernando (Cádiz, Spain), University of Cádiz (Cádiz, Spain). Scheduled travel to Santiago; field trips to Jerez. Students typically earn 8 semester credits per term.
Sessions • Jun–Jul (summer).
Eligibility Requirements • Minimum age 18; open to freshmen, sophomores, juniors, seniors; 3.3 GPA; 3 letters of recommendation; good academic standing at home school; 1 year of college course work in Spanish.
Living Arrangements • Students live in host family homes. Quarters are shared with host institution students, students from other programs. Meals are taken with host family, in residences.
Costs (2005) • $4100; includes tuition, housing, all meals, insurance, excursions, books and class materials, student support services. $100 application fee. $1700 deposit required.
For More Information • Ms. Carolyn Ortmayer, Study Abroad Coordinator, Davidson College, Box 7155, Davidson, NC 28035-7155; *Phone:* 704-894-2250; *Fax:* 704-894-2120. *E-mail:* abroad@davidson.edu. *World Wide Web:* http://www.davidson.edu/international/

VILLANOVA UNIVERSITY
INTENSIVE SPANISH LANGUAGE AND LITERATURE

Hosted by University of Cádiz
Academic Focus • Spanish language and literature.
Program Information • Students attend classes at University of Cádiz (Cádiz, Spain). Field trips to Madrid, Granada, Toledo, Avila, El Escorial, Segovia. Students typically earn 6 semester credits per term.
Sessions • Jun–Aug (summer).
Eligibility Requirements • Minimum age 18; open to freshmen, sophomores, juniors, seniors; 2.75 GPA; 2 letters of recommendation; good academic standing at home school; 1 year of college course work in Spanish.
Living Arrangements • Students live in host family homes, hotels. Meals are taken as a group, with host family, in restaurants.

SPAIN
Cádiz

Costs (2005) • $4050; includes tuition, housing, all meals, excursions, student support services. $450 nonrefundable deposit required. Financial aid available for students from sponsoring institution.
For More Information • Dr. Salvatore Poeta, Professor, Villanova University, 800 Lancaster Avenue, Middleton Hall, Villanova, PA 19085; *Phone:* 610-519-6412; *Fax:* 610-519-7649. *E-mail:* salvatore. poeta@villanova.edu. *World Wide Web:* http://www. internationalstudies.villanova.edu/

CÓRDOBA

INTERNATIONAL HOUSE CÓRDOBA
IDIOMA Y CULTURA

Hosted by Academia Hispánica
Academic Focus • Cultural studies, Spanish language and literature, Spanish studies.
Program Information • Students attend classes at Academia Hispánica (Córdoba, Spain). Field trips to local historic and artistic sites, museums; optional travel to Seville, Granada at an extra cost.
Sessions • 2 week sessions, year-round.
Eligibility Requirements • Minimum age 17; open to precollege students, freshmen, sophomores, juniors, seniors, graduate students, adults.
Living Arrangements • Students live in locally rented apartments, host family homes, hotels. Meals are taken on one's own, with host family, in residences, in restaurants.
Costs (2006) • €500 for 2 weeks; includes tuition, excursions, books and class materials. €150 deposit required.
For More Information • International House Córdoba, Rodriguez Sánchez 15, 14003 Córdoba, Spain; *Phone:* +34 957-448 002; *Fax:* +34 957-448 119. *E-mail:* info@academiahispanica.com. *World Wide Web:* http://www.academiahispanica.com/

INTERNATIONAL HOUSE CÓRDOBA
INTENSIVE PLUS

Hosted by Academia Hispánica
Academic Focus • Cultural studies, Spanish language and literature, Spanish studies.
Program Information • Students attend classes at Academia Hispánica (Córdoba, Spain). Field trips to local historic and artistic sites, museums; optional travel at an extra cost.
Sessions • 1, 2 week sessions, year-round.
Eligibility Requirements • Minimum age 17; open to precollege students, freshmen, sophomores, juniors, seniors, graduate students, adults; no foreign language proficiency required.
Living Arrangements • Students live in locally rented apartments, host family homes, hotels, apartments. Meals are taken on one's own, with host family, in residences, in restaurants.
Costs (2006) • €465 for 1 week; (€445 for each additional week); includes tuition, books and class materials. €150 deposit required.
For More Information • International House Córdoba, Rodriguez Sánchez 15, 14003 Córdoba, Spain; *Phone:* +34 957-448 002; *Fax:* +34 957-488 119. *E-mail:* info@academiahispanica.com. *World Wide Web:* http://www.academiahispanica.com/

INTERNATIONAL HOUSE CÓRDOBA
INTENSIVE SPANISH CÓRDOBA

Hosted by Academia Hispánica
Academic Focus • Cultural studies, Spanish language and literature, Spanish studies.
Program Information • Students attend classes at Academia Hispánica (Córdoba, Spain). Field trips to local historic and artistic sites, museums; optional travel to Seville, Granada at an extra cost.
Sessions • 2 to 4 week sessions, year-round.
Eligibility Requirements • Minimum age 17; open to precollege students, freshmen, sophomores, juniors, seniors, graduate students, adults; no foreign language proficiency required.
Living Arrangements • Students live in locally rented apartments, host family homes, hotels, apartments. Meals are taken on one's own, with host family, in residences, in restaurants.

Costs (2006) • €290 for 2 weeks; €420 for 3 weeks; €538 for 4 weeks; includes tuition, excursions, books and class materials. €150 deposit required.
For More Information • International House Córdoba, Rodriguez Sánchez 15, 14003 Cordoba, Spain; *Phone:* +34 957-448 002; *Fax:* +34 957-488 119. *E-mail:* info@academiahispanica.com. *World Wide Web:* http://www.academiahispanica.com/

INTERNATIONAL HOUSE CÓRDOBA
PREPARACIÓN PARA DELE

Hosted by Academia Hispánica
Academic Focus • Cultural studies, Spanish language and literature, Spanish studies.
Program Information • Students attend classes at Academia Hispánica (Córdoba, Spain). Field trips to local historic and artistic sites, museums; optional travel to Seville, Granada at an extra cost.
Sessions • 5 weeks.
Eligibility Requirements • Minimum age 17; open to precollege students, freshmen, sophomores, seniors, graduate students, adults.
Living Arrangements • Students live in locally rented apartments, host family homes, hotels, apartments. Meals are taken on one's own, with host family, in residences, in restaurants.
Costs (2006) • €970 for 5 weeks; includes tuition, excursions, books and class materials. €150 deposit required.
For More Information • International House Córdoba, Rodriguez Sánchez 15, 14003 Córdoba, Spain; *Phone:* +34 957-448 002; *Fax:* +34 957-448 119. *E-mail:* info@academiahispanica.com. *World Wide Web:* http://www.academiahispanica.com/

LANGUAGE LINK
ACADEMIA HISPÁNICA (IH) OF CÓRDOBA, SPAIN

Hosted by Academia Hispánica
Academic Focus • Spanish language and literature.
Program Information • Students attend classes at Academia Hispánica (Córdoba, Spain). Field trips to Granada, Seville, local sites of interest. Students typically earn 6–15 semester credits per term.
Sessions • Year-round, start dates every other Monday for beginners.
Eligibility Requirements • Minimum age 14; open to precollege students, freshmen, sophomores, juniors, seniors, graduate students, adults; no foreign language proficiency required.
Living Arrangements • Students live in locally rented apartments, host family homes. Quarters are shared with host institution students. Meals are taken on one's own, with host family, in residences, in restaurants.
Costs (2005) • $359 per week; includes tuition, housing, some meals, books and class materials, student support services, cultural activities.
For More Information • Ms. Kay G. Rafool, Director, Language Link, PO Box 3006, Peoria, IL 61612-3006; *Phone:* 800-552-2051; *Fax:* 309-692-2926. *E-mail:* info@langlink.com. *World Wide Web:* http://www.langlink.com/

GRANADA

ACADEMIC PROGRAMS INTERNATIONAL (API)
(API)–GRANADA, SPAIN

Hosted by University of Granada
Academic Focus • Art history, civilization studies, history, international business, Latin American studies, Spanish language and literature, Spanish studies.
Program Information • Students attend classes at University of Granada (Granada, Spain). Scheduled travel to Madrid; field trips to Toledo, El Escorial, Córdoba, Sevilla, Madrid, Cabo de Gata, Las Alpujarras. Students typically earn 6 semester credits per term.
Sessions • May–Jul (summer), Jun–Jul (summer 2).
Eligibility Requirements • Minimum age 18; open to freshmen, sophomores, juniors, seniors, graduate students, adults; 2.75 GPA; 1 letter of recommendation; good academic standing at home school; official transcript from home university; 1 year of college course work in Spanish.

Living Arrangements • Students live in host institution dormitories, host family homes. Quarters are shared with host institution students. Meals are taken on one's own, with host family, in residences, in restaurants.

Costs (2006–2007) • $3700–$6700; includes tuition, all meals, insurance, excursions, student support services, airport pick-up, ground transportation, mobile phone, on-line services, on-site director; wireless access in API office. $150 nonrefundable deposit required. Financial aid available for all students: scholarships.

For More Information • Ms. Jennifer C. Allen, Director, Academic Programs International (API), 107 East Hopkins, San Marcos, TX 78666; *Phone:* 800-844-4124; *Fax:* 512-392-8420. *E-mail:* api@academicintl.com. *World Wide Web:* http://www.academicintl.com/

ALMA COLLEGE
SUMMER PROGRAM OF STUDIES IN GRANADA, SPAIN

Hosted by ENFOREX

Academic Focus • Cultural studies, Spanish language and literature.

Program Information • Students attend classes at ENFOREX (Granada, Spain). Field trips to local sites. Students typically earn 3–9 semester credits per term.

Sessions • Apr–Aug (4 to 14 weeks).

Eligibility Requirements • Minimum age 18; open to freshmen, sophomores, juniors, seniors, graduate students, adults; 2.5 GPA; 2 letters of recommendation; good academic standing at home school; no foreign language proficiency required.

Living Arrangements • Students live in locally rented apartments, host family homes. Quarters are shared with students from other programs. Meals are taken on one's own, with host family, in residences.

Costs (2005) • $3200–$7700; includes tuition, housing, all meals, insurance, excursions, books and class materials, international student ID, student support services, e-mail access, on-site orientation, airport pick-up. $50 application fee. $200 refundable deposit required.

For More Information • Ms. Julie Elenbaas, Office Associate, International Education, Alma College, 614 West Superior Street, Alma, MI 48801-1599; *Phone:* 989-463-7055; *Fax:* 989-463-7128. *E-mail:* intl_studies@alma.edu. *World Wide Web:* http://international.alma.edu/

AMERICAN INSTITUTE FOR FOREIGN STUDY (AIFS)
AIFS–GRANADA, SPAIN–UNIVERSITY OF GRANADA

Hosted by University of Granada

Academic Focus • Art history, geography, history, literature, sociology, Spanish language and literature.

Program Information • Students attend classes at University of Granada (Granada, Spain). Scheduled travel to 3 day London stopover; field trips to weekend in Seville and Cordoba, cultural activities, welcome party, Alhambra and Albaicin, Cathedral and Royal Chapel of Granada, Costa del Sol, poet Garcia Lorca's house, farewell party with Flamenco show; optional travel to 4-day optional tour of Spain including Madrid, Toledo, Segovia, El Escorial and Valley of the Fallen for a supplemental fee of $599 at an extra cost. Students typically earn 6–9 semester credits per term.

Sessions • May–Jun (summer), May–Jul.

Eligibility Requirements • Minimum age 17; open to precollege students, freshmen, sophomores, juniors, seniors; 2.0 GPA; no foreign language proficiency required.

Living Arrangements • Students live in host institution dormitories, program-owned apartments, host family homes, hotels. Quarters are shared with host institution students. Meals are taken as a group, in residences.

Costs (2007) • 4 weeks: $4139, 6 weeks: $5299; includes tuition, housing, some meals, insurance, excursions, student support services, On-site Resident Director, Phone Card to call the U.S., Computer Facilities/Internet. $95 application fee. $395 nonrefundable deposit required. Financial aid available for all students: scholarships.

For More Information • Mr. David Mauro, Admissions Advisor, American Institute For Foreign Study (AIFS), 9 West Broad Street, Stamford, CT 06902-3788; *Phone:* 800-727-2437 Ext. 5163; *Fax:* 203-399-5597. *E-mail:* dmauro@aifs.com. *World Wide Web:* http://www.aifsabroad.com/

ARCADIA UNIVERSITY
SUMMER IN GRANADA, SPAIN

Hosted by University of Granada

Academic Focus • Spanish language and literature, Spanish studies.

Program Information • Students attend classes at University of Granada (Granada, Spain). Field trips; optional travel. Students typically earn 3–6 semester credits per term.

Sessions • Jun–Jul (summer).

Eligibility Requirements • Open to sophomores, juniors, seniors; 3.0 GPA; 1 letter of recommendation; no foreign language proficiency required.

Living Arrangements • Students live in host family homes. Quarters are shared with host institution students. Meals are taken with host family, in residences.

Costs (2005) • Contact sponsor for cost. $35 application fee. $500 nonrefundable deposit required. Financial aid available for all students: scholarships, loans.

For More Information • Arcadia University, Center for Education Abroad, 450 South Easton Road, Glenside, PA 19038; *Phone:* 866-927-2234; *Fax:* 215-572-2174. *E-mail:* cea@arcadia.edu. *World Wide Web:* http://www.arcadia.edu/cea/

DON QUIJOTE
INTENSIVE SPANISH COURSE IN GRANADA

Hosted by Don Quijote

Academic Focus • Romance languages, Spanish language and literature, Spanish studies.

Program Information • Students attend classes at Don Quijote (Granada, Spain). Field trips to historic sites, important cities in Spain; optional travel to Morocco at an extra cost. Students typically earn 4 semester credits per term.

Sessions • Minimum 1 week sessions begin every Monday.

Eligibility Requirements • Minimum age 18; open to freshmen, sophomores, juniors, seniors, graduate students, adults; no foreign language proficiency required.

Living Arrangements • Students live in host institution dormitories, program-owned apartments, host family homes. Quarters are shared with host institution students, students from other programs. Meals are taken on one's own, with host family, in residences.

Costs (2006) • Contact sponsor for cost. €65 application fee. €500 deposit required. Financial aid available for all students: scholarships.

For More Information • Ms. Carmen Cantarino, USA Director, Don Quijote, Plaza San Marcos 7, 37002 Salamanca, Spain; *Phone:* +34 923-268874; *Fax:* +34 923-260674. *E-mail:* usa@donquijote.org. *World Wide Web:* http://www.donquijote.org/

DON QUIJOTE
INTENSIVE TOURISM

Hosted by Don Quijote

Academic Focus • Romance languages, Spanish language and literature, Spanish studies, tourism and travel.

Program Information • Students attend classes at Don Quijote (Granada, Spain). Field trips to historic sites, cultural attractions. Students typically earn 4 semester credits per term.

Sessions • 4 week courses start Jan, Apr, Oct.

Eligibility Requirements • Minimum age 18; open to freshmen, sophomores, juniors, seniors, graduate students, adults; intermediate Spanish.

Living Arrangements • Students live in host institution dormitories, program-owned apartments, host family homes. Quarters are shared with host institution students, students from other programs. Meals are taken on one's own, in residences.

Costs (2006) • €1001; includes tuition, books and class materials, lab equipment, student support services, guided cultural tour and welcome dinner, student discount card, level test, tutor, end-of-course certificate. €65 application fee. €500 nonrefundable deposit required. Financial aid available for all students: scholarships.

For More Information • Ms. Carmen Cantarino, USA Director, Don Quijote, Plaza San Marcos 7, 37002 Salamanca, Spain; *Phone:* +34 923-268874; *Fax:* +34 923-260674. *E-mail:* usa@donquijote.org. *World Wide Web:* http://www.donquijote.org/

SPAIN
Granada

ENFOREX–SPANISH IN THE SPANISH WORLD
SPANISH INTENSIVE COURSE GRANADA
Hosted by ENFOREX

Academic Focus • Dance, Spanish language and literature, Spanish studies, teaching.

Program Information • Students attend classes at ENFOREX (Granada, Spain). Field trips to Alhambra, Córdoba, Sierra Nevada; optional travel to Seville, Barcelona, Madrid, Salamanca at an extra cost. Students typically earn 4 semester credits per term.

Sessions • Year-round.

Eligibility Requirements • Minimum age 14; open to precollege students, freshmen, sophomores, juniors, seniors, graduate students, adults; no foreign language proficiency required.

Living Arrangements • Students live in host institution dormitories, locally rented apartments, program-owned apartments, host family homes, hotels. Quarters are shared with host institution students, students from other programs. Meals are taken as a group, on one's own, with host family, in residences.

Costs (2005) • €1080 per month; includes tuition, housing, all meals, excursions, books and class materials, international student ID, student support services. €65 application fee. €250 nonrefundable deposit required.

For More Information • Mr. Domenico Oppizzio, Marketing and Promotion, ENFOREX–Spanish in the Spanish World, Alberto Aguilera, 26, 28015 Madrid, Spain; *Phone:* +34 91-594-3776; *Fax:* +34 91-594-5159. *E-mail:* promotion@enforex.es. *World Wide Web:* http://www.enforex.com/

EUROPEAN HERITAGE INSTITUTE
YEAR-ROUND PROGRAMS IN GRANADA
Hosted by Don Quijote

Academic Focus • Business administration/management, commerce, Spanish language and literature, Spanish studies.

Program Information • Students attend classes at Don Quijote (Granada, Spain). Field trips to areas around Granada. Students typically earn 3–6 semester credits per term.

Sessions • 1 to 15 week sessions begin weekly, year-round.

Eligibility Requirements • Minimum age 18; open to freshmen, sophomores, juniors, seniors, graduate students, adults; 2.25 GPA; 2 letters of recommendation; no foreign language proficiency required.

Living Arrangements • Students live in host institution dormitories, locally rented apartments, host family homes, residence center. Quarters are shared with students from other programs. Meals are taken on one's own, with host family, in residences, in restaurants.

Costs (2005) • $1581 for 4 weeks; $2958 for 8 weeks; $4732 for 12 weeks; includes tuition, housing, some meals, excursions, books and class materials, student support services. $300 refundable deposit required.

For More Information • Dr. Antonio Masullo, Professor, European Heritage Institute, 2708 East Franklin Street, Richmond, VA 23223; *Phone:* 804-643-0661; *Fax:* 804-648-0826. *E-mail:* info@europeabroad. org. *World Wide Web:* http://www.europeabroad.org/

INTERNATIONAL STUDIES ABROAD
GRANADA, SPAIN–INTENSIVE SPANISH LANGUAGE MONTH
Hosted by University of Granada

Academic Focus • Civilization studies, Spanish language and literature.

Program Information • Students attend classes at University of Granada (Granada, Spain). Optional travel to Madrid, Toledo at an extra cost. Students typically earn 5 semester credits per term.

Sessions • Jan, Feb, Mar, Apr, May, Sep, Oct, Nov.

Eligibility Requirements • Minimum age 18; open to freshmen, sophomores, juniors, seniors, graduate students, adults; 2.5 GPA; good academic standing at home school; transcripts; no foreign language proficiency required.

Living Arrangements • Students live in host family homes, hotels. Quarters are shared with host institution students, students from other programs. Meals are taken with host family, in residences.

Costs (2005–2006) • Contact sponsor for cost. $200 deposit required. Financial aid available for all students: scholarships, loans, U.S. federal financial aid.

For More Information • Spain Site Specialist, International Studies Abroad, 901 West 24th Street, Austin, TX 78705; *Phone:* 800-580-8826; *Fax:* 512-480-8866. *E-mail:* isa@studiesabroad.com. *World Wide Web:* http://www.studiesabroad.com/

INTERNATIONAL STUDIES ABROAD
GRANADA, SPAIN–SUMMER SESSIONS, INTENSIVE SPANISH LANGUAGE
Hosted by University of Granada

Academic Focus • Civilization studies, Spanish language and literature.

Program Information • Students attend classes at University of Granada (Granada, Spain). Scheduled travel to Madrid; field trips to Córdoba, El Escorial, Sevilla, Cabo de Gata or Nerja; optional travel at an extra cost. Students typically earn 5–6 semester credits per term.

Sessions • Jun (summer), Jul–Jul (summer 2), Aug–Aug (summer 3).

Eligibility Requirements • Minimum age 18; open to freshmen, sophomores, juniors, seniors, graduate students, adults; 2.5 GPA; good academic standing at home school; transcripts; no foreign language proficiency required.

Living Arrangements • Students live in host family homes, hotels. Quarters are shared with host institution students. Meals are taken with host family, in residences.

Costs (2006) • $3350; includes tuition, housing, all meals, insurance, excursions, books and class materials, student support services, tutors, ground transportation, laundry, Internet access. $200 deposit required. Financial aid available for all students: scholarships, loans, U.S. federal financial aid.

For More Information • Spain Site Specialist, International Studies Abroad, 901 West 24th Street, Austin, TX 78705; *Phone:* 800-580-8826; *Fax:* 512-480-8866. *E-mail:* isa@studiesabroad.com. *World Wide Web:* http://www.studiesabroad.com/

LANGUAGE LIAISON
LEARN SPANISH IN GRANADA
Hosted by Language Liaison

Academic Focus • Spanish language and literature.

Program Information • Students attend classes at Language Liaison (Granada, Spain). Field trips; optional travel at an extra cost. Students typically earn 3–15 semester credits per term.

Sessions • New programs begin weekly, year-round.

Eligibility Requirements • Minimum age 16; open to precollege students, freshmen, sophomores, juniors, seniors, graduate students, adults; no foreign language proficiency required.

Living Arrangements • Students live in host family homes, hotels. Meals are taken on one's own, with host family, in residences, in restaurants.

Costs (2005) • Contact sponsor for cost. $175 application fee. Financial aid available for all students: scholarship research service.

For More Information • Ms. Nancy Forman, President, Language Liaison, PO Box 1772, Pacific Palisades, CA 90272; *Phone:* 800-284-4448; *Fax:* 310-454-1706. *E-mail:* learn@languageliaison. com. *World Wide Web:* http://www.languageliaison.com/

LINGUA SERVICE WORLDWIDE
VACATION 'N LEARN SPANISH IN SPAIN
Hosted by Don Quijote

Academic Focus • Spanish language and literature, Spanish studies.

Program Information • Students attend classes at Don Quijote (Granada, Spain). Optional travel to cultural sites around Spain at an extra cost. Students typically earn 3 semester credits for 3 weeks, 6 semester credits for 5 weeks.

Sessions • Classes held year-round, beginning on Mondays, minimum session length is 2 weeks.

Eligibility Requirements • Minimum age 16; open to precollege students, freshmen, sophomores, juniors, seniors, graduate students, adults; no foreign language proficiency required.

Living Arrangements • Students live in host institution dormitories, locally rented apartments, host family homes, hotels. Quarters are shared with host institution students. Meals are taken with host family.

Costs (2006–2007) • Contact sponsor for cost. $100 application fee.

For More Information • Assistant Director, Lingua Service Worldwide, 75 Prospect Street, Suite 4, Huntington, NY 11743; *Phone:* 800-394-5327; *Fax:* 631-271-3441. *E-mail:* linguaservice@att.net. *World Wide Web:* http://www.linguaserviceworldwide.com/

NORTHERN ARIZONA UNIVERSITY
SUMMER STUDY ABROAD IN SPAIN

Hosted by University of Granada
Academic Focus • Spanish studies.
Program Information • Students attend classes at University of Granada (Granada, Spain). Field trips to Córdoba, Las Alpujarras. Students typically earn 7 semester credits per term.
Sessions • Jun (summer).
Eligibility Requirements • Open to freshmen, sophomores, juniors, seniors, adults; 2.5 GPA; 2 letters of recommendation; good academic standing at home school; minimum 2.75 GPA in Spanish; 1 year of college course work in Spanish.
Living Arrangements • Students live in host family homes. Quarters are shared with host institution students. Meals are taken with host family, in residences.
Costs (2005) • $2975; includes tuition, housing, all meals, excursions, international student ID, student support services, airport pick-up in Madrid. $125 application fee. Financial aid available for all students: scholarships, loans.
For More Information • International Office, Northern Arizona University, NAU Box 5598, Flagstaff, AZ 86011-5598; *Phone:* 928-523-2409; *Fax:* 928-523-9489. *E-mail:* international.office@nau.edu. *World Wide Web:* http://internationaloffice.nau.edu/

SEVEN CONTINENTS' EXCHANGE PROGRAMS
SEVEN CONTINENTS' EXCHANGE PROGRAMS AT THE UNIVERSITY OF GRANADA, SPAIN

Hosted by University of Granada
Academic Focus • Bilingual education, culinary arts, dance, music, Spanish language and literature, Spanish studies.
Program Information • Students attend classes at University of Granada (Granada, Spain). Scheduled travel to Córdoba, Montilla, Seville, Jerez; field trips to the coast, mountains, historic monuments in Andalucia, bullfights, wine and cuisine tours; optional travel to Morocco, Portugal, other destinations in Spain at an extra cost. Students typically earn 8–20 semester credits per term.
Sessions • May–Sep (programs begin monthly).
Eligibility Requirements • Minimum age 16; open to precollege students, freshmen, sophomores, juniors, seniors, graduate students, adults; no foreign language proficiency required.
Living Arrangements • Students live in locally rented apartments, host family homes. Meals are taken on one's own, with host family, in restaurants.
Costs (2005) • $2475 for 1 month; includes tuition, housing, all meals, excursions, lab equipment, student support services, travel and lodging for excursions, certificates. $250 nonrefundable deposit required. Financial aid available for all students: scholarships.
For More Information • Mr. Domenico M. Vene, President, Seven Continents' Exchange Programs, 671 East Beverwyck, Suite 1, Paramus, NJ 07653-8163; *Phone:* 201-444-8687; *Fax:* 201-444-8687. *E-mail:* info@mediterranean-heritage.org. *World Wide Web:* http://www.mediterranean-heritage.org/7continents/. Students may also apply through Mediterranean World Heritage Association, Bruselas 11, 3G, 18008 Granada, Spain.

UNIVERSITY OF DELAWARE
SUMMER SESSION IN GRANADA, SPAIN

Hosted by University of Granada
Academic Focus • Music, Spanish language and literature, Spanish studies.
Program Information • Students attend classes at University of Granada (Granada, Spain). Scheduled travel to Madrid; field trips to Segovia, Córdoba, Toledo, Seville, Costa del Sol; optional travel to Europe at an extra cost. Students typically earn 6 semester credits per term.
Sessions • May–Jul (summer).

Eligibility Requirements • Open to freshmen, sophomores, juniors, seniors, adults; 2.0 GPA; 1 letter of recommendation; no foreign language proficiency required.
Living Arrangements • Students live in host family homes. Quarters are shared with host institution students. Meals are taken with host family, in residences.
Costs (2005) • Contact sponsor for cost. $200 nonrefundable deposit required. Financial aid available for all students: scholarships.
For More Information • Center for International Studies, University of Delaware, 186 South College Avenue, Newark, DE 19716-1450; *Phone:* 888-831-4685; *Fax:* 302-831-6042. *E-mail:* studyabroad@udel.edu. *World Wide Web:* http://www.udel.edu/studyabroad/

UNIVERSITY OF DELAWARE
WINTER SESSION IN GRANADA, SPAIN

Hosted by University of Granada
Academic Focus • Spanish language and literature, Spanish studies.
Program Information • Students attend classes at University of Granada (Granada, Spain). Scheduled travel to Madrid; field trips to Córdoba, Alhambra, Seville, Cartuja Monastery, Toledo, Segovia; optional travel to Europe at an extra cost. Students typically earn 6–7 semester credits per term.
Sessions • Jan–Feb (winter).
Eligibility Requirements • Open to freshmen, sophomores, juniors, seniors, adults; 2.0 GPA; 1 letter of recommendation; 1 year of college course work in Spanish.
Living Arrangements • Students live in host family homes. Quarters are shared with host institution students. Meals are taken with host family, in residences.
Costs (2005) • Contact sponsor for cost. $200 nonrefundable deposit required. Financial aid available for all students: scholarships.
For More Information • Center for International Studies, University of Delaware, 186 South College Avenue, Newark, DE 19716-1450; *Phone:* 888-831-4685; *Fax:* 302-831-6042. *E-mail:* studyabroad@udel.edu. *World Wide Web:* http://www.udel.edu/studyabroad/

LAS PALMAS DE GRAN CANARIA

LINGUA SERVICE WORLDWIDE
VACATION 'N LEARN SPANISH IN SPAIN

Hosted by Gran Canaria School of Languages
Academic Focus • Spanish language and literature, Spanish studies.
Program Information • Students attend classes at Gran Canaria School of Languages (Las Palmas, Spain). Optional travel to cultural sites around Spain at an extra cost. Students typically earn 3 semester credits for 3 weeks, 6 semester credits for 5 weeks.
Sessions • Classes held year-round, beginning on Mondays; minimum session length is 2 weeks.
Eligibility Requirements • Minimum age 16; open to precollege students, freshmen, sophomores, juniors, seniors, graduate students, adults; no foreign language proficiency required.
Living Arrangements • Students live in host institution dormitories, locally rented apartments, host family homes, hotels. Quarters are shared with host institution students. Meals are taken with host family.
Costs (2006–2007) • Contact sponsor for cost. $100 application fee.
For More Information • Assistant Director, Lingua Service Worldwide, 75 Prospect Street, Suite 4, Huntington, NY 11743; *Phone:* 800-394-5327; *Fax:* 631-271-3441. *E-mail:* linguaservice@att.net. *World Wide Web:* http://www.linguaserviceworldwide.com/

MADRID

ACADEMIC PROGRAMS INTERNATIONAL (API)
(API)–ANTONIO DE NEBRIJA UNIVERSITY, MADRID, SPAIN

Hosted by Antonio de Nebrija University

SPAIN
Madrid

Academic Focus • Cultural studies, political science and government, social sciences, Spanish language and literature, Spanish studies.

Program Information • Students attend classes at Antonio de Nebrija University (Madrid, Spain). Field trips to El Escorial, Madrid, Salamanca, Segovia, Toledo, Barcelona. Students typically earn 6 semester credits per term.

Sessions • Jun-Jul (summer).

Eligibility Requirements • Minimum age 18; open to freshmen, sophomores, juniors, seniors, graduate students, adults; 2.75 GPA; 1 letter of recommendation; good academic standing at home school; official transcript from home university; no foreign language proficiency required.

Living Arrangements • Students live in host institution dormitories, host family homes. Quarters are shared with host institution students, students from other programs. Meals are taken on one's own, with host family, in residences, in restaurants.

Costs (2006–2007) • $3850-$3900; includes tuition, housing, all meals, insurance, excursions, student support services, airport pick-up, ground transportation, mobile phone, on-line services, on-site director; wireless access in API office. $150 nonrefundable deposit required. Financial aid available for all students: scholarships.

For More Information • Ms. Jennifer C. Allen, Director, Academic Programs International (API), 107 East Hopkins, San Marcos, TX 78666; *Phone:* 800-844-4124; *Fax:* 512-392-8420. *E-mail:* api@academicintl.com. *World Wide Web:* http://www.academicintl.com/

ACADEMIC STUDIES ABROAD
ACADEMIC STUDIES ABROAD–MADRID, SPAIN

Hosted by Complutense University of Madrid

Academic Focus • Spanish language and literature, Spanish studies.

Program Information • Students attend classes at Complutense University of Madrid (Madrid, Spain). Scheduled travel to Barcelona, Seville; field trips to Avila, Toledo. Students typically earn 6 semester credits per term.

Sessions • Jun-Jul (summer).

Eligibility Requirements • Minimum age 18; open to freshmen, sophomores, juniors, seniors; 2.5 GPA; college transcript; no foreign language proficiency required.

Living Arrangements • Students live in host family homes. Quarters are shared with host institution students. Meals are taken with host family, in residences.

Costs (2006) • $3695; includes tuition, housing, all meals, insurance, excursions, international student ID, student support services, cell phone, laundry. $150 refundable deposit required. Financial aid available for all students: scholarships.

For More Information • Mr. Lee Frankel, Director, Academic Studies Abroad, 434 Massachusetts Avenue, Suite 501, Boston, MA 02118; *Phone:* 617-437-9388; *Fax:* 617-437-9390. *E-mail:* lee@academicstudies.com. *World Wide Web:* http://www.academicstudies.com

ACCENT INTERNATIONAL CONSORTIUM FOR ACADEMIC PROGRAMS ABROAD
SUMMER IN MADRID

Hosted by Don Quijote

Academic Focus • Art history, Spanish language and literature, Spanish studies.

Program Information • Students attend classes at Don Quijote (Madrid, Spain). Field trips to Segovia, La Granja, Avila. Students typically earn 6 semester credits per term.

Sessions • Jun-Jul (summer).

Eligibility Requirements • Minimum age 18; open to freshmen, sophomores, juniors, seniors, graduate students, adults; no foreign language proficiency required.

Living Arrangements • Students live in locally rented apartments, host family homes. Quarters are shared with host institution students, students from other programs. Meals are taken on one's own, in residences.

Costs (2005) • $3200; includes tuition, housing, excursions, international student ID, student support services. $250 nonrefundable deposit required.

For More Information • ACCENT International Consortium for Academic Programs Abroad, 870 Market Street, Suite 1026, San Francisco, CA 94102; *Phone:* 415-835-3744; *Fax:* 415-835-3749. *E-mail:* info@accentintl.com. *World Wide Web:* http://www.accentintl.com/

ALMA COLLEGE
SUMMER PROGRAM OF STUDIES IN MADRID, SPAIN

Hosted by ENFOREX

Academic Focus • Cultural studies, Spanish language and literature.

Program Information • Students attend classes at ENFOREX (Madrid, Spain). Field trips to sites around Madrid. Students typically earn 3-9 semester credits per term.

Sessions • Apr-Aug (4 to 14 weeks).

Eligibility Requirements • Minimum age 18; open to freshmen, sophomores, juniors, seniors, graduate students, adults; 2.5 GPA; 2 letters of recommendation; good academic standing at home school; no foreign language proficiency required.

Living Arrangements • Students live in locally rented apartments, host family homes. Quarters are shared with students from other programs. Meals are taken on one's own, with host family, in residences.

Costs (2005) • $3200-$7700; includes tuition, housing, all meals, insurance, excursions, books and class materials, international student ID, student support services, Metro pass; e-mail access; on-site orientation; telephone card, airport pick-up; Forocio membership. $50 application fee. $200 refundable deposit required.

For More Information • Ms. Julie Elenbaas, Office Associate, International Education, Alma College, 614 West Superior Street, Alma, MI 48801-1599; *Phone:* 989-463-7055; *Fax:* 989-463-7126. *E-mail:* intl_studies@alma.edu. *World Wide Web:* http://international.alma.edu/

BOSTON UNIVERSITY
MADRID INTERNSHIP PROGRAM

Held at Instituto Internacional en España

Academic Focus • Spanish language and literature, Spanish studies.

Program Information • Classes are held on the campus of Instituto Internacional en España (Madrid, Spain). Faculty members are drawn from the sponsor's U.S. staff and local instructors hired by the sponsor. Scheduled travel to Granada, Córdoba; field trips to Toledo, Segovia. Students typically earn 8 semester credits per term.

Sessions • May-Jul (summer).

Eligibility Requirements • Open to sophomores, juniors, seniors, graduate students, adults; 1 letter of recommendation; good academic standing at home school; essay; writing sample in Spanish; approval of participation; minimum GPA of 3.0 in major and overall; 2.5 years of college course work in Spanish.

Living Arrangements • Students live in host family homes. Meals are taken on one's own, with host family, in residences, in restaurants.

Costs (2005) • $6000; includes tuition, housing, all meals, insurance, excursions, internship placement, limited reimbursements for cultural activities. $50 application fee. $400 nonrefundable deposit required. Financial aid available for all students: scholarships, loans.

For More Information • Division of International Programs, Boston University, 232 Bay State Road, Boston, MA 02215; *Phone:* 617-353-9888; *Fax:* 617-353-5402. *E-mail:* abroad@bu.edu. *World Wide Web:* http://www.bu.edu/abroad/

BOSTON UNIVERSITY
MADRID LANGUAGE AND LIBERAL ARTS PROGRAM

Held at Instituto Internacional en España

Academic Focus • Liberal studies, social sciences, Spanish language and literature, Spanish studies.

Program Information • Classes are held on the campus of Instituto Internacional en España (Madrid, Spain). Faculty members are drawn from the sponsor's U.S. staff and local instructors hired by the sponsor. Scheduled travel to Granada, Córdoba; field trips to Toledo, Segovia. Students typically earn 8 semester credits per term.

Sessions • May-Jul (summer).

Eligibility Requirements • Open to freshmen, sophomores, juniors, seniors, graduate students, adults; 3.0 GPA; 1 letter of recommenda-

SPAIN
Madrid

tion; good academic standing at home school; essay; writing sample in Spanish; approval of participation; transcript; 1 year of college course work in Spanish.

Living Arrangements • Students live in host family homes. Meals are taken on one's own, with host family, in residences.

Costs (2005) • $6000; includes tuition, housing, all meals, insurance, excursions, limited reimbursements for cultural activities. $50 application fee. $400 nonrefundable deposit required. Financial aid available for all students: scholarships, loans.

For More Information • Division of International Programs, Boston University, 232 Bay State Road, Boston, MA 02215; *Phone:* 617-353-9888; *Fax:* 617-353-5402. *E-mail:* abroad@bu.edu. *World Wide Web:* http://www.bu.edu/abroad/

CENTER FOR INTERNATIONAL STUDIES
SUMMER STUDY IN MADRID, SPAIN

Hosted by Suffolk University–Madrid Campus

Academic Focus • Full curriculum.

Program Information • Students attend classes at Suffolk University–Madrid Campus (Madrid, Spain). Scheduled travel to Paris; field trips to Barcelona, Seville, Toledo. Students typically earn 6 semester credits per term.

Sessions • May–Jul (summer).

Eligibility Requirements • Minimum age 18; open to freshmen, sophomores, juniors, seniors, graduate students, adults; 2.5 GPA; 1 letter of recommendation; good academic standing at home school; personal statement; no foreign language proficiency required.

Living Arrangements • Students live in host institution dormitories, program-owned apartments, host family homes. Quarters are shared with host institution students. Meals are taken on one's own, in residences, in restaurants.

Costs (2005) • $4850; includes tuition, housing, some meals, insurance, excursions, international student ID, student support services, airport reception. $50 application fee. $500 nonrefundable deposit required. Financial aid available for all students: scholarships.

For More Information • Mr. Jeff Palm, Program Director, Center for International Studies, 25 New South Street, #105, Northampton, MA 01060; *Phone:* 413-582-0407; *Fax:* 413-582-0327. *E-mail:* jpalm@cisabroad.com. *World Wide Web:* http://www.cisabroad.com/

CENTER FOR STUDY ABROAD (CSA)
UNIVERSITY COMPLUTENSE MADRID (SPAIN)

Hosted by Complutense University of Madrid

Academic Focus • Spanish language and literature, Spanish studies.

Program Information • Students attend classes at Complutense University of Madrid (Madrid, Spain). Optional travel. Students typically earn 3–4 semester credits per term.

Sessions • Summer.

Eligibility Requirements • Minimum age 17; open to precollege students, freshmen, sophomores, juniors, seniors, graduate students, adults; no foreign language proficiency required.

Living Arrangements • Quarters are shared with students from other programs. Meals are taken on one's own, in central dining facility, in restaurants.

Costs (2005–2006) • Contact sponsor for cost. $45 application fee.

For More Information • Ms. Alima K. Virtue, Program Director, Center for Study Abroad (CSA), 325 Washington Avenue South #93, Kent, WA 98032; *Phone:* 206-726-1498; *Fax:* 253-850-0454. *E-mail:* info@centerforstudyabroad.com. *World Wide Web:* http://www.centerforstudyabroad.com/

DON QUIJOTE
INTENSIVE BUSINESS–MADRID

Hosted by Don Quijote

Academic Focus • International business, Romance languages, Spanish language and literature, Spanish studies.

Program Information • Students attend classes at Don Quijote (Madrid, Spain). Field trips to historic sites, cultural attractions. Students typically earn 4 semester credits per term.

Sessions • 4 week courses start every Monday.

Eligibility Requirements • Minimum age 18; open to freshmen, sophomores, juniors, seniors, graduate students, adults; intermediate Spanish.

Living Arrangements • Students live in host institution dormitories, host family homes. Quarters are shared with host institution students, students from other programs. Meals are taken on one's own, in residences.

Costs (2006) • €1001; includes tuition, books and class materials, lab equipment, student support services, guided cultural tour; welcome dinner, student discount card, level test, tutor, end-of-course certificate. €65 application fee. €500 nonrefundable deposit required. Financial aid available for all students: scholarships.

For More Information • Ms. Carmen Cantarino, USA Director, Don Quijote, Plaza San Marcos 7, 37002 Salamanca, Spain; *Phone:* +34 923-268874; *Fax:* +34 923-260674. *E-mail:* usa@donquijote.org. *World Wide Web:* http://www.donquijote.org/

DON QUIJOTE
INTENSIVE SPANISH COURSE IN MADRID

Hosted by Don Quijote

Academic Focus • Romance languages, Spanish language and literature, Spanish studies.

Program Information • Students attend classes at Don Quijote (Madrid, Spain). Field trips to historic sites, important cities in Spain. Students typically earn 4 semester credits per term.

Sessions • Minimum 1 week sessions begin every Monday.

Eligibility Requirements • Minimum age 18; open to freshmen, sophomores, juniors, seniors, graduate students, adults; no foreign language proficiency required.

Living Arrangements • Students live in host institution dormitories, program-owned apartments, host family homes. Quarters are shared with host institution students, students from other programs. Meals are taken on one's own, with host family, in residences.

Costs (2006) • Contact sponsor for cost. €65 application fee. €500 deposit required. Financial aid available for all students: scholarships.

For More Information • Ms. Carmen Cantarino, USA Director, Don Quijote, Plaza San Marcos 7, 37002 Salamanca, Spain; *Phone:* +34 923-268874; *Fax:* +34 923-260674. *E-mail:* usa@donquijote.org. *World Wide Web:* http://www.donquijote.org/

ENFOREX–SPANISH IN THE SPANISH WORLD
SPANISH INTENSIVE COURSE MADRID

Hosted by ENFOREX

Academic Focus • Dance, Spanish language and literature, Spanish studies, teaching.

Program Information • Students attend classes at ENFOREX (Madrid, Spain). Field trips to El Prado, El Escorial, Salamanca; optional travel to Seville, Barcelona, Salamanca at an extra cost. Students typically earn 4 quarter credits per term.

Sessions • Year-round.

Eligibility Requirements • Minimum age 14; open to precollege students, freshmen, sophomores, juniors, seniors, graduate students, adults; no foreign language proficiency required.

Living Arrangements • Students live in host institution dormitories, program-owned apartments, host family homes, hotels. Quarters are shared with host institution students, students from other programs. Meals are taken as a group, on one's own, with host family, in residences.

Costs (2005) • €1280 per month; includes tuition, housing, all meals, excursions, books and class materials, international student ID, student support services. €65 application fee. €250 nonrefundable deposit required.

For More Information • Mr. Domenico Oppizzio, Marketing and Promotion, ENFOREX–Spanish in the Spanish World, Alberto Aguilera, 26, 28015 Madrid, Spain; *Phone:* +34 91-594-3776; *Fax:* +34 91-594-5159. *E-mail:* promotion@enforex.es. *World Wide Web:* http://www.enforex.com/

SPAIN
Madrid

ESCUELA INTERNACIONAL
INTENSIVE SPANISH LANGUAGE AND CULTURE–ALCALÁ DE HENARES

Hosted by Escuela Internacional
Academic Focus • Spanish language and literature, Spanish studies.
Program Information • Students attend classes at Escuela Internacional (Alcalá de Henares, Spain). Field trips to El Prado, Palacio Real, Segovia, Toledo, El Escorial, Avila; optional travel to Seville, Granada, Córdoba, Barcelona at an extra cost. Students typically earn 4 semester credits for 4 weeks.
Sessions • 2 to 32 week durations begin every Monday.
Eligibility Requirements • Minimum age 17; open to precollege students, freshmen, sophomores, juniors, seniors, graduate students, adults; no foreign language proficiency required.
Living Arrangements • Students live in locally rented apartments, host family homes, hotels. Quarters are shared with host institution students. Meals are taken on one's own, with host family, in residences, in restaurants.
Costs (2005) • €1029 for 4 weeks; includes tuition, housing, all meals, excursions, books and class materials, student support services, all activities. €65 application fee.
For More Information • Ms. Midori Ishizaka, Director of Marketing, Escuela Internacional, C/Talamanca, 10, 28807 Alcalá de Henares (Madrid), Spain; *Phone:* +34 91-883-1264; *Fax:* +34 91-883-1301. *E-mail:* info@escuelai.com. *World Wide Web:* http://www.escuelai.com/

ESCUELA INTERNACIONAL
SPANISH LANGUAGE–ALCALÁ DE HENARES

Hosted by Escuela Internacional
Academic Focus • Spanish language and literature, Spanish studies.
Program Information • Students attend classes at Escuela Internacional (Alcalá de Henares, Spain). Field trips to Madrid, El Prado, Palacio Real, Segovia, Toledo, El Escorial, Avila; optional travel to Seville, Granada, Córdoba, Barcelona at an extra cost. Students typically earn 5 quarter credits for 4 weeks.
Sessions • 2 to 32 week durations begin every Monday.
Eligibility Requirements • Minimum age 17; open to precollege students, freshmen, sophomores, juniors, seniors, graduate students, adults; no foreign language proficiency required.
Living Arrangements • Students live in locally rented apartments, host family homes, hotels. Quarters are shared with host institution students. Meals are taken on one's own, with host family, in residences, in restaurants.
Costs (2005) • €1029 for 4 weeks; includes tuition, housing, all meals, excursions, books and class materials, student support services, all activities. €65 application fee.
For More Information • Ms. Midori Ishizaka, Director of Marketing, Escuela Internacional, C/Talamanca, 10, 28807 Alcalá de Henares (Madrid), Spain; *Phone:* +34 91-883-1264; *Fax:* +34 91-883-1301. *E-mail:* info@escuelai.com. *World Wide Web:* http://www.escuelai.com/

ESTUDIA FUERA
STUDY ABROAD PROGRAMS

Hosted by Antonio de Nebrija University, College for International Studies, University Camilo José Cela, University Francisco de Vitoria
Academic Focus • Full curriculum.
Program Information • Students attend classes at Antonio de Nebrija University (Madrid, Spain), College for International Studies (Madrid, Spain), University Camilo José Cela (Madrid, Spain), University Francisco de Vitoria (Madrid, Spain). Optional travel to Ibiza, Sevilla, Cadiz, Toledo, Barcelona, Alicante, Paris, London at an extra cost. Students typically earn 3–6 semester credits per term.
Sessions • 13 to 26 weeks.
Eligibility Requirements • Minimum age 16; open to precollege students, freshmen, sophomores, juniors, seniors, graduate students, adults; no foreign language proficiency required.
Living Arrangements • Students live in host institution dormitories, locally rented apartments, program-owned apartments, host family homes, hotels. Quarters are shared with host institution students, students from other programs. Meals are taken with host family.

Costs (2005–2006) • $6005–$9445; includes tuition, housing, all meals, books and class materials, lab equipment, student support services, cultural activities. $100 application fee.
For More Information • Academic Counsellor, Estudia Fuera, Calle Fernandez de la Hoz 53, Estudio 1, Madrid 28003, Spain; *Phone:* +34 91-308-3112; *Fax:* +34 91-319-2130. *E-mail:* info@estudiafuera.com. *World Wide Web:* http://www.estudiafuera.com/

EUROPEAN HERITAGE INSTITUTE
YEAR-ROUND PROGRAMS IN MADRID

Hosted by Don Quijote
Academic Focus • Business administration/management, commerce, Spanish language and literature, Spanish studies.
Program Information • Students attend classes at Don Quijote (Madrid, Spain). Field trips to sites around Madrid. Students typically earn 3–6 semester credits per term.
Sessions • 1 to 15 week sessions begin every Monday, year-round; 12 week internships held monthly.
Eligibility Requirements • Minimum age 18; open to freshmen, sophomores, juniors, seniors, graduate students, adults; 2.25 GPA; 2 letters of recommendation; no foreign language proficiency required.
Living Arrangements • Students live in host institution dormitories, locally rented apartments, host family homes, hotels, a residence center. Quarters are shared with host institution students. Meals are taken on one's own, with host family, in restaurants.
Costs (2005) • $1800 for 4 weeks; $3200 for 8 weeks; $4732 for 12 weeks; includes tuition, housing, some meals, excursions, books and class materials, student support services. $300 refundable deposit required. Financial aid available for students from sponsoring institution: scholarships, loans.
For More Information • Dr. Antonio Masullo, Professor, European Heritage Institute, 2708 East Franklin Street, Richmond, VA 23223; *Phone:* 804-643-0661; *Fax:* 804-648-0826. *E-mail:* info@europeabroad.org. *World Wide Web:* http://www.europeabroad.org/

INTERNATIONAL HOUSE MADRID
INTENSIVE SPANISH COURSE

Hosted by International House Madrid
Academic Focus • Spanish language and literature.
Program Information • Students attend classes at International House Madrid (Madrid, Spain). Scheduled travel to Barcelona, Seville, Pamplona; field trips to El Escorial, Toledo, Segovia, Avila, Chinchon, Salamanca, El Prado and Reina Sofia museums, Barcelona, Seville; optional travel to Granada, Córdoba, Sevilla, San Sebastián, Barcelona, Valencia at an extra cost. Students typically earn 3 semester credits for 3 weeks.
Sessions • 2 to 12 week sessions, year-round.
Eligibility Requirements • Minimum age 16; open to precollege students, freshmen, sophomores, juniors, seniors, graduate students, adults; no foreign language proficiency required.
Living Arrangements • Students live in host institution dormitories, locally rented apartments, program-owned apartments, host family homes, hotels. Quarters are shared with host institution students, students from other programs. Meals are taken as a group, on one's own, with host family, in residences, in central dining facility, in restaurants.
Costs (2003–2004) • €350 for 2 weeks; includes tuition, housing, some meals, excursions, books and class materials, international student ID, student support services, welcome and farewell party. €180 refundable deposit required. Financial aid available for students: scholarships.
For More Information • Ms. Carmen Traver, Commercial Coordinator, International House Madrid, Zurbano, 8, 28010 Madrid, Spain; *Phone:* +34 91-3197224; *Fax:* +34 91-3085321. *E-mail:* ctraver@ihmadrid.com. *World Wide Web:* http://www.ihmadrid.com/

INTERNATIONAL HOUSE MADRID
SPANISH, CULTURE, AND BUSINESS (SCB)

Hosted by International House Madrid
Academic Focus • Business administration/management, Spanish language and literature, Spanish studies, tourism and travel.

Program Information • Students attend classes at International House Madrid (Madrid, Spain). Scheduled travel to Andalucía; field trips to Toledo, Segovia. Students typically earn 3 semester credits for 3 weeks.
Sessions • Year-round.
Eligibility Requirements • Minimum age 18; open to seniors, graduate students, adults; fluency in Spanish.
Living Arrangements • Students live in host institution dormitories, locally rented apartments, host family homes. Meals are taken as a group, on one's own, with host family, in residences, in central dining facility, in restaurants.
Costs (2003–2004) • €2465 for 12 weeks; includes tuition, books and class materials, student support services. €200 deposit required. Financial aid available for all students: scholarships.
For More Information • Ms. Helena Mazo, Director, Spanish Department, International House Madrid, Zurbano, 8, 28010 Madrid, Spain; *Phone:* +34 91-3197224; *Fax:* +34 91-3085321. *E-mail:* hmazo@ihmadrid.com. *World Wide Web:* http://www.ihmadrid.com/

INTERNATIONAL STUDIES ABROAD
MADRID, SPAIN–SPANISH LANGUAGE AND CULTURE
Hosted by Complutense University of Madrid
Academic Focus • Art, history, international business, music, Spanish language and literature, Spanish studies.
Program Information • Students attend classes at Complutense University of Madrid (Madrid, Spain). Field trips to Granada, Toledo, El Escorial, Valencia. Students typically earn 6–7 semester credits per term.
Sessions • Jun-Jul (summer).
Eligibility Requirements • Minimum age 18; open to freshmen, sophomores, juniors, seniors, adults; 2.5 GPA; good academic standing at home school; contact sponsor if GPA is under 2.5; no foreign language proficiency required.
Living Arrangements • Students live in host family homes. Quarters are shared with host institution students. Meals are taken with host family, in residences.
Costs (2005–2006) • Contact sponsor for cost. $200 deposit required.
For More Information • Spain Site Specialist, International Studies Abroad, 901 West 24th Street, Austin, TX 78705; *Phone:* 800-580-8826; *Fax:* 512-480-8866. *E-mail:* isa@studiesabroad.com. *World Wide Web:* http://www.studiesabroad.com/

INTERNATIONAL STUDIES ABROAD
MADRID, SPAIN–SPANISH LANGUAGE AND ELECTIVES
Hosted by Antonio de Nebrija University
Academic Focus • Art history, Spanish language and literature, Spanish studies.
Program Information • Students attend classes at Antonio de Nebrija University (Madrid, Spain). Field trips. Students typically earn 5-6 semester credits per term.
Sessions • May-Jun (summer).
Eligibility Requirements • Minimum age 18; open to freshmen, sophomores, juniors, seniors, adults; 2.5 GPA; good academic standing at home school; no foreign language proficiency required.
Living Arrangements • Students live in host family homes. Quarters are shared with host institution students. Meals are taken with host family, in residences.
Costs (2005–2006) • Contact sponsor for cost. $200 deposit required. Financial aid available for all students: scholarships.
For More Information • Spain Site Specialist, International Studies Abroad, 901 West 24th Street, Austin, TX 78705; *Phone:* 800-580-8826; *Fax:* 512-480-8866. *E-mail:* isa@studiesabroad.com. *World Wide Web:* http://www.studiesabroad.com/

LANGUAGE LIAISON
LEARN SPANISH IN MADRID
Hosted by Language Liaison
Academic Focus • Spanish language and literature.
Program Information • Students attend classes at Language Liaison (Madrid, Spain). Field trips; optional travel at an extra cost. Students typically earn 3-15 semester credits per term.
Sessions • New programs begin weekly, year-round.

Eligibility Requirements • Minimum age 16; open to precollege students, freshmen, sophomores, juniors, seniors, graduate students, adults; no foreign language proficiency required.
Living Arrangements • Students live in host family homes, hotels. Meals are taken on one's own, with host family, in residences, in restaurants.
Costs (2005) • Contact sponsor for cost. $175 application fee. Financial aid available for all students: scholarship research service.
For More Information • Ms. Nancy Forman, President, Language Liaison, PO Box 1772, Pacific Palisades, CA 90272; *Phone:* 800-284-4448; *Fax:* 310-454-1706. *E-mail:* learn@languageliaison.com. *World Wide Web:* http://www.languageliaison.com/

LANGUAGE LINK
EUREKA OF MADRID, SPAIN
Hosted by Eureka, School of Spanish Language
Academic Focus • Spanish language and literature.
Program Information • Students attend classes at Eureka, School of Spanish Language (Madrid, Spain). Field trips to cultural attractions of Madrid. Students typically earn 6–15 semester credits per term.
Sessions • Classes every Monday, year-round.
Eligibility Requirements • Minimum age 18; open to freshmen, sophomores, juniors, seniors, graduate students, adults; no foreign language proficiency required.
Living Arrangements • Students live in program-owned apartments, host family homes, hotels. Quarters are shared with host institution students. Meals are taken as a group, in central dining facility.
Costs (2005) • $386 per week; includes tuition, housing, some meals, books and class materials, student support services. $50 application fee.
For More Information • Ms. Kay G. Rafool, Director, Language Link, PO Box 3006, Peoria, IL 61612-3006; *Phone:* 800-552-2051; *Fax:* 309-692-2926. *E-mail:* info@langlink.com. *World Wide Web:* http://www.langlink.com/

LINGUA SERVICE WORLDWIDE
VACATION 'N LEARN SPANISH IN SPAIN
Hosted by Estudio Sampere
Academic Focus • Spanish language and literature, Spanish studies.
Program Information • Students attend classes at Estudio Sampere (Madrid, Spain). Optional travel to cultural sites around Spain at an extra cost. Students typically earn 3 semester credits for 3 weeks, 6 semester credits for 5 weeks.
Sessions • Classes held year-round, beginning on Mondays, minimum session length is 2 weeks.
Eligibility Requirements • Minimum age 16; open to precollege students, freshmen, sophomores, juniors, seniors, graduate students, adults; no foreign language proficiency required.
Living Arrangements • Students live in host institution dormitories, locally rented apartments, host family homes, hotels. Quarters are shared with host institution students. Meals are taken with host family.
Costs (2006–2007) • Contact sponsor for cost. $100 application fee.
For More Information • Assistant Director, Lingua Service Worldwide, 75 Prospect Street, Suite 4, Huntington, NY 11743; *Phone:* 800-394-5327; *Fax:* 631-271-3441. *E-mail:* linguaservice@att.net. *World Wide Web:* http://www.linguaserviceworldwide.com/

LYCOMING COLLEGE
SUMMER STUDY ABROAD (SPAIN)
Hosted by Estudio Sampere
Academic Focus • History, Spanish language and literature, Spanish studies.
Program Information • Students attend classes at Estudio Sampere (Madrid, Spain). Scheduled travel; field trips; optional travel at an extra cost. Students typically earn 8 semester credits per term.
Sessions • May-Aug (summer).
Eligibility Requirements • Open to sophomores, juniors, seniors; major in Spanish; 2.5 GPA; 1 letter of recommendation; good academic standing at home school; 2 years of college course work in Spanish.

SPAIN
Madrid

Living Arrangements • Students live in host family homes. Quarters are shared with students from other programs. Meals are taken with host family, in residences.
Costs (2005) • $4050 for 4 weeks; includes tuition, housing, all meals, insurance, excursions, books and class materials, student support services.
For More Information • Dr. Barbara Buedel, Coordinator of Study Abroad Program, Lycoming College, Campus Box 2, 700 College Place, Williamsport, PA 17701-5192; *Phone:* 570-321-4210; *Fax:* 570-321-4389. *E-mail:* buedel@lycoming.edu. *World Wide Web:* http://www.lycoming.edu/

MICHIGAN STATE UNIVERSITY
INTERNSHIPS IN MADRID
Held at CAPA
Academic Focus • International affairs, liberal studies, public policy, social sciences, social services, Spanish language and literature, Spanish studies.
Program Information • Classes are held on the campus of CAPA (Madrid, Spain). Faculty members are local instructors hired by the sponsor. Field trips to cultural sites in and around Madrid. Students typically earn 10 semester credits per term.
Sessions • May–Jul (summer).
Eligibility Requirements • Open to juniors, seniors; 2.5 GPA; good academic standing at home school; curriculum vitae; cover letter; statement of purpose at application; 3 years of college course work in Spanish.
Living Arrangements • Students live in host family homes, apartment or townhouse. Meals are taken on one's own, with host family, in residences, in restaurants.
Costs (2005) • $3769; includes housing, some meals, insurance, excursions, books and class materials, student support services.

$100 application fee. $200 nonrefundable deposit required. Financial aid available for students from sponsoring institution: scholarships, loans.
For More Information • Mr. Mark Davis, Coordinator, Michigan State University, Office of Study Abroad, 109 International Center, East Lansing, MI 48824-1035; *Phone:* 517-432-1315; *Fax:* 517-432-2082. *E-mail:* mdavis@msu.edu. *World Wide Web:* http://studyabroad.msu.edu/

MODERN LANGUAGE STUDIES ABROAD
MLSA–SPANISH AT THE UNIVERSITY
Hosted by Complutense University of Madrid
Academic Focus • Spanish language and literature.
Program Information • Students attend classes at Complutense University of Madrid (Madrid, Spain). Students typically earn 9 semester credits per term.
Sessions • Jun–Jul (summer).
Eligibility Requirements • Open to freshmen.
Costs (2007) • $5955.
For More Information • Modern Language Studies Abroad, *World Wide Web:* http://www.mlsa.com/

MODERN LANGUAGE STUDIES ABROAD
MLSA–SUMMER STUDY AT UNIVERSITY COMPLUTENSE OF MADRID-GRADUATE-UNDERGRADUATE
Hosted by Complutense University of Madrid
Academic Focus • Civilization studies, cultural studies, drama/theater, education, Latin American studies, music, music history, Spanish language and literature, Spanish studies, teaching.
Program Information • Students attend classes at Complutense University of Madrid (Madrid, Spain). Scheduled travel to Pamplona,

south of Spain, France; field trips to Toledo, Segovia, El Escorial, south of Spain, France, Avila, Pamplona, Barcelona, Ruta del Quijote; optional travel at an extra cost. Students typically earn 4-10 semester credits per term.
Sessions • Jun-Jul (summer).
Eligibility Requirements • Minimum age 17; open to precollege students, freshmen, sophomores, juniors, seniors, graduate students, adults; no foreign language proficiency required.
Living Arrangements • Students live in host institution dormitories, locally rented apartments, host family homes. Quarters are shared with host institution students. Meals are taken as a group, in residences, in central dining facility.
Costs (2006) • $1985 (minimum); includes tuition, housing, all meals, excursions, international airfare, lab equipment, student support services. $100 application fee.
For More Information • Dr. Celestino Ruiz, Professor of Spanish, Modern Language Studies Abroad, PO Box 548, Frankfort, IL 60423; *Phone:* 815-464-1800; *Fax:* 815-464-9458. *E-mail:* mlsa@sprintmail.com. *World Wide Web:* http://www.mlsa.com/

NEW YORK UNIVERSITY
NYU IN MADRID
Hosted by NYU in Madrid
Academic Focus • Art history, civilization studies, cultural studies, drama/theater, film and media studies, history, Spanish language and literature.
Program Information • Students attend classes at NYU in Madrid (Madrid, Spain). Scheduled travel to Córdoba, Granada, Toledo, Burgos, Leon; field trips to Córdoba, Granada, Toledo, Burgos, Leon. Students typically earn 8 semester credits per term.
Sessions • Jun-Jul (summer).
Eligibility Requirements • Minimum age 18; open to freshmen, sophomores, juniors, seniors; 3.0 GPA; good academic standing at home school; personal statement for non-New York University students; college course work in Spanish required for advanced Spanish courses.
Living Arrangements • Students live in locally rented apartments, host family homes. Quarters are shared with host institution students. Meals are taken on one's own, with host family, in residences, in restaurants.
Costs (2006) • $6704; includes tuition, housing, some meals, excursions, student support services, program fee, cultural activities. $25 application fee. $300 nonrefundable deposit required. Financial aid available for students from sponsoring institution: loans.
For More Information • Office of Summer Sessions, New York University, 7 East 12th Street, 6th Floor, New York, NY 10003; *Phone:* 212-998-2292; *Fax:* 212-995-4642. *E-mail:* summer.info@nyu.edu. *World Wide Web:* http://www.nyu.edu/global/studyabroad.html

SAINT LOUIS UNIVERSITY, MADRID CAMPUS
SAINT LOUIS UNIVERSITY, MADRID CAMPUS
Hosted by Saint Louis University Madrid Campus
Academic Focus • Arabic, biological/life sciences, business administration/management, communications, engineering, English, fine/studio arts, French language and literature, German language and literature, liberal studies, mathematics, physical sciences, Portuguese, social sciences, Spanish language and literature.
Program Information • Students attend classes at Saint Louis University Madrid Campus (Madrid, Spain). Scheduled travel to Spain, Europe, north Africa, Canary Islands; Balearic Islands; South America; field trips to Segovia; El Escorial, Toledo, Salamanca, Cuenca, Galicia; the Pyrenees; Granada; optional travel to other areas of Europe, north Africa, Greece, Argentina; Brazil; Mexico; South Africa at an extra cost. Students typically earn 3-6 semester credits per term.
Sessions • May-Jul (summer).
Eligibility Requirements • Minimum age 19; open to precollege students, freshmen, sophomores, juniors, seniors, graduate students, adults; 3.0 GPA; transcripts; 1 year of college course work in Spanish.
Living Arrangements • Students live in host institution dormitories, locally rented apartments, program-owned apartments, host family homes. Quarters are shared with host institution students.

Meals are taken as a group, on one's own, with host family, in residences, in central dining facility.
Costs (2005) • $420 per credit hour; includes tuition, insurance, student support services, computer services. $45 application fee. $200 nonrefundable deposit required. Financial aid available for all students: scholarships, work study, loans.
For More Information • Ms. Phyllis Chaney, Director of Admission, Saint Louis University, Madrid Campus, Avda Del Valle, 34, 28003 Madrid, Spain; *Phone:* +34 91-554-5858; *Fax:* +34 91-554-6202. *E-mail:* admissions@madrid.slu.edu. *World Wide Web:* http://spain.slu.edu/

STATE UNIVERSITY OF NEW YORK COLLEGE AT BROCKPORT
INTERNSHIPS IN SPAIN
Hosted by University Francisco de Vitoria
Academic Focus • Business administration/management, information science, journalism, law and legal studies, Spanish studies.
Program Information • Students attend classes at University Francisco de Vitoria (Madrid, Spain). Field trips. Students typically earn 12 credits per term.
Sessions • May-Jul (summer).
Eligibility Requirements • Minimum age 18; open to juniors, seniors, graduate students; course work in some Spanish; 2.5 GPA; 2 letters of recommendation; good academic standing at home school; resume; some Spanish.
Living Arrangements • Students live in host family homes. Meals are taken with host family, in residences.
Costs (2006–2007) • $10,750; includes tuition, housing, some meals, excursions, international student ID, student support services. $200 nonrefundable deposit required. Financial aid available for all students: scholarships, loans, regular financial aid, grants.
For More Information • Dr. John Perry, Director, International Education, State University of New York College at Brockport, 350 New Campus Drive, Brockport, NY 14420; *Phone:* 800-298-SUNY; *Fax:* 585-637-3218. *E-mail:* overseas@brockport.edu. *World Wide Web:* http://www.brockport.edu/studyabroad/

SYRACUSE UNIVERSITY
ENGINEERING INTERNSHIPS AND RESEARCH PROJECTS IN MADRID
Hosted by Syracuse University Center–Madrid
Academic Focus • Electrical engineering, engineering, mechanical engineering.
Program Information • Students attend classes at Syracuse University Center–Madrid (Madrid, Spain). Students typically earn 3-7 semester credits per term.
Sessions • May-Jul (summer).
Eligibility Requirements • Minimum age 18; open to sophomores, juniors, seniors, graduate students; 1 letter of recommendation; good academic standing at home school; no foreign language proficiency required.
Living Arrangements • Students live in host family homes. Meals are taken with host family, in residences.
Costs (2005) • $4000 for 3 credits; $7000 for 7 credits; includes tuition, housing, some meals, international student ID. $55 application fee. $350 nonrefundable deposit required. Financial aid available for all students: loans, need-based tuition grants.
For More Information • Ms. Daisy Fried, Associate Director, Syracuse University, 106 Walnut Place, Syracuse, NY 13244-4170; *Phone:* 800-251-9674; *Fax:* 315-443-4593. *E-mail:* dipasum@syr.edu. *World Wide Web:* http://suabroad.syr.edu/

SYRACUSE UNIVERSITY
MANAGEMENT INTERNSHIPS IN MADRID
Hosted by Syracuse University Center–Madrid
Academic Focus • Accounting, business administration/management, finance, management information systems.
Program Information • Students attend classes at Syracuse University Center–Madrid (Madrid, Spain). Field trips. Students typically earn 6 semester credits per term.
Sessions • May-Jul (summer).

SPAIN
Madrid

Eligibility Requirements • Open to sophomores, juniors, seniors, graduate students, adults; major in management or a related field; course work in management; 1 letter of recommendation; good academic standing at home school; fluency in Spanish.

Living Arrangements • Students live in host family homes. Meals are taken with host family, in residences.

Costs (2005) • $7335; includes tuition, housing, some meals, excursions, international student ID, student support services. $55 application fee. $350 nonrefundable deposit required. Financial aid available for all students: loans, need-based tuition grants.

For More Information • Ms. Daisy Fried, Associate Director, Syracuse University, 106 Walnut Place, Syracuse, NY 13244-4170; *Phone:* 800-251-9674; *Fax:* 315-443-4593. *E-mail:* dipasum@syr.edu. *World Wide Web:* http://suabroad.syr.edu/

SYRACUSE UNIVERSITY
SUMMER IN SPAIN: A CULTURAL, LINGUISTIC, AND HISTORICAL JOURNEY

Hosted by Syracuse University Center–Madrid

Academic Focus • Anthropology, Spanish language and literature.

Program Information • Students attend classes at Syracuse University Center–Madrid (Madrid, Spain). Scheduled travel to San Sebastián, Balearic Islands, Santillana del Mar, Mallorca, Barcelona; field trips to Toledo, Segovia, Seville, Mérida. Students typically earn 6–7 semester credits per term.

Sessions • May–Jul (summer).

Eligibility Requirements • Minimum age 18; open to freshmen, sophomores, juniors, seniors, graduate students, adults; 1 letter of recommendation; good academic standing at home school; no foreign language proficiency required.

Living Arrangements • Students live in host family homes, hotels. Meals are taken with host family, in residences.

Costs (2006) • $7655 for 6 credits; $8380 for 7 credits; includes tuition, housing, some meals, excursions, international student ID, student support services. $55 application fee. $350 nonrefundable deposit required. Financial aid available for all students: loans, need-based tuition grants.

For More Information • Mrs. Daisy Fried, Associate Director, Syracuse University, 106 Walnut Place, Syracuse, NY 13244-4170; *Phone:* 800-251-9674; *Fax:* 315-443-4593. *E-mail:* dipasum@syr.edu. *World Wide Web:* http://suabroad.syr.edu/

SYRACUSE UNIVERSITY
SUMMER INTERNSHIPS IN SPAIN

Hosted by Syracuse University Center–Madrid

Academic Focus • Business administration/management.

Program Information • Students attend classes at Syracuse University Center–Madrid (Madrid, Spain). Students typically earn 6–7 semester credits per term.

Sessions • May–Jul (summer).

Eligibility Requirements • Open to freshmen, sophomores, juniors, seniors; 1 letter of recommendation; good academic standing at home school; no foreign language proficiency required.

Living Arrangements • Students live in host family homes. Meals are taken with host family, in residences.

Costs (2005) • $7240 for 6 credits; $7965 for 7 credits; includes tuition, housing, some meals, international student ID, student support services. $55 application fee. $350 nonrefundable deposit required. Financial aid available for all students: loans, need-based tuition grants.

For More Information • Mrs. Daisy Fried, Associate Director, Syracuse University, 106 Walnut Place, Syracuse, NY 13244-4170; *Phone:* 800-251-9674; *Fax:* 315-443-4593. *E-mail:* dipasum@syr.edu. *World Wide Web:* http://suabroad.syr.edu/

UNIVERSITY OF CALIFORNIA SAN DIEGO EXTENSION
SPANISH IMMERSION PROGRAM: MADRID, SPAIN

Hosted by Elemadrid

Academic Focus • Spanish language and literature.

Program Information • Students attend classes at Elemadrid (Madrid, Spain). Field trips to Toledo, El Escorial. Students typically earn 4 quarter credits for 2 weeks, 2 quarter credits for each additional week.

Sessions • 2 to 12 week sessions, year-round.

Eligibility Requirements • Minimum age 18; open to freshmen, sophomores, juniors, seniors, graduate students, adults; no foreign language proficiency required.

Living Arrangements • Students live in host institution dormitories, host family homes, hotels. Quarters are shared with host institution students, students from other programs. Meals are taken with host family, in residences.

Costs (2006) • Contact sponsor for cost. $125 application fee. Financial aid available for all students: loans.

For More Information • Ms. Natalie Bruce, Travel Study Coordinator, University of California San Diego Extension, Department of Arts, Humanities and Languages, 0170A, 9500 Gilman Drive, San Diego, CA 92093-0170; *Phone:* 858-964-1050; *Fax:* 858-964-1099. *E-mail:* travelstudy@ucsd.edu. *World Wide Web:* http://www.extension.ucsd.edu/travelstudy/

UNIVERSITY OF NEW ORLEANS
MADRID SUMMER SEMINARS

Held at Suffolk University–Madrid Campus

Academic Focus • Comparative literature, creative writing, history, Spanish language and literature, Spanish studies.

Program Information • Classes are held on the campus of Suffolk University-Madrid Campus (Madrid, Spain). Faculty members are drawn from the sponsor's U.S. staff and local instructors hired by the sponsor. Field trips to Toledo, Burgos, León. Students typically earn 6 semester credits per term.

Sessions • Jul (summer).

Eligibility Requirements • Minimum age 18; open to sophomores, juniors, seniors, graduate students, adults; 2.5 GPA; good academic standing at home school; no foreign language proficiency required.

Living Arrangements • Students live in host institution dormitories. Quarters are shared with students from other programs. Meals are taken as a group, in central dining facility.

Costs (2005) • $3800; includes tuition, housing, all meals, insurance, excursions, student support services. $150 application fee. $150 refundable deposit required. Financial aid available for all students: scholarships, work study, loans.

For More Information • Mr. William Lavendar, Coordinator, University of New Orleans, PO Box 582, New Orleans, LA 70148; *Phone:* 504-280-7457; *Fax:* 504-280-7317. *E-mail:* wlavend@uno.edu. *World Wide Web:* http://inst.uno.edu/

UNIVERSITY STUDIES ABROAD CONSORTIUM
SPANISH AND ART HISTORY STUDIES: MADRID, SPAIN

Hosted by University Rey Juan Carlos

Academic Focus • Art, art history, history, Spanish language and literature, Spanish studies.

Program Information • Students attend classes at University Rey Juan Carlos (Madrid, Spain). Field trips to Toledo; Segovia, Pedraza, El Valle de los Caídos, El Escorial, La Mancha; optional travel to The Camino de Santiago at an extra cost. Students typically earn 5–10 semester credits per term.

Sessions • May–Jun (summer), Jul (summer 2).

Eligibility Requirements • Minimum age 18; open to freshmen, sophomores, juniors, seniors, graduate students, adults; 2.5 GPA; no foreign language proficiency required.

Living Arrangements • Students live in locally rented apartments, host family homes. Quarters are shared with host institution students. Meals are taken on one's own, with host family, in residences, in restaurants.

Costs (2007) • $2780 for 1 session; $5460 for 2 sessions; includes tuition, housing, some meals, insurance, excursions, student support services. $100 application fee. $200 refundable deposit required. Financial aid available for all students: scholarships, loans.

For More Information • University Studies Abroad Consortium, USAC/323, Reno, NV 89557-0093; *Phone:* 775-784-6569; *Fax:* 775-784-6010. *E-mail:* usac@unr.edu. *World Wide Web:* http://usac.unr.edu/

VILLANOVA UNIVERSITY
STUDIES IN INTERNATIONAL BUSINESS AND INTERNSHIP PROGRAM: MADRID

Hosted by Universidad Portificia Canillas de Madrid (ICADE)

Academic Focus • International business.

Program Information • Students attend classes at Universidad Portificia Canillas de Madrid (ICADE) (Madrid, Spain). Field trips to El Prado, Toledo, El Escorial, Segovia. Students typically earn 6 semester credits per term.

Sessions • 6 weeks.

Eligibility Requirements • Minimum age 18; open to sophomores, juniors, seniors; major in business; 3.0 GPA; 2 letters of recommendation; good academic standing at home school; 2 years of college course work in Spanish.

Living Arrangements • Students live in locally rented apartments, host family homes. Meals are taken with host family, in residences.

Costs (2005) • $7500; includes tuition, housing, some meals, excursions, cell phone rental, internship placement, metro pass. $450 nonrefundable deposit required. Financial aid available for students from sponsoring institution: loans.

For More Information • Dr. Ken Taylor, Villanova University, 800 Lancaster Avenue, Department of Economics, Villanova, PA 19085; *Phone:* 610-519-6412; *Fax:* 610-519-7649. *E-mail:* kenneth.taylor@villanova.edu. *World Wide Web:* http://www.internationalstudies.villanova.edu/

MÁLAGA

EF INTERNATIONAL LANGUAGE SCHOOLS
SPANISH IN MÁLAGA

Hosted by Cervantes School

Academic Focus • Spanish language and literature.

Program Information • Students attend classes at Cervantes School (Málaga, Spain). Field trips to Marbella, Seville, Tangiers, Flamenco Museum; optional travel at an extra cost. Students typically earn 15–18 quarter credits per term.

Sessions • Program length 2 to 52 weeks, year round.

Eligibility Requirements • Minimum age 16; open to precollege students, freshmen, sophomores, juniors, seniors, graduate students, adults; no foreign language proficiency required.

Living Arrangements • Students live in program-owned apartments, host family homes. Quarters are shared with host institution students. Meals are taken on one's own, with host family.

Costs (2006–2007) • $1050 for 2 weeks; includes tuition, housing, some meals, books and class materials, student support services. $145 application fee. Financial aid available for all students: scholarships.

For More Information • Ms. Varvara Kirakosyan, Director of Admissions, EF International Language Schools, One Education Street, Cambridge, MA 02141; *Phone:* 800-992-1892; *Fax:* 800-590-1125. *E-mail:* ils@ef.com. *World Wide Web:* http://www.ef.com/

ESCUELA INTERNACIONAL
INTENSIVE SPANISH LANGUAGE AND CULTURE–MÁLAGA

Hosted by Escuela Internacional

Academic Focus • Spanish language and literature, Spanish studies.

Program Information • Students attend classes at Escuela Internacional (Málaga, Spain). Field trips to Granada, Nerja, Sevilla, White Villages, Córdoba; optional travel to Morocco at an extra cost. Students typically earn 4 semester credits for 4 weeks.

Sessions • 2 to 32 week durations begin every Monday.

Eligibility Requirements • Minimum age 17; open to precollege students, freshmen, sophomores, juniors, seniors, graduate students, adults; no foreign language proficiency required.

Living Arrangements • Students live in locally rented apartments, host family homes, hotels. Quarters are shared with host institution students. Meals are taken on one's own, with host family, in residences, in restaurants.

Costs (2005) • €1169 for 4 weeks; includes tuition, housing, all meals, excursions, books and class materials, student support services. €65 application fee.

For More Information • Ms. Midori Ishizaka, Director of Marketing, Escuela Internacional, C/Talamanca, 10, 28807 Alcalá de Henares (Madrid), Spain; *Phone:* +34 91-883-1264; *Fax:* +34 91-883-1301. *E-mail:* info@escuelai.com. *World Wide Web:* http://www.escuelai.com/

ESCUELA INTERNACIONAL
SPANISH LANGUAGE–MÁLAGA

Hosted by Escuela Internacional

Academic Focus • Spanish language and literature, Spanish studies.

Program Information • Students attend classes at Escuela Internacional (Málaga, Spain). Field trips to Granada, Nerja, Sevilla, White Villages, Córdoba; optional travel to Morocco at an extra cost. Students typically earn 5 quarter credits for 4 weeks.

Sessions • 2 to 32 week durations begin every Monday.

Eligibility Requirements • Minimum age 17; open to precollege students, freshmen, sophomores, juniors, seniors, graduate students, adults; no foreign language proficiency required.

Living Arrangements • Students live in locally rented apartments, host family homes, hotels. Quarters are shared with host institution students. Meals are taken on one's own, with host family, in residences, in restaurants.

Costs (2005) • €1169 for 4 weeks; includes tuition, housing, all meals, excursions, books and class materials, student support services. €65 application fee.

For More Information • Ms. Midori Ishizaka, Director of Marketing, Escuela Internacional, C/Talamanca, 10, 28807 Alcalá de Henares (Madrid), Spain; *Phone:* +34 91-883-1264; *Fax:* +34 91-883-1301. *E-mail:* info@escuelai.com. *World Wide Web:* http://www.escuelai.com/

INTERNATIONAL STUDIES ABROAD
MÁLAGA, SPAIN–INTENSIVE SPANISH LANGUAGE MONTH

Hosted by University of Málaga

Academic Focus • Spanish language and literature, Spanish studies.

Program Information • Students attend classes at University of Málaga (Málaga, Spain). Students typically earn 6 semester credits per term.

Sessions • Month-long sessions available Feb, Mar, Apr, May, Aug, Sep, Oct, Nov, Dec.

Eligibility Requirements • Minimum age 18; open to freshmen, sophomores, juniors, seniors; 2.5 GPA; good academic standing at home school; no foreign language proficiency required.

Living Arrangements • Students live in host family homes. Meals are taken with host family.

Costs (2005) • Contact sponsor for cost. $200 deposit required.

For More Information • Malaga Site Specialist, International Studies Abroad, 901 West 24th Street, Austin, TX 78705; *Phone:* 800-580-8826; *Fax:* 512-480-8866. *E-mail:* isa@studiesabroad.com. *World Wide Web:* http://www.studiesabroad.com/

INTERNATIONAL STUDIES ABROAD
MÁLAGA, SPAIN–SPANISH LANGUAGE AND CULTURE SUMMER

Hosted by University of Málaga

Academic Focus • Art history, Spanish language and literature, Spanish studies.

Program Information • Students attend classes at University of Málaga (Málaga, Spain). Field trips to Madrid, Toledo, Granada, Sevilla, El Escorial, Ronda. Students typically earn 6–8 semester credits per term.

Sessions • Jun-Jul (summer), Jul-Aug (summer 2).

Eligibility Requirements • Minimum age 18; open to freshmen, sophomores, juniors, seniors; 2.5 GPA; good academic standing at home school; no foreign language proficiency required.

Living Arrangements • Students live in host family homes. Meals are taken with host family.

Costs (2005) • Contact sponsor for cost. $200 deposit required.

For More Information • Malaga Site Specialist, International Studies Abroad, 901 West 24th Street, Austin, TX 78705; *Phone:* 800-580-8826; *Fax:* 512-480-8866. *E-mail:* isa@studiesabroad.com. *World Wide Web:* http://www.studiesabroad.com/

SPAIN
Málaga

LANGUAGE LIAISON
LEARN SPANISH AT LA BRISA

Hosted by Language Liaison
Academic Focus • Spanish language and literature.
Program Information • Students attend classes at Language Liaison (La Brisa, Spain). Field trips; optional travel at an extra cost. Students typically earn 3-15 semester credits per term.
Sessions • Classes begin weekly, year-round.
Eligibility Requirements • Minimum age 17; open to precollege students, freshmen, sophomores, juniors, seniors, graduate students, adults; no foreign language proficiency required.
Living Arrangements • Students live in locally rented apartments, host family homes, hotels. Meals are taken on one's own, with host family, in residences, in restaurants.
Costs (2005) • Contact sponsor for cost. $175 application fee. Financial aid available for all students: scholarship research service.
For More Information • Ms. Nancy Forman, President, Language Liaison, PO Box 1772, Pacific Palisades, CA 90272; *Phone:* 800-284-4448; *Fax:* 310-454-1706. *World Wide Web:* http://www.languageliaison.com/

LANGUAGE LIAISON
LEARN SPANISH IN MÁLAGA

Hosted by Language Liaison
Academic Focus • Spanish language and literature.
Program Information • Students attend classes at Language Liaison (Málaga, Spain). Field trips; optional travel at an extra cost. Students typically earn 3-15 semester credits per term.
Sessions • New programs begin weekly, year-round.
Eligibility Requirements • Minimum age 16; open to precollege students, freshmen, sophomores, juniors, seniors, graduate students, adults; no foreign language proficiency required.
Living Arrangements • Students live in host family homes, hotels. Meals are taken on one's own, with host family, in residences, in restaurants.
Costs (2005) • Contact sponsor for cost. $175 application fee. Financial aid available for all students: scholarship research service.
For More Information • Ms. Nancy Forman, President, Language Liaison, PO Box 1772, Pacific Palisades, CA 90272; *Phone:* 800-284-4448; *Fax:* 310-454-1706. *E-mail:* learn@languageliaison.com. *World Wide Web:* http://www.languageliaison.com/

LINGUA SERVICE WORLDWIDE
VACATION 'N LEARN SPANISH IN SPAIN

Hosted by Malaca Instituto
Academic Focus • Spanish language and literature, Spanish studies.
Program Information • Students attend classes at Malaca Instituto (Málaga, Spain). Optional travel to cultural sites around Spain at an extra cost. Students typically earn 3 semester credits for 3 weeks, 6 semester credits for 5 weeks.
Sessions • Classes held year-round, beginning on Mondays, minimum session length is 2 weeks.
Eligibility Requirements • Minimum age 16; open to precollege students, freshmen, sophomores, juniors, seniors, graduate students, adults; no foreign language proficiency required.
Living Arrangements • Students live in host institution dormitories, locally rented apartments, host family homes, hotels. Quarters are shared with host institution students. Meals are taken with host family.
Costs (2006–2007) • Contact sponsor for cost. $100 application fee.
For More Information • Assistant Director, Lingua Service Worldwide, 75 Prospect Street, Suite 4, Huntington, NY 11743; *Phone:* 800-394-5327; *Fax:* 631-271-3441. *E-mail:* linguaservice@att.net. *World Wide Web:* http://www.linguaserviceworldwide.com/

LINGUA SERVICE WORLDWIDE
VACATION 'N LEARN SPANISH IN SPAIN

Hosted by Instituto Alhambra
Academic Focus • Spanish language and literature, Spanish studies.
Program Information • Students attend classes at Instituto Alhambra (Málaga, Spain). Optional travel to cultural sites around Spain at an extra cost. Students typically earn 3 semester credits for 3 weeks, 6 semester credits for 5 weeks.
Sessions • Classes held year-round, beginning on Mondays, minimum session length is 2 weeks.
Eligibility Requirements • Minimum age 16; open to precollege students, freshmen, sophomores, juniors, seniors, graduate students, adults; no foreign language proficiency required.
Living Arrangements • Students live in host institution dormitories, locally rented apartments, host family homes, hotels. Quarters are shared with host institution students. Meals are taken with host family.
Costs (2006–2007) • Contact sponsor for cost. $100 application fee.
For More Information • Assistant Director, Lingua Service Worldwide, 75 Prospect Street, Suite 4, Huntington, NY 11743; *Phone:* 800-394-5327; *Fax:* 631-271-3441. *E-mail:* linguaservice@att.net. *World Wide Web:* http://www.linguaserviceworldwide.com/

MARBELLA

ALMA COLLEGE
SUMMER PROGRAM OF STUDIES IN MARBELLA, SPAIN

Hosted by ENFOREX
Academic Focus • Cultural studies, Spanish language and literature.
Program Information • Students attend classes at ENFOREX (Marbella, Spain). Field trips to local sites. Students typically earn 3-9 semester credits per term.
Sessions • Apr–Aug (4 to 14 weeks).
Eligibility Requirements • Minimum age 18; open to freshmen, sophomores, juniors, seniors, graduate students, adults; 2.5 GPA; 2 letters of recommendation; good academic standing at home school; no foreign language proficiency required.
Living Arrangements • Students live in locally rented apartments, host family homes. Quarters are shared with students from other programs. Meals are taken on one's own, with host family, in residences.
Costs (2005) • $3200–$7700; includes tuition, housing, all meals, insurance, excursions, books and class materials, international student ID, student support services, e-mail access, on-site orientation, airport pick-up. $50 application fee. $200 refundable deposit required.
For More Information • Ms. Julie Elenbaas, Office Associate, International Education, Alma College, 614 West Superior Street, Alma, MI 48801-1599; *Phone:* 989-463-7055; *Fax:* 989-463-7128. *E-mail:* intl_studies@alma.edu. *World Wide Web:* http://international.alma.edu/

ENFOREX–SPANISH IN THE SPANISH WORLD
SPANISH INTENSIVE COURSE MARBELLA

Hosted by ENFOREX
Academic Focus • Dance, Spanish language and literature, Spanish studies, teaching.
Program Information • Students attend classes at ENFOREX (Marbella, Spain). Field trips to Granada, Córdoba, Puerto Banus; optional travel to Seville, Granada, Barcelona, Salamanca at an extra cost. Students typically earn 4 semester credits per term.
Sessions • Year-round.
Eligibility Requirements • Minimum age 14; open to precollege students, freshmen, sophomores, juniors, seniors, graduate students, adults; no foreign language proficiency required.
Living Arrangements • Students live in host institution dormitories, program-owned apartments, host family homes, hotels. Quarters are shared with host institution students, students from other programs. Meals are taken as a group, on one's own, with host family, in residences.
Costs (2005) • €1280 per month; includes tuition, housing, all meals, excursions, books and class materials, lab equipment, international student ID, student support services. €65 application fee. €250 nonrefundable deposit required.
For More Information • Mr. Antonio Anadón, Director of Spanish Department, ENFOREX–Spanish in the Spanish World, Alberto

Aguilera, 26, 28015 Madrid, Spain; *Phone:* +34 91-594-3776; *Fax:* +34 91-594-5159. *E-mail:* promotion@enforex.es. *World Wide Web:* http://www.enforex.com/

LANGUAGE LIAISON
LEARN SPANISH IN MARBELLA

Hosted by Language Liaison
Academic Focus • Spanish language and literature.
Program Information • Students attend classes at Language Liaison (Marbella, Spain). Field trips; optional travel at an extra cost. Students typically earn 3-15 semester credits per term.
Sessions • New programs begin weekly, year-round.
Eligibility Requirements • Minimum age 16; open to precollege students, freshmen, sophomores, juniors, seniors, graduate students, adults; no foreign language proficiency required.
Living Arrangements • Students live in host family homes, hotels. Meals are taken on one's own, with host family, in residences, in restaurants.
Costs (2005) • Contact sponsor for cost. $175 application fee. Financial aid available for all students: scholarship research service.
For More Information • Ms. Nancy Forman, President, Language Liaison, PO Box 1772, Pacific Palisades, CA 90272; *Phone:* 800-284-4448; *Fax:* 310-454-1706. *E-mail:* learn@languageliaison. com. *World Wide Web:* http://www.languageliaison.com/

MENORCA

BOSTON UNIVERSITY
MEDITERRANEAN ARCHAEOLOGICAL FIELD SCHOOL

Academic Focus • Archaeology.
Program Information • Faculty members are drawn from the sponsor's U.S. staff and local instructors hired by the sponsor. Field trips to cultural monuments, museums, historic sites. Students typically earn 8 semester credits per term.
Sessions • May-Jul (summer).
Eligibility Requirements • Open to freshmen, sophomores, juniors, seniors; 3.0 GPA; 1 letter of recommendation; good academic standing at home school; essay; approval of participation; transcript; no foreign language proficiency required.
Living Arrangements • Students live in hotels. Meals are taken as a group, in central dining facility, in restaurants.
Costs (2005) • $6250; includes tuition, housing, all meals, insurance, excursions. $50 application fee. $400 nonrefundable deposit required. Financial aid available for all students: scholarships, loans.
For More Information • Division of International Programs, Boston University, 232 Bay State Road, Boston, MA 02215; *Phone:* 617-353-9888; *Fax:* 617-353-5402. *E-mail:* abroad@bu.edu. *World Wide Web:* http://www.bu.edu/abroad/

NERJA

LANGUAGE LIAISON
SPANISH IN MÁLAGA–NERJA

Hosted by Language Liaison
Academic Focus • Spanish language and literature.
Program Information • Students attend classes at Language Liaison (Nerja, Spain). Field trips; optional travel at an extra cost. Students typically earn 3-15 semester credits per term.
Sessions • New programs begin weekly, year-round.
Eligibility Requirements • Minimum age 16; open to precollege students, freshmen, sophomores, juniors, seniors, graduate students, adults; no foreign language proficiency required.
Living Arrangements • Students live in locally rented apartments, program-owned apartments, host family homes, hotels. Meals are taken on one's own, with host family, in residences, in restaurants.
Costs (2005) • Contact sponsor for cost. $175 application fee. Financial aid available for all students: scholarship research service.
For More Information • Ms. Nancy Forman, President, Language Liaison, PO Box 1772, Pacific Palisades, CA 90272; *Phone:* 800-284-4448; *Fax:* 310-454-1706. *E-mail:* learn@languageliaison. com. *World Wide Web:* http://www.languageliaison.com/

LINGUA SERVICE WORLDWIDE
VACATION 'N LEARN SPANISH IN SPAIN

Hosted by Escuela de Idiomas Nerja
Academic Focus • Spanish language and literature, Spanish studies.
Program Information • Students attend classes at Escuela de Idiomas Nerja (Nerja, Spain). Optional travel to cultural sites around Spain at an extra cost. Students typically earn 3 semester credits for 3 weeks, 6 semester credits for 5 weeks.
Sessions • Classes held year-round, beginning on Mondays, minimum session length is 2 weeks.
Eligibility Requirements • Minimum age 16; open to precollege students, freshmen, sophomores, juniors, seniors, graduate students, adults; no foreign language proficiency required.
Living Arrangements • Students live in host institution dormitories, locally rented apartments, host family homes, hotels. Quarters are shared with host institution students. Meals are taken with host family.
Costs (2006–2007) • Contact sponsor for cost. $100 application fee.
For More Information • Assistant Director, Lingua Service Worldwide, 75 Prospect Street, Suite 4, Huntington, NY 11743; *Phone:* 800-394-5327; *Fax:* 631-271-3441. *E-mail:* linguaservice@att. net. *World Wide Web:* http://www.linguaserviceworldwide.com/

OVIEDO

AHA INTERNATIONAL AN ACADEMIC PROGRAM OF THE UNIVERSITY OF OREGON
OVIEDO, SPAIN: MIDWEST CONSORTIUM FOR STUDY ABROAD AND NORTHWEST COUNCIL ON STUDY ABROAD (NCSA)

Hosted by University of Oviedo
Academic Focus • Art history, history, Romance languages, Spanish language and literature, Spanish studies, translation.
Program Information • Students attend classes at University of Oviedo (Oviedo, Spain). Field trips to Covadonga, Gijón, Oviedo museums and local pre-Romanesque architectural sites. Students typically earn 6-12 quarter credits per term.
Sessions • Jul-Aug (summer), Sep (fall intensive).
Eligibility Requirements • Open to sophomores, juniors, seniors; 2 letters of recommendation; good academic standing at home school; official transcripts; 2 admission essays; no foreign language proficiency required.
Living Arrangements • Students live in host institution dormitories. Quarters are shared with host institution students, students from other programs. Meals are taken on one's own, in central dining facility, in restaurants.
Costs (2005–2006) • $2380 for summer term; $2240 for fall intensive term; includes tuition, housing, insurance, excursions, books and class materials, international student ID, student support services, on-site orientation. $50 application fee. $200 refundable deposit required. Financial aid available for all students: scholarships, loans, home institution financial aid.
For More Information • Mr. Richard Browning, Associate Director for University Programs, AHA International An Academic Program of the University of Oregon, 221 NW 2nd Avenue, Suite 200, Portland, OR 97209; *Phone:* 503-295-7730; *Fax:* 503-295-5969. *E-mail:* mail@aha-intl.org. *World Wide Web:* http://www.aha-intl.org/

TEMPLE UNIVERSITY
TEMPLE IN SPAIN

Hosted by University of Oviedo
Academic Focus • Film and media studies, Spanish language and literature.
Program Information • Students attend classes at University of Oviedo (Oviedo, Spain). Field trips to Madrid, Toledo, Segovia, Avila; optional travel to student-chosen sites at an extra cost. Students typically earn 6 semester credits per term.
Sessions • Jun-Jul (summer).
Eligibility Requirements • Open to sophomores, juniors, seniors; 2.5 GPA; 1 letter of recommendation; good academic standing at home school; official transcripts; 1 year of college course work in Spanish.

SPAIN
Oviedo

Living Arrangements • Students live in host institution dormitories, host family homes. Quarters are shared with host institution students. Meals are taken on one's own, with host family, in residences, in central dining facility.
Costs (2005) • $3300–$4600; includes tuition, housing, some meals, excursions, program fee. $30 application fee. $200 nonrefundable deposit required. Financial aid available for students from sponsoring institution: scholarships, loans.
For More Information • Ms. Erin Joslyn, Study Abroad Coordinator, Temple University, International Programs, 200 Tuttleman Learning Center, 1809 North 13th Street, Philadelphia, PA 19122; *Phone:* 215-204-0720; *Fax:* 215-204-0729. *E-mail:* study.abroad@temple.edu. *World Wide Web:* http://www.temple.edu/studyabroad/

PALMA DE MALLORCA

CIEE
CIEE STUDY CENTER AT UNIVERSITAT DE LES ILLES BALEARS, PALMA DE MALLORCA, SPAIN
Hosted by University of the Balearic Islands
Academic Focus • Cultural studies, hotel and restaurant management, Spanish language and literature, Spanish studies, tourism and travel.
Program Information • Students attend classes at University of the Balearic Islands (Palma de Mallorca, Spain). Field trips to museums, theaters and fairs. Students typically earn 6 semester credits per term.
Sessions • Jun–Jul (summer).
Eligibility Requirements • Minimum age 18; open to sophomores, juniors, seniors; 2.75 GPA; 1 letter of recommendation; good academic standing at home school; no foreign language proficiency required.
Living Arrangements • Students live in host family homes. Meals are taken with host family, in residences.
Costs (2006) • $4650; includes tuition, housing, all meals, insurance, excursions, student support services, resident director, on-site pick-up, orientation, cultural activities, pre-departure advice. $30 application fee. $300 nonrefundable deposit required. Financial aid available for all students: scholarships, minority student scholarships.
For More Information • Information Center, CIEE, 7 Custom House Street, 3rd Floor, Portland, ME 04101; *Phone:* 800-40-STUDY; *Fax:* 207-553-7699. *E-mail:* studyinfo@ciee.org. *World Wide Web:* http://www.ciee.org/isp/

INTERNATIONAL HOUSE PALMA DE MALLORCA
INTENSIVE SPANISH COURSE
Hosted by International House Palma de Mallorca
Academic Focus • Spanish language and literature, Spanish studies.
Program Information • Students attend classes at International House Palma de Mallorca (Palma de Mallorca, Spain). Field trips to Old Quarter and Cathedral, Sollen, Castello de Bellver, Santa Maria market; optional travel to Valencia, Madrid, Barcelona at an extra cost. Students typically earn 3–8 semester credits per term.
Sessions • Classes held year-round.
Eligibility Requirements • Minimum age 16; open to precollege students, freshmen, sophomores, juniors, seniors, graduate students, adults; no foreign language proficiency required.
Living Arrangements • Students live in host institution dormitories, locally rented apartments, program-owned apartments, host family homes, hotels. Quarters are shared with host institution students, students from other programs. Meals are taken on one's own, in residences, in central dining facility, in restaurants.
Costs (2006) • €670 for 2 weeks; €1340 for 4 weeks; €2560 for 8 weeks; includes tuition, housing, some meals, excursions, books and class materials, student support services. €200 nonrefundable deposit required.
For More Information • Ms. Carmen Sánchez, Marketing Manager, International House Palma de Mallorca, Trafalgar, 14, Barcelona 08010, Spain; *Phone:* +34 93-268 4511; *Fax:* +34 93-268 0239. *E-mail:* spanish@bcn.ibes.com. *World Wide Web:* http://www.ihes.com/bcn/

LANGUAGE LIAISON
LEARN SPANISH IN PALMA DE MALLORCA
Hosted by Language Liaison
Academic Focus • Spanish language and literature.
Program Information • Students attend classes at Language Liaison (Palma de Mallorca, Spain). Field trips; optional travel at an extra cost. Students typically earn 3–15 semester credits per term.
Sessions • Classes begin weekly, year-round.
Eligibility Requirements • Minimum age 17; open to precollege students, freshmen, sophomores, juniors, seniors, graduate students, adults; no foreign language proficiency required.
Living Arrangements • Students live in locally rented apartments, host family homes, hotels. Meals are taken on one's own, with host family, in residences, in restaurants.
Costs (2005) • Contact sponsor for cost. $175 application fee. Financial aid available for all students: scholarship research service.
For More Information • Ms. Nancy Forman, President, Language Liaison, PO Box 1772, Pacific Palisades, CA 90272; *Phone:* 800-284-4448; *Fax:* 310-454-1706. *E-mail:* learn@languageliaison.com. *World Wide Web:* http://www.languageliaison.com/

SALAMANCA

ACADEMIC PROGRAMS INTERNATIONAL (API)
(API)–SALAMANCA, SPAIN
Hosted by University of Salamanca
Academic Focus • Art history, civilization studies, communications, European studies, history, international business, linguistics, Spanish language and literature, Spanish studies, teaching.
Program Information • Students attend classes at University of Salamanca (Salamanca, Spain). Scheduled travel to Madrid; field trips to Toledo, Avila, Segovia, El Escorial, Santander, La Granja, San Sebastian, Bilbao, Madrid countryside equestrian excursion. Students typically earn 5–10 semester credits per term.
Sessions • May–Jul (summer), Jun–Jul (summer 2); Jul–Aug (summer 3).
Eligibility Requirements • Minimum age 18; open to freshmen, sophomores, juniors, seniors, graduate students, adults; 2.75 GPA; 1 letter of recommendation; good academic standing at home school; official transcript from home university; no foreign language proficiency required.
Living Arrangements • Students live in host institution dormitories, locally rented apartments, host family homes. Quarters are shared with host institution students, students from other programs. Meals are taken on one's own, with host family, in residences.
Costs (2006–2007) • $3800–$6700; includes tuition, housing, all meals, insurance, excursions, student support services, airport pick-up, ground transportation, mobile phone, on-line services, on-site director; wireless access in API office. $150 nonrefundable deposit required. Financial aid available for all students: scholarships.
For More Information • Ms. Jennifer C. Allen, Director, Academic Programs International (API), 107 East Hopkins, San Marcos, TX 78666; *Phone:* 800-844-4124; *Fax:* 512-392-8420. *E-mail:* api@academicintl.com. *World Wide Web:* http://www.academicintl.com/

ACADEMIC STUDIES ABROAD
ACADEMIC STUDIES ABROAD–SALAMANCA, SPAIN
Hosted by University of Salamanca
Academic Focus • Spanish language and literature, Spanish studies.
Program Information • Students attend classes at University of Salamanca (Salamanca, Spain). Scheduled travel to Avila, Segovia, Toledo; field trips to Madrid, Santander. Students typically earn 6 semester credits per term.
Sessions • May–Jul (summer).
Eligibility Requirements • Minimum age 18; open to freshmen, sophomores, juniors, seniors; 2.5 GPA; college transcript; no foreign language proficiency required.
Living Arrangements • Students live in host family homes. Quarters are shared with host institution students. Meals are taken with host family, in residences.
Costs (2006) • $3495; includes tuition, housing, all meals, insurance, excursions, international student ID, student support

services, cell phone, laundry. $150 refundable deposit required. Financial aid available for all students: scholarships.

For More Information • Mr. Lee Frankel, Director, Academic Studies Abroad, 434 Massachusetts Avenue, Suite 501, Boston, MA 02118; *Phone:* 617-437-9388; *Fax:* 617-437-9390. *E-mail:* lee@ academicstudies.com. *World Wide Web:* http://www.academicstudies. com

ALMA COLLEGE
SUMMER PROGRAM OF STUDIES IN SALAMANCA, SPAIN
Hosted by ENFOREX
Academic Focus • Cultural studies, Spanish language and literature.
Program Information • Students attend classes at ENFOREX (Salamanca, Spain). Field trips to local sites. Students typically earn 3–9 semester credits per term.
Sessions • Apr–Aug (4 to 14 weeks).
Eligibility Requirements • Minimum age 18; open to freshmen, sophomores, juniors, seniors, graduate students, adults; 2.5 GPA; 2 letters of recommendation; good academic standing at home school; no foreign language proficiency required.
Living Arrangements • Students live in locally rented apartments, host family homes. Quarters are shared with students from other programs. Meals are taken on one's own, with host family, in residences.
Costs (2005) • $3200–$7700; includes tuition, housing, all meals, insurance, excursions, books and class materials, international student ID, student support services, e-mail access, on-site orientation, airport pick-up. $50 application fee. $200 refundable deposit required.
For More Information • Ms. Julie Elenbaas, Office Associate, International Education, Alma College, 614 West Superior Street, Alma, MI 48801-1599; *Phone:* 989-463-7055; *Fax:* 989-463-7128. *E-mail:* intl_studies@alma.edu. *World Wide Web:* http://international. alma.edu/

AMERICAN INSTITUTE FOR FOREIGN STUDY (AIFS)
AIFS–SALAMANCA, SPAIN–UNIVERSITY OF SALAMANCA
Hosted by University of Salamanca
Academic Focus • Spanish language and literature.
Program Information • Students attend classes at University of Salamanca (Salamanca, Spain). Scheduled travel to 3-day London stopover; field trips to overnight visit to Madrid, day visit to Segovia, cultural activities, walking tours, museums visits, cooking courses, guided tours; day visit to Pena de Francia mountains for 6 week students only; optional travel to 3-day optional visit to Lisbon, Portugal for a supplement of $379. Students typically earn 4 semester credits week students can earn up to 4 credits; 6 week students can earn up to 8 credits.
Sessions • Jun–Jul (summer), Jun–Aug.
Eligibility Requirements • Minimum age 17; open to precollege students, freshmen, sophomores, juniors, seniors; 2.0 GPA; no foreign language proficiency required.
Living Arrangements • Students live in host institution dormitories, program-owned apartments, host family homes, hotels. Quarters are shared with host institution students. Meals are taken as a group, in residences.
Costs (2007) • 4 weeks: $3999, 6 weeks: $5139; includes tuition, housing, some meals, insurance, excursions, student support services, On-site Resident Director; Phone Card to call the U.S. $95 application fee. $395 nonrefundable deposit required. Financial aid available for all students: scholarships.
For More Information • Mr. David Mauro, Admissions Advisor, American Institute For Foreign Study (AIFS), 9 West Broad Street, Stamford, CT 06902-3788; *Phone:* 800-727-2437 Ext. 5163; *Fax:* 203-399-5597. *E-mail:* dmauro@aifs.com. *World Wide Web:* http:// www.aifsabroad.com/

AUGUSTA STATE UNIVERSITY
SALAMANCA PROGRAM
Hosted by University of Salamanca
Academic Focus • Spanish language and literature.
Program Information • Students attend classes at University of Salamanca (Salamanca, Spain). Scheduled travel to Madrid, Barcelona,

Palma de Mallorca, Seville, Granada, Paris; field trips to Toledo, Segovia; optional travel to Pamplona, León, Zamora, Portugal, Ciudad Rodrigo, La Alberca, Cáceres, Trujillo at an extra cost. Students typically earn 6–9 semester credits per term.
Sessions • Jun–Aug (summer).
Eligibility Requirements • Minimum age 18; open to freshmen, sophomores, juniors, seniors, graduate students; 2.5 GPA; 2 letters of recommendation; good academic standing at home school; minimum 3.0 GPA in Spanish; 1.5 years of college course work in Spanish.
Living Arrangements • Students live in host family homes. Quarters are shared with host institution students. Meals are taken with host family, in residences.
Costs (2006) • $4995–$5295; includes tuition, housing, all meals, insurance, excursions, international airfare, books and class materials, student support services, laundry while in Salamanca. $200 nonrefundable deposit required. Financial aid available for students from sponsoring institution: scholarships, loans.
For More Information • Dr. Jana Sandarg, Program Director, Augusta State University, Department of Languages, Literature and Communications, Augusta, GA 30904-2200; *Phone:* 706-737-1500; *Fax:* 706-667-4770. *E-mail:* jsandarg@aug.edu. *World Wide Web:* http://www.aug.edu/salamanca

More About the Program
This program gives more for the money than most other programs, even with the $250 out-of-state fee. Students learn Spanish, culture, and customs by living with a family. Classes are taught by faculty members at the University of Salamanca, not professors from the States or local institutes. There are excursions to Madrid, Toledo, Segovia, Pamplona (running of the bulls), Barcelona, Palma de Mallorca, and Paris.

Price includes airfare from Atlanta (students can deduct $850 if arranging their own airfare), tuition, books, housing, laundry, all meals, insurance, and excursions. Alternate departure or return dates are available. Orientation, postprogram reunion, and on-site tutoring are provided.

CENTER FOR STUDY ABROAD (CSA)
SPANISH LANGUAGE AND CULTURE, SALAMANCA–UNIVERSITY OF SALAMANCA
Hosted by University of Salamanca
Academic Focus • Spanish language and literature, Spanish studies.
Program Information • Students attend classes at University of Salamanca (Salamanca, Spain). Optional travel at an extra cost. Students typically earn 4–10 semester credits per term.
Sessions • Classes begin weekly, year-round.
Eligibility Requirements • Minimum age 17; open to precollege students, freshmen, sophomores, juniors, seniors, graduate students, adults; no foreign language proficiency required.
Living Arrangements • Students live in host institution dormitories, locally rented apartments, host family homes. Quarters are shared with students from other programs. Meals are taken on one's own, with host family, in residences, in central dining facility.
Costs (2005) • Contact sponsor for cost. $45 application fee.
For More Information • Ms. Alima K. Virtue, Program Director, Center for Study Abroad (CSA), 325 Washington Avenue South #93, Kent, WA 98032; *Phone:* 206-726-1498; *Fax:* 253-850-0454. *E-mail:* info@centerforstudyabroad.com. *World Wide Web:* http://www. centerforstudyabroad.com/

COLEGIO DELIBES
SPANISH LANGUAGE COURSES FOR FOREIGN STUDENTS
Hosted by Colegio Delibes
Academic Focus • Business administration/management, Spanish language and literature, Spanish studies, translation.
Program Information • Students attend classes at Colegio Delibes (Salamanca, Spain). Optional travel to Avila, Segovia, Madrid, Toledo, León, Burgos, Portugal at an extra cost.
Sessions • 2 to 36 weeks, year-round.

SPAIN
Salamanca

Eligibility Requirements • Minimum age 16; open to precollege students, freshmen, sophomores, juniors, seniors, graduate students, adults; good academic standing at home school; no foreign language proficiency required.

Living Arrangements • Students live in host institution dormitories, locally rented apartments, program-owned apartments, host family homes, hotels, a student residence. Quarters are shared with host institution students. Meals are taken on one's own, with host family, in residences.

Costs (2005–2006) • Contact sponsor for cost. €150 refundable deposit required.

For More Information • Ms. Sonia Fajardo Rique, Secretary, Colegio Delibes, Av. Italia, 21, 37007 Salamanca, Spain; *Phone:* +34 923-120460; *Fax:* +34 923-120489. *E-mail:* delibes@colegiodelibes.com. *World Wide Web:* http://www.colegiodelibes.com/

DON QUIJOTE
INTENSIVE SPANISH COURSE IN SALAMANCA

Hosted by Don Quijote

Academic Focus • Romance languages, Spanish language and literature, Spanish studies.

Program Information • Students attend classes at Don Quijote (Salamanca, Spain). Field trips. Students typically earn 4 semester credits per term.

Sessions • Minimum 1 week sessions begin every Monday.

Eligibility Requirements • Minimum age 18; open to freshmen, sophomores, juniors, seniors, graduate students, adults; no foreign language proficiency required.

Living Arrangements • Students live in host institution dormitories, program-owned apartments, host family homes. Quarters are shared with host institution students, students from other programs. Meals are taken on one's own, with host family, in residences.

Costs (2006) • Contact sponsor for cost. €65 application fee. €500 nonrefundable deposit required. Financial aid available for all students: scholarships.

For More Information • Ms. Carmen Cantarino, USA Director, Don Quijote, Plaza San Marcos 7, 37002 Salamanca, Spain; *Phone:* +34 923-268874; *Fax:* +34 923-260674. *E-mail:* usa@donquijote.org. *World Wide Web:* http://www.donquijote.org/

ENFOREX–SPANISH IN THE SPANISH WORLD
SPANISH INTENSIVE COURSE SALAMANCA

Hosted by ENFOREX

Academic Focus • Dance, Spanish language and literature, Spanish studies, teaching.

Program Information • Students attend classes at ENFOREX (Salamanca, Spain). Field trips to Museo del Prado, El Escorial, Granada; optional travel to Seville, Granada, Barcelona, Salamanca at an extra cost. Students typically earn 4 quarter credits per term.

Sessions • Year-round.

Eligibility Requirements • Minimum age 14; open to precollege students, freshmen, sophomores, juniors, seniors, graduate students, adults; no foreign language proficiency required.

Living Arrangements • Students live in host institution dormitories, program-owned apartments, host family homes, hotels. Quarters are shared with host institution students, students from other programs. Meals are taken as a group, on one's own, with host family, in residences.

Costs (2005) • €1080 per month; includes tuition, housing, all meals, excursions, books and class materials, lab equipment, international student ID, student support services. €65 application fee. €250 nonrefundable deposit required.

For More Information • Mr. Antonio Anadón, Director of Spanish Department, ENFOREX–Spanish in the Spanish World, Alberto Aguilera, 26, 28015 Madrid, Spain; *Phone:* +34 91-594-3776; *Fax:* +34 91-594-5159. *E-mail:* promotion@enforex.es. *World Wide Web:* http://www.enforex.com/

ESCUELA INTERNACIONAL
INTENSIVE SPANISH LANGUAGE AND CULTURE–SALAMANCA

Hosted by Escuela Internacional

Academic Focus • Spanish language and literature, Spanish studies.

Program Information • Students attend classes at Escuela Internacional (Salamanca, Spain). Field trips to Madrid, Segovia, Avila, Toledo; optional travel to Madrid, Portugal, Seville, Santiago de Compostela at an extra cost. Students typically earn 4 semester credits for 4 weeks.

Sessions • 2 to 32 week durations begin every Monday.

Eligibility Requirements • Minimum age 17; open to precollege students, freshmen, sophomores, juniors, seniors, graduate students, adults; no foreign language proficiency required.

Living Arrangements • Students live in locally rented apartments, host family homes, hotels. Quarters are shared with host institution students. Meals are taken on one's own, with host family, in residences, in restaurants.

Costs (2005) • €993 for 4 weeks; includes tuition, housing, all meals, excursions, books and class materials, student support services, all activities. €65 application fee.

For More Information • Ms. Midori Ishizaka, Director of Marketing, Escuela Internacional, C/Talamanca, 10, 28807 Alcalá de Henares (Madrid), Spain; *Phone:* +34 91-883-1264; *Fax:* +34 91-883-1301. *E-mail:* info@escuelai.com. *World Wide Web:* http://www.escuelai.com/

ESCUELA INTERNACIONAL
SPANISH LANGUAGE–SALAMANCA

Hosted by Escuela Internacional

Academic Focus • Spanish language and literature, Spanish studies.

Program Information • Students attend classes at Escuela Internacional (Salamanca, Spain). Field trips to Madrid, Segovia, Avila, Toledo, Sierra de Francia; optional travel to Portugal, Seville, Madrid at an extra cost. Students typically earn 5 quarter credits for 4 weeks.

Sessions • 2 to 32 week durations begin every Monday.

Eligibility Requirements • Minimum age 17; open to precollege students, freshmen, sophomores, juniors, seniors, graduate students, adults; no foreign language proficiency required.

Living Arrangements • Students live in locally rented apartments, host family homes, hotels. Quarters are shared with host institution students. Meals are taken on one's own, with host family, in residences, in restaurants.

Costs (2005) • €993 for 4 weeks; includes tuition, housing, all meals, excursions, books and class materials, student support services, all activities. €65 application fee.

For More Information • Ms. Midori Ishizaka, Director of Marketing, Escuela Internacional, C/Talamanca, 10, 28807 Alcalá de Henares (Madrid), Spain; *Phone:* +34 91-883-1264; *Fax:* +34 91-883-1301. *E-mail:* info@escuelai.com. *World Wide Web:* http://www.escuelai.com/

EUROPEAN HERITAGE INSTITUTE
YEAR-ROUND PROGRAMS IN SALAMANCA

Hosted by Don Quijote

Academic Focus • Spanish language and literature, Spanish studies.

Program Information • Students attend classes at Don Quijote (Salamanca, Spain). Field trips to areas around Salamanca. Students typically earn 3–6 semester credits per term.

Sessions • 1 to 15 week sessions begin weekly, year-round.

Eligibility Requirements • Minimum age 18; open to freshmen, sophomores, juniors, seniors, graduate students, adults; 2.25 GPA; 2 letters of recommendation; no foreign language proficiency required.

Living Arrangements • Students live in host institution dormitories, locally rented apartments, host family homes. Quarters are shared with host institution students. Meals are taken on one's own, with host family, in residences, in restaurants.

Costs (2005) • $1581 for 4 weeks; $2958 for 8 weeks; $4732 for 12 weeks; includes tuition, housing, some meals, excursions, books and class materials, international student ID, student support services. $300 refundable deposit required.

For More Information • Dr. Antonio Masullo, Professor, European Heritage Institute, 2708 East Franklin Street, Richmond, VA 23223; *Phone:* 804-643-0661; *Fax:* 804-648-0826. *E-mail:* info@europeabroad.org. *World Wide Web:* http://www.europeabroad.org/

INTERNATIONAL STUDIES ABROAD
SALAMANCA, SPAIN: INTENSIVE MONTHS, LANGUAGE AND CULTURE

Hosted by University of Salamanca

Academic Focus • Art history, cultural studies, history, international business, Spanish language and literature, Spanish studies.

Program Information • Students attend classes at University of Salamanca (Salamanca, Spain). Optional travel to Madrid, Toledo, Segovia at an extra cost. Students typically earn 4–6 semester credits per term.

Sessions • Intensive month periods begin on or around the first of each month: Jan–May, Sep–Nov.

Eligibility Requirements • Minimum age 18; open to freshmen, sophomores, juniors, seniors, graduate students, adults; 2.5 GPA; good academic standing at home school; transcripts; no foreign language proficiency required.

Living Arrangements • Students live in locally rented apartments, host family homes. Quarters are shared with host institution students, students from other programs. Meals are taken with host family, in residences.

Costs (2005–2006) • Contact sponsor for cost. $200 deposit required. Financial aid available for all students: scholarships, loans, U.S. federal financial aid.

For More Information • Salamanca Site Specialist, International Studies Abroad, 901 West 24th Street, Austin, TX 78705; *Phone:* 800-580-8826; *Fax:* 512-480-8866. *E-mail:* isa@studiesabroad.com. *World Wide Web:* http://www.studiesabroad.com/

INTERNATIONAL STUDIES ABROAD
SALAMANCA, SPAIN–LANGUAGE AND CULTURE (SUMMER SESSIONS)

Hosted by University of Salamanca

Academic Focus • Art history, cultural studies, history, international business, Spanish language and literature, Spanish studies.

Program Information • Students attend classes at University of Salamanca (Salamanca, Spain). Scheduled travel to Madrid, Toledo; field trips to El Escorial, Avila, Segovia, Santander; La Granja; optional travel at an extra cost. Students typically earn 6–10 semester credits per term.

Sessions • Summer.

Eligibility Requirements • Minimum age 18; open to freshmen, sophomores, juniors, seniors, graduate students, adults; 2.5 GPA; good academic standing at home school; transcripts; no foreign language proficiency required.

Living Arrangements • Students live in locally rented apartments, host family homes. Quarters are shared with students from other programs. Meals are taken with host family, in residences.

Costs (2005) • Contact sponsor for cost. $200 deposit required. Financial aid available for all students: scholarships, loans, U.S. federal financial aid.

For More Information • Salamanca Site Specialist, International Studies Abroad, 901 West 24th Street, Austin, TX 78705; *Phone:* 800-580-8826; *Fax:* 512-480-8866. *E-mail:* isa@studiesabroad.com. *World Wide Web:* http://www.studiesabroad.com/

JAMES MADISON UNIVERSITY
SUMMER PROGRAM IN SALAMANCA

Hosted by University of Salamanca

Academic Focus • Art, art history, economics, international business, political science and government, Spanish language and literature, Spanish studies.

Program Information • Students attend classes at University of Salamanca (Salamanca, Spain). Scheduled travel to Seville, Toledo; field trips to Barcelona, Madrid. Students typically earn 9 semester credits per term.

Sessions • May–Jul (summer).

Eligibility Requirements • Minimum age 18; open to sophomores, juniors, seniors; 2.0 GPA; 1 letter of recommendation; good academic standing at home school; 2 years of college course work in Spanish.

Living Arrangements • Students live in host family homes. Quarters are shared with host institution students. Meals are taken on one's own, with host family, in residences, in restaurants.

Costs (2005) • $5762 for Virginia residents; $8282 for nonresidents; includes tuition, housing, some meals, excursions, books and class

materials, international student ID. $400 nonrefundable deposit required. Financial aid available for students from sponsoring institution: scholarships.

For More Information • Mr. Felix Wang, Director, James Madison University, Office of International Programs, MSC 5731, 1077 South Main Street, Harrisonburg, VA 22807; *Phone:* 540-568-6419; *Fax:* 540-568-3310. *E-mail:* studyabroad@jmu.edu. *World Wide Web:* http://www.jmu.edu/international/

LANGUAGE LIAISON
LEARN SPANISH IN SALAMANCA

Hosted by Language Liaison

Academic Focus • Spanish language and literature.

Program Information • Students attend classes at Language Liaison (Salamanca, Spain). Field trips; optional travel at an extra cost. Students typically earn 3–15 semester credits per term.

Sessions • New programs begin weekly, year-round.

Eligibility Requirements • Minimum age 16; open to precollege students, freshmen, sophomores, juniors, seniors, graduate students, adults; no foreign language proficiency required.

Living Arrangements • Students live in host family homes, hotels. Meals are taken on one's own, with host family, in residences, in restaurants.

Costs (2005) • Contact sponsor for cost. $175 application fee. Financial aid available for all students: scholarship research service.

For More Information • Ms. Nancy Forman, President, Language Liaison, PO Box 1772, Pacific Palisades, CA 90272; *Phone:* 800-284-4448; *Fax:* 310-454-1706. *E-mail:* learn@languageliaison.com. *World Wide Web:* http://www.languageliaison.com/

LINGUA SERVICE WORLDWIDE
VACATION 'N LEARN SPANISH IN SPAIN

Hosted by Estudio Sampere

Academic Focus • Spanish language and literature, Spanish studies.

Program Information • Students attend classes at Estudio Sampere (Salamanca, Spain). Optional travel to cultural sites around Spain at an extra cost. Students typically earn 3 semester credits for 3 weeks, 6 semester credits for 5 weeks.

Sessions • Classes held year-round, beginning on Mondays; minimum session length is 2 weeks.

Eligibility Requirements • Minimum age 16; open to precollege students, freshmen, sophomores, juniors, seniors, graduate students, adults; no foreign language proficiency required.

Living Arrangements • Students live in host institution dormitories, locally rented apartments, host family homes, hotels. Quarters are shared with host institution students. Meals are taken with host family.

Costs (2006–2007) • Contact sponsor for cost. $100 application fee.

For More Information • Assistant Director, Lingua Service Worldwide, 75 Prospect Street, Suite 4, Huntington, NY 11743; *Phone:* 800-394-5327; *Fax:* 631-271-3441. *E-mail:* linguaservice@att.net. *World Wide Web:* http://www.linguaserviceworldwide.com/

LINGUA SERVICE WORLDWIDE
VACATION 'N LEARN SPANISH IN SPAIN

Hosted by Don Quijote

Academic Focus • Spanish language and literature, Spanish studies.

Program Information • Students attend classes at Don Quijote (Salamanca, Spain). Optional travel to cultural sites around Spain at an extra cost. Students typically earn 3 semester credits for 3 weeks, 6 semester credits for 5 weeks.

Sessions • Classes held year-round, beginning on Mondays, minimum session length is 2 weeks.

Eligibility Requirements • Minimum age 16; open to precollege students, freshmen, sophomores, juniors, seniors, graduate students, adults; no foreign language proficiency required.

Living Arrangements • Students live in host institution dormitories, locally rented apartments, host family homes, hotels. Quarters are shared with host institution students. Meals are taken with host family.

Costs (2006–2007) • Contact sponsor for cost. $100 application fee.

SPAIN
Salamanca

For More Information • Assistant Director, Lingua Service Worldwide, 75 Prospect Street, Suite 4, Huntington, NY 11743; *Phone:* 800-394-5327; *Fax:* 631-271-3441. *E-mail:* linguaservice@att. net. *World Wide Web:* http://www.linguaserviceworldwide.com/

LINGUA SERVICE WORLDWIDE
VACATION 'N LEARN SPANISH IN SPAIN

Hosted by Colegio de España
Academic Focus • Spanish language and literature, Spanish studies.
Program Information • Students attend classes at Colegio de España (Salamanca, Spain). Optional travel to cultural sites around Spain at an extra cost. Students typically earn 3 semester credits for 3 weeks, 6 semester credits for 5 weeks.
Sessions • Classes held year-round, beginning on Mondays, minimum session length is 2 weeks.
Eligibility Requirements • Minimum age 16; open to precollege students, freshmen, sophomores, juniors, seniors, graduate students, adults; no foreign language proficiency required.
Living Arrangements • Students live in host institution dormitories, locally rented apartments, host family homes, hotels. Quarters are shared with host institution students. Meals are taken with host family.
Costs (2006–2007) • Contact sponsor for cost. $100 application fee.
For More Information • Assistant Director, Lingua Service Worldwide, 75 Prospect Street, Suite 4, Huntington, NY 11743; *Phone:* 800-394-5327; *Fax:* 631-271-3441. *E-mail:* linguaservice@att. net. *World Wide Web:* http://www.linguaserviceworldwide.com/

SAN SEBASTIAN

LACUNZA-INTERNATIONAL HOUSE–SAN SEBASTIAN
INTENSIVE COURSES

Hosted by Lacunza-International House–San Sebastian
Academic Focus • Spanish language and literature.
Program Information • Students attend classes at Lacunza-International House–San Sebastian (San Sebastian, Spain). Field trips to the Bilbao Guggenheim Museum, nature reserves, Pamplona, Chillida-Leku museum, rafting, canoeing, Port Aventura, Biarritz, skiing (winter), The Pyrenees, surfing; optional travel to Madrid, weekend skiing, Barcelona, trekking in the Pyranees, Asturias at an extra cost. Students typically earn no academic credit granted.
Sessions • 4 week courses offered year-round.
Eligibility Requirements • Minimum age 17; open to precollege students, freshmen, sophomores, juniors, seniors, graduate students, adults; interest in learning Spanish; no foreign language proficiency required.
Living Arrangements • Students live in locally rented apartments, host family homes. Quarters are shared with students from other programs. Meals are taken on one's own, with host family, in residences, in restaurants.
Costs (2006) • €150 per week; includes tuition, books and class materials, student support services, use of facilities, student card. €50 application fee. €250 nonrefundable deposit required.
For More Information • Ms. Marta Asensio, Admissions Officer, Lacunza-International House–San Sebastian, Camino de Mundaiz n-8, Entlo D, 20012 San Sebastian, Spain; *Phone:* +34 943-326680; *Fax:* +34 943-326822. *E-mail:* info@lacunza.com. *World Wide Web:* http://www.lacunza.com/

LANGUAGE LIAISON
LEARN SPANISH IN SAN SEBASTIAN

Hosted by Language Liaison
Academic Focus • Spanish language and literature.
Program Information • Students attend classes at Language Liaison (San Sebastian, Spain). Field trips; optional travel at an extra cost. Students typically earn 3–15 semester credits per term.
Sessions • New programs begin weekly, year-round.
Eligibility Requirements • Minimum age 16; open to precollege students, freshmen, sophomores, juniors, seniors, graduate students, adults; no foreign language proficiency required.

Living Arrangements • Students live in host family homes, hotels. Meals are taken on one's own, with host family, in residences, in restaurants.
Costs (2005) • Contact sponsor for cost. $175 application fee. Financial aid available for all students: scholarship research service.
For More Information • Ms. Nancy Forman, President, Language Liaison, PO Box 1772, Pacific Palisades, CA 90272; *Phone:* 800-284-4448; *Fax:* 310-454-1706. *E-mail:* learn@languageliaison. com. *World Wide Web:* http://www.languageliaison.com/

LANGUAGE LINK
LACUNZA (IH) OF SAN SEBASTIAN, SPAIN

Hosted by Lacunza-International House–San Sebastian
Academic Focus • Spanish language and literature.
Program Information • Students attend classes at Lacunza-International House–San Sebastian (San Sebastian, Spain). Field trips to Pamplona, Bilbao, France, local sites of interest. Students typically earn 6–15 semester credits per term.
Sessions • Year-round, start dates every other Monday for beginners.
Eligibility Requirements • Minimum age 14; open to precollege students, freshmen, sophomores, juniors, seniors, graduate students, adults; no foreign language proficiency required.
Living Arrangements • Students live in locally rented apartments, host family homes. Quarters are shared with host institution students. Meals are taken on one's own, with host family, in residences, in restaurants.
Costs (2005) • $390 per week; includes tuition, housing, some meals, books and class materials, student support services, cultural activities.
For More Information • Ms. Kay G. Rafool, Director, Language Link, PO Box 3006, Peoria, IL 61612-3006; *Phone:* 800-552-2051; *Fax:* 309-692-2926. *E-mail:* info@langlink.com. *World Wide Web:* http://www.langlink.com/

LINGUA SERVICE WORLDWIDE
VACATION 'N LEARN SPANISH IN SPAIN

Hosted by Lacunza-International House–San Sebastian
Academic Focus • Spanish language and literature, Spanish studies.
Program Information • Students attend classes at Lacunza-International House–San Sebastian (San Sebastian, Spain). Optional travel to cultural sites around Spain at an extra cost. Students typically earn 3 semester credits for 3 weeks, 6 semester credits for 5 weeks.
Sessions • Classes held year-round, beginning on Mondays, minimum session length is 2 weeks.
Eligibility Requirements • Minimum age 16; open to precollege students, freshmen, sophomores, juniors, seniors, graduate students, adults; no foreign language proficiency required.
Living Arrangements • Students live in host institution dormitories, locally rented apartments, host family homes, hotels. Quarters are shared with host institution students. Meals are taken with host family.
Costs (2006–2007) • Contact sponsor for cost. $100 application fee.
For More Information • Assistant Director, Lingua Service Worldwide, 75 Prospect Street, Suite 4, Huntington, NY 11743; *Phone:* 800-394-5327; *Fax:* 631-271-3441. *E-mail:* linguaservice@att. net. *World Wide Web:* http://www.linguaserviceworldwide.com/

UNIVERSITY STUDIES ABROAD CONSORTIUM
CULTURAL STUDIES AND SPANISH AND BASQUE LANGUAGE: SAN SEBASTIAN, SPAIN

Hosted by University of the Basque Country–San Sebastian Campus
Academic Focus • Anthropology, Basque studies, business administration/management, cultural studies, film and media studies, international business, marketing, Spanish language and literature, Spanish studies.
Program Information • Students attend classes at University of the Basque Country–San Sebastian Campus (San Sebastian, Spain). Field trips to France, Basque provinces: Bizkaia, Pyrénées mountains, Gernika; optional travel to Madrid, Toledo at an extra cost. Students typically earn 6–12 semester credits per term.

Sessions • May-Jun (summer), Jun-Jul (summer 2).
Eligibility Requirements • Minimum age 18; open to freshmen, sophomores, juniors, seniors, graduate students, adults; 2.5 GPA; no foreign language proficiency required.
Living Arrangements • Students live in locally rented apartments, host family homes. Quarters are shared with host institution students. Meals are taken on one's own, with host family, in residences, in restaurants.
Costs (2007) • $3090-$3740 for 1 session; $6730 for 2 sessions; includes tuition, housing, some meals, insurance, excursions, student support services, some entries to museums and cultural events. $100 application fee. $200 refundable deposit required. Financial aid available for all students: scholarships, loans.
For More Information • University Studies Abroad Consortium, USAC/323, Reno, NV 89557-0093; *Phone:* 775-784-6569; *Fax:* 775-784-6010. *E-mail:* usac@unr.edu. *World Wide Web:* http://usac.unr.edu/

SANTANDER

INTERNATIONAL STUDIES ABROAD
SANTANDER: SPANISH LANGUAGE AND CULTURE PROGRAM (SUMMER)
Hosted by Menendez Pelayo International University
Academic Focus • Latin American literature, Spanish language and literature, Spanish studies.
Program Information • Students attend classes at Menendez Pelayo International University (Santander, Spain). Scheduled travel to Madrid, Toledo, El Escorial; field trips to Santillana del Mar, Comillas, Potes, Picos de Europa, Bilbao; Castro Uriales; San Sebastian; optional travel. Students typically earn 5-6 semester credits per term.
Sessions • Jun-Jul (summer).

Eligibility Requirements • Minimum age 18; open to freshmen, sophomores, juniors, seniors, adults; 2.5 GPA; good academic standing at home school; contact sponsor if GPA is lower than 2.5; no foreign language proficiency required.
Living Arrangements • Students live in locally rented apartments, host family homes. Quarters are shared with students from other programs. Meals are taken with host family, in residences, in central dining facility.
Costs (2005–2006) • Contact sponsor for cost. $200 deposit required.
For More Information • Santander Site Specialist, International Studies Abroad, 901 West 24th Street, Austin, TX 78705; *Phone:* 800-580-8826; *Fax:* 512-480-8866. *E-mail:* isa@studiesabroad.com. *World Wide Web:* http://www.studiesabroad.com/

MICHIGAN STATE UNIVERSITY
SPANISH LANGUAGE, LITERATURE, AND CULTURE IN SANTANDER
Hosted by Menendez Pelayo International University
Academic Focus • Spanish language and literature.
Program Information • Students attend classes at Menendez Pelayo International University (Santander, Spain). Field trips to places of interest near Santander. Students typically earn 9 semester credits per term.
Sessions • May-Jul (summer).
Eligibility Requirements • Minimum age 18; open to freshmen, sophomores, juniors, seniors; 2.5 GPA; good academic standing at home school; approval of faculty director; interview, essay, statement of purpose at application; 2.5 years of college course work in Spanish.
Living Arrangements • Students live in host family homes. Meals are taken with host family, in residences.
Costs (2005) • $2208 (estimated); includes housing, all meals, insurance, excursions, student support services. $100 application

SPAIN
Santander

fee. $200 nonrefundable deposit required. Financial aid available for students from sponsoring institution: scholarships, loans.
For More Information • Mr. Mark Davis, Coordinator, Michigan State University, Office of Study Abroad, 109 International Center, East Lansing, MI 48824-1035; *Phone:* 517-432-1315; *Fax:* 517-432-2082. *E-mail:* mdavis@msu.edu. *World Wide Web:* http://studyabroad.msu.edu/

UNIVERSITY OF MIAMI
ART HISTORY AND SPANISH LANGUAGE IN CANTABRIA

Hosted by University of Cantabria
Academic Focus • Art history, Spanish studies.
Program Information • Students attend classes at University of Cantabria (Santander, Spain). Field trips. Students typically earn 6 semester credits per term.
Sessions • Jul (summer).
Eligibility Requirements • Minimum age 18; open to sophomores, juniors, seniors, graduate students; good academic standing at home school; no foreign language proficiency required.
Living Arrangements • Students live in host institution dormitories, host family homes. Quarters are shared with students from other programs. Meals are taken as a group, with host family, in residences.
Costs (2005) • $5672; includes tuition, housing, all meals, excursions, student support services. $40 application fee. $500 nonrefundable deposit required. Financial aid available for students from sponsoring institution: scholarships, loans.
For More Information • Ms. Glenda Hayley, Director, International Education and Exchange Programs, University of Miami, 5050 Brunson Drive, Allen Hall Room 212, PO Box 248005, Coral Gables, FL 33124-1610; *Phone:* 305-284-3434; *Fax:* 305-284-4235. *E-mail:* ieep@miami.edu. *World Wide Web:* http://www.studyabroad.miami.edu/

UNIVERSITY OF MIAMI
SUMMER LANGUAGE PROGRAM IN SANTANDER

Hosted by University of Cantabria
Academic Focus • Spanish language and literature.
Program Information • Students attend classes at University of Cantabria (Santander, Spain). Students typically earn 6 semester credits per term.
Sessions • Jun–Jul (summer).
Eligibility Requirements • Minimum age 18; open to freshmen, sophomores, juniors, seniors; 3.0 GPA; 2 letters of recommendation; personal interview; no foreign language proficiency required.
Living Arrangements • Students live in host institution dormitories, host family homes. Quarters are shared with students from other programs. Meals are taken on one's own, with host family, in residences, in central dining facility.
Costs (2006) • $3161; includes tuition, housing, some meals, student support services. $40 application fee. $500 nonrefundable deposit required. Financial aid available for students from sponsoring institution: scholarships, loans.
For More Information • Ms. Kefryn Block, Coordinator, University of Miami, International Education and Exchange Programs, 5050 Brunson Drive, Allen Hall 212, PO Box 248005, Coral Gables, FL 33124-1610; *Phone:* 305-284-3434; *Fax:* 305-284-4235. *E-mail:* ieep@miami.edu. *World Wide Web:* http://www.studyabroad.miami.edu/

SEGOVIA

AHA INTERNATIONAL AN ACADEMIC PROGRAM OF THE UNIVERSITY OF OREGON
SEGOVIA, SPAIN: MIDWEST CONSORTIUM FOR STUDY ABROAD (MCSA) AND THE NORTHWEST COUNCIL ON STUDY ABROAD (NCSA)

Hosted by AHA Segovia Center
Academic Focus • Art history, European studies, international affairs, political science and government, Romance languages, Spanish language and literature, Spanish studies.
Program Information • Students attend classes at AHA Segovia Center (Segovia, Spain). Field trips to the Route of the Castles,

museums of Madrid (including El Prado), La Granja, Salamanca. Students typically earn 6–12 semester credits per term.
Sessions • Jun–Jul (summer).
Eligibility Requirements • Open to sophomores, juniors, seniors; 2 letters of recommendation; good academic standing at home school; language proficiency report; transcripts; 2 admission essays; 2 years of college course work in Spanish.
Living Arrangements • Students live in host family homes. Meals are taken with host family, in residences.
Costs (2005–2006) • $3920; includes tuition, housing, all meals, insurance, excursions, books and class materials, international student ID, student support services, on-site orientation. $50 application fee. $200 refundable deposit required. Financial aid available for students: scholarships, loans, home institution financial aid.
For More Information • Mr. Richard Browning, Associate Director for University Programs, AHA International An Academic Program of the University of Oregon, 221 NW 2nd Avenue, Suite 200, Portland, OR 97209; *Phone:* 503-295-7730; *Fax:* 503-295-5969. *E-mail:* mail@aha-intl.org. *World Wide Web:* http://www.aha-intl.org/

KENTUCKY INSTITUTE FOR INTERNATIONAL STUDIES
SPAIN

Academic Focus • Spanish language and literature, Spanish studies.
Program Information • Faculty members are drawn from the sponsor's U.S. staff. Scheduled travel to Madrid; field trips to Toledo, Salamanca; optional travel at an extra cost. Students typically earn 6 semester credits per term.
Sessions • May–Jul (summer).
Eligibility Requirements • Minimum age 18; open to freshmen, sophomores, juniors, seniors, graduate students; 2.0 GPA; 1 letter of recommendation; 12 credit hours of college course work in Spanish.
Living Arrangements • Students live in host family homes. Meals are taken with host family, in residences.
Costs (2006) • $3200; includes housing, some meals, insurance, excursions, international airfare, international student ID, instructional expenses. $150 application fee. Financial aid available for all students: scholarships.
For More Information • Ms. Nancy Martin, Coordinator, Kentucky Institute for International Studies, PO Box 9, Murray, KY 42071-0009; *Phone:* 270-762-3091; *Fax:* 270-762-3434. *E-mail:* kiismsu@murraystate.edu. *World Wide Web:* http://www.kiis.org/

KENTUCKY INSTITUTE FOR INTERNATIONAL STUDIES
SPAIN (SESSION II)

Academic Focus • Spanish language and literature, Spanish studies.
Program Information • Faculty members are drawn from the sponsor's U.S. staff. Scheduled travel to Madrid; field trips to Toledo, Salamanca; optional travel to Avila at an extra cost. Students typically earn 3–6 semester credits per term.
Sessions • Jun–Aug (summer).
Eligibility Requirements • Minimum age 18; open to sophomores, juniors, seniors, graduate students; 2.0 GPA; 1 letter of recommendation; 18 credit hours of college course work in Spanish.
Living Arrangements • Students live in host family homes. Meals are taken in residences.
Costs (2006) • $3200; includes housing, some meals, insurance, excursions, international airfare, international student ID, instructional expenses. $150 application fee. Financial aid available for all students: scholarships.
For More Information • Ms. Nancy Martin, Coordinator, Kentucky Institute for International Studies, PO Box 9, Murray, KY 42071-0009; *Phone:* 270-762-3091; *Fax:* 270-762-3434. *E-mail:* kiismsu@murraystate.edu. *World Wide Web:* http://www.kiis.org/

MOUNT SAINT MARY COLLEGE
MOUNT SAINT MARY COLLEGE IN SEGOVIA, SPAIN

Hosted by Center of Hispanic Studies
Academic Focus • Spanish language and literature.
Program Information • Students attend classes at Center of Hispanic Studies (Segovia, Spain). Scheduled travel to Madrid, Toledo. Students typically earn 6 semester credits per term.

Sessions • May–Jun (summer).

Eligibility Requirements • Minimum age 17; open to freshmen, sophomores, juniors, seniors, graduate students, adults; 2.0 GPA; 2 letters of recommendation; good academic standing at home school; 1 recommendation from a faculty member from home institution; interview with program coordinator; 0.5 years of college course work in Spanish.

Living Arrangements • Students live in host family homes. Quarters are shared with host institution students. Meals are taken with host family, in residences.

Costs (2005) • $4000; includes tuition, housing, all meals, excursions, international airfare, student support services. $200 application fee. $1000 nonrefundable deposit required. Financial aid available for students from sponsoring institution: loans.

For More Information • Dr. Jerome L. Wyant, Associate Dean for Curriculum, Mount Saint Mary College, Aquinas Hall, 330 Powell Avenue, Newburgh, NY 12550; *Phone:* 845-569-3259; *Fax:* 845-562-6762. *E-mail:* wyant@msmc.edu. *World Wide Web:* http://www.msmc.edu/

SEVILLE

ACADEMIC PROGRAMS INTERNATIONAL (API)
(API)–SEVILLE, SPAIN

Hosted by University of Seville

Academic Focus • Civilization studies, Spanish language and literature, Spanish studies.

Program Information • Students attend classes at University of Seville (Seville, Spain). Scheduled travel to Madrid; field trips to Toledo, El Escorial, Córdoba, Cadiz, Granada, Jerez, Madrid. Students typically earn 6 semester credits per term.

Sessions • May–Jun (summer), Jun–Jul (summer 2).

Eligibility Requirements • Minimum age 18; open to sophomores, juniors, seniors; 2.75 GPA; 1 letter of recommendation; good academic standing at home school; official transcript from home university; 1 year of college course work in Spanish.

Living Arrangements • Students live in host institution dormitories, host family homes. Quarters are shared with host institution students. Meals are taken on one's own, with host family, in residences, in central dining facility, in restaurants.

Costs (2006–2007) • $3800–$3850; includes tuition, housing, all meals, insurance, excursions, student support services, airport pick-up, ground transportation, mobile phone, on-line services, on-site director; wireless access in API office. $150 nonrefundable deposit required. Financial aid available for all students: scholarships.

For More Information • Ms. Jennifer C. Allen, Director, Academic Programs International (API), 107 East Hopkins, San Marcos, TX 78666; *Phone:* 800-844-4124; *Fax:* 512-392-8420. *E-mail:* api@academicintl.com. *World Wide Web:* http://www.academicintl.com/

ACADEMIC PROGRAMS INTERNATIONAL (API)
(API)–SEVILLE UPO PROGRAM

Hosted by Pablo de Olavide University

Academic Focus • International business, Spanish language and literature, Spanish studies.

Program Information • Students attend classes at Pablo de Olavide University (Seville, Spain). Scheduled travel to Madrid, Lagos, Portugal; field trips to El Escorial, Toledo, Cordoba, Jerez, La Rabida. Students typically earn 6 semester credits per term.

Sessions • May–Jul (summer).

Eligibility Requirements • Minimum age 18; open to freshmen, sophomores, juniors, seniors; 2.75 GPA; 1 letter of recommendation; good academic standing at home school; official transcript from home university; no foreign language proficiency required.

Living Arrangements • Students live in host institution dormitories, host family homes. Quarters are shared with students from other programs. Meals are taken on one's own, with host family, in residences.

Costs (2006–2007) • $3800–$3850; includes tuition, housing, all meals, insurance, excursions, student support services, airport reception, ground transportation, mobile phone, on-line service,

on-site director; wireless access in API office. $150 nonrefundable deposit required. Financial aid available for all students: scholarships.

For More Information • Ms. Jennifer C. Allen, Director, Academic Programs International (API), 107 East Hopkins, San Marcos, TX 78666, San Marcos, TX 78666; *Phone:* 800-844-4124; *Fax:* 512-392-8420. *E-mail:* api@academicintl.com. *World Wide Web:* http://www.academicintl.com/

THE CENTER FOR CROSS-CULTURAL STUDY
JANUARY TERM IN SEVILLE, SPAIN

Hosted by The Center for Cross-Cultural Study

Academic Focus • Anthropology, civilization studies, history, Spanish language and literature.

Program Information • Students attend classes at The Center for Cross-Cultural Study (Seville, Spain). Field trips to Ronda, Ubeda, Córdoba, Baeza. Students typically earn 4 semester credits per term.

Sessions • Jan (winter).

Eligibility Requirements • Minimum age 16; open to precollege students, freshmen, sophomores, juniors, seniors, graduate students, adults; 1 letter of recommendation; good academic standing at home school; minimum 3.0 GPA in Spanish; 1 year of college course work in Spanish.

Living Arrangements • Students live in host family homes. Quarters are shared with host institution students. Meals are taken with host family, in residences.

Costs (2007) • $2675; includes tuition, housing, all meals, insurance, excursions, student support services, laundry, activities, study tours, email and high-speed Internet access. $50 application fee. $300 nonrefundable deposit required. Financial aid available for all students: scholarships.

For More Information • Dr. Judith M. Ortiz, Director, U.S., The Center for Cross-Cultural Study, 446 Main Street, Amherst, MA 01002-2314; *Phone:* 800-377-2621; *Fax:* 413-256-1968. *E-mail:* admin@cccs.com. *World Wide Web:* http://www.cccs.com/

THE CENTER FOR CROSS-CULTURAL STUDY
SUMMER PROGRAM IN SEVILLE, SPAIN

Hosted by The Center for Cross-Cultural Study

Academic Focus • Art history, business administration/management, cultural studies, drama/theater, history, international business, political science and government, Spanish language and literature, Spanish studies, teaching English as a second language.

Program Information • Students attend classes at The Center for Cross-Cultural Study (Seville, Spain). Field trips to Ronda, La Rabida monastery and beach, Córdoba. Students typically earn 4 semester credits per term.

Sessions • May–Jun (summer), Jun–Jul (summer term 2); May–Jul (summer term 7).

Eligibility Requirements • Minimum age 16; open to precollege students, freshmen, sophomores, juniors, seniors, graduate students, adults; 1 letter of recommendation; good academic standing at home school; minimum 3.0 GPA in Spanish; no foreign language proficiency required.

Living Arrangements • Students live in host family homes. Quarters are shared with host institution students. Meals are taken with host family, in residences.

Costs (2007) • $2975 for 4 weeks; $5640 for 7 weeks; includes tuition, housing, all meals, insurance, excursions, student support services, laundry, activities, study tours, email and high-speed Internet access. $50 application fee. $300 nonrefundable deposit required. Financial aid available for all students: scholarships.

For More Information • Dr. Judith M. Ortiz, Director, U.S., The Center for Cross-Cultural Study, 446 Main Street, Amherst, MA 01002-2314; *Phone:* 800-377-2621; *Fax:* 413-256-1968. *E-mail:* admin@cccs.com. *World Wide Web:* http://www.cccs.com/

CENTRO DE LENGUAS E INTERCAMBIO CULTURAL (CLIC)
ACCREDITED SUMMER PROGRAM

Hosted by CLIC International House

Academic Focus • Business administration/management, history, language studies, Spanish language and literature, Spanish studies.

SPAIN
Seville

Program Information • Students attend classes at CLIC International House (Seville, Spain). Students typically earn 12 semester credits per term.
Sessions • May–Jul (summer).
Eligibility Requirements • Minimum age 18; open to precollege students, freshmen, sophomores, juniors, seniors, graduate students, adults; no foreign language proficiency required.
Living Arrangements • Students live in host family homes. Quarters are shared with host institution students. Meals are taken with host family.
Costs (2005) • €2690; includes tuition, housing, all meals, student support services. €150 nonrefundable deposit required.
For More Information • Ms. Eva White, Head of Administration, Centro de Lenguas e Intercambio Cultural (CLIC), C/Albareda, 19, 41001 Sevilla, Spain; *Phone:* +34 95450-2131; *Fax:* +34 95456-1696. *E-mail:* eva@clic.es. *World Wide Web:* http://www.clic.es/. Students may also apply through Benedictine College, 1020 North 2nd Street, Atchison, KS 66002.

CIEE
CIEE STUDY CENTER IN SEVILLE, SPAIN–INTERNSHIP

Held at CIEE Study Center
Academic Focus • Spanish language and literature.
Program Information • Classes are held on the campus of CIEE Study Center (Seville, Spain). Faculty members are local instructors hired by the sponsor. Field trips to Granada, Córdoba, Hálica, Carmona, Madrid. Students typically earn 6 semester credits per term.
Sessions • Jun–Jul (summer).
Eligibility Requirements • Minimum age 18; open to sophomores, juniors, seniors; 2.75 GPA; 2 letters of recommendation; good academic standing at home school; evaluation should be from a language professor; 2.5 years of college course work in Spanish.
Living Arrangements • Students live in host family homes. Meals are taken with host family, in residences.
Costs (2006) • $4900; includes tuition, housing, all meals, insurance, excursions, student support services, pre-departure advising, resident staff, orientation, cultural activities, on-site pick-up. $30 application fee. $300 nonrefundable deposit required. Financial aid available for all students: minority student scholarships.
For More Information • Information Center, CIEE, 7 Custom House Street, 3rd Floor, Portland, ME 04101; *Phone:* 800-40-STUDY; *Fax:* 207-553-7699. *E-mail:* studyinfo@ciee.org. *World Wide Web:* http://www.ciee.org/isp/

CIEE
CIEE STUDY CENTER IN SEVILLE, SPAIN–LANGUAGE AND CULTURE PROGRAM

Hosted by CIEE Study Center
Academic Focus • Social sciences, Spanish language and literature.
Program Information • Students attend classes at CIEE Study Center (Seville, Spain). Field trips to Granada, Córdoba, Hálica, Carmona, Madrid. Students typically earn 3 semester credits per term.
Sessions • May–Jun (summer), Session II early June-late June; Session III late June-late July.
Eligibility Requirements • Minimum age 18; open to sophomores, juniors, seniors; 2.75 GPA; 1 letter of recommendation; good academic standing at home school; no foreign language proficiency required.
Living Arrangements • Students live in host family homes. Meals are taken on one's own, with host family, in residences, in restaurants.
Costs (2006) • $2500 for 1 session; $4900 for 2 sessions; $7300 for 3 sessions; includes tuition, housing, all meals, insurance, excursions, student support services, pre-departure advising, resident staff, orientation, cultural activities, on-site pick-up. $30 application fee. $300 nonrefundable deposit required. Financial aid available for all students: minority student scholarships.
For More Information • Information Center, CIEE, 7 Custom House Street, 3rd Floor, Portland, ME 04101; *Phone:* 800-40-STUDY; *Fax:* 207-553-7699. *E-mail:* studyinfo@ciee.org. *World Wide Web:* http://www.ciee.org/isp/

COLLEGE CONSORTIUM FOR INTERNATIONAL STUDIES–BROWARD COMMUNITY COLLEGE AND ST. BONAVENTURE UNIVERSITY
SUMMER IN SPAIN

Hosted by International College of Seville
Academic Focus • Anthropology, Spanish language and literature, Spanish studies.
Program Information • Students attend classes at International College of Seville (Seville, Spain). Field trips to Córdoba, La Rabida monastery, Ronda, Jerez; optional travel to Madrid, Portugal at an extra cost. Students typically earn 6 semester credits per term.
Sessions • Jun–Jul (summer).
Eligibility Requirements • Minimum age 18; open to freshmen, sophomores, juniors, seniors, graduate students, adults; 2.5 GPA; 3 letters of recommendation; good academic standing at home school; no foreign language proficiency required.
Living Arrangements • Students live in locally rented apartments, host family homes. Quarters are shared with host institution students. Meals are taken on one's own, with host family, in residences, in restaurants.
Costs (2006) • $2625; includes tuition, housing, all meals, insurance, excursions, student support services, cell phones; internet access. Financial aid available for students from sponsoring institution: scholarships, loans.
For More Information • Dr. David Moore, Associate Vice President for International Education, College Consortium for International Studies–Broward Community College and St. Bonaventure University, 225 East Las Olas Boulevard, Ft. Lauderdale, FL 33301; *Phone:* 954-201-7707; *Fax:* 954-201-7708. *E-mail:* dmoore@broward.edu. *World Wide Web:* http://www.ccisabroad.org/. Students may also apply through St. Bonventure University, St. Bonaventure, NY 14778.

DON QUIJOTE
INTENSIVE SPANISH COURSE IN SEVILLE

Hosted by Don Quijote
Academic Focus • Romance languages, Spanish language and literature, Spanish studies.
Program Information • Students attend classes at Don Quijote (Seville, Spain). Field trips to historic sites, important cities in Spain. Students typically earn 4 semester credits per term.
Sessions • Minimum 1 week sessions begin every Monday.
Eligibility Requirements • Minimum age 18; open to freshmen, sophomores, juniors, seniors, graduate students, adults; no foreign language proficiency required.
Living Arrangements • Students live in host institution dormitories, program-owned apartments, host family homes. Quarters are shared with host institution students, students from other programs. Meals are taken on one's own, with host family, in residences.
Costs (2006) • Contact sponsor for cost. €65 application fee. €500 deposit required. Financial aid available for all students: scholarships.
For More Information • Ms. Carmen Cantarino, USA Director, Don Quijote, Plaza San Marcos 7, 37002 Salamanca, Spain; *Phone:* +34 923-268874; *Fax:* +34 923-260674. *E-mail:* usa@donquijote.org. *World Wide Web:* http://www.donquijote.org/

EUROPEAN HERITAGE INSTITUTE
YEAR-ROUND PROGRAMS IN SEVILLE

Hosted by Don Quijote
Academic Focus • Spanish language and literature, Spanish studies.
Program Information • Students attend classes at Don Quijote (Seville, Spain). Field trips to areas around Seville. Students typically earn 3-6 semester credits per term.
Sessions • 1 to 15 week sessions begin weekly, year-round.
Eligibility Requirements • Minimum age 18; open to freshmen, sophomores, juniors, seniors, graduate students, adults; 2.25 GPA; 2 letters of recommendation; no foreign language proficiency required.
Living Arrangements • Students live in host institution dormitories, locally rented apartments, host family homes. Quarters are shared with host institution students. Meals are taken on one's own, with host family, in residences, in restaurants.

Costs (2005) • $1581 for 4 weeks; $2958 for 8 weeks; $4732 for 12 weeks; includes tuition, housing, some meals, excursions, books and class materials, international student ID, student support services. $300 refundable deposit required.

For More Information • Dr. Antonio Masullo, Professor, European Heritage Institute, 2708 East Franklin Street, Richmond, VA 23223; *Phone:* 804-643-0661; *Fax:* 804-648-0826. *E-mail:* info@europeabroad.org. *World Wide Web:* http://www.europeabroad.org/

INTERNATIONAL STUDIES ABROAD
SEVILLA: SPANISH LANGUAGE, CULTURE, AND BUSINESS PROGRAM

Hosted by International University 'Menéndez Pelayo'–Seville

Academic Focus • Civilization studies, economics, international business, marketing, Spanish language and literature.

Program Information • Students attend classes at International University 'Menéndez Pelayo'-Seville (Seville, Spain). Scheduled travel to Madrid, Toledo, El Escorial; field trips to Granada, Ronda, Córdoba; optional travel at an extra cost. Students typically earn 6–8 semester credits per term.

Sessions • May–Jul (summer), Jun–Aug (summer 2).

Eligibility Requirements • Minimum age 18; open to freshmen, sophomores, juniors, seniors, adults; 2.5 GPA; good academic standing at home school; contact sponsor if GPA is lower than 2.5; no foreign language proficiency required.

Living Arrangements • Students live in locally rented apartments, host family homes. Quarters are shared with host institution students. Meals are taken with host family, in residences.

Costs (2005–2006) • Contact sponsor for cost. $200 deposit required.

For More Information • Sevilla Site Specialist, International Studies Abroad, 901 West 24th Street, Austin, TX 78705; *Phone:* 800-580-8826; *Fax:* 512-480-8866. *E-mail:* isa@studiesabroad.com. *World Wide Web:* http://www.studiesabroad.com/

INTERNATIONAL UNIVERSITY STUDIES (IUS)
INTERNATIONAL UNIVERSITY STUDIES (IUS)

Hosted by International University Studies (IUS)

Academic Focus • Archaeology, history, Israeli studies, sociology, Spanish language and literature, Spanish studies.

Program Information • Students attend classes at International University Studies (IUS) (Seville, Spain). Field trips to Córdoba, Haelra.

Sessions • May–Jul (summer), Jan (winter).

Eligibility Requirements • Minimum age 16; open to precollege students, freshmen, sophomores, juniors, seniors, graduate students, adults; 2.5 GPA; 2 letters of recommendation; good academic standing at home school; beginner to advanced Spanish required for summer term; advanced Spanish required for winter term.

Costs (2005) • $2300; includes tuition, housing, all meals, insurance, excursions, lab equipment, international student ID, student support services, program-generated study materials. $350 nonrefundable deposit required.

For More Information • Ms. Ann Persoff, Admissions and Processing Office, International University Studies (IUS), Calle Vidvio, 35, 41007 Sevilla, Spain; *Phone:* 877-449-3615; *Fax:* +34 954-546198. *E-mail:* admissions@iustospain.com. *World Wide Web:* http://www.iustospain.com/

LANGUAGE LINK
CLIC OF SEVILLE, SPAIN

Hosted by Centro de Lenguas e Intercambio Cultural (CLIC)

Academic Focus • Spanish language and literature.

Program Information • Students attend classes at Centro de Lenguas e Intercambio Cultural (CLIC) (Seville, Spain). Field trips to Granada. Students typically earn 6–30 semester credits for 3 weeks (30 maximum per year).

Sessions • Year-round, start dates every other Monday for beginners.

Eligibility Requirements • Minimum age 13; open to precollege students, freshmen, sophomores, juniors, seniors, graduate students, adults; no foreign language proficiency required.

Living Arrangements • Students live in host institution dormitories, locally rented apartments, host family homes. Quarters are shared with host institution students. Meals are taken on one's own, with host family, in residences, in restaurants.

Costs (2005) • $350 per week; includes tuition, housing, some meals, books and class materials, student support services, cultural activities.

For More Information • Ms. Kay G. Rafool, Director, Language Link, PO Box 3006, Peoria, IL 61612-3006; *Phone:* 800-552-2051; *Fax:* 309-692-2926. *E-mail:* info@langlink.com. *World Wide Web:* http://www.langlink.com/

LINGUA SERVICE WORLDWIDE
VACATION 'N LEARN SPANISH IN SPAIN

Hosted by Centro de Lenguas e Intercambio Cultural (CLIC)

Academic Focus • Spanish language and literature, Spanish studies.

Program Information • Students attend classes at Centro de Lenguas e Intercambio Cultural (CLIC) (Seville, Spain). Optional travel to cultural sites around Spain at an extra cost. Students typically earn 3 semester credits for 3 weeks, 6 semester credits for 5 weeks.

Sessions • Classes held year-round, beginning on Mondays, minimum session length is 2 weeks.

Eligibility Requirements • Minimum age 16; open to precollege students, freshmen, sophomores, juniors, seniors, graduate students, adults; no foreign language proficiency required.

Living Arrangements • Students live in host institution dormitories, locally rented apartments, host family homes, hotels. Quarters are shared with host institution students. Meals are taken with host family.

Costs (2006–2007) • Contact sponsor for cost. $100 application fee.

For More Information • Assistant Director, Lingua Service Worldwide, 75 Prospect Street, Suite 4, Huntington, NY 11743; *Phone:* 800-394-5327; *Fax:* 631-271-3441. *E-mail:* linguaservice@att.net. *World Wide Web:* http://www.linguaserviceworldwide.com/

STATE UNIVERSITY OF NEW YORK AT NEW PALTZ
SUMMER SPANISH LANGUAGE STUDIES

Academic Focus • Spanish language and literature.

Program Information • Faculty members are drawn from the sponsor's U.S. staff and local instructors hired by the sponsor. Field trips to Madrid, Toledo, Segovia, Córdoba, Oviedo. Students typically earn 6 semester credits per term.

Sessions • Jul (summer).

Eligibility Requirements • Minimum age 18; open to freshmen, sophomores, juniors, seniors, graduate students; 2.5 GPA; 1 letter of recommendation; good academic standing at home school; 1 year of college course work in Spanish.

Living Arrangements • Students live in host institution dormitories, locally rented apartments, hotels. Meals are taken as a group, in residences, in restaurants.

Costs (2006) • $3600 for New York residents; $5100 for nonresidents; includes tuition, housing, all meals, excursions, student support services, administrative fee. $25 application fee. $300 nonrefundable deposit required. Financial aid available for students from sponsoring institution: scholarships, loans.

For More Information • Center for International Programs, State University of New York at New Paltz, 1 Hawk Drive, New Paltz, NY 12561-2443; *Phone:* 845-257-3125; *Fax:* 845-257-3129. *E-mail:* studyabroad@newpaltz.edu. *World Wide Web:* http://www.newpaltz.edu/studyabroad/

SWEET BRIAR COLLEGE
SUMMER IN SPAIN

Academic Focus • Full curriculum.

Program Information • Faculty members are drawn from the sponsor's U.S. staff and local instructors hired by the sponsor. Field trips; optional travel to Morocco at an extra cost. Students typically earn 6 semester credits per term.

Sessions • May–Jun (summer).

Eligibility Requirements • Minimum age 18; open to freshmen, sophomores, juniors, seniors, graduate students, adults; 2 letters of recommendation; good academic standing at home school; 1 year of college course work in Spanish.

SPAIN
Seville

Living Arrangements • Students live in host family homes. Meals are taken with host family.
Costs (2006) • $4400; includes tuition, housing, all meals, insurance, excursions, books and class materials, international student ID, student support services. $50 application fee. $250 nonrefundable deposit required. Financial aid available for all students: scholarships.
For More Information • Ms. Lynn Ann McGuern, Director, Sweet Briar College, Sweet Briar, VA 24595; *Phone:* 434-381-6281; *Fax:* 434-381-6293. *E-mail:* jys@sbc.edu

TRINITY CHRISTIAN COLLEGE
SEMESTER IN SPAIN

Held at Trinity Christian College
Academic Focus • Spanish language and literature, Spanish studies.
Program Information • Classes are held on the campus of Trinity Christian College (Seville, Spain). Faculty members are local instructors hired by the sponsor. Field trips to Córdoba, Toledo, Italica, Granada. Students typically earn 4-8 semester credits per term.
Sessions • May-Jul (summer).
Eligibility Requirements • Minimum age 18; open to freshmen, sophomores, juniors, seniors, graduate students, adults; 2.5 GPA; 2 letters of recommendation; good academic standing at home school; good health; high school diploma; 1 year of college course work in Spanish.
Living Arrangements • Students live in host family homes. Quarters are shared with host institution students. Meals are taken with host family, in residences.
Costs (2007) • $2600; includes tuition, housing, all meals, insurance, excursions, books and class materials, student support services, laundry and linens, cell phone. $40 application fee. $100 nonrefundable deposit required.

For More Information • Ms. Debra Veenstra, Semester in Spain Coordinator, Trinity Christian College, 6601 West College Drive, Palos Heights, IL 60463; *Phone:* 800-748-0087; *Fax:* 708-239-3986. *E-mail:* spain@trnty.edu. *World Wide Web:* http://www.semesterinspain.org/

UNIVERSITY OF WISCONSIN–PLATTEVILLE
SUMMER SESSION IN SEVILLE

Hosted by Spanish American Institute of International Education
Academic Focus • History, Spanish language and literature, Spanish studies.
Program Information • Students attend classes at Spanish American Institute of International Education (Seville, Spain). Field trips to museums, galleries, historic sites in and around Seville, churches; optional travel to Portugal, Granada at an extra cost. Students typically earn 6 semester credits per term.
Sessions • May-Jul (summer), Jun-Jul (summer 2).
Eligibility Requirements • Minimum age 18; open to freshmen, sophomores, juniors, seniors; 2.0 GPA; 2 letters of recommendation; good academic standing at home school; 1 year of college course work in Spanish.
Living Arrangements • Students live in host family homes. Meals are taken on one's own, with host family, in residences, in restaurants.
Costs (2005) • $3695 for Wisconsin and Minnesota residents; $3995 for nonresidents; includes tuition, housing, some meals, insurance, excursions, books and class materials, international student ID, student support services. $25 application fee. $400 nonrefundable deposit required. Financial aid available for students from sponsoring institution: scholarships, loans, federal and state grants.
For More Information • Ms. Donna Anderson, Director, Study Abroad Programs, University of Wisconsin–Platteville, Institute for

study • faith • immersion • service

Semester in Spain

- Fall or Spring semesters, Summer terms
- Beginning, Intermediate or Advanced Spanish courses
- Earn 12-20 credits per semester, or 4-8 credits for summer terms
- Live and learn in beautiful Seville while studying Spanish at your level
- Experience Spanish life and culture while living with a Spanish host - 3 meals/day and laundry included
- Excursions to Cordoba, Grenada, Toledo and more!

For more information or an application, contact us at:
E-mail: spain@trnty.edu
Phone: 1-800-748-0087
Mail: Semester in Spain
Trinity Christian College
6601 W. College Drive
Palos Heights, IL 60463
Web: www.semesterinspain.org

Improve your **vision** with Semester in Spain

Study Abroad Programs, 111 Royce Hall, 1 University Plaza, Platteville, WI 53818-3099; *Phone:* 800-342-1725; *Fax:* 608-342-1736. *E-mail:* studyabroad@uwplatt.edu. *World Wide Web:* http://www.uwplatt.edu/studyabroad/

TENERIFE

DON QUIJOTE
INTENSIVE SPANISH COURSE IN TENERIFE
Hosted by Don Quijote
Academic Focus • Romance languages, Spanish language and literature, Spanish studies.
Program Information • Students attend classes at Don Quijote (Tenerife, Spain). Field trips. Students typically earn 4 semester credits per term.
Sessions • Minimum 1 week sessions begin every Monday.
Eligibility Requirements • Minimum age 18; open to freshmen, sophomores, juniors, seniors, graduate students, adults; no foreign language proficiency required.
Living Arrangements • Students live in host institution dormitories, program-owned apartments, host family homes. Quarters are shared with host institution students, students from other programs. Meals are taken on one's own, with host family, in residences.
Costs (2006) • Contact sponsor for cost. €65 application fee. €500 deposit required. Financial aid available for all students: scholarships.
For More Information • Ms. Carmen Cantarino, USA Director, Don Quijote, Plaza San Marcos 7, 37002 Salamanca, Spain; *Phone:* +34 923-268874; *Fax:* +34 923-260674. *E-mail:* usa@donquijote.org. *World Wide Web:* http://www.donquijote.org/

EUROPEAN HERITAGE INSTITUTE
YEAR-ROUND PROGRAMS IN TENERIFE
Hosted by Don Quijote
Academic Focus • Spanish language and literature.
Program Information • Students attend classes at Don Quijote (Tenerife, Spain). Field trips to sites around Tenerife. Students typically earn 3-6 semester credits per term.
Sessions • 1 to 15 week sessions begin weekly, year-round.
Eligibility Requirements • Minimum age 18; open to freshmen, sophomores, juniors, seniors, graduate students, adults; 2.25 GPA; 2 letters of recommendation; no foreign language proficiency required.
Living Arrangements • Students live in host institution dormitories, locally rented apartments, host family homes, hotels, a residence center. Quarters are shared with host institution students. Meals are taken on one's own, with host family, in restaurants.
Costs (2005) • $1800 for 4 weeks; $3220 for 8 weeks; $4732 for 12 weeks; includes tuition, housing, some meals, excursions, books and class materials, student support services. $300 refundable deposit required.
For More Information • Dr. Antonio Masullo, Professor, European Heritage Institute, 2708 East Franklin Street, Richmond, VA 23223; *Phone:* 804-643-0661; *Fax:* 804-648-0826. *E-mail:* info@europeabroad.org. *World Wide Web:* http://www.europeabroad.org/

TOLEDO

ARCADIA UNIVERSITY
SUMMER IN TOLEDO, SPAIN
Hosted by Fundación José Ortega y Gasset
Academic Focus • Art history, liberal studies, social sciences, Spanish language and literature, Spanish studies.
Program Information • Students attend classes at Fundación José Ortega y Gasset (Toledo, Spain). Field trips to Madrid, Segovia, El Escorial; optional travel to Andalucia or Avila/Salamanca (weekend trip) at an extra cost. Students typically earn 6-9 semester credits per term.
Sessions • Jun-Jul (summer).
Eligibility Requirements • Open to sophomores, juniors, seniors, graduate students, adults; 3.0 GPA; 1 letter of recommendation; 1 year of college course work in Spanish.
Living Arrangements • Students live in host institution dormitories, host family homes. Quarters are shared with students from other programs. Meals are taken on one's own, with host family, in residences, in central dining facility.
Costs (2005) • $4500; includes tuition, housing, all meals, insurance, excursions, international student ID, student support services, pre-departure guide, transcript, orientation. $35 application fee. $500 nonrefundable deposit required. Financial aid available for all students: scholarships, loans.
For More Information • Arcadia University, Center for Education Abroad, 450 South Easton Road, Glenside, PA 19038-3295; *Phone:* 866-927-2234; *Fax:* 215-572-2174. *E-mail:* cea@arcadia.edu. *World Wide Web:* http://www.arcadia.edu/cea/

NORTHERN ILLINOIS UNIVERSITY
SPANISH LANGUAGE AND CULTURE IN TOLEDO, SPAIN
Hosted by University of Castilla-La Mancha
Academic Focus • Spanish language and literature, Spanish studies.
Program Information • Students attend classes at University of Castilla-La Mancha (Toledo, Spain). Field trips to Segovia, the Route of Don Quixote, Madrid. Students typically earn 3-6 semester credits per term.
Sessions • Jun-Jul (summer).
Eligibility Requirements • Minimum age 18; open to juniors, seniors, graduate students; 2.75 GPA; good academic standing at home school; approval of NIU Chair of Department of Foreign Languages; 3 years of college course work in Spanish.
Living Arrangements • Students live in host institution dormitories, host family homes. Quarters are shared with students from other programs. Meals are taken as a group, with host family, in central dining facility.
Costs (2005) • $3185-$3540; includes tuition, housing, all meals, insurance, excursions, international student ID, student support services. $200 nonrefundable deposit required. Financial aid available for students from sponsoring institution: loans.
For More Information • Ms. Rita Withrow, Program Assistant, Northern Illinois University, Study Abroad Office, Williston Hall 417, DeKalb, IL 60115; *Phone:* 815-753-0700; *Fax:* 815-753-0825. *E-mail:* niuabroad@niu.edu. *World Wide Web:* http://www.niu.edu/niuabroad/

UNIVERSITY OF MINNESOTA
INTERNATIONAL PROGRAM IN TOLEDO
Hosted by Fundación José Ortega y Gasset
Academic Focus • Anthropology, archaeology, art history, drama/theater, economics, European studies, history, interdisciplinary studies, Latin American studies, political science and government, Spanish language and literature, Spanish studies, women's studies.
Program Information • Students attend classes at Fundación José Ortega y Gasset (Toledo, Spain). Field trips to the route of Don Quixote, El Escorial, Segovia, Madrid, Aranjuez, Cúenca; optional travel at an extra cost. Students typically earn 3-9 semester credits per term.
Sessions • May-Jun (summer), Jun-Jul (summer 2).
Eligibility Requirements • Minimum age 18; open to freshmen, sophomores, juniors, seniors, graduate students, adults; 2.5 GPA; good academic standing at home school; 2 years of college course work in Spanish.
Living Arrangements • Students live in host family homes, the Residencia San Juan de la Penitencia. Quarters are shared with host institution students, students from other programs. Meals are taken as a group, with host family, in residences, in central dining facility.
Costs (2006) • Contact sponsor for cost; includes tuition, housing, all meals, insurance, excursions. Financial aid available for students from sponsoring institution: scholarships, loans.
For More Information • Learning Abroad Center, University of Minnesota, 230 Heller Hall, 271 19th Avenue South, Minneapolis, MN 55455; *Phone:* 888-700-UOFM; *Fax:* 612-626-8009. *E-mail:* umabroad@umn.edu. *World Wide Web:* http://www.umabroad.umn.edu/. Students may also apply through Centro de Estudios Internacionales, Fundación Ortega y Gasset, Callejón de San Justo S/N, 45001 Toledo, Spain.

SPAIN
Toledo

UNIVERSITY OF NOTRE DAME
TOLEDO SUMMER PROGRAM

Held at Fundación José Ortega y Gasset
Academic Focus • Spanish studies.
Program Information • Classes are held on the campus of Fundación José Ortega y Gasset (Toledo, Spain). Faculty members are drawn from the sponsor's U.S. staff. Field trips to Madrid, Segara, Aranjuez. Students typically earn 3 semester credits per term.
Sessions • May–Jun (summer).
Eligibility Requirements • Open to sophomores, juniors, seniors; good academic standing at home school; no foreign language proficiency required.
Living Arrangements • Students live in host institution dormitories. Quarters are shared with students from other programs. Meals are taken on one's own, in central dining facility.
Costs (2004–2005) • $3080; includes tuition, housing, all meals, excursions. Financial aid available for students from sponsoring institution: scholarships, loans.
For More Information • Dr. Claudia Kselman, Associate Director, University of Notre Dame, 158 Hurley Building, Notre Dame, IN 46556; *Phone:* 574-631-5882; *Fax:* 571-631-5711. *E-mail:* kselman.2@nd.edu. *World Wide Web:* http://www.nd.edu/~intlstud/

UBEDA

UNIVERSITY OF NORTH CAROLINA AT WILMINGTON
SUMMER STUDY IN SPAIN

Held at SAFA School of Education
Academic Focus • Spanish language and literature.
Program Information • Classes are held on the campus of SAFA School of Education (Ubeda, Spain). Faculty members are drawn from the sponsor's U.S. staff. Scheduled travel to Toledo; field trips to Granada, Sevilla, Madrid, Malaga, Cordoba, Cazorla National Park; optional travel to various parts of Spain at an extra cost. Students typically earn 6 semester credits per term.
Sessions • May–Jun (summer).
Eligibility Requirements • Minimum age 18; 2.0 GPA; 2 letters of recommendation; good academic standing at home school; 1.5 years college course work in Spanish.
Living Arrangements • Students live in host family homes. Meals are taken with host family, in residences.
Costs (2005) • $3180 for North Carolina residents; includes tuition, housing, all meals, insurance, excursions, international airfare. $200 nonrefundable deposit required. Financial aid available for students from sponsoring institution: scholarships, loans.
For More Information • Ms. Elizabeth A. Adams, Director, Education Abroad, University of North Carolina at Wilmington, 601 South College Road, Wilmington, NC 28403-5965; *Phone:* 910-962-3685; *Fax:* 910-962-4053. *E-mail:* studyabroad@uncw.edu. *World Wide Web:* http://www.uncw.edu/intprogs/

VALENCIA

DON QUIJOTE
INTENSIVE SPANISH COURSE IN VALENCIA

Hosted by Don Quijote
Academic Focus • Romance languages, Spanish language and literature, Spanish studies.
Program Information • Students attend classes at Don Quijote (Valencia, Spain). Field trips to historic sites, important cities in Spain. Students typically earn 4 semester credits per term.
Sessions • Minimum 1 week sessions begin every Monday.
Eligibility Requirements • Minimum age 18; open to freshmen, sophomores, juniors, seniors, graduate students, adults; no foreign language proficiency required.
Living Arrangements • Students live in host institution dormitories, program-owned apartments, host family homes. Quarters are shared with host institution students, students from other programs. Meals are taken on one's own, with host family, in residences.
Costs (2005) • Contact sponsor for cost. €65 application fee. €500 deposit required. Financial aid available for all students: scholarships.

For More Information • Ms. Carmen Cantarino, USA Director, Don Quijote, Plaza San Marcos 7, 37002 Salamanca, Spain; *Phone:* +34 923-268874; *Fax:* +34 923-260674. *E-mail:* usa@donquijote.org. *World Wide Web:* http://www.donquijote.org/

ENFOREX–SPANISH IN THE SPANISH WORLD
SPANISH INTENSIVE COURSE VALENCIA

Hosted by ENFOREX
Academic Focus • Dance, Spanish language and literature, Spanish studies.
Program Information • Students attend classes at ENFOREX (Valencia, Spain). Field trips to Sagunto, Alicante; optional travel to Ibiza at an extra cost. Students typically earn 4 quarter credits per term.
Sessions • Year-round.
Eligibility Requirements • Minimum age 14; open to precollege students, freshmen, sophomores, juniors, seniors, graduate students, adults; no foreign language proficiency required.
Living Arrangements • Students live in host institution dormitories, program-owned apartments, host family homes, hotels. Quarters are shared with host institution students, students from other programs. Meals are taken as a group, on one's own, with host family, in residences.
Costs (2005) • €1280 per month; includes tuition, housing, all meals, books and class materials, international student ID, student support services. €65 application fee. €250 nonrefundable deposit required.
For More Information • Mr. Antonio Anadón, Director of Spanish Department, ENFOREX–Spanish in the Spanish World, Alberto Aguilera, 26, 28015 Madrid, Spain; *Phone:* +34 91-594-3776; *Fax:* +34 91-594-5159. *E-mail:* promotion@enforex.es. *World Wide Web:* http://www.enforex.com/

EUROPEAN HERITAGE INSTITUTE
ACADEMIC SUMMER IN VALENCIA

Hosted by Institute of Spanish Studies
Academic Focus • Full curriculum.
Program Information • Students attend classes at Institute of Spanish Studies (Valencia, Spain). Field trips to Valencia, Gandia, Sagunto, Pensicola. Students typically earn 6 semester credits per term.
Sessions • May–Jun (summer), Jun–Jul (summer 2).
Eligibility Requirements • Minimum age 18; open to freshmen, sophomores, juniors, seniors, graduate students, adults; 2.5 GPA; 1 letter of recommendation; no foreign language proficiency required.
Living Arrangements • Students live in host institution dormitories, locally rented apartments, host family homes. Quarters are shared with students from other programs. Meals are taken on one's own, with host family, in residences, in central dining facility, in restaurants.
Costs (2005) • $3100; includes tuition, housing, all meals, excursions, books and class materials, student support services, fees. $300 refundable deposit required.
For More Information • Dr. Antonio Masullo, Professor, European Heritage Institute, 2708 East Franklin Street, Richmond, VA 23223; *Phone:* 804-643-0661; *Fax:* 804-648-0826. *E-mail:* info@europeabroad.org. *World Wide Web:* http://www.europeabroad.org/

EUROPEAN HERITAGE INSTITUTE
YEAR-ROUND PROGRAMS IN VALENCIA

Hosted by Don Quijote
Academic Focus • Spanish language and literature, Spanish studies.
Program Information • Students attend classes at Don Quijote (Valencia, Spain). Field trips to areas around Valencia. Students typically earn 3-6 semester credits per term.
Sessions • 1 to 15 week sessions held year-round.
Eligibility Requirements • Minimum age 18; open to freshmen, sophomores, juniors, seniors, graduate students, adults; 2.25 GPA; 2 letters of recommendation; no foreign language proficiency required.
Living Arrangements • Students live in host institution dormitories, locally rented apartments, host family homes. Quarters are

shared with host institution students. Meals are taken on one's own, with host family, in residences, in restaurants.
Costs (2005) • $3100 for 4 weeks; $5800 for 8 weeks; includes tuition, housing, some meals, excursions, books and class materials, international student ID, student support services. $300 refundable deposit required.
For More Information • Dr. Antonio Masullo, Professor, European Heritage Institute, 2708 East Franklin Street, Richmond, VA 23223; *Phone:* 804-643-0661; *Fax:* 804-648-0826. *E-mail:* info@europeabroad. org. *World Wide Web:* http://www.europeabroad.org/

INSTITUTE OF SPANISH STUDIES
SUMMER SESSIONS ABROAD IN VALENCIA, SPAIN

Hosted by Institute of Spanish Studies
Academic Focus • Civilization studies, geography, history, literature, Spanish language and literature.
Program Information • Students attend classes at Institute of Spanish Studies (Valencia, Spain). Field trips to Sagunto, beaches, Peñiscola; optional travel to Mallorca at an extra cost. Students typically earn 9 semester credits per term.
Sessions • May–Jun (summer), Jun–Jul (summer 2).
Eligibility Requirements • Open to freshmen, sophomores, juniors, seniors, graduate students, adults; 2.5 GPA; 2 letters of recommendation; good academic standing at home school; no foreign language proficiency required.
Living Arrangements • Students live in host family homes. Quarters are shared with host institution students. Meals are taken with host family.
Costs (2006) • $3100; includes tuition, housing, all meals, insurance, excursions, international student ID, student support services. $300 refundable deposit required.
For More Information • Mr. Arturo Sanchez, Director, Institute of Spanish Studies, El Bachiller 13, 46010 Valencia, Spain; *Phone:* +34 96-369 6168; *Fax:* +34 96-361 5189. *E-mail:* arturo@spanish-studies. com. *World Wide Web:* http://www.spanish-studies.com/. Students may also apply through Longwood College, International Affairs, 201 High Street, Farmville, VA 23909.

INTERNATIONAL STUDIES ABROAD
VALENCIA, SPAIN–SPANISH LANGUAGE AND CULTURE

Hosted by University of Valencia
Academic Focus • Spanish language and literature, Spanish studies.
Program Information • Students attend classes at University of Valencia (Valencia, Spain). Field trips to El Escorial, Granada, Madrid, Toledo, Barcelona, Ubeda/Baeza. Students typically earn 6–8 semester credits per term.
Sessions • May–Jun (summer), Jun–Jul (summer 2).
Eligibility Requirements • Minimum age 18; open to freshmen, sophomores, juniors, seniors, adults; 2.5 GPA; good academic standing at home school; 1 year of college course work in Spanish.
Living Arrangements • Students live in host family homes. Quarters are shared with host institution students. Meals are taken with host family, in residences.
Costs (2005–2006) • Contact sponsor for cost. $200 deposit required. Financial aid available for all students: scholarships.
For More Information • Spain Site Specialist, International Studies Abroad, 901 West 24th Street, Austin, TX 78705; *Phone:* 800-580-8826; *Fax:* 512-480-8866. *E-mail:* isa@studiesabroad.com. *World Wide Web:* http://www.studiesabroad.com/

LANGUAGE LIAISON
SPANISH IN SPAIN–VALENCIA

Hosted by Language Liaison
Academic Focus • Spanish language and literature.
Program Information • Students attend classes at Language Liaison (Valencia, Spain). Field trips to cultural sites; optional travel. Students typically earn 3–15 semester credits per term.
Sessions • New programs begin weekly, year-round.
Eligibility Requirements • Minimum age 14; open to precollege students, freshmen, sophomores, juniors, seniors, graduate students, adults; no foreign language proficiency required.

Living Arrangements • Students live in host institution dormitories, locally rented apartments, host family homes. Meals are taken as a group, with host family, in residences, in central dining facility, in restaurants.
Costs (2005) • Contact sponsor for cost. $175 application fee. Financial aid available for all students: scholarship research service.
For More Information • Ms. Nancy Forman, President, Language Liaison, PO Box 1772, Pacific Palisades, CA 90272; *Phone:* 800-284-4448; *Fax:* 310-454-1706. *E-mail:* learn@languageliaison. com. *World Wide Web:* http://www.languageliaison.com/

LINGUA SERVICE WORLDWIDE
VACATION 'N LEARN SPANISH IN SPAIN

Hosted by Centro Internacional de Lengua y Cultura Española (CLICE)
Academic Focus • Spanish language and literature, Spanish studies.
Program Information • Students attend classes at Centro Internacional de Lengua y Cultura Española (CLICE) (Valencia, Spain). Optional travel to cultural sites around Spain at an extra cost. Students typically earn 3 semester credits per term.
Sessions • Classes held year-round, beginning on Mondays, minimum session length is 2 weeks.
Eligibility Requirements • Minimum age 16; open to precollege students, freshmen, sophomores, juniors, seniors, graduate students, adults; no foreign language proficiency required.
Living Arrangements • Students live in host institution dormitories, locally rented apartments, host family homes, hotels. Quarters are shared with host institution students. Meals are taken with host family.
Costs (2006–2007) • Contact sponsor for cost. $100 application fee.
For More Information • Assistant Director, Lingua Service Worldwide, 75 Prospect Street, Suite 4, Huntington, NY 11743; *Phone:* 800-394-5327; *Fax:* 631-271-3441. *E-mail:* linguaservice@att. net. *World Wide Web:* http://www.linguaserviceworldwide.com/

UNIVERSITY AT ALBANY, STATE UNIVERSITY OF NEW YORK
LANGUAGE AND CULTURE STUDIES IN VALENCIA

Hosted by A.I.P. Language Institute
Academic Focus • Spanish language and literature, Spanish studies.
Program Information • Students attend classes at A.I.P. Language Institute (Valencia, Spain). Field trips; optional travel to Madrid, Barcelona, Ibiza at an extra cost. Students typically earn 15 semester credits per term.
Sessions • Jun–Aug (summer).
Eligibility Requirements • Open to freshmen, sophomores, juniors, seniors, graduate students, adults; 2.5 GPA; 2 letters of recommendation; good academic standing at home school; advanced Spanish for advanced levels of study; no foreign language proficiency requirement for other tracks.
Living Arrangements • Students live in host family homes. Meals are taken with host family, in residences.
Costs (2005) • Contact sponsor for cost. $150 nonrefundable deposit required. Financial aid available for students from sponsoring institution: all customary sources.
For More Information • University at Albany, State University of New York, Office of International Education, LI 66, Albany, NY 12222; *Phone:* 518-442-3525; *Fax:* 518-442-3338. *E-mail:* intled@ uamail.albany.edu. *World Wide Web:* http://www.albany.edu/ studyabroad/

VALLADOLID

INTERNATIONAL HOUSE VALLADOLID
INTENSIVE SPANISH VALLADOLID

Hosted by International House Valladolid
Academic Focus • Spanish language and literature, Spanish studies.
Program Information • Students attend classes at International House Valladolid (Valladolid, Spain). Field trips to Salamanca, Segovia, Burgos, Avila.
Sessions • Year-round; minimum 2 weeks.

Eligibility Requirements • Minimum age 16; open to precollege students, freshmen, sophomores, juniors, seniors, graduate students, adults; no foreign language proficiency required.

Living Arrangements • Students live in host family homes, hotels. Meals are taken on one's own, with host family, in residences, in restaurants.

Costs (2006) • €305 for 2 weeks; 559Ç for 4 weeks; 1639Ç for 12 weeks; includes tuition, books and class materials, lab equipment, IH study folder and student information handbook. €32 application fee. €200 nonrefundable deposit required.

For More Information • Mr. William B. Ott, Director, International House Valladolid, Plaza Mayor 3-1 Izquierda, 47001 Valladolid, Spain; *Phone:* +34 942-233664; *Fax:* +34 942-236016. *E-mail:* william@ihvalladolid.com. *World Wide Web:* http://www.ihvalladolid.com

VEJER DE LA FRONTERA

INTERNATIONAL HOUSE LA JANDA
GENERAL SPANISH INTENSIVE COURSE

Hosted by International House La Janda

Academic Focus • Spanish language and literature, Spanish studies.

Program Information • Students attend classes at International House La Janda (Vejer, Spain). Field trips to Sevilla, Granada, Tarifa, Morocco.

Sessions • 2 to 8 week sessions, year-round.

Eligibility Requirements • Minimum age 17; open to precollege students, freshmen, sophomores, juniors, seniors, graduate students, adults; no foreign language proficiency required.

Living Arrangements • Students live in locally rented apartments, program-owned apartments, host family homes, hotels. Quarters are shared with host institution students. Meals are taken as a group, on one's own, with host family, in residences.

Costs (2005) • €118 per week; includes tuition. €35 application fee. €150 deposit required.

For More Information • Ms. Caroline Trustram, Head of Administration, International House La Janda, Colegio De Espanol La Janda IH Vejer, Vejer de la Frontera, 11150 Cadiz, Spain; *Phone:* +34 956-447060; *Fax:* +34 956-447378. *E-mail:* info@lajanda.org. *World Wide Web:* http://www.lajanda.org/

LANGUAGE LINK
LA JANDA OF VEJER DE LA FRONTERA, SPAIN

Hosted by La Janda

Academic Focus • Spanish language and literature.

Program Information • Students attend classes at La Janda (Vejer de la Frontera, Spain). Field trips to Seville, Cadiz, Córdoba, Granada. Students typically earn 6–15 semester credits per term.

Sessions • Classes begin every Monday, year-round.

Eligibility Requirements • Minimum age 14; open to precollege students, freshmen, sophomores, juniors, seniors, graduate students, adults; no foreign language proficiency required.

Living Arrangements • Students live in locally rented apartments, program-owned apartments, host family homes. Quarters are shared with host institution students. Meals are taken on one's own, with host family, in residences, in restaurants.

Costs (2005) • $390 per week; includes tuition, housing, some meals, student support services.

For More Information • Ms. Kay G. Rafool, Director, Language Link, PO Box 3006, Peoria, IL 61612-3006; *Phone:* 800-552-2051; *Fax:* 309-692-2926. *E-mail:* info@langlink.com. *World Wide Web:* http://www.langlink.com/

$\mathcal{S}$WEDEN

CITY-TO-CITY

LANGUAGE LIAISON
LEARN SWEDISH IN SWEDEN

Hosted by Language Liaison
Academic Focus • Swedish.
Program Information • Students attend classes at Language Liaison (Stockholm). Optional travel at an extra cost. Students typically earn 3-15 semester credits per term.
Sessions • Classes begin weekly, year-round.
Eligibility Requirements • Minimum age 18; open to freshmen, sophomores, juniors, seniors, graduate students, adults; no foreign language proficiency required.
Living Arrangements • Students live in host family homes, residence center. Meals are taken as a group, in central dining facility.
Costs (2005) • Contact sponsor for cost. $175 application fee. Financial aid available for all students: scholarship research service.
For More Information • Ms. Nancy Forman, President, Language Liaison, PO Box 1772, Pacific Palisades, CA 90272; *Phone:* 800-284-4448; *Fax:* 310-454-1706. *E-mail:* learn@languageliaison.com. *World Wide Web:* http://www.languageliaison.com/

LUND

MICHIGAN STATE UNIVERSITY
LOGISTICAL PACKAGING IN SWEDEN

Hosted by Lund University
Academic Focus • Packaging.
Program Information • Students attend classes at Lund University (Lund, Sweden). Field trips to manufacturing sites, Stockholm. Students typically earn 3 semester credits per term.
Sessions • Jun (summer).
Eligibility Requirements • Minimum age 18; open to sophomores, juniors, seniors; major in agriculture and natural resources; course work in packaging; 2.35 GPA; good academic standing at home school; faculty approval; no foreign language proficiency required.
Living Arrangements • Students live in host institution dormitories, hotels. Meals are taken as a group, on one's own, in central dining facility, in restaurants.
Costs (2005) • $1632 (estimated); includes housing, some meals, insurance, excursions, student support services. $100 application fee. $200 nonrefundable deposit required. Financial aid available for students from sponsoring institution: scholarships, loans.
For More Information • Ms. Yvonne Squiers, Secretary, Michigan State University, Office of Study Abroad, 109 International Center, East Lansing, MI 48824-1035; *Phone:* 517-353-8920; *Fax:* 517-432-2082. *E-mail:* squiers@msu.edu. *World Wide Web:* http://studyabroad.msu.edu/

STOCKHOLM

UNIVERSITY OF KANSAS
HEALTH CARE AND SOCIAL POLICIES IN SWEDEN

Academic Focus • Sociology.
Program Information • Faculty members are drawn from the sponsor's U.S. staff. Scheduled travel to Helsinki, Finland; field trips to Uppsala. Students typically earn 3 semester credits per term.
Sessions • Jun (summer).
Eligibility Requirements • Minimum age 21; open to freshmen, sophomores, juniors, seniors, graduate students, adults; 2.5 GPA; 2 letters of recommendation; good academic standing at home school; no foreign language proficiency required.
Living Arrangements • Students live in hotels. Meals are taken as a group, on one's own, in restaurants.
Costs (2005) • $3550; includes tuition, housing, some meals, excursions, student support services, medical evacuation and repatriation services. $38 application fee. $300 nonrefundable deposit required. Financial aid available for students from sponsoring institution: scholarships, loans.
For More Information • Mr. David Wiley, Program Coordinator, University of Kansas, Office of Study Abroad, Lippincott Hall, 1410 Jayhawk Boulevard, Room 108, Lawrence, KS 66045-7515; *Phone:* 785-864-3742; *Fax:* 785-864-5040. *E-mail:* osa@ku.edu. *World Wide Web:* http://www.ku.edu/~osa/

 WITZERLAND

CITY-TO-CITY

MICHIGAN STATE UNIVERSITY
ENVIRONMENTAL SCIENCE

Academic Focus • Physical sciences.
Program Information • Faculty members are drawn from the sponsor's U.S. staff. Scheduled travel to Lucerne, Lauterbrunnen, St. Moritz, Locarno, Zermatt; field trips to museums, natural sites (mountains). Students typically earn 6 semester credits per term.
Sessions • Jul–Aug (summer).
Eligibility Requirements • Minimum age 18; open to juniors, seniors; 2.0 GPA; good academic standing at home school; faculty approval; interview; good physical condition; no foreign language proficiency required.
Living Arrangements • Students live in hotels, hostels; campsites. Meals are taken as a group, in restaurants.
Costs (2005) • $2477 (estimated); includes housing, some meals, insurance, excursions, student support services. $100 application fee. $200 nonrefundable deposit required. Financial aid available for students from sponsoring institution: scholarships, loans.
For More Information • Ms. Yvonne Squiers, Secretary, Michigan State University, Office of Study Abroad, 109 International Center, East Lansing, MI 48824-1035; *Phone:* 517-353-8920; *Fax:* 517-432-2082. *E-mail:* squiers@msu.edu. *World Wide Web:* http://studyabroad.msu.edu/

UNIVERSITY OF SOUTHERN MISSISSIPPI
SWITZERLAND STUDIES

Academic Focus • Hospitality services.
Program Information • Faculty members are drawn from the sponsor's U.S. staff and local instructors hired by the sponsor. Scheduled travel; field trips. Students typically earn 4–6 semester credits per term.
Sessions • May (summer).
Eligibility Requirements • Minimum age 18; open to sophomores, juniors, seniors, graduate students, adults; 2.0 GPA; good academic standing at home school; no foreign language proficiency required.
Living Arrangements • Students live in host institution dormitories, locally rented apartments, hotels. Meals are taken as a group, on one's own, in central dining facility, in restaurants.
Costs (2005) • $4999 for undergraduate students; $5299 for graduate students; includes tuition, housing, excursions, international airfare, student support services. $200 nonrefundable deposit required. Financial aid available for students from sponsoring institution: scholarships, loans.
For More Information • Director, Switzerland Studies Program, University of Southern Mississippi, 118 College Drive #10047, Hattiesburg, MS 39406-0001; *Phone:* 601-266-4344; *Fax:* 601-266-5699. *E-mail:* holly.buckner@usm.edu. *World Wide Web:* http://www.usm.edu/internationaledu/

FRIBOURG

AMERICAN COLLEGE PROGRAM AT THE UNIVERSITY OF FRIBOURG
SURVEY OF INTERNATIONAL ORGANIZATIONS

Hosted by American College Program at the University of Fribourg
Academic Focus • Interdisciplinary studies, international business, law and legal studies, political science and government.
Program Information • Students attend classes at American College Program at the University of Fribourg (Fribourg, Switzerland). Scheduled travel to Strausbourg; field trips to Geneva, Bern, Zurich, Strasbourg. Students typically earn 6–9 semester credits per term.
Sessions • Jul–Aug (summer).
Eligibility Requirements • Open to freshmen, sophomores, juniors, seniors, graduate students, adults; 3.0 GPA; 2 letters of recommendation; good academic standing at home school; no foreign language proficiency required.
Living Arrangements • Students live in host institution dormitories. Quarters are shared with host institution students. Meals are taken on one's own, in central dining facility, in restaurants.
Costs (2006) • $3650; includes tuition, housing, some meals, excursions, international airfare, books and class materials, international student ID, student support services. $500 nonrefundable deposit required. Financial aid available for all students: scholarships, work study.
For More Information • Mr. Andrej N. Lushnycky, Executive Director, American College Program at the University of Fribourg, Avenue de Beauregard 13, Case Postal 102, 1701 Fribourg, Switzerland; *Phone:* +41 26-300-8190; *Fax:* +41 26-300-9690. *E-mail:* acp@unifr.ch. *World Wide Web:* http://www.unifr.ch/acp/

GENEVA

NEW YORK UNIVERSITY
INTERNATIONAL HEALTH POLICY AND PROSPECTS IN GENEVA

Hosted by NYU at Geneva

Academic Focus • Health-care management.

Program Information • Students attend classes at NYU at Geneva (Geneva, Switzerland). Students typically earn 4 semester credits per term.

Sessions • May–Jun (summer).

Eligibility Requirements • Open to graduate students; Bachelor's Degree; no foreign language proficiency required.

Living Arrangements • Students live in hotels. Meals are taken as a group, in restaurants.

Costs (2005) • $3226; includes tuition. Financial aid available for students from sponsoring institution: scholarships, loans.

For More Information • Dr. Charles Nicolson, Director, Academic Services, New York University, Robert F. Wagner Graduate School, N.Y.U., 295 Lafayette Street, Rooom 2209, New York, NY 10012-9604; *Phone:* 212-998-7418; *Fax:* 212-995-4164. *E-mail:* charles.nicolson@nyu.edu. *World Wide Web:* http://www.nyu.edu/global/studyabroad.html

SCHOOL FOR INTERNATIONAL TRAINING, SIT STUDY ABROAD
SWITZERLAND: INTERNATIONAL STUDIES, ORGANIZATIONS, AND SOCIAL JUSTICE

Academic Focus • International affairs.

Program Information • Faculty members are drawn from the sponsor's U.S. staff and local instructors hired by the sponsor. Scheduled travel; field trips to cultural events. Students typically earn 8 semester credits per term.

Sessions • Jun–Jul (summer).

Eligibility Requirements • Open to freshmen, sophomores, juniors, seniors; 2.5 GPA; 2 letters of recommendation; good academic standing at home school; no foreign language proficiency required.

Living Arrangements • Students live in hotels, guest houses. Meals are taken in residences, in restaurants.

Costs (2005–2006) • $7574; includes tuition, housing, all meals, insurance, excursions. $50 application fee. $400 nonrefundable deposit required. Financial aid available for all students: scholarships.

For More Information • SIT Study Abroad, School for International Training, SIT Study Abroad, PO Box 676, Kipling Road, Brattleboro, VT 05302-0676; *Phone:* 888-272-7881; *Fax:* 802-258-3296. *E-mail:* studyabroad@sit.edu. *World Wide Web:* http://www.sit.edu/studyabroad/

SYRACUSE UNIVERSITY
GRADUATE INTERNSHIPS IN INTERNATIONAL ORGANIZATIONS: GENEVA, SWITZERLAND

Academic Focus • International affairs.

Program Information • Faculty members are drawn from the sponsor's U.S. staff. Students typically earn 6 semester credits per term.

Sessions • May–Jul (summer).

Eligibility Requirements • Open to juniors, seniors, graduate students; 1 letter of recommendation; good academic standing at home school; no foreign language proficiency required.

Living Arrangements • Students live in host institution dormitories. Meals are taken on one's own, in restaurants.

Costs (2005) • $7167; includes tuition, housing, some meals, international student ID. $55 application fee. $350 nonrefundable deposit required. Financial aid available for all students: loans, need-based tuition grants.

For More Information • Mrs. Daisy Fried, Associate Director, Syracuse University, 106 Walnut Place, Syracuse, NY 13244-4170; *Phone:* 800-251-9674; *Fax:* 315-443-4593. *E-mail:* dipasum@syr.edu. *World Wide Web:* http://suabroad.syr.edu/

UNIVERSITY OF DELAWARE
WINTER SESSION IN GENEVA, SWITZERLAND

Academic Focus • Economics.

Program Information • Faculty members are drawn from the sponsor's U.S. staff. Field trips to local businesses, Zurich, Vienna, Paris, Munich; optional travel to Europe at an extra cost. Students typically earn 6 semester credits per term.

Sessions • Jan–Feb (winter).

Eligibility Requirements • Open to freshmen, sophomores, juniors, seniors, adults; 2.0 GPA; 1 letter of recommendation; no foreign language proficiency required.

Living Arrangements • Students live in hotels. Meals are taken on one's own, in restaurants.

Costs (2005) • Contact sponsor for cost. $200 nonrefundable deposit required. Financial aid available for all students: scholarships.

For More Information • Center for International Studies, University of Delaware, 186 South College Avenue, Newark, DE 19716-1450; *Phone:* 888-831-4685; *Fax:* 302-831-6042. *E-mail:* studyabroad@udel.edu. *World Wide Web:* http://www.udel.edu/studyabroad/

VILLANOVA UNIVERSITY
STUDIES IN INTERNATIONAL BUSINESS AND INTERNSHIP: GENEVA

Held at University of Geneva

Academic Focus • International business.

Program Information • Classes are held on the campus of University of Geneva (Geneva, Switzerland). Faculty members are drawn from the sponsor's U.S. staff and local instructors hired by the sponsor. Field trips to tour of Geneva. Students typically earn 6 semester credits per term.

Sessions • Jun–Aug (summer).

Eligibility Requirements • Minimum age 18; open to sophomores, juniors, seniors; major in business; 3.0 GPA; 2 letters of recommendation; good academic standing at home school; no foreign language proficiency required.

Living Arrangements • Students live in host institution dormitories. Quarters are shared with students from other programs. Meals are taken on one's own, in residences.

Costs (2005) • $7500; includes tuition, housing, excursions. $450 nonrefundable deposit required. Financial aid available for students from sponsoring institution: loans.

For More Information • Mr. Sohail Chaudhry, Professor, Villanova University, 800 Lancaster Avenue, Department of Decision Information Technologies, Villanova, PA 19085; *Phone:* 610-519-6412; *Fax:* 610-519-7649. *E-mail:* sohail.chaudhry@villanova.edu. *World Wide Web:* http://www.internationalstudies.villanova.edu/

VILLANOVA UNIVERSITY
STUDIES IN INTERNATIONAL ORGANIZATION AND INTERNSHIP: GENEVA

Held at University of Geneva

Academic Focus • Political science and government.

Program Information • Classes are held on the campus of University of Geneva (Geneva, Switzerland). Faculty members are local instructors hired by the sponsor. Field trips to Geneva tour. Students typically earn 6 semester credits per term.

Sessions • Jun–Aug (summer).

Eligibility Requirements • Minimum age 18; open to sophomores, juniors, seniors; 3.0 GPA; 2 letters of recommendation; good academic standing at home school; no foreign language proficiency required.

Living Arrangements • Students live in host institution dormitories. Quarters are shared with students from other programs. Meals are taken on one's own, in residences.

Costs (2005) • $7500; includes tuition, housing, excursions. $450 nonrefundable deposit required. Financial aid available for students from sponsoring institution: loans.

For More Information • Mr. Markus Kreuzer, Assistant Professor, Villanova University, 800 Lancaster Avenue, Department of Political Science, Villanova, PA 19085; *Phone:* 610-519-6412; *Fax:* 610-519-7649. *E-mail:* markus.kreuzer@villanova.edu. *World Wide Web:* http://www.internationalstudies.villanova.edu/

SWITZERLAND
Geneva

WIDENER UNIVERSITY SCHOOL OF LAW
GENEVA, SWITZERLAND SUMMER LAW INSTITUTE

Held at Graduate Institute of International Studies
Academic Focus • Law and legal studies.
Program Information • Classes are held on the campus of Graduate Institute of International Studies (Geneva, Switzerland). Faculty members are drawn from the sponsor's U.S. staff and local instructors hired by the sponsor. Field trips to hiking, picnics, rafting, visits to legal institutions; optional travel at an extra cost. Students typically earn 6 semester credits per term.
Sessions • Jun-Jul (summer).
Eligibility Requirements • Open to graduate students; good academic standing at home school; must be enrolled in an accredited law school or a law school graduate; no foreign language proficiency required.
Living Arrangements • Students live in host institution dormitories, locally rented apartments, hotels. Quarters are shared with students from other programs. Meals are taken on one's own, in residences, in restaurants.
Costs (2005) • $7900; includes tuition, housing, some meals, excursions, international airfare, books and class materials, student support services. $100 application fee. Financial aid available for all students: loans.
For More Information • Ms. Peggie Wyant, Coordinator, International Programs, Widener University School of Law, 4601 Concord Pike, Room 418 Law Building, Wilmington, DE 19803; *Phone:* 302-477-2248; *Fax:* 302-477-2257. *E-mail:* mawyant@mail.widener. edu. *World Wide Web:* http://www.law.widener.edu/go/summer/

LAUSANNE

LANGUAGE LIAISON
LEARN FRENCH OR GERMAN IN SWITZERLAND–LAUSANNE

Hosted by Language Liaison
Academic Focus • French language and literature, German language and literature.
Program Information • Students attend classes at Language Liaison (Lausanne, Switzerland). Optional travel at an extra cost. Students typically earn 3-15 semester credits per term.
Sessions • New programs begin weekly, year-round.
Eligibility Requirements • Minimum age 16; open to precollege students, freshmen, sophomores, juniors, seniors, graduate students, adults; no foreign language proficiency required.
Living Arrangements • Students live in locally rented apartments, host family homes, hotels. Meals are taken on one's own, with host family.
Costs (2005) • Contact sponsor for cost. $175 application fee. Financial aid available for all students: scholarship research service.
For More Information • Ms. Nancy Forman, President, Language Liaison, PO Box 1772, Pacific Palisades, CA 90272; *Phone:* 800-284-4448; *Fax:* 310-454-1706. *E-mail:* learn@languageliaison. com. *World Wide Web:* http://www.languageliaison.com/

UNIVERSITY OF MIAMI
INTENSIVE FRENCH LANGUAGE PROGRAM IN SWITZERLAND

Hosted by University of Lausanne
Academic Focus • French language and literature.
Program Information • Students attend classes at University of Lausanne (Lausanne, Switzerland). Field trips to local cultural and historical sites. Students typically earn 6 semester credits per term.
Sessions • Jul-Aug (summer).
Eligibility Requirements • Minimum age 18; open to sophomores, juniors, seniors; 2 letters of recommendation; good academic standing at home school; 1 year of college course work in French.

Living Arrangements • Students live in host institution dormitories. Quarters are shared with students from other programs. Meals are taken on one's own, in central dining facility.
Costs (2005) • $5972; includes tuition, housing, student support services. $40 application fee. $500 nonrefundable deposit required. Financial aid available for students from sponsoring institution: loans.
For More Information • University of Miami, International Education and Exchange Programs, 5050 Brunson Drive, Allen Hall Room 212, PO Box 248005, Coral Gables, FL 33124-1610; *Phone:* 305-284-3434; *Fax:* 305-284-4235. *E-mail:* ieep@miami.edu. *World Wide Web:* http://www.studyabroad.miami.edu/

LUGANO

COLLEGE CONSORTIUM FOR INTERNATIONAL STUDIES–CENTRAL WASHINGTON UNIVERSITY
SWITZERLAND PROGRAM

Hosted by Franklin College Switzerland
Academic Focus • Full curriculum.
Program Information • Students attend classes at Franklin College Switzerland (Lugano, Switzerland). Students typically earn 3-6 semester credits per term.
Sessions • May-Jun; Jul-Aug (two 4-week sessions).
Eligibility Requirements • Open to sophomores, juniors, seniors; 2.5 GPA; good academic standing at home school; sophomore standing or above; no foreign language proficiency required.
Living Arrangements • Students live in host institution dormitories. Quarters are shared with host institution students. Meals are taken on one's own, in residences, in central dining facility.
Costs (2006) • $2900; includes tuition, housing, insurance, student support services. $50 application fee. $300 deposit required. Financial aid available for students from sponsoring institution: scholarships, loans, grants.
For More Information • Ms. Harmony DeFazio, Study Abroad Advisor, College Consortium for International Studies–Central Washington University, Study Abroad and Exchange Programs, 400 East University Way, Ellensburg, WA 98926-7408; *Phone:* 509-963-3615; *Fax:* 509-963-1558. *E-mail:* defazioh@cwu.edu. *World Wide Web:* http://www.ccisabroad.org/

FRANKLIN COLLEGE SWITZERLAND
FRANKLIN COLLEGE SWITZERLAND

Hosted by Franklin College Switzerland
Academic Focus • Full curriculum.
Program Information • Students attend classes at Franklin College Switzerland (Sorengo, Switzerland). Field trips to Milan, Torino, Lugano and environs, Zurich, Lucerne; optional travel to Florence, Venice, Munich, Zurich, Geneva, Rome, Nice, Paris at an extra cost. Students typically earn 6 semester credits per term.
Sessions • May-Jul (summer), Jul-Aug (summer 2).
Eligibility Requirements • Minimum age 18; open to freshmen, sophomores, juniors, seniors, adults; 2.5 GPA; good academic standing at home school; no foreign language proficiency required.
Living Arrangements • Students live in host institution dormitories, locally rented apartments, program-owned apartments. Quarters are shared with host institution students. Meals are taken in residences, in central dining facility.
Costs (2005) • $3175 per session; includes tuition, housing, student support services. $40 application fee. $150 nonrefundable deposit required.
For More Information • Ms. Karen Ballard, Director of Admissions, Franklin College Switzerland, U.S. Office, Suite 411, 91-31 Queens Boulevard, Elmhurst, NY 11373-5506; *Phone:* 718-335-6800; *Fax:* 718-335-6733. *E-mail:* info@fc.edu. *World Wide Web:* http://www. fc.edu/

 # TANZANIA

CITY-TO-CITY

UNIVERSITY OF DELAWARE
WINTER SESSION IN TANZANIA

Academic Focus • Photography, wildlife studies.
Program Information • Faculty members are drawn from the sponsor's U.S. staff. Scheduled travel to Serengeti, Ngorongoro and Monyara reserves. Students typically earn 6 semester credits per term.
Sessions • Jan (winter).
Eligibility Requirements • Open to freshmen, sophomores, juniors, seniors; 2.0 GPA; 1 letter of recommendation.
Living Arrangements • Students live in campsites. Meals are taken as a group, in central dining facility.
Costs (2005) • Contact sponsor for cost. $200 nonrefundable deposit required. Financial aid available for all students: scholarships.
For More Information • Center for International Studies, University of Delaware, 186 South College Avenue, Newark, DE 19716-1450; *Phone:* 888-831-4685; *Fax:* 302-831-6042. *E-mail:* studyabroad@udel.edu. *World Wide Web:* http://www.udel.edu/studyabroad/

DAR ES SALAAM

UNIVERSITY OF PENNSYLVANIA
PENN-IN-DAR ES SALAAM

Hosted by University of Dar Es Salaam
Academic Focus • African studies, Swahili.
Program Information • Students attend classes at University of Dar Es Salaam (Dar es Salaam, Tanzania). Field trips to cultural sites throughout Dar es Salaam. Students typically earn 2 course units per term.
Sessions • Jul–Aug (summer).
Eligibility Requirements • Open to freshmen, sophomores, juniors, seniors, graduate students; 1 letter of recommendation; good academic standing at home school; no foreign language proficiency required.
Living Arrangements • Students live in host family homes. Meals are taken with host family, in residences.
Costs (2005) • $7700; includes tuition, housing, all meals, insurance, excursions, international airfare. $50 application fee. $300 nonrefundable deposit required. Financial aid available for students from sponsoring institution: scholarships, loans.
For More Information • Penn Summer Abroad, University of Pennsylvania, 3440 Market Street, Suite 100, Philadelphia, PA 19104-3335; *Phone:* 215-746-6900; *Fax:* 215-573-2053. *E-mail:* summerabroad@sas.upenn.edu. *World Wide Web:* http://www.sas.upenn.edu/summer/

THAILAND

CITY-TO-CITY

UNIVERSITY OF CALIFORNIA, SANTA BARBARA, WILDLANDS STUDIES
THAILAND ECOSYSTEMS AND CULTURES

Academic Focus • Asian studies, ecology, environmental science/studies, geography, wildlife studies.
Program Information • Faculty members are drawn from the sponsor's U.S. staff and local instructors hired by the sponsor. Scheduled travel to wildland field locations. Students typically earn 15 quarter credits per term.
Sessions • Jan–Mar (winter).
Eligibility Requirements • Minimum age 18; open to freshmen, sophomores, juniors, seniors; course work in biology or environmental studies; good academic standing at home school; application essay; no foreign language proficiency required.
Living Arrangements • Students live in field study sites. Meals are taken as a group.
Costs (2007) • $1995; includes tuition. $75 application fee.
For More Information • Mr. Crandall Bay, Director, Wildlands Studies Program, University of California, Santa Barbara, Wildlands Studies, 3 Mosswood Circle, Cazadero, CA 95421; *Phone:* 707-632-5665; *Fax:* 707-632-5665. *E-mail:* wildlands@sonic.net. *World Wide Web:* http://www.wildlandsstudies.com/

BANGKOK

KNOWLEDGE EXCHANGE INSTITUTE (KEI)
BANGKOK INTERNSHIP PROGRAM

Hosted by Mahidol University
Academic Focus • Accounting, actuarial science, advertising and public relations, anatomy, biochemistry, biological/life sciences, biomedical sciences, botany, brokerage, business administration/management, chemical sciences, commerce, communication services, communications, community service, computer science, conservation studies, criminal justice, earth sciences, East Asian studies, ecology, economics, entrepreneurship, environmental health, environmental science/studies, ethnic studies, finance, forestry, geology, health-care management, hospitality services, hotel and restaurant management, information science, international business, law and legal studies, management information systems, marine sciences, marketing, mathematics, medicine, meteorology, natural resources, nursing, nutrition, pharmacology, physical sciences, physics, political science and government, psychology, public administration, public health, science, social services, social work, Thai, tourism and travel, veterinary science, wildlife studies, zoology.
Program Information • Students attend classes at Mahidol University (Bangkok, Thailand). Scheduled travel to Chiang Mai, Ko Samai; field trips to Bangkok, Naikhon Pathom, Ko Si Chaing. Students typically earn 6 semester credits per term.
Sessions • Jun–Aug (summer).
Eligibility Requirements • Open to freshmen, sophomores, juniors, seniors, graduate students, adults; 2.2 GPA; 2 letters of recommendation; good academic standing at home school; no foreign language proficiency required.
Living Arrangements • Students live in host institution dormitories, program-owned apartments, host family homes. Quarters are shared with host institution students, students from other programs. Meals are taken on one's own, with host family, in residences, in restaurants.
Costs (2006) • $3450; includes tuition, housing, insurance, excursions, student support services, mobile telephone. $50 application fee. $500 nonrefundable deposit required. Financial aid available for all students: scholarships, loans.
For More Information • Mr. Eduard Izraylovsky, Director, Knowledge Exchange Institute (KEI), 111 John Street, Suite 800, New York, NY 10038; *Phone:* 800-831-5095; *Fax:* 212-528-2095. *E-mail:* info@knowledgeexchange.org. *World Wide Web:* http://www.knowledgeexchange.org/

KNOWLEDGE EXCHANGE INSTITUTE (KEI)
COMPUTER SCIENCE AND SOFTWARE ENGINEERING

Hosted by Mahidol University
Academic Focus • Asian studies, Chinese language and literature, communication services, computer science, East Asian studies, graphic design/illustration, information science, interdisciplinary studies, Japanese, liberal studies, mathematics, statistics, telecommunications, Thai.
Program Information • Students attend classes at Mahidol University (Bangkok, Thailand). Scheduled travel; field trips. Students typically earn 6 quarter credits per term.
Sessions • Jun–Aug (summer), Jul–Aug (summer 2).
Eligibility Requirements • Open to freshmen, sophomores, juniors, seniors, graduate students, adults; 2.2 GPA; 2 letters of recommendation; good academic standing at home school; no foreign language proficiency required.

Living Arrangements • Students live in host institution dormitories, program-owned apartments, program-owned houses, host family homes. Quarters are shared with host institution students, students from other programs. Meals are taken on one's own, in residences, in central dining facility, in restaurants.

Costs (2006) • $3900; includes tuition, housing, insurance, excursions, books and class materials, lab equipment, student support services. $50 application fee. $500 nonrefundable deposit required. Financial aid available for all students: scholarships, loans.

For More Information • Mr. Eduard Izraylovsky, Director, Knowledge Exchange Institute (KEI), 111 John Street, Suite 800, New York, NY 10038; *Phone:* 800-831-5095; *Fax:* 212-528-2095. *E-mail:* info@knowledgeexchange.org. *World Wide Web:* http://www.knowledgeexchange.org/

KNOWLEDGE EXCHANGE INSTITUTE (KEI)
ENVIRONMENTAL AND ECOLOGICAL STUDIES
Hosted by Mahidol University

Academic Focus • Asian studies, biochemistry, biological/life sciences, botany, chemical sciences, Chinese language and literature, conservation studies, earth sciences, East Asian studies, ecology, environmental health, environmental science/studies, fisheries studies, forestry, geology, interdisciplinary studies, Japanese, liberal studies, marine sciences, mathematics, meteorology, natural resources, oceanography, physical sciences, physics, science, statistics, Telugu, wildlife studies, zoology.

Program Information • Students attend classes at Mahidol University (Bangkok, Thailand). Scheduled travel; field trips. Students typically earn 6 quarter credits per term.

Sessions • Jun–Aug (summer), Jul–Aug (summer 2).

Eligibility Requirements • Open to freshmen, sophomores, juniors, seniors, graduate students, adults; 2.2 GPA; 2 letters of recommendation; good academic standing at home school; no foreign language proficiency required.

Living Arrangements • Students live in host institution dormitories, program-owned apartments, program-owned houses, host family homes. Quarters are shared with host institution students, students from other programs. Meals are taken on one's own, in residences, in central dining facility, in restaurants.

Costs (2006) • $3900; includes tuition, housing, insurance, excursions, books and class materials, lab equipment, student support services. $50 application fee. $500 nonrefundable deposit required. Financial aid available for all students: scholarships, loans.

For More Information • Mr. Eduard Izraylovsky, Director, Knowledge Exchange Institute (KEI), 111 John Street, Suite 800, New York, NY 10038; *Phone:* 800-831-5095; *Fax:* 212-528-2095. *E-mail:* info@knowledgeexchange.org. *World Wide Web:* http://www.knowledgeexchange.org/

KNOWLEDGE EXCHANGE INSTITUTE (KEI)
PRE-MEDICINE, HEALTH, AND BIOMEDICAL SCIENCE
Hosted by Mahidol University

Academic Focus • Anatomy, Asian studies, biochemistry, biological/life sciences, biomedical sciences, chemical sciences, Chinese language and literature, East Asian studies, environmental health, health-care management, interdisciplinary studies, Japanese, liberal studies, mathematics, nursing, nutrition, pre-dentistry, premedical studies, public health, science, statistics, Telugu.

Program Information • Students attend classes at Mahidol University (Bangkok, Thailand). Scheduled travel; field trips. Students typically earn 6 quarter credits per term.

Sessions • Jun–Aug (summer), Jul–Aug (summer 2).

Eligibility Requirements • Open to freshmen, sophomores, juniors, seniors, graduate students, adults; 2.2 GPA; 2 letters of recommendation; good academic standing at home school; no foreign language proficiency required.

Living Arrangements • Students live in host institution dormitories, program-owned apartments, program-owned houses, host family homes. Quarters are shared with host institution students, students from other programs. Meals are taken on one's own, in residences, in central dining facility, in restaurants.

Costs (2006) • $3900; includes tuition, housing, insurance, excursions, books and class materials, lab equipment, student support services. $50 application fee. $500 nonrefundable deposit required. Financial aid available for all students: scholarships, loans.

For More Information • Mr. Eduard Izraylovsky, Director, Knowledge Exchange Institute (KEI), 111 John Street, Suite 800, New York, NY 10038; *Phone:* 800-831-5095; *Fax:* 212-528-2095. *E-mail:* info@knowledgeexchange.org. *World Wide Web:* http://www.knowledgeexchange.org/

KNOWLEDGE EXCHANGE INSTITUTE (KEI)
PSYCHOLOGY, SOCIOLOGY, AND HUMAN BEHAVIOR
Hosted by Mahidol University

Academic Focus • Biological/life sciences, Chinese studies, communications, community service, criminal justice, cultural studies, East Asian studies, ethics, ethnic studies, health-care management, intercultural studies, interdisciplinary studies, liberal studies, peace and conflict studies, philosophy, psychology, public policy, science, social sciences, social services, social work, sociology, statistics, Thai.

Program Information • Students attend classes at Mahidol University (Bangkok, Thailand). Scheduled travel; field trips. Students typically earn 6 quarter credits per term.

Sessions • Jun–Aug (summer), Jul–Aug (summer 2).

Eligibility Requirements • Open to freshmen, sophomores, juniors, seniors, graduate students, adults; 2.2 GPA; 2 letters of recommendation; good academic standing at home school; no foreign language proficiency required.

Living Arrangements • Students live in host institution dormitories, program-owned apartments, program-owned houses, host family homes. Quarters are shared with host institution students, students from other programs. Meals are taken on one's own, in residences, in central dining facility, in restaurants.

Costs (2006) • $3900; includes tuition, housing, insurance, excursions, books and class materials, lab equipment, student support services. $50 application fee. $500 nonrefundable deposit required. Financial aid available for all students: scholarships, loans.

For More Information • Mr. Eduard Izraylovsky, Director, Knowledge Exchange Institute (KEI), 111 John Street, Suite 800, New York, NY 10038; *Phone:* 800-831-5095; *Fax:* 212-528-2095. *E-mail:* info@knowledgeexchange.org. *World Wide Web:* http://www.knowledgeexchange.org/

KNOWLEDGE EXCHANGE INSTITUTE (KEI)
SCIENCE, MATHEMATICS, AND ENGINEERING
Hosted by Mahidol University

Academic Focus • Asian studies, biochemistry, biological/life sciences, biomedical sciences, botany, chemical sciences, Chinese language and literature, earth sciences, East Asian studies, ecology, engineering, interdisciplinary studies, Japanese, liberal studies, mathematics, meteorology, physical sciences, physics, science, statistics, Telugu, zoology.

Program Information • Students attend classes at Mahidol University (Bangkok, Thailand). Scheduled travel; field trips. Students typically earn 6 quarter credits per term.

Sessions • Jun–Aug (summer), Jul–Aug (summer 2).

Eligibility Requirements • Open to freshmen, sophomores, juniors, seniors, graduate students, adults; 2.2 GPA; 2 letters of recommendation; good academic standing at home school; no foreign language proficiency required.

Living Arrangements • Students live in host institution dormitories, program-owned apartments, program-owned houses, host family homes. Quarters are shared with host institution students, students from other programs. Meals are taken on one's own, in residences, in central dining facility, in restaurants.

Costs (2006) • $3900; includes tuition, housing, insurance, excursions, books and class materials, lab equipment, student support services. $50 application fee. $500 nonrefundable deposit required. Financial aid available for all students: scholarships, loans.

For More Information • Mr. Eduard Izraylovsky, Director, Knowledge Exchange Institute (KEI), 111 John Street, Suite 800, New York, NY 10038; *Phone:* 800-831-5095; *Fax:* 212-528-2095. *E-mail:* info@knowledgeexchange.org. *World Wide Web:* http://www.knowledgeexchange.org/

KNOWLEDGE EXCHANGE INSTITUTE (KEI)
SOUTHEAST ASIAN BUSINESS, LAW, AND DIPLOMACY
Hosted by Mahidol University

THAILAND
Bangkok

Academic Focus • Accounting, advertising and public relations, Asian studies, business administration/management, Chinese studies, commerce, communication services, community service, criminal justice, cultural studies, East Asian studies, economics, entrepreneurship, finance, human resources, information science, intercultural studies, interdisciplinary studies, international affairs, international business, Japanese, labor and industrial relations, law and legal studies, liberal studies, management information systems, marketing, natural resources, peace and conflict studies, political science and government, public administration, public policy, statistics, Thai.
Program Information • Students attend classes at Mahidol University (Bangkok, Thailand). Scheduled travel; field trips. Students typically earn 6 quarter credits per term.
Sessions • Jun–Aug (summer), Jul–Aug (summer 2).
Eligibility Requirements • Open to freshmen, sophomores, juniors, seniors, graduate students, adults; 2.2 GPA; 2 letters of recommendation; good academic standing at home school; no foreign language proficiency required.
Living Arrangements • Students live in host institution dormitories, program-owned apartments, program-owned houses, host family homes. Quarters are shared with host institution students, students from other programs. Meals are taken on one's own, in residences, in central dining facility, in restaurants.
Costs (2006) • $3900; includes tuition, housing, insurance, excursions, books and class materials, lab equipment, student support services. $50 application fee. $500 nonrefundable deposit required. Financial aid available for all students: scholarships, loans.
For More Information • Mr. Eduard Izraylovsky, Director, Knowledge Exchange Institute (KEI), 111 John Street, Suite 800, New York, NY 10038; *Phone:* 800-831-5095; *Fax:* 212-528-2095. *E-mail:* info@knowledgeexchange.org. *World Wide Web:* http://www.knowledgeexchange.org/

KNOWLEDGE EXCHANGE INSTITUTE (KEI)
SOUTHEAST ASIAN STUDIES AND LANGUAGES

Hosted by Mahidol University
Academic Focus • Ancient history, anthropology, area studies, art, Asian languages, Asian studies, Chilean studies, Chinese language and literature, civilization studies, communication services, communications, community service, comparative history, comparative literature, conservation studies, creative writing, cultural studies, East Asian studies, economics, environmental science/studies, ethics, ethnic studies, geography, history, intercultural studies, interdisciplinary studies, international affairs, Japanese, Japanese studies, language studies, law and legal studies, liberal studies, literature, mathematics, music, peace and conflict studies, philosophy, political science and government, religious studies, social services, social work, sociology, Thai.
Program Information • Students attend classes at Mahidol University (Bangkok, Thailand). Scheduled travel; field trips. Students typically earn 6 quarter credits per term.
Sessions • Jun–Aug (summer), Jul–Aug (summer 2).
Eligibility Requirements • Open to freshmen, sophomores, juniors, seniors, graduate students, adults; 2.2 GPA; 2 letters of recommendation; good academic standing at home school; no foreign language proficiency required.
Living Arrangements • Students live in host institution dormitories, program-owned apartments, program-owned houses, host family homes. Quarters are shared with host institution students, students from other programs. Meals are taken on one's own, in residences, in central dining facility, in restaurants.
Costs (2006) • $3900; includes tuition, housing, insurance, excursions, books and class materials, lab equipment, student support services. $50 application fee. $500 nonrefundable deposit required. Financial aid available for all students: scholarships, loans.
For More Information • Mr. Eduard Izraylovsky, Director, Knowledge Exchange Institute (KEI), 111 John Street, Suite 800, New York, NY 10038; *Phone:* 800-831-5095; *Fax:* 212-528-2095. *E-mail:* info@knowledgeexchange.org. *World Wide Web:* http://www.knowledgeexchange.org/

KNOWLEDGE EXCHANGE INSTITUTE (KEI)
SOUTHEAST ASIAN TOURISM AND HOSPITALITY

Hosted by Mahidol University
Academic Focus • Advertising and public relations, Asian studies, business administration/management, Chinese studies, cultural studies, East Asian studies, food service, hospitality services, hotel and restaurant management, intercultural studies, international business, Japanese, Thai, tourism and travel.
Program Information • Students attend classes at Mahidol University (Bangkok, Thailand). Scheduled travel; field trips. Students typically earn 6 quarter credits per term.
Sessions • Jun–Aug (summer), Jul–Aug (summer 2).
Eligibility Requirements • Open to freshmen, sophomores, juniors, seniors, graduate students, adults; 2.2 GPA; 2 letters of recommendation; good academic standing at home school; no foreign language proficiency required.
Living Arrangements • Students live in host institution dormitories, program-owned apartments, program-owned houses, host family homes. Quarters are shared with host institution students, students from other programs. Meals are taken on one's own, in residences, in central dining facility, in restaurants.
Costs (2006) • $3900; includes tuition, insurance, excursions, books and class materials, lab equipment, student support services. $50 application fee. $500 nonrefundable deposit required. Financial aid available for all students: scholarships, loans.
For More Information • Mr. Eduard Izraylovsky, Director, Knowledge Exchange Institute (KEI), 111 John Street, Suite 800, New York, NY 10038; *Phone:* 800-831-5095; *Fax:* 212-528-2095. *E-mail:* info@knowledgeexchange.org. *World Wide Web:* http://www.knowledgeexchange.org/

MICHIGAN STATE UNIVERSITY
POLITICAL AND ECONOMIC DEVELOPMENT IN SOUTHEAST ASIA

Held at Asia Institute of Technology
Academic Focus • Asian studies, international affairs, political science and government.
Program Information • Classes are held on the campus of Asia Institute of Technology (Bangkok, Thailand). Faculty members are drawn from the sponsor's U.S. staff and local instructors hired by the sponsor. Scheduled travel to Laos; field trips to Laos, Bangkok, Chiang Mai, Phuket. Students typically earn 8 semester credits per term.
Sessions • May–Jun (summer).
Eligibility Requirements • Open to sophomores, juniors, seniors; 2.0 GPA; good academic standing at home school; no foreign language proficiency required.
Living Arrangements • Students live in host institution dormitories. Meals are taken on one's own, in central dining facility, in restaurants.
Costs (2005) • Contact sponsor for cost. $100 application fee. $200 nonrefundable deposit required. Financial aid available for students from sponsoring institution: scholarships, loans.
For More Information • Ms. Yvonne Squiers, Secretary, Michigan State University, Office of Study Abroad, 109 International Center, East Lansing, MI 48824-1035; *Phone:* 517-353-8920; *Fax:* 517-432-2082. *E-mail:* squiers@msu.edu. *World Wide Web:* http://studyabroad.msu.edu/

UNIVERSITY STUDIES ABROAD CONSORTIUM
INTERNATIONAL BUSINESS AND POLITICAL STUDIES: BANGKOK, THAILAND

Hosted by Rangsit University
Academic Focus • Accounting, Asian studies, business administration/management, communications, economics, finance, hotel and restaurant management, international business, marketing, philosophy, political science and government, psychology, Thai, tourism and travel.
Program Information • Students attend classes at Rangsit University (Pathum Thani, Thailand). Field trips to Bangkok, JJ Park weekend market; optional travel to historic and cultural sites, Ayuthaya, Kanchanaburi, Rayong, Huahi, Hong Kong, Angkor Wat at an extra cost. Students typically earn 15 semester credits per term.
Sessions • May–Aug (summer).
Eligibility Requirements • Minimum age 18; open to freshmen, sophomores, juniors, seniors, graduate students, adults; 2.5 GPA; no foreign language proficiency required.

Living Arrangements • Students live in host institution dormitories. Quarters are shared with host institution students. Meals are taken on one's own, in central dining facility.
Costs (2007) • $2980; includes tuition, insurance, excursions, student support services. $100 application fee. $200 refundable deposit required. Financial aid available for all students: scholarships, loans.
For More Information • University Studies Abroad Consortium, USAC/323, Reno, NV 89557-0093; *Phone:* 775-784-6569; *Fax:* 775-784-6010. *E-mail:* usac@unr.edu. *World Wide Web:* http://usac.unr.edu/

CHIANG MAI

LEXIA INTERNATIONAL
LEXIA SUMMER IN CHIANG MAI
Hosted by Payap University
Academic Focus • Anthropology, area studies, art history, Asian studies, civilization studies, comparative history, cultural studies, economics, ethnic studies, geography, history, interdisciplinary studies, international affairs, liberal studies, literature, political science and government, social sciences, sociology, Thai.
Program Information • Students attend classes at Payap University (Chiang Mai, Thailand). Field trips to Chiang Rai, Bangkok. Students typically earn 8–10 semester credits per term.
Sessions • Jun–Aug (summer).
Eligibility Requirements • Minimum age 18; open to freshmen, sophomores, juniors, seniors, graduate students, adults; 2.5 GPA; 2 letters of recommendation; no foreign language proficiency required.
Living Arrangements • Students live in host institution dormitories, host family homes. Quarters are shared with host institution students. Meals are taken on one's own, with host family, in residences.
Costs (2006) • $5950; includes tuition, housing, some meals, insurance, excursions, international student ID, student support services, transcript, computer access. $40 application fee. $300 nonrefundable deposit required. Financial aid available for all students: scholarships, work study.
For More Information • Lexia International, 23 South Main Street, Hanover, NH 03755; *Phone:* 800-775-3942; *Fax:* 603-643-9899. *E-mail:* info@lexiaintl.org. *World Wide Web:* http://www.lexiaintl.org/

UNIVERSITY OF WISCONSIN–EAU CLAIRE
THAILAND: ETHNIC MINORITIES, THE ENVIRONMENT AND SUSTAINABILITY
Held at Payap University
Academic Focus • Ethnic studies.

Program Information • Classes are held on the campus of Payap University (Chiang Mai, Thailand). Faculty members are local instructors hired by the sponsor. Scheduled travel to Hmong village, NGO; field trips to 1 traditional Hmong village, 1 agricultural NGO. Students typically earn 6 semester credits per term.
Sessions • Jun–Jul (summer).
Eligibility Requirements • Open to sophomores, juniors, seniors; 2.3 GPA; good academic standing at home school; no foreign language proficiency required.
Living Arrangements • Students live in host institution dormitories. Meals are taken on one's own, in restaurants.
Costs (2005) • $2262 for Wisconsin and Minnesota residents; $3162 for nonresidents; includes tuition, housing, some meals, insurance, excursions, student support services. $30 application fee. $150 nonrefundable deposit required. Financial aid available for all students: scholarships, loans.
For More Information • Ms. Colleen Marchwick, Study Abroad Coordinator, University of Wisconsin–Eau Claire, Center for International Education, 111 Schofield Hall, Eau Claire, WI 54702-4004; *Phone:* 715-836-4411; *Fax:* 715-836-4948. *E-mail:* studyabroad@uwec.edu. *World Wide Web:* http://www.uwec.edu/Cie/

NOGKHAI

SANTA BARBARA CITY COLLEGE
FILM STUDIES AND PRODUCTION IN THAILAND
Held at First Global Community College
Academic Focus • Film and media studies.
Program Information • Classes are held on the campus of First Global Community College (Nongkhai, Thailand). Faculty members are drawn from the sponsor's U.S. staff. Scheduled travel to Bangkok; field trips. Students typically earn 6 semester credits per term.
Sessions • Jun–Jul (summer).
Eligibility Requirements • Minimum age 18; open to precollege students, freshmen, sophomores, juniors, seniors, graduate students, adults; good academic standing at home school; no foreign language proficiency required.
Living Arrangements • Students live in hotels. Meals are taken on one's own, in restaurants.
Costs (2006) • $2500; includes housing, some meals, excursions, international student ID, student support services. $200 refundable deposit required. Financial aid available for all students: scholarships, loans.
For More Information • Ms. Naomi Sullwold, Program Assistant, Santa Barbara City College, 721 Cliff Drive, Santa Barbara, CA 93109; *Phone:* 805-965-0581 Ext. 2494; *Fax:* 805-963-7222. *E-mail:* smithe@sbcc.edu. *World Wide Web:* http://www.sbcc.cdu/studyabroad/

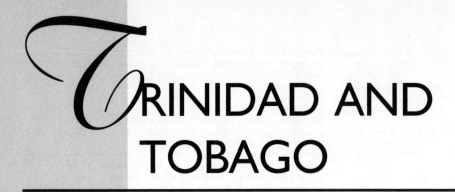RINIDAD AND TOBAGO

CITY-TO-CITY

JAMES MADISON UNIVERSITY
SUMMER PROGRAM IN TRINIDAD AND TOBAGO

Academic Focus • Public health.

Program Information • Faculty members are drawn from the sponsor's U.S. staff. Field trips. Students typically earn 3 semester credits per term.

Sessions • May (summer).

Eligibility Requirements • Minimum age 18; open to sophomores, juniors, seniors, graduate students; major in a health-related field; 2.0 GPA; 1 letter of recommendation; good academic standing at home school; no foreign language proficiency required.

Living Arrangements • Students live in locally rented apartments. Meals are taken as a group, in central dining facility, in restaurants.

Costs (2005) • $1558 for Virginia residents; $2438 for nonresidents; includes tuition, housing, some meals, excursions, international student ID. $400 nonrefundable deposit required.

For More Information • Mr. Felix Wang, Director, James Madison University, Office of International Programs, MSC 5731, 1077 South Main Street, Harrisonburg, VA 22807; *Phone:* 540-568-6419; *Fax:* 540-568-3310. *E-mail:* studyabroad@jmu.edu. *World Wide Web:* http://www.jmu.edu/international/

TURKEY

ISTANBUL

KENTUCKY INSTITUTE FOR INTERNATIONAL STUDIES
TURKEY

Academic Focus • History, law and legal studies, political science and government.
Program Information • Faculty members are drawn from the sponsor's U.S. staff and local instructors hired by the sponsor. Students typically earn 3-6 semester credits per term.
Sessions • Jun-Jul (summer).
Eligibility Requirements • Minimum age 18; open to freshmen, sophomores, juniors, seniors, graduate students; 2.0 GPA; 1 letter of recommendation; no foreign language proficiency required.
Living Arrangements • Students live in host institution dormitories, hotels. Meals are taken on one's own, in restaurants.
Costs (2006) • $3390; includes housing, some meals, insurance, excursions, international airfare, international student ID, instructional costs. $150 application fee. Financial aid available for all students: scholarships.
For More Information • Ms. Nancy Martin, Coordinator, Kentucky Institute for International Studies, PO Box 9, Murray, KY 42071-0009; *Phone:* 270-762-3091; *Fax:* 270-762-3434. *E-mail:* kiismsu@murraystate.edu. *World Wide Web:* http://www.kiis.org/

LEXIA INTERNATIONAL
LEXIA SUMMER IN ISTANBUL

Hosted by Bosphorus University
Academic Focus • Anthropology, archaeology, architecture, area studies, art, art history, business administration/management, comparative history, cultural studies, economics, film and media studies, geography, history, international affairs, Middle Eastern studies, political science and government, religious studies, sociology, Turkish studies, visual and performing arts.
Program Information • Students attend classes at Bosphorus University (Istanbul, Turkey). Field trips. Students typically earn 8-10 semester credits per term.
Sessions • Jun-Aug (summer).
Eligibility Requirements • Minimum age 18; open to freshmen, sophomores, juniors, seniors, graduate students, adults; 2.5 GPA; 2 letters of recommendation; no foreign language proficiency required.
Living Arrangements • Students live in locally rented apartments. Quarters are shared with host institution students. Meals are taken on one's own, in residences, in central dining facility, in restaurants.
Costs (2006) • $6450; includes tuition, housing, insurance, excursions, international student ID, student support services, computer access, transcript. $40 application fee. $300 nonrefundable deposit required. Financial aid available for all students: scholarships, work study.
For More Information • Lexia International, 23 South Main Street, Hanover, NH 03755; *Phone:* 800-775-3942; *Fax:* 603-643-9899. *E-mail:* info@lexiantl.org. *World Wide Web:* http://www.lexiaintl.org/

TEMPLE UNIVERSITY
TEMPLE IN TURKEY

Hosted by Istanbul Culture University
Academic Focus • History, religious studies.
Program Information • Students attend classes at Istanbul Culture University (Istanbul, Turkey). Field trips to Pergamum, Gallipoli, Troy, Ephesus; Sardis. Students typically earn 6 semester credits per term.
Sessions • Jul-Aug (summer).
Eligibility Requirements • Minimum age 19; open to sophomores, juniors, seniors; 2.5 GPA; 1 letter of recommendation; good academic standing at home school; official transcripts; essay; no foreign language proficiency required.
Living Arrangements • Students live in host institution dormitories, hotels. Meals are taken on one's own, in residences.
Costs (2005) • $3200-$4600; includes tuition, housing, some meals, program fee, local travel. $30 application fee. $200 nonrefundable deposit required. Financial aid available for students from sponsoring institution: scholarships, loans.
For More Information • Ms. Erin Joslyn, Study Abroad Coordinator, Temple University, International Programs, 200 Tuttleman Learning Center, 1809 North 13th Street, Philadelphia, PA 19122; *Phone:* 215-204-0720; *Fax:* 215-204-0729. *E-mail:* study.abroad@temple.edu. *World Wide Web:* http://www.temple.edu/studyabroad/

TURKEY
Istanbul

UNIVERSITY OF KANSAS
LAW IN INSTANBUL

Hosted by University of Bahcesehir

Academic Focus • Law and legal studies.

Program Information • Students attend classes at University of Bahcesehir (Istanbul, Turkey). Field trips to Izmir, Ephesus, Troy. Students typically earn 4-6 semester credits per term.

Sessions • Jul (summer).

Eligibility Requirements • Open to graduate students; good academic standing at home school; completed first year of law curriculum at ABA-accredited law school; no foreign language proficiency required.

Living Arrangements • Students live in hotels. Meals are taken on one's own, in central dining facility, in restaurants.

Costs (2005) • $4000; includes tuition, housing, some meals, excursions, books and class materials, emergency medical evacuation and repatriation insurance. $38 application fee. $300 nonrefundable deposit required. Financial aid available for students from sponsoring institution: scholarships.

For More Information • Ms. Justine Hamilton, Program Coordinator, University of Kansas, Office of Study Abroad, Lippincott Hall, 1410 Jayhawk Boulevard, Room 108, Lawrence, KS 66045-7515; *Phone:* 785-864-3742; *Fax:* 785-864-5040. *E-mail:* osa@ku.edu. *World Wide Web:* http://www.ku.edu/~osa/

TURKS AND CAICOS ISLANDS

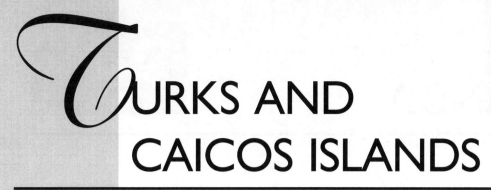

SOUTH CAICOS

THE SCHOOL FOR FIELD STUDIES
TURKS AND CAICOS: MARINE PROTECTED AREAS: MANAGEMENT TECHNIQUES AND POLICIES

Hosted by Center for Marine Resource Studies

Academic Focus • Biological/life sciences, ecology, marine sciences.

Program Information • Students attend classes at Center for Marine Resource Studies (South Caicos, Turks and Caicos Islands). Optional travel to Grand Turk, Salt Cay. Students typically earn 4 semester credits for 4 weeks.

Sessions • Jun–Jul (summer), Jul–Aug (summer 2).

Eligibility Requirements • Minimum age 16; open to precollege students, freshmen, sophomores, juniors, seniors; 2 letters of recommendation; good academic standing at home school; high school students must have completed their junior year.

Living Arrangements • Students live in a field station. Quarters are shared with host institution students. Meals are taken as a group, in central dining facility.

Costs (2007) • $3880; includes tuition, housing, all meals, lab equipment, student support services, some excursions, emergency evacuation insurance. $45 application fee. $450 deposit required. Financial aid available for all students: scholarships, loans.

For More Information • Admissions Counselor, The School for Field Studies, 10 Federal Street, Suite 24, Salem, MA 01970-3876; *Phone:* 800-989-4418; *Fax:* 978-741-3551. *E-mail:* admissions@fieldstudies.org. *World Wide Web:* http://www.fieldstudies.org/

$\mathcal{U}$GANDA

KAMPALA

SCHOOL FOR INTERNATIONAL TRAINING, SIT STUDY ABROAD
UGANDA AND RWANDA: PEACE AND CONFLICT STUDIES IN THE LAKE VICTORIA BASIN

Held at Makerere University

Academic Focus • Peace and conflict studies.

Program Information • Classes are held on the campus of Makerere University (Kampala, Uganda). Faculty members are drawn from the sponsor's U.S. staff and local instructors hired by the sponsor. Scheduled travel to the International Tribunal on Genocide in Arusha, Tanzania, Kigali, Rwanda, western and southwestern Uganda; field trips to cultural events. Students typically earn 6 semester credits per term.

Sessions • Jun–Jul (summer).

Eligibility Requirements • Open to sophomores, juniors, seniors; 2.5 GPA; 2 letters of recommendation; good academic standing at home school; background in peace and conflict resolution, social justice and human rights; no foreign language proficiency required.

Living Arrangements • Students live in host family homes, hotels. Meals are taken as a group, with host family, in residences, in restaurants.

Costs (2005–2006) • $5138; includes tuition, housing, all meals, insurance, excursions. $50 application fee. $400 nonrefundable deposit required. Financial aid available for all students: scholarships.

For More Information • SIT Study Abroad, School for International Training, SIT Study Abroad, PO Box 676, Kipling Road, Brattleboro, VT 05302-0676; *Phone:* 888-272-7881; *Fax:* 802-258-3296. *E-mail:* studyabroad@sit. edu. *World Wide Web:* http://www.sit.edu/studyabroad/

KRAINE

CITY-TO-CITY

MICHIGAN STATE UNIVERSITY
IN SEARCH OF A NEW DEMOCRACY

Hosted by Lviv Institute of Internal Affairs, Odessa State University
Academic Focus • Criminal justice, social sciences, social work.
Program Information • Students attend classes at Lviv Institute of Internal Affairs (Lviv), Odessa State University (Odessa). Field trips to museums, historic sites, churches, the Carpathian Mountains, Black Sea coast. Students typically earn 9 semester credits per term.
Sessions • May–Jun (summer).
Eligibility Requirements • Minimum age 18; open to freshmen, sophomores, juniors, seniors; 2.0 GPA; good academic standing at home school; faculty approval; no foreign language proficiency required.
Living Arrangements • Students live in host family homes. Meals are taken with host family, in residences.
Costs (2005) • $1975 (estimated); includes housing, all meals, insurance, excursions, student support services. $100 application fee. $200 nonrefundable deposit required. Financial aid available for students from sponsoring institution: scholarships, loans.
For More Information • Ms. Yvonne Squiers, Secretary, Michigan State University, Office of Study Abroad, 109 International Center, East Lansing, MI 48824-1035; *Phone:* 517-353-8920; *Fax:* 517-432-2082. *E-mail:* squiers@msu.edu. *World Wide Web:* http://studyabroad.msu.edu/

L'VIV

UNIVERSITY OF KANSAS
SUMMER UKRANIAN LANGUAGE AND AREA STUDIES

Hosted by Ivan Franko National University of L'viv
Academic Focus • Ukrainian, Ukrainian studies.
Program Information • Students attend classes at Ivan Franko National University of L'viv (L'viv, Ukraine). Scheduled travel to Kiev, Olesko, the Carpathian Mountains, Mukacheve and Uzhorod; field trips to Olesko. Students typically earn 6 semester credits per term.
Sessions • Jun–Jul (summer).
Eligibility Requirements • Minimum age 18; open to juniors, seniors, graduate students, adults; 2.5 GPA; 2 letters of recommendation; good academic standing at home school; program is targeted at graduate students, but undergraduates with appropriate profile may be eligible; 3 years college course work in Russian or 1 year in Ukrainian.
Living Arrangements • Students live in host family homes. Meals are taken as a group, on one's own, with host family, in residences, in central dining facility, in restaurants.
Costs (2005) • $3250; includes tuition, housing, all meals, excursions, student support services, medical evacuation and repatriation services. $38 application fee. $300 nonrefundable deposit required. Financial aid available for students from sponsoring institution: scholarships, loans.
For More Information • Ms. Justine Hamilton, Program Coordinator, University of Kansas, Office of Study Abroad, Lippincott Hall, 1410 Jayhawk Boulevard, Room 108, Lawrence, KS 66045-7515; *Phone:* 785-864-3742; *Fax:* 785-864-5040. *E-mail:* osa@ku.edu. *World Wide Web:* http://www.ku.edu/~osa/

$\mathcal{U}$NITED ARAB EMIRATES

DUBAI

AMERICAN INTERCONTINENTAL UNIVERSITY
AMERICAN UNIVERSITY IN DUBAI

Hosted by American University in Dubai

Academic Focus • Advertising and public relations, Arabic, art, business administration/management, commercial art, communications, computer science, design and applied arts, engineering, fine/studio arts, information science, intercultural studies, interior design, international business, liberal studies, marketing, Middle Eastern studies, photography.

Program Information • Students attend classes at American University in Dubai (Dubai, United Arab Emirates). Optional travel to other Middle East destinations at an extra cost. Students typically earn 10–15 quarter credits per term.

Sessions • Jun–Aug (summer), Aug–Sep (summer 2).

Eligibility Requirements • Open to freshmen, sophomores, juniors, seniors, graduate students, adults; 2.0 GPA; good academic standing at home school; advisor/dean and study abroad office approval; college transcripts; no foreign language proficiency required.

Living Arrangements • Students live in host institution dormitories. Quarters are shared with host institution students. Meals are taken on one's own, in central dining facility.

Costs (2004) • $1363 for 1 class; $5123 for 4 classes; includes tuition, student support services. $150 refundable deposit required.

For More Information • American InterContinental University, Study Abroad Programs, 3150 West Higgins Road, Suite 105, Hoffman Estates, IL 60195; *Phone:* 800-255-6839; *Fax:* 847-885-8422. *E-mail:* studyabroad@aiuniv.edu. *World Wide Web:* http://www.studyabroad.aiuniv.edu/

ENEZUELA

CARACAS

LANGUAGE LIAISON
SPANISH IN VENEZUELA–CARACAS

Hosted by Language Liaison
Academic Focus • Spanish language and literature.
Program Information • Students attend classes at Language Liaison (Caracas, Venezuela). Field trips; optional travel at an extra cost. Students typically earn 3–15 semester credits per term.
Sessions • New programs begin weekly, year-round.
Eligibility Requirements • Minimum age 17; open to precollege students, freshmen, sophomores, juniors, seniors, graduate students, adults; no foreign language proficiency required.
Living Arrangements • Students live in locally rented apartments, host family homes, hotels. Meals are taken on one's own, with host family, in residences, in restaurants.
Costs (2005) • Contact sponsor for cost. $175 application fee. Financial aid available for all students: scholarship research service.
For More Information • Ms. Nancy Forman, President, Language Liaison, PO Box 1772, Pacific Palisades, CA 90272; *Phone:* 800-284-4448; *Fax:* 310-454-1706. *E-mail:* learn@languageliaison.com. *World Wide Web:* http://www.languageliaison.com/

MÉRIDA

LANGUAGE LIAISON
SPANISH IN MÉRIDA

Hosted by Language Liaison
Academic Focus • Spanish language and literature.
Program Information • Students attend classes at Language Liaison (Mérida, Venezuela). Field trips; optional travel at an extra cost. Students typically earn 3–15 semester credits per term.
Sessions • Classes begin weekly, year-round.
Eligibility Requirements • Minimum age 17; open to precollege students, freshmen, sophomores, juniors, seniors, graduate students, adults; no foreign language proficiency required.
Living Arrangements • Students live in locally rented apartments, host family homes, hotels. Meals are taken on one's own, with host family, in residences, in restaurants.
Costs (2005) • Contact sponsor for cost. $175 application fee. Financial aid available for all students: scholarship research service.
For More Information • Ms. Nancy Forman, President, Language Liaison, PO Box 1772, Pacific Palisades, CA 90272; *Phone:* 800-284-4448; *Fax:* 310-454-1706. *E-mail:* learn@languageliaison.com. *World Wide Web:* http://www.languageliaison.com/

STATE UNIVERSITY OF NEW YORK COLLEGE AT CORTLAND
SUMMER STUDY ABROAD IN MÉRIDA, VENEZUELA

Hosted by VEN-USA–Institute of International Studies and Modern Languages
Academic Focus • Anthropology, communications, Latin American studies, Spanish language and literature, teaching English as a second language.
Program Information • Students attend classes at VEN-USA–Institute of International Studies and Modern Languages (Mérida, Venezuela). Optional travel to the Caribbean, Canaima/Angel Falls, Amazonas region, Caracas, Los Nevados, Jaji, Bailadores at an extra cost. Students typically earn 6–8 semester credits per term.
Sessions • May–Jun (summer), Jun–Aug (summer 2).
Eligibility Requirements • Minimum age 18; open to freshmen, sophomores, juniors, seniors, graduate students; 2.5 GPA; 2 letters of recommendation; good academic standing at home school.
Living Arrangements • Students live in host family homes. Meals are taken with host family, in residences.
Costs (2005) • $5500; includes tuition, housing, all meals, insurance, excursions, international airfare, books and class materials, international student ID, student support services, passport fees. $20 application fee. $200 nonrefundable deposit required. Financial aid available for students from sponsoring institution: scholarships, loans.
For More Information • Ms. Liz McCartney, Assistant Director, Office of International Programs, State University of New York College at Cortland, PO Box 2000, Cortland, NY 13045; *Phone:* 607-753-2209; *Fax:* 607-753-5989. *E-mail:* cortlandabroad@cortland.edu. *World Wide Web:* http://www.cortlandabroad.com/

VENEZUELA
Mérida

UNIVERSITY OF MINNESOTA
STUDY ABROAD IN VENEZUELA

Hosted by VEN-USA–Institute of International Studies and Modern Languages

Academic Focus • Botany, civilization studies, ecology, history, international business, Latin American studies, literature, political science and government, science, Spanish language and literature, teaching English as a second language.

Program Information • Students attend classes at VEN-USA-Institute of International Studies and Modern Languages (Mérida, Venezuela). Field trips to La Mucuy, Sierra Nevada. Students typically earn 6–10 semester credits per term.

Sessions • May-Jun (summer), Jun-Aug (summer 2).

Eligibility Requirements • Minimum age 18; open to freshmen, sophomores, juniors, seniors, graduate students, adults; 2.5 GPA; good academic standing at home school; no foreign language proficiency required.

Living Arrangements • Students live in host family homes. Quarters are shared with host institution students. Meals are taken with host family, in residences.

Costs (2006) • Contact sponsor for cost; includes tuition, housing, all meals, insurance, excursions. Financial aid available for students from sponsoring institution: scholarships, loans.

For More Information • Learning Abroad Center, University of Minnesota, 230 Heller Hall, 271 19th Avenue South, Minneapolis, MN 55455; *Phone:* 888-700-UOFM; *Fax:* 612-626-8009. *E-mail:* umabroad@umn.edu. *World Wide Web:* http://www.umabroad.umn. edu/. Students may also apply through Venusa, C.P.S.A., Institute of International Studies, 6542 Hypoluxo Road, PMB #324, Lake Worth, FL 33467.

IETNAM

CITY-TO-CITY

CITY COLLEGE OF SAN FRANCISCO
PASSAGE TO VIETNAM AND LAOS

Academic Focus • Asian studies.
Program Information • Faculty members are drawn from the sponsor's U.S. staff. Scheduled travel to Hanoi, Vientiane; field trips to Luong Prabang, Lao Cai, Sapa. Students typically earn 3 semester credits per term.
Sessions • Dec–Jan (winter break).
Eligibility Requirements • Minimum age 18; open to freshmen, sophomores, juniors, seniors, adults; 2.0 GPA; no foreign language proficiency required.
Living Arrangements • Students live in hotels. Meals are taken as a group, in restaurants.
Costs (2005–2006) • $2750; includes housing, all meals, excursions, international airfare, international student ID, student support services. $250 nonrefundable deposit required. Financial aid available for students from sponsoring institution: scholarships, loans.
For More Information • Ms. Jill Heffron, Study Abroad Coordinator, City College of San Francisco, 50 Phelan Avenue, Box C212, San Francisco, CA 94112; *Phone:* 415-239-3778; *Fax:* 415-239-3804. *E-mail:* studyabroad@ccsf.edu. *World Wide Web:* http://www.ccsf.edu/studyabroad/

UNIVERSITY OF SOUTHERN MISSISSIPPI
THE VIETNAM WAR

Academic Focus • History.
Program Information • Faculty members are drawn from the sponsor's U.S. staff and local instructors hired by the sponsor. Scheduled travel; field trips. Students typically earn 4 semester credits per term.
Sessions • Dec (winter).
Eligibility Requirements • Minimum age 18; open to sophomores, juniors, seniors, graduate students, adults; 2.0 GPA; good academic standing at home school; no foreign language proficiency required.
Living Arrangements • Students live in hotels. Meals are taken as a group, on one's own, in restaurants.
Costs (2004) • $3799 for undergraduate students; $3999 for graduate students; includes tuition, housing, some meals, excursions, international airfare, student support services. $200 nonrefundable deposit required. Financial aid available for students from sponsoring institution: scholarships, loans.
For More Information • Director, The Vietnam War, University of Southern Mississippi, 118 College Drive #10047, Hattiesburg, MS 39406-0001; *Phone:* 601-266-4344; *Fax:* 601-266-5699. *E-mail:* holly.buckner@usm.edu. *World Wide Web:* http://www.usm.edu/internationaledu/

HO CHI MINH CITY

CENTER FOR STUDY ABROAD (CSA)
VIETNAM NATIONAL UNIVERSITY

Hosted by Vietnam National University
Academic Focus • Asian studies, full curriculum, Vietnamese.
Program Information • Students attend classes at Vietnam National University (Ho Chi Minh City, Vietnam). Scheduled travel to local sites, Hanoi; field trips; optional travel at an extra cost. Students typically earn 4–10 semester credits per term.
Sessions • Classes begin weekly, year-round.
Eligibility Requirements • Minimum age 18; open to precollege students, freshmen, sophomores, juniors, seniors, graduate students, adults; no foreign language proficiency required.
Living Arrangements • Students live in hotels. Quarters are shared with students from other programs. Meals are taken on one's own, in residences, in restaurants.
Costs (2005) • Contact sponsor for cost. $45 application fee.
For More Information • Ms. Alima K. Virtue, Program Director, Center for Study Abroad (CSA), 325 Washington Avenue South #93, Kent, WA 98032; *Phone:* 206-726-1498; *Fax:* 253-850-0454. *E-mail:* info@centerforstudyabroad.com. *World Wide Web:* http://www.centerforstudyabroad.com/

YEMEN

SANA'A

LANGUAGE LIAISON
ARABIC IN YEMEN

Hosted by Language Liaison
Academic Focus • Arabic.
Program Information • Students attend classes at Language Liaison (Sana'a, Yemen). Field trips; optional travel at an extra cost. Students typically earn 3–15 semester credits per term.
Sessions • New programs begin weekly, year-round.
Eligibility Requirements • Minimum age 18; open to freshmen, sophomores, juniors, seniors, graduate students, adults; no foreign language proficiency required.
Living Arrangements • Meals are taken as a group, in central dining facility.
Costs (2005) • Contact sponsor for cost. $175 application fee. Financial aid available for all students: scholarship research service.
For More Information • Ms. Nancy Forman, President, Language Liaison, PO Box 1772, Pacific Palisades, CA 90272; *Phone:* 800-284-4448; *Fax:* 310-454-1706. *E-mail:* learn@languageliaison.com. *World Wide Web:* http://www.languageliaison.com/

INDEXES

Field of Study

AFRICAN-AMERICAN STUDIES

AFRICAN LANGUAGES AND LITERATURES

AFRICAN STUDIES

ART ADMINISTRATION
England
Germany

FIELD OF STUDY
Art Administration

ASIAN STUDIES

FIELD OF STUDY
Asian Studies

BIBLICAL STUDIES

BILINGUAL EDUCATION

BIOCHEMISTRY

BIOLOGICAL/LIFE SCIENCES

BIOMEDICAL SCIENCES

BOTANY

BUSINESS ADMINISTRATION/MANAGEMENT

FIELD OF STUDY
Conservation and Natural Resources

ECONOMICS

EDUCATION

FIELD OF STUDY
Education

FIELD OF STUDY
Geography

HORTICULTURE SERVICES OPERATIONS AND MANAGEMENT, GENERAL

HOSPITALITY SERVICES

INTERDISCIPLINARY STUDIES

LAW AND LEGAL STUDIES

MANAGEMENT INFORMATION SYSTEMS

FIELD OF STUDY
Management Information Systems

FIELD OF STUDY
Political Science and Government

Guatemala

Italy

FIELD OF STUDY
Romance Languages and Literatures

FIELD OF STUDY
Social Sciences, General

SOCIAL WORK

SOCIOLOGY

FIELD OF STUDY
Visual and Performing Arts, General

$\mathcal{P}$rogram Sponsors

PROGRAM SPONSORS
Bemidji State University

LIVING ROUTES–STUDY ABROAD IN ECOVILLAGES

LONDON COLLEGE OF FASHION

LOYOLA UNIVERSITY NEW ORLEANS

LYCOMING COLLEGE

LYNN UNIVERSITY

MARQUETTE UNIVERSITY

MICHIGAN STATE UNIVERSITY

PROGRAM SPONSORS
Organization for Tropical Studies

PROGRAM SPONSORS
University of North Carolina at Wilmington

$\mathcal{H}$ost Institutions

HOST INSTITUTIONS
Brazil